THE OXFORD HANDBOOK OF

SYNESTHESIA

THE OXFORD HANDBOOK OF

SYNESTHESIA

Edited by

JULIA SIMNER

and

EDWARD M. HUBBARD

OXFORD

UNIVERSITY PRESS

Great Clarendon Street, Oxford, OX2 6DP,
United Kingdom

Oxford University Press is a department of the University of Oxford.
It furthers the University's objective of excellence in research, scholarship,
and education by publishing worldwide. Oxford is a registered trade mark of
Oxford University Press in the UK and in certain other countries

Published in the United States of America by Oxford University Press
198 Madison Avenue, New York, NY 10016, United States of America

British Library Cataloguing in Publication Data
Data available

Library of Congress Control Number: 2013936563

ISBN 978–0–19–960332–9

Printed in China by
C&C Offset Printing Co. Ltd

Oxford University Press makes no representation, express or implied, that the
drug dosages in this book are correct. Readers must therefore always check
the product information and clinical procedures with the most up-to-date
published product information and data sheets provided by the manufacturers
and the most recent codes of conduct and safety regulations. The authors and
the publishers do not accept responsibility or legal liability for any errors in the
text or for the misuse or misapplication of material in this work. Except where
otherwise stated, drug dosages and recommendations are for the non-pregnant
adult who is not breast-feeding.

Links to third party websites are provided by Oxford in good faith and
for information only. Oxford disclaims any responsibility for the materials
contained in any third party website referenced in this work.

For my two children: the blue one (*Indigo*) and the
brown one (*Tommy Bruno*)

JS

For my Mom and Dad, *Karen L. Gray* and
Frederick L. Hubbard

EMH

ACKNOWLEDGMENTS

We are very grateful for the helpful and encouraging editorial support of Charlotte Green and Martin Baum of Oxford University Press. Special thanks are owed to our contributors and reviewers, who have shared their enormous expertise so generously. Finally we are grateful to Iain Botwood, Jean Simner, and Lisa Williams, who supported our efforts with good humor and tolerance throughout this process.

Julia Simner, University of Edinburgh
Edward M. Hubbard, University of Wisconsin-Madison

Contents

PART III ATTENTION AND PERCEPTION

PART IV CONTEMPORARY AND HISTORICAL APPROACHES

PART V NEUROLOGICAL BASIS OF SYNESTHESIA

PART VI COSTS AND BENEFITS: CREATIVITY, MEMORY, AND IMAGERY

PART VII CROSS-MODALITY IN THE GENERAL POPULATION

PART VIII PERSPECTIVES ON SYNESTHESIA

Contributors

Carrie Allison Autism Research Centre, University of Cambridge, Department of Psychiatry, Cambridge, UK

Bryan D. Alvarez Psychology, University of California, Berkeley, CA, USA

Julian E. Asher Department of Psychiatry, Section of Developmental Psychiatry, University of Cambridge, Cambridge, UK

Michael J. Banissy Department of Psychology, Goldsmiths, University of London, London, UK

Simon Baron-Cohen Autism Research Centre, University of Cambridge, Department of Psychiatry, Cambridge, UK

Greta Berman The Juilliard School, New York, NY, USA.

Randolph Blake Vanderbilt University, Nashville, TN, USA; Seoul National University, Seoul, Korea

Colin Blakemore Department of Physiology, Anatomy and Genetics, University of Oxford, Oxford, UK; Centre for the Study of the Senses, Institute of Philosophy, School of Advanced Study, University of London, London, UK

David Brang Department of Psychology, Northwestern University, Evanston, IL, USA

Alicia Callejas Department of Neurology, Washington University School of Medicine, Saint Louis, MO, USA

Duncan A. Carmichael Institute for Adaptive and Neural Computation, School of Informatics, Edinburgh, UK

Roi Cohen Kadosh Department of Experimental Psychology, University of Oxford, Oxford, UK

Christine Cuskley Linguistics and English Language, Language Evolution and Computation Unit, University of Edinburgh, Edinburgh, UK

Richard E. Cytowic George Washington University, Washington DC, USA

Sean A. Day Department of English and Journalism; Department of Behavioural and Social Sciences; Trident Technical College, Charleston, SC, USA

Anne G. De Volder Université catholique de Louvain, Institute of Neuroscience (IoNS), Brussels, Belgium

Patricia Lynne Duffy United Nations Language and Communications Programme, New York, USA

Chris D. Frith Wellcome Trust Centre for Neuroimaging at UCL, London, UK; Interacting Minds Centre, Aarhus University, Aarhus, Germany; All Souls College, Oxford, UK

Laura C. Gibson Department of Psychology, Neuroscience & Behaviour, McMaster University, Hamilton, ON, Canada

Peter Hancock Psychology, School of Natural Sciences, University of Stirling, Stirling, UK

Avishai Henik Department of Psychology, Ben-Gurion University of the Negev, Beer-Sheva, Israel

Edward M. Hubbard Department of Educational Psychology, University of Wisconsin-Madison, Madison, WI, USA

Wan-Yu Hung MIT International Design Centre, Singapore University of Technology and Design, Singapore

Lutz Jäncke Division Neuropsychology, Psychological Institute, University of Zurich, Zurich, Switzerland

Ashok S. Jansari School of Psychology, University of East London, London, UK

Michelle Jarick Department of Psychology, Grant MacEwan University, Edmonton, AB, Canada

Jörg Jewanski Department Musikhochschule, University of Münster, Münster, Germany

Donielle Johnson Autism Research Centre, University of Cambridge, Department of Psychiatry, Cambridge, UK

Clare Jonas School of Psychology, University of East London, London, UK

Brian L. Keeley Philosophy Field Group, Pitzer College, Claremot, CA, USA

Chai-Youn Kim Department of Psychology, Korea University, Seoul, Korea

Simon Kirby Linguistics and English Language, Language Evolution and Computation Unit, University of Edinburgh, Edinburgh, UK

Bruno Laeng Department of Psychology, University of Oslo, Oslo, Norway

Christopher T. Lovelace Department of Psychology, Shepherd University, Shepherdstown, WV, USA

Juan Lupiáñez Department of Experimental Psychology, Universidad de Granada, Granada, Spain

Mary-Ellen Lynall Department of Physiology, Anatomy and Genetics, University of Oxford, Oxford, UK

Lawrence E. Marks John B. Pierce Laboratory, New Haven, CT, USA; School of Public Health and Department of Psychology, Yale University, New Haven, CT, USA

Jason B. Mattingley Queensland Brain Institute & School of Psychology, The University of Queensland, St Lucia, QLD, Australia

Daphne Maurer Department of Psychology, Neuroscience & Behaviour, McMaster University, Hamilton, ON, Canada

Beat Meier Department of Psychology and Center for Cognition, Learning, and Memory, University of Bern, Bern, Switzerland.

Kevin J. Mitchell Smurfit Institute of Genetics and Institute of Neuroscience, Trinity College Dublin, Dublin, Ireland

Christine Mohr Institute of Psychology, University of Lausanne, Switzerland

Aleksandra Mroczko-Wąsowicz Max-Planck-Institute for Brain Research, Frankfurt, Germany; Institute of Philosophy of Mind and Cognition, National Yang Ming University, Taipei, Taiwan

Neil G. Muggleton Institute of Cognitive Neuroscience and Department of Psychology, University College London, London, UK; Institute of Cognitive Neuroscience, National Central University, Jhongli, Taiwan; Laboratories for Cognitive Neuroscience, National Yang-Ming University, Taipei, Taiwan

Catherine M. Mulvenna Department of Psychiatry, Yale University School of Medicine, New Haven, CT, USA

Fiona N. Newell School of Psychology and Institute of Neuroscience, Trinity College Dublin, Dublin, Ireland

Tanja C. W. Nijboer Department of Experimental Psychology, Utrecht University, Utrecht, The Netherlands

Danko Nikolić Max-Planck-Institute for Brain Research, Frankfurt; Frankfurt Institute for Advanced Studies, Frankfurt, Germany

Cesare Parise Crossmodal Research Laboratory, Department of Experimental Psychology, University of Oxford, Oxford, UK; Max Planck Institute for Biological Cybernetics, and Bernstein Centre for Computational Neuroscience, Tuebingen, Germany; Department of Cognitive Neuroscience, and Cognitive Interaction Technology Center of Excellence, University of Bielefeld, Bielefeld, Germany

Mark C. Price Psychology Faculty, University of Bergen, Bergen, Norway

V. S. Ramachandran Department of Psychology, University of California, San Diego, La Jolla, CA, USA

Marie Rehme Hannover Medical School, Hannover, Germany

Laurent Renier Université catholique de Louvain, Institute of Neuroscience (IoNS), Brussels, Belgium

Anina N. Rich Department of Cognitive Science & ARC Centre of Excellence in Cognition & its Disorders, Macquarie University, Sydney, NSW, Australia

Lynn C. Robertson Psychology, University of California, Berkeley, CA, USA; Research Service, Veterans Administration, Martinez, CA, USA

Nicolas Rothen School of Psychology and Sackler Centre for Consciousness Science, University of Sussex, Brighton, UK

Romke Rouw Department of Psychology, University of Amsterdam, Amsterdam, The Netherlands

Noam Sagiv Centre for Cognition and Neuroimaging, Brunel University, London, UK

Julia Simner Department of Psychology, University of Edinburgh, Edinburgh, UK

Monika Sobczak-Edmans Centre for Cognition and Neuroimaging, Brunel University, London, UK

Ferrinne Spector Department of Psychology, Edgewood College, Madison, WI, USA

Charles Spence Crossmodal Research Laboratory, Department of Experimental Psychology, University of Oxford, Oxford, UK

Mary Jane Spiller School of Psychology, University of East London, London, UK

Carol Steen Touro College, New York, NY, USA.

Elias Tsakanikos Department of Psychology, Roehampton University, London, UK

Cretien van Campen Synesthetics Netherlands, Utrecht, The Netherlands

Tessa M. van Leeuwen Department of Neurophysiology, Max Planck Institute for Brain Research, Frankfurt am Main, Germany

Argiro Vatakis Cognitive Research Systems Institute (CSRI), Athens, Greece

Vincent E. Walsh Institute of Cognitive Neuroscience and Department of Psychology, University College London, London, UK

Jamie Ward School of Psychology, University of Sussex, Brighton, UK; Sackler Centre for Consciousness Science, University of Sussex, Brighton, UK

Peter H. Weiss Cognitive Neurology, Department of Neurology, University Hospital Cologne, Köln, Germany

Markus Zedler Hannover Medical School, Hannover, Germany

OVERVIEW OF TERMINOLOGY AND FINDINGS

JULIA SIMNER
EDWARD M. HUBBARD

So why write a handbook of synesthesia? The answer is that there has probably never been a better time to write one. The modest aims of this book were to try to capture a snap-shot of our collective knowledge on synesthesia as it stands two hundred years after the very first scientific study, by Georg Tobias Ludwig Sachs in 1812. In this first work, Sachs described in his doctoral thesis the colors he saw in his mind's eye each time he thought of letters of the alphabet, of numbers, or of days of the week, or when he heard the notes of the musical scale. It is not known how these descriptions were received by his examiners—they would almost certainly have sounded rather alien. But Sachs' words represented the first written scholastic description of synesthesia at a time when the name "synesthesia" did not even exist, and this took place exactly two centuries ago. But this seemingly long time-line is something of a red herring: the last two hundred years have been typified by a distinct *lack* of research into synesthesia. This much is true except for two particularly fervent periods of study—the first surge took place in the final decades of the nineteenth century, and the second, a bigger, stronger, more powerful tsunami of a surge, has taken place since the last two decades of the twentieth century, and continues to grow stronger and more focused to the current day. Never before in its history has synesthesia been the focus of so many investigations—by psychologists, neuroscientists, philosophers, historians, artists, literary scholars, musicians, designers, and many more. This brings us neatly to the second reason for writing this book, and specifically, for choosing an Oxford Handbook format. This has allowed us to draw together the thoughts from a wide range of different scholars and artists because, perhaps more than any other topic of study, synesthesia is multidisciplinary. It is multidisciplinary not only because it interests both scientists and artists alike, but because it unites different facets of experience as a *sine qua non*. Synesthesia has been described as a "merging of the senses," with more than 150 different manifestations reported depending on what is "merged" (sound with color, taste with shape, touch with smell, and so on). Hence, each manifestation of synesthesia unites a different pair of modalities, with each modality bringing its own interested party. So one synesthete might see colors (of interest to vision scientists) when thinking of numbers (interesting for numerical cognition) while another might taste flavors in the mouth (interesting to gustatory psychophysicists) when reading words (of interest to psycholinguists). Another still might experience letters and numbers as distinct personality types (interesting for personality researchers) or as having their own particular location in space (interesting in visuo-spatial terms). And then there are the secondary qualities of synesthesia which draw their own interested parties: that it might help or hinder memory, require attention, be linked with creativity and metaphor, be genetically inherited, give an insight into consciousness, indicate differences in brain structure, or that it might reflect the types of implicit cross-sensory integration found in all people. With each facet of this *quintessentially* multifaceted condition comes a specialist subfield, and we hope to have reflected a broad range of those subfields within this handbook. Advances in synesthesia research have painted a detailed story about the development, inheritance, psychology, history, art, and neuroscience of synesthesia, and provided a contemporary source of study for a new generation of scholars. The aim of this book is to bring together this body of knowledge into one definitive handbook, to provide an overview of the field in an accessible form. Our contributors have written their chapters with a broad readership in mind, and our six-pronged target audience includes academics, students, artists, clinicians, educators, and the general public (synesthete and non-synesthete alike).

The final reason to write a handbook of synesthesia is because it is quite simply a fascinating subject—an astonishing phenomenon. It's difficult to imagine any other condition drawing so much interest from those who do not experience it. This fascination comes partly from a challenge: there is something uniquely challenging about the possibility that other people might not experience the world in qualitatively the same way. Most people have an intrinsic feeling that "reality" is fixed, that it is exactly as we see it, that it could not be different in somebody else's shoes. And this is because our sensations feel unambiguous: sound is noisy (not colorful!) taste is flavorsome (not pointed!). But neuropsychologists have long since known that reality is a construct we create by filtering stimuli through the individuality of our brain. This means that subtle differences in brain structure or function can allow some people to experience the world in different ways. Nowhere is this more obvious than in the case of synesthesia. So our aim with this handbook is to show these differences, to illustrate how they are brought about, and to demonstrate their consequences for cognition, social interaction, artistic expression, and so on. Most importantly, we hope to demystify what is, for the average non-synesthete, something rather mysterious. We should probably declare at this point that neither editor is a synesthete, although a number of our contributors are. Some of these contributors have given first-hand accounts of their experiences, and those that have, allow us an insight into a fundamentally different world of experience. As non-synesthetes, we find our fascination comes from the obvious "differentness" of these experiences, but as scholars, it also comes from a knowledge of the elegance in the systems that underlie them. Two hundred years of (on–off) research have allowed us to understand that the experiences of synesthetes—sometimes seemingly chaotic or at least superficially unexpected—are driven by an underlying set of interlocking cogs each moving in a predictable manner; these provide the synesthete with a different class of perception but in a way that we can come to understand. We hope that some of this underlying elegance emerges through the chapters of this book.

A Note on Terminology

In this section we provide an overview of the terminology that is to be found in this handbook, with cited references pointing the reader back to source materials. *Synesthesia* is a neuropsychological condition which gives rise to extraordinary sensations. As well as the usual impressions one would experience from everyday stimuli such as music, writing, eating foods, and so on, *synesthetes* (i.e., individuals with synesthesia) experience additional, otherwise unrelated sensations such as colors, moving shapes, unusual textures, and so on. Synesthesia is often defined as a "merging of the senses," suggesting that the stimulus itself and the unusual second unstimulated experience must both be sensory in nature (e.g., sound triggering the experience of colors). However, the limitations of this sensory definition are becoming more apparent as we learn about an increasing number of potential variants involving conceptual elements (e.g., word meanings, personifications) and this has led to a careful re-evaluation of definitional criteria (e.g., Cohen Kadosh and Terhune 2012; Eagleman 2012; Simner 2012a, 2012b; see also Lynall and Blakemore, Chapter 47, this volume). Despite these difficulties, definitions of synesthesia tend to share a set of core facts: that a small percentage of the population report these extraordinary experiences (colors, tastes, shapes, etc.) triggered by everyday activities (reading, eating, moving, etc.) and that these experiences are felt consciously and explicitly, and have been there, often, for as long as the synesthete can remember. In this handbook, we have taken an inclusive, descriptive approach, rather than a strict, proscriptive one, and the reader will note that different authors use the term *synesthesia* in slightly different ways.

By convention, the trigger that elicits synesthesia is referred to as the *inducer*, and the additional synesthetic experience itself is known as the *concurrent* (Grossenbacher 1997). In general, different variants of synesthesia are typically named by linking the inducer and concurrent, often with a hyphen or an arrow, with the inducer typically listed first and the concurrent second, so that a synesthete who experiences colors in response to letters or numbers (collectively referred to as *graphemes*) would be said to experience *grapheme-color synesthesia*. However, other authors may refer to this same form of synesthesia as *colored graphemes*, *color-grapheme synesthesia*, *graphemic color synesthesia*, or *color-graphemic synesthesia*. One way to tell which variant is being described is with a knowledge of which are most common; so *color-grapheme* does not describe a form of synesthesia in which looking at colors elicits the conscious percept of graphemes because that almost never exists (likewise neither shapes triggering taste, colors triggering sound, space triggering number percepts, etc.; but see Cohen Kadosh and Henik, Chapter 6, this volume). In all cases throughout this handbook, we hope that the particular variant described will be clear from context.

A diversity of terminological usage is to be expected in the early days of a science, and might be especially true in the case of synesthesia, which is a multivariant condition, incorporating a number of extremely diverse phenomenological experiences. Different authors estimate that there are between 65 (Day 2005, 2012) and 150 (Cytowic and Eagleman 2009) different manifestations of synesthesia. Within any one of these variants (although more practically, within those variants that trigger color, given that these dominate the science literature) synesthesia has also been classified according to the nature of the inducer and the nature of the concurrent. This is best understood with reference again to grapheme-color synesthesia. Grapheme-color synesthetes can have *lower synesthesia* or *higher synesthesia* (Ramachandran and Hubbard 2001) depending on whether, respectively, they are triggered by low-level perceptual features of the inducer (e.g., the curvature of the number 3, the angularity of 4) or by their higher-level conceptual features (the fact that 4 is equivalent in magnitude to IV or to ❖). Grapheme-color synesthetes can also be said to have *projector synesthesia* or *associator synesthesia* (Dixon et al. 2004) depending on whether, respectively, they experience their concurrent color projected into the outside world, or only within their mind's eye.

The choice of description for differing forms and subdivisions of synesthesia depends, in part, on the degree to which different authors are "splitters," who prefer to break the forms of synesthesia down into fine-grained categories, or "lumpers" who prefer identifying broad phenomenological similarities across synesthetes. For example, in another form of synesthesia, numbers and other ordinal sequences including months of the year and days of the week are associated with specific spatial locations (Galton 1880a, 1880b; Seron et al. 1992). "Lumpers" would refer to this as *sequence-space synesthesia* (Simner 2009), or as *spatial sequence synesthesia* (Eagleman, 2009), or *visuo-spatial forms* (Sagiv et al. 2006). "Splitters," however, would prefer different terms to reflect the particular subvariant under discussion. So when triggered by numbers, for example, this form of synesthesia is typically described as *number form synesthesia* (Hubbard et al. 2005) and when triggered by temporal sequences like months and days of the week, as *time-space synesthesia* (Smilek et al. 2007). These terminological differences may reflect a simple difference between lumping (*sequence-space synesthesia*) and splitting (*number form synesthesia; time-space synesthesia*), but may also reflect the fact that synesthetes report quite different experiences, with number forms being the most common of the sequence-space forms, and others, like alphabet forms, or forms for shoe sizes (Cytowic 1989, 2002) or sequential pure bred dog names (Hubbard et al. 2009) being much rarer. As the association with space is more likely for certain sequences than others, a complete theory of sequence-space synesthesia will not only have to account for these common associations, but also the dissociations. One way to avoid the subjective application of splitting or lumping rules is to identify patterns across large numbers of synesthetes and to use sophisticated statistical tools to determine the clusters of types (e.g., Novich et al. 2011). However, even within these clusters, there may be important subdivisions, and this is reflected in the names that authors use to describe synesthesia. Here, we have allowed authors to use their own preferred choice of nomenclature for any given variant. In part, this is a simple preference to avoid being prescriptive about terminology at this particular stage of research, but it also reflects a broader goal of allowing terminological differences to highlight different interpretations and emphases on different aspects of synesthesia.

We close this terminological overview by describing the neuroscientific methodologies referenced throughout this book. One of the most direct methods allows visualization of brain structure, including *magnetic resonance imaging* (MRI). Quantitative measurements of the volume elements or *voxels* that make up an imaging dataset allow researchers to measure differences in the cortical *gray matter* (the brain's grayish tissue, composed primarily of nerve cell bodies and their dendrites) and underlying *white matter* (the brain's pale-colored tissue, composed primarily of myelin-covered nerve cell fibers). This type of measurement is called *voxel-based morphometry* (VBM: see Weiss, Chapter 26, this volume) and *diffusion tensor imaging* (DTI), which measures the flow of water along the myelinated axons that make up long-range anatomical white matter tracts in the brain (see Rouw, Chapter 25, this volume). However, in many cases we are interested in measuring how brain responses change under various experimental conditions. Methods that measure functional responses (rather than anatomical structure) are broadly referred to as *functional neuroimaging,* and include methods such as *positron emission tomography* (PET), *single-photon emission tomography* (SPECT), and *functional magnetic resonance imaging* (fMRI). Functional neuroimaging methods permit relatively precise localization of function (i.e., "what happens where"), but often with poor timing information (i.e., poor "when" information; for a fuller discussion of these methods, see Hubbard, Chapter 24, this volume). Conversely, methods that measure the summed electrical activity of large numbers of neurons under the scalp are referred to as *electrophysiological* methods, including *electroencephalography* (EEG) and a more recent variant that measures the slight magnetic fields generated by this electrical activity, *magnetoencephalography* (MEG). These methods provide precise timing information (to the millisecond, or 1/1000 of a second) but provide only coarse spatial localization (see Jäncke, Chapter 28, this volume). One limitation of both classes of methods is that they are limited to correlational data. Changes in some stimulus feature or some psychological state are associated with changes in neuroimaging or electrophysiological responses, but these methods do not permit causal inferences. To do so, we need methods that allow us to modify neural activity directly, and to measure the consequences of this modification. One common method to do so is *transcranial magnetic stimulation* (TMS), which uses strong, rapidly varying magnetic fields to elicit or interfere with neural activity (see Muggleton and Tsakanikos, Chapter 29, this volume). However the true power of cognitive neuroscience as applied to synesthesia is not found in the use of any one method, but rather is highlighted by the use of converging methods, in which the strengths and limitations of any one method are balanced by other methods (for a review of this approach applied to grapheme-color synesthesia, see Hubbard et al. 2011). Much like in the study of synesthesia itself, the use of multiple cases, multiple methods and multiple perspectives provides much richer insights than any one perspective or method alone ever could. It is this spirit of integration that, we hope, permeates this entire volume.

STRUCTURE OF THE HANDBOOK

The eight parts of this handbook represent basic divisions into themes that have arisen in contemporary synesthesia scholarship. Part I covers the origins of synesthesia, asking where it comes from in a genetic and developmental sense, and how many people might experience it. Part II takes a closer look at how numbers, letters, and words play a role in synesthetic experiences—these are particularly important triggers of synesthesia and account for some 80% to 90% of all known types. Part III looks at two subdisciplines—attention and perception—asking whether synesthetes need to pay attention to stimuli in order to experience their unusual sensations, whether these sensations are "perceptual" or "percept-like," whether synesthesia is automatic, how synesthesia reflects the real-world binding of features, and whether this can cause emotional affect if there is a clash between synesthetic and real-world perception. In Part IV we look at contemporary and historical approaches to the study of synesthesia, examining in turn the methodologies employed through the last three centuries, as well as considering two additional contemporary modes of study. In Part V we examine the neurological basis of synesthesia, considering functional and structural brain differences, looking at both white and gray matter, and also taking a neurodevelopmental perspective. In this section we also consider the relationship between synesthesia and mirror neurons, and look at methods that closely track the time-course of synesthesia in neurophysiological terms, as well as those that can inform us by causing temporary "virtual lesions" in the brains of synesthetes. In Part VI we consider the costs and benefits of synesthesia in terms of memory and imagery, in creativity, art, literature, and design. We also look at how synesthesia may be implicated in cases of prodigy or extreme human ability, of the type found in savant individuals. In Part VII we look at synesthesia-like cross-sensory mappings in the general population, and ask how they might influence perception, speech processing, linguistic metaphor, and even the very evolution of language. We also ask how synesthesia might be artificially created via technologies designed for populations who have lost one sensory faculty (e.g., technologies exploiting sound to help blind people). Finally, in Part VIII we take a step back to give a broader overview of the issues raised in this handbook. We look at the topic of synesthesia and consciousness, and ask fundamental questions about cross-modality, cognition, and the senses. This section also includes a first-person description of synesthesia from someone who is not only a synesthete himself, but who has spent over 20 years seeking out synesthetes in order to elicit their experiences, and provide them with a forum to describe their unusual sensations. Perhaps this chapter, more than any other in this handbook, can give the layperson an insight into the rich, fascinating, unexpected, and extra-ordinary world of the synesthete.

REFERENCES

Cohen-Kadosh, Roi, and Avishai Henik. 2013. Numbers, synesthesia and directionality. In *The Oxford Handbook of Synesthesia*, ed. Julia Simner and Edward M. Hubbard, 103–122 . Oxford: Oxford University Press.

Cohen Kadosh, Roi and Devin B. Terhune. 2012. Redefining synaesthesia? *British Journal of Psychology* 103 (1):20–23.

Cytowic, Richard E. 1989. *Synesthesia: A Union of the Senses*. 1st ed. New York: Springer-Verlag.

——. 2002. *Synesthesia: A Union of the Senses*. 2nd ed. Cambridge, MA: MIT Press

Cytowic, Richard E., and David M. Eagleman. 2009. *Wednesday Is Indigo Blue: Discovering the Brain of Synesthesia*. Cambridge, MA: MIT Press.

Day, Sean A. 2005. Some demographic and socio-cultural aspects of synaesthesia. In *Synesthesia: Perspectives from Cognitive Neuroscience*, ed. Lynn C. Robertson and Noam Sagiv, New York: Oxford University Press.

——. 2012. Types of synesthesia. Synesthesia.<http://www.daysyn.com/Types-of-Syn.html>.

Dixon, Mike J., Daniel Smilek, and Philip M. Merikle. 2004. Not all synaesthetes are created equal: projector versus associator synaesthetes. *Cognitive, Affective, and Behavioral Neuroscience* 4:335–343.

Eagleman, David M. 2009. The objectification of overlearned sequences: A new view of spatial sequence synesthesia, *Cortex* 45 (10):1266–1277.

——. 2012. Synaesthesia in its protean guises. *British Journal of Psychology* 103 (1):16–19.

Galton, Francis 1880a. Visualised numerals. *Nature* 21 (543):494–495.

——. 1880b. Visualised numerals. *Nature* 21 (533):252–256.

Grossenbacher, Peter G. 1997. Perception and sensory information in synaesthetic experience. In *Synaesthesia: Classic and Contemporary Readings*, ed. Simon Baron-Cohen and John E. Harrison, 148–172. Oxford: Blackwell.

Hubbard, Edward M. 2013. Synesthesia and functional imaging. In *The Oxford Handbook of Synesthesia*, ed. Julia Simner and Edward M. Hubbard, 475–499 . Oxford: Oxford University Press.

Hubbard, Edward M., David Brang, and Vilayanur S. Ramachandran. 2011. The cross-activation theory at 10. *Journal of Neuropsychology* 5 (2):152–177.

Hubbard, Edward M., Manuela Piazza, Philippe Pinel, and Stanislas Dehaene. 2005. Interactions between number and space in parietal cortex, *Nature Reviews Neuroscience* 6 (6):435–448.

Hubbard, Edward M., Mariagrazia Ranzini, Manuela Piazza, and Stanislas Dehaene. 2009. What information is critical to elicit interference in number-form synesthesia? *Cortex* 45 (10):1200–1216.

Jäncke, Lutz. 2013. The timing of neurophysiological events in synesthesia. In *The Oxford Handbook of Synesthesia*, ed. Julia Simner, and Edward M. Hubbard, 558–569. Oxford: Oxford University Press.

Lynall, Mary-Ellen, and Colin Blakemore. 2013. What synesthesia isn't. In *The Oxford Handbook of Synesthesia*, ed. Julia Simner, and Edward M. Hubbard, 959–998 . Oxford: Oxford University Press.

Muggleton, Neil G., and Elias Tsakanikos. 2013. The use of transcranial magnetic stimulation in the investigation of synesthesia. In *The Oxford Handbook of Synesthesia*, ed. Julia Simner and Edward M. Hubbard, 583 . Oxford: Oxford University Press.

Novich, Scott D., Sherry Cheng, and David M. Eagleman. 2011. Is synesthesia one condition or many? A large-scale analysis reveals subgroups. *Journal of Neuropsychology* 5:353–371.

Ramachandran, Vilayanur S., and Edward M. Hubbard. 2001. Synaesthesia—a window into perception, thought and language. *Journal of Consciousness Studies* 8 (12):3–34.

Rouw, Romke. 2013. Synesthesia, hyperconnectivity, and diffusion tensor imaging. In *The Oxford Handbook of Synesthesia*, ed. Julia Simner and Edward M. Hubbard, 500–518 . Oxford: Oxford University Press.

Sagiv, Noam, Julia Simner, James Collins, Brian Butterworth, and Jamie Ward. 2006. What is the relationship between synaesthesia and visuo-spatial number forms? *Cognition* 101 (1):114–128.

Seron, Xavier, Mauro Pesenti, Marie-Pascale Noel, Gérard Deloche, and Jacques-André Cornet. 1992. Images of numbers: or 'When 98 is upper left and 6 sky blue'. *Cognition* 44 (1–2):159–196.

Simner, Julia. 2009. Synaesthetic visuo-spatial forms: Viewing sequences in space. *Cortex* 45:1138–1147.

——. 2012a. Defining synaesthesia. *British Journal of Psychology* 103 (1)1–15.

——. 2012b. Defining synaesthesia: A response to two excellent commentaries. *British Journal of Psychology* 103 (1):24–27.

Smilek, Daniel, Alicia Callejas, Mike J. Dixon, and Philip M. Merikle. 2007. Ovals of time: Time-space associations in synaesthesia. *Consciousness and Cognition* 16 (2):507–519.

Weiss, Peter H. 2013. Can grey matter studies inform theories of (grapheme-colour) synesthesia? In *The Oxford Handbook of Synesthesia*, ed. Julia Simner and Edward M. Hubbard, 519–529 . Oxford: Oxford University Press.

PART I

ORIGINS OF SYNESTHESIA

CHAPTER 1

THE PREVALENCE OF SYNESTHESIA

The consistency revolution

DONIELLE JOHNSON, CARRIE ALLISON, AND
SIMON BARON-COHEN

A BRIEF HISTORY OF SYNESTHESIA RESEARCH

Traditionally, the term synesthesia describes a condition in which the stimulation of one sensory modality automatically evokes a perception in an unstimulated modality (e.g., the sound of a bell leads the synesthete to experience the color pink; Baron-Cohen, Wyke, and Binnie 1987; Bor, Billington, and Baron-Cohen 2007; Marks 1975; Sagiv 2005). While this definition describes a cross-sensory association, synesthetic experiences can also be intrasensory (e.g., the letter "g" triggers a blue photism when read). The stimulus (bell or "g") that triggers the synesthetic perception is referred to as an *inducer*, while the resulting experience or *percept* (blue) is called the *concurrent* (Grossenbacher 1997; Grossenbacher and Lovelace 2001). Not all inducers are sensory, however. Grossenbacher and Lovelace (2001) used the term *synesthetic conception* to refer to synesthetic experiences in which inducers are concepts. For example, in "time-space" synesthesia months take on locations in space, and this can occur whether the months are read, heard, or even thought about (Grossenbacher and Lovelace 2001).

Throughout this chapter, when we use the term synesthesia we are referring to genuine, developmental synesthesia. Developmental synesthetes generally report having synesthesia for as long as they can remember and cannot provide an explanation or learning account of their experiences (Baron-Cohen et al. 2007). Genuine synesthesia does not arise voluntarily, nor is it learned through training, acquired through drug use, or induced (solely) by any neurological pathology.[1]

Learned or acquired associations (e.g., in those familiar with the number-color coding on cross-stitch needles) can be difficult to distinguish from genuine synesthesia. Over-rehearsal can lead to a high level of performance similar to synesthetes on tests designed to assess synesthesia (i.e., the synesthetic Stroop test; discussed in more detail later). Non-synesthetes have also been shown to experience learned or trained associations as automatically as true synesthetes do (Elias et al. 2003; Meier and Rothen 2009). This in turn has led some to suggest that synesthesia itself is merely learned. However, a learning account of synesthesia cannot explain why siblings with synesthesia reared in essentially identical environments (or at least exposed to the same alphabet teaching materials or children's books) report different colors for the same inducer, or experience different variants of synesthesia altogether (Barnett et al. 2008).

Metaphors, too, can seem synesthetic. It is not uncommon, for example, for non-synesthete artists and musicians to ascribe colors or other characteristics to pieces. A composer might refer to a musical piece as heavy and blue because of its tone or the mood it evokes, not because it literally triggers a heavy, blue percept for him or her. Synesthetic metaphors are not exclusively used by artists. Many people describe wine or cheese as "sharp" or "robust." However, the use of metaphor and imagery should be distinguished from true synesthesia, in which percepts are induced automatically and involuntarily (Baron-Cohen and Harrison 1999; Simpson and McKellar 1955). Having established what we consider as synesthesia in this article, we will now review the recent history of research into this phenomenon.

Despite its popularity in the late nineteenth century, by the mid 1930s there was a considerable reduction in the psychological literature on synesthesia (Marks 1975). The problem for researchers then and now is that synesthesia is an internal, subjective experience. Although some early studies incorporated objective verification (Calkins 1893, and see later), most relied on descriptions and reports given by synesthetes themselves. In the belief that it would restore objectivity to the field of psychology, the school of behaviorism, which emerged in the 1920s and 1930s, rejected the study of subjective, mental phenomena, or required rigorous independent evidence of their existence. One casualty of this was synesthesia research. With few or no objective tests to validate self-reports from synesthetes and thereby distinguish them from people with a vivid imagination or a faculty for generating striking pseudo-synesthetic metaphors, the condition was "[no longer] considered amenable to scientific investigation" (Harrison and Baron-Cohen 1997, 4). When behaviorism was supplanted by cognitivism in the latter half of

---

[1] Several substances and conditions have been associated with acquired synesthesia: hallucinogenic drugs, including 3,4,5-trimethoxyphenethylamine (mescaline; Simpson and McKellar 1955), psilocybin ('magic mushrooms'; Duffy 2001), lysergic acid diethylamide (LSD; Harrison and Baron-Cohen 1997), and cannabis (Cytowic 1989); epileptic seizures (Duffy 2001); migraines (Podoll and Robinson 2002); and optic nerve and optic chiasm lesions (Jacobs et al. 1981). Multiple sclerosis has also been associated with acquired synesthesia (Jacobs et al. 1981).

the twentieth century, however, new methods were introduced to assess the genuineness of synesthesia. This ushered in a synesthesia "renaissance" characterized by rigorous empirical investigation which continues to this day.

Since the earliest days of synesthesia research, we have moved beyond merely proving that synesthesia exists. Much of this progress can be attributed to advancements stemming from a relatively simple but powerful test developed (or re-discovered, see later) in the 1980s. This test allows researchers to quickly determine whether a person is a genuine synesthete, and ultimately opens the door for a more thorough examination of the condition. In this chapter we will describe the creation and development of this test, now known as the Test of Genuineness (TOG) and discuss reasons why its central tenet, assessing the consistency of synesthetes' reports, became the first "gold standard" method for authenticating reported synesthesia (Rich, Bradshaw, and Mattingley 2005; Simner et al. 2006; Ward and Mattingley 2006). We will also consider recent examinations of synesthesia's other features and show that together, consistency tests, behavioral tasks, and neuroimaging methods are helping researchers establish prevalence rates, shed light on neural and cognitive mechanisms underlying the phenomenon, and use synesthesia research to inform our understanding of typical cognition.

Synesthetic Consistency and the First Test of Genuineness

Early investigators meticulously recorded the experiences of synesthetes, primarily providing detailed case descriptions and reproducing drawings of reported percepts when possible. A comparison of early studies reveals differences of opinion regarding definitions (Phillips 1897), prevalence rates (Calkins 1895; Phillips 1897), heritability (Flournoy 1893), and what might be considered typical manifestations of the same form of synesthesia (e.g., what constitutes "normal" number-form visualizations for synesthetes; Galton 1883; Phillips 1897; see later). However, the constancy of synesthetic percepts is one point of agreement: for any particular synesthete, the synesthetic experience is typically the same for any given trigger (e.g., if the letter "A" is red for a synesthete, it will tend to always be red for that synesthete, over days, months, years, and even decades).[2] In one early study, for example, Dresslar (1903) aimed to assess the stability of a young woman's synesthesia over a period of 8 years. Whether she chose color words from a dictionary or used artistic media to convey her percepts, her choices for 29 proper names were nearly

---

[2] It is important to note that some have questioned whether consistency over time should be an essential criterion of synesthesia (Simner 2012). Perhaps percepts might change slightly over time (e.g., changes in saturation), or some genuine synesthetes have experiences that are not consistent, which causes them to fail tests relying solely on consistency. Overall, however, the idea that synesthesia is generally characterized by consistency is widely accepted throughout the field.

invariable. Ginsberg (1923) assessed the consistency of his own tone–color associations over a 5-month period. The majority of the pairings remained the same and the ones that varied only did so slightly. For example, "deep brown, almost black" was reported as "blackish brown" at time two, and "deep brown, with blue tinge; almost maroon" changed to "dark purple" (Ginsberg 1923, 586). In *Inquiries into Human Faculty*, Galton (1883) noted the consistency of number forms, and Mary Calkins remarked on the "stability" of synesthesia in her 1895 study (91).

Contemporary researchers extended earlier work by introducing features that would increase the reliability and objectivity of the consistency testing paradigm. Baron-Cohen and colleagues (1987) used the first contemporary consistency test in their seminal case study of word-color synesthete EP. The researchers presented the synesthete with a list of triggering words and noted her reported synesthetic color for each one. They then repeated the process after the passing of time and noted the number of identical responses across the testing sessions. Next, they compared the synesthete's performance to that of a control participant who was asked to invent analogous color associations for each word. Their comparison showed that the synesthete was far superior in the consistency of her responses. They concluded that her performance was evidence of genuine synesthesia and this test became known as the Test of Genuineness. Enabling researchers to objectively infer the genuineness of synesthesia, the TOG became the first reliable way to draw a distinction between synesthetes and non-synesthetes.

The original TOG included a list of 103 randomly selected words. There were 50 meaningful words (animals, names of places, objects, occupations, and abstract terms), the 7 days of the week, 20 first names, and the 26 letters of the English alphabet. After each word was read aloud by an experimenter, EP was asked to provide a detailed description of the percept each word induced. Three hours later without warning, she was asked to provide descriptions for ten words selected randomly from the original list. Ten weeks later she was tested again, but on the entire list this time. EP was 100% consistent on both retests.

EP's control, an intelligent 27-year-old lawyer with a good memory, completed the same protocol. However, unlike EP she was informed of the impending retests and was instructed to use a strategy to remember her word-color pairings. When tested 3 hours later, she reported the same description for only three of ten words. Ten weeks later, she gave consistent responses for 17 items, most of which were predictable associations (e.g., word = "table," reported color = "brown").

Baron-Cohen et al. (1993) replicated earlier findings with a larger group consisting of nine synesthetes and nine control participants. This time, the TOG stimuli were 117 items: 40 words describing occupations, objects, places, or animals; the 7 days of the week; 20 first names; the 26 letters of the alphabet; eight abstract, emotionally neutral terms; eight pronouns and prepositions; and eight nonsensical words. Again, the experimenter read each word aloud and participants were asked to give verbal descriptions of the colors they experienced for each one. In this study, synesthetes' responses were 92.3% consistent when retested 1 year later. Despite a warning and a shorter test–retest interval (1 week), control participants were only 37.6% consistent in their pairings. Of note, this study introduced a longer test–retest interval for potential synesthetes compared to controls. This "stacking the deck" in favor of control participants has become an important feature of more recent demonstrations of genuineness (Simner et al. 2006; Ward and Simner 2003; Ward, Simner, and Auyeung 2005). The fact that control participants invariably have lower consistency scores despite their advantages is taken as further confirmation of the genuineness of synesthesia.

A significant shortcoming of the original TOG was its scoring protocol. Scoring criteria and procedures varied across Baron-Cohen and colleagues' first TOG studies (1987, 1993, 1996), making it difficult to compare results across the three. Perhaps more importantly, consistency was not quantifiable in any great depth. Responses were verbal color names (e.g., "a" = "red," "b" = "light green") and these were either taken as consistent over time (or similar enough that independent raters agreed that they were consistent) or inconsistent. In their 1996 study, Baron-Cohen and colleagues transitioned from relying on verbal descriptions to using color swatches, and asked each participant to select the swatch closest to their percept for several items. Two independent judges then reviewed participants' choices from 309 color swatches, but what constituted an "exact," "nearly exact," or "inconsistent" pairing was not systematically outlined and these labels did not correspond to specific numerical values.

THE REVISED TEST OF GENUINENESS

Asher et al. (2006) introduced the Revised Test of Genuineness for visual synesthesia (TOG-R). The test featured new materials, a more precise scoring system, and a method of phenotyping synesthetes. The test stimuli were 51 words (days of the week, months, names, nouns, verbs, articles) and 48 sounds lasting 1 to 3 seconds (instrumental sounds, naturally occurring and manmade environmental sounds, and vocal exclamations). The sounds were recorded onto two CDs and the tracks were presented in a different, randomized order on each. Synesthetes chose their color responses from what the group termed the Cambridge Synesthesia Charts, which consisted of 238 numbered color swatches printed onto three A4 sheets (see Figure 1.1). In addition to these colors, synesthetes could indicate white, transparent, and translucent if they experienced these particular concurrents.

To validate the TOG-R, 26 synesthetes who experienced colors from words and/or sounds and 23 control participants were tested. Synesthetes were instructed to listen to each track and choose the color swatch that most closely matched their induced color. They were instructed to choose up to two dominant colors for sounds inducing multiple concurrents and indicate non-inducing stimuli. Synesthetes were given at least a one-month delay between testing sessions. Non-synesthete controls listened to each sound and chose one color by free association. Similar to the TOG protocol, they were told to try to remember their color choices for the retest session. After an average of 5 months, synesthetes were significantly more consistent than the control participants,

FIGURE 1.1 Excerpts of Cambridge Synaesthesia Colour Charts A, B, and C used in Asher et al. (2006). Reprinted from *Cortex*, 42 (2), Julian E. Asher, Michael R.F. Aitken, Nasr Farooqi, Sameer Kurmani, and Simon Baron-Cohen, Diagnosing and Phenotyping Visual Synaesthesia: a Preliminary Evaluation of the Revised Test of Genuineness (TOG-R), pp. 137–146, Copyright (2006), with permission from Elsevier.

who experienced only a week-long interval between test sessions (synesthetes: 71.3% consistent, range 57.2–85.3%; control participants: 33% consistent, range 14–52.3%). The distribution of the scores suggested the TOG-R could be used to accurately distinguish synesthetes from non-synesthetes.

The TOG-R used a more precise scoring algorithm than the original TOG. Consistency scores were based on a point system where the number of points depended on the proximity of color swatches chosen (see Figure 1.2, each block represents a color swatch on the charts shown in Figure 1.1). An exact or nearly exact match at time two (i.e., within one swatch either above, below, left, or right of the swatch chosen at time one) was given three points. Two points were awarded if: the retest swatch was within one swatch diagonally or two swatches above, below, left, or right of the initial swatch; no color was reported for a stimulus at both times; and white or transparent was chosen during the test and either white, transparent, or any of the five lightest neutrals were chosen at retest. If two choices did not meet criteria for two or three points, one point was awarded if: they were within the same (of seven) color groups as determined by their cyan, magenta, yellow, black proportions; and white or transparent was chosen at time one and a neutral at time two. Participants received no points for choosing colors in different color groups.

1	1	1	1	1	1	1
1	1	1	2	1	1	1
1	1	2	3	2	1	1
1	2	3	EXACT 3 MATCH	3	2	1
1	1	2	3	2	1	1
1	1	1	2	1	1	1
1	1	1	1	1	1	1

FIGURE 1.2 TOG-R scoring protocol. Reprinted from *Cortex*, 42 (2), Julian E. Asher, Michael R.F. Aitken, Nasr Farooqi, Sameer Kurmani, and Simon Baron-Cohen, Diagnosing and Phenotyping Visual Synaesthesia: a Preliminary Evaluation of the Revised Test of Genuineness (TOG-R), pp. 137–146, Copyright (2006), with permission from Elsevier.

The TOG-R added a new dimension to color synesthesia diagnosis by enabling Asher and colleagues to systematically divide synesthetes into component phenotypes. Based on the range of sound stimuli that evoked their percepts, synesthetes were categorized as "broad-band" or "narrow-band." The eight "broad-band" synesthetes reported percepts to 80% to 100% of the stimuli, including words and sounds. Eighteen synesthetes classified as "narrow-band" synesthetes reported percepts to 37% to 71% of stimuli.

STRENGTHS AND WEAKNESSES OF CONSISTENCY TESTING

The TOG has become perhaps the most widely used paradigm in synesthesia research for a number of reasons. First, regardless of the variant assessed, consistency test results tend to be robust, that is, mean scores for synesthetes typically do not overlap non-synesthete scores (Asher et al. 2006; Baron-Cohen et al. 1993, 1996; Ward, Simner, and Auyeung 2005). Consistency tests are easily administered and completed, and modifications in the test are allowing researchers to obtain relatively fine-grained information about exactly how consistent synesthetes are. We saw earlier that in some versions of the task, participants are asked to describe their color experiences in their own words, while other versions assess synesthetes using color charts (Asher et al. 2006; Baron-Cohen et al. 1996) or computerized color palettes (Eagleman et al. 2007; Simner et al. 2009). This change in the basic protocol has increased the precision of color selection and ensured more systematic similarity calculations. Color charts and computerized palettes have also made the test more accessible for those with poorer communication skills (e.g., children) and thus have facilitated its use in a wider range of populations.

Another strength of the test is its flexible format. The stimuli used in Baron-Cohen and colleagues' 1987 case study varied from those used in the 1993 study, which differed still from those used in 1996. Despite modified lists of potential inducers, the first versions of the TOG reliably distinguished "colored hearing" synesthetes from controls. Since then, the TOG has been adapted to diagnose various forms of synesthesia. This includes object-personality synesthesia, a form in which inanimate objects such as shapes and pieces of furniture have personalities (Smilek et al. 2007), and mirror-touch synesthesia, in which an individual experiences tactile sensations upon seeing other people being touched (Banissy et al. 2009). Ward (2004) relied on the consistency principle to diagnose synesthesia induced by emotional stimuli (e.g., names of acquaintances and "highly emotional" words such as anger and love). A consistency test was also used to test a rare form of synesthesia in which the synesthete experiences tastes in response to words he reads, thinks about, hears, or says aloud himself (referred to as lexical-gustatory synesthesia; Ward and Simner 2003). Tests of number-form synesthesia, a variant in which numbers are experienced in various spatial configurations, have also relied on the consistency criterion (Cytowic 2002; Sagiv et al. 2006). Typically, these tests involve asking participants to draw or describe the spatial patterns experienced for numbers, letters, days, and/or months. Individuals with number-form synesthesia consistently draw or describe the same patterns when retested without warning at a later time (Sagiv et al. 2006). The TOG has appeared in some form or other in almost every scientific article on synesthesia published in the last two decades.

Even studies assessing features other than consistency usually include some element of consistency testing to inform experimental design, develop test stimuli, or verify genuineness before an experiment. For example, Asher et al. (2009) employed the TOG and TOG-R in a genetic study. The authors diagnosed and phenotyped 43 families of auditory-visual synesthetes prior to analyses. Moreover, given that consistency tests are also suitable for use in remote-testing protocols (Asher et al. 2006; Barnett et al. 2008) and studies involving large samples (Rich, Bradshaw, and Mattingley 2005; Simner et al. 2005, 2006), they are ideal tools for prevalence studies (see later).

Despite its strengths, consistency testing has significant limitations. The test works on the assumption that synesthetic associations are generally consistent so any associations that change over time work to lower a person's overall consistency score. There are indeed instances where authentic, synesthetic percepts *have* changed over time (Cytowic 2002; Eagleman et al. 2007; Riggs and Karwoski 1934) or have been described slightly differently upon retest (Jordan 1917). Synesthesia in children may be particularly likely to change. After using consistency tests to diagnose and observe the development of grapheme-color synesthesia in 6- and 7-year-olds for 12 months, Simner and colleagues (2009) asserted that synesthetic consistency develops, with pairings becoming more permanent over time. Child synesthetes showed greater internal consistency than their peers with both average and superior memories, but were notably less consistent than adult synesthetes. Thus, scoring synesthetes on the basis of permanent inducer–concurrent pairs could contribute to false negative diagnoses, especially when synesthete scores are not compared to scores of well-matched controls.

False positive diagnoses are also possible with this type of test. Although unlikely, participants completing the test remotely could save copies of their responses and use them again during retest. The risk of this is higher in studies where control participants are informed of retest sessions. Non-synesthetes with deeply rooted associations could also achieve consistency scores indistinguishable from those of true synesthetes. The threat of TOG false positives is reduced in studies that supplement the test with interviews or self-report questionnaires (Simner et al. 2006; Ward, Huckstep, and Tsakanikos 2006).

In studies that provide synesthetes with hundreds or thousands of color choices, participants are sometimes overwhelmed by the sheer number from which to choose. Frustration is often reported as well—not being able to find the "right color" or feeling as though there are too few can be unpleasant for synesthetes (see Asher et al. 2006). One way to prevent participant fatigue in consistency testing is to decrease the number of potential inducers. Versions with fewer items are just as diagnostically accurate as longer ones as long as the test contains a sufficient number of items to prevent successful memory-recall by non-synesthete controls (Asher et al. 2006; Baron-Cohen, Wyke, and Binnie 1987; Simner et al. 2006). In addition to limiting the number of items, consistency tests could further minimize participant frustration by providing a way to indicate attributes such as texture, luster, and luminosity. These features can be as important as the color of the concurrent to synesthetes, and selection can be challenging without a way to convey them (Eagleman and Goodale 2009).

Finally, although consistency tests substantiate personal anecdotes, they do not tell us much about the way synesthesia works. Indeed, the last decade has seen a shift from focusing on internal consistency to investigating other characteristics, and in the following section we present a review of alternative methodologies that rely on other features to demonstrate genuineness. These methods have shown us not only that synesthesia is genuine, but also what its fundamental properties might be.

ASSESSING OTHER FEATURES OF SYNESTHESIA

The methods reviewed here are a selection of those that have been used to demonstrate authenticity and elucidate the mechanisms involved in synesthesia. Modified Stroop tasks are commonly used to demonstrate the automatic, involuntary nature of synesthetic associations (Cytowic 2002; Wollen and Ruggiero 1983). In a traditional Stroop test, participants asked to name the print color of a color word are slower to name it if the print color does not match the semantics of the word (e.g., the word "blue" shown in red print; Stroop 1935). In the variant of the Stroop test used to assess grapheme-color synesthesia, inducing graphemes are printed in colors that are congruent, incongruent, or neutral (e.g., black) with respect to the synesthete's percepts. For example, if the synesthete sees the letter "q" as pink, a "q" printed in pink is congruent with her percept while a "q" printed in yellow is incongruent. Compared to congruent or neutral presentations, synesthetes take longer to name the color of a grapheme if it is printed in an incongruent color (Blake et al. 2005; Mills, Boteler, and Oliver 1999). This difference in response times, arising from the interference between the synesthetic and printed colors of the stimulus, is referred to as the synesthetic Stroop effect.

Incongruent cross-modal pairs can induce the same interference effect in other types of synesthesia as well. Beeli, Esslen, and Jäncke (2005) reported a synesthete who experienced tastes for musical intervals. She identified tonal intervals more quickly than non-synesthete musicians when the tastes applied to her tongue matched her synesthetic experience for the interval, but she performed more slowly in incongruent trials. Control participants' reaction times did not vary as a function of interval-taste congruence. In another study, sound-color synesthetes also exhibited the Stroop effect. When asked to name the color of a computerized patch while ignoring tones presented through headphones, they showed an interference effect for incongruent tone-color pairings (Ward, Huckstep, and Tsakanikos 2006).

Since interference effects are not ordinarily seen in controls some have recommended the use of Stroop tasks to diagnose synesthetes (Odgaard, Flowers, and Bradman 1999). However, synesthetic Stroop task results should be interpreted cautiously since non-synesthetes are sometimes indistinguishable from genuine cases. In fact, non-synesthetes can show "synesthesia-like" interference if they have well-established color associations for numbers (e.g., those highly familiar with the number-color coding on cross-stitch needles, or children with colored alphabetic refrigerator magnets; Elias et al. 2003; Hancock 2006), or if color associations have been recently formed during an experimental training period (Meier and Rothen 2009). Thus, the synesthetic Stroop test demonstrates the automaticity of associations, but cannot distinguish synesthetes from those with synesthesia-like associations formed through training or long-term exposure (Kim, Blake, and Palmeri 2006; Sagiv 2005).

Notwithstanding Stroop-type effects in highly trained non-synesthetes, the consensus among researchers is that synesthesia is something other than everyday long-term memory associations. Some synesthetes appear to have concurrents that are highly similar to veridical real-world percepts. One commonly cited study is Ramachandran and Hubbard's (2001) experiment involving an embedded shapes task. In the task, graphemes are arranged in a matrix such that the matrix appears to have a shape embedded within it (e.g., a triangle of Ss within a random array of 5s). Synesthetes identify the embedded shapes more accurately than controls and it has been suggested that they are facilitated by the differences in synesthetic color between the shape and the background array (Ramachandran and Azoulai 2006; although see Rothen and Meier 2009 and

Rich and Mattingley, Chapter 14, this volume, for a thorough dissection of this finding). Synesthetic colors also appear to affect apparent motion perception (Ramachandran and Azoulai 2006) and "interact" with physically printed colors to influence motion perception (Kim, Blake, and Palmeri 2006). In one experiment, Kim, Blake, and Palmeri (2006) found that for two synesthetes but not for controls, the perceived direction of motion in an ambiguous display was biased by the location of inducing graphemes in successive frames (see Kim and Blake, Chapter 15, this volume).

Neuroimaging studies confirm synesthesia's authenticity by demonstrating that synesthetic experiences are embodied by differences in the brains of synesthetes. Using positron emission tomography, Paulesu et al. (1995) showed visual association cortex activation in synesthetes in response to spoken words. This was the first group study of the synesthetic brain using functional neuroimaging. Focusing on colored hearing but employing functional magnetic resonance imaging (fMRI), Nunn et al. (2002) found that synesthetes who associated spoken words with colors showed left hemispheric visual cortex activation, specifically in the V4/V8 region. This pattern of activation in the human "color center" was not seen when synesthetes listened to tones, nor was it observed in control participants who were first trained to associate colors with words and then instructed to visualize colors when hearing word matches in the scanner. This result contests the claim that synesthesia is akin to non-synesthetic mental imagery. Unlike controls, synesthetes who associate *written* letters with colors also show V4/V8 activation, although in this case differential brain activity appears to be bilateral (Sperling et al. 2006). Blakemore and colleagues (2005) used fMRI to assess mirror-touch synesthesia. Mirror-touch synesthete C showed significantly greater somatosensory activation than non-synesthete controls when observing people being touched. Rouw and Scholte (2007) used diffusion tensor imaging to demonstrate that grapheme-color synesthetes have white matter structure abnormalities not seen in matched, non-synesthete controls. For a final example, an electrophysiological study by Brang et al. (2008) revealed that when the synesthetic color (e.g., blue) of an achromatic grapheme (e.g., "2") is congruent to a color contextually primed by a sentence (e.g., "The sky is ... "), synesthetes show different brainwave responses than control participants.

In summary, both behavioral and neuroimaging methodologies stand alongside the TOG in providing adequate and ample evidence for the genuineness of synesthesia. In the next section we outline how the TOG can be used to study fundamental properties of synesthesia beyond the mere fact that it is genuine. One such property is its prevalence within the population.

PREVALENCE OF SYNESTHESIA

Remarking on the universality of the condition, Ginsberg claimed that everyone has synesthesia in some form. Instead of discriminating between synesthetes and non-synesthetes he proposed that, "in 15% of the population [synesthesia] is so intense as to be more noticeable than in the other 85%" (1923, 589). Could it be true that most of us have associations on the less-pronounced-and-detectable end of a synesthetic spectrum? Or, is it that we are all born with synesthesia but for most of us being a synesthete is a transient developmental stage (Baron-Cohen 1996; Maurer 1997)? Do we all have the potential to become synesthetes but the condition manifests itself only in some of us for some reason? And what are the factors that influence the development of synesthesia or cause synesthetes to retain the ability that the majority of people lose? Answers to these questions rely in part on knowing the prevalence of synesthesia, a figure that has been discussed and debated for at least 100 years (Calkins 1893; Galton 1883; Simner and Holenstein 2007; Simner et al. 2006). Table 1.1 reviews estimates for the prevalence of all forms of synesthesia as well as the most common forms (those involving color associations for letters, digits, and words; Blake et al. 2005; Day 2005; Harrison and Baron-Cohen 1997; Rich, Bradshaw, and Mattingley 2005; Ward and Simner 2005).

Why have estimates been so divergent? Almost all of the studies listed in Table 1.1 depended on self-referred samples and were thus susceptible to a self-referral bias. If we count synesthetes by relying on them to come forward for testing, we will of course omit all of those synesthetes who do not make the effort to present themselves. One exception is the study by Simner and colleagues (2006), which avoided the self-referral bias and yielded the most reliable estimate of the prevalence of synesthesia to date: at least 4.4% of the population (described in detail later). Differences in prevalence estimates might also stem from other sampling biases, methodological dissimilarities across studies, differences in the variants of interest, and composition of cohorts.

A related issue is that synesthesia's heterogeneous manifestations and unknown etiologies make it difficult to propose accurate diagnostic criteria or a standard definition. It will be challenging to reliably establish the population prevalence until standard terminology is developed and consistently implemented. Investigators often struggle to define what does and does not count as synesthesia, and estimates fluctuate when certain variants are consequently omitted from some studies but included in others. Often, a crucial deciding factor is whether or not the variant can be subjected to consistency testing. Self-reported variants that seem obscure or unstable tend to be excluded from discussions of prevalence only to be included once their consistency can be proven. One example is ordinal linguistic personification (OLP), a variant in which genders, personalities, cognitive attributes, and other animate qualities are assigned to linguistic units from ordinal sequences (e.g., to letters, numbers, names of days; Simner and Holenstein 2007), for example, 7 might be a jovial woman, 8 a young man, etc. Demonstrating that OLP synesthetes' inducer–concurrent associations were not only consistent but also automatic, and often present with other forms, Simner and Holenstein argued that OLP should be considered as genuine as the more prototypical manifestations of synesthesia. However, the status of OLP as a distinct variant remains unresolved. At one time, number forms occupied this same category of ambiguous synesthetic phenomena (Sagiv et al. 2006) and even color associations for days of the week were dismissed as non-synesthetic (Baron-Cohen et al. 1996). How to categorize new or suspected variants is an important question for future prevalence research.

Table 1.1 Prevalence estimates for "lexical–color" or any variant of synesthesia in adult samples between 1893 and 2006[a]

Variant(s) assessed	Study	Variant as defined by study	N	Percentage
Colors induced by lexical stimuli	Flournoy (1893)[b]	Colored hearing	370	16.7
	Baron-Cohen et al. (1996)	Word-color	55000	0.05
	Mulvenna et al. (2004)[c]	Grapheme-color	445	0.9
	Simner et al. (2006)	Day-color	500	2.8
	Simner et al. (2006)	Colored letters and numbers	1190	1.1
	Simner et al. (2006)	Colored letters and numbers	500	1.4
	Simner et al. (2006)	Month-color	500	1
Any variant	Bleuler and Lehmann (1881)[d]	Double sensations	600	12.5
	Cytowic (1989)[e]	Any	–	0.004
	Ginsberg (1923)	Any	–	15
	Cytowic (1994)[f]	Any	–	0.001
	Emrich (2001)[e]	Any	–	0.24
	Ramachandran and Hubbard (2001a)	Any	–	0.5
	Cytowic (2002)	Any	–	0.05
	Rich, Bradshaw, and Mattingley (2005)[g]	Any	–	0.024
	Simner et al. (2006)	Any	500	4.4

[a] Table excludes estimates from single-sex samples (i.e., Calkins 1893, 1895; Rose 1909) and subpopulations of interest (e.g., art students; Domino 1989)
[b] Cited in Phillips (1897)
[c] Cited in Hancock (2006)
[d] Cited in Ostwald (1964)
[e] Cited in Cytowic (2002)
[f] Cited in Baron-Cohen et al. (1996)
[g] Cited in Simner et al. (2006)

Fortunately, these challenges have not stopped researchers from attempting to determine prevalence, typically by measuring percept stability through a TOG in a large sample. Although earlier prevalence studies relied on self-referral, they were instrumental in bringing the issue of prevalence to the attention of researchers and showing how the TOG could be used to investigate it. Baron-Cohen and colleagues (1996) conducted the seminal study in this regard, when they assessed population prevalence by counting responses to newspaper advertisements asking word-color and sound-color synesthetes to contact their research group. Those who made contact were then given the TOG to confirm their reports. The advertisements were placed in publications read by two large, distinct populations within Cambridge, UK. Of 32 affirmative responses, 26 people met TOG criteria. Based on these results and the circulation figures of the publications, the group concluded that *at least* 1 in 2000 people (0.05%) had a form of synesthesia.

They were able, for the first time, to provide a reliable lower-end estimate (an "at least" number) of the prevalence of synesthesia within the population.

In what is considered the most accurate population prevalence study to date, Simner and colleagues (2006) attempted to minimize the self-referral bias by individually surveying participants from a large population of university students and museum-goers rather than asking synesthetes to present themselves. Participants were given a questionnaire about synesthesia and those indicating any form were given a list of appropriate stimuli (e.g., a list of letters to test letter-color synesthesia, a set of tastes to test taste-shape and taste-color synesthesia, and 40 scents to assess smell-color synesthesia) and asked to describe their concurrents in a series of TOGs. Twenty-two synesthetes with nine distinct variants were diagnosed using these individualized consistency tests. As noted earlier, this corresponded to a 4.4% population prevalence across the range of variants tested. To date, this is the only population prevalence study that has systematically confirmed the genuineness of each reported variant. It should be noted that even this study would not meet the stringent criteria of epidemiology since students and museum-goers are clearly not representative of the entire population. That is, they are not a random sample and as such, the researchers will inevitably have introduced biases, even unwittingly. It will be important for future studies of prevalence to use a clear screening instrument, which will likely involve a test of consistency, in a *truly random* population. This could be done by following a birth cohort (every child born in a given period in a given geographical area) or by exploiting a census of the adult population (one adult randomly selected from every household in a defined geographical area).

Most studies focus on determining the prevalence for a particular type. The first contemporary prevalence study of synesthesia focused on the grapheme-color variant. Later, Simner et al. (2006) found grapheme-color synesthesia to be even more common, identifying seven grapheme-color synesthetes in a group of 500. They replicated this estimate in a larger sample of 1190 children and adults (grapheme-color prevalence: 1.1%). Using computerized consistency tests to investigate grapheme-color associations in children, Simner et al. (2009) suggested 1.3% ($N = 615$) of 6- and 7-year-olds are synesthetes. Moving away from the grapheme-color variant, Banissy et al. 2009 assessed the prevalence of mirror-touch synesthesia in a sample of 567 undergraduates.[3] By testing respondents indicating mirror-touch synesthesia on a screening questionnaire, they concluded that the variant affected 1.6% of the population. Given that the estimated prevalence of grapheme-color synesthesia is 1.1% to 1.4%, mirror-touch synesthesia may be another common form. Mann et al. (2009) reported a prevalence of 26% for time-space synesthesia in a sample of 50 undergraduates. These single-variant prevalence studies often verify each participant's reports, and thus may yield more accurate estimates than studies that verify only a subset then extrapolate the prevalence for all types of synesthesia.

---

[3] Of note, the sample solely consisted of undergraduates so the results may not generalize to the population.

Synesthesia has long been considered to be a predominantly female condition with female to male ratios ranging from 1.6:1 (Simner et al. 2009), 2:1 (Galton 1883; Ward and Simner 2005), 2.2:1 (Uhlich 1957, cited in Ward and Simner 2005), 2.5:1 (Cytowic 1989, cited in Cytowic 2002), 3:1 (Day 2005), 5:1 (Emrich 2001, cited in Ward and Simner 2005), 5.5:1 (Baron-Cohen et al. 1996), 6:1 (Barnett et al. 2008), to 6.2:1 (Rich, Bradshaw, and Mattingley 2005). However, the existence of this female bias continues to be disputed. Simner et al. (2006) found a 1:1 female to male ratio, suggesting that the supposed predominance of female synesthetes in past studies might be attributed to or exaggerated by the self-referral bias; there are known differences in self-reporting behavior among males and females, with women being more likely to come forward to report atypical behavior even if that behavior exists equally across the sexes (Simner et al. 2006). This argument is strengthened by the fact that when family members of participants in Ward and Simner's (2005) self-referred sample were asked about their experiences, the sex bias was reduced from 3.7:1 (original ratio) to 2:1 (ratio including family members; Ward and Simner 2005). Barnett et al. (2008) reported a 6:1 female to male ratio that did not change with the assessment of family members, suggesting the sex difference cannot be explained by methodological artifacts alone. However, a portion of the data contributing to this ratio appears to come from unverified self-report, making it difficult to determine its accuracy. The true sex ratio will be better established in a truly random population study.

Conclusion

Synesthesia research has advanced significantly from early explorations of the phenomenon. The current consensus is that synesthesia is much more common than once thought, with a complex genetic basis likely involving "multiple modes of inheritance" (Asher et al. 2009, 279). Family studies constrain the list of possible underlying mechanisms of synesthesia, showing that various forms can exist within one family, with phenotypes differing even among close relatives (e.g., a taste-shape synesthete whose children experience "lexical-color" synesthesia; Barnett et al. 2008). This finding suggests there is some common basis for most, if not all, of these anomalous experiences.

A universally recognized diagnostic method still does not exist and subjective experiences still evade direct measurement. However, numerous tools now exist to assess synesthesia's distinctive correlates and assert its genuineness. To date, empirically authenticated features include: remarkable test–retest reliability over years (year-long test–retest interval: Baron-Cohen et al. 1993; 2-year interval: Simner and Holenstein 2007; 5-year interval: Jordan 1917; 8-year interval: Phillips 1897; 30-year interval: Simner and Logie 2007), activity in the human color center upon hearing words (Nunn et al. 2002), larger pupillary diameter while viewing incongruent pairings during Stroop tests (Paulsen and Laeng 2006), and outperformance of controls on embedded shape identification (Ramachandran and Hubbard 2001; Ward et al. 2009).

A foreseeable next step is uncovering how frequently synesthesia occurs in subpopulations of interest. Is the rate of synesthesia higher in child populations and what is the mechanism behind associations that anecdotally cease to exist in the transition from childhood to adulthood (Marks 1975; Simner et al. 2009)? Or, how often do synesthesia and epilepsy co-occur (Baron-Cohen et al. 2007; Cytowic 2002)? Of particular interest is the prevalence of synesthesia in the autistic population—one in which sensory atypicalities, including synesthetic experiences have been reported (Asher et al. 2009; Baron-Cohen et al. 2007; Kemner et al. 1995; see Cesaroni and Garber 1991, for reports of "multichannel receptivity" in autism spectrum conditions). Future research should address these questions.

Acknowledgements

DJ was supported by the Gates Foundation, and SBC and CA by the MRC, during the period of this work. We are grateful to Bhismadev Chakrabarti, Simon Fisher, and Teresa Tavassoli for discussions, and to Maria Wyke for early inspiration.

References

Asher, Julian, Michael R. F. Aitken, Nasr Farooqi, Sameer Kurmani, and Simon Baron-Cohen. 2006. Diagnosing and phenotyping visual synaesthesia—a preliminary evaluation of the revised test of genuineness (TOG-R). *Cortex* 42:137–146.

Asher, Julian, Janine A. Lamb, Denise Brocklebank, Jean-Baptiste Cazier, Elena Maestrini, Laura Addis, Mallika Sen, Simon Baron-Cohen, and Anthony P. Monaco. 2009. A whole-genome scan and fine-mapping linkage study of auditory-visual synaesthesia reveals evidence of linkage to chromosomes 2q24, 5q33, 6p12, and 12p12. *American Journal of Human Genetics* 84:279–285.

Banissy, Michael J., Roi Cohen Kadosh, Gerrit W. Maus, Vincent Walsh, and Jamie Ward. 2009. Prevalence, characteristics and a neurocognitive model of mirror-touch synaesthesia. *Experimental Brain Research* 198 (2–3):261–272.

Barnett, Kylie J., Ciara Finucane, Julian Asher, Gary Bargary, Aiden P. Corvin, Fiona N. Newell, and Kevin J. Mitchell. 2008. Familial patterns and the origins of individual differences in synaesthesia. *Cognition* 106 (2):871–893.

Baron-Cohen, Simon. 1996. Is there a phase of synaesthesia in normal development? *Psyche* 2 (27).

Baron-Cohen, Simon, Daniel Bor, Jac Billington, Julian Asher, Sally Wheelwright, and Chris Ashwin. 2007. Savant memory in a man with colour-number synaesthesia and Asperger Syndrome. *Journal of Consciousness Studies* 14:237–251.

Baron-Cohen, Simon, Lucy Burt, Fiona Laittan-Smith, John E. Harrison, and Patrick Bolton. 1996. Synaesthesia: Prevalence and familiarity. *Perception* 25:1073–1079.

Baron-Cohen, Simon, and John Harrison. 1999. Synaesthesia: A challenge for developmental cognitive neuroscience. In *Neurodevelomental Disorders*, ed. Helen Tager-Flusberg, 491–504. Cambridge, MA: MIT Press.

Baron-Cohen, Simon, John Harrison, Laura H. Goldstein, and Maria Wyke. 1993. Coloured speech perception: Is synaesthesia what happens when modularity breaks down? *Perception* 22:419–426.

Baron-Cohen, Simon, Maria Wyke, and Colin Binnie. 1987. Hearing words and seeing colours: An experimental investigation of a case of synaesthesia. *Perception* 16:761–767.

Beeli, Gian, Michaela Esslen, and Lutz Jäncke. 2005. When coloured sounds taste sweet. *Nature* 434:38.

Blake, Randolph, Thomas J. Palmeri, Rene Marois, and Chai-Youn Kim. 2005. On the perceptual reality of synesthetic color. In *Synaesthesia: Perspectives from Cognitive Neuroscience*, ed. Lynn Robertson and Noam Sagiv, 47–73. New York: Oxford University Press.

Blakemore, S.-J., D. Bristow, G. Bird, C. Frith, and J. Ward. 2005. Somatosensory activations during the observation of touch and a case of vision-touch synaesthesia. *Brain* 128:1571–1583.

Bor, Daniel, Jac Billington, and Simon Baron-Cohen. 2007. Savant memory for digits in a case of synaesthesia and Asperger syndrome is related to hyperactivity in the lateral prefrontal cortex. *Neurocase* 13 (5–6):311–319.

Brang, David, L. Edwards, Vilayanur S. Ramachandran, and Seana Coulson. 2008. Is the sky 2? Contextual priming in grapheme-color synaesthesia. *Psychological Science* 19 (5):421–428.

Calkins, Mary W. 1893. A statistical study of pseudo-chromesthesia and of mental-forms. *American Journal of Psychology* 5:439–466.

———. 1895. Synaesthesia. *American Journal of Psychology* 7:90–107.

Cesaroni, Laura, and Malcolm Garber. 1991. Exploring the experience of autism through firsthand accounts. *Journal of Autism and Developmental Disorders* 21 (3):303–313.

Cytowic, Richard E. 1989. *Synaesthesia: A Union of the Senses.* 1st ed. New York: Springer-Verlag.

———. 2002. *Synaesthesia: A Union of the Senses.* 2nd ed. Cambridge, MA: MIT Press.

Day, Sean. 2005. Some demographic and socio-cultural aspects of synesthesia. In *Synaesthesia: Perspectives from Cognitive Neuroscience*, ed. Lynn Robertson and Noam Sagiv, 11–33. Oxford: Oxford University Press.

Domino, George. (1989). Synaesthesia and creativity in fine arts students: An empirical look. *Creativity Research Journal*, 2, 17–29.

Dresslar, F. B. 1903. Are chromaesthesias variable?—A study of an individual case. *American Journal of Psychology* 14:632–646.

Duffy, Patricia Lynne. 2001. *Blue Cats and Chartreuse Kittens.* New York: Time Books.

Eagleman, David M., and Melvyn A. Goodale. 2009. Why color synesthesia involves more than color. *Trends in Cognitive Sciences* 13 (7):288–292.

Eagleman, David M., Arielle D. Kagan, Stephanie S. Nelson, Deepak Sagaram, and Anand K. Sarma. 2007. A standardized test battery for the study of synesthesia. *Journal of Neuroscience Methods* 159 (1):139–145.

Elias, Lorin J., Deborah M. Saucier, Colleen Hardie, and Gordon E. Sarty. 2003. Dissociating semantic and perceptual components of synaesthesia: Behavioural and functional neuroanatomical investigations. *Cognitive Brain Research* 16 (2):232–237.

Flournoy, Theodore. 1893. *Des phenomenes de synopsie.* Paris: Felix Alcan.

Galton, Francis. 1883. *Inquiries into human faculty and its development.* London: Dent & Sons.

Ginsberg, Leon. 1923. A case of synaesthesia. *American Journal of Psychology* 34:582–589.

Grossenbacher, Peter G. 1997. Perception and sensory information in synaesthetic experience. In *Synaesthesia: classic and Contemporary Readings*, ed. Simon Baron-Cohen and John E. Harrison, 148–172. Oxford: Blackwell.

Grossenbacher, Peter G., and Christopher T. Lovelace. 2001. Mechanisms of synesthesia: cognitive and physiological constraints. *Trends in Cognitive Sciences* 5:36–41.

Hancock, Peter. 2006. Monozygotic twins' colour-number association: A case study. *Cortex* 42 (2):147–150.

Harrison, John, and Simon Baron-Cohen. 1997. Synaesthesia: an introduction. In *Synaesthesia: Classic and Contemporary Readings*, ed. Simon Baron-Cohen and John E. Harrison, 3–16. Oxford: Blackwell.

Jacobs, Lawrence, Alice Karpik, Diana Bozian, and Svend Gothgen. 1981. Auditory-Visual Synaesthesia: Sound-Induced Photisms. *Archives of Neurology* 38:211–216.

Jordan, David S. 1917. The colors of letters. *Science* 46 (1187):311–312.

Kemner, Chantal, Marinus N. Verbaten, Juliane M. Cuperus, Gert Camfferman, and Herman van Engeland. 1995. Auditory event-related brain potentials in autistic children and three different control groups. *Biological Psychiatry* 38:150–165.

Kim, Chai-Youn, and Randolph Blake. 2013. Revisiting the perceptual reality of synesthetic colour. In *The Oxford Handbook of Synesthesia*, ed. Julia Simner and Edward M. Hubbard, 283–316. Oxford: Oxford University Press.

Kim, Chai-Youn, Randolph Blake, and Thomas J. Palmeri. 2006. Perceptual interaction between real and synesthetic colors. *Cortex* 42 (2):195–203.

Mann, Heather, Jason Korzenko, Jonathan S. A. Carriere, and Michael J. Dixon. 2009. Time–space synaesthesia—a cognitive advantage? *Consciousness and Cognition* 18:619–627.

Marks, Lawrence E. 1975. On coloured-hearing synaesthesia. *Psychological Bulletin* 82 (3):303–331.

Maurer, Daphne. 1997. Neonatal synaesthesia: implications for the processing of speech and faces. In *Synaesthesia: Classic and Contemporary Readings*, ed. Simon Baron-Cohen and John E. Harrison, 224–242. Oxford: Blackwell.

Meier, B., and N. Rothen. 2009. Training grapheme-colour associations produces a synaesthetic Stroop effect, but not a conditioned synaesthetic response. *Neuropsychologia* 47 (4):1208–1211.

Mills, Carol B., Edith H. Boteler, and Glenda K. Oliver. 1999. Digit synaesthesia: A case study using a Stroop-type test. *Cognitive Neuropsychology* 16 (2):181–191.

Nunn, J., L. Gregory, R. Morris, M. Brammer, E. Bullmore, J. Harrison, S. Williams, Simon Baron-Cohen, and J. Gray. 2002. Functional magnetic resonance imaging of synaesthesia: activation of colour vision area V8 by spoken words. *Nature Neuroscience* 5:371–375.

Odgaard, Eric C., John H. Flowers, and H. L. Bradman. 1999. An investigation of the cognitive and perceptual dynamics of a colour-digit synaesthete. *Perception* 28:651–664.

Ostwald, Peter F. (1964). Color hearing. *Archives of General Psychiatry,* 11:40–47.

Paulesu, Eraldo, John Harrison, Simon Baron-Cohen, John Watson, Laura Goldstein, John Heather, Richard Frakowiak, and Christopher Frith. 1995. The physiology of coloured hearing. A positron emission tomography activation study of coloured-word synaesthesia. *Brain* 118:661–676.

Paulsen, Helle G., and Bruno Laeng. 2006. Pupillometry of grapheme-color synaesthesia. *Cortex* 42 (2):290–294.

Phillips, D. E. 1897. Genesis of number-forms. *American Journal of Psychology* 8:506–527.

Podoll, Klaus and Derek Robinson. 2002. Auditory-visual synaesthesia in a patient with basilar migraine. *Journal of Neurology* 249:476–477.

Ramachandran, Vilayanur S., and Shai Azoulai. 2006. Synesthetically induced colors evoke apparent-motion perception. *Perception* 35 (11):1557–1560.

Ramachandran, Vilayanur S., and Edward M. Hubbard. 2001. Psychophysical investigations into the neural basis of synaesthesia. *Proceedings of the Royal Society of London B* 268:979–983.

Rich, Anina N., John L. Bradshaw, and Jason B. Mattingley. 2005. A systematic, large-scale study of synaesthesia: Implications for the role of early experience in lexical-colour associations. *Cognition* 98 (1):53–84.

Rich, Anina N., and Jason B. Mattingley. 2013. The role of attention in synesthesia. In *The Oxford Handbook of Synesthesia*, ed. Julia Simner and Edward M. Hubbard, 265–282. Oxford: Oxford University Press.

Riggs, Lorrin A., and Theodore Karwoski. 1934. Synaesthesia. *British Journal of Psychology* 25:29–41.

Rose, K. B. (1909). Some statistics on synaesthesia. *American Journal of Psychology*, 22, 529–539.

Rouw, Romke, and H. S. Scholte. 2007. Increased structural connectivity in grapheme-color synesthesia. *Nature Neuroscience* 10 (6):792–797.

Sagiv, Noam. 2005. Synaesthesia in perspective. In *Synaesthesia: Perspectives from Cognitive Neuroscience*, ed. Lynn Robertson and Noam Sagiv, 3–10. New York: Oxford University Press.

Sagiv, Noam, Julia Simner, James Collins, Brian Butterworth, and Jamie Ward. 2006. What is the relationship between synaesthesia and visuo-spatial number forms? *Cognition* 101 (1):114–128.

Simner, Julia. 2012. Defining synaesthesia. *British Journal of Psychology* 103:1–15.

Simner, Julia, Jenny Harrold, Harriet Creed, Louise Monro, and Louise Foulkes. 2009. Early detection of markers for synaesthesia in childhood populations. *Brain* 132:57–64.

Simner, Julia, and Emma Holenstein. 2007. Ordinal linguistic personification as a variant of synesthesia. *Journal of Cognitive Neuroscience* 19 (4):694–703.

Simner, Julia, and Robert H. Logie. 2007. Synaesthetic consistency spans decades in a lexical-gustatory synaesthete. *Neurocase* 13 (5–6):358–365.

Simner, Julia, Catherine Mulvenna, Noam Sagiv, Elias Tsakanikos, Sarah A. Witherby, Christine Fraser, Kirsten Scott, and Jamie Ward. 2006. Synaesthesia: The prevalence of atypical cross-modal experiences. *Perception* 35 (8):1024–1033.

Simner, Julia, Jamie Ward, Monika Lanz, Ashok Jansari, Krist Noonan, Louise Glover, and David A. Oakley. 2005. Non-random associations of graphemes to colours in synaesthetic and non-synaesthetic populations. *Cognitive Neuropsychology* 22 (8):1069–1085.

Simpson, Lorna, and Peter McKellar. 1955. Types of synaesthesia. *Journal of Mental Science* 101:141–147.

Smilek, Daniel, Kelly A. Malcolmson, Jonathan S. A. Carriere, Meghan Eller, Donna Kwan, and Michael Reynolds. 2007. When '3' is a jerk and 'T" is a king: Personifying inanimate objects in synesthesia. *Journal of Cognitive Neuroscience* 19 (6):981–992.

Sperling, Julia M., David Prvulovic, David E. J. Linden, Wolf Singer, and Aglaja Stirn. 2006. Neuronal correlates of colour-graphemic synaesthesia: A fMRI study. *Cortex* 42 (2):295–303.

Stroop, John R. 1935. Studies in interference in serial verbal reactions. *Journal of Experimental Psychology* 18:643–661.

Ward, Jamie. 2004. Emotionally mediated synaesthesia. *Cognitive Neuropsychology* 21 (7):761–772.

Ward, Jamie, Brett Huckstep, and Elias Tsakanikos. 2006. Sound-colour synaesthesia: To what extent does it use cross-modal mechanisms common to us all? *Cortex* 42 (2):264–280.

Ward, Jamie, Clare Jonas, Zoltan Dienes, and Anil Seth. 2009. Grapheme-colour synaesthesia improves detection of embedded shapes, but without pre-attentive 'pop-out' of synaesthetic colour. *Proceedings of the Royal Society B: Biological Sciences* 277 (1684):1021–1026.

Ward, Jamie, and Jason B. Mattingley. 2006. Synaesthesia: An overview of contemporary findings and controversies. *Cortex* 42 (2):129–136.

Ward, Jamie, and Julia Simner. 2003. Lexical-gustatory synaesthesia: linguistic and conceptual factors. *Cognition* 89 (3):237–261.

——. 2005. Is synaesthesia an X-linked dominant trait with lethality in males? *Perception* 34 (5):611–623.

Ward, Jamie, Julia Simner, and Vivian Auyeung. 2005. A comparison of lexical-gustatory and grapheme-colour synaesthesia. *Cognitive Neuropsychology* 22 (1):28–41.

Wollen, Keith A., and Frank T. Ruggiero. 1983. Coloured-letter synaesthesia. *Journal of Mental Imagery* 7:83–86.

CHAPTER 2

THE GENETICS AND INHERITANCE OF SYNESTHESIA

JULIAN E. ASHER AND
DUNCAN A. CARMICHAEL

EARLY EVIDENCE FOR GENETIC TRANSMISSION OF SYNESTHESIA: PREVALENCE, SEX BIAS, AND FAMILIALITY

Synesthesia is a neurodevelopmental condition characterized by anomalous sensory perception and associated alterations in cognitive function due to interference from synesthetic percepts. For synesthetes, a stimulus ("inducer") in one modality triggers an automatic, consistent sensation ("concurrent") in another modality. For example, in auditory-visual synesthesia, sound triggers the perception of color (Baron-Cohen, Wyke, and Binnie 1987; Ward, Huckstep, and Tsakanikos 2006). For many synesthetes, the synesthetic experience crosses modalities (e.g., sound-to-color) while for other synesthetes, the inducer and synesthetic concurrent occur in different facets of the same modality; in visual grapheme-color synesthesia, for example, reading black-on-white text triggers the perception of color (Mattingley et al. 2001; Ramachandran and Hubbard 2001). While synesthetic inducers vary widely (e.g., sounds, tastes, graphemes), the resulting percepts are almost always visual, most often in the form of color although visually salient texture and movement have also been described (Asher et al. 2006; Baron-Cohen, Wyke, and Binnie 1987; Simner et al. 2006).

The focus of this chapter is on the genetics of synesthesia, which has important implications for its underlying etiology. This etiology can also be illuminated by examining the co-occurrence of synesthesia with other cognitive phenotypes. Using neuroimaging techniques, alterations in white matter have been observed which could indicate the existence of overall increased connectivity in the brains of synesthetes (Rouw and Scholte 2007). Studies also show that anomalous activation occurs in brain regions involved in color processing when color-experiencing synesthetes are exposed to syn-esthetic triggers (e.g., Nunn et al. 2002). Although many synesthetes report their syn-esthesia to be neutral or even pleasant, a growing body of evidence indicates that the simultaneous perception of normal and synesthetic percepts can result in perceptual and cognitive dysfunction, with particularly strong effects on linguistic (Mattingley et al. 2001) and numerical (Green and Goswami, 2007) processing. Conversely, synesthesia has also been implicated in "positive" cognitive variation, including superior perform-ance on certain perceptual tests (Ramachandran and Hubbard 2001; see Kim and Blake, Chapter 15, this volume) and improved recall (Smilek et al. 2002; see Meier and Rothen, Chapter 35, this volume). One of the most interesting connections is between synesthe-sia and different forms of eidetic ("photographic") memory (Glicksohn, Steinbach, and Elimalach-Malmilyan 1999; Luria 1968), including absolute ("perfect") musical pitch (Rizzo and Eslinger 1989), and with heightened visual memory and imagery more gen-erally (see Price, Chapter 37, this volume). Synesthesia has also been implicated in cases of savantism (Baron-Cohen et al. 2007; Simner, Mayo, and Spiller 2009; see Spiller and Jansari, Chapter 36, this volume). We shall return later to examine these findings in our discussion of candidate genes.

The tendency of synesthesia to cluster in families was first reported in 1883 by Sir Francis Galton (Galton, 1883), 71 years after synesthesia was first described in the sci-entific literature (by Sachs in 1812; see Jewanski, Day, and Ward 2009). Despite this early observation, the genetics of synesthesia remained unexplored for most of the twentieth century. During the early part of the last century, the techniques required to investigate the role of genes were simply unavailable; then later, following the development of genetic techniques, scientific resources were initially focused on identifying genes associated with more pathological conditions. Towards the very end of the twentieth century, how-ever, the first attempts were made to investigate the hereditary nature of synesthesia.

The development of suitable diagnostic methodologies to verify genuine synesthetes played a key role in enabling researchers to investigate the genetics of synesthesia. These methodologies relied (and still rely to this day) on the consistency of synesthetes' reports about their percepts for any given trigger. Consistency is considered to be a hall-mark of authenticity because for synesthetes, the particular concurrent triggered by a given inducer (e.g., the very specific shade of red triggered by the letter "A") tends to stay the same over time—even over very long time periods such as years and decades (e.g., Simner and Logie, 2008; see Johnson, Allison, and Baron-Cohen, Chapter 1, this vol-ume, for review). In contrast, non-synesthetes who invent analogous mappings by free association tend to be far less consistent over time, and this difference forms the basis of what has become known as the Test of Genuineness (TOG; Asher et al. 2006; Baron-Cohen, Wyke, and Binnie 1987; Baron-Cohen et al. 1993). The use of the TOG (or later versions; e.g., the Revised Test of Genuineness (TOG-R); Asher et al. 2006) to identify synesthetes remains central to the study of synesthesia in general, and to studies of its familiality.

At the birth of modern synesthesia research in the final decades of the twentieth century, there was little empirical evidence regarding either the prevalence of synesthesia or the ratio at which it occurs across the sexes, both of which are important for investigations of inheritance. Using the TOG, studies aimed to establish the prevalence and gender ratio as a starting point to explore the underlying genetics of the phenomenon. However, subsequent estimates of the prevalence of synesthesia varied rather widely. Studies estimating prevalence by self-referral methods (i.e., asking synesthetes to come forward through advertising media) estimated its prevalence at 0.05% to 1% of the population (Barnett et al. 2008; Baron-Cohen et al. 1996; Simner et al. 2006), while studies directly testing samples of the population without relying on synesthetes' self-motivation found it to be as high as 4% (Simner et al. 2006; see Johnson Allison, and Baron-Cohen, Chapter 1, this volume, for an evaluation of previous prevalence methodologies). The use of different definitions of "synesthesia" for the various prevalence studies further complicated matters; many of the earlier studies (e.g., Baron-Cohen et al. 1996) focused on what was at the time the most well-known phenotype (auditory-visual synesthesia, including music-color synesthesia which is now known to be a relatively uncommon phenotype) while the later studies included a much wider range of phenotypes (notably the most common variant, day-color synesthesia; e.g., Simner et al. 2006). Given recent evidence of clustering amongst synesthetic phenotypes and, specifically, the evidence that that auditory-visual and day-color synesthesia may be entirely separate phenomena (Novich, Cheng, and Eagleman 2011), revisiting prevalence figures for different clusters of synesthesia would now be warranted. However, while the prevalence of synesthesia has been controversial (for review, see Johnson, Allison, and Baron-Cohen, Chapter 1, this volume) the results of modern familiality studies provided clear evidence for a strong genetic component in synesthesia by showing greater than 40% prevalence amongst the first- or second-degree relatives of known synesthetes (Barnett et al. 2008; Baron-Cohen et al. 1996; Ward and Simner, 2005).[1]

Initial pedigree analyses of multiplex families (families containing multiple synesthetes; Bailey and Johnson 1997; Baron-Cohen et al. 1996) supported the theory that synesthesia may be a highly penetrant Mendelian disorder showing a major gene effect and a dominant mode of inheritance. By way of background, we provide here a brief overview of this terminology and then describe how such a theory was informed by early data on the relative proportion of female to male synesthetes. Simply put, a Mendelian disorder is a condition caused by a mutation in a single gene. Penetrance refers to the proportion of people possessing a particular variant of the gene in question who exhibit the phenotype (if the variant has a penetrance of 35%, only 35% of the people with that

---

[1] The extent to which synesthesia occurs in multiple family members may not be obvious because the condition can appear in different manifestations within the same family (e.g., a sister with colored words may have a brother whose words trigger taste; e.g., Ward and Simner 2003). Indeed, data from a large-scale familiality study performed in Ireland with systematic screening of the first-degree relatives of synesthetic probands revealed 11% of "non-synesthete" relatives to be synesthetes of a different phenotype than the probands (Barnett et al. 2008). This means that reports from probands may underestimate the extent of familiality in synesthesia if they focus on one variant only.

variant will show the phenotype). A condition is considered highly penetrant if a majority of people with that variant express the associated phenotype. To understand how these relate to inheritance and sex biases, we must also understand the inheritance of chromosomes.

Chromosomes are strings of nucleic acids and protein which carry genetic information in the form of genes. Humans possess 23 pairs of chromosomes, and inherit one chromosome per pair from each parent (for more information on this inheritance, see later in this chapter). As a consequence, we possess two copies (known as *alleles*) of the same gene, one on each chromosome—one inherited from our father, and one from our mother. In Mendelian terms, an allele can be *dominant* or *recessive*. If the possession of a single allele is sufficient to cause the expression of a trait in the phenotype, that allele is dominant. A condition with a dominant mode of inheritance only requires one of the two alleles in a particular pair to cause the phenotype to be expressed, so in effect, only one parent needs to carry the allele and pass it on to their offspring. If a pair of alleles consists of a dominant and a recessive copy, the dominant allele will mask the effect of the recessive allele in the phenotype. So for conditions that have a recessive mode of inheritance, the offspring must inherit a recessive copy from both parents before its effect can be expressed in the resulting phenotype.

The inheritance of synesthesia initially appeared to be linked to the X chromosome because more females seemed to be affected than males and there was a notable absence of confirmed cases of father-to-son (i.e., male-to-male) transmission. Females inherit two X chromosomes, while males inherit only one, this coming from their mother. Early studies suggested that there were six times more female synesthetes than male synesthetes (Baron-Cohen et al. 1996), and an initial meta-analysis performed by Bailey and Johnson in 1997 concluded that the available data at that time best fitted an X-linked dominant mode of inheritance. Because X-linked dominant inheritance alone cannot explain a female:male ratio greater than 3:1, the heavily skewed female presence was accounted for by suggesting that the putative "synesthesia gene" may be lethal in males causing death *in utero* (Bailey and Johnson 1997; Baron-Cohen et al. 1996). This could occur because males are hemizygous (meaning they possess only one copy of the X chromosome) and if that single copy were defective it could result in lethality.

However, more recent prevalence studies using different methodologies, and meta-analyses with larger data sets (e.g., Simner et al. 2006; Ward and Simner 2005) indicate that the female:male ratio may be far lower than previously believed (perhaps as low as 2:1 or even 1:1), calling the X-linked mode of inheritance into question. Furthermore, Ward and Simner (2005) showed that the male/female make-up of synesthetes within families does not support a model of male lethality: female synesthetes are just as likely to give birth to a son as to a daughter, and there was no difference in their number of brothers/sisters, aunts/uncles, or female/male cousins (see also Barnett et al. 2008). It was also suggested that the mode of inheritance was likely to be more complex, with skipped generations indicating reduced penetrance (Barnett et al. 2008; Simner et al. 2006; Ward and Simner 2005). Nonetheless, the enduring possibility of an elevated number of female synesthetes in sex comparisons (if not 1:1, then anywhere between 2:1

and 6:1 depending on methodology; and we return to this later) and the historical failure to detect any confirmed cases of male-to-male transmission made it imperative to directly test for the involvement of the X chromosome.

At present, the search for genes underpinning synesthesia is still in its infancy. Empirical evidence linking specific areas of the genome to synesthesia has been limited to a small handful of recent papers. Since the relative paucity of empirical studies precludes an extensive literature review, this chapter will focus on an in-depth discussion of the current literature, with particular emphasis on the seminal paper by Asher et al. (2009), the first genome-wide scan examining the genetic basis of synesthesia. We begin with an overview of the genetic concepts that are relevant to the findings reviewed in these family linkage studies.

What Is "Linkage" and Why Is It Important?

The initial phase of sexual reproduction involves a stage called *meiosis*, which takes place in the ovaries and testes. The cells produced by meiosis are gametes (eggs or sperm). In meiosis, 23 pairs of chromosomes—half having originated from each parent—exchange fragments of DNA and are recombined. This results in the formation of a new and unique set of chromosomes containing genes from both parents. Unlike normal cells, gametes have only half the usual number of chromosomes: only 23, rather than 46. (When sexual intercourse subsequently occurs, these combine with the gamete chromosomes from the sexual partner, and genes from both parties are then inherited by the resulting offspring. In this way, genes from all four grandparents are inherited by the child.) In meiosis, the proximity of genes to each other on a given chromosome governs the likelihood of whether those genes become separated or remain together during the process of recombination. The closer together genes are located, the more likely they are to remain together on the newly formed chromosome. This likelihood of being inherited together is referred to as "genetic linkage."

In genetic studies, linkage is commonly measured as a "log of odds" (LOD) ratio, which gives a statistical measure of the likelihood of genes remaining adjacent on the newly formed chromosome.[2] For example, a LOD score of 2 would indicate odds of 100:1 that linkage did not occur by chance and a LOD score of 3 would indicate odds of 1000:1. Linkage can be used to identify particular locations on a chromosome which

---

[2] As in any statistical analysis, it is necessary to ensure that the results obtained in a linkage study are not due to chance and the logarithm of the odds (LOD) score, introduced by Morton (1955), is a statistical measure of the evidence for linkage. LOD scores are calculated by comparing the likelihood of two alternative hypotheses: the likelihood of observing the genotypes obtained from the study at each meiosis under the hypothesis of linkage, to the likelihood of observing that genotype under the null hypothesis of no linkage, in a likelihood ratio. If the likelihood ratio ("odds") is greater than 1 it is said to support linkage. This is normally expressed as Z, the LOD score. The probability of linkage in a set of families can be calculated by summing the LOD scores across the sample.

contain genes responsible for a particular phenotype. *Microsatellites*, short sequences of repeating base-pairs of DNA distributed throughout the genome, can be used as genetic markers in familial linkage studies. In the same way that different family members can possess different versions of certain gene alleles, versions of microsatellites will also vary per family member. If we compare the microsatellites of affected versus non-affected family members, we can see which microsatellites are different and importantly, on which chromosomes these differences appear. Because of the principles governing genetic linkage, we can deduce that the locations at which the microsatellites differ are also likely to be the locations at which the genes causing the phenotype under investigation (e.g., synesthesia) are found. The implication is that the genes responsible for producing the phenotype will be in close proximity to the particular microsatellite markers found in affected family members.

FAMILY-BASED LINKAGE STUDIES

Evidence of linkage to chromosomes 2, 5, 6, and 12 (2q24, 5q33, 6p12, and 12p12)

Asher et al. (2009) conducted the first whole-genome scan for susceptibility genes linked to synesthesia. This study was conducted in a sample of 196 individuals who experience color synesthesia triggered by sounds and/or by spoken words (referred to henceforth as "auditory-visual synesthesia") from 43 multiplex families. Families were recruited in two waves, with 19 families recruited during the initial recruitment period (Wave 1), and 24 families recruited during the second recruitment period (Wave 2). Of particular interest, the sample included two families reporting male-to-male transmission of synesthesia (see Figure 2.1) and we return to this later in the chapter. Before starting the genome scan, Asher et al. confirmed the power of this sample to detect a major gene effect via computer simulations (SLINK; Weeks, Ott, and Lathrop, 1990) using the best available data on prevalence and mode of inheritance.

The sample was phenotyped using the TOG or TOG-R (Asher et al. 2006; Baron-Cohen et al. 1996). Phenotyping revealed 121 affected individuals and 68 unaffected individuals; seven individuals were treated as phenotype unknown (five children who were too young to undergo diagnostic testing and two reported synesthetes who were not available for testing). Genomic DNA was extracted from blood samples (Wave 1) or buccal swabs (Wave 2). Following extraction, DNA samples underwent whole-genome amplification—the production of larger usable samples of DNA from minute quantities.

Four hundred and ten highly polymorphic microsatellite markers were used in the genome scan. Asher et al. conducted a multipoint non-parametric linkage (NPL) analysis which estimates allele-sharing among all affected family members. NPL analysis makes no assumptions about the mode of inheritance, which makes it more sensitive

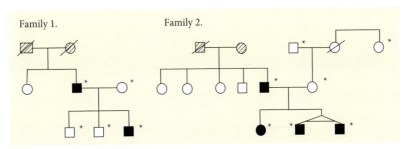

FIGURE 2.1 Pedigrees of families reporting male-to-male transmission of auditory-visual synesthesia. Hatched = phenotype unknown. Asterisk indicates an individual from whom DNA was obtained. Reprinted from *The American Journal of Human Genetics*, 84 (2), Julian E. Asher, Janine A. Lamb, Denise Brocklebank, Jean-Baptiste Cazier, Elena Maestrini, Laura Addis, Mallika Sen, Simon Baron-Cohen, and Anthony P. Monaco, A Whole-Genome Scan and Fine-Mapping Linkage Study of Auditory-Visual Synesthesia Reveals Evidence of Linkage to Chromosomes 2q24, 5q33, 6p12, and 12p12, pp. 279–285, Copyright (2009), with permission from Elsevier.

to linkage than parametric analysis (where a mode of inheritance must be specified) but it is less powerful as the candidate regions identified tend to be larger. The analysis detected 15 potential candidate regions with a LOD score >1 on 11 chromosomes (see Figure 2.2). Single-point NPL LOD scores for the linkage peaks were calculated using the same set of parameters. These regions were then fine mapped at higher density with additional microsatellites. Further NPL analysis of the fine-mapped regions identified four candidate regions with LOD >2. Suggestive linkage under the Lander and Kruglyak criteria (LOD >2.2; Lander and Kruglyak 1995) was detected at two of these regions, on chromosomes 5q33 (LOD = 2.3, p = 0.0006) and 6p12.3 (LOD = 2.37, p = 0.0005). All regions with LOD scores >2 were supported by single-point LOD scores >1 from a minimum of three markers.

In addition, Asher et al conducted a multipoint heterogeneity LOD (HLOD) score analysis using models derived from the best available estimates following pedigree analysis. HLOD analysis has greater power to detect linkage in the context of substantial genetic heterogeneity than either traditional parametric or NPL analyses. Given the lack of consensus regarding the prevalence of auditory-visual synesthesia in published prevalence studies (Baron-Cohen et al. 1996; Simner et al. 2006) a conservative estimate (genotype frequency = 0.01) was used for disease allele frequency in the analysis. Pedigree analysis of the sample revealed a dominant inheritance pattern (see Figure 2.3); but because skipping of generations has been observed both in this sample and in previous prevalence studies, initial penetrance for the dominant model was set at a variety of levels (see Asher et al. 2009 for details). Three models provided the best fit: dominant (penetrance = 0.65), dominant (penetrance = 0.90), and recessive (penetrance = 0.75). HLOD analysis was conducted using fine-mapping data whenever this was available and data from the primary genome scan data for the remainder of the genome.

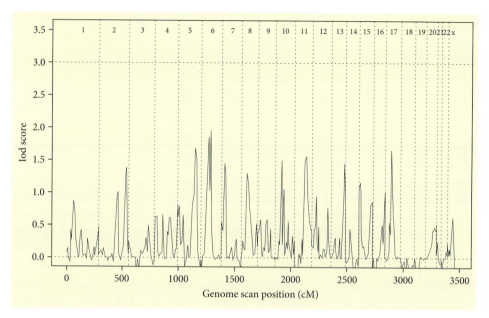

FIGURE 2.2 Results of the whole-genome scan. Generated by NPL analysis using MERLIN 1.1a with the exponential function. Reprinted from *The American Journal of Human Genetics*, 84 (2), Julian E. Asher, Janine A. Lamb, Denise Brocklebank, Jean-Baptiste Cazier, Elena Maestrini, Laura Addis, Mallika Sen, Simon Baron-Cohen, and Anthony P. Monaco, A Whole-Genome Scan and Fine-Mapping Linkage Study of Auditory-Visual Synesthesia Reveals Evidence of Linkage to Chromosomes 2q24, 5q33, 6p12, and 12p12, pp. 279–285, Copyright (2009), with permission from Elsevier.

Genome-wide empirical *p*-values for the HLOD analysis were calculated, correcting for multiple testing by estimating the null distribution over all genetic models in each simulation. Under the null hypothesis of no linkage anywhere in the genome, 1000 replicates were generated, retaining original pedigree structures and missing data patterns in order to reflect the real data. In accordance with the Lander and Kruglyak recommendation, thresholds were calculated for suggestive linkage (1000 LOD scores of equal or greater size in 1000 simulations), significant linkage (50 LOD scores of equal or greater size in 1000 simulations), and highly significant linkage (1 LOD score of equal or greater size observed in 1000 simulations) across the entire marker set. These simulations generated the following empirical genome-wide significance thresholds: 2.03 for suggestive linkage, 2.97 for significant linkage (*p* <0.05), and 5.70 for highly significant linkage (*p* <0.001). The empirical *p*-value for a peak in the analysis was set by counting how often a simulated unlinked LOD score of greater or equal value is seen in 1000 simulations.

The HLOD analysis detected one region of significant linkage on chromosome 2q24.1 (HLOD = 3.025, empirical genome-wide *p* = 0.047) and three regions of suggestive linkage on chromosomes 6p12.3 (HLOD = 2.272, empirical genome-wide *p* = 0.275), 12p12.1 (HLOD = 2.849, empirical *p* = 0.073), and 9q33.1 (HLOD = 2.473, empirical *p* = 0.188). A total of 23 regions with HLOD >1 were detected, 12 of which were also detected by the

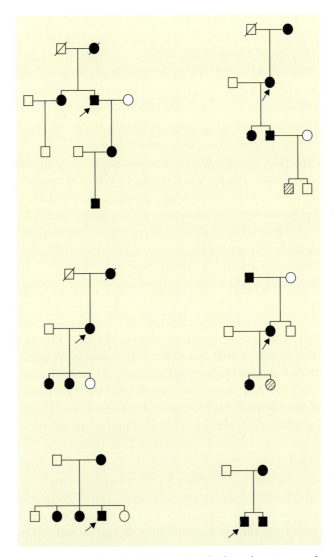

FIGURE 2.3 Representative sample of pedigrees. Hatched = phenotype unknown. Deceased individuals are included for information only with phenotypes based on clinical interview, and were excluded from the analysis. Reprinted from *The American Journal of Human Genetics*, 84 (2), Julian E. Asher, Janine A. Lamb, Denise Brocklebank, Jean-Baptiste Cazier, Elena Maestrini, Laura Addis, Mallika Sen, Simon Baron-Cohen, and Anthony P. Monaco, A Whole-Genome Scan and Fine-Mapping Linkage Study of Auditory-Visual Synesthesia Reveals Evidence of Linkage to Chromosomes 2q24, 5q33, 6p12, and 12p12, pp. 279–285, Copyright (2009), with permission from Elsevier.

NPL analysis (including the suggestive linkage peak on chromosome 6). The linkage results on chromosomes 2, 6, and 12 were supported by single-point HLOD scores based on the same parameters. The result on chromosome 9 was only supported by a single marker in the single-point analysis, indicating a possible statistical artifact, and hence this locus was not considered a candidate region. Additional support for the HLOD results came from an additional set of NPL analyses focusing on the subsets of families contributing to each HLOD peak (see Figure 2.4). This analysis reveals a significant LOD score increase over the initial NPL analysis, indicating that the presence of significant heterogeneity at these loci was likely to have diminished the linkage signal in these regions and providing strong support for the HLOD result.

In sum, Asher et al.'s pioneering genome-wide scan for susceptibility genes for auditory-visual synesthesia identified four candidate regions, with significant linkage to chromosome 2q and suggestive linkage to chromosomes 5q, 6p, and 12p under the criteria proposed by Lander and Kruglyak (1995). Notably, the results failed to support previous suggestions of linkage to the X chromosome, and we discuss this in further detail later. While the resolution of this genome scan makes identifying potential candidate genes within the candidate regions challenging, the uncertainty about the etiology of synesthesia makes the genetic locations of these regions of particular interest. We review this next, following Asher et al. (2009).

The marker with the highest LOD score in the region of significant linkage on chromosome 2q (D2S142, with HLOD = 3.025) has previously been linked to autism (IMGSAC 2001). This is particularly interesting in light of the fact that sensory abnormalities are a significant feature of autism-spectrum disorders (ASD; Ashwin et al. 2009; Belmonte et al. 2004), with synesthesia itself sometimes reported as a symptom (Harrison and Hare 2004). Moreover, a recent study at the University of Cambridge indicates a possible increased prevalence of synesthesia among people with ASD (S. Baron-Cohen, personal communication). Furthermore, neuroimaging studies have revealed that auditory stimuli trigger responses in both auditory and visual brain regions in both autistic individuals (Kemner et al. 1995) and auditory-visual synesthetes (Nunn et al. 2002). Studies have also shown increased neural connectivity in the brains of people with ASD (Courchesne et al. 2005), which is particularly notable given recent evidence for increased connectivity in the brains of synesthetes (Rouw and Scholte 2007; see Rouw, Chapter 25, this volume). Finally, recent studies also suggest that savantism, long connected with ASD, may in some cases result from the combination of ASD and synesthesia together (Baron-Cohen et al. 2007; Simner, Mayo, and Spiller 2009; see Spiller and Jansari, Chapter 36, this volume).

There are a number of interesting candidate genes on chromosome 2. *TBR1* (MIM[3] 604616) induces the transcription of genes regulated by the T-box element that are thought to be integral in embryo development (Bulfone et al. 1995; Hsueh et al. 2000; Smith 1999). These genes include reelin (*RELN* (MIM 600514)), which is central in the development of the cerebral cortex; the brains of *tbr1* knockout mice develop abnormalities in laminar cortical organization, which could in theory play a role in the altered neural connectivity of synesthetes (Hevner, Miyashita-Lin, and Rubenstein 2002; Hevner

---

[3] Information on specific genes can be found online in the Mendelian Inheritance in Man (MIM) database (<http://www.ncbi.nlm.nih.gov/omim>); the MIM numbers used here refer to the unique identifier each gene has been assigned in this database.

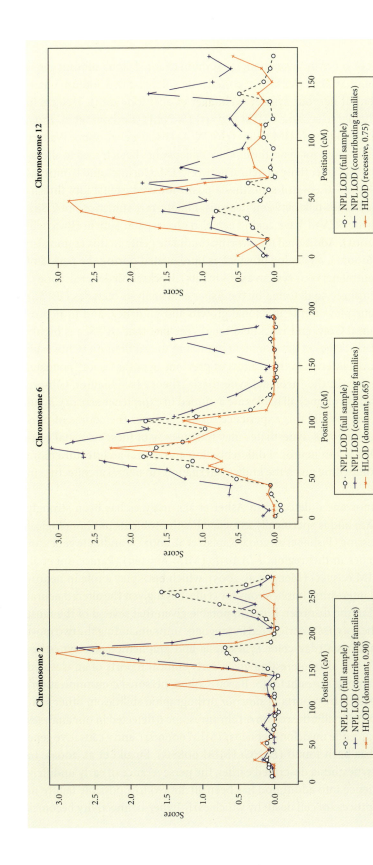

FIGURE 2.4 Increase in NPL during subset analysis. Dashed black = NPL (full sample); blue = NPL (contributing families); dashed and dotted red = HLOD (chromosome 2 = dominant, 0.90; chromosome 6 = dominant, 0.65; chromosome 12 = recessive, 0.75). Contributing families are those showing linkage to the HLOD peak. Reprinted from *The American Journal of Human Genetics*, 84 (2), Julian E. Asher, Janine A. Lamb, Denise Brocklebank, Jean-Baptiste Cazier, Elena Maestrini, Laura Addis, Mallika Sen, Simon Baron-Cohen, and Anthony P. Monaco, A Whole-Genome Scan and Fine-Mapping Linkage Study of Auditory-Visual Synesthesia Reveals Evidence of Linkage to Chromosomes 2q24, 5q33, 6p12, and 12p12, pp. 279–285, Copyright (2009), with permission from Elsevier.

et al. 2001). Another set of genes in this region, the sodium channel alpha subunit genes *SCN1A* (MIM 182389) and *SCN2A* (MIM 182390) encode voltage-gated sodium channels throughout the central nervous system (Whitaker et al. 2000, 2001). Defects in these genes have been linked to seizures (MIM 607745) (*SCN2A*) (Berkovic et al. 2004; Herlenius et al. 2007) and epilepsy (MIM 604233) (*SCN1A*) (Escayg et al. 2000; Wallace et al. 2001). This has implications for synesthesia since epilepsy has been traced to alterations in the excitability and connectivity of neural networks (McCormick and Contreras 2001) and the "disinhibition" theory of synesthesia posits lowered excitability thresholds leading to increased cross-talk between neurons. Finally, rare mutations of *TBR1*, *SCN2A*, and a nearby gene *SCN3A* have again been also observed in autism (Bacchelli et al. 2003; Weiss et al. 2003). Additional noteworthy candidate genes in this region also include *ERMN* (MIM 610072), an analog of which is upregulated during the period of active myelination of central nervous system axons in rats (Brockschnieder et al. 2006).

The region on chromosome 5q detected by the Asher et al analysis includes *DPYSL3* (MIM 601168). This gene plays a role in axonal growth and guidance, and in neuronal differentiation (Quinn, Gray, and Hockfield 1999). The fact that *DPYSL3* is highly expressed in the very early stages of development but not in the adult brain (Choi et al. 2005) makes it of potential interest in the context of previous hypotheses for "neonatal synesthesia" (Maurer 1993). In the "neonatal synesthesia" theory (see Maurer, Gibson, and Spector, Chapter 3, this volume) all babies are assumed to experience sensory input in an undifferentiated way. While this experience disappears over the course of normal development in most people, synesthetes may retain some of these neonatal connections. The role of *DPYSL3* in neuronal differentiation and neural architecture more generally is therefore compelling given the known alternations in neural architecture in synesthetes.

The region on chromosome 6 detected in Asher et al.'s analyses has been strongly linked to dyslexia (*DYX2*) and is specifically associated with problems in phonological and orthographic processing (Fisher et al. 2002; Kaplan et al. 2002). Candidate genes for dyslexia include two genes in this region, *KIAA0319* (MIM 609269) (Paracchini et al. 2006) and *DCDC2* (MIM 605755) (Meng et al. 2005), which both play a role in neuronal migration. This has interesting implications for synesthesia given the altered neural architecture implicated in the disorder. It is also notable given that several of the most common synesthetic phenotypes are triggered by language units, including the two most common forms of synesthesia (day-color synesthesia and grapheme-color synesthesia; Simner et al. 2006). It is also interesting given early clinical reports of an elevated prevalence of dyslexia among synesthetes (S. Baron-Cohen, personal communication) although this is complicated by reports of *superior* orthographic abilities in other synesthetes (Linn et al. 2008). Finally, the region on chromosome 6 detected in our analyses has also been linked to juvenile myoclonic epilepsy (MIM 606904), and a causative gene involved in apoptosis has been found (*EFHC1* (MIM 608815); Suzuki et al. 2004). In the neonatal theory of synesthesia described earlier, the perseverance of early undifferentiated sensory experience into adulthood has been attributed to a possible failure in apoptosis (the normal process of cell death by which early hyper-connectivity becomes "pruned" in development; see Maurer, Gibson, and Spector, Chapter 3, and Mitchell, Chapter 27, this volume). The mutation of these epilepsy-linked genes in chromosome 6 seen in epileptic families lowers the gene's apoptotic effect causing problems in neuronal pruning in development; a similar effect in synesthetes could contribute to the retention of early synesthetic pathways.

The region identified on chromosome 12 contains *GRIN2B* (MIM 138252), the N-methyl-D-aspartate (NMDA) receptor 2B subunit gene. NMDA receptors may play a central role in long-term potentiation and the consolidation of learning and memory (Shimizu et al. 2000), a finding of particular interest in light of studies which have shown a connection between synesthesia and improve recall. Over-expression of this gene in mice has resulted in enhanced learning and memory (Tang et al. 1999). *GRIN2B* has been further linked to autism (McCauley et al. 2005), which is particularly notable given our earlier discussions of improved memory, savantism, and autism in synesthesia.

Evidence of linkage to chromosome 16 (16q12.2–23.1)

Further research into the genetic basis of synesthesia has highlighted a region of interest on chromosome 16. Tomson et al. (2011) conducted a family-based linkage study investigating a different form of synesthesia, a phenotype they called *colored sequence synesthesia* in which linguistic inducers that fall in sequences (e.g., days, letters, numbers, months) trigger the perception of color. There is some potential phenotypic overlap with the Asher et al. (2009) study (e.g., synesthetes with colored letters; these often experience color for spoken words—although spoken words can also be triggered by phonemes). Testing five families (n = 48), Tomson et al. discovered linkage to a region of chromosome 16 (16q12.2–23.1) in two of the five families. Within this region, six candidate genes were selected for further analysis on the basis of having functions that may play a role in the development of abnormal neural connectivity between regions of the cortex. However, further sequencing of these genes did not reveal any evidence to suggest that they contributed to the development of synesthesia in this subgroup. While these results must be interpreted cautiously given the small size of the sample and hence the lack of statistical power, this result is certainly of interest.

The fact that separate familial linkage studies investigating different phenotypes of synesthesia identified linkage on distinct regions of different chromosomes raises a broader issue worthy of further discussion. Is there a single synesthesia genotype that lends itself to a general predisposition to developing synesthesia, with differences in sensory input or other environmental factors contributing to the development of a particular phenotype? Or do specific genes contribute directly to the occurrence of particular synesthesia phenotypes? It has been demonstrated that certain types of synesthesias tend to co-occur more than others (Simner et al. 2006) and synesthesia may be classified according to broader groupings (Novich, Cheng, and Eagleman 2011). Novich and colleagues considered the co-occurrence within individuals of 22 different types of synesthesias in a group of 12,127 synesthetes who had been verified using a type of TOG via the online interface at <http://www.synesthete.org> (Eagleman et al. 2007). Novich, Cheng, and Eagleman (2011) reported five distinct clusters of synesthesia forms, in that a person possessing more than one type of synesthesia is more likely to have types within the same cluster, rather than across clusters. They labeled these five clusters *colored music synesthesias*, *colored sequence synesthesias* (see earlier), *non-visual sequela synesthesias* (colors triggered by physical touch or some emotional component), *spatial sequence synesthesia* (where sequenced units are experienced as having spatial locations), and *colored sensation synesthesias* (whose inducers are non-visual; e.g., taste).

The findings of this study suggest that what we think of as "synesthesia" may in fact encompass several distinct phenomena each with their own patterns of expression. This has important implications for our hypotheses about the genetic roots of synesthesia which are more likely, therefore, to be multifaceted. Specifically, Novich, Cheng, and Eagleman (2011) suggest that each group of synesthesias may have independent underlying neural pathways, the development of which may be driven by distinct sets of genes. Importantly then, although there was likely to have been a partial overlap in the populations of synesthetes sampled by Tomson et al. (2011) and by Asher et al. (2009), there was also a key difference, the importance of which is now magnified by the findings of Novich, Cheng, and Eagleman: Asher et al.'s sample included music-color synesthetes, while Tomson et al.'s sample were solely triggered by language sequences. The findings by Novich and colleagues tell us that these may represent qualitatively and meaningfully different forms (in the terminology of Novich and colleagues, *colored music synesthesia* and *colored sequence synesthesia*), each with their own genetic mechanism. While further empirical evidence will be required before firm conclusions can be drawn, it is clear that the relationship between genotype and phenotype is unlikely to be straightforward.

WHY DOESN'T X MARK THE SPOT?

We end our chapter with a re-evaluation of what was perhaps the most important early hypothesis about the genetic roots of synesthesia. Early studies had suggested that there may be a major locus on the X chromosome, due to an absence of confirmed male-to-male transmission and a female:male ratio of up to 6:1. However, neither Asher et al. (2009) nor Tomson et al. (2011) found evidence for a major locus on the X chromosome and so these findings indicate a need to revisit our early understanding of the mode of inheritance of synesthesia.

The early assumption about an absence of male-to-male transmission has been subsequently refuted by the verification of two cases of male-to-male transmission of synesthesia in the study by Asher et al. (2009). While it is possible that these two families may carry a very rare autosomal mutation and that the majority of cases of synesthesia are in fact X-linked, the results of the genome scan indicate that this is unlikely to be the case. It is also possible that the marker density was insufficient to detect significant linkage to a locus on the X chromosome; increased marker density (e.g., with an approach known as single-nucleotide polymorphism (SNP)-based high-density genotyping) would indeed increase the amount of information obtained from the chromosome (Sawcer et al. 2004). However, studies directly comparing the results of microsatellite and SNP-based genome scans indicate that while the increased information content may raise unremarkable LOD scores to the level of suggestive linkage, or suggestive scores to the level of genome-wide significance, it has not resulted in the detection of significant linkage in areas where the microsatellite scan failed to do so (Middleton et al. 2004; Sawcer et al. 2005). This suggests that increased marker density would be unlikely to reveal a major locus on the X chromosome, though it might reveal stronger linkage in the region where the maximum LOD score was obtained.

In the absence of evidence for a major locus on the X chromosome, an alternate explanation for earlier observed high female:male ratios must be found. We noted earlier that is possible that the female predominance observed in previous studies of synesthesia does not in fact reflect the true ratio among affected persons (Simner et al. 2006; Ward and Simner 2005). Simner and colleagues have suggested that an especially high female skew may emerge when synesthetes are asked to self-refer for study (e.g., Baron-Cohen et al. 1996), since women have been shown to be more likely to come forward to report atypical behavior (Dindia and Allen 1992). Furthermore, when prevalence was assessed without the potential for self-referral, there was a non-significant difference across the sexes (Simner et al. 2006). However, the complete absence of female predominance seems highly unlikely given the consistency of a small but persistent female bias across multiple studies (Simner et al. 2009). Simner and colleagues have pointed out a repeated trend in the direction of a female bias of approximately 2:1 (e.g., Simner et al. 2006, 2009) and suggest that poor power alone in previous statistical tests makes it possible that a female bias (perhaps of around 2:1) may re-emerge in larger sample testing.[4] Furthermore, referral bias usually accounts for only a slight variation (10%) in response rates (Dindia and Allen 1992) again making it likely that high early estimates were at least pointing in the right direction.

Assuming a slight but significant female bias may yet be found in future large-scale testing, a number of genetic factors could account for this. Synesthesia may be a complex trait involving multiple genes with relatively small individual genetic effect, or it may be subject to multiple modes of inheritance or locus heterogeneity. If synesthesia

---

[4] Studies showing an apparent female bias without self-referral have not, thus far, been entirely free of the potential for this confound. Barnett et al. (2008) report a female bias of approximately 6:1 in a study that looked at both self-referred probands, and their family members who were directly contacted by the researchers. However, Barnett and colleagues were only able to objectively assess all first-degree family members for 17 out of 53 probands, which meant that 81 of their 92 synesthetes were either objectively unconfirmed cases or self-referred (J. Simner, personal communication). A similarly high female bias of approximately 4:1 (based on the members of n = 5 families) reported in Tomson et al. (2011) has now been corrected by erratum to 2.7:1. This brings it in line with an earlier study by Ward and Simner (2005) who showed a female:male ratio of 2:1 when they also attempted to eliminate a referral bias by looking within the families of synesthetes (n = 85 families). However, Simner and colleagues point out that this type of ratio may yet be an overestimate from self-referral, since families with a lone synesthete are less likely to come to the attention of researchers if that synesthete is male (Simner et al. 2006).

is an oligogenic or complex trait subject to a threshold of liability, the families with father-to-son transmission may represent cases in which threshold was reached without any contributions from mutations on the X chromosome, whereas the other families represent cases in which a mutation or mutations on the X chromosome plays a role in reaching threshold. Greater prevalence of the X chromosome mutation(s) would account for the X-linked transmission pattern observed in the majority of synesthetic families. Additionally, the threshold may differ between the sexes, with one sex requiring fewer disease-causing factors to display the phenotype (Carter 1976). In the context of a complex disorder, the findings on the X chromosome could reflect the existence of a locus with limited effect. Finally, a specific hypothesis has been proposed by Mitchell (Chapter 27, this volume) who points to a priori sex differences in connectivity, with women's brains showing greater overall connectivity across the entire brain. Mitchell suggests that a condition such as synesthesia, which results from atypical hyper-connectivity may certainly be expected to be greater in females than males.

SUMMARY AND FUTURE DIRECTIONS

The findings reviewed here have important implications for our overall understanding of synesthesia, as they indicate that its genetic basis is rather more complex than originally believed. Separate linkage studies (Asher et al. 2009; Tomson et al. 2011) conclude that rather than being caused by a single gene at a single locus with a single mode of inheritance, synesthesia is more likely to arise from the effects of multiple genes at multiple loci with different modes of inheritance. The discovery of multiple peaks with relatively small genetic effects combined with the detection of significant linkage on chromosome 2q and suggestive linkage to chromosomes 5q, 6p, and 12p (Asher et al. 2009) is consistent with a complex disorder with considerable genetic heterogeneity. This conclusion is further reinforced by the discovery of linkage to a region on chromosome 16, found in participants exhibiting a different, yet possibly overlapping, phenotype (Tomson et al. 2011).This could potentially mean that there are a number of causative loci, with different loci producing the clinical phenotype in particular families. This would be consistent with findings in other neurodevelopmental disorders such as specific language impairment (MIM 606711) (Newbury, Bishop, and Monaco 2005) and dyslexia (MIM 127700) (Paracchini, Scerri, and Monaco 2007) where both gene–environment and gene–gene (epistatic) interactions are believed to play an important role.

Given the evidence for substantial genetic heterogeneity, it is likely that the development of meaningful *endophenotypes* will play a key role in future research. A genetic endophenotype is a well-defined, quantifiable measure describing one subdimension of a complex disease phenotype. Increasing phenotypic homogeneity through the use of endophenotypes has been shown to increase the power to find susceptibility genes (Buxbaum et al. 2004; Shao et al. 2002). It will be necessary to revisit the phenotypic data to identify subdomains of the synesthetic phenotype that may serve as useful

endophenotypes, ideally by providing quantitative measures. The amount of information generated by more recent tests of genuineness (e.g., the TOG-R; or the tests at
<http://www.synesthete.org>) makes this test a logical candidate for use in endopheno-
typing. However, it is notable that while the use of endophenotypes can produce more
statistically reliable data they do not necessarily have a simpler genetic architecture than
the underlying disease, and that the genetic effect sizes observed with endophenotypes
are not necessarily larger than those observed with the global disease phenotype (Flint
and Munafo 2007); care will need to be taken to ensure adequate statistical power to
detect genes of small effect.

Even with this additional data, it may not be possible to specify a single mode of inheritance for synesthesia. The recent evidence from Novich and colleagues based on a large
sample of synesthetes has shown that types of synesthesias can be clustered together in
certain subtypes and different varieties of synesthesias are more likely to co-occur in
affected individuals if they belong to the same subgroup (Novich, Cheng, and Eagleman
2011). This conclusion raises the possibility that multiple genotypes may be responsible
for the expression of distinct groups of different phenotypes. Indeed, we cannot currently say for certain whether Asher et al. (2009) and Tomson et al. (2011) have identified different loci that contribute some proportion of genetic effect to an overarching
"synesthesia genotype" or whether they are loci central to quite distinct subgenotypes.
For this reason, further investigation into the subtleties of the relationship between phenotypes should prove to be a fruitful line of inquiry. The use of additional phenotyping methods, notably neuroimaging, to define subphenotypes within the synesthetic
population with greater precision would provide important additional information and
facilitate the search for susceptibility genes.

Even if most cases are due to oligogenic inheritance, it is possible (even probable given
what has been seen in other neurodevelopmental disorders) that there are individual
families (e.g., as in specific language impairment; Fisher et al. 1998) or subgroups of families (e.g., as in Tourette's syndrome (MIM 137580; Abelson et al. 2005) and ASD (MIM
209850; Martin and Ledbetter 2007)) which show Mendelian inheritance of a mutation
although genome scans indicate that the overall inheritance of the disease is genetically
complex. While they are likely to be considerably rarer than those showing more complex
inheritance, the detailed analysis of families with known chromosomal abnormalities or
detectable copy number variants may facilitate the identification of candidate genes and
the delineation of pathways which play an important role in the etiological process.

Scientific exploration of the role played by genes in human cognition has only recently
begun. Formerly an obscure condition, synesthesia has attracted growing interest for
its potential to advance our understanding of both typical and atypical human cognition and perception. A greater understanding of the neural mechanisms underlying
synesthesia has important implications for other neurodevelopmental disorders, many
of which (e.g., ASD (Harrison and Hare 2004); Williams–Beuren syndrome (MIM
194050; Levitin et al. 2005)) involve abnormal sensory perception. Moreover, as synesthetic perception occurs in the absence of direct sensory stimulation, it may offer insight
into how the human brain integrates sensory data into conscious perception, and may

even illuminate the neural basis of consciousness (Gray et al. 2002; see Sagiv and Frith, Chapter 45, this volume). The eventual identification and functional characterization of susceptibility genes linked to synesthesia will yield fundamental insights into the role of genetics in human cognition and perception.

ACKNOWLEDGEMENTS

DAC was supported in part by grants EP/F500385/1 and BB/F529254/1 for the University of Edinburgh, School of Informatics Doctoral Training Centre in Neuroinformatics and Computational Neuroscience (<http://www.anc.ed.ac.uk/dtc>) from the UK Engineering and Physical Sciences Research Council (EPSRC), UK Biotechnology and Biological Sciences Research Council (BBSRC), and the UK Medical Research Council (MRC).

REFERENCES

Abelson, Jesse F., Kenneth Y. Kwan, Brian J. O'Roak, Danielle Y. Baek, Althea A. Stillman, Thomas M. Morgan, *et al.* 2005. Sequence variants in SLITRK1 are associated with Tourette's syndrome. *Science* 310 (5746):317–320.

Asher, Julian E., Janine A. Lamb, Denise Brocklebank, Jean-Baptiste Cazier, Elena Maestrini, Laura Addis, Mallika Sen, Simon Baron-Cohen, and Anthony P. Monaco. 2009. A whole-genome scan and fine-mapping linkage study of auditory-visual synesthesia reveals evidence of linkage to chromosomes 2q24, 5q33, 6p12, and 12p12. *American Journal of Human Genetics* 84 (2):279–285.

Asher, Julian E., Michael R. F. Aitken, Nasr Farooqi, Sameer Kurmani, and Simon Baron-Cohen. 2006. Diagnosing and phenotyping visual synaesthesia: A preliminary evaluation of the revised test of genuineness (TOG-R). *Cortex* 42 (2):137–146.

Ashwin, Emma, Chris Ashwin, Danielle Rhydderch, Jessica Howells, and Simon Baron-Cohen. 2009. Eagle-eyed visual acuity: An experimental investigation of enhanced perception in autism. *Biological Psychiatry* 65 (1):17–21.

Bacchelli, E., F. Blasi, M. Biondolillo, J. A. Lamb, E. Bonora, G. Barnby, J. Parr, *et al.* 2003. Screening of nine candidate genes for autism on chromosome 2q reveals rare nonsynonymous variants in the cAMP-GEFII gene. *Molecular Psychiatry* 8 (11):916–924.

Bailey, Mark E. S., and Keith J. Johnson. 1997. Synaesthesia: Is a genetic analysis feasible? In *Synaesthesia: Classic and Contemporary Readings*, ed. Simon Baron-Cohen and John Harrison, 182–207. Oxford: Blackwells.

Barnett, Kylie, Fiona N. Newell, Ciara Finucane, Julian E. Asher, Aiden P. Corvin, and Kevin J. Mitchell. 2008. Familial patterns and the origins of individual differences in synaesthesia. *Cortex* 106 (2):871–893.

Baron-Cohen, Simon, Daniel Bor, Jaclyn Billington, Julian Asher, Sally Wheelwright, and Chris Ashwin. 2007. Savant memory in a man with colour form-number synaesthesia and Asperger syndrome. *Journal of Consciousness Studies* 14:237–252.

Baron-Cohen, Simon, Lucy Burt, Fiona Smith-Laittan, John Harrison, and Patrick Bolton. 1996. Synaesthesia: Prevalence and familiality. *Perception* 25 (9):1073–1079.

Baron-Cohen, Simon, John Harrison, Laura H. Goldstein, and Maria Wyke. 1993. Coloured speech perception: Is synaesthesia what happens when modularity breaks down? *Perception* 22:419–426.

Baron-Cohen, Simon, Maria A. Wyke, and Colin Binnie. 1987. Hearing words and seeing colours: An experimental investigation of a case of synaesthesia. *Perception* 16 (6):761–767.

Belmonte, Matthew K., Greg Allen, Andrea Beckel-Mitchener, Lisa M. Boulanger, Ruth A. Carper, and Sara J. Webb. 2004. Autism and abnormal development of brain connectivity. *Journal of Neuroscience* 24 (42): 9228–9231.

Berkovic, Samuel F., Sarah E. Heron, Lucio Giordano, Carla Marini, Renzo Guerrini, Robert E. Kaplan, Antonio Gambardella, *et al.* 2004. Benign familial neonatal-infantile seizures: Characterization of a new sodium channelopathy. *Annals of Neurology* 55 (4):550–557.

Brockschnieder, Damian, Helena Sabanay, Dieter Riethmacher, and Elior Peles. 2006. Ermin, a myelinating oligodendrocyte-specific protein that regulates cell morphology. *Journal of Neuroscience* 26 (3):757–762.

Bulfone, Alessandro, Susan M. Smiga, Kenji Shimamura, Andrew Peterson, Luis Puelles, and John L. R. Rubenstein. 1995. T-brain-1: A homolog of Brachyury whose expression defines molecularly distinct domains within the cerebral cortex. *Neuron* 15 (1):63–78.

Buxbaum, J. D., J. Silverman, M. Keddache, C. J. Smith, E. Hollander, N. Ramoz, and J. G. Reichert. 2004. Linkage analysis for autism in a subset families with obsessive-compulsive behaviors: Evidence for an autism susceptibility gene on chromosome 1 and further support for susceptibility genes on chromosome 6 and 19. *Molecular Psychiatry* 9 (2):144–150.

Carter, C. O. 1976. Genetics of common single malformations. *British Medical Bulletin* 32 (1):21–26.

Choi, Yoon-La, Chong Jai Kim, Tatsuya Matsuo, Carlo Gaetano, Rita Falconi, Yeon-Lim Suh, Seok-Hyung Kim, *et al.* 2005. HUlip, a human homologue of unc-33-like phosphoprotein of Caenorhabditis elegans; immunohistochemical localization in the developing human brain and patterns of expression in nervous system tumors. *Journal of Neuro-Oncology* 73 (1):19–27.

Courchesne, Eric, Elizabeth Redcay, John T. Morgan, and Daniel P. Kennedy. 2005. Autism at the beginning: Microstructural and growth abnormalities underlying the cognitive and behavioral phenotype of autism. *Developmental Psychopathology* 17 (3):577–597.

Dindia, Kathryn, and Mike Allen. 1992. Sex differences in self-disclosure: A meta-analysis. *Psychological Bulletin* 112 (1):106–124.

Eagleman, David M., Arielle D. Kagan, Stephanie S. Nelson, Deepak Sagaram, and Anand K. Sarma. 2007. A standardized test battery for the study of synesthesia. *Jounal of Neuroscience Methods* 159:139–145.

Escayg, Andrew, Bryan T. MacDonald, Stéphanie Baulac, Gilles Huberfeld, Isabelle An-Gourfinkel, Alexis Brice, Eric LeGuern, *et al.* 2000. Mutations of SCN1A, encoding a neuronal sodium channel, in two families with GEFS+2. *Nature Genetics* 24 (4):343–345.

Fisher, Simon E., Clyde Francks, Angela J. Marlow, I. Laurence MacPhie, Dianne F. Newbury, Lon R. Cardon, Yumiko Ishikawa-Brush, *et al.* 2002. Independent genome-wide scans identify a chromosome 18 quantitative-trait locus influencing dyslexia. *Nature Genetics* 30 (1):86–91.

Fisher, Simon E., Faraneh Vargha-Khadem, Kate E. Watkins, Anthony P. Monaco, and Marcus E. Pembrey. 1998. Localisation of a gene implicated in a severe speech and language disorder. *Nature Genetics* 18 (2):168–170.

Flint, Jonathon, and Marcus R. Munafo. 2007. The endophenotype concept in psychiatric genetics. *Psychological Medicine* 37 (2):163–180.

Galton, Francis. (1883). *Inquiries into Human Faculty and its Development.* London: Macmillan.

Glicksohn, Joseph, Iris Steinbach, and Sigal Elimalach-Malmilyan. 1999. Cognitive dedifferentiation in eidetics and synaesthesia: Hunting for the ghost once more. *Perception* 28 (1):109–120.

Gray, Jeffrey, Susan Chopping, Julia Nunn, David Parslow, Lloyd Gregory, Steve Williams, Michael J. Brammer, and Simon Baron-Cohen. 2002. Implications of synaesthesia for functionalism. *Journal of Consciousness Studies* 9:5–31.

Green, Jennifer A., and Usha Goswami. 2007. Synesthesia and number cognition in children. Cognition 106 (1):463–473.

Harrison, John, and Dougal Julian Hare. 2004. Brief report: Assessment of sensory abnormalities in people with autistic spectrum disorders. *Journal of Autism and Developmental Disorders* 34 (6):727–730.

Herlenius, Eric, Sarah E. Heron, Bronwyn E. Grinton, Deborah Keay, Ingrid E. Scheffer, John C. Mulley, and Samuel F. Berkovic. 2007. SCN2A mutations and benign familial neonatal-infantile seizures: The phenotypic spectrum. *Epilepsia* 48 (6):1138–1142.

Hevner, Robert F., Emily Miyashita-Lin, and John L. Rubenstein. 2002. Cortical and thalamic axon pathfinding defects in Tbr1, Gbx2, and Pax6 mutant mice: Evidence that cortical and thalamic axons interact and guide each other. *Journal of Comparative Neurology* 447 (1):8–17.

Hevner, Robert F., Limin Shi, Nick Justice, Yi-Ping Hsueh, Morgan Sheng, Susan Smiga, Alessandro Bulfone, André M. Goffinet, Anthony T. Campagnoni, and John L. R. Rubenstein. 2001. Tbr1 regulates differentiation of the preplate and layer 6. *Neuron* 29 (2):353–366.

Hsueh, Yi-Ping, Ting-Fang Wang, Fu-Chia Yang, and Morgan Sheng. 2000. Nuclear translocation and transcription regulation by the membrane-associated guanylate kinase CASK/LIN-2. *Nature* 404 (6775):298–302.

IMGSAC. 2001. A genomewide screen for autism: Strong evidence for linkage to chromosomes 2q, 7q, and 16p. *American Journal of Human Genetics* 69 (3):570–581.

Jewanski, Jörg, Sean A. Day, and Jamie Ward. 2009. A colorful albino: The first documented case of synaesthesia, by Georg Tobias Ludwig Sachs in 1812. *Journal of the History of Neurosciences* 18:293–303.

Johnson, Donielle, Carrie Allison, and Simon Baron-Cohen. 2013. The prevalence of synesthesia: The consistency revolution. In *The Oxford Handbook of Synesthesia*, ed. Julia Simner and Edward M. Hubbard, 3–22. Oxford: Oxford University Press.

Kaplan, D. E., J. Gayan, J. Ahn, T.-W. Won, D. L. Pauls, R. K. Olson, J. C. DeFries, *et al.* 2002. Evidence for linkage and association with reading disability on 6p21.3–22. *American Journal of Human Genetics* 70 (5):1287–1298.

Kemner, Chantal, Marinus N. Verbaten, Juliane M. Cuperus, Gert Camfferman, and Herman van Engeland. 1995. Auditory event-related brain potentials in autistic children and three different control groups. *Biological Psychiatry* 38 (3):150–165.

Kim, Chai-Youn, and Randolph Blake. 2013. Revisiting the perceptual reality of synesthetic colour. In *The Oxford Handbook of Synesthesia*, ed. Julia Simner and Edward M. Hubbard, 283–316. Oxford: Oxford University Press.

Lander, Eric, and Leonid Kruglyak. 1995. Genetic dissection of complex traits: Guidelines for interpreting and reporting linkage results. *Nature Genetics* 11 (3):241–247.

Levitin, Daniel J., Kristen Cole, Alan Lincoln, and Ursula Bellugi. 2005. Aversion, awareness, and attraction: Investigating claims of hyperacusis in the Williams syndrome phenotype. *Journal of Child Psychology and Psychiatry* 46 (5):514–523.

Linn, A., P. Hancock, J. Simner, and M. Akeroyd. 2008. Cognitive advantages in tickertape synaesthesia. Paper presented at the 4th Annual Meeting of the UK Synaesthesia Association, Edinburgh, March.

Luria, Aleksandr. 1968. *The Mind of a Mnemonist*. Cambridge, MA: Harvard University Press.

Martin, Christa L., and David H. Ledbetter. 2007. Autism and cytogenetic abnormalities: Solving autism one chromosome at a time. *Current Psychiatry Reports* 9 (2):141–147.

Mattingley, Jason B., Anina N. Rich, Greg Yelland, and John L. Bradshaw. 2001. Unconscious priming eliminates automatic binding of colour and alphanumeric form in synaesthesia. *Nature* 410 (6828):580–582.

Maurer, Daphne. 1993. Neonatal synesthesia: Implications for the processing of speech and faces. In *Developmental Neurocognition: Speech and Face Processing in the First Year of Life*, ed. Benedicte de Boysson-Bardies, Scania de Schonen, Peter Jusczyk, Peter McNeilage, and John Morton, 109–124. Dordrecht: Kluwer Academic Publishers.

Maurer, Daphne, Laura C. Gibson, and Ferrinne Spector. 2013. Synesthesia in infants and very young children. In *The Oxford Handbook of Synesthesia*, ed. Julia Simner and Edward M. Hubbard, 45–63. Oxford: Oxford University Press.

Meier, Beat, and Nicolas Rothen. 2013. Synesthesia and memory. In *The Oxford Handbook of Synesthesia*, ed. Julia Simner and Edward M. Hubbard, 692–706. Oxford: Oxford University Press.

McCauley, Jacob L., Chun Li, Lan Jiang, Lana M. Olson, Genea Crockett, Kimberly Gainer, Susan E. Folstein, Jonathan L. Haines, and James S. Sutcliffe. 2005. Genome-wide and ordered-subset linkage analyses provide support for autism loci on 17q and 19p with evidence of phenotypic and interlocus genetic correlates. *BMC Medical Genetics* 6:1.

McCormick, David A., and Diego Contreras. 2001. On the cellular and network bases of epileptic seizures. *Annual Review of Physiology* 63:815–846.

Meng, Haiying, Shelley D. Smith, Karl Hager, Matthew Held, Jonathan Liu, Richard K. Olson, Bruce F. Pennington, *et al.* 2005. DCDC2 is associated with reading disability and modulates neuronal development in the brain. *Proceedings of the National Academy of Sciences of the United States of America* 102 (47):17053–17058.

Middleton, F. A., M. T. Pato, K. L. Gentile, C. P. Morley, X.-Z. Zhao, A. F. Eisener, A. Brown, *et al.* 2004. Genomewide linkage analysis of bipolar disorder by use of a high-density single-nucleotide-polymorphism (SNP) genotyping assay: A comparison with microsatellite marker assays and finding of significant linkage to chromosome 6q22. *American Journal of Human Genetics* 74 (5):886–897.

Mitchell, Kevin J. 2013. Synesthesia and cortical connectivity: a neurodevelopmental perspective. In *The Oxford Handbook of Synesthesia*, ed. Julia Simner and Edward M. Hubbard, 530–557. Oxford: Oxford University Press.

Morton, Newton E. 1955. Sequential tests for the detection of linkage. *American Journal of Human Genetics* 7 (3):277–318.

Newbury, Dianne F., Dorothy V. Bishop, and Anthony P. Monaco. 2005. Genetic influences on language impairment and phonological short-term memory. *Trends in Cognitive Sciences* 9 (11):528–534. doi: S1364-6613(05)00262-7 [pii] 10.1016/j.tics.2005.09.002

Novich, Scott D., Sherry Cheng, and David M. Eagleman. 2011. Is synesthesia one condition or many? A large-scale analysis reveals subgroups. *Journal of Neuropsychology* 5:353–371.

Nunn, J. A., L. J. Gregory, M. J. Brammer, S. C. R. Williams, D. M. Parslow, M. J. Morgan, R. G. Morris, E. T. Bullmore, S. Baron-Cohen, and J. A. Gray. 2002. Functional magnetic resonance imaging of synesthesia: Activation of V4/V8 by spoken words. *Nature Neuroscience* 5 (4):371–375.

Paracchini, Silvia, Thomas Scerri, and Anthony P. Monaco. 2007. The genetic lexicon of dyslexia. *Annual Review of Genomics and Human Genetics* 8 (1):57–79.

Paracchini, Silvia, Ankur Thomas, Sandra Castro, Cecilia Lai, Murugan Paramasivam, Yu Wang, Brendan J. Keating, *et al.* 2006. The chromosome 6p22 haplotype associated with dyslexia reduces the expression of KIAA0319, a novel gene involved in neuronal migration. *Human Molecular Genetics* 15 (10):1659–1666.

Price, Mark C. 2013. Synesthesia, imagery, and performance. In *The Oxford Handbook of Synesthesia*, ed. Julia Simner and Edward M. Hubbard, 728–757. Oxford: Oxford University Press.

Quinn, Christopher C., Grace E. Gray, and Susan Hockfield. 1999. A family of proteins implicated in axon guidance and outgrowth. *Journal of Neurobiology* 41 (1):158–164.

Ramachandran, Vilayanur S., and Edward M. Hubbard. 2001. Psychophysical investigations into the neural basis of synaesthesia. *Proceedings of the Royal Society B: Biological Sciences* 268 (1470):979–983.

Rizzo, Matthew, and Paul J. Eslinger. 1989. Colored hearing synesthesia: An investigation of neural factors. *Neurology* 39 (6):781–784.

Rouw, Romke. 2013. Synesthesia, hyper-connectivity and diffusion tensor imaging. In *The Oxford Handbook of Synesthesia*, ed. Julia Simner and Edward M. Hubbard, 500–518. Oxford: Oxford University Press.

Rouw, Romke, and H. Steven Scholte. 2007. Increased structural connectivity in grapheme-color synesthesia. *Nature Neuroscience* 10 (6):792–797.

Sagiv, Noam, and Chris D. Frith. 2013. Synesthesia and consciousness. In *The Oxford Handbook of Synesthesia*, ed. Julia Simner and Edward M. Hubbard, 924–940. Oxford: Oxford University Press.

Sawcer, Stephen, Maria Ban, Mel Maranian, Tai Wai Yeo, Alastair Compston, Andrew Kirby, Mark J. Daly, *et al.* 2005. A high-density screen for linkage in multiple sclerosis. *American Journal of Human Genetics* 77 (3):454–467.

Sawcer, Stephen J., Mel Maranian, Sara Singlehurst, TaiWai Yeo, Alastair Compston, Mark J. Daly, Philip L. De Jager, *et al.* 2004. Enhancing linkage analysis of complex disorders: An evaluation of high-density genotyping. *Human Molecular Genetics* 13 (17):1943–1949.

Shao, Yujun, Raiford, Kimberly L. Raiford, Chantelle M. Wolpert, Heidi A. Cope, Sarah A. Ravan, Allison A. Ashley-Koch, Ruth K. Abramson, *et al.* 2002. Phenotypic homogeneity provides increased support for linkage on chromosome 2 in autistic disorder. *American Journal of Human Genetics* 70 (4):1058–1061.

Shimizu, Eiji, Ya-Ping Tang, Claire Rampon, and Joe Z. Tsien. 2000. NMDA receptor-dependent synaptic reinforcement as a crucial process for memory consolidation. *Science* 290 (5494), 1170–1174.

Simner, Julia, and Robert H. Logie. 2008. Synaesthetic consistency spans decades in a lexical–gustatory synaesthete. *Neurocase* 13 (5,6):358–365

Simner, Julia, Catherine Mulvenna, Noam Sagiv, Elias Tsakanikos, Sarah A. Witherby, Christine Fraser, Kirsten Scott, and Jamie Ward. 2006. Synaesthesia: The prevalence of atypical cross-modal experiences. *Perception* 35 (8):1024–1033.

Simner, Julia, Neil Mayo, and Mary Jane Spiller. 2009. A foundation for savantism? Visuo-spatial synaesthetes present with cognitive benefits. *Cortex* 45 (10) 1246–1260.

Simner, Julia, Jenny Harrold, Harriet Creed, Louise Monro, and Louise Foulkes. 2009. Early detection of markers for synaesthesia in childhood populations. *Brain* 132 57–64.

Smilek, Daniel, Mike J. Dixon, Cera Cudahy, and Philip M. Merikle. 2002. Synesthetic color experiences influence memory. *Psychological Science* 13 (6):548–552.

Smith, Jim. 1999. T-box genes: What they do and how they do it. *Trends in Genetics* 15 (4): 154–158.

Spiller, Mary Jane, and Ashok S. Jansari. 2013. Synesthesia and savantism. In *The Oxford Handbook of Synesthesia*, ed. Julia Simner and Edward M. Hubbard, 707–727. Oxford: Oxford University Press.

Suzuki, Toshimitsu, Antonio V. Delgado-Escueta, Kripamoy Aguan, Maria E. Alonso, Jun Shi, Yuji Hara, Motohiro Nishida, *et al.* 2004. Mutations in EFHC1 cause juvenile myoclonic epilepsy. *Nature Genetics* 36 (8):842–849.

Tang, Ya-Ping, Eitaroh Shimizu, Gilles R. Dube, Claire Rampon, Geoffrey A. Kerchner, Ming-Lei Zhuo, Guosong Liu, and Joe Z. Tsien. 1999. Genetic enhancement of learning and memory in mice. *Nature* 401 (6748):63–69.

Tomson, Steffie N., Nili Avidan, Kwanghyuk Lee, Anand K. Sarma, Rejnal Tushe, Dianna M. Milewicz, Molly Bray, Suzanne M. Lealc, and David M. Eagleman. 2011. The genetics of colored sequence synesthesia: Suggestive evidence of linkage to 16q and genetic heterogeneity for the condition. *Behavioural Brain Research* 223:48–52.

Wallace, R. H., I. E. Scheffer, S. Barnett, M. Richards, L. Dibbens, R. R. Desai, T. Lerman-Sagie, *et al.* 2001. Neuronal sodium-channel alpha1-subunit mutations in generalized epilepsy with febrile seizures plus. *American Journal of Human Genetics* 68 (4):859–865.

Ward, Jamie, Brett Huckstep, and Elias Tsakanikos. 2006. Sound-colour synaesthesia: To what extent does it use cross-modal mechanisms common to us all? *Cortex* 42 (2):264–280.

Ward, Jamie, and Julia Simner. 2003. Lexical-gustatory synaesthesia: Linguistic and conceptual factors. *Cognition* 89:237–261.

———. 2005. Is synaesthesia an X-linked dominant trait with lethality in males? *Perception* 34 (5):611–623.

Weeks, Daniel, Jürg Ott, and G. Mark Lathrop. 1990. SLINK: A general simulation program for linkage analysis. *American Journal of Human Genetics* 47:A204.

Weiss, L. A., A. Escayg, J. A. Kearney, M. Trudeau, B. T. MacDonald, M. Mori, J. Reichert, J. D. Buxbaum, and M. H. Meisler. 2003. Sodium channels SCN1A, SCN2A and SCN3A in familial autism. *Molecular Psychiatry* 8(2):186–194.

Whitaker, William R., Jeffrey J. Clare, Andrew J. Powell, Yu Hua Chen, Richard L. M. Faull, and Piers C. Emson. 2000. Distribution of voltage-gated sodium channel alpha-subunit and beta-subunit mRNAs in human hippocampal formation, cortex, and cerebellum. *Journal of Comparative Neurology* 422 (1):123–139.

Whitaker, William R., Richard L. M. Faull, Henry J. Waldvogel, Christopher J. Plumpton, Piers C. Emson, and Jeffrey J. Clare. 2001. Comparative distribution of voltage-gated sodium channel proteins in human brain. *Brain Research. Molecular Brain Research* 88 (1–2):37–53. doi: S0169328X00002898.

CHAPTER 3

SYNESTHESIA IN INFANTS AND VERY YOUNG CHILDREN

DAPHNE MAURER, LAURA C. GIBSON,
AND FERRINNE SPECTOR

The perceptual validity of synesthesia has been established through behavioral (Asher et al. 2006; Jarick et al. 2009; Novich, Cheng, and Eagleman 2011; Ward, Huckstep, and Tsakanikos 2006; Ward and Mattingley 2006; Ward, Simner, and Auyeung 2005) and neuroimaging (Hubbard et al. 2005; Nunn et al. 2002; Paulesu et al. 1995; Rouw and Scholte 2007; Rouw, Scholte, and Colizoli 2011) evidence; however, its cause and developmental origins remain unclear. Several theories have been proposed as to the origins of synesthesia, such as the neonatal synesthesia theory (Maurer 1993; Maurer and Maurer 1988; Maurer and Mondloch 2004), the cross-activation theory (Hubbard, Brang, and Ramachandran 2011; Ramachandran and Hubbard 2001b), the disinhibited feedback theory (Grossenbacher and Lovelace 2001), and the re-entrant feedback model (Smilek et al. 2001), each generating predictions about normal and atypical cross-sensory development.

THE DEVELOPMENTAL ORIGINS OF SYNESTHESIA

Typical brain development is characterized by two distinct processes: first, the exuberant generation of connections between neurons via the production of synapses, and second, the strengthening of stimulated connections and the pruning away of unused connections—the result being (relatively) distinct sensory areas each specialized to process one type of dominant input (reviewed in Maurer, Gibson, and Spector, 2012). Anatomical tracing, a method in which groups of neurons are labeled with a substance (e.g., a fluorescent dye) such that the pathways connected to, and ultimately structures targeted by, the labeled neurons are visible, has documented this developmental process in numerous species. Studies using this methodology show that the timing of exuberance and pruning varies across species and sensory modalities (Bourgeois and Rakic 1993; Dehay, Bullier, and Kennedy 1984; Huttenlocher 1984). In humans, this pattern of formation and subsequent pruning of synaptic connections has also been revealed by increases in measurements of glucose utilization over sensory cortical areas during the first 3 to 4 years of life—presumably reflecting the flourishing of exuberant connections in sensory areas—followed by a subsequent decline beginning at about age 9—presumably reflecting experience-dependent pruning (Chugani 1994; Chugani and Phelps 1986; Chugani, Phelps, and Mazziotta 1987). Similarly, studies of resting state metabolism (synchronous increases and decreases in neuronal activity across the brain in the absence of stimulation) and white matter tracks (connections between neurons with axons sheathed in myelin, which speeds neural conduction) indicate that between 7 to 9 years of age and adulthood, the strength of local connectivity diminishes (Fair et al. 2009; Supekar, Musen, and Menon 2009).

The exuberant connections early in development include ones between cortical areas that receive input from different sensory systems (e.g., originating from auditory versus visual versus tactile receptors), and these connections appear to be functional. For example, in newborns, unlike adults, sound amplifies the somatosensory potential evoked by tactile stimulation of the wrist (Wolff et al. 1974). In other words, our early neural response to touch is exaggerated when accompanied by sound. Another example comes from the evoked responses elicited by human speech: in young infants, human speech elicits event-related potentials over both the auditory *and visual* cortices, unlike adults, for whom speech elicits evoked responses only over the auditory cortex (Neville 1995). This pattern of cross-activation by speech diminishes over the first 3 years of life (Neville 1995), suggesting that the connections between auditory and visual cortices are gradually being pruned away. Similarly, at 3 months of age, exposure to speech in comparison to a baseline quiet period causes increases in oxygenated hemoglobin and decreases in deoxygenated hemoglobin not only in the temporal, language-specialized cortex, as is true in adults, but also in the visual cortex (Homae et al. 2011). Neuroimaging (positron emission tomography) data also suggest more widespread activation by visual stimulation during infancy (Tzourio-Mazoyer et al. 2002): when activation evoked by Christmas tree lights is compared to that evoked by a human face, there is differential activity at 2 months of age, not only in areas geographically close to what will become the face area in the fusiform gyrus, but also in a number of other areas, including the right inferior parietal cortex (which is active during many forms of synesthesia; Rouw et al. 2011), the left inferior frontal cortex, and left temporal gyrus, which will later form the core of the language network. Similarly, there is evidence that different pathways in the visual cortex are not initially segregated. For example, adults process color and motion in distinct, parallel ventral and dorsal pathways within the extrastriate visual cortex. This causes motion for adults to be "color-blind," in the sense that adults can discern the direction of moving stripes only if they are of contrasting luminance but not if they vary only in color. Unlike adults, infants 2 to 4 months old can discern the direction of movement of stripes defined by either color or luminance (Dobkins and Anderson

2002). These results suggest that the motion and color pathways in the visual cortex are not initially as segregated as they will become.

The observation of functional cross-sensory connections in infants, combined with anatomical evidence for increased cross-modal connectivity in synesthetes (Rouw et al. 2011), supports the "neonatal synesthesia hypothesis": that the perception of typical infants is influenced more strongly by cross-modal activation than the perception of non-synesthetic adults, perhaps even to the point that an inducer in one modality can induce a conscious synesthetic percept in another modality or along another dimension (Maurer 1993; Maurer and Maurer 1988; Maurer and Mondloch 2004; Maurer, Gibson, and Spector 2012; Spector and Maurer 2009). Indeed, three recent studies provide empirical evidence for synesthetic-like cross-modal correspondences in young infants (see section entitled "Manifestations of synesthesia-like perception in infants and young children").

The neonatal synesthesia hypothesis proposes that all infants experience a form of synesthesia, but that these cross-sensory percepts are largely eliminated in most people via experience-dependent neural pruning as they develop through childhood into adulthood. This pruning leaves behind remnants that are largely inhibited but nevertheless influence intuitive cross-modal associations (Spector and Maurer 2009). For example, even non-synesthetic adults might sense that higher pitch matches brighter light in some way. The hypothesis suggests that those who experience synesthesia as adults, in contrast, experience less-than-normal synaptic pruning among and between sensory cortices during development, causing some of the functional cross-modal hyperconnectivity observed in infancy to persist into adulthood (Maurer 1993; Maurer and Mondloch 2004; Maurer et al. 2012; Spector and Maurer 2009). In addition, there may be less inhibition of the remaining connections. Consistent with this hypothesis, synesthetes report having experienced their synesthesia "all their lives" and often experience more than one form of synesthesia (Simner et al. 2006), an outcome predicted by less overall pruning and inhibition throughout the brain. Also, consistent with this hypothesis is neuroimaging evidence of activation by black letters and digits in adults with colored grapheme synesthesia of color area V4, which lies contiguous to the visual word form area. Also activated is a network involving other extrastriate visual areas, posterior parietal areas involved in binding color and shape, the insula, the precentral gyrus, and the frontal lobe (Hubbard et al. 2005; Rouw et al. 2011). That these activations result from hyperconnectivity is supported by evidence for increased white and gray matter in much of the same network (Rouw and Scholte 2007, 2010; Weiss and Fink 2009). Although much less extensive, there is similar neuroimaging and anatomical evidence for hyperconnectivity in other forms of synesthesia (Hänggi et al. 2008; reviewed in Hubbard, Brang, and Ramachandran 2011; Rouw et al. 2011).

In the typically developing child, the initial exuberant connections are reshaped by experience so that those that are frequently activated become stronger and those that are rarely used are pruned. The best evidence for this experience-dependent pruning comes from comparisons of typical adults with those who missed auditory or visual input because of deafness or blindness, respectively. In adults who are congenitally blind, unlike adults with normal vision, auditory, tactile, and language input increase activation in the visual cortex. Interference with this activation by transcranial magnetic stimulation (TMS; a method in which magnetic stimulation is applied to the scalp to depolarize neurons in the underlying cortex, effectively disrupting the normal processing of affected cortical structures) degrades accuracy in responding to those inputs (Collignon et al. 2009; Kupers et al. 2007; Lewis, Saenz, and Fine 2010; Pascual-Leone and Hamilton 2001; Pascual-Leone and Torres 1993; Stilla et al. 2008). Indeed, in adult cats whose eyes were removed at birth, neurons in the visual cortex are tuned precisely to auditory rather than visual inputs (other modalities have not been tested) (Yaka, Yinon, and Wollberg 1999). Similarly, in adults who are congenitally deaf, unlike normally hearing adults, visual input increases activation of the auditory cortex (Finney 2003; Finney, Fine, and Dobkins 2001).

Together, these studies suggest that in typical development, dominant input from a single sensory system leads to the specialization of sensory cortical areas through the strengthening and refinement of the synapses it drives. It also leads to the pruning away of other synapses that respond to the less frequent or less coherent input from other sensory modalities. Remnants of the initial cross-sensory connections do remain but they have minimal impact because their influence is dampened by neuronal inhibition. They nevertheless can influence our cross-modal associations (Spector and Maurer 2009). Unlike typical adults, synesthetes appear to have a genetic predisposition for the pruning process to be less complete and for the remaining connections to be uninhibited (Hubbard, Brang, and Ramachandran 2011; Ramachandran and Hubbard 2001a, 2001b). Instead, or in addition, the synesthete may develop less than the normal amount of modulation of the remaining hyperconnectivity by feedback from higher cortical areas (Grossenbacher and Lovelace 2001; Smilek et al. 2001).

Regardless of the origins of synesthesia in adults, the implication is that synesthesia will be a normal phase in typical development, either before experience-dependent pruning is complete, or before inhibition has emerged and been consolidated. Two predictions follow: (1) even in the typical, non-synesthetic adult, functional remnants of cross-sensory and cross-dimensional connections should still exist because of incomplete pruning or inhibition; (2) to the extent that contiguous brain areas are organized systematically by specific stimulus properties (e.g. neurons are contiguous that have the same orientation or color tuning in the visual cortex or the same tuning to auditory frequency in the auditory cortex), there may be similarities in the cross-modal and cross-dimensional associations of typical children and adults and the conscious percepts of synesthetes. In the next section, we present evidence for similarities between the perception of adults with synesthesia and the perception of typical infants and toddlers. We then summarize the two studies documenting changes in the nature of synesthesia during development and in the final section, consider their implications for the neonatal synesthesia hypothesis.

Manifestations of Synesthesia-Like Perception in Infants and Young Children

Evidence of functional hyperconnectivity in early development and of the slow development of inhibitory processes (discussed in the previous section) suggests that young children's perception should resemble that of adults with synesthesia. In this section, we summarize investigations of whether cross-modal and cross-dimensional percepts that are commonly elicited in adults with synesthesia can be observed early in development.

Synesthesia-like perception in infants

Wagner and Dobkins (2011) recently provided the first direct evidence for synesthetic perception in typical infants. They did so by testing for the infant equivalent of colored grapheme synesthesia, which they reasoned would be manifest as the elicitation of a colored percept by basic shapes. Specifically, they presented infants with arrays of triangles on some trials and arrays of circles on other trials, in each case against a background that was half red (or yellow) and half green (or blue). The researchers hypothesized that if either shape evoked a particular color for an infant, that shape would be easier to see against some colors than against others. For example, if an infant perceived red when looking at the triangle, it would be easier for that infant to see the triangle against a green background than against a red background. In this case, the infant should look consistently at the green side when shown triangles, both on trials when the green background was on the right side of the panel and trials when it was on the left side of the panel. Consistent with this hypothesis, infants behaved as though the shapes were colored by exhibiting non-random responses across trials—a result suggesting that synesthetic binding of color and shape is present at 2 months of age for red/green. The same pattern of results was observed in slightly older infants for yellow/blue backgrounds (as expected, given the slower development of yellow/blue channels). This pattern diminished with increasing age, as would be expected if experience-dependent pruning has begun to shape inputs into visual cortical neurons.

Other studies have looked for cross-modal associations in infants that match typical synesthetic percepts in adults with synesthesia. One common form of synesthesia is colored hearing, in which specific pitches evoke specific colors and often shapes as well. Although these pitch to color associations are largely idiosyncratic, higher pitches usually evoke visual percepts of sharp, pointy shapes that are smaller in size and located higher in space, and lower pitches usually evoke percepts of round, amoeboid shapes that are of larger size and located lower in space (Marks 1974, 1975; Melara and O'Brien 1987). To test whether these associations are present early in development, Walker and colleagues (2010) presented 3- to 4-month-old infants with two audiovisual combinations. In one combination, a visual display showed a shape morphing from round and amoeboid to sharp and pointy, while a whistle changed from low to high pitch (congruent condition) or from high to low pitch (incongruent condition). In a second combination, an orange ball moved up and down the screen while the pitch of the whistle increased and decreased, respectively (congruent condition), or while the whistle first decreased and then increased (incongruent condition). In both experiments, infants looked longer at the congruent displays, a preference that the authors interpreted as a familiarity preference—an interpretation suggesting infants experience common synesthesia-like pitch/shape and pitch/height associations. Even if the authors' assumption of a familiarity preference is unwarranted, the results do indicate that 3- to 4-month-old infants systematically relate pitch and shape, as well as pitch and location. In a separate experiment, Peña and colleagues (Peña, Mehler, and Nespor 2011) found that 4-month-old infants also associate sound with size: when they heard a consonant-vowel pairing with higher pitch vowels such as /i/ (as in feet), they looked longer at the smaller of two geometric shapes, and when they heard the pairing with lower pitch vowels such as /a/ (as in cat), they looked longer at the larger object. These associations may be based on pitch, because the "smaller" sounds had a higher pitch than the "larger" sounds. As it is unlikely that infants have learned these associations from the statistics of the environment (e.g., there is no obvious connection between pointed shapes and higher pitch), these associations may represent natural biases that result from the initial hyperconnectivity of the auditory and visual systems and that persist as conscious percepts in adults with audiovisual synesthesia. Remnants of these associations appear to exert unconscious influences in non-synesthetic adults (Spector and Maurer 2009).

Even when pitch is matched between sound contrasts, infants show systematic associations between sound and shape. Typical adults tend to associate words with rounded vowels (e.g. the phoneme /o/, as in code, or /u/, as in rule) with round, amoeboid shapes, and words with non-rounded vowels (e.g., the phoneme /i/, as in feet) with pointed shapes (Köhler 1929; Lindauer 1990; Ramachandran and Hubbard 2001b). There are additional systematic associations of these shapes to specific consonants (Nielsen and Rendall 2011). Infants just 4 months old make similar sound symbolic matches: when presented with words matched to ameboid shapes (*kiki*) versus jagged shapes (*bubu*) by 98% of English-speaking adults, infants look longer on trials with the incongruent mapping than on trials with the congruent mappings (Orturk, Krehm, and Vouloumanos 2013). Unlike adults, presentation of just the vowel contrast (*kiki* versus *kuku*) or just the consonant contrast (*bubu* versus *kuku*) is insufficient to elicit the congruency effect. By toddlerhood, children explicitly match words with rounded vowels (e.g. go-gaa, maa-boo-maa, go-go, do-do) with round, amoeboid shapes and words with non-rounded vowels (e.g. tee-tay; tuh-kee-tee, gee gee, dee-dee) with sharp, pointy shapes (Maurer, Pathman, and Mondloch, 2006), and do so even when the stimuli contrast only in vowels (*bibi* versus *bobo*) (Spector and Maurer, 2013). It is possible that these associations are based in experience. Having been exposed to language since they were in the womb, it is possible that children become sensitive to the statistical regularities of English semantics, and may have learned that sharp objects often have names with non-rounded vowels (e.g., the last syllable of spiky) and round objects often have names with rounded vowels (e.g., round, amoeboid). Although that explanation is plausible for the data from toddlers and adults, it seems unlikely to explain the results from 4-month-old infants. Future research could test for the associations at even younger ages and test whether the same relationships hold for synesthetes for whom specific sounds induce specific shapes, as would be predicted if the infants' and toddlers' associations are a consequence of neonatal synesthesia.

Some cross-modal correspondences seen in synesthetic adults can be explained as a manifestation of a common code for magnitude, such that more intense stimuli in one modality induce more intense percepts in another modality. For example, adults with colored hearing synesthesia report that louder sounds induce brighter percepts (Marks 1974, 1975). Similarly, newborn infants habituated to a brighter light exhibit less heart-rate response to the presentation of a louder noise, while those habituated to a darker light show less heart-rate response to a softer noise (Lewkowicz and Turkewitz 1980)—as if they transfer habituation from visual to auditory intensity.

In sum, it is clear that infants experience a number of functional cross-sensory connections, some of which cannot readily be explained by learning and manifest as synesthesia-like perception.

Synesthesia-like perceptions in toddlers

With toddlers, we have investigated a number of other correspondences that are common in synesthetes. According to the neonatal synesthesia hypothesis, the initial hyperconnectivity should be most prominent during infancy, but remnants of it should persist into toddlerhood, and, to a lesser extent, even adulthood. While studies with infants make it easier to sort out the role of experience versus intrinsic wiring, studies of toddlers and older children can be easier to interpret because the child understands verbal instructions.

In addition to the evidence for colored percepts elicited by shapes during infancy (see earlier section entitled "The developmental origins of synesthesia"), there is evidence for color associations to some letters in toddlers that parallel the colored percepts elicited by letters in adults with colored grapheme synesthesia. Thus, both typical toddlers and adults with colored grapheme synesthesia associate X and Z with black, I and O with white, and C with yellow at rates far exceeding chance (Spector and Maurer 2008, 2011). For toddlers, like typical synesthetes with colored graphemes, these associations were observed when they were presented with both the letter shape and sound or just the letter shape, but not when they just heard the sound of the letter. Certain other common associations in colored grapheme synesthesia appear to result from learning to read because there is a ready explanation based on literacy (G is green for English-speaking synesthetes) and because typical toddlers are random while older children who have learned to read make the expected association. This is the developmental pattern for English-speaking children for A/red; G/green; B/blue; and Y/yellow (Spector and Maurer 2008, 2011). Combined, the results suggest that there are some natural associations between shapes and colors that influence toddlers' cross-dimensional associations and the actual percepts of adults with colored grapheme synesthesia (Day 2005; Rich, Bradshaw, and Mattingley 2005; Simner et al. 2006). Not surprisingly, remnants of this organization are also evident in the letter/color associations of typical adults without synesthesia (Rich, Bradshaw, and Mattingley 2005; Simner et al. 2006).

Toddlers also associate pitch to surface lightness in the same way as adults with colored hearing synesthesia. Although the exact color elicited by a particular pitch varies among adults with colored hearing, almost universally they report that higher pitches induce percepts of lighter colors: a higher pitched C induces a lighter color than a lower pitched C (Marks 1974, 1975; Ward, Huckstep, and Tsakanikos 2006). A similar pattern is observed in toddlers. This was evident when 2.5- to 3-year-old toddlers observed a display of two balls, one white and one gray, bouncing in synchrony with one another and accompanied by a higher or lower pitched tone (Mondloch and Maurer 2004). When asked which ball was making which tone, the toddlers consistently matched the lighter-colored white ball to the higher pitched tone, and the darker, gray ball to the lower pitched tone. This association is unlikely to have developed through experience with the statistics of the environment, because lighter colored stimuli do not consistently produce higher-pitched sounds than darker stimuli (e.g., white cats do not have higher-pitched meows than black cats). Instead, it is possible that this pairing reflects a natural bias induced by cortical connectivity between neighboring sensory cortices that influences the synesthetic percepts of adults with colored hearing and the cross-modal matches of young children. Remnants of the connections appear to influence the perception of non-synesthetic adults: they also match higher pitches to lighter colors, and are more accurate at judging pitch or lightness when the luminance of a paired distracter is congruent (Marks 1987).

Adults with colored hearing also commonly report that exposure to pitch induces visual images, with higher pitches inducing visual photisms that are smaller in size than those induced by lower pitched sounds (Marks 1975; see section "Synesthesia-like perception in infants"). This association is evident in toddlers: when asked which of two bouncing white balls was making a higher- or lower-pitched sound, 2.5- to 3-year-olds matched the higher pitch with the smaller ball, and the lower pitch with the larger ball (Mondloch and Maurer 2004). It is possible that this association arises with exposure to regularities in the environment because larger organisms tend to produce lower-pitched sounds: the roar of a lion is lower pitched than the squeak of a mouse. However, the association may also reflect a natural bias based in cortical connectivity that is reinforced and strengthened with experience. A role for experience is supported by the fact that children exhibit stronger evidence of making the association at older ages (Marks, Hammeal, and Bornstein 1987).

In sum, in addition to evidence of functional hyperconnectivity in human infants, behavioral evidence lends support to the hypothesis that all infants experience synesthesia-like percepts. The similarity of cross-sensory associations in adults with synesthesia, toddlers, and non-synesthetic adults suggests that remnants of the early hyperconnectivity persist to influence cross-modal and cross-dimensional associations, whether or not it is sufficiently strong to influence conscious perception (as it does in adult syn-esthetes). Many of these cross-sensory associations cannot be explained by learning, and as such, likely reflect natural biases arising from unpruned and uninhibited exuber-ant neural connections between contiguous brain areas.

LONGITUDINAL OBSERVATIONS OF
DEVELOPING SYNESTHETES

One of the most common forms of synesthesia is colored graphemes (Day 2005; Novich, Cheng, and Eagleman 2011; Simner et al. 2006; Ward, Simner, and Auyeung 2005). However, as letters and numbers are culturally-learned stimuli, it is likely that colored-grapheme synesthesia cannot have been present since birth despite the impression of synesthetes that they have had it "all their lives." Instead, it is likely that it was originally manifest as a robust association between color and basic shapes or between color and the sound of words, as suggested by the finding that infants appear to perceive circles versus triangles as differentially colored (Wagner and Dobkins 2011) and the finding that toddlers' associations between letters and colors are driven systematically by the jaggedness of the shape (Spector and Maurer 2008, 2011) (see section "Manifestations of synesthesia-like perception in infants and young chil-dren"). Indeed, one adult with colored grapheme synesthesia and colored hearing has preserved pictures she drew as a pre-schooler of the sound of words: it appears that before she learned to read she drew a unique design for each word (Duffy 2001). The sample reproduced in the book resembles a swirling kaleidoscope of three- and four-sided shapes in red, purple, blue, and yellow, overlaid with blue circles and yellow curved lines.

Two longitudinal studies on the development of colored grapheme synesthesia illus-trate how the phenomenon changes as children learn to read. Simner and colleagues (Simner et al. 2009) asked a large sample (615) of 6- to 7-year-old British children to choose the best of 13 possible colors for the 26 letters of the English alphabet and the ten numerals from 0 to 9 on an initial test, and on a surprise retest 10 seconds later. Follow-up tests 1 year later with the 46 children who were significantly more consist-ent than their peers during the first session pointed to eight children who appeared to have colored grapheme synesthesia, or 1.3% of the sample: their color choices were more consistent over 12 months than those of their peers after 10 seconds during the first ses-sion. Interestingly, across the 12 months, the putative synesthetes became more consist-ent, moving from having on average 10.5 stable grapheme-to-color associations (29%) during the first session to16.9 stable associations (43%) during the second session 1 year later. Even so, at age 8, more than half of the graphemes were not consistently colored for these putative synesthetes, a far larger proportion than lack color for adults with colored grapheme synesthesia (Mills et al. 2002).

A similar picture emerges from our longitudinal study of three pre-school English-speaking children of mothers with colored grapheme synesthesia (Spector and Maurer, unpublished data). Because synesthesia tends to run in families, we knew that the likelihood that these children would have some form of synesthesia was higher than in the general population. Moreover, all three children were making comments from the start of our observations suggesting that they experienced some colored graphemes. Over 1 to 2 years, beginning at age 3.5, 3.75, or 4.5 years, the three children were asked to choose from among 96 crayons, the best one or ones to color the 26 letters of the alphabet, the digits 0 to 9, and four basic shapes. Once the child had colored all of those stimuli, with no more than one given per day, the cycle was repeated, with a total of six cycles for one child, and three cycles for the other two children. As a baseline against which to evaluate consistency, we tested non-synesthetic control children on two cycles of the same task at the age corresponding to each synesthete's 1st and 2nd cycle, and, for the child with six cycles, between the 5th and 6th cycles, with four controls for each time point and stimulus. Each control child was tested with ten of the stimuli.

From the first test, each putative synesthete reported having very specific color associations to the graphemes. Parents recorded comments like: "This is definitely blue, but not dark blue, this blue"; "The right green is not in this box, but this is as close as I can find"; "This letter is always gray like rain clouds." Such comments are reminiscent of reports of how specific and adamant adult synesthetes are about their synesthetic colors. The three putative synesthetes were far more consistent (55%) than their age-matched controls (0%), but less consistent than adults synesthetes (Baron-Cohen et al. 1996). Moreover, consistency between later cycles (cycles five to six, or for the children with only three cycles, cycles two to three; age 4.5 to 5.5 years: 75%) was much higher than between the first two cycles (age 3.75 to 4.75 years: 40%), perhaps because learning to read altered the neural representation of the letters. Most of the inconsistencies during the first two cycles were small, such as purple changing to red or a letter colored yellow changing to half yellow/half orange. Tests of letter knowledge indicated that children progressed from some basic letter knowledge at the beginning of testing to complete letter and letter-sound knowledge by the end of testing. Like studies of color-shape associations in typical toddlers (Spector and Maurer 2011), these data suggest that there may be intrinsic connections between graphemes and color that are modified as children learn to read and those graphemes take on meaning.

At the initial meeting, all children were tested on immediate and delayed recall for letters, numbers, colors, objects, and shapes. On the immediate test, two of the three synesthetic children showed a much higher rate of recall than age-matched controls (see Table 3.1). After a 5-minute delay, only one synesthetic child showed a much higher rate of recall than controls (see Table 3.1). It is important to note that the synesthetic children who did not perform better on the memory tests appeared bored with the task (perhaps because their procedure was much longer than that for controls), and thus their performance may be more reflective of a lack of attentiveness than a lack of memory. However, the evidence of superior memory in some of the children is consistent with

Table 3.1 Correct responses on a memory task consisting of immediate and delayed recall for four each of colors, letters, objects, numbers, and shapes. Memory scores for synesthetic children (GK, BP, and ED) are presented in raw scores (number correct). Memory scores for controls are the mean of correct responses across the three controls for each synesthetic child

Immediate	Colors	Letters	Objects	Numbers	Shapes	Overall
GK	4	2	4	4	2	3.2
Control average	2.75	3.25	4	3	3.25	3.25
BP	4	4	4	2	4	3.6
Control average	0	1.5	2.25	1.5	2.25	1.5
ED	4	3	4	4	4	3.8
Control average	2	1.75	2.5	1.25	2.5	2
Delay	Colors	Letters	Objects	Numbers	Shapes	Overall
GK	3	0	0	0	0	0.6
Control average	2.75	2.25	4	3.5	3.75	3.25
BP	0	4	4	2	4	2.8
Control average	0	0.8	0.8	0.4	0.8	0.56
ED	0	2	0	0	0	0.4
Control average	0.5	0.75	1.25	0.75	1	0.85

evidence that adult synesthetes have a better memory for stimuli related to their synesthesia (Yaro and Ward 2007) or, in some cases, more generally (Gross et al. 2011).

In sum, although synesthetes report having their particular forms of synesthesia "all their lives," longitudinal data on the general population of 6- to 7-year-olds and on preschool children growing up in synesthetic homes suggests that the nature of synesthesia changes as children enter and progress through school, at least for colored grapheme synesthesia: their color associations to graphemes become more consistent and more graphemes induce consistent choices. It is not clear whether these changes represent the emergence of synesthetic percepts that are greater in number, stronger, or more salient and/or an increase in the stability of the color induced, which may be as strong perceptually at all ages. Children's comments in our longitudinal study favor the latter hypothesis because they described very specific colors from the start, much like synesthetic adults.

RECONSIDERATION OF THE NEONATAL SYNESTHESIA HYPOTHESIS

Studies of typical infants and young children (see "Manifestations of synesthesia-like perception in infants and young children" section) provide support for the neonatal synesthesia hypothesis: before they learn to read, typical children associate some shapes to specific colors and make systematic cross-modal associations that are not explained easily by mere learning of the statistical regularities in the environment. In at least some cases, these associations match common percepts induced in adults with synesthesia. Studies of emerging colored grapheme synesthesia (see section "Manifestations of synesthesia-like perception in infants and young children") also provide support by showing that its manifestation in pre-literature children has many of its later hallmarks: highly specific induced colors and consistency over time. What seems paradoxical is that the consistency increases with age and learning to read and that, like so many other forms of synesthesia (e.g., ordinal space synesthesia for days of the weeks or months of the year; gustatory synesthesia induced by words), it involves a culturally learned inducer that children learn postnatally.

An evolutionary perspective is useful in thinking about this paradox. Such culturally learned stimuli developed fairly recently, long after the brain had evolved to process color, shape, touch, flavor, etc., processing systems that are well-conserved across mammalian species. Dehaene and Cohen (2011) have hypothesized that the neural representation of such cultural stimuli makes use of existing cortical specialization by recycling neuronal architecture best suited for the types of computations needed. In the case of reading and writing, they speculate that the neural recycling took advantage of brain areas already adept at processing objects and faces. Support for this hypothesis comes from their findings for the visual word form area in the left temporal cortex, which sits next to color area V4, that is active in colored hearing and colored grapheme synesthesia. In typical adults (synesthetes have not been studied), the visual word form area responds more to strings of letters than to line drawings of objects, scrambled words, or scrambled objects. This specialization for letter processing/reading is evident in adults who know how to read, whether they learned as adults or children, but not in illiterate adults (Dehaene et al. 2010). At the same time, the visual word form area responds to other objects—to faces, houses, tools, and patterns of checks—but the response to at least some of these categories is smaller in literate than in illiterate adults, as would be expected if reading is making use of neurons that would otherwise be used to process objects. From this perspective, colored grapheme synesthesia would not be expected to emerge in its adult form before the child has begun to learn to read so that hyperconnectivity between the reshaped visual word form area/fusiform gyrus and color area V4 can be manifest. Before the child learns to read, the same hyperconnectivity could be manifest in other forms, such as colored facial features, shapes, or sounds. Consistent with the neuronal recycling account, graphemes that are encountered most frequently have the strongest representation in the visual word form area (Dehaene and Cohen 2011) and elicit correspondingly brighter synesthetic percepts in adults with colored grapheme synesthesia (Beeli, Esslen, and Jäncke 2007; Cohen Kadosh, Henik, and Walsh 2009; Simner 2007; Smilek et al. 2007). For similar reasons, graphemes learned early (1, 2, 3) or learned in association with specific colors, such as those on fridge magnets (Witthoft and Winawer 2006), may be strongly represented in the visual word form area and elicit especially strong or consistent colors in those individuals with the hyperconnectivity leading to colored grapheme synesthesia. Similarly, culturally based ordinal sequences, such as the days of the week or the months of the year, may be represented in the right parietal cortex because its pre-existing properties make it best suited to represent them by neuronal recycling—and as they become represented there, they easily become linked to other properties represented in the parietal cortex in those with hyperconnectivity, namely, spatial position and/or colored shapes (Hubbard et al. 2005).

Remnants of neonatal synesthesia are evident in typical adults (Spector and Maurer 2009) as intuitive cross-modal associations and subsequent influences on behavior. These remnants may be sufficiently strong to induce synesthetic percepts after the use of drugs that reduce inhibition (e.g., lysergic acid diethylamide (LSD)) or after hypnosis (Cohen Kadosh et al. 2009). Nevertheless, they appear insufficient to support the induction of synesthesia through training without altered states of consciousness. Non-synesthetic adults can learn to associate a specific color to a specific letter through many hours of training or through years of linking numbers to colors in activities such as cross-stitch needlepoint (e.g., one cross-stitching system uses the number 3 to denote red thread and the number 7 to denote yellow etc.; Elias et al. 2003; Meier and Rothen 2009; Rothen, Wantz, and Meier 2011). Nonetheless, these individuals do not experience those colors perceptually, although they may show congruency effects in a Stroop-type task: trainees are slower to name the font color of digits if these colors conflict with their learned associations (i.e., slower to name the font color of digit 3 if this is yellow versus red). This is much like the interference found in genuine synesthetes—who are slower for colors that conflict with their synesthesia—even though the non-synesthetic trainees do not experience synesthetic percepts (Elias et al. 2003; Meier and Rothen 2009).

Recent evidence of unexpected plasticity in the adult brain (reviewed in Bavelier et al. 2010) suggests that there are manipulations that might increase the efficacy of the remnants of the original hyperconnectivity. For example, pharmacological interventions that reduce neural inhibition (e.g., Rösser et al. 2008), engaging in aerobic exercise (e.g., Colcombe and Kramer 2003), and playing action video games (e.g., Li et al. 2011) all appear to induce heightened plasticity in the adult brain. However, it is not clear that doing so would be desirable—after all, the function of experience-dependent pruning is to tune the individual's brain to match the stimuli in his or her environment. It leads to sensory cortices that are relatively specialized and efficient for specific functions. Sudden strengthening of the residual hyperconnectivity—unlike spending years of development learning about a world formed of a combination of "real" and synesthetic percepts—might lead to a loss of sensitivity to the building blocks of perception.

In summary, we have shown that infants and young children exhibit functional hyperconnectivity between the senses, much of which is reminiscent of the cross-modal associations observed in synesthetic adults. The recent research findings reviewed in this chapter lend cogent support to the hypothesis that all individuals experience something like synesthesia as infants, with remnants of these cross-modal associations still observable in adulthood, either explicitly in synesthetes or implicitly in all other people.

References

Asher, Julian E., Michael R.F. Aitken, Nasr Farooqi, Sameer Kurmani, and Simon Baron-Cohen. 2006. Diagnosing and phenotyping visual synaesthesia: A preliminary evaluation of the revised test of genuineness (TOG-R). *Cortex* 42:137–146.

Baron-Cohen, Simon, Lucy Burt, Fiona Smith-Laittan, John Harrison and Patrick Bolton. 1996. Synaesthesia: prevalence and familiality. *Perception* 25:1073–1079.

Bavelier, Daphne, Dennis M. Levi, Roger W. Li, Yang Dan, and Takao K. Hensch. 2010. Removing brakes on adult brain plasticity: From molecular to behavioral interventions. *The Journal of Neuroscience* 30:14964–14971.

Beeli, Gian, Michaela Esslen, and Lutz Jäncke. 2007. Frequency correlates in grapheme-color synaesthesia. *Psychological Science* 18:788–792. doi: 10.1111/j.1467-9280.2007.01980.x.

Bourgeois, Jean-Pierre, and Rakic, Pasko. 1993. Changes of synaptic density in the primary visual cortex of the macaque monkey from fetal to adult stage. *The Journal of Neuroscience* 13:2801–2820.

Chugani, Harry T. 1994. Development of regional brain glucose metabolism in relation to behavior and plasticity. In *Human Behavior and the Developing Brain*, ed. Geraldine Dawson and Kurt W. Fischer, 153–175. New York: Guilford Press.

Chugani, Harry T., and Michael E. Phelps. 1986. Maturational changes in cerebral function in infants determined by 18FDG positron emission tomography. *Science* 23:840–843. DOI: 10.1126/science.3945811.

Chugani, Harry T., Michael E. Phelps, and John C. Mazziotta. 1987. Positron emission tomography study of human brain functional development. *Annals of Neurology* 22:487–497.

Cohen Kadosh, Roi, Avishai Henik, Andres Catena, Vincent Walsh, and Luis J. Fuentes. 2009. Induced cross-modal synaesthetic experience without abnormal neuronal connections. *Psychological Science* 20:258–265.

Cohen Kadosh, Roi, Avishai Henik, and Vincent Walsh. 2009. Synaesthesia: Learned or lost? *Developmental Science* 12:484–491.

Colcombe, Stanley, and Arthur F. Kramer. 2003. Fitness effects on the cognitive function of older adults: A meta-analytic study. *Psychological Science* 14:125–130.

Collignon, Olivier, Geneviève Charbonneau, Maryse Lassonde, and Franco Lepore. 2009. Early visual deprivation alters multisensory processing in peripersonal space. *Neuropsychologia* 47:3236–3243.

Day, Sean. 2005. Some demographic and socio-cultural aspects of synesthesia. In *Synesthesia: Perspectives from Cognitive Neuroscience*, ed. Lynn C. Robertson and Noam Sagiv, 11–33. Oxford: Oxford University Press.

Dehaene, Stanislas, and Laurent Cohen. 2011. The unique role of the visual word form area in reading. *Trends in Cognitive Sciences* 15:254–262.

Dehaene, Stanislas, Felipe Pegado, Lucia W. Braga, Paulo Ventura, Gilberto Nunes Filho, Antoinette Jobert, Ghislaine Dehaene-Lambertz, Régine Kolinsky, José Morais, and Laurent Cohen. 2010. How learning to read changes the cortical networks for vision and language. *Science (New York, N.Y.)*, 330 (6009):1359–1364. doi:10.1126/science.1194140.

Dehay, Colette, Jean Bullier, and Henry Kennedy. 1984. Transient projections from the fronto-parietal and temporal cortex to areas 17, 18 and 19 in the kitten. *Experimental Brain Research* 57:208–212.

Dobkins, Karen R., and Christina M. Anderson. 2002. Color-based motion processing is stronger in infants than in adults. *Psychological Science* 13:76–80.

Duffy, Patricia L. 2001. *Blue Cats and Chartreuse Kittens: How Synesthetes Color Their World*. New York: Times Books.

Elias, Lorin J., Deborah M. Saucier, Colleen Hardie, and Gordon E. Sarty. 2003. Dissociating semantic and perceptual components of synaesthesia: Behavioural and functional neuro-anatomical investigations. *Cognitive Brain Research* 16:232–237.

Fair, Damien A., Alexander L. Cohen, Jonathan D. Power, Nico U. F. Dosenbach, Jessica A. Church, Francis M. Miezin, Bradley L. Schlaggar, Steven E. Petersen. 2009. Functional brain networks develop from a "local to distributed" organization. *PLoS Computational Biology* 5 (5):e1000381. doi:10.1371/journal.pcbi.1000381.

Finney, Eva M., Brett A. Clementz, Gregory Hickok, and Karen R. Dobkins. 2003. Visual stimuli activate auditory cortex in deaf subjects: Evidence from MEG. *Neuroreport* 14:1425–1427.

Finney, Eva M., Ione Fine, and Karen R. Dobkins. 2001. Visual stimuli activate auditory cortex in the deaf. *Nature Neuroscience* 4:1171–1173. doi:10.1038/nn763.

Gross, Veronica C., Sandy Neargarder, Catherine L. Caldwell-Harris, and Alice Cronin-Golomb. 2011. Superior encoding enhances recall in color-graphemic synesthesia. *Perception* 40:196. doi:10.1068/p6647.

Grossenbacher, Peter G. and Christopher T. Lovelace. 2001. Mechanisms of synesthesia: Cognitive and physiological constraints. *Trends in Cognitive Sciences* 5:36–41.

Hänggi, Jürgen, Gian Beeli, Mathias S. Oechslin, and Lutz Jäncke. 2008. The multiple synaes-thete E.S.: Neuroanatomical basis of interval-taste and tone-colour synaesthesia. *Neuroimage* 43:192–203. doi:10.1016/j.neuroimage.2008.07.018.

Homae, Fumitaka, Hama Watanabe, Tamami Nakano, Gentaro Taga. 2011. Large-Scale brain networks underlying language acquisition in early infancy. *Frontiers in Psychology* 2:93. doi:10.3389/fpsyg.2011.00093.

Hubbard, Edward M., A. Cyrus Arman, Vilayanur S. Ramachandran, and Geoffrey M. Boynton. 2005. Individual differences among grapheme-color synesthetes: Brain-behavior correla-tions. *Neuron* 45:975–985. doi:10.1016/j.neuron.2005.02.008.

Hubbard, Edward M., David Brang, and Vilayanur S. Ramachandran. 2011. The cross-activation theory at 10. *Journal of Neuropsychology* 5:152–177. doi:10.1111/j.1748-6653.2011.02014.

Hubbard, Edward M., Manuela Piazza, Philippe Pinel, and Stanislas Dehaene. 2005. Interactions between number and space in parietal cortex. *Nature Reviews Neuroscience* 6:435–448. doi:10.1038/nrn1684.

Huttenlocher, Peter R. 1984. Synapse elimination and plasticity in developing human cerebral cortex. *American Journal of Mental Deficiency* 88:488–496.

Jarick, Michelle, Mike J. Dixon, Emily C. Maxwell, Michael E. R. Nicholls, and Daniel Smilek. 2009. The ups and downs (and lefts and rights) of synaesthetic number forms: Validation from spatial cueing and snarc-type tasks. *Cortex* 45:1190–1199. doi:10.1016/j.cortex.2009.04.015.

Köhler, W. 1929. *Gestalt Psychology*. New York: Liveright.

Kupers, R., M. Pappens, A. Maertens de Noordhout, J. Schoenen, M. Ptito, and A. Fumal. 2007. rTMS of the occipital cortex abolishes braille reading and repetition priming in blind sub-jects. *Neurology* 68:691–693. doi:10.1212/01.wnl.0000255958.60530.11.

Lewis, Lindsay B., Melissa Saenz, and Ione Fine. 2010. Mechanisms of cross-modal plasticity in early blind subjects. *Journal of Neurophysiology* 104:2995–3008. doi:10.1152/jn.00983.2009.

Lewkowicz, David J., and Gerald Turkewitz. 1980. Cross-modal equivalence in early infancy: Auditory-visual intensity matching. *Developmental Psychology* 16:597–607. doi:10.1037/0012-1649.16.6.597.

Li, Roger W., Charlie Ngo, Jennie Nguyen, and Dennis M. Levi. 2011. Video-game play induces plasticity in the visual system of adults with amblyopia. *PLoS Biology* 9:e1001135. doi:10.1371/journal.pbio.1001135.

Lindauer, Martin S. 1990. The effects of the physiognomic stimuli taketa and maluma on the meanings of neutral stimuli. *Bulletin of the Psychology Society* 28:151–154.

Marks, Lawrence E. 1974. On associations of light and sound: The mediation of brightness, pitch, and loudness. *The American Journal of Psychology* 87:173–188.

——. 1975. On colored-hearing synesthesia: Cross-modal translations of sensory dimensions. *Psychological Bulletin* 82:303–331. doi:10.1037/0033–2909.82.3.303.

——. 1987. On cross-modal similarity: Auditory-visual interactions in speeded discrimination. *Journal of Experimental Psychology: Human Perception and Performance* 13:384–394. doi:10.1037/0096-1523.13.3.384.

Marks, Lawrence E., Robin J. Hammeal, and Marc H. Bornstein. 1987. Perceiving similarity and comprehending metaphor. *Monographs of the Society for Research in Child Development* 52:1–102.

Maurer, Daphne. 1993. Neonatal synesthesia: Implications for the processing of speech and faces. In *Developmental Neurocognition: Speech and Face Processing in the First Year of Life*, ed. Bénédicte de Boysson-Bardies, Scania de Schonen, Peter Jusczyk, Peter McNeilage, and John Morton, 109–124. Dordrecht: Kluver.

Maurer, Daphne, and Charles Maurer. 1988. *The World of the Newborn*. New York: Basic Books.

Maurer, Daphne, and Catherine J. Mondloch. 2004. Neonatal synesthesia: A re-evaluation. In *Synesthesia: Perspectives from Cognitive Neuroscience*, ed. Lynn C. Robertson and Noam Sagiv, 193–213. New York: Oxford University Press.

Maurer, Daphne, Laura C. Gibson, and Ferrine Spector. 2012. Infant synaesthesia: New insights into the development of multisensory perception. In *Multisensory Development*, ed. Andrew J. Bremner, David J. Lewkowicz, and Charles Spence. 229–250. New York: Oxford University Press.

Maurer, Daphne, Thanujeni Pathman, and Catherine J. Mondloch. 2006. The shape of boubas: Sound-shape correspondences in toddlers and adults. *Developmental Science* 9:316–322. doi:10.1111/j.1467-7687.2006.00495.x.

Meier, Beat, and Nicolas Rothen. 2009. Training grapheme-colour associations produces a synaesthetic Stroop effect, but not a conditioned synaesthetic response. *Neuropsychologia* 47:1208–1211. doi:10.1016/j.neuropsychologia.2009.01.009.

Melara, Robert D., and Thomas P. O'Brien. 1987. Interaction between synesthetically corresponding dimensions. *Journal of Experimental Psychology: General* 116:323–336. doi:10.1037/0096-3445.116.4.323.

Mills, Carol Bergfeld, Meredith L. Viguers, Shari K. Edelson, Amanda T. Thomas, Stephanie L. Simon-Dack, and Joanne A. Innis. 2002. The color of two alphabets for a multilingual synesthete. *Perception* 31:1371–1394. doi:10.1068/p3429.

Mondloch, Catherine J., and Daphne Maurer. 2004. Do small white balls squeak? Pitch-Object correspondences in young children. *Cognitive, Affective, & Behavioral Neuroscience* 4:133–136. doi:10.3758/CABN/4.2.133.

Neville, Helen J. 1995. Developmental specificity in neurocognitive development in humans. In *The Cognitive Neurosciences*, ed. Michael S. Gazzaniga, 219–231. Cambridge, MA: The MIT Press.

Nielsen, Alan, and Drew Rendall. 2011. The sound of round: Evaluating the sound-symbolic role of consonants in the classic takete-maluma phenomenon. *Canadian Journal of Experimental Psychology* 65:115–124. doi: 10.1037/a0022268.

Novich, Scott, Sherry Cheng, and David M. Eagleman. 2011. Is synaesthesia one condition or many? A large-scale analysis reveals subgroups. *Journal of Neuropsychology* 5:353–371. doi:10.1111/j.1748-6653.2011.02015.x.

Nunn, Julia A., L. J. Gregory, M. Brammer, S. C. R. Williams, D. M. Parslow, M. J. Morgan, R. G. Morris, *et al.* 2002. Functional magnetic resonance imaging of synesthesia: Activation of V4/V8 by spoken words. *Nature Neuroscience* 5:371–375. doi:10.1038/nn818.

Orturk, Ozge, Madelaine Krehm, and Athena Vouloumanos. 2013. Sound symbolism in infancy? Evidence for sound-shape cross-modal correspondences in 4-month-olds. *Journal of Experimental Child Psychology* 114 (2):173–186. doi:10.1016/j.jecp.2012.05.004.

Pascual-Leone, Alvaro, and Roy Hamilton. 2001. The metamodal organization of the brain. *Progress in Brain Research* 134:1–19. doi:10.1016/S0079-6123(01)34028-1.

Pascual-Leone, Alvaro, and Fernando Torres. 1993. Plasticity of the sensorimotor cortex representation of the reading finger in braille readers. *Brain* 116:39–52. doi:10.1093/brain/116.1.39.

Paulesu, Eraldo, J. Harrison, S. Baron-Cohen, J. D. G. Watson, L. Goldstein, J. Heather, R. S. J. Frackowiak, and C. D. Frith. 1995. The physiology of coloured hearing A PET activation study of colour-word synaesthesia. *Brain* 118:661–676. doi:10.1093/brain/118.3.661.

Peña, Marcela, Jacques Mehler, and Marina Nespor. 2011. The role of audiovisual processing in early conceptual development. *Psychological Science* 22:1419–1421. doi:10.1177/0956797611421791.

Ramachandran, Vilayanur S., and Edward M. Hubbard. 2001a. Psychophysical investigations into the neural basis of synaesthesia. *Proceedings of the Royal Society B: Biological Sciences* 268:979–983. doi:10.1098/rspb.2000.1576.

———. 2001b. Synaesthesia—A window into perception, thought and language. *Journal of Consciousness Studies* 8:3–34.

Rich, Anina N., Bradshaw, John L., and Mattingley, Jason B. 2005. A systematic, large-scale study of synaesthesia: Implications for the role of early experience in lexical-colour associations. *Cognition* 98:53–84. doi:10.1016/j.cognition.2004.11.003.

Rösser, N., P. Heuschmann, H. Wersching, C. Breitenstein, S. Knecht, and A. Flöel. 2008. Levodopa improves procedural motor learning in chronic stroke patients. *Archives of Physical Medicine and Rehabilitation* 89:1633–1641. doi:10.1016/j.apmr.2008.02.030.

Rothen, Nicolas, Andrea-Laura Wantz, and Beat Meier. 2011. Training synaesthesia. *Perception* 40:1248–1250. doi:10.1068/p6984.

Rouw, Romke and H. Steven Scholte. 2007. Increased structural connectivity in grapheme-color synesthesia. *Nature Neuroscience* 10:792–797. doi:10.1038/nn1906.

———. 2010. Neural basis of individual differences in synesthetic experiences. *The Journal of Neuroscience* 30:6205–6213. doi:10.1523/JNEUROSCI.3444-09.2010.

Rouw, Romke, H. Steven Scholte, and Olympia Colizoli, O. 2011. Brain areas involved in synaesthesia: A review. *Journal of Neuropsychology* 5:214–242. doi:10.1111/j.1748-6653.2011.02006.x.

Simner, Julia. 2007. Beyond perception: Synaesthesia as a psycholinguistic phenomenon. *Trends in Cognitive Sciences* 11:23–29. doi:10.1016/j.tics.2006.10.010.

Simner, Julia, Jenny Harrold, Harriet Creed, Louise Monro, and Louise Foulkes. 2009. Early detection of markers for synaesthesia in childhood populations. *Brain* 132:57–64. doi:10.1093/brain/awn292.

Simner, Julia, Catherine Mulvenna, Noam Sagiv, Elias Tsakanikos, Sarah A. Witherby, Christine Fraser, Kirsten Scott, and Jamie Ward. 2006. Synaesthesia: The prevalence of atypical cross-modal experiences. *Perception* 38:1024–1033. doi:10.1068/p5469.

Smilek, Daniel, Jonathan S. A. Carriere, Mike J. Dixon, and Philip M. Merikle. 2007. Grapheme frequency and color luminance in grapheme-color synaesthesia. *Psychological Science* 18:793–795. doi:10.1111/j.1467-9280.2007.01981.

Smilek, Daniel, Mike J. Dixon, Cera Cudahy, and Philip M. Merikle. 2001. Synaesthetic photisms influence visual perception. *Journal of Cognitive Neuroscience* 13:930–936. doi:10.1162/089892901753165845.

Spector, Ferrine, and Daphne Maurer. 2008. The colour of Os: Naturally biased associations between shape and colour. *Perception* 37:841–847. doi:10.1068/p5830.

——. 2009. Synesthesia: A new approach to understanding the development of perception. *Developmental Psychology* 45:175–189. doi:10.1037/a0021437.

——. 2011. The colors of the alphabet: Naturally-biased associations between shape and color. *Journal of Experimental Psychology. Human Perception and Performance* 37:484–495.

——. 2013. Early sound symbolism for vowel sounds. *i-Perception* 4:239–241.

Stilla, Randall, Rebecca Hanna, Xiaoping Hu, Erica Mariola, Gopikrishna Deshpande, and K. Sathian. 2008. Neural processing underlying tactile microspatial discrimination in the blind: A functional magnetic resonance imaging study. *Journal of Vision* 8:13.1–19. doi:10.1167/8.10.13.

Supekar, Kaustubh, Mark Musen, and Vinod Menon. 2009. Development of large-scale functional brain networks in children. *PLoS Biology* 7:e1000157. doi:10.1371/journal.pbio.1000157.

Tzourio-Mazoyer, Nathalie, Scania De Schonen, Fabrice Crivello, Bryan Reutter, Yannick Aujard, and Bernard Mazoyer. 2002. Neural correlates of woman face processing by 2-month-old infants. *Neuroimage* 15:454–461. doi:10.1006/nimg.2001.0979.

Wagner, Katie, and Karen R. Dobkins. 2011. Synaesthetic associations decrease during infancy. *Psychological Science* 22:1067–1072. doi:10.1177/0956797611416250.

Walker, Peter, J. Gavin Bremner, Uschi Mason, Jo Spring, Karen Mattock, Alan Slater, and Scott P. Johnson. 2010. Preverbal infants' sensitivity to synaesthetic cross-modality correspondences. *Psychological Science* 21:21–25. doi:10.1177/0956797609354734.

Ward, Jamie, Brett Huckstep, and Elias Tsakanikos. 2006. Sound-colour synaesthesia: To what extent does it use cross-modal mechanisms common to us all? *Cortex* 42:264–280. doi.org/10.1016/S0010-9452(08)70352-6.

Ward, Jamie, and Jason B. Mattingley. 2006. Synaesthesia: An overview of contemporary findings and controversies. *Cortex* 42:129–136. doi:10.1016/S0010-9452(08)70336-8.

Ward, Jamie, Julia Simner, and Vivian Auyeung. 2005. A comparison of lexical-gustatory and grapheme-colour synaesthesia. *Cognitive Neuropsychology* 22:28–41. doi:10.1080/02643290442000022.

Weiss, Peter H., and Gereon R. Fink. 2009. Grapheme-colour synaesthetes show increased grey matter volumes of parietal and fusiform cortex. *Brain* 132:65–70. doi:10.1093/brain/awn304.

Witthoft, Nathan, and Jonathan Winawer. 2006. Synesthetic colors determined by having colored refrigerator magnets in childhood. *Cortex* 42:175–183. doi:10.1016/S0010-9452(08)70342-3.

Wolff, P. H., Matsumiya, Y., Abroms, I. F., van Velzer, C., and Lombroso, C. T. 1974. The effect of white noise on the somatosensory evoked response in sleeping newborn infants. *Electroencephalography and Clinical Neurophysiology* 37:269–274.

Yaka, Rami, Uri Yinon, and Zvi Wollberg. 1999. Auditory activation of cortical visual areas in cats after early visual deprivation. *European Journal of Neuroscience* 11:1301–1312.

Yaro, Caroline, and Jame Ward. 2007. Searching for Shereshevskii: What is superior about the memory of synaesthetes? *Quarterly Journal of Experimental Psychology* 60:681–695. doi:10.1080/17470210600785208.

CHAPTER 4

SYNESTHESIA IN SCHOOL-AGED CHILDREN

JULIA SIMNER AND EDWARD M. HUBBARD

Synesthesia is an inherited condition with a neurological basis, which gives rise to a type of "merging of the senses." There are many different forms of synesthesia (perhaps over 150; Cytowic and Eagleman 2009; Day 2005). A synesthete might see shapes when hearing music, for example, or experience tastes in the mouth when speaking. Or she might feel sensations of touch against the skin of the hand when eating food, or hear sounds when looking at colors, and so on. Unlike other chapters in this compendium, the current article tackles a subject not well explored within synesthesia research. Although great advances have been made in understanding the psychological and neurological characteristics of synesthesia in adults, comparatively less is known about the manifestation of synesthesia in children and especially in children of an age that would place them within the schooling system. The period beforehand from birth to age 5 has been admirably treated by Daphne Maurer and her colleagues over the last 15 years and a review of this body of work is given by those authors in Chapter 3. In contrast, here we pick up the story at age 5 years and explore how the characteristics of synesthesia might manifest in the developing child and adolescent. We cover not only the psychological and neurological aspects (i.e., how synesthesia operates and how it is supported by developing brain networks) but also the ways in which children with synesthesia might be received within the schooling system. We base our arguments firstly on the small number of recent empirical studies that have covered synesthesia within this age group, but we also extend our discussions to include first-hand reports from children and parents, which have been received in our labs over the last decade. The story this paints is one of a variable and sometimes difficult journey taken by synesthetic children and their parents through the schooling system, largely because very little is known about synesthesia by the average non-synesthete adult and hence by the average educator. As a result we shall see that synesthetic children sometimes encounter resistance from teachers when giving simple descriptions about their perceptual worlds. We shall end by addressing what changes might be considered in order that children with synesthesia, their parents, their educators, and educational policymakers, might be better equipped to deal with the particular experiences of the synesthetic child.

How Prevalent Is Synesthesia in Schools?

Questions about the prevalence of synesthesia have occupied scientists for over one hundred years (e.g., Hall 1883; see Johnson, Allison, and Baron-Cohen, Chapter 1, this volume). We now know that in adults, synesthesia is found in at least 4.4% of the population, based on a study that counted individuals with a range of different types of manifestations of the condition (Simner et al. 2006). One particularly common variant is grapheme-color synesthesia (i.e., colored letters and/or digits) and this is found in 1% to 2% of the adult population (Simner et al. 2006). However, one recurrent question has been whether synesthesia might be more commonly found among children compared to adults. In recent years one particularly plausible mechanism has been proposed that might provide a reasonable scientific basis for such a claim. Here we will review this proposal and ask what it might mean for the prevalence of synesthesia in childhood.

Psychologists Daphne Maurer, Simon Baron-Cohen, and their colleagues (Baron-Cohen et al. 1996; Maurer 1993; Maurer and Mondloch 2005; see Maurer, Gibson, and Spector, Chapter 3, this volume) have proposed a developmental theory that has become known as the *neonatal synesthesia hypothesis*. This hypothesis takes two well-accepted assumptions—that all children have more highly connected brains than adults, and that adult synesthetes also have hyperconnected brains—and extends these facts in two ways. Firstly, it proposes that early hyperconnected brains may cause synesthesia-like experiences in all children. Secondly, it proposes that this early synesthesia might be maintained into adulthood on rare occasions due to some synesthetic genetic predisposition. One suggestion is that this predisposition may interfere with the normal processes of cell death and elimination of synapses which slowly prune away abundant childhood connections in the average person. This failure would explain why some adults have synesthesia—this representing unusually enduring states of early childhood connectivity.

The neonatal synesthesia account is plausible given that the brains of adult synesthetes do show greater connectivity (Rouw and Scholte 2007; see Part V of this volume), and that a genetic inheritance for synesthesia is highly likely (Asher et al. 2009; Tomson et al. 2011; see also Asher and Carmichael, Chapter 2, this volume). As a result, the neonatal synesthesia hypothesis is widely accepted within the synesthesia research community, and this theory is fully reviewed by Maurer, Gibson, and Spector in Chapter 3 of this volume. For the purposes of the current chapter, our interests lie in what this might mean for the prevalence of synesthesia among children. The conclusion would be that if synesthesia is found pervasively in all neonates, it is likely to be highly prevalent in young children, until such an age as the normal pruning process has run its course (around adolescence; Huttenlocher and Dabholkar 1997). This would necessarily mean that synesthesia is found in a greater proportion of the childhood population compared to the adult population. Next we explore whether there is there independent evidence for this assumption.

A number of early studies in the historical literature made the claim that synesthesia is indeed more common in children (English 1923; Galton 1883; Hall 1883; Lenzberg 1923; Révész 1923; Riggs and Karwoski 1934; Werner 1940) and these claims have been cited or repeated in later works (e.g., Cytowic 2002; Hurley and Noë 2007; Marks 1975; Shanon 2003), giving them currency into the twenty-first century. For example, Cytowic and Eagleman (2009) pointed out that if nineteenth- and early twentieth-century reports were to be believed, children would be roughly three times more likely than adults to be synesthetic. However, these historical reports are unreliable and should be treated with caution. Not one of these earlier studies had strongly robust empirical evidence to support their claims and indeed, a number were based simply on intuition. These "best guesses" would have been based on the number of adult and child synesthetes brought to the attention of the researcher, although we know that this method of assessing prevalence is highly susceptible to the failings of human reasoning. Researchers, like all humans, are more likely to remember cases that seem especially remarkable (e.g., someone who is not only a synesthete, but both a synesthete *and* a child!). In this way, early studies may have a skewed notion of the commonness of childhood synesthesia.

Where these historical assertions were put to the test, the methodologies used were unreliable. For example, the psychologist G. Stanley Hall asked 53 children whether musical notes were colored, and got an affirmative response from 21 of them, thereby concluding that 40% of children have synesthesia (Hall 1883). This is a dubious method for several reasons. Firstly, we know that cross-sensory metaphors link sound and color in all people (e.g., minor notes might feel "blue," major notes might sound "bright," higher notes might sound "lighter" in color than lower notes, and so on) and this is something different from true, inherited synesthesia. Hence it is possible that these children were simply non-synesthetes who—like all people—are able to make a sound-color association by metaphorical thinking (e.g., Ward, Huckstep, and Tsakanikos 2006; see Simner, Chapter 8, this volume). Second, we know from independent studies that the classification of synesthesia cannot come simply from the word of the participant alone, as it did in this historical investigation. In 2006, we conducted a large-scale prevalence study for synesthesia in adults (Simner et al. 2006) which included independent tests to compare with personal reports. We found that for every one synesthete who claimed to have synesthesia, there were *five non-synesthetes* who also claimed to have synesthesia. Some of these latter were simply artistically minded or creative individuals who mistook synesthesia for a heightened appreciation of color, and others were calling on normal cross-sensory (non-synesthetic) metaphorical associations. Others still were what we might think of as malingerers, who later fully retracted their claims on further questioning 6 months later. In other words, we might give only small credence to studies that simply take the report of the participant, rather than providing independent evidence.

Despite earlier unreliable methodologies, there are certain facts that do speak to the idea that synesthesia might be more common in children. One is the plausibility of the neonatal synesthesia hypothesis described earlier, which gives a credible explanation for *why* children may be more commonly synesthetic. The second comes from a large number of anecdotal accounts, in which non-synesthetic adults have reported synesthesia in childhood that died out, although the reverse pattern (i.e., developmental synesthesia spontaneously appearing in adulthood) has not been found (i.e., not without some external cause such as drug use or disease). If these anecdotal reports are to be believed, this would mean that cases are indeed more abundant in childhood. Finally, one recent empirical study has provided the first robust data that might point towards a higher number of cases of synesthesia in children versus adults. In this study (Simner et al. 2009) we looked at the prevalence of one particular type of synesthesia in two age groups (ages approximately 6.5 and 7.5 years) and found a numerical trend for greater numbers in the younger age group. We describe this study briefly in the following paragraphs.

The type of synesthesia under investigation was grapheme-color synesthesia, in which reading, hearing, saying, or thinking about letters, numbers, and words generates synesthetic sensations of color (e.g., Simner, Glover, and Mowat 2006). Simner *et al.* (2009) aimed to find out how many children age 6.5 and 7.5 years have grapheme-color synesthesia. We randomly sampled 615 children (6.5 years = 338 and 7.5 years = 277) from 21 different primary schools in the UK, with permission granted from both head-teachers and individual parents. Every child was tested for synesthesia with an objective test of genuineness. This test identified synesthetes using a method first devised in the 1980s (Baron-Cohen, Wyke, and Binnie 1987; see Johnson, Allison, and Baron-Cohen, Chapter 1, this volume) which has since become the behavioral "gold standard" test of genuineness (e.g., Baron-Cohen et al. 1987; Baron-Cohen et al. 1996; Brang and Ramachandran 2010; Palmeri et al. 2002; Rich, Bradshaw, and Mattingley 2005; Ward and Simner 2003; Ward et al. 2010). This test closely examined how consistently each child paired colors with graphemes (i.e., letters and digits). We know that synesthetes are highly consistent in the colors they pair with graphemes when asked on different occasions: for example, if a synesthete describes the letter A as colored red, say, then he/she will tend to repeat that it is red if asked again some time later. Non-synesthetes are far less consistent and they may say that A is red on one occasion, but switch to another color when asked again. Hence, in our study of synesthesia in childhood, we aimed to identify child synesthetes as those who were significantly more consistent in their pairings of colors with graphemes, when compared to the average child.

For our test, each of the 615 children played a computer "game," which presented a large grapheme on the left side of the computer screen (e.g., the letter "k," approximately 5 cm high) and a palette of 13 colors on the right side (black, dark blue, brown, dark green, grey, pink, purple, orange, red, white, light blue, light green, yellow). The screen set-up also includes a timer clock-face, and is shown in Figure 4.1.

Children were seated in front of the screen and were asked to pick from the color palette whichever they considered to be the "best" color for each grapheme; they were told,

FIGURE 4.1 Screen shot of the test of consistency presented to children in Simner et al. (2009). Left side shows one of 36 randomly presented graphemes (a–z and 0–9) and right side shows a randomizing electronic color palette. Figure by the author JS (synesthesia testing tool used in Simner et al. (2006) and Simner et al. (2009)) licensed under the Creative Commons Attribution-NonCommercial-NoDerivs 3.0 Unported License. To view a copy of this license, visit <http://creativecommons.org/licenses/by-nc-nd/3.0/> or send a letter to Creative Commons, 171 Second Street, Suite 300, San Francisco, California 94105, USA.

of course, that there was no right or wrong answer. Each time the child selected a color (e.g., k green) the grapheme disappeared from the left-hand side of the screen and was replaced by another grapheme, and then the game continued. In the course of the test, every letter of the alphabet and every digit from 0 to 9 was shown to the child in a random order, and every grapheme was paired by the child to its own color. When all the letters and digits had been shown once, the game paused and children were told they'd done well and were to simply carry on as before as soon as the test began again, approximately 10 seconds later. Unbeknownst to the children, the same set of letters (a–z) and digits (0–9) were presented again, a second time, but in a different random order. This meant that by the end of the test, each child had paired a color to each letter or digit, twice— once before the 10-second break and once after. In order to give an initial indication about whether each child might be synesthetic, we simply compared the colors given for each letter before and after the 10-second break, to see whether they matched. For the average child, they matched only around three times out of 36 graphemes (approximately 8% of the time). However, there were 47 children who showed a significantly higher proportion of matching colors—on average they were almost three times more consistent than the rest. These were the children we focused on most carefully because they were performing differently for one of two reasons: either they had better memories than the average child (and so were able to give the same color to each letter on that basis alone) or they were children with synesthesia, who were responding on the basis of their synesthetic colors,[1] since these colors would be relatively stable. Nonetheless, we could not be certain at that stage which children were which (i.e., which simply had high memories and which were true synesthetes). For this reason, we returned to our children a year later and repeated the same test again. We came without warning and conducted the test as before. This time, however, we compared how consistently children colored the graphemes across the 12 months that had passed. While a non-synesthetic child with a high memory span could perform consistently in her color choices over 10 seconds, she could not maintain this high consistency over 12 months; only a synesthete could do this. In other words, by considering the consistency of these 47 children, first over 10 seconds, and then over 12 months, we were able to tease apart the synesthetes (who perform well in both tests) from the high-memory non-synesthetes (who perform well over 10 seconds only). Hence, in our study, young child synesthetes were required to outperform their peers in what would be a hugely challenging task for non-synesthetes, and on this basis we were able to identify eight grapheme-color synesthetes from the 615 children tested.

This finding of eight child grapheme-color synesthetes places the prevalence of grapheme-color synesthesia in children aged 6.5- to 7.5 years at 1.3%. Taken as an indication of synesthesia in childhood, this would imply that there are over 170,000 synesthetic children age 0 to 17 years in the UK alone, and over 930,000 in the USA. Furthermore, it would suggest that the average primary school in England and Scotland (n = 168 pupils) contains 2.2 grapheme-color synesthetes at any time, while the average-sized US primary school (n = 396 pupils) contains 5.1 (see Simner et al. 2009 for references to national statistics on UK/US education). We point out that this estimate covers only grapheme-color synesthesia, which is just one of up to 150 different variants of the condition identified to date (Cytowic and Eagleman 2009; Day 2005). This makes the projected combined figure for all variants of synesthesia considerably higher.

We might also consider that our prevalence figure in children is a necessary underestimate, because its methodology relies on the assumption that synesthetes are consistent in their grapheme-colors. Although this tends to be true of adult synesthetes, who have consistent colors for around 90% to 100% of letters and digits (Dixon et al. 2000; Rich, Bradshaw, and Mattingley 2005; Simner, Glover, and Mowat 2006; Simner and Ward 2006; Smilek, Dixon, et al. 2002; Smilek, Moffatt, et al. 2002; Yaro and Ward 2007) this is far less true of children. We shall see later in this chapter that fixed, consistent synesthetic colors are not yet fully achieved in children at the age we tested them, and that, instead, they have consistent colors for only 30% to 50% of letters/digits. In other words, a test of genuineness based on consistency would identify the majority of adult synesthetes tested, but a proportionally smaller number of child synesthetes (i.e., only those that happen to have already developed consistent associations at the time of

---

[1] Although synesthetes' colors are highly specific (e.g., Ward, Simner, and Auyeung, 2005) prior studies have shown that a presentation of our condensed palette allows for a successful assessment of synesthesia that is practical for testing those with limited attention, such as children (Day 2005; Simner et al. 2006; Simner et al. 2009).

testing). For this reason, the estimate of prevalence given for children age 6.5 to 7.5 years in Simner et al. (2009) should be taken only as a reliable lower cut-off, and the true figure may yet be higher.

One final consideration to end this section brings us back to the question of whether synesthesia is found more commonly in children versus adults. Although child and adult prevalence figures cannot be directly compared (because the consistency methodology identifies proportionately more adults; see earlier in this section) there is evidence to suggest there may be higher numbers of child synesthetes when we look more closely at our data. Of the 615 children we tested, some were aged 6.5 years at initial testing and some were aged 7.5 years. After identifying the synesthetes, we found that the ratio of synesthetes ages 6.5 versus 7.5 years was 2.5:1. In other words, there were two-and-a-half times more synesthetes in the younger population compared to the older population. This ratio could not be verified statistically because the sample size was a little too small. However, this type of numerical difference fits with earlier assumptions about prevalence in childhood and about the loss of synesthesia with age. In the following section we look more closely at how synesthesia develops over time.

THE GROWTH OF SYNESTHESIA IN CHILDHOOD

Adult synesthetes tend to claim that they have had synesthesia for as long as they can remember, and that their colors do not change over time. However, the majority of synesthesias (approximately 88%; Simner et al. 2006) are triggered by language units such as letters and words, and these are culturally acquired symbols. As such, these types of synesthesia could not have existed in infancy since they require knowledge learned during language and literacy acquisition (although they may have been present in other forms; see Duffy 2001). This means that variants such as grapheme-color synesthesia must form at some point during childhood development, at, or subsequent to, the acquisition of letters and digits. It is important to add here that although grapheme-color synesthesia can be triggered by either written language, spoken language, or both (e.g., by reading A, and/or by hearing "A"), it is always triggered by processes tied to the written letter A, rather than the sound alone. This much we can tell from considering the synesthetic coloring of letters with more than one spoken pronunciation. Hence, grapheme-color synesthetes will have the same (or very similar) color for the letter C whether it is pronounced /k/ as in *car*, or /s/ as in *cite*.[2] The fact that it doesn't matter whether the letter is spoken or read derives from normal psychological mechanisms, which automatically mentally activate the spellings of words even when those words are heard or spoken (e.g., Seidenberg and Tanenhaus 1979). Given this, a grapheme-color synesthete must be familiar with written letters in order for their synesthesia to develop, and this familiarity

---

[2] Those synesthetes for whom the color significantly changes according to pronunciation would be termed "phoneme-color synesthetes" (see Simner 2007).

is acquired as a protracted process during schooling years. As such, we asked how the development of synesthesia might take place during this time.

In our study described earlier (Simner et al. 2009), we identified eight grapheme-color synesthetes from among 615 children by comparing their colors for graphemes across 12 months: we tested the children once when they were 6.5 to 7.5 years old, and then again a year later when they were around 7.5 to 8.5 years. Within these two testing sessions, however, we also looked at how consistently the children colored letters and digits over 10 seconds. When we compared their scores for the 10-second retest in the first session to their scores for the 10-second retest in the second session, we found an interesting pattern of development characterized by increasing consistency. Specifically, we found that they had a stable color over 10 seconds for around 29% of letters and digits at age 6.5 to 7.5, but for around 47% 1 year later at age 7.5 to 8.5 years. In other words, child synesthetes appear to show increasing stability in their letter/digit colors as they grow older. Put differently, the type of consistency that characterizes adult synesthesia, where, typically, adult synesthetes are consistent about their colors for between 90% to 100% of letters and digits, is a trait that develops over time. Interestingly, the same movement from less fixed colored alphabet to a more fixed colored alphabet has also been shown in a sample of much younger synesthetes. Daphne Maurer and colleagues describe in Chapter 3, this volume, how three pre-school synesthetes (ages 3.5, 3.75, and 4.5 years respectively) paired colors to letters using crayons in a way that became more consistent as they grew older, across approximately 1 to 2 years.

In summary, in the earliest stages of development, synesthetic associations (e.g., A = red) may be relatively chaotic pairings, where the colors of letters and numbers can change over even very short time periods such as 10 seconds. Nonetheless, by age 6.5 years, approximately one-third of graphemes have stabilized enough that the color associated to the letter or digit does not change. One year later, this stable characteristic has spread to approximately half of graphemes. In other words, the memories of adult synesthetes which suggest their synesthesia is unchanging throughout a lifetime overlook their necessary stages of development which started in the early schooling years.

Neural Development of Synesthesia

Numerous studies of adult synesthetes have suggested that grapheme-color synesthesia arises through a process of "cross-activation" between brain regions involved in recognition of graphemes and words (the "visual word form area" or VWFA for short), and an adjacent brain region involved in color processing called V4 (Hubbard et al. 2005; Nunn et al. 2002; Rouw and Scholte 2007; see Hubbard, Chapter 24, this volume). However, we noted earlier that since grapheme-color synesthesia is intimately tied to knowledge of these culturally acquired symbols, it could not have existed as such in infancy. Based on observations of adult synesthetes, the development of the VWFA would make a plausible candidate for observation during synesthesia's "growth."

Although neuroimaging data suggests that left-hemisphere language areas are already well organized for the perception of spoken language even in pre-verbal infants (Dehaene-Lambertz, Hertz-Pannier, and Dubois 2006; Dehaene-Lambertz et al. 2006), it is only later, during the process of learning to recognize letters and numerals, that the types of representations required to drive grapheme-color synesthesia can be established.

A small number of imaging studies have examined the development of reading skills in young children, and suggest a reorganization of the ventral visual areas in response to the pressures of learning to read (see McCandliss et al. 2003). With experience, the VWFA becomes particularly specialized for recognizing letters and words (for reviews see Dehaene and Cohen 2007; McCandliss et al. 2003) across a range of language backgrounds (e.g., Bolger et al. 2005). This specialization seems to be due to developments in reading proficiency, rather than maturation per se (Shaywitz et al. 2002) and in particular is due to learning letter-speech sound correspondences (Brem et al. 2010). Consistent with this, recent work suggests that, prior to learning to read, the brain region that becomes the VWFA may be driven by early sensitivity to auditory input (Balsamo et al. 2006). This would predict there may be some contiguity in the development of colored graphemes from colored speech. That literacy acquisition is dependent to some extent on the system for spoken language has been seen in other regions, also (see van Atteveldt et al. 2004 for evidence of the integration of speech sounds and letters in the superior temporal gyrus, for example) but connections between spoken representations and letter forms are particularly linked to functional changes in the VWFA. Such regions may therefore provide interesting areas of study, although any direct observation of synesthesia's neural development would require the difficult task of very early identification of randomly sampled child synesthetes, as well as improved imaging techniques in early childhood (see Dehaene and Cohen 2007).

Advantages and Disadvantages of Synesthesia for Children

Synesthesia is a mixed condition with a complex profile of assets and deficits, although the majority of research to date has pointed to mostly *positive* attributes associated with synesthesia. The range of these advantages are covered by those chapters in Part VI of this volume on synesthesia's costs and benefits, and these describe studies on adult synesthetes which show the condition may be linked to superior memory (under certain conditions), superior creativity, superior musicality, and superior imagery, and even, in rare cases, to the exceptional skills of savants (e.g., extreme mnemonists). A small number of studies in adults have suggested minor costs associated with the condition, such as a marginally slower speed of mental calculation for some synesthetes under some circumstances. In particular, the study in question (Ward, Sagiv, and Butterworth 2009) looked at sequence-space synesthetes (also known as visuo-spatial synesthetes; see Cohen Kadosh and Henik, Chapter 6; Price, Chapter 37, this volume) who experience numbers in particular spatial arrays. For example, a sequence-space synesthete might "see" the numbers 1 to 10 ascending at chest height in front of the body then bending at 45° right up to 20, and so on. Ward, Sagiv, and Butterworth (2009) found that these individuals were around 500 ms slower than non-synesthetes when performing mental multiplication, for example, although their accuracy was not affected. This deficit for multiplication is likely to be because the average person tends to rely on verbal rote retrieval for multiplication (e.g., "7 times 7 is 49; 8 times 8 is 64 … "), while sequence-space synesthetes rely more heavily on the visual cues provided by their mental number line, and this slows calculations. In general, however, the majority of adult studies show synesthetes with benefits rather than costs, and we direct the reader to Part VI of this compendium for further details.

Here, we describe the small amount of research investigating costs and benefits in childhood synesthesia. The key study in this area was conducted in Cambridge by psychologists Jennifer Green and Usha Goswami. They asked a pivotal question about the effects of childhood synesthesia on numeracy, literacy, and memory, and tested a group of six child grapheme-color synesthetes, age 7 to 15 years, who experience colors when reading or thinking about numbers (Green and Goswami 2008). These children showed both assets and deficits compared to the average child. First, they were less accurate in recalling a series of numbers from memory (e.g., nine digits in a 3×3 grid), but only when those numbers were presented in colors that conflicted with their synesthesia. For example, a child for whom the number 6 is synesthetically blue would have no difficulty recalling that number from memory if it had been presented in blue font, and no difficulty if it had been presented as regular black-on-white text. Difficulties would arise however, if the number had been presented in the color *other than* the synesthete's blue (e.g., red, or yellow, or green). A very small number of the synesthete children also showed difficulties in a task in which they had to ignore the colors of two digits, and simply indicate which was the largest (e.g., 7–3 in red and blue respectively). Two synesthete children were slower to respond if the colors of the digits conflicted with their synesthesia, although it is difficult to interpret these results since there was no control group to provide a comparison condition, and no statistical tests to demonstrate whether these findings were meaningful or due to chance variation. However, both studies are suggestive of a processing cost when child synesthetes read digits presented in colors that conflict with their synesthesia, and the same has been reported in adult studies (e.g., Cohen Kadosh and Henik 2006; Smilek, Dixon, et al. 2002).

Despite these apparently mild deficits which are found in rather unusual circumstances (when children must manipulated digits in color), there were also a number of possible advantages found in the group of child synesthetes studied in this research.

The children were given three tests, of mathematical reasoning, spatial reasoning, and vocabulary, and they apparently out-performed the average child in all three. First, in the test of mathematical reasoning, Green and Goswami (2008, 471) report that of eight child synesthetes tested, "all synesthetes except one" scored higher than the national mean (in fact, we believe five scored higher than the mean, two scored the average mark, and one scored below average). A consideration of the data shows that this equates to a near-significant advantage for synesthetic children compared to the average child (one-sample t = 2.08 and p = 0.08), at least according to our own statistical evaluation of their data.[3] A significant advantage for synesthetes was also found when we analyzed their data for the synesthetes' test of spatial reasoning (one-sample t = 3.1875, p = 0.01) and for their test of vocabulary (one-sample t = 2.79, p = 0.02). From their data (and our statistics concur), Green and Goswami concluded that synesthetes scored extremely highly on these measures, sometimes extraordinarily so.

Green and Goswami's (2008) study suggests that being born with synesthesia will endow cognitive advantages that manifest themselves in the types of tests administered during schooling. However, there is reason for caution when interpreting these results. We point out that it is difficult to draw strong conclusions about the average child synesthete from these data, because the children tested by Jennifer Green and her colleague were probably not "average child synesthetes." Although it is unclear how these children were recruited, it appears they were not randomly sampled from the broad range of child synesthetes at large. Instead, they are likely to have been brought to the attention of the researchers by their parents. These parents are themselves likely to be synesthetes (since the condition is heritable; see Asher et al. 2009; Ward and Simner 2005), and are almost certain to have had some long-standing knowledge of synesthesia, in order to recognize the condition in their children. Moreover, these parents may be highly motivated individuals, given that they took time to refer their children for testing by psychologists for the advancement of science. In other words, the children in this study were likely to be children from family environments led by motivated parents with an interest in scientific research, and in particular, with an interest in synesthesia. For all these reasons, both the children themselves, and the children's synesthesia, may be non-representative of what we might expect from the average child synesthete, randomly sampled. Instead, it is possible that their high scores in mathematics, reasoning, and vocabulary were somehow due to an upbringing within a motivated family environment, where synesthesia is known and likely discussed. We should probably, therefore, take these findings as an interesting first step in the question of how synesthesia might affect childhood cognition, and await future studies on a wider range of more randomly sampled participants.

---

[3] The finding here, that child synesthetes were better, rather than worse at mathematics might be compared alongside the reverse finding from a group of adult synesthetes (Ward, Sagiv, and Butterworth 2009; see earlier discussion). However, the adults tested by Jamie Ward and colleagues had a different variant of synesthesia (numbers in space) compared to the child synesthetes here (with numbers in color).

LIVING WITH SYNESTHESIA: SYNESTHETES' EXPERIENCES IN SCHOOLS

The authors of this chapter are two non-synesthetes who might therefore be hesitant to describe the experiences of children with synesthesia, since neither of us has been such a child. Nonetheless, there are two sources of information we might draw on in this regard. We first direct the reader to the first-hand reports described by synesthete Sean Day, Chapter 44, in this volume, as well as the first-hand reports cited within that chapter, including the scores of first-hand reports gathered by Sean Day over the last 25 years (see Day 2005). These will provide the interested reader with a broad understanding of how the average synesthete experiences the world. Second, we can reflect on how those experiences might translate themselves into a schooling environment, drawing on the very large number of reports we have received to our labs from the parents of child synesthetes, and from those children themselves.

We begin our discussion with the qualification that the majority of parents who contact our lab will be those whose children are experiencing difficulties, and therefore, what follows may be a somewhat skewed description of the situation. After all, parents with well-settled, successfully-integrated children would have less need to call on the advice of an academic. We therefore assume that a large, silent, perhaps majority of children with synesthesia are operating well within the schooling system. Nonetheless, even where children show no apparent surface disadvantages from synesthesia, we have learned that there is, often, still an underlying sense of malaise when the child first discovers that her experiences are simply not typical of her peers, and this appears to be a general experience reported by very many synesthetes. Hence one key problem for childhood synesthetes is the lack of knowledge about their condition within the schooling system. Indeed, a key motivation for our research in childhood synesthesia has come from the numbers of parents who have contacted our lab, from both Europe and North America, seeking simply to convince their child's teacher that synesthesia is a genuine phenomenon. In this regard, the education sector is almost 30 years behind scientific study, where evidence of genuineness was first established in the 1980s (Baron-Cohen et al. 1987).

Let us consider one case study, for example. The first author of this chapter has been contacted within the last month by the mother of a child synesthete, 11-year-old AW, who reports a number of synesthesias including colors from letters, digits, and sounds, as well as a variant known as "mirror-touch" synesthesia (see Banissy, Chapter 30, this volume). In this latter variant, synesthetes experience sensations of touch when they see touch applied to another person's body, and this can also manifest as pain experienced by the synesthete, if witnessing the pain of another person. AW has three specific difficulties: firstly, she experiences information overload at school when her synesthetic colors distract her from a task at hand. Second, she has experienced sensations of pain when observing accidents in the school yard. Third, and perhaps most importantly, her accounts have met with disbelief from her teachers. This has been an exhausting experience for both AW and her mother, who explains that AW "knows that no one believes her at school, and that certain members of staff are very strong minded about her [synesthesia-related] behavior and unsupportive. I think that I am fighting a losing battle trying to get some of them to try and understand, because [synesthesia] all sounds so abstract and weird to them." We have selected this comment to repeat here because it is representative of the very many almost identical reports we receive on a regular basis. In other words, there is a lack of information for educators, which spills over into difficulties for the synesthetic child, who may be experiencing day-to-day problems that need to be addressed.

Reports to our lab also suggest that in many cases, because they are greeted with a negative response from their peers and teachers, synesthetes quickly learn to not discuss their experiences (see Steen and Berman, Chapter 34, this volume, for a first-hand account of this). Indeed, many synesthetes remain silent about their experiences from an early age, either because a lack of widespread knowledge means they are simply unaware that others do not share their experiences (as reported, for example, by our synesthetes JS, LS, KK, IB), or because early attempts to describe them met with disbelief (reported, for example, by our synesthetes KD, DM, BH, EK, SS, CC), or because they simply had no forum at school in which to discuss them (reported, for example, by our synesthetes LW, DM). One study conducted in our lab (Simner, in preparation) has shown empirically the very low levels of awareness of synesthesia in schools in the UK. In this study, which was run in 2007, 20 head-teachers and 20 learning support teachers were asked: whether they had ever heard the term "synesthesia," whether they could define it, whether their school had a provision to identify children with synesthesia, and whether it had one to cater for their educational and/or welfare needs. Additionally, we interviewed representatives from the offices for Learning Support/Special Educational Needs in two sample cities in the UK, to determine whether any city- or county-wide provisions existed (at the time of study in 2007). In questionnaire responses, only 5% of head-teachers and 29% of learning support educators had heard the term "synesthesia," and only 14% of learning support educators could provide an accurate definition. None of the schools sampled had any systematic provision to identify children with synesthesia or to cater for their educational and/or welfare needs (although one learning support educator described an improvised approach for one child who had reported digit-color synesthesia). The learning support officers in city-wide and country-wide administration confirmed there was no systematic provision at either level. By the time our chapter goes to press, this study will be 6 years old, and we are hopeful that sufficient improvements may have occurred in the public understanding of synesthesia over the last half decade to paint a more positive picture at the current time.

Any lack of support for synesthetes in schools has likely arisen from a failure to transmit knowledge between scientists and educators. While scientific studies on synesthesia have proliferated during the past decade, virtually no attention has been given to childhood issues. The current chapter presents the first united summary of empirical studies of childhood synesthesia, of its prevalence in schools, its development over time, of the schooling experience, and of the associated awareness among educators. Our central aim in this chapter has been to provide information about childhood synesthesia so that it might reach not only scientists, but also parents, teachers, and policymakers. Where this information has been absent, children with synesthesia have experienced derision and even reprimand (Day 2005) when expressing simple descriptions about their perceptual world. Where negative feedback has not been experienced, synesthetes have been able to profit from, or adapt to their sensations, or simply enjoy their differences. We are aiming for a state in which synesthetes can describe their sensations to a receptive audience, and receive a response appropriate to their needs. In the final section, we provide several suggestions for parents and educators, to make them better equipped to deal with the particular experiences of the synesthetic child. These suggestions are addressed also towards education policymakers (see also Cawley 2010).

SUGGESTIONS FOR PARENTS AND EDUCATORS

- *Help your child to celebrate her synesthesia.* Your child will benefit from realizing that she is a rather special member of the population and that her synesthesia is tied to very many cognitive benefits. Synesthetes can be more creative, have better perception, better memories and are "gifted" in many ways. Your child may feel alienated when first realizing she is unusual among his or her peers. However, with your help, she may begin to view synesthesia as a positive attribute. Maechler (2012) has pointed out that children are open to synesthesia when they find a space to experience it.
- *Foster a community.* You can help your child realize that although she is somewhat rare in the population, she is certainly not alone. We saw earlier in this chapter that the average UK primary school has 2.2 grapheme-color synesthetes at any time, and yet more synesthetes when all variants of synesthesia are considered. Encourage your child's school to consider an assembly on synesthesia, or a class project, which might foster better understanding (although of course, the school would want to be mindful not to "reveal" any child synesthetes who may not feel comfortable). Make contact with other synesthetes via national synesthesia associations, which have emerged in many countries over the last decade or more, details of which are given at the end of this chapter. These societies tend to hold annual general meetings, in which synesthetes can gather and meet, and where they can learn about the latest scientific information on synesthesia. Some societies (e.g., the American Synesthesia Association) host email discussion groups where synesthetes can share their experiences, post questions, or ask advice from academics.
- *Assess yourself.* Parents suspecting their child may be a synesthete should ask themselves whether they are also synesthetes, because evidence suggests it is (often) an

inherited trait. The key point to keep in mind is that although synesthesia appears to be largely inherited, the *particular manifestation* of the condition may vary from parent to child. For example, a child with colored letters may have a parent who tastes words, or who sees time mapped out in space, and so on. Open a dialogue with your child to discover synesthesias you may share in a different way. If you are unsure whether you also experience synesthesia, you can test yourself at the widely used online testing forum at <http://www.synesthete.org>. This provides relatively immediate feedback on your status as a synesthete. Because this site is, at present, tailored to adult synesthetes it may fail to detect synesthesia that genuinely exists in children (because it relies on consistency, a trait we have seen grows only slowly over time in children).

- *Encourage the benefits.* Help your child to use his or her synesthesia in beneficial ways. For example, if school work requires your child to remember a series of digits (a date in history or; the decimal places of pi etc.), you could suggest she use her synesthesia as an aide-memoire. It is known, for example, that synesthetes with colored numbers can improve their recall for digits by remembering the colors that accompany them. So encourage your child to use this information in his or her school work (and equally, with questions of spelling and so on). In this way, you can begin to explore with your child the ways in which her synesthesia could aid in day-to-day life.

- *Educate the educators.* If, as a parent, you are experiencing a lack of interest or support from your child's school, one suggestion is to source relevant articles (e.g., this chapter, or Simner et al. 2009) to present to your child's teacher, head-teacher, or learning support officer. These individuals will welcome new information, and be in a better position to respond to the needs of your child. We point out that in our recent study examining the attitudes of learning support staff towards synesthesia, we found that although awareness of synesthesia was overall low, every learning support staff member we surveyed was highly progressive in his/her attitude to learning more about the condition, and all requested further information. This is a very positive basis on which to build support for your child.

National synesthesia associations and synesthesia Web communities

UK: <http://www.uksynaesthesia.com/>.
USA: <http://synesthesia.info/>.
Germany: <http://www.synaesthesie.org>.
Australia and New Zealand: <http://synesthesia.com.au/wp/>.
Belgium: <http://www.doctorhugo.org/synaesthesia/>.
Netherlands: <http://www.synesthesie.nl/>.

References

Asher, Julian E., and Duncan A. Carmichael. 2013. Genetics and inheritance of synesthesia. In *Oxford Handbook of Synesthesia*, ed. Julia Simner and Edward M. Hubbard, 23–45. Oxford: Oxford University Press.

Asher, Julian E., Janine A. Lamb, Denise Brocklebank, Jean-Baptiste Cazier, Elena Maestrini, Laura Addis, Mallika Sen, Simon Baron-Cohen, and Anthony P. Monaco. 2009. A whole-genome scan and fine-mapping linkage study of auditory-visual synesthesia reveals evidence of linkage to chromosomes 2q24, 5q33, 6p12, and 12p12. *American Journal of Human Genetics* 84:279–285.

Balsamo, L. M., B. Xu, and W. D. Gaillard. 2006. Language lateralization and the role of the fusiform gyrus in semantic processing in young children. *Neuroimage* 31:1306–1314.

Banissy, Michael J. 2013. Synesthesia, mirror-neurons, and mirror-touch. In *The Oxford Handbook of Synesthesia*, ed. Julia Simner and Edward M. Hubbard, 584–603. Oxford: Oxford University Press.

Baron-Cohen, Simon, Lucy Burt, Fiona Smith-Laittan, John Harrison, and Patrick Bolton. 1996. Synaesthesia: prevalence and familiarity. *Perception* 25:1073–1079.

Baron-Cohen, Simon, Maria A. Wyke, and Colin Binnie. 1987. Hearing words and seeing colors and an experimental investigation of a case of synesthesia. *Perception* 16:761–767.

Brang, David, and Vilayanur S. Ramachandran. 2010. Visual field heterogeneity, laterality, and eidetic imagery in synesthesia. *Neurocase* 16:169–174.

Brem, Silvia, Silvia Bach, Karin Kucian, Tomi K. Guttorm, Ernst Martin, Heikki Lyytinen, Daniel Brandeis, and Ulla Richardson. 2010. Brain sensitivity to print emerges when children learn letter–speech sound correspondences. *Proceedings of the National Academy of Sciences of the United States of America* 107:7939–7944.

Bolger, Donald J., Charles A. Perfetti, and Walter Schneider 2005. Cross-cultural effect on the brain revisited: universal structures plus writing system variation. *Human Brain Mapping* 25:92–104.

Cawley, Valentine. 2010. The synaesthete: A new type of "gifted student" and how to teach them. International Conference on Learner Diversity 2010. *Procedia Social and Behavioral Sciences* 7:574–579.

Cohen Kadosh, Roi, and Avashai Henik. 2006. Color congruity effect: Where do colors and numbers interact in synaesthesia? *Cortex* 42:259–263.

———. 2013. Numbers, synesthesia, and directionality. In *The Oxford Handbook of Synesthesia*, ed. Julia Simner and Edward M. Hubbard, 103–122. Oxford: Oxford University Press.

Cytowic, Richard E. 2002. *Synesthesia: A Union of the Senses*. 2nd ed. Cambridge, MA: MIT Press.

Cytowic, Richard, E. and David M. Eagleman. 2009. *Wednesday is Indigo Blue: Discovering the Brain of Synaesthesia*. Cambridge, MA: MIT Press.

Day, Sean A. 2005. Some demographic and socio-cultural aspects of synaesthesia. In *Synesthesia: Perspectives from Cognitive Neuroscience*, ed. Lynn C. Robertson and Noam Sagiv, 11–33. New York: Oxford University Press.

———. 2013. Synesthesia: A first-person perspective. In *The Oxford Handbook of Synesthesia*, ed. Julia Simner and Edward M. Hubbard, 903–923. Oxford: Oxford University Press.

Dehaene, Stanislas and Laurent Cohen. 2007. Cultural recycling of cortical maps. *Neuron* 56:384–398.

Dehaene-Lambertz, Ghislaine, Lucie Hertz-Pannier, and Jessica Dubois. 2006. Nature and nurture in language acquisition: Anatomical and functional brain-imaging studies in infants. *Trends in Neuroscience* 29:367–373.

Dehaene-Lambertz, Ghislaine, Lucie Hertz-Pannier, Jessica Dubois, Sebastien Mériaux, Alexis Roche, Mariano Sigman, and Stanislas Dehaene. 2006. Functional organization of perisylvian activation during presentation of sentences in preverbal infants. *Proceedings of the National Academy of Sciences of the United States of America* 103:14240–14245.

Dixon, Mike J., Daniel Smilek, Cera Cudahy, and Philip M Merikle. 2000. Five plus two equals yellow. *Nature* 406:365.

Duffy, Patricia L. 2001. *Blue Cats and Chartreuse Kittens*. New York: Time Books Henry Holt and Company.

English, Horace B. 1923. Colored hearing. *Science* 57:444.

Galton, Francis. 1883. *Inquiries into Human Faculty and its Development*. London: Macmillan.

Green, Jennifer A. K. and Usha Goswami. 2008. Synesthesia and number cognition in children. *Cognition* 106:463–473.

Hall, G. Stanley. 1883. The contents of children's minds. *Princeton Review* 249–272.

Hubbard, Edward M. 2013. Synesthesia and functional imaging. In *The Oxford Handbook of Synesthesia*, ed. Julia Simner and Edward M. Hubbard, 475–499. Oxford: Oxford University Press.

Hubbard, Edward M., A. Cyrus Arman, Vilayanur S. Ramachandran, and Geoffrey M. Boynton, 2005. Individual differences among grapheme-color synesthetes: Brain-behavior correlations. *Neuron* 45:975–985.

Hurley, Susan, and Alva Noë. 2007. Can hunter-gatherers hear colour? In *Common Minds: Themes from the Philosophy of Phillip Pettit*, ed. Geoffrey Brennan, Robert Goodin, Frank Jackson, and Michael Smith, 55–83. Oxford: Oxford University Press.

Huttenlocher, Peter R., and Arun S. Dabholkar. 1997. Regional differences in synaptogenesis in human cerebral cortex. *Journal of Comparative Neurology* 387:167–178.

Johnson, Donielle, Carrie Allison, and Simon Baron-Cohen. 2013. The prevalence of synesthesia: The consistency revolution. In *The Oxford Handbook of Synesthesia*, ed. Julia Simner and Edward M. Hubbard, 3–22. Oxford: Oxford University Press.

Lenzberg, Karl. 1923. Zur Theorie der Sekundärempfindungen und zur Bleulerschen Theorie im besonderen. *Zeitschrift fur angewandte Psychologie* 21:283–307.

Maechler, Marc-Jacques. (2012). *Synaesthesia. Children*. <http://www.synaesthesia.com/en/Information/kinder>.

Marks, Lawrence E. 1975. On colored-hearing synesthesia: Cross-modal translations of sensory dimensions. *Psychological Bulletin* 82:303–331.

Maurer, Daphne. 1993. Neonatal synesthesia: Implications for the processing of speech and faces. In *Developmental Neurocognition: Speech and Face Processing in the First Year of Life*, ed. Benedicte de Boysson-Bardies, Scania de Schonen, Peter Jusczyk, Peter McNeilage, and John Morton, 109–124. Dordrecht: Kluwer Academic Publishers.

Maurer, Daphne, Laura C. Gibson, and Ferrinne Spector. 2013. Synesthesia in infants and very young children. In *The Oxford Handbook of Synesthesia*, ed. Julia Simner and Edward M. Hubbard, 46–63 . Oxford: Oxford University Press.

Maurer, Daphne, and Catherine. J. Mondloch. 2005. Neonatal synesthesia: A reevaluation. In *Synesthesia: Perspectives from Cognitive Neuroscience*, ed. Lynn C. Robertson and Noam Sagiv, 193–213. New York: Oxford University Press.

McCandliss, Bruce D., Laurent Cohen, and Stanislas Dehaene. 2003. The visual word form area: Expertise for reading in the fusiform gyrus. *Trends in Cognitive Sciences* 7:293–299.

Nunn, J. A., L. J. Gregory, M. J. Brammer, S. C. R. Williams, D. M. Parslow, M. J. Morgan, R. G. Morris, E. T. Bullmore, S. Baron-Cohen, and J. A. Gray. 2002. Functional magnetic resonance imaging of synaesthesia: activation of V4/V8 by spoken words. *Nature Neuroscience* 5:371–375.

Palmeri, Thomas J., Randoph Blake, Rene Marois, Marci A. Flanery, and William Whetsell, Jr. 2002. The perceptual reality of synesthetic colors. *Proceedings of the National Academy of Sciences of the United States of America* 99:4127–4131.

Price, Mark C. 2013. Synesthesia, imagery, and performance. In *The Oxford Handbook of Synesthesia*, ed. Julia Simner and Edward M. Hubbard, 728–757. Oxford: Oxford University Press.

Riggs, L. A., and Karwoski, T. 1934. Synaesthesia. *British Journal of Psychology* 25:29–41.

Révész, Géza. 1923. Über audition colorée. *Zeitschrift fur angewandte Psychologie* 21:308–332.

Rich, Anina N., John L. Bradshaw, and Jason B. Mattingley. 2005. A systematic, large-scale study of synaesthesia: Implications for the role of early experience in lexical-colour associations. *Cognition* 98:53–84.

Rouw, Romke, and H. Steven Scholte. 2007. Increased structural connectivity in grapheme-color synesthesia. *Nature Neuroscience* 10:792–797.

Seidenberg, Mark S., and Michael K. Tananhaus. 1979. Orthographic effects on rhyme monitoring, *Journal of Experimental Psychology: Human Learning and Memory* 5:546–554.

Shanon, Benny. 2003. Three stories concerning synaesthesia and a commentary on Ramachandran and Hubbard. *Journal of Consciousness Studies* 10:69–74.

Shaywitz, Bennett. A, Sally E. Shaywitz, Kenneth R. Pugh, W. Einar Mencl, Robert K. Fulbright, Pawel Skudlarski, R. Todd Constable, *et al.* 2002. Disruption of posterior brain systems for reading in children with developmental dyslexia. *Biological Psychiatry* 52:101–110.

Simner, Julia. 2007. Beyond perception: synaesthesia as a psycholinguistic phenomenon. *Trends in Cognitive Science* 11:23–29.

——. 2013. The 'rules' of synesthesia. In *The Oxford Handbook of Synesthesia*, ed. Julia Simner and Edward M. Hubbard, 149–164. Oxford: Oxford University Press.

——. In preparation. *Awareness of Synaesthesia in Schools.*

Simner, Julia, Louise Glover, and Alice Mowat. 2006. Linguistic determinants of word colouring in grapheme-colour synaesthesia. *Cortex* 42:281–289.

Simner, Julia, Jennifer Harrold, Harriet Creed, Louise Monro, and Louise Foulkes. 2009. Early detection of markers for synaesthesia in childhood populations. *Brain* 132:57–64.

Simner, Julia, Catherine Mulvenna, Noam Sagiv, Elias Tsakanikos, S. Athene Witherby, Christine Fraser, Kirsten Scott, and Jamie Ward. 2006. Synaesthesia: The prevalence of atypical cross-modal experiences. *Perception* 35:1024–1033.

Simner, Julia, and Jamie Ward. 2006. The taste of words on the tip of the tongue. *Nature* 444: 438.

Smilek, D., B A. Moffatt, J. Pasternak, B. N. White, M. J. Dixon, and P. M. Merikle. 2002. Synaesthesia: a case study of discordant monozygotic twins. *Neurocase* 8:338–342.

Smilek, Daniel, Mike J. Dixon, Cera Cudahy, and Philip M. Merikle. 2002. Synesthetic color experiences influence memory. *Psychological Science* 13:548–552.

Steen, Carol, and Greta Berman. 2013. Synesthesia and the artistic process. In *The Oxford Handbook of Synesthesia*, ed. Julia Simner and Edward M. Hubbard, 671–691. Oxford: Oxford University Press.

Tomson, Steffie N., Nili Avidan, Kwanghyuk Lee, Anand K. Sarma, Rejnal Tushe, Dianna M. Milewicz, Molly Bray, Suzanne M. Leal, and David M. Eagleman. 2011. The genetics of colored sequence synesthesia: Suggestive evidence of linkage to 16q and genetic heterogeneity for the condition. *Behavioural Brain Research* 223:48–52.

van Atteveldt, Nienke, Elia Formisano, Rainer Goebel, and Leo Blomert. 2004. Integration of letters and speech sounds in the human brain. *Neuron* 43:271–282.

Ward, Jamie, Brett Huckstep, and Elias Tsakanikos. 2006. Sound-colour synaesthesia: to what extent does it use cross-modal mechanisms common to us all? *Cortex* 42: 264–280.

Ward, Jamie, Clare Jonas, Zoltan Dienes, and Anil Seth. 2010. Grapheme-colour synaesthesia improves detection of embedded shapes, but without pre-attentive "pop-out" of synaesthetic colour. *Proceedings of the Royal Society B: Biological Sciences* 277:1021–1026.

Ward, Jamie, Noam Sagiv, and Brian Butterworth. 2009. The impact of visuo-spatial number forms on simple arithmetic. *Cortex* 45:12661–1265.

Ward, Jamie, and Julia Simner. 2003. Lexical-gustatory synaesthesia: linguistic and conceptual factors. *Cognition* 89:237–261.

——. 2005. Is synaesthesia an X-linked dominant trait with lethality in males? *Perception* 34:611–623.

Ward, Jamie, Julia Simner, and Vivien Auyeung. 2005. A comparison of lexical-gustatory and grapheme-colour synaesthesia. *Cognitive Neuropsychology* 22:28–41.

Werner, Heinz. 1940. *Comparative Psychology of Mental Development*. New York: Harper.

Yaro, Caroline, and Jamie Ward. 2007. Searching for Shereshevskii: what is superior about the memory of synaesthetes? *Quarterly Journal of Experimental Psychology* 60:681–695.

CHAPTER 5

SYNESTHESIA, ALPHABET BOOKS, AND FRIDGE MAGNETS

PETER HANCOCK

INTRODUCTION

Where do the colors of synesthesia come from? Where tastes, or other synesthetic associations, come from is an equally pertinent question, but harder to answer due to the relative infrequency of these forms of synesthesia. The origins of color bindings are obscure, partly because most synesthetes simply report that the colors have "always" been that way, with some even taking offence at the suggestion that they are learned. This chapter surveys evidence, some of it anecdotal, relating to why the colors are as they are; there is more on the "rules" of synesthesia in Chapter 8, by Julia Simner, in this volume.

There would appear to be four possible explanations for grapheme-color bindings. One is that the associations are learned, perhaps through some childhood book or toy, but the memory is lost through childhood amnesia. The second is that there are natural associations, that "A" is somehow "obviously" red, but the colors become synesthesia in only a minority of individuals, due to a mixture of genetic and developmental reasons. The third, given that synesthesia runs in families, is that colors are in some way taught by parent to child. The last is that the colors are entirely arbitrary, produced by random connections in the developing brain. Each of these possibilities makes testable predictions.

OBJECTIVE ASSOCIATIONS

The best way to determine if the origin of colors is learned is to find the source of the association. There are two reported cases in the literature that do so with a high degree of certainty (but see also Rich, Bradshaw, and Mattingley 2005), and these coincidentally appeared in the same special issue of the journal *Cortex*. Witthoft and Winawer (2006) report the case of AED, where the colors originate from alphabet fridge magnets. Figure 5.1 shows a reproduction of AED's synesthetic colors and of the fridge magnets; the hues are highly correlated, $\rho = 0.96$, $p < 0.0001$. In her case there is an intriguing further twist, in that she moved to Russia when 3 years old and learned the Cyrillic alphabet. She has colors for Cyrillic letters too, and an analysis of the patterns showed that a total of 40 (upper and lower case) showed a clear match to visually similar Roman letters, with a near perfect correlation between the hues. This is despite the fact that visually similar letters may sound completely different, such as "p" in Cyrillic which is an "r" sound. On the other hand, there are some Cyrillic characters that have no visually similar Roman character, but do have phonetic equivalents, such as f/ф. There were ten such letters that also showed a near perfect hue match to their phonetic Roman equivalents. The implication is that AED formed her colors for the Cyrillic alphabet from the nearest equivalents in the Roman letters, by shape or sound.

FIGURE 5.1 AED's synesthetic colors (top) and the fridge magnet letters she played with as a child (bottom). Note that G and H are missing, but if the pattern repeats they would be red and orange. Reprinted from *Cortex*, 42 (2), Nathan Witthoft and Jonathan Winawer, *Synesthetic Colors Determined by Having Colored Refrigerator Magnets in Childhood*, pp. 175–183, Copyright (2006), with permission from Elsevier.

The original set of fridge magnets were upper-case letters in a simple font. Witthoft and Winawer (2006) go on to show that, while the colors appear to derive from the fridge magnets, the more a letter differs from the font of the magnets, the lower the saturation of the perceived colors. Lower-case letters, letters in a cursive font, and the Cyrillic letters were all less saturated than upper-case Times font letters. They then demonstrated that the synesthetic colors have their origin in low-level visual mechanisms, using a lightness constancy illusion. This is the mechanism by which the human visual system compensates for the effects of shadows. A scene can be constructed where two patches have identical gray levels, but one that appears to be in a shadow is perceived to be far brighter than the one that is not shadowed. AED was tested by asking her to adjust a color patch to match her synesthetic color of a letter that was either in the shadow or in the bright area of the scene. Control participants performed a similar task with actually colored letters, while AED also did the task with colored oval shapes that did not generate any synesthetic color for her. The result showed that AED's synesthetic colors were susceptible to the illusion, though not as strongly as true colors in the scene. Witthoft and Winawer speculate that synesthetic colors are generated by downward connections from letter recognition areas to early color processing areas, thereby missing some of the lowest level lightness constancy processing. Whatever the mechanism, the degree to which her synesthetic colors match the fridge magnet set implies that her colors derived from this source (see now also Witthoft and Winawer 2013 for further cases).

I reported another case of an enduring number-color association where the origins of the colors are known (Hancock 2006). The case concerns a pair of monozygotic twins, RH and TH, who were attending the Psychology Department playgroup at the University of Stirling. The playgroup leader observed RH, then aged 3, responding unusually to a number naming game on the computer; for example, when presented with the digit "8," he said "orange." His brother, TH, made the same pairings, though only when asked. I recorded the colors and it soon became apparent that they derived from an "Early Learning Centre" number jigsaw they played with at home. However, they also reported colors for letters and, while they played with an equivalent letter jigsaw, the colors did not match and no other source for them could be traced. Their mother also has grapheme-color associations, though with different colors from those of the boys. Although she has no memory of where her colors come from, she reports having come across a set of toy bricks in a school where the colors were "correct."

I recorded RH's and TH's colors again when aged 6, 11, and 12, simply by asking them to name them. The results are reported in Table 5.1, along with those in a recent retest. At age 12, at least 5 years after they had last seen the jigsaw, I also conducted a synesthetic Stroop test (Odgaard, Flowers, and Bradman 1999; Wollen and Ruggiero 1983). For this, I asked them independently to pick the best color for each number, using the color picker from Adobe Photoshop®. The colors they chose are reproduced in Figure 5.2, along with those from the jigsaw. The accuracy of the match for each of them is immediately apparent; the probability of a match this good by chance is less than 0.001 for both (six color names used, nine out of ten correct for RH, eight out of ten for TH). I then set up the synesthetic Stroop reaction time experiment, with

Table 5.1 Colors for letters and numbers reported by TH and RH.
(Age in years:months, Dk = dark, Lt = light)

	TH				RH			
Age	6:7	11:3	12:2	18	6:7	11:3	12:2	18
1	Pink	Pink	Pink	Pink	Dk green	Pink	Red	Pink
2	Dk blue	Lt blue	Blue	Blue	Lt blue	Lt blue	Blue	Lt blue
3	Yellow	Red	Red	Yellow	Yellow	Yellow	Gold	Yellow
4	Red	Red	Red	Red	Red	Red	Blue	Red
5	Green	–	Green	–	Lt green	Orange	Green	Dk green
6	Pale blue	Dk blue	Dk blue	Blue	Dk blue	Dk blue	Blue	Dk blue
7	Lt green	Lt green	Nice green	Green	Dk green	Green	Green	Lt green
8	Orange	Orange	Orange	Orange	Lt pink	Orange	Orange	Orange
9	Lt blue	Royal blue	Dk blue	Blue	Orange	Lt blue	Blue	Lt blue
0	Pink	Pink	Pink	Pink	Dirty pink	Pink	Pink	Pink
A	Red	Red	Red	Red	Red	Red	Red	Red
B	Brown	Brown	Brown	–	Orange	Orange	Brown	Red/orange
C	Yellow	Yellow	Yellow	–	Pink	Red	Yellow/red	Yellow
D	Blue	Blue	Blue	–	Red	Red	Red	–
E	Orange	Yellow	Yellow	–	Brown	Brown	Brown	Brown
F	Purple	Brown	Brown	–	Orange	Orange	Orange	Orange
G	Green	Lt blue	Orange	–	Green	Green	Green	–
H	Red	Red	Red	–	Red	Red	Red	Red
I	Blue	Yellow	Yellow	–	Orange	Yellow	Yellow	Yellow
J	Blue	Pink	Pink	–	Purple	Pink	–	–
K	Pink	Pink	Red	–	Pink	Pink	Red	–
L	Red	Red	Red	–	Red	Red	Red	–
M	Red	Red	Red	Red	Red	Red	Red	Red
N	Orange	Brown	Brown	–	Orange	Brown	Brown	–
O	Orange	Orange	Orange	Orange	Orange	Orange	Orange	Orange
P	Blue	Blue	Blue	Blue	Blue	Blue	Blue	–
Q	Gray	Yellow	Black	–	White	Pink	Pink	–
R	Red	Dk blue	Blue	Blue	Pink	Dk blue	Dk blue	Dk blue
S	Dk green	Dk green	Green	–	Red	Dk green	Green	Yellow
T	Lt green	Lt green	Green	Green	Green	Lt green	Green	Green
U	Red	–	White	–	Brown	Orange	–	–
V	Gray	–	Orange	–	Brown	Orange	–	–
W	Gray	Gray/blue	Brown	–	Yellow	Brown	–	–
X	Black	Red	Black	–	White	Red	–	–
Y	Red	Yellow	Black	–	Yellow	Yellow	–	–
Z	Black	–	Red	–	Brown	Brown	–	–

FIGURE 5.2 Colors chosen by RH (top two rows) and TH (middle two rows), with a repro-
duction of the colors used in the jigsaw (bottom two rows). Reprinted from *Cortex*, 42 (2),
Peter Hancock, Monozygotic Twins' Colour-Number Association: A case study, pp. 147–150,
Copyright (2006), with permission from Elsevier.

the task being to speak the name of the font-color in which a digit is displayed on-
screen. Unbeknown to them, I created incongruous versions of each number for each
of them, by swapping discordant pairs, e.g., "1" became blue and "2" became pink.
Over a few days, both were tested 24 times for each number-color combination. The
results showed a significant effect of incongruence—they named the synesthetically
"wrong" colors slower than the "correct" ones. The statistics did not indicate a difference between the boys, though it was apparent the effect was being driven by RH, who
showed a bigger effect than TH.

This case is apparently unique in that it was first recorded at such a young age—around
the early limit of memory for most people. So far as RH and TH are concerned, the numbers have simply always been that color, and it wasn't until after completing the Stroop
task that they were shown the jigsaw. Now aged 18, I asked them again about their colors.
The results are shown in Table 5.1, along with their reports from age 6, 11, and 12. For TH,
the color associations are fading, though the ones that remain are highly consistent. RH
has more remaining colors and again these are highly consistent. Note that the three

changes in the number colors since the age of 12 are actually reversions to the original. RH commented that listing them was now essentially a memory task but also that when he was recently cutting out colored letters for a banner the ones with incongruent colors (i.e., with font-colors that conflicted with his synesthetic colors) "felt wrong." However, neither of them reports the photisms or automatic percepts often experienced by people with synesthesia; in the terminology of Ward et al. (2007) they might be "know-associators." The number 8 simply is orange, rather than any other color. Despite this, they pass the two tests often regarded as a marker of true synesthesia: a long-lasting association, now more than 12 years (the "Test of Genuineness"; Baron-Cohen, Wyke, and Binnie 1987), and a measurable Stroop effect for incongruent colors.

Some might wish to argue that RH and TH do not exhibit synesthesia, having "merely" a long-lasting association. This is the argument of Elias et al. (2003), who describe a case of an individual who learned color associations from cross-stitch sewing patterns, where numbers refer to colors of threads. They showed that in this case also, a measurable Stroop effect could be detected, similar to that shown by a color-grapheme synesthete, though the two could be distinguished by the pattern of functional magnetic resonance imaging activation. The issue is further complicated by the discovery that it is possible to induce color transfer to novel graphemes after only 10 minutes of exercise (Mroczko et al. 2009) and to hypnotize suitably suggestible participants into behaving as if they have a strong number-color association. Cohen Kadosh et al. (2009) demonstrated that their hypnotized participants were prone to errors in detecting a digit when placed on a background that matched its induced color, the implication being that they were projecting the color onto the display. Cohen Kadosh et al. argue that this finding challenges the suggestion that synesthesia is caused by hyperconnectivity between brain regions, since there is no reason to suppose their participants developed extra connectivity in the relatively short time-scale of the experiment. However, it seems possible that while their hypnotism reduced inhibition between normally separate brain regions, natural synesthetes still have stronger than usual connections, rather than similarly reduced inhibition. The Cohen Kadosh et al. finding does further blur the boundary of what is classified as synesthesia. RH and TH pass objective tests for synesthesia, their colors have "always" been that way and they have a family history, but they are clearly associators, rather than projectors. AED, by contrast, is classed as a projector synesthete (Witthoft and Winawer 2006); she sees colors on the surfaces of letters, so we therefore have evidence for a clear origin for colors from both ends of the scale of synesthetic experience.

SUBJECTIVE EXPLANATIONS FOR ASSOCIATIONS

While some synesthetes state that their colors have always been there and object to the notion that they may have been learned, others are interested in what the origins may be and have clearly spent time thinking about it. My requests for examples, obtained from synesthesia mailing lists, and by appealing for synesthetes from a university population,

Table 5.2 Colors reported by PD, along with those currently used by the book band scheme in the UK, the most common colors from Day (2005) and from Rich et al. (2005). (RGBY for the numbers 6 and 7 mean that red, green, blue, and yellow were perceived about equally.)

	1	2	3	4	5	6	7	8	9
PD	Blue	Red	Yellow	Brown	Green	Orange	Purple	Maroon	Yellow
Book band	Pink	Red	Yellow	Blue	Green	Orange	Turquoise	Purple	Gold
Day	Gray	Blue	Yellow	Blue	Red	Dark blue	Green	Yellow-green	Brown
Rich	White Black	Blue	Green	Red Blue	Yellow	RGBY	RGBY	Brown green	Brown

have produced a few interesting cases, necessarily anecdotal. For example, KR: "My Friday is black and I assume it's black because as a child I was able to stay up late at night and play outside well past dark. Saturdays are a vivid medium blue—maybe the color of the sky because I spent so much time outdoors on Saturdays? Sundays are medium brown, the color of church pews." VE commented: "I do remember playing with magnetic alphabet letters when I was young, but remember being annoyed that they were not the right colors!" However, she went on to say: "I do know that my colors for days of the week almost completely matched with the TV magazine my mum used to buy (with the exception of Thursday and Sunday)." PD speculated that his number colors derived from those used in a reading scheme that he enjoyed working through at school. Table 5.2 shows his reported colors and those from the current book banding scheme in the UK; he matches on five of nine digits (allowing yellow for gold, there is nothing metallic about the color used in the scheme), compared with matching only one of the commonest colors reported by Day (2005) and none of those reported by Rich, Bradshaw, and Mattingley (2005)

The most complete description came from WG:

I have a definite memory of having a "number board," as an infant (early 1950s). It was plastic and a long oval, wider at one end, with 10 circular holes in it and removable discs, 1 being smallest, 10 largest. The discs were different colours and, with a bit of vagueness about 5, the colours of those discs are the colours I see for those numbers: 1 (red), 2 (blue), 3 (green), 4 (yellow), 5 (I think it was red. I see it now as orange), 6 (white), 7 (blue), 8 (green), 9 (yellow), 10 (red). I strongly suspect some letters' colours come from alphabet blocks but have no definite memories of this. At my primary school there was a circular disc on the wall showing the church's year divided into coloured sections with, fairly obviously, Advent blue, Epiphany purple, Trinity green, Christmas and Easter thin red segments which is how I think of these. I think that is also why I think of a year as a circle, divided into 12 coloured segments (months) although, oddly perhaps, the year in my mind goes anti-clockwise.

I strongly suspect the one on the classroom wall would go clockwise. We were often asked to underline nouns in red so the word "noun" is red to me. For the same reason, "verb" is blue, "adjective" yellow and "adverb" purple.

I know why I envisage most months of the year as I do but not when I first did or what the actual trigger was. January gray (cold, dreary), Feb white (snow), March green and yellow (daffodils), April dark blue (Easter usually comes then and although "Easter" is a red word, "Sunday," the main day of Easter, is a dark blue word), May pink (cherry blossom), June yellow (sun), July orange (hotter sun), August yellow (sun and parched grass), September green (cooler countryside), October brown (autumn leaves), November black (dark and depressing), December red (Christmas).

I have attempted to locate a copy of the number board to confirm the colors, without success. However, while all the examples given are interesting, and clearly suggest the possibility of synesthetic colors coming from some association, the more striking finding is that very few synesthetes have any idea why their colors are as they are. Rich, Bradshaw, and Mattingley (2005) report that only 5% of their sample of 192 synesthetes believed their colors came from sources such as colored letters, while 6% specifically report now having different pairings to those seen as a child. If TH and RH are in any way typical, this may be because any associations are learned during the period of childhood amnesia; they were only picked up because of observant staff in the university playgroup. However, all is not lost, because it may be possible to pick up commonalities in the colors experienced by different synesthetes that give a clue to common origins.

STATISTICAL ASSOCIATIONS

There have now been three large-scale studies looking for common color associations in synesthesia. Fortunately, all three use the same standardized set of 11 basic color terms: black, white, red, green, yellow, blue, brown, gray, orange, pink, and purple from Berlin and Kay (1969). Rich, Bradshaw, and Mattingley (2005) report on 150 grapheme-color synesthetes, Simner et al. (2005) report on 70, while Day (2005) reports 172, though these are from a variety of sources and may not pass a consistency Test of Genuineness (see Johnson, Allison, and Baron-Cohen, Chapter 1, this volume). Day (2004) gives a more complete account of observed frequencies for each letter. A summary of the most frequent responses is given in Table 5.3. Perhaps the most immediately striking finding, since it is the first letter, is the tendency of "A" to be red: 43% for both Day and Simner et al., 36% for Rich, Bradshaw, and Mattingley. The common explanation for this is that "A" is for apple on children's spelling charts, and apples are red. Note, though, that apples may also be green and green does not figure in the list for synesthetes, though it does for Simner et al.'s controls. Similarly, "D" is for dog and dogs are brown, so is "D" for between 30% and 45% of synesthetes. There is an evident tendency for letters to take on the color for which they form the start of the name, so "R" is often red (35–40% of cases) and "Y"

Table 5.3 Color choices for synesthetes and controls from three studies, see the section "Associations in non-synesthetes" for explanation of the categories of controls. (Multiple colors are listed in order of frequency. Day (2004): the most frequent responses are reported, with no significance testing. Rich, Bradshaw, and Mattingley (2005) the significant and "trend" associations are listed. Simner et al. (2005), significant associations.)

	Synesthetes			Controls			
	Day	Rich, Bradshaw, and Mattingley	Simner et al.	Rich, Bradshaw, and Mattingley	Simner et al. required choice	Simner et al. free choice	Simner et al. random order
A	Red 44%	Red	Red		Red	Green	Red, green
B	Blue, brown	Blue	Blue, brown	Blue	Blue	Blue, brown	Blue
C	Yellow	Yellow, pink	Yellow, pink		Yellow, orange	White, gray	
D	Brown, green	Brown	Brown, blue	Brown	Green, brown	Blue, brown	Green, blue
E	Yellow, green, blue		Green, yellow		Gray, green		Gray, green
F	Brown, green		Brown, green, orange	Green	Green, purple		
G	Green, brown	Green	Brown, green	Green	Green	Green	Green
H	Brown		Yellow, green	Brown	Black	Red, brown	
I	White, black	White	White, black	White	White, blue	Blue	Blue, white
J	Brown, purple, red	Orange	Red, orange, purple			Pink	
K	Brown, yellow					Pink	
L	Yellow, blue		Gray	Yellow	Yellow	Yellow	Yellow
M	Red, brown		Red, brown		Purple	Purple, brown, pink	Pink
N	Brown, green		Brown		White	Blue	Orange
O	White	White	White, Black	Orange	Orange	Orange	Orange, White
P	Blue, green, pink, purple	Pink	Blue, pink	Purple, pink	Purple, pink	Purple, pink	Purple, pink
Q	Yellow, gray, purple		Purple, gray, pink		Black	Orange	Purple
R	Red 32%, green	Red	Red, green		Red, brown	Red	Red
S	Yellow, red		Yellow, red		Yellow	Red, gray	Yellow, red
T	Green, blue		Black, blue		Brown	Green, blue, brown	Blue
U	Yellow, brown		Gray, white	Gray	Black	Yellow	
V	Gray, purple, green	Purple	Purple	Purple	Purple	Purple	Purple
W	Green, brown, blue		Blue, orange	White	White	White	White
X	Black, gray	Black, gray	Black, gray	Black, gray	Black, gray	Black	Black, gray
Y	Yellow 44%	Yellow	Yellow, gray	Yellow	Yellow	Yellow	Yellow
Z	Black, gray	Black	Black	Black	Black, white	Black	Black

is yellow for 40–45%, while "B" is often blue or brown. Equally striking is the tendency for some letters to be "colorless" in the sense of being either white or black. In particular, "O" is white for around half of those studied, while "I" is often either white or black. The letters "X" and "Z" are also often black, for around 25% to 30% of cases. This would seem to rule out the final possibility given earlier, that the associations are entirely random, since chance, if the 11 colors were equally frequent, would be around 9%.

Origins of the Observed Patterns

Rich, Bradshaw, and Mattingley (2005) looked to see whether they could find any relationship between the colors reported by their synesthetes and alphabet books that they might have seen in childhood. They identified 136 possible books, only 38 of which had colored letters, or an obviously colored object as illustration, and 20 had colored numbers. They found some commonality between the books, so "A" was associated with red in 43%, and green with "H" (24%) and "S" (23%). They found just one of their sample of 150 synesthetes whose alphabet colors matched those in a book with high consistency and four whose numbers matched a book. The colors in this book also matched those used in the "Cuisenaire rods" system that was commonly used to teach simple arithmetic in the 1960s and 1970s, see Table 5.4. Looking only at synesthetes likely to have used this system in school, they found a trend for "5" to be yellow. However, overall, they conclude there is little evidence for colors to have come from early exposure to such sources. So we need other explanations for the consistencies shown in Table 5.3.

Associations in Non-synesthetes

To test for natural associations, Simner et al. (2005) used three English-speaking control groups: one (required-choice) were asked to write down the first color that came to mind for each letter and number, the second (free-choice) were instructed to give a color only if it came easily to mind. A third group saw the letters in a random order, and gave a required-choice response. Rich, Bradshaw, and Mattingley's (2005) control group were required-choice. The results in Table 5.3 show some obvious parallels between the controls and the synesthetes such as "B" being blue or brown and "Y" being yellow,

Table 5.4 Colors used by the Cuisenaire rods number teaching system

1	2	3	4	5	6	7	8	9	10
White	Red	Light green	Lavender	Yellow	Dark green	Black	Brown	Blue	Orange

along with some evident differences, for example, the controls gave white for "W" and orange for "O," which are not typical of synesthetes. Note that the common response of purple for "V" is assumed to be due to the English word violet, which gets classed as purple. Despite some apparent differences between the first two control groups, Simner et al. show that their responses are more similar than expected by chance. The overlap between all three groups of controls and the synesthetes is also significant, with 16 matches from the required-choice group, against an expectation of five by chance. It would seem that there are one or more underlying causes in common between the synesthetes and the controls.

One possibility is that "A" is red because it is the first letter, and red is an obvious color name in that it easily comes to mind when thinking of colors (compared to, say, turquoise). To test this, Simner et al. used the ease of generation ranking of color names given by Battig and Montague (1969). Blue is top of this list, with red second. Simner et al. (2005) found a near-significant correlation between the colors in the required-choice group and the ease of generation list, suggesting that these participants may have had a tendency to offer the next easiest color name as they went through the list. Neither synesthetes nor free-choice controls showed a relationship, and no group showed a correlation between list-order and the frequency of occurrence of color names in English, which differ from ease of generation; black and white being actually the most common.

LETTER FREQUENCY EFFECTS

Simner et al. (2005) did however find a significant correlation for the synesthetes between the frequency of graphemes in the English language and the frequency of color terms. Thus high frequency letters, such as "E," "T," and "A" tend to be associated with high-frequency color names such as black, white, and red, $\rho = 0.37$, $p <0.02$. There was a somewhat stronger correlation between letter frequency and the order in which color names enter the language, $\rho = 0.47$, $p <0.01$ (Berlin and Kay 1969). This ordering derives from studies across human languages, and indicates that the simplest distinction is between white and black, followed by red and then green and yellow. Shanon (1982) showed that this ordering correlated with colors given for numbers by his sample of 18 synesthetes.

This finding of a correlation between letter frequency and color was replicated for a group of German-speaking synesthetes by Beeli, Esslen, and Jäncke (2007). They found that more frequent letters tended to have more saturated colors, though the correlation is weak ($r = 0.15$) and there is a notable outlier in "E," which has nearly twice the frequency of any other letter in German. Simner and Ward (2008) reanalyzed these data to show that they are consistent with the explanation that frequent letters are associated with frequent color names, as in the previous paragraph.

Beeli, Esslen, and Jäncke (2007) also found a relationship between the luminance of their synesthetes' colors and number frequency. Thus zero is the most frequent digit and is commonly white and therefore most luminant. One is the next most frequent digit, and is commonly either white or black, producing a lower average luminance. Two comes next and is typically colored, often red. They report a strong overall correlation between luminance and frequency of digits in the language ($r = 0.58$). Smilek et al. (2007) performed a similar analysis on a set of data from 55 synesthetes and confirmed a strong correlation between number frequency and luminance and also found a small correlation for letters, with the most frequent being brightest. Smilek et al. were able to perform the same analysis for a set of 254 non-synesthetes who had completed their color assignment test and found the same tendency, albeit much more weakly. That is, non-synesthetes also tended to give brighter colors for more frequent letters and numerals.

COLOR NAMES

Table 5.3 suggests an association between a color and the first letter of its name, such as "R" being red. Simner et al. (2005) showed that, for both synesthetes and control participants, these associations are more common than would be expected by chance. The effect is surprisingly weak however, given the patterns in Table 5.3, with their average synesthete having only two such letters. An obvious further test of this hypothesis would be to study synesthetes who have different native languages. Zedler et al. (2005) tested 71 German-speaking synesthetes and found a pattern remarkably similar to those reported in Table 5.3; significant associations being A with red (49%), I with white (36%), K (46%) and R (40%) with brown, S with yellow (51%), and V (41%) and X (46%) with gray. There is no evidence for color names here; for example, G is not yellow "gelb". However, Simner et al. (2005) tested a non-synesthetic German control group and found, for example, a tendency to attribute purple to the letter "L," presumably because the word for purple in German is "lila." There are some studies of bilingual synesthetes, such as AED, see earlier section. Barnett et al. (2009) looked for patterns of similarity across a group of 21 bi- or multi-lingual synesthetes. They found that colors were not related to word meaning so much as to the visual form. Thus January is janvier in French, Januar in German, and Eanáir in Irish and the degree of color agreement between languages was significantly lower where the first letter differed. Where the first letter is the same, agreement for the colors of months was higher than that for days of the week, which in turn was higher than for numbers. Barnett et al. follow Rich, Bradshaw, and Mattingley (2005) in speculating that this relates to the age at which the items are learned. Numbers are learned early, followed by days of the week, and finally months. The suggestion is that, while numbers are learned early, and pick up their own idiosyncratic colors as discussed earlier, months are learned in their written form, by which time colors for letters have been established, with a tendency for the month to inherit the color of their first letter. Days of the week are learned earlier than months and are therefore less likely to inherit the first letter color.

WHY O IS WHITE

One of the common observations from these studies is that some letters, such as "I," "O," and "X" are often colorless—i.e., white or black, as are the numbers "o" and "1." Spector and Maurer (2008) tested presumed non-synesthetes of varying ages, including pre-literate toddlers, to see whether they showed consistent associations for these typically "colorless" (i.e., achromatic) letters. They had to decide which side of a box a plastic letter would be found, where one side of the box was black and the other white. Around 80% of the toddlers picked black for "X" and white for "O," exactly the same proportion as older children, and similar to adult choices. However, given the choice of red and green for "A" and "G," the toddlers chose at random, while older children chose red for "A" and green for "G" 80% of the time, and adults almost always. Given only the sound of "X" and "O," toddlers had no preference, implying it is the shape of the letters that has the association. Spector and Maurer (2011) extended these results, showing that toddlers preferred white for "I" and black for "Z" but were at chance for "B" and "Y," which older children and adults tended to associate with blue and yellow respectively. They also showed that toddlers associated rounded shapes with white and jagged ones with black and also that they associate "C" with yellow, but not with white, while "T," "E," and "M" showed no color association. Overall, their results indicate that the toddlers associate angular things, such as "X" and "Z," with black, and non-angular ones, such as "O" and "I" with white. Why "C" is yellow is unclear.

A number of studies have shown that the relationship between letter shape and associated colors continues into adult synesthesia. For example, Brang et al. (2011) found a significant correlation between letter shape similarity and color similarity for about half their sample of synesthetes, with the correlation stronger for projectors than for associators. Thus the letters "D" and "B" are more similar than "D" and "V," with data coming from an earlier study on the confusability of letters, and amongst synesthetes, "D" and "B" are both often brown, while "V" has a tendency to be purple.

AGE OF LEARNING

Rich, Bradshaw, and Mattingley (2005) suggested that the earlier that an item sequence is learned, the more likely the items are to have idiosyncratic colors. Thus letters are learned before days of the week, which in turn precede the sequence of months. Their data confirm that words for months are more likely to have the same color as their initial letter than words for days. However, it may be possible to go further back and investigate the effects of the order in which individual letters and digits are learned. Thus Beeli, Esslen, and Jäncke (2007) report a relationship between digit frequency and luminosity of associated colors, but it is surely the case that most children will learn digits in the same order, 1, 2, 3, so the ordering might be that of learning, rather than frequency. The exception to this will be zero, which is a relatively sophisticated concept and yet has the highest average luminosity. However, the Spector and Maurer results show that pre-literate toddlers tend to associate the letter "O" with white, and the letter "O" and the digit "0" are obviously similar. Both are commonly white for synesthetes, hence the high average luminosity for the digit "0."

With letters, it is less obvious which will be learned early. "E" may be the common-est letter, but "A" is the first in the alphabet. Treiman et al. (1998) collect three sets of data about which letters young children know, taken from different studies in the USA. Hancock and Simner (in preparation) combined the youngest age group from each set to give an average rank order of learning and, perhaps unexpectedly, "O" and "X" are top of the list. We performed a rank correlation between the order of letter learning and the Berlin and Kay (1969) ordering of entry of colors into language (see earlier), using the Simner et al. (2005) commonest colors reported by synesthetes. Thus "A" is commonly red, and red is in the second rank of colors, while "A" is the third best known letter; "C" is commonly yellow, yellow is in the third rank of colors, and "C" is twelfth best known. The correlation is highly significant, $\rho = 0.61$, $p = 0.001$. Using the most frequent colors from Day (2004), the correlation is also significant, $\rho = 0.51$, $p = 0.008$. This echoes the report by Shanon (1982) that the common colors for numbers and for days of the week correlate with the Berlin and Kay color ordering. More work is needed to investigate these relationships, but it appears that there is a tendency for early-learned letters to be associated with simpler color concepts.

INHERITED COLORS

The third possibility for the origin of colors suggested earlier is that they are learned from a parent or other older family member. Anecdotally, this does not seem to be the case, with reports of synesthetic siblings arguing about the "correct" colors. Barnett et al. (2008) sought to trace patterns of synesthesia within families and report that they could see no consistent pattern of associations within the ten families that they identified as having multiple members with linguistic-color synesthesia. Overall there is no evidence that family members agree more than would be expected by the general agreement between synesthetes described previously.

A NON-COLOR EXAMPLE

Finally, there is some evidence for origins of associations other than colors. Ward and Simner (2003) report a case of lexical-gustatory synesthete, JIW, for whom specific tastes are induced by words. For example, "this" tastes of "bread soaked in tomato soup"

(241). Ward and Simner show that tastes are associated with phonemes, rather than whole words, but that the order and combination of phonemes affects the concurrent. Of interest here is that many of the associations have a semantic or phonological relationship to the taste, or to the word that describes it. For example, "blue" tastes "inky" and "bar" of "milk chocolate," while "Barbara" tastes of "rhubarb" and "Sydney" of "kidney." These relationships are significantly more frequent than expected by chance and linked particularly to the foods that he experienced most often in childhood. It therefore seems likely that, in this case, the associations were learned during language acquisition.

Conclusions

The introduction proposed four possible explanations for the observed color-grapheme bindings. Overall, it seems that while synesthetic colors are idiosyncratic in detail, there are apparent underlying patterns that explain some of them, thus ruling out the fourth possibility, that they are entirely random. There is clear evidence for the first explanation, that they *can* be learned from pairings observed in childhood, but limited evidence that they often are. There is a variety of evidence for the second explanation, that there are "natural" pairings. Letters tend to take on the color for which they are the start of the color name; for example "Y" is often yellow. Pre-literate toddlers classify "O" and "I" as white and "X" and "Z" as black, as do many synesthetes. Similar shaped letters have similar colors. Digits and letters that occur frequently tend to be brighter and more saturated. Frequent letters, and those learned early, tend to take on colors that are also learned early. How these various factors may combine, even on average, remains to be explained. There is no evidence for the third explanation, that colors are learned from synesthetic relatives.

While some associations may be identifiable, others reflect the complexities of synesthetic percepts. Odgaard, Flowers, and Bradman (1999) report a study of L, who sees 9 as being pink and 8 as purple. However, her colors for some double-digit numbers do not fit comfortably onto a standard color wheel. For example, she described 98 as a "hollow sphere of orange and grayish purple that is as real a color as red or green," but which she had "never seen anywhere in the world" (663). Ramachandran and Hubbard (2001) mention someone who is color blind, and perceives some colors only when seeing numbers. It does not seem possible for such a concurrent to be learned if it has no external perceptual existence. Studies also indicate that the colors experienced are much more sophisticated than the usual categorization into 11 basic colors admits. Thus Simner et al. (2005) report that their synesthetes gave 54 different descriptions of green, such as jade green and lettuce green, compared with only five from their control group. While the statistical patterns presented may account for some of the observed pairings it seems unlikely that they will adequately explain the full variety of synesthetic experience.

REFERENCES

Barnett, Kylie J., Joanne Feeney, Michael Gormley, and Fiona N. Newell. 2009. An Exploratory study of linguistic–colour associations across languages in multilingual synaesthetes. *The Quarterly Journal of Experimental Psychology* 62 (7):1343–1355. doi:10.1080/17470210802483461.

Barnett, Kylie J., Ciara Finucane, Julian E. Asher, Gary Bargary, Aiden P. Corvin, Fiona N. Newell, and Kevin J. Mitchell. 2008. Familial patterns and the origins of individual differences in synaesthesia. *Cognition* 106 (2):871–893. doi:10.1016/j.cognition.2007.05.003.

Baron-Cohen, Simon, Maria A. Wyke, and Colin Binnie. 1987. Hearing words and seeing colours: An experimental investigation of a case of synaesthesia. *Perception* 16 (6):761–767. doi:10.1068/p160761.

Battig, William F., and William E. Montague. 1969. Category norms for verbal items: A replication and extension of the Connecticut category norms. *Journal of Experimental Psychology* 80:1–46.

Beeli, Gian, Michaela Esslen, and Lutz Jäncke. 2007. Frequency correlates in grapheme-color synaesthesia. *Psychological Science* 18 (9):788–792. doi:10.1111/j.1467-9280.2007.01980.x.

Berlin, Brent, and Paul Kay. 1969. *Basic Color Terms: Their Universality and Evolution.* Berkeley, CA: University of California Press.

Brang, David, Romke Rouw, Vilayanur S. Ramachandran, and Seana Coulson. 2011. Similarly shaped letters evoke similar colors in grapheme–color synesthesia. *Neuropsychologia* 49 (5):1355–1358. doi:10.1016/j.neuropsychologia.2011.01.002.

Cohen Kadosh, Roi, Avishai Henik, Andres Catena, Vincent Walsh, and Luis J. Fuentes. 2009. Induced cross-modal synaesthetic experience without abnormal neuronal connections. *Psychological Science* 20 (2):258–265. doi:10.1111/j.1467-9280.2009.02286.x.

Day, Sean. 2004. Trends in synesthetically colored graphemes and phonemes–2004 revision. < http://www.daysyn.com/Day2004Trends.pdf >.

——. 2005. Some demographic and socio-cultural aspects of synesthesia. In *Synesthesia: Perspectives from Cognitive Neuroscience,* ed. Lynn C. Robertson and Noam Sagiv, 11–33. New York: Oxford University Press.

Elias, Lorin J., Deborah M. Saucier, Colleen Hardie, and Gordon E. Sarty. 2003. Dissociating semantic and perceptual components of synaesthesia: Behavioral and functional neuroanatomical investigations. *Cognitive Brain Research* 16 (2):232–237. doi:10.1016/S0926-6410(02)00278-1.

Hancock, Peter J. B. 2006. Monozygotic twins' colour-number association: A case study. *Cortex: A Journal Devoted to the Study of the Nervous System and Behavior* 42 (2):147–150. doi:10.1016/ S0010-9452(08)70338-1.

Johnson, Donielle, Carrie Allison, and Simon Baron-Cohen. 2013. The prevalence of synesthesia: The consistency revolution. In *The Oxford Handbook of Synesthesia,* ed. Julia Simner and Edward M. Hubbard, 3–22. Oxford: Oxford University Press.

Mroczko, Aleksandra, Thomas Metzinger, Wolf Singer, and Danko Nikolić. 2009. Immediate transfer of synesthesia to a novel inducer. *Journal of Vision* 9 (12). doi:10.1167/9.12.25.

Odgaard, Eric C., John H. Flowers, and H. Lynn Bradman. 1999. An investigation of the cognitive and perceptual dynamics of a color–digit synesthete. *Perception* 28:651–664.

Ramachandran, Vilayanur S., and Edward M. Hubbard. 2001. Synaesthesia—a window into perception, thought and language. *Journal of Consciousness Studies* 8 (12):3–34.

Rich, Anina N., John L. Bradshaw, and Jason B. Mattingley. 2005. A systematic, large-scale study of synaesthesia: Implications for the role of early experience in lexical-colour associations. *Cognition* 98 (1):53–84. doi:10.1016/j.cognition.2004.11.003.

Shanon, Benny. 1982. Colour associates to semantic linear orders. *Psychological Research* 44 (1):75–83. doi:10.1007/BF00308557.

Simner, Julia. 2013. The 'rules' of synesthesia. In *The Oxford Handbook of Synesthesia*, ed. Julia Simner and Edward M. Hubbard, 149–164. Oxford: Oxford University Press.

Simner, Julia, and Jamie Ward. 2008. Synaesthesia, color terms, and color space: Color claims came from color names in Beeli, Esslen, and Jäncke (2007). *Psychological Science* 19 (4):412–414. doi:10.1111/j.1467-9280.2008.02101.x.

Simner, Julia, Jamie Ward, Monika Lanz, Ashok Jansari, Krist Noonan, Louise Glover, and David A. Oakley. 2005. Non-random associations of graphemes to colours in synaesthetic and non-synaesthetic populations. *Cognitive Neuropsychology* 22 (8):1069–1085. doi:10.1080/02643290500200122.

Smilek, Daniel, Jonathan S. A. Carriere, Mike J. Dixon, and Philip M. Merikle. 2007. Grapheme frequency and color luminance in grapheme-color synaesthesia. *Psychological Science* 18 (9):793–795. doi:10.1111/j.1467-9280.2007.01981.x.

Spector, Ferrinne, and Daphne Maurer. 2008. The colour of Os: Naturally biased associations between shape and colour. *Perception* 37 (6):841–847. doi:10.1068/p5830.

——. 2011. The colors of the alphabet: Naturally-biased associations between shape and color. *Journal of Experimental Psychology: Human Perception and Performance* 37 (2):484–494. doi:10.1037/a0021437.

Treiman, Rebecca, Ruth Tincoff, Kira Rodriguez, Angeliki Mouzaki, and David J. Francis. 1998. The foundations of literacy: Learning the sounds of letters. *Child Development* 69 (6):1524–1540. doi:10.1111/j.1467-8624.1998.tb06175.x.

Ward, Jamie, Ryan Li, Shireen Salih, and Noam Sagiv. 2007. Varieties of grapheme-colour synaesthesia: A new theory of phenomenological and behavioural differences. *Consciousness and Cognition: An International Journal* 16 (4):913–931. doi:10.1016/j.concog.2006.09.012.

Ward, Jamie, and Julia Simner. 2003. Lexical-gustatory synaesthesia: Linguistic and conceptual factors. *Cognition* 89 (3):237–261. doi:10.1016/S0010-0277(03)00122-7.

Witthoft, Nathan, and Jonathan Winawer. 2006. Synesthetic colors determined by having colored refrigerator magnets in childhood. *Cortex: A Journal Devoted to the Study of the Nervous System and Behavior* 42 (2):175–183. doi:10.1016/S0010-9452(08)70342-3.

——. 2013. Learning, memory, and synesthesia. *Psychological Science* 24:258–65.

Wollen, Keith A., and Frank T. Ruggiero. 1983. Colored-letter synesthesia. *Journal of Mental Imagery* 7 (2):83–86.

Zedler, Markus, Udo Schneider, Mine Büyükoktay, and Hinderk M. Emrich. 2005. The A is Red – Genuine Synaesthetic's Letter-Colour Chart. Paper presented at 1st Congreso Int. Sinestesia y Arte, Cuevas de Almanzora, Spain.

PART II

SYNESTHESIA, LANGUAGE, AND NUMBERS

CHAPTER 6

NUMBERS, SYNESTHESIA, AND DIRECTIONALITY

ROI COHEN KADOSH AND AVISHAI HENIK

SYNESTHESIA AND NUMBERS

The influence of synesthesia on numerical cognition was discussed by Francis Galton as early as 1880 in his seminal paper entitled "Visualized numerals" (Galton 1880). Galton describes the processing of numerical information by number-space synesthetes (people who see numbers in an organized array in external space; see Figure 6.1) as "the power of mentally seeing numerals, of holding them fast in the field of view, of perusing them when there, and working sums by mental imagery in the same form as that in which they are usually carried on with pen and paper" (252). Several aspects of the phenomena discussed by Galton are echoed in current research today. For example, the first participant in Galton's sample describes his experience as follows: "If words such as fifty-six be spoken, I most clearly, easily and instantly visualize the figures. I do so almost automatically. . . . I find it quite impossible to think of the date of a year without remembering and visualizing the figures" (252). This report describes a typical synesthete's inability to repress his or her synesthetic sensations, and we might think of this as "automaticity" in the phenomenon. Skill and automaticity are of major interest in the cognitive literature in general and in discussions of synesthesia in particular. It is pretty clear from synesthetes' reports and empirical studies that there is an intimate connection between numbers and the synesthetic experience attached to them, be it color or location in space, and this intimate, irrepressible connection gives rise to the notion of automaticity. We would like to discuss this aspect in more detail. Before we do that we need to turn to a brief exposition of two phenomena in the area of numerical cognition: (1) comparative judgment and the distance effect, and (2) the numerical Stroop-like effect.

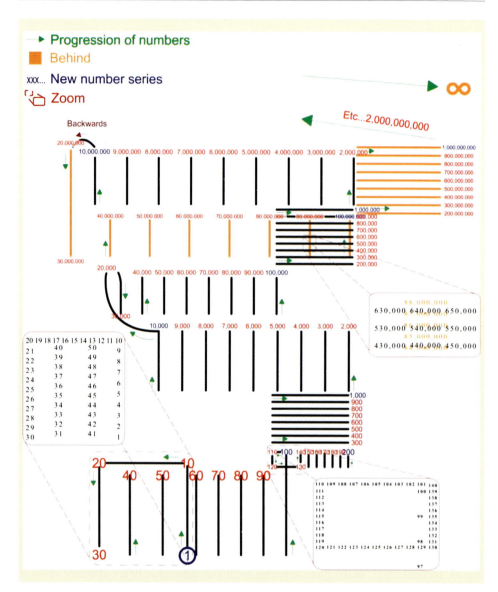

FIGURE 6.1 A detailed description of the explicit synesthetic experiences of a number-space synesthete, SM. The beginning of the numerical sequence starts at the digit 1 (circled in blue). Progression of numbers is indicated by the green arrows. A change in the overall representation occurs at the numbers 100 and 200 (in blue). The representation continues to change after 1000 (in blue). The zoom windows show a more detailed representation.

NUMERICAL COGNITION: BASIC TASKS AND EFFECTS

Comparative judgment and the distance effect

In a comparative judgment task, participants are presented with two digits (e.g., 3 5) and are asked to decide which one is larger. In an early paper, Moyer and Landauer (1967) suggested that performance is modulated by the distance between the compared stimuli. Specifically, reaction time (RT) declines as the distance between the two stimuli increases. For example, it takes longer to decide that 8 is larger than 6 than to decide that 8 is larger than 2. This distance effect has since been reported in numerous studies in adults (Banks, Mermelstein, and Yu 1982; Cohen Kadosh, Henik, et al. 2005; Dehaene 1989; Dehaene, Dupoux, and Mehler 1990; Duncan and McFarland 1980; Henik and Tzelgov 1982; Kaufmann et al. 2005; Moyer 1973; Moyer and Bayer 1976; Nuerk, Weger, and Willmes 2001; Schwarz and Ischebeck 2000; Tzelgov, Meyer, and Henik 1992), in children (Holloway and Ansari 2008; Landerl and Kölle 2009; Sekular and Mierkiewicz 1977), and in primates (Brannon 2006; Nieder and Dehaene 2009). Moyer and Landauer (1967) suggested that people convert written or auditory numbers into analogue magnitudes. The digits (representing external magnitude) automatically arouse an internal array of magnitudes, which has become known as the "mental number line" (Dehaene 1992). It has been postulated that the source of the distance effect is the spatial overlap between representations of numbers on the mental number line.

A related effect is the size effect. When two pairs of digits have the same numerical distance, smaller numbers are compared faster than larger numbers. For example, comparative judgments of 2 and 4 yield faster responses than comparative judgments of 6 and 8. It was suggested that this is related to the nature of the number line. If this line is logarithmic in nature then the larger the numbers the closer they are on the line, which in turns make the comparison more difficult and slows down responding.

Researchers suggested that the distance effect (as well as the size effect) indicates that the numerical magnitude of the presented numbers is activated automatically. This is because the distance between the two numbers has nothing to do with the decision, as, for all the examples given, one digit is larger than the other whether it is more or less distant from the other member of the pair. However, discussions of automaticity have not always accepted such cases as indicative of automaticity and we will have more to say about this in what follows.

Numerical Stroop-like effect

An essential part of arithmetic is related to understanding the numerical symbolic system. Digits are symbols that convey specific quantities, magnitudes, etc. However, digit symbols have their own physical features (e.g., physical font size) that may modulate their effect. Accordingly, in a comparative judgment task it is possible to manipulate not only the difference in numerical values between two digits but also the difference in physical sizes. These physical sizes could be employed to ask questions about digit representation and usage. For example, in our culture 8 represents a larger magnitude than 3; hence, the appearance of 8 as physically smaller than 3 might produce a conflict. Psychologists have been using similar conflict situations to study automaticity and selective attention. The paradigmatic experiments were first conducted by Stroop and the results published in 1935 (MacLeod 1991; Stroop 1935).

In 1975, Alan Paivio (1975) noticed that the physical sizes of pictures slowed down comparisons when they conflicted with the real-life size relationship between the pictures. For example, picturing an elephant smaller than a mouse might hinder comparisons. In 1982, we (Henik and Tzelgov 1982) carried the reasoning behind Paivio's experiments one step further and examined both the effect of physical size on numerical comparisons and the effect of numerical values on comparisons of physical sizes. This enabled us to examine how automatic (i.e., processed even when not part of the task requirement) the numerical values were. In a numerical Stroop task, we presented participants with two digits that could differ in both the numerical values and the physical sizes. The participants were asked to compare the numbers based on their physical size (physical comparison) or their numerical value (numerical comparison). The two dimensions could be incongruent (e.g., 3 5), congruent (e.g., 3 5), or neutral—the two digits differed only in the relevant dimension (e.g., 3 5 for numerical comparisons and 3 3 for physical comparisons). We showed that physical sizes affected numerical comparisons and more important from the perspective of numerical cognition, that numerical size affected physical comparisons. The difference in RT (or in error rate) between incongruent and congruent conditions has become known as the size congruity effect. Facilitation due to congruency between the two dimensions is indicated by faster RTs to congruent than neutral trials, and interference is indicated by the difference between incongruent and neutral trial RTs. In recent years this effect has been employed to study proficiency with number systems, and automaticity in numerical processing (Butterworth 2000; Cohen Kadosh and Henik 2006b; Cohen Kadosh et al. 2007; Gebuis et al. 2009; Girelli, Lucangeli, and Kaufmann et al. 2006; Rubinsten et al. 2002; Szűcs et al. 2007).

We point out that one has to be proficient with the numerical system in order to show a size congruity effect when asked to pay attention to the physical size and ignore the numerical values. Several researchers have suggested this as a mark of automaticity because the numerical values are activated even when they are not relevant to the task and when it is clear that they need to be ignored. Note that this is different from the comparative judgments described earlier. There, the distance is irrelevant but numerical values are relevant, since participants are asked to decide which digit is larger numerically.

Automaticity

How automatic is the effect of synesthesia on numerical processing? Several studies used the logic already discussed and asked if the effect of color, in digit-color synesthesia, appears even when the color is irrelevant to the task at hand. For example, Cohen Kadosh and Henik (2006a) designed a color congruity task in which colors replaced the physical sizes of the digits. Synesthete MM experiences 2 as synesthetically yellow and 8 as synesthetically green, hence, presenting 2 in yellow and 8 in green font creates a congruent condition whereas presenting 2 in green and 8 in yellow font creates an incongruent condition.

MM produced a congruity effect—she responded slower to incongruent than to congruent trials. This effect suggests that the appearance of numbers activates synesthetic colors even when these are irrelevant to the task at hand. Moreover, the relative magnitudes of the digits may modulate the color congruity effect. When asked to compare the numerical values of the digits, MM produced a larger congruity effect when the numerical distance between the numbers was smaller, rather than when it was larger. This pattern of results is similar to what is found when color is replaced by physical size in non-synesthetes (Cohen Kadosh, Henik, and Rubinsten 2008; Henik and Tzelgov 1982; Schwarz and Ischebeck 2003; Tzelgov et al. 2000) suggesting that colors are attached to detailed representations of numerical values and these are in turn activated and modulate performance in these situations.

In addition, the size effect seems also to modulate the synesthetic experience. That is, when a digit-color synesthete, IS, had to name the color of a digit in one experiment, or to name the numerical value in another experiment, the size of the numerical value modulated performance. For example, in examining digits colored incongruently in their neighboring digit's synesthetic color (e.g., 1 in the color of 2), it took longer for IS to name the ink when those digits were numerically smaller than when they were numerically larger (i.e., RT for 1 in the color of 2 > RT for 7 in the color of 8). These results support the existence of a mental number line with a vaguer numerical representation as numbers increase in size (see also the section on bidirectionality for additional arguments that in this synesthete colors can evoke numerical representation automatically).

Berteletti and colleagues (Berteletti, Hubbard, and Zorzi 2010) studied NM, another digit-color synesthete. NM experiences colors for digits but not for dot patterns. Berteletti and colleagues presented NM with digits or dot patterns (in canonical or random arrangements) in congruent or incongruent colors and asked him to name the color and ignore the digits or dot patterns. They reported a significant congruency effect both for the digits and the dot patterns. Importantly, NM never experienced photisms in conjunction with dot patterns but in spite of this, he did show a congruency effect that was similar to the digit congruency effect. This pattern of results is reminiscent of a study of synesthete IS by Cohen Kadosh and Henik (2006c). IS is also a digit-color synesthete and declared that he never saw lines in colors. Nevertheless, in a comparative judgment task of long and short colored lines, he showed a "synesthetic" congruency effect that was similar to his digit-color congruency effect. Interestingly, IS reported after this experiment that suddenly colors began triggering the experience of digits, which indicates that the effect of color of digit can be conscious under some conditions. This is similar to previous cases, in which synesthetes reported new types of synesthesia that they did not experience before, when their attention was brought to bear on the issue (Tyler 2004).

It seems that automaticity also characterizes number-space synesthetes. One of Galton's participants described this experience:

> The representation I carry in my mind of the numerical series is quite distinct to me, so much so that I cannot think of any number but I at once see it (as it were) in its peculiar place in the diagram. My remembrance of dates is also nearly entirely dependent on a clear mental vision of their loci in the diagram. (Galton 1880, 253)

A century later, Seron and colleagues (Seron et al. 1992) presented a few cases of individuals who were also automatically able to "see" numbers in precise locations in mental space. More recently, several works provided additional empirical data supporting the genuineness of number-space synesthesia (which has also been referred to as *visuo-spatial forms*, or a type of *sequence-space synesthesia*; see Simner 2009, for an overview of this phenomenon, and Jonas and Jarick, Chapter 7, this volume). In those studies participants with number-space synesthesia exhibited a significant congruency effect when asked to compare numbers presented congruently or incongruently with their relative number-space location (Gertner, Henik, and Cohen Kadosh 2009; Hubbard et al. 2009; Piazza, Pinel, and Dehaene 2006; Sagiv et al. 2006). For example, for synesthetes who experiences small numbers on the right and large numbers on the left, presenting 1 on the left and 8 on the right will be incongruent, while the opposite numerical presentation would be congruent. Apparently, similar to digit-color synesthetes, for individuals with number-space synesthesia, numbers automatically trigger a conscious sense of spatially-defined arrays that modulate performance in simple number comparison tasks.

Spalding and Zangwill (1950) described a patient (AL) who lost his number-space synesthesia as a result of a left-sided occipito-parietal gunshot wound. Prior to the injury, his number-space started with 1 on the left, continued in a straight line to 10 on the right, then up to 12, a turn to the left up to 15, up to 20 and so on. He also had spatial representations for months, days of the week, and the alphabet. After the injury, his synesthetic experience was not clear and was difficult to recall.

RELIANCE ON VISION MIGHT TAKE ITS TOLL

What are the consequences of this vivid imagery? Galton thought that number-space was of service to the synesthetes at least for simple arithmetic. For example, one of the descriptions in the article discusses synesthetes using their number-space synesthesia for simple multiplication but not for multiplication of large numbers. The patient AL, described by Spalding and Zangwill (1950), complained that his arithmetic abilities were compromised by the injury and that this was due to the fact that he could not use the number-space any more. However, several results suggest that reliance on number-space synesthesia might compromise performance. Ward and colleagues (Ward, Sagiv, and Butterworth 2009) tested basic arithmetic operations in number-space synesthetes and found that the existence of number-space synesthesia modulates arithmetical processing. In particular, number-space synesthetes were significantly slower on multiplication (not subtraction or addition) than those without number-space synesthesia (among them those that do have other types of synesthesia). It was suggested that multiplication relies on different cognitive strategies and brain areas (Dehaene et al. 2004). Accordingly, the authors suggested that an over-reliance on number-space synesthesia (useful when solving subtraction) and/or an under-reliance on the use of verbal facts (which are needed in multiplication) impaired the performance in multiplication (Ward, Sagiv, and Butterworth 2009; but see Simner, Mayo, and Spiller 2009, for an alternative explanation).

In another study, Gertner and colleagues (Gertner, Henik, and Cohen Kadosh 2009) asked number-space synesthetes and controls to compare digits that were presented either congruently or incongruently with their number-space. For example, if for a given synesthete numbers are represented from left to right, then presenting 4 on the left of the screen and 6 on the right would constitute a congruent condition whereas presenting 6 on the left and 4 on the right would create an incongruent condition. The synesthetes exhibited a sizeable distance effect only when the displayed numbers were congruent with their number-space. In contrast, the controls exhibited a distance effect regardless of congruency or presentation type. The findings suggest that number-space synesthesia impairs the ability to represent numbers in a flexible manner according to task demands.

Hubbard and colleagues reported a strong spatial effect in button-pressing (see below), but with no congruency effect in another number-space synesthete. Their research suggests constraints with respect to the elicitation of number-space synesthesia. They tested synesthete DG for whom numbers between 1 and 12 were represented vertically with the smaller numbers at the bottom and the larger numbers at the top. In a comparative judgment task (in which participants indicate which number is numerically larger), DG responded faster to small pairs (e.g., 2 4) with a bottom-button response and to large pairs (e.g., 7 9) with top-button response. The congruency within the pair (e.g., 4 above

2 or 9 above 7) did not modulate performance. The authors suggested that the lack of congruency effect might be due to the use of a fixed distance of 2 units for all presented number pairs. The fixed distance might have prevented access to numerical magnitude (e.g., made ordinal information more salient) and this in turn did not give rise to the spatial congruency effect. As predicted, DG showed no such spatial effect when numbers were presented horizontally. In further experiments the authors presented single digits and asked participants to decide on the digit's parity (i.e., is it odd or even?) or to compare it with a standard (i.e., is it larger or smaller than 5). The authors were looking for a type of SNARC (spatial numerical association of response code) effect; this is the tendency for people in general to respond faster to small numbers with their left hand as compared to right hand, and to respond faster to large numbers with their right hand as compared to left hand (Dehaene, Bossini, and Giraux 1993; Fias and Fischer 2004; Gevers and Lammertyn 2005; Hubbard, Piazza, et al. 2005). The authors did not find a SNARC effect in their synesthete subjects. Accordingly, they suggested that: "interference elicited by synesthetic number forms—at least in DG's case—requires explicit representation of spatial information, and may require explicit access to numerical magnitude information in order to clearly emerge."

INDIVIDUAL DIFFERENCES

One other insight by Galton that we should bear in mind is related to individual differences. In his words:

> The power of seeing vivid images in the mind's eye changes between individuals … it is certainly not possessed by all metaphysicians, who are too apt to put forward generalizations based solely on the experiences of their own special ways of thinking, in total disregard of the fact that the mental operations of other men may be conducted in very different ways to their own. (Galton 1880, 252)

Two points are raised by Galton: (1) individuals differ in the ability to see vivid images, and (2) most people have the tacit assumption that their mental operations are the same as those of anyone else. The synesthesia literature, too, shows evidence of individual differences. Hubbard and colleagues (Hubbard, Arman, et al. 2005) studied individual differences among synesthetes in their synesthetic experiences and in their corresponding brain functions (see also Dixon, Smilek, and Merikle 2004). They found that functional magnetic resonance imaging (fMRI) results and performance on behavioral tasks were correlated; participants with better performance on behavioral tasks (e.g., texture segregation) presented larger fMRI activation in early visual areas. The authors suggested that these results support the hypothesis that grapheme-color synesthesia is due to cross-activation between grapheme-selective and color-selective brain areas. Moreover, these results stress the heterogeneity among synesthetes. Similarly, we have discussed individual differences with respect to awareness of the existence of cross-modal connections

(Cohen Kadosh and Henik 2007). Commonly, one of the differences between synesthetes and non-synesthetes is that synesthetes are aware of the connection between graphemes and colors. We suggested that people vary in awareness to particular cross-modal relationships; from low levels of awareness that characterize non-synesthetes to high levels of awareness characterizing some synesthetes. (This is also the case for whether synesthesia is experienced in a bidirectional fashion, see the section about bidirectionality.)

With respect to Galton's second point, most synesthesia researchers are very familiar with the astonishment conveyed by synesthetes when they first realize that they are "different" from others who surround them. "Doesn't everyone see numbers in color?" was the response of a synesthetic colleague of ours the very first time he heard about our research into digit-color synesthesia. This aspect of synesthesia might provide a window to study the social aspects of mental experience, which is one area that has, to our knowledge, received very little research attention thus far.

BIDIRECTIONALITY IN SYNESTHESIA

For many years the idea that synesthesia is unidirectional has been endorsed as though it were an undisputed law (Brugger et al. 2004; Cohen Kadosh, Sagiv, et al. 2005). For example, it has been claimed that in grapheme-color synesthesia a grapheme will trigger the experience of a color but not vice versa for the same individual. Rare descriptions of the phenomenology of some synesthetes who experience bidirectionality between the inducer and concurrent have been largely neglected (Baron-Cohen et al. 1996). In addition, the possible confound of bidirectionality in some experimental designs has not been taken into account (Dixon et al. 2000). In what follows, we summarize the evidence for bidirectionality in grapheme-color and other forms of synesthesia. We consider different neural mechanisms and conclude by outlining the implications of bidirectionality for our understanding of synesthesia.

EVIDENCE FOR BIDIRECTIONALITY

Peter Brugger and colleagues (Brugger et al. 2004) have shown that synesthesia can be bidirectional by examining whether synesthetes' identification of colors adheres to the SNARC effect—the tendency for subjects to respond faster to small numbers with their left hand as compared to their right hand and to large numbers with their right hand as compared to their left hand (Dehaene, Bossini, and Giraux 1993; Fias and Fischer 2004; Gevers and Lammertyn 2005; Hubbard, Piazza, et al. 2005). In this experiment digit-color synesthetes were asked to respond to a color patch, which appeared at the centre of the screen, with their left or right hand. If synesthesia is unidirectional, and the color patch does not evoke a numerical representation, then the response hand should not modulate the performance. However, if color can activate an associated number then a SNARC effect should be observed for colors. That is, responding to colors that are associated with small numbers should be faster with the left hand than with the right hand, and responding to colors that are associated with large numbers should be faster with the right hand as compared to the left hand. Brugger et al. (2004) observed the latter scenario and thereby provide evidence that synesthesia can be bidirectional. It should be noted that the synesthetes in this study did not report that they experience synesthesia in a bidirectional way. It follows that these results reflect implicit bidirectionality; the bidirectionality is not available to conscious access.

In a second study involving the random generation of color names (Knoch et al. 2005), the same group used an established effect to identify further evidence for bidirectionality in synesthesia. The task was modeled after random number generation tasks. In the latter subjects are asked to produce a random sequence of numbers. Previous studies have shown that subjects tend to produce too few repetitions of a particular digit on consecutive trials (e.g., 5 followed by 5) (*repetition avoidance*), and tend to arrange consecutive responses in steps of one (e.g., 5 followed by 6 or vice versa) to a greater extent than a random system (*counting bias*). The latter bias indicates interference from over-learned and highly automatized rules that characterize forwards and backwards counting (Brugger 1997). In the color generation task, 20 digit-color synesthetes were asked to name their synesthetic colors. If synesthesia is bidirectional then a similar bias as observed with numbers should be observed with colors. For example, the synesthetes should show a counting bias in their color generation such as producing colors that represent consecutive numbers more often than a random system. Importantly, this bias should not be observed in non-synesthetes. This would be because on naming a color associated with, say, the digit 4, the color associated with either digit 3 or digit 5 would have a higher probability of occurrence on the subsequent trial due to the postulated bidirectional automaticity of digit–color associations. This is exactly what the researchers found (Figure 6.2). These results provide robust evidence for implicit bidirectionality among synesthetes.

Further evidence for bidirectionality comes from a study using a numerical comparison task (Cohen Kadosh, Sagiv, et al. 2005). In this study, numbers were presented in different colors. Two grapheme-color synesthetes and controls were asked to decide which of two digits was numerically larger whilst ignoring the color dimension. We hypothesized that due to bidirectionality the presented color would trigger its corresponding numerical value. We defined the color distance as the difference between the digits that induce the two presented colors for each synesthete. For example, the two colors evoked by the digits 2 and 7 represent a color distance of five units. In participants with synesthesia, we expected facilitation of performance whenever the colors indicated a larger distance than the actual numerical values (e.g., the digits 4 and 5 printed in the colors induced by 2 and 7, respectively). In contrast, if synesthesia is strictly unidirectional there should be no facilitative effect of color on the time taken to make a magnitude judgment. This prediction departs from classical unidirectional models of synesthesia,

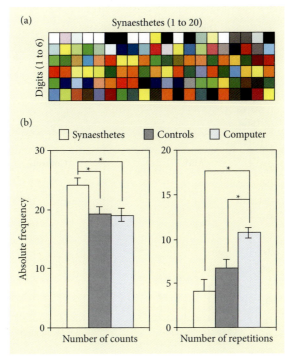

FIGURE 6.2 Synesthetic colors (a) and random color generation performances of synesthetes and controls (b). In (a) the columns correspond to 20 grapheme-color synesthetes; the rows to individually associated colors for the digits 1 (top)–6 (bottom). In (b) the figures show the mean number of counts (left panel) and of repetitions (right panel) for sequences generated by synesthetes, controls, and a computer. *P < 0.01. Error bars indicate one standard error of mean (SEM). Reprinted from *Cognitive Brain Research*, 25 (1), Daria Knoch, Lorena R.R. Gianotti, Christine Mohr, and Peter Brugger, Synesthesia: When colors count, pp. 372–374, Copyright (2005), with permission from Elsevier.

which would predict only an interference effect or no effect at all whenever the colors do not match the digits but no bidirectional facilitation effect. Again, the observed results provide further support for bidirectionality in synesthetes. When the colors represented numbers with a larger numerical distance the processing time was faster than when the colors represented a smaller numerical distance. This effect was not found in the controls (see Figure 6.3). While we presented these results in the context of automaticity, we would like to stress that the results here indicate not only evidence for bidirectionality, but also for automaticity, which is considered one of the conditions for synesthesia (Ward and Mattingley 2006).

Further cognitive studies on digit-color synesthetes (Cohen Kadosh and Henik 2006c; Gebuis, Nijboer, and van der Smagt 2009a; Johnson, Jepma, and de Jong 2007) extended these findings and have shown: (1) that bidirectionality can also occur with other tasks such as priming, attentional blink, and Stroop-like paradigms; (2) that color can still evoke number-processes even when a vivid number experience is absent; (3) that the

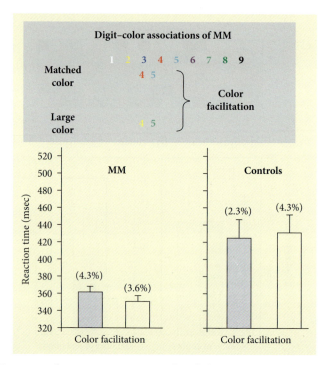

FIGURE 6.3 Upper panel represents an example of the synesthete MM's color–grapheme associations, and the experimental conditions of matched color and large color. Lower panel represent mean RT in milliseconds and error percentage (in parentheses) as a function of matched color (gray), and large color distance (white) for synesthete MM and naïve controls. Error bars depict 1 SEM. Adapted from Roi Cohen Kadosh, Gali Elinger, Avishai Henik, David E. J. Linden, Lynn C. Robertson, and Noam Sagiv, "When Blue is Larger than Red: Colors Influence Numerical Cognition in Synthesia," *Journal of Cognitive Neuroscience*, 17:11 (November, 2005), pp. 1766–1773. © 2005 by the Massachusetts Institute of Technology, with permission.

effect of color on numerical processing, which indicates bidirectionality, is of the same magnitude as the effect of number on color. The latter effect has been used in previous studies to test the genuineness of (unidirectional) synesthesia (Mattingley et al. 2001); and (4) that in some rare cases some people even report explicit bidirectionality.

IS BIDIRECTIONALITY RESTRICTED ONLY TO DIGIT-COLOR SYNESTHESIA?

The studies that we described so far have shown that bidirectionality is present in grapheme-color synesthesia, although there are marked individual differences in this dimension. For instance, some synesthetes display explicit bidirectionality, some exhibit implicit bidirectionality, and some do not present it at all (Cohen Kadosh and Henik 2006c, 2007; Johnson, Jepma, and de Jong 2007). However, these findings were observed only with digit-color synesthetes. One possibility is that bidirectionality is restricted to this type of synesthesia, which might offer further interesting insights into the developmental and neural mechanism of synesthesia. Another possibility is that it is a general characteristic, and with the right paradigm or analysis, it might be possible to uncover it also in other forms of synesthesia. Recent studies support the latter option. For example, Weiss and colleagues (Weiss, Kalckert, and Fink 2009) have shown that colors can implicitly influence lexical search in letter-color synesthesia. However, this finding is still consistent with the possibility that bidirectionality is restricted to grapheme-color synesthesia. Critically, there is evidence against this interpretation. Goller, Otten, and Ward (2008) reported on two auditory-visual synesthetes who show an indication of implicit bidirectional experience (e.g., 1877). Furthermore, these phenomenological reports have been supported at the neural level (see the section "Bidirectionality at the neural level").

Bidirectionality at the Neural Level

As the study of bidirectionality in synesthesia is relatively young, there are only a few studies that have examined its neural basis. To the best of our knowledge there are no studies that examined anatomical differences between bidirectional synesthesia and unidirectional synesthesia (in gray matter volume, or fractional anisotropy, which have been examined elsewhere for synesthetes; Weiss and Fink 2009; Rouw and Scholte 2007). Instead, there are several studies that examined how bidirectional synesthesia affects brain activation by using fMRI and event-related potentials (ERPs). Cohen Kadosh, Cohen Kadosh, and Henik (2007) examined the case of IS, a synesthete who at the time of testing reported that he experienced bidirectionality at the explicit level. Following a cognitive task in the scanner, he displayed a behavioral effect that provided evidence of the existence of bidirectionality processing; that is, color affected physical size comparisons between a pair of vertical lines, even though numerical information had not been presented, and given that color normally lacks any ordinal or cardinal information. At the neural level, color stimuli activated the region of the fusiform gyrus that had been activated with the presentation of numerical digits in a different experimental run, as well as in previous studies (Hubbard, Arman, et al. 2005; Pesenti et al. 2000). In addition, using ERPs, the researchers found that the presentation of color modulates the N170 component, an ERP component that has been shown to be associated with orthographic processing (Bentin et al. 1999). These effects were not present in non-synesthetes. Taken together, these fMRI and ERP findings converge on the conclusion that colors activate digits even in the absence of digit presentation.

Gebuis and colleagues (Gebuis, Nijboer, and Van der Smagt 2009b) examined 14 grapheme-color synesthetes who did not report bidirectionality, on a priming task in which color patches primed graphemes or graphemes primed colors patches. The former priming task, in which subjects had to name the number (e.g., TWO), aimed to uncover neural processing that relates to implicit bidirectionality. The latter priming task, in which subjects were asked to name the color patch (e.g., GREEN), aimed to examine the neural processing that relates to unilateral synesthesia. At the behavioral level the researchers found similar priming effects in both tasks. By using ERPs to examine the bidirectionality at the neural level they found that the priming effect in both tasks modulates the same ERP components, which appeared around 300 ms after stimulus presentation (P3a and P3b components). These results led the authors to conclude that the neural basis of implicit bidirectional processing in synesthesia is similar to the processing of unidirectional synesthesia (Gebuis, Nijboer, and Van der Smagt 2009b), although different brain areas could have contributed to the similar ERP effects.

Last, Goller, Otten, and Ward (2008) examined two synesthetes with explicit bidirectionality between audition and vision. They found that the two synesthetes differed from other synesthetes with unilateral auditory-visual experience, but also from each other. One synesthete (JR) showed a greater amplitude of visual P1 (80–120 ms) and another synesthete (SL) showed a negative-going later deflection (230–270 ms), which tended to be positive in other participants. These differences have been attributed to individual differences in the timing of synesthetic experiences (Dixon, Smilek, and Merikle 2004; Ward et al. 2007).

Together the previous findings provide strong support that bidirectionality occurs also at the level of the brain. The differences in the timing of such an experience (Cohen Kadosh, Cohen Kadosh, and Henik 2007; Gebuis, Nijboer, and Van der Smagt 2009b; Goller, Otten, and Ward 2008), and possibly also in the specific brain areas involved (Cohen Kadosh, Cohen Kadosh, and Henik 2007) may be due to different factors, including the type of synesthesia, explicit versus implicit bidirectionality, and the experimental task, which might lead to different cognitive strategies. Future studies should try to use tasks that involve automatic processing, and compare different populations to examine these potential factors (Cohen Kadosh and Walsh 2009).

POSSIBLE REASONS FOR BIDIRECTIONALITY

An intriguing question is what are the reasons for bidirectionality? One suggestion is that this experience is due to a long-term association between the inducer and the concurrent, and this is because unidirectional effects, but not bidirectional effects, can be observed in non-synesthetes after a limited amount of training. That is, a training on color-number associations over 5 days can lead to a unilateral synesthetic effect, but not a bidirectional synesthetic effect (Cohen Kadosh, Sagiv, et al. 2005). However, this explanation might provide only partial explanation if any, as it is unclear why some synesthetes display explicit bidirectionality, some display implicit bidirectionality, and some exhibit neither (Cohen Kadosh and Henik 2007; Johnson, Jepma, and de Jong

2007). Another possibility is that these differences are due to quantitative differences in the brain mechanism that underlies synesthesia (e.g., excess connectivity (Bargary and Mitchell 2008; Ramachandran and Hubbard 2001a; Rouw and Scholte 2007), or degree of disinhibition (Cohen Kadosh et al. 2009; Grossenbacher and Lovelace 2001), etc.). For example, a larger degree of disinhibition in two connected brain regions can lead not only to digits triggering color, but also vice versa, as in this case the regions for processing digits might be disinhibited as well. Another possibility is that these individual differences are due to qualitative differences, such as additional or different brain areas that subserve the synesthetic experience. Finally, it may be that both qualitative and quantitative differences give rise to individual differences among synesthetes. How such potential differences might have emerged is a question that is still waiting for an answer.

THE IMPORTANCE OF BIDIRECTIONALITY RESEARCH

Aside from providing a more complete picture of the synesthetic experience in some subjects, what is the added value of studying bidirectionality? We suggest that understanding why some features reach awareness, whereas others affect performance at the implicit level only, or not at all, can provide a promising line of research that will add important insights into the brain mechanisms of synesthesia and perceptual awareness. For example, studying explicit bidirectionality may strengthen our understanding of why grapheme-color associations are only implicit in non-synesthetes (Cohen Kadosh and Henik 2007). Synesthesia research is often promoted as a phenomenon that can lend great insights into the nature of consciousness (Ramachandran and Hubbard 2001b). This is done by comparing synesthetes and non-synesthetes. However, comparing synesthetes with explicit bidirectionality, implicit bidirectionality, and only unidirectional processing will undoubtedly provide important supplementary evidence for the different mechanisms that might be involved in perceptual awareness (Cohen Kadosh and Henik 2007). Of course, if it appears that bidirectionality is subserved by different brain mechanisms than those involved in the comparison between synesthetes and non-synesthetes, it will provide a complicated picture (although not an unreasonable one), which suggests that perceptual awareness is subserved by different and diffuse brain mechanisms (Dehaene et al. 2006). However, if only a limited number of brain areas are involved, and these modulate the synesthetic bidirectionality as well as the differences between synesthetes and non-synesthetes, it will provide robust support for the localistic idea of perceptual awareness (Tong 2003).

Finally, an improved understanding of bidirectionality in synesthesia and its brain mechanisms may have important implications for the issue of individual differences. At the moment it might be that synesthetes with different degrees of bidirectionality increase the amount of variance in empirical data, and thereby obscure some results that might have been observed otherwise. We therefore think that a better understanding of bidirectionality, similar to other features of synesthesia (e.g., projectors vs associators; see Dixon, Smilek, and Merikle 2004;van Leeuwen, Chapter 13, this volume), is fundamental for a better understanding of the neurocognitive basis of synesthesia.

ACKNOWLEDGMENTS

We would like to thank Devin B. Terhune for helpful comments. RCK is supported by the Wellcome Trust (WT88378).

REFERENCES

Banks, William P., Robin Mermelstein, and Howard K. Yu. 1982. Discrimination among perceptual and symbolic stimuli. *Memory & Cognition* 10:265–275.

Bargary, Gary, and Kevin J. Mitchell. 2008. Synaesthesia and cortical connectivity. *Trends in Neurosciences* 31:335–342.

Baron-Cohen, Simon, Lucy Burt, Fiona Smith-Laittan, John Harrison, and Patrick Bolton. 1996. Synaesthesia: prevalence and familiality. *Perception* 25:1073–1079.

Bentin, S., Y. Mouchetant-Rostaing, M. H. Giard, J. F. Echallier, and J. Pernier. 1999. ERP manifestations of processing printed words at different psycholinguistic levels: Time course and scalp distribution. *Journal of Cognitive Neuroscience* 11:235–260.

Berteletti, Ilaria, Edward M. Hubbard, and Marco Zorzi. 2010. Implicit versus explicit interference effects in a number-color synesthete. *Cortex* 46 (2):170–177.

Brannon, Elizabeth M. 2006. The representation of numerical magnitude. *Current Opinion in Neurobiology* 16:222–229.

Brugger, Peter. 1997. Variables that influence the generation of random sequences: An update. *Perceptual and Motor Skills* 84:627–661.

Brugger, Peter, Daria Knoch, Christine Mohr, and Lorena Gianotti. 2004. Is digit-color synaesthesia strictly unidirectional? Preliminary evidence for an implicitly colored number space in three synaesthetes. *Acta Neuropsychologica* 2:252–258.

Cohen Kadosh, Roi, Kathrin Cohen Kadosh, and Avishai Henik. 2007. The neuronal correlate of bi-directional synaesthesia: A combined ERP and fMRI study. *Journal of Cognitive Neuroscience* 19:2050–2059.

Cohen Kadosh, Roi, Kathrin Cohen Kadosh, David E. J. Linden, Wim Gevers, Andrea Berger, and Avishai Henik. 2007. The brain locus of interaction between number and size: A combined functional magnetic resonance imaging and event-related potential study. *Journal of Cognitive Neuroscience* 19:957–970.

Cohen Kadosh, Roi, and Avishai Henik. 2006a. Color congruity effect: Where do colors and numbers interact in synesthesia? *Cortex* 42:259–263.

——. 2006b. A common representation for semantic and physical properties: A cognitive-anatomical approach. *Experimental Psychology* 53:87–94.

———. 2006c. When a line is a number: Color yields magnitude information in a digit-color synesthete. *Neuroscience* 137:3–5.

———. 2007. Can synaesthesia research inform cognitive science? *Trends in Cognitive Sciences* 11:177–184.

Cohen Kadosh, Roi, Avishai Henik, and Orly Rubinsten. 2008. Are Arabic and verbal numbers processed in different ways? *Journal of Experimental Psychology: Learning, Memory and Cognition* 34:1377–1391.

Cohen Kadosh, Roi, Avishai Henik, Andrés Catena, Vincent Walsh, and Luis J. Fuentes. 2009. Induced cross-modal synesthetic experience without abnormal neuronal connections. *Psychological Science* 20:258–265.

Cohen Kadosh, Roi, Avishai Henik, Orly Rubinsten, Harald Mohr, Halit Dori, Vincent van de Ven, Marco Zorzi, Talma Hendler, Rainer Goebel, and David E. J. Linden. 2005. Are numbers special? The comparison systems of the human brain investigated by fMRI. *Neuropsychologia* 43:1238–1248.

Cohen Kadosh, Roi, Noam Sagiv, David E. J. Linden, Lynn C. Robertson, Gali Elinger, and Avishai Henik. 2005. When blue is larger than red: Colors influence numerical cognition in synesthesia. *Journal of Cognitive Neuroscience* 17:1766–1773.

Cohen Kadosh, Roi, and Vincent Walsh. 2009. Numerical representation in the parietal lobes: Abstract or not abstract? *Behavioral and Brain Sciences* 32:313–373.

Dehaene, Stanislas. 1989. The psychophysics of numerical comparison: A reexamination of apparently incompatible data. *Perception & Psychophysics* 45:557–566.

———. 1992. Varieties of numerical abilities. *Cognition* 44:1–42.

Dehaene, Stanislas, Serge Bossini, and Pascal Giraux. 1993. The mental representation of parity and number magnitude. *Journal of Experimental Psychology: General* 122:371–396.

Dehaene, Stanislas, Jean-Pierre Changeux, Lionel Naccache, Jérôme Sackur, and Claire Sergent. 2006. Conscious, preconscious, and subliminal processing: A testable taxonomy. *Trends in Cognitive Sciences* 10:204–211.

Dehaene, Stanislas, Emmanuel Dupoux, and Jacques Mehler. 1990. Is numerical comparison digital? Analogical and symbolic effects in two-digit number comparison. *Journal of Experimental Psychology: Human Perception and Performance* 16:626–641.

Dehaene, Stanislas, Nicolas Molko, Laurent Cohen, and Anna J. Wilson. 2004. Arithmetic and the brain. *Current Opinion in Neurobiology* 14:218–224.

Dixon, Mike J., Daniel Smilek, Cera Cudahy, and Philip M. Merikle. 2000. Five plus two equals yellow. *Nature* 406:365.

Dixon, Mike J., Daniel Smilek, and Philip M. Merikle. 2004. Not all synaesthetes are created equal: Projector versus associator synaesthetes. *Cognitive, Affective, & Behavioral Neuroscience* 4:335–343.

Duncan, Edward M., and Carl E. McFarland. 1980. Isolating the effect of symbolic distance and semantic congruity in comparative judgements: an additive factors analysis. *Memory & Cognition* 2:95–110.

Fias, Wim, and Martin H. Fischer. 2004. Spatial representation of numbers. In *Handbook of mathematical cognition*, ed. Jamie I. D. Campbell, 43–54. New York: Psychology Press.

Galton, Francis. 1880. Visualised numerals. *Nature* 21:252–256.

Gebuis, Titia, Roi Cohen Kadosh, Edward de Haan, and Avishai Henik. 2009. Automatic quantity processing in 5-year olds and adults. *Cognitive Processing* 10:133–142.

Gebuis, Titia, Tanja C. W. Nijboer, and Maarten J. Van der Smagt. 2009a. Of colored numbers and numbered colors: Interactive processes in grapheme-color synesthesia. *Experimental Psychology* 56:180–187.

Gebuis, Titia, Tanja C. W. Nijboer, and Maarten J. Van der Smagt. 2009b. Multiple dimensions in bi-directional synesthesia. *European Journal of Neuroscience* 29:1703–1710.

Gertner, Limor, Avishai Henik, and R. Cohen Kadosh. 2009. When 9 is not on the right: Implications from number-form synaesthesia. *Consciousness and Cognition* 18:366–374.

Gevers, Wim, and Jan Lammertyn. 2005. The hunt for SNARC. *Psychology Science* 47:10–21.

Girelli, Luisa, Daniela Lucangeli, and Brian Butterworth. 2000. The development of automaticity in accessing number magnitude. *Journal of Experimental Child Psychology* 76:104–122.

Goller, Aviva I., Leun J. Otten, and Jamie Ward. 2008. Seeing sounds and hearing colors: An event-related potential study of auditory-visual synaesthesia. *Journal of Cognitive Neuroscience* 21:1869–1881.

Grossenbacher, Peter G., and Christopher T. Lovelace. 2001. Mechanisms of synesthesia: cognitive and physiological constraints. *Trends in Cognitive Sciences* 5:36–41.

Henik, Avishai, and Joseph Tzelgov. 1982. Is three greater than five: The relation between physical and semantic size in comparison tasks. *Memory & Cognition* 10:389–395.

Holloway, Ian D., and Daniel Ansari. 2008. Domain-specific and domain-general changes in children's development of number comparison. *Developmental Science* 11:644–649.

Hubbard, Edward M., A. Cyrus Arman, Vilayanur S. Ramachandran, and Geoffrey M. Boynton. 2005. Individual differences among grapheme-color synesthetes: Brain-behavior correlations. *Neuron* 45:975–985.

Hubbard, Edward M., Manuela Piazza, Philippe Pinel, and Stanislas Dehaene. 2005. Interactions between number and space in parietal cortex. *Nature Reviews Neuroscience* 6:435–448.

Hubbard, Edward M., Mariagrazia Ranzini, Manuela Piazza, and Stanislas Dehaene. 2009. What information is critical to elicit interference in number-form synaesthesia? *Cortex* 45:1200–1216.

Johnson, Addie, Marieke Jepma, and Ritske de Jong. 2007. Colours sometimes count: Awareness and bi directionality in grapheme-colour synaesthesia. *Quarterly Journal of Experimental Psychology* 60:1406–1422.

Jonas, Clare and Michelle Jarick. 2013. Synesthesia, sequences, and space. In *The Oxford Handbook of Synesthesia*, ed. Julia Simner and Edward M. Hubbard, 123–148. Oxford: Oxford University Press.

Kaufmann, Liane, Florian Koppelstaetter, Margarete Delazer, Christian Siedentopf, Paul Rhomberg, Stefan Golaszewski, Stefan Felber, and Anja Ischebeck. 2005. Neural correlates of distance and congruity effects in a numerical Stroop task: An event-related fMRI study. *NeuroImage* 25:888–898.

Kaufmann, Liane, Florian Koppelstaetter, Christian Siedentopf, Ilka Haala, Edda Haberlandt, Lothar-Bernd Zimmerhackl, Stefan Felber, and Anja Ischebeck. 2006. Neural correlates of the number-size interference task in children. *NeuroReport* 17:587–591.

Knoch, Daria, Lorena R. R. Gianotti, Christine Mohr, and Peter Brugger. 2005. Synesthesia: When colors count. *Cognitive Brain Research* 25:372–374.

Landerl, Karin, and Christina Kölle. 2009. Typical and atypical development of basic numerical skills in elementary school. *Journal of Experimental Child Psychology* 103:546–565.

MacLeod, Colin M. 1991. Half a century of research on the Stroop effect: An integrative review. *Psychological Bulletin* 109:163–203.

Mattingley, Jason B., Anina N. Rich, Greg Yelland, and John L. Bradshaw. 2001. Unconscious priming eliminates automatic binding of color and alphanumeric form in synaesthesia. *Nature* 410:580–582.

Moyer, Robert S. 1973. Comparing objects in memory: Evidence suggesting an internal psychophysics. *Perception & Psychophysics* 13:180–184.

Moyer, Robert S., and Richard H. Bayer. 1976. Mental comparison and the symbolic distance effect. *Cognitive Psychology* 8:228–246.

Moyer, R. S., and Thomas K. Landauer. 1967. Time required for judgment of numerical inequality. *Nature* 215:1519–1520.

Nieder, Andreas, and Stanislas Dehaene. 2009. Representation of number in the brain. *Annual Review of Neuroscience* 32:185–208.

Nuerk, Hans-Cristoph, Ulrich Weger, and Klaus Willmes. 2001. Decade breaks in the mental number line? Putting the tens and units back in different bins. *Cognition* 82:B25–B33.

Paivio, Allan. 1975. Perceptual comparisons through the mind's eye. *Memory & Cognition* 3:635–647.

Pesenti, Mauro, Marc Thioux, Xavier Seron, and Anne De Volder. 2000. Neuroanatomical substrates of Arabic number processing, numerical comparison, and simple addition: A PET study. *Journal of Cognitive Neuroscience* 12:461–479.

Piazza, M., P. Pinel, and S. Dehaene. 2006. Objective correlates of an unusual subjective experience: A single-case study of number–form synaesthesia. *Cognitive Neuropsychology* 23:1162–1173.

Ramachandran, V.S., and E. M. Hubbard. 2001a. Psychological investigations into the neural basis of synaesthesia. *Proceedings of the Royal Society of London B: Biological Sciences* 268:979–983.

——. 2001b. Synaesthesia – A window into perception, thought and language. *Journal of Consciousness Studies* 8:3–34.

Rouw, Romke, and H. Steven Scholte. 2007. Increased structural connectivity in grapheme-color synesthesia. *Nature Neuroscience* 10:792–797.

Rubinsten, Orly, Avishai Henik, Andrea Berger, and Sharon Shahar-Shalev. 2002. The development of internal representations of magnitude and their association with Arabic numerals. *Journal of Experimental Child Psychology* 81:74–92.

Sagiv, Noam, Julia Simner, James Collins, Brian Butterworth, and Jamie Ward. 2006. What is the relationship between synaesthesia and visuo-spatial number forms? *Cognition* 101:114–128.

Schwarz, Wolfgang, and Anya Ischebeck. 2000. Sequential effects in number comparison. *Journal of Experimental Psychology: Human Perception and Performance* 26:1606–1621.

——. 2003. On the relative speed account of the number-size interference in comparative judgment of numerals. *Journal of Experimental Psychology: Human Perception and Performance* 29:507–522.

Sekular, Robert, and Diane Mierkiewicz. 1977. Children's judgement of numerical inequality. *Child Development* 48:630–633.

Seron, Xavier, Mauro Pesenti, Marie-Pascale Noel, Gérard Deloche and Jacques-André Cornet. 1992. Images of numbers, or 'When 98 is upper left and 6 sky blue'. *Cognition* 44:159–196.

Simner, Julia. 2009. Synaesthetic visuo-spatial forms: Viewing sequences in space. *Cortex* 45:1138–1147.

Simner, Julia, Neil Mayo, and Mary-Jane Spiller. 2009. A foundation for savantism? Visuo-spatial synaesthetes present with cognitive benefits. *Cortex* 45:1246–1260.

Spalding, J. M. K., and O. L. Zangwill. 1950. Disturbance of number-form in a case of brain injury. *Journal of Neurology, Neurosurgery and Psychiatry* 13:24–29.

Stroop, John R. 1935. Studies of interference in serial verbal reactions. *Journal of Experimental Psychology* 18:643–662.

Szucs, Dénes, Fruzsina Soltész, Éva Jármi, and Valéria Csépe. 2007. The speed of magnitude processing and executive functions in controlled and automatic number comparison in children: An electro-encephalography study. *Behavioral and Brain Functions* 3:23.

Tong, Frank. 2003. Primary visual cortex and visual awareness. *Nature Reviews Neuroscience* 4:219–229.

Tyler, Christopher. 2004. Varieties of synesthetic experience. In *Synesthesia: Perspectives from Cognitive Neuroscience*, ed. Lynn C. Robertson and Noam Sagiv, 34–44. New York: Oxford University Press.

Tzelgov, Joseph, Joachim Meyer, Avishai Henik. 1992. Automatic and intentional processing of numerical information. *Journal of Experimental Psychology: Learning, Memory and Cognition* 18:166–179.

Tzelgov, Joseph, Vered Yehene, Lital Kotler, Ariel Alon. 2000. Automatic comparisons of artificial digits never compared: Learning linear ordering relations. *Journal of Experimental Psychology: Learning, Memory and Cognition* 26:103–120.

van Leeuwen, Tessa M. 2013. Individual differences in synesthesia. In *The Oxford Handbook of Synesthesia*, ed. Julia Simner and Edward M. Hubbard, 241–264. Oxford: Oxford University Press.

Ward, Jamie, Ryan Li, Shireen Salih, Noam Sagiv. 2007. Varieties of grapheme-colour synaesthesia: A new theory of phenomenological and behavioural differences. *Consciousness and Cognition* 16:913–931.

Ward, Jamie, and Jason B. Mattingley. 2006. Synaesthesia: an overview of contemporary findings and controversies. *Cortex* 42:129–136.

Ward, Jamie, Noam Sagiv, and Brian Butterworth. 2009. The impact of visuo-spatial number forms on simple arithmetic. *Cortex* 45:1261–1265.

Weiss, P. H., and G. R. Fink. 2009. Grapheme-colour synaesthetes show increased grey matter volumes of parietal and fusiform cortex. *Brain* 132:65–70.

Weiss, P. H., A. Kalckert, and G. R. Fink. 2009. Priming letters by colors: evidence for the bidirectionality of grapheme-color synesthesia. *Journal of Cognitive Neuroscience* 21:2019–2026.

CHAPTER 7

SYNESTHESIA, SEQUENCES, AND SPACE

CLARE JONAS AND MICHELLE JARICK

The various ways in which numerals are visualized is but a small subject, nevertheless it is one that is curious and complete in itself.

(Sir Francis Galton 1880a, 252)

INTRODUCTION

History

Sequence-space synesthesia is an umbrella term used to describe a particular group of synesthetes who share a peculiar experience: some ordinal sequences (e.g., letters, numbers, days, months) are perceived in a spatial arrangement, such that each member of the sequence induces the sensation of a very specific location in space. Other general terms for this phenomenon include *spatial-form synesthesia* and *visuo-spatial synesthesia*, with some authors using individual terms for different subtypes such as *time-space synesthesia* (triggered by days, months, etc.) and *number-space synesthesia/number forms* (triggered by numbers; see Simner 2009, in the special issue of *Cortex* on spatial-form synesthesia). Spatial-form synesthesia has been estimated to occur in 29% of individuals who would otherwise have no other type of synesthesia (Sagiv et al. 2006).[1] This makes number forms by far the most commonly self-reported type. The next most common form of synesthesia, day-color, is ten times less prevalent (Simner et al. 2006).

---

[1] This prevalence estimate may be rather high since the criterion used to provide objective evidence of synaesthesia in that study was not particularly stringent (see later).

In sequence-space synesthesia, as in other types of synesthesia, the synesthetic experience (known as the "concurrent"; here, the spatial form) has been reported to occur either in the mind's eye or out in the external world. However, the stimuli that give rise to synesthesia (known as "inducers"; here, numbers, letters, months of the year, etc.) are cognitive constructs learned during language development, and this fact has caused some debate over whether the sequence-space experience is truly a form of synesthesia. This debate stems from the general tendency to describe the majority of synesthesias in purely sensory terms (see Simner 2012). Recently it has become increasingly apparent, however, that this is a mistake, since experiences which are undoubtedly synesthetic are showing themselves to have conceptual features. For instance, number-color synesthesia (Cohen Kadosh and Henik 2006; Gevers, Imbo, et al. 2010) hinges on links between colors and number magnitude, rather than purely sensory components. Other forms of synesthesia may also be conceptually induced too; for example, lexical-gustatory synesthesia, in which words trigger taste sensations, can be induced by the relatively conceptual construct of word meaning (and so can arise in "tip of the tongue" states when other more concrete information like pronunciation or spelling is not available; Simner and Ward 2006).

The fact that sequence-space synesthesia often co-occurs with other forms of synesthesia and shares their defining characteristics (being automatic[2] cross-modal pairings, established at an early age without conscious effort, consistent across time, etc.), suggests that spatial forms are indeed likely to be a form of synesthesia in their own right (e.g., Sagiv et al. 2006; Smilek et al. 2007). In this chapter we review sequence-space synesthesia, first according to its possible inducers, and then by assessing its behavioral and neural characteristics. In doing this we ask what methodological approaches might be suited to studying it, and what these methods might tell us about its nature.

Inducers in sequence-space synesthesia

Number

The first scientific reports of spatial-forms, made by Francis Galton (1880a, 1880b), were specifically centered on individuals seeing spatial numbers. In his 1880b paper, Galton remarks on several characteristics of these synesthetic number forms that are consistent with other forms of synesthesia: the forms have been present for as long as the synesthete can remember, they are idiosyncratic, and they are consistent over time.[3] These assertions are supported by Sagiv et al. (2006), who added that unlike most other forms of synesthesia, number forms were reported equally often by men and women, at a prevalence of approximately 12%. Additionally, Sagiv et al. studied

---

[2] But see later, and Price and Mattingley (2013).
[3] But see Simner (2012) for a discussion of why consistency may not be a reliable standard by which to recognize synaesthesia.

the orientations and shapes of the number-forms in their sample of self-reported synesthetes and showed that the majority of forms were straight lines that tended to run in a left-to-right direction, while others were vertically oriented, or aligned in patterns such as zigzags. In modern Western societies, the synesthetic number form tends to have a bend, break, or other salient feature at 10 (Jarick, Dixon, Stewart, et al. 2009; Sagiv et al. 2006), perhaps reflecting the very common use of the decimal system in counting. The role of culture in the layout of synesthetic number forms is further supported by Galton's (1880a) observation that in Victorian Britain, where the duodecimal system was more prominent than the decimal, salient features in the synesthetic number forms were located at 12 (Jonas et al. 2011; Piazza et al. 2006). Not all synesthetes have such simple spatial forms, however. Phillips (1897) reports a variety of complex shapes, and we reproduce some of his examples in Figure 7.1. Examples of the prominence of the number 12 in historical synesthetic number forms may also be seen in this figure.

The finding that synesthetic number-forms are commonly oriented horizontally means they correspond with the mental number line (MNL). This is a mental representation of number found in the general population that implicitly locates small numbers on the left and large numbers on the right, at least in those whose mother tongue is written from left to right (e.g., Dehaene, Bossini, and Giraux 1993; Fischer et al. 2003; see later). This representation, linking two otherwise separate modalities (number, space) is one example of a number of cross-modal associations found to exist implicitly in the general population (e.g., Cohen Kadosh, Cohen Kadosh, and Henik 2007; Ward, Banissy, and Jonas 2008). For example, people tend to associate tactile roughness with low visual luminance, and interestingly, a similar effect is found explicitly in people with touch-color synesthesia (Ward, Banissy, and Jonas 2008). Thus, in this respect sequence-space synesthesia is similar to other forms of synesthesia in having an implicit counterpart in the general population.

Time

Spatial-form synesthesia for time units (referred to as time-space synesthesia) can be triggered by hours, days, months, years, and even centuries. However, most research has centered on days within a week and months within a year. The prevalence of time-space synesthesia was previously estimated at around 20% (Sagiv et al. 2006). It should be noted however, that the true prevalence rate might be much lower (or higher) since although Sagiv et al. used an independent test to verify time-space synesthetes (and other sequence-space synesthetes), details of this test are scantly reported. Specifically, their estimate was based on verifying synesthetes with a test of consistency over time. This is a standard approach built on the assumption that genuine synesthetic sequence-space arrays do not change greatly over time compared to those of controls asked to invent sequence-space layouts. Sagiv et al. asked their participants to draw or describe their sequence-space associations on two separate occasions but did not state exactly how these assessments were used to get a measure of consistency. Brang et al. (2010) on the other hand tested consistency by asking participants on two separate occasions

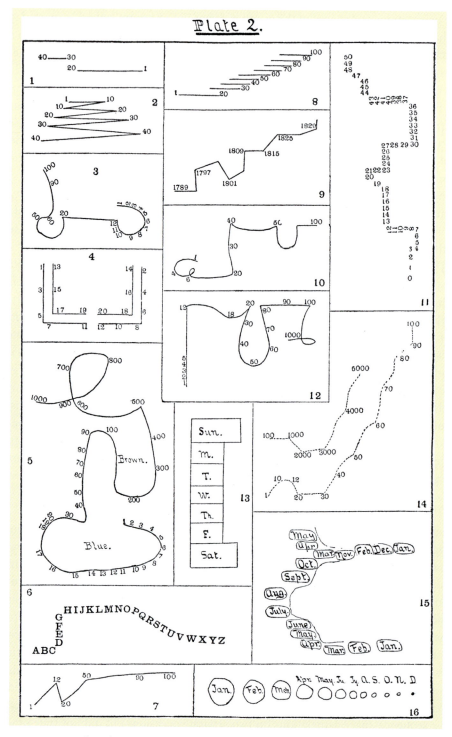

FIGURE 7.1 Examples of sequence-space synesthesia. For further examples see also Figure 47.1, Lynall and Blakemore, Chapter 47, this volume. Reproduced from Phillips, D. E. Genesis of Number-Forms, *The American Journal of Psychology*, 8(4), p. 513 © 1897, University of Illinois Press.

to visualize their months of the year on a computer screen and to indicate the location of each month with a mouse click. This conservative method resulted in a much lower prevalence of only 2.2% for synesthetes with month forms.

Hour forms most often appear in the shape of a clock face (Jarick, Dixon, Stewart, et al. 2009; Peabody 1915), as one might predict based on environmental cues. Day and month forms are commonly found to be oval, round, or rectangular in nature (Brang et al. 2010; Seymour 1980), but straight lines running left-to-right are also common (Eagleman 2009; Peabody 1915). One unusual aspect of time-space synesthesia for months, in comparison to other forms of synesthesia more generally, is that the synesthetic concurrent (i.e., the calendar) can move: either the calendar moves around the synesthete, or the synesthete around the calendar, so that the month of interest is always the closest or most central in visual space (e.g., Jarick, Dixon, Stewart, et al. 2009).

The alphabet

Letter-based spatial sequences (referred to as alphabet-form synesthesia) have received little attention. Past research has acknowledged the existence of alphabet forms (e.g., Hubbard et al. 2009) but usually only through passing mention as an adjunct to the already described spatial time and numbers (e.g., Spalding and Zangwill 1950). Although research on alphabet forms is scarce, Sagiv et al. (2006) report the prevalence of alphabet-forms to be similar to other spatial forms at approximately 15% (albeit relying on the drawing method critiqued earlier).

Peabody's (1915) study indicated that the most likely alphabet form was a straight left-to-right line, similar to synesthetic number forms. This observation has recently been supported by Jonas et al. (2011). In addition, Jonas et al. found that where alphabets do have direction changes, gaps, or line breaks, those features tend to fall at the middle of the alphabet, or are dictated by "The Alphabet Song" (a mnemonic commonly learned by English-speaking children that separates the alphabet into chunks of two to seven letters). Specifically gaps or direction changes in the alphabet form tended to fall where the song has a pause. However, the alphabet-song effect was also observed in synesthetes who had not learned the song (i.e., German speakers), indicating that it is likely to be speech patterns of alphabet recitation that influence the eventual layout of the alphabet form, and the alphabet song itself.

Other sequences

Though we have focused on the most common types of sequences (for number, time, and alphabet) these are not the only inducers for sequence-space synesthesia. Seymour (1980) reported that the planets of the solar system, the color spectrum, and the signs of the zodiac might also induce spatial associations. Hubbard et al. (2009) have provided evidence from a single verified number form synesthete (DG) whose additional spatial associations extend to over 58 varied sequence patterns, such as historical periods, pure breed dog names (which are based on an alphabet-to-year sequencing), and FM radio stations to name a few (see Figure 7.2 for examples). The prevalence of spatial associations for sequences that do not include numbers, time units,

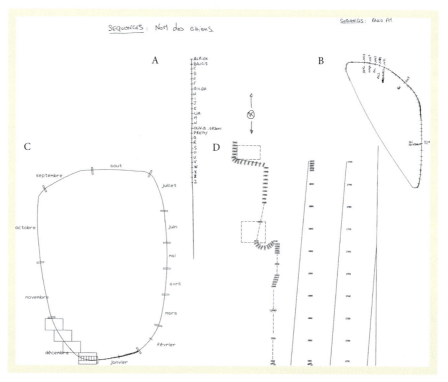

FIGURE 7.2 Examples of synesthete DG's spatial forms (Hubbard et al. 2009). In panel c is the typical spatial calendar experienced by some time-space synesthetes. Panel a is the unique representation of pure breed dog names, along with FM radio stations (panel b) and historical periods or years (panel d). Images used with Permission of Edward M. Hubbard, unpublished observations.

or the alphabet still remain unclear as DG's reports are the only available accounts so far. However, researchers will undoubtedly make more of an attempt to explore these other sequence-space associations as the characteristics inherent in other spatial forms become clear.

OBJECTIVELY VERIFYING SEQUENCE-SPACE SYNESTHESIA

Consistency testing

Consistency has typically been considered the gold-standard test for verifying synesthesia (Baron Cohen et al. 1993; but see Simner 2012). For experiments on sequence-space synesthesia, we noted earlier that consistency tended to be measured by asking synesthetes to draw their spatial associations on separate occasions (e.g., weeks, or months, or years apart) and then by simply assessing whether the two drawings at the different time points were similar or different (e.g., Sagiv et al. 2006). The basis of this methodology is the assumption that true synesthetic sequence-space arrays will tend to stay the same over time. This technique is of course open to experimenter bias due to the subjective nature of the assessments made (i.e., are two pictorial representations the same or different?). Of late, consistency has instead been assessed by asking participants to indicate where a member of the spatial form (e.g., July) is located in several ways: in two-dimensional (2D) space on a blank screen via a mouse click (e.g., Brang et al. 2010), by gaze fixation (Jonas et al. 2011), using a laser pointer mounted on a 360° compass (Smilek et al. 2007), or positioning the months in virtual space (Eagleman 2009). These methods use pixel or angle distance to measure variability in order to provide a more accurate and objective test of consistency compared to the subjective drawing method.

   Evidence for consistency of synesthesia is most compelling if the time between test and retest is long (i.e., a year or more). However, for time-space synesthesia, this type of consistency testing may not be a useful paradigm since although the overall spatial form may be consistent, the synesthetic viewpoint across the spatial form can change (and we discuss this in more detail later). There is therefore the strong possibility that a synesthete might change their mental vantage point and view their sequence from a different perspective from the initial test. Therefore, it might be necessary in this case to rely more strongly on the second defining feature of synesthesia—automaticity—using, for example, spatial cueing tasks.

Spatial cueing effects

Synesthesia is said to be "automatic" if the synesthetic concurrent can rapidly and involuntarily influence the individual's perception, attention, or behavior. Smilek et al. (2007) used a classic Posner-type cueing paradigm to examine whether month names could rapidly cue synesthetes' spatial attention. This cueing paradigm measures participants' response times (RTs) to detect a target (e.g., a cross) presented to the left or right following a central month cue. The centrally presented month cue serves to direct the synesthetes' attention according to where it would be found in the sequence-space form. For example, if the month cue were *July*, and if July falls in the left side of space in that particular synesthete's spatial form, then this cue should direct attention to the left side of the screen. In Smilek et al.'s version of the cueing task, the month cue was presented for either a very short (150 ms) or relatively long (600 ms) period of time before the target appeared. On half the trials, the target would appear in the location synesthetically cued by the month name (*valid* trials), and on the other half of the trials, the target appeared in the synesthetically uncued location (*invalid* trials; see Figure 7.3). The results of the cueing task showed that three of their four synesthetes performed in accordance with

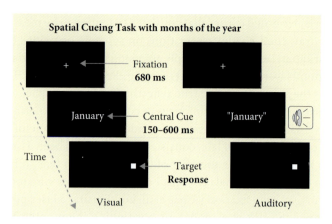

FIGURE 7.3 Schematic of a typical trial in the spatial cueing task used by Jarick and colleagues (Jarick, Dixon, Maxwell, et al. 2009; Jarick, Dixon, Stewart, et al. 2009; Jarick, Dixon, and Smilek 2011; Jarick et al. 2011), but adopted from Smilek et al. (2007). Valid trials occurred when the target position (left or right) was congruent with the location of January in synesthetic space (in this example, January would be to the right of the synesthete).

their synesthetic experiences. That is, each synesthete responded significantly faster when the target landed in the synesthetically valid location compared to the invalid location. Importantly, these cueing effects were observed even at the shortest stimulus onset asynchrony (SOA) between the cue and the target. Thus, not only were month names cueing the synesthetes' attention to spatial locations, they seemed to influence attention rapidly, within 150 ms, suggesting time-space associations can occur automatically. Moreover, using the same cueing paradigm, Jarick et al. (2011) replicated and extended Smilek et al.'s finding by demonstrating that a sequence-space synesthete (L) showed these cueing effects even when the task was loaded up with invalid trials (80% of the time the cue predicted the synesthetically "wrong" location). This finding by Jarick et al. was important because it demonstrated the resiliency of synesthetic spatial forms. In order to perform well in the revised cueing task, L should have developed a strategy opposite to her spatial form, however the results show that she could not. Therefore, the rapid and resilient cueing effects observed by Smilek et al. (2007) and Jarick et al. (2011) were unlikely to be due to the synesthetes employing any form of strategy, and suggest that at least for some synesthetes (e.g., L), spatial forms could occur automatically and without conscious control (but see later, and Price and Mattingley 2013).

Recently, it has been established that for at least one time-space synesthete, the spatial form (for months or hours) is not solely induced by visual month (or hour) names, but also by aurally presented months (or hours) as well. Furthermore, it was shown that each type of cue name (visual or auditory) elicits a different mental vantage point.[4] Jarick, Dixon, Maxwell, et al. (2009) presented this fascinating case (L) who sees her spatial

---

[4] To understand the term 'mental vantage point," the reader can imagine a pen lying on a table. It is possible to mentally picture the scene from various angles (e.g., directly above the table, from the side

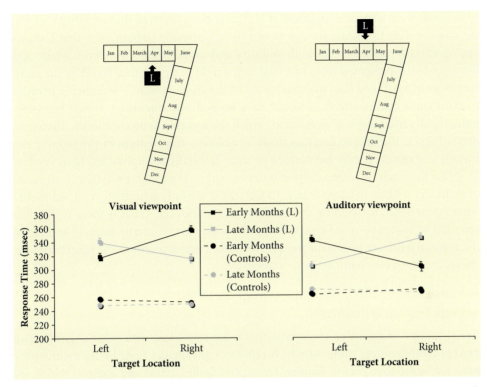

FIGURE 7.4 Response time data from Jarick, Dixon, Stewart, et al. (2009) demonstrating L's cueing effects for both visually presented months and auditory months. The dotted lines are the response times from non-synesthetes showing no cueing effects when presented with months. The errors bars are 95% confidence intervals.

calendar from opposite viewpoints dependent on whether the month is written or spoken. The authors implemented the same cueing paradigm as Smilek et al. (2007) in which a centrally presented month name was followed by a target cross on either the left- or right-hand side of the computer screen. Participants had to passively read the month name and then respond as to whether the target appeared on the left or right. Using this paradigm, Jarick, Dixon, Maxwell, et al. showed opposite cueing effects for visual cues compared to aural cues, which corresponded to L's different mental vantage points (see Figure 7.4). For example, L responded significantly faster to detect a target on the left following the visual cue *January* (which is located in her left mental space for visual month-names), but detected targets faster on the right following the spoken word *January* (which is located in her *right* mental space for heard month-names, see Figure 7.4).

of the table, by the tip of the pen). These different angles are potential mental vantage points. In L's case, when she *hears* the name of a month, she views months in the first half of the calendar year on her right and months in the second half of the year on her left. Conversely, when she *sees* the name of a month, she sees the first half of the year on the left and the second half on the right.

In a follow-up experiment, Jarick et al. (2011) demonstrated that auditory and visual months elicit L's mental vantage points in an automatic fashion, such that L shows cueing-effects consistent with both auditory and visual perspectives even when cues were randomly presented from one trial to the next (e.g., one trial could be the auditory month "April" and then next trial could be the visual month "November"). In order to show these cueing-effects, L would have needed to immediately switch her viewpoint rapidly from one trial to the next, which she was able to do effortlessly. Therefore, depending on the unique qualities of the synesthete, the medium of the inducer can literally and rapidly change her outlook on time. It should be emphasized, however, that L's ability to switch between viewpoints dependent on the inducer modality (i.e., visual or auditory) is likely to be quite rare. In fact, she is the only synesthete reported to date whose experience is based on the modality of the inducer. What is more commonly reported by sequence-space synesthetes is the ability to voluntarily zoom in and out of their spatial forms, or to take the perspective of the current month of the year (therefore, always changing viewpoint as the months go by).

Is spatial cueing an appropriate paradigm to test sequence-space synesthesia?

Certain forms of sequence-space synesthesia are associated with other cognitive and perceptual differences, some of which represent advantages (e.g., better memory for personal and public events; Simner, Mayo, and Spiller 2009) and some of which are disadvantageous (e.g., slowing of some forms of mental arithmetic; Ward, Sagiv, and Butterworth 2009). Skill with mental imagery is an obvious advantage that one would predict synesthetes to have, since synesthesia could be considered an involuntary form of mental imagery. Self-reports from a group of sequence-space synesthetes studied by Price, Solberg, and Blakstad (2010) suggest that synesthetes might make greater use of mental imagery in a general sense, compared with non-synesthetes. Price (2009a) also showed that spatial-form synesthetes report greater abilities with visual (but not spatial) imagery. Self-reports, however, only allow insight into subjective experience. In order to test whether synesthetes' ideas about their own experience are objectively true, Simner, Mayo, and Spiller (2009) ran a battery of tests on spatial manipulation and visual memory, which demonstrated that sequence-space synesthetes outperformed non-synesthetes on both visual memory and spatial abilities. Indeed, Price and Mattingley (2013) have recently argued that heightened mental imagery ability may be the catalyst that gives rise to the "automatic" cueing effects demonstrated in synesthetes using the spatial cueing task.

Cueing effects can occur via two different attentional systems: endogenous and exogenous. Endogenous cueing is said to occur voluntarily, where the participant is cued to one direction or the other by the meaning of the cue (e.g., the word LEFT), whereas exogenous cueing is said to occur reflexively (automatically, outside of the participant's control, e.g., flash of light to the left). In examining the cueing effects seen in Hubbard et al. (2009), Jarick and colleagues (Jarick, Dixon, and Smilek 2011; Jarick, Dixon, Stewart, et al. 2009; Jarick et al. 2011) and Smilek et al. (2007), Price and Mattingley (2013) described four features of synesthetes' behavior that are incompatible with the account of sequence-space synesthesia as a property of exogenously (involuntary) cueing, or that are more compatible with endogenous (voluntary) cueing explanations. Firstly, endogenous cueing effects usually remain for long SOAs while exogenous cueing effects do not sustain in this manner. Secondly, synesthetes' RTs to cues have also been rather long, making it possible that synesthetes are endogenously cued. Thirdly, cueing effects have been larger than those typically seen in exogenous cueing paradigms and are in fact more like endogenous cueing. Finally, there is evidence that the stronger the cueing effect in a given sequence-space study, the longer the incongruent RT (with no effect on *congruent* RT). This, again, is unlike exogenous cueing in which congruent cues shorten RTs and incongruent cues lengthen RTs (thought of as a "cost" for incongruent cues and a "benefit" for congruent cues). Furthermore, Price and Mattingley speculate that synesthetes are placed in a situation with very strong demand characteristics—they are effectively being asked to prove they are "special" compared to non-synesthetes—and therefore may, consciously or unconsciously, make use of their mental imagery skills in order to meet the experimenter's expectations.

In light of Price and Mattingley's fair evaluation of the cueing effects found in sequence-space synesthetes thus far, research is still at a crossroads as far as describing with great precision what sequence-space synesthetes really experience and to what degree the experiences vary across individuals. It is unlikely, though possible, that time units, digits, or letters are experienced by synesthetes as if they were real objects in the environment. What is more plausible is to describe the synesthetic experience as something in between "seeing-as-real" and a product of the imagination (and this experience no doubt lies on a continuum from more object-like to more imagination-like; Brang et al. 2010). Thus, each synesthetic experience is unique and could encompass properties of visualization that a non-synesthete might not even be capable of. Because of this, it is possible that tests of attention (i.e., spatial cueing tasks) might not correspond to the typical endogenous and exogenous cueing characteristics previously shown in non-synesthetes. Perhaps it is a hybrid of endogenous and exogenous properties, such that it follows the endogenous properties of being a slightly slower process and driven by internal representations, with the exogenous properties of being involuntary and resilient to strategic manipulation. For these reasons, synesthetes should be assessed using multiple paradigms, whereby researchers can compare and contrast the converging or diverging results.

SNARC effects

In 1993, Dehaene and colleagues were investigating how parity (oddness and evenness of numbers) is mentally coded in the general population when they made a surprising discovery. When they presented a range of numbers on a computer screen and asked participants to judge whether the number was odd or even (a parity judgment task), small magnitudes were responded to more quickly when the response was made to the left hand (or left side of space) and large magnitudes were responded to more quickly with the right hand (or right side of space). Dehaene, Bossini, and Giraux (1993) referred to this finding as the spatial-numerical association of response codes (SNARC) effect, after the eponymous character in Lewis Carroll's poem *The Hunting of the Snark*. This effect has also been found for the other sequences we have mentioned, mainly units of time and letters of the alphabet (Dehaene, Bossini, and Giraux 1993; Dodd et al. 2008; Gevers, Reynvoet, and Fias 2003; Price 2009a; Price and Mentzoni 2008).

Dehaene, Bossini, and Giraux interpreted the SNARC effect as showing that numbers are directly and *implicitly* linked with space in the general population, on a mental number line (MNL, as we described earlier). By analogy, SNARC type effects with other sequences would be demonstrating a similarly implicit "mental time line" or "mental alphabet line." We pointed out earlier that synesthetic spatial forms could be interpreted as an explicit version of these implicit links. For instance if prompted with the numbers 1 through 10, a synesthete might actually see these numbers in a line right in front of them, whereas a non-synesthete would not, although she may still show a SNARC effect as an indication of a similar but implicit line.

An alternative interpretation of the SNARC effect which has recently started to garner attention suggests that this effect is not visuo-spatial but rather verbal-spatial (Bae et al. 2009; Fischer 2006; Santens and Gevers 2008). By this account, the behavior of participants in SNARC-type experiments is explained through "polarity-matching," as follows. Any opposing pair of words (e.g., left–right, large–small, early–late) is divided such that one is categorized as negative (left, small, and early in this example) and one is categorized as positive (right, large, and late in this example). When carrying out a SNARC-type experiment, it is these verbal categories that determine reaction times to particular stimulus–response pairings. For example, small numbers receive fast responses with the left hand because small and left are both categorized as negative, while they receive slow responses with the right hand because of a clash between the negative-categorized "small" label and the positive-categorized "right" label. Given this latter interpretation of the SNARC effect in the general population, there are two possible ways in which *synesthetic* spatial forms would now be interpreted. First, they may be unique expressions of a direct link between a sequence and space that have no implicit counterpart in the general population. Alternatively, they may be a conscious elaboration on the general, implicit verbal link between polarities. Given these interpretations, and other more general features of the SNARC effect, there are three general predictions that can be made regarding synesthetes' behavior on SNARC-type tasks, and we describe these next.

Firstly, because spatial forms take on idiosyncratic shapes and directions, synesthetes may show atypical directionality in SNARC effects—for example, a vertical SNARC effect in a synesthete with a vertical number form (Jarick, Dixon, Maxwell, et al. 2009). Secondly, because spatial forms are explicit rather than implicit, SNARC effects (typical or atypical) may be stronger for synesthetes than for non-synesthetes. Finally, we hypothesize that synesthetes have a different susceptibility to influences of mental imagery or environmental cueing on SNARC effects than non-synesthetes, though the direction of this difference is not immediately clear. They may be more susceptible to environmental manipulations because of their increased skill at mental imagery (Price

2009a) or less susceptible because spatial forms appear to involve direct and invariant links between sequences and space in a phenomenological sense at least (Gertner, Henik, and Cohen Kadosh 2009). We explore these predictions in the next section.

Are there atypical SNARC effects in synesthetes with idiosyncratic forms?

If SNARC effects can reveal the implicit spatial linearity of numbers in the general population, we might expect it to also reveal the more idiosyncratic arrangements of sequence-space synesthetes. Several studies have addressed this prediction in number-form synesthetes using the SNARC paradigm, showing mixed results. The first study, by Pizza et al. (2006), found that a synesthete with a number form running in a right-to-left direction showed a non-significant trend towards a typical left-to-right SNARC effect. A significant left-to-right SNARC effect would be expected if the synesthete's number form did not affect his reaction times in the experiment (i.e., he would be behaving in the same way as a non-synesthete). Two more recent studies (Hubbard et al. 2009; Jarick, Dixon, Maxwell, et al. 2009) have tested synesthetes with vertical number forms, using both horizontal and vertical versions of the SNARC paradigm. The horizontal version was simply the original paradigm used by Dehaene, Bossini, and Giraux (1993), with the response keys located on the left and right of a response pad. In the vertical SNARC test, the response keys are to the top and bottom of the response pad. Hubbard et al. (2009) found a similar result to Piazza et al. (2006): their synesthete with a vertical number form showed a non-significant trend towards a left-to-right horizontal SNARC effect, but no vertical SNARC effect. However, Jarick and colleagues (Jarick, Dixon, Maxwell, et al. 2009) found a strong vertical SNARC effect but not a horizontal left-to-right SNARC effect in their synesthete (L) whose number form ran vertically from bottom to top. One possible explanation for these two contradictory findings is that synesthetes may differ in the strength of activation of their synesthetic number lines, just as non-synesthetes differ in the extent to which they show a SNARC effect (see Bull and Benson 2006 for a discussion of variation in SNARC effect strength related to the ratio of the lengths of the second and fourth fingers). Alternatively, as Hubbard et al. point out, a simple difference in the instructions given in each study might have led to the differences in results. Specifically, Hubbard et al. gave instructions concentrating on the *hands* used to respond, while Jarick et al. gave instructions concentrating on the *buttons* used to respond.

Turning to other types of sequences, only one study (Price and Mentzoni 2008) has considered the SNARC effect in sequence-space synesthetes for time units. Participants in Price and Mentzoni's experiment were presented with month names in the centre of an otherwise blank screen and had to make a rapid judgment regarding the month. In the first experiment, the task was to judge whether the month was in the first or the second half of the calendar year, and in the second experiment the task was to judge whether the month was odd or even (e.g., January, as the first month, is "odd," while April, as the fourth month, is "even"). Each task required responses using lateralized button-presses. For all four synesthetes tested, responses conformed to the idiosyncrasies of their month-space mappings. In other words, if a synesthete's month form had early months on the right and later months on the left, her right-hand responses were faster for early months and her left-hand responses were faster for later months.

For sequences such as the alphabet, data is just beginning to surface. One study (Jonas 2011) has investigated the SNARC effect for alphabet-forms. Fourteen non-synesthetes, and 14 alphabet-form synesthetes for whom the alphabet runs horizontally left-to-right, were asked to make lateralized button-presses to indicate whether a letter was lower-case or upper-case. The SNARC-type effect for these alphabet forms was predicted to be horizontally left-to-right, as in the non-synesthete group. However, neither group showed a significant SNARC-type effect. This null finding is possibly due to the study design, since SNARC effects for the alphabet have only been elicited in the general population when alphabetical order is important to the task (e.g., deciding if a letter comes before or after M in the alphabet; Dehaene, Bossini, and Giraux 1993; Dodd et al. 2008; Gevers, Reynvoet, and Fias 2003). Another possibility for the lack of SNARC effect could be the depth of processing required for the alphabet task. For instance the original SNARC task requires participants to evaluate digits based a semantic level analysis (i.e., whether the digit is odd or even) which is a fairly deep level of processing, while the alphabet task asked participants to judge letters based on a superficial attribute (i.e., whether the letter is in upper or lower case) which requires only surface level processing. Perhaps if participants were required to process the meaning of the letters (e.g., whether the letter is a consonant or vowel, as in Gevers, Reynvoet, and Fias 2003) then an alphabet SNARC effect might have emerged.

Do synesthetes show stronger SNARC effects than non-synesthetes?

Studies examining the strength of the SNARC effect in synesthetes typically have shown performance differences between synesthete(s) and non-synesthetic controls, but again the evidence is mixed. For instance, we noted earlier that Piazza et al. showed a typical left-to-right SNARC effect for non-synesthetes, but no (or very weak) effect for a number form synesthete with an opposite (right-to-left) number form. This diminished left-to-right SNARC for the synesthete actually suggests a stronger right-to-left SNARC effect, since his right-to-left number line should have cancelled out a left-to-right SNARC effect. Likewise, Jarick, Dixon, Maxwell, et al. (2009) reported vertical SNARC effects for two synesthetes who experienced vertical number forms and significant horizontal SNARC effects for controls, but the SNARC effects were equally as strong in synesthetes and controls. Hubbard et al. (2009) did not make a direct comparison in the same way as Jarick, Dixon, Maxwell, et al. (2009a), so it is difficult to assess the strength of their synesthete's results compared to non-synesthetes. In addition to single-case studies, there is one group study of sequence-space synesthetes with number forms that run horizontally left-to-right, which should give rise to typical SNARC effects (Jonas et al. 2013). In this study, 20 synesthetes were compared to 26 non-synesthetes. When a direct comparison of the strength of the SNARC effect was made between the two groups there was no significant difference. Thus far, we might summarize as follows: when the synesthetic number form runs left-to-right, the SNARC effect is no stronger than that of controls. When it runs in reverse, the left-to-right SNARC effect is weak or absent, and when it runs vertically, a vertical SNARC is present, but is no stronger than the horizontal effect in non-synesthetes.

Price and Mentzoni (2008) examined the SNARC effect for months of the year and reported that when making lateralized judgments about month order (early or late) time-space synesthetes showed stronger SNARC-type effects than non-synesthetes. Time-space synesthetes also showed marginally significant ($p = 0.07$) stronger SNARC effects than non-synesthetes when making parity judgments. These results were found using side-by-month position ANOVA analyses. However, in a later reanalysis (using a regression method suggested by Lorch and Myers 1990), Price (2009a) found that non-synesthetes did not show a significant SNARC effect when making order judgments (e.g., does April come before July?), but did show a significant SNARC effect when making parity judgments (e.g., is April an odd or even month?). In comparison, synesthetes showed a significant SNARC effect in both tasks. Here, the depth-of-processing hypothesis could also apply, such that order judgments (superficial attributes) did not show a SNARC effect, where parity judgments (semantic evaluation) did show a SNARC effect.

Putting these studies together, it remains unclear what influence spatial forms might have on the strength of SNARC and SNARC-type effects. However, the research is still in its infancy and many of these studies on sequence-space synesthesia examine single cases. Future studies will likely contain larger sample sizes with greater generalization power, while also considering individual variation within and between synesthetes to find more conclusive answers.

Do synesthetes show polarity-matching behaviors? Can their SNARC effect be manipulated?

Indirect evidence suggests that synesthetes may be susceptible to attempts to manipulate the SNARC effect in some direction *other* than the spatial form would predict. To objectively show that mental imagery in non-synesthetes could alter their SNARC effects, Price (2009a) asked participants to imagine a number line such that it ran right-to-left instead of left-to-right. Price found that non-synesthetes were able to reverse the direction of the SNARC effect based on the imagined number line. In that study, Price also found that sequence-space synesthetes self-reported superior mental imagery ability compared to non-synesthetes. From these findings Price argued that synesthetes may in fact be unconsciously using mental imagery when completing SNARC-type tasks, rather than the SNARC effect being a consequence of their spatial forms. A good test of Price's speculation would be to ask synesthetes to use mental imagery counter to their spatial forms and then to evaluate whether they showed the same effects as non-synesthetes also using mental imagery. However, more direct evidence that synesthetes are susceptible to attempts to manipulate their SNARC effect comes from Jonas et al. (2013).

Following a paradigm used by Gevers, Santens, et al. (2010), Jonas et al. (2013) asked 20 non-synesthetes, and 19 synesthetes with left-to-right horizontal number forms, to complete a parity-matching task. This differed from the technique used by Dehaene, Bossini, and Giraux (1993) in that participants were asked to respond to lateralized labels reading *LEFT* and *RIGHT* on the screen, rather than simply pressing a button on the left or the right. The labels could appear in their canonical positions (*LEFT* on the left and *RIGHT* on the right) or non-canonical positions (*LEFT* on the right and *RIGHT* on the left), and this congruency varied on a trial-by-trial basis. Response buttons were located below each position where a label could appear (Figure 7.5). Before beginning a block of trials, participants were given the rule: "When you see an even number, press the button that is closest to the label that says right and when you see an odd number, press the button that is closest to the label that says left." Under these rules, if a participant saw the number 4 with the labels in the non-canonical position, they would press the button to their left (nearest the label that said *RIGHT*). The rule was reversed halfway through the experiment and the order in which the rules were given was counterbalanced across participants.

In Gevers, Santens, et al. (2010), non-synesthete participants were shown to alter their behavior based on where the labels were on screen. When labels were in their canonical positions, participants exhibited typical SNARC behavior, responding more quickly with their left hand to small numbers and with their right hand to large numbers. When the labels were in their non-canonical positions, this behavior was reversed—in effect, the SNARC effect followed the verbal labels *LEFT* and *RIGHT* around the screen, providing support for the verbal polarity-matching account of the link between number and space. In Jonas et al. (2013) this effect was replicated for non-synesthetes and, perhaps surprisingly, extended to synesthetes. Jonas et al. have put forward several possible reasons for this. Firstly, and following Gevers, Santens, et al. (2010), sequence-space synesthesia might depend on a verbal link (low (number) = LEFT, high (number) = RIGHT) when completing parity judgment tasks (but not necessarily when completing other tasks relating to number). If so, it is possible that only these synesthetes, with their

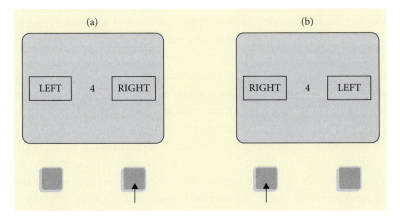

FIGURE 7.5 Illustration of two trials, (a) canonical and (b) non-canonical, in the task carried out by participants in Gevers, Santens, et al. (2010) and Jonas et al. (2013). Participants have been given the rule: "When you see an even number, press the button that is closest to the label that says right and when you see an odd number, press the button that is closest to the label that says left." Arrows indicate the button that should be pressed in each trial—always nearest the label that says *RIGHT* because the number presented is even.

left-to-right number lines, have a verbal basis for their experiences, perhaps because their forms match cultural norms (left = low = negative valence). Alternatively, it is possible that *every* synesthete has a verbal basis for their number/space associations, and that those with right-to-left forms simply clash with culture-dependent experiences (such as direction of written language; Dehaene, Bossini, and Giraux 1993). Each of these explanations has the same practical outcome: the SNARC paradigm may not be a good way to verify sequence-space synesthesia. We assess this idea in the next two sections.

An evaluation of SNARC-type findings in sequence-space synesthesia

The SNARC methodology allows us to evaluate the possibility that everyone has a MNL but that only synesthetes are able to perceive theirs consciously. This question, of whether synesthetic number forms reflect implicit non-synesthetic experiences, could be evaluated from three directions. In a phenomenological sense, there are superficial differences between sequence-space forms and the MNL: the association between number and space in the general population appears to be implicit and malleable (Bächtold, Baumüller, and Brugger 1998; Ristic, Wright, and Kingstone 2006), whereas number-forms are reported to be consciously experienced and invariant. In a behavioral sense, however, although synesthetes outperform non-synesthetes in tests of consistency (e.g., Hubbard et al. 2009) they tend to behave like non-synesthetes in SNARC-type tests: they do not necessarily show atypical directionality (Hubbard et al. 2009; Piazza et al. 2006; but see Jarick, Dixon, Maxwell, et al. 2009 for a counter-example), nor stronger SNARC effects (Jarick, Dixon, Maxwell, et al. 2009; Jonas et al. 2013), and synesthetes are susceptible to manipulations of their SNARC effect (Jonas et al. 2013). When it comes to letters and time, synesthetes are more consistent than non-synesthetes (Brang et al. 2010; Jonas et al. 2011; Smilek et al. 2007) and have shown stronger spatial cueing effects. They show the same strength or stronger SNARC-type effects as non-synesthetes (Jonas 2011; Price 2009a) but the directionality is in line with their spatial forms (Price 2009a).

Given the evidence presented, we might ask whether the SNARC task is an appropriate paradigm to test sequence-space synesthesia at all. This question has been raised by Price and Mattingley (2013), who suggest that the subtle nature of the synesthetic number form may not be appropriately gauged by the simple division into left and right responding that SNARC-type tasks require. They also suggest, as we have noted earlier, that SNARC effects in synesthetes are no stronger than those seen in non-synesthetes. Finally, Price and Mattingley theorize that mental imagery ability (higher among sequence-space synesthetes than in the general population) may influence the strength and direction of SNARC and cueing effects. Jonas et al. (2013) add that since synesthetes and non-synesthetes both appear to be susceptible to labeling manipulations (see earlier), the link between number and space that is tapped by SNARC task appears to be verbal rather than visuo-spatial. While everyone makes verbal links between number and space, synesthetes may have additional, visuo-spatial links that cannot be elicited in SNARC-type paradigms (Gevers, Santens, at al. 2010). Therefore, perhaps SNARC paradigms should not be used to test synesthetic associations between sequences and space. We now consider other options for objectively verifying sequence-space synesthesia.

The future of objective verification

For all three verification methods we have described, individual differences between synesthetes and within synesthetes pose certain difficulties. For instance, changes in vantage points could potentially result in poor consistency over time, mixed cueing effects or weak SNARC effects. Furthermore, consistency testing has only been managed in 2D space—but some synesthetes report that their spatial forms occupy three dimensions. Cueing and SNARC tests require fairly blunt divisions into left and right (or top and bottom)—but synesthetes' spatial forms generally have sequence members occupying much more specific spaces, for example, February may be perceived as behind, above, and to the right of January. Finally, SNARC tests may not tap synesthetic links between sequences and space, but verbal links that are common to everyone. However, the experiments that test this verbal linkage hypothesis have only been carried out with numbers, so it is possible that they may still be of use in verifying time-space or alphabet-space synesthesia.

There are several possibilities for overcoming these problems. The Synesthesia Battery (Eagleman et al. 2007) uses avatars in virtual reality environments to allow participants to place sequence elements in the space around the avatar's body. However, no reports have yet been made on whether this measure can distinguish between self-reported synesthetes and non-synesthetes. More recently, Jamie Ward (personal communication) has suggested tracking synesthetes' body movements and finger locations as they point to sequence elements. The latter of these techniques is likely to be easier for participants to intuitively grasp as pointing to the locations of elements is a common behavior when describing synesthesia informally. Recording these three-dimensional (3D) layouts may also make it easier to predict accurately where a synesthete with a temporally moving calendar would place days, months, etc. at various different times. When using cueing tasks, it might be more accurate to measure eye movements (e.g., saccades, fixations) in 3D space, as opposed to button-press responses with reference to a 2D computer screen. Even further, it might be possible to cue synesthetes to more specific locations using 3D goggles or in a 3D virtual space.

THE NEURAL BASIS OF SPATIAL-FORM SYNESTHESIA

There are three neural models of synesthesia in general, which we might apply here to spatial forms: the cross-activation, disinhibition, and re-entrant theories. They will only be briefly covered here as they will be described in more detail in other chapters.

The cross-activation theory put forth by Ramachandran and Hubbard (2001) suggests that the unusual coupling between the inducer and concurrent in synesthesia (e.g., letter A is light blue, January is 30° to the left) is due to direct neural pathways (i.e., white matter tracts) connecting areas responsible for the inducer (e.g., letter A, months) and concurrent (e.g., light blue, spatial location). According to this theory, these excess connections are formed prior to birth in all individuals, but are typically pruned throughout development in non-synesthetes. For synesthetes however, it is proposed that these extra connections fail to be pruned (Hubbard and Ramachandran 2005).

The second neural model is the disinhibition theory, proposed by Grossenbacher and Lovelace (2001). This theory claims that pathways between brain areas involved in the inducer-concurrent coupling could be disinhibited in synesthetes, but inhibited in the majority of the population. For instance, perhaps we all have an excess of connections between the intraparietal sulci that process spatial representations and the inferior parietal/temporal areas that process sequences and the concept of time such as time units themselves. Yet, the reason we do not experience sequences in a spatial form is due to the inhibitory connections that prevent activation of those connecting pathways. For time-space synesthetes, however, these inhibitory connections may not be in place, and this allows for cross-talk between regions that elicit the experience of time units in space. An intriguing aspect of this theory is that it would be possible for non-synesthetes to experience time units in space given the disinhibition of those inhibitory pathways (e.g., via psychedelic drugs; Shanon 2003).

Lastly, the re-entrant theory exists somewhere in between the cross-activation and disinhibition theories. Smilek et al. (2001) suggested that the synesthetic coupling of inducer and concurrent was due to aberrant "re-entrant processing." That is, information regarding the inducer is aberrantly fed back to the brain areas that are processing the concurrent. Therefore, it is not only the perceptual qualities of the inducer (i.e., the sight or sound of the stimulus) that can elicit the synesthetic experience, but also the conceptual qualities of the inducer (meaning of the stimulus). This theory is important as it could explain how meaning alone could shape the synesthetic experience (Dixon and Smilek 2005).

Currently there is not enough evidence to confidently say which theory (or theories) is equipped to explain the neural basis of sequence-space synesthesia, and the models themselves are not mutually exclusive. In addition, Eagleman (2009) has developed a "reification" theory to specifically account for sequence-space synesthesia. This will be discussed in more detail in the following sections.

The role of parietal cortex

In non-synesthetes the neural architecture underlying quantity and distance between numbers has been localized to the parietal lobes using functional magnetic resonance imaging (fMRI). In numerical cognition tasks, such as judging which of two presented numbers is larger or smaller while the distance between them varies (the numerical distance effect), fMRI has shown a connection between task performance and parietal activation, specifically involving the intraparietal sulcus (IPS; Pinel et al. 2001). Interestingly, the activation observed had occasionally spread to dorsal regions that reflect spatial attention mechanisms. The IPS has also been implicated in tasks of spatial processing, such that the posterior portion of the IPS is active when non-synesthetes make eye-movements (i.e., saccades) to regions out in external space (Sereno, Pitzalis, and Martinez 2001). Indeed, Göbel et al. (2006) suggest a link between the parietal lobes (specifically areas of the IPS) and the MNL in non-synesthetes.

If numbers and space associate in the parietal cortex for the general population (for review see Hubbard et al. 2005), a reasonable assumption might be that sequence-space synesthesia relies on similar, but exaggerated, brain mechanisms. Yet, the picture for spatial-form synesthetes may be more complex. Tang, Ward, and Butterworth (2008) conducted an fMRI experiment with a group of number form synesthetes and non-synesthete controls using tasks that involve processing number magnitude or number order. Synesthetes showed similar brain activation to non-synesthetes on the former task, but increased activity was seen in the posterior IPS of synesthetes during the number order task. This research provided two important pieces of the synesthetic puzzle. First, synesthetic number forms seem to primarily activate the IPS in synesthetes. Second, synesthetic number forms are ordinal in nature; i.e., they encode information about the order in which numbers are represented rather than information about the relative magnitudes of numbers.

Unfortunately there has not yet been brain imaging work concentrating on other sequence-forms (such as time-space or alphabet-form synesthesias). We can, however, speculate that since parietal lobe activation was linked to the ordinal nature of the number-forms, it might extend to processing the ordinality of time units or letters as well (for an alternative explanation see Eagleman 2009; Makioka 2009).

The role of temporal cortex

We saw earlier that it is not uncommon for synesthetes to report that they can "move around" their synesthetic space, taking on a variety of vantage points (Jarick, Dixon, and Smilek 2009; Seron et al. 1992). This ability to move around within the synesthetic space prompted Eagleman (2009) to propose that the spatial coordinates attached to each of the sequence members do not have to be strictly tied to the synesthete's body; in fact, it might even be more common for sequence members to be linked to *each other* in their own coordinate system, much as any real-world object has its own coordinate system. Consequently, Eagleman proposed the *reification hypothesis*, which suggests that the sequences experienced by synesthetes are converted into imagined objects that exist in peri-personal space or in their "mind's eye." Price (2009a) put forth a similar hypothesis to explain why sequence-space synesthetes have superior visual imagery ability. Perhaps spatial forms are "holistic visual depictions, rather than parietally mediated spatial representations" (Price 2009a, 1240). In essence, Price believes it could be the case that spatial forms are not *spatial* at all, but rather *visual* by-products of a superior visual memory in synesthetes. According to Eagleman (2009) and Price (2009a), in order to understand the neural substrate of the synesthetic experience, one first needs to understand how spatial forms are processed in comparison to real objects and then examine how visual imagery might provide the glue that binds sequences with the representation of real objects to result in external spatial forms. Therefore, to get an accurate picture of the neural architecture underlying synesthetic spatial forms, we should look for clues not only in parietal cortex, but in the inferior and middle temporal lobes.

In non-synesthetes, Pariyadath, Churchill, and Eagleman (2008) used event-related fMRI to show that overlearned sequences (such as letters, months, days, and numbers) resulted in brain activation predominantly in the middle temporal gyrus and temporo-parietal junction compared to scrambled sequences or non-sequences. Thus, Pariyadath, Churchill, and Eagleman (2008) concluded that the middle temporal gyrus was the "sequence area" in the brain. Following this, Eagleman's (2009) reification theory suggested a link between the sequence area and object representation in the temporal lobes in that sequence-forms are the product of crosstalk between those two areas. Eagleman speculated that the strength of the synesthetic experience might have a direct correlation with the strength of connections between the "sequence area" and object reification, most likely localized to the right middle temporal gyrus (Eagleman, 2009). Thus far, this is still only a hypothesis, but an intriguing possibility nonetheless.

CONCLUSION

Extensive informal interviews with a variety of sequence-space synesthetes may lead one to speculate that there are classifiable differences among them. For instance, just as there are "associators" and "projectors" among grapheme-color synesthetes (i.e., those who experience visual concurrents in the mind's eye versus projected externally into space; Dixon, Smilek, and Merikle 2004), this distinction appears true of sequence-form synesthetes as well. Likewise, the classification of being a "higher" or "lower" synesthete (whose inducers are either conceptual versus perceptual; Ramachandran and Hubbard 2001) might also apply to sequence-space synesthetes. It may well be that for some individuals the explicit awareness of a spatial location might only be elicited by the month name itself (e.g., actually seeing or hearing the word *January*—"lower"). For others (specifically "higher" synesthetes) activating the concept or meaning of a time unit such as a month may be enough to activate the spatial location. Researchers have come to recognize the importance of adequately discriminating synesthetes from non-synesthetes, and of correctly subtyping different experiences. Brang et al. (2010) have taken an important step in differentiating synesthetes from non-synesthetes using a standard consistency task and a cognitive measure. An ongoing challenge to researchers will be to find ways to empirically differentiate between the different subtypes of synesthetes suggested by self-reports. It could be the case that once objective measures are available we will be able to show that, like their grapheme-color counterparts, not all sequence-space synesthetes are created equal. By correctly subtyping different synesthetes, researchers may ultimately be able to place them on a continuum that ranges from non-synesthetic (effortful assignment of time units to space), to extreme synesthetic (effortless, automatic assignments of time units to space).

Researchers in different laboratories have revealed that sequence-space synesthetes have specialized cognitive abilities (e.g., superior memory, imagery ability) that may confer a cognitive advantage over non-synesthetes (Brang et al. 2010; Mann et al. 2009; Price 2009a; Simner, Mayo, and Spiller 2009). This leads to the question of "Which came first?" Did the skill lead to the synesthesia or did the synesthesia lead to the skill? One possibility is that individuals with superior visuo-spatial and memory abilities use these abilities to develop conscious associations between sequences and space (the skill leads to synesthesia). Alternatively having sequence-space synesthesia could provide an additional memory cue (much like the method of Loci) that confers a cognitive advantage over those without vivid sequence-space mappings (synesthesia leads to the skill). Deciding on which alternative remains a challenge for cognitive neuroscience, but could shed light on spatial and memory abilities in the general population.

Besides being an intriguing phenomenon within itself, synesthesia can also inform us about mechanisms in the non-synesthetic mind, giving insights into perception, consciousness, memory, and development, amongst others. One area where synesthesia might inform us about the general population is in numerical cognition. Number-form synesthesia research in general contradicts the notion of a linear MNL, showing that many explicit (at least) number-forms often take on an idiosyncratic structure (e.g., spirals, ovals, staircases, rectangles, etc.). Another crucial difference between implicit number-space mappings and explicit number-forms is the extent to which they arise automatically. Furthermore, Jarick, Dixon, and Smilek (2011) show that at least for one number-form synesthete (L), the synesthetic experience occurs rapidly (in less than 150 ms). While the representations are active, L can rapidly take on a variety of mental vantage points (Jarick, Dixon, and Smilek 2011). These features point to synesthetic number forms being elicited automatically. Thus, studying the neural architecture underlying synesthesia could ultimately help to uncover the mechanisms responsible for automatic processes.

Another central question in the numerical cognition literature is how we represent two-digit numbers (e.g., 12). One theory suggests that numbers are represented as a whole (12; holistic model), while the competing theory argues numbers are represented in single digits (1 and 2; parallel model). Research on synesthetic number forms supports the holistic model, since number forms tend to form a continuous pattern from 1 to thousands and beyond. Each whole number (single, double, or triple digits) occupies a distinct spatial position along the number form (e.g., 1, 2, 3 .... 21, 22, 23 .... 31, 32, 33 ... etc.). Indeed, some synesthetes have reported that numbers are sometimes added or represent additional space if they become significant. For example, a synesthete reported that she realized one day that negative numbers had been added to her number form, and another reported that as years became more relevant to her, they occupied more space. Therefore, research with sequence-space synesthetes supports a holistic model (e.g., representing 12 as "12") as opposed to a parallel model (e.g., representing 12 as "1" and "2" separately).

Typically, synesthesia research has been dedicated to understanding synesthesia exclusively, but much of the knowledge acquired can also be applied to other realms of psychology. The study of synesthesia arguably is the study of individual variation—it shows what is possible in a small, extraordinary segment of the population. Bringing synesthesia research into other subdisciplines of cognitive research will widen the understanding of scientists in both areas.

References

Bächtold, Daniel, Martin Baumüller, and Peter Brugger. 1998. Stimulus-response compatibility in representational space. *Neuropsychologia* 36:731–735.

Bae, Gi Yeul, Jong Moon Choi, Yang Seok Cho, and Robert W. Proctor. 2009. Transfer of magnitude and spatial mappings to the SNARC effect for parity judgments. *Journal of Experimental Psychology: Learning, Memory and Cognition* 35:1506–1521.

Baron Cohen, Simon, John Harrison, Laura H. Goldstein, and Maria Wyke. 1993. Colored speech-perception—is synaesthesia what happens when modularity breaks down? *Perception* 22:419–426.

Bull, Rebecca and Philip J. Benson. 2006. Digit ratio (2D:4D) and the spatial representation of magnitude. *Hormones and Behaviour* 50:194–199.

Brang, David, Ursina Teuscher, Vilayanur S. Ramachandran, and Seana Coulson. 2010. Temporal sequences, synesthetic mappings, and cultural biases: The geography of time. *Consciousness and Cognition* 19:311–320.

Cohen Kadosh, Roi, Kathrin Cohen Kadosh, and Avishai Henik. 2007. The neuronal correlate of bidirectional synesthesia: A combined event-related potential and functional magnetic resonance Imaging study. *Journal of Cognitive Neuroscience* 19:2050–2059.

Cohen Kadosh, Roi, and Avishai Henik. 2006. When a line is a number: Color yields magnitude information in a digit-color synesthete. *Neuroscience* 137:3–5.

——. 2007. Can synaesthesia research inform cognitive science? *Trends in Cognitive Sciences* 11:177–184.

Dehaene, Stanislas, Serge Bossini, and Pascal Giraux. 1993. The mental representation of parity and number magnitude. *Journal of Experimental Psychology: General* 122:371–396.

Dixon, Mike J., and Daniel Smilek. 2005. The importance of individual differences in grapheme-color synaesthesia. *Neuron* 45:821–823.

Dixon, Mike J., Daniel Smilek, and Philip Merikle. 2004. Not all synaesthetes are created equal: Projector versus associator synaesthetes. *Cognitive, Affective, & Behavioral Neuroscience* 4:335–343.

Dodd, Michael D., Stefan Van der Stigchel, M. Adil Leghari, Gery Fung and Alan Kingstone. 2008. Attentional SNARC: There's something special about numbers (let us count the ways). *Cognition* 108:810–818.

Eagleman, David M. 2009. The objectification of overlearned sequences: A new view of spatial sequence synesthesia. *Cortex* 45:1266–1277.

Eagleman, David M., Arielle D. Kagan, Stephanie S. Nelson, Deepak Sagaram, and Anand K. Sarma. 2007. A standardized test battery for the study of synesthesia. *Journal of Neuroscience Methods* 159:139–145.

Fischer, Martin H. 2006. The future for SNARC could be stark… *Cortex* 42:1066–1068.

Fischer, Martin H., Alan D. Castel, Michael D. Dodd, and Jay Pratt. 2003. Perceiving numbers causes spatial shifts of attention. *Nature Neuroscience* 6:555–556.

Galton, Francis. 1880a. Visualised numerals. *Nature* 21:252–256.

——. 1880b. Visualised numerals. *Nature* 21:494–495.

Gertner, Limor, Avishai Henik, and Roi Cohen Kadosh. 2009. When 9 is not on the right: Implications from number form synaesthesia. *Consciousness & Cognition* 18:366–374.

Gevers, Wim, Ineke Imbo, Roi Cohen Kadosh, Wim Fias, and Robert J. Hartsuiker. 2010. Bidirectionality in synesthesia evidence from a multiplication verification task. *Experimental Psychology* 57:178–184.

Gevers, Wim, Bert Reynvoet, and Wim Fias. 2003. The mental representation of ordinal sequences is spatially organized. *Cognition* 87:B87–B95.

Gevers, Wim, Seppe Santens, Elisah Dhooge, Qi Chen, Lisa van den Bossche, Wim Fias, and Tom Verguts. 2010. Verbal-spatial and visuospatial coding of number-space interactions. *Journal of Experimental Psychology: General* 139:180–190.

Göbel, Silke M., Marco Calabria, Alessandro Farnè, and Yves Rossetti. 2006. Parietal rTMS distorts the mental number line: Simulating 'spatial' neglect in healthy subjects. *Neuropsychologia* 44:860–868.

Grossenbacher, Peter G., and Christopher T. Lovelace. 2001. Mechanisms of synesthesia: cognitive and physiological constraints. *Trends in Cognitive Sciences* 5:36–41.

Hubbard, Edward M., Manuela Piazza, Philippe Pinel, and Stanislas Dehaene. 2005. Interactions between number and space in parietal cortex. *Nature Reviews Neuroscience* 6:435–448.

Hubbard, Edward M., and Vilayanur S. Ramachandran. 2005. Neurocognitive mechanisms of synesthesia. *Neuron* 48:509–520.

Hubbard, Edward M., Mariagrazia Ranzini, Manuela Piazza, and Stanislas Dehaene. 2009. What information is critical to elicit interference in number-form synaesthesia? *Cortex* 45:1200–1216.

Jarick, Michelle, Mike J. Dixon, Emily C. Maxwell, Michael E. R. Nicholls, and Daniel Smilek. 2009. The ups and downs (and lefts and rights) of synaesthetic number forms: Validation from spatial cueing and SNARC-type tasks. *Cortex* 45:1190–1199.

Jarick, Michelle, Michael J. Dixon, and Daniel Smilek. 2011. 9 is always on top: Assessing the automaticity of synaesthetic number-forms. *Brain and Cognition* 77:96–105.

Jarick, Michelle, Mike J. Dixon, Mark T. Stewart, Emily C. Maxwell, and Daniel Smilek. 2009. A different outlook on time: Visual and auditory month names elicit different mental vantage points for a time-space synaesthete. *Cortex* 45:1217–1228.

Jarick, Michelle, Candice Jensen, Michael J. Dixon, and Daniel Smilek. 2011. The automaticity of vantage point shifts within a synaesthetes' spatial calendar. *Journal of Neuropsychology* 5:333–352.

Jonas, Clare N. 2011. *Effects of synaesthetic colour and space on cognition*. PhD thesis, University of Sussex.

Jonas, Clare N., Mary Jane Spiller, Ashok Jansari, and Jamie Ward. 2013. Comparing implicit and explicit number-space associations: visuospatial and verbal SNARC effects. Article under review.

Jonas, Clare N., Alisdair J. G. Taylor, Sam Hutton, Peter H. Weiss, and Jamie Ward. 2011. Visuospatial representations of the alphabet in synaesthetes and non-synaesthetes. *Journal of Neuropsychology* 5:302–322

Lorch, Robert F., and Jerome L. Myers. 1990. Regression analyses of repeated measures data in cognition research. *Journal of Experimental Psychology: Learning, Memory, and Cognition* 16:149–157.

Lynall, Mary-Ellen, and Colin Blakemore. 2013. What synesthesia isn't. In *The Oxford Handbook of Synesthesia*, ed. Julia Simner and Edward M. Hubbard, 959–998. Oxford: Oxford University Press.

Makioka, Shogo. 2009. A self-organizing learning account of number-form synaesthesia. *Cognition* 112:397–414.

Mann, Heather, Jason Korzenko, Jonathan S. A. Carriere, and Mike J. Dixon, M. 2009. Time-space synaesthesia—A cognitive advantage? *Consciousness and Cognition* 18:619–627.

Pariyadath, Vani, Sara J. Churchill, and David M. Eagleman. 2008. Why overlearned sequences are special: distinct neural networks in the right hemisphere for ordinal sequences. *Nature Precedings* <http://hdl.handle.net/10101/npre.2008.2452.1>.

Peabody, Charles. 1915. Certain further experiments in synaesthesia. *American Anthropologist* 17:143–155.

Phillips, D. E. 1897. Genesis of number-forms. *The American Journal of Psychology* 8:506–527.

Piazza, M., P. Pinel, and S. Dehaene. 2006. Objective correlates of an unusual subjective experience: A single-case study of number-form synaesthesia. *Cognitive Neuropsychology* 23:1162–1173.

Pinel, Philippe, Stanislas Dehaene, Denis Rivière and Denis LeBihan. 2001. Modulation of parietal activation by semantic distance in a number comparison task. *Neuroimage* 14 (5):1013–1026.

Price, Mark C. 2009a. Spatial forms and mental imagery. *Cortex* 45:1229–1245.

——. 2009b. What kind of mental images are spatial forms? *Cognitive Processing* 10 (Suppl 2):S276–S278.

Price, Mark C., and Jason B. Mattingley. 2013. Automaticity in sequence-space synaesthesia: A critical appraisal of the evidence. *Cortex* 49:1165–1186.

Price, Mark C., and Rune A. Mentzoni. 2008. Where is January? The month-SNARC effect in sequence-form synaesthetes. *Cortex* 44:890–907.

Price, Mark C., Tormod Elias Solberg, and Oskar Blakstad. 2010. Self-report and behavioural measures of spatial forms. Talk given at the 2010 Meeting of the UK Synaesthesia Association, Brighton, UK, March.

Ramachandran, Vilayanur S., and Edward M. Hubbard. 2001. Synaesthesia – A window into perception, thought and language. *Journal of Consciousness Studies* 8:3–34.

Ristic, Jelena, Alissa Wright, and Alan Kingstone. 2006. The number line effect reflects top-down control. *Psychonomic Bulletin & Review* 13:862–868.

Sagiv, Noam, Julia Simner, James Collins, Brian Butterworth, and Jamie Ward. 2006. What is the relationship between synaesthesia and visuo-spatial number forms? *Cognition* 101:114–128.

Santens, Seppe, and Wim Gevers. 2008. The SNARC effect does not imply a mental number line. *Cognition* 108:263–270.

Sereno, M. I., A. Pitzalis, and A. Martinez. 2001. Mapping of contralateral space in retinotopic coordinates by a parietal cortical area in humans. *Science* 294:1350–1354.

Seron, Xavier, Mauro Pesenti, Marie-Pascale Noel, Gérard Deloche and Jacques-André Cornet. 1992. Images of numbers, or when 98 is upper left and 6 sky blue. *Cognition* 44:159–196.

Seymour, Philip H. K. 1980. Internal representation of the months—an experimental analysis of spatial forms. *Psychological Research* 42:255–273.

Shanon, Benny. 2003. Three stories concerning synaesthesia: A commentary on Ramachandran and Hubbard. *Journal of Consciousness Studies* 10:69–74.

Simner, Julia. 2009. Synaesthetic visuo-spatial forms: Viewing sequences in space. *Cortex* 45:1138–1147.

Simner, Julia. 2012. Defining synaesthesia. *British Journal of Psychology* 103:1–15.

Simner, Julia, Neil Mayo, and Mary Jane Spiller. 2009. A foundation for savantism? Visuo-spatial synaesthetes present with cognitive benefits. *Cortex* 45:1246–1260.

Simner, Julia, Catherine Mulvenna, Noam Sagiv, Elias Tsakanikos, Sarah A. Witherby, Christine Fraser, Kirsten Scott, and Jamie Ward. 2006. Synaesthesia: The prevalence of atypical cross-modal experiences. *Perception* 35:1024–1033.

Simner, Julia, and Jamie Ward. 2006. The taste of words on the tip of the tongue. *Nature* 444:438.

Smilek, Daniel, Alicia Callejas, Mike J. Dixon, and Philip M. Merikle. 2007. Ovals of time: Time-space associations in synaesthesia. *Consciousness and Cognition* 16:507–519.

Smilek, Daniel, Michael J. Dixon, Cera Cudahy, and Philip M. Merikle. 2001. Synaesthetic photisms influence visual perception. *Journal of Cognitive Neuroscience* 13:930–936.

Spalding, J. M. K., and O. L. Zangwill. 1950. Disturbance of number-form in a case of brain injury. *Journal of Neurology, Neurosurgery and Psychiatry* 13:24–29.

Tang, Joey, Jamie Ward, and Brian Butterworth. 2008. Number forms in the brain. *Journal of Cognitive Neuroscience* 20:1–10.

Ward, Jamie, Michael J. Banissy, and Clare N. Jonas. 2008. Haptic perception and synaesthesia. In *Human Haptic Perception: Basics and Applications*, ed. Martin Grünwald, 259–265. Basel, Switzerland: Birkhauser-Verlag.

Ward, Jamie, Noam Sagiv, and Brian Butterworth. 2009. The impact of visuo-spatial number forms on simple arithmetic. *Cortex* 45:1261–1265.

CHAPTER 8

....

THE "RULES" OF SYNESTHESIA

....

JULIA SIMNER

The last 20 years have seen a rapid growth in the number of scientific studies on synesthesia and, to some extent, our views on synesthesia have undergone a sea change. Earlier studies in the historical literature (e.g., Jordan 1917), and even up to the late twentieth century, were based largely around the assumption that synesthetic associations were random and idiosyncratic—that these sensations were largely individual to each synesthete, and that there were no apparent guiding rules. Hence if one synesthete experienced the letter A as the color red, another might experience it as blue, and yet another still as yellow, without any obvious guiding principle. In recent years, however, an emerging body of work has carefully considered the pattern of experiences across a range of synesthesias, and shown not only that individual synesthetes' sensations are sometimes "logical" and rule-abiding, but that in some cases, these associations are shared across synesthetes. This chapter aims to describe these studies, and to show the ways in which synesthetic associations are predictable rather than random. To date, something approximating 150 different variants of synesthesia have been identified by science writers (e.g., Cytowic and Eagleman 2009; Day 2005), and this review covers examples of just those that have, thus far, been recognized as rule-based. However, it is likely that a very large number of other variants, too, may come to be seen as systematic in their own ways.

So what types of rules are we exploring? To some extent, every scientific paper written about synesthesia has uncovered some type of "rule" about how it functions. This is because the nature of psychological science is to shine a light on psychological functions in order to reveal their underlying mechanisms. However, the types of rules under consideration here relate to the particular pairing of the synesthetic trigger with the synesthetic sensation. At its most fundamental level, synesthesia can be considered an unusual pairing across modalities, of a type that is not explicitly experienced in the average person.[1] For example, some synesthetes might have a pairing between sound and color in that hearing sounds triggers colored photisms (known as *music-color synesthesia*; e.g., Ward, Huckstep, and Tsakanikos 2006). Alternatively, other synesthetes might have a pairing between words and tastes, in that reading words floods the mouth with flavors (known as *lexical-gustatory synesthesia*; e.g., Ward and Simner 2003). In each type of synesthesia, we can characterize the condition as linking a particular triggering stimulus (termed the *inducer*) with a particular synesthetic sensation (termed the *concurrent*; Grossenbacher and Lovelace 2001). Hence music-color synesthesia, for example, is induced by music and triggers the concurrent of color. These classifications of inducer and concurrent are important to our discussion in that our interest focuses on the "rules" of synesthesia that emerge within these pairings. In other words, there is something non-random in the type of concurrent for any given inducer, and I explore this issue here (see also Hancock, Chapter 5, this volume).

I noted earlier that the rules linking inducers and concurrents are often shared across synesthetes, and this means that different synesthetes show underlying similarities, even if they appear superficially different. In addition, and of particular interest for theories of the evolution and development of synesthesia, we shall see later that some of these underlying rules can also be found operating in the population at large. All people, not just synesthetes, can make intuitive matchings across the senses. For example, most people agree that high-pitch sounds pair better in some way with lighter colors, compared to dark colors (Hubbard 1996; Marks 1974, 1982, 1987; Melara 1989; Ward, Huckstep, and Tsakanikos 2006). When we closely inspect these intuitive associations made by the average person, we discover that they share a great deal in common with the pairings made by synesthetes, and I shall explore this further towards the end of the chapter. First however, I address the rules that have been shown to operate in synesthetes.

I divide my review according to the level at which each rule of synesthesia appears to be operating: either involving lower-level perceptual features of the inducer/concurrent, or higher-level cognitive features. This division is based loosely on the historical distinction made in psychological science between perception and cognition. In as much as it is possible to draw such a distinction (for discussion, see Barsalou 2008), we can consider *perception* to be closely tied to sensation, in that it acts on stimuli received directly through the senses (e.g., how things look, how they sound) while *cognition* is more closely tied to mental states involving abstraction, learning, reasoning, and language. At each level, I will look at relationships that hold between the inducer and concurrent.

Finally, I point out that, in uncovering the underlying patterns in synesthetic associations, researchers have been demonstrating "rules" that are, in most cases, unknown to synesthetes themselves. In other words, it is somewhat rare that

---

[1] I use the term "average person" throughout this chapter to denote non-synesthetes, who represent the modal average of the population. This wording does not imply that synesthetes are "above" or "below" average (i.e., they are not better or worse) but that they are simply something other than the average in statistical terms.

synesthetes could voice the rules that guide their system, and most synesthetes have no conscious knowledge whatsoever of any systematicity in their synesthesia at all. In the rare cases where synesthetes do have conscious access to these "rules," I flag this within the text.

PERCEPTUAL/SENSORY RULES OF SYNESTHESIA

A useful starting point for a discussion of non-random associations comes from a consideration of music-color synesthesia. This variant was first recognized in the literature 200 years ago (Sachs 1812; see Jewanski, Day, and Ward 2009, Jewanski, Chapter 19, this volume). In this early study, the doctoral student Georg Tobias Ludwig Sachs self-reported several variants of his own synesthesia, which included colored music. In fact, the variant of "colored music" described by Sachs was twofold: first, he experienced colors from the timbres of different musical instruments. (Timbre is the aspect of sound unrelated to pitch and loudness, which allows us to distinguish between the same notes on different instruments; e.g., a piano versus a trumpet.) Colored timbre has since been reported in other synesthetes also (e.g., Cutsforth 1925; Masson 1952; Whitchurch 1922; Zigler 1930). Ward, Huckstep, and Tsakanikos (2006) have shown that the relationship between timbre and color can be captured by an understanding of the three distinct components of color: hue (e.g., redness, greenness, etc.), saturation (or chroma; i.e., the depth/vividness or the color), and luminance (lightnesss/brightness of color). In their study of ten sound-color synesthetes, Ward, Huckstep, and Tsakanikos showed that the timbre of musical inducers was related to, specifically, the saturation of colors, in that musical notes from the piano and strings had significantly higher saturation (i.e., were "literally, more colorful"; Ward, Huckstep, and Tsakanikos 2006, 270) than pure tone sine waves.

The second variant of music-color synesthesia experienced by Georg Sachs (1812; see Jewanski, Day, and Ward 2009) was a color for each note of the musical scale.[2] Sachs' native language German, like English, uses letters of the alphabet to denote musical notes, and for Sachs, the colors for notes were not random, but dictated by their designating letter. Hence, both the letter A in writing and the note designated by A in the musical scale were colored the same for Sachs. In other words, for individuals with both colored music and colored letters (this latter known as *grapheme-color synesthesia*), the colors from letters appear to be able to migrate to the printed musical notes (or vice versa; Carroll and Greenberg 1961; Haack and Radocy 1981; Langfeld 1914; Riggs and Karwoski 1934; Rogers 1987; Ward, Tsakanikos, and Bray 2006).

---

[2] Ward, Huckstep, and Tsakanikos (2006) also describe other potential variants of "colored music" not covered here. These include color from loudness, tempo, emotional response, consonance/dissonance, and the key or tonality of a piece (e.g., C major). See also Marks (1975).

In addition to the influence from written musical transcription, there is an additional rule that can dictate the coloring of notes in music-color synesthesia. Early studies suggested that for synesthetes, high-pitched sounds might be lighter/brighter in color, and low-pitched sounds might be darker in color (e.g., Cutsforth 1925; Riggs and Karwoski 1934; Whitchurch 1922; Zigler 1930). These historical observations were tested directly by Ward, Huckstep, and Tsakanikos (2006), and subsequently supported. Ward and colleagues showed that, for their ten music-color synesthetes, the synesthetic color experienced from heard notes increased monotonically in lightness with pitch. Ward and colleagues also found a significant relationship with saturation, in that saturation peaked at the mid-range pitches presented to synesthetes (in that study, a semitone below "middle C"). An example of how higher pitch triggers lighter colors is illustrated in Figure 8.1 (top), which shows the colors seen by music-color synesthete LMH for ascending notes on the musical scale. The fact that the effects found in this study were significant across a group of synesthetes suggests that synesthetes were not acting entirely idiosyncratically, but rather, that there were shared rules underlying their synesthesia (linking pitch and timbre with luminance and saturation, respectively). Finally, a link between pitch and luminance can also unite

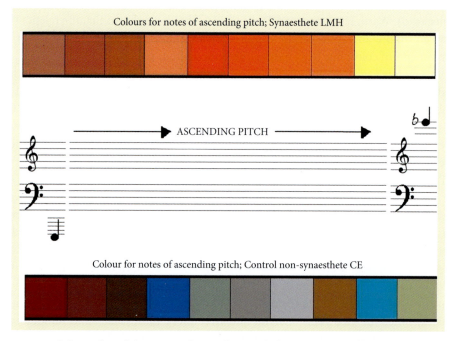

FIGURE 8.1 Colors selected for notes of ascending pitch by synesthete LMH and control subject, CE. Figure by Julia Simner and Jamie Ward (synesthetic and non-synesthetic color choices, based on the data described in Ward, Huckstep, and Tsakanikos (2006)) licensed under the Creative Commons Attribution-NonCommercial-NoDerivs 3.0 Unported License. To view a copy of this license, visit <http://creativecommons.org/licenses/by-nc-nd/3.0/> or send a letter to Creative Commons, 444 Castro Street, Suite 900, Mountain View, California, 94041, USA.

different forms of synesthesia. Fernay, Reby, and Ward (2012) have recently shown that a voice-color synesthete also related pitch and color lightness when asked to indicate the color of vowels varying in their fundamental frequency (i.e., higher pitch vowels were lighter in color).

Another variant in which features of luminance and saturation are systematically related to the inducer is touch-color synesthesia. In this, colors are triggered by tactile sensations against the skin. Although these synesthetic colors appear to be superficially random, both my own research group (Simner and Ludwig 2012) and that of Jamie Ward (Ward, Banissy, and Jonas 2008) have suggested an underlying systematicity. In our study, for example, we presented a range of tactile stimuli that varied incrementally in hardness (from hard to soft), roughness (from rough to smooth) and roundness (from round to pointed). We found that our synesthete, EB, mapped softer objects to significantly more luminant colors, and that she also mapped rougher objects to more saturated colors. In other words, there was an underlying systematicity to the synesthesia experienced by EB, and similar findings were reported by Ward, Banissy, and Jonas (2008; who tested EB and an additional synesthete).

I end this section by reviewing additional perceptual influences on the relationship between inducers and concurrents. Eagleman (2010), for example, has recently shown that color concurrents in grapheme-color synesthesia are dictated, to some extent, by the visual form of letters that induce those colors. Specifically, he demonstrated that letters similar in shape (i.e., those that resemble each other in rotation; e.g., N, Z) generate similar synesthetic colors—more similar in fact than the colors generated by differently shaped letters (e.g., B, X). A similar finding has come from Brang and Ramachandran (2011) who showed, too, that visually similar letters trigger visually similar colors (see also Hubbard et al. 2005; Jürgens, Mausfeld, and Nikolić 2010). Watson, Akins, and Enns (2012) show that this type of letter–color mappings works at the level of individual dimensions of color, in that letter shape is linked to, specifically, color hue (rather than luminance or saturation). Watson, Akins, and Enns elicited the colors of letters from 54 grapheme-color synesthetes and compared pairs of letters according to differences in their shape and in their synesthetic hue. They found that a greater distance in one dimension correlated with a greater distance in the other—in other words, letter shape and color hue were significantly linked. (With a similar method, Watson and colleagues found that hue was also linked to letter ordinality, and that luminance was linked to letter frequency.) Other influences of letter-shape have also been shown by Carol Mills and her colleagues (Mills et al. 2002; Mills et al. 2009; Witthoft and Winawer 2006) who showed that visual similarities in letters dictate how colors are transferred across alphabets for bilingual synesthetes. Letters that look similar across alphabets, such as the Cyrillic letter И and the Roman letter N, tended to be colored similarity for an English-Russian synesthetic bilingual. In this way, and across a range of studies, synesthetic systems appear to be built up non-randomly, with perceptual rules that link inducers and concurrents in predictable ways. In the next section I turn to synesthetic rules based on higher-level, cognitive features.

COGNITIVE AND LINGUISTIC RULES

Studies on the prevalence of synesthesia show that the most common variants by far are those that are triggered by language units, such as graphemes (i.e., units of written language), phonemes (i.e., units of spoken language), and words. These linguistic variants account for as many as 88% of all synesthesias (Simner et al. 2006) and are of special interest to synesthesia researchers because they can be studied using tools from the rich history of research into psycholinguistics. The assumption here, and one that has been borne out with research (see Simner 2007), is that the same cognitive processes that aid in human language comprehension and production are also at work in generating synesthetic experiences. In other words, linguistic synesthesias do not appear to be driven by novel rules specific only to synesthetes, but rather, they are driven by general psycholinguistic processes of language production/comprehension. These processes have, in effect, been commandeered by the synesthetic system to systematically (rather than randomly) produce cross-modal synesthetic sensations.

One example of a general psycholinguistic feature found pervasively in synesthesia is linguistic frequency. Frequency describes the commonness with which a language unit is encountered in the linguistic environment. For example, some words (e.g., *pen*) are more frequent than others (e.g., *pun*), as are some syntactic constructions (e.g., active voice is more frequent than passive). The human language system is highly sensitive to linguistic frequency, and a great deal of the language system is built around this feature. For example, frequency lies at the heart of the mental process of "lexical access" (in which word meanings are retrieved from the "mental lexicon") and so high-frequency words are accessed faster than low-frequency words (Rubenstein, Garfield, and Millikan 1970). In the same way that linguistic frequency plays a central role in language processing, so it also plays a role in the system of associations that bring together inducers and concurrents in synesthesia, and I describe this next.

Two early studies identifying the role of frequency in synesthesia were Simner et al. (2005) and Rich, Bradshaw, and Mattingley (2005). Together, these studies showed that in grapheme-color synesthesia, the highest frequency letters and digits tend to pair with the highest frequency colors terms. For example, Rich and colleagues noted that the highest frequency color word ("white") within their respective sets of alphabet and color names, is most commonly associated by synesthetes with the highest frequency number word (the number "one"). Equally, the high-frequency letter A, tends to be paired with the highest frequency chromatic color (red). This observation was empirically verified by Simner et al. (2005) who showed significant correlations between the frequency of letter inducers, and the frequency of their concurrent colors (high-frequency letters pair with high-frequency color terms).

The role of frequency in grapheme-color synesthesia was further illustrated by Gian Beeli, Daniel Smilek, and their colleagues (Beeli, Esslen, and Jäncke 2007; Smilek, Carriere, et al. 2007). These studies showed that the linguistic frequency of grapheme inducers (letters and digits) was significantly correlated with the luminance and saturation of concurrent colors: high-frequency letters and digits tend to generate colors that are lighter, and the colors of high-frequency letters are also more vivid. This mediation of frequency was true both for the English-speaking synesthetes tested by Smilek et al., as well as the German-speaking participants tested in the Beeli collaboration.

The role of frequency in synesthesia has been also demonstrated in languages other than English. Hung (2011) examined Mandarin Chinese synesthetes who experience colors for Chinese characters (i.e., the Chinese logographic word-unit; e.g., 木 meaning *tree*) and Chinese Bopomo (the traditional Chinese phonetic alphabet system; e.g., ㄅ, ㄆ). For synesthetes within that sample, high-frequency characters (e.g., 木 *tree*) tend to combine with high-frequency color terms (e.g., red), while lower-frequency characters (e.g., 凳 *stool*) tend to pair with lower-frequency color-terms (e.g., purple). A similar effect was also found for high- and low-frequency Bopomo letters. Indeed, Hung (2011) reveals a number of ways in which colors are generated by non-random rules for Chinese synesthetes, and I direct the reader to her full review in this volume (Chapter 11).

Another variant of synesthesia whose inducer/concurrent relationships are based, to some extent, on frequency, is lexical-gustatory synesthesia (e.g., Simner and Ward 2006; Ward and Simner 2003; Ward, Simner, and Auyeung 2005). In this variant, reading words, saying words, hearing words, and even thinking about words can trigger a flood of flavor in the mouth (e.g., for synesthete JIW, the word *jail* tastes of bacon; see Simner 2011 for review). From synesthete to synesthete, tastes can be generated either by a subset of words in the language, or by all words (e.g., Simner and Haywood 2009). Some words generate particularly strong flavor concurrents which can last for several minutes, while other concurrent tastes are weaker and more fleeting (Ward and Simner 2003). Simner and Haywood (2009) and Gendle (2007) have shown that the linguistic frequency of triggering words determines the likelihood of there being a synesthetic taste, in that low-frequency words are less likely to generate a taste than high-frequency words. Furthermore, Ward, Simner, and Auyeung (2005; also Simner and Haywood 2009) show that the frequency of the inducer also determines the *intensity* of the concurrent taste, in that high-frequency words generate more strongly tasting concurrents than lower-frequency words. In two ways, then, the nature of the concurrent is to some extent predicted by the linguistic frequency of the inducer.

One recent study, Simner, Gartner, and Taylor (2011), has shown the role played by frequency in the variant of synesthesia known as *sequence-personality synesthesia* or *ordinal linguistic personification* (OLP; see Sobczak-Edmans and Sagiv, Chapter 12, this volume). In OLP synesthesia, individuals experience sequenced units (e.g., letters, digits, days of the week, months of the year) as triggering a gender or personality type (Flournoy 1893; Simner and Holenstein 2007; Simner and Hubbard 2006; Smilek, Malcolmson, et al. 2007). For example, the letter A might be a bossy older female while the letter B might be a young male child. Simner, Gartner, and Taylor (2011) showed that the frequency of the inducer dictates the personality type of the concurrent. Specifically, we looked at personality traits as they had been defined by Goldberg (1990, 1992), Costa and McCrae (1992), and others, who classify personality along five dimensions, which

Costa and McCrae term *Extraversion, Agreeableness, Conscientiousness, Neuroticism,* and *Openness to experience.* In our synesthesia study, we showed that these personality factors are linked to linguistic frequency, in that synesthetes tend to associate high-frequency letters with synesthetic personalities that are high Agreeable and low Neurotic. In other words, common letters tend to take on personalities that are highly agreeable while low-frequency letters tend to take the on personalities that are highly neurotic. It was not possible in our study to determine *why* this particular set of pairings occurred, although it might be a manifestation of "hedonic matching," in which positive traits are paired together. For example, it could be argued that high frequency (associated with familiarity) is a positive trait, which therefore comes to be associated with the more positive personality trait of agreeableness.

In summary, across a series of studies in synesthesia research, we have seen that one of the most important determinants of synesthetic sensations in language-triggered synesthesias is the linguistic frequency of the inducer. We saw its influence in letter-color synesthesia (letter frequency determines luminance, saturation and hue-category; Beeli, Esslen, and Jäncke 2007; Smilek et al. 2007; Simner and Ward 2008; Simner et al. 2005), in lexical-gustatory synesthesia (word frequency determines likelihood and intensity of tastes; Gendle 2007; Simner and Haywood 2009; Ward, Simner, and Auyeung 2005) and in OLP synesthesia (letter-frequency determines concurrent personalities; Simner, Gartner, and Taylor 2011). This sensitivity to linguistic frequency is reviewed further by Simner (2007), and has been found across a range of variants.

I turn now to other ways in which the association between inducer and concurrent is systematic for synesthetes. We saw earlier that there is a relationship in OLP between inducer and concurrent based on frequency, and related to this, Smilek, Malcolmson, et al. (2007) have shown that concurrent personalities are linked to the familiarity of the inducer object: familiar objects were given more social/relational personifications (e.g., *fatherly/popular*) while novel objects were given more physical/personal ones (e.g., *heavy-set/organized*). OLP synesthesia is systematic and non-random in other ways, too. Simner and Holenstein (2007) showed that synesthetic personalities are also influenced by the life experience of the synesthete, since the personality concurrents tend to reflect the society that is contemporary to the synesthete. Historical studies, for example, describe concurrents that are "housekeepers" or "society girls" (Flournoy 1893) while modern accounts describe more contemporary personality-types (e.g., "a sociable type whose mobile phone is always ringing"; Simner, Gartner, and Taylor 2011, p. 285).

Other effects of culture and environment have been seen in another type of synesthesia, known as *visuo-spatial forms* (or *sequence-space synesthesia*; see Jonas and Jarick, Chapter 7, this volume, and Simner 2009 for overview). In this variant, numbers (as well as other sequenced units such as letters, days, months) are "seen" in particular spatial arrays (e.g., in ellipses, lines, zig-zags, and so on). Earlier reports of this phenomenon from synesthetes in Victorian Britain (reported by Galton 1880) suggested these "number lines" tended to bend at the number 12, rather than at the number 10 which is more commonly found today. This appears to reflect the fact that the decimal monetary system was introduced in Britain only in 1971, before which a duodecimal system was in place. Hence, this over-familiarity to the number 12 (and subsequently, the number 10) may have influenced the particular form that concurrents took from the nineteenth to the twentieth/twenty-first centuries (Sagiv et al. 2006). One final influence of environment might also be seen in sequence-space synesthesia: number-forms and alphabet-forms tend to run left-to-right in English-speaking synesthetes, and this mirrors the direction that text unfolds in that language (Sagiv et al. 2006).

I end this section by describing one particular rule that guides synesthetic associations, but is rare in that it is often known *consciously* by synesthetes. This rule applies to individuals with grapheme-color synesthesia, who experience not only colored letters, but colored words. Importantly, the ways in which words come to be colored tends to be systematic, in that words tend to be dominated by the color of the initial letter (Baron-Cohen et al. 1993; Ward, Simner, and Auyeung 2005) or the initial vowel (e.g., Ward, Simner, and Auyeung 2005). Take, for example, a synesthete for whom the letters A, B, and C are colored red, blue, and green respectively. This synesthete is likely to report that the word *cab* has all three colors but that the color of the letter C tends to dominate. Hence, in a forced-choice, single-response task, the synesthete will reply that the word *cab* is green. Simner, Glover, and Mowat (2006) show that this rule for the coloring of words is generally true for approximately 60% to 70% of grapheme-color synesthetes. For a further 20%, words are colored by their initial vowel (so the word *cab* would be predominately red). Again, in both cases, synesthetes tend to be able to voice this rule. However, for the type of synesthete who is particularly sensitive to vowels, we have been able to show a more subtle manifestation of their word-coloring rule (Simner et al. 2006). In English, the initial letters of words tend to fall within stressed syllables (e.g., similar to *canon* [CA-non] rather than *cadet* [ca-DET]). Since stressed syllables are particularly important in decoding speech, we hypothesized that synesthetes sensitive to initial vowels might in fact be sensitive to vowels in stressed syllables, rather than to any vowel that comes first in a word. We showed that this was true, at least for our case-study JW. For JW, words such as *canon* take on the synesthetic color of the letter A, while words such as *cadet* take the synesthetic color of the letter E; in other words, the stressed syllable dominates. Although JW was overall familiar with the fact that her words were colored by vowels, she was not aware of this fine-grained rule linked to syllabic stress. As such, this rule reflects most of those covered in this chapter, in being largely unknown to the synesthete.

SYNESTHETIC RULES IN THE GENERAL POPULATION

I end this chapter by considering the ways in which the rules of synesthesia, which pair inducers with concurrents for synesthetes, can also be seen in operation within the general population. To complement this section, I draw the reader's attention to those chapters in this volume where Lawrence Marks (Chapter 38), and Cesare Parise and Charles Spence (Chapter 39) describe in full the area I briefly review here. We shall see that the average non-synesthetic person makes systematic, intuitive, rule-based pairings across the senses and I focus here on those examples where the preferences of the general population mirror the rule-based pairings of synesthetes.

We saw earlier that the synesthetic colors perceived by music-color synesthetes can be systematically tied to the acoustic features of the inducer sound. Jamie Ward and others have shown that higher-pitch sounds tend to trigger more luminant (lighter) colors (e.g., Ward, Huckstep, and Tsakanikos 2006). Additionally, these researchers have shown striking similarities when comparing synesthetes and non-synesthetes on the same color-picking task (Ward, Huckstep, and Tsakanikos 2006). Ward and colleagues asked a group of ten music-color synesthetes and ten control non-synesthetes to select colors from an electronic palette for a range of sounds played over headphones. Synesthetes selected colors triggered by their synesthesia and controls picked whatever color they felt "went best" with each sound. Although synesthetes differed from controls in several ways (their colors were more consistent over time, and were "seen" explicitly, in space or the mind's eye) both groups appeared to be selecting colors non-randomly, and both were following a rule which paired lighter colors to higher pitch. This rule can be seen in action in Figure 8.1, where the colors selected by a synesthete are shown alongside those selected by a control participant: in both cases, the colors get lighter as the paired sound gets higher. A similar link between pitch and luminance was also shared between a synesthete and non-synesthetes in a study of voice-color synesthesia (Fernay, Reby, and Ward 2012). Both populations linked increasing fundamental frequency in vowels with increasing color luminance, and also with higher vertical position (higher pitch being higher in space).

Another area in which synesthetic associations are mirrored in the general population comes in the coloring of letters and digits. Grapheme-color synesthetes "see" colors when exposed to graphemes, which is an experience rather unfamiliar to the average person. Nonetheless, when we compared their colors with those picked by non-synesthetes, we found similar choices across groups. In our study (Simner et al. 2005) approximately 400 non-synesthetes were asked to write down a color for each letter of the alphabet according to their feeling or intuition. Although our non-synesthetes said the task made little sense to them, they tended to agree with each other on the color for each letter. For example, although people might choose any color for the letter A, they were significantly likely to choose the color red above all other colors (and this was true whether they received the letters in alphabetical order, or in a random order). Further inspection showed that these color choices were based on a set of rules, and that some of these rules also captured the particular colors experienced by synesthetes. For example, both synesthetes and non-synesthetes had a tendency to pair colors with the initial letter of the color name (e.g., G = green; R = red). A later study showed that both groups are sensitive to linguistic frequency, since higher-frequency letters and digits tend to be paired with more luminant colors, both for synesthetes and non-synesthetes alike (Smilek et al. 2007).

Evidence of shared mechanisms in synesthetes and non-synesthetes also comes from a consideration of touch-color synesthesia. We saw previously that touch-color associations in synesthetes are driven by rules which pair soft-hardness with the luminance of the synesthetic color (softer objects are colored lighter), and rough–smoothness with its saturation (rougher objects are more saturated). In our study in 2012 (Simner and Ludwig 2012; see also Ward, Banissy, and Jonas 2008) we found that the touch–color mappings of a touch-color synesthetes patterned like those of non-synesthetes in two ways. Firstly, both our synesthete and controls significantly mapped softer objects to more luminant colors, and both mapped qualities of rough–smoothness to qualities of saturation.[3]

Despite these similarities, the experiences of synesthetes still differ in important ways. Synesthetes experience their synesthetic sensations (e.g., colors) at a conscious level, in that they are aware of them in everyday life. In questionnaire studies, synesthetes report that their touch–color associations feel more certain, more automatic, and are more specific and detailed than those of controls (e.g., Simner and Ludwig 2012; Simner et al. 2005). Synesthetes also tend to be highly consistent over time (e.g., Baron-Cohen, Wyke, and Binnie 1987; but see Simner 2012) while the pairings of non-synesthetes are more changeable and subject to variation. In other words, synesthetes differ from the general population in the phenomenology of their associations, but their underlying mechanisms appear be similar or the same. I end this section by directing the reader to the six excellent chapters in Part VII of this volume, on cross-modality in the general population. These chapters discuss the many ways in which non-synesthetes make cross-sensory and cross-modal associations, not only in explicit forced-choice matching tasks, but also in the day-to-day use of language and cognition.

SUMMARY AND CONCLUSIONS

The previous sections have shown a number of ways in which synesthetes and non-synesthetes rely on shared rules in the integration of the senses. In grapheme-color synesthesia, for example, as in other variants, synesthetes' associations tend to be shared

---

[3] It is interesting to note that for the synesthete in that study, EB, smoothness–saturation mapping were in the opposite direction to those of controls (EB mapped more saturated colors to rougher rather than smoother surfaces). In this way, the synesthete relies on broadly the same types of underlying rules as non-synesthetes, although the directionality differed. This type of fluidity is also found within groups of non-synesthetes. For example, some non-synesthetes match increasing loudness to increasing lightness, whereas others systematically match it to increasing darkness. Moreover, some non-synesthetes change the direction of their mapping over time (Marks 1974). In other words, there is a separation between whether two dimensions come to be associated in cross-modal mapping, and the directionality that mapping takes.

both from synesthete to synesthete (Day 2005; Rich, Bradshaw, and Mattingley 2005; Simner et al. 2005) and between synesthetes and non-synesthetes (Simner et al. 2005). Some of these associations are based on shared cognitive rules, for example, relating to linguistic frequency (e.g., common letters pair with common color terms; Simner et al. 2005) while others stem from lower-level perceptual features, for example, in the visual form of graphemes (e.g., Brang and Ramachandran 2011). These underlying rules can bring together purely sensory inducers and concurrents, such as pitch and luminance, or they can unite higher-level cognitive dimensions, such as graphemes and personality-types. Where these rules are shared by synesthetes and non-synesthetes, we see similar underlying mechanisms, but radically different phenomenology: synesthetes are aware of their cross-modal sensations, while for non-synesthetes, these are experienced only implicitly. The examples shown here are just a subset of the ways in which synesthetic associations have been shown to be rule based, although other studies show yet *more* variants where rules guide the pairings (e.g., in taste-shape synesthesia sweeter flavors have rounder shape concurrents; Cytowic and Wood 1982; for similar effects in non-synesthetes see Simner et al. 2013).

In summary, we have seen that synesthetic experiences of colors, tastes, and other modalities come to be associated to the inducing stimulus in non-random ways, and in ways that reflect, to some extent the intuitive cross-modal correspondences of non-synesthetes. But what can we conclude from these similarities across the populations? At the very least, they appear to show that synesthesia relies not on specialized mechanisms specific only to synesthetes, but to more universal mechanisms of general perception and cognition. We might also conclude that all people are synesthetic to some extent, in as much as we all share an ability to integrate cross-modal information in fixed ways. Finally, I point out that researchers have proposed an explanation for the similarity between synesthetes and non-synesthetes, and this explanation speaks to the very roots of synesthesia. The early chapters in this compendium describe the development of synesthesia, and one key theory is the "neonatal synesthesia hypothesis" (Baron-Cohen 1996; Baron-Cohen, Wyke, and Binnie 1987; Baron-Cohen et al. 1996; Maurer 1993). This account suggests that all humans may be born with explicit, synesthetic cross-modal perception, but that this dies out in most people during childhood. Hence the average person would be left with only implicit associations into adulthood. In synesthetes, however, these early explicit cross-modal experiences may be maintained (perhaps due to some genetic predisposition) and so would endure into adulthood. In other words, the explicit experiences of synesthetes would be echoed by similar, but implicit experiences in the general population, and both of these might trace back to a shared infantile state. We can think of this theory as being one particular manifestation of what we have described elsewhere as the *Continuity Hypothesis* (Ludwig and Simner 2013). This theory, first posited by Simon Baron-Cohen and colleagues (e.g., Harrison and Baron-Cohen 1997) states that synesthetes and non-synesthetes occupy opposite ends of a shared continuum of cross-modality, with synesthetes experiencing consciously what non-synesthetes feel only intuitively. Overall, what is clear is that the synesthetic experiences are not, apparently, a breed apart from the everyday experiences of all people.

Instead, a broad spectrum of people share a set of underlying rules which systematically support cross-modal correspondences, felt either explicitly in synesthetes, or implicitly by everyone else.

REFERENCES

Baron-Cohen, Simon. 1996. Is there a normal phase of synaesthesia in development? *Psyche* 2 (27).

Baron-Cohen, Simon, Lucy Burt, Fiona Laittan-Smith, John E. Harrison, and Patrick Bolton. 1996. Synaesthesia: Prevalence and familiarity. *Perception* 25:1073–1079.

Baron-Cohen, Simon, John Harrison, Laura H. Goldstein, and Maria Wyke. 1993. Coloured speech perception: Is synaesthesia what happens when modularity breaks down? *Perception* 22:419–426.

Baron-Cohen, Simon, Maria Wyke, and Colin Binnie. 1987. Hearing words and seeing colours: an experimental investigation of a case of synaesthesia. *Perception* 16:761–767.

Barsalou, Lawrence W. 2008. Grounded cognition. *Annual Review of Psychology* 59:617–645.

Beeli, Gian, Michaela Esslen, and Lutz Jäncke. 2007. Frequency correlates in grapheme-color synaesthesia. *Psychological Science* 18:788–792.

Brang, David, and Vilayanur S. Ramachandran. 2011. Similarly shaped letters evoke similar colors in grapheme-color synesthesia. *Neuropsychologia* 49:1355–1358.

Carroll John B., and Joseph H. Greenberg. 1961. Two cases of synaesthesia for color and musical tonality associated with absolute pitch. *Perceptual and Motor Skills* 13:48.

Costa, Paul T., and Robert R. McCrae. 1992. *NEO Personality Inventory-Revised (NEO-PI-R) and NEO Five-Factor Inventory (NEO-FFI) professional manual.* Odessa, FL: Psychological Assessment Resources.

Cytowic, Richard, E. and David M. Eagleman. 2009. *Wednesday is indigo blue: Discovering the brain of synaesthesia.* Cambridge, MA: MIT Press.

Cytowic, Richard E. and Frank B. Wood. 1982. Synaesthesia II: Psychophysical relations in the synaesthesia of geometrically shaped taste and colored hearing. *Brain and Cognition* 1:36–49.

Cutsforth, Thomas D. 1925. The role of emotion in a synaesthetic subject. *American Journal of Psychology* 36:527–543.

Day, Sean. 2005. Some demographic and socio-cultural aspects of synaesthesia. In *Synesthesia: Perspectives from Cognitive Neuroscience*, ed. Lynn C. Robertson and Noam Sagiv, 11–33. New York: Oxford University Press.

Eagleman, David M. 2010. What has large-scale analysis taught us? Paper presented at the 5th Meeting of the UK Synaesthesia Association. Brighton, University of Sussex, UK, March.

Fernay, Louise, David Reby and Jamie Ward. (2012). Visualized voices: A case study of audio-visual synesthesia. *Neurocase* 18:50–56.

Flournoy, Théodore. 1893. *Des phénomènes de synopsie.* Paris: Félix Alcan.

Galton, Francis. 1880. Visualised numerals. *Nature* 21:252–256.

Gendle, Mathew H. 2007. Word-gustatory synesthesia: A case study. *Perception* 36:495–507.

Goldberg, Lewis R. 1990. An alternative 'description of personality': The Big-Five factor structure. *Journal of Personality and Social Psychology* 59:1216–1229.

——. 1992. The development of markers for the Big-Five factor structure. *Psychological Assessment* 4:26–42.

Grossenbacher, Peter G., and Christoper T. Lovelace. 2001. Mechanisms of synesthesia: Cognitive and physiological constraints. *Trends in Cognitive Sciences* 5:36–41.

Haack Paul A., and Rudolf E. Radocy. 1981. A case study of a chromesthetic. *Journal of Research in Music Education* 29:85–90.

Hancock, Peter. 2013. Synesthesia, alphabet books, and fridge magnets.In *The Oxford Handbook of Synesthesia*, ed. Julia Simner and Edward M. Hubbard, 83–99. Oxford: Oxford University Press.

Harrison, John E., and Simon Baron-Cohen. 1997. Synesthesia: A review of psychological theories. In *Synesthesia: Classic and Contemporary Readings*, ed. Simon Baron-Cohen and John E. Harrison, 109–122. Oxford: Blackwell.

Hubbard, Timothy L. 1996. Synesthesia-like mappings of lightness, pitch and melodic interval. *American Journal of Psychology* 109:219–238.

Hubbard, Edward M., Pearl Ambrosio, Shai Azoulai, and Vilayanur S. Ramachandran. 2005. Grapheme and letter name based patterns in synesthetic colors. *Cognitive Neuroscience Society Abstracts.*

Hung, Wan-Yu. 2011. *An investigation into the underlying linguistic cues of Chinese synaesthesia.* PhD thesis, University of Edinburgh.

——. 2013. Synesthesia in non-alphabetic languages. In *The Oxford Handbook of Synesthesia*, ed. Julia Simner and Edward M. Hubbard, 205–221. Oxford: Oxford University Press.

Jürgens, Uta T., Rainer Mausfeld, and Danko Nikolić. 2010. Grapheme–colour synaesthesia: Similar shapes take similar colours. Paper presented at the 5th Meeting of the UK Synaesthesia Association. Brighton, University of Sussex, UK, March.

Jewanski, Jörg. 2013. Synesthesia in the nineteenth century: Scientific origins. In *The Oxford Handbook of Synesthesia*, ed. Julia Simner and Edward M. Hubbard, 369–398. Oxford: Oxford University Press.

Jewanski, Jörg, Sean A. Day, and Jamie Ward. 2009. A colorful albino: The first documented case of synaesthesia, by Georg Tobias Ludwig Sachs in 1812. *Journal of the History of the Neurosciences* 18:293–303.

Jonas, Clare and Michelle Jarick. 2013. Synesthesia, sequences, and space. In *The Oxford Handbook of Synesthesia*, ed. Julia Simner and Edward M. Hubbard, 123–148. Oxford: Oxford University Press.

Jordan, David S. 1917. The colors of letters. *Science* 46:311–312.

Langfeld H. S. 1914. Note on a case of chromesthesia. *Psychological Bulletin* 11:113–114.

Ludwig, Vera U., and Julia Simner. 2013. What color does that feel? Tactile-visual mapping and the development of cross-modality. *Cortex* 49:1089–1099.

Marks, Lawrence E. 1974. On associations of light and sound: The mediation of brightness, pitch, and loudness. *American Journal of Psychology* 87:173–188.

——. 1982. Bright sneezes and dark coughs, loud sunlight and soft moonlight. *Journal of Experimental Psychology: Human Perception and Performance* 8:177–193.

——. 1987. On cross-modal similarity: Auditory-visual interactions in speeded discrimination. *Journal of Experimental Psychology: Human Perception and Performance* 13:384–394.

——. 2013. Weak synesthesia in perception and language. In *The Oxford Handbook of Synesthesia*, ed. Julia Simner and Edward M. Hubbard, 761–789. Oxford: Oxford University Press.

Masson, David L. 1952. Synesthesia and sound spectra. *Word* 8:39–41.

Maurer, Daphne. 1993. Neonatal synesthesia: Implications for the processing of speech and faces. In *Developmental Neurocognition: Speech and Face Processing in the First Year of Life,* ed. Bénédicte de Boysson-Bardies, Scania de Schonen, Peter Jusczyk, Peter McNeilage, and John Morton, 109–124. Dordrecht: Kluwer Academic Publishers.

Melara, Robert D. 1989. Dimensional interaction between color and pitch. *Journal of Experimental Psychology: Human Perception and Performance* 15:69–79.

Mills, Carol B., Shari R. Metzger, Catherine. A. Foster, Melaina N. Valentine-Gresko, and Stephanie Ricketts. 2009. Development of color-grapheme synesthesia and its effect on mathematical operations. *Perception* 38:591–605.

Mills, Carol B., Meredith L. Viguers, Shari K. Edelson, Amanda T. Thomas, Stephanie L. Simon-Dack, and Joanne A. Innis. 2002. The color of two alphabets for a multilingual synesthete. *Perception* 13:1371–1394.

Rich, Anina N., John L. Bradshaw, and Jason B. Mattingley. 2005. A systematic, large-scale study of synaesthesia: implications for the role of early experience in lexical-colour associations. *Cognition* 98:53–84.

Riggs, Lorrin A., and Theodore Karwoski. 1934. Synaesthesia. *British Journal of Psychology* 25:29–41.

Rogers, George L. 1987. Four cases of pitch-specific chromesthesia in trained musicians with absolute pitch. *Psychology of Music* 15:198–207.

Rubenstein, Herbert, Lonnie Garfield, and Jane A. Millikan. 1970. Homographic entries in the internal lexicon. *Journal of Verbal Learning and Verbal Behavior* 9:487–494.

Sachs, Georg T. L. 1812. *Historiae naturalis duorum leucaetiopum: Auctoris ipsius et sororis eius.* Erlangen. <http://mdz10.bib-bvb.de/~db/0001/bsb00012567/images/>.

Sagiv, Noam, Julia Simner, J. Collins, Brian Butterworth, and Jamie Ward. 2006. What is the relationship between synaesthesia and visuo-spatial number forms? *Cognition* 101: 114–128.

Simner, Julia. 2007. Beyond perception: Synaesthesia as a psycholinguistic phenomenon. *Trends in Cognitive Science* 11:23–29.

——. 2009. Synaesthetic visuo-spatial forms: Viewing sequences in space. *Cortex* 45:138–1147.

——. 2011. Lexical-gustatory synesthesia and food- and diet-related behavior. In *Handbook of Behavior, Diet and Nutrition*, ed. Victor R. Preedy, 1397–1408. Berlin: Springer.

——. 2012. Defining synaesthesia. *British Journal of Psychology* 103:1–15.

Simner, Julia, Sarah L. Bates, Becky G. Wood, and Jamie Ward. 2013. Multisensory tools rehabilitate taste function. Manuscript under review.

Simner, Julia, Oliver Gartner, and Michelle D. Taylor. 2011. Cross-modal personality attributions in synaesthetes and non-synaesthetes. *Journal of Neuropsychology* 5:283–301.

Simner, Julia, Louise Glover, and Alice Mowat. 2006. Linguistic determinants of word colouring in grapheme-colour synaesthesia, *Cortex* 42:281–289.

Simner, Julia, and Sarah L. Haywood. 2009. Tasty non-words and neighbours: The cognitive roots of lexical-gustatory synaesthesia. *Cognition* 110:171–181.

Simner, Julia, and Emma Holenstein. 2007. Ordinal linguistic personification: The systematic attribution of animate qualities to the linguistic units of ordinal sequences. *Journal of Cognitive Neuroscience* 19:694–703.

Simner, Julia, and Edward M. Hubbard. 2006. Variants of synesthesia interact in cognitive tasks: Evidence for implicit associations and late connectivity in cross-talk theories. *Neuroscience* 143:805–814.

Simner, Julia and Vera U. Ludwig. 2012. The colour of touch: A case of tactile-visual synaesthesia. *Neurocase* 18:167–180.

Simner Julia, Catherine Mulvenna, Noam Sagiv, Elias Tsakanikos, S. Athene Witherby, Christine Fraser, Kirsten Scott, and Jamie Ward. 2006. Synaesthesia: The prevalence of atypical cross-modal experiences. *Perception* 35:1024–1033.

Simner Julia, and Jamie Ward. 2006. The taste of words on the tip of the tongue. *Nature* 444 (7118):438.

——. 2008. Synaesthesia, color terms, and color space: Color claims came from color names in Beeli, Esslen, and Jäncke 2007. *Psychological Science* 19:412–414.

Simner, Julia, Jamie Ward, Monika Lanz, Ashok Jansari, Kris Noonan, Louise Glover, and David A. Oakley, 2005. Non-random associations of graphemes to colours in synaesthetic and non-synaesthetic populations. *Cognitive Neuropsychology* 22:1069–1085.

Smilek, Daniel, Jonathan S. A. Carriere, Michael J. Dixon, and Philip M. Merikle. 2007. Grapheme frequency and color luminance in grapheme-color synaesthesia. *Psychological Science* 18:793–795.

Smilek, Daniel, Kelly A. Malcolmson, Jonathan S. A. Carriere, Meghan Eller, Donna Kwan, and Michael Reynolds. 2007. When '3' is a jerk and 'T' is a king: Personifying inanimate objects in synaesthesia. *Journal of Cognitive Neuroscience* 19:981–992.

Sobczak-Edmans, Monika, and Noam Sagiv. 2013. Synesthetic personification: The social world of graphemes. In *The Oxford Handbook of Synesthesia*, ed. Julia Simner and Edward M. Hubbard, 222–238 . Oxford: Oxford University Press.

Ward, Jamie, Michael J. Banissy, and Clare N. Jonas. 2008. Haptic perception and synaesthesia. In *Human Haptic Perception*, ed. Martin Grunewald, 259–265. Basel: Springer Publishers.

Ward, Jamie, Brett Huckstep, and Elias Tsakanikos. 2006. Sound-colour synaesthesia: To what extent does it use cross-modal mechanisms common to us all? *Cortex* 42:264–280.

Ward Jamie, Elias Tsakanikos, and Alice Bray. 2006. Synaesthesia for reading and playing musical notes. *Neurocase* 12:27–34.

Ward, Jamie, and Julia Simner. 2003. Lexical-gustatory synaesthesia: linguistic and conceptual factors. *Cognition* 89:237–261.

Ward, Jamie, Julia Simner, and Vivien Auyeung. 2005. A comparison of lexical-gustatory and grapheme-colour synaesthesia. *Cognitive Neuropsychology* 22:28–41.

Watson, Marcus R., Kathleen A. Akins, and James T. Enns. 2012. *Psychonomic Bulletin and Review* 19:211–217.

Whitchurch, Anna K. 1922. Synaesthesia in a child of three and a half years. *American Journal of Psychology* 33:302–303.

Witthoft, Nathan, and Jonathan Winawer. 2006. Synesthetic colors determined by having colored refrigerator magnets in childhood. *Cortex* 42:175–183.

Zigler, Michael J. 1930. Tone shapes: A novel type of synaesthesia. *Journal of General Psychology* 3:277–286.

CHAPTER 9

COLORED ALPHABETS IN BILINGUAL SYNESTHETES

ALEKSANDRA MROCZKO-WĄSOWICZ AND
DANKO NIKOLIĆ

INTRODUCTION

In this chapter, we explore how grapheme-color synesthesia might be expressed in second languages. Grapheme-color synesthesia is one of the most common forms of synesthesia. In this, the triggers (or "inducers") for synesthetic colors are the linguistic symbols known as graphemes (the smallest distinct entities of the written language). These graphemes might trigger colors whether or not they are read from text or heard from speech (or even if they are merely thought about).[1] Graphemes are a more common type of a synesthetic inducer than phonemes, and grapheme-color synesthesia can be triggered by letters and numerals, and less often by punctuations, Braille signs, or musical notation. According to Ward and Cytowic (2010), phonemes are inducers in only about 10% of the cases of all forms of synesthesia, while graphemes are responsible for about 68% of cases.

In early research, synesthesia was considered as being merely a linguistic metaphor or a learned association. However, later investigations provided a more accurate picture. Evidence indicated that the neural representations of synesthetic colors

---

[1] An alternative form of synesthesia is phoneme-color synesthesia in which the colors are triggered by phonemes (the smallest distinct entities of spoken language) (Henderson 1985; Simner 2006). It is possible to distinguish between grapheme-color synesthesia and phoneme-color synesthesia by considering the extent to which the synesthetic color is related to the spelling of the word. For example, if a synesthete experiences a different synesthetic color when hearing the /s/ sound in the words "site" and "cite," it is clear that the color is linked to the spelling, and thus, this would be grapheme-color synesthesia. Alternatively, if the synesthete experiences the same synesthetic color when they hear the /s/ sound, whether this is the word "site" or "cite," it is clear that the color is independent of the spelling and related only to the sound; in this case, we have phoneme-color synesthesia.

resemble those activated during color vision under standard perceptual conditions: specifically, functional magnetic resonance imaging studies detected activation in areas V4/V8 during synesthetic experiences (Hubbard et al. 2005; Nunn et al. 2002; Sperling et al. 2006; but see Van Leeuwen et al. 2010 for a discussion). Furthermore, psychophysics experiments indicated that these experiences have color opponent properties (Nikolić, Lichti, and Singer 2007), just like veridical colors. Both of these pieces of evidence suggest the involvement of neurons responsible for color perception. Interference between the color of the ink and the synesthetic color can be seen in Stroop-type tests, which suggested that synesthetic associations are uncontrollable (Mattingley et al. 2001; Mroczko et al. 2009; Nikolić, Lichti, and Singer 2007; Odgaard, Flowers, and Bradman 1999; Smilek and Dixon 2002). In a synesthetic Stroop task, grapheme-color synesthetes must name the font-color of presented graphemes (e.g., the letter A in the font-color red) while ignoring their synesthetic colors. Such tasks show that synesthetes are slower to respond when the font color clashes with the synesthetic color (e.g., when required to name red font coloring for letters that are synesthetically green). This type of interference in speeded tasks suggests that synesthetic associations are automatically elicited and cannot easily be suppressed.

Synesthetic associations remain consistent throughout the lifetime (Baron-Cohen, Wyke, and Binnie 1987), whereas non-synesthetes trained with letter-color associations can lose up to 70% of the consistency after only a week (Ward and Cytowic 2010). Hence, long-term stability of synesthetic associations seems to be the best available test for the authenticity of synesthesia. The Stroop test is commonly used too, but has less diagnostic capability as it only provides evidence of the existence of an involuntary association, but does not offer any information of whether this association reflects synesthesia or another mental phenomenon (e.g., rehearsed learning). The majority of associations detected by a Stroop test are not synesthetic. For example, a learned link between the shape of a smiley face with its yellow color will produce a Stroop effect although this association is unrelated to synesthesia (Nikolić, Lichti, and Singer 2007).

Here, we review known evidence about the interaction between synesthesia and the acquisition of a second language. We will show that synesthetic colors can pass from the primary language to the secondary language. Our discussion relates to cases in which a second language is learned later in life than the primary language. It seems that cross-linguistic transfer may be specific to such situations, because those who are bilingual from birth may not have a distinction between a "primary" language, which serves as a source for transfer, and a "secondary" language, which builds on that base. Research on bilingual people has uncovered distinct representations in the brain for a mother tongue and for a later-acquired foreign language (Paivio and Lambert 1981; Smith 1991). It is thus interesting to know whether these differences have implications for synesthesia associated with the writing systems of these different languages.

Cross-Linguistic Transfer When Learning a Second Language

Studies have shown that English-speaking synesthetes can also experience synesthesia for the graphemes of scripts that do not use the Latin alphabet, and which are learned later in life (Mills, Boteler, and Oliver 2002; Rich, Bradshaw, and Mattingley 2005; Witthoft and Winawer 2006). This phenomenon might be thought of as a cross-linguistic transfer from a first language to a second language (Simner 2007). According to the "scaffolding" hypothesis of Simner (2007), synesthetic colors from a second language may be mapped onto the existing colors of the first language.

For example, Witthoft and Winawer (2006) described a case of an American girl with grapheme-color synesthesia, who moved to Russia at the age of three. In the US, she first associated Latin letters to colors from a set of colored refrigerator magnets. Later, while learning the Cyrillic alphabet, she experienced synesthetic colors too, which were evidently transferred from her Latin letters. The transfer was based largely on the visual resemblance across alphabets, e.g., similarly looking English "N" and Cyrillic "И" were associated to the same shade of red. In cases where a Cyrillic grapheme did not bear a visual resemblance to a Latin grapheme, phonetic similarity became the basis on which colors were transferred. For example, English "F" and Cyrillic "Ф" (pronounced /f/) were both violet. Other evidence indicated that visual similarity was a stronger cue for the transfer of color than was phonetic similarity: visual counterparts in the two alphabets correlated positively in both hue and saturation of their colors, while phonetic equivalents shared only the hue (Witthoft and Winawer 2006).

A similar case, reported by Rich, Bradshaw, and Mattingley (2005), was of an English–Greek bilingual who acquired Greek as a second language after puberty. Her synesthetic colors elicited by Greek symbols were related to the shapes and sounds of Latin letters. Much like in the case in Witthoft and Winawer (2006), shape similarity took precedence over phonetic similarity. Lowercase Greek letters, which are more similar in shape to Latin letters (compared to uppercase Greek letters), often evoked the same synesthetic colors across languages, even if their Greek counterparts were pronounced differently. For example, "β" is pronounced similar to "V" in English, but triggers the brown-like color of her Latin "B" rather than the gray of her "V." Greek letters that did not bear any visual resemblance to Latin letters elicited colors that were determined by similarity in pronunciation. For example, the letter "ψ," which is pronounced as /psi/ ("psee"), elicits an experience of a pink, the same color associated to the letter "P" in the Latin alphabet.

In a similar fashion, Mills, Boteler, and Oliver (2002) studied in detail a native English-speaking multilingual synesthete who was also a college professor of the Russian language, which she started learning in high school. Her colors for Cyrillic letters appeared to be adopted from their visual and phonetic equivalents in the Latin alphabet. Her

Cyrillic and Latin letter-color pairings became permanently acquired. In the study by Mills and colleagues, this synesthete performed a Stroop-type task, in which she had to name the print color of letters printed either congruently with her synesthetic colors (e.g., in red print, for a letter that is synesthetically red) or incongruently (e.g., the same letter printed in green). This type of "synesthetic Stroop" is used to show that synesthetic colors are automatically generated since they can slow naming times where real and synesthetic colors clash (i.e., in the incongruent condition). In her Stroop task, irrespective of whether the synesthete had to name the print color of the Latin or Cyrillic letter, the synesthete's naming times were approximately the same. This task provided evidence that cross-linguistic equivalents evoke identical colors, which interfere with naming print colors in the same way. Also, the consistency of responses over a period of 2.5 to 5 years indicated that her synesthesia for Cyrillic letters was almost as vivid and stable as it was for Latin letters.

Steven and Blakemore (2004) studied idiopathic synesthesia in six late-blind synesthetes who had been without normal vision for over 10 years. Prior to the impairment of vision, all of them had experienced spatially patterned colored hearing for letters, numbers, and time-related words such as days of the week and months. They perceived these colors when hearing or even thinking about the inducers, and had these experiences for as long as they could remember. The authors showed that these experiences were highly consistent over a period of 2 months. Five subjects had been using Braille for more than 40 years, i.e., since the age of primary school, but only one of these five individuals had developed full colored-Braille synesthesia. For him, Braille characters that were similar in shape evoked similar colors; we describe this case next.

This synesthete was reported to see Braille characters as colored dots either while touching them or just from thinking about touching them, i.e., by mentally simulating this action and reflecting on the corresponding sensation (see Mroczko-Wąsowicz and Werning 2012). These experiences were specific to tactile inputs forming Braille symbols, since other textures did not evoke synesthetic colors (e.g., object surfaces, or spatial dots arranged in shapes not related to Braille). Similarly, synesthesia was not triggered for Latin graphemes made up of Braille dots. Moreover, his Braille colors were generally determined by the spatial pattern of dots, and not by the specific meaning of a Braille character in any given context. To explain this, in Braille the same geometric arrangements of dots can have three different meanings: for example, the letter I, the number 9, and the musical note "A"-quaver. For this subject, the shape conveying these three different meanings triggered the same color irrespective of the meaning implied by any given context. Also, much like in grapheme-color synesthesia (Brang, Coulson, and Ramachandran 2011; Jürgens and Nikolić 2012; Watson, Akins, and Enns 2012), and as noted earlier, Braille characters that were similar in shape evoked similar synesthetic colors.

All these case studies show highly similar patterns of cross-linguistic transfer across different individuals. Hence, we can conclude that the described rules of transfer (e.g., the frequent priority of shape similarity over phonetic similarity) might be general and representative for synesthetes as a population. However, one limitation of such case

studies is that no insights are offered about the learning mechanisms that take place during the transfer of synesthesia. These learning mechanisms can probably be best investigated under the controlled conditions of a laboratory.

Cross-Linguistic Transfer in
Laboratory Conditions

One study that sheds light on the speed and effort with which such cross-linguistic
transfer can occur was done by Mroczko et al. (2009). We were interested in the amount
of practice required to adopt a novel inducer for an old synesthetic association. Hence,
we replicated in the laboratory the natural phenomenon of cross-linguistic transfer. We
introduced to monolingual grapheme-color synesthetes special graphemes with novel
shapes but without any corresponding sound. We assigned each new grapheme a meaning by linking it to existing Latin letters (and Arabic numerals) which triggered synesthesia for the synesthete. The main measure was of the time needed for the synesthesia
of one writing system to transfer to the novel graphemes of the second writing system.
It was unknown whether the transfer would require exposure to the new graphemes for
just a few minutes, or maybe for weeks, or even months.

The answer has implications for understanding the fundamental nature of synesthesia. One of the most important issues of the current debate on the phenomenon of synesthesia is about the nature of its associations. The question is whether novel synesthetic
associations can be explained by the creation of novel synaptic connections between
neurons representing the inducer and the concurrent—which might be referred to as a
"low-level" hypothesis. Alternatively, it might be that synesthetic associations occur at
a "higher," distributed level of organization, in which associations are formed in a more
elaborated ways than accounted for by simply direct synaptic connections. The high-
level hypothesis is closer to the level at which the semantic structure of knowledge operates—i.e., associations between conceptual contents rather than neurons—and where
attentional mechanisms, interpretation and context have a predominant role. The two
levels are also often referred to as perceptual and conceptual respectively, as it is often
assumed that perception is an earlier and hence, more rudimentary and automatic stage
of information processing than is the activation and processing of semantic information. The low-level hypothesis is frequently discussed together with the assumption that
there is a neuron coding for letter "A," in one brain area, and another neuron coding
for red color, in another brain area, and that in cases of grapheme-color synesthesia, a
direct physical connection is created from the "A"-neuron to the red-color neuron. As a
result, an activation of the former produces inevitable activation of the latter (Cytowic
and Wood 1982; Harrison and Baron-Cohen 1997; Ramachandran and Hubbard 2001b;
see also Grossenbacher and Lovelace 2001 for the alternative version that involves local
disinhibition). Discussion of the high-level hypothesis typically leaves unspecified the

nature of associations in terms of neuronal connectivity (individual neurons or some form of a widespread representation at the network level), but is instead concerned with the dynamics of the semantic organization of the human mind. It also states that synesthetic associations result as a consequence of the interpretation of the meaning that an inducer may have for a synesthete, and this may change dynamically depending on the context (Dixon et al. 2006; Mausfeld 2002; Rich and Mattingley 2003; Ward, Tsakanikos, and Bray 2006).

In our study on the transfer of synesthesia we reasoned that if synesthetic associations originate at the semantic level of representation, the transfer should occur quickly, requiring only a few minutes to learn the meaning of a new grapheme. Semantic associations are known to be learned quickly (Bloom 2000; Markson and Bloom 1997). But, if the synesthetic associations occur at the low, perceptual level, longer transfer times would be expected, because the system would have to undergo perceptual learning, which is a comparatively slower process (Goldstone 1998; Kami and Sagi 1993). Hence, the speed of transfer is indicative of the type of representation (high versus low level). We designed our study to distinguish between these two hypotheses.

Here, we tested native speakers of German with grapheme-color synesthesia. We aimed to induce a transfer of synesthetic colors from their native Latin alphabet to a set of never-seen-before Glagolitic graphemes (Franolić and Zagar 2008), which we introduced to them using a writing exercise in order to teach the orthography and the meaning of the graphemes—i.e., the semantic correspondence between a new Glagolitic grapheme and a familiar Latin/Arabic one. No sounds associated with the graphemes were presented in the study. Glagolitsa is an ancient Eastern European alphabet and numbering system that was ideal for our study, because German subjects would be completely unfamiliar with this alphabet prior to the writing exercise. Furthermore, Glagolitsa has the required exotic appearance, as only few letters bear any resemblance to other known graphemes (see Figure 9.1).

In total, 16 synesthetes were trained under laboratory conditions to use the Glagolitic alphabet. The training was implemented as a short writing exercise that consisted of two phases. In the first phase the subjects learned how to write a Glagolitic grapheme and in the second phase the subjects were asked to write a list of 20 German words or number

FIGURE 9.1 The correspondence between the graphemes of Latin and square Glagolitic alphabets.

sequences while substituting one Latin/Arabic grapheme with its Glagolitic counterpart. The entire procedure lasted less than 10 minutes. As predicted by the semantic hypothesis, immediately after learning the meaning of a new grapheme, most of our subjects (88%) reported experiencing synesthetic colors associated to this grapheme. The associated colors were, in all cases, identical to those linked previously to the corresponding Latin/Arabic graphemes. Furthermore, Stroop-type tests (Nikolić, Lichti, and Singer 2007; Odgaard, Flowers and Bradman 1999) indicated that these associations had become automaticized. Moreover, we also found that synesthetic associations transferred to Glagolitsa even when presented in the handwriting of the experimenter. Thus, not only did the Glagolitic letters written by the subject induce perceptions of colors but this also happened equally well when handwritten by another person. This indicates that subjects learned a category of stimuli rather than only individual exemplars, or particular motor coordinates.

Overall, we concluded that our results support the "high-level" hypothesis of synesthetic associations. That is, synesthetic associations are induced by the conceptual content related to a grapheme. We came to this conclusion on two bases. First, the transfer time to the new grapheme was fast, which is consistent with the speed with which the meaning of a new symbol can be learned (a single trial; Bloom 2000; Markson and Bloom 1997). In contrast, low-level perceptual learning requires typically thousands of trials (Ahissar and Hochstein 1997; Ball and Sekuler 1981; Seitz and Watanabe 2005). Second, the association generalized to the exemplars never seen before, which is consistent with learning of a semantic category and is inconsistent with specific perceptual learning (for a different view see Bayne 2009 where recognizing that something belongs to a certain category, kind, or type is considered as a property of high-level perception). Thus, the newly created synesthetic associations to Glagolitic letters must have been induced via existing synesthetic color-associations linked to conceptual contents represented by Latin letters. In other words, after training, a Glagolitic letter would activate the same semantic content that is normally activated by a Latin letter. This feature has to be first conceptually recognized by the synesthete (Simner 2007) for the concurrent phenomenal aspect to be included into an overall unified synesthetic experience (Mroczko-Wąsowicz 2011).

Hence, synesthesia may be a phenomenon in which concepts become associated with perceptual experiences, so called *ideaesthesia* (Jürgens and Nikolić 2012; Nikolić 2009; Nikolić et al. 2011; Rothen et al. 2012). In the most common variant of such a conceptual synesthesia, namely grapheme-color synesthesia, the color is associated to a letter by its similarity to other letters, i.e., letters of similar shapes tend to elicit similar colors. The formation of novel associations between graphemes and colors, created within minutes, is too rapid to be accounted for by low-level sensory cross-wiring between grapheme and color brain areas. Additionally, the dimensions of similarity used to create these associations are more abstract than what would be expected from elementary features processed in the grapheme area. Therefore, a better explanation seems to be provided by high-level conceptual mechanisms guiding the creation and assignment of synesthetic concurrents (Jürgens and Nikolić 2012).

Finally, our results suggest that in natural cases of cross-language transfer, too, the synesthetic associations to new graphemes are likely to be established quickly, possibly even during the first encounter of the new alphabet. In other words, synesthetic associations do not seem to be created from scratch but are instead inherited from existing associations, the original colors being passively adopted from the original synesthesia. As mentioned earlier, not all of the synesthetes tested in our study on cross-linguistic transfer (Mroczko et al. 2009) reported experiencing color associations for the novel characters. Nonetheless, the subjects who did not report associations subjectively still showed the same Stroop effect. One can speculate on the reasons for this difference in subjective experiences. Although all subjects were given equal amount of practice, it may well be that, for some individuals, the given time and effort was not enough to create new synesthetic associations sufficiently strong to be consciously experienced. Thus, it is possible that some subjects would confirm the acquisition of novel synesthetic associations subjectively only after additional training.

WHAT DETERMINES THE TRANSFER?

Not every synesthete will transfer synesthesia to a new language. For example, in our study two subjects reported not seeing colors when presented with Glagolitic graphemes. Similarly, not every multilingual synesthete has synesthesia for all languages and writing systems (Ramachandran and Hubbard 2003; Rich, Bradshaw, and Mattingley 2005). Whether a transfer will take place or not may depend on different factors. Rich, Bradshaw, and Mattingley (2005) reported a tendency for cross-linguistic transfer to occur more often if a person is fluent in the second language (88% for fluent versus 73% for non-fluent). Still, the fluency in a second language does not guarantee a transfer. Furthermore, the cross-linguistic transfer is not the only way to acquire a new synesthetic association. Some monolingual synesthetes perceive colors for completely unfamiliar writing systems. In the results recently presented by Hung, Simner, and Shillcock (2009) as well as Jürgens and Nikolić (2012) synesthetic associations were acquired quickly—even immediately—for newly seen graphemes.

THE RULES AND IDIOSYNCRASIES FOR THE SELECTION OF GRAPHEME-COLOR PAIRINGS IN SYNESTHESIA

It is important to know whether synesthetic associations are completely random or whether some rules can be established. On the surface at least, each synesthete appears to have his/her own individual associations. This means that the synesthetic colors of any two randomly chosen grapheme-color synesthetes most likely do not match. This normally happens even if the synesthetes are family members or twins (Cytowic 2002; Grossenbacher and Lovelace 2001; Rich, Bradshaw, and Mattingley 2005). Nonetheless, certain regularities between synesthetic associations have been detected. Studies examining large numbers of grapheme-color synesthetes reveal that they may share some noteworthy tendencies to associate particular letters with specific colors; e.g., "A" is likely red, "B" tends to be blue, and "C" has a propensity to be yellow (Baron-Cohen et al. 1993; Day 2005; Marks 1975; Ramachandran and Hubbard 2003; Rich, Bradshaw, and Mattingley 2005; Simner et al. 2005). Beeli, Esslen, and Jäncke (2007) presented a statistical analysis of synesthetic colors reported by 16 subjects for all Latin letters and Arabic numerals. Distributions of colors were not random but varied systematically across different graphemes. The variations were to some extent explained by the frequencies of use of the letters. More recently, evidence has accumulated showing that graphemes of similar shapes tend to induce similar colors (Brang, Coulson, and Ramachandran 2011; Jürgens and Nikolić 2012; Watson, Akins, and Enns 2012). At the same time, however, color associations are to a large degree individual. Flournoy (1893) investigated 250 synesthetes for similarities in their "chosen" colors. He found that only two of them experienced identical colors and only for vowels "A," "E," "I," "O," and "U." These two synesthetic individuals happened to be siblings. Hence, although synesthetic associations are generally idiosyncratic, apparently, sometimes young synesthetes who interact during the acquisition of associations (i.e., most likely siblings) may influence each other's associations (Cytowic 2002; Rich, Bradshaw, and Mattingley 2005). It is unclear whether these individuals had a shared model for synesthetic associations (e.g., a book with colored letters) or whether one child suggested to the other the color that a given letter should be associated to.

By gathering statistics of letter-color preferences from 70 synesthetes, Simner et al. (2005) determined a "prototypical model" of a synesthetic alphabet, which showed which colors were most likely to be associated with which letters. In that alphabet some letters have a single color significantly associated with them: red "A," white "I" and "O," black "X" and "Z," gray "L," brown "N," and violet "V." Other letters are shown as having two or three colors because they each had more than one significant color tendency across synesthetes. Interestingly, the letter "K" had no significant tendency, at least in that study. Given their data, among English speaking synesthetes this letter could apparently take almost any color with about equal likelihood.

In addition, Simner and colleagues (2005) found several linguistic rules that determine the assignment of synesthetic colors in Latin alphabet: (1) frequent graphemes associated with frequent color words (e.g., more frequent "a" is red, whereas less frequent "v" is purple); (2) synesthetic letter-color associations reflect first-letter priming (e.g., "r" tends to be red and "g" tends to be green); (3) frequent letters correspond to colors occurring early in the Berlin and Kay's (1969) typology of color terms across languages (see also Simner, Chapter 8, this volume). This typology describes the fact that black and white are the most common colors across language systems, followed by red, yellow, green, blue, and brown (equal frequency), orange, violet, gray, and pink. Simner et al. (2005) found that this ordering tended to map onto graphemes from high to low frequency, at least in the synesthetes tested in that study.

Currently, it is unclear to what degree grapheme-color associations can be imposed from the environment, i.e., how susceptible synesthetic children are towards internalizing pairings suggested in color books, for example, or other educational toys. Witthoft and Winawer (2006) reported a case of a synesthete for whom refrigerator magnets served as the model for the grapheme-color pairings. Other similar cases have been reported too (Hancock 2006; Smilek, Dixon, and Merikle 2005; Ward and Mattingley 2006). However, this mode of synesthesia acquisition may be the exception rather than the rule. For most synesthetes, no such environmental sources can be found. For example, the Gattegno's learning system of colored letters (and sounds that are associated with them) is often used by teachers to teach children the alphabet (Gattegno 1962, 1963). If all grapheme-color synesthetes developed their colors on the basis of such a colored alphabet, synesthetes from the same generation should have the same or very similar associations. Rich, Bradshaw, and Mattingley (2005) shed light on this issue in an interesting study that analyzed the relation between environmental learning systems and synesthesias in Australia, using an extensive survey. The researchers compared letter-color combinations used in Australian alphabet schoolbooks between 1900 and 1989 with the color associations reported by 150 grapheme-color synesthetes born between 1914 and 1986. No clear dependencies were found. Only one individual had synesthetic colors consistent with those in an alphabet book. This indicates that suggestions from the environment have very little influence on the attribution of synesthetic associations.

Overall, evidence suggests that the selection of graphemic and chromatic pairings in synesthetic associations is based on a process that is driven partly by internal cognitive rules. Also, there is not one but a number of rules a synesthete might follow, and, at each particular learning instance, the synesthete may happen to follow any of them. Some combinations may appear random, but these can be also based on an ad hoc rule, used only once (i.e., to establish only one inducer-concurrent association).

SYNESTHESIA AND THE SUCCESS IN LANGUAGE LEARNING

One important question is whether synesthesia sometimes helps or distracts in the learning of a new language. The answer seems to depend on various factors such as whether different languages use the same alphabet, whether graphemes are assigned to phonemes in the same way (phonemic versus morpho-phonemic alphabets), and whether the inducers in synesthesia are primarily graphemes or phonemes. In short, if the rules by which synesthetic associations are established in the first language can also be used in the second language, synesthesia is likely to facilitate acquisition of the new language. Otherwise, synesthesia may produce confusion and hence interfere with the language learning.

Synesthesia can help learn a language-related skill

Learning a second language involves not only learning new vocabulary but also a different spelling system, and the acquisition of unfamiliar pronunciation and intonation. Dittmar (2007) suggested that synesthetic letter-color associations may sometimes be used to learn pronunciation and intonation in a foreign language. She supported this point by describing a case of a multilingual synesthete for whom hearing a foreign language produces experiences of specific colored three-dimensional shapes. These additional experiences helped the subject to improve her pronunciation in a new language. According to the self-report, her synesthesia enabled her to produce proper pronunciation and intonation in the second language, if she focused on how the speech sounds ought to *look*, in a synesthetic sense. This made it possible for her to sound like a native speaker. Hence, thanks to synesthesia she was able to hide her accent, even in foreign languages that she only began learning recently.

Synesthesia may help also in learning correct spelling. Galton (1883) described a case of a synesthete who learned how to spell correctly based on the synesthetic color induced by the entire word, as a result of the combination of the colors of individual letters. If the nuance of the color of the word was right, the spelling of the word was also correct. Likewise, synesthesia has been reported to improve typing speed. Day (2005) described a grapheme-color synesthete who substituted the letters on the computer keyboard with his synesthetic colors. That way, he was much faster finding the needed keys and thus, typed faster.

Synesthesia can also cause difficulties in learning foreign languages

If synesthesia is used to develop learning strategies that are not flexible, the acquisition of a foreign language may become more difficult than it would be without synesthesia. For example, an important issue is whether the inducer is a grapheme or a phoneme (Simner 2007). In French, the English sound "o" may be written with different letters or combinations of letters, such as "o," "au," "eau," or "ot." The color experience associated with the sound "o" will not help a phoneme-color synesthete to learn the appropriate spellings in French, but may instead produce confusion if the person is used to rely on synesthesia for ensuring correct spelling.

Mills et al. (2002) described a native English speaker and a multilingual synesthete who perceives colors for both graphemes and phonemes and who reported significant difficulties in learning French. Although French uses the same Latin alphabet that she learned in her native English, the way sounds were built from the combinations of letters was considerably different across the two languages, which caused difficulties. Learning Russian was much easier to her even though this language employs a different writing system than her native language. The advantage of Russian was that each phoneme has one Cyrillic letter, a property that fitted well within the framework of her synesthesia. Interestingly, when she later learned another Slavic language, Polish, which sounds similar to Russian but is written in Latin, she experienced this as a disorientating situation, comparable to when learning French.

A unique case of difficulty in language learning arose in the case of German grapheme-color and word-color synesthetes when the German government reformed spelling rules in 1996, and then again made minor changes in 2006. Synesthetes found themselves needing to reorganize their synesthesias in accordance to the new rules. For example, the word "einbleuen" changed to "einbläuen," and the word "daß" into "dass." As would be expected, these changes were not always easily accepted by synesthetes (Dittmar 2007) and may have led to extra difficulties in spelling and reading.

CONCLUSIONS

The main issue of this chapter, namely the interaction between synesthesia and the acquisition of a second language, was examined from different perspectives. We have described how, despite differences in the way that different languages may be represented in the brain (shown from psycholinguistic studies on bilinguals), synesthetic experiences can come to be associated with the writing systems of both languages. Multilingual synesthetes commonly acquire graphemic-chromatic associations for all writing systems that they use. We then discussed the mechanisms by which colors become linked to graphemes, and the consequences that synesthesia may have for language-related skills, including cases in which it accelerates or impedes the learning of a second language.

We have shown that the graphemes of a second language usually inherit colors from the first language, a phenomenon known as cross-linguistic transfer. The two most universally used rules relate to the similarity in shapes across the alphabets and their phonetic similarity. Interestingly, as many studies suggest, shape resemblance takes priority over phonetic match. In controlled laboratory conditions it could be demonstrated that this type of transfer of colors from one writing system to another can be made quickly, within minutes.

When colors are newly created, i.e., without a model from another writing system, other rules may apply, relating to the shapes of graphemes: graphemes of similar shapes get similar colors. Other sources for the particular letter-color pairings found in synesthetes sometimes come from the environment, in the form of an alphabet book or an educational toy with colored letters, whose colors are then adopted by synesthetes. Nonetheless, this external way of acquiring synesthesia seems to be relatively rare in comparison to the application of internal rules, as most synesthetes do not seem to use such environmental models for creating their associations.

Whether synesthesia enhances or distracts the learning of a new language may depend on numerous factors, such as whether the native and the foreign language use the same alphabet, whether graphemes are assigned to phonemes unambiguously, and whether the core synesthetic inducers are graphemes or phonemes. Synesthesia has the tendency to facilitate the acquisition of a new language if the rules by which letter-coloring is established in the first language match those in the second language. If there is a discrepancy, synesthesia may generate confusion and may hence slow down the learning process.

REFERENCES

Ahissar, Merav, and Shaul Hochstein. 1997. Task difficulty and the specificity of perceptual learning. *Nature* 387:401–406.

Ball, Karlene, and Robert Sekuler. 1981. Adaptive processing of visual motion. *Journal of Experimental Psychology: Human Perception and Performance* 7:780–794.

Baron-Cohen, Simon, John Harrison, Laura H. Goldstein, and Maria Wyke. 1993. Coloured speech perception: Is synaesthesia what happens when modularity breaks down? *Perception* 22:419–426.

Baron-Cohen, Simon, Maria A. Wyke, and Colin Binnie. 1987. Hearing words and seeing colors: An experimental investigation of a case of synesthesia. *Perception* 16:761–767.

Bayne, Tim. 2009. Perception and the reach of phenomenal content. *Philosophical Quarterly*, 59(236):385–404.

Beeli, Gian, Michaela Esslen, and Lutz Jäncke. 2007. Frequency correlates in grapheme-color synaesthesia. *Psychological Science* 18:788–792.

Berlin, Brent and Paul Kay. 1969. *Basic Color Terms: Their Universality and Evolution* Berkeley, CA: University of California Press.

Bloom, Paul. 2000. *How Children Learn the Meanings of Words.* Cambridge, MA: MIT Press.

Brang, David, Seana Coulson, and Vilayanur S. Ramachandran. 2011. Similarly shaped letters evoke similar colors in grapheme-color synesthesia. *Neuropsychologia* 49:1355–1358.

Cytowic, Richard E., and Frank B. Wood. 1982. Synesthesia: I. A review of major theories and their brain basis. *Brain Cognition* 1:23–35.

Cytowic, Richard E. 2002. *Synesthesia: A Union of the Senses.* Cambridge, MA: MIT Press, 2002.

Day, Sean. 2005. Some demographic and socio-cultural aspects of synesthesia. In *Synesthesia: Perspectives from Cognitive Neuroscience*, ed. Lynn C. Robertson and Noam Sagiv, 11–33. Oxford: Oxford University Press.

Dittmar, Alexandra, ed. 2007. *Synästhesien. Roter Faden durchs Leben?* Essen: Verlag Die blaue Eule.

Dixon, Mike J., Daniel Smilek, Patricia L. Duffy, Mark P. Zanna, and Philip M. Merikle. 2006. The role of meaning in grapheme-colour synaesthesia. *Cortex*, 42:243–252.

Flournoy, Théodore. 1893. *Des phénomènes de synopsie.* Paris: Félix Alcan.

Franolić, Branko, and Mateo Zagar. 2008. *A Historical Outline of Literary Croatian and the Glagolitic Heritage of Croatian Culture.* London and Zagreb: Erasmus and CSYPN.

Galton, Francis. 1883. *Inquiries into Human Faculty and its Development.* London: Macmillan.

Gattegno, Caleb. 1962. *Words in Color*. Chicago, IL: Learning materials.

——. 1963. *Teaching Foreign Languages in Schools: The Silent Way*. Reading, UK: Educational Explorers.

Goldstone, Robert L. 1998. Perceptual learning. *Annual Review of Psychology* 49:585–612.

Grossenbacher, Peter G., and Christopher T. Lovelace. 2001. Mechanisms of synesthesia: Cognitive and physiological constraints. *Trends in Cognitive Sciences* 5:36–41.

Hancock, Peter. 2006. Monozygotic twins' colour-number association: A case study. *Cortex* 42:147–150.

Harrison, John E., and Simon Baron-Cohen. 1997. Synaesthesia: A review of psychological theories. In *Synaesthesia. Classic and Contemporary Readings*, ed. Simon Baron-Cohen and John E. Harrison, 109–122. Cambridge: Blackwell.

Hubbard, Edward M., A. Cyrus Arman, Vilayanur S. Ramachandran, and Geoffrey M. Boynton. 2005. Individual differences among grapheme-color synesthetes: Brain-behavior correlations. *Neuron* 45:975–985.

Hung, Wan-Yu, Simner, Julia, and Richard Shillcock. 2009. Immediate acquisition of new synaesthetic associations. Presentation at the *Third International Congress on Synaesthesia, Science and Art*. Granada, Spain, 26–29 April.

Jürgens, Uta M. and Danko Nikolić. 2012. Ideaesthesia: Conceptual processes assign similar colours to similar shapes. *Translational Neuroscience* 3 (1):22–27.

Kami, Avi, and Dov Sagi. 1993. The time course of learning a visual skill. *Nature* 365:250–252.

Marks, Lawrence E. 1975. On coloured-hearing synaesthesia. *Psychological Bulletin* 82 (3):303–331.

Markson, Lori, and Paul Bloom. 1997. Evidence against a dedicated system for word-learning in children. *Nature* 385:813–815.

Mattingley, Jason B., Anina N. Rich, Greg Yelland, and John L. Bradshaw. 2001. Unconscious priming eliminates automatic binding of colour and alphanumeric form in synaesthesia. *Nature* 410:580–582.

Mausfeld Rainer 2002. The physicalistic trap in perception theory. In *Perception and the Physical World*, ed. Dieter Heyer and Rainer Mausfeld, 75–112. Chichester, UK: Wiley.

Mills, Carol B., Meredith L. Viguers, Shari K. Edelson, Amanda T. Thomas, Stephanie L. Simon-Dack, and Joanne A. Innis. 2002. The color of two alphabets for a multilingual synesthete. *Perception* 31:1371–1394. doi:10.1068/p3429.

Mroczko-Wąsowicz, Aleksandra. 2011. The Unity of Consciousness and the Phenomenon of Synesthesia [Die Einheit des Bewusstseins und das Phänomen der Synästhesie]. Doctoral dissertation, Johannes Gutenberg University of Mainz.

Mroczko, Aleksandra, Thomas Metzinger, Wolf Singer, and Danko Nikolić. 2009. Immediate transfer of synesthesia to a novel inducer. *Journal of Vision* 9 (12):1–8.

Mroczko-Wąsowicz, Aleksandra, and Markus Werning. 2012. Synesthesia, sensory-motor contingency, and semantic emulation: how swimming style-color synesthesia challenges the traditional view of synesthesia. *Frontiers in Psychology* 3(279): 1–12. doi.10.3389/fpsyg.2012.00279.

Nikolić, Danko. 2009. Is synaesthesia actually ideaesthesia? An inquiry into the nature of the phenomenon. In *Proceedings of the Third International Congress on Synaesthesia, Science and Art*. Granada: Spain, 26–29 April.

Nikolić, Danko, Philipp Lichti, and Wolf Singer. 2007. Color opponency in synaesthetic experiences. *Psychological Science* 18 (6):481–486.

Nikolić, Danko, Uta M. Jürgens, Nicolas Rothen, Beat Meier, and Aleksandra Mroczko, A. 2011. Swimming-style synesthesia. *Cortex* 47 (7):874–879.

Nunn, J. A., L. J. Gregory, M. J. Brammer, S. C. R. Williams, D. M. Parslow, M. J. Morgan, R. G. Morris, E. T. Bullmore, S. Baron-Cohen, and J. A. Gray. 2002. Functional magnetic resonance imaging of synesthesia: Activation of V4/V8 by spoken words. *Nature Neuroscience* 5 (4):371–375.

Odgaard, Eric C., John H. Flowers, and H. Lynn Bradman. 1999. An investigation of the cognitive and perceptual dynamics of a colour-digit synaesthete. *Perception* 28:651–664.

Paivio, Allan, and Wallace Lambert. 1981. Dual coding and bilingual memory. *Journal of Verbal Learning and Verbal Behaviour* 200:532–539.

Ramachandran, Vilayanur S., and Edward M. Hubbard. 2001. Psychophysical investigations into the neural basis of synaesthesia. *Proceedings of the Royal Society B: Biological Sciences* 268:979–983.

——. 2003. The phenomenology of synaesthesia. *Journal of Consciousness Studies* 10 (8):49–57.

Rich, Anina N., John L. Bradshaw, and Jason B. Mattingley. 2005. A systematic, large-scale study of synaesthesia: Implications for the role of early experience in lexical-colour associations. *Cognition* 98 (1):53–84.

Rich, Anina N., and Jason B. Mattingley. 2003. The effects of stimulus competition and voluntary attention on colour-graphemic synaesthesia. *NeuroReport* 14 (14):1793–1798.

Rothen Nicolas, Danko Nikolić, Uta M. Jürgens, Aleksandra Mroczko-Wąsowicz, Josephine Cock, and Beat Meier. 2012. Psychophysiological evidence for the genuineness of swimming-style colour synaesthesia. *Consciousness and Cognition* 22 (1):35–46.

Seitz, Aaron, and Takeo Watanabe. 2005. A unified model for perceptual learning. *Trends in Cognitive Sciences* 9:329–334.

Simner, Julia. 2007. Beyond perception: Synaesthesia as a psycholinguistic phenomenon. *Trends in Cognitive Sciences* 11:23–29.

——. 2013. The 'rules' of synesthesia. In *The Oxford Handbook of Synesthesia*, ed. Julia Simner and Edward M. Hubbard, 149–164. Oxford: Oxford University Press.

Simner, Julia, Jamie Ward, Monika Lanz, Ashok Jansari, Krist Noonan, Louise Glover, and David A. Oakley. 2005. Non-random associations of graphemes to colours in synaesthetic and non-synaesthetic populations. *Cognitive Neuropsychology* 22 (8):1069–1085.

Smilek, Daniel, and Mike J. Dixon. 2002. Towards a synergistic understanding of synaesthesia. Combining current experimental findings with synaesthetes' subjective descriptions. *Psyche* 8 (1). <http://www.theassc.org/files/assc/2529.pdf>.

Smilek, Daniel, Mike J. Dixon, and Philip M. Merikle. 2005. Synaesthesia: Discordant male monozygotic twins. *Neurocase* 11:363–370.

Smith, Marilyn C. 1991. On the recruitment of semantic information for word fragment completion: Evidence from bilingual priming. *Journal of Experimental Psychology: Learning, Memory, and Cognition* 17:234–244.

Sperling, Julia M., David Prvulovic, David E. J. Linden, Wolf Singer, and Aglaja Stirn. 2006. Neuronal correlates of colour-graphemic synaesthesia: A fMRI study. *Cortex* 42 (2):295–303.

Steven, Megan. S., and Colin Blakemore. 2004. Visual synaesthesia in the blind. *Perception* 33:855–868.

Van Leeuwen, Tessa M., Karl M. Petersson, and Peter Hagoort. 2010. Synaesthetic colour in the brain: Beyond colour areas. A functional magnetic resonance imaging study of synaesthetes and matched controls. *PLoS ONE* 5(8):e12074.

Ward, Jamie, and Richard Cytowic. 2010. Synesthesia and language. In *Concise Encyclopedia of Brain and Language*, ed. Harry Whitaker, 495–500. Oxford: Elsevier.

Ward, Jamie, and Jason B. Mattingley. 2006. Synaesthesia: An overview of contemporary findings and controversies. *Cortex* 42:129–136.

Ward, Jamie, Elias Tsakanikos, and Alice Bray. 2006. Synaesthesia for reading and playing musical notes. *Neurocase* 12 (1):27–34.

Watson Marcus R., Kathleen A. Akins, James T. Enns. 2012. Second-order mappings in grapheme-color synesthesia. *Psychonomic Bulletin and Review* 19 (2):211–217.

Witthoft, Nathan, and Jonathan Winawer. 2006. Synesthetic colors determined by having colored refrigerator magnets in childhood. *Cortex* 42 (2):175–183.

CHAPTER 10

....

SYNESTHESIA, MEANING, AND MULTILINGUAL SPEAKERS

....

FIONA N. NEWELL

OVERVIEW

....

Although the topic of synesthesia has received a lot of attention in recent years, largely as a consequence of the significant contribution from brain imaging over the last two decades, the condition has been known for some time. For example, it is argued that the Irish scientist Robert Boyle (1664) may have provided the first documented case of synesthesia (Larne 2006).[1] In his essay entitled "Experiments and Considerations Touching Colours," Boyle recounts a curious case that was, in turn, related to him by his colleague, anatomist Dr J. Finch. Boyle reports that, during his travels across Europe, Dr Finch met with a blind man who reportedly could discriminate colors through touch. Boyle stated that "the Doctor desir'd to be told by him what kind of Discrimination he had of Colours by his Touch, to which he gave a reply, . . . That all the difference was more or less Asperity, for says he, Black feels as if you were feeling Needles points, or some harsh Sand, and Red feels very Smooth." According to Boyle, this man became completely blind at the age of 2 years as a result of contracting smallpox. Although the account shares several of the hallmarks of synesthesia, whether or not we can definitively state that this is the first case of synesthesia reported in the literature is not clear as the information available is insufficient. However, the account does compare with more recent reports, and with one study in particular, in which a number of late-blind synesthetes were also found to experience colors elicited by the sounds and feel of letters (see Steven and Blakemore 2004).

---

[1] Indeed, Larne further suggested that some of the storyline in Jonathan Swift's *Gulliver's Travels*, published in 1726, may have been inspired by Boyle's account of this blind man who could feel colors.

Synesthesia is an involuntary sensory cross-activation that occurs when a trigger stimulus, known as the inducer, activates an unusual specific experience in a submodality or in another modality, known as the concurrent (Grossenbacher and Lovelace 2001). One of the most common forms of synesthesia is known as grapheme-color synesthesia and it occurs when letters or words trigger a color. Despite a great deal of research activity into the area of synesthesia in recent years, several questions remain outstanding about the cognitive origins of the synesthetic response, not least of which is the question of when, during the information processing of the veridical stimulus, a synesthetic response arises. There are likely many levels of representation involved in letter/word recognition but it is currently unclear what the nature is of the representation of the inducing stimulus that results in a synesthetic experience. Is synesthesia triggered by low-level, featural properties of the inducing stimulus or does a considerable amount of information processing have to occur before the concurrent is evoked, such that synesthesia is triggered at a much later stage related perhaps to semantic memory or linguistic meaning? Or perhaps synesthesia is triggered by a mid-stage representation, which is neither completely sensory-driven nor one which is entirely top-down but influenced by both processes (e.g., Fensche et al. 2006; Wilson and Farah 2003). For example, a multisensory representation, which is invariant to specific visual or auditory features but related to its cognitive category or concept (see, e.g., Rosch 1975) may be sufficient to trigger synesthesia. Alternatively, a high-level representation determined by linguistic processing may be required (see Simner 2007). Our knowledge about how letters and words are perceived, and how and when these stimuli are represented in the (neurotypical) human brain may provide some clues to this problem.

In this chapter, I will review recent findings from studies on perceptual processing in general, and on grapheme-color synesthesia in particular, which have provided some insight into this issue. Specifically, by appealing to evidence from two separate lines of research we can address this in several ways. First, recent investigations on how the visual, auditory, and tactile sensory systems integrate information in the neurotypical brain to provide a coherent perception of the world can offer some clues as to when the synesthetic experience is triggered. Second, by examining the extent to which a synesthetic response is invariant to changes in the low-level sensory properties of the encoded stimulus, or to different sensory inputs that nevertheless have a common, conceptual link, we can also target when synesthesia may be evoked. Finally, if synesthesia is triggered by lexical meaning, then we should find color consistency to words sharing the same meaning across languages in multilingual synesthetes. The current literature suggests that many levels of representation, from low-level pattern recognition to abstract concepts and lexical semantics all have the propensity to induce a synesthetic experience. Our research has investigated the precise nature of the multisensory influences on the evoked synesthetic colors to letters and words and on the degree to which the synesthetic colors are consistently evoked to words presented in different languages, but which share the same meaning (i.e., lexical semantics). Our findings have suggested that the synesthetic color is triggered by a multisensory representation of the encoded stimulus perhaps linked to its concept, but that, contrary to recent suggestions, a higher-level representation determined by lexical meaning does appear to be necessary to trigger the synesthetic response. I will review evidence in support of this claim in the following sections.

Are Some Cross-Modal Associations Innate?

More and more often it is claimed that arbitrary associations across the senses are common to all, and are not just peculiar to the condition of synesthesia (see, e.g., Marks 1987; Parise and Spence 2009; also see relevant chapter in this volume) suggesting that synesthesia may be built on perceptual or cognitive processes common to us all. These observations should not be that surprising to us since we regularly use cross-sensory descriptions to connote meaning. Colors are often used to describe subtle emotional or attentional states: we talk about being "tickled pink," "feeling blue," "being green with envy," or being in a "brown study." Tastes can be used to describe the dispositions of others: somebody can be described as being very "sweet." And finally, metaphors such as something going "smoothly" or of someone "chilling out" representing the use of tactile sensations to describe meaning.

But the extent to which these cross-modal associations are innate or acquired as the individual constructs meaning from their sensory world, is not known. Interestingly, this is a question reminiscent of that posed by William Molyneux to John Locke in 1688 (see Molyneux 1688/1978), and mused over by George Berkeley more than 300 years ago (Berkeley 1709). It is tempting to assume that evidence for universal cross-modal correspondences, such as those found when an unfamiliar visual shape is matched with an unfamiliar sound, as demonstrated by Kohler (1929) in the Bouba/Kiki effect, or those related to metaphors as previously described (see also Ramachandran and Hubbard 2001a, 2001b, 2005) suggests "innate" mechanisms. However, recent studies have cast doubt on this assumption. In a recent report based on an analysis of the etiology of languages, specifically the structure of word order, the authors concluded that language has evolved based on lineage-specific or cultural-specific influences (Dunn et al. 2011). Their findings challenge the notion that language has universal tendencies, as argued by the Chomskyan approach to linguistics (Chomsky 1965). In a separate study Held et al. (2011) investigated interactions between vision and touch in a group of individuals who had had their sight restored. Held and colleagues found no evidence that recently sighted individuals could immediately match object shape across vision and touch, but that this ability was rapidly acquired. Their evidence suggests that the visual brain is not wired such that cross-modal correspondences (object shape in this case) are directly perceived, but argues that these correspondences are built up (albeit very rapidly) following learning (Held 2011). Berkeley (1709) also predicted these findings by arguing that the "ideas" or connections between vision and touch are not innate but built up with experience.

How Do the Senses Develop as Separate But Sufficiently Interconnected Systems?

During the course of development, particularly in the first few years of life, the infant rapidly learns to make sense from the "blooming, buzzing confusion" (James 1890/1981) that is its world. Although at birth the sensory systems in the cortex are not sufficiently differentiated, the development of separate functional areas within the sensory areas of the brain are rapidly shaped by experience-dependent processes. In other words, brain structure is linked to the statistical properties of stimulation from the baby's environment, such as the high probability of a co-occurrence of a particular visual stimulus (e.g., mother's face) with a particular auditory stimulus (mother's voice) or the feel of an object shape (e.g., a toy) and its visual appearance. The assumption is made that experience affects both the rapid neural proliferation within and across sensory systems, and the pruning of transient connections between sensory areas in the neonate brain during normal development. For example, comparative studies have revealed that during the synaptic pruning phase, transient neuronal projections to the occipital cortex from the auditory cortex of the normally sighted cat are eliminated (e.g., Dehay, Kennedy, and Bullier 1988). This process is highly dependent on early experience however, since, for example, visual deprivation can alter the degree to which the intact sensory systems interact, both in animals (see, e.g., Wallace and Stein 2007; Wallace et al. 2004) and in humans (e.g., Gori et al. 2010; Hötting, Rösler, and Röder 2004; Pasqualotto and Newell 2007). The challenge for the perceptual system is, however, to allow for the functional and structural differentiation of the senses but at the same time maintain sufficient, intersensory connectivity to allow the infant to perceive a coherent percept of their multisensory world. We can speculate that this developmental process of consolidating the intra- and intersensory systems, reflects a critical period of development (see, e.g., Hensch and Fagiolini 2005), which is particularly sensitive to environmental influences.

Coupled with the rapid, postnatal changes in brain structure are the concomitant effects on behavior. For example, young infants show a remarkable ability to share information across the senses for the purpose of object perception, such as shape matching across vision and touch (Meltzoff and Borton 1979; Sann and Streri 2007) and even person recognition based on matching voices to faces (Bahrick, Netto, and Hernandez-Reif 1998). Interestingly, however, this initial ability to integrate information across the senses appears to decline rapidly in the first year of life, a processes known as "perceptual narrowing" (Lewkowicz and Ghazanfar 2009) and evidence suggests that efficient multisensory perception seems to re-emerge only relatively later in life: for some sensory interactions such as vision and touch this may possibly be as late as around 8 years of age

(Gori et al. 2008; see also Nardini, Bedford, and Mareschal 2010; Nardini et al. 2008, for further evidence of late integration). This seemingly "U"-shaped function during development suggests that the earliest, transient intersensory connections in the neonate brain may be functional (thus allowing for the observation of cross-modal abilities) but following the neuronal restructuring of the brain, cross-modal associations need to be re-established based on learned natural associations from the environment.

Thus, there are grounds for speculating that the apparent initial ability of the neonate to integrate information across the senses is attributable to the undifferentiated structure of their sensory cortices and that this ability declines with postnatal experience as the cortices become specialized around the specific nature of the encoded sensory information (through processes involving neuronal proliferation and/or pruning). Subsequently, as the infant is exposed to extensive stimulation across the senses from the environment, cross-modal correspondences are acquired from the environment and re-established in neuronal circuits such that, in late childhood, adult-like levels of efficiency in multisensory perception emerge (Burr and Gori 2012). Given the developmental goal of the sensory systems, we might further speculate that it is within this critical period (or perhaps sensory-specific critical *periods*) in which cross-modal correspondences shape the brain, that the acquisition of more permanent synesthetic associations may be acquired. Moreover, it may be a critical period during which the biological substrates underpinning synesthesia may emerge (see, e.g., Maurer 1993; Maurer and Mondloch 2005) or become embedded (Rich, Bradshaw, and Mattingley 2005). This may be particularly true for some forms of synesthesia, such as grapheme-color synesthesia, as the child acquires written language around the age of 5 or 6 years (Simner et al. 2009). However, other forms of synesthesia may have a different developmental trajectory, likely dependent on when the infant is exposed to the inducing stimulus or when it is first acquired. Moreover, given the recent evidence on the development of multisensory integration (see, e.g., Bremner, Lewkowicz, and Spence 2012), it is possible that the developmental trajectories associated with synesthesia may be inextricably linked to the maturity both of the underlying sensory system itself and the structural connectivity between sensory systems in the brain.

ARE CROSS-MODAL CORRESPONDENCES BETWEEN GRAPHEMES AND COLORS UNIVERSALLY ACQUIRED?

During middle to late childhood, one of the most challenging cross-modal tasks for the child to acquire is the ability to associate arbitrary visual shapes and symbols (letters) and combinations of these shapes (words) to their sounds and, in turn, their associated meaning. Letter and word recognition represents a perceptual and cognitive expertise system, similar to the face perception system but different in its phylogenetic heritage (i.e., given the relative youthfulness of written language in human history, we are unlikely to have evolved a dedicated system to the perception of letters or words). Unlike the recognition of other stimuli, letter and word recognition takes years to acquire such that even by the age of 11, children still are not as proficient as adults at reading and writing (Jeon et al. 2010). Moreover, the nature by which letters are represented in the brain changes with age (see, e.g., Burgund and Abernathy 2008) and level of literacy (Dehaene et al. 2010). The relatively long time it takes to gain proficiency at this task is perhaps not surprising given the perceptual challenges involved: not only do specific cross-modal associations have to be maintained in memory but these representations should have the flexibility to generalize across different instances of the visual form (i.e., from upper to lower case, or variations in typeface or handwriting) or verbal form (e.g., different age of speaker, or different accents or even languages). This raises the issues of what is the precise nature of the representation of visual letters and associated sounds in memory, how are these representations sufficiently specific to discriminate between different letters but at the same time invariant to incidental changes in their visual or acoustic features; and when in information processing is the encoded stimulus associated with its meaning (semantic or linguistic).

The study of grapheme-color synesthesia may offer some insight into the nature of the underlying grapheme form in memory that is required to induce the synesthetic response. For example, if the color is induced by particular sensory properties of the encoded stimulus, such as letter font or case, then this will allow us to make assumptions about the underlying (perceptual) nature of the representation. On the other hand, if the synesthetic color is triggered by the semantic meaning of the stimulus, rather than any of the associated low-level perceptual features, then this finding can help deduce the nature of such an abstract representation in memory.

Although the colors induced by graphemes were thought to be idiosyncratic and peculiar to each individual synesthete, recent studies have suggested that this may not be the case as certain patterns linking the form of the grapheme to a particular color have emerged across synesthetes. For example, some recent studies have observed remarkable inter-synesthete agreements on the nature of the color induced by particular letters, such that A tends to be red, B tends to be blue, C tends to be yellow, and I and 1 and O and 0 are often black or white (see, e.g., Barnett et al. 2008; Rich, Bradshaw, and Mattingley 2005; Simner et al. 2005). Brang et al. (2011) reports that graphemes which are more visually similar to each other are more likely to trigger similar colors. Furthermore, letter frequency has been shown to be associated with common characteristics of the color concurrent, such as hue, saturation and luminance (Beeli, Esslen, and Jäncke 2007; Watson, Akins, and Enns 2012) and color terms (see, e.g., Simner et al. 2005). These findings suggest that the associations established in grapheme-color synesthesia, whilst exhibited only by some individuals, are based in part on cognitive mechanisms that are common to everyone. Indeed, a recent study on consistent letter-color correspondences in pre-literal children supports this idea (Spector and Maurer 2011). Spector and Maurer speculate that these consistent correspondences may be determined by learned regularities from the environment (e.g., sharp objects are scary, and dark is scary, therefore sharp-like shapes are dark). Although this is a plausible mechanism, other environmental influences may *not* be predictive of color associations in synesthetes. For example, Rich, Bradshaw, and Mattingley (2005) failed to find evidence that known letter-color correspondences presented in children's books were consistently adopted by synesthetes. Moreover, evidence that monozygotic twins can be discordant for synesthesia rules out a purely genetic (innate) basis for the condition (e.g., Smilek, Dixon, and Merikle 2005; Smilek et al. 2002) although it may be the general trait, rather than a specific subtype which is inherited (Barnett et al. 2008).

A recent model of synesthesia has suggested that correspondences occur due to exuberant cross connections between neighboring brain regions (Hubbard and Ramachandran 2005). In the case of grapheme-color synesthesia in particular, the cortical regions activated in word recognition and in the perception of color are thought to be anatomically adjacent to each other, providing some support to this model. However, what is not known is how letters and words are represented in the visual areas of the brain, i.e., what their perceptual characteristics are. Furthermore, the extent to which evidence supports the idea that letters and words are subserved by a distinct neural system is disputed (see later in chapter). Without this knowledge, we cannot be clear whether or not grapheme-color synesthesia is underpinned by distinct sensory processes or more higher-level multisensory representations possibly linked to meaning. If the evidence is in favor of higher-level representations mediating synesthesia, then current models of synesthesia may need to be revised. In the following section, I will review the evidence for the idea that letter and word representations involve distinct perceptual and neural processes to the perception of other objects and introduce some challenges that such a model represents regarding our understanding of how visual (or auditory) patterns are ultimately associated with lexical meaning for the purpose of language comprehension.

How Specific is the Representation of Letters and Words in Memory?

Similar to general object recognition, letter and word recognition appears to be invariant to incidental changes in visual form such as type face (i.e., font) and case (e.g., Rudnicky and Kolers 1984), although this may depend on the context (Sanocki 1987). Letter recognition is, however, known to be sensitive to orientation in the image plane, such as when the page on which a letter is written is gradually turned upside-down (Cooper and Shepard 1973). Moreover, similar to the recognition of objects from line drawings at least (Biederman and Cooper 1991a) certain orthographic features, such as the letter vertices, are more diagnostic of letter identity than others, such as line segments (Lanthier et al. 2009; Szwed et al. 2009). However, unlike general object recognition (Biederman and Cooper 1991b), the perception of letters is disrupted by mirror-view changes in the image (Cooper and Shepard 1973; Pegado et al. 2011). Taken together, this behavioral evidence suggests that the extent to which the representations of letters in memory may be invariant to incidental changes may be constrained by the visual features available (see, e.g., Grainger, Rey, and Dufau 2008) and the context in which the letter is presented (Sanocki 1987).

Support for the idea that letter and word recognition involves an expert system comes from evidence suggesting that there exists a distinct cortical region underlying these processes. An area in the left-hemispheric inferotemporal region, specifically the left-fusiform cortex (or BA37) has been identified as the visual word form area (VWFA). The blood oxygen level-dependent (BOLD) activation in the brain tends to be greater to alphabetical strings than for other types of visual input such as checkerboard patterns or non-letter like meaningless shapes, or pseudoletters with equivalent visual complexity (Price, Wise, and Fracowiak 1996; Burgund, Guo, and Aurback 2009). Activation in the VWFA region is also thought to be correlated with literacy (Dehaene et al. 2010) and is known to develop with reading expertise (e.g., Cohen and Dehaene 2004; Cohen et al. 2002). It is also thought that activation within this region develops around familiar letter patterns such that greater activation is found for Hebrew letter forms in readers of Hebrew than non-readers and to alphabetical letters than Chinese letters in those unfamiliar with Chinese logographs (Baker et al. 2007).

However, recent findings that both real and readable pseudo-words activate the VWFA have, raised questions about the precise functional role of this brain region with regard to visual word recognition (Mechelli, Gorno-Tempini, and Price 2003) leading some to cast doubt on its existence as a specific neural module within the visual system (see, e.g., Price and Devlin 2003). Price and Devlin reported that damage in this area is not specifically implicated in cases of alexia (i.e., a condition in which word recognition is impaired), and that its functional role is not limited to visual letter or word recognition. For example, they report that the VWFA region is also activated by various naming tasks involving colors or pictures, and other types of word processing such as Braille recognition or repetition of auditory words. Similarly, Joseph et al. (2006) tested letter-specificity on VWFA activation and reported very similar BOLD responses to letter naming and object naming, suggesting that the functional role of the left fusiform area is not specific to letters per se, although may reflect general processing of letters and objects. Therefore, although the VWFA subserves the perception of words, and thus represents the neural locus of word recognition in the brain, it clearly also serves other perceptual functions. In light of the behavioral and neuroimaging evidence, and indeed the debate on the existence of a specific neural substrate dedicated to letter and word perception, it is clear that we are not yet at the stage of understanding what is the nature of the underlying representation of a letter or a word in memory and the associated neural structures supporting the perception of letters and words in the neurotyical brain. Moreover, our understanding is limited on how much processing of the sensory information related to letters or words is required before the letter is perceived, and is available to conscious awareness.

In the following section I will review research on grapheme-color synesthesia which has helped elucidate this issue.

What Information Induces the Color in Grapheme-Color Synesthesia?

Some recent reports have suggested that the synesthetic color response may be triggered by low-level features in either the visual or auditory input. For example, Hubbard, Manohar, and Ramachandran (2006) reported that the contrast between a visual grapheme against the background is related to the strength of the color experienced by a particular synesthete, and Asano and Yokosawa (2011) reported that similar acoustic features across (visually dissimilar) characters were likely to induce the same color experience in Japanese grapheme-color synesthetes. Furthermore, several studies have now shown that similarity of visual features across letters is associated with similarity in color dimensions related to the synesthetic experience (e.g., Brang et al. 2011; Watson, Akins, and Enns 2012). Visual similarity across graphemes in different typescripts is also reported to be related to the colors induced (Witthoft and Winawer 2006). Moreover, synesthete colors are sensitive to letter orientation and to the typicality of the written font (Ramachandran and Hubbard 2003; Witthoft and Winawer 2006). In the individuals tested, these limitations likely arise from general principles of perceptual processing which are not specific to grapheme-color synesthesia per se. In contrast, a number of other reports have suggested that different processes underpin the perception of the induced color in synesthesia, on the one hand, and the perception of a veridical color stimulus, on the other. For example, on the basis of findings from several experiments in which color perception was investigated in four synesthetes, Hong and Blake (2008) argued that the properties of the induced color experience are unlikely to be same as those associated with early visual mechanisms involved in the perception of veridical colors (Hong and Blake 2008). In support of this conclusion, van Leeuwen, Petersson and Hagoort (2010) conducted a functional magnetic resonance imaging study on 21 grapheme-color synesthetes and reported that color experiences in synesthesia did not necessarily activate the same visual areas in the brain associated with the processing of low-level properties of color. Others have reported that activation of "color" regions in the visual brain to the synesthetic color are not necessarily confined to area V4, normally activated in color perception (see Rouw, Scholte, and Colizoli 2011 for a review). Yet, grapheme-color synesthesia confers perceptual benefits in normal color processing (see, e.g., Banissy, Walsh, and Ward 2009).

These seemingly contradictory findings have led some researchers to speculate that there may be a distinction in grapheme color synesthesia, based on the nature of representation of the inducing stimulus required to trigger the color response

(Ramachandran and Hubbard 2001; Ward et al. 2007). For some synesthetes, those with so-called "lower synesthesia," the color response may be triggered by a low-level, feature-based exemplar of the inducing stimulus whereas for other synesthetes with so-called "higher-synesthesia," the response may be linked to more higher-level processing related to concepts or lexical meaning. This distinction between lower and higher synesthesia is helpful in highlighting the fact that different cognitive mechanisms may underpin the synesthetic experience across individuals. However, it does not help elucidate the precise cognitive processes involved nor the nature of the perceptual/conceptual representation required. Moreover, the distinction may hide the fact that for many, the synesthetic experience may be related to a combination of lower- and higher-level processing, or the level of processing may be dependent on the nature of the synesthetic associations within the same individual. In other words, it remains possible that individuals lie on a continuum relating to the nature of the representation necessary to trigger a synesthetic response. Furthermore, it means that despite evidence for this bimodal classification, the answer to the question of what cognition representation drives synesthesis is still unresolved.

In an attempt to assess the limits to which synesthetic responses to letters are induced by low-level perceptual, or higher-level cognitive processing of letter and word forms (e.g., concepts derived from categories or constructs involved in language processing and production), we recently tested the role of cross-modal influences in two different studies. In the first of these, Bargary et al. (2009), presented a number of grapheme-color synesthetes with a series of spoken word stimuli and asked our participants to report the word heard and the color induced by each word. To investigate whether cross-modal information influences the nature of the color induced by the spoken words, in one condition we presented a video clip of an actor silently speaking a word which was incongruent to the heard word. We thus introduced a "McGurk" condition in which the viseme (i.e., the visual representation of the mouth articulating the spoken word) affected the nature of the auditory word perceived. What was surprising to us was that this manipulation changed the color response, such that the color was induced by the perceived illusory word (i.e., the "McGurk" word) and not by the actual auditory word. We argued that this result suggested that there are strong cross-modal influences on the synesthetic response, and that grapheme-color synesthesia does not appear to be linked to processing in one specific modality alone. Furthermore, our results suggest a relatively late activation of the synesthetic response, most likely associated with knowledge-driven or conceptual representation of the word rather than any low-level, sensory specific component of the input. The results of this particular study do not allow us to determine how "late" this representation may be and whether the synesthetic trigger is more related to concepts or lexical meaning. Moreover, the neural locus of this representation which triggers the synesthetic experience in this case remains unknown.

Associations between vision and audition, however, are built up during the acquisition of written language. In a more recent study, we tested the extent to which cross-modal percepts mediate the synesthetic response by presenting letters in an unfamiliar modality, namely touch (Kilroy 2006). Previous studies on how letters are recognized through touch found that although tactile letter recognition is not as efficient as visual recognition (Bliss and Hämäläinen 2005), it can be rapidly acquired (Hunt, Edwards, and Quest 1988; Hunt et al. 1989). We tested five female synesthetes (mean age of 49 years, range between 21 and 63 years) and five sex- and age-matched non-synesthete control participants. We were specifically interested in the following issues: whether or not letter recognition through an unfamiliar modality could induce synesthetic colors in grapheme-color synesthetes, at what stage in information processing do these synesthetic responses arise, and do the colors induced by tactile letter processing resemble those induced by the visual presentations of the letters? For example, during tactile exploration, which is necessarily serial and offers features of the letter shape in a piecemeal fashion, colors could be induced by *components* of letters rather than the integrated letter as a whole. Alternatively, the synesthetic color may be induced only once the entire letter is recognized.

In our study, we used a device known as the virtual haptic display (VHD; see Chan et al. 2007) to present virtual tactile letters. The VHD operates by translating black and white visual images into topographic, two-dimensional, tactile pixel (taxel) arrays which are realized once the participant moves a carriage over the location of the image boundary. These taxels are either raised or depressed at any one time representing black and white pixel colors of the visual image respectively. Tactile exploration of the image (which is not seen by the participant) occurs based on a single finger only and the virtual letter could span the surface of the VHD with a tactile area of 160 mm^2. The task for each participant was to recognize the virtual letter displayed, using the VHD, and to report, as fast as possible the (first) color associated with the shape by choosing the corresponding matching color on a color picker. All participants received practice on letter recognition using the VHD with a set of letters which were not subsequently tested in the experiment. A criterion response of over 60% correct letter identification was required during practice before the test could begin. The target letters were A, C, D, H, J, K, M, and Z. Each letter appeared twice, with the only constraint being that the same letter could not appear in succession. There was no time limit to this task but participants were asked to complete it as quickly as possible. The entire test took approximately 1 hour on average per participant. The average amount of time spent on letters that were correctly identified was over 100 seconds while the average time spent on letters that were incorrectly identified was 150 seconds. In a procedure adopted from Ward et al. (2006) we found that synesthetes were more consistent in their color choices to these tactile stimuli (54.78 ± 6.57) than controls (132.38 ± 9.82) (p <0.05).

First our data suggest evidence that a sensory modality which does not represent an "expert system" for letter or word recognition was sufficient to induce color in response to letters. Second, we found that the color was evoked upon identification of the letter only and not by other tactile information such as feature recognition. In all cases, when the letter could not be identified, the color was not induced. Interestingly, the evoked

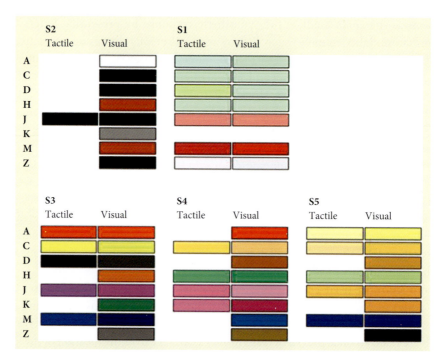

FIGURE 10.1 A representation of the synesthetic colors from five synesthetes (S1–S5). Right columns show the colors generated from a visual exposure to letters, and the left columns show the colors generated from a tactile exposure.

color was associated with the perceived letter even when letter identification was incorrect. For example, if the letter was "A" but it was recognized as "R" the elicited color was to the letter "R." There was one exception to this. Participant S2, twice reported the color of the (correct) letter even though she reported identifying a different, incorrect letter. Unfortunately, S2 has a limited range of color concurrents, therefore it is difficult to determine the reliability of this experience. Finally, the color elicited to the tactile presentation of the letter was generally the same as the color experienced to the visual presentation of the letter (see Figure 10.1). The result of this experiment is consistent with that reported by Bargary et al. (2009) that multisensory influences in the processing of the encoded stimulus can trigger the synesthetic response. Moreover, these studies suggest that colors are induced once the letter has been perceived, possibly at the decision level when recognition has occurred. However, it is worth noting that these results are equivocal as to whether the color response in grapheme-color synesthesia is triggered by the concept of the letter, commonly accessed by either of these sensory modalities, or, in other cases, by the lexical semantics related to word meaning (remembering that grapheme-color synesthetes experience colors from both letters and words). The following section reviews recent findings on the role of meaning in synesthetic responses.

Do Multisensory or Later (Language-Driven) Representations Trigger Synesthesia?

As discussed, previous research in grapheme-color synesthesia suggests that the color experience can be induced when the letter or word is read, heard or felt. Some studies have also suggested that the color may be experienced when just the concept is induced, and therefore is not dependent on the perceptual content of the trigger (Rich, Bradshaw, and Mattingley 2005). In other words, it may not be necessary for the referred sensory modality to be stimulated by the inducer from the environment, but instead it may be evoked by the mere thought of the inducing stimulus. Moreover, the concept of the inducing stimulus may interact with other cognitive processes. For example, in a case study involving the digit-color synesthete C, Dixon et al. (2000) reported that priming with a congruent synesthetic color facilitated the perception of the associated inducing stimulus (see also Brang et al., 2008; Ghirardelli et al. 2010, for similar findings). Specifically, for synesthete C, Dixon et al. presented a color patch following the presentation of an arithmetic problem (e.g., $4 + 3 =$). They reported that when the color of the patch was congruent with the synesthetic color induced by the solution (i.e., 7) this facilitated the time it took for C to solve the problem, relative to when the color was incongruent. This finding, according to Dixon et al. argues for a link between the concurrent color and the conceptual representation of the inducing stimulus, since the actual inducing stimulus was never physically presented. This experience may be mediated, for example, through top-down feedback from other higher-order regions of the brain implicated in semantic memory (Grossenbacher and Lovelace 2001).

The extent to which a concurrent is triggered by conceptual representations as a general principle for all synesthetic associations cannot be determined from these studies. However, recent studies involving larger numbers of participants suggest that for the majority of synesthetes with one variant at least (colored months, see later), the meaning of the inducing stimulus is not necessarily that which triggers the associated synesthetic color (see, e.g., Barnett et al. 2008; Rich, Bradshaw, and Mattingley 2005). For example, in a comprehensive survey of a large population of synesthetes with colored letters and words, Rich, Bradshaw, and Mattingley (2005) found varying influences on what triggered the color response, and that these influences largely depended on the nature of the word stimuli themselves, even within the same synesthete. For example, colors induced by months of the year could often be predicted by the color associated with the initial letter in the word overall (e.g., the color of "February" tended to be the color of "F"). Put differently, there was nothing about the meaning of words such as "February" ("March," "April," etc.) which triggered color; instead, color was determined by the word-form. In contrast, Rich, Bradshaw, and Mattingley found that colors induced by days of the week were likely to be idiosyncratic and not determined by the component letters. In other words, for days of the week at least, the color was induced by the lexical meaning of the word. Rich and her colleagues argued that since months of the year are learned later than days of the week during language acquisition, the colors induced by months are more likely to be associated with a general principle (found for most other words) that the color of the first letter dominates the word. In contrast, colors induced by stimuli learned early in life (predating literacy perhaps, or in contrast, when phonemic awareness is less advanced) are more likely to be associated with word meaning.

In line with this argument, another interesting observation made by Rich and her colleagues was that the color induced by a number word (e.g., "seven") was more likely to match the color of the corresponding digit (i.e., "7") than its own first letter (i.e., "s"). This match between number word and digit was also more likely than a match between the digit and the initial letter itself (i.e., the color induced by the digit "7" and the letter "s" are likely to differ). In other words, the color induced by the number digit was more related to that of the entire number word, than any visual feature (component letter) of the number word. This raises two possibilities for the nature of the association between the digit and number word. First, the color may be elicited by the lexical meaning (i.e., the denoted magnitude) of the number, since both the word "seven" and the digit "7" relate to the same numeric value. The second possibility is that the color is induced by a common auditory, not visual, percept of both the word and digit form of the number. However, Rich, Bradshaw, and Mattingley (2005) also noted that color words are more likely to trigger the denoted color ("green" is green) when compared with the colors induced by similar sounding words (e.g., "greed," "Greek," and "greet" are red). Furthermore, Simner (2012) reported that shared acoustic properties across words associated with different semantic constructs (e.g., "one" or "won") do not trigger the same color experiences for grapheme-color synesthetes. Taken together with the evidence from number words and their similarly colored digits, these findings suggest that this type of synesthesia is more likely to be mediated by higher-level constructs (i.e., meaning related to linguistic processing), rather than any perceptual representations. However, the finding that months of the year, and other words, are colored by the initial grapheme (e.g., "February" and "fan" are the color of the letter F) suggests that semantic meaning does not solely trigger colors in words, and that other factors may need to be considered. For example, the association between synesthetic colors and words may be mediated by audition, especially when these associations were acquired early in life. (The association between the names of colors and the written form of these colors is learned relatively later in life, suggesting that the association between the written word and color may be mediated by other factors by that point.) These studies, therefore, do not provide clear predictions about the precise nature of the word percept or concept which triggers the synesthetic color, but do suggest a role for the age at which the stimuli were acquired, and possibly, the learning modality. In an attempt to understand how age of acquisition and the representation which triggers synesthesia interact, we tested cross-linguistically. Specifically, we looked at the similarity of synesthetic colors induced by words sharing the same meaning across languages (which are associated with the same, higher-level linguistic category) but not necessarily having the same visual or auditory form (Barnett et al. 2009). We tested 21 multilingual synesthetes whose mother tongue was English and second language (L2) was typically acquired early in life (most were bilingual from birth, some acquired the second language prior to acquiring literacy). Thus, our study was unlike previous reports which had investigated the transfer of synesthete colors across languages, since these typically involved participants who acquired L2 later in life, usually after puberty, and therefore after the written form of the word was acquired (see Mills et al. 2002). When L2 is learned later in life, a typical finding is that the colors induced by letters and words in the second language are heavily influenced by orthographic patterns found in L1 (Simner 2007).

In our sample, the second (and other) languages included French, German, Italian, Spanish, and Irish. We tested the consistency of the synesthetic colors induced by each word within three sequences (days of the week, numbers, and months of the year) presented in different languages: in other words, we tested whether the synesthetic color was the same, similar, or different for a word presented in two (or more) languages familiar to the participant. None of the 21 synesthetes tested had the same synesthetic color across all words which shared the same meaning (e.g., "Monday"/"lundi"/"An Luan" or "February"/"fevrier"/"Feabhra" in English, French, and Irish respectively).[2] Moreover, the colors induced by words in the second language were not necessarily fully consistent with those in the first (which shared the same lexical meaning) when either the initial word letter was the same (i.e., orthographic percept) or the initial phoneme was the same (i.e., auditory percept). On the other hand, the colors induced by these types of word-sequences across languages were not completely arbitrary either, since words (days, weeks, and months) which shared visual or auditory properties were more likely to induce the same color response than words which did not share these perceptual properties. For example, the words "March" and "Marta" in English and Irish respectively, were judged (by independent raters) as being more visually similar than "May" and "Bealtaine." Correspondingly, color consistency scores were higher to March/Marta than to May/Bealtaine. Moreover, shared orthographic properties, specifically the same first letter in the spelling, were more likely to induce the same color across languages than shared initial phonemes.

Finally, we found some evidence consistent with previous reports that the age in which a word is learned may affect the factors that influence the synesthetic color association. Although we found that colors induced to words across languages were unrelated to the age at which the language was acquired, this was not necessarily the case for months of the year. For those sequence words, the age at which the second (or third etc.) language was acquired affected the consistency of the colors experienced,

---

[2] For one synesthete the colours were consistent across English, French, and German to "months" only but inconsistent across "numbers" and "days." For another synesthete, colours were consistent across English Irish and French to "days" only but neither "months" nor "numbers" triggered a colour in any language.

such that for languages learned later, the colors induced by months of the year were more likely to be consistent with those induced by the same stimuli in the primary language. This finding is consistent with the earlier proposal by Rich, Bradshaw, and Mattingley (2005) that the later the concept (or language) is acquired, the more likely the color is elicited by general principles such as the initial letter of the word, rather than a unique association not predicted by visual or auditory word features (see also Simner 2007).

A FINAL WORD: THE ROLE OF VISION IN GRAPHEME-COLOR SYNESTHESIA

Although there is strong evidence in support of late perceptual, multisensory representations playing a role in the synesthetic experience, it remains an open issue as to whether these representations may be dominated by vision, even if only at the initial processing of the encoded grapheme or word. For example, visual processing (of either the inducer or concurrent or both) is more frequently involved across all types of synesthesia than any other modality (see Day 2012). In studies of grapheme-color synesthesia, it is possible that the spoken version of a word or letter, or even its tactile form, maybe be recoded into its visual counterpart, and that it is the visual representation which triggers synesthesia. Indeed visual coding or recoding would have to be assumed in order to adopt the model that synesthesia arises from hyperconnectivity between adjacent cortical areas (Hubbard and Ramachandran, 2005). Furthermore, synesthetes appear to have heightened abilities in visual imagery: Barnett and Newell (2008) found that synesthetes report more vivid visual imagery generally, than either their first degree non-synesthete relatives or unrelated non-synesthete controls. Also, visual imagery may mediate shape processing in other modalities (see, e.g., Lacey and Sathian 2012 for a discussion of shape processing in touch). Moreover, in an electroencephalogram study we found differences between synesthetes and non-synesthetes in the early sensory components of the visual evoked potential to visual stimuli which did not elicit a synesthetic response. Taken together, these findings suggest general differences in visual perception between synesthetes and non-synesthetes and which might account for the role of vision in eliciting the synesthetic response.

In contrast, however, other evidence suggests that vision, per se, may not be necessary. Previous studies on grapheme-color synesthesia in blind individuals (Steven and Blakemore 2004), suggest that synesthetic responses are robust to long-term visual deprivation. Steven and Blakemore reported that for one of their participants at least, Braille letter recognition was sufficient to induce a color response. Braille letters, moreover, bear little resemblance to their alphabetical counterparts, therefore it is unlikely that shared spatial features mediated these responses (in cases where the visual form was learned prior to the onset of blindness).

CONCLUSIONS

Based on current evidence, it appears that there is not a single or general principle of cognitive processing which explains how and when colors are triggered by graphemes. On the one hand, some studies have suggested that both the concurrent and inducer may share low-level properties with their corresponding veridical percepts (e.g., Banissy, Walsh, and Ward 2009), and that early visual processing differences, likely residing in primary occipital cortices (Barnett et al. 2009) are associated with grapheme-color synesthesia. Moreover, others have reported a role for low-level visual features in the grapheme, in that common features tend to be associated with more similar colors (e.g., Brang et al. 2011; Watson, Atkins, and Enns 2012). However, other evidence suggests that the representation linked to the synesthetic response is not likely to be based solely on low-level, unisensory features: colors induced by early-acquired sequences, such as days of the week, tend to be related to word meaning rather than the perception of the component letters. Others have argued that these findings may be accounted for by individual differences in what they term "lower/higher synesthesia" across synesthetes (Ramachandran and Hubbard 2001b). In any case, the evidence from multisensory studies (e.g., involving the McGurk effect) suggest that a considerable amount of information processing of the inducing stimulus is conducted before the synesthetic experience arises. Moreover, these multisensory modes of input are not limited to those acquired and commonly used during the lifetime, since tactile letter recognition is also sufficient to elicit the synesthetic response.

Evidence that synesthesia is triggered by a more multisensory representation is compatible with a growing literature on widespread cross-sensory interactions in the neurotypical brain. For example, until recently, the traditional view was that sensory systems were fully differentiated and that sensory information converged in association cortices only once a significant amount of unisensory processing of information had occurred (Ghazanfar and Schroeder 2006). However, an increasing number of studies have reported evidence for early sensory convergence, including cross-sensory modulation in primary sensory cortices (see Foxe and Schroeder 2005 for a review). For example, there is evidence for tactile influences on visual object regions (Amedi et al 2001), vocal modulation of fusiform face area, (von Kriegstein et al. 2005), and even visual modulation of auditory cortices during speech (Calvert et al. 1997). However, the results are non-committal regarding the neural mechanism supporting these interactions in synesthesia: i.e., they do not differentiate between models that appeal specifically to cortical hyperconnectivity (Hubbard and Ramachandran 2005), disinhibition (Grossenbacher and Lovelace 2001), or lack of cortical specialization.

Cross-modal associations between visual letter and word forms and their auditory counterparts form the basis of reading abilities. However, little is known about where in the brain these information sources merge. It was previously thought that visual and auditory words activated different regions of the sensory brain, and integration occurred in later, more associative brain regions (see, e.g., Burton et al. 2005; van Atteveldt et al. 2004). For example, activation in the VWFA of the brain was reported to be specific to visual, written input (Cohen et al. 2004) and not responsive to spoken words (Dehaene et al. 2010), with a neighboring region known as the lateral inferotemporal multimodal area (LIMA) responsive to both visual and auditory inputs. Joseph et al. (2006) reported activation in the left hemisphere which was specific to letter naming in both the insula and inferior parietal lobule, which, they argued may subserve a recoding from vision to audition of graphemes to phonemes. However, other evidence suggests that, contrary to these findings, auditory input can also modulate activation within the VWFA region of the brain (Yoncheva et al. 2010) and, moreover, that these cross-modal influences may be related to an increase in reading proficiency during language acquisition (e.g., Bolger et al. 2008). Furthermore, others have suggested a symmetrical effect of visual modulation on auditory cortex when congruent written letters are presented during auditory speech (see van Atteveldt, Roebroeck, and Goebel 2009 for a review). Evidence for cross-modal interactions in the VWFA suggest the possibility that the representation of the letter or word which triggers the color experience in grapheme-color synesthesia may reside in, or be moderated by, this cortical area. Further research is required, however, to elucidate these multisensory interactions within this cortical region, specifically in the synesthete brain. However, evidence that the VWFA may have a multisensory capacity would lend further support to the idea that synesthesia may arise between adjacent functional brain regions (Hubbard and Ramachandran 2005).

Although, broadly speaking, there is no consistent evidence to help us make conclusions about when synesthesia is triggered during information processing, or even pinpoint the key cortical area(s) that underpin this phenomenon, this is largely because research into synesthesia is a relatively young field and there has not yet been the opportunity to investigate these issues in depth. Further research is required to understand the level of representation linked to the synesthetic experience and to provide insight into the extent to which synesthesia is associated with principles of perceptual or cognitive processing common to us all. Only until further behavioral and neuroimaging studies have elucidated the precise properties (perceptual, cognitive, and neurophysiological) of the inducing stimulus necessary to trigger a synesthetic response will we be in a position to develop a strong model of how synesthesia occurs. The complementary and rapidly growing research field in multisensory perceptual processing in the neurotypical brain may be a rich source of evidence that could inform models of synesthesia. Indeed, research developments in both fields will provide us with a better understanding of cognitive processing in the human brain more generally.

REFERENCES

Amedi, Amir, Rafael Malach, Talma Hendler, Sharon Peled, and Ehud Zohary. 2001. Visuo-haptic object-related activation in the ventral visual pathway. *Nature Neuroscience* 4:324–330.
Asano, Michiko, and Kazuhiko Yokosawa. 2011. Synesthetic colors are elicited by sound quality in Japanese synesthetes. *Consciousness and Cognition* 4:1816–1823.

Bahrick, Lorraine E., Dianelys Netto, and Maria Hernandez-Reif. 1998. Intermodal perception of adult and child faces and voices by infants. *Child Development* 69(5):1263–1275.

Baker, Chris I., Jia Liu, Lawrence L. Wald, Kenneth K. Kwong, Thomas Benner, and Nancy Kanwisher. 2007. Visual word processing and experiential origins of functional selectivity in human extrastriate cortex. *Proceedings of the National Academy of Sciences of the United States of America* 104:9087–9092.

Banissy, Michael J., Vincent Walsh, and Jamie Ward. 2009. Enhanced sensory perception in synaesthesia. *Experimental Brain Research* 196:565–571.

Bargary, Gary, Kylie J. Barnett, Kevin J. Mitchell, and Fiona N. Newell. 2009. Colored-speech synaesthesia is triggered by multisensory, not unisensory, perception. *Psychological Science* 20:529–533.

Barnett, Kylie J., Joanne Feeney, Michael Gormley, and Fiona N. Newell. 2009. An exploratory study of linguistic-colour associations across languages in multilingual synaesthetes. *The Quarterly Journal of Experimental Psychology* 62:1343–1354

Barnett, Kylie J., Ciara Finucane, Julian E. Asher, Gary Bargary, Aiden P. Corvin, Fiona N. Newell, and Kevin J. Mitchell. 2008. Familial patterns and the origins of individual differences in synaesthesia. *Cognition* 106 (2):871–893.

Barnett, Kylie J., John J. Foxe, Sophie Molholm, Simon P. Kelly, Shani Shalgi, Kevin J. Mitchell, and Fiona N. Newell. 2008. Differences in early sensory-perceptual processing in synesthesia: A visual evoked potential study. *Neuroimage* 43:605–613.

Barnett, Kylie J., and Fiona N. Newell. 2008 Synaesthesia is associated with enhanced, self-rated visual imagery. *Consciousness and Cognition* 17 (3):1032–1039.

Beeli, Gian, Michaela Esslen, and Lutz Jäncke. 2007. Frequency correlates in grapheme-color synaesthesia. *Psychological Science* 18:788–792.

Berkeley, George. (1709). *An essay towards a new theory of vision*. Printed by Aaron Rhames, for Jeremy Pepyat, Dublin, Ireland.

Biederman, Irving, and Eric E. Cooper. 1991a. Priming contour-deleted images: evidence for intermediate representations in visual object recognition. *Cognitive Psychology* 23:393–419.

——. 1991b. Evidence for complete translational and reflectional invariance in visual object priming. *Perception* 20:585–593.

Bliss, Irina, and Keikki Hämäläinen H. 2005. Different working memory capacity in normal young adults for visual and tactile letter recognition task. *Scandinavian Journal of Psychology* 46:247–251.

Bolger, Donald J., Jane Hornickel, Nadia E. Cone, Douglas D. Burman, James R. Booth. 2008. Neural correlates of orthographic and phonological consistency effects in children. *Human Brain Mapping* 29:1416–1429.

Boyle, Robert. 1664. *Experiments and Considerations Touching Colours*. Printed for Henry Herringman at the Anchor on the Lower walk of the New Exchange, London, UK.

Brang, D., L. Edwards, V. S. Ramachandran, and S. Coulson. 2008. Is the sky 2? Contextual priming in grapheme-color synaesthesia. *Psychological Science* 5:421–428.

Brang, David, Romke Rouw, Vilayanur S. Ramachandran, and Seana Coulson. 2011. Similarly shaped letters evoke similar colors in grapheme-color synesthesia. *Neuropsychologia* 49:1355–1358.

Bremner, Andrew J., David J. Lewkowicz, and Charles Spence, eds. 2012. *Multisensory Development*. Oxford: Oxford University Press.

Burgund, E. Darcy, and Alana E. Abernathy. 2008. Letter-specific processing in children and adults matched for reading level. *Acta Psychologia* 129:66–71.

Burgund, E. Darcy, Yi Guo, and Elyse L. Aurbach. 2009. Priming for letters and pseudoletters in mid-fusiform cortex: examining letter selectivity and case invariance. *Experimental Brain Research* 193:591–601.

Burr, David C., and Monica Gori. 2012. Multisensory integration develops late in humans. In *The Neural Bases of Multisensory Processes*, ed. Micah M. Murray, and Mark T. Wallace, 345–362. Boca Raton, FL: CRC Press.

Burton, Martha W., Paul C. Locasto, Donna Krebs-Noble, and Rao P. Gullapalli. 2005. A systematic investigation of the functional neuroanatomy of auditory and visual phonological processing. *Neuroimage* 26:647–661.

Calvert, Gemma A., Edward T. Bullmore, Michael J. Brammer, Ruth Campbell, Steven C. R. Williams, Philip K. McGuire, Peter W. R. Woodruff, Susan D. Iversen, and Anthony S. David. 1997. Activation of auditory cortex during silent lipreading. *Science* 276:593–596.

Chan, Jason S., Thorsten Maucher, Johannes Schemmel, Dana Kilroy, Fiona N. Newell, and Karlheinz Meier. 2007. The virtual haptic display: a device for exploring 2-D virtual shapes in the tactile modality. *Behavioural Research Methods* 39:802–810.

Chomsky, Noam 1965. *Aspects of the Theory of Syntax*. Cambridge MA: MIT Press.

Cooper, Lynn A., and Roger N. Shepard. 1973. The time required to prepare for a rotated stimulus. *Memory and Cognition* 1:246–250.

Cohen, Laurent, and Stanislas Dehaene. 2004. Specialization within the ventral stream: the case for the visual word form area. *Neuroimage* 22:466–476.

Cohen, Laurent, Antoinette Jobert, Denis Le Bihan, and Stanislas Dehaene. 2004. Distinct unimodal and multimodal regions for word processing in the left temporal cortex. *Neuroimage* 23 (4):1256–1270.

Cohen, Laurent, Stéphane Lehéricy, Florence Chochon, Cathy Lemer, Sophie Rivaud, and Stanislas Dehaene. 2002. Language-specific tuning of visual cortex? Functional properties of the visual word form area. *Brain* 125:1054–1069.

Day, Sean. 2012. *Synesthesia*. <http://www.daysyn.com>.

Dehaene, Stanislas, Felipe Pegado, Lucia W. Braga, Paulo Ventura, Gilberto Nunes Filho, Antoinette Jobert, Ghislaine Dehaene-Lambertz, Régine Kolinsky, José Morais, and Laurent Cohen. 2010. How learning to read changes the cortical networks for vision and language. *Science (New York, N.Y.)*, 330 (6009):1359–1364.

Dehay, Collette, Henry Kennedy, and Jean Bullier. 1988. Characterization of transient cortical projections from auditory, somatosensory, and motor cortices to visual areas 17, 18, and 19 in the kitten. *Journal of Computational Neurology* 272:68–89.

Dixon, Mike J., Daniel Smilek, Cera Cudahy, and Philip M. Merikle. 2000. Five plus two equals yellow. *Nature* 406:365.

Dunn, Michael, Simon J. Greenhill, Stephen C. Levinson, and Russell Gray. 2011. Evolved structure of language shows lineage-specific trends in word-order universals. *Nature* 473 (7345):79–82

Fenske, Mark J., Elissa Aminoff, Nurit Gronau, and Moshe Bar. 2006. Top-down facilitation of visual object recognition: object-based and context-based contributions. *Progress in Brain Research* 155:3–21.

Foxe, John J., and Charles E. Schroeder. 2005. The case for feedforward multisensory convergence during early cortical processing. *Neuroreport* 16:419–423.

Ghazanfar, Asif A. and Charles E. Schroeder. 2006. Is neocortex essentially multisensory? *Trends in Cognitive Science* 10 (6):278–285.

Ghirardelli, Thomas G., Carol Bergfield Mills, Monica K. Zilioli, Leah P. Bailey, and Paige K. Kretschmar. 2010. Synesthesia affects verification of simple arithmetic equations. *Journal of General Psychology* 137:175–189.

Grainger Jonathan, Arnaud Rey, and Stéphane Dufau. 2008. Letter perception: from pixels to pandemonium. *Trends in Cognitive Sciences* 12:381–387.

Grossenbacher, Peter G., and Christopher T. Lovelace. 2001. Mechanisms of synesthesia: Cognitive and physiological constraints. *Trends in Cognitive Sciences*, 5:36–41.

Gori, Monica, Michela Del Viva, Giulio Sandini, and David C. Burr. 2008. Young children do not integrate visual and haptic form information. *Current Biology* 18:694–698.

Gori, Monica, Giulio Sandini, Cristina Martinoli, and David Burr. 2010. Poor haptic orientation discrimination in nonsighted children may reflect disruption of cross-sensory calibration. *Current Biology* 20:223–225.

Held, Richard, Yuri Ostrovsky, Beatrice de Gelder, Tapan Gandhi, Suma Ganesh, Umang Mathur, and Pawan Sinha. 2011. The newly sighted fail to match seen with felt. *Nature Neuroscience* 14:551–553.

Hensch, Takao K., and Michela Fagiolini. 2005. Excitatory-inhibitory balance and critical period plasticity in developing visual cortex. *Progress in Brain Research* 147:115–124.

Hong, Sang Wook, and Randolph Blake. 2008. Early visual mechanisms do not contribute to synesthetic color experience. *Vision Research* 48 (8):1018–1026.

Hötting, Kirsten, Frank Rösler, and Brigitte Röder. 2004. Altered auditory-tactile interactions in congenitally blind humans: An event-related potential study. *Experimental Brain Research* 159:370–381.

Hubbard, Edward M., Sanjay Manohar, and Vilayanur S. Ramachandran. 2006. Contrast affects the strength of synesthetic colors. *Cortex* 42:184–194.

Hubbard, Edward M., and Vilayanur S. Ramachandran. 2005. Neurocognitive mechanisms of synesthesia. *Neuron* 48:509–520.

Hunt, Lester J., Heidi Edwards, and Kathryn Quest. 1988. Haptic identification of letters using the left or right hand. *Perceptual and Motor Skills* 66:403–406.

Hunt, Lester J., Mary Janssen, Jerry Dagostino, and Barbara Gruber. 1989. Haptic identification of rotated letters using the left or right hand. *Perceptual and Motor Skills* 68:899–906.

James, William. 1981. *The Principles of Psychology*. Cambridge, MA: Harvard University Press. (Originally published in 1890.)

Jeon, Seong Taek, Joshua Hamid, Daphne Maurer, and Terri L. Lewis. 2010. Developmental changes during childhood in single-letter acuity and its crowding by surrounding contours. *Journal of Experimental Child Psychology* 107:423–437.

Joseph, Jane E., Michael A. Cerullo, Alison B. Farley, Nicholas A. Steinmetz, and Catherine R. Mier. 2006. fMRI correlates of cortical specialization and generalization for letter processing. *Neuroimage* 32:806.

Kilroy, D. 2006. Letter recognition by tactile perception and synaesthesia. Unpublished dissertation, Trinity College Dublin.

Köhler, Wolfgang (1929). Gestalt Psychology. New York: Liveright.

Lacey, Simon and Krish Sathian. 2012. Representation of object form in vision and touch. In *The Neural Bases of Multisensory Processes*, ed. Mark T. Murray and Micah M. Wallace, 179–188. Boca Raton, FL: CRC Press.

Lanthier, Sophie N., Evan R. Risko, Jennifer A. Stolz, and Derek Besner. 2009. Not all visual features are created equal: early processing in letter and word recognition. *Psychonomic Bulletin and Review* 16:67–73.

Larne, A. J. 2006. A possible account of synaesthesia dating from the seventeenth century. *Journal of the History of the Neurosciences: Basic and Clinical Perspectives* 15:245–249.

Lewkowicz, David J., and Asif A. Ghazanfar. 2009. The emergence of multisensory systems through perceptual narrowing. *Trends in Cognitive Sciences* 13:470–478.

Marks, Lawrence E. 1987. On cross-modal similarity: Auditory-visual interactions in speeded discrimination. *Journal of Experimental Psychology: Human Perception and Performance* 13:384–394.

Maurer, Daphne. 1993. Neonatal synesthesia: Implications for the processing of speech and faces. In *Developmental Neurocognition: Speech and Face Processing in the First Year of Life*, ed. Benedicte de Boysson-Bardies, Scania de Schonen, Peter Jusczyk, Peter McNeilage, and John Morton, 109–124. Dordrecht: Kluwer Academic Publishers.

Maurer, Daphne, and Catherine J. Mondloch. 2005. Neonatal synesthesia: A re-evaluation. In *Synesthesia: Perspectives from Cognitive Neuroscience*, ed. Lynn C. Robertson and Noam Sagiv, 193–213. New York: Oxford University Press.

Meltzoff, Andrew N., and Richard W. Borton. 1979. Intermodal matching by human neonates. *Nature* 282:403–404.

Mechelli, Andrea, Maria Luisa Gorno-Tempini, and Cathy, J. Price. 2003. Neuroimaging studies of word and pseudoword reading: consistencies, inconsistencies, and limitations. *Journal of Cognitive Neuroscience* 15 (2):260–271.

Mills, Carol Bergfeld, Meredith L. Viguers, Shari K. Edelson, Amanda T. Thomas, Stephanie L. Simon-Dack, and Joanne A. Innis. 2002. The color of two alphabets for a multilingual synesthete. *Perception* 31:1371–1394. doi:10.1068/p3429.

Molyneux, William. 1978. Letter to John Locke, 7 July. In *The Correspondence of John Locke*, 9 vols., ed. E.S. de Beer, vol. 3, no. 1064. Oxford: Clarendon Press. (Originally published in 1688.)

Nardini, Marko, Rachael Bedford, and Denis Mareschal. 2010. Fusion of visual cues is not mandatory in children. *Proceedings of the National Academy of Sciences of the United States of America* 107:17041–17046.

Nardini, Marko, Peter Jones, Rachael Bedford, and Oliver Braddick. 2008. Development of cue integration in human navigation. *Current Biology* 18:689–693.

Parise, Cesare V., and Charles Spence. 2009. "When birds of a feather flock together": synesthetic correspondences modulate audiovisual integration in non-synesthetes. *PLoS ONE* 4:e5664.

Pasqualotto, Achille, and Fiona N. Newell. 2007. The role of visual experience on the representation and updating of novel haptic scenes. *Brain and Cognition* 65:184–194.

Pegado, Felipe, Kimihiro Nakamura, Laurent Cohen, and Stanislas Dehaene. 2011. Breaking the symmetry: mirror discrimination for single letters but not for pictures in the visual word form area. *Neuroimage* 55:742–749.

Price, Cathy J., and Joseph T. Devlin. 2003. The myth of the visual word form area. *Neuroimage* 19:473–481.

Price, Cathy J., Richard J. S. Wise, and Richard S. J. Frackowiak. 1996. Demonstrating the implicit processing of visually presented words and pseudowords. *Cerebral Cortex* 6 (1):62–70.

Ramachandran, Vilayanur S., and Hubbard, E. M. 2001a. Psychophysical investigations into the neural basis of synaesthesia. *Proceedings of the Royal Society B: Biological Sciences* 268:979–983.

———. 2001b. Synaesthesia—a window into perception, thought and language. *Journal of Consciousness Studies* 8:3–34.

———. 2005. Hearing colours and tasting shapes. *Scientific American* 16:16–23.

Rich, Anina N., John L. Bradshaw, and Jason B. Mattingley. 2005. A systematic, large-scale study of synaesthesia: implications for the role of early experience in lexical-colour associations. *Cognition* 98:53–84.

Rosch, Eleanor. 1975. Cognitive representations of semantic categories. *Journal of Experimental Psychology: General* 104:192–233.

Rouw, Romke, Steven H. Scholte, and Olympia Colizoli. 2011. Brain areas involved in synaesthesia: A review. *Journal of Neuropsychology* 5:214–242.

Rudnicky, Alexander I., and Paul A. Kolers. 1984. Size and case of type as stimuli in reading. *Journal of Experimental Psychology: Human Perception and Performance* 10:231–249.

Sann, Coralie, and Arlette Streri. 2007. Perception of object shape and texture in human newborns: Evidence from cross-modal transfer tasks. *Developmental Science* 10:399–410.

Sanocki, Thomas. 1987. Visual knowledge underlying letter perception: Font-specific, schematic tuning. *Journal of Experimental Psychology: Human Perception and Performance* 13:267–278.

Simner, Julia. 2007. Beyond perception: Synaesthesia as a psycholinguistic phenomenon. *Trends in Cognitive Sciences* 11:23–29.

———. 2012. Defining synaesthesia. *British Journal of Psychology* 103:1–15.

Simner, Julia, Jennifer Harrold, Harriet Creed, Louise Monro, and Louise Foulkes. 2009. Early detection of markers for synaesthesia in childhood populations. *Brain* 132:57–64.

Simner, Julia, Jamie Ward, Monika Lanz, Ashok Jansari, Krist Noonan, Louise Glover, and David A. Oakley. 2005. Non-random associations of graphemes to colours in synaesthetic and non-synaesthetic populations. *Cognitive Neuropsychology* 22(8):1069–1085.

Smilek, D., B. A. Moffatt, J. Pasternak, B. N. White, Michael J. Dixon, and Philip M. Merikle. 2002. Synaesthesia: a case study of discordant monozygotic twins. *Neurocase* 8:338–342.

Smilek, Daniel, Michael J. Dixon, and Philip M. Merikle. 2005. Synaesthesia: discordant male monozygotic twins. *Neurocase* 11:363–370.

Spector, Ferrine and Daphne Maurer. 2011. The colors of the alphabet: Naturally-biased associations between shape and color. *Journal of Experimental Psychology. Human Perception and Performance* 37:484–495.

Steven, Megan S., and Colin Blakemore. 2004. Visual synaesthesia in the blind. *Perception* 33:855–868.

Swift, Jonathan. 1726. *Gulliver's Travels: Travels into Several Remote Nations of the World.* London: J. Motte.

Szwed, Marcin, Laurent Cohen, Emelie Qiao, and Stanislas Dehaene. 2009. The role of invariant line junctions in object and visual word recognition. *Vision Research* 49:718–725.

van Atteveldt, Nienke, Elia Formisano, Rainer Goebel, and Leo Blomert. 2004. Integration of letters and speech sounds in the human brain. *Neuron* 43:271–282.

van Atteveldt, Nienke, Alard Roebroeck, and Rainer Goebel. 2009. Interaction of speech and script in human auditory cortex: insights from neuro-imaging and effective connectivity. *Hearing Research* 258:152–164.

van Leeuwen, Tessa M., Karl M. Petersson, and Peter Hagoort. 2010. Synaesthetic colour in the brain: Beyond colour areas. A functional magnetic resonance imaging study of synaesthetes and matched controls. *PLoS ONE* 5:e12074.

von Kriegstein, Katharina, Andreas Kleinschmidt, Philipp Sterzer, and Anne-Lise Giraud. 2005. Interaction of face and voice areas during speaker recognition. *Journal of Cognitive Neuroscience* 17:367–376.

Wallace, Mark T., and Barry E. Stein. 2007. Early experience determines how the senses will interact. *Journal of Neurophysiology* 97:921–926.

Wallace, Mark T., Thomas J. Perrault Jr, W. David Hairston, and Barry E. Stein. 2004. Visual experience is necessary for the development of multisensory integration. *Journal of Neuroscience* 24:9580–9584.

Ward, Jamie, Brett Huckstep and Elias Tsakanikos. 2006. Sound-colour synaesthesia: to what extent does it use cross-modal mechanisms common to us all? *Cortex* 42: 264–280.

Ward, Jamie, Ryan Li, Shireen Salih, and Noam Sagiv. 2007. Varieties of grapheme-colour synaesthesia: A new theory of phenomenological and behavioural differences. *Consciousness and Cognition* 16: 913–931.

Watson, Marcus R., Kathleen A. Akins, and James T. Enns. 2012. Second-order mappings in grapheme-color synesthesia. *Psychonomic Bulletin and Review* 19:211–217.

Wilson, Kevin D., and Martha J. Farah. 2003. When does the visual system use viewpoint-invariant representations during recognition? *Cognitive Brain Research* 3:399–415.

Witthoft, Nathan, and Jonathan Winawer. 2006. Synesthetic colors determined by having colored refrigerator magnets in childhood. *Cortex* 42:175–183.

Yoncheva, Yuliya N., Jason D. Zevin, Urs Maurer, and Bruce D. McCandliss. 2010. Auditory selective attention to speech modulates activity in the visual word form area. *Cerebral Cortex* 20:622–632.

CHAPTER 11

SYNESTHESIA IN NON-ALPHABETIC LANGUAGES

WAN-YU HUNG

In studies of synesthesia and languages, links have often been drawn mapping the underlying mechanisms of synesthesia to the mechanisms of language processing (e.g., Simner 2007; Simner, Glover, and Mowat 2006; Ward, Simner, and Auyeung 2005). People who experience colors for words, for instance, usually report a tie between the color of a word and the color of its first letter (e.g., *cat* taking the color of *c*), and this relationship mirrors the special role that initial letters play in the retrieval of word meaning (Simner 2007; Simner, Glover, and Mowat 2006; Ward, Simner, and Auyeung 2005). The bulk of evidence has been gathered from studies on alphabetic languages over the past two decades including English (e.g., Baron-Cohen, Wyke, and Binnie 1987; Simner 2007; Simner, Glover, and Mowat 2006; Ward, Simner, and Auyeung 2005), German, French, Spanish, Italian, Irish Gaelic (Barnett et al. 2009), and Russian (Mills et al. 2002; Witthoft and Winawer 2006). However, little is known about whether such relationship between synesthesia and language processing can be generalized to non-alphabetic languages. This question of how synesthesia works in non-alphabetic languages has been largely ignored until recently when two synesthesia research labs, one at the University of Edinburgh (Hung 2010; Simner, Hung, and Shillcock 2011) and the other at Baylor College of Medicine, Texas (Eagleman 2008; Eagleman et al. 2007), began to extend their reach into the Chinese population. This new line of research asks an important question about synesthesia and language: whether synesthesia shows similar traits across different languages (or language types), or alternatively, whether it is governed by rules that are language-specific and so *not* shared across languages (Simner 2007; Simner, Hung, and Shillcock 2011). The aim of this chapter is thus to provide an overview of the current understanding of synesthesia in Chinese. This chapter begins with a brief introduction to the Chinese language followed by a review of evidence both from anecdotal reports and from current empirical investigations of synesthesia in Chinese.

THE CHINESE LANGUAGE

Features of the Chinese language

Chinese has many different dialects spoken in different regions of China and also in certain south-east Asian countries including Taiwan, Malaysia, and Singapore (DeFrancis 1984). This chapter focuses on synesthesia in Mandarin Chinese because this constitutes the largest spoken Chinese dialect worldwide. The basic constituents of Mandarin Chinese are characters, and these characters are recognized by their non-alphabetic, square-like configurations. In contrast to alphabetic words which comprise linear strings of letters, Chinese characters are constructed from strokes which are usually fashioned in a compact pattern that fits within a square area (e.g., 家 *home*). Unlike letters of alphabetic words, individual strokes within a character never function as a phonemic unit of pronunciation, and many of the stroke patterns are thought to have evolved from ancient pictographs that denoted objects by representing their physical features (e.g., 木 *tree*). For this reason, reading Chinese characters lacks the "grapheme-to-phoneme" conversion rules typical in alphabetic languages, which assign phonology to a written word based on the sound of its component letters (e.g., $b \rightarrow$ [b]; Coltheart and Rastle 1994). Given this, learning character pronunciation requires an engagement of rote memory to help establish the pairing of sound and form.

One critical feature of the characters in Mandarin Chinese is that all of them are pronounced monosyllabically, in that they comprise an onset and a rhyme (e.g., 媽 *mother* [ma], containing an onset [m] and a rhyme [a]). Mandarin Chinese is also a tonal language in that four main tones are used to distinguish between characters (first tone = high, second tone = rising, third tone = falling-then-rising, fourth tone = falling). For instance, the syllable [ma] pronounced with the first tone means 媽 *mother*, but could also mean 麻 *hemp*, 馬 *horse*, or 罵 *to scold* if the syllable is pronounced with the second, third, or fourth tone respectively. As such, tones serve as a prosodic, supra-segmental feature of characters, and this feature has been shown to be important for the recognition of characters (Wang 1973). Research has found that Chinese children who underperformed in discriminating same/different tones in homophones would also tend to underperform in naming aloud written characters, which suggests that character reading ability is positively correlated with sensitivity to character tones (Chan and Siegel 2001; So and Siegel 1997).

Since the early twentieth century, several spelling systems have been developed and introduced into Chinese speaking countries as an aid to teaching Chinese. Although different systems are used in some places, there are two major systems: Hanyu Pinyin (known in Chinese as 漢語拼音) and Bopomo (known as 注音). Chinese children typically learn one spelling system early on in their kindergarten and primary education, with Pinyin most used in China and Bopomo in Taiwan. In Pinyin, character pronunciation is represented by English letters, with the addition of a digit (from 1 to 4) at the end to indicate character tone (e.g., 媽 *mother* [ma1], 麻 *hemp* [ma2], 馬 *horse* [ma3], 罵 *to scold* [ma4]; Howie 1976). The alternative, Bopomo, uses traditional Chinese phonetic alphabet (e.g., ㄅ, ㄆ, ㄇ) for transcription, and diacritics at the end for tone-marking (e.g., no diacritic marking = high tone, [ˊ] = rising tone, [ˇ] = falling-then-rising tone, [ˋ] = falling tone). In this system, the examples [ma1–4] from Pinyin are written as [ㄇㄚ], [ㄇㄚˊ], [ㄇㄚˇ], [ㄇㄚˋ], respectively. Later in this chapter, we will revisit these two spelling systems and discuss what role these spellings may play in the synesthetic coloring of characters (and relatedly, whether characters written in Pinyin and Bopomo spellings might trigger their own colors in synesthesia).

While simple pictographs constitute the bases of many ancient Chinese texts, modern Chinese has evolved in a fashion such that the majority of characters (about 80%) are compounds composed of two further morphemic subcomponents known as radicals. The "phonetic radical" provides information about the pronunciation of the characters, and the "semantic radical" provides information about its meaning. For instance, the character 櫻, *cherry blossom*, consists of a phonetic radical on the right, 嬰 [ying1], that indicates the character is to be pronounced as [ying1], and a semantic radical on the left, 木 *tree*, that shows the character is a type of tree/plant. In this case, since the phonetic radical provides full information about the pronunciation of the character, this is known as a "regular" character (Hsiao and Shillcock 2006). However, not all characters take their exact pronunciation from their phonetic radicals. Some characters only take the rhyme of their phonetic radical (e.g., 騙 [pian4] = 馬 + 扁 [bian3]), while others may take a completely different pronunciation (e.g., 調 [diao4] = 言 + 周 [zhou1]). These latter kinds of characters are thus termed "irregular" (Hsiao and Shillcock 2006). Moreover, although many compound characters have the two types of radicals placed side by side, with the semantic radical on the left and the phonetic radical on the right, the reverse is also possible (i.e., with a phonetic radical on the left and a semantic radical on the right; 鸚 *parrot* [ying1] = 嬰 [ying1] + 鳥 *bird*). Finally, many Chinese radicals can also stand alone in their own right as legal characters; for instance, the phonetic radical 嬰 [ying1] in the earlier examples is also a character in its own right meaning *infant*. This chapter will later return to these various features of characters and review the roles they play in the synesthetic coloring of Chinese.

Chinese character recognition

The following sections give a concise overview of some key research about language processing in Chinese character recognition, and this forms the theoretical ground for later sections of this chapter where I review current evidence of how these features play a role in synesthesia in Chinese. Chinese character recognition involves both the processing of character orthography (written form) and character phonology (pronunciation). Since this fact forms the basis of hypotheses I present later in this chapter, I review studies below on both Chinese orthography recognition and phonology recognition.

The fact that written Chinese is a logographic system (i.e., a system in which character meaning is often transparent from its orthography) has led some researchers to speculate that characters may have a direct relationship between their meaning and written form (Chen, d'Arcais, and Cheung 1995; Leck, Weekes, and Chen 1995; Liu 1995; Wang 1973). This contrasts with alphabetic languages in which component graphemes are directly mapped onto phonemes rather than meaning (e.g., $b \rightarrow$ [b]; Coltheart et al. 1979; Coltheart and Rastle 1994). It has thus been suggested that characters are the basic recognizable units in written Chinese and hence are read holistically without having to be mentally decomposed into smaller units (Tan and Perfetti 1998; Wang 1973; Yu et al. 1990). For instance, the character 木 might be known immediately as *tree* because it looks like tree. Evidence shows that Chinese readers seldom differ in reaction time for naming characters with certain different substructures, such as different spatial arrangements of their constituent radicals (e.g., whether the radicals are positioned in a horizontal fashion with one radical on the left and another on the right such as 王 + 里 = 理, or whether the radicals are posed in a vertical fashion with one radical on the top and another at the bottom such as 小 + 大 = 尖; Yu et al. 1990).

However, conflicting evidence has shown that other subcomponents of a character *may* influence the reaction time of character naming, such as the number of strokes in a character: characters with fewer strokes tended to be named faster (Peng and Wang 1997; Tan and Perfetti, 1998; Shen and Zhu 1994). Phonetic regularity, too, has been shown to have an effect on character naming: regular characters (i.e., those which sound completely the same with their phonetic radical) were named faster than irregular characters (i.e., those with some form of phonetic variation; Seidenberg 1985). Nonetheless, it is important to note that these subcharacter effects were not found in high-frequency characters (i.e., characters that are very commonly used in writing and/or speaking), and this suggests that their component radicals are "lexicalized" into a single unit, which in turn cancels out any subcharacter effects (Peng and Wang 1997; Seidenberg 1985; Shen and Zhu 1994). Given this frequency effect, researchers have proposed that previously found null effects of stroke number (Chen and Yung, 1989) and phonetic regularity (Yu et al. 1990) may be due to these earlier studies only using high-frequency characters in their experiments (Taft and Zhu 1997).

Although it remains debatable whether it is individual strokes or radicals that constitute the earliest perceptual/cognitive unit in character recognition, evidence has shown that radicals can exert clear "psychologically real" effects on Chinese speakers when they read characters. In other words, radicals may influence the way in which characters are read. By manipulating the number of radicals in a character and meanwhile controlling its overall stroke number, Chen, Allport and Marshall (1996) found that character naming speed was in fact dictated by the number of radicals, not the number of strokes, within a character. Characters with fewer radicals tended to be named faster than those with more radicals (e.g., a two-radical character such as 日 + 月 = 明 versus a three-radical character such as 口 + 日 + 日 = 唱). It is believed that any previous absence of a radical effect in prior studies may have been due to confounding the number of radicals with the number of strokes (i.e., characters that have more radicals usually happen to have more strokes). This special status of radicals as "psychologically real" units in character recognition will be relevant for the later parts of this chapter when I review the current evidence on how synesthesia works in Chinese characters.

Research has also shown that different radicals may have different weights in character recognition depending on their position within the character. For instance, characters are recognized faster and more accurately if they contain a high-frequency radical on the right side compared to on the left (Taft and Zhu 1997). This suggests that right-side radicals may have "heavier weights" in character recognition than do left-side radicals. Nonetheless, the other side of the coin may equally be true if we consider that left-side radicals are usually in an optimal viewing position since eye fixations during single-character reading tend to exert a leftward drift from the centre of the whole character (Hsiao and Cottrell 2009). This chapter will return to this issue of radical position when reviewing synesthesia in Chinese characters.

In addition to the relative position of radicals in a character, radicals' phonetic properties may also play a role in character recognition. Given that pronunciations are never related to constituent strokes (e.g., none of the strokes in 馬 horse indicates the pronunciation [ma3]; Leong 1973; Wang 1973) researchers previously believed that character meaning might be accessed without, or prior to, accessing any information about phonology, pointing especially to pictographs that denote objects visually (e.g., 木 tree; 馬 horse; 火 fire; Wang 1973; for reviews, see Hung and Tzeng 1981; Liu 1995; Perfetti and Zhang 1995; Tan and Perfetti 1998). This view, however, has gradually lost its appeal since the early 1990s in the face of growing evidence that phonological processing is an immediate, automatic part of character recognition (for reviews, see Cheng and Shih 1988; Hung, Tzeng, and Tzeng 1992; Tan and Perfetti 1997, 1998). In one character-naming study with 20 native Chinese speakers, Perfetti and Zhang (1991) found that participants' performance in character-naming was significantly speeded when the target character was shown immediately after a character with the same pronunciation (e.g., target character: 視 watch [shi4]; homophonic character: 事 matter [shi4]), compared with when presented after a visually similar but phonetically different character (現 now [xian4]), or a semantically-related but visually and phonetically different character (看 see [kan4]), or a completely different control character (清 clear [qing1]). Similar phonetic facilitation has also been reported in English; for example, masking a target word (e.g., made) with a homophonic non-word (e.g., mayd) can also speed naming (Perfetti, Bell, and Delaney 1988). Given this role of phonology in character recognition, the following section will review evidence for what role phonological qualities (phonetic spellings, phonetic radicals) may play in synesthesia in Chinese characters.

How Does Synesthesia Operate
in Chinese Characters?

Research on synesthesia in Chinese is still in an early stage with limited empirical evidence, and currently (at the point of writing this chapter) there are only two empirical research projects investigating synesthetic coloring in Chinese characters. Thus, a substantial part of the following sections will focus on studies from these two groups (in Edinburgh and Texas), and I will review their findings as well as their methods for the "diagnosis" of Chinese synesthetes.

"Diagnosis" of Chinese synesthetes

Many studies in English use consistency over time as a gold standard for diagnosing synesthesia (Baron-Cohen, Wyke, and Binnie 1987; Cytowic 1989; Rich, Bradshaw, and Mattingley 2005; Simner and Logie 2007; Simner et al. 2005; Ward and Simner 2003). In such studies, synesthetes list their colors or other sensory associations for a list of stimuli (e.g., a = red, b = blue, c = yellow, etc.) and are then asked to repeat these associations some considerable time later. Synesthetes are highly consistent in their reports (e.g., if a is red, it is always red),[1] compared with controls asked to invent analogous associations who recall these from memory and are often highly inconsistent (e.g., a = red at time 1 but green at time 2). Two Chinese studies reviewed here also applied this methodology to identify Chinese synesthetes, albeit with slightly different materials for testing different types of synesthesia. In their tests for Chinese number-color synesthetes (i.e., those who see colors in response to Chinese number characters, e.g., 一 *one*, 二 *two*), Eagleman and colleagues (2007; Eagleman 2008) developed a computerized test using ten Chinese number characters (from 零 *zero* to 九 *nine*) as trigger stimuli, each presented three times randomly in one single session (rather than over a lengthy time interval) for the assessment of consistency. By comparing against the performance of non-synesthete controls using the same stimuli, the authors identified Chinese number-color synesthetes as those who selected significantly more consistent colors throughout the test (Eagleman et al. 2007).

Simner, Hung, and Shillcock (2011) examined synesthetic coloring in Chinese focusing on Chinese characters. A range of common characters were used in their test of consistency, including characters that indicate concrete objects (e.g., 球 *ball*, 友 *friend*),

---

[1] Traditionally, it has been assumed that colours are consistent over time not only in their category (e.g., red) but also in their particular shade (i.e., saturation, hue, luminance). However, since many consistency studies elicit colours by verbal response ("A is red"), it is not entirely clear whether colour shading might change over time. For the purpose of this chapter, we continue to assume that synaesthetic colours tend to remain wholly similar over time.

abstract concepts (e.g., 力 *strength*, 言 *speech*) as well as concepts about time (e.g., 今 *today*, 年 *year*). Simner, Hung, and Shillcock identified genuine Chinese synesthetes by conducting a test of consistency over a longer period of time. Their aim was to clearly separate synesthetes from non-synesthetes, who might be able to perform the consistency test well over short time intervals, but not over longer ones. In this test, Simner and colleagues first identified a group of "potential synesthetes" as those participants who self-reported synesthesia (by contact via their online information website). The authors named these as "potential synesthetes" because their reported synesthesia had not yet been verified with objective assessments. To do this, Simner and colleagues gave each participant a surprise retest of their synesthetic associations 6 months after their first test. The consistency scores of these potential synesthetes were then compared individually with the consistency scores of a group of non-synesthetes performing an analogous task with a retest after only 2 weeks. It is a common practice to "stack the deck" against synesthetes in this way, in order to test them more conservatively (e.g., Ward and Simner 2003). Based on this method, only potential synesthetes who showed significantly more consistency than the controls were considered to be genuine synesthetes (Simner, Hung, and Shillcock 2011). These two studies form the earliest efforts in synesthesia research to identify Chinese synesthetes in a systematic way.

In an additional study that applied this test of consistency with 831 school children in Taiwan aged between 12 and 15, Hung found that character-color synesthesia could have a prevalence of about 1 in 100 in the Chinese population (Hung 2010), which would make it comparable to the estimated prevalence of grapheme-color synesthesia in the English-speaking population (Simner et al. 2006). Boys were found to be approximately as likely as girls to experience colors for characters; although there was a non-significant numerical trend with a female to male ratio of 2:1. This ratio is consistent with the numerical trends for grapheme-color synesthesia in English, which have been shown to be in a range between 1.1:1 and 2:1 (Simner et al. 2006; Simner et al. 2009; Ward and Simner 2005). Further investigations with participants from a wider age range are needed before conclusive estimates can be given about the prevalence, as well as the sex ratio, of character-color synesthesia in Chinese. That said, this data provide clues to the number of Chinese character-color synesthetes in the world (with an estimate of 1.3 million), making it likely to be the single largest group of synesthetes worldwide.

Synesthetic coloring in Chinese; a rule-based system

We saw earlier that a Chinese character can be read holistically (e.g., if high frequency) and/or via its subcharacter components (e.g., phonetic components and radicals). The following sections will consider synesthetic coloring by these two means. From a holistic view, we ask whether and how character frequency and character meaning might influence synesthetic coloring. From a subcharacter point of view we ask whether coloring might be influenced by a character's phonetic spelling (Pinyin/Bopomo spelling) and/or its component radicals.

Synesthetic coloring based on subcharacter components

Effects of phonetic spellings: initial letters and initial vowels

A possible link between the way a character is colored in Chinese synesthesia, and the way that character is spelled in the phonetic writing system was first mentioned in an anecdotal self-report from an English grapheme-color synesthete who speaks Chinese as a second language (L2) (Duffy 2001). In that report, Duffy (2001) described experiencing a transfer of her synesthetic colors in her native language (English) to Chinese when she mentally transcribed the pronunciation of character sounds into Pinyin spellings using letters of the alphabet ("seeing" characters being spelled out in colored letters in her "mind's eye"). This suggested that the color of a character may be related to the color of its associated Pinyin (or indeed Bopomo) spelling. Simner, Hung, and Shillcock (2011) put this idea to formal testing by asking a group of native Chinese synesthetes (i.e., first-language Chinese, L1, $n = 4$) and a group of second-language Chinese synesthetes (L2, $n = 3$) to indicate their synesthetic colors for a set of characters and their associated phonetic spellings (e.g., 方 and *fang1*). The authors confirmed that phonetic spellings can influence the coloring of characters, since some synesthetes showed systematic associations between the coloring of characters and the coloring of their spelled counterparts. This association usually meant that characters took on the color of the first letter or the first vowel in their phonetic spelling (e.g., the character 方 [fang1] tends to take on the color of the letter *f* or *a*).

However, not all synesthetes who see colors for characters experience the influence of phonetic spellings, and this is true especially for synesthetes who are native speakers of Chinese. Although some native (L1) speakers did show an influence of the first letter or first vowel, this only happened when words were presented to the synesthete in their phonetic Pinyin/Bopomo spellings (e.g., [fang1] took the color of *f* or *a*), but this happened considerably less often when words were presented in their character form. For *second*-language (L2) Chinese synesthetes, however, the coloring was often determined by the initial letters (or vowels) of the characters irrespective of how they were presented (i.e., whether in the form of Pinyin spellings or characters). In other words, Pinyin/Bopomo spellings had far less effect for native, compared to second-language speakers. This is likely to be because L2 synesthesia may be based on the L1 synesthesia, which is largely dominated by colored letters. Furthermore, research in bilingualism has suggested that reading Chinese as a second language involves unconsciously translating it into one's first language (Thierry and Wu 2007) and this would further reinforce the effect of spelling. In contrast, for native speakers, Pinyin/Bopomo spellings would typically have been learned only long ago in childhood rather than being in current use. It therefore appears that Chinese synesthetes may have developed a different mechanism for the coloring of characters, in addition to the mechanism for coloring phonetic spellings.

The presence of first letter/vowel effects in the coloring of characters or phonetic spellings reflects their similar role in the synesthetic coloring of alphabetic languages (e.g., for English synesthetes, *cat* tends to take on the color of *c* or *a*; Simner 2007; Simner, Glover, and Mowat 2006; Ward, Simner, and Auyeung 2005). In English, it is possible to tell whether this effect is graphemic or phonemic, since English letters can have more than one possible pronunciation (e.g., the letter *c* sometimes corresponds to the sound [s] such as in the word *cite*, and sometimes to the sound [k] as in *cat*). This fact allows graphemic and phonemic influences to be teased apart. If the word-color is based on graphemes, then words such as *cat* and *cite* (which have the same grapheme but different pronunciation) would both colored the same. However, if word-color is based on phonemes, these words would be colored differently (since they begin with different phonemes). In Chinese, it is not possible to dissociate these two components of phonetic spelling using this method because both Pinyin and Bopomo systems use consistent 1:1 grapheme-to-phoneme mappings, such that the same Pinyin/Bopomo symbol always corresponds to the same phoneme (e.g., the Pinyin symbol *c* is always pronounced as [tsh]). It remains unclear whether the effects shown above of phonetic spelling in Chinese character coloring are visual/graphemic or phonological, and further research is needed to untangle these two factors (Simner, Hung, and Shillcock 2011).

Effects of character tones

There has been speculation that lexical tone might also play a role in determining character colors, given its special status in character recognition in providing critical supra-segmental speech information. So far there is no clear evidence that lexical tone is involved in synesthetic word-coloring. In the same study by Simner, Hung, and Shillcock (2011) which looked into the role of phonetic spellings (see earlier), the authors also found that character colors did not systematically vary with the four character tones (e.g., 梯 [ti1], 提 [ti2], 體 [ti3], 替 [ti4]). There was no evidence that tone-matched characters (e.g., 梯 [ti1], 方 [fang1]) were more likely to be colored the same than characters paired randomly. Although this finding was found to be true both for their L1 and L2 Chinese synesthetes, their small sample size means this finding has limited implications. To verify this provisional null effect of tone, further research with a larger number of Chinese speaking synesthetes is necessary. Future research may also examine whether character tones would influence other attributes of colors such as brightness and saturation.

We saw earlier that the first letters/vowels in phonetic spellings consistently played an important role both in the coloring of characters and their phonetic spellings for the L2 synesthetes, but not for the L1 synesthetes (for whom these letters usually influenced the coloring of spelled words only). This raises the question as to what determines the L1 (native speaker) synesthetes' coloring for characters. The following sections shift the focus to the morphological structures of characters. Since radicals constitute the morphemic elements of characters (e.g., the character 櫻 [ying1], *cherry blossom*, consists of two radicals: a semantic radical 木 [mu4] *tree* and a phonetic radical 嬰 [ying1] *infant*), the next section reviews evidence on how component radicals in a character might influence the coloring of that character.

Effects of radicals

In one recent study, I and my colleagues (Hung 2010; see also Hung et al., in preparation) revealed that the radicals in a character sometimes determine the coloring of
that character, according to certain rules. We tested 22 Chinese-speaking synesthetes
(Asian: $n = 12$, Caucasian: $n = 1$, mixed ethnicity: $n = 1$, ethnicity undisclosed: $n = 8$;
female: $n = 16$, male: $n = 3$, gender undisclosed: $n = 3$) by giving each synesthete a series
of individual characters (e.g., 櫻 [ying1] *cherry blossom*) and their component radicals
(e.g., 木 [mu4] *tree*; 嬰 [ying1] *infant*) in two separate blocks. Along with each char-
acter/radical, participants were presented with a digital color wheel on screen and
from which each was asked to select the color that best matched their synesthetic color
experiences. The relationship between the colors of characters and the colors of their
component radicals was then assessed. Specifically, we examined the three ingredients
of each synesthetic color: its hue, saturation and brightness, and asked whether these
ingredients were influenced by the location of the radicals within the character (e.g.,
left versus right), or by the function the radicals (e.g., semantic versus phonetic). The
results showed that there was a significant influence of radicals on the coloring of characters: left radicals were more likely to determine the hue of the character's synesthetic
color, whereas right radicals determined the brightness. Moreover, the saturation of
synesthetic colors tended to be determined by semantic radicals when they were positioned on the left in a character. For instance, the character 櫻 tended to trigger a color
whose hue was determined by the left radical 木, whose brightness was determined by
the right radical 嬰, and whose saturation was determined by the left-semantic radical
(which is also 木).

This study shows that the synesthetic coloring of a character can be influenced by various subcomponents within it. However, further research is required to understand how
the radicals interact in the make-up of character colors. This kind of composite coloring driven by morphemic units has also been found in other languages. In one study in
German, for instance, compound words (e.g., *Fährmann* = *ferry* + *man*) tended to produce more than one dominant color (Simner 2007; see also <http://www.uni-erfurt.de/
psycholinguistik/Kubitza.html>), and this suggests, as in Chinese, that different components of a word can have an influence on the overall coloring of the word. That said,
this composite coloring in German may be subject to word frequency since it tended to
be absent in *high-frequency* compound words, which were usually associated with one
dominant color only. This tendency has been explained as high-frequency compounds
(e.g., *Bahnhof* = *station*) being lexicalized as a single unit (i.e., mentally encoded as a
non-divisible word), and so this in turn would generate a single dominant color for the
word as a whole (Simner 2007). Thus, it seems that the determining factors of synesthetic coloring for a word may also come from the word itself as a whole (and likewise
for the character itself as a whole in Chinese). The next section reviews influences from
the holistic level of the character, where I consider a character's overall visual configuration, its character frequency, and its meaning.

Synesthetic coloring for the character as a whole

Effects of visual configuration

In a study that looked into synesthetic coloring for sequential units such as letters of the alphabet and numbers, Eagleman (2008) found that for letters/numbers consisting of a simple shape such as a circle, line or cross (e.g., Q and X, 0 and 1), the synesthetic coloring tended to be colorless (clear or white). A similar trend was also found in the coloring of Chinese number characters such as 一 (*one*) and 十 (*ten*), which again have simple shapes, and whose synesthetic colors again tended to be achromatic. This achromaticity was not true for complex number characters such as 零 (*zero*). Thus, it has been suggested that the overall visual configuration of a character may play a role in determining the synesthetic coloring of the character.

Effects of frequency

Previous studies in grapheme-color synesthesia have suggested that familiarity with letters may influence synesthetic colors since high-frequency (i.e., common) letters tend to be associated with high-frequency color terms (e.g., $a \rightarrow red$; Simner and Ward 2008; Simner et al. 2005) and have brighter and more saturated colors (Beeli, Esslen, and Jäncke 2007) than infrequent letters. A comparable frequency effect was found in the coloring of Chinese characters in which high-frequency characters were also found to be more likely associated with high-frequency color terms (e.g., 人 *people* → red), albeit that this tendency was significant only for certain individual synesthetes, rather than as a group (Hung, 2010).

Effects of meaning

While previous studies on grapheme-color synesthesia have shown that the coloring of letters can be driven by meaning associations (e.g., $d \rightarrow dog \rightarrow$ brown, $r \rightarrow red \rightarrow$ red; Rich, Bradshaw, and Mattingley 2005; Simner et al. 2005), one study by Hung (2010) showed that a comparable link with meaning may also exist in the synesthetic coloring of characters. In that study, nine Chinese synesthetes completed a questionnaire about their colors for 60 characters, among which half referred to an abstract concept with no real-world color (e.g., 今 *today*, 年 *year*) while the other half referred to a concrete object that had a distinct real-world color (e.g., 田 *farm field* = green, 刀 *knife* = silver). Five hundred and eighty-one non-synesthetic Chinese speakers were also tested to serve as controls and they performed an analogous task using free-associations (i.e., "Please freely associate a color to each of the following characters"). For both groups, Hung measured the frequency of each color associated with each test characters, as well as the overall frequency of that color in the responses as a whole (e.g., how often "red" was associated with the character 田 *farm field*, and how often "red" was given as a response overall). This overall frequency was then used as a baseline for assessing whether, for each character individually, any of its associated colors occurred more often than chance would predict. The results showed that both synesthetes and non-synesthetes had significant coloring preferences for certain characters. In the case of concrete words, these colors were often the same as the real-world color (e.g., 田 *farm field* → green). An implication is that synesthetic coloring can be driven by character meaning, and this was also found in the non-synesthetes' coloring task. However, it is to be noted that synesthetes and non-synesthetes differed in the extent to which their coloring was influenced by meaning. Non-synesthetes showed significant coloring preferences for 57 (out of 60) characters, whereas a comparable preference existed only for 11 characters for the synesthetes. This high result in the control group may appear counter-intuitive at first sight given that only half of the test characters involved real-world colors (e.g., 田 *farm field* = green). The extra preferences may be accounted for by the fact that many of the supposedly abstract characters in fact had culturally stereotyped colors, or connotations of related objects with a distinct color. For example, the character 年 (*year*) was significantly associated with red for our non-synesthetes probably because they tended to associate the concept of year with the concept of Chinese new year, a time in which red is predominantly used for festive decors as a representation of good luck and fortune. Non-synesthetes also appeared to color characters based on the associated gender classification in a way that feminine characters tended to be red whereas masculine characters were blue (e.g., 媽 *mother*, 姊 *older sister*, 妹 *younger sister* = red; 爸 *father*, 兄 *older brother*, 弟 *younger brother* = blue). Other factors, too, served as a shared source for making color associations in non-synesthetes. For instance, the character 社 (*society*), which had been pre-selected to be neutral in color, was significantly associated with black for the non-synesthetes. One possibility is that this association stemmed from the vocabulary 黑社會 (*gang*), which is a common three-character word in daily use in which the character 社 (*society*) is immediately preceded by a color character 黑 that means black. Conversely, for our nine synesthetes, far fewer characters had a shared significant coloring preference across the group, and this seems consistent with existing knowledge that synesthetic associations are often idiosyncratic (e.g., synesthetes tend to disagree with one another on their synesthetic experience in response to the same trigger).

The previous sections have shown that the synesthetic coloring of characters involves various aspects of different Chinese linguistic systems all working together, ranging from character meaning to character frequency, as well as component radicals and phonetic spellings. The Pinyin spelling is especially important for L2 Chinese synesthetes whose first language uses letters of the alphabet, given that Pinyin also uses the same alphabet for spelling. This finding is of particular interest because it suggests a potential transfer of synesthetic coloring from one linguistic system to another. As such, the next section reviews how synesthetic coloring can migrate from Chinese to an alphabetic language such as English.

Synesthetic coloring transferrable across Chinese and English

Many synesthetes who speak more than one language report experiencing synesthesia for later-acquired languages in addition to their first language (e.g., an English–Russian grapheme-color synesthete reported experiencing colors both for the English alphabet and the Cyrillic alphabet; Mills et al. 2002; Witthoft and Winawer 2006). However, this issue of whether synesthesia necessarily crosses to a later-acquired language remains debatable. Ramachandran and Hubbard (2003) reported the case of a Chinese–English bilingual synesthete (L1 in Chinese) who experienced synesthesia only in Chinese and not in English. Interestingly, our evidence, as mentioned earlier, suggests that synesthetic transfer is possible even between an alphabetic language and a non-alphabetic language; we saw that for second-language (L2) Chinese synesthetes, the colors of Chinese characters tend to be heavily influenced by the colors of their corresponding phonetic spellings (Simner, Hung, and Shillcock 2011). Previous studies have shown that synesthetic transfer can be established on a visual and/or a phonetic basis: letters of different alphabet systems that look or sound alike can induce similar synesthetic response (e.g., the same colors for English: *b* and Cyrillic: *b*; or for English *f* [f] and Cyrillic: *Φ* [f]; Mills et al. 2002; Witthoft and Winawer 2006).

To examine whether a comparable form of transfer may also exist in the colors experienced by Chinese–English bilingual synesthetes, Hung (2010) examined the relationship between the coloring of the Chinese Bopomo alphabet and the coloring of the English alphabet in a Chinese–English bilingual synesthete (L1 in Chinese) who reported seeing colors for both systems. By using a computerized test that incorporated a digitized color wheel, the synesthete was able to represent his synesthetic colors in a color space for letters of both alphabets. His color responses were then compared across languages for letters that look alike, or sound alike. Results showed that his colors for visually-alike letters (e.g., Bopomo: ㄨ versus English: *X*) were significantly closer than for letters that were randomly matched (e.g., Bopomo: ㄨ versus English: *A*), but no such relationship was significant in phonetically-alike letters (e.g., Bopomo: ㄆ [ph] versus English: *P*). Since this particular synesthete learned to speak English (around 12 years old) much later than when he started to learn the Bopomo alphabet (around 6 years old), it is possible that his synesthetic colors for the English alphabet were derived from his colors for Bopomo letters. Further research is required to determine the direction of his synesthetic transfer.

Despite growing interest in how synesthesia can transfer across languages, little is known about how quickly it can transfer to a newly-acquired language. Methodological constraints make it difficult to trace and determine accurately the onset of synesthetic transfer on the basis of memory. A study by Mroczko et al. (2009) looked into this issue of timing and revealed that synesthesia can transfer to newly-acquired linguistic symbols after only a short period of learning. However, studies elsewhere have indicated that synesthetic associations thus established may be compromised in their stability over time compared with those that were established early on (Smilek et al. 2007). To further examine how fast linguistically-induced synesthesia may transfer to a newly acquired language, Hung (2010) recruited a group of English monolingual grapheme color synesthetes (*n* = 8) who had no prior knowledge of the Chinese language, and tested them with the Chinese Bopomo alphabet by asking whether they experienced any color for this alphabet on the very first encounter without any learning practice. The synesthetes all reported experiencing colors for the Bopomo alphabet, but the experience was found to be significantly less intense than those reported by L1 Chinese synesthetes. This result provides another line of evidence that may complement previous findings that newly established synesthetic associations may be more unstable over time. Further research is required to test how the colors of Bopomo established this way might be consistent over time for these English synesthetes, both with and without any further practice. This study also showed that visual and/or phonetic features were critical in establishing the color of Bopomo letters in this group of English synesthetes. The colors of many Bopomo letters could be traced to their colors for English letters that were visually and/or phonetically comparable. This finding is consistent with existing knowledge that synesthetic transfer can occur on the basis of visual and/or phonetic similarity (e.g., Witthoft and Winawer 2006).

These conclusions are limited to language-related synesthesia, and it remains to be seen whether synesthetic transfer may also happen beyond the realm of language, for instance, to non-linguistic symbols as simple as basic shapes and patterns. Future studies may include simple shapes that are visually comparable to Bopomo as triggers (e.g., simple shape: << versus Bopomo: 《); this would allow us to examine whether shapes, like letters, would also take on the colors of their visual counterparts in Bopomo. If synesthetic transfer goes beyond language to visual shapes, this could have important implications for identifying the key factors of synesthesia.

Conclusion

In summary, this chapter has shown that synesthetic coloring in Chinese is a genuine phenomenon and that it may affect as many as 1 in 100 people among the Chinese population, with a non-significant trend towards a female to male ratio of about 2:1. A number of factors have been found to play a role in the synesthetic coloring of Chinese characters, including characters' phonetic spellings, component radicals, overall visual configuration, linguistic frequency, as well as meaning. Synesthesia may transfer across languages, even between languages of very different systems such as Chinese and English. The transfer between Chinese and English is established based on similarities in visual/phonetic features, and this applies even for mono-lingual English synesthetes who have no prior exposure to the Chinese writing system. Taken together, this chapter aimed to provide a summary of work so far available on the mechanisms of synesthesia in Chinese.

References

Barnett, Kylie J., Joanne Feeney, Michael Gormley, and Fiona N. Newell. 2009. An exploratory study of linguistic-colour associations across languages in multilingual synaesthetes. *Quarterly Journal of Experimental Psychology* 62 (7):1343–1355.

Baron-Cohen, Simon, Maria A. Wyke, and Colin Binnie. 1987. Hearing words and seeing colors and an experimental investigation of a case of synesthesia. *Perception* 16:761–767.

Beeli, Gian, Michaela Esslen, and Lutz Jäncke. 2007. Frequency correlates in grapheme-color synaesthesia. *Psychological Science* 18:788–792.

Chan, Carol K. K., and Linda S. Siegel. 2001. Phonological processing in reading Chinese among normally achieving and poor readers. *Journal of Experimental Child Psychology* 80 (1):23–43.

Chen, Hsuan-Chih, Giovanni B. Flores d'Arcais, and Sim-Ling Cheung. 1995. Orthographic and phonological activation in recognizing Chinese characters. *Psychological Research-Psychologische Forschung* 58 (2):144–153.

Chen, May Jane, and Yiu Fai Yung. 1989. Reading Chinese: a holistic or piecemeal process? In *Cognition in Individual and Social Contexts*, ed. Adrienne F. Bennet and Kevin M. McConkey, 91–102. Amsterdam: Elsevier.

Chen, Y. P., D. A. Allport, and J. C. Marshall. 1996. What are the functional orthographic units in Chinese word recognition: The stroke or the stroke pattern? *Quarterly Journal of Experimental Psychology Section a: Human Experimental Psychology* 49 (4):1024–1043.

Cheng, C. M., and S. I. Shih. 1988. The nature of lexical access in Chinese: Evidence from experiments on visual and phonological priming in lexical judgment. In *Cognitive Aspects of the Chinese Language*, ed. In-Mao Liu, Hsuan-Chih Chen, and May Jane Chen, 1–14. Hong Kong: Asian Research Service.

Coltheart, Max, Derek Besner, Jon Torfi Jonasson, and Eileen Davelaar. 1979. Phonological encoding in the lexical decision task. *Quarterly Journal of Experimental Psychology* 31 (3):489–507.

Coltheart, Max, and Kathleen Rastle. 1994. Serial processing in reading aloud: Evidence for dual-route models of reading. *Journal of Experimental Psychology: Human Perception and Performance* 20 (6):1197–1211.

Cytowic, Richard E. 1989. Synesthesia and mapping of subjective sensory dimensions. *Neurology* 39 (6):849–850.

DeFrancis, John. 1984. *The Chinese Language: Fact and Fantasy*. Honolulu: University of Hawaii Press.

Duffy, Patricia L. 2001. *Blue Cats and Charteuse Kittens*. New York: Henry Holt & Company, 2001.

Eagleman, David M. 2008. A large-scale analysis of synaesthetic correspondences. Paper presented at the UK Synaesthesia Association Annual General Meeting and Conference, Edinburgh, UK, March

Eagleman, David M., Arielle D. Kagan, Stephanie S. Nelson, Deepak Sagaram, and Anand K. Sarma. 2007. A standardized test battery for the study of synesthesia. *Journal of Neuroscience Methods* 159: 139–145.

Howie, John M. 1976. *Acoustical Studies of Mandarin Vowels and Tones*. New York: Cambridge University Press.

Hsiao, Janet H. W., and Garrison W. Cottrell. 2009. Not all visual expertise is holistic, but it may be leftist: The case of Chinese character recognition. *Psychological Science* 20 (4):455–463.

Hsiao, Janet H. W., and Richard Shillcock. 2006. Analysis of a Chinese phonetic compound database: Implications for orthographic processing. *Journal of Psycholinguistic Research* 35 (5):405–426.

Hung, Daisy L., and Ovid J. L. Tzeng. 1981. Orthographic variations and visual information-processing. *Psychological Bulletin* 90 (3):377–414.

Hung, Daisy L., Ovid J. L. Tzeng, and Angela K. Y. Tzeng. 1992. Automatic activation of linguistic information in Chinese character recognition. In *Orthography, Phonology, Morphology, and Meaning*, ed. Ram Frost and Leonard Katz, 119–130. Amsterdam: North-Holland.

Hung, Wan-Yu. 2010. An investigation into the underlying linguistic cues of synaesthesia in Chinese. PhD thesis, University of Edinburgh.

Hung, Wan-Yu, Julia Simner, Richard Shillcock, and David Eagleman. In preparation. Synaesthesia in Chinese characters: The role of radicals.

Leck, K. J., B. S. Weekes, and M. J. Chen. 1995. Visual and phonological pathways to the lexicon—evidence from Chinese readers. Memory & Cognition 23 (4):468–476.

Leong, Che Kan 1973. Reading in Chinese with reference to reading practices in Hong Kong. In *Comparative Reading: Cross-National Studies of Behavior and Processes in Reading and Writing*, ed. John Downing, 383–402. New York: Macmillan.

Liu, In-Mao. 1995. Script factors that affect literacy: Alphabetic vs. logographic languages. In *Scripts and Literacy*, ed. Insup Taylor and David R. Olson, 145–162. Dordrecht: Kluwer Academic Publishers.

Mills, Carol B., Meredith L. Viguers, Shari K. Edelson, Amanda T. Thomas, Stephanie L. Simon-Dack, and Joanne A. Innis. 2002. The color of two alphabets for a multilingual synesthete. *Perception* 31:1371–1394. doi:10.1068/p3429.

Mroczko, Aleksandra, Thomas Metzinger, Wolf Singer, and Danko Nikolić. 2009. Immediate transfer of synesthesia to a novel inducer. *Journal of Vision* 9 (12): 1–8.

Peng, D. L., and C. Wang. 1997. Basic processing unit of Chinese character recognition: Evidence from stroke number effect and radical number effect. *Acta Psychologica Sinica* 29 (1):8–16.

Perfetti, C. A., L. C. Bell, and S. M. Delaney. 1988. Automatic (prelexical) phonetic activation in silent word reading—evidence from backward-masking. *Journal of Memory and Language* 27 (1):59–70.

Perfetti, C. A., and S. Zhang. 1991. Phonological processes in reading Chinese characters. *Journal of Experimental Psychology: Learning Memory and Cognition* 17 (4):633–643.

——. 1995. The universal word identification reflex. In *The Psychology of Learning and Motivation*, ed. Douglas Medin, 159–189. New York: Academic Press.

Ramachandran, Vilayanur S., and Edward M. Hubbard. 2003. Hearing colors, tasting shapes. *Scientific American* 16:53–59.

Rich, Anina N., John L. Bradshaw, and Jason B. Mattingley. 2005. A systematic, large-scale study of synaesthesia: Implications for the role of early experience in lexical-colour associations. *Cognition* 98 (1):53–84.

Seidenberg, M. S. 1985. The time course of phonological code activation in 2 writing systems. *Cognition* 19 (1):1–30.

Shen, Liemin., and Xiaoping Zhu. 1994. The effects of stroke number and character frequency during Chinese character recognition. [In Chinese.] *Journal of Psychological Science* 17 (4):245–247.

Simner, Julia. 2007. Beyond perception: Synaesthesia as a psycholinguistic phenomenon. *Trends in Cognitive Science* 11:23–29.

Simner, Julia, Louise Glover, and Alice Mowat. 2006. Linguistic determinants of word colouring in grapheme-colour synaesthesia, *Cortex* 42:281–289.

Simner, Julia, Jenny Harrold, Harriet Creed, Louise Monro, and Louise Foulkes. 2009. Early detection of markers for synaesthesia in childhood populations. *Brain* 132:57–64.

Simner, Julia, Wan-Yu Hung, and Richard Shillcock. 2011. Synaesthesia in a logographic language: Evidence from Chinese. *Consciousness and Cognition* 20 (4):1376–1392.

Simner, Julia, and Robert H. Logie. 2007. Synaesthetic consistency spans decades in a lexical-gustatory synaesthete. *Neurocase* 13:358–365.

Simner, Julia, Catherine Mulvenna, Noam Sagiv, Elias Tsakanikos, Sarah A. Witherby, Christine Fraser, Kirsten Scott, and Jamie Ward. 2006. Synaesthesia: The prevalence of atypical cross-modal experiences. *Perception* 38:1024–1033. doi:10.1068/p5469.

Simner, Julia, and Jamie Ward. 2008. Synaesthesia, color terms, and color space: Color claims came from color names in Beeli, Esslen, and Jäncke. 2007. *Psychological Science* 19 (4):412–414.

Simner, Julia, Jamie Ward, Monika Lanz, Ashok Jansari, Krist Noonan, Louise Glover, and David A. Oakley. 2005. Non-random associations of graphemes to colours in synaesthetic and non-synaesthetic populations. *Cognitive Neuropsychology* 22 (8):1069–1085.

Smilek, Daniel, Kelly A. Malcolmson, Jonathan S. A. Carriere, Meghan Eller, Donna Kwan, and Michael Reynolds. 2007. When 3 is a jerk and T' is a king: Personifying inanimate objects in synesthesia. *Journal of Cognitive Neuroscience* 19: 981–992.

So, Dominica, and Linda S. Siegel. 1997. Learning to read Chinese: Semantic, syntactic, phonological and working memory skills in normally achieving and poor Chinese readers. *Reading and Writing* 9 (1):1–21.

Taft, Marcus, and Xiaoping Zhu. 1997. Submorphemic processing in reading Chinese. *Journal of Experimental Psychology: Learning Memory and Cognition* 23 (3):761–775.

Tan, Li Hai, and Charles A. Perfetti. 1997. Visual Chinese character recognition: Does phonological information mediate access to meaning? *Journal of Memory and Language* 37 (1):41–57.

——. 1998. Phonological codes as early sources of constraint in Chinese word identification: A review of current discoveries and theoretical accounts. *Reading and Writing* 10 (3–5):165–200.

Thierry, Guillaume, and Yan Jing Wu. 2007. Brain potentials reveal unconscious translation during foreign-language comprehension. *Proceedings of the National Academy of Sciences of the United States of America* 104 (30):12530–12535.

Wang, William S. Y. 1973. Chinese language. *Scientific American* 228 (2):50–60.

Ward, Jamie, and Julia Simner. 2003. Lexical-gustatory synaesthesia: linguistic and conceptual factors. *Cognition* 89 (3):237–261.

——. 2005. Is synaesthesia an X-linked dominant trait with lethality in males? *Perception* 34 (5):611–623.

Ward, Jamie, Julia Simner, and Vivian Auyeung. 2005. A comparison of lexical-gustatory and grapheme-colour synaesthesia. *Cognitive Neuropsychology* 22 (1):28–41.

Witthoft, Nathan, and Jonathan Winawer. 2006. Synesthetic colors determined by having colored refrigerator magnets in childhood. *Cortex* 42 (2):175–183.

Yu, Bolin, Ling Feng, Heqi Cao, and Wenling Li. 1990. Visual perception of Chinese characters effect of perceptual task and Chinese character attributes. *Acta Psychologica Sinica* 22 (2):141–148.

CHAPTER 12

SYNESTHETIC PERSONIFICATION

The social world of graphemes

MONIKA SOBCZAK-EDMANS AND NOAM SAGIV

INTRODUCTION

Native speakers of some languages think of houses as masculine, kitchens as feminine, and living-rooms as masculine. This is the case in Polish—one of many languages in which grammatical gender is assigned to nouns. Grammatical gender and other noun classes vary across languages. English does not have grammatical genders. French and Spanish have two—masculine and feminine, while language such as Polish or German have three (also including a neutral category). Some languages (e.g., Sesotho) have up to 20 noun classes (Sera et al. 2002). To a German or Polish speaker, moons are masculine, whereas to a Spanish speaker moons are feminine. If you are a native English speaker, moons and most other nouns depicting inanimate objects are probably genderless to you, unless you are bilingual. However, some individuals do attribute genders to certain words (e.g., the weekdays or month names) or even to graphemes (e.g., a or 3), regardless of whether their language has grammatical genders at all (and irrespective of the specific grammatical genders attributed to the word in other languages). This automatic attribution of gender is common among synesthetes, where it seems to be as involuntary as synesthetic colors and in many cases relatively stable over time. Moreover, synesthetes who experience this unusual form of personification often attribute not only genders but also a whole range of social and personal attributes. These may include personality traits (*B is shy*), family relationships (*B is A's child*), mental states (*K knows when to stop or say no*), moods (*K is happy*), and more. These features can be attributed to letters, numbers, other sequences, concepts, and certain objects.

It is now recognized that such instances of personification may qualify as a type of synesthesia in their own right (Amin et al. 2011; Simner and Holenstein 2007). Simner and Holenstein argued that its characteristics are in line with modern definitions of synesthesia. For example, Hubbard (2007) defines synesthesia as a condition in which stimulation of one sensory or cognitive stream induces an involuntary and idiosyncratic experience in one or more additional modalities or streams. These associations between a trigger and a synesthetic sensation (known as the "inducer" and "concurrent" respectively) remain consistent over time.[1] Grapheme personification fulfils these same requirements: the inducer and concurrent belong to different cognitive streams; the correspondences are idiosyncratic, involuntarily elicited, and consistent over time (although some synesthetes report that their graphemes' personalities may develop with time or be subject to mood swings).

Variants of synesthesia involving some sort of personification have been described using partially-overlapping terminologies. Mary Calkins (1893) used the term *dramatization* to describe the personification of graphemes among synesthetes. Contemporary studies also describe several other instances of personification, with inducing stimuli including inanimate objects, body parts, weekdays, months, seasons, etc. Some attempts have been made to name and characterize the phenomenon with greater precision. Julia Simner and Emma Holenstein (2007) emphasized the ordinal and linguistic nature of most inducers that evoke synesthetic personifications (letters, numbers, weekdays, months, seasons etc.), labeling it *ordinal linguistic personification*. Given that the range of reported synesthetic inducers is wider than just ordinal linguistic sequences and includes everyday objects, Simner, Gartner, and Taylor (2011) recently suggested the new term *sequence-personality synesthesia*. A different feature of this phenomenon has been highlighted in a different designation—*social synesthesia* (Amin et al. 2011), in which emphasis is placed not on the nature of the inducer but rather on the social aspect, since it involves concepts from social cognition/perception such as personality traits, mental states, moods, social roles, etc. For clarity, in this chapter, we will refer to this variant of synesthesia as sequence-personality synesthesia or simply *personification*.

HISTORICAL BACKGROUND

Historical reports on synesthetic personification appeared as early as the nineteenth century. Two prominent figures in the field of psychology at that time were both interested in personification and synesthesia: American psychologist and philosopher Mary Calkins and Swiss psychologist—and friend of Carl Jung—Theodore Flournoy. The first

---

[1] For further discussion on the issue of defining synesthesia, please see Macpherson (2007), Simner (2012), or Sagiv, Ilbeigi, and Ben-Tal (2011).

studies of synesthetic personification were mostly exploratory and descriptive, primarily resulting in phenomenological descriptions of these synesthetic experiences (Calkins 1893; Flournoy 1893; Patrick 1893). In a group study of the "dramatization" of letters, numbers, and musical notes, Calkins (1895) attempted to identify the rules governing this type of synesthesia. In that particular sample, personifications for numbers were found to be twice as frequent as personifications for letters. Calkins hypothesized that numbers are more likely than letters to be the subject of emotional associations due to the greater level of "intellectual engagement" involved in number processing compared to letter processing. In her research, Calkins noted that synesthetes not only attribute personalities to graphemes, but also tend to like and dislike them. For example, she observed that the numbers 2 and 5 are often perceived as more likable than prime numbers such as 7, 11, and 13, and this may result from "the actual experience of facility in the use of even numbers, and of difficulties with the unyielding indivisibility of prime numbers" (Calkins 1895, 101). In the twentieth century, sequence-personality synesthesia is mentioned (though not identified as a distinct phenomenon) by the eminent Russian neuropsychologist Aleksander Luria in *The Mind of a Mnemonist* (1969), an elaborate case study of Solomon Shereshevskii, a synesthete who had at least five other different types of synesthesia. In the chapter dedicated to mental images, there is a passage in which Shereshevskii describes his personifications:

> Take the number 1. This is a proud, well-built man; 2 is a high-spirited woman; 3 is a gloomy person (why, I don't know); 6 a man with a swollen foot; 7 a man with a moustache; 8 a very stout woman—a sack within a sack. As for the number 87, what I see is a fat woman and a man twirling his moustache. (Luria 1969, 31)

The historical accounts of sequence-personality synesthesia provided some observations about its phenomenology, but systematic empirical studies were not carried out. Although a cognitive mechanism underlying affective associations (positive versus negative) to graphemes was suggested (Calkins 1895), there was no widely accepted framework for explaining personification in synesthesia.

CHARACTERISTICS OF SEQUENCE-PERSONALITY SYNESTHESIA

Contemporary investigations into sequence-personality synesthesia have focused not only on providing phenomenological descriptions of synesthetic personifications (Cytowic 2002; Day 2005; Sagiv 2005), but have also aimed to objectively assess the synesthetic reports of personification by testing for their involuntary character and consistency over time—both considered core qualities of synesthesia (e.g., Rich et al. 2005). In other words, studies have aimed to show that these personifications automatically come to mind rather than being generated by conscious effort, and that they tend to stay the same over time for any given synesthete (e.g., if 6 is a busy mother, it tends to always be so—at least for that particular synesthete). A number of recent studies have employed behavioral congruity paradigms as well as consistency tests similar to those used to study other forms of synesthesia (see later). Neuroimaging methods have also been employed to uncover the neural basis of the phenomenon.

Automaticity and the involuntary nature of personification

Most paradigms used to objectively assess the automaticity and involuntary nature of personification rely on the fact that personifications tend to be consistent over time, at least in some cases. In other words, some synesthetes show relatively consistent mappings between (at least) some inducers (e.g., graphemes) and concurrents (e.g., gender). Thus before turning to examine the automaticity of personification, the consistency of inducer–concurrent pairings needs to be demonstrated. Indeed the consistency of these reports has been confirmed in both single case studies (Simner and Holenstein 2007; Smilek et al. 2007) and group studies (Amin et al. 2011; Simner, Gartner, and Taylor 2011). In these studies, synesthetes are asked to describe their personifications for a list of stimuli, such as letters and numbers, and their reports (e.g., A is a bossy man, B is a happy mother…) are stored by the experimenter. The synesthete is then unexpectedly recalled for retesting some time later and given the same task. Their reports in this retest tend to mirror those they gave previously, even when the two testing sessions were separated by many months or even years. Given this method to establish that associations are consistent over time, other studies have next aimed to use this consistency to also demonstrate that the associations are automatic and involuntary, using innovative variants of the Stroop (1935) and Navon (1977) paradigms, as shown in Table 12.1.

In a Stroop interference test, the automaticity of synesthetic experiences is verified by comparing the average reaction times to stimuli that are either congruent or incongruent with the synesthetic experience. For example, in one Stroop task used by

Table 12.1 Behavioral assessment of the automaticity of personification in synesthesia

Study	Personification type	Testing method	Study size
Amin 2005	Grapheme-gender	Navon figure (stick figure gender discrimination task)	Group study (6 synesthetes)
Simner and Holenstein 2007	Letter-gender	Stroop paradigm (name gender discrimination task)	Single case (AP)
Smilek et al. 2007	Grapheme-personality	Tracking eye movement	Single case (TE)
Amin et al. 2011	Grapheme-gender	Priming paradigm (face gender discrimination)	Group study (5 synesthetes)

Amin et al. (2011), synesthetes saw a grapheme such as the letter A, which for their particular synesthete is feminine. This grapheme was followed by either a female face (in congruent trials) or a male face (in incongruent trials). Participants were asked to judge whether the presented face was a female or a male. Synesthetes were expected to be slower in responding to incongruent trials than when responding to congruent trials (Dixon et al. 2000; Smilek et al. 2001). As predicted, synesthetes had significantly slower average reaction times where the synesthetic gender of the letter-prime conflicted with the semantic gender of the face (i.e., on incongruent trials) compared with when synesthetic and semantic genders matched (i.e., on congruent trials) even though the grapheme primes were irrelevant to the task. This effect was not found in non-synesthetes, even when they chose the letters that were most masculine/feminine in their opinion to be included on experimental trials (rather than being randomly assigned to letter-gender pairing chosen by one of the synesthetes). The results from this study provide evidence that synesthetic gender-grapheme associations are involuntary and automatically elicited, a finding that differentiates synesthetic personification from the types of grapheme-gender associations that non-synesthetes may come up with if invited to do so.

In another Stroop type task, Simner and Holenstein (2007) presented a synesthetic participant, AP, with boy and girl names and asked her to press buttons marked either "male" or "female" to indicate the semantic gender of each name (e.g., Brian = male). Their aim was to assess whether semantic gender judgments can be affected by synesthetic genders, and whether this occurs automatically. In their materials, the semantic gender of the name was congruent with the synesthetic gender of its initial letter in half of the trials (e.g., Brian, where B is masculine); while in the other half of the trials it was incongruent (e.g., Mark, where M is feminine). Simner and Holenstein compared congruent and incongruent reaction times to see whether the synesthetic gender associated with the first letter interferes with semantic gender judgments for whole name. A congruency effect was indeed observed; reactions times were faster when the synesthetic gender of the first letter matched the name gender, suggesting that synesthetic genders are automatically generated and cannot easily be suppressed.

Simner and Holenstein (2007) could employ this type of Stroop-like paradigm only after they verified that for their synesthete AP, the genders of words (in this case names) are likely to take the gender of the first letter (a similar effect is noted in grapheme-color synesthesia, where the color of initial letters spreads throughout the whole word, giving the word its color; Rich et al. 2005). To determine this, AP was also asked to indicate how feminine/masculine a particular name felt to her (e.g., Betsy) on a scale from extremely female to extremely male. Target stimuli were names whose initial letter's synesthetic gender was either congruent or incongruent with semantic gender of the name. The experiment showed that AP's semantic masculinity/femininity was influenced by the synesthetic genders: AP perceives as more feminine female names starting with a female synesthetic gender (congruent condition) compared with female names starting with a male synesthetic gender (incongruent condition). This same pattern was found with male names. For example, if presented with the name Betsy, AP thought of Betsy as less feminine, because for her, the synesthetic gender of B is male and this interferes with semantic gender. Although this type of letter-to-word transfer applies to the genders of names, it may not apply to linguistic sequences such as days of the week, months of the year. Such frequently used words are often associated with their own synesthetic gender (or color for that matter), which is independent of the gender associated with the first letter.

An alternative way of testing for the automaticity of grapheme-gender is a variant of the Navon-figures task. In this type of task, participants are presented with a larger recognizable "global" shape (e.g., the letter T) composed of smaller different "local" shapes (e.g., copies of the letter S). In the synesthetic version, participants saw (global) male or female stick figures made of (local) grapheme elements (Amin 2005; Sagiv et al. 2006). Crucially, the gender synesthetes associated with the graphemes making up the stick figures was either congruent or incongruent with the gender depicted by the stick figure. The task was to determine the gender of the stick figure. A congruity effect was observed here too; synesthetes were slower to decide what the stick figure gender was if it was composed of letters with the opposite gender. Thus, synesthetes find it hard to ignore the gender associated with graphemes, even when it is irrelevant and sometimes detrimental to the task.

Finally, Smilek et al. (2007) used eye-tracking to show that synesthete TE's eye movement are biased by the emotional valence attributed to personified graphemes. TE fixated less often (but for a longer duration) on graphemes she considered to be more negative compared with more positive grapheme personalities. Together, these studies provide compelling objective evidence not only for automaticity but also for the reality of synesthetic personifications; i.e., grapheme personifications are not confabulatory in origin.

Prevalence of sequence-personality synesthesia

While sequence-personality synesthesia is recognized as one of the most common synesthesia types (Cytowic and Eagleman 2009; Simner, Gartner, and Taylor 2011), as yet, no large-scale study of the general population has been conducted that would provide an estimate of its prevalence. In 2007, Simner and Holenstein carried out a survey of 219 individuals. In this group they found three synesthetic personifiers, suggesting that about 1 in 73 people have personifications for ordinal sequences or objects. A similar prevalence (about 1.4%) can be found in a historical text showing that among 75 men and women, there was one female synesthete associating personalities to numbers (Patrick 1893).

Among the population of synesthetes, personification is fairly common: 33% of the 248 synesthetes studied by Amin et al. (2011) reported experiencing genders and/or personalities to graphemes. More than three-quarters of the synesthetes who attribute personalities and genders to graphemes also personified objects, such as fruit and vegetables, computers, household objects, and others. Graphemes and objects are personified on a daily basis, and the attribution of social and affective characteristics is conceptually driven although some of the synesthetes testified that color,[2] shape, number parity, and sound of graphemes may play a role in determining the specific associations of person-alities and genders. For example, in the questionnaire employed by Amin et al. (2011), 26% of synesthetes indicated that grapheme shape influenced the gender associated with them (e.g., rounded letters might be thought of as more feminine). According to self-reports gathered by Amin et al. (2011), sequence-personality synesthesia has been experienced by individuals when they were as young as 7 years old—around the time they acquire reading and writing skills. This is consistent with Hunt's (2005) hypothesis explaining synesthesia as a "semantically significant state of consciousness" that devel-ops in mid-childhood (when children learn to read and write).

Categories of inducers and concurrents

Although synesthetic experiences can be induced by many different types of stimuli—emotions, flavors, musical sounds, temperature, and others—the most common induc-ers are linguistic constructs. We can differentiate between two different types of inducers in personification: linguistic inducers, such as graphemes, weekdays, months, and non-linguistic inducers, including body parts, inanimate objects, geometrical shapes, plants, colors, spatial concepts (e.g., left–right) and so on. Linguistic inducers, in contrast to non-linguistic inducers, often have a conventional order (e.g., alphabetical sequence) that may influence how synesthetes personify them (e.g., neighboring letters might have friendships or kinship relations, Simner and Holenstein 2007). Similarly, anecdotal evi-dence suggests that personified non-linguistic inducers (e.g., inanimate objects) tend to have some sort of relationship with their own kind; for example, coffee mugs might miss a broken mug from the same set (Amin et al. 2011). Another synesthete tested by Sobczak, Sagiv, and Williams (2011) described a family of mushrooms consisting of mother mushroom, father mushroom, and their children, which she perceived as hav-ing mental lives and interactions. A similar picture can be seen in linguistic inducers: for example, one of the synesthetes we tested noted that: "The personalities of all my letters and numbers centre around a "pecking order" based on age and leadership relation-ships.... All are "nice" personalities, quiet, confident, respectful, staying within their order. No moods. i.e., my letters, numbers, months and days have more "relationship" to one another than personalities."

   This description and our discussion of personification thus far show that the concur-rent experiences are not purely sensory (i.e., they are not colors, tastes, and so on), but rather, they are conceptual properties (e.g., personality types). Moreover, they are at times social descriptions and this suggests that, in sequence-personality synesthesia, the con-currents belong to the interpersonal domain: they may reflect individual characteristics

---

[2] This is consistent with Simner and Hubbard's (2006) observation that graphemes' colors and genders interact. For example, they found that synesthetes are slower to state the synesthetic gender of letters if these are printed in colors from other letters with mis-matching (but not matching) genders.

(gender, personality, physical appearance, cognitive abilities, occupation, mental states, moods, attitudes, interests, inclinations) as well as "social interactions" between inducers (e.g., emotive and behavioral responses to other units; Amin et al. 2011; Simner and Holenstein 2007). Smilek et al. (2007) classified the social and affective characteristics attributed in sequence-personality synesthesia into four more specific types: physical (gender, physical appearance), personal (cognitive abilities, occupation, personality, mental states, moods, attitudes, interests, inclinations), relation (emotive and behavioral responses to other units), and social role (occupation, familial and non-familial relationships). From a comparison between the social attributes to graphemes in the historical and contemporary literature, it can be concluded that although synesthesia is congenital, life experiences can influence the personality traits that are being attributed to graphemes and other sequences (Simner and Holenstein 2007). Concurrents such as "society girl," "policy girl," "housekeeper" (in Patrick 1893, 509) are rather uncommon among synesthetes today.

Theories of Sequence-Personality Synesthesia

After establishing the genuineness of sequence-personality synesthesia, researchers are attempting to provide an explanatory framework for the phenomenon. In order to explain how it arises, researchers look at the underlying neural mechanisms in addition to the phenomenological characteristics and behavioral consequences. One neurobiological framework for understanding sequence-personality synesthesia focuses on the *cross-activation hypothesis* (e.g., Hubbard, Brang, and Ramachandran 2011), whereas a more functional alternative approach describes the condition as a by-product of the developmental mechanisms for social cognition. These two approaches will be discussed next.

Neural cross-talk and neural over-excitation as models for sequence-personality synesthesia

It has been suggested that synesthesia occurs when activation of the brain areas associated with processing the inducers (e.g., graphemes) also results in activation of the brain areas associated with processing the concurrent (e.g., color); this process has been termed cross-activation (Hubbard, Brang, and Ramachandran 2011). Cross-activation may result from either direct (Hubbard and Ramachandran 2005; Rich and Mattingley 2002) and/or indirect "cross-talk" between brain areas (Grossenbacher and Lovelace 2001; Smilek et al. 2001). This may be facilitated by either structural or functional differences in connectivity in synesthetes' brains. The functional model of cross-talk assumes that there are no structural differences in the brains of synesthetes and non-synesthetes, with synesthetic cross-activations arising as a result of disinhibition of otherwise normal pathways (e.g., Ward, Huckstep, and Tsakanikos 2006; Cohen Kadosh et al. 2009). Conversely, the structural explanation of synesthetic cross activation highlights anatomical differences between the synesthetic and non-synesthetic brain; i.e., an additional feedforward neural pathway connecting the particular brain areas involved in processing the inducers and concurrents in a given type of synesthesia.

While functional neuroimaging studies showed that such an explanation for grapheme-color synesthesia is plausible (Hubbard et al. 2005), more recent studies provided direct evidence for hyper-connectivity (Rouw and Scholte 2007; Weiss and Fink 2009) using diffusion tensor imaging. These studies suggest that there are structural differences between synesthetes' and non-synesthetes' brains. However, future developmental neuroimaging studies seem to be necessary in order to clarify whether hyper connectivity precedes functional specialization and what the role of learning and practice is.

Could sequence-personality synesthesia also be explained within this framework? Simner and Hubbard (2006) argue that sequence-personality synesthesia is likely to arise as a result of cross-talk between the left inferior parietal lobule (in particular the angular gyrus) and temporo-parietal junction that mediate sequence information, and the "social brain" regions associated with mental states and personality trait attribution, such as the amygdala, somatosensory cortex, frontal, and parietal regions. It is suggested that the angular gyrus is a crucial area in inducing cross-modal pairings in sequence-personality synesthesia due to its importance in processing ordinal sequence information, which has been well documented in neuropsychological studies of semantic agnosia and acalculia (Cappelletti, Butterworth, and Kopelman 2001; Dehaene and Cohen 1997; Turconi and Seron 2002). Synesthetic concurrents in this variant of synesthesia include social and affective associations, therefore it is likely that neural correlates involved in generating these experiences overlap with the neural systems underlying social cognition. Previous neuroimaging experiments (e.g., Castelli et al. 2002; Martin and Weisberg 2003; Schultz et al. 2003) provided evidence that personification of non-randomly moving shapes (similar to Heider and Simmel's 1944 animations) activates some of the same brain areas that have been found to be active during interaction with or observation of other human beings. The inferior frontal cortex is crucial for personality judgments (Heberlein and Saxe 2005). Additionally, the temporo-parietal junction, posterior cingulate cortex/precuneus, the amygdala, prefrontal cortex, and fusiform gyrus may also play a role in generating social and affective concurrents reported in sequence-personality synesthesia.

The first case study examining empirically the neural substrates of sequence mapping synesthesia provided only partial support for these predictions. Amin et al. (2011) tested AA—a 38-year-old female synesthete who attributes genders to letters—using functional magnetic resonance imaging. The study identified the medial part of the superior parietal lobule—the precuneus—as a possible brain region mediating the attribution of gender to letters. Aiming to establish whether personifications in synesthesia arise automatically, Amin et al. asked AA to perform a letter repetition detection task (rather than to focus on the synesthetic experiences of genders). Given that the synesthetic gender of letters was irrelevant to the task, the authors argue that the observed differences in precuneus activity when AA was presented with letters with genders and letters without genders may indeed reflect automatic processes associated with synesthetic personification. As the precuneus is associated with self-referential processing (information related to oneself) as well as with mental imagery (e.g., Cavanna and Trimble 2006), Amin et al. proposed two corresponding possible mechanisms for synesthetic personification. One possibility is that synesthesia is an extraordinary manifestation of mental imagery that is elicited automatically, and has well defined inducers and concurrences. The second hypothesis emphasizes self-referential functions; this variant of synesthesia may represent an unusual projection of one's own mental states onto graphemes and/or objects.

A similar explanation for the precuneus activation has been also proposed in another case study of a synesthete who personifies inanimate objects (Sobczak, Sagiv, and Williams 2011). The self-projection hypothesis is in line with current theory in social neuroscience on how we get to know the minds of others: we never perceive the minds of others directly since mental states are unobservable constructs, but we infer intentions, feelings and personality traits of others using self-referential accounts, by accessing our own mental states that serve as a model of the minds of others, and then project them on the target (Mitchell 2008). Could this suggest that the attribution of social and affective characteristics to graphemes in synesthesia is merely an extension of normal social cognition, in which projection of one's own mental states includes not only other humans but also non-humans entities as targets? The hypothesis that sequence-personality synesthesia is a misattribution of self-referential processing will be presented further in the following section.

Personification in synesthesia as a misattribution of self-referential processing

According to the neonatal synesthesia hypothesis (e.g., Maurer and Mondloch 2005), all newborn babies experience synesthesia or, at the very least, some sort of sensory confusion; they experience unisensory stimuli with all their senses as a consequence of having a cortex that is not fully developed. This ability disappears with the development of the nervous system as cortical areas acquire functional specialization. Could this also apply to synesthetic personification? Young children assign life and conscious mental states to non-living objects and concepts; this was referred to as "animism" in the early literature (Piaget 1929). Animistic thought in early childhood gradually decreases during cognitive development. According to this model of development, a child's progression from perceiving all functional objects as endowed with conscious life, goes through a stage of assigning these attributes only to objects that are in motion; subsequently, conscious life is only assigned to things that move on their own accord, and finally, animate characteristics are only attributed to living things. After this stage, the animistic mode of cognition (similar to that of personification) is almost completely replaced by logical reasoning, and human-like qualities are rarely attributed explicitly to inanimate objects.

Piaget (1929) studied animistic thought in children and hypothesized that the excessive animistic mode of thinking (including personification) serves as a mechanism for constructing reality with the self as a model. This is in line with contemporary accounts of the way in which we construct social reality. The discovery of mirror neurons demonstrates this well. Mirror neurons fire both when we observe others performing an action and when we perform the same action ourselves. This constitutes a neural, mirror-like mechanism that has been suggested to facilitate the understanding of the actions, emotions and feelings of other people, presumably through a simulation process (for a review, see Bastiaansen et al. 2009). Personification in synesthetic adults may represent an excessive manifestation of the human tendency to perceive reality using the self as a model. This in turn derives from younger children's animistic thought which children use as an undeveloped filter through which they learn about the social world. In other words, synesthetic personification could represent a residual expression of childhood animism.[3]

The brain areas associated with self-referential processing such as the insula, the precuneus, the inferior frontal cortex, and the posterior cingulate, have been found to be involved in implementation of animistic thought[4] (Sobczak 2009; Sobczak, Sagiv, and Williams 2010). Furthermore, evidence from neuropsychology suggests that lesions of the right (and sometimes left) parietal cortex may result in peculiar misattributions of agency, which might itself sometimes involve animistic attributions. Specifically, patients with such lesions frequently display delusional misidentifications of body parts, thinking that their left arm or left leg does not belong to them. They often attribute their limbs to other people—their wife, examiner, or fellow patient. This condition—somatoparaphrenia is a subtype of asomatognosia (unawareness of one's limb ownership). Interestingly, some patients also assign personalities to their limbs and give misidentified arms or legs nicknames such as "George," "Toby," "Silly Billy," "Floppy Joe," etc. (Critchley 1955, 286). Misattribution of animacy and agency has also been found after frontal lobe damage. For example, Feinberg and Keenan (2005) describe a peculiar case of personification known as "phantom child syndrome" which is thought to represent a delusional reduplication of self. The patient believed that he is in the process of adopting a child with "problems." Such patients deny that they have certain problems themselves, instead attributing them to the "phantom child.

In summary, evidence from neuroimaging and neuropsychology is consistent with the idea that misattribution of the self could explain both benign synesthetic personification as well as some pathological forms of personification. However, this framework

---

[3] The tendency to personify may be crucial for the development of normal social cognition. Indeed Amin et al. (2011) point out that synesthetic personification may be a small price to pay given the benefits of the "personification instinct".

[4] A similar pattern is found in synesthetes and non-synesthetes who are prompted to personify visually presented object images.

for understanding personification remains tentative and needs to be tested directly in future studies involving synesthetes.

SIMILARITIES AND DIFFERENCES BETWEEN SYNESTHETIC PERSONIFICATIONS AND NON-SYNESTHETIC PERSONIFICATIONS

Personification and animism involving the attribution of human-like social and affective characteristics to non-human entities can be observed not only in synesthesia, but also in non-synesthetes' everyday life. Examples include personification of objects, both in childhood and in adulthood (Piaget 1929; Bouldin and Pratt 1999; Epley et al. 2008), the attribution of masculine/feminine genders to nouns in many languages, as well as the attribution of agency, personality traits and moods to body parts (usually limbs) following brain injury. Personification is also widespread in various cultures as metaphors, and in folk legends and myths (Guthrie 1993). For example, according to one Russian superstition, if you drop a fork (masculine) a male guest will visit your house, but if you drop a spoon (feminine)—this will be a female guest (Corbett 1991). Personification is also utilized in design and "human factors engineering," in which social rules are used when designing human–computer interactions (Nass et al. 1997), as well as in advertising and marketing (Ouwersloot and Tudorica 2001). Young children often think of inanimate objects as if they were humans, endowing them with life-like features (animism). It has been suggested that children's tendency to personify is a normal stage in cognitive development (Piaget, 1929), but can also be linked with social isolation; solitary children frequently create imaginary friends. Often these imaginary companions exist entirely in their imaginations, but sometimes the focus of their imaginations are physical objects such as dolls or other toys that have ascribed to them elaborate personalities and biographies (Bouldin and Pratt 1999). Additionally, among adults, loneliness and inability to create social bonds may be compensated by attaching social and affective characteristics to animals, inanimate objects and also religious agents (Epley et al. 2008).

In many languages, nouns have masculine/feminine grammatical genders that influence the way people think about inanimate objects: objects with feminine grammatical genders are thought to be more feminine, and objects with masculine grammatical gender are perceived as more masculine (Boroditsky, Schmidt, and Phillips 2003). This effect can already be observed in children of 8 to 9 years, who, when asked to assign voices to inanimate objects (presented together with their labels), ascribe voices to presented objects congruent with their grammatical genders (Sera, Berge, and de Castillo 1994). Boroditsky and her colleagues found that the adjectives used to describe nouns tend to be feminine when the noun concerned has feminine grammatical gender and more masculine when the noun has masculine gender. Furthermore, adjectives usually associated more with femininity (such as calm, friendly, good, happy, kind) tended to be used for descriptions of rounded shapes, whereas adjectives associated with masculinity (e.g., angry, brave, frustrated, jealous, nervous, and resentful) were used when describing a spiky shape (Lyman 1979). Thus, shapes may be associated, at least implicitly, with some social and affective characteristics. Additionally, musical sounds can evoke attributions of moods (Odbert, Karwoski, and Eckersson 1942), and letters can induce associations of personality traits (Simner, Gartner, and Taylor 2011).

In this last respect, Simner and her colleagues examined whether synesthetes and non-synesthetes exhibited similar patterns of letter-personality correspondences. While non-synesthetes' (forced) personifications of letters were less elaborated and less consistent over time compared with synesthetes, both groups seem to share the underlying rules for the personality trait attribution to letters. Using Goldberg's Big Five personality traits questionnaire (Saucier 1994), Simner, Gartner, and Taylor found that both synesthetes and non-synesthetes tend to associate frequently occurring letters (e.g., the letter A compared with the letter Z) with personalities low in neuroticism and high in agreeableness; the main difference between the groups is therefore that in synesthetes, the personality-letter associations occur explicitly, whereas in non-synesthetes, they are implicit.

SUMMARY

In this chapter, we have attempted to provide a broad overview of personification in synesthesia, including the phenomenology, as well as behavioral and neural characteristics. Sequence-personality synesthesia appears to be consistent over time. Furthermore, the associations between inducer and concurrent are automatically and involuntarily elicited. The variety of inducers in this variant of synesthesia include linguistic (graphemes, weekdays, months, etc.) and non-linguistic inducers (inanimate objects, colors, body parts, etc.). The concurrent synesthetic experiences have affective and social characteristics, and fall into the following general groups: physical, personal, relational, and social role descriptions. Several lines of evidence suggest that some forms of personification occur in non-synesthetes too; examples include childhood animistic thought, mild forms of personification in everyday life, personifications of body parts, as well as gender attributions to linguistic constructs (i.e., grammatical gender). Synesthetes and non-synesthetes alike think of the letters that are more frequently used as rather agreeable and not neurotic. However, non-synesthetes do so only implicitly, compared with synesthetes, for whom these pairings occur involuntarily and they are aware of them explicitly in everyday life. A similar pattern is found when considering object personification; many synesthetes tend to spontaneously personify inanimate objects; non-synesthetes usually do not, but when prompted to personify both activate similar brain regions. Preliminary neuroimaging evidence suggests that sequence-personality synesthesia depends on the posterior parts of parietal cortex, namely precuneus, which is involved in mental imagery and self-referential processing. Synesthetic personification may therefore represent a special case of mental imagery or the involuntary projection of one's own mental states onto graphemes and/or inanimate objects. As in other forms of synesthesia, it is conceivable that cross-activation of brain areas could underlie personification (e.g., cross-talk between the angular gyrus and some of the "social brain" areas). At the developmental level, it has been proposed that sequence-personality synesthesia may represent a residual expression of childhood animism, an early stage in social cognitive development. Although there are many differences between the accounts described here for sequence-personality synesthesia, they all seem to point to the observation that (as in other types of synesthesia) this variant may be utilizing a universal mechanism (e.g., Sagiv and Ward 2006). Admittedly, the study of synesthetic personification using cognitive neuroscience methods is only in its infancy. It would therefore be wise to regard these frameworks for understanding synesthetic personification as tentative, at least until further evidence becomes available.

REFERENCES

Amin, Maina. 2005. Documenting a new type of synaesthesia: The personification of alpha-numeric symbols. MSc dissertation, Birkbeck College and University College London Programme in Cognitive Neuropsychology.

Amin, Maina, Olufemi Olu-Lafe, Loes E. Claessen, Monika Sobczak-Edmans, Jamie Ward, Adrian L. Williams, and Noam Sagiv. 2011. Understanding grapheme personification: A social synaesthesia? *Journal of Neuropsychology* 5 (2):255–282.

Bastiaansen, Jojanneke A. C. J., Marc Thioux, and Christian Keysers. 2009. Evidence for mirror systems in emotions. *Philosophical Transactions of the Royal Society B: Biological Sciences* 364:2391–2304.

Bouldin, Paula, and Chris Pratt .1999. Characteristics of preschool and school-age children with imaginary companions. *Journal of Genetic Psychology* 160 (4):397–310.

Boroditsky, Lera, Lauren Schmidt, and Webb Phillips. 2003. Sex, syntax, and semantics. In *Language in Mind: Advances in the study of Language and Cognition*, ed. Dedre Gentner and Susan Goldin-Meadow, 61–78. Cambridge, MA: MIT Press.

Calkins, Mary W. 1893. A statistical study of pseudo-chromesthesia and of mental-forms. *American Journal of Psychology* 5:439–466.

———. 1895. Synaesthesia. *American Journal of Psychology* 7:90–107.

Cappelletti, Marinella, Brian Butterworth, and Michael Kopelman. 2001. Spared numerical abilities in a case of semantic dementia. *Neuropsychologia* 39:1224–1239.

Castelli, Fulvia, Chris Frith, Francesca Happé, and Uta Frith. 2002. Autism, Asperger syndrome and brain mechanisms for the attribution of mental states to animated shapes. *Brain* 125:1839–1849.

Cavanna, Andrea E., and Michael R. Trimble. 2006. The precuneus: A review of its functional anatomy and behavioural correlates. *Brain* 129:564–583.

Cohen Kadosh, Roi, Avishai Henik, Andres Catena, Vincent Walsh, and Luis J. Fuentes. 2009. Induced cross-modal synaesthetic experience without abnormal neuronal connections. *Psychological Science* 20 (2):258–265.

Cytowic, Richard E. 2002. *Synesthesia: A Union of the Senses.* Cambridge, MA: MIT Press.

Cytowic, Richard, E. and David M. Eagleman. 2009. *Wednesday is Indigo Blue: Discovering the Brain of Synaesthesia*. Cambridge, MA: MIT Press.

Corbett, Greville. 1991. *Gender*. Cambridge: Cambridge University Press.

Critchley, Macdonald. 1955. Personification of paralysed limbs in hemiplegics. *British Medical Journal* 2:284–285.

Day, Sean. 2005. Some demographic and socio-cultural aspects of synesthesia. In *Synaesthesia: Perspectives from Cognitive Neuroscience*, ed. Lynn C. Robertson and Noam Sagiv, 11–33. Oxford: Oxford University Press.

Dehaene, Stanislas, and Laurent Cohen. 1997. Cerebral pathways for calculation: Double dissociation between rote verbal and quantitative knowledge of arithmetic. *Cortex* 33:219–250.

Dixon, Mike J., Daniel Smilek, Cera Cudahy, and Philip M. Merikle. 2000. Five plus two equals yellow. *Nature* 406:365.

Epley, Nicholas, Scott Akalis, Adam Waytz, and John T. Cacioppo. 2008. Creating social connection through inferential reproduction. *Psychological Science* 19 (2):114–120.

Feinberg, Todd E., and Julian P. Keenan. 2005. Where in the brain is self? *Consciousness and Cognition* 14 (4):661–678.

Flournoy, Théodore. 1893. *Des phénomènes de synopsie*. Paris: Félix Alcan.

Guthrie, Stewart E. 1993. *Faces in the Clouds: A New Theory of Religion*. New York: Oxford University Press.

Grossenbacher, Peter G., and Christopher T. Lovelace. 2001. Mechanisms of synesthesia: Cognitive and physiological constraints. *Trends in Cognitive Sciences* 5:36–41.

Heberlein, Andrea S., and Rebecca R. Saxe. 2005. Dissociation between emotion and personality judgments: Convergent evidence from functional neuroimaging. *Neuroimage* 28: 770–777.

Heider, F., and M. Simmel. 1944. An experimental study of apparent behavior. *American Journal of Psychology* 57:243–259.

Hubbard, Edward M. 2007. Neurophysiology of synesthesia. *Current Psychiatry Reports* 9: 193–199.

Hubbard, Edward M., A. Cyrus Arman, Vilayanur S. Ramachandran, and Geoffrey M. Boynton. 2005. Individual differences among grapheme-color synesthetes: Brain-behavior correlations. *Neuron* 45:975–985.

Hubbard, Edward M., David Brang, and Vilayanur S. Ramachandran. 2011. The cross-activation theory at 10. *Journal of Neuropsychology* 5:152–177.

Hubbard, Edward M., and Vilayanur S. Ramachandran. 2005. Neurocognitive mechanisms of synesthesia. *Neuron* 48:509–520.

Hunt, Harry T. 2005. Synaesthesia, metaphor and consciousness – a cognitive-developmental perspective. *Journal of Consciousness Studies* 12:26–45.

Luria, Aleksandr R. 1969. *The Mind of a Mnemonist: A Little Book about a Vast Memory*. London: Cape.

Lyman, Bernard. 1979. Representation of complex emotional and abstract meanings by simply forms. *Perceptual and Motor Skills* 49:839–842.

Martin, Alex, and Jill Weisberg. 2003. Neural foundations for understanding social and mechanical concepts. *Cognitive Neuropsychology* 20:575–587.

Maurer, Daphne, and Mondloch, Catherine J. 2005. Neonatal synesthesia: A reevaluation. In *Synaesthesia: Perspectives from Cognitive Neuroscience*, ed. Lynn C. Robertson and Noam Sagiv, 193–213. New York: Oxford University Press.

Macpherson, Fiona. 2007. Synaesthesia, functionalism, and phenomenology. In: *Cartographies of the Mind. Philosophy and Psychology in Intersection*, ed. Massimo Marraffa, Mario De Caro, and Francesco Ferretti, 65–80. Dordrecht: Springer Verlag.

Mitchell, Jason. 2008. Contributions of functional neuroimaging to the study of social cognition. *Current Directions in Psychological Science* 17:142–146.

Nass, Clifford I., Youngme Moon, John Morkes, Eun-Young Kim, and B. J. Fogg. 1997. Computers are social actors: A review of current research. In *Human Values and the Design of Computer Technology*, ed. Batya Friedman, 137–162. Cambridge, MA: Cambridge University Press.

Navon, David. 1977. Forest before trees: the precedence of global features in visual perception. *Cognitive Psychology* 9:353–383.

Odbert, H. S., T. F. Karwoski, and A. B. Eckerson. 1942. Studies in synesthetic thinking: I. Musical and verbal associations of color and mood. *The Journal of General Psychology* 26:153–173.

Ouwersloot, Hans and Anamaria Tudorica. 2001. Brand personality creation through advertising. *MAXX Working Paper Series*. Maastricht: Maastricht Academic Center for Research in Services.

Patrick, George T. W. 1893. Number forms. *Popular Science Monthly*. 42:508–510.

Piaget, Jean. 1929. *The Child's Conception of the World*. New York: Harcourt Brace.

Rich, Anina N., John L. Bradshaw, and Jason B. Mattingley. 2005. A systematic, large-scale study of synaesthesia: Implications for the role of early experience in lexical-colour associations. *Cognition* 98 (1):53–84.

Rich, Anina N., and Jason B. Mattingley. 2002. Anomalous perception in synaesthesia: A cognitive neuroscience perspective. *Nature Reviews Neuroscience* 3:43–52.

Rouw, Romke, and H. Steven Scholte. 2007. Increased structural connectivity in grapheme-color synesthesia. *Nature Neuroscience* 10:792–797.

Sagiv, Noam. 2005. Synaesthesia in perspective. In *Synaesthesia: Perspectives from Cognitive Neuroscience*, ed. Lynn C. Robertson and Noam Sagiv, 3–10. New York: Oxford University Press.

Sagiv, Noam, Alireza Ilbeigi, and Oded Ben-Tal. 2011. Reflections on synaesthesia, perception, and cognition. *Intellectica* 55:81–94.

Sagiv Noam, and Jamie Ward. 2006. Cross-modal interactions: Lessons from synesthesia. *Progress in Brain Research* 155:259–271.

Sagiv, Noam, Olufemi Olu-Lafe, Maina Amin, and Jamie Ward. 2006. A neurocognitive perspective on animism. Presented at the 13th Meeting of the Cognitive Neuroscience Society, San Francisco, CA, 8–11 April.

Saucier, G. 1994. Mini-markers: A brief version of Goldberg's unipolar Big-Five markers. *Journal of Personality Assessment* 63:506–516.

Schultz, Robert T., David J. Grelotti, Ami Klin, Jamie Kleinman, Christiaan Van der Gaag, René Marois, and Pawel Skudlarski. 2003. The role of the fusiform face area in social cognition: Implications for the pathobiology of autism. *Philosophical Transactions of the Royal Society B: Biological Sciences* 358:415–427.

Sera, Maria, Christian Berge, and Javier del Castillo. 1994. Grammatical and conceptual forces in the attribution of gender by English and Spanish speakers. *Cognitive Development* 9:261–292.

Sera, Maria D., Chryle Elieff, James Forbes, Melissa C. Burch, Wanda Rodriguez, and Diane Dubois. 2002. When language affects cognition and when it does not: An analysis of grammatical gender and classification. *Journal of Experimental Psychology: General* 131:377–397.

Simner, Julia, Oliver Gartner, and Michelle D. Taylor. 2011. Cross-modal personality attribu-
    tions in synaesthetes and non-synaesthetes. *Journal of Neuropsychology* 5 (2):283–201.
Simner, Julia, and Emma Holenstein. 2007. Ordinal linguistic personification as a variant of
    synesthesia. *Journal of Cognitive Neuroscience* 19 (4):694–703.
Simner, Julia and Edward M. Hubbard. 2006. Variants of synesthesia interact in cognitive tasks:
    Evidence for implicit associations and late connectivity in cross-talk theories. *Neuroscience*
    143:805–814.
Simner, Julia. 2012. Defining synaesthesia. *British Journal of Psychology* 103:1–15.
Smilek, Daniel, Michael J. Dixon, Cera Cudahy, and Philip M. Merikle. 2001. Synaesthetic pho-
    tisms influence visual perception. *Journal of Cognitive Neuroscience* 13:930–936.
Smilek, Daniel, Kelly A. Malcolmson, Jonathan S. A. Carriere, Meghan Eller, Donna Kwan, and
    Michael Reynolds. 2007. When 3 is a jerk and T' is a king: personifying inanimate objects in
    synesthesia. *Journal of Cognitive Neuroscience* 19:981–992.
Sobczak, Monika. 2009. The neural correlates of personification. MSc thesis, MSc Programme
    in Functional Neuroimaging, Brunel University, London.
Sobczak, Monika, Noam Sagiv, and Adrian L. Williams. 2010. Reflections of the self: A neuroim-
    aging investigation of the link between animistic thought and self-processing. Presented at
    the 14th Association for the Scientific Study of Consciousness Meeting, Toronto, Ontario,
    Canada, 24–27 June.
——. 2011. Automatic attributions of human qualities to graphemes and linguistic sequences
    in synaesthesia: An fMRI study. Presented at the 15th Association for the Scientific Study of
    Consciousness meeting, Kyoto, Japan, 9–12 June.
Stroop, John R. 1935. Studies in interference in serial verbal reactions. *Journal of Experimental
    Psychology* 18:643–661.
Turconi, Eva, and Xavier Seron. 2002. Dissociation between order and quantity meanings in a
    patient with Gerstmann syndrome. *Cortex* 38:911–914.
Ward, Jamie, Brett Huckstep, and Elias Tsakanikos. 2006. Sound-colour synaesthesia: To what
    extent does it use cross-modal mechanisms common to us all? *Cortex* 42 (2):264–280.
Weiss, Peter H., and Gereon R. Fink. 2009. Grapheme-colour synaesthetes show increased grey
    matter volumes of parietal and fusiform cortex. *Brain* 132 (1):65–70.

PART III

ATTENTION AND PERCEPTION

CHAPTER 13

INDIVIDUAL DIFFERENCES IN SYNESTHESIA

TESSA M. VAN LEEUWEN

INTRODUCING DIFFERENT SYNESTHETES

When synesthetes exemplify their rich inner experiences, it immediately becomes clear that every synesthete is unique. One synesthete would, for example, describe the days of the week as side-by-side blocks, oriented in a circle in head-centered space. But another synesthete would experience blue-orange shimmering colors for specific musical chords—as did composer Messiaen, for example, who explicitly noted his synesthetic colors in his sheet music (Bernard 1986). These are examples of different types of synesthesia, namely time-space and music-color synesthesia. Dozens of types exist (Day 2011). Besides variations in type, individual variability also exists among synesthetes who experience the same form of synesthesia. There is idiosyncrasy for instance in the specific combinations of synesthesia *inducer* (i.e. trigger) and *concurrent* (i.e. resultant sensation) across synesthetes (Grossenbacher and Lovelace 2001; Hochel and Milán 2008). I am a grapheme-color synesthete and I experience the grapheme 3 as a bright shade of green and 4 as dark red, but for other grapheme-color synesthetes, other color combinations would occur (although trends may exist; see Beeli, Esslen, and Jäncke 2007; Simner and Ward 2008; Simner et al. 2005; Smilek et al. 2007). Synesthetes are very particular about their letter-color combinations, and will firmly disagree with one another about which color a letter should be; I cannot imagine that the number 3 would be any other color than this one particular shade of green (Cytowic 1995; Ramachandran and Hubbard 2001a, 2003a). Individual differences in the experience of textures for graphemes have also been reported for grapheme-color synesthesia (Eagleman and Goodale 2009). For instance, the surface of a grapheme could look shiny and metallic, or soft like a flannel blanket.

For grapheme-color synesthesia, individual differences between synesthetes (in addition to the idiosyncrasy described earlier) have led to the recognition of several divisions among synesthetes (Dixon and Smilek 2005; Dixon, Smilek, and Merikle

2004; Hubbard et al. 2005; Ramachandran and Hubbard 2001a). The two major distinctions are between "projector" and "associator" synesthetes, and between "higher" and "lower" synesthetes (see later). In this chapter I review the literature on these individual differences between synesthetes and their relevance for experimental outcomes in synesthesia research. For instance, how do individual differences in synesthesia relate to the mechanism of synesthesia in the brain? My focus is on grapheme-color synesthesia; this is the form of synesthesia that has received the most attention in the literature, as it is one of the most prevalent forms (Day 2011; Simner et al. 2006). Distinctions on the basis of individual differences are currently only well-documented for grapheme-color synesthesia. It is however possible that similar distinctions may exist for other forms of synesthesia; this is actually likely to be the case (Cytowic 1993; Ward and Simner 2003).

All grapheme-color synesthetes experience colors for letters and/or digits (e.g. the letter J may elicit the color orange). The colors are elicited in an automatic fashion (Beeli, Esslen, and Jäncke 2005; Dixon, Smilek, and Merikle 2004; Dixon et al. 2000; Mattingley et al. 2001; Odgaard, Flowers, and Bradman 1999; Wollen and Ruggiero 1983), are consistent over time (e.g. Baron-Cohen, Wyke, and Binnie 1987; Simner and Logie 2007; but see Niccolai et al. 2012; Simner 2012, for a discussion on consistency as a defining feature), and are usually highly specific in nature and described in great detail by the synesthete (e.g. Motluk 1996; Tyler 2005). Despite these shared characteristics, however, not all grapheme-color synesthetes are alike. The first distinction is the "projector-associator" distinction which concerns the spatial location where *concurrent* synesthetic colors are perceived (Dixon and Smilek 2005; Dixon, Smilek, and Merikle 2004; Smilek et al. 2001). Figure 13.1 illustrates "projector" and "associator" synesthesia. Projector and associator synesthetes do not differ in the type of inducers that elicit synesthesia, but rather, it is the way the colors appear that is different. Projector synesthetes describe their colors as "being out there on the page" or on a "mental screen" in the peripersonal space around them, whereas associator synesthetes report their colors are located "in the mind's eye," in "the inner eye," or that they know what the color is but do not experience this anywhere at all (Dixon, Smilek, and Merikle 2004; Ward et al. 2007).

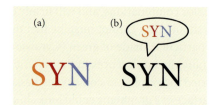

FIGURE 13.1 Projector and associator synesthesia. (a) For projectors, the synesthetic color appears as an overlay on the grapheme. (b) For associator synesthetes, the color appears 'in the mind's eye' and does not have a particular place in space.

The color experiences of projector synesthetes (Figure 13.1a) have been described in several different ways: as existing in external space and being superimposed on the text (Ward et al. 2007); as transparent overlays on the printed letter (Skelton, Ludwig, and Mohr 2009); as being externally co-localized with a grapheme (van Leeuwen, den Ouden, and Hagoort 2011) or as being "in the outside world" (Rouw and Scholte 2007). Even when the synesthetic color is experienced as an overlay on the grapheme, the physical ink color on the paper is still perceived. Smilek et al. (2001) were the first to make an explicit mention of a synesthete who "projected [her color] onto the digit" (933). In their paper, synesthete C was given the task of searching for a target digit (2 or 4, synesthetically eliciting red and blue, respectively) among distractors (a group of 8's, eliciting a black color). All digits were displayed in dark grey, but crucially, the background color of the search display was either congruent or incongruent with the synesthetic color of the target digit. Thus, if the target were a 2, a red background would constitute a congruent background and if the background were blue this would be an incongruent trial (and vice versa for target digit 4). The synesthete participant C was slower in identifying the target digit when the background of the display was congruent with the synesthetic color of the target. The same effect of background color occurred when C was asked to identify digits that were presented very briefly (here, C was less accurate at identifying digits on congruent-color trials). On the basis of these results, Smilek et al. (2001) concluded that synesthetic colors could influence the perception of the digits. This entails the assumption that during the process of digit recognition the synesthetic color is already elicited and the background color can then affect the perception of the digit. These early effects may not be true for all synesthetes (Dixon and Smilek 2005; Smilek and Dixon 2002).

Associator synesthetes experience their colors quite differently from projector synesthetes (Figure 13.1b). Judging from the literature, associator synesthesia is also more common than projector synesthesia, as projectors are usually the minority in group studies. Associator synesthesia has been described as a strong internal association of the color (van Leeuwen, den Ouden, and Hagoort 2011), as occurring "in the head" (Dixon, Smilek, and Merikle 2004), or as appearing in an internalized space (Ward et al. 2007). For some associator synesthetes (known as "know-associators"; Ward et al. 2007), the color association is more like simply "knowing" that a color belongs to a grapheme. Dixon et al. (2004) compare associator synesthesia to the general sensation shared by all people of knowing that a traffic light stop-sign is red, even when seeing a black and white picture of a traffic light. For synesthetes the association with the color is automatic and the colors are also highly specific in nature; this is true of both projector and associator synesthetes. Associator synesthesia could also be likened to the way some people without synesthesia can form a clear mental image of a scene from memory. If you have visited a lake during your summer holidays, you might have a vivid memory of sailboats with white sails; when you visualize this scene it is highly specific in nature but occurs "in the mind's eye" and is not present in a perceptual sense. Later I discuss how the differences between projector and associator synesthetes may

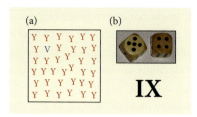

FIGURE 13.2 Lower and higher synesthesia. (a) For lower synesthetes, a search display with black letters on a white background may appear as shown here, i.e., as colored according to their synesthesia. The way this effect is depicted in (a) is probably not completely realistic; there is evidence the synesthetic colors do not appear all at once but only around the 'spotlight' of attention (Ward et al. 2010). (b) Examples of inducers of higher synesthesia: dice patterns and Roman numerals which elicit the same colors as their numerical counterpart.

affect the outcomes of synesthesia experiments, but first I describe a second type of individual difference in synesthesia.

The second distinction among grapheme-color synesthetes is between "lower" and "higher" synesthetes (Hubbard et al. 2005; Ramachandran and Hubbard 2001a, 2001b, 2003a, 2003b). Here, synesthetes are classified not according to their experience of the concurrent, but on the basis of the level of processing of the inducer, and relatedly, on the type of inducer that elicits synesthesia. In "lower" synesthetes, synesthetic colors are evoked at a relatively early visual processing stage, and so for grapheme-color synesthetes, colors are elicited on the basis of the *shape* of the grapheme (rather than by its identity as one given grapheme over another; Ramachandran and Hubbard 2001a, 2001b). Given this, synesthetic colors can lead to early perceptual effects (Kim and Blake 2005; Kim, Blake, and Palmeri 2006; Nikolić, Lichti, and Singer 2007; Palmeri et al. 2002; Ramachandran and Hubbard 2001a, 2001b; Smilek, Dixon, and Merikle 2003). One such early phenomenon is the "pop-out" effect in which synesthetes are asked to locate a target item (e.g. letter V) among an array of distractors (e.g. Ys). Lower synesthetes perform this task particularly fast and accurately, since the synesthetic color of the target may allow it to "pop out" from the differently colored distractor items (illustrated in Figure 13.2a; see also Figure 14.7 in Rich and Mattingley, Chapter 14, this volume, for a different example with a target 2 among distractor 5s). Importantly, for lower synesthetes, the target's color can pop out even before the target has been fully identified as a grapheme. In "higher" synesthetes, in contrast, these early effects do not occur to the same extent because it is not the shape but the concept (meaning) of the grapheme that elicits the synesthetic color (Hubbard et al. 2005; Ramachandran and Hubbard 2003a). For higher synesthetes for instance, Roman numerals (e.g. IX) or dice patterns (see Figure 13.2b) may sometimes elicit the same colors as the numerical digit (e.g. 9) that represents the same magnitude and position in the numerical sequence (Ramachandran and Hubbard 2001a, 2003a; Ward and Sagiv 2007; Ward et al. 2007). It should be noted that Grossenbacher and Lovelace (2001) have proposed a similar distinction, i.e. between "perceptual" and "conceptual" synesthetes. This classification is dependent on whether the inducers of synesthesia are perceived sensory stimuli (perceptual) or the meaning of the stimulus (conceptual).

EVIDENCE FROM BEHAVIORAL EXPERIMENTS

During the past decades many studies have characterized synesthetic experiences, and any failures to replicate findings with different subject groups or individual cases have gradually led to the recognition that not all grapheme-color synesthetes are the same. Let us take a look at the different experimental paradigms that have been used and how the outcomes have revealed individual differences between synesthetes. One of the most important experimental findings in the synesthesia literature is that synesthetic color experiences can influence the reaction times of judgments on real color (Dixon, Smilek, and Merikle 2004; Dixon et al. 2000; Mattingley et al. 2001; Odgaard, Flowers, and Bradman 1999; Palmeri et al. 2002; Smilek et al. 2001; van Leeuwen, Petersson, and Hagoort 2010; Wollen and Ruggiero 1983). An influential type of task in which interference from synesthetic colors has been found is the synesthetic Stroop task (Elias et al. 2003; Dixon, Smilek, and Merikle 2004; Odgaard, Flowers, and Bradman 1999; Palmeri et al. 2002; Wollen and Ruggiero 1983). In a regular Stroop task (Stroop 1935), color words (e.g. "red") are displayed in ink colors that are either congruent (red ink) or incongruent (e.g. green ink) with the colors that the words indicate. Participants are asked to name the ink colors in which the words are printed; in the incongruent condition, the automatic process of reading words causes interference between the written color words and the ink-naming decision. Color naming times for the incongruent condition ("red" in green ink) are therefore slower.

In synesthesia research, similar logic was used to show the automaticity of synesthetic colors. In "synesthetic Stroop tasks," graphemes are displayed in a color that is either congruent or incongruent with the synesthetic color of the grapheme. It has been demonstrated repeatedly that synesthetes are slower to name the ink color of the grapheme when this color does not match the synesthetic color associated with the grapheme (Dixon, Smilek, and Merikle 2004; Elias et al. 2003; Mills, Boteler, and Oliver 1999; Odgaard, Flowers, and Bradman 1999; Palmeri et al. 2002; Wollen and Ruggiero 1983). This Stroop-type effect indicated that synesthetic colors are elicited automatically and cannot be suppressed even when they are detrimental to the task at hand—otherwise the participants would have been able to suppress their synesthetic colors in the incongruent condition in the Stroop experiment. That synesthesia is elicited automatically was also demonstrated in priming studies (Mattingley et al. 2001; van Leeuwen, Petersson, and Hagoort 2010) in which a grapheme eliciting synesthesia (e.g. the color orange) was followed by a congruently (orange) or incongruently (e.g. yellow) colored patch. Synesthetes were slower to indicate the color of the patch in the incongruent condition. Later on we will see how a Stroop-type task was used by Dixon et al. (2004) to show relative differences in automaticity between projector and associator synesthesia.

Although Stroop and priming effects indicate that synesthetic colors occur automatically, this does not prove that the colors perceived by the synesthetes are actually *perceptual* in nature. Perceptual effects occur early in visual color processing and are elicited immediately and pre-attentively (Treisman and Gelade 1980). Given these features of veridical perceptual colors, we might argue that lower synesthetes (triggered by perceptual inducers) may perform as if their colors, too, are relatively perceptual in nature. For example, all people are fast to resolve visual search "pop-out" tasks, in which targets and distractors are presented in actual colored ink (e.g. a blue letter V among red Ys). Importantly, we saw earlier that lower synesthetes perform well even when presented with *monochrome* stimuli. In other words, their synesthetic colors seem to act in a similar way to real-world colors. (More information about the perceptual reality of synesthetic colors can be found in Kim and Blake, Chapter 15, this volume.) Alternatively, previous findings might be interpreted in a way that does *not* require us to think synesthetic colors are like real-word colors. For example, the observed Stroop interference in the types of studies described earlier could be explained by an automatic semantic (rather than perceptual) association between the grapheme and the color, such that the synesthetic color is somehow a semantic concept, and it is this *semantic* activation that interferes with the color decision.

Several experimenters followed up on the reports of Stroop interference and aimed to demonstrate perceptual, and not just semantic, effects of synesthesia. For this, they used tasks which have been interpreted as showing early visual processing, and these tasks showed that synesthetic colors played a role during these early steps of visual information analysis. Ramachandran and Hubbard (2001a) for instance, had two synesthetes (JC and ER) perform a perceptual grouping task. They presented the synesthetes with square matrices, in which graphemes were presented in rows and columns. The graphemes could be grouped either horizontally or vertically; non-synesthetic participants preferentially grouped the graphemes on the basis of their similarity in shape (for instance, grouping 3s with 8s). The synesthetes, however, preferentially grouped the graphemes on the basis of their synesthetic color. The authors argue that perceptual grouping effects are a good indication of whether a given feature is genuinely perceptual or not. It is for instance possible to segregate tilted lines from a background of vertical lines, but Ts will not segregate from Ls in a display. The Ts would not differ enough perceptually from the Ls for a grouping structure to become easily apparent. If we argue that the synesthetes were able to group the display according to synesthetic color because these colors appeared early during visual processing, we could in hindsight speculate—with caution—that these synesthetes were lower synesthetes.

Several other tasks were deployed to demonstrate the perceptual reality of synesthetic colors. We saw earlier that synesthetic color can increase the efficiency of visual search in "pop out" paradigms (Palmeri et al. 2002; Ramachandran and Hubbard 2001a; Smilek, Dixon, and Merikle 2003; Ward et al. 2010). We noted that synesthetes were faster than controls to locate the hidden target digit among an array of distractors (see Figure 13.2a, which was presented achromatically in these studies), indicating relatively fast elicitation of synesthetic colors. We should qualify however that the results of this "pop out" study were different from a true, *immediate* "pop-out" effect, as found when displays are presented in colored ink. In other words, when searching for a blue V among red Ys in a colored display, people immediately spot the target item, irrespective of the number of distractors. In contrast, synesthetes viewing achromatic displays (and relying on synesthetic colors), although better than controls, were still affected by the number of distractors in the display (see also later papers on visual search: Laeng 2009; Laeng, Svartdal, and Oelmann 2004; Sagiv, Heer, and Robertson 2006; Ward et al. 2010). Nonetheless, "pop-out" effects suggest that synesthetic colors can improve performance even before overt recognition of the grapheme, and this is an indication of lower synesthesia (where synesthetic colors are elicited on the basis of the shape of the grapheme). Similarly, in a "crowding task," where target digits are flanked with distractor digits, synesthetic color again appears to precede recognition and improve performance (Hubbard et al. 2005; Ramachandran and Hubbard 2001b). Furthermore, synesthetic colors can help to protect the ability to identify graphemes from different types of masking (Smilek et al. 2001; Wagar et al. 2002). In masking paradigms, a stimulus is immediately followed by a masking stimulus, which makes the first stimulus very difficult to detect. Synesthetic colors can also induce apparent motion (Kim, Blake, and Palmeri 2006) and the watercolor illusion (Kim and Blake 2005), which again makes them similar to real colors. Synesthetic colors may even adhere to early visual color-opponency mechanisms (Nikolić, Lichti, and Singer 2007). Witthoft and Winawer (2006) have demonstrated that synesthetic colors are subject to ordinary lightness constancy mechanisms, and for some synesthetes, the visual contrast of the graphemes influences the strength of their synesthetic percept (Hubbard, Manohar, and Ramachandran 2006). Together these studies suggest that, for the particular synesthetes tested at least, synesthesia is indeed perceptual in nature and is elicited at a rather early stage of grapheme processing. Synesthesia may even happen pre-attentively: before overt attention is completely deployed to the grapheme and awareness is complete (Carriere et al. 2009; Palmeri et al. 2002; Ramachandran and Hubbard 2001a; Smilek, Dixon, and Merikle 2003). Carriere et al. (2009), for example, have shown that graphemes which were colored congruently with their synesthetic color can attract attention in synesthetes.

Synesthetes who do not experience perceptual and early effects of their synesthetic colors, however, have also been encountered (Edquist et al. 2006; Hong and Blake 2008; Hubbard et al. 2005; Mattingley et al. 2001; Rothen and Meier 2009; Sagiv, Heer, and Robertson 2006) In Hubbard et al. (2005), several synesthetes did not show superior in performance (compared to control participants) on a crowding task. The authors suggest these synesthetes might be higher synesthetes, meaning that their synesthesia is not elicited on the basis of the shape of the grapheme, but only after awareness is complete and grapheme identity has been established. This was one of the first studies in which stable individual differences between synesthetes were found (Dixon and Smilek 2005; Hubbard et al. 2005). In group studies by Edquist et al. (2006), Gheri et al., (2008), and Rothen and Meier (2009), synesthetes as a group did not perform significantly better than controls on visual search tasks similar to the display in Figure 13.2a (displayed in monochrome in the studies). The lack of overall effect indicates that synesthetes were not significantly helped by their colors. The colors may have been elicited not at an early stage, but at a later semantic grapheme processing stage (suggesting higher synesthesia), similar to the processing stage at which control subjects perform the visual search. Or perhaps the synesthetic colors were elicited early but were not located in the same spatial location as the graphemes (possibly again suggesting associator synesthesia). Rothen and Meier (2009), however, did find that *some individual* synesthetes showed faster target detection in visual search displays. As the earlier studies on synesthesia often included only one or two synesthetes, Rothen and Meier support an earlier suggestion (Dixon and Smilek 2005; Hubbard et al. 2005; Hubbard and Ramachandran 2005) that differing findings in case studies could possibly be ascribed to individual differences between synesthetes. The results of case studies might therefore not be representative for all synesthetes; in fact, in retrospect, lower synesthesia might even be quite rare even though the findings from lower synesthetes in early case studies directed much subsequent research. In another visual search study by Sagiv et al. (2006) two synesthetes again showed no evidence for early "pop-out" effects.

Additional evidence against an early generation of colors, at least for some synesthetes, came from a priming study by Jason Mattingley and colleagues (a group study including 15 grapheme-color synesthetes). Mattingley et al. (2001) showed that when synesthesia-inducing graphemes were only shown to participants for a very short time, priming effects for subsequently presented colored patches were lost. The synesthetic colors no longer affected the reaction times of the color decisions. The graphemes were shown so briefly that they were not consciously perceived: this implies that awareness of the grapheme is necessary for synesthesia to be elicited in these synesthetes, which might contradict the early perceptual findings that were discussed earlier in other synesthetes. The debate about the level of awareness of the grapheme that is necessary to elicit synesthesia continues until today, and is closely coupled to the discussion about the role of attention in synesthesia (Mattingley, Payne, and Rich 2006; Ward et al. 2007; Ward et al. 2010; see also Smilek, Dixon, and Merikle 2005, for a review). From the earlier-mentioned results, however, it becomes clear that not all synesthetes experience early effects of synesthesia occurring completely prior to awareness of the grapheme, and that individual differences between synesthetes influence experimental outcomes.

By now, more synesthetes have been identified for whom their synesthesia is elicited on the basis of the concept of the inducers. For instance, days of the week can induce a color sensation. It is not always the first letter of the actual word that induces the color—as is the case for most other words in many individuals with grapheme-color synesthesia—but often the concept of "Wednesday" or the position of the item in the sequence of week-days (Ramachandran and Hubbard 2001a; Sagiv et al. 2006). This type of synesthesia for ordinal sequences and concepts would be considered "higher" synesthesia because it is not elicited on the basis of perceptual properties of the inducers. Dixon et al. (2000) and Jansari et al. (2006) have shown that synesthesia can also be elicited when grapheme-color synesthetes only think about the inducing stimulus and do not perceive it on paper. When synesthetes performed simple mental arithmetic (e.g.

2 + 5) the synesthetic color of the answer (7) was enough to induce Stroop interference (Dixon et al. 2000). Furthermore, synesthetes who experience synesthesia for abstract representations of numerosity such as dice patterns and finger counting have been identified by Ward and Sagiv (2007) and Ward et al. (2007). For these synesthetes, it is again the concept of the number that determines the color, and this is clear because the same color can be generated by different surface forms of the same number (e.g. by 2, II: and ⚅). Indeed, for the majority of synesthetes it is the identity (meaning) of a grapheme that influences its synesthetic color (Dixon et al. 2006; Myles et al. 2003; Ramachandran and Hubbard 2001a). This effect can be demonstrated in ambiguous figures or displays in which a shape can be read as either a letter or a digit depending on the context (e.g. S and 5, 2 and Z). In these cases, the top-down, context-driven interpretation of the grapheme tends to determine which color is perceived (Ramachandran and Hubbard 2001a) and even directs Stroop-type interference effects (Dixon et al., 2006; Myles et al., 2003). In Navon-type displays (e.g. where a large number 5 is created from smaller 3s), attention to either the local or global level of the display makes the synesthetic color switch accordingly (Rich and Mattingley 2003). Context effects have also been reported to play a role in synesthetes for whom the synesthetic color is believed to arise from the *shape* of the grapheme. An example is synesthete C (mentioned previously), for whom her synesthetic colors made it more difficult to discern a grapheme against a background that had the same color as her synesthesia (Smilek et al. 2001), indicating the synesthetic colors were elicited early during visual processing. However, C also reported that ambiguous stimuli can have a different color depending on their interpretation (Myles et al. 2003). Hence, the distinction between lower and higher synesthesia might not be clear-cut in all cases. The authors have captured the role of shape, color, and the meaning of graphemes in a re-entrant model of synesthesia, in which the shape, color, and meaning of the grapheme are interacting in an iterative way during grapheme processing (Carriere et al. 2009; Smilek et al. 2001).

How Individual Differences Are Assessed

Synesthesia is a subjective phenomenon by nature, which makes it a difficult phenomenon to study because the synesthesia is only experienced by the synesthetes themselves. Subjective reports of synesthetes have always been important in synesthesia research to generate hypotheses about the properties and neural underpinnings of synesthesia (Smilek and Dixon 2002). Similarly, detailed subjective reports are crucial to assess the influence of individual differences in synesthesia on experimental outcomes. Often, individual differences in synesthesia are therefore assessed by asking the synesthetes to describe their synesthesia in detail, relying on their subjective report alone. However, because not all synesthetes might use the same words to describe their experiences, it is very important to ask the right questions. It has been demonstrated that simply asking the question "How do the colors appear?" with the answer possibilities "out there in space," "in my mind's eye," or "neither," does not always yield good test–retest reliability (Edquist et al. 2006). More elaborate question-naires including more questions and a Likert-scale have therefore been developed to classify synesthetes more objectively, at least for the projector-associator distinction (Rouw and Scholte 2007). On these questionnaires, synesthetes indicate how much they agree with specific statements that either correspond to a projector viewpoint ("My synesthetic colors take on the same shape as the letter that is on the paper") or an associator viewpoint ("I do not actually see the letter in color, but I know which color belongs to the letter"). Skelton et al. (2009) developed an illustrated questionnaire to distinguish projector from associator synesthetes which yields better stable classifi-cation results over time. In the on line test for synesthesia known as the Synesthesia Battery (Eagleman et al. 2007), a section on the projector-associator distinction is also included. An elaborate account of how to ask the right questions to classify synesthetes is given by Mohr (Chapter 22, this volume).

To provide more objective evidence for the projector-associator distinction, inde-pendent from subjective reports, Dixon and colleagues investigated whether projec-tors and associators showed different patterns of performance on synesthetic Stroop tasks (Dixon, Smilek, and Merikle 2004). In their study, synesthetes performed two such tasks. In the first, they named the font colors of graphemes on a screen, and expe-rienced interference from their synesthetic colors in the incongruent condition (e.g. in naming green font for a grapheme that was synesthetically red). In the second Stroop task, participants named their synesthetic colors for each grapheme, experiencing interference from the font colors on the screen. The authors hypothesized that for pro-jectors, the projected synesthetic colors may be more difficult to ignore than the inter-nally experienced colors would be for associators. The projected synesthetic colors are spatially closer to the grapheme or even overlapping with it, and this is what makes them harder to ignore. Dixon et al. (2004) were able to show that projector synesthetes experienced more reaction time interference from synesthetically induced colors than from real colors, while for associator synesthetes this pattern was reversed. The reaction time results confirmed an earlier classification of projector versus associator made on the basis of subjective descriptions of the synesthetes' experiences. This convergence of behavioral findings and self-report provides evidence for stable individual differences between synesthetes. The authors interpret the effects in terms of relative automaticity of the synesthetic colors. They argue that because the projectors experience more inter-ference from their synesthetic colors than associators, their synesthesia is elicited more automatically.

Ward et al. (2007) have replicated these "dual-Stroop" results of Dixon and colleagues, although the behavioral patterns did not match the classification on the basis of subjec-tive reports in all cases. Nonetheless, the study provides more evidence that patterns of reaction times on Stroop tasks can be a useful tool in classifying subtypes of synesthetes. The study by Dixon et al. (2004) is therefore crucial to the projector/associator distinc-tion literature.

SAME OR DIFFERENT DISTINCTIONS?

Reviewing the outcomes of synesthesia experiments, individual differences between grapheme-color synesthetes become clear immediately. During the past years, two different naming conventions have emerged for distinctions between synesthetes, and these have been used side by side. Often, the definitions for these terms have also been quite unclear. The different reports about perceptual, early effects of synesthesia and the more conceptual (semantic), later effects suggest, at least on the surface, that the projector/associator distinction (for the concurrent) and the lower/higher distinction (for the inducer) could be very strongly related (Dixon and Smilek 2005; Hubbard and Ramachandran 2005). If this were the case, we would predict that early perceptual triggering of synesthetic colors (lower synesthesia) would occur mainly in projector synesthetes and not in associator synesthetes. Indeed, the examples of lower synesthesia resemble the findings of Smilek et al. (2001) for their projector synesthete C, for whom synesthetically colored graphemes were more difficult to discern against a background that was colored identical to her synesthetic color. Wagar et al. (2002) also showed that masking effects were less severe in projector synesthete C, possibly because the (brief) presentation of the grapheme already elicited a color for C, which made the masking stimulus that followed the grapheme less effective in masking the processing of the grapheme. It is likely that early triggering of synesthesia from low-level inducers in several case studies (Kim and Blake 2005; Kim, Blake, and Palmeri 2006; Palmeri et al. 2002; Ramachandran and Hubbard 2001a, 2001b) were observed in participants who were actually projector synesthetes (judging from the descriptive reports in e.g. crowding experiments). Similarly, synesthetes without any superior performance in visual search tasks (i.e. those who show no "lower synesthesia" effects), might simultaneously be associator synesthetes who do not perceive the color in the same place as the to-be-detected target. Indeed Rothen and Meier (2009), who showed no benefits of synesthesia in such tasks, mentioned that all participating synesthetes were associator synesthetes. Ward et al. (2010) tested a mixed group of projectors and associators on a visual search task. The participants were shown a black and white search array in which a shape, made up out of graphemes, was hidden amongst other graphemes. During the task, some synesthetes reported seeing or using their synesthetic colors, and this was more frequently reported by the projector synesthetes; moreover, these synesthetes performed better on the search task. Therefore, several studies suggest that the projector/associator distinction and the lower/higher distinction may covary and this has been noted by several authors (Dixon and Smilek 2005; Hubbard and Ramachandran 2005).

However, it was not mentioned in all studies whether the synesthetes who participated were projector or associator synesthetes. In retrospect it is therefore not always possible to say whether particular findings are in line with the prediction. Other authors have suggested that the projector/associator distinction and the lower/higher distinction are orthogonal and have little relationship to each other (Ward et al. 2007). In their study, Ward and colleagues extensively tested synesthetes on projector/associator characteristics and higher/lower characteristics. This elaborate and important paper is described in detail in the following paragraphs.

Ward et al. (2007) investigated whether for individual synesthetes, the higher/lower distinction would map onto the associator/projector distinction—in other words, whether higher synesthetes are all associators and lower synesthetes are projectors. Ward and colleagues were the first to address this question with direct empirical testing. The synesthetes in that study performed a crowding task to assess the extent to which their synesthesia resembled "lower" synesthesia, and were asked about the presence of "higher" properties such as synesthesia for dice patterns or number words. Because the distribution of higher properties was seemingly unrelated to projector/associator status, the authors conclude that the two distinctions are not the same and are orthogonal to each other.

An important finding by Ward et al. (2007) in this paper is that not all projector synesthetes experience their colors in the same way, and that there are individual differences between associator synesthetes, also. There are, for instance, not only projector synesthetes who perceive their colors as overlaid on the graphemes, but also projectors for whom the colors appear on a "mental screen" that is placed a certain distance away from them in peripersonal space. On the Stroop tasks, these "mental screen projectors" behaved as associators. When modeling activations in the brain, however, these synesthetes grouped with the projectors (van Leeuwen, den Ouden, and Hagoort 2011). Similarly, there are associator synesthetes who "see" their colors, and those who "know" their colors (Ward and Sagiv 2007). The individual differences *within* the projector and associator subgroups suggest that projectors and associators may not simply represent two separate subgroups of synesthetes, but instead represent two ends of a continuum. Because the individual differences between synesthetes can be so subtle, it is always valuable to collect detailed subjective reports of synesthetic experience (by means of a standardized questionnaire) in addition to more objective experimental tests.

In the Brain

In recent years, many neuroimaging studies have contributed to a better understanding of the neural mechanisms of synesthesia, although many questions still remain. Also here, it is important to take individual differences between synesthetes into account in order to understand the full neural underpinnings of synesthesia. Several different questions have intrigued researchers in the neuroimaging field. For instance, which brain areas are active during synesthesia, and how do these areas interact? How does this relate to individual differences? Most of the neuroimaging studies have focused on grapheme-color synesthesia, since this is one of the more prevalent forms.

One of the first questions that arose about synesthesia in the brain was whether synesthetic colors "behave" like real colors in the brain. During (real) color perception, the visual system and in particular visual area V4 becomes active, an area located at the back of the brain that is important for color perception. Many imaging studies have by now shown that synesthetic colors can indeed also activate visual color area V4 (Hubbard et al. 2005; Nunn et al. 2002; Rouw and Scholte 2007; Sperling et al. 2006; van Leeuwen, Petersson, and Hagoort 2010). Besides area V4, the superior parietal lobule (SPL) is also believed to be essential in eliciting grapheme-color synesthesia (Esterman et al. 2006; Hubbard 2007; Muggleton et al. 2007; van Leeuwen, Petersson, and Hagoort 2010; Weiss and Fink 2009; Weiss, Zilles, and Fink 2005). The SPL is important for combining different types of incoming sensory information, for instance, information provided by seeing and hearing a stimulus.

As a potential neural mechanism of synesthesia, aberrant cross-activation between brain areas is proposed. Researchers think that somehow, brain areas are cross-activating each other in an abnormal way in synesthesia, leading to the additional experiences that characterize synesthesia. The cross-activation hypothesis therefore led to the question of *how* color area V4 becomes active during synesthesia. One question pertains to the "hardware" of cross-activation: would there be anatomical or functional differences in the brains of synesthetes (Bargary and Mitchell 2008; Hänggi et al. 2008; Jäncke et al. 2009; Rouw and Scholte 2007, 2010; Weiss and Fink 2009)? Another main question is via which route of cross-activation area V4 becomes active during synesthesia experiences (e.g. Beeli, Esslen, and Jäncke 2008; Brang et al. 2010; van Leeuwen, den Ouden, and Hagoort 2011). Competing hypotheses exist: one debate is whether cross-activation of color area V4 results from *direct* influences from grapheme areas on color areas within the visual system (cross-wiring model; Hubbard, Brang, and Ramachandran 2011; Ramachandran and Hubbard 2001a), or whether cross-activation is induced *indirectly* through higher-order multimodal areas like parietal lobe (disinhibited feedback model; Grossenbacher and Lovelace 2001). In the brain, initial sensory processing areas (visual and auditory cortex, for instance) forward information to higher-order cortical areas, where information is integrated (Robertson 2003). Next, these higher order areas also return feedback to lower-hierarchy areas, to inform them of processing steps that have been taken. The disinhibited feedback model proposes that aberrant feedback from the multi-modal region SPL is sent back to color areas lower in the hierarchy, activating V4 in a top-down manner. Figure 13.3 summarizes the two models. It is possible that mechanisms of cross-activation may not be similar for all synesthetes (van Leeuwen, den Ouden, and Hagoort 2011). In this section I discuss imaging studies related to these questions—which areas are active, by which route is V4 activated?—which have revealed individual differences between synesthetes in the brain. The interested reader can also see Part V of this volume, which describes the neuroimaging methods and neuroscientific data on synesthesia in greater detail.

V4 activity during grapheme-color synesthesia has been shown in many studies, but in several other studies, activity in color areas was not found or the location did not correspond to V4 (Paulesu et al. 1995; Rich et al. 2006; Weiss, Zilles, and Fink 2005). It is

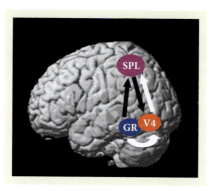

FIGURE 13.3 Cross-wiring and disinhibition theories. This figure shows the position in the brain of the areas involved in grapheme processing (Gr), color area V4, and the superior parietal lobule (SPL). The essential interactions proposed by the cross-wiring theory are depicted with white arrows, those of the disinhibition theory with black arrows.

possible that these differences between studies are influenced by individual differences between synesthetes. Hubbard and colleagues (2005) were the first to show a stable correlation between brain activity in area V4 and individual differences on a behavioral task. In their functional magnetic resonance imaging (fMRI) study, synesthetes with low performance on a crowding task showed less activation of color area V4 during synesthesia (see Hubbard, Chapter 24, this volume for more information on fMRI). The authors interpret the performance on the crowding task as an indication of lower synesthesia (better performance than controls) or higher synesthesia (no improvement compared to controls). This study then, for the first time, linked individual differences between synesthetes to differences in brain activity. The authors, advocating the cross-wiring theory, suggest that for lower synesthetes direct cross-wiring to area V4 at the level of the fusiform gyrus in the visual system (grapheme processing area) may cause synesthesia. For higher synesthetes, the cross-wiring may happen at the level of a higher-order brain area, the angular gyrus. In a study by Sperling et al. (2006), four grapheme-color synesthetes participated who experienced their colors "in the mind's eye." Two of these synesthetes experienced a "flat screen of color" while two reported the colors resembled the shape of the letter. Only for the two synesthetes who reported a screen of color, was activity in area V4/V8 found. This finding further strengthens the finding that individual differences in subjective synesthetic color experience are related to color area activation.

Rouw and Scholte (2007) investigated anatomical differences in synesthetes' brains. They deployed diffusion tensor imaging and investigated the structure of white matter in the brain. White matter consists of the connecting fibers between neurons (more about this technique can be found in Rouw, Chapter 25, this volume). Rouw and Scholte (2007) showed that synesthetes, compared to non-synesthetes, have more coherently structured white matter in frontal brain areas, in left superior parietal cortex, and in inferior temporal cortex (located near color areas). This suggests that in synesthetes, the "hardware" connections in some places of the brain are stronger. Using an extensive questionnaire, the authors classified the participating synesthetes as either projector or associator synesthetes, and moreover obtained a graded "projector/associator score" for each synesthete. Correlating these scores with the measure of white matter coherence in the brain, it was found the more the synesthetes agreed with a projector viewpoint, the more coherent the white matter structure was in inferior temporal cortex. In the other two brain areas this correlation was not found. The authors suggest a link between the subjective experience of synesthesia and white matter structure in the vicinity of color areas.

In a later study, Rouw and Scholte (2010) investigated differences in functional activations (using fMRI) and in brain structure between a large group of projectors (N = 16) and a large group of associators (N = 26). This time, differences in grey matter function and structure were investigated using fMRI and the voxel-based morphometry (VBM) technique, respectively. With VBM, the local density of grey matter, consisting mainly of the actual neuron cell bodies, can be assessed. Some effects were shared between projector and associator synesthetes, for example in the posterior SPL. But differences were also found: for projector synesthetes, increased functional activations and increased grey matter density were found in brain areas related to sensory experience, such as visual, auditory, and motor cortex. In contrast, for associators, increased activity and grey matter structure were found in the hippocampus and parahippocampal gyrus, brain structures that play a role in memory. The "outside world" versus "in the mind's eye" experiences of projectors and associators appear to be mediated by different brain areas. It should be noted that although parietal lobe activity was found for both associators and projectors, associators showed more activity than projectors in SPL in a previous study (van Leeuwen, Petersson, and Hagoort 2010). Even though SPL is involved in both types of synesthesia, its role could be different for each group.

To understand the neural mechanisms of synesthesia, we need to know more than just the anatomical location of the crucially involved areas. We also need to know how these areas become active and how they interact. Unfortunately, not all neuroimaging techniques are capable of identifying these interactions. We recently (van Leeuwen, den Ouden, and Hagoort 2011) applied the powerful method of dynamic causal modeling (Stephan et al. 2010) to investigate the directed interactions (effective connectivity) within the network of areas involved in grapheme-color synesthesia. With dynamic causal modeling (DCM), it is possible to infer the direction of interactions between brain regions. It models the hidden neural dynamics of a system of interacting brain regions and can be applied to fMRI data. It is possible to compare different models using Bayesian model selection (Stephan et al. 2009) to assess which model is more likely given the data: one of the models will explain the data the best. In our DCM study we focused on the two neural theories summarized in Figure 13.3. We deployed DCM to test the hypothesis that the different subjective experiences of projector and associator synesthetes are due to differences in the interactions within the synesthesia network (consisting of the grapheme processing area, V4, and SPL).

Synesthetes underwent an fMRI scan during free viewing of synesthesia-inducing graphemes (letters and numbers), non-synesthesia inducing control graphemes (letters and symbols), false font stimuli (rare symbols), and colored control graphemes (colored letters and numbers; van Leeuwen, Petersson, and Hagoort 2010). For the DCM analyses, the locations of the letter shape area (LSA) involved in grapheme processing, color area V4, and SPL were individually identified for 15 synesthetes (ten projectors, five associators) and were included in the two DCMs (Figure 13.4a and b). The inputs to both models were the same. In Model 1 (Figure 13.4a), synesthesia-inducing graphemes exerted modulatory effects on the bottom-up processing pathway (Ramachandran and Hubbard 2001a), i.e. synesthesia could influence the strength of the connections from grapheme area LSA to V4 and from V4 to SPL. The modulatory effect on the connection from LSA to V4 modeled a direct, bottom-up effect of synesthesia on activity in V4 (cross-wiring theory). In Model 2 (Figure 13.4b), synesthesia-inducing graphemes exerted modulatory effects on the top-down processing pathway, i.e. synesthesia could influence the strength of the connections from LSA to SPL and from SPL to V4. Thus, in this case, synesthesia indirectly induced synesthesia-related activity in V4 (disinhibited feedback theory, Grossenbacher and Lovelace 2001). Overall across synesthetes, there was no strong preference for one or the other model (Figure 13.4c). However, when separated according to the participants' synesthetic experience (projector versus associator), for the projectors the bottom-up model was a much more likely explanation of the data (99.6%). In contrast, for the associators, the top-down model was better (98.1%).

These results reconcile the direct (cross-wiring) and indirect (disinhibition) cross-activation accounts of synesthesia by showing how modulation of coupling in different parts of the synesthesia network results in different synesthetic experiences. This study is yet another example of stable individual differences between synesthetes and directly relates those to different activation pathways in the brain. The model preferences of projectors and associators are more easily interpreted when we think of their subjective experiences: for projectors, the colors are projected at the spatial location of the grapheme itself (or at least out in space), suggesting a direct link between the (retinotopic) grapheme and color areas in visual cortex. For associators, the "in the mind's eye" experience is more resembling of mental imagery, which is always initiated in a top-down manner in the brain. The fast activation of color areas in the case of projector synesthesia is in line with findings by Brang et al. (2010), who showed that V4 is already activated 5 ms after the grapheme area for projector synesthetes. They used magnetoencephalography, a technique with good time resolution but poorer spatial resolution. Similarly, our findings fit well with the findings from dual-Stroop tasks (Dixon, Smilek, and Merikle 2004; Ward et al. 2007) which suggest that projector synesthesia is more automatic than associator synesthesia. The direct versus indirect activation of area V4 may explain this relative difference in automaticity. Also, in a recent study by Neufeld and colleagues (Neufeld et al. 2012) stronger connectivity of the left inferior parietal cortex with the left primary auditory and right primary visual cortex was found in a group of auditory-visual synesthetes, supporting the disinhibition theory. These synesthetes were all classified as associator synesthetes, strengthening the suggestion that associator synesthesia may rely more on top-down processing than projector synesthesia.

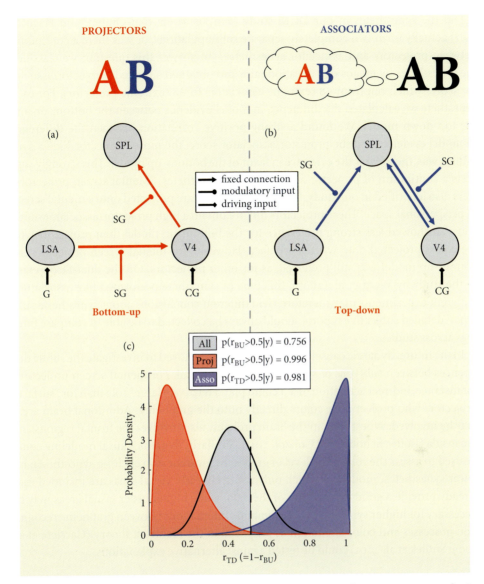

FIGURE 13.4 Dynamic causal modeling study of projector and associator synesthesia. Projector synesthesia (left) and associator synesthesia (right). (a, b) Two DCMs to test for bottom-up (a, red) versus top-down (b, blue) modulation by synesthesia-inducing graphemes (SG) within the letter shape area (LSA)/V4/SPL synesthesia-network. G = all grapheme stimuli, CG = colored graphemes. LSA and V4 are located in the fusiform gyrus (visual system). (c) Bayesian model selection (Stephan et al. 2009): shaded areas represent the probability of the winning model to be better than the alternative model, given the data. $r_{TD} = 1 - r_{BU}$, where r denotes the probability of the observed data to be generated by that model given the models that are present. BU = bottom-up, TD = top-down. Reproduced with permission from Van Leeuwen et al. (2011).

Did the synesthetes in our DCM study (van Leeuwen, den Ouden, and Hagoort 2011) actually form two completely separate subpopulations, or was there a continuum between projectors and associator synesthetes? To answer this question we classified the synesthetes by means of a questionnaire and obtained a graded "projector/associator score" which ran from −8 (extreme associator) to +8 (extreme projector). For each synesthete we calculated the difference in model evidence between the bottom-up and the top-down model. We found a strong positive correlation between the difference in model evidence and the projector/associator score: the more "projector-like" a synesthete was, the greater the evidence in favor of the bottom-up model. This strongly suggests a continuum of projector and associator synesthetes. "Mental screen projectors" were also identified in our study, for whom the colors are projected onto a mental screen in peripersonal space. These projectors did not obtain a high projector/associator score, and also showed less strong preference for the bottom-up model than projectors who see colors projected onto written typeface. However, for mental screen projectors the bottom-up model was still preferred, as for other projectors. On the dual-Stroop task in the study by Ward et al. (2007), this type of synesthete performed like associators. Different experiments may therefore yield different conclusions about synesthesia subtypes; detailed subjective reports should always be collected to be able to compare findings across studies.

In the future, dynamic causal modeling could be deployed to investigate the subtle differences between subtypes of synesthetes in more detail. For mental screen projectors, for instance, indirect activation of V4 could play a relatively larger role than for "surface" projectors who project their colors directly onto the grapheme. Additional brain areas may be involved; synesthesia in the brain probably also involves the frontal regions and the insula (Rouw, Scholte, and Colizoli 2011). Similarly, dynamic causal modeling could be used to assess the role of the level of grapheme awareness in eliciting synesthesia; for lower synesthetes, models in which only relatively early visual areas are included may already provide a good explanation of the data, while higher order visual areas may be necessary for higher synesthetes. The dynamic interactions between grapheme recognition processes and color elicitation as proposed in the reentrant theory (Carriere et al. 2009; Smilek et al. 2001) could be tested against alternative explanations.

DISCUSSION

There is a great body of evidence that individual differences between synesthetes are real and are very important for the correct interpretation of experimental results. If individual differences between synesthetes and detailed subjective reports are not taken into account in synesthesia research, failures to replicate results will significantly hamper our progress in understanding the phenomenon. Correctly classifying synesthetes as projectors, associators, higher, or lower synesthetes prior to each study greatly pays off in terms of gained information. The different mechanisms underlying different subtypes are all providing crucial pieces of information to obtain the full picture of synesthesia. Even when only one subtype of synesthetes is included in a study, it is still useful to discuss the findings in the known context of this subtype; if only "know" associators are included in a visual search study, it is most likely not productive to expect "pop-out" effects for this group.

Collecting objective measures of individual differences in combination with subjective reports will yield the best results. Not all recent experimental papers about synesthesia have looked into individual differences, either because the number of projectors or lower synesthetes was too small or because synesthetes were not classified (e.g. Hänggi, Wotruba, and Jäncke 2011; Nijboer and Van der Stigchel 2009). In the case of Weiss and Fink (2009), correlation of projector-associator status with differences in brain structure did not yield any significant effects; negative findings can however also be informative of the mechanisms underlying individual differences in synesthesia. Finally, there are indications of projector and associator distinctions in other variants such as taste-color synesthesia, in which the location of the experienced colors can vary between being in the mouth, or projected into external space (for a short review see Ward and Simner 2003). Whether individual differences between synesthetes will be equally important for our understanding of the neural mechanisms of other forms of synesthesia, is a question for the future.

REFERENCES

Bargary, Gary, and Kevin J. Mitchell. 2008. Synaesthesia and cortical connectivity. *Trends in Neurosciences* 31 (7):335–342.

Baron-Cohen, Simon, Maria A. Wyke, and Colin Binnie. 1987. Hearing words and seeing colors; An experimental investigation of a case of synesthesia. *Perception* 16:761–767.

Beeli, Gian, Michaela Esslen, and Lutz Jäncke. 2005. When coloured sounds taste sweet. *Nature* 434:38.

——. 2007. Frequency correlates in grapheme-color synaesthesia. *Psychological Science* 18:788–792.

——. 2008. Time course of neural activity correlated with colored-hearing synesthesia. *Cerebral Cortex* 18 (2):379–385.

Bernard, Jonathan W. 1986. Messiaen's synaesthesia: The correspondence between color and sound structure in his music. *Music Perception* 4 (1):41–68.

Brang, David, Edward M. Hubbard, Seana Coulson, Minxiong Huang, and Vilayanur S. Ramachandran. 2010. Magnetoencephalography reveals early activation of V4 in grapheme-color synesthesia. *NeuroImage* 53 (1):268–274.

Carriere, Jonathan S. A., Daniel Eaton, Michael G. Reynolds, Mike J. Dixon, and Daniel Smilek. 2009. Grapheme-color synesthesia influences overt visual attention. *Journal of Cognitive Neuroscience* 21 (2):246–258.

Cytowic, Richard E. 1993. *The Man Who Tasted Shapes*. Cambridge, MA: MIT Press.

——. 1995. Synesthesia: Phenomenology and neuropsychology. A review of current knowledge. *Psyche* 2 (10). <http://psyche.cs.monash.edu.au/v2/psyche-2-10-cytowic.html>.

Day, Sean. 2011. *Types of synesthesia*. <http://www.daysyn.com/Types-of-Syn.html>.

Dixon, Mike J., and Daniel Smilek. 2005. The importance of individual differences in grapheme-color synesthesia. *Neuron* 45:821–823.

Dixon, Mike J., Daniel Smilek, Cera Cudahy, and Philip M. Merikle. 2000. Five plus two equals yellow. *Nature* 406:365.

Dixon, Mike J., Daniel Smilek, Patricia L. Duffy, Mark P. Zanna, and Philip M. Merikle. 2006. The role of meaning in grapheme-colour synaesthesia. *Cortex* 42 (2):243–252.

Dixon, Mike J., Daniel Smilek, and Philip M. Merikle. 2004. Not all synaesthetes are created equal: Projector versus associator synaesthetes. *Cognitive, Affective, and Behavioral Neuroscience* 4:335–343.

Eagleman, David M., and Melvyn A. Goodale. 2009. Why color synesthesia involves more than color. *Trends in Cognitive Sciences* 13 (7):288–292.

Eagleman, David M., Arielle D. Kagan, Stephanie S. Nelson, Deepak Sagaram, and Anand K. Sarma. 2007. A standardized test battery for the study of synesthesia. *Journal of Neuroscience Methods* 159: 139–145.

Edquist, Jessica, Anina N. Rich, Cobie Brinkman, and Jason B. Mattingley. 2006. Do synaesthetic colours act as unique features in visual search? *Cortex* 42: 222–231.

Elias, Lorin J., Deborah M. Saucier, Colleen Hardie, and Gordon E. Sarty. 2003. Dissociating semantic and perceptual components of synaesthesia: Behavioural and functional neuroanatomical investigations. *Cognitive Brain Research* 16:232–237.

Esterman, Michael, Timothy Verstynen, Richard B. Ivry, and Lynn C. Robertson. 2006. Coming unbound: Disrupting automatic integration of synesthetic color and graphemes by transcranial magnetic stimulation of the right parietal lobe. *Journal of Cognitive Neuroscience* 18 (9):1570–1576.

Gheri, C., S. Chopping, and M. J. Morgan. 2008. Synaesthetic colours do not camouflage form in visual search. *Proceedings of the Royal Society B: Biological Sciences* 275 (1636):841–846.

Grossenbacher, Peter G., and Christopher T. Lovelace. 2001. Mechanisms of synesthesia: Cognitive and physiological constraints. *Trends in Cognitive Sciences* 5 (1):36–41.

Hänggi, Jürgen, Gian Beeli, Mathias S. Oechslin, and Lutz Jäncke. 2008. The multiple synaesthete ES: Neuroanatomical basis of interval-taste and tone-colour synaesthesia. *NeuroImage* 43 (2):192–203.

Hänggi, Jürgen, Diana Wotruba, and Lutz Jäncke. 2011. Globally altered structural brain network topology in grapheme-color synesthesia. *The Journal of Neuroscience* 31 (15):5816–5828.

Hochel, Matej, and Emilio G. Milan. 2008. Synaesthesia: The existing state of affairs. *Cognitive Neuropsychology* 25: 93–117.

Hong, Sang Wook, and Randolph Blake. 2008. Early visual mechanisms do not contribute to synesthetic color experience. *Vision Research* 48 (8):1018–1026.

Hubbard, Edward M. 2007. A real red-letter day. *Nature Neuroscience* 10 (6):671–672.

Hubbard, Edward M., A. Cyrus Arman, Vilayanur S. Ramachandran, and Geoffrey M. Boynton. 2005. Individual differences among grapheme-color synesthetes: Brain-behavior correlations. *Neuron* 45:975–985.

Hubbard, Edward M., David Brang, and Vilayanur S. Ramachandran. 2011. The cross-activation theory at 10. *Journal of Neuropsychology* 5 (2):152–177.

Hubbard, Edward M., Sanjay Manohar, and Vilayanur S. Ramachandran. 2006. Contrast affects the strength of synesthetic colors. *Cortex* 42:184–194.

Hubbard, Edward M., and Vilayanur S. Ramachandran. 2005. Neurocognitive mechanisms of synesthesia. *Neuron* 48:509–520.

Jäncke, Lutz, Gian Beeli, Cornelia Eulig, and Jürgen Hanggi. 2009. The neuroanatomy of graph-eme-color synesthesia. *European Journal of Neuroscience* 29 (6):1287–1293.

Jansari, Ashok S., Mary Jane Spiller, and Steven Redfern. 2006. Number synaesthesia: When hearing 'four plus five' looks like gold. *Cortex* 42:253–258.

Kim, Chai-Youn, and Randolph Blake. 2005. Watercolor illusion induced by synesthetic colors. *Perception* 34 (12):1501–1507.

———. 2013. Revisiting the perceptual reality of synesthetic color. In *The Oxford Handbook of Synesthesia*, ed. Julia Simner and Edward M. Hubbard, 283–316. Oxford: Oxford University Press.

Kim, Chai-Youn, Randolph Blake, and Thomas J. Palmeri. 2006. Perceptual interaction between real and synesthetic colors. *Cortex* 42 (2):195–203.

Laeng, Bruno. 2009. Searching through synaesthetic colors. *Attention Perception & Psychophysics* 71 (7):1461–1467.

Laeng, Bruno, Frode Svartdal, and Hella Oelmann. 2004. Does color synesthesia pose a para-dox for early-selection theories of attention? *Psychological Science* 15 (4):277–281.

Mattingley, Jason B., Jonathan M. Payne, and Anina N. Rich. 2006. Attentional load attenuates synaesthetic priming effects in grapheme-colour synaesthesia. *Cortex* 42 (2):213–221.

Mattingley, Jason B., Anina N. Rich, Greg Yelland, and John L. Bradshaw. 2001. Unconscious priming eliminates automatic binding of colour and alphanumeric form in synaesthesia. *Nature* 410:580–582.

Mills, Carol B., Edith H. Boteler, and Glenda K. Oliver. 1999. Digit synaesthesia: A case study using a Stroop-type test. *Cognitive Neuropsychology* 16 (2):181–191.

Mohr, Christine. 2013. Synesthesia in space versus the "mind's eye": How to ask the right ques-tions. In *The Oxford Handbook of Synesthesia*, ed. Julia Simner and Edward M. Hubbard, 440–458. Oxford: Oxford University Press.

Motluk, Alison. 1996. Two synaesthetes talking colour. In *Synaesthesia: Classic and Contemporary Readings*, ed. John Harrison and Simon Baron-Cohen, 269–277. Oxford: Blackwell Publishers.

Muggleton, Neil, Elias Tsakanikos, Vincent Walsh, and Jamie Ward. 2007. Disruption of synaes-thesia following TMS of the right posterior parietal cortex. *Neuropsychologia* 45: 1582–1585.

Myles, Kathleen M., Mike J. Dixon, Daniel Smilek, and Philip M. Merikle. 2003. Seeing double: The role of meaning in alphanumeric colour synaesthesia. *Brain and Cognition* 53:342–345.

Neufeld, Janina, Christopher Sinke, Markus Zedler, Wolfgang Dillo, Hinderk M. Emrich, Stefan Bleich, and Gregor R. Szycik 2012. Disinhibited feedback as a cause of synesthe-sia: Evidence from a functional connectivity study on auditory-visual synesthetes. *Neuropsychologia* 50 (7):1471–1477.

Niccolai, Valentina, Tessa M. Van Leeuwen, Janina Jennes, and Petra Stoerig. 2012. Modality and variability of synesthetic experience. *American Journal of Psychology* 125 (1):81–94.

Nijboer, Tanja C. W., and Stefan van der Stigchel. 2009. Is attention essential for inducing syn-esthetic colors? Evidence from oculomotor distractors. *Journal of Vision* 9 (6):9.

Nikolić, Danko, Philipp Lichti, and Wolf Singer. 2007. Color opponency in synaesthetic experi-ences. *Psychological Science* 18 (6):481–486.

Nunn, J. A., L. J. Gregory, M. J. Brammer, S. C. R. Williams, D. M. Parslow, M. J. Morgan, R. G. Morris, E. T. Bullmore, S. Baron-Cohen, and J. A. Gray. 2002. Functional magnetic resonance imaging of synesthesia: Activation of V4/V8 by spoken words. *Nature Neuroscience* 5 (4):371–375.

Odgaard, Eric C., John H. Flowers, and H. Lynn Bradman. 1999. An investigation of the cogni-tive and perceptual dynamics of a colour-digit synaesthete. *Perception* 28:651–664.

Palmeri, Thomas J., Randolph Blake, René Marois, Marci A. Flanery, and William Jr Whetsell. 2002. The perceptual reality of synesthetic colors. *Proceedings of the National Academy of Sciences of the United States of America* 99 (6):4127–4131.

Paulesu, E., J. Harrison, S. Baron-Cohen, J. D. G. Watson, L. Goldstein, J. Heather, R. S. J. Frackowiak, and C. D. Frith. 1995. The physiology of coloured hearing A PET activation study of colour-word synaesthesia. *Brain* 118:661–676.

Ramachandran, Vilayanur S., and Edward M. Hubbard. 2001a. Synaesthesia: A window into perception, thought and language. *Journal of Consciousness Studies* 8 (12):3–34.

——. 2001b. Psychophysical investigations into the neural basis of synaesthesia. *Proceedings of the Royal Society London B: Biological Sciences* 268:979–983.

——. 2003a. The phenomenology of synaesthesia. *Journal of Consciousness Studies* 10 (8):49–57.

——. 2003b. Hearing colors, tasting shapes. *Scientific American* 16:53–59.

Rich, Anina N., and Jason B. Mattingley. 2003. The effects of stimulus competition and voluntary attention on colour-graphemic synaesthesia. *NeuroReport* 14 (14):1793–1798.

——. 2013. The role of attention in synesthesia. In *The Oxford Handbook of Synesthesia*, ed. Julia Simner and Edward M. Hubbard, 265–282. Oxford: Oxford University Press.

Rich, Anina N., Mark A. Williams, Aina Puce, Ari Syngeniotis, Matthew A. Howard, Francic McGlone, and Jason B. Mattingley. 2006. Neural correlates of imagined and synaesthetic colours. *Neuropsychologia* 44 (14):2918–2925.

Robertson, Lynn C. 2003. Binding, spatial attention and perceptual awareness. *Nature Reviews Neuroscience* 4:93–102.

Rothen, Nicolas, and Beat Meier. 2009. Do synesthetes have a general advantage in visual search and episodic memory? A case for group studies. *PLoS ONE* 4:e5037.

Rouw, Romke. 2013. Synesthesia, hyper-connectivity and diffusion tensor imaging. In *The Oxford Handbook of Synesthesia*, ed. Julia Simner and Edward M. Hubbard, 500–518. Oxford: Oxford University Press.

Rouw, Romke, and H. Steven Scholte. 2007. Increased structural connectivity in grapheme-color synesthesia. *Nature Neuroscience* 10 (6):792–797.

——. 2010. Neural basis of individual differences in synesthetic experiences. *Journal of Neuroscience* 30 (18):6205–6213.

Rouw, Romke, H. Steven Scholte, and Olympia Colizoli. 2011. Brain areas involved in synaesthesia: A review. *Journal of Neuropsychology* 5 (2):214–242.

Sagiv, Noam, Jeffrey Heer, and Lynn Robertson. 2006. Does binding of synesthetic color to the evoking grapheme require attention? *Cortex* 42 (2):232–242.

Sagiv, Noam, Julia Simner, James Collins, Brian Butterworth, and Jamie Ward. 2006. What is the relationship between synaesthesia and visuo-spatial number forms? *Cognition* 101 (1):114–128.

Simner, Julia. 2012. Defining synaesthesia. *British Journal of Psychology* 103:1–15.

Simner, Julia, and Robert H. Logie. 2007. Synaesthetic consistency spans decades in a lexical-gustatory synaesthete. *Neurocase* 13 (5–6):358–365.

Simner Julia, Catherine Mulvenna, Noam Sagiv, Elias Tsakanikos, S. Athene Witherby, Christine Fraser, Kirsten Scott, and Jamie Ward. 2006. Synaesthesia: The prevalence of atypical cross-modal experiences. *Perception* 35:1024–1033.

Simner, Julia, and Jamie Ward. 2008. Synaesthesia, color terms, and color space—Color claims came from color names in Beeli, Esslen, and Jäncke (2007). *Psychological Science* 19 (4):412–414.

Simner, Julia, Jamie Ward, Monika Lanz, Ashok Jansari, Krist Noonan, Louise Glover, and David A. Oakley. 2005. Non-random associations of graphemes to colours in synaesthetic and non-synaesthetic populations. *Cognitive Neuropsychology* 22(8):1069–1085.

Skelton, Richard, Casimir Ludwig, and Christine Mohr. 2009. A novel, illustrated questionnaire to distinguish projector and associator synaesthetes. *Cortex* 45: 721–729.

Smilek, Daniel, Jonathan S.A. Carriere, Mike J. Dixon, and Philip M. Merikle. 2007. Grapheme frequency and color luminance in grapheme-color synaesthesia. *Psychological Science* 18 (9):793–795.

Smilek, Daniel, and Mike J. Dixon. 2002. Towards a synergistic understanding of synaesthesia. Combining current experimental findings with synaesthetes' subjective descriptions. *Psyche* 8 (1). <http://www.theassc.org/files/assc/2529.pdf>.

Smilek, Daniel, Mike J. Dixon, Cera Cudahy, and Philip M. Merikle. 2001. Synaesthetic photisms influence visual perception. *Journal of Cognitive Neuroscience* 13 (7):930–936.

Smilek, Daniel, Mike J. Dixon, and Philip M. Merikle. 2003. Synaesthetic photisms guide attention. *Brain and Cognition* 53:364–367.

———. 2005. Binding of graphemes and synesthetic colors in grapheme-color synesthesia. In *Synesthesia: Perspectives from Cognitive Neuroscience*, ed. Lynn C. Robertson and Noam Sagiv, 74–89. New York: Oxford University Press.

Sperling, Julia M., David Prvulovic, David E.J. Linden, Wolf Singer, and Aglaja Stirn. 2006. Neuronal correlates of colour-graphemic synaesthesia: A fMRI study. *Cortex* 42:295–303.

Stephan, Klaas E., Will D. Penny, Jean Daunizeau, Rosalyn J. Moran, and Karl J. Friston. 2009. Bayesian model selection for group studies. *NeuroImage* 46 (4):1004–1017.

Stephan, K. E., W. D. Penny, R. J. Moran, H. E. M. den Ouden, J. Daunizeau, and K. J. Friston. 2010. Ten simple rules for dynamic causal modeling. *NeuroImage* 49 (4):3099–3109.

Stroop, John R. 1935. Studies of interference in serial verbal reactions. *Journal of Experimental Psychology* 18:643–662.

Treisman, Anne M., and Garry Gelade. 1980. Feature-integration theory of attention. *Cognitive Psychology* 12 (1):97–136.

Tyler, Christopher W. 2005. Varieties of synesthetic experience. In *Synesthesia: Perspectives from Cognitive Neuroscience*, ed. Lynn Robertson and Noam Sagiv, 34–46. New York: Oxford University Press.

van Leeuwen, Tessa M., Hanneke E. M. den Ouden, and Peter Hagoort. 2011. Effective Connectivity determines the nature of subjective experience in grapheme-color synesthesia. *Journal of Neuroscience* 31 (27):9879–9884.

van Leeuwen, Tessa M., Karl Magnus Petersson, and Peter Hagoort. 2010. Synaesthetic colour in the brain: Beyond colour areas. A functional magnetic resonance imaging study of synaesthetes and matched controls. *PLoS ONE* 5 (8):e12074.

Wagar, B. M., M. J. Dixon, D. Smilek, and C. Cudahy. 2002. Colored photisms prevent object-substitution masking in digit-color synesthesia. *Brain and Cognition* 48 (2–3):606–611.

Ward, Jamie, Clare Jonas, Zoltan Dienes, and Anil Seth. 2010. Grapheme-colour synaesthesia improves detection of embedded shapes, but without pre-attentive 'pop-out' of synaesthetic colour. *Proceedings of the Royal Society B: Biological Sciences* 277 (1684):1021–1026.

Ward, Jamie, Ryan Li, Shireen Salih, and Noam Sagiv. 2007. Varieties of grapheme-colour synaesthesia: A new theory of phenomenological and behavioural differences. *Consciousness and Cognition* 16: 913–931.

Ward, Jamie, and Noam Sagiv. 2007. Synaesthesia for finger counting and dice patterns: a case of higher synaesthesia? *Neurocase* 13 (2):86–93.

Ward, Jamie, and Julia Simner. 2003. Lexical-gustatory synaesthesia: linguistic and conceptual factors. *Cognition* 89 (3):237–261.

Weiss, Peter H., and Gereon R. Fink. 2009. Grapheme-colour synaesthetes show increased grey matter volumes of parietal and fusiform cortex. *Brain* 132 (1):65–70.

Weiss, Peter H., Karl Zilles, and Gereon R. Fink. 2005. When visual perception causes feeling: enhanced cross-modal processing in grapheme-color synesthesia. *NeuroImage* 28 (4):859–868.

Witthoft, Nathan, and Jonathan Winawer. 2006. Synesthetic colors determined by having colored refrigerator magnets in childhood. *Cortex* 42 (2):175–183.

Wollen, Keith A., and Frank T. Ruggiero. 1983. Colored-letter synesthesia. *Journal of Mental Imagery* 7 (2):83–86.

CHAPTER 14

THE ROLE OF ATTENTION IN SYNESTHESIA

ANINA N. RICH AND JASON B. MATTINGLEY

INTRODUCTION

Synesthesia is a condition in which individuals report unusual sensory, cognitive, or affective experiences associated with seen, heard, felt, smelled, tasted, or even imagined stimuli, in the absence of any disorder (Mattingley 2009). A key issue in the last decade of research on synesthesia has been the extent to which these unusual experiences, particularly those involving experiences of color, are influenced by an individual's attentional state. In particular, there is debate as to whether the inducing stimulus needs to be selectively attended or identified for synesthesia to arise. Here, we review the empirical studies that address this question.

Attention is argued to be fundamental for conscious perception (Posner 1994). It allows us to select what is relevant and ignore irrelevancies. Attention is driven by a dynamic interplay between events in the environment that might be important (e.g. a sudden flash or sound) and what our internal goals require (e.g. reading rather than gazing out the window). It plays a critical role in determining what reaches awareness: what we "see," "hear," and "feel" depends on how we attend to the stimuli around us. Anecdotal reports from synesthetes suggest that attention might play an analogous role in the way synesthetic experiences get bound to the stimuli or events that trigger them. For example, many grapheme-color synesthetes, for whom letters, numbers, and words elicit experiences of color, report that the color of a word is often determined by the color induced by its initial letter (e.g. if the letter C is experienced as yellow, then so is CAT, CAR, CRATE, and so on). If the person is asked to attend to individual letters within the word, however, each letter tends to trigger its own individual color. In addition, ambiguous symbols, such as "I" elicit different colors depending on their context, for example, as a letter (klmno) or as a number (12345; e.g. Myles et al. 2003). Similarly, when synesthetes view compound letters (large forms composed of smaller elements), as exemplified by Navon-type stimuli (Figure 14.1), the reported synesthetic

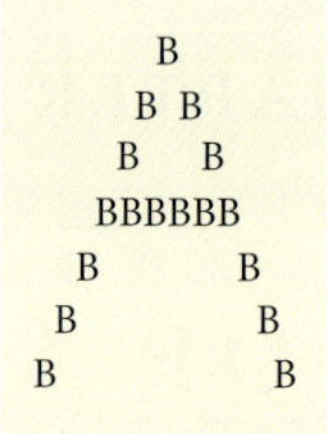

```
        B
       B B
      B    B
      BBBBBB
    B        B
   B          B
  B            B
```

FIGURE 14.1 An example of "local-global" stimuli: synesthetes typically report seeing the color of the letter to which they are currently attending.

color changes depending on whether attention is focused on the "local" or the "global" form (e.g. Palmeri et al. 2002). From these subjective reports, it appears that attention plays an important part in synesthetic experiences. In fact, many synesthetes report that when they are reading for meaning, they are barely aware of their colors at all. One of our synesthetes described it like this: "It's kind of like looking at your own nose—if you try, you can see it clearly, but you don't walk around the whole time 'seeing' your nose. But it's always there and you can see it, just that you don't unless you're attending to it" (Rich, Bradshaw, and Mattingley 2005, 68). Importantly, despite the apparent influence of attention on synesthetic experiences, synesthetes indicate that their experiences occur involuntarily and without effort.

On the basis of these subjective reports, it seems that the synesthetic experience is determined by the inducer that is currently being attended, but once the inducer *is* attended, the experience is triggered involuntarily. This leads to a number of testable predictions. First, synesthetes' experiences should only arise when they are able to attend to the inducing stimulus. Under conditions in which the stimulus is not the focus of attention, the synesthetic percept should be attenuated or eliminated. Second, synesthetes should be unable to prevent their synesthesia from occurring, even if it interferes with a current task. There are other subjective reports, however, that give rise to an alternative hypothesis. Ramachandran and Hubbard's (2001a) synesthete reported that a shape composed of repeated instances of a single digit "popped out" from within a cluttered display of another digit, because of the unique synesthetic color of the target elements. For example, a triangle shape composed of repeated instances of 2s popped out from within a cluttered display of number 5s (see Figure 48.2 in Ramachandran and Brang, Chapter 48, this volume). Similarly, a synesthete studied by Palmeri et al. (2002) felt he could find a target digit rapidly because the synesthetic color caused it to "pop out" from the surrounding distractors. This is the type of description we would expect when people are asked to search multielement displays that contain target items defined by their unique chromaticity (hereafter termed "actual" or "display" colors, to distinguish them from synesthetic colors). When we view cluttered displays with actual color, and one color is different from the others, the focus of attention can be guided very efficiently—in fact, in some circumstances, we can detect the presence or absence of a uniquely colored target without needing to search at all. Do synesthetic colors guide attention in the same way as display colors? If so, then they must be elicited prior to attentive processing of the inducing stimulus.

As we will see later, the synesthesia literature contains some apparently conflicting results regarding the need for attention and awareness of inducer identity. One explanation for this conflict has been that grapheme-color synesthetes are not all the same. The differences in the way synesthetes describe their experiences have been interpreted as reflecting different underlying brain processes. Dixon and colleagues (Dixon, Smilek, and Merikle 2004; Dixon et al. 2004; Smilek and Dixon 2002; Smilek et al. 2001) have divided grapheme-color synesthetes into "projectors" and "associators" depending on where they perceive their synesthetic colors ("out in space" versus "in the mind's eye," respectively). Ward et al. (2007) proposed a further division between projector synesthetes who experience their colors projected onto the inducer and those for whom the colors appear elsewhere in space, suggesting that it might be the spatial frame of reference that underlies the variability in subjective experience and task performance.

A second major distinction has been proposed by Ramachandran and Hubbard (2001b), who suggest that "lower" synesthetes have synesthetic colors elicited by the perceptual input, whereas "higher" synesthetes have their colors elicited by the concept. For example, number-color synesthesia might be elicited by, say, either the curvatures of the number 2, or by its numerical magnitude or quantity. These authors have also proposed distinct neural mechanisms for these two subtypes: whereas higher synesthetes are assumed to have anomalous parietal lobe function, lower synesthetes are thought to possess extra functional or anatomical connectivity between the visual word form area and the human color area (V4).

For both distinctions, there seems to be general agreement that associators and higher synesthetes may require attentive processing of the inducer because of the involvement of more conceptual-level mechanisms. The debate is whether projectors and/or lower synesthetes (these distinctions may not directly map onto each other; Ward et al. 2007), who seem to be less common, can experience synesthesia without attentive processing of the inducing stimulus. If so, this would provide key evidence that they form a separate group of synesthetes, with fundamentally different cognitive and perhaps neural mechanisms underlying their experiences. Here, we will consider the evidence for whether synesthetes' performance on objective tests truly indicates pre-attentive synesthesia, as we review the empirical literature on the role of attention and awareness in synesthesia.

MEASURING SYNESTHESIA: HOW MUCH PROCESSING OF AN INDUCER IS NECESSARY FOR SYNESTHETIC CONGRUENCY EFFECTS TO ARISE?

Taking synesthetes' own subjective reports as a starting point, we and other investigators have developed behavioral tasks to measure the influence of attention on synesthetic experiences. Most of this work has concentrated on grapheme-color synesthesia, since this form of the condition is among the most common (Rich, Bradshaw, and Mattingley

2005; Simner et al. 2006), and in many respects is the most amenable to experimental manipulation. The color experiences are typically highly consistent and can be matched fairly well using computer-generated color palettes. It is therefore relatively easy to construct stimuli that resemble an individual's own synesthetic experience, and these stimuli can then be manipulated to obtain objective measures of the phenomenon.

One widely used objective measure of synesthesia is the synesthetic congruency task. Participants are asked to name the display color of items that induce synesthesia (letters; e.g. Wollen and Ruggiero 1983), or are accompanied by a stimulus that induces synesthesia (sounds; e.g. Chiou, Stelter, and Rich 2012; Ward, Huckstep, and Tsakanikos 2006). On "congruent" trials, the synesthetic color elicited by the stimulus matches the display color to be named. On "incongruent" trials, the synesthetic color elicited by the stimulus is different from the display color (Figure). If synesthetic colors arise involuntarily, incongruent trials should cause conflict between the display color to be identified and the synesthetic color triggered by the letter or sound, relative to congruent trials where the colors match. This should give rise to slower and more error-prone color-naming responses on incongruent than congruent trials. The synesthetic congruency effect then is the size of the difference in reaction time to name the colors on congruent and incongruent trials. Synesthetes are typically slower to name the display color on incongruent than congruent trials, whereas non-synesthetic controls show no differences between the conditions.

There are substantial individual differences in the magnitude of the synesthetic congruency effect (as there are with all reaction time tasks), but at a group level the difference between incongruent and congruent trials is robust, and has been replicated under many different conditions (e.g. Mattingley, Payne, and Rich 2006; Mattingley et al. 2001; Rich and Mattingley 2003, 2010; Dixon et al. 2000; Chiou, Stelter, and Rich 2012; Ward, Huckstep, and Tsakanikos 2006). It is not clear whether the effect is caused by interference from incongruent synesthetic colors (the common interpretation), facilitation by congruent synesthetic colors, or a combination of both, as it has proven difficult to find

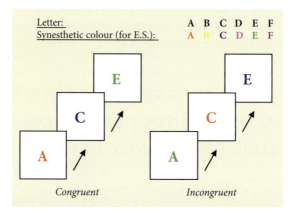

FIGURE 14.2 The synesthetic congruency task for grapheme-color synesthetes. Example stimuli for synesthete ES. Reproduced from Rich, A. N. and Mattingley, J. B., Anomalous perception in synaesthesia: a cognitive neuroscience perspective. *Nature Reviews Neuroscience*, 3 (1), pp. 43–52 © 2002, The Authors, with permission.

an appropriate baseline or neutral condition. It is also important to note that the synesthetic congruency effect itself does not tell us about the mechanisms underpinning synesthesia. Similar effects can occur from training non-synesthetes on arbitrary pairings between shapes and colors (MacLeod 1991) or in non-synesthetes with deliberately learned associations (Elias et al. 2003). The effect could also operate at different levels of processing (e.g. from perception through to response selection). What the synesthetic congruency effect gives us, however, is a useful index by which to measure the effect of synesthetic colors on behavior without asking participants directly.

We used a version of the synesthetic congruency task in which the letter and the target color were separated (a priming paradigm; Figure 14.3) to address the question of whether synesthetes need to have explicit awareness of an inducing stimulus for their synesthetic colors to arise (Mattingley et al. 2001). We presented brief, irrelevant letter primes prior to a color patch to be named (Figure 14.3). The synesthetic color elicited by the prime could be congruent or incongruent with the color of the subsequent target patch. We varied awareness by using primes of different durations sandwiched between a forward and backward mask. At the long duration (500 ms), the prime was clearly visible, and synesthetes were slower to name the color of the target on incongruent than congruent trials, demonstrating a reliable synesthetic congruency effect. When the prime was masked from awareness with shorter presentation durations (28 and 56 ms), however, the effect disappeared. These findings imply that explicit awareness of the identity of an inducing stimulus is necessary for synesthetic colors to be elicited.

In our masked priming experiment (Mattingley et al. 2001), we physically changed the stimuli (by reducing duration) to manipulate the extent to which the inducing primes were processed. We have also modified this priming paradigm to enable us to examine

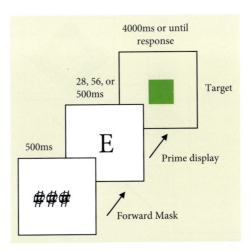

FIGURE 14.3 The synesthetic priming task. Example of a congruent trial sequence using stimuli from synesthete ES. Note the color patch actually formed a pattern mask but is represented as a solid square for illustrative purposes. From Mattingley, J.B. & Rich, A.N. (2004). *Behavioural and brain correlates of multisensory experience in synaesthesia*. In Handbook of Multisensory Integration, G.Calvert, C.Spence, B.Stein (Eds.), Cambridge, MA: MIT Press.

processing limitations caused by attention without changing the physical stimuli. We presented the same synesthetic priming task, where participants were asked to name the color patch as quickly as possible, but this time we introduced a task during the prime display to divert attention from the inducer (Mattingley, Payne, and Rich 2006). As before, the synesthetic color elicited by the prime could be congruent or incongruent with the subsequent color patch. During the 400 ms prime display, we had participants perform an easy (low-load) or difficult (high-load) gap discrimination task on a diamond-shaped frame that surrounded the letter prime (Figure 14.4). The rationale here was that the high load would divert more attentional resources from the letter prime then the low load, changing the processing of the letter without changing the physical duration. Under high load, synesthetes showed a smaller congruency effect than under low load, suggesting that any synesthetic colors induced by the prime were attenuated when attentional resources were diverted from the inducing letter. Even under high load, however, there was still an effect of congruency. This may be because in the high-load condition sufficient residual attentional resources were available to process the prime. Alternatively, perhaps attention modulates synesthetic experiences but is not critical for them to occur. We return to these competing hypotheses later.

A similar modulation of synesthetic experience by attention was reported by Sagiv, Heer, and Robertson (2006). They asked two (projector) synesthetes to name the colors of dots presented either centrally or peripherally on the left and right sides of a display, while ignoring digits presented in the peripheral locations. The synesthetic color elicited by the digits could either be congruent or incongruent with the color of the dots.

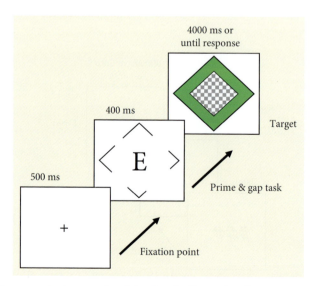

FIGURE 14.4 The synesthetic attentional load task. Example of a congruent trial sequence using stimuli from synesthete ES. Reprinted from *Cortex*, 42 (2), Jason B. Mattingley, Jonathan M. Payne, and Anina N. Rich, Attentional Load Attenuates Synaesthetic Priming Effects in Grapheme-Colour Synaesthesia, pp. 213–221, Copyright (2006), with permission from Elsevier.

When the dots were peripheral, the attentional window had to be wide to perform the task, and so included the digits. In contrast, when the dots were central, the synesthetes could maintain a narrow attentional window, effectively excluding the digits. There was a smaller congruency effect when participants maintained a narrow attentional window, again suggesting attention to the inducer is important.

We have also found that attention reduces the congruency effect when there is both congruent and incongruent information within a single stimulus. We presented synesthetes with local–global stimuli like that shown in Figure 14.1, and colored the letters congruently at one level and incongruently at the other (e.g. a global "A" made up of local "B"s, presented in the color elicited synesthetically by "A"). Synesthetes showed smaller congruency effects if they could attend to the congruently colored level throughout a block relative to blocks in which the congruent level varied. These findings are consistent with subjective reports that synesthetic colors change when the focus of attention is switched between different letters (local versus global) within a single display (e.g. Palmeri et al. 2002).

In all three studies reviewed there were residual congruency effects even when attention was diverted. This might indicate synesthesia can arise without attention. However, it might also reflect that the task did not consume all the available attentional resources. This is a difficult issue to address because it is hard to demonstrate that a stimulus is completely unattended. One task that does provide a measure of the extent to which attentional resources are available to process a particular stimulus is the "attentional blink" task (Raymond, Shapiro, and Arnell 1992).

In a classic attentional blink experiment, there are two targets (T1 and T2) embedded in a central stream of brief stimuli. Participants can readily detect or identify either of these targets alone, but when required to identify both there is a marked decrement in performance on T2 if it follows T1 within about 500 ms. This impairment is thought to arise because the attentional resources required to identify T2 are still tied up processing T1 (Chun and Potter 1995; Raymond, Shapiro, and Arnell 1992). The advantage of the attentional blink task for testing the role of attention in synesthesia is that we can measure the extent to which synesthetes are aware of, or able to attend to, an inducing letter, by presenting it as T2.

We modified the classic attentional blink task to examine whether an inducing letter could elicit a synesthetic color in the absence of attention. In contrast with a study which looked at synesthetes' subjective reports in a task that aimed but failed to elicit an attentional blink (Johnson, Jepma, and De Jong 2007), we induced an attentional blink and then examined the effect of a T2 letter on subsequent color naming times (Rich and Mattingley 2005, 2010). Our task was composed of three separate blocks with identical stimuli (Figure 14.5a). The purpose was to: (1) map the attentional blink (*T1/T2*); (2) verify the synesthetic congruency effect when the letter was attended (*T2/color-naming*); and (3) test for the synesthetic congruency effect when the letter was not attended (*T1/color-naming*). In the *T1/T2* task, we asked participants to identify a white grating (T1) and detect the presence of a black letter (T2) embedded in a stream of black nonsense characters. The T2 letter was present on 50% of trials. We varied the number of nonsense distractors that separated T1 and T2, and the congruency between the synesthetic color elicited by T2 and a color patch that appeared at the end of the stream (Figure 14.5a). When participants tried to identify both T1 and T2, both synesthetes and non-synesthetic controls showed a decrement in performance on T2 when it followed T1 by 230 or 350 ms, a classic attentional blink (Figure 14.5b). In the *T2/color-naming* task, we wanted to verify that we would still get synesthetic congruency effects from an identified letter, despite the intervening distractors. We asked participants to detect the T2 letter as well as naming the color patch as rapidly as possible. When synesthetes attended to the letter, we found a robust synesthetic congruency effect, regardless of where the letter appeared in the stream (Figure 14.5c, black bars). The critical block was the *T1/color-naming* task, where participants identified T1 (ignoring the T2 letter) and named the color as quickly as possible. In this block, we tested whether a letter presented during the period of the attentional blink would still induce a synesthetic congruency effect. The results showed that a letter presented 350 ms after T1 failed to induce a synesthetic

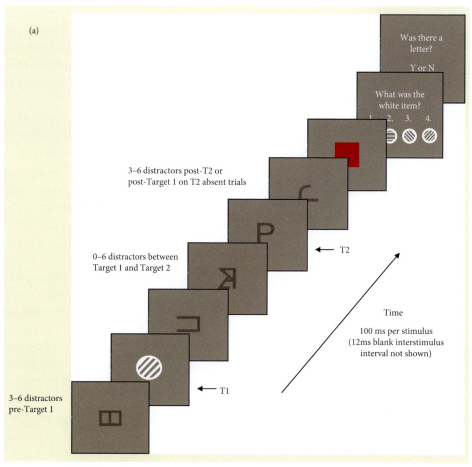

FIGURE 14.5 (*Continued*)

congruency effect (Figure 14.5c, white bars); in other words, the congruency effect disappeared in the middle of the blink.

The lack of a congruency effect in the middle of the attentional blink (350 ms post-T1) was the first demonstration that synesthetic colors can be completely suppressed by a manipulation of attention. This is consistent with the notion that synesthesia arises only in the presence of focused attention to the inducer.

The experiments reviewed thus far show that attention can be a powerful modulator of the synesthetic congruency effect, and indeed can be the critical determinant of whether such an effect occurs. Some authors argue, however, that the results of group

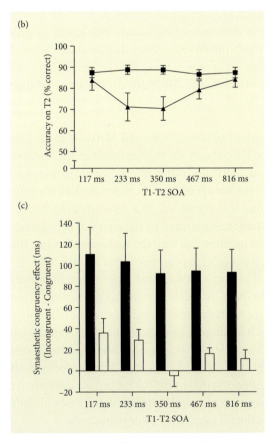

FIGURE 14.5 The synesthetic attentional blink task. (a) Schematic of trial in which T1 is a white grating and T2 is a letter ("P" in this example). Note the T2 letter could elicit a synesthetic color congruent or incongruent with the color patch at the end of the stream. (b) The attentional blink (*T1/T2* task) for 12 synesthetes. (c) Color naming-time data from the same synesthetes showing the magnitude of the synesthetic congruency effect (incongruent–congruent) when the letter was attended (black bars; *T2/color naming* task) versus ignored (white bars; *T1/color naming* task). Adapted from *Cognition*, 114 (3), Anina N. Rich and Jason B. Mattingley, Out of sight, out of mind: The attentional blink can eliminate synaesthetic colours, pp. 320–328, Copyright (2010), with permission from Elsevier.

studies mask different behavioral effects from distinct subgroups of grapheme-color synesthetes (Dixon, Smilek, and Merikle 2004; Hubbard et al. 2005). To date, most studies that have attempted to distinguish between subtypes of synesthesia have used subjective report to categorize individuals. This is not ideal because subjective report can be unreliable. For example, we found that some synesthetes gave different responses on different occasions, when asked whether their synesthetic colors appear "out there in space" versus "in the mind's eye," which would lead to changes in categorization of those individuals (Edquist et al. 2006). Dixon, Smilek, and Merikle (2004) have proposed a way to distinguish objectively between "projector" and "associator" synesthetes using two versions of the synesthetic congruency task. They found that projectors showed greater effects of synesthetic colors on display color-naming times (the synesthetic congruency effect described earlier) compared with a task in which synesthetes were instead asked to name their synesthetic colors and ignore display colors. In contrast, associators showed more interference from display colors when trying to name their synesthetic colors. This difference may reflect a categorical distinction that is based on different underlying mechanisms. Alternatively, the apparent dichotomy could reflect variation on a more continuous dimension such as the intensity or automaticity of the synesthetic experience.

Smilek and colleagues (Smilek, Dixon, and Merickle 2003; Smilek et al. 2001) have argued that projector synesthetes show synesthesia in the absence of awareness of the inducer, implying a (categorically) different mechanism to that of associator synesthetes. In their studies, a projector synesthete, C, was asked to identify a briefly presented, masked black digit that was presented on a colored background. C was poorer at the task when the synesthetic color elicited by the digit was congruent with the background color than when it was incongruent with the background color. The authors argued that C's synesthetic color must emerge prior to explicit identification of the digit in order for this camouflage effect to occur. In a second experiment, they presented multiple digits in a search array and asked C to locate the target digit. Again, C's search was less efficient on congruent than incongruent trials (Smilek et al. 2001). This pattern was stronger in a second study with a different projector synesthete. On the basis of these findings, Smilek, Dixon, and Merickle (2003) suggested that synesthetic colors can arise prior to awareness of the identity of the inducer, at least in projector synesthetes (Dixon, Smilek, and Merikle 2004). Although these results have proven difficult to replicate (Blake et al. 2005), they provide some evidence that different processes might underpin the projector–associator distinction in grapheme-color synesthesia.

To summarize, there is clear evidence that synesthesia, as measured by the synesthetic congruency effect, is strongly modulated by selective attention. In all the studies reviewed here, limiting attention to an inducing stimulus reduced the congruency effect and, in the case of the attentional blink, eliminated the effect entirely. We have also provided evidence that masked inducers do not elicit synesthesia, at least for most synesthetes. These data are consistent with the notion that synesthetic colors arise only when sufficient attentional resources are available to bring the inducing stimulus into awareness.

DO SYNESTHETIC COLORS GUIDE BEHAVIOR LIKE DISPLAY COLORS?

Recall the case of the synesthete for whom embedded shapes "popped out" of a cluttered display of achromatic inducers (Ramachandran and Hubbard 2001a). The implication is that the synesthetic color for the target items (e.g. a triangle of 2s with a random array of 5s) acted like a unique display color, drawing attention to the location of the target shape. If synesthetic colors can influence the deployment of attention in this manner, it suggests that they arise very early in processing of the inducer, without relying on attentive processes.

In the classic visual search literature, "pre-attentive" or "pop-out" effects of color are well documented. If an item is uniquely colored relative to other items in a display, it pops out, such that participants can detect its presence rapidly and without an effortful search (Treisman and Gelade 1980). As a result, reaction times (RTs) in both target-present and target-absent trials are practically unaffected by the number of distractors in the display, yielding relatively flat search slopes in plots of RT over set size (Friedman-Hill and Wolfe 1995; Treisman and Gelade 1980). Color information can also be used to guide attention effectively, making an inefficient search—such as looking for a conjunction of features—more efficient. For example, participants can restrict their attention to just red items when looking for a conjunction target of a "red horizontal line" among green horizontal and red vertical lines (Wolfe and Horowitz 2004). This makes the search more efficient than one would predict based on a serial search in which participants attend to each item in turn. If synesthetic colors can guide attention like display colors, this could provide evidence that they are elicited prior to attentive processing and identification of the inducer.

In the now well-known "embedded figures" task first presented by Ramachandran and Hubbard (2001a), two synesthetes were asked to identify a shape made up of a single letter repeated in a cluttered display containing two different distractor letters (a triangle of 2s in an array of 5s; see Figure 48.2 in Ramachandran and Brang, Chapter 48, this volume). The synesthetes were more accurate than controls in this task. In related papers, the authors refer to this as "pop-out" (Ramachandran and Hubbard 2001b), which has led to the interpretation that the effect arises pre-attentively. Subsequently, these authors replicated an advantage for five out of six synesthetes over controls, but showed that in no case was performance as good as if the displays were actually colored (Hubbard et al. 2005).

The embedded figures effect has recently been replicated in a large group of 36 synesthetes. Ward et al. (2010) confirmed the original result, with synesthetes more accurate than controls overall, but the proportion of correct trials was much lower than would be predicted if display colors had defined the shape (41.4% for synesthetes compared with 31.5% for controls). In addition, there was no clear link between reports of seeing the graphemes as colored during the task and synesthetes' objective performance. Rather, the participants' descriptions suggested that the synesthetic color appeared as they moved their attention around the display. Rothen and Meier (2009) also tried to replicate the embedded figures effect. In contrast to Ward et al. (2010), they did not find any significant advantage in accuracy for 13 synesthetes relative to controls.

The claim of "pop-out" suggests that synesthetes' response times in the embedded figures task should be relatively unaffected by increases in the number of distractors. Recently we examined the search efficiency of synesthetes in a modified embedded figures task in which we varied the number of distracting elements (set-size) and used a two-alternative forced choice decision between two embedded figures that were identical except for their orientation (a triangle pointing to the left versus right; Figure 14.6) (Rich and Karstoft, in press). Synesthetes were more accurate than controls in identifying which target shape appeared in the display, replicating the original effect, but there was no difference between the groups in reaction times, which increased significantly as the number of distractor elements increased (mean slopes ~13.5 ms/item for both synesthetes and controls). Thus, we have no evidence that the shapes "popped-out" or were identified without attentive processing of items in the display.

All things considered, although the evidence implies a slight advantage for synesthetes in identifying embedded shapes defined by their synesthetic color, it does not resemble the pop-out effect associated with real color targets. We therefore need to look for alternative explanations for the effect, rather than interpreting these results as evidence for pre-attentive synesthesia. One possibility is that synesthetes are able to use their colors to aid in decision-making ("target" versus "distractor") or in grouping similar items together. In particular, it may be that synesthesia helps in rejecting distractors more rapidly. Palmeri et al. (2002) showed results consistent with this notion from a synesthete, WO. They presented WO with an achromatic search display of a single target 2 among multiple distractor 5s, or a target 8 among distractor 6s (Figure 14.7). For WO, 2 elicited orange, different from the less vivid green of the 5s, whereas both 8 and 6 elicited a bluish color. In each case, participants were asked to indicate the presence or absence of the target digit. Although WO showed an advantage over non-synesthetes when the synesthetic color of the target was unique (2 among 5s), his search slope was

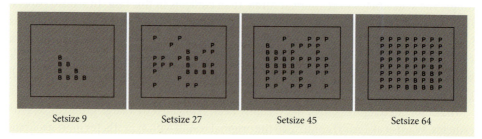

| Setsize 9 | Setsize 27 | Setsize 45 | Setsize 64 |

FIGURE 14.6 Example displays for the four setsizes of the modified embedded figures task for a synesthete who experiences B as orange and P as white. The task was to determine whether the triangle formed by the target letters pointed to the left or the right. From Rich, A.N. and Karstoft, K.-I. (in press). Exploring the benefit of synaesthetic colours: testing for "pop-out" in individuals with grapheme-colour synaesthesia. *Cognitive Neuropsychology.*

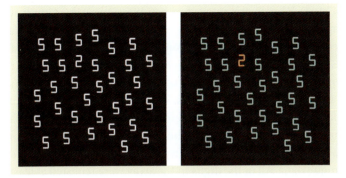

FIGURE 14.7 Example visual search displays from Palmeri et al. (2002). Achromatic display (left) and a colored display using WO's synesthetic colors (right). Reproduced with permission from *Proceedings of the National Academy of Sciences USA*, 99 (6) The perceptual reality of synesthetic colors, Thomas J. Palmeri, Randolph Blake, Rene Marois, Marci A. Flanery, and William Whetsell Jr., figure 3a pp. 4127–4131 © 2002, National Academy of Sciences, U.S.A.

not flat, unlike classic "pop-out." This advantage depended on the synesthetic colors of the distractors—when Palmeri et al. (2002) replaced the distractors with characters that did not elicit colors or with targets and distractors of similar synesthetic colors (i.e. 6 and 8), WO's advantage disappeared. This suggests that it is not synesthesia from the (unattended) target that draws WO's attention to the target location. Rather something about the synesthesia induced by the distractors seems important. Perhaps as the synesthete moves attention around the display, attended distractors are able to be rejected more rapidly because they elicit a synesthetic color different from that of the target. Sagiv, Heer, and Robertson (2006) also used a visual search task in which only the target induced synesthesia (an L among rotated Ts), and found no advantage compared with a condition in which neither the target nor the distractors induced synesthesia (an inverted L among rotated Ts). These results are consistent with the interpretation that synesthetic colors induced by attended distractor elements can occasionally allow for more efficient target search.

Other explanations for synesthetic advantages in search relate to the chance appearance of a target close to fixation. Laeng, Svartdal, and Oelmann (2004) observed nearly flat search slopes for trials in which the target was present, even though the synesthete they tested had the same positive search slope as controls on target-absent trials. On further investigation, Laeng and colleagues found that the target-present advantage occurred only when the target fell within the central region of the display, which was the region within which her attention was focused at the beginning of the trial.

Despite a few case studies showing an advantage for synesthetes in traditional visual search tasks (Laeng 2009; Laeng, Svartdal, and Oelmann 2004; Palmeri et al. 2002), this does not seem to occur for most synesthetes. In fact, the majority of studies that have employed visual search tasks have failed to show any differences between synesthetes and non-synesthetes. For example, in one of our studies, we tested 14 synesthetes and matched controls (Edquist et al. 2006) with displays much like those of

Palmeri et al. (2002). We also presented chromatic versions of the stimuli, with each digit colored appropriately for the individual synesthetes. For the colored displays, both synesthetes and controls showed flat search slopes, as expected. In contrast, for the achromatic displays, we found no evidence that synesthetes were more efficient than controls.

Gheri, Chopping, and Morgan (2008) used a slightly different approach, but also failed to find any advantage for synesthetes. They based their manipulation on an effect known as "color camouflage," in which heterogeneously colored elements interfere with search for a unique shape target. Gheri, Chopping, and Morgan (2008) presented achromatic digits in a 4×4 array of 16 items to a group of synesthetes, and had them search for a single unique digit. All of the digits in the array were repeated at least once, except for the target digit. Thus, for example, in the set 3, 6, 6, 7, 6, 7, 5, 6, 3, 7, 5, 6, 3, 5, 7, 8, the digit 8 would be the target. In the "unique" condition, the synesthetic experience elicited by all the non-target digits was a single, common color (e.g. red), while the synesthetic experience for the target digit was a different color (e.g. green). In the "non-unique" condition, most of the non-target items elicited different synesthetic color experiences from each other, creating synesthetic heterogeneity. For this condition, at least one of the non-target items elicited the same color as the target. The authors reasoned that having more than one item in the array that elicits the target color should slow search for the target itself, analogous to the color camouflage effect with actually colored displays. Consistent with the results of our previous study (Edquist et al., 2006), Gheri, Chopping, and Morgan (2008) found that synesthetic colors did not behave like display colors; their synesthetes were no faster than non-synesthetes when the target was uniquely colored, and no slower than non-synesthetes when one or more distractor items shared the target color.

Overall, then, the results from visual search tasks suggest that some synesthetes can use their colors to improve search efficiency, but this seems to be related to rejecting distractors or grouping items, rather than attracting attention towards the target. In vision, having attention captured by a peripheral event often leads to an eye movement to the stimulus (Van der Stigchel and Theeuwes 2007). One recent study has investigated whether this type of oculomotor capture effect can arise for peripheral stimuli that elicit synesthetic colors. Nijboer and Van der Stigchel (2009) had eight synesthetes perform a task that required them to make single saccades to peripheral colored dots. On some trials, there was also a digit or non-digit distractor at another location in the periphery. These distractor stimuli were either colored the same as the target, or were achromatic but evoked the same synesthetic color as the target dot. The authors found occasional saccadic capture by colored distractors, as expected, but the achromatic distractors chosen to elicit synesthetic colors had no such effect. Again, this illustrates the difference between display colors, which are perceived without the need for selective attention, and synesthetic colors, which only arise with substantial processing of the inducer.

To summarize, some synesthetes appear to benefit from their color experiences when trying to detect target items in achromatic displays. The inconsistency of these effects and the fact that they clearly do not reflect pre-attentive pop-out, however, suggests that synesthesia might facilitate "grouping" of like items or more efficient rejection of distractors (Palmeri et al. 2002; Sagiv, Heer, and Robertson 2006; Ward et al. 2010). In embedded figures tasks (Figure 14.6; and Figure 48.2 in Ramachandran and Brang, Chapter 48, this volume), the color of the target letters might enhance perceptual grouping once attended, thus enabling more accurate recognition of the global shape. Similarly, in traditional visual search tasks, some synesthetes might use their colors strategically to group like-colored distractors and thus reject them more efficiently.

There has been much debate over whether discrepant findings on the role of attention and awareness in grapheme-color synesthesia might be due to the existence of distinct subtypes of synesthesia. Although this is possible, the balance of evidence suggests that attention is a powerful modulator for all synesthetes, and that directing attention to an inducer is critical for synesthesia to arise. Synesthetes who are able to use their colors to improve performance seem to do so via post-attentive strategies such as rejecting distractors, or grouping similar items, more efficiently.

CONCLUSION

Identifying the role of attention in synesthesia is crucial for developing models of the phenomenon and how it relates to general aspects of cognition. Here, we have reviewed the data that contribute to the debate about synesthesia and attention. To summarize, studies using synesthetic congruency as a measure have demonstrated a powerful modulatory role for attention in synesthesia. In particular, when attentional resources are not available, there are minimal or no synesthetic congruency effects. Although there is some inconsistency in the visual search findings, results that have shown an advantage for synesthetes suggest the benefit is from post-attentive processes, such as grouping of similar items. Although pre-attentive synesthesia is an intriguing possibility, we do not believe there is compelling evidence for its existence. Instead, current evidence suggests that synesthetic color experiences arise relatively late in visual processing. For instance, in recent studies we have shown that synesthetic color signals are not influenced by low-level processes responsible for color constancy (Erskine, Mattingley, and Arnold 2012) and that the variance associated with repeated matching of synesthetic colors is similar to that for matching colors recalled from memory (Arnold et al. 2012). Synesthesia seems to operate under the same constraints as visual feature binding, with selective attention playing a critical role. This brings synesthetic binding in line with current theories on the way we put together information more generally for conscious perception: selective attention seems critically involved in binding object features and the inputs from different sensory modalities for conscious perception.

ACKNOWLEDGEMENTS

ANR was supported by an Australian Research Council (ARC) Postdoctoral Fellowship (DP0984494). JBM was supported by an ARC Australian Laureate Fellowship (FL110100103). We thank Margery Pardey for comments on the manuscript.

REFERENCES

Arnold, Derek. H., Signy V. Wegener, Francesca Brown, and Jason B. Mattingley. 2012. Precision of synesthetic color matching resembles that for recollected colors rather than physical colors. *Journal of Experimental Psychology. Human Perception and Performance* 38(5):1078–1084.

Blake, Randolph, Thomas J. Palmeri, Rene Marois, and Chai-Youn Kim. 2005. On the perceptual reality of synesthetic color. In *Synaesthesia: Perspectives from Cognitive Neuroscience*, ed. Lynn C. Robertson and Noam Sagiv, 47–73. New York: Oxford University Press.

Chiou, Rocco, Marleen Stelter, and Anina N. Rich. 2012. Beyond colour perception: Auditory-visual synaesthesia induces experiences of geometric objects in specific locations. *Cortex*. Advance online publication. doi:10.1016/j.cortex.2012.04.006.

Chun, Marvin M., and Mary C. Potter. 1995. A two-stage model for multiple target detection in rapid serial visual presentation. *Journal of Experimental Psychology: Human Perception and Performance* 21:109–127.

Dixon, Mike J., Daniel Smilek, Cera Cudahy, and Philip M. Merikle. 2000. Five plus two equals yellow. *Nature* 406:365.

Dixon, Mike J., Daniel Smilek, and Philip M. Merikle. 2004. Not all synaesthetes are created equal: Projector versus associator synaesthetes. *Cognitive, Affective, & Behavioral Neuroscience* 4:335–343.

Dixon, Mike J., Daniel Smilek, Brandon M. Wagar, and Philip M. Merikle. 2004. Grapheme-colour synaesthesia: When 7 is yellow and d is blue. In *Handbook of Multisensory Integration*, ed. Gemma A. Calvert, G., Charles Spence, and Barry E. Stein, 837–849. Cambridge, MA: MIT Press.

Edquist, Jessica, Anina N. Rich, Cobie Brinkman, and Jason B. Mattingley. 2006. Do synaesthetic colours act as unique features in visual search? *Cortex* 42:222–231.

Elias, Lorin J., Deborah M. Saucier, Colleen Hardie, and Gordon E. Sarty. 2003. Dissociating semantic and perceptual components of synaesthesia: Behavioural and functional neuroanatomical investigations. *Cognitive Brain Research* 16:232–237.

Erskine, Holly, Jason B. Mattingley, and Derek H. Arnold. 2013. Synaesthesia and colour constancy. *Cortex*. 49:1082–1088.

Friedman-Hill, Stacia, and Jeremy M. Wolfe. 1995. Second-order parallel processing: Visual search for the odd item in a subset. *Journal of Experimental Psychology: Human Perception and Performance* 21:531–551.

Gheri, C., S. Chopping, and M. J. Morgan. 2008. Synaesthetic colors do not camouflage form in visual search. *Proceedings of the Royal Society of London B: Biological Sciences* 275:841–846.

Hubbard, Edward M., A. Cyrus Arman, Vilayanur S. Ramachandran, and Geoffrey M. Boynton. 2005. Individual differences among grapheme-color synesthetes: Brain-behavior correlations. *Neuron* 45(6):975–985.

Johnson, Addie, Marieke Jepma, and Ritske De Jong. 2007. Colours sometimes count: Awareness and bidirectionality in grapheme-colour synaesthesia. *The Quarterly Journal of Experimental Psychology* 60:1406–1422.

Laeng, Bruno. 2009. Searching through synaesthetic colors. *Attention Perception & Psychophysics* 71 (7):1461–1467.

Laeng, Bruno, Frode Svartdal, and Hella Oelmann. 2004. Does color synesthesia pose a paradox for early-selection theories of attention? *Psychological Science* 15 (4):277–281.

MacLeod, Colin M. 1991. Half a century of research on the Stroop effect: An integrative review. *Psychological Bulletin* 109:163–203.

Mattingley, Jason B. (2009). Attention, automaticity and awareness in synaesthesia. Annals of the New York Academy of Sciences. 1156, 141–167.

Mattingley, Jason B., Jonathan M. Payne, and Anina N. Rich. 2006. Attentional load attenuates synaesthetic priming effects in grapheme-colour synaesthesia. *Cortex* 42 (2):213–221.

Mattingley, Jason B., Anina N. Rich, Greg Yelland, and John L. Bradshaw. 2001. Unconscious priming eliminates automatic binding of colour and alphanumeric form in synaesthesia. *Nature* 410:580–582.

Myles, Kathleen M., Mike J. Dixon, Daniel Smilek, and Philip M. Merikle. 2003. Seeing double: The role of meaning in alphanumeric-colour synaesthesia. *Brain and Cognition* 53 (2):342–345.

Nijboer, Tanja C. W., and Stefan van der Stigchel. 2009. Is attention essential for inducing synesthetic colors? Evidence from oculomotor distractors. *Journal of Vision* 9 (6):9.

Palmeri, Thomas J., Randolph Blake, René Marois, Marci A. Flanery, and William Whetsell Jr. 2002. The perceptual reality of synesthetic colors. *Proceedings of the National Academy of Sciences of the United States of America* 99 (6):4127–4131.

Posner, Michael I. 1994. Attention: The mechanisms of consciousness. *Proceedings of the National Academy of Sciences of the United States of America* 91:7398–7403.

Ramachandran, V. S., and David Brang. 2013. From molecules to metaphor: Outlooks on synesthesia research. In *The Oxford Handbook of Synesthesia*, ed. Julia Simner and Edward M. Hubbard, 999–1024. Oxford: Oxford University Press.

Ramachandran, Vilayanur S., and Edward M. Hubbard. 2001a. Psychophysical investigations into the neural basis of synaesthesia. *Proceedings of the Royal Society B: Biological Sciences* 268:979–983.

——. 2001b. Synaesthesia—A window into perception, thought and language. *Journal of Consciousness Studies* 8 (12):3–34.

Raymond, Jane E., Kimron L. Shapiro, and Karen M. Arnell. 1992. Temporary suppression of visual processing in an rsvp task: An attentional blink? *Journal of Experimental Psychology: Human Perception and Performance* 18:849–860.

Rich, Anina N., John L. Bradshaw, and Jason B. Mattingley. 2005. A systematic, large-scale study of synaesthesia: implications for the role of early experience in lexical-colour associations. *Cognition* 98 (1):53–84.

Rich, Anina N. and Karen-Inge Karstoft. In press. Exploring the benefit of synaesthetic colours: testing for "pop-out" in individuals with grapheme-colour synaesthesia. *Cognitive Neuropsychology.*

Rich, Anina N., and Jason B. Mattingley. 2003. The effects of stimulus competition and voluntary attention on colour-graphemic synaesthesia. *NeuroReport* 14 (14):1793–1798.

——. 2005. Can attention modulate color-graphemic synesthesia? In *Synesthesia: Perspectives from Cognitive Neuroscience*, ed. Lynn C. Robertson and Noam Sagiv, 108–123. Oxford: Oxford University Press.

———. 2010. Out of sight, out of mind: The attentional blink can eliminate synaesthetic colours. *Cognition* 114:320–328.

Rothen, Nicolas, and Beat Meier. 2009. Do synesthetes have a general advantage in visual search and episodic memory? A case for group studies. *PLoS ONE* 4:e5037.

Sagiv, Noam, Jeffrey Heer, and Lynn C. Robertson. 2006. Does binding of synesthetic color to the evoking grapheme require attention? *Cortex* 42 (2):232–242.

Simner, Julia, Catherine Mulvenna, Noam Sagiv, Elias Tsakanikos, S. Athene Witherby, Christine Fraser, Kirsten Scott, and Jamie Ward. 2006. Synaesthesia: The prevalence of atypical cross-modal experiences. *Perception* 35:1024–1033.

Smilek, Daniel, and Mike J. Dixon. 2002. Towards a synergistic understanding of synaesthesia. Combining current experimental findings with synaesthetes' subjective descriptions. *Psyche* 8 (1). <http://www.theassc.org/files/assc/2529.pdf>.

Smilek, Daniel, Mike J. Dixon, Cera Cudahy, and Philip M. Merikle. 2001. Synaesthetic photisms influence visual perception. *Journal of Cognitive Neuroscience* 13:930–936.

Smilek, Daniel, Mike J. Dixon, and Philip M. Merikle. 2003. Synaesthetic photisms guide attention. *Brain and Cognition* 53 (2):364–367.

Treisman, Anne M., and Garry Gelade. 1980. A feature-integration theory of attention. *Cognitive Psychology* 12 (1):97–136.

Van der Stigchel, Stefan, and Jan Theeuwes. 2007. The relationship between covert and overt attention in endogenous cuing. *Perception and Psychophysics* 69:719–713.

Ward, Jamie, Brett Huckstep, and Elias Tsakanikos. 2006. Sound-colour synaesthesia: To what extent does it use cross-modal mechanisms common to us all? *Cortex* 42 (2):264–280.

Ward, Jamie, Clare Jonas, Zoltan Dienes, and Anil Seth. 2010. Grapheme-colour synaesthesia improves detection of embedded shapes, but without pre-attentive 'pop-out' of synaesthetic colour. *Proceedings of the Royal Society B: Biological Sciences* 277 (1684):1021–1026.

Ward, Jamie, Ryan Li, Shireen Salih, and Noam Sagiv. 2007. Varieties of grapheme-colour synaesthesia: A new theory of phenomenological and behavioural differences. *Consciousness and Cognition* 16:913–931.

Wolfe, Jeremy M., and Todd S. Horowitz. 2004. What attributes guide the deployment of visual attention and how do they do it? *Nature Reviews Neuroscience* 5:1–7.

Wollen, Keith A., and Frank T. Ruggiero. 1983. Colored-letter synesthesia. *Journal of Mental Imagery* 7 (2):83–86.

CHAPTER 15

REVISITING THE PERCEPTUAL REALITY OF SYNESTHETIC COLOR

CHAI-YOUN KIM AND RANDOLPH BLAKE

INTRODUCTION

Emerging over the past decade is the view that synesthesia is not attributable to over-learned semantic associations, florid imagination, metaphorical thinking, or, for that matter, frank hallucination (see Box 15.1). Instead, some forms of synesthesia are thought to be mediated by at least some of the same neural processes engaged during ordinary perception. A growing number of papers report evidence that purportedly supports this view, and we see it endorsed in some of the most widely read publications in this field of study (e.g., Cytowic 2002; Ramachandran and Hubbard 2003). This chapter takes a critical look at the various lines of reasoning used to arrive at this conclusion concerning the perceptual nature of synesthesia.

Rather than comprehensively reviewing studies bearing on this question, this chapter focuses on: (1) distilling from this literature some of the general strategies that have been utilized to examine the perceptual reality of synesthesia, and (2) evaluating limitations to those strategies and, hence, the validity of results obtained from them. We will focus primarily, but not exclusively, on color-graphemic synesthesia because it represents a common, widely studied form of this beguiling condition and because it is the form of synesthesia we are most familiar with from our own work. Our chapter is motivated, in part, by a provocative paper questioning much of the evidence often cited in favor of the perceptual basis of color reports by people with color-graphemic synesthesia (Gheri et al. 2008). That paper challenges those of us interested in synesthesia to think carefully about the reasoning underlying the tests we use to assess whether or not color-graphemic synesthesia includes a genuine perceptual component. This chapter is our attempt to grapple with that challenge.

Box 15.1

Synesthetic experiences in the visual domain (e.g., a "colored" achromatic letter) are sometimes referred to as "photisms" (e.g., Witthoft and Winawer 2006). This is an interesting word choice, for Webster's unabridged dictionary defines photoism as "A luminous image or appearance of a hallucinatory character." Is visual synesthesia a form of hallucination? When, for example, LR (a synesthete tested by us on many tasks) describes seeing this character—A—as vivid red, is she hallucinating? In one sense of that term, she is: the visual stimulus ordinarily "appropriate" for this perceptual experience would be the character A printed in real colored ink, but that's not what LR is looking at when she reports seeing "A" as red. Yet, she insists that "A" looks as red as "A." In that sense, she seems to be hallucinating: she describes seeing something that is not really there (Collerton, Perry, and McKeith 2005). Yet in other ways, those "photisms" do not resemble hallucinations. For one thing, LR readily acknowledges that she knows that the letter "A" is really "A" and not "A." This is not always the case in other contexts where hallucinations occur. For example, some, but not all, schizophrenia patients describe hearing voices and believe that those voices are real to the extent that they act on those beliefs. In schizophrenia, these hallucinatory experiences are attributable to deficits in core speech perception (Hoffman et al. 1999). For another thing, there is a fundamental distinction between synesthesia and the hallucinatory experiences of, say, schizophrenic patients. In the former, there is an external stimulus triggering the unusual sensory experience whereas in the latter there is not. Moreover, hallucinations in schizophrenia are accompanied by decreased activity in sensory brain areas that would ordinarily respond to an external stimulus of the sort described by the patients (Aleman et al. 2001; Shergill et al. 2003), but, as summarized in our chapter, synesthetic experiences can be accompanied by increases in brain activations in at least some of the sensory areas appropriate for the experience being reported. Finally, hallucinations tend to have a narrative quality that incorporates recent events, prejudices, and even cultural symbols. Synesthesia, however, does not come with a story nor is it so attuned to the vagaries of daily events.

So, we are disinclined to characterize synesthetic experiences as hallucinations. If anything, synesthesia may have more in common with imagery, willfully generated forms of sensory experience (Tong 2003). Indeed, self-rated visual imagery tends to be stronger in people with synesthesia (Barnett and Newell 2008), and simply imagining an inducer can trigger a synesthetic experience (Dixon et al. 2000). Still, there is indirect evidence implying that synesthesia is not merely a form of extra vivid mental imagery (Rich et al. 2006; Steven and Blakemore 2004; Steven, Hansen, and Blakemore 2006; but also see Price, Chapter 37, this volume). Nonetheless, the correlation between imagery and synesthesia means investigators must be mindful of it and control for its influence in studies of synesthesia where salience, vividness, or intensity could be controlling factors (Barnett and Newell 2008).

To be clear, by "genuine perceptual component" we mean that at least some of the mechanisms mediating synesthetic experiences are the same mechanisms involved in non-synesthetically induced analogues of those experiences. In the case of color-graphemic synesthesia, for example, do the purported experiences of color influence performance on tasks known to be sensitive to the presence of color? Does synesthetic color behave like real color on tests where color appearance depends on the spatial and temporal context in which colored stimuli are presented, including contexts that produce illusions of color or after-effects of color? Is the reported experience of synesthetic color accompanied by neural activation within sensory brain areas believed to be involved in color perception?

From the outset, we wish to stress that this question of the perceptual nature of synesthesia is different from the question of whether synesthesia can be experienced when stimuli inducing synesthesia fall outside of awareness (e.g., Ramachandran and Hubbard 2001) or outside the focus of attention (e.g., Mattingley et al. 2001; Sagiv, Heer, and Robertson 2006).[1] Answers to these two questions do not tell us whether or not synesthesia is perceptual in nature.

STRATEGIES FOR EVALUATING THE PERCEPTUAL REALITY OF SYNESTHETIC EXPERIENCES

Most investigators of synesthesia are themselves not synesthetes; for us, our first peek into the world of synesthesia comes from conversations with individuals who do have the condition. The verbal descriptions of their synesthetic experiences sound both familiar and incredible: familiar because we can easily understand what is meant when the person says, for example, that the letter A appears red, and incredible because the letter provoking that description is obviously black and not red. Of course, as psychologists we have been taught not to place too much stock in people's verbal reports of their mental experiences—those reports can be misleading, not because people lie but because they—we—are very good at fabricating plausible accounts that bear little relation to the actual causes of our mental experiences and our behaviors (Nisbett and Wilson 1977). Consequently, those of us interested in this mystery of the mental representations associated with synesthesia must resort to indirect techniques. So, what kinds of indirect measures allow us to evaluate the bases for the beguiling verbal descriptions offered by synesthetes? What, in other words, can we do to convince ourselves that the letter A indeed looks like A?

Fortunately when it comes to color, we have a variety of strategies to use in pursuit of an answer to this question. We divide these strategies into two broad groups, one comprising strategies based on behavioral performance measures obtained using perceptual and/or cognitive tasks and the other comprising strategies using indirect measures based on oculomotor responses, brain imaging, or electrophysiology.

---

[1] Readers interested in those questions will want to see the chapters by Rich and Mattingley (Chapter 14) and by Alvarez and Robertson (Chapter 16), in this volume.

BEHAVIORAL MEASURES

In the following sections we consider strategies that exploit: (1) well-established tasks where real colors exert robust effects on performance, and (2) visual phenomena where contextual factors influence color appearance. The best tasks are ones where participants do not know the expected outcome on the task, to preclude response bias or, in the worst case, blatant cheating to confirm an expected outcome. Moreover, as others have opined (Gheri, Chopping, and Morgan 2008), we must also be mindful of the possibility that experimenter bias could influence the outcomes of behavioral tests of synesthesia, for testing is rarely if ever done blind. While not a foolproof antidote to experimenter bias, computer-based, forced-choice testing together with written, not verbal, instructions can go some way toward minimizing this contaminating effect. It is imperative, of course, that participants in these studies be given no clues about the expected outcome or the hypothesis under test.

Performance enhancement

It is well known that appropriately created color differences among spatially distributed objects in the visual scene can promote robust segmentation of a figure from its background. One of the most widely studied versions of this phenomenon is visual search wherein observers judge as quickly as possible whether or not a specific target is present amongst an array of distractors (e.g., Treisman and Gelade 1980). When the target conspicuously differs in color from the distractors, observers can quickly spot it and respond, a phenomenon sometimes dubbed pop-out. In principle, these kind of visual search tasks lend themselves nicely to the study of color-graphemic synesthesia using digits and/or letters as targets and distractors, for the potential conspicuity of the target owing to its synesthetic color can be systematically varied relative to the synesthetic color(s) of the distractors. For example, a visual search task might use an achromatic display of distractor 5s with a single embedded target digit 2 (see Figure 14.7, in Rich and Mattingley, Chapter 14, this volume; the right-hand side of the figure shows how the achromatic display is "seen" by synesthete WO, who experiences green on the digit 5 and orange on the digit 2; Palmeri et al. 2002). If synesthetic color promotes figure/ground segmentation, it is not unreasonable to expect that visual search will be consistently faster (with no loss in accuracy) when targets differ in perceived color from distractors. When target and distractors comprise characters with identical color associations, however, this benefit should disappear. The same pattern of results would be predicted for accuracy (percentage correct) on tasks where shapes are defined by the configuration of alphabetic characters appearing within a larger array of other characters.

Versions of these kinds of tasks involving the use of achromatic inducers have been employed in a number of studies, including single-subject case studies and group studies. Some of those studies report faster or more accurate search performance by synesthetes relative to normal controls (Hubbard et al. 2005; Kim and Blake 2005; Laeng, Svartdal, and Oelmann 2004; Palmeri et al. 2002; Ramachandran and Hubbard 2001; Smilek, Dixon, and Merikle 2003; Smilek et al. 2001), whereas other studies find that synesthetes enjoy no significant advantage over control subjects (Edquist et al. 2006; Gheri, Chopping, and Morgan 2008) and one recent study found a small performance advantage for some but not all of the 13 synesthetes tested (Rothen and Meier 2009). Two research groups have found that synesthesia does not produce speeded search when only the target, but not the distractors, has an associated color (Palmeri et al. 2002; Sagiv, Heer, and Robertson 2006). Laeng (2009) found that search efficiency can be enhanced when the synesthetic colors of a target and distractors are "nearly complementary" (p. 1461) resembling pop-out search. In reviewing this confusing literature, Rothen and Meier (2009) speculate that individual differences among synesthetes might underlie the conflicting patterns of results with, perhaps, so-called projector synesthetes (whose synesthetic colors are seen projected into space) being more likely than associators (whose colors appear in the mind's eye) to enjoy enhanced visual search owing to the vividness and external localization of their color experiences.[2] From this Rothen and Meier conclude that the diverse nature of synesthesia can be more appropriately understood from results of group studies, not single-case reports. To this we would add the recommendation that studies using visual search employ a full array of conditions that include mixtures of synesthetic and real colors in which the synesthetic colors are congruent with or incongruent with the real colors—with this array of conditions, investigators have the opportunity to look for performance improvement and performance impairment within the same set of trials. At the same time, it is also important to be mindful of the overall angular size of the array of target and distractors as well as the angular subtense of those individual items. Acuity falls off with eccentricity, and the loss of spatial resolution for alphanumeric characters located off fixation is bound to adversely affect their clarity. We cannot expect a small alphanumeric character imaged away from fixation to induce a synesthetic color if its features are unresolvable—the character may be visible but indistinguishable and, therefore, ineffective as an inducer. This constraint does not apply, of course, to real colored graphemes unless it is imaged far enough into the periphery where color vision itself is reduced. It would be informative to see results from a visual search task in which letters are rendered equally readable based on their sizes and retinal eccentricity (Anstis 1974), but this would require careful fixation and, hence, eye movement monitoring.

Another strategy for exploring whether color-graphemic synesthesia enhances performance capitalizes on visual crowding, the impairment in identification of a peripherally viewed target stimulus when that target is surrounded by flanking stimuli

---

[2] Using diffusion tensor imaging, Rouw and Scholte (2007) found stronger connectivity in projectors relative to associators within brain areas in close proximity to color areas and a region believed to be involved in visual word processing. For more on the distinction between projectors and associators, see van Leeuwen (Chapter 13, this volume).

(Bouma 1970). When flankers and target differ in color, this crowding effect is weakened, i.e., target identification performance improves (Kooi et al. 1994). Hubbard et al. (2005) created crowding displays in which target and flankers were achromatic letters specially selected such that the associated synesthetic color of the target differed from that of its surrounding flankers. Three out of six color-graphemic synesthetes were more accurate than control observers when tested using these achromatic crowding displays; coincidentally or not, these three synesthetic participants also performed significantly better than controls on the embedded figures task described in the next paragraph. Hubbard et al. (2005) did not test the synesthetes on a condition where the associated synesthetic color of the target and crowding flankers was identical, an even more revealing comparison. They did note, however, that the improvement in performance associated with synesthetic color was still significantly weaker than the improvement produced by actual color differences.

While not explicitly assessing performance enhancement, some perceptual tasks ask whether color associations enable people with synesthesia to perceptually organize a visual display differently than do individuals without synesthesia and, thereby, react to that display in a qualitatively different way. To give an example, Ramachandran and Azoulai (2006) created an apparent motion (AM) display that would produce motion in a given direction only if synesthetic color contributed to solution of the "motion correspondence" problem. To understand this, let us consider the task used by Ramachandran and Azoulai, who created an AM animation of four frames. Each frame comprised achromatic numerals whose locations were spatially jittered from frame to frame. In addition, a small cluster of the numerals within each frame differed from the "background" numerals and formed a virtual shape (e.g., a vertical bar); this shape fell at neighboring locations in the successive frames of the animation. When a similar task is performed with real colors, the perceived experience is that of a bar moving laterally. In this version, people without color-graphemic synesthesia experienced no sense of coherent motion when viewing the AM display and, instead, saw individual letters jittering around idiosyncratically. The synesthetic individual tested by Ramachandran and Azoulai, however, did spontaneously report seeing a bar moving laterally, with its direction of motion perfectly correlated with the direction of the shift in the positions of the characters. These subjective reports were substantiated in a four-choice categorization task: observers were required to indicate the direction of motion—up, down, left, or right—where on each trial the correct answer was defined by the correspondence between the successive positions of the cluster of numerals forming the virtual bar. Control participants performed at chance level[3] but the synesthete performed the task without mistakes. It would have been good if Ramachandran and Azoulai had also tested their synesthetic observer using achromatic digits all of which have the same color association, to show that this benefit disappears under that condition. Still, this kind of display, together with an appropriately designed forced-choice task, offers a compelling way to test for the

---

[3] Without color, the strong local motion signals produced by the positional jitter overwhelm motion associated with spatio-temporal displacement of the form-defined bar.

involvement of color in synesthesia: individuals with synesthesia who genuinely experience colors when viewing the digits comprising the AM animation should—and apparently do—benefit from a potent AM cue (Papathomas, Gorea, and Julesz 1991) that is unavailable to individuals without synesthesia. In this respect, the display created by Ramachandran and Azoulai in which there is, potentially, an objectively correct answer is superior to displays that use inherently ambiguous AM sequences to ask whether synesthetic color can induce judgment biases in perceived direction of motion (Kim, Blake, and Palmeri 2006)—the Ramachandran and Azoulai display is less susceptible to effects of response bias.

There are other examples of tasks where color influences spatial grouping, including perception of form based on figural grouping (e.g., Gorea and Papathomas 1993) and figural coherence in binocular rivalry (Kim and Blake 2007; Papathomas, Kovács, and Conway 2005). Guided by those findings, investigators have created synesthetic versions of displays used in these tasks to learn whether colors associated with letters and numbers behave comparably to real colors. The answer to that question appears to be "yes" both in the case of a figural grouping task (Hubbard, Manohar, and Ramachandran 2006; Hubbard et al. 2005) and global coherence on a binocular rivalry tracking task (Kim, Blake, and Palmeri 2006).[4] In both instances, however, synesthetic colors produced significantly weaker grouping than did real colors and, in the case of Hubbard et al. (2006) grouping based on synesthesia disappeared at low contrast levels of the inducers.

Finally, we should mention that another version of the enhancement strategy is simply to ask whether people with a given form of synesthesia perform better than non-synesthetic observers on conventional tasks that measure sensory acuity for the modality in which synesthesia is experienced. Do color-graphemic synesthetes, for example, exhibit better color vision than non-synesthetes or synesthetes whose experiences are confined to another modality? While not a widely employed strategy, those studies that have asked the question report an affirmative answer: individuals in whom color is a concurrent synesthetic experience tend to perform better on conventional tests of color discrimination (Yaro and Ward 2007) and individuals for whom touch is a concurrent experience tend to have better tactile acuity (Banissy, Walsh, and Ward 2009). This enhanced discrimination could result from more refined category boundaries within a given stimulus dimension owing to the enriched experiences that come with synesthesia or, alternatively, to inherent differences in brain connectivity between synesthetes and non-synesthetes and, for that matter, between different categories of synesthetes.

Performance impairment

Turning now to the opposite side of the coin, one can imagine tasks where synesthetic colors, if genuinely perceptual in nature, should impair performance under appropriate

---

[4] Paffen and colleagues have also found that the likelihood of binocular rivalry is increased when the two eyes receive inducers that generate different synesthetic colors (Paffen, van der Smagt, and Nijboer 2011).

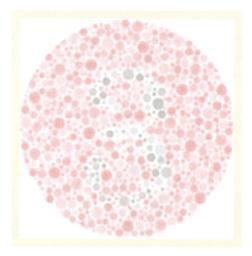

FIGURE 15.1 This stimulus, a variant of the classic Ishihara test plate, presents a numeral embedded within a background of texture elements whose colors ("pinkish") match the synesthetic color experienced by WO. When tested with this and other comparably designed test plates, he very quickly and accurately names the test figure even when, according to his self-report, the background perfectly matches his experience of the numeral's synesthetic color.

conditions. Is it possible, for example, to camouflage an ordinarily visible grapheme by embedding it in comparably shaped texture elements whose colors are matched to that induced by the grapheme? Using specially constructed test plates like the one shown in Figure 15.1 we tried but failed to render inducers invisible to color-graphemic synesthetes, even though our observers verified that the color matches were accurate. This negative result, however, may simply mean that synesthetes must first be aware of the identity of an inducer before that inducer can inherit its characteristic color (e.g., Rich and Mattingley 2005).

Using a variant of this masking strategy, Smilek et al. (2001) measured digit identification accuracy by briefly flashing a black digit against a uniformly colored background, with the background color either being congruent or incongruent with the synesthetic color of the digit experienced by their single synesthetic subject. This individual made significantly more errors on congruent versus incongruent trials; non-synesthetic control participants did not have significantly different error rates for the two categories of trials. Stronger interference on congruent trials was also observed on a second task that used reaction time (RT) in a visual search paradigm. On the other hand, Sagiv et al. (2006) found the opposite pattern of results in the single synesthete that they tested, i.e., RTs were actually faster on trials where the target's associated color was congruent with the background color. Adding to the confusion, Cohen Kadosh et al. (2009) reported that interference on congruent trials could be induced temporarily in non-synesthetic participants through the use of hypnotic suggestion associating particular colors and digits. So while the logic underlying this particular interference task seems straightforward, the results certainly are not.

One well-known interference effect observed in color-graphemic synesthesia is the so-called synesthetic Stroop effect, wherein words are printed in colors either congruent or incongruent with a synesthete's associated colors for those words. It is repeatedly found that color naming is slower and more error-prone for the words portrayed in an incongruent color (e.g., Dixon et al. 2000; Myles et al. 2003).[5] Several groups have argued that this synesthetic Stroop effect could, in fact, stem from semantic interference and not the perceptual experience of color (e.g., Palmeri et al. 2002). An account based exclusively on semantic confusion, however, is difficult to reconcile with the findings of Nikolić, Lichti, and Singer(2007) that synesthetically induced Stroop interference is greatest when the real and synesthetic colors presented on a given trial constitute opponent pairs (e.g., red/green) rather than non-opponent pairs (e.g., blue/red). In a control experiment, these authors demonstrated that this effect of opponency was not related to color naming per se, as evidenced by results on a shape/color version of the Stroop task (yellow lemon versus red lemon). Nikolić and colleagues believe their results point to the involvement of color opponent mechanisms in the synesthetic Stroop task.

At this stage, the jury is still out on the verdict of whether the color associations implicated in the Stroop effect are genuinely perceptual. Still, it is safe to conclude that the Stroop effect can confirm whether someone purporting to experience colors when viewing achromatic characters is indeed a color-graphemic synesthete—a genuine synesthete should exhibit the synesthetic Stroop effect. The converse, however, is not necessarily true: with extensive practice associating specific colors and alphanumeric characters, someone who does not experience synesthesia can still exhibit a synesthetic Stroop effect (Elias et al. 2003). The Stroop task, incidentally, has the virtue of not requiring performance comparison between groups (synesthetic versus non-synesthetic), because response times are compared within an individual for congruent and incongruent test stimuli. It is also possible to use the pupillary reflex to assess the synesthetic Stroop effect, capitalizing on the fact that the appearance of an unexpected or incongruent stimulus can evoke a brief, measurable increase in pupil size (Paulsen and Laeng 2006).

Another interference strategy was developed by Gheri et al. (2008) capitalizing on the observation that identification of a unique item among an array of distractors is slowed when the item and distractors are drawn in different, random colors. Gheri et al. reasoned that color-graphemic synesthetes should be impaired on such a task when the array items were actually randomly colored and, if synesthetic colors are perceptual, also when the items were achromatic and generated different synesthetic experiences. Non-synesthetes, of course, would exhibit impairment only on the real color condition. Evidently this task was quite difficult because the search times averaged almost 6 seconds, unusually slow times for a task where one must find the unique numeral among

---

[5] See Beeli, Esslen, and Jä ncke (2005) for a clever adaptation of the Stroop task to a case of tone-evoked taste sensations.

an array of 16 numerals. In any event, synesthetes performed no worse than non-syn-esthetes on both versions of the task, leading Gheri et al. to conclude that synesthetic colors are not perceptual, at least in the individuals they tested. Note, however, that the logic underlying their interference condition predicts that synesthetes' responses should be slower than those made by control participants if synesthetic color has a perceptual component; as noted earlier, search times were quite slow for all observers, raising the possibility of ceiling effects. Would the same pattern of results be found if the number of distractors was varied or if a dependent variable other than reaction time were used (e.g., accuracy with brief presentation)? Moreover, the individuals tested by Gheri et al. were characterized as colored hearing synesthetes, not color-graphemic synesthetes, in an earlier study in which they participated (Nunn et al. 2002). It is true that Gheri and colleagues confirmed that these individuals exhibited stable associations between colors and achromatic numerals, but the authors did not specify whether these individuals "saw" the numerals in color or, instead, associated a given color when thinking about a given numeral. The participants studied by Gheri and colleagues thus may not have possessed the type of synesthesia that influences color appearance target and distractor items defining visual search arrays.[6]

Contextual effects

The vision literature is replete with examples of stimulus conditions where one's percep-tual experience of color depends on the context—spatial and temporal—in which the colored stimulus appears, and among these are conditions that produce vivid illusions in perceived color. These contextual phenomena offer a potentially revealing window onto the determinants of color-graphemic synesthesia, in part because we can make educated guesses about the neural mechanisms underlying at least some of those phe-nomena. The following paragraphs describe several examples where such phenomena have been employed in studies of color-graphemic synesthesia.

To start, consider chromatic adaptation wherein exposure to a given color alters the color appearance of a subsequently viewed patch of color. To give an example, exposure to a patch of green light causes subsequently viewed yellow light to appear slightly red-dish, and to eliminate that reddish appearance requires adding a given amount of green light to the mixture to restore it to equilibrium yellow. This technique, called hue cancel-lation, provides a precise quantitative measure of the magnitude of chromatic adapta-tion (Hurvich and Jameson 1957). The neural concomitants of these short-lasting shifts in color appearance are generally thought to arise very early within the visual path-ways, probably from gain changes in the cone receptors and in the opponent process

---

[6] As mentioned in an earlier section, Gheri et al. also measured search speed under a condition where synesthetic color should have facilitated performance, but they found no facilitation relative to performance by non-synesthetic controls. Again, the question of type of synesthesia may be pertinent here as well.

mechanism they innervate (Hurvich and Jameson 1957; Jameson and Hurvich 1972). What happens when the real colored adaptation field is replaced with a dense array of graphemes all of which have the same color association (Figure 15.2)? Does adaptation to this field of synesthetic color produce a temporary shift in the ratio of red to green necessary to achieve equilibrium yellow? Hong and Blake (2008) found that it did *not*, even though same dense array of graphemes did produce robust adaptation when those graphemes were presented in real colors. Moreover, it did not matter whether those real colors were congruent or not with the synesthetic color of the graphemes. In a related set of measurements, Hong and Blake found that the red/green ratio yielding equilibrium yellow did not shift when the nulling target itself was a grapheme whose associated

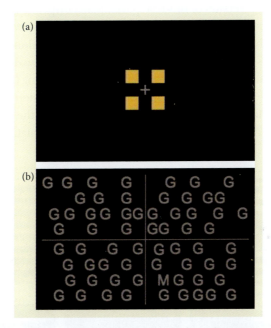

FIGURE 15.2 Displays used to induce and measure color adaptation using a nulling technique. (a) The test display comprised four small squares each composed of red and green light, and the observer could adjust the amount of green light necessary to make the mixture appear neither red nor green: equilibrium yellow. (b) The adaptation display consisted of 16 gray letters, 15 being distractors and one being the target; all 16 letters had the same associated synesthetic color for a given observer ("red"). During the 5-minute adaptation period, the observer maintained fixation on the central cross and reported for each display the quadrant containing the "target" letter; this response triggered presentation of another 16-character display with the target and distractors rearranged. Even though the adapting field appeared "red" to the observers, their equilibrium yellow settings were unaffected by the prolonged period of exposure to this adaptation display. Adaptation to real colored versions of these arrays produced a robust shift in equilibrium yellow. Reprinted from *Vision Research*, 48 (8), Hong, Sang Wook, and Randolph Blake, Early visual mechanisms do not contribute to synesthetic color experience, pp. 1018–1026, Copyright (2008), with permission from Elsevier.

color was either green or was red, implying that the synesthetic color did not enter into the equation when making these judgments. Evidently, then, color experiences associated with synesthesia have no impact on color judgments dependent on neural processes believed to arise within peripheral stages of the visual pathway. On the other hand, results from a related strategy that isolates cortical color adaptation reveals that color associated with graphemes can impact color/form adaptation, and it is to that strategy that we turn next.

The upper panel in Figure 15.3 shows the configuration used to induce (green and red bars) and observe (black/white bars) the well-known McCollough effect (McCollough 1965), a form of adaptation characterized by the long-lasting experience of desaturated, illusory color the hue of which depends on the orientation of the contours of the test pattern. In the original version of this test, participants inspect alternately the red horizontal and green vertical gratings; after a few minutes they switch to the black-and-white gratings, which now look greenish on the horizontal sections and pinkish on the vertical sections. This orientation-contingent color aftereffect provides a nifty means for testing the perceptual reality of synesthetic colors without tipping off participants about the expected outcome. The lower panel shows a synesthetic version of the induction and test stimuli for the McCollough effect (Blake et al. 2005). Here the oriented contours of the induction pattern are formed from closely spaced, achromatic letters that can be

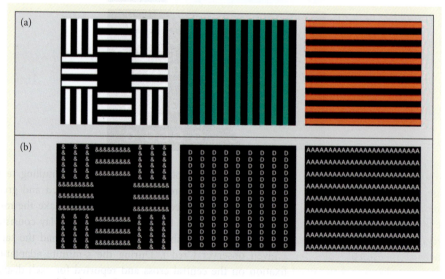

FIGURE 15.3 (a) The configuration used to induce and observe the conventional McCollough effect. After being adapted to the green/black vertical (middle) and red/black horizontal gratings (right-hand side), observers report faint pink on the horizontal, faint green on the vertical part of the white/black test pattern (left-hand side). (b) A synesthetic version of the induction and test stimuli for the McCollough effect. For LR, who "sees" green on the letter D and red on the letter A, those stimuli shown in the middle and on the right-hand side serve as adapting stimuli. The test pattern was made with "&" which doesn't induce any synesthetic color for LR.

appropriately selected for their associated colors (e.g., A = red and D = green); the test pattern comprises closely spaced characters that have no color association. Following prolonged inspection of the inducing "gratings" does the synesthetic observer experience faint pink and green colors on the appropriate parts of the test figure? For LR, a participant in our studies, the answer is "yes"—not only did she spontaneously report the appropriate hues without prompting, she also experienced this adaptation aftereffect only when the inducing patterns and test pattern were presented to the same eye, matching the absence of interocular transfer seen with the conventional McCollough effect. And like the conventional McCollough effect, her synesthetic version was restricted to the region of the visual field where the adapting stimuli were imaged, and the effect lasted several days. Unfortunately, the McCollough effect remains a conundrum in vision science: its boundary conditions have been studied in some detail, but there is still no uniformly accepted explanation for why it occurs or what brain regions might give rise to it. Still, we recommend this test as a foolproof means for assessing the nature of the color experiences of color-graphemic synesthetes, for expected responses are not obvious and the stimulus selectivity for eye and visual field are additional signatures of the reality of the effect. Moreover, it is possible to measure this aftereffect without relying on verbal descriptions, using a nulling technique modeled after the one developed by Vul and colleagues (Vul and MacLeod 2006; Vul, Krizay, and MacLeod 2008).

Another illusion that has been used to study color synesthesia is lightness constancy wherein the perceived variations in surface illumination influence the perceived lightness of objects located in that scene. A compelling example of this illusion is the checker-shadow display devised by Adelson (2000) and reproduced with permission in Figure 15.4. Witthoft and Winawer (2006) used this and related displays in conjunction with a color/brightness matching procedure to learn whether colors associated

FIGURE 15.4 The squares marked A and B look very different in lightness but are indeed the same shade of gray. Withoft and Winawer (2006) asked a synesthete whether the induced synesthetic color was influenced by the brightness setting by presenting an inducing letter on the squares A and B. ©1995, Edward H. Adelson.

with synesthesia were susceptible to the illusion. Testing one color-graphemic synesthete categorized as a projector, they found that this person's color/brightness settings depended on whether the character appeared directly illuminated (e.g., the letter
A in Figure 15.4) or appeared to fall within an apparent shadow (e.g., the letter B in
Figure 15.4). This influence was not as great, however, as when the letters were actually
colored, leading Witthoft and Winawer to conclude that, "it is likely that the synesthetic color is not available to some of the earliest constancy mechanisms" (182). That
conclusion could explain why Hong and Blake (2008) failed to find evidence for synesthetically mediated brightness induction using a much simpler stimulus configuration
devoid of three-dimensional cues that imply illumination and shading, a configuration more likely to engage very low-level constancy mechanisms only. And in a variant of this lightness constancy task, Nijboer and colleagues (Nijboer, Satris, and van
der Stigchel 2011) asked whether the color appearance associated with a given grapheme was susceptible to the real color of the background against which that grapheme
appeared, i.e., whether simultaneous color contrast could be induced in a synesthetic
color. They attempted to answer this question by having observers adjust the color of
an achromatic grapheme that appeared against a background matched to the grapheme's color and to one that was opposite in color to the grapheme's color; for purposes
of comparison, non-synesthetic individuals performed identical matches in which
the grapheme was actually colored to match the associated color of a given synesthete.
Results from these measurements gave an affirmative answer to this question (i.e.,
matched color depended on the background color) but, oddly, the shift in perceived
color of the grapheme was in the opposite direction to that experienced by the control
observers viewing real colored graphemes placed on colored backgrounds. Nijboer and
colleagues speculated that high-level visual memory associated with synesthesia might
have something to do with this counter-intuitive result. This conundrum needs to be
sorted out before we can place faith in simultaneous color contrast as a useful strategy
for assessing the perceptual reality of synesthetic color.

We end this section with another color illusion produced by spatial context, this
one being color assimilation wherein an achromatic region of a surface appears
colored because that region is bounded by a real colored border (Broerse, Vladusich,
and O'Shea 1999; Pinna 2005). Nowadays called the watercolor illusion, this spread
of illusory color is compelling, surprising and puzzling to naïve observers (and, for
that matter, to some seasoned vision scientists). To experience the illusion for yourself, compare the interiors of the two figures shown in Figure 15.5a. As you will see,
the interior region of the left-hand figure looks faintly yellow/gold and in the right-
hand figure the interior looks white with a faint tint of purple. In fact, the two interior regions are identical, and it's the color of the inner border defining the figure that
induces the illusory, spreading color. Shown in Figure 15.5b are two figures where the
borders that ordinarily promote color induction are replaced by two adjacent rings of
achromatic letters, with the letters forming a given ring all having a given color association. When first shown achromatic configurations like that illustrated in Figure 15.5b,

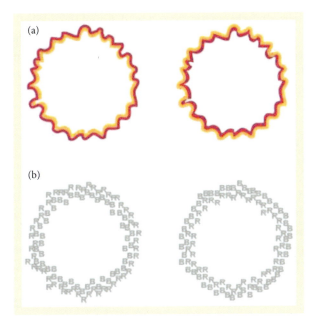

FIGURE 15.5 (a) The watercolor effect. When an orange contour is surrounded by a purple contour, the enclosed area looks yellowish (left-hand side). When a purple contour is surrounded by an orange contour, however, this illusory color spreading is not experienced (right-hand side). (b) An example display for a synesthetic version of the watercolor test. For a synesthete LR, the letter "B" appears orange and the letter "R" appears purple. LR sees the watercolor illusion induced within the left-hand circle but not within the right-hand circle. Reproduced from *Perception* 34(12), Watercolor illusion induced by synesthetic color, Kim, Chai-Youn, and Randolph Blake, pp. 1501–1507 © 2005, Pion, with permission Pion Ltd, London: www.pion.co.uk and www.envplan.com.

the projector synesthetes in our lab spontaneously described the interior regions as faintly colored, and their reports varied depending on the inducing characters forming the interior border (Kim and Blake 2005). It is noteworthy that these individuals had not seen real color versions of this display ever before, and they were puzzled by what they saw. When next shown real color versions of the displays, they described the same illusion with the interior color being less washed out than in the synesthetic version. These verbal reports were supplemented by an indirect task that capitalized on the propensity of illusory colored surfaces to stand out when presented among other forms that do not induce color spreading. Observers were required to indicate the location of an oddball target among four equally sized shapes whose borders were defined by characters that, for the synesthetes, had color associations. The task did not require judging color, only the one shape whose letter configuration differed from the other three. However, color spreading associated with the oddball shape on some trials tended to draw attention it and, thus, speed performance on the task. Again, this speeding was also found for synesthetes, but not for age-matched control observers, using displays where the achromatic characters defining the oddball target had a different associated color than the achromatic characters defining the interior of the other three shapes. The synesthetes, in other words, were faster than normal observers spotting an oddball target whose interior region was described as different from the interiors of the other three shapes.

Precision of color matching

We close this section on behavioral strategies by describing a task that to date has not been utilized in published work on color-graphemic synesthesia but that would seem to have promise as a means for quantitatively assessing the preciseness of the color associations experienced in this condition. Specifically, we can ask whether the synesthetic colors associated with different inducers can be reproduced with the precision known to be achieved when people with normal color vision perform a color discrimination task. In one version of this kind of task, a person is given control of the hue, saturation, and brightness of a test patch displayed on a video monitor and is instructed to adjust those settings until the test patch appears identical to a comparison stimulus also displayed on the monitor. People are remarkably accurate (as evidenced by the near-equivalence of test and comparison values) and reliable (as evidenced by the variance among repeated test settings). Indeed, performance of this task appears to be limited primarily by an individual's wavelength discrimination ability, which is known to be quite good except at extremes of the wavelength spectrum (Wright and Pitt 1934).

Now suppose we ask a color-graphemic synesthete to use this matching procedure to reproduce the colors evoked by different achromatic inducers (i.e., letters or numbers). We would not be able to score the accuracy of those matches, of course, because we would have no objectively "correct" color against which to score the accuracy of the settings. But we could derive the variance from repeated color matches, and we could compare those variance estimates with the variance associated with matches using real colors. We have implemented this procedure in synesthete LR in our laboratory, and find that her synesthetic color matches are highly reliable with repeated measurement. An example of this consistency can be seen in Figure 15.6a, which shows, in CIE color space, color matches produced on three different occasions when tested using the alphabetic characters A, B, C, D, E, and F. For purposes of comparison, we also asked LR to produce color matches for five different real colors portrayed by a symbol with the same average contour length as the alphabetic letters we used to assess her synesthetic colors (the symbol had no synesthetic association whatsoever for LR). Those results are summarized in Figure 15.6b. Comparison of the two sets of results—synesthetic and real color matches—reveals remarkable consistency over time with the between-session variability of synesthetic settings rivaling the within-session variability for real color matches. If her judgments were based on categorical labeling, this level of matching consistency would be unimaginable (Chapanis and Overbey

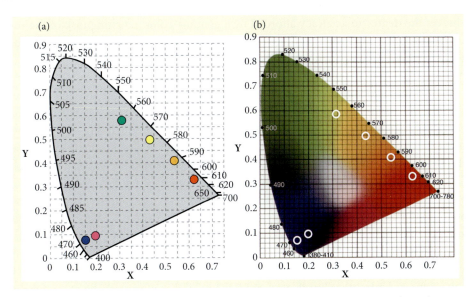

FIGURE 15.6 (a) Synesthetic color matching results from a synesthete LR for achromatic alphabetic characters A, B, C, D, E, and F. (b) Real color matching results from the same synesthete for non-inducing symbols in physical colors consistent with her reported synesthetic colors for A, B, C, D, E, and F. Note the remarkable similarity between the synesthetic and real color matching results. Each data point is the average of four settings obtained on each of three weekly test sessions; the error bars cannot be plotted because they are smaller than the plotting symbols. We are very grateful to Sang-Wook Hong for writing the MatLab code to implement this test and supervising the testing.

1971). Instead, her performance implies fine-grained color resolution for these synesthetic colors.[7]

So, measuring the reliability of color matches is one strategy for testing the claim that synesthetic colors are genuinely perceptual in character. In fact, however, no studies to date have gone to the trouble of assessing reliability using refined color matching tasks like the one exemplified in the data of Figure 15.6; instead, most rely on categorical, subjective reports. There are several standardized, web-based tests that provide reasonable estimates of reliability (Asher et al. 2006; Eagleman et al. 2007), but neither of these

---

[7] A key concept in colorimetry, the science of quantifying and physically describing human color vision, is metamerism: two color samples differing in spectral power distributions that appear to be identical constitute a metameric match. Are we to conclude that a synesthetic color and its matched, real color counterpart are metameric? It is certainly true that, following careful color adjustments, the person achieves a setting where the colors are deemed to be equivalent and, yet, the stimuli differ in their spectral content. There is, however, a fundamental difference between synesthetic color matches and the metameric matches measured in colorimetry: people cannot tell the difference between true metameric matches (e.g., pure "yellow" light cannot be distinguished from the "yellow" produced by an appropriate mixture of red and green lights), but a synesthete never confuses a synesthetically colored inducer and a real colored character that matches the synesthetic color.

achieves the degree of accuracy afforded by a genuine color matching task of the sort described earlier. And none of these tests, including color matching, captures the surface appearance accompanying color experiences such as luster, sheen, or matte appearance described by some synesthetes (Eagleman and Goodale 2009).

Compelling evidence for high reliability still does not constitute unequivocal evidence for the perceptual reality of synesthetic colors. One could reasonably argue that the appropriate benchmark for gauging the basis of the reproducibility of synesthetic colors should be repeated matches from memory made by non-synesthetic individuals who have spent years associating particular colors with particular letters. This benchmark is all the more relevant when we take into account the tendency for synesthetes to exhibit superior performance on standardized tests of memory (e.g., Cytowic 1997).[8] Unfortunately it will be very difficult to identify people whose color associations have the richness and long history of associations reported by synesthetes, whose color experiences typically date back to early childhood. Nor have we been able to find non-synesthetic volunteers willing to spend the time embedding these associations in their memory. Unless that hurdle is cleared, the reliability of synesthetic color matches must remain suggestive but not definitive with respect to the perceptual nature of the condition.

Interim Conclusions

As the previous sections document, there are strategies for going beyond simple phenomenological reports to learn whether color associations reported by color-graphemic synesthetes behave as if they have a genuine perceptual component. Moreover, versions of some of these strategies can minimize the potential, contaminating influence of bias resulting from expectations on the part of the participant(s), owing to the technique itself (e.g., genuine forced-choice testing) or to the counterintuitive nature of the phenomenon being employed (e.g., the McCollough effect). Some strategies depend on comparison of test performance of synesthetes to non-synesthetic control participants, and in those instances it is important to ensure that non-synesthetic individuals forming the comparison group are equally motivated, equally attentive, and as well trained on the task as the synesthetes, for otherwise group differences cannot be interpreted definitively. It is also desirable to utilize tasks where it is possible to test synesthetes under conditions where their color associations could plausibly improve their performance and conditions where their color associations could interfere with performance.

---

[8] Synesthetes report that their novel sensory experiences enhance their memory abilities, but in reality the causal arrow could point in the opposite direction.

INDIRECT MEASURES

To circumvent potential problems inherent in behavioral measures (e.g., response bias), one can turn to indirect measures of physiological responses that accompany synesthesia. Here the general strategy is to ask whether those measurements are equivalent to physiological responses measured in response to real stimulation (e.g., color) that mimics the induced experiences (color-graphemic synesthesia). In the following sections, we consider several physiological responses that have been used to address this question; these include: (1) saccades and pupil reflex, (2) hemodynamic responses measured using magnetic resonance imaging (MRI), and (3) event-related brain potentials measured using scalp electrodes.[9]

Our purpose is not to review the extensive set of studies utilizing those kinds of indirect measures but, rather, to show specifically how those indirect measures are used to examine the perceptual reality of synesthetic experience. This is a narrower question than asking about the neural bases of synesthesia (Bargary and Mitchell 2008; Grossenbacher and Lovelace, 2001).[10]

Oculomotor responses

When it comes to presentation of real colored stimuli, the eyes themselves exhibit telltale signs of reactions to color. So, for example, saccadic eye movements are affected by the variety of colors among potential eye movement targets (Ludwig and Gilchrist 2003). Pupillary reflexes, too, can show sensitivity to stimulus color (Gamlin et al. 1998). There are a couple of studies that have asked whether synesthetic colors evoke comparable oculomotor responses.[11]

---

[9] These measures can produce suggestive correlations between synesthesia and neural activity, but not the causal relationship. One technique that potentially can point to causality is Transcranial Magnetic Stimulation (TMS), a non-invasive means for producing neural activity using magnetic induction to induce weak currents into targeted regions of the brain (Hallett 2000). However, TMS can hardly be used in the study bearing on the question of the perceptual reality of synesthetic color, since it cannot be applied selectively to the color-related brain regions along the ventral visual processing stream (e.g., hV4, V8). Thus existing studies of the effect of TMS on synesthesia have targeted posterior parietal areas in an attempt to learn whether those areas are involved in color-shape binding (Eastermann et al. 2006; Muggleton et al. 2007), which is not within the scope of the current chapter. One recent study targeted the primary visual cortex which can be accessed by TMS and found enhanced cortical excitability (threefold lower phosphene threshold in synesthetes than in non-synesthetes) In this study, another technique that can point to causality—transcranial direct current stimulation (TDCS)—was also exploited to demonstrate modulation of synesthetic experience (Terhune et al. 2011).

[10] For more on the neural theories of synesthesia, see Part V in this volume.

[11] For more detailed discussions on this topic, see Nijboer and Laeng (Chapter 17, this volume).

Using a visual saccade paradigm, Nijboer and van der Stigchel (2009) revised the paradigm of Ludwig and Gilchrist to ask whether similarity between real and synesthetic color can affect oculomotor responses during visual search. In their study, color-graphemic synesthetes were instructed to make eye-movements to a real colored target. When that target was accompanied by a single distractor whose physical hue was identical to that of the target, many erroneous eye movements were made towards the distractor. In contrast, presentation of a synesthetically colored distractor did not trigger erroneous eye movements; it, instead, behaved like an achromatic, non-inducing symbol. In a second study, however, Carriere and colleagues showed that the interaction between real and synesthetic color can indeed influence oculomotor responses during visual search (Carriere et al. 2009). These researchers exploited the well-established synesthetic color congruity effect and showed that synesthetes rapidly fixated and identified the congruently colored target letters, but showed difficulty in identifying incongruently colored letters.

These seemingly contradictory results may be due to methodological differences. In Nijboer and van der Stigchel's study, synesthetes had to hold their fixation very carefully on a central fixation point and were asked to make only one eye movement to the target, whereas in Carriere et al.'s study synesthetes visually explored the search array freely until they detect the target. In line with different viewing conditions, the two studies employed different independent variables: Nijboer and van der Stigchel focused on percentage of capture by the distractor whereas Carriere et al. used probability of target fixation within the first two saccades. Regardless of the methodological differences, do those two studies tell us anything definitive about the perceptual reality of synesthetic color? Both groups discussed their findings in relation to the role of attention in synesthetic color experience, an issue distinguishable from the question of the perceptual reality of synesthesia as mentioned earlier in this chapter. Nijboer and van der Stigchel showed that unattended inducing stimulus failed to induce synesthetic color, and Carriere et al. showed that attentional bias favoring the congruently colored inducing grapheme can modulate synesthetes' performance during visual search task. Of course, an alternative, more sceptical interpretation of Nijboer and van der Stigchel's finding is that synesthetic color is not perceptually equivalent to real color.

For the past 15 years or so, investigation into the neural mechanisms has been a centre of attention in the field of synesthesia research. Regarding the perceptual reality, the question becomes whether neural mechanisms engaged during genuine color perception are also engaged during synesthetic color experience. To answer this question, several different techniques with relative advantages and disadvantages have been utilized, and it is those techniques that we turn to in the next several sections.

Brain imaging using MRI

The most frequently used technique for studying neural responses associated with synesthetic experience is functional MRI (fMRI), and most of those fMRI studies—but not all (see, e.g., Beauchamp and Ro 2008; Blakemore et al. 2005; Tang, Ward, and Butterworth 2008) have focused on color synesthesia induced by viewing graphemes or listening to sounds. The general strategy has been to compare areas of activation associated with color synesthesia with activations in cortical areas believed to be involved in genuine color perception.[12] There is general agreement that this complex of areas includes primary visual cortex (V1) and extrastriate areas comprising the ventral occipital cortex (Wandell and Winawer 2011), with additional, higher-level processing spilling into the inferotemporal cortex (Shapley and Hawken, 2011). Are these same areas active when a synesthete experiences color induced by achromatic inducers or by sound? As the next several paragraphs indicate, the answer to this question is not unequivocal.

In a study targeting primary visual cortex, Aleman and colleagues observed increased activation in V1 when their colored hearing synesthete listened to color-inducing words relative to activations measured when she listened to non-inducing tones (Aleman et al. 2001). From this result, however, we cannot be certain that the V1 activations were causally related to the experience of color. After all, synesthetes can experience vivid color imagery when an associated color is retrieved from memory, and it is quite likely that visual imagery is associated with activation in early visual brain regions (Kosslyn et al. 1999). So perhaps the activations in the synesthete studied by Aleman and colleagues were arising from the conceptual association between inducing stimulus and color. This hypothesis cannot explain, however, why a blind synesthete who does not show V1 activations during visual imagery does show V1 activations when listening to color inducing words but not when listening to frequency matched, non-inducing words (Steven, Hansen, and Blakemore 2006). Further complicating the story, a study of 13 auditory word-color synesthetes (described later) failed to find significant V1 activations but did find reliable activations in extrastriate areas (Nunn et al. 2002).

More frequently pinpointed in fMRI studies of synesthesia are color-responsive regions in the ventral extrastriate cortex including hV4 and V8. Some of those studies find selective activation of these areas when synesthetes experience color (Hubbard et al. 2005; Nunn et al. 2002; Rouw and Scholte 2007; Sperling et al. 2006; Weiss et al. 2001). Studies showing hV4/V8 involvement in synesthetic color experience vary in terms of the number of synesthetes tested (ranging from 1 (Weiss et al. 2001) to 18 (Rouw and Scholte, 2007)), the type of synesthesia (colored hearing or color-graphemic), and the way color-responsive areas are identified (whole brain analysis (Nunn et al. 2002), anatomically defined, or functionally defined (Hubbard et al. 2005)). However, they all conclude that at least some of the brain regions involved in genuine color perception are also associated with synesthetic color perception (see, e.g., Figure 15.7). To quote Nunn

---

[12] Neural events involved in genuine color vision, of course, are inaugurated in the retina and then conveyed to the lateral geniculate nucleus (LGN), so the cortex is certainly not the first stage of visual processing associated with color perception. It is highly unlikely, however, that retinal mechanisms are involved in generating color experiences during synesthesia (aside from signaling features of the inducer). Whether the LGN is involved has not yet been studied, although the ability to image this structure (e.g., O'Connor et al. 2002) makes such a study possible.

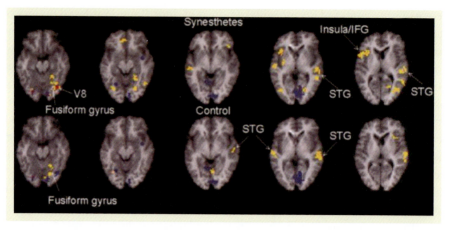

FIGURE 15.7 BOLD responses to real color stimuli and synesthesia inducing stimuli. Areas showing greater activation for synesthesia-inducing words than for non-inducing tones are presented in yellow. Areas showing greater activation for physically colored stimuli than for achromatic stimuli are presented in blue. For colored-hearing synesthetes, areas associated with induced synesthetic color (yellow) and real color (blue) showed intersection (red; *upper panel*). For non-synesthetes who don't experience any color when hearing words, however, such intersection was not observed (*lower panel*). Reprinted by permission from Macmillan Publishers Ltd: *Nature Neuroscience*, 5 (4), Nunn, J. A., L. J. Gregory, M. Brammer, S. C. R. Williams, D. M. Parslow, Michael J. Morgan, R. G. Morris, E. T. Bullmore, S. Baron-Cohen, and J. A. Gray, Functional magnetic resonance imaging of synesthesia: activation of V4/V8 by spoken words, pp. 371–375, copyright (2002).

et al. (2002), "differences between synesthetes and controls in activation of a color-selective region by spoken words, lend such phenomena an authenticity beyond reasonable doubt" (373). For that matter, there is also evidence for correlation between the blood oxygen level-dependent (BOLD) signal intensities in these color-selective visual areas and perceptual characteristics of synesthetic color experiences. Specifically, Hubbard et al. (2005) found a positive correlation between performance in synesthetic color tasks—spatial crowding and segregation of figure from background—and BOLD signal intensity in hV4. In other words, synesthetes whose color experience exerts a stronger influence on color-related visual tasks showed greater activation in hV4 when viewing color-inducing stimuli.

Complicating this tidy story however are a handful of studies that fail to find activations related to synesthesia in color-responsive areas in early visual cortex. For example, Weiss and colleagues tested color-graphemic synesthetes and found increased activation in the left intraparietal cortex associated with synesthesia, but not in the ventral visual processing areas (Weiss, Zilles, and Fink 2005). However, their results need to be interpreted with caution. Weiss and colleagues designed their fMRI experiments "to depict where in the human brain the hypothesized *binding* of alphanumeric form and synesthetic color occurs" (860). To do that, they manipulated both physical color (presence or absence) and synesthetic color (induced or not-induced). Thus the lack of early visual area activation was based on the contrast between inducing stimuli with or without physical color and non-inducing stimuli with or without physical color. In all the studies successfully showing early visual area involvement in synesthetic color, only the contrast between inducing stimuli and non-inducing stimuli without physical color was considered.

But even if activations are observed in color-selective visual cortical areas of synesthetes experiencing color, this does not necessarily mean that the activated neurons are also those activated when those individuals view genuinely colored stimuli. For one thing, a voxel may contain anywhere from tens of thousands to more than a million neurons depending on the voxel's volume. Moreover, a typically localized color area includes multiple voxels. In the extreme case scenario, what if a subset of neurons within a color area subserves real color processing while another subset of neurons within the same area subserves synesthetic color processing, with little or no overlap between the subsets? To examine whether synesthetic and real color arise from activation of the same neurons, a technique called repetition suppression (aka repetition attenuation or fMR-adaptation) can be exploited: BOLD responses are generally reduced in amplitude following repeated presentation of the same stimulus (Grill-Spector, Henson, and Martin 2006). Using this technique, van Leeuwen and colleagues (van Leeuwen, Petersson, and Hagoort 2010) measured brain activations in carefully localized regions in the brains of color-graphemic synesthetes and matched control observers. In both groups of observers, as expected, two real colored targets presented one after the other produced weakened BOLD signals in color-responsive areas when and only when the two targets were the same color—this repetition suppression effect merely validates the technique. When the first target was an achromatic letter that induced a color identical to a second, real colored letter, repetition suppression was not observed in color-selective areas but was seen in the superior parietal lobule, an area uniquely activated using a synesthesia localizer. These authors concluded that, "synesthetic color experiences are mediated by higher-order visual pathways that lie beyond the scope of classical, ventral-occipital visual areas" (1). This potentially important conclusion would be stronger if the experiment had included conditions to rule out the possibility that activations in color-selective areas are generally weak for synesthetically induced colors. One such condition could involve presentation of two successive synesthetic colors, sometimes identical and sometimes different. Also in the critical condition of this study, the first letter of a pair was always an achromatic inducing grapheme, followed by a real color letter. Reversing the order of the two—real color followed by synesthetic color—might reveal the existence of a significant but weak repetition suppression effect.

Although not a repetition suppression study, Rich and colleagues (Rich et al. 2006) have also reported fMRI results that call into question the involvement of color-selective cortical areas in synesthesia. They compared brain regions activated during synesthetic color experience, during real color perception, during color imagery, and during color naming. From those comparisons, it appears that the brain regions involved in synesthetic color experience are adjacent to, but not identical with, the real color responsive areas which, themselves, are associated with color imagery. Synesthetic color experiences were uniquely associated with activations in the lingual gyrus, an occipito-temporal region thought to be importantly involved in color naming. In general, the results of Rich et al. suggest that internally generated color experience in synesthesia is mediated by differential neural mechanisms than those involved in visual imagery of color.

In a recent study, Hupé and colleagues (Hupé, Bordier, and Dojat 2012) questioned the involvement of hV4 in synesthetic color experience. By contrasting brain responses to multicolored mondrians with those to achromatic mondrians, they localized color-sensitive brain regions including hV4. Next, they contrasted responses within those localized areas produced by synesthetic color-inducing graphemes and by pseudo fonts that did not induce synesthesia, and they failed to find significant differences between the two categories of stimuli. Hupé and colleagues reckoned that previous studies showing hV4 activation associated with synesthetic color managed to achieve statistical significance only by relaxing their statistical threshold. While not quarrelling with their statistical reasoning, we do question whether their design was optimal for maximizing BOLD responses associated with synesthetic color experiences. In Hupé and colleagues' study, mondrian stimuli were large (8× 6 degrees in visual angle) and multicolored, whereas the individual graphemes inducing synesthesia and the pseudo fonts were much smaller (approximately 1 degree), and only a single color experience was induced at a time during the stimulus sequence. It is possible, therefore, that the synesthesia-inducing stimuli were too weak to produce robust BOLD signal changes in the localized color area. In fact, one sees some hints of greater activation of hV4 in response to inducers compared to non-inducers, although this difference did not achieve their strict criterion for statistical significance. It is doubtful whether this negative result will overturn the current view that neural correlates of color-graphemic synesthesia include activity within visual cortex, but the study does raise important issues about statistical power and corrections for multiple comparisons.

Before leaving this section, we want to mention a study that uses MRI brain imaging to identify anatomical differences between synesthetes and normal controls and, intriguingly, among different synesthetic individuals.[13] Rouw and Scholte (2010) used voxel-based morphometry (VBM) to study the brains of 42 non-synesthetes and 42 synesthetes, some being projectors who see colors on object surfaces in the world and others being associators who see colors in the mind's eye. The investigators found increased gray matter volume at the posterior superior parietal cortex in synesthetes compared to non-synesthetes. Moreover, the projector-type synesthetes were different from non-synesthetes within gray matter volumes at the early visual processing streams including V1, whereas the associator-type synesthetes were different from non-synesthetes in

---

[13] Several more studies utilizing structural brain imaging methods have showed differences between synesthetic brains from non-synesthetic brains, which suggest the neural bases of synesthesia (Hänggi, Wotruba, and Jäncke 2011; Jäncke et al. 2009; Weiss and Fink 2009). Readers interested in those questions will want to see Rouw, Chapter 25, in this volume.

gray-matter volume in the hippocampus, a brain region associated with memory. These findings, together with the results of Rouw and Scholte (2007) mentioned in footnote 2, provide an intriguing picture of the possible neural bases for these two types of synesthesia, with stronger connectivity between areas within early visual areas of individuals who see their colors localized on surfaces in the world. The extent to which synesthesia engages the same neural mechanisms as real color vision, in other words, may depend on the type of synesthesia.

Event-related potentials

The spatial resolution of modern fMRI makes it well suited for identifying brain areas involved in synesthesia, but the sluggishness of the BOLD signal means the technique is not so good for revealing the fine-grained temporal evolution of synesthetic experiences. But why would high temporal resolution matter when it comes to addressing the question of the perceptual reality of synesthesia? Because, in principle, neural signals arising within the first few hundred milliseconds following stimulus presentation are likely to reflect initial sensory/perceptual processing. For this reason, some investigations of synesthesia have turned to event-related potentials (ERPs), i.e., stimulus triggered, task dependent waveforms seen in the scalp-recorded electroencephalogram (EEG) signal reflecting neural activity measurable on the millisecond scale (Luck 2005). Woodman (2010) provides an excellent overview of ERPs, including the origins of the signal, the limitations in its measurement and the dissection of the various components of the ERP. For our purposes, it is useful to keep in mind that the early components of the ERP appearing within 200 ms of the onset of a stimulus are generally attributed to sensory/perceptual processing; later components, which can arise up to several seconds later, are attributed to deployment of attention, stimulus recognition and evaluation, reaction to unexpected or incongruent stimuli, and complex cognitive activity such as mental arithmetic and memory rehearsal. It is also worth noting that to obtain reliable ERP measurements of these components requires many trial repetitions and, then, signal averaging to pull out those components from the noise inherent in EEG recordings. With those aspects of ERP in mind, we turn to the handful of studies that have used ERP to evaluate the unfolding time course of neural responses associated with synesthesia.

To our knowledge, the first ERP study on synesthesia was performed by Schiltz and colleagues (Schiltz et al. 1999). They reported unusually large amplitude late components of the ERP (300–600 ms) in color-graphemic synesthetes following very brief presentation of an achromatic letter or number. These large signals were observed at electrode sites associated with frontal and central brain sites but not occipital sites, suggesting to the authors some form of inhibitory control possibly in response to the distracting quality of synesthetic color. These ERP measurements were obtained within the context of an oddball task based on memory for alphanumeric characters, so it is doubtful whether the results provide evidence for unique perceptual processing associated with synesthesia.

In a more elaborate study using ERP, Beeli et al. (2008) measured auditory evoked potentials in 16 colored-hearing synesthetes (which they defined for the purposes of their study as those who experience colors when hearing tones or spoken utterances) and 16 non-synesthetic control participants. Results revealed that the P1, N1, and P2 components, while clearly present in both groups, were longer in latency and smaller in amplitude in synesthetes relative to controls. Using a source localization technique, the researchers estimated the sources of these differences to be increased activation in the inferior temporal region including hV4 of the synesthetes. In fact, the N1 difference was measurable just 122 ms following onset of the auditory stimulus, implying to Beeli and colleagues that, "synesthetic perceptions are automatic and fast" (382). The involvement of early auditory-evoked components in synesthetic color experience was again reported in a subsequent study using a refined oddball paradigm (Goller, Otten, and Ward 2008).

It is noteworthy that the two ERP studies showing an association between synesthetic color experience and early ERP components tested individuals exhibiting "colored-hearing synesthesia," not color-graphemic synesthesia (or perhaps at least not color-graphemic synesthesia in isolation; see Simner 2007 for a discussion of how color-graphemic synesthetes are sometimes classified as "colored hearing" synesthetes). There might be methodological advantages to testing this type of synesthesia, because the inducer (sound) and the concurrent (color) are in different modalities and, therefore, are less likely to involve neural interference of the sort that could occur when an achromatic character evokes a concurrent experience of color (Hubbard 2007).

Later components of the ERP can reflect an influence of synesthesia, too. Brang et al. (2008) measured ERPs while synesthetes and control subjects read sentences (e.g., "Is the sky __?") ending in a color word (e.g., "blue"), a color patch (e.g., o) or a grapheme that evoked a color association for the synesthetes only; the colors of these sentence-ending stimuli were either congruent or incongruent with the first part of the sentence (e.g., in the sentence "Is the sky 2?" the digit would be contextually congruent for a synesthete if it induced "blue" but would be incongruent if it induced "brown"). ERPs were time-locked to the onset of the final item in the sentence. Besides finding an effect of synesthetic congruence on early, perception-related ERP components including N1 (in synesthetes, not controls), Brang et al. also found that the achromatic digits viewed by the synesthetes, but not controls, produced a significant reduction in the negativity of the N400 component that is known to be sensitive to contextual priming. From this pattern of results the authors concluded "the color-induction process in grapheme-color synesthesia is automatic and suggests that the concurrent color sensation is treated by the brain as a meaningful stimulus subject to con-textual integration processes" (Brang et al. 2008, 424). In a follow-up study by the same group of researchers, the modulation of N1 component observed when synesthetes viewed an achromatic inducing grapheme was extended to the condition where non-synesthetic controls viewed physically colored graphemes either congruent or incongruent with the semantic context in a sentence (Brang et al. 2011). Importantly, such modulation of N1 component was not found when non-synesthetes viewed a colored patch or colored words. These results point to the similarity of synesthetes' experiences when viewing achromatic graphemes with non-synesthetes' experiences when viewing real-color graphemes, supporting the perceptual reality of synesthetic color experience.

Another tactic for studying synesthesia using ERPs is to assess whether signal components in synesthetes differ from those in non-synesthetes in response to basic sensory stimulation that itself does not evoke synesthetic experiences. So, for example, Barnett and colleagues (2008) used simple gratings and geometric forms tailored to bias ERP responses in favor of magnocellular pathway or parvocellular pathway activation. They found differences in early sensory-generated ERP components between linguistic-color synesthetes and normal controls, even though none of the visual stimuli evoked synesthetic experiences. The most pronounced difference was in a very early component arising less than 100 ms after onset of a high spatial frequency grating that, according to Barnett et al., activated parvocellular mechanisms only. The parvocellular pathway, of course, is the one associated with color vision. This represents an interesting, complimentary approach to the study of synesthesia, although the creation of stimuli that selectively isolate subpathways within a given modality can be tricky (e.g., Callaway 2005). Still, the approach reminds us of a suggestion discussed earlier in this chapter that people with a given form of synesthesia perform better than non-synesthetic observers on conventional tasks that measure sensory acuity for the modality in which synesthesia in experienced. This enhanced discrimination ability might result from inherent differences in brain connectivity between synesthetes and non-synesthetes (recall footnote 2).

Closing Comments

A paper we published several years ago (Kim, Blake, and Palmeri 2006) concluded, "Based on recent work in a number of laboratories it is now impossible to dispute that at least some forms of synesthesia entail mental experiences that have a genuine perceptual reality" (195). We acknowledge that this is a very strong claim, as others subsequently reminded us (Gheri et al. 2008), but we remain comfortable standing behind it. That said, the purpose of this chapter was not simply to weigh the evidence for—and against—this position but, instead, to identify and critique strategies deployed to test the claim. Hopefully readers are now convinced that some strategies for assessing the perceptual nature of synesthesia rest on firmer ground than do others: preferred strategies are ones that are relatively immune to response bias and expectations, and ideally ones that rest on foundational findings in perception science. We have also tried to emphasize that the question of the perceptual reality of synesthesia is distinct from the question of whether or not attention and/or awareness are essential to the phenomena. Research on synesthesia has matured considerably over the last dozen or so years, with less emphasis on case studies of one or two people and more emphasis on large subject samples that are constructed with possible subtypes of synesthesia in mind. Informal testing and clever demonstrations are giving way to more rigorous, subtle tests based on strategies that disguise the purpose and expected outcomes of the tests from those being tested. There remains, however, one bias that will be difficult to overcome: positive results are more likely to be published than negative results, and this bias can unwittingly tip the balance of evidence in favor of the "perceptual reality" hypothesis. But this sword has two edges: many existing studies, especially in the field of brain imaging, are "statistically underpowered" to use Hubbard's phrase (Hubbard 2007). To overcome this, studies using fMRI should include independent functional localizers and, when dealing with vision, retinotopic mapping; these allow investigators to focus their analyses of BOLD signal to identified brain regions. But even when armed with valid strategies, experience teaches us that not all synesthetes yield the same pattern of results, even when tested in the same laboratory under identical conditions. Individual differences in the type of synesthesia could plausibly contribute to the seemingly contradictory results currently plaguing the literature (e.g., Smilek et al. 2001 versus Sagiv, Heer, and Robertson 2006) Case studies of single individuals have played a useful role in bringing this fascinating condition into the laboratory. Now it is time to tackle the subtleties of synesthesia using group studies that employ multiple tasks (e.g., Hubbard et al. 2005) that can potentially shed light on individual differences, their possible relation to the categories of synesthesia and, perhaps, to the genetic bases of the condition (e.g., Asher et al. 2009; Tomson et al. 2011).

Finally, we need to continue placing some stock in what people with synesthesia tell us they are experiencing. A grapheme-color synesthete who describes seeing the letter A as A—and who can repeatedly match that color with high reliability—is in a unique position to know what she's experiencing and to know what it's like to have a comparable experience when viewing a real-colored letter. We are not recanting our introductory comment about the limitations of verbal reports, for it is indeed imperative to buttress those claims with carefully designed tests of performance that are sensitive to the concurrent reportedly experienced by the person. But it would be near-sighted indeed to limit our imagination of what might be possible for the human brain to conjure up in the way of perceptual experiences just because we ourselves do not have first-hand access to those experiences.

ACKNOWLEDGMENTS

This work was supported by the Korea Research Foundation Grant funded by the Korean Government (KRF-2009–332-H00011) to C-Y. K. and by the World Class University program through the National Research Foundation of Korea funded by the Ministry of Education, Science and Technology (R32–10142) to R.B.

REFERENCES

Adelson, Edward H. 2000. Lightness perception and lightness illusions. In *The new cognitive neuroscience,* ed. Michael S. Gazzaniga, 339–351. Cambridge, MA: MIT Press.

Aleman, André, Geert-Jan M. Rutten, Margriet M. Sitskoorn, Geraud Dautzenberg, and Nick F. Ramsay. 2001. Activation of striate cortex in the absence of visual stimulation: An fMRI study of synesthesia. *Neuroreport* 12 (13):2827–2830.

Anstis, Stuart M. 1974. A chart demonstrating variations in acuity with retinal position. *Vision Research* 14:589–592.

Asher, Julian E., Michael R. F. Aitken, Nasr Farooqi, Sameer Kurmani, and Simon Baron-Cohen. 2006. Diagnosing and phenotyping visual synaesthesia: a preliminary evaluation of the revised test of genuineness (TOG-R). *Cortex* 42 (2):137–146.

Asher, Julian E., Janine Lamb, Denise Brocklebank, Jean-Baptiste Cazier, Elena Maestrini, Laura Addis, Mallika Sen, Simon Baron-Cohen, and Anthony P. Monaco. 2009. A whole-genome scan and fine-mapping linkage study of auditory-visual synaesthesia reveals evidence of linkage to chromosomes 2q24, 5q33, 6p12, and 12p12. *The American Journal of Human Genetics* 84(2):279–285.

Banissy, Michael J., Vincent Walsh, and Jamie Ward. 2009. Enhanced sensory perception in synaesthesia. *Experimental Brain Research* 4: 565–571.

Bargary, Gary, and Kevin J. Mitchell. 2008. Synaesthesia and cortical connectivity. *Trends in Neuroscience* 31(7):335–342.

Barnett, Kylie J., John J. Foxe, Sophie Molholm, Simon P. Kelly, Shani Shalgi, Kevin J. Mitchell, and Fiona N. Newell. 2008. Differences in early sensory-perceptual processing in synesthesia: A visual evoked potential study. *NeuroImage* 43:605–613.

Barnett, Kylie J., and Fiona N. Newell. 2008. Synaesthesia is associated with enhanced, self-rated visual imagery. *Consciousness and Cognition* 17 (3):1032–1039.

Beauchamp, Michael S., and Tony Ro. 2008. Neural substrates of sound–touch synesthesia after a thalamic lesion. *Journal of Neuroscience* 28 (50):13696–13702.

Beeli, Gian, Michaela Esslen, and Lutz Jä ncke. 2008. Time course of neural activity correlated with colored-hearing synesthesia. *Cerebral Cortex* 18:379–385.

Blake, Randolph, René Marois, Thomas J. Palmeri, and Chai-Youn Kim. 2005. On the perceptual reality of synesthetic color. In *Synesthesia: Perspectives from Cognitive Neuroscience*, ed. Lynn C. Robertson and Noam Sagiv, 47–73. New York: Oxford University Press.

Blakemore, Sarah-Jane, Davina Bristow, Geoffrey Bird, Christopher Frith, and Jamie Ward. 2005. Somatosensory activations during the observation of touch and a case of vision-touch synaesthesia. *Brain* 128(7):1571–1583.

Bouma, Herman. 1970. Interaction effects in parafoveal letter recognition. *Nature* 226 (5241):177–178.

Brang, David, L. Edwards, Vilayanur S. Ramachandran, and Seana Coulson. 2008. Is the sky 2? Contextual priming in grapheme-color synaesthesia. *Psychological Science* 19:421–428.

Brang, David, Stanley Kanai, Vilayanur S. Ramachandran, and Seana Coulson. 2011. Contextual priming in grapheme-color synesthetes and yoked controls: 400 msec in the life of a synesthete. *Journal of Cognitive Neuroscience* 23 (7):1681–1696.

Broerse, Jack, Tony Vladusich, and Robert P. O'Shea. 1999. Colour at edges and colour spreading in McCollough effect. *Vision Research* 39:1305–1320.

Callaway, Edward M. 2005. Neural substrates within primary visual cortex for in- teractions between parallel visual pathways. *Progress in Brain Research* 149:59–64.

Carriere, Jonathan S. A., Daniel Eaton, Michael G. Reynolds, Michael J. Dixon, and Daniel Smilek. 2009. Grapheme-color synesthesia influences overt visual attention. *Journal of Cognitive Neuroscience,* 21 (2):246–258.

Chapanis, Alphonse, and Charles M. Overbey. 1971. Absolute judgments of colors using natural color names. *Perception and Psychophysics* 9:356–360.

Cohen Kadosh, Roi, Avishai Henik, Andres Catena, Vincent Walsh, and Luis J. Fuentes. 2009. Induced cross-modal synaesthetic experience without abnormal neuronal connections. *Psychological Science* 20 (2): 258–265.

Collerton, Daniel, Elaine Perry, and Ian McKeith. 2005. Why people see things that are not there: A novel perception and attention deficit model for recurrent complex visual hallucinations. *Behavioral and Brain Sciences* 28 (6):737–757.

Cytowic, Richard E. 1997. Synesthesia: phenomenology and neuropsychology. In *Synesthesia: Classic and Contemporary Readings,* ed. Simon Baron-Cohen and John E. Harrison, 17–39. Oxford: Blackwell.

——. 2002. *Synesthesia: A Union of the Senses.* Cambridge: MA, MIT Press.

Cytowic, Richard E., and David M. Eagleman. 2009. *Wednesday is Indigo Blue: Discovering the Brain of Synesthesia.* Cambridge, MA: MIT Press.

Dixon, Mike J., Daniel Smilek, Cera Cudahy, and Philip M. Merikle. 2000. Five plus two equals yellow. *Nature* 406:365.

Eagleman, David M., Arielle D. Kagan, Stephanie S. Nelson, Deepak Sagaram, and Anand K. Sarma. 2007. A standardized test battery for the study of synesthesia. *Journal of Neuroscience Methods* 159:139–1345.

Eagleman, David M., and Melvin A. Goodale. 2009. Why color synesthesia involves more than color. *Trends in Cognitive Sciences* 13 (7):288–292.

Easterman, Michael, Timothy Verstynen, Richard B. Ivry, and Lynn C. Robertson. 2006. Coming unbound: Disrupting automatic integration of synesthetic color and graphemes by TMS of the right parietal lobe. *Journal of Cognitive Neuroscience* 18:1570–1576.

Edquist, Jessica, Anina N. Rich, Cobie Brinkman, and Jason B. Mattingley. 2006. Do synesthetic colors act as unique features in visual search? *Cortex* 42:222–231.

Elias, Lorin J., Deborah M. Saucier, Colleen Hardie, and Gordon E. Sarty. 2003. Dissociating semantic and perceptual components of synaesthesia: Behavioural and functional neuroanatomical investigations. *Cognitive Brain Research* 16:232–237.

Gamlin, Paul D. R., Hongyu Zhang, Alistair Harlow, and John L. Barbur. (1998). Pupil responses to stimulus color, structure and light flux increments in the rhesus monkey. *Vision Research* 38 (21):3353–3358.

Gheri, Carolina, Susan Chopping, and Michael J. Morgan. 2008. Synaesthetic colors do not camouflage form in visual search. *Proceedings of the Royal Society of London B: Biological Sciences* 275:841–846.

Goller, Aviva I., Leun J. Otten, and Jamie Ward. 2008. Seeing sounds and hearing colors: An event-related potential study of auditory-visual synesthesia. *Journal of Cognitive Neuroscience* 21:1869–1881.

Gorea, Andrei, and Thomas V. Papathomas. 1993. Double-opponency as a generalized concept in texture segregation illustrated with color, luminance and orientation defined stimuli. *Journal of the Optical Society of America A* 10:1451–1462.

Grill-Spector, Kalanit, Richard Henson, and Alex Martin. 2006. Repetition and the brain: Neural models of stimulus-specific effects. *Trends in Cognitive Sciences* 10:15–23.

Grossenbacher, Peter G., and Chrostopher T. Lovelace. 2001. Mechanisms of synesthesia: Cognitive and physiological constraints. *Trends in Cognitive Sciences* 5:36–41

Hallett, Mark. 2000. Transcranial magnetic stimulation and the human brain. *Nature* 406:147–150.

Hänggi, Jürgen, Diana Wotruba, and Lutz Jäncke. 2011. Globally altered structural brain network topology in grapheme-color synesthesia. *Journal of Neuroscience* 31 (15):5816–5828.

Hong, Sang Wook, and Randolph Blake. 2008. Early visual mechanisms do not contribute to synesthetic color experience. *Vision Research* 48 (8): 1018–1026.

Hoffman, Ralph E., Jill Rapaport, Carolyn M. Mazure, and Donald M. Quinlan. 1999. Selective speech perception alterations in schizophrenic patients reporting hallucinated "voices." *American Journal of Psychiatry* 156:393–399.

Hubbard, Edward M. 2007. Neurophysiology of synesthesia. *Current Psychiatry Reports* 9 (3):193–199.

Hubbard, Edward M., A. Cyrus Arman, Vilayanur S. Ramachandran, and Geoffrey M. Boynton. 2005. Individual differences among grapheme-color synesthetes: Brain-behavior correlations. *Neuron* 45 (6):975–985.

Hubbard, Edward M., Sanjay Manohar, and Vilayanur S. Ramachandran. 2006. Contrast affects the strength of synesthetic colors. *Cortex* 42 (2):183–194.

Hupé, Jean-Michael, Cécile Bordier, and Michel Dojat. 2012. The neural bases of grapheme-color synesthesia are not localized in real-color sensitive areas. *Cerebral Cortex* 22:1622–1633.

Hurvich, Leo M., and Dorothea Jameson.1957. An opponent-process theory of color vision. *Psychological Review* 64:384–404.

Jameson, Dorothea, and Leo M. Hurvich. 1972. Color adaptation: Sensitivity, contrast, afterimages. In *Handbook of Sensory Physiology Vol. VII/4*, ed. Dorothea Jameson and Leo M. Hurvich, 568–581. New York: Springer.

Jäncke, Lutz, Gian Beeli, Cornelia Eulig, and Jürgen Hänggi. 2009. The neuroanatomy of grapheme-color synesthesia. *European Journal of Neuroscience* 29:1287–1293.

Kim, Chai-Youn, and Randolph Blake. 2005. Watercolor illusion induced by synesthetic color. *Perception* 34 (12):1501–1507.

——. 2007. Illusory colors promote interocular grouping during binocular rivalry. *Psychonomic Bulletin & Review* 14 (2):356–362.

Kim, Chai-Youn, Randolph Blake, and Thomas J. Palmeri. 2006. Perceptual interaction between real and synesthetic colors. *Cortex* 42 (2):195–203.

Kooi, Frank L., Alex Toet, Srimant P. Tripathy, and Dennis M. Levi. 1994. The effect of similarity and duration on spatial interaction in peripheral vision. *Spatial Vision* 8:255–279.

Kosslyn, Stephen M., Alvaro Pascual-Leone, Olivier Felician, Susana Camposano, Julian P. Keenan, William L. Thompson, Giorgio Ganis, Katherine E. Sukel, and Nathaniel M. Alpert. 1999. The role of area 17 in visual imagery: Convergent evidence from PET and rTMS. *Science* 284:167–170.

Laeng, Bruno. 2009. Searching through synaesthetic colors. *Attention, Perception, & Psychophysics* 71 (7):1461–1467.

Laeng, Bruno, Frode Svartdal, and Hella Oelmann. 2004. Does color synesthesia pose a paradox for early-selection theories of attention? *Psychological Science* 15 (4):277–281.

Luck, Steven J. 2005. *An introduction to the event-related potential technique*. Cambridge, MA: MIT Press.

Ludwig, Casimir J. H., and Iain D. Gilchrist. 2003. Target similarity affects saccade curvature away from irrelevant onsets. *Experimental Brain Research* 152:60–69.

Mattingley, Jason B., Anina N. Rich, Greg Yelland, and John L. Bradshaw. 2001. Unconscious priming eliminates automatic binding of colour and alphanumeric form in synaesthesia. *Nature* 410:580–582.

McCollough, Celeste. 1965. Color adaptation of edge-detectors in the human visual system. *Science* 149 (3688):1115–1116.

Muggleton, Neil, Elias Tsakanikos, Vincent Walsh, and Jamie Ward. 2007. Disruption of synaesthesia following TMS of the right posterior parietal cortex. *Neuropsychologia* 45:1582–1585.

Myles, Kathleen M., Mike J. Dixon, Daniel Smilek, and Philip M. Merikle. 2003. Seeing double: The role of meaning in alphanumeric-colour synaesthesia. *Brain and Cognition* 53 (2):342–345.

Nikolić, Danko, Philipp Lichti, and Wolf Singer. 2007. Color opponency in synaesthetic experiences. *Psychological Science* 18 (6):481–486.

Nijboer, Tanja C. W., and Bruno Laeng. 2013. Synaesthesia, eye-movements, and pupillometry. In *Oxford Handbook of Synaesthesia*, ed. Julia Simner and Edward M. Hubbard, 334–346. Oxford: Oxford University Press.

Nijboer, Tanja. C. W., Gabriela Satris, and Stefan van der Stigchel. 2011. The influence of synesthesia on eye movements: No synesthetic pop-out in an oculomotor target selection task. *Consciousness and Cognition* 20 (4):1193–1200.

Nijboer, Tanja C. W., and Stefan van der Stigchel. 2009. Is attention essential for inducing synesthetic colors? Evidence from oculomotor distractors. *Journal of Vision* 9 (6):1–9.

Nisbett, Richard E., and Timothy D. Wilson. 1977. Telling more than we can know: Verbal reports on mental processes. *Psychological Review* 84 (3):231–259.

Nunn, Julia A., Lloyd J. Gregory, Michael Brammer, Steven C. R. Williams, David M. Parslow, Michael J. Morgan, Robin G. Morris, Edward T. Bullmore, Simon Baron-Cohen, and Jeffrey A. Gray. 2002. Functional magnetic resonance imaging of synesthesia: activation of V4/V8 by spoken words. *Nature Neuroscience* 5:371–375.

O'Connor, Daniel H., Miki M. Fukui, Mark A. Pinsk, and Sabine Kastner. 2002. Attention modulates responses in the human lateral geniculate nucleus. *Nature Neuroscience* 5 (11):1203–1209.

Paffen, Chris L. E., Maarten J. van der Smagt, and Tanja C. W. Nijboer. 2011. Colour-grapheme synaesthesia affects binocular vision. *Frontiers in Psychology* 2 (314):1–6.

Palmeri, Thomas J., Randolph Blake, René Marois, Marci A. Flanery, and William Whetsell Jr. 2002. The perceptual reality of synesthetic colors. *Proceedings of the National Academy of Sciences of the United States of America* 99 (6):4127–4131.

Papathomas, Thomas V., Andrei Gorea, and Bela Julesz. 1991. Two carriers for motion perception: Color and luminance. *Vision Research* 31 (11):1883–1892.

Papathomas, Thomas V., Illona Kovács, and Tiffany Conway. 2005. Interocular grouping in binocular rivalry: Basic attributes and combinations. In *Binocular Rivalry*, ed. David Alais and Randolph Blake, 155–168. Cambridge, MA: MIT Press.

Paulsen, Helle G., and Bruno Laeng. 2006. Pupillometry of grapheme-color synaesthesia. *Cortex* 42:290–294.

Pinna, Baingio, 2005. The role of Gestalt principle of similarity in the watercolour illusion. *Spatial Vision* 21:1–8.

Ramachandran, Vilayanur S., and Shai Azoulai. 2006. Synesthetically induced colors evoke apparent-motion perception. *Perception* 35 (11):1557–1560.

Ramachandran, Vilayanur S., and Edward M. Hubbard. 2001. Psychophysical investigations into the neural basis of synaesthesia. *Proceedings of the Royal Society of London B: Biological Sciences* 268 (1470):979–983.

——. 2003. Hearing colors, tasting shapes. *Scientific American* 288 (5):53–59.

Rich, Anina N., and Jason B. Mattingley. 2005. Can attention modulate color-graphemic syn-esthesia? In *Synesthesia: Perspectives from Cognitive Neuroscience*, ed. Lynn C. Robertson, and Noam Sagiv, 108–123. New York: Oxford University Press.

——. 2013. The role of attention in synaesthesia. In *Oxford Handbook of Synaesthesia*, ed. Julia Simner and Edward M. Hubbard, 265–282. Oxford: Oxford University Press.

Rich, Anina N., Mark A. Williams, Aina Puce, Ari Syngeniotis, Matthew A. Howard, Rancis McGlone, and Jason B. Mattingley. 2006. Neural correlates of imagined and synaesthetic colours. *Neuropsychologia* 44 (14):2918–2925.

Rothen, Nicolas, and Beat Meier. 2009. Do synesthetes have a general advantage in visual search and episodic memory? A case for group studies. *PLoS ONE* 4 (4): e5037. doi:10.1371/journal.pone.0005037.

Rouw, Romke. 2013. Synaesthesia, hyper-connectivity and diffusion tensor imaging. In *Oxford Handbook of Synaesthesia*, ed. Julia Simner and Edward M. Hubbard, 500–518. Oxford: Oxford University Press.

Rouw, Romke, and H. Steven Scholte. 2007. Increased structural connectivity in grapheme-color synesthesia. *Nature Neuroscience* 10:792–797.

——. 2010. Neural basis of individual differences in synesthetic experiences. *Journal of Neuroscience* 30 (18):6205–6213.

Sagiv, Noam, Jeffrey Heer, and Lynn C. Robertson. 2006. Does binding of synesthetic color to the evoking grapheme require attention? *Cortex* 42 (2):232–242.

Schiltz, Kolja, Karen Trocha, Bernardina M. Wieringa, Hinderk M. Emrich, Sönke Johannes, and Thomas F. Münte. 1999. Neurophysiological aspects of synesthetic experience. *Journal of Neuropsychiatry and Clinical Neurosciences* 11:58–65.

Shapley, Robert, and Michael J. Hawken. 2011. Color in the cortex: single- and double opponent cells. *Vision Research* 51:701–717.

Shergill, Sukhwinder S., Michael J. Brammer, Rimmei Fukuda, Steven C. R. Williams, Robin, M. Murray, and Philip K. McGuire. 2003. Engagement of brain areas implicated in process-ing inner speech in people with auditory hallucinations. *The British Journal of Psychiatry* 183:525–531.

Simner, Julia. 2007. Beyond perception: Synaesthesia as a psycholinguistic phenomenon. *Trends in Cognitive Sciences* 11:23–29.

Smilek, Daniel, Mike J. Dixon, Cera Cudahy, and Philip M. Merikle. 2001. Synaesthetic pho-tisms influence visual perception. *Journal of Cognitive Neuroscience* 13 (7):930–996.

Smilek, Daniel, Mike J. Dixon, and Philip M. Merikle. 2003. Synaesthetic photisms guide atten-tion. *Brain and Cognition* 53 (2):364–367.

Sperling, Julia M., David Prvulovic, David E. J. Linden, Wolf Singer, and Aglaja Stirn. 2006. Neuronal correlates of graphemic colour synaesthesia: A fMRI study. *Cortex* 42: 295–303.

Steven, Megan S., and Colin Blakemore. 2004. Visual synaesthesia in the blind. *Perception* 33 (7):855–868.

Steven, Megan S., Peter C. Hansen, and Colin Blakemore. 2006. Activation of color-selective areas of the visual cortex in a blind synesthete. *Cortex* 42 (2): 304–308.

Tang, Joey, Jamie Ward, and Brian Butterworth. 2008. Number forms in the brain. *Journal of Cognitive Neuroscience* 20 (9):1547–1556.

Terhune, Devin B., Sarah Tai, Alan Cowey, Tudor Popescu, and Roi Cohen Kadosh. 2011. Enhanced cortical excitability in grapheme-color synesthesia and its modulation. *Current Biology* 21: 2006–2009.

Tomson, Steffie N., Nili Avidan, Kwanghyuk Lee, Anand K. Sarma, Rejnal Tushe, Dianna M. Milewicz, Molly Bray, Suzanne M. Leal, and David M. Eagleman. 2011. The genetics of colored sequence synesthesia: Suggestive evidence of linkage to 16q and genetic heterogeneity for the condition. *Behavioral Brain Research* 223:48–52.

Tong, Frank. 2003. Primary visual cortex and visual awareness. *Nature Reviews Neuroscience* 4:219–229.

Treisman, Anne M., and Garry Gelade. 1980. A feature-integration theory of attention. *Cognitive Psychology* 12 (1):97–136.

van Leeuwen, Tessa M., Karl M. Petersson, and Peter Hagoort. 2010. Synaesthetic colour in the brain: Beyond color areas. A functional magnetic resonance imaging study of synaesthetes and matched controls. *PLoS ONE* 5 (8): e12074. doi:10.1371/journal.pone.0012074

Vul, Edward, Erin Krizay, and Donald I. A. MacLeod. 2008. The McCollough effect reflects permanent and transient adaptation in early visual cortex. *Journal of Vision* 8 (12):4.1–12. <http://journalofvision.org/8/12/4/> doi:10.1167/8.12.4.

Vul, Edward, and Donald I. A. MacLeod. 2006. Contingent aftereffects distinguish conscious and preconscious color processing. *Nature Neuroscience* 9:873–874.

Wandell, Brian A., and Jonathan Winawer. 2011. Imaging retinoptic maps in the human brain. *Vision Research* 51:718–737.

Weiss, Peter H., and Gerone R. Fink. 2009. Grapheme-colour synaesthetes show increased grey matter volumes of parietal and fusiform cortex. *Brain* 132:65–70.

Weiss, Peter H., N. Jon Shah, Ivan Toni, Karl Zilles, and Gerone R. Fink. 2001. Associating colours with people: a case of chromatic-lexical synaesthesia. *Cortex* 37:750–753.

Weiss, Peter H., Karl Zilles, and Gereon R. Fink. 2005. When visual perception causes feeling: enhanced cross-modal processing in grapheme-color synesthesia. *NeuroImage* 28:859–868.

Witthoft, Nathan, and Jonathan Winawer. 2006. Synesthetic colors determined by having colored refrigerator magnets in childhood. *Cortex* 42 (2):175–183.

Woodman, Geoffrey F. 2010. A brief introduction to the use of event-related potentials in studies of perception and attention. *Attention, Perception, & Psychophysics* 72:2031–2046.

Wright, William D., and Frederick. H. G. Pitt. 1934. Hue-discrimination in normal colour-vision. *Proceedings of the Physical Society* 46:459–473.

Yaro, Caroline, and Jamie Ward. 2007. Searching for Shereshevskii: What is superior about the memory of synaesthetes? *The Quarterly Journal of Experimental Psychology* 60 (5):681–695.

CHAPTER 16

SYNESTHESIA AND BINDING

BRYAN D. ALVAREZ AND LYNN C. ROBERTSON

INTRODUCTION

Many synesthetic experiences such as colors triggered by letters, numbers, sequences, auras, flavors, spoken words, and touch are perceived by some synesthetes as projected in specific locations in the external world. Of these many varieties, colored graphemes (e.g., letters and numbers) have been studied most extensively and the combined knowledge collected from grapheme-color synesthetes will form the basis for this chapter. Our aim is to understand when and how synesthetic experiences can be bound by attention to a specific location in space, similar to the way that typical features including colors are bound on a daily basis.

One fascinating paradox that remains unanswered in the study of grapheme-color synesthesia is how it is possible for a synesthete who perceives synesthetically colored letters to experience print and synesthetic color simultaneously, appearing in the same place without the two colors blending together. As an example, imagine looking at this text printed in black ink, but also seeing "orange" in the same place at the same time. A grapheme-color synesthete that projects color onto text might describe seeing a synesthetic orange color appearing in the same place as the black printed letters but the colors would remain distinct. Likewise, synesthetes that see their colors in their mind's eye still report the dual experience of print color and synesthetic colors that do not interact. Synesthetes sometimes may describe the synesthetic color in various ways: as a transparency, as "filling in" the letter, or as being in the mind's eye. However, no length of description can capture the full experience for one who does not have synesthesia. The black color of the text in this example is the normal form of color that is triggered by different wavelengths reflected from printed pigments and received by the retina. We will refer to this color as "print color." The other form of color is synesthetic color, which in this example arises when *shape* (of a grapheme) triggers hue selective networks to produce the phenomenological experience of color. We will refer to synesthetic color (and other synesthetic experiences) as "concurrents" to maintain the tradition within the field (Dixon and Smilek 2005). For the same reason, the stimulus (e.g., a grapheme) that triggers synesthetic color will be called the "inducer."

Are synesthetic colors bound in perception, and if so are they bound through the same mechanisms as print colors? The answers to these questions are still unknown and are complex because of individual differences between synesthetes, and also the level of binding in question. This chapter will give an overview of what is known about this issue and summarize current models for synesthetic binding. It will build upon the synesthetic binding model originally proposed by Robertson (2003) to explain the mechanism of perceptual binding of synesthetic color in grapheme-color synesthesia, especially those unusual cases in which synesthetic and print colors appear to be in the same place simultaneously. We will first summarize how perceptual binding is thought to occur normally in typical brains, and then discuss how the same mechanism may account for binding of synesthetic color and graphemes in at least some grapheme-color synesthetes. We will also review existing theories that incorporate the need for attention into synesthetic experience and will briefly suggest how this binding theory may account for other forms of synesthesia. Although it is not fully understood whether synesthetic color is bound like print color, current evidence suggest that if synesthetic color *is* bound, it is bound through the same attention-dependent integration of feature maps that occurs in other forms of binding, making synesthesia an excellent model for understanding binding in the average human brain.

WHAT A SYNESTHETIC BINDING MODEL NEEDS TO ACCOUNT FOR

Any account of synesthetic binding must acknowledge many years of research showing that synesthetic experiences are automatic, consistent, and can be perceptual-like in nature (not just memories, metaphors, or make-believe). A model of synesthetic binding must also take into consideration evidence that synesthetic color and print color are not represented in exactly the same way. For example, synesthetic color does not "pop out" in visual search like printed color (Palmeri et al. 2002; Sagiv, Heer, and Robertson 2006), nor does it show effects as robust or consistent between subjects as printed color (Hubbard et al. 2005) or rely on exactly the same neural mechanisms (van Leeuwen, Petersson, and Hagoort 2010). Synesthetic color normally requires attention to the inducer, to be perceptually bound with it, to be spatially localized, and to be perceived consciously (for a review of attention see Rich and Mattingley, Chapter 14, this volume). A role for attention in synesthetic experience has been supported with only rare exception, possibly due to individual differences in a handful of synesthetes (Smilek, Dixon, and Merikle 2005; Wagar et al. 2002). Lastly, a binding model of synesthesia must account for the synesthetic paradox where synesthetic (grapheme) inducers and printed (color) concurrents can appear co-localized simultaneously. Ideally, this model should also account for individual differences in subjective experience amongst grapheme-color synesthetes, and be able to account for perceptual binding in other forms of synesthesia if and when it exists. To date, no single theory can meet all of these criteria perfectly, which leaves open the opportunity for exploration into a very important aspect of synesthesia research, namely the perceptual binding of synesthetic concurrents.

WHAT IS PERCEPTUAL BINDING?

After visual information leaves the retina, it is segmented into many different types of features, including hue, luminance, size, shape, motion, etc. (DeYoe and Van Essen 1988; Livingstone and Hubel 1988). The brain must then bind these many segmented features correctly into different objects. For example, imagine you just woke up for an early breakfast and you want to have a sip of orange juice before adding creamer to your coffee. You reach for the orange cylindrical glass of juice while avoiding the blue creamer carton. As you look out upon the table, your brain segments orange from blue, cylinder from rectangle, tall from short, and many other featural dimensions of the objects before you. Quickly, the brain then "binds" these individual features into their correct objects and in the correct locations to give you an accurate view of the layout before you. If there had been a problem with the binding, you might have unexpectedly taken a sip of cream instead.

So how is this "binding" achieved? Decoding the mechanisms underlying this "binding problem" (Robertson 2003) presents a challenge for researchers, and finding an adequate model for the study of binding in humans has been a priority. Decades ago, behavioral studies revealed that features in a display could be bound in perception incorrectly, and these were termed "illusory conjunctions" (Treisman and Schmidt 1982). In an illusory conjunction, features (e.g., color and shape) are perceived to be conjoined in a way that is not consistent with their real-world properties. For example, in a real-world display of colored printed letters, an orange "O" and a blue "B" might appear to the observer incorrectly in the opposite colors of orange "B" and blue "O" under special circumstances. For cognitively healthy subjects, these circumstances are not easily achieved, and typically require both colored letters to be presented simultaneously in close proximity for extremely brief periods of time. In rare cases of bilateral brain damage to the parietal lobes, illusory conjunctions are much more common as will be discussed later. Intrusion errors, replacing one color with another that is not present at all (e.g., seeing a green "B"), are far more rare than illusory conjunctions, suggesting that the problem is a misbinding of existing features rather than a generalized error of reporting arbitrarily incorrect features. Binding errors seldom occur in feature search tasks with only one dimension of difference (e.g., searching for a blue "B" amongst orange "B"s (only the color is different) or a blue "B" amongst blue "O"s (only the shape is different)). Instead, it is when attention is limited by the complexity and diversity of a scene that binding becomes a problem (Treisman 1999). This research supports the idea that the binding problem is one of conjoining the right features into the correct object representations when multiple features of the same domain (e.g., orange versus blue color and cylinder versus rectangular shape in the breakfast example) are competing for attention.

The question of binding has been central to an influential theory of attention, namely Feature Integration Theory (FIT; Treisman and Gelade 1980). According to FIT, spatial attention is required to bind features (e.g., color, shape) of a multi-itemed display into correctly bound objects. FIT has received strong support by those researching the deficits in attention suffered by brain damaged patients. When attentional mechanisms are severely impaired by a stroke or other brain damage, illusory conjunctions can become quite common even under free viewing conditions. One of the most striking cases of a binding problem was studied in patient RM, a 58-year-old man who suffered nearly symmetrical bilateral parieto-occipital lesions resulting in Balint's syndrome (Friedman-Hill, Robertson, and Treisman 1995; Robertson 2004; Robertson et al. 1997). RM could perceive an object but could not localize it to a spatial location. In other words, he could not bind spatial information correctly with object features present in a scene. Furthermore, when RM was presented with an array of objects he would describe seeing only one and could not shift his attention to search for others. In fact, his spatial abilities were so poor that he could not correctly discriminate the horizontal position of a target (whether it was on the left or right of a screen) even when it was presented alone with no distracters. As a result, and consistent with FIT, he was often unable to bind features such as color and shape together in perception. For instance, when shown two letters X and O colored in red and blue respectively, he frequently reported illusory conjunctions (i.e., reversed colors) even with up to 10 seconds of viewing time. RM also exhibited similar illusory conjunctions of color and size, and motion and shape (Bernstein and Robertson 1998). Despite RM's problem binding features accurately in space, he could identify (but not localize) targets in a feature search display (e.g., a red dot among several blue dots) when the target only differed from distracters in terms of one feature. RM's unique case supports the theoretical view that features undergo a certain degree of processing prior to awareness and without spatial attention (Treisman and Gelade 1980). However, attention is needed to correctly bind features into the correct representation and in the correct location in space. RM's data also make a strong case for the role of the parietal cortex in spatial attention and feature binding.

Another more common attentional problem called visual spatial neglect interferes with binding only on one side of space (Cohen Kadosh and Rafal 1991) and most often occurs with a unilateral lesion of the cortex that interferes with fronto-parietal or cortico-subcortical communication (see Bartolomeo, De Schotten, and Doricchi 2007). Visual neglect is different from hemianopsia caused by lesions in primary visual cortex, in which a patient is blind in one visual field but is still aware that the blind side of space exists and can accommodate accordingly. A patient with neglect cannot attend to the neglected part of the visual field and appears to have no awareness of its existence.

Studies of patients with neglect have contributed to understanding some of the subtleties of the binding problem and its relationship to attention. Stimuli presented to the
neglected visual field of a patient may not reach awareness but information is still processed and integrated to a certain degree. For example, van Vleet and Robertson (2009)
showed that patients' performance was affected equally in a visual *feature* priming task
(Figure 16.1) where features were presented to the neglected versus normal visual fields.

Performance between neglected and normally perceived sides was also equal between
conditions when the stimulus presentation time made the display easily visible (75%
corrected hit rate) versus hardly visible (25% corrected hit rate). When the same task
involved a target embedded in a conjunction search display (where attention and correct binding would be necessary), patients with neglect performed well in the conjunction condition (Figure 16.2) when detection was thresholded at 75% (easy condition),
but performed very poorly when the detection threshold was adjusted to 25% detection
(hard condition). This difference was not due to differences in difficulty between search

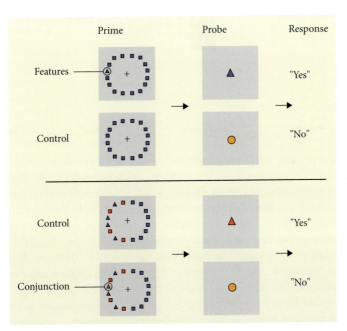

FIGURE 16.1 Schematic representation of the priming experiment of van Vleet and Robertson
(2009, figure 2). Feature, conjunction, or associated neutral primes were presented at threshold presentation time that resulted in 75% (easy) or 25% (hard) correct responses for each
participant as determined using an adaptive staircase procedure. Primes were followed by a
probe presented at central fixation; participants were instructed to make a speeded verbal discrimination ("yes" or "no"), indicating whether the probe was the target or not. Reproduced
from Thomas M. Van Vleet and Lynn C. Robertson, Implicit representation and explicit
detection of features in patients with hemispatial neglect, *Brain*, 2009, 132 (7), pp. 1889,
by permission of Oxford University Press [http://ukcatalogue.oup.com/]. For permission to
reuse this material, please visit http://www.oup.co.uk/academic/rights/permissions

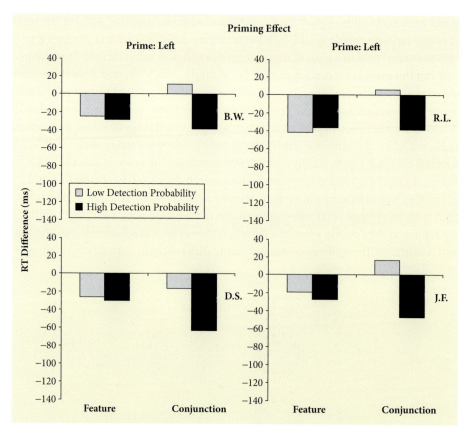

FIGURE 16.2 The priming effect per condition (feature or conjunction prime/high threshold presentation time (TPT) or low TPT) in van Vleet and Robertson (2009). Experiment 1: RT to relevant probe presented at central fixation when preceded by a conjunction or feature prime minus when it was preceded by a neutral conjunction or feature display. Results show that there was no significant effect of attention on magnitude of feature priming whereas in the conjunction prime condition, only primes presented at the high TPT duration produced a significant priming effect compared with the low TPT condition. Reproduced from Thomas M. Van Vleet and Lynn C. Robertson, Implicit representation and explicit detection of features in patients with hemispatial neglect, *Brain*, 2009, 132 (7), pp. 1889, by permission of Oxford University Press [http://ukcatalogue.oup.com/]. For permission to reuse this material, please visit http://www.oup.co.uk/academic/rights/permissions.

displays because difficulty was equated using an adaptive staircase procedure for each condition. Rather, these results suggest that patients with neglect can represent features equally well whether the features are perceived explicitly or only represented implicitly, but cannot implicitly represent conjunctions within their neglected field when detection is hard.

Overall, research has taught us that the visual system can represent features implicitly, even when they are presented briefly, below detection thresholds, or among multiple objects. However, to correctly bind different features in the correct spatial locations in a quickly presented display, attention must be utilized. When attention is redirected or lacking, illusory conjunctions occur.

A drawback to interpreting the findings from neglect patients is that they often suffer severe and extensive brain damage that affects motivation, basic perceptual abilities, and other factors beyond attentional control. To better understand the normal binding process what is needed is a healthy group of subjects that bind features in a way that is consistent with normal binding, but also distinguishable enough to isolate from normal perception in control populations.

BACKGROUND ON BINDING IN SYNESTHESIA

One reason synesthesia, and grapheme-color in particular, is such an interesting model to help understand the binding problem is that these synesthetes experience an unusual binding of color to form that is more easily induced and stable than illusory conjunctions. Unlike patients with neglect or Balint's syndrome, synesthetes are cognitively and neurologically normal. Synesthetic color can coexist with print color but remains distinct from it in most cases, so synesthetes experience normal binding of both print color and synesthetic color separately. Thus, studying the underlying networks involved when isolating synesthetic color specifically may be a way to reveal the underlying mechanisms of binding more generally. Esterman et al. (2006) proposed the term "hyper-binding" to suggest that synesthetes have additional binding of features not found in non-synesthetes. We expand upon this concept now and clarify the binding model for grapheme-color synesthetes, suggesting that when synesthetic color is bound it may be through the same binding mechanisms as normal feature binding, with the feature of synesthetic color simply arising through an atypical route (e.g., hue induced by shape; see Robertson 2003).

Before explaining synesthetic binding in more detail, it is important to mention two caveats. The first caveat is that not all grapheme-color synesthetes may bind color to form in the same way, and in fact some (or most) may not bind color at all, or may not bind it to an external spatial location in the same way print color appears to be bound. The difference here has been proposed by some to be between projector and associator synesthetes; the former seem to experience synesthetic color externally on the page, and the later experience their concurrent colors only in their "mind's eye." However, we remain agnostic to the exact nature of this phenomenological distinction. The second caveat is that our binding model may not apply to all forms of synesthesia, but may offer an explanation for phenomenological experiences of at least some forms of synesthesia besides grapheme-color, in which the concurrent experience appears to be attention dependent or bound to a spatial location. Since the majority of research on synesthesia has focused on grapheme-color types we will describe this pool of research as it reflects on a binding model and speculate about other forms of synesthesia afterwards.

SYNESTHETIC BINDING PART I: REPRESENTATION OF FEATURES

The case where synesthetic and print colors appear in the same place at the same time without blending implies that these two forms of color maintain separate feature representations. Importantly, however, the two color signals may combine when synesthetic and print colors are the same (Alvarez and Robertson *in press*), implying that they converge at some point in visual processing. How can a model of synesthetic binding account for both competition and convergence of print and synesthetic hues depending on their similarity? At least one answer involves the unique way that synesthetic color is induced. Here we will begin with a summary of early visual processing and then summarize higher-order attention-based systems to fully represent the binding of synesthetic color.

Grapheme-induced color cannot form until, during, or after graphemes, or at least their components (Brang et al. 2010), are represented. It has also been suggested that synesthetic color may not arise until after the meaning of the grapheme is registered by higher cortical areas that feed back to earlier visual areas (Grossenbacher and Lovelace 2001; Smilek et al. 2001). However, the normal process of color formation begins much earlier with trichromatic cone receptors in the retina leading to an opponent system in the lateral geniculate nucleus of the thalamus (LGN; De Valois, Abromov, and Jacobs 1966), and transitioning into double opponent systems in area V1 that maintain color constancy (Conway 2001). Hue-selective cortical columns within early visual areas have been identified and named in areas V1 ("blobs"; Xiao et al. 2007), V2 ("thin stripes"; Xiao, Wang, and Felleman 2003), and V4 ("globs"; Conway and Tsao 2009; Tanigawa, Lu, and Roe 2010). It is not known exactly how these hue-selective columns interact to produce perceived hue, although blobs in V1 have been shown to connect anatomically to thin stripes in V2 (Livingstone and Hubel 1984) and thin stripes project to large patches in V4 (Felleman and Van Essen 1991). It is likely that color blending occurs at some stage before V4 and that multiple hue-selective columns in this region can be active simultaneously without blending to represent the experience of a multicolored world.

BRAIN-BASED MODELS OF SYNESTHETIC COLOR

There are several different theories of how synesthetic color is induced and what cortical areas are involved, which are relevant to understanding synesthetic binding. Color and letter networks may be connected via direct projections between hue-selective and grapheme-selective cortical maps (Brang et al. 2010; Hubbard 2007; Rouw and Scholte 2007) and the presence of these direct anatomical and functional pathways may vary between synesthetes (van Leeuwen, den Ouden, and Hagoort, 2011). Synesthetic color is likely influenced functionally via cortical disinhibition or unmasking from a higher-order nexus (Cohen Kadosh and Walsh 2008; Grossenbacher and Lovelace 2001), or via re-entrant feedback from more anterior areas of the temporal lobes involving letter meaning (Smilek et al. 2001). Finally, synesthetic color may be perceptually bound via direct (Felleman and Van Essen 1991) or indirect pathways between occipito-parietal regions such as area V4 and the intraparietal sulcus (IPS) (Esterman et al. 2006; Robertson 2003; van Leeuwen et al. 2011).

Brain-based studies of grapheme-color synesthesia offer much support for the involvement of ventral color-selective visual areas in representing synesthetic color. Functional magnetic resonance imaging (fMRI), positron emission tomography (PET), and magnetoencephalography (MEG) studies consistently show increased activation in color-selective area V4 when synesthetes are presented with achromatic printed graphemes or spoken words (Brang et al. 2010; Hubbard et al. 2005; Nunn et al. 2002; Paulesu et al. 1995; Sperling et al. 2006; Steven, Hansen, and Blakemore 2006; van Leeuwen, Petersson, and Hagoort 2010) in contrast to a non-grapheme baseline. Some fMRI studies that do not report V4 activation during synesthetic viewing presented graphemes in baseline conditions, which may have negated the effects (Aleman et al. 2001; Weiss, Zilles, and Fink 2005). EEG and MEG studies have shown that synesthetic concurrent-related increases in activity can occur quickly (e.g., by 114 ms) after stimulus onset within the ventral stream (Beeli, Esslen, and Jäncke 2008; Brang et al. 2010), and neuroanatomical studies (diffusion tensor imaging (DTI), voxel-based morphometry (VBM)) have provided some evidence that ventral stream areas, including area V4, have differences in white matter coherence and cortical thickness and/or surface area in synesthetes (Rouw and Scholte 2007, 2010; Weiss and Fink 2008).

Brang et al. (2010) propose a cascaded cross-tuning model of synesthetic color processing to explain how synesthetic color arises (Figure 16.3). The team collected MEG data from four grapheme-color synesthetes, all of whom experienced color projected onto the page (projector synesthetes). MEG allows for millisecond temporal resolution and millimeter spatial resolution, making it an excellent tool to analyze the functional activation of synesthetic activity in real time. The color-selective region V4 of the ventral occipital cortex and grapheme-selective region (posterior temporal grapheme area (PTGA)) just anterior to V4, were first localized. Next, achromatic graphemes that induced synesthetic color concurrents were presented to synesthetes while MEG data were recorded. Activity within the PTGA region of interest (ROI) differed significantly from baseline early on for synesthetes (105 –109 ms) and for a group of matched non- synesthete controls (115 –119 ms) with the onset and amount of activity not varying between the groups. However, synesthetes also showed significant activity within area V4 (111–114 ms onset) while controls did not at any point in time. Thus, both groups processed graphemes similarly whereas graphemes also triggered color activity early and automatically only in synesthetes. The team suggests that direct projections from PTGA to V4 account for the rapid parallel activation of color as graphemes are being processed. According to their cascaded cross-tuning model (illustrated in Figure 16.3), synesthetic color first begins to emerge when the

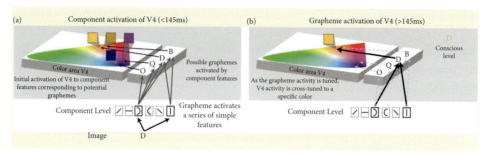

FIGURE 16.3 Cascaded cross-tuning model of synesthesia proposed by Brang et al. (2010). (a) Initial processing. As in hierarchical feature models of grapheme processing, visual input prior to 145 ms activates component features (line segments, curves, etc.) and partially activates graphemes comprised of those features. Horizontal connections between grapheme units and V4 afford partial activations of associated colors. (b) Subsequent processing. A competitive activation process results in the activation of the grapheme most consistent with bottom-up and top-down activations as well as its associated color. The synesthete's conscious experience of an orange D reflects only the final stage of activation. Reprinted from *NeuroImage*, 53 (1), D. Brang, E. M. Hubbard, S. Coulson, M. Huang, and V. S. Ramachandran, Magnetoencephalography reveals early activation of V4 in grapheme-color synesthesia, pp. 268–274, Copyright (2010), with permission from Elsevier.

components of a grapheme are processed and trigger a broad range of hue maps via direct projections to area V4. As grapheme components are assembled into a completed letter shape, increased interaction between PTGA and V4 leads to a convergence on a single grapheme shape and a single hue map, creating a specific and consistent shape-induced synesthetic color. This idea has support from a recent finding that a subsection of V4 does contain hue-selective maps in macaques (Tanigawa, Lu, and Roe 2010) and from developmental theories suggesting that synesthesia arises from a lack of cortical pruning during infant development (Maurer and Mondloch 2005).

Like all studies, the study by Brang et al. (2010) has some limitations that can be addressed in the future. The team used a relatively small sample of synesthetes, all of whom were classified by self-report as projectors based on their phenomenology. Inferring activity patterns across all grapheme-color synesthetes based on data from a subset of projectors alone is not trivial. Researchers differ in their opinions of whether grapheme-color synesthetes should be classified categorically (Dixon and Smilek 2005; Rouw and Scholte 2007, 2010) or on one or more continuums (Hubbard et al. 2005; Ward 2011; Ward et al. 2007) based on the phenomenological experience of synesthetic color and other factors. Thus, different synesthetes may show the same patterns of cascaded cross-tuning found by Brang et al. (2010) but to lesser degrees, or show completely different patterns of activity altogether. It will be fascinating to see the patterns of activity that emerge from similar brain-imaging studies of other types of grapheme-color synesthetes and other varieties of synesthesia more generally.

In sum, the perception of print color begins with processes that respond to different wavelengths of light at the retina, whereas synesthetic color emerges from something other than wavelength opponent processing and occurs during and after the inducer (e.g., grapheme) has been processed. Visual area V4 in the ventral stream of the cortex may serve as the (or one) locus at which synesthetic and print colors converge and share hue-selective maps that determine perceived color.

SYNESTHETIC BINDING PART II: BINDING OF SYNESTHETIC COLOR TO SPACE

As discussed earlier, results from cognitive and neurophysiological studies have shown that attention is required to conjoin features in complex scenes. However, simple features can be encoded as object representations pre-attentively, as shown by van Vleet and Robertson (2009) and by studies of patient RM. EEG and MEG studies show that synesthetic mechanisms begin very early in cortical processing of letter shapes, as described in the previous section. The majority of studies suggest that synesthesia requires attention to be spatially bound or perceived, although in a handful of rare cases synesthesia has been suggested to operate pre-attentively (Smilek, Dixon, and Merikle 2005; Wagar et al. 2002). How is it possible to account for these different reports?

The study by Brang et al. (2010) showed activation of color-selective regions in synesthetes' brains in response to achromatic graphemes, but a further measure of behavior will be needed in future studies to tell whether this activation requires attention in the emergence of the synesthetically bound percept. It may be that the onset of V4 activity coupled with grapheme activation in PTGA explains the early emergence of a synesthetic color representation, but this does not mean that it is bound to the grapheme at this stage or fully brought into awareness until it has interacted with other brain regions associated with attention, such as the parietal cortex and other regions of the brain.[1]

Activation of parietal cortex is ubiquitous with synesthesic experience in the neurophysiology literature where parietal activity has been shown using every form of brain imaging tool that has been used to study it.[2] Of special note among these studies are those using TMS because they offer direct evidence that decreased activation of the

[1] The pulvinar nucleus of the thalamus is directly involved in sustained attention and also projects to nearly every area of the cortex. The thalamus and other subcortical regions may play an important role in synesthetic representation and even development.

[2] (PET/fMRI: Aleman et al. 2001, inferior parietal lobe (IPL); Neufeld, et al. 2012, left inferior parietal cortex (IPC); Nunn et al. 2002, left angular gyrus; Paulesu et al. 1995, right parietal lobe; Rouw and Scholte, 2010, left IPS; Steven et al. 2006, bilateral IPL, superior parietal lobe (SPL); van Leeuwen et al. 2011, left IPL; Weiss et al. 2005, left intraparietal sulcus (IPS). EEG: Beeli et al. 2008 using LORETA for 7 mm voxel resolution, left precuneus, right IPS; Jäncke and Langer 2011, left parietal lobe. TMS: Esterman et al. 2006, right angular gyrus (AG); Muggleton et al. 2007, right AG; Rothen et al. 2010 bilateral parito-occipital junction. DTI/VBM: Rouw and Scholte 2007, left posterior parietal cortex (PPC); Rouw and Scholte 2010, left SPL; Weiss and Fink 2008, left IPS; although see Jäncke et al. 2009 for a contrary finding).

parietal cortex can suppress synesthetic concurrents. The direct involvement of the parietal cortex in synesthesia fits well with related ideas of attention-dependent perceptual binding (e.g., Robertson et al. 1997; Treisman and Gelade 1980). Consistently, behavioral data collected from synesthetes suggest a critical role of awareness and attention for the induction of colors from grapheme shapes (Laeng, Svartdal, and Oelmann 2004; Mattingley, Payne, and Rich 2006; Mattingley et al. 2001; Rich and Mattingley 2003, 2010; Sagiv, Heer, and Robertson 2006; Smilek et al. 2001).

Synesthetic color likely requires attention to be spatially bound and may be bound through the same mechanism as print color. But if this is true, how do we address the paradox of synesthetic and print color appearing in the same place at the same time without blending? Synesthetic and print colors may rely on similar mechanisms for binding, but these mechanisms are not identical, and although the differences may be subtle, they are important when addressing the paradox.

Van Leeuwen et al. (2010) examined the extent of the overlap in brain activity between synesthetic and print color using an fMRI method that shows repetition suppression. Repetition suppression occurs when the brain adapts to repeated exposures of a stimulus and compensates with a decrease in activity over trials in regions that represent the repeated stimulus. Van Leeuwen and colleagues hypothesized that if synesthetic and print color mechanisms overlapped exactly then repeating a stimulus that induced *synesthetic* color would create repetition suppression effects in regions that represent the *printed* color of a subsequent target. However, there was no evidence of repetition suppression effects, induced by synesthetic color in ROIs that represented the printed color. The lack of a repetition suppression effect suggests that synesthetic and print colors do not share the exact same neural substrates, although van Leeuwen and colleagues were careful to stay agnostic to the degree that the two color systems may partially overlap.

This study may be interpreted in multiple ways assuming the null result is representative of no true effect. One possibility is that synesthetic and print colors exist as entirely separate feature maps. This idea cannot be ruled out, but it seems unlikely since van Leeuwen and colleagues (and many other groups prior) report significant overlap (but not repetition suppression) in activity between synesthetic and print colors, particularly in color-selective region V4. It is more likely that synesthetic and print color overlap partially but not to the extent that they would produce equal repetition suppression effects in functional imaging measures (a method that has a low signal to noise ratio).

There are behavioral data that do suggest at least a partial overlap between print and synesthetic color. For instance, Alvarez and Robertson (in press) conducted a behavioral study similar in design to that used by van Leeuwen and colleagues to study repetition suppression effects, but which now measured how a preceding stimulus (the prime) changed response time. In the study by Alvarez and Robertson, 13 synesthetes were presented with four types of primes; those that triggered print color only (e.g., red "Ω"), synesthetic color only[3] (e.g., a black "A"), both print and synesthetic colors simultaneously

---

[3] Black in this case is considered a neutral color because none of the chosen primes induced black synesthetically and no probe was ever colored in black. Thus, printed black primes acted as a baseline condition for all subjects.

(e.g., a red "A"), or primes that triggered no colors (e.g., black "Ω," to serve as a baseline). Primes were followed immediately by centrally presented circles acting as the target probes, which were congruent or incongruent in color to the prime (e.g., red "A" followed by either a red or green probe). Participants named the color of the probes out loud as quickly and accurately as they could. Synesthetes were faster to name congruent probes compared to incongruent probes replicating previous reports of synesthetic priming effects (Mattingley et al. 2001; Spruyt et al. 2009). Most importantly, the size of the priming effect (difference between congruent and incongruent reaction times) was significantly larger for the prime that induced both synesthetic and print colors (e.g., a red "A") than the priming effect induced by either synesthetic or print color alone (e.g., black "A," or red "Ω"). These findings suggest that synesthetic and print colors converge during cortical processing, for example by utilizing the same feature map of hue. When synesthetic and print hues are very similar or equal they sum to create an amplified neural signal for that hue, leading to the measured increase in the size of the priming effect. One alternative to this account would be that either print or synesthetic colors prime the color name and that a different name slows response time. In fact, pairwise comparisons revealed that synesthetic priming was highly significant while print color priming did not reach significant levels (showing a trend). Thus, in this case synesthetic color would act as a strong naming prime, while print color would not, resulting in similar priming effects across synesthetic-only and print-plus-synesthetic-color conditions.

To summarize, in most every case, synesthetic color arises after the point at which separate wavelengths blend in normal color vision, meaning that if synesthetic and print color do converge, they cannot blend, even in the extreme case where they share a single spatial location. If a letter is printed in a color different from the synesthetic color it induces, the two hues will activate different hue-selective maps allowing for dual representation of color, but if synesthetic and print colors are the same/similar they will co-activate the same hue-selective map and create an amplified color signal. To the extent that synesthetic color is spatially bound, it is likely done through the same attention-dependent mechanism through which print color is bound. Studies suggest that the parietal cortex plays a key role in this binding of synesthetic and/or print color to shape.

APPLYING THE SYNESTHETIC BINDING MODEL TO OTHER TYPES OF SYNESTHESIA

This chapter has focused on the available research on grapheme-color synesthesia as a means of understanding a model of perceptual binding of synesthetic concurrents. Many other varieties of synesthetic experience have been reported to be externalized as well, including projected colors triggered by music (Cytowic and Eagleman 2009), locations of sequences such as weekdays, months, or numbers (Eagleman 2009; Galton 1880; Sagiv et al. 2006), colored auras that are projected onto a face or body (Cytowic and Eagleman 2009), synesthetic flavors that are experienced as existing on the tongue (Beeli, Esslen, and Jäncke 2005), words that are visualized as floating in space or spilling out of a speaker's mouth (Linn et al. 2008), and touch that is experienced mirrored from another person's body and physically felt on the body of the synesthete as is the case with mirror touch synesthesia (Blakemore et al. 2005; see Banissy, Chapter 30, this volume). Variations of all of these synesthetic forms involve concurrents that are projected into an external spatial location for the synesthete. There are multiple reference frames of space (body centered, head centered, eye centered, near space, far space, allocentric, etc.) and these different synesthetic experiences seem to rely on different reference frames to exist, most (but not all) of which are within the peripersonal space on or within arm's reach of the body.

In almost all of these forms of synesthesia, the synesthetic concurrents are likely triggered through atypical pathways of feature representation. But for any of these synesthetic concurrents to be bound, the mechanisms of binding probably work similarly to the attention-dependent ones that bind non-synesthetic features. Understanding these mechanisms and the subtly of their differences has great potential to inform research on perceptual binding in general and address a host of other questions in cognitive psychology and neuroscience. Such questions might address the representation and integration of low-level and high-level features, the role of cortico-subcortical interactions in sensory experience, the importance of feedback and context on sensory perception, and the role of individual differences in development in perception.

References

Aleman, Andre, Geert-Jan M. Rutten, Margriet M. Sitskoorn, Geraud Dautzenberg, and Nick F. Ramsay. 2001. Activation of striate cortex in the absence of visual stimulation: An fMRI study of synaesthesia. *Neuroreport* 12 (13):2827–2830.

Alvarez B.D, and L. C. Robertson. In press. The interaction of synesthetic and print color and its relation to visual imagery. *Attention, Perception, & Psychophysics*.

Banissy, Michael J. 2013. Synesthesia, mirror-neurons, and mirror-touch. In *The Oxford Handbook of Synesthesia*, ed. Julia Simner and Edward M. Hubbard, 584–603 . Oxford: Oxford University Press.

Bartolomeo, Paolo, Michel T. De Schotten, and Fabrizzio Doricchi. 2007. Left unilateral neglect as a disconnection syndrome. *Cerebral Cortex* 17 (11):2479–2490.

Beeli, Gian, Michaela Esslen, and Lutz Jäncke. 2005. Synaesthesia: When coloured sounds taste sweet. *Nature* 434 (7029):38–38. doi:10.1038/434038a.

——. 2008. Time course of neural activity correlated with coloured-hearing synaesthesia. *Cerebral Cortex* 18 (2):379–385.

Bernstein, Lori J., and Lynn C. Robertson. 1998. Illusory conjunctions of colour and motion with shape following bilateral parietal lesions. *Psychological Science* 9 (3):167–175.

Blakemore, Sarah-Jane, Davina Bristow, Geoffrey Bird, Christopher Frith, and Jamie Ward. 2005. Somatosensory activations during the observation of touch and a case of vision-touch synaesthesia. *Brain* 128 (7):1571–1583. doi:10.1093/brain/awh500.

Brang, David, Edward M. Hubbard, Seana Coulson, Minxiong Huang, and Vilayanur S. Ramachandran. 2010. Magnetoencephalography reveals early activation of V4 in grapheme-colour synaesthesia. *NeuroImage* 53 (1):268–274.

Cohen, Asher, and Robert D. Rafal. 1991. Attention and feature integration: Illusory conjunctions in a patient with a parietal lobe lesion. *Psychological Science* 2 (2):106–110.

Cohen Kadosh, Roi, and Vincent Walsh. 2008. Synaesthesia and cortical connections: Cause or correlation? *Trends in Neurosciences* 31 (11):549–501.

Conway, Bevil R. 2001. Spatial structure of cone inputs to colour cells in alert macaque primary visual cortex (V-1). *The Journal of Neuroscience* 21 (8):2768–2783.

Conway, Bevil R., and Doris Y. Tsao. 2009. Colour-tuned neurons are spatially clustered according to colour preference within alert macaque posterior inferior temporal cortex. *Proceedings of the National Academy of Sciences of the United States of America* 106 (42):18034–18039.

Cytowic, Richard E., and David Eagleman. 2009. *Wednesday is Indigo Blue: Discovering the Brain of Synaesthesia*. Cambridge, MA: MIT Press.

De Valois, Russell L., Israel Abramov, and Gerald H. Jacobs. 1966. Analysis of response patterns of LGN cells. *Journal of the Optical Society of America* 56 (7):966–977.

DeYoe, E. A, and D. C. Van Essen. 1988. Concurrent processing streams in monkey visual cortex. *Trends in Neurosciences* 11 (5):219–226.

Dixon, Mike J., and Daniel Smilek. 2005. The importance of individual differences in grapheme-colour synaesthesia. *Neuron* 45 (6):821–823.

Eagleman, David M. 2009. The objectification of overlearned sequences: A new view of spatial sequence synaesthesia. *Cortex* 45 (10):1266–1277.

Esterman, Michael, Timothy Verstynen, Richard B. Ivry, and Lynn C. Robertson. 2006. Coming unbound: Disrupting automatic integration of synaesthetic colour and graphemes by transcranial magnetic stimulation of the right parietal lobe. *Journal of Cognitive Neuroscience* 18 (9):1570–1576.

Felleman, Daniel J., and David C. Van Essen. 1991. Distributed hierarchical processing in the primate cerebral cortex. *Cerebral Cortex* 1 (1):1–47.

Friedman-Hill, S. R., L. C. Robertson, and A. Treisman. 1995. Parietal contributions to visual feature binding: evidence from a patient with bilateral lesions. *Science* 269 (5225): 853–855.

Galton, Francis. 1880. Visualized numerals. *Nature* 21: 252–256.

Grossenbacher, Peter G., and Christopher T. Lovelace. 2001. Mechanisms of synaesthesia: Cognitive and physiological constraints. *Trends in Cognitive Sciences* 5 (1):36–41.

Hubbard, Edward M. 2007. Neurophysiology of synaesthesia. *Current Psychiatry Reports* 9 (3):193–199.

Hubbard, Edward M., A. Cyrus Arman, Vilayanar S. Ramachandran, and Geoffrey M. Boynton. 2005. Individual differences among grapheme-colour synaesthetes: Brain-behavior correlations. *Neuron* 45 (6):975–985.

Laeng, Bruno, Frode Svartdal, and Hella Oelmann. 2004. Does colour synaesthesia pose a paradox for early-selection theories of attention? *Psychological Science* 15 (4):277–281.

Linn, A., P. Hancock, J. Simner, and M. Akeroyd. Cognitive advantages in tickertape synaesthesia. Paper presented at the 4th Annual Meeting of the UK Synaesthesia Association, Edinburgh, March.

Livingstone, Margaret, and David Hubel. 1988. Segregation of form, colour, movement, and depth: anatomy, physiology, and perception. *Science* 240 (4853):740–749.

———. 1984. Anatomy and physiology of a colour system in the primate visual cortex. *The Journal of Neuroscience* 4 (1):309–56.

Mattingley, Jason B., Jonathan M. Payne, and Anina N. Rich. 2006. Attentional load attenuates synaesthetic priming effects in grapheme-colour synaesthesia. *Cortex* 42 (2):213–221.

Mattingley, Jason B., Anina N. Rich, Greg Yelland, and John L. Bradshaw. 2001. Unconscious priming eliminates automatic binding of colour and alphanumeric form in synaesthesia. *Nature* 410:580–582.

Maurer, Daphne, and Catherine J. Mondloch. 2005. Neonatal synaesthesia: A reevaluation. In *Synaesthesia: Perspectives from Cognitive Neuroscience*, ed. Lynn C. Robertson and Noam Sagiv, 193–213. New York: Oxford University Press.

Muggleton, Neil, Elias Tsakanikos, Vincent Walsh, and Jamie Ward. 2007. Disruption of synaesthesia following TMS of the right posterior parietal cortex. *Neuropsychologia* 45 (7):1582–1585.

Nunn, J. A., L. J. Gregory, M. Brammer, S. C. R. Williams, D. M. Parslow, M. J. Morgan, R. G. Morris, E. T. Bullmore, S. Baron-Cohen, and J. A. Gray. 2002. Functional magnetic resonance imaging of synaesthesia: activation of V4/V8 by spoken words. *Nature Neuroscience* 5 (4):371–375.

Palmeri, Thomas J., Randolph Blake, René Marois, Marci A. Flanery, and William Whetsell Jr. 2002. The perceptual reality of synaesthetic colours. *Proceedings of the National Academy of Sciences of the United States of America* 99 (6):4127–4131.

Paulesu, E., J. Harrison, S. Baron-Cohen, J. D. G. Watson, L. Goldstein, J. Heather, R. S. J. Frackowiak, and C. D. Frith. 1995. The physiology of coloured hearing A PET activation study of colour-word synaesthesia. *Brain* 118 (3):661–676.

Rich, Anina N., and Jason B. Mattingley. 2003. The effects of stimulus competition and voluntary attention on colour-graphemic synaesthesia. *Neuroreport* 14 (14):1793–1798.

——. 2010. Out of sight, out of mind: The attentional blink can eliminate synaesthetic colours. *Cognition* 114 (3):320–328. doi:10.1016/j.cognition.2009.10.003.

——. 2013. The role of attention in synesthesia. In *The Oxford Handbook of Synesthesia*, ed. Julia Simner and Edward M. Hubbard, 265–282 . Oxford: Oxford University Press.

Robertson, Lynn. C. 2003. Binding, spatial attention and perceptual awareness. *Nature Reviews Neuroscience* 4 (2):93–102.

——. 2004. *Space, Objects, Minds, and Brains: Essays in Cognitive Neuroscience*. New York: Psychology Press.

Robertson, Lynn, Anne Treisman, Stacia Friedman-Hill, and Marcia Grabowecky. 1997. The interaction of spatial and object pathways: Evidence from Balint's syndrome. *Journal of Cognitive Neuroscience* 9 (3):295–317.

Rouw, Romke, and H. Steven Scholte. 2007. Increased structural connectivity in grapheme-colour synaesthesia. *Nature Neuroscience* 10 (6):792–797.

——. 2010. Neural basis of individual differences in synaesthetic experiences. *The Journal of Neuroscience* 30 (18):6205–6213.

Sagiv, Noam, Jeffrey Heer, and Lynn C. Robertson. 2006. Does binding of synaesthetic colour to the evoking grapheme require attention? *Cortex* 42 (2):232–242.

Sagiv, Noam, Julia Simner, James Collins, Brian Butterworth, and Jamie Ward. 2006. What is the relationship between synaesthesia and visuo-spatial number forms? *Cognition* 101 (1):114–128.

Smilek, Daniel, Mike J. Dixon, Cera Cudahy, and Philip M. Merikle. 2001. Synaesthetic photisms influence visual perception. *Journal of Cognitive Neuroscience* 13 (7):930–936.

Smilek, Daniel, Mike J. Dixon, and Philip M. Merikle. 2005. Binding of graphemes and synaesthetic colours in colour-graphemic synaesthesia. In *Synaesthesia: Perspectives from Cognitive*

Neuroscience, ed. Lynn C. Robertson and Noam Sagiv, 74–89. New York: Oxford University Press.

Sperling, Julia M., David Prvulovic, David E. J. Linden, Wolf Singer, and Aglaja Stirn. 2006. Neuronal correlates of colour-graphemic synaesthesia: A fMRI study. *Cortex* 42 (2):295–303.

Spruyt, Adriaan, Johannes Koch, Heleen Vandromme, Dirk Hermans, and Paul Eelen. 2009. A time course analysis of the synaesthetic colour priming effect. *Canadian Journal of Experimental Psychology* 63 (3):211–215. doi:37/a0015299.

Steven, Megan S., Peter C. Hansen, and Colin Blakemore. 2006. Activation of colour-selective areas of the visual cortex in a blind synaesthete. *Cortex* 42 (2):304–308.

Tanigawa, Hisashi, Haidong D. Lu, and Anna W. Roe. 2010. Functional organization for colour and orientation in macaque V4. *Nature Neuroscience* 13 (12):1542–1548.

Treisman, Anne. 1999. Solutions to the binding problem: Review progress through controversy summary and convergence. *Neuron* 24:105–110.

Treisman, Anne M., and Garry Gelade. 1980. A feature-integration theory of attention. *Cognitive Psychology* 12 (1):97–136.

Treisman, Anne, and Hilary Schmidt. 1982. Illusory conjunctions in the perception of objects. *Cognitive Psychology* 14 (1):107–141.

van Leeuwen Tessa M., Karl M. Petersson, and Peter Hagoort. 2010. Synaesthetic colour in the brain: Beyond colour areas. A functional magnetic resonance imaging study of synaesthetes and matched controls. *PLoS ONE* 5 (8):e12074. doi:10.1371/journal.pone.0012074.

van Leeuwen, Tessa M., Hanneke E. M. den Ouden, and Peter Hagoort. 2011. Effective connectivity determines the nature of subjective experience in grapheme-colour synaesthesia. *The Journal of Neuroscience* 31 (27):9879–9884.

van Vleet, Thomas M., and Lynn C. Robertson. 2009. Implicit representation and explicit detection of features in patients with hemispatial neglect. *Brain* 132 (7):1889–1897.

Wagar, Brandon M., Mike J. Dixon, Daniel Smilek, and Cera Cudahy. 2002. Coloured photisms prevent object-substitution masking in digit-colour synaesthesia. *Brain and Cognition* 48 (2–3):606–611.

Ward, Jamie. How many different types of grapheme-colour synaesthesia are there? Presented at the annual meeting of the UK Synaesthesia Association, University of East London, London, 26–27 March.

Ward, Jamie, Ryan Li, Shireen Salih, and Noam Sagiv. 2007. Varieties of grapheme-colour synaesthesia: A new theory of phenomenological and behavioural differences. *Consciousness and Cognition* 16 (4):913–931. doi:10.1016/j.concog.2006.09.012.

Weiss, Peter H., and Gereon R. Fink. 2008. Grapheme-colour synaesthetes show increased grey matter volumes of parietal and fusiform cortex. *Brain* 132 (1):65–70.

Weiss, Peter H., Karl Zilles, and Gereon R. Fink. 2005. When visual perception causes feeling: Enhanced cross-modal processing in grapheme-colour synaesthesia. *NeuroImage* 28 (4):859–868.

Xiao, Youping, Alexander Casti, Jun Xiao, and Ehud Kaplan. 2007. Hue maps in primate striate cortex. *NeuroImage* 35 (2):771–786.

Xiao, Youping, Yi Wang, and Daniel J. Felleman. 2003. A spatially organized representation of colour in macaque cortical area V2. *Nature* 421 (6922):535–539.

CHAPTER 17

SYNESTHESIA, EYE-MOVEMENTS, AND PUPILLOMETRY

TANJA C.W. NIJBOER AND BRUNO LAENG

EYE MOVEMENTS AND ATTENTION

Eye movements can provide important information about how synesthetic elements influence target selection. This target selection is known to be controlled by attentional processes. Our visual environment is packed with multiple objects, but only a subset of these objects can be attended to at any given time, and thus receive more (thorough) processing. When one wants to inspect a certain subset of objects or a specific spatial region, one can shift attention to this spatial location. This is mostly done by moving the eyes to the attended location. This process gives rise to what is known as "*overt attention*." Alternatively, one can also keep the eye straight ahead and pay attention to a spatial location or an object in the periphery of vision, giving rise to what is known as "*covert attention*."

There is now ample evidence that eye movements and attention are highly related (Corbetta 1998). Eye movements can be categorized into several distinct types. Two involuntary and automatic types are the *vestibulo-ocular* and *optokinetic reflexes*, which are both essential for keeping the eyes still with respect to the visual environment when one moves. Additionally, there are three types of eye movements that are linked to higher cognitive processes, such as target selection. First, *saccadic eye movements* are fast eye movements that are crucial to bring a selected target onto the fovea; second, (smooth) *pursuit* allows a moving target to be followed with the eyes; and third, the *vergence system* allows for maintaining the eyes on a target when it moves towards or away from the observer or when a new target at a different depth needs to be focused on.

Saccadic eye movements and fixations have frequently been used to investigate both covert and overt attentional processes. It has been strongly argued that investigating covert attention in isolation is not very useful (Findlay and Gilchrist 2003) but that covert attention should be considered as part of an integrated attentional system which includes both covert and overt attention. That is, optimal attentional processing takes place at the site of fixation (i.e., overt attention), while the next fixation location in the visual field's periphery is previewed by covert processes.

One influential model of attention with its focus on the central role of overt orienting is the pre-motor theory of attention (Rizzolatti, Riggio, and Sheliga 1994; Rizzolatti et al. 1987). Rizzolatti et al. (1987) argued that the (overt) oculomotor and covert attention mechanisms both utilize the same motor control circuits. The pre-motor theory proposes that covert attention to a visual location involves the mechanisms for saccade programming, but the actual motor reaction is interrupted. Rizzolatti and colleagues proposed that both motor planning and visual perception mediate visuo-spatial attention. Therefore, allocation of attention through spatial cueing results in more accurate and faster processing of information in the space surrounding the cued region irrespective of whether a saccadic eye movement is necessary or not. Put simply, the eyes do not need to move in order for attention to shift to any particular place in space. Evidence in favor of the pre-motor theory comes from studies demonstrating close links between the programming of saccadic eye movements and shifts of visual spatial attention. Attentional shifts towards saccade target locations are triggered during saccade preparation even before the eyes have begun to move (Hoffman and Subramaniam 1995; Irwin and Gordon 1998), resulting in superior performance to visual (Deubel and Schneider 1996), auditory (Rorden and Driver 1999), or tactile stimuli (Rorden et al. 2002) at this location. Moreover, saccade trajectories, the paths that the eye movement makes through space as a function of time, are strongly affected by the focus of visual attention (Sheliga et al. 1995). Such findings, together with the fact that overlapping fronto-parietal areas are activated both during covert shifts of visual attention and during saccade preparation (Corbetta, 1998), support the pre-motor theory of attention, since they imply that the control of eye movements and the control of visual spatial attention are based on common mechanisms.

In sum, attention allows us to select which part of the visual information will become available for further or more detailed analysis. The fovea provides the primary mechanism for such selection to occur (i.e., overt attention). Items that are not fixated receive greatly reduced processing in terms of acuity. Covert attention on the other hand might yet play an important role in selecting which locations in space, which objects, or which visual features might be relevant to fixate next. Any feature or location that is relevant for the observer and attracts covert attention will therefore guide the oculomotor system to behaviorally relevant items.

WHAT CAN EYE MOVEMENTS TELL US ABOUT SYNESTHESIA?

The choice of eye movements we make is driven by a unique balance between issues in perception and issues in cognition. In other words, when viewing a static scene, eye movements generally are driven both by "bottom-up," perceptual properties of the stimulus, such as color and shape, as well as by "top-down" cognitive processes, such as knowledge and expectations (Henderson, 2003). For example, while driving, our eyes may be captured by a flashing billboard when our goal is to keep our eyes on the road. There are ample ways to investigate visual perception and attention using eye movements. As mentioned earlier, several different types of eye movements can be distinguished. Saccadic eye movements in particular are of most interest to investigate a wide range of cognitive and perceptual processes. Saccadic eye movements incorporate several unique features that give important insight in cognitive functions, such as when saccades are launched (i.e., saccade latency), where they land (i.e., landing position), the pattern of locations (i.e., scan path), and how long the eye stays at a certain location (i.e., fixation duration).

Very few studies have investigated either perceptual or attentional processes in synesthesia by means of eye movements. One recent study by Nijboer and Van der Stigchel (2009) investigated the role of visual attention in the induction of a synesthetic color experience by means of eye movements. In other words, that study looked at the eye movements of synesthetes in order to answer questions about how attention might play a role in triggering synesthetic color. Like other studies on attention in synesthesia, this research asked whether synesthetic colors are triggered either before or after attention falls on the inducer (the "inducer" being the element which triggers the color, e.g., a letter or a number). An "oculomotor distractor paradigm" was used (Walker et al. 1997), in which a target and a single distractor were presented simultaneously and participants were required to make a single eye movement to the target while ignoring the distractor. Usually, when a distractor resembles a target, the distractor evokes strong interference (Ludwig and Gilchrist 2002, 2003); in such cases, the number of erroneous eye movements directed to the distractor is usually higher (Ludwig and Gilchrist 2002). This type of erroneous eye-movement is known as "capture" by the distractor, in that the distractor "wins" the competition over the target and captures attention. In the study by Nijboer and Van der Stigchel (2009), synesthetes were instructed to make an eye movement to a colored target, while a single irrelevant distractor was presented in half of the trials (see Figure 17.1). These distractors could either be digits that were colored the same as the target, or achromatic digits that induced the same *synesthetic* hue. Alternatively, the distractors were chromatic or achromatic nongraphemes, which did not induce a synesthetic experience.

The crucial comparison was the percentage of capture by the achromatic digit distractor (which triggered synesthetic color) compared to the achromatic non-digit distractor (which did not trigger synesthetic color). The results showed that whereas both the chromatic distractors influenced the target selection process, achromatic distractors did not; the percentage of capture by the achromatic digit as well as non-digit were comparable to each other, and were lower than the percentage of capture by chromatic distractors.

These findings were taken as evidence that the synesthetic hue was either absent or not strong enough to distract eye movements away from the target when a "synesthetic distractor" was present. The authors of that study concluded that this absence might relate to a question of how much attention had been allocated to the synesthetic distractors.

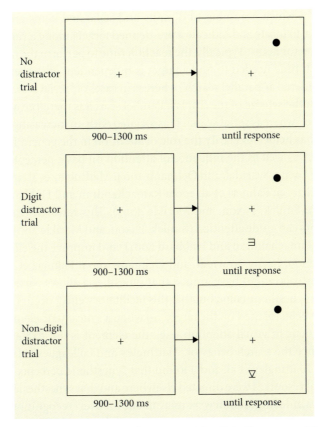

FIGURE 17.1 Trial sequences for the no distractor trials, digit distractor trials, and non-digit distractor trials. Participants first fixated a central cross after which a target element (the dot) was presented. This target was either presented alone (no distractor condition) or together with a distractor, which could either be a digit or a non-digit.

Since the inducing grapheme was a task-irrelevant distractor (in other words, it was not necessary to attend to the distractor in order to complete the task), participants may not have attended sufficiently to the distractors to trigger a synesthetic color (see Rich and Mattingley, Chapter 14, this volume, for a further discussion of issues in attention and synesthesia). In other words, because these inducing graphemes were mere distractors, the amount of attention allocated to them was most probably lower than in studies where graphemes were targets.

An experimental paradigm that has been extensively used both in the study of gaze control and in the study of synesthesia is "visual search." Visual search has been perhaps the most exploited of all attentional tasks since its introduction by Anne Treisman and her colleagues (e.g., Treisman and Gelade 1980). Visual search mimics an attentional process that is common in daily living; searching the environment for an object (as, for example, when looking for a pen on a cluttered desk, looking for a friend's face in a crowd, or for one's car in a car park). In a typical visual search experiment, a display is presented to participants in which a number of discrete and separated items are presented and participants have to locate and indicate a pre-defined target among a varying number of non-target distractor items. Typically, the reaction time to perform the task is measured. When the search time needed to find a target is independent of the set size of the display this is considered a "parallel search" whereas in cases of "serial search," search times do increase with the set size of the display. Parallel search is therefore associated with a flat "search slope," whereas serial search is associated with an increasing "search slopes." This paradigm has helped to clarify the role of attention in the generation of the synesthetic experience as well as the influence of attention on basic perceptual tasks (Hong and Blake 2008; Laeng, Svartdal, and Oelmann 2004; Mattingley et al. 2001; Nijboer and Van der Stigchel 2009; Palmeri et al. 2002; Ramachandran and Hubbard 2001; Rothen and Meier 2009; Smilek, Dixon, and Merikle 2003). This research has suggested that synesthetic colors can guide attention (Smilek, Dixon, and Merikle 2003), cause perceptual grouping (Ramachandran and Hubbard 2001), and improve the efficiency of visual search (Laeng 2009; Laeng, Svartdal, and Oelmann 2004; Palmeri et al. 2002). Sagiv, Heer, and Robertson (2006) have argued that synesthesia allows participants to guide search based on synesthetic color, but that this facilitatory effect occurs only after attention has already been focused on the target. So when a synesthetic element is presented outside of the focus of visual attention (e.g., the element is not fixated), this element does not influence the search behavior. Mattingley and colleagues (Mattingley, Payne, and Rich 2006; Mattingley et al. 2001) found that synesthetic percepts were attenuated when attentional resources were directed elsewhere and that synesthesia was completely eliminated when inducing stimuli were unavailable for overt recognition.

Another recent study by Nijboer, Satris, and Van der Stigchel (2011), combined the visual search paradigm with an oculomotor target selection task. The study assessed the possibility that the synesthetic element could induce pop-out in a comparable manner to normal color. Pop-out is the phenomenon characterized by a fast and automatic allocation of attention to a salient object in the scene; at a phenomenological level, the object appears to "pop out" from the rest of the scene (Treisman and Sato 1990). For example a green dot immediately captures attention when it is surrounded by red dots, and not when it is surrounded by green diamonds. In the oculomotor target selection task, participants viewed an array of digits with varying set sizes and were required to make an eye movement to the "odd one out" (e.g., a target "2" among multiple distractors "5"s). Target and distractor stimuli were presented as either all colored (chromatic), all gray (achromatic) or achromatic with one chromatic distractor (mixed) (see Figure 17.2).

Target and distractors were always differently colored in a synesthetic sense. Participants were not allowed to freely move their eyes across the different elements in the scene, but were only allowed to execute one eye movement to locate the target element. This should be no problem when the target has a distinct color with respect to the other elements, but would be difficult when there was no distinct feature that allowed for a fast detection of the target. This experiment would therefore reveal whether synesthetic colors resulted in a similar search benefit as physical colors do. To this end, it was investigated whether search slopes for synesthetes in the achromatic condition resembled search

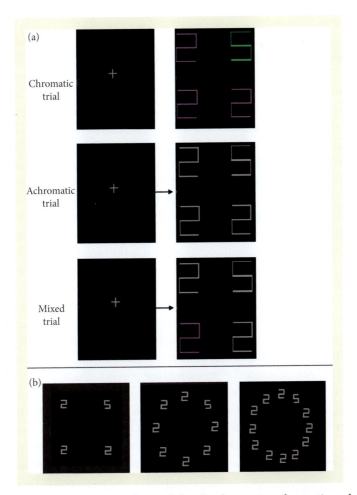

FIGURE 17.2 (a) Examples of a stimulus trial for the chromatic, achromatic and mixed configurations (each with a set size of 4). Specific hues used were set by individual synesthetes at the start of the experiment; (b) Stimulus configurations for set sizes 4, 8, and 12.

slopes in the chromatic condition. In the chromatic condition, the target had a unique physical color in the visual scene. A pop-out effect was expected in both synesthetes and controls, resulting in fast reaction times and high accuracy, irrespective of set size.

However, if synesthetic percepts arise pre-attentively, then the achromatic condition would also show a pop-out effect for synesthetes, because the target would elicit a synesthetic color experience and this would aid in making a fast and accurate eye movement. Alternatively, if the binding of form and color in synesthesia requires attention, then the achromatic conditions would not elicit a synesthetically colored target pre-attentively. In this case, no pop-out effect would be seen in the achromatic condition for both synesthetes and controls.

The mixed condition, in which the target is achromatic and one distractor is chromatic, allowed for a direct comparison between the strength of physically and synesthetically colored elements. If the amount of erroneous eye movements executed to the physically colored element was similar for synesthetes and controls, this would indicate that the presence of a synesthetic target does not modulate the strength of the pop-out effect. Results revealed that synesthetes and control participants showed comparable patterns in accuracy and saccade latencies for the different conditions. Highest accuracies and shortest latencies were obtained for the chromatic condition, compared to achromatic and mixed condition. In the chromatic condition, where the target had a unique physical color in the visual scene, we found that there was no effect of set size. This indicates that the physically colored target resulted in a pop-out effect. As expected, this effect was similar for the synesthetes and the control group. Such a pop-out effect was absent in the achromatic condition in which all elements were gray. In contrast to the chromatic condition, accuracy decreased with increasing set size; this was expected for the control group, but a null finding for the synesthetes additionally indicates that a synesthetic element does not elicit a synesthetic color when it is the target in an oculomotor target selection task. Moreover, the groups did not significantly differ on the percentage capture by the real color distractor in the mixed condition (in which one chromatic distractor was presented). Furthermore, the percentage capture was not influenced by set size. Again, none of the synesthetes outperformed the controls in the achromatic condition. The high percentage capture in the mixed condition revealed that the real color distractor was more salient than the synesthetic target. In other words, the presence of the synesthetic target did not influence the strength of the pop-out effect.

Another recent study did, however, find evidence that synesthesia can influence overt visual attention. Carriere et al. (2009) revealed that synesthetes fixate congruently colored letters more often and for longer durations than incongruently colored letters. Furthermore, they observed in a subsequent visual search task that synesthetes rapidly fixated and identified the congruently colored target letters, but had problems in identifying incongruently colored letters. The apparent inconsistency between the earlier studies and the study of Carriere et al. (2009) might be explained by methodological differences between the two studies. In the oculomotor target selection task as well as the oculomotor distractor task by Nijboer and colleagues (Nijboer and van der Stigchel 2009; Nijboer, Satris, and van der Stigchel 2011), participants were not allowed to freely move their eyes across the different elements in the scene, but were only allowed to execute one eye movement to locate the target element. Although participants were actively searching for a synesthetic target, they were restricted in the elements that they could select as the target location for their eye movement. This was no problem when the target had a distinct color with respect to the other elements, but was difficult when there was no distinct feature that allowed for a fast detection of the target.

On the basis of the earlier mentioned reasoning, it appears that synesthetic percepts are not available to distinguish the synesthetic target from synesthetic distractors when they are presented in the periphery. This explanation is also consistent with the results of Laeng and colleagues (2004) since they only observed fast reaction times to synesthetic targets when the target was within a few degrees of visual angle from fixation. In contrast to normal colors, synesthetic colors only arise early enough to effectively distinguish achromatic graphemes from each other when they are fixated. Because it is known that best attentional processing takes place at the site of fixation (Findlay and Gilchrist, 2003), the need for visual attention and full recognition of the grapheme for synesthesia is becoming unambiguously apparent. In conjunction with other research that manipulated attentional resources (Mattingley, Payne, and Rich 2006; Mattingley et al. 2001), synesthesia seems to require visual attention and full recognition to bind form and color. According to this view, synesthesia only influences oculomotor behavior when the grapheme is fully recognized.

WHAT CAN PUPILLOMETRY TELL US ABOUT SYNESTHESIA?

The measurement of the diameter of the eyes' pupils (in short, "pupillometry") has been part of the tool kit of psychology for at least the last 50 years (Laeng, Sirois, and Gredebäck 2012). A large number of studies have established that, although the eye's pupil normally constricts or dilates in direct relationship to the light energy of ambient light (Loewenfeld 1993), pupillary responses can also occur when people are engaged in cognitive tasks, despite constant illumination (Beatty and Lucero-Wagoner 2000; Goldwater 1972; Hess and Polt 1960, 1964). In general then, pupil size increases when one views attention-grabbing stimuli but also during mental effort (Kahneman 1973; Kahneman and Beatty 1966).

Pupillometry has also been recently shown to be a valid method for the study of cognitive conflict; that is, when contradicting interpretations or readings of the same visual stimuli are simultaneously possible. For example, Einhäuser et al. (2008) showed that, when viewing bistable images (e.g., the Necker cube), pupillary dilations predicted switches between conscious percepts. Another well-known task in which rival information is simultaneously present and competes for a response is the Stroop task. In its classic form, participants are requested to name the color in which written words are printed (or to name their font color, if presentation is on screen). Although participants are instructed to disregard the meaning of the written words and concentrate instead on their display colors, participants cannot avoid reading the words. This gives an inevitable interfering effect, which is particularly noticeable when the words denote color terms different from the word colors (e.g., when the word red appears in blue font). Interestingly, a few studies have examined the pupil correlates of the Stroop task (Brown et al. 1999; Laeng et al. 2011; Siegle, Steinhauer, and Thase 2004). These have replicated the Stroop color effect measuring eye responses: larger pupil dilations were recorded when word meaning and word color mismatched, compared to when they did not.

Paulsen and Laeng (2006) were the first to investigate with pupillometry the phenomenon of synesthetic Stroop. This is a variant of the classic Stroop task, which we can understand using the example of grapheme-color synesthesia. As previously mentioned, the most common form of synesthesia is grapheme-color synesthesia, where each specific grapheme elicits a specific color (e.g., the letter A might be red). This form of synesthesia makes it possible to elicit Stroop-like situations where the (objective, externally observable) ink color of an alphanumeric symbol can differ from the (subjective, not externally observable) synesthetic photism (e.g., Mattingley et al. 2001). For example, a synesthete might be slow to name the blue font of a letter A, if that letter is synesthetically red. This would be considered the "incongruent" condition, and reaction times are measured in comparison with a "congruent" condition, where synesthetic and font colors match. Instead of using the traditional method of decision times or reaction times, Paulsen and Laeng (2006) examined a group of four grapheme-color synesthetes' physiological reactions by the method of pupillometry. However, they did not request their participants to name colors but simply to passively view the letters and numbers presented on a computer screen.

Because pupil size can be a reliable marker of processing load, "wrong" (incongruent) pairings of color and form should arouse attention and elicit physiological effects, and this should be measurable as changes in pupil dilation. There were two other comparison conditions, where the same symbols are colored either congruently or "neutrally" (i.e., presented in a neutral, standard, black print color). The incongruent items shown to a particular synesthete were those items that were congruent for the other synesthetes, so that each synesthete served as a control participant for the other synesthetes. As expected, Paulsen and Laeng (2006) found that incongruently-colored alphanumeric symbols elicited larger pupil dilation than congruently-colored or the neutral black-colored symbols (see Figure 17.3). The pupillary changes in such a synesthetic Stroop situation are therefore similar to the pupillary changes that can be observed in the classic

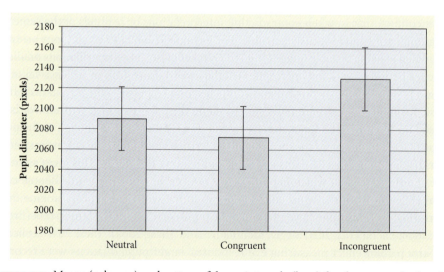

FIGURE 17.3 Means (columns) and 95% confidence intervals (bars) for three synesthetic color conditions (neutral = black, congruent and incongruent). Pupil diameters are expressed in number of pixels. Reprinted from *Cortex*, 42 (2), Helle Gaare Paulsen and Bruno Laeng, Pupillometry of Grapheme-Color Synaesthesia, pp. 290–294, Copyright (2006), with permission from Elsevier.

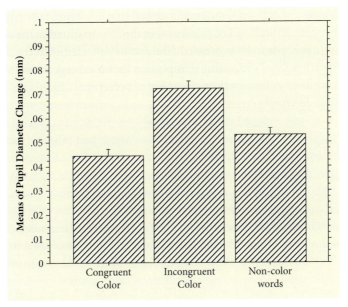

FIGURE 17.4 Means (columns) and 95% confidence intervals (bars) for color–word conditions (congruent, and incongruent and non-color words). Pupil diameters are expressed as change (in mm) from baseline. Reproduced from *Cognitive Processing*, 12 (1), Laeng, B., Ørbo, M., Holmlund, T., and Miozzo, M., Pupillary Stroop effects pp. 13–21 © 2010, The Authors.

word-color Stroop task (see Figure 17.4; note that the conditions are re-ordered in this figure).

One interesting aspect of these findings is that the pupil's change in diameter can clearly be used as an index of a private color experience as well as cognitive conflict. Moreover, the changes in pupil diameter were observed in the synesthetes as a group as well as when each synesthete was analyzed individually. Thus, pupillometry could offer a unique and valuable tool for exploring the private phenomenology of a synesthete even in conditions where the synesthete reports no "awareness" of subjective colors (similar to blindsight patients' pupillary responses to shapes or faces, Tamietto et al. 2009; Weiskrantz, Cowey, and Barbur 1999).

CONCLUSIONS

Eye-tracking methodology provides data-rich information that can be relevant for understanding the role of attentional processing in a specific cognitive task. This information can provide a record of the allocation of overt attention, by examining fixations' locations, durations, and other dynamic parameters of eye movements (e.g., saccades' onset or velocity). It can also be a record of the amount of cognitive resources or attentional load ("effort"; in Kahneman's terms) that a specific task requires, due to competition between stimuli and responses (as in the Stroop situation) or of the amount of information that needs to be processed. The results collected with these methods so far confirm that attentional processing is important for the emergence of the synesthetic experience to occur as well as for the occurrence of perceptual advantages due to synesthetic colors (e.g., in visual searches).

References

Beatty, Jackson, and Brennis Lucero-Wagoner. 2000. The pupillary system. In *Handbook of Psychophysiology*, ed. John T. Cacioppo, Louis G. Tassinary, and Gary C. Berntson, 142–162. Cambridge: Cambridge University Press.

Brown, Gregory G., Sandra S. Kindermann, Greg J. Siegle, Eric Granholm, Eric C. Wong, and Richard B. Buxton. 1999. Brain activation and pupil response during covert performance of the Stroop color word task. *Journal of the International Neuropsychological Society* 5:308–319.

Carriere, Jonathan. S. A., Daniel Eaton, Michael G. Reynolds, Mike J. Dixon, and Daniel Smilek. 2009. Grapheme-color synesthesia influences overt visual attention. *Journal of Cognitive Neuroscience* 21(2):246–258.

Corbetta, Maurizio. 1998. Frontoparietal cortical networks for directing attention and the eye to visual locations: Identical, independent, or overlapping neural systems? *Proceedings of the National Academy of Sciences of the United States of America* 95:831–838.

Deubel, Heiner, and Werner X. Schneider. 1996. Saccade target selection and object recognition: Evidence for a common attentional mechanism. *Vision Research* 36 (12):1827–1837.

Einhäuser, Wolfgang, James Stout, Christof Koch, and Olivia Carter. 2008. Pupil dilation reflects perceptual selection and predicts subsequent stability in perceptual rivalry. *Proceedings of the National Academy of Sciences of the United States of America* 105:1704–1709.

Findlay, John M., and Iain D. Gilchrist. 2003. *Active Vision: The Psychology of Looking and Seeing*. New York: Oxford University Press.

Goldwater, Bram C. 1972. Psychological significance of pupillary movements. *Psychological Bulletin* 77:340–355.

Henderson, John M. 2003. Human gaze control during real-world scene perception. *Trends in Cognitive Sciences* 7:498–504.

Hess, Eckhard H., and James M. Polt. 1960. Pupil size as related to interest value of visual stimuli. *Science* 132:349–350.

Hess, Eckhard H., and James M. Polt. 1964. Pupil size in relation to mental activity during simple problem solving. *Science* 140:1190–1192.

Hoffman, James E., and Baskaran Subramaniam. 1995. The role of visual attention in saccadic eye movements. *Perception and Psychophysics* 37 (6):787–795.

Hong, Sang Wook, and Randolph Blake. 2008. Early visual mechanisms do not contribute to synesthetic color experience. *Vision Research* 48 (8):1018–1026.

Irwin, David E., and Gordon, Robert D. 1998. Eye movements, attention, and transsaccadic memory. *Visual Cognition* 5:127–155.

Kahneman, Daniel. 1973. *Attention and Effort*. Englewood Cliffs, NJ: Prentice-Hall.

Kahneman, Daniel, and Jackson Beatty. 1966. Pupil diameter and load on memory. *Science* 154:1583–1585.

Laeng, Bruno. 2009. Searching through synaesthetic colors. *Attention, Perception and Psychophysics* 71 (7):1461–1467.

Laeng, Bruno, Marte Ørbo, Terje Holmlund, and Michele Miozzo. 2011. Pupillary Stroop effects. *Cognitive Processing* 12:13–21.

Laeng, Bruno, Sylvain Sirois, and Gustaf Gredebäck. 2012. Pupillometry: A window to the preconscious? *Perspectives on Psychological Science* 7 (1):18–27.

Laeng, Bruno, Frode Svartdal, and Hella Oelmann. 2004. Does color synesthesia pose a paradox for early-selection theories of attention? *Psychological Science* 15:277–281.

Loewenfeld, Irene. 1993. *The Pupil: Anatomy, Physiology, and Clinical Applications.* Detroit, MI: Wayne State University Press.

Ludwig, Casimir J. H., and Iain D. Gilchrist. 2002. Stimulus-driven and goal-driven control over visual selection. *Journal of Experimental Psychology: Human Perception and Performance* 28 (4):902–912.

Ludwig, Casimir J. H., and Iain D. Gilchrist. 2003. Target similarity affects saccade curvature away from irrelevant onsets. *Experimental Brain Research* 152:60–69.

Mattingley, Jason B., Jonathan M. Payne, and Anina N. Rich. 2006. Attentional load attenuates synaesthetic priming effects in grapheme-colour synaesthesia. *Cortex* 42:213–221.

Mattingley, Jason B., Anina N. Rich, Greg Yelland, and John L. Bradshaw. 2001. Unconscious priming eliminates automatic binding of colour and alphanumeric form in synaesthesia. *Nature* 410:580–582.

Nijboer, Tanja C. W., Gabriela Satris, and Stefan Van der Stigchel. 2011. The influence of synesthesia on eye movements: No synesthetic pop-out in an oculomotor target selection task. *Consciousness and Cognition* 20 (4):1193–1200.

Nijboer, Tanja C. W., and Stefan van der Stigchel. 2009. Is attention essential for inducing synesthetic colors? Evidence from oculomotor distractors. *Journal of Vision* 9 (6):1–9.

Palmeri, Thomas J., Randolph Blake, René Marois, Marci A. Flanery, and William Whetsell Jr. 2002. The perceptual reality of synesthetic colors. *Proceedings of the National Academy of Sciences of the United States of America* 99:4127–4131.

Paulsen, Helle G., and Bruno Laeng. 2006. Pupillometry of grapheme-color synaesthesia. *Cortex* 42:290–294.

Ramachandran, Vilanayur S., and Edward M. Hubbard. 2001. Psychophysical investigations into the neural basis of synaesthesia. *Proceedings of the Royal Society of London B: Biological Sciences* 268:979–983.

Rich, Anina N., and Jason B. Mattingley. 2013. The role of attention in synesthesia. In *The Oxford Handbook of Synesthesia,* ed. Julia Simner and Edward M. Hubbard, 265–282 . Oxford: Oxford University Press.

Rizzolatti, Giacomo, Lucia Riggio, Isabella Dascola, and Carlo Umilta. 1987. Reorienting attention across the horizontal and vertical meridians: Evidence in favor of a premotor theory of attention. *Neuropsychologia* 25:31–40.

Rizzolatti, Giacomo, Lucia Riggio, and Boris M. Sheliga. 1994. Space and selective attention. In *Attention and Performance XIV,* ed. Carlo Umilta and Morris Moscovitch, 231–265. Cambridge, MA: MIT Press.

Rorden, Chris, and John Driver. 1999. Does auditory attention shift in the direction of an upcoming saccade? *Neuropsychologia* 37:357–377.

Rorden, Chris, Kristen Greene, Gregory M. Sasine, and Gordon C. Baylis. 2002. Enhanced tactile performance at the destination of an upcoming saccade. *Current Biology* 12:1429–1434.

Rothen, Nicolas, and Beat Meier. 2009. Do synesthetes have a general advantage in visual search and episodic memory? *PLoS One* 4 (4):e5037.

Sagiv, Noam, Jeffrey Heer, and Lynn C. Robertson. 2006. Does binding of synesthetic color to the evoking grapheme require attention? *Cortex* 42:232–242.

Sheliga, Boris M., Lucia Riggio, Laila Craighero, and Giacomo Rizzolatti. 1995. Spatial attention-determined modifications in saccade trajectories. *Neuroreport* 6:585–588.

Siegle, Greg J., Stuart R. Steinhauer, and Michael E. Thase. 2004. Pupillary assessment and computational modelling of the Stroop task in depression. *International Journal of Psychophysiology* 52:63–76.

Smilek, Daniel, Mike J. Dixon, and Philip M. Merikle. 2003. Synaesthetic photisms guide attention. *Brain and Cognition* 53:364–367.

Tamietto, Marco, Lorys Castelli, Sergio Vighetti, Paolo Perozzo, Giuliano Geminiani, Laurence Weiskrantz, and Beatrice de Gelder. 2009. Unseen facial and bodily expressions trigger fast emotional reactions. *Proceedings of the National Academy of Sciences of the United States of America* 106:17661–17666.

Treisman, Anne M., and Garry Gelade. 1980. A feature-integration theory of attention. *Cognitive Psychology* 12 (1):97–136.

Treisman, Anne M., and Sharon Sato. 1990. Conjunction Search Revisited. *Journal of Experimental Psychology: Human Perception and Performance* 16 (3):459–478.

Walker, Robin, Heiner Deubel, Werber X. Schneider, and John M. Findlay. 1997. Effect of remote distractors on saccade programming: evidence for an extended fixation zone. *Journal of Neurophysiology* 78 (2):1108–1119.

Weiskrantz, L., Cowey, A., and Barbur, J. L. 1999. Differential pupillary constriction and awareness in the absence of striate cortex. *Brain* 122:1533–1538.

....

CHAPTER 18

SYNESTHESIA, INCONGRUENCE, AND EMOTIONALITY

....

ALICIA CALLEJAS AND JUAN LUPIÁÑEZ

INTRODUCTION

....

When speaking with a wide range of synesthetes, one gets the impression that synesthesia has an emotional quality, at least for some synesthetes. A synesthetic experience is associated with a sensation of certitude and a conviction that the experienced phenomenon is real and valid (Cytowic 1993, 1989, 2002); a sense that one's experiences are "the right ones." As Richard Cytowic describes it, "Synesthesia is emotional. Synesthetes have an unshakable conviction and sense of validity that what they perceive is real. They trust their synesthetic perceptions. A 'eureka' sensation, as when the light bulb of insight goes off, often accompanies the parallel sense" (Cytowic 2002, 69). For example, a synesthete for whom the letter A (i.e., the inducer) induces the experience of green (i.e., its concurrent), it may feel absolutely clear that the letter A should be green, above any other color, and that the "greenness" of the letter A is as certain and "correct" as the angles in its uppercase written form. This emotional component is one of the defining factors in Cytowic's list of characteristics of synesthesia (Cytowic 1989). Given that synesthetic perception occurs in an involuntary manner and it is difficult to suppress, these perceptions will happen independently of the "real-life" features of the inducer (e.g., whether a letter is written in black ink, or green, or red) and independently of whether the qualities of the stimulus (e.g., this ink color) do or do not match the synesthetic experience. Therefore a letter that is associated with the experience of green will keep inducing such a sensation independently of the color in which the letter is shown, be it black, green, or red. The resulting match or mismatch between the perceptual features of the inducer and the subjective features of the concurrent provides the grounds for whether there is "congruence" or "incongruence" between real-life and synesthetic dimensions, which will in turn induce certain emotional reactions of either a positive or negative nature, respectively.

It is common to encounter reports from synesthetes describing this sense of discomfort, caused by the inconsistency between their synesthetic experience and the real-world perceptual features of the stimulus. Synesthetes usually talk about it as a feeling of things being "wrong," out of order, or incorrect. As one synesthete described it to us: "It is wrong, it's like coming into a room and finding all the chairs upside-down and everything out of place. I can't stand it. It is just wrong." This reaction has been reported in varying intensities ranging from just a mild discomfort to a fairly strong aversive emotional response.

These emotions elicited by the congruency or incongruency between "synesthetic" and "real" perception is different from cases where emotions serve as the actual inducer of synesthetic experiences (Ramachandran et al. 2012; Ward 2004) or as the actual concurrent (Hochel et al. 2009; Ramachandran and Brang 2008). Emotion in these latter types of synesthesia is different in that it represents an integral part of the synesthetic relationship (i.e., emotion either induces a synesthetic experience or is the concurrent experience itself). In contrast, our interest here is in emotion as a by-product of *any type of* inducer–concurrent relationship (i.e., a by-product of the mere existence of synesthesia). Nonetheless, we will devote a few lines to emotion as inducer/concurrent, before scrutinizing the emotional reactions that emerge as a by-product in the rest of the chapter.

EMOTIONS IN SYNESTHESIA

Emotions have been reported as inducers of synesthetic experiences of color in several studies. In most early studies the available information is sparse, and therefore inferences must be made about what dimension of the inducer was the one responsible for the experience of a concurrent. Two studies published in the early twentieth century (Raines 1909; Whipple 1900) reported cases of synesthetes where certain emotions had color or certain affectively toned names had colors. Cutsforth (1925) reported a case in which stimuli coming from different senses such as sounds, smells, or days of the week were colored based on affective influences. For example, a tone would only evoke a color when it was so intense that it became unpleasant. Collins (1929) also reported on a synesthete who saw colors for people but such experience only happened with individuals that the synesthete knew, or who had a strong personality. Additionally, new colors would be experienced for people who did not originally evoke them, as the person became better known to the synesthete. Last, Riggs and Karwoski (1934) reported a case in which a young synesthete also experienced colors associated with people but the colors were perceived projected on the people. They concluded that the color was determined by the degree to which the person was known to the synesthete and was not based on the physical features of the person.

More recently, Ward (2004) described a case of a synesthete who experienced synesthetic colors (also called photisms) for stimuli with an emotional connotation.

Specifically she experiences colors for people's names or faces, especially as she becomes acquainted with them. Ward reported high consistency in the colors she attributed to inducers when these inducers were presented to her across a 4-month interval. A synesthetic Stroop experiment was also performed where the synesthete had to either name the color in which a set of words were presented or the photism that she perceived for them. These words were shown half of the time in a congruent color (i.e., the color she reported to experience as a photism) and half of the time in an incongruent color. As expected, she was much faster naming the ink color when it was congruent with her photism than when it was not. Similarly, photism naming was also faster when ink color was congruent. Ward also reported a set of analyses to show that words with an emotional connotation were more likely to have a photism associated with them (e.g., people's first names versus foods, animals, or color names).

A more recent study also reporting colors evoked by emotions was conducted by Ramachandran et al. (2012) in which a single case was also reported. This individual was diagnosed with Asperger's syndrome as a child and when growing up, he was prompted to use colors to code people's emotions in an effort to learn to recognize them better. Since then, he started experiencing the colors, as well as auras around individuals in an automatic manner. Researchers used a target detection paradigm to show the authenticity of these aura experiences, a paradigm that has been used before to test color-grapheme synesthesia (Smilek et al. 2001). While a person stood in front of a projector screen, letters were flashed within or outside of the space reported to cover the aura for that person. The letters could be presented either in the same color as that person's aura or in a different one. Results showed that when the letter was presented inside the aura space in the same color as that of the aura, this synesthete was much slower to discriminate its identity than when it was presented outside of the aura space, or inside it but in a different color.

Emotions have also been the target of a synesthetic experience. That is, the experience of a stimulus can trigger a synesthetic emotion. Back in 1909, Raines reported a case where letters elicited an emotional response and a personality feature (e.g., D would be stupid while N was agreeable and C was good-natured). More recently, Ramachandran and Brang (2008) described the case of two synesthetes for which textures elicited emotions. While touching denim evoked strong depression, a tennis ball induced a feeling of happiness. Both synesthetes showed great consistency in a test–retest with an 8-month interval. Additionally, the authors recorded the synesthetes' facial expressions when touching the items as well as skin conductance response, and showed that the magnitude of the latter correlated with the valence judgment of the former, given by independent blind raters. Last, Hochel et al. (2009) reported on a synesthete with a complex set of inducers–concurrents where colors, faces, scenes, letters, numbers, names places, concepts, sounds, etc. elicited emotions, and letters also elicited photisms. Additionally, the photisms elicited by the letters would in turn also elicit emotions. That is, he experienced emotions associated with colors regardless of whether they were "real colors" or photisms. In a series of experiments they presented white colored numbers surrounded by a square frame that could be colored either matching the photism elicited by the number (congruent condition) or not matching the photism but inducing the same valence emotion (e.g., both the color and the photism elicited positive emotions), or not matching the photism and inducing a different emotion (i.e., a photism eliciting a negative emotion and a frame color eliciting a positive emotion). The authors reported that, for this synesthete, the perception of a stimulus in an incongruent color did not hinder his performance as long as the emotion elicited by the incongruent color was consistent with the emotion elicited by the stimulus' photism. That is, the concurrent emotion seemed stronger than the concurrent photism that induced the emotion.

Affective Reactions to Synesthetic Experiences

As outlined earlier, positive and negative emotions can also be elicited by the congruency or incongruency between any synesthetic and "real" perception. Nevertheless, although these affective reactions are quite usual amongst synesthetes, not many empirical studies have tried to achieve an understanding of this phenomenon, or to test whether it can be reliably replicated and measured under experimental conditions. Although this situation can happen in many types of synesthesia where a physical inducer presents features different from those experienced by a given synesthete (e.g., Beeli, Esslen, and Jäncke 2005), it is most commonly found and easiest to study in grapheme-color synesthesia due to the large number of synesthetes with this type of synesthesia and to the ease in manipulating the features of the inducer stimulus.

As Ramachandran and Hubbard (2001) point out, finding that emotional reactions could happen as a by-product of a synesthetic experience is highly interesting from a neuroscientific viewpoint. It supports their "cross-wiring theory" that proposes an abnormal cross-talk between brain regions that are in close proximity to each other and which process the information related to the inducer or the concurrent. In the case of grapheme-color synesthesia, the cross-talk would happen between a region related to visual shape (for the letter) and the color processing region. The emotional reactions associated with synesthetic perceptions could be explained in terms of the crosswiring hypothesis since this cross-talk can happen in part in the temporal lobe (e.g., fusiform gyrus for shape) and it is known that information processed in the temporal lobe gets relayed to the amygdala and other parts of the limbic system (Amaral et al. 1992; LeDoux 1992) which are involved in the processing of emotions and assigning valence to the stimuli that the organism is interacting with.

The first step in the analysis of what we might call these "side effect emotions" is to ask a simple question: Can we objectively measure them? With this goal a parallel is made with the logic established in the literature (Cytowic 2002; Dixon et al. 2000; Ramachandran and Hubbard 2001), where synesthesia is first shown to be an empirically detectable phenomenon (different than associations or metaphors), and is then further analyzed only when this prerequisite is met. To this end, we tried to determine whether these reactions reported by synesthetes are reproducible in an experimental setting to then test whether they are just affective memory associations, or if they are automatically elicited by the perception of an incongruently colored grapheme. That is, a grapheme presented in a color different from the elicited photism. Lastly, if we found that they are automatically elicited we would want to check whether the emotions are as automatic as the synesthetic photisms themselves.

We extensively studied a synesthete who reports strong negative emotions associated with the experience of incongruently colored stimuli. MA's reactions are so strong that when participating in a synesthetic Stroop-type experiment (in which she was presented with letters colored either congruently to her synesthesia, or incongruently, and she was required to simply name the color of the font), her discomfort could be overtly perceived as an increase in hand perspiration, a difficulty to stay calmed and sit still, etc.

We first tried to reproduce the reported disliking with an indirect behavioral task in which MA had to rate the valence of a set of words (i.e., whether they were positive or negative) on the basis of their semantic meaning (for details on the procedure see Callejas, Acosta, and Lupiáñez 2007). For example, the average person rates the word "love" as positive, semantically speaking, while "hate" is rated as negative, and "table" is neutral. In order to test the influence of the synesthetic colors and given that MA perceives a single color for each word, we manipulated the physical color in which the words were presented so it would either match or clash with her photism for that word. This manipulation provided us with "congruent words" (where the physical color of the stimulus matched the synesthetic percept induced by it) and "incongruent words" (where physical and synesthetic colors differed). Both conditions were compared to an "absence-of-color condition" where all words were presented in black given that informal reports by synesthetes point to black being considered a neutral color; a topic that will be discussed in a later section. The congruency between physical and synesthetic color modulated the emotional rating that MA gave to the words, whereas it did not affect ratings for a group of non-synesthetes. This was true not only for the incongruently colored words, which were rated by MA as negative, but also for the congruently colored ones which she rated as positive.

Interestingly, however, this congruency effect was independent of the semantic valence of words (e.g., whether the word was "love" or "hate") since both variables did not interact. Figure 18.1 shows the same ratings from MA and the group of non-synesthetes but broken down by the semantic valence of the words that were presented as well as the congruency of the color. We can see that on average (gray and white bars), negative words were rated as more negative than positive words which were rated more positively than neutral words. Therefore, MA seemed to use two sources of information in order to determine word valence: word meaning and congruency between the presented color and the experienced photism. Needless to say, the same was clearly not true for the control participants who showed no effect of congruency (gray and white bars on left side of figure).

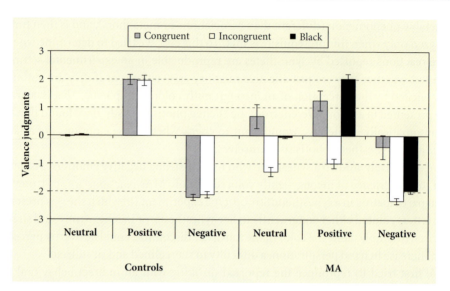

FIGURE 18.1 Valence ratings. Mean valence ratings for the control group and MA broken down by word valence (X-axis) and word color-photism congruence (gray and white bars). Words could have a positive valence (e.g. 'love'), neutral valence (e.g. 'table'), or a negative valence (e.g. 'danger'). Black bars represent MA's results from a different experiment in which all words were presented in black ink. Error bars represent the standard error of the mean.

When the color of the font clashed with the photism causing what we expect to be negative emotions in MA, she rated positive words (e.g., "love") as more negative and gave a more accurate rating (more similar to controls' ratings) for negative words. In contrast, when the color of the font matched the photism causing positive emotions in MA, she rated negative words (e.g., "hate") as more positive and gave a more accurate rating for positive words. As a result we found an overall less extreme rating in MA than the control group. It is worth noting though that the main effect of word valence was still significant both for the control group as well as for MA. Thus, all participants were following the instructions that emphasized ignoring the color and concentrating on the word meaning.

Even though the main effect of this experiment showed that MA was following the instructions and rating the words according to their semantic valence, in a separate control experiment we showed that when words were presented in a neutral color (e.g., all positive, neutral, and negative words presented in black ink), her valence ratings did not differ from those of the control group. As expected, when only one source of emotional information was present (i.e., the semantics of the word), MA's performance was comparable to that of the control participants (black bars in Figure 18.1 depicting MA's ratings in the control experiment versus the gray/white bars of the control participants). These results suggest that MA is using two sources of information to judge the emotionality of the words (word semantics and synesthetic congruency) when words are given non-black coloring.

MEMORY ASSOCIATIONS VERSUS AUTOMATIC AFFECTIVE REACTIONS TO SYNESTHETIC EXPERIENCES

One way to test whether affective reactions to synesthetic incongruence are experienced automatically is to use a paradigm in which a competition is created between the access to word meaning (known to be automatic) and the access to synesthetically induced emotions, and to then check whether the latter has an effect on the former.

Using a modified Stroop task (Stroop 1935) we were able to achieve this goal (Callejas, Acosta, and Lupiáñez 2007). In a classical Stroop task, participants are told to ignore the meaning of a word and to name its font color (e.g., name the font color of the word "red" written in green ink). Hence, in a regular Stroop task, the irrelevant dimension of the stimulus is the word meaning and the relevant dimension is the color in which the word is presented. Here we asked participants to categorize word valence. Therefore, the irrelevant dimension was the color in which the word was presented and ultimately, the congruency between that color and the photism for that word—whether this would lead to a positive or negative affective reaction. The relevant dimension was the semantic (emotional) meaning of the word. Consequently the color in which the word is presented should only affect MA's valence categorization if checking the consistency between color and photism and developing an emotional state based on that consistency is as automatic as processing the semantic meaning of the word. That is, our prediction stated that if affective reactions are automatic, when a speeded response is required, an interaction between semantic word valence categorization and synesthetic congruence should be found.

Results showed that, unlike controls, MA's responses were affected by color (Figure 18.2, gray and white bars on right side of figure). She took much longer to categorize positive words that were incongruently colored and tended to take longer to categorize negative words that were congruently colored (Figure 18.2, right side of top panel). That is, she found it easier to categorize words where the semantic emotion matched the emotion produced by the color-photism congruency (e.g., "love" in its synesthetically appropriate color) than words where they did not match (e.g., "love" in a synesthetically clashing color). This was true whether the semantics of the word were positive (as in the earlier "love" example) or negative (e.g., "hate" in a synesthetically clashing color was also fast to categorize). To more clearly demonstrate this, we coded a new variable called "correspondence" where we clumped together positive words in the "right" color and negative words in the "wrong" color to give a "corresponding" condition. Conversely, we also clumped positive words in the "wrong" color and negative words in the "right" color to give a "non-corresponding" condition. Corresponding trials were faster than non-corresponding trials. Again, MA's performance in a control experiment where all words were presented in black was comparable to that of the

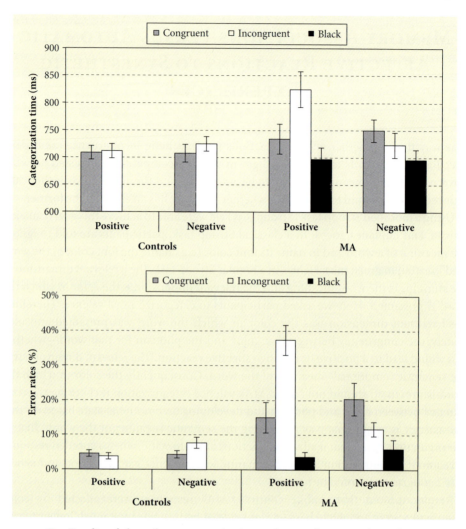

FIGURE 18.2 Results of the valence categorization task as a function of word valence and color-photism congruence. (a) Mean RT data for controls and MA in the categorization experiment (gray and white bars) and for MA in the control experiment (black bars). (b) Mean error rate data for controls and MA in the categorization experiment (gray and white bars) and for MA in the control experiment (black bars). Error bars represent the standard error of the mean.

control group (black bars in Figure 18.2) both for reaction time (RT) data (top panel), as well as accuracy (bottom panel).

Previous studies have shown that the perception of the synesthetic photism associated with a particular word is highly automatic (Dixon et al. 2000; Lupiáñez and Callejas 2006). Affective priming studies in non-synesthetes have also shown participants' ability to automatically extract semantic meaning from words, even when they do not have to be consciously evaluated (Fazio et al. 1986). Therefore, only if the affective reaction associated with the match-mismatch between a word's photism and the presented color happens automatically would one expect it to interact with the automatic evaluation of the words' semantic connotation. And only if that affective reaction is strong enough, would it influence such automatic processing of words. Moreover, since feedback was provided after each trial, only if this affective reaction is sufficiently strong, would top-down control mechanisms in charge of goal-driven behavior fail to suppress it in order to give an accurate categorization of the words based only on their semantic meaning.

These results, although robust, must be taken with caution since they are based on a single case. It is well accepted that not all synesthetes are equal and not all of them experience synesthesia in the same manner (Dixon and Smilek 2005; Dixon, Smilek, and Merikle 2004; Hubbard and Ramachandran 2005; Hubbard et al. 2005; Ramachandran and Hubbard 2001; Smilek and Dixon 2002). We checked whether these results are common to other synesthetes by running these experiments in three more synesthete participants who experience colors in their mind's eye. The synesthete group as a whole replicated the findings reported for MA although, as also shown in other group studies (Mattingley and Rich 2004), we also found individual differences. The most striking case was that of PSV who, despite reporting very strong emotions associated with her synesthetic experiences, did not show a congruency effect.

PSV did show a strong congruency effect on a Stroop task. That is, longer RTs when naming the color of a synesthetically incongruently colored letter, compared with when the color of the letter matched her photism. Therefore, the lack of emotional reactions could not be due to a lack of interference between photism and color. In the valence categorization task the dimension of the stimulus PSV had to respond to (emotional meaning of the words) is orthogonal to the congruence manipulation (matching between the presented color and elicited photisms). Since she did not have to respond with a color name but with a valence category, maybe it was easier for her to inhibit the irrelevant information and focus on the required task. In the Stroop task, since the dimension to be ignored shared a response code with the dimension to be attended, strong interference was observed instead.

If this hypothesis is correct, promoting color processing would modulate the effect of color-photism congruency on the emotionality processing of the words, or vice versa. To test this idea we presented the same words but now asked PSV to categorize the accuracy of their coloring according to her photisms. Now color was the attended dimension of the stimulus and emotional valence of words was the ignored one. MA also took part in this experiment. Since MA did show a behavioral effect in previous experiments, we expected her to also show the same congruency effect here. Since access to word meaning has been shown to be highly automatic (Mari-Beffa et al. 2000) we expected it to be processed regardless of its role in the task. On the other hand, photisms may be easily ignored when the task is more demanding and they are irrelevant. If this is the case, since photism processing was promoted here, we expected it to interact with word semantics and produce the typical inversed congruency effect for negative words.

PSV's performance did not differ in pattern from MA's (see Figure 18.3). They both took longer to categorize non-corresponding conditions ("wrong-colored" positive

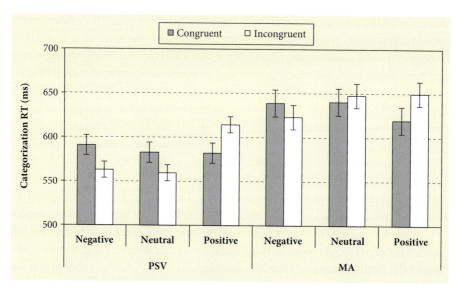

FIGURE 18.3 Reaction times for PSV and MA as a function of word valence and color congruence. Participants had to decide whether words were displayed in their right color (i.e., congruently with their photism) or in a wrong color (i.e., incongruently with their photism). Error bars represent the standard error of the mean.

words and "right-colored" negative words) than corresponding conditions ("right-colored" positive words and "wrong-colored" negative words). This result demonstrates that when the affective reaction produced by the perception of a colored word agrees with the valence of the word itself, PSV finds it easier to respond than in the non-corresponding conditions. Her subjective reports confirming the unpleasantness she feels when looking at wrongly colored words points to the possibility that the affective reaction is always present, even though it may not always be behaviorally measurable.

Assessing the fit between the environment and the subjective experience of synesthesia, as well as the affective reaction associated with such an assessment, is a strong and highly automatic side effect of, at least, some grapheme-color synesthesias. Synesthetes seem to automatically assess the fit between the physical world and their internal coloring schema. Apparently this evaluation happens even when it is not relevant to the current task. As Cytowic describes it, "synesthesia can perhaps be looked on as a shorthand way of calculating valence and salience, of attaching meaning to things" (Cytowic 2002, 11). A congruency effect, independent of emotionality, is usually taken as an index of the true experience of synesthesia. That is, many studies show faster RTs to congruently colored words than incongruently colored words as proof that the participant experiences synesthesia. Here we show that this robust effect can be reversed when the experimental manipulation turns an incongruently colored word (e.g., "hate" colored "wrongly") into a more consistent stimulus by aligning the result of the affective reaction produced by the color-photism congruence with the intrinsic semantic valence of the word.

Therefore emotion is part of the set of subjective experiences known as synesthesia and its effects on behavior may be as clear and robust as those produced by the concurrent itself. These results show that the "synesthetic" valence of the words—whether the perceptual features of the inducer match those of the subjective synesthetic experience—is activated automatically.

CONTEXTUAL EFFECTS ON SYNESTHETICALLY INDUCED AFFECTIVE REACTIONS

Informal reports suggest that the affective reaction induced by incongruently colored stimuli may be permeable to contextual influences. Previous reports have shown that the experience of synesthesia can be modulated by the context in which the inducer happens (Dixon et al. 2006; Myles et al. 2003). The very same perceptual shape could be experienced as a letter "S" or a number "5" depending on the context (i.e., HPSOA or 37564). These authors found that the photism changed according to the way the inducer was interpreted. More importantly, by combining the color elicited by each grapheme (i.e., by the letter or by the number) with the context in which it was presented (i.e., letter context or number context) they showed that the very same perceptual shape printed in the same ink color could give rise to shorter color naming times when it was perceived as congruent (e.g., when interpreted as a letter) than when it was incongruent (e.g., the same perceptual shape interpreted as a number).

Given these findings whereby the strong vivid experience of a synesthetic color can be manipulated by the contextual cues that modulate the interpretation of the identity of ambiguous grapheme shapes, we wanted to test whether the affective reaction resulting from the perception of an incongruently colored item could also be manipulated by the context in which the inducer was presented. A straightforward example of this situation would be that of synesthetes reading a letter written by a friend with a blue ink ball pen or a newspaper printed in black ink. If a word is presented in a context in which all words are uniformly colored, even though not in their "right" color, it is possible that synesthetes interpret that as a color-independent context and therefore try to avoid or control the affective reactions elicited by the incongruence. In order to test this, we systematically manipulated the color and context of a set of neutral and emotional words.

As described earlier when all words were consistently colored in black, MA showed the same pattern of results as control participants in the emotional categorization task (Callejas, Acosta, and Lupiáñez 2007). That is, she correctly assessed the words as being semantically positive/negative/neutral even though black was not the photism of any of the presented words and strictly speaking it was an incongruent color. To test whether previous results were due to black being a neutral color or words appearing in an achromatic context we manipulated the context. In an achromatic context, all words were shown in black ink (no color context). In the chromatic context words were presented in one of three different colors (congruent, incongruent, and black) all mixed together within each block of the experiment. If black is neutral because it lacks a hue then in the chromatic context we should still find an accurate assessment of black colored words even when they are preceded or followed by a colored word. Conversely, if context determines whether a black word is perceived as "neutrally colored" then we would expect to find the same pattern of results for black than for the incongruent color condition.

Participants rated words on a scale from very positive to very negative. Ratings for control participants did not differ depending on the context but MA showed an intriguing pattern. Black words were rated significantly higher than incongruently colored words but much lower than congruently colored words. Therefore, a neutral color under no coloring conditions (i.e., black words in an achromatic context) becomes an incongruent color under chromatic conditions (i.e., in the color context). Last, when comparing MA's results for black colored words across contexts we found that word rating was more accurate in the achromatic context. Therefore for MA, black is not a universally neutral color.

We next tested which feature of black allows it to be interpreted as a neutral color in an achromatic context. Since black is the absence of hue and gray is a brighter version of it, we tested whether neutrality was determined by absence of hue irrespective of brightness. If lack of hue is critical, gray or white would behave as black does in an achromatic context. However, if black is neutral because it is the most common color in printed documents and thus the "incongruent" color that synesthetes are most used to deal with, we would expect to find that gray would be considered an incongruent color irrespective of its context. Again we ran the same experiment but now words were presented either in a chromatic context where congruent, incongruent and gray colored words were mixed within each block or in an achromatic context where only gray words were presented. In the chromatic context, MA rated congruently colored words as the most positively ones, incongruent words were more negative and gray words were the most negative. In the achromatic context MA tended to rate all words more negatively than the control participants did. Therefore, while black was highly influenced by context, gray was not since it was experienced as an incongruent color in all situations.

Last, we manipulated the color of the background so that the gray words would be perceived as white to test how subjective perception and not wave length affects MA's color preferences. We found that gray-perceived words were rated more negative than white-perceived words by MA while control participants did not show any effect of subjective color. Thus, we showed that the very same color-photism mismatch influenced valence ratings differently based on the subjective color experience. This is consistent with MA's reports. After finishing the gray perception experiment she informed us that most of the colors of the words were wrong but after finishing the white perception experiment she commented that it was not so bad since "white is not such a bad color." This is an interesting demonstration that the evaluation of the color-photism fit is not a fixed process but one that is affected by different factors and that not all "wrong colors" are equally wrong.

If synesthetes like MA claim such strong aversive reactions to wrongly colored words, how can they cope with black printed stimuli? Do they lose their synesthesia? Do they lose the emotional reaction associated with the synesthetic experience? The experiment with black stimuli in a chromatic context showed that the synesthetic experience is not lost and neither is the affective reaction as measured by the influence of congruency on the valence ratings. If the synesthetic photism is still experienced in a color context, it is presumably also experienced in an achromatic context. If we assume that there is a mechanism involved in assessing the match between external features of the stimuli and the internally experienced phenomena (e.g., the color in which a word is presented and the photism elicited by such a word) then the fact that different samples of achromatic shades (black, gray) elicit different responses, points to the assessment process as being flexible. And it seems that one of the factors that can influence this process is the amount of practice with such stimuli. Therefore, the result we found with black ink could be explained by the fact that black is the most used color for printed books, newspapers, etc. and printed books do not usually show black print mixed up with other colors.

To summarize, black is only processed as a neutral color under certain conditions. This might be due to extensive practice with black printed material. As already noted by Dixon et al. (2006), meaning has an important role in synesthesia and not only in the process of experiencing one color or another as the synesthetic concurrent but, as shown here, also when categorizing a stimulus as congruent or incongruent with the internal perception. Two factors seem to have a crucial influence on these processes. Context influences how a color is categorized (especially for black) and subjective interpretation of the perceived wave length also seems to play a role (i.e., gray versus perceived-as-white color). Some other factors influencing the affective reaction might be personality traits or the amount of practice with the presented colors.

Synesthetic Emotions Can Condition Co-occurring Events

As shown earlier, affective reactions experienced as a side effect of synesthesia are real and quite strong (at least in some synesthetes). Additionally, some synesthetes report that synesthesia determines or at least influences the way they behave, the clothes they wear, or even how to spell their name so that the resulting synesthetic experience is pleasant.

We next questioned whether the affective reaction resulting from synesthetically congruent or incongruent experiences could be strong enough to affect attitude formation about a stimulus that was otherwise neutral. Attitude formation has long been studied in social psychology and is thought to occur through classical conditioning where the object for which an attitude will be formed (conditioned stimulus, CS) is encountered repeatedly paired with a stimulus that has a positive or negative valence (unconditioned stimulus, US). Early research seemed to back up this idea (Razran 1938; Staats and Staats 1958) and researchers even proposed that such a mechanism happens without awareness of the CS–US pairings. Olson and Fazio (2001) carried out a study based on an implicit learning paradigm to test whether attitudes form implicitly. After a conditioning phase they asked volunteers to rate some of the stimuli presented, among which were the positively and negatively conditioned stimuli (CS+ and CS−). Images paired with positive attributes were rated as more positive than those paired with negative attributes, although a subsequent awareness test showed that participants were not aware of the CS–US pairings shown in the conditioning phase.

Inspired by this experiment we sought to study whether the negative affective reaction associated with a synesthetically incongruently colored stimulus could be strong enough to serve as a US− (i.e., a negatively valent unconditioned stimulus) and whether the positive affective reaction associated with a congruently colored stimulus would be able to act as a US+ (i.e., a positively valent unconditioned stimulus). We devised a task in which a 3×3 grid appeared on the screen. Each of the 9 slots created by the grid was identified by a number located on its upper right corner. A colored target image was presented among distracters in one of the slots and participants had to report the slot number in which it was presented. Therefore, the slot number had to be processed and the answer entered as quickly and as accurately as possible via the number-keys of the computer keyboard. Participants were told the experiment studied their ability to transpose a grid-like spatial arrangement into a linear one.

Target stimuli were cartoon figures derived from two sets (see later). Distracters were nonsense images designed to have a set of perceptual features organized in different distributions (see Figure 18.4). In preparing the materials, we took the cartoon figures and randomly divided them into seven pairs. We used the colors evoked by MA's numbers 1 to 9 to color the seven pairs (two numbers are seen by MA as yellow and two as red and therefore the same cartoon image was used for both numbers). Once colored, we normalized the cartoon figures with a separate sample of participants who were asked to rate them on a 7-point pleasantness scale ranging from −3 (very negative) to +3 (very positive). One cartoon figure from each pair was assigned to the CS+ and one to the CS− according to the outcome of this norming so that the group of CS+ and CS− cartoons had similar baseline pleasantness ratings.

During congruent trials, the slot numbers were presented in the same color as the photism they elicit and a cartoon belonging to the CS+ (i.e., those to be positively conditioned) was used as target. For example, for a congruent trial where the target was presented in slot 6, all slot numbers were colored congruently with MA's photism and the blue cartoon figure shown on Figure 18.4 as associated with number 6 was shown inside slot 6. During incongruent trials slot numbers were presented in a clashing color and a cartoon figure assigned to the CS− (i.e., those to be negatively conditioned) was presented as target. For an incongruent trial where the target was in slot 6, all slot numbers were colored incongruently and the red cartoon figure shown on Figure 18.4 as associated with number 6 was shown inside slot 6. Thus, by manipulating the color-photism correspondence for the slot numbers and the color of the cartoon figures we created

MA's colours	CS+	CS−	Distracters

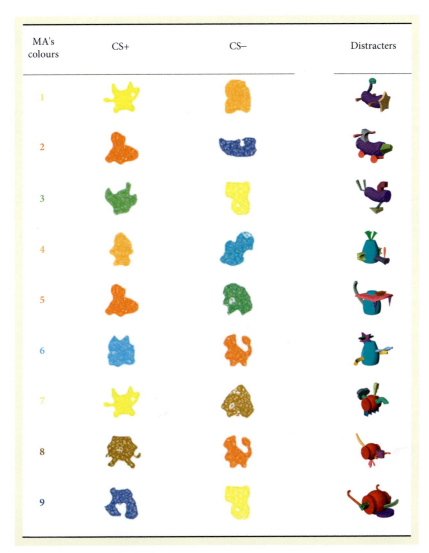

FIGURE 18.4 MA's colors for numbers 1 to 9 and the cartoon images associated with each number (in the experiment, Pokémon images were used, colored as the cartoons shown here). A representative subset of the distracters used is also presented.

congruent and incongruent conditions. If this congruence/incongruence was experienced with sufficient strength it could give rise to a significant emotional response that would act as a US (US+ for congruent trials and US− for incongruent trials) that would condition the target stimulus. This conditioned response could then be measured as an attitude towards that stimulus.

We asked MA to rate the valence of each image in a 7-point scale (−3 to +3), as we had requested from non-synesthetes during norming. Her mean valence of the images was 1.20 for items in the CS+ group and 1.20 for those in the CS− (in other words, MA showed no preference for either group of images). However, after the conditioning/visual search phase MA rated CS+ cartoon figures as more pleasant (mean rating = 1.49) than CS− cartoon figures (mean rating = −0.31). A t-test confirmed that this difference was statistically significant. Control participants did not show a difference between their ratings for CS+ and CS− stimuli. Therefore a reliable conditioning effect was found since MA rated those cartoons shown in incongruent trials (where numbers were colored incongruently with the photism they elicited) as more negative than those cartoons paired with a number in its "right" color.

We can conclude that the affective reaction triggered by an incongruently colored stimulus such as a red 6, acted as a US and conditioned an attitude towards an otherwise neutral item (i.e., the red cartoon associated with number 6). These results have interesting implications for the understanding of how synesthesia influences the way synesthetes go about their normal daily lives. If a few hundred trials showing an image paired with a certain incongruence results in a negative attitude towards that image, a lifetime of encounters with incongruent stimuli paired with different objects (e.g., a brand name in an incongruent color) could be determining their attitudes towards situations or objects. Although the results from this experiment should be taken with caution since they were performed on a single synesthete, it is not uncommon to hear from synesthetes who change the way they spell their name, or change their name altogether only because they do not identify with the color they see for the letters forming it, the personality of their initial, etc. which underlines the fact that synesthetes behavior is to some extent influenced by their synesthetic perceptions and their emotional impressions.

Proposal of a Bi-Dimensional Assessment Hypothesis

The results presented here lead to the conclusion that, at least for the synesthetes we studied, synesthetic affective reactions seem to be strong enough to have an influence on valence categorization and rating of emotional words, and even to condition neutral stimuli, thus influencing attitudes towards them. In the following section, we suggest a model that could account for these results. We propose that a comparison mechanism that we term synesthetic assessment (SynA) is continuously checking for inconsistencies between perceptual and synesthetic experience. Certain factors, which we will discuss, modulate whether the results of this synesthetic assessment influence performance or not.

We suggest that SynA modulates performance by adding evidence biasing emotional judgments. In our tasks, where positive, negative and neutral valence words had to be evaluated, participants have to perform a semantic categorization. A semantic assessment process (SemA) checks the meaning of the word and informs about its positive or negative semantic dimension. At the same time, the SynA process informs about the synesthetic dimension of the word and its relationship to the external world. These two

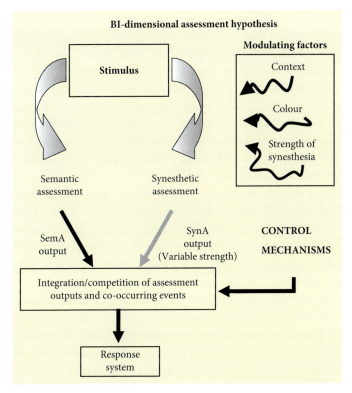

FIGURE 18.5 Depiction of the bi-dimensional assessment hypothesis proposed to explain the affective reactions found in synesthetes when perceiving a stimulus colored congruently or incongruently with their internal experience.

assessment processes are then compared, and its outcome can be positive (i.e., when internal and external features match) or negative (i.e., when internal and external features do not match). In a later stage, information from the two assessment processes is integrated and ultimately the result of this integration is relayed to the response mechanisms.

As shown in Figure 18.5, when a positive word is presented in a congruent color, the outcome of the SemA is positive and the result of the SynA is also positive. When the same positive word is instead presented in a synesthetically clashing color, while the SemA is still producing the same outcome, the SynA is now returning a negative result (the external color does not match the internally experienced photism), and thus a negative affective reaction is elicited. When in the next stage of processing these two sources of information are combined, the result can be a coherent one (both processes yielding the same outcome) or an incoherent one (each process yielding an outcome of different sign). For coherent outcomes, information is sent to the execution modules and a fast response is performed. For incoherent outcomes a control mechanism has to bias the competition so that the outcome of the stimulus dimension to which the participant has to respond is the one that ultimately gets relayed to the execution modules. Therefore, longer RTs and more errors are expected under these circumstances.

In the case of negative words presented in a congruent color, this model predicts that the response will be longer than for congruently colored positive words. Although intuition would predict that because words are colored congruently they are processed faster, this model proposes that, given the automaticity of word reading, what is crucial is the coherence between information coming from different assessment processes. In the case of the negative congruently colored word, the SemA would yield a negative outcome while the SynA would yield a positive one. A conflicting situation is encountered and control processes have to bias the competition. Therefore, this model would propose that negative incongruently colored words would be easier to respond to because both SemA and SynA provide similar outcomes.

As shown in this chapter, the results are not as clear-cut as predicted by a simple version of the model, since different factors have been shown to influence the outcome such as the context in which the information is presented, the color that is used or the strength of the synesthesia experience. In order to account for differences across synesthetes we propose that, although the SynA process is present in all synesthetes, it might be more active in some synesthetes and therefore influence their performance to greater levels. Its effect can also depend on the strength and specificity of the synesthetic associations of each synesthete. The noisier results found for negative words (e.g., RTs in the categorization task) can also be explained by the strength of both assessment processes. Negative stimuli seem to have a greater impact on processing than positive stimuli (Baumeister et al. 2001; Cacioppo and Gardner 1999; Taylor 1991) and it may be that the outcome of the SemA when categorizing negative words is stronger than the outcome of the SynA. Only if synesthesia is strong enough would the SynA outcome influence the SemA.

Our context experiments informed us that not all colors are "equally incongruent" and that other factors, such as the context in which the task is performed, can also influence performance. We propose that the SynA process is a complex one that not only takes into account the photism and physical color, but also other factors that aid in the synesthete's effort to adapt to his/her environment (i.e., whether the context of the task invites color processing, whether plenty of colors are present or not, whether reading a printed book, etc.). Adaptation to the environment would then act by weakening the strength of the SynA outcome. Last, the fact that attitudes can be formed as a result of pairing a neutral stimulus with a synesthetically incongruent one supports the claim that this SynA process is ubiquitous. Nevertheless, the demands of the task being performed could influence the outcome of the process and make it more available to conscious report while in other situations it would just be acting implicitly on behavior without the synesthete noticing it.

CONCLUSIONS

For many synesthetes, synesthesia often has an emotional component. Synesthetes report a strong feeling of certainty associated with their synesthetic experiences and, in many cases, a sense of discomfort when their sensory experiences do not match their internal synesthetic ones. This emotional side of synesthesia can be quite strong and can influence the way synesthetes interact with the environment, and can also influence their attitudes towards certain stimuli based on their synesthetic relationship to them. Different emotions can also be synesthetically elicited as concurrents to stimuli such as colors and letters. Equally, synesthesic photisms can arise from emotions as inducers (e.g., colors elicited by people depending on whether the synesthete likes the person). Altogether these experiences speak about the emotional nature of synesthesia and should be taken into account in order to fully understand this phenomenon and its implications to the everyday life of people experiencing it.

References

Amaral, David G., Joseph L. Prince, Ala Pitanen, and S. Thomas Carmichael. 1992. Anatomical organization of the primate amygdaloid complex. In *The Amygdala: Neurobiological Aspects of Emotion, Memory and Mental Dysfunction*, ed. John P. Aggelton, 1–66. New York: Wiley.

Baumeister, Roy F., Ellen Bratslavsky, Catrin Finkenauer, and Kathleen Vohs. 2001. Bad is stronger than good. *Review of General Psychology* 5:323–370.

Beeli, Gian, Michaela Esslen, and Lutz Jäncke. 2005. Synaesthesia: When coloured sounds taste sweet. *Nature* 434 (7029):38.

Cacioppo, John T., and Wendi L. Gardner. 1999. Emotion. *Annual Review of Psychology* 50:191–214.

Callejas, Alicia, Alberto Acosta, and Juan Lupiáñez. 2007. Green love is ugly: Emotions elicited by synesthetic grapheme-colour perceptions. *Brain Research* 1127:99–107.

Collins, Mary. 1929. A case of synaesthesia. *Journal of General Psychology* 2:12–27.

Cutsforth, Thomas D. 1925. The rôle of emotion in a synaesthetic subject. *The American Journal of Psychology* 36:527–543.

Cytowic, Richard E. 1989. *Synaesthesia: A Union of the Senses*. 1st ed. New York: Springer Verlag.

——. 1993. *The Man Who Tasted Shapes*. New York: Putnam.

——. 2002. *Synaesthesia: A Union of the Senses*. 2nd ed. Cambridge, MA: MIT Press.

Dixon, Mike J., and Daniel Smilek. 2005. The importance of individual differences in grapheme-colour synaesthesia. *Neuron* 45 (6):821–823.

Dixon, Mike J., Daniel Smilek, and Philip Merikle. 2004. Not all synaesthetes are created equal: Projector versus associator synaesthetes. *Cognitive, Affective and Behavioral Neuroscience* 4 (3):335–343.

Dixon, Mike J., Daniel Smilek, Cera Cudahy, and Philip M. Merikle. 2000. Five plus two equals yellow. Mental arithmetic in people with synaesthesia is not coloured by visual experience. *Nature* 406: 365.

Dixon, Mike J., Daniel Smilek, Patricia L. Duffy, Mark P. Zanna, and Philip M. Merikle. 2006. The role of meaning in grapheme-colour synaesthesia. *Cortex* 42 (2):243–252.

Fazio, Russell H., David M. Sanbonmatsu, Martha C. Powell, and Frank R. Kardes. 1986. On the automatic activation of attitudes. *Journal of Personality and Social Psychology* 50:229–238.

Hochel, M., E. G. Milán, J. L. M. Martín, A. González, E. D. García, F. Tornay, and J. Vila. 2009. Congruence or coherence? Emotional and physiological responses to colours in synaesthesia. *European Journal of Cognitive Psychology* 21 (5):703–723.

Hubbard, Edward M., and Vilayanur S. Ramachandran. 2005. Neurocognitive mechanisms of synaesthesia. *Neuron* 48 (3):509–520.

Hubbard, Edward M., A. Cyrus Arman, Vilayanur S. Ramachandran, and Geoffrey M. Boynton. 2005. Individual differences among grapheme-colour synesthetes: Brain-behaviour correlations. *Neuron* 45:975–985.

LeDoux, Joseph E. 1992. Brain mechanisms of emotion and emotional learning. *Current Opinion in Neurobiology* 2 (2):191–197.

Lupiáñez, Juan, and Alicia Callejas. 2006. Automatic perception and synaesthesia: evidence from colour and photism naming in a Stroop-negative priming task. *Cortex* 42 (2):204–212.

Mari-Beffa, Paloma, Luis J. Fuentes, Andrés Catena, and George Houghton. 2000. Semantic priming in the prime task effect: Evidence of automatic semantic processing of distractors. *Memory and Cognition* 28 (4):635–647.

Mattingley, Jason B., and Anina N. Rich. 2004. Behavioral and brain correlates of multisensory experience in synaesthesia. In *Handbook of Multisensory Processes*, ed. Gemma A. Calvert, Charles Spence, and Barry E. Stein, 851–865. Cambridge, MA: MIT Press.

Myles, Kathleen M., Mike J. Dixon, Daniel Smilek, and Philip M. Merikle. 2003. Seeing double: The role of meaning in alphanumeric-colour synaesthesia. *Brain and Cognition* 53:342–345.

Olson, Michael A., and Russell H. Fazio. 2001. Implicit attitude formation through classical conditioning. *Psychological Science* 12 (5):413–417.

Raines, Thomas H. 1909. Report of a case of psychochromesthesia. *Journal of Abnormal Psychology* 4:249–260.

Ramachandran, Vilayanur S., and David Brang. 2008. Tactile-emotion synesthesia. *Neurocase* 14 (5):390–399.

Ramachandran, Vilayanur S., and Edward M. Hubbard. 2001. Synaesthesia - A window into perception, thought and language. *Journal of Consciousness Studies* 8 (12):3–34.

Ramachandran, Vilayanur S., Luke Miller, Margaret S. Livingstone, and David Brang. (2012). Colored halos around faces and emotion-evoked colors: A new form of synesthesia. *Neurocase* 18 (4):352–358.

Razran, G. H. S. 1938. Conditioning away social bias by the luncheon technique. *Psychological Bulletin* 37:481–485.

Riggs, Lorrin A., and Theodore Karwoski. 1934. Synaesthesia. *British Journal of Psychology* 25:29–41.

Smilek, Daniel, and Mike J. Dixon. 2002. Towards a synergistic understanding of synaesthesia: combining current experimental findings with synaesthetes' subjective descriptions. *Psyche* 8 (1).

Smilek, Daniel, Mike J. Dixon, Cera Cudahy, and Philip M. Merikle. 2001. Synaesthetic photisms influence visual perception. *Journal of Cognitive Neuroscience* 13 (7):930–936.

Staats, Arthur W., and Carolyn K. Staats. 1958. Attitudes established by classical conditioning. *Journal of Abnormal and Social Psychology* 11:187–192.

Stroop, John R. 1935. Studies of interference in serial verbal reactions. *Journal of Experimental Psychology* 18:643–662.

Taylor, Shelley E. 1991. Asymmetrical effects of positive and negative events: the mobilization-minimization hypothesis. *Psychological Bulletin* 110:67–85.

Ward, Jamie. 2004. Emotionally mediated synaesthesia. *Cognitive neuropsychology* 21 (7):761–772.

Whipple, Guy M. 1900. Two cases of synaesthesia. *American Journal of Psychology* 11: 377–404.

PART IV

....

CONTEMPORARY AND HISTORICAL APPROACHES

....

CHAPTER 19

SYNESTHESIA IN THE NINETEENTH CENTURY

Scientific origins

JÖRG JEWANSKI

SYNESTHESIA BEFORE THE NINETEENTH CENTURY

In this chapter I examine the history of synesthesia reporting, beginning in 1812 with the first known description of synesthesia, and progressing through the turn of the twentieth century, where the number of reports starts to diminish but see chapters by Lovelace (Chapter 21) and Cytowic (Chapter 20), this volume, who describe a resurgence of reporting at the end of the twentieth century. I follow through to the end of World War I and, specifically, to Wheeler (1920), and its précis in Wheeler and Cutsforth (1922), who gave the most extensive overview of its kind in the literature up to that date. The research described in this chapter was conducted in collaboration with Sean A. Day, Julia Simner, and Jamie Ward. I focus particularly cases of synesthesia reported within the scientific and medical literature, rather than potential cases within music, visual arts, and poetry. These latter are difficult to disentangle from symbolic and metaphorical movements during this period linking different senses.

Synesthesia is likely as old as mankind. Hence, there is no reason why there should not be many cases of synesthesia before the nineteenth century, although we have no sources of information about them. We know of many theorists from the time of the ancient Greeks up to the middle of the eighteenth century, who compared colors and tones or tone intervals mostly in parallel with comparisons to the planets, elements, epoques, or sometimes even with taste qualities. Those authors include, for example, Girolamo Cardanus, Gioseffo Zarlino, Athanasius Kircher, Marin Mersenne, Isaac Beckmann, Cureau de la Chambre, Isaac Newton, and Louis-Bertrand Castel, the latter famous for his *clavecin oculaire* (color organ). In these writings, it is possible to detect a type of analogical thinking in which the authors make associations across different dimensions, for example, color and tone based on structure, and in particular, by uniting elements which arise naturally in sets of the same number (Jewanski 1995a, 1999, 2006, 2007, 2010a, 2010b). A typical example can be found in the natural scientist Athanasius Kircher, who in 1646, divided colors, the intensities of colors, the brightness of light, tastes, elements, ages of human beings, steps of science, steps of being, and musical tones, into five parts apiece. These were then brought together into an order from bright to dark, from pleasant to unpleasant, from young to old, or from high to low, for example, the brightest light matched with the most intense taste, and so on. This has nothing to do with neurological synesthesia, but with the notion of a complete harmony of the world. This type of analogical thinking was an accepted method of science up to the end of the seventeenth century used for obtaining new knowledge, and which should clearly be distinguished from synesthesia as a "condition." However, there are several examples for possible cases of synesthesia before 1800 (Jewanski, Day, and Ward 2009), where, for example, the color scarlet was "like" the sound of a trumpet Locke (1690, book III, chapter IV, § 11, p. 199). However, such cases seem to be explained more obviously via the common ability to construct intermodal analogies (Behne 1991), which all people can do and which is not the type of involuntary association that typifies synesthesia. At our present state of knowledge, the first documented case of synesthesia was reported in 1812, and I describe this, and subsequent cases, in more detail in the following sections.

REPORTED CASES

Cases of synesthesia in the nineteenth century can be divided into two epochs. The first consists of single case studies and goes up to 1873; the second consists of larger scale studies and starts in 1876. I review both in the following sections.

Single case studies 1812–1873

Currently, the first known convincing account of synesthesia is the case of Georg Tobias Ludwig Sachs (1786–1814), given as a self-description in his medical dissertation about albinism, published in Latin in 1812 (Jewanski, Day, and Ward 2009, 2012; Sachs 1812). There are only three and a half pages about synesthesia inside his book (§ 157–160, pp. 80–84; German translation in Schlegel 1824, 98–102; English translation in Jewanski, Day, and Ward 2009, 297–298; version in Latin/German/English/Spanish in Jewanski, Day, and Ward 2012, 57–67). In this, Sachs describes his multiple synesthesias and gives examples of his color synesthesia for letters of the alphabet, for tones of the musical scale, for numbers and for days of the week. In this work he also alludes to a possible second case by claiming "I recently found a trace of it in a very famous man" although the identity of this man was never revealed.

The second identified case of synesthesia, historically speaking, is mentioned only in two sentences within a letter dated 12 January 1848. This letter was included in William Krohn's bibliography on synesthesia (1892), but not evaluated either by him or by anyone else until the present day. This case represents the first female synesthete, the first child (Jewanski et al. 2013b), the first synesthete outside of Europe, and the first synesthete in the US. She was the 8-year-old Ellen Tucker Emerson (1839–1909), the second of four children of the poet Ralph Waldo Emerson and his second wife Lidian Jackson. Ralph Waldo Emerson was a friend of the philosopher Henry David Thoreau, who wrote in a letter to Emerson: "I was struck by Ellen's asking me, yesterday, [...] if I did not use '*colored* words.' She said that she could tell the color of a great many words, and amused the children at school by so doing" (1848, 745). Although only two sentences, we can be quite certain that Ellen was a synesthete: colored words are typical indicators of synesthesia, as is her wondering whether others do not also do this. And since Thoreau was "struck," we can assume it was not just the amusing game of a child; Thoreau was hearing this type of report apparently for the first time, and it was something unusual to him. What other explanations can be given for an 8-year-old girl talking about colored words other than her being a synesthete? Finally, Ellen Tucker Emerson is the first synesthete of whom we have a photograph (Figure 19.1).

FIGURE 19.1 Ellen Tucker Emerson (1839–1909), the first synesthete of whom we have a photo, 1872. Courtesy of the Concord Free Public Library.

At our present state of knowledge, we have suggested that the next case of a synesthete after 1812 Sachs is the case mentioned earlier that Emerson dated 1848, and so we appear to have a gap of 36 years between them (Jewanski et al. 2011a). However, there is no reason why there should not be many synesthetes between 1812 and 1848 although there are three main problems in finding them:

(1) The first and the perhaps second case were hidden in a book about albinism, the third in a private letter, the fourth in a book review (see later). Perhaps there are more hidden cases in books or articles about medicine, anatomy, biology, psychology, physiology, physics, and so on, where again the title does not give us a clue to this content.

(2) During the first half of the nineteenth century, opportunities to trace back accounts through bibliographies and references were limited. This is because many medical, psychological, and physiological weekly, monthly, or annual journals and reviews reporting new research were founded after 1848. Many reviews, for example, about another synesthesia report in the Nussbaumer articles (1873, see later) were published in journals such as Medizinische Neuigkeiten für praktische Ärzte [Medical news for medical practitioners] first published in 1851; Centralblatt für die Medicinischen Wissenschaften [Essential journal for medical sciences] first published in 1863; Jahresbericht über die Leistungen und Fortschritte in der gesammten Medicin [Annual report of the efforts and progresses in the whole medicine] first published in 1867.

(3) Although we now have more possibilities for finding sources, e.g., via databases on the Internet, there was no name for synesthesia between 1812 and 1848. Since it is difficult to find something which has no name, our modern research abilities are restricted.

With one exception, all scientific papers about synesthesia up to 1873 deal with the description of one or two new cases see Table 19.1. This exception is the article written by Charles-Auguste- Édouard Cornaz, who became a famous surgeon with numerous publications to his name. Cornaz was the first to discover and summarize the case of Sachs, and to give a name to the phenomenon in 1848, *hyperchromatopsie*, because the condition was assumed to cause the perception of too many colors. Cornaz was also the first to give an explanation of the condition, to classify it in a context, to ask a set of basic research questions, to publish an article (1851a) with the name of the phenomenon as the title, to provide a bibliography with five titles (Anonymous 1849a; Cornaz 1848; Sachs 1812, 1824; Wartmann 1849a, 1849b (who summarized Sachs based on Cornaz 1848), and the first science author about synesthesia who was not himself a synesthete. Cornaz published his article as a booklet (1851b), which became the first monograph on synesthesia.

Cornaz's work also led to the discovery of new cases (Anonymous 1849a; Wartmann 1850). His study about hyperchromatopsia was reviewed or reported several times in medical journals and handbooks in Belgium, France, Germany, and Switzerland, and helped to make synesthesia known and accepted as a serious research topic

Table 19.1 Summary of reported cases of synesthesia between 1812 and 1873

The first known synesthetes 1812–1873

Source	No. of cases	Brief description
Sachs 1812, translated Schlegel 1824	1	Multiple synesthesia: (1) the alphabet; (2) tones of a musical scale; (3) numbers; and (4) days of a week
Sachs 1812	1?	Sachs: "I recently found a trace of it in a very famous man." We do not know more
Thoreau 1848	1	Word-to-color-synesthesia
Anonymous 1849a	1	Letter-to-color-synesthesia
Wartmann 1850	2	Both synesthetes have perception of colors, but we do not know what the trigger stimulus is for case 1. Concerning case 2 these seem to be the same triggers as Sachs: "but without his letters of the alphabet necessarily producing the same colours." We do not know more
Perroud 1863	1	Letter-to-color-synesthesia
Chabalier 1864	1	Vowel-to-color-synesthesia
Kaiser 1872, 1882	1	Number-to-color- and word-to-color-synesthesia
Nussbaumer 1873a, 1873b, 1873c, 1873d, 1873e	2	Two brothers with music-to-color-synesthesia
Lussana 1873, 1883	2	Two brothers with voice-to-color-synesthesia
Hudson 1873	1	Number-form-synesthesia. She also visualized the alphabet pictorially

internationally within the scientific community (Jewanski et al. 2012, 2013a). In contrast, because Sachs only gave a self-description of his own synesthesia, he did not generate basic questions and was apparently no longer interested in the phenomenon. After his initial thesis there is only one more scientific paper from him: a study about the sensation of color unrelated to synesthesia (Sachs 1814). In comparison, Cornaz became the first researcher on synesthesia, proper see Figure 19.2.

Today, we know of 14 cases of synesthesia up to 1873 or perhaps 15 if we include Sachs' "very famous man." In general, until 1873, studies about synesthesia were rare. This situation changed with studies by Fidelis Alois Nussbaumer (1873a, 1873b, 1873c, 1873d, 1873e; see Jewanski, Day, and Ward 2010). Nussbaumer was the first to develop a questionnaire about synesthesia, including 19 questions, designed for himself and his brother, as well as being the first to describe colored hearing in detail. He was also the first to give a description of synesthesia that was very detailed, and this centered on a self-description of his and his brother's synesthesia. Nussbaumer noted that his synesthesia persisted in his dreams, that it was neither pleasant nor unpleasant, and that with full concentration on something different he could get rid of it. He also noted that the sensation was inside his head, where it starts at the temple as a band of colors, which spread to the middle of the forehead. Whereas Sachs and his anonymous reviewer (1849b) did not write about the reaction of their circle of acquaintances to synesthesia, and while we know that the 8-year-old Ellen amused the children at school when describing the color of a word,

1825-1911

FIGURE 19.2 Charles-Auguste Édouard Cornaz, the first researcher on synesthesia. Reproduced from M. de Tribolet. 1912. Edouard Cornaz 1825–1911. Notice biographique. *Bulletin de la société Neuchâteloise des sciences naturelles* 39: 20–48, page 25. Courtesy of the Société Neuchâteloise des Sciences Naturelles, Switzerland.

Nussbaumer is the first to report being laughed at by his parents and siblings when he was a child who talked about colored tones (1873a, 7).

For the first time in history, famous scientists began to get to grips with synesthesia: Nussbaumer published a reference letter written for him by the professor of zootomy Carl Bernard Brühl 1872 in which Brühl commended the work carried out by Nussbaumer. Later, Nussbaumer also published a critical commentary by Moritz Benedikt (1873), a professor of electrotherapy and the pathology of nerves. Due to Brühl's letter in particular, Nussbaumer's papers were reported and reviewed in Germany and Austria, and eventually found their way to the US, where they were reviewed in a medical journal, and even integrated into a practical treatise for the use of medical students and practitioners (see Jewanski, Day, and Ward 2010). This was the largest reception synesthesia had received until this date, and one wonders whether Nussbaumer was even aware of it. At this point the phenomenon became a real topic within science: with one blow, synesthesia became popular. Nearly every article with new cases and new theories published between 1873 and 1880 was initiated by Nussbaumer's articles. The negative aspect of his popularity for the modern reviewer is that from then on, nearly every history

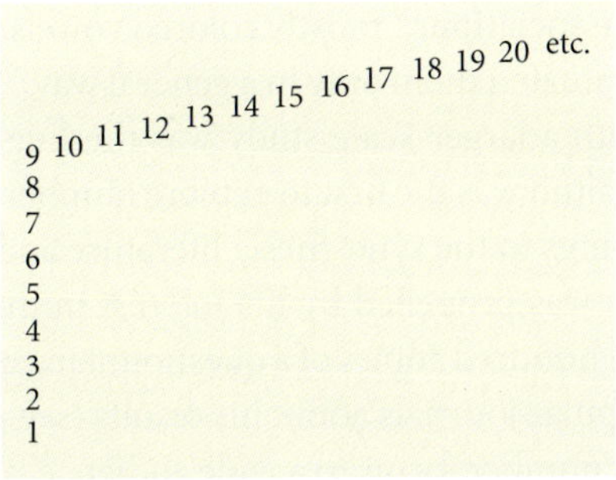

```
                                        18 19 20 etc.
                            15 16 17
                   13 14
          11 12
   9 10
   8
   7
   6
   5
   4
   3
   2
   1
```

FIGURE 19.3 The first visual representation of what a synesthete sees: "The nine digits *will* ascend in a straight line before my mind's eye, and the larger numbers *will* slant off at a queer angle." Reproduced from H. R. Hudson. 1873, Idiosyncrasies. *The Atlantic monthly: A magazine of literature, art and politics* 31 (184):197–201, page 199.

about synesthesia started with him, because Nussbaumer did not write about earlier cases. So the older cases went into oblivion and were rediscovered mainly by Suarez de Mendoza (1890), while Fidelis Alois Nussbaumer became the most popular synesthete in the nineteenth century (Jewanski, Day, and Ward 2010).

With one exception, all the single case studies up to 1873 had synesthesia triggering color: this exception is the poet Hannah Reba Hudson, who described her "number-form" synesthesia. Via her, we get the first visual representation of what a synesthete "sees" (Figure 19.3).

Larger-scale studies since 1876

During the last two decades of the nineteenth century, several larger-scale studies were conducted, above all by Galton (see papers from 1880 to 1882; also Bleuler and Lehmann 1881; Calkins 1892, 1893, 1895; Flournoy 1892, 1893). In addition to these, a number of single-case studies were also published, compare Wheeler (1920) and Mahling (1926, 1927). The forerunner was by the German psychologist Gustav Theodor Fechner (1876), who asked several people within his circle of friends and acquaintances about combinations of letters mainly vowels and colors. He got four people to answer; two of them seem to be synesthetes because of their very special descriptions of colors. In the appendix of his book, Fechner gave an evaluation of 73 people, who had connected vowels with colors, but he did not differentiate between synesthesia and normal non-synesthetic association. Three years later, Fechner, in collaboration with the academic-philosophical society in Leipzig, published a request in journals for readers to send him an answer regarding whether any had color associations for vowels, numbers, days of the week, and musical keys. Fechner did not evaluate the data from this inquiry, but allocated his materials to Hermann Steinbrügge, who evaluated them in 1887. Altogether, Fechner found 347 cases of "color associations," mostly colored vowels. Steinbrügge did not keep the questionnaires and evaluated them only in a general way.

The next researcher with a larger-scale study was the English polymath Sir Francis Galton. In his research, Galton was the first to explore number forms in detail he was the first to link Hudson's writings to the synesthesia literature and to find patterns. Galton's interest in number-forms was propelled by his interest in mental imagery. In 1879/80 Galton distributed several hundred copies of a questionnaire, and then published several articles in science and popular journals about his results (see papers from 1880 to 1881). This broadcast the idea of number forms to a wide audience, and broadened knowledge about them 1883. It is within these works that the first colored printed photisms of synesthetes appear (Figure 19.4).

In addition to cases of number forms, Galton found "many curious cases of color association with the various numerals" and "many different ways in which dates, days of the week, and months of the year are apt to be visualised" (1880a, 252). Although Galton did not focus on them in his following articles, from now on we know of a steadily increasing number of reported synesthetes. Altogether, Galton received answers from 107 men, around 180 women, and several hundred short reports from schoolchildren (Burbridge 1994, 447). For Galton, several visual phenomena came under the umbrella of synesthesia, like visual memory of scenes, hypnogogic imagery, visual hallucinations, as well as number forms.

The first large scale study focusing on synesthesia in its entirety was conducted in 1881 by the Swiss medical students Eugen Bleuler who became a famous psychiatrist and Karl Lehmann who became a famous researcher on hygiene. They found 76 synesthetes, many more than all the cases together before 1881. Their book became a milestone in the history of synesthesia. Together with Nussbaumer's papers (1873), it is the most cited study on synesthesia in the nineteenth century. Because of its international reception, references to Bleuler and Lehmann initiated nearly every following study about synesthesia. Their seminal paper was reported/reviewed several times in medical periodicals, and even in *The Times* (Anonymous 1882).

Influenced by Bleuler and Lehmann, the Swiss psychologist Théodore Flournoy started collecting his own observations (1890). With his cousin Edouard Claparède, who later became a famous psychologist, Flournoy developed a questionnaire 2 years later Claparède and Flournoy (1892) and subsequently published the results without Claparède (Flournoy 1892, 1893; cf. Philippe 1894). Next to Galton's British work and Bleuler and Lehmann's study in Germany, Flournoy's book from France and Calkins's articles in the US (see later) became the most important statistical studies on synesthesia during the entire nineteenth century.

EARLY HYPOTHESES WITHIN THESE WRITINGS

The phenomenon we today name synesthesia had different names during the nineteenth century; and the term synesthesia or a variant of it as we understand it today was not in

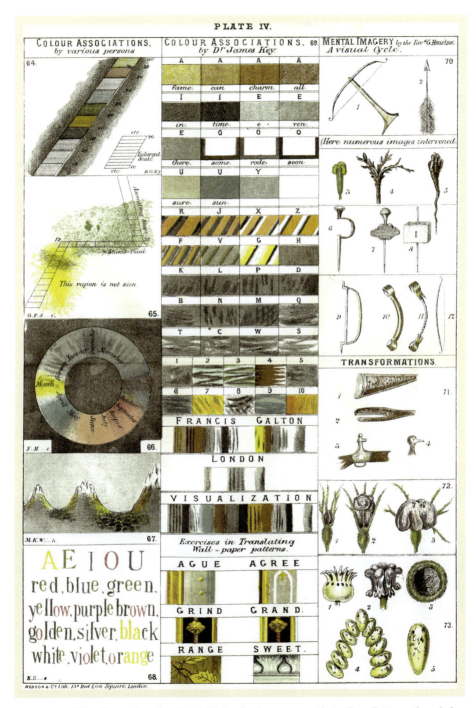

FIGURE 19.4 The first colored print (1883) of what a synesthete "sees." Reproduced from F. Galton. (1883). Inquiries into human faculty and its development, plate IV. London: Macmillan.

use before (Millet 1892). For easier understanding and to avoid confusion, in this section, I will employ the term synesthesia, although nearly none of the described authors used it.

Origin

Although Sachs never ventured an explanation of synesthesia, his opening sentence implies that he considered it a product of the mind, and not of the eye: "Although I am unwilling to speak anything about the *minds* of our albinos, yet I should nevertheless state some observations" (1812, 80).

1848–1866

A first period of theories about the origin of synesthesia started in 1848 and ended in 1866. The focus of debate in this time-frame can be summarized as the conflict between eye-based- and brain-based-theories, with a chronological development favoring the latter. For Cornaz (1848), synesthesia was a disease of the eye, the opposite of Daltonism color-blindness. One year later, inside a review of Cornaz's book, synesthesia was regarded rather differently:

> The editorial board would like to derive the roots of these assonant associations from a type of fortuitous pairing, namely following the law of *simultaneous impressions*. This would be similar to coincidental coordinated movements, although the coordination for colors and tones takes on a rather subjective identity. To understand this we must look at a certain unit in consciousness; even smells are thus noted to occasionally spread to other senses and sensory impressions. (Anonymous 1849b)

This was a positive approach and quite different to that of Cornaz. Two years later, Cornaz asked if synesthesia was "just a simple memory relationship in the coincidence that presents itself to the mind between an object and one color or another? We don't think so at all: however, this hypothesis is at least possible" (1851a, 8). Cornaz again rejected the idea that the condition might arise from the brain, because he saw no reason that memory association should tend to be limited to sequences, e.g., letters, numbers, days, which are the most common triggers of synesthesia.

Whereas most of Cornaz's commentators during the 1850s accepted his explanations uncritically because of the lack of more information, at least two argued against an eye-based explanation. The ophthalmic surgeon William White Cooper wrote: "In the present state of our knowledge we are not in a position to offer any satisfactory explanation of this singular anomaly of vision. That its seat is not in the eye but in the sensorium is however most probable" (1852, 1462). Another author classified it "more into psychology than Ophthalmology. [...] this strange phenomenon is likely to be based on a mapping between a sensuous perception and a certain psychological conception" (Anonymous 1852a).

Perroud, a medical doctor, discussed several eye-based explanations, but rejected them in favor of a brain-based explanation:

> For subjects with this abnormal condition, letters are not really colored, but simply awaken an idea of their associated color, which surrounds the letter like a reflection. This characteristic prevents hyperchromatopsia i.e., synesthesia from being an illusion or hallucination, and requires us to classify it as an aberration in the intellectual faculty which allows us to associate an idea to a sensation, or another idea. (1863, 40–41)

Chabalier, another medical doctor, also believed that the phenomenon was not related to the eyes: "It takes place not only when the printed letter is objectively submitted to the perception of the visual organ, but [also] well away from any material impression, when the idea of the letter is presented to the mind" (1864, 98). He also considered the similarities and differences between synesthesia, illusions and hallucinations, and regarded synesthesia as a form of illusion which needs an exterior object to develop rather than hallucination which develops from a purely intellectual undertaking. So he linked synesthesia to an illusion because the perceiver is aware of its false nature. The philosopher Joseph-Pierre Durand also argued that whilst hyperchromatopsia appears to be the opposite of color-blindness, it reflects the functioning of the mind and eyes respectively (1866).

1873–1880

The most important historical significance of the Nussbaumer cases in 1873 was their impact on new theories, which started directly thereafter. Brühl (1873) wrote that maybe heterotopy tissue located in the wrong place within the body could be an explanation, but his theory was not adopted by anyone else. Jakob Hock (1873), an ophthalmologist, conducted an innovative experiment in which he failed to observe any changes in the retina or optic nerve of Nussbaumer upon striking a tuning fork, which would have led to a synesthetic perception. One wonders why it took so long to conduct this experiment, because an eye-based theory, developed by Cornaz 1848, was exactly 25 years old by that point. Schöler 1873, a reviewer for a medical journal, argued against the physiological, objective validity of Nussbaumer's synesthesia because of five reasons: (1) the rareness of this ability, (2) the vague and fluctuating names of the colors, (3) the dependence on concentration, (4) the non-existing projection into the field of seeing, and (5) the discrepancy with the colors seen by his brother. However, exactly these arguments became accepted features of synesthesia in the later nineteenth century.

Nussbaumer's brother, a clockmaker, for the first time in history, drew a connection between synesthesia and art:

> I don't know if it makes sense, but I will say this: If I were a painter and musician, then I could make colors exactly for each different tone, and find musical tones for each color, including all possible dissonances; and people would then adjudge that we are gifted by Nature to find and present the relationship between light and sound. (Cited in Nussbaumer 1873a, 31)

This idea was developed by William Schooling, initiated by Gruber (1892), who thought of a new art form named *Color-music*, a pure art of colors only without music, because synesthesia shows that "color is capable [...] of suggesting ideas" (1895, 126). The art itself is independent from neurological synesthesia and this proposal might be seen as the roots of later *abstract films visual music* especially from the 1910s to 1930s, with film directors such as Walter Ruttmann, Viking Eggeling, or Oskar Fischinger (Jewanski and Düchting 2009, 337–348). Another connection between synesthesia and art was made by the psychologist Lillien J. Martin (1909), who examined "aesthetic synesthesia," which involves a mixture of sensation and imagination. In this, the stimulus is an artwork, perceived through the eye paintings, sculptures, architecture, and the triggered sensation is, for example, a smell, taste, temperature and so on dependent upon the content of the artwork.

Returning to the scientific theories of synesthesia, Nussbaumer pointed towards a possible physiological basis, popular in his time, which was that of the "doctrine of specific nerve energies." This had been developed by the physiologist Johannes Peter Müller (1826), who had explained that sensory experiences were assumed to be aligned to different "energies" of nerves associated with specific sensory organs, and where these nerves were linked to one and only one sensory organ. In other words, one sensory organ had one associated sensation, such that the ear can only hear, the eye only see, and so on. With the arrival of Nussbaumer cases, this doctrine was discussed in a new way. Nussbaumer himself was aware of the problem posed by synesthesia for the one-to-one mappings of the "nerve energies" theory. He regarded synesthesia as a "simultaneous, direct stimulation of several respectively different perception-mediating sensory nerves. This happens by means of a stimulation [irritation], or indirect stimulation of different sensory nerves as a result of the transfer of excitation of directly stimulated sensory nerves to other perception-mediating nerve fibres lying close by" (Nussbaumer 1873a, 5). In making this point, his proposal was somewhat controversial. John Orne Green (1873), a medical journal reviewer, stated that Nussbaumer attacked Müller's very axiom. Others did not agree. Johannes Ranke, a professor of physiology, explained synesthesia as an atavistic phenomenon. He suggested that the borders between the senses are not as clearly separated as generally believed. In infants and primitive animal organisms, the senses were undifferentiated within a "common feeling" (1875, 160). He argued that specific energies of the senses were learned via a process of sensory differentiation, but this need not be absolute, as the Nussbaumer brothers show.

Whereas the Nussbaumer cases were widely discussed, an article by the famous physiologist Filippo Lussana (1873) was more marginally received. His explanation was in terms of intimate associations between language, music, and color such that each is independently capable of conveying different ideas and feelings. These associations are assumed to be present in all people, rather than limited to synesthesia. For him, synesthesia and metaphor were essentially different manifestations of the same mechanism. Lussana underpinned this by referring to the anatomical closeness of regions in the brain specialized for color, music, and language (see Figure 19.5) and reiterated his explanation 10 years later (1883).

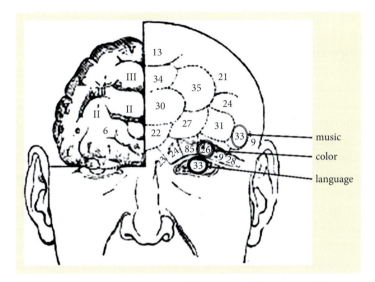

FIGURE 19.5 The first figure (Lussana 1873) of the anatomical closeness of regions in the brain for music, color, and language, which is the physiological basis for synesthesia. Adapted from F. Lussana. 1873. *Fisiologia dei colori*, p. 122. Padone: Sacchetto.

In addition to these physiological theories, during the same period, the first theories based on mental associations were raised by the medical doctor Antonio Berti (1865), who regarded synesthesia as an accidental association of ideas, and by the medical doctor Heinrich Kaiser, who considered synesthesia as associations from earliest childhood, which become automatic because of their long use over a lifetime (1872, 197). Two years later, the physiologist and psychologist Wilhelm Wundt did not broach the issue of synesthesia, but in general regarded analogies between the senses as analogies of sensations which are based on a "relationship of underlying feelings" (1874, 552). His idea was later transferred to apply to synesthesia research by Itelson (1897) and Wehofer (1912).

Since 1881

The scientific papers up to Beuler and Lehmann (1881) who themselves did not provide an explanation about the origin of synesthesia, but tended to report a physiological one (53–58), defended by Bleuler in 1913 are well defined (Jewanski et al. 2011b). Initiated by the popularity of their book, a nearly unmanageable number of articles and books were published during the next decades. Some were printed several times in various journals in the same language, and some were translated and reprinted in different languages. Some appeared in popular magazines, the first of which was the American *The Popular Science Monthly*, a magazine founded in 1872 and existing to this day. This magazine disseminates scientific knowledge to educated laymen, and many important scientists have contributed articles to it. In this way, synesthesia became very popular from the early 1880s not only within the scientific community but also amongst the general public at large.

The next key stage in the dissemination of information was a *Congrès International de Psychologie Physiologique,* held in Paris in 1889, which led to extensive research about synesthesia, especially in France. Within this congress, a committee was formed to conduct research about synesthesia (Gruber 1890; Varigny et al. 1890). Following this, several books about synesthesia were published in France, more so than in any other country; these included: Suarez de Mendoza (1890, enlarged edition 1899), Millet (1892 dissertation), Flournoy (1893), Benoist (1899, dissertation), Lemaître (1901), and Laures (1908).

In Russia, research on synesthesia started with Kovalevskij (1884; cf. Dorso-Sidoroff 2012; Vanechkina et al. 2005), and in Sweden with Klinckowström (1891, in French) and Wahlstedt (1891, in Swedish). These authors were well informed about their German, French, Swiss, and Italian fellow psychologists' and physiologists' theories and reports of that period. In South America research on synesthesia started with a huge empirical study by Mercante (1908, 1909). Both his articles were merged to a book, published in Spain in 1910, which became the first book about synesthesia in that country.

A number of papers also summarized the literature about synesthesia, beginning in 1882 with the bibliography of the German musicologist Friedrich Mahling (1926), the most extensive up till today. Mahling listed 188 titles up to 1899, an average of ten titles per year. Within the period 1900 to 1920, he listed 170 titles, an average of eight per year. Altogether although some novels about synesthesia are included, Mahling listed 358 titles for the period 1882 to 1920. Most of these offer an explanation about the origin of synesthesia. While the American psychologist Raymond H. Wheeler (1920) provided the most extensive discussion about theories on synesthesia up to his time, Mahling's discussion, an enlargement of the second part of his unpublished musicological dissertation of 1923, is the most extensive up to today, see "Bibliographies."

Starting in 1872, four main theories can be described, each of them appearing 1 year apart:

(1) Learned association theories, first developed by Kaiser (1872). These were supported by Schenkl (1881), and Quincke (1890), who explained synesthesia as a "fading rest of unregulated associations of imaginations in children" (Quincke 1890, 442), Calkins (1893), Binet (1892, translated into English (1893a) and German (1893b)), or Dresslar (1903).

(2) Physiological theories, first conceived by Nussbaumer (1873) and Lussana (1873). These were based on an anatomical closeness of regions in the brain for music, color, and language. This was adopted as a two-way influence or overlapping of nerves, in France by Pedrono (1882a, 1882b), and Millet (1892); in Germany by Grützner (1888), and Deichmann (1889); in the US by Krohn (1892), the first American scientific paper on synesthesia, and by many other authors (Mahling 1926, 201–210).

(3) Analogous-impact theories (wirkungsanaloge Theorien): Wundt's 1874 theory of an analogy of underlying feelings (see section "1873–1880"), was transferred to synesthesia by Itelson (1897) and Wehofer (1912).

(4) Atavistic theories, first developed by Ranke (1875). These were based on Darwinistic principles, and were championed by Nordau (1892, 217–122; Hilbert

1897, 12), based on the example of the piddock (*Pholas dactylus*), which had only one sensory organ for all sensations.

Other new theories were developed after the 1880s, the most important of which were all-embracing theories which include several approaches. Flournoy (1893, 18–45) proposed three laws: First, *law of affective association*, when two sensations are united because they match in their hedonic quality (e.g., pleasant sounds matching with pleasant colors); second, *law of habitual association*, when two sensations are united, because they habitually co-occur; third, *law of opportune association* (association privilégiée), when many connections gain a footing in our mind at their first appearance, because they come at a suitable time. Hennig (1896) considered two theories, first, a theory of "physiological photisms," which are a direct and necessary reaction to a stimulus, and second, "psychological photisms," which are involuntary and invented by the brain to provide more a concrete association for abstract objects. The origin of the latter is based on association: a special theory was developed by Ruths (1898), who proposed that when creating, reproducing and perceiving music, the domain of the ear is first activated, but also, over time, this spreads to other psychological domains. Urbantschitsch (1888) hypothesized that the senses do not react totally separately, but rather, that they might influence each other during perception. As well as these synthesized theories, psychoanalytical theories were also developed. Based on Sigmund Freud's psychoanalytical theories, some authors (Hug-Hellmuth 1912; Pfister 1912) explained synesthesia via early sexual experiences, which were of such a strong impression that accompanying sensations of sound or colors were fixed permanently in memory as synesthetic associations.

Wheeler (1920) regarded physiological theories as the most important, and this was based on nine assumptions:

> 1 the almost simultaneous presence of secondary with primary sensations at the point of origin; 2 the close proximity of brain areas involved in synaesthesis; 3 the stimulating influence of drugs; 4 the irreversibility of synaesthesis; 5 the destructive influence of fatigue or the reverse effect; 6 the disappearance of synaesthesis in adolescence or in senescence; 7 the dependence of attributes of secondary sensations upon the properties of the stimulus of the primary sensation; 8 the appearance of synaesthesis in early childhood at a time when meaningful associations are not yet formed; 9 the spontaneity and suddenness with which synaesthesis begins. (Wheeler 1920, 38).

Mahling (1926) reported that the most frequent acceptance in the literature came with theories based on associations, analogous impact, and physiology.

Is synesthesia congenital?

Sachs (1812) did not write down how long his synesthesia had existed for. In 1850, Wartmann reported that one of his synesthetes "was affected by it in childhood" (cited in Cornaz 1851a, 5). This phrase, although only written inside a private letter, is the first time that synesthesia was regarded as something that can affect an individual for a lifetime. Later, Cornaz asked:

> Is this state congenital? Is it *always* congenital? Can it disappear with age? These are points we can't resolve. It's likely that this state dates back to birth […]. It's possible that with age, reason little by little diminishes the vivacity of these coloured perceptions. (Cornaz 1851a, 8)

Perroud (1863) did not believe that synesthesia was always congenital, because his own case, a 30-year-old man, reported having it for only 12 to 15 years. One year later, Chabalier argued that synesthesia may emerge in childhood rather than being present from birth and that it may be biased by color associations in alphabet books (1864, 102). With the discovery of the Nussbaumer brothers in 1873, who were both synesthetes, a congenital theory of synesthesia became obvious. This theory was supported by Bleuler and Lehmann (1881, 49), who examined 76 synesthetes, many of them relatives, and came to the conclusion that synesthesia was indeed congenital. Galton, who analyzed mainly number-forms, concluded: "These forms are survivals of a very early mental stage, and must have originated before the child learnt his letters. There is no nursery book or diagram that could suggest their fantastic shapes" (Galton 1880b, 495). Laignel-Lavastine (1901) found nine synesthetes out of ten individuals inside one particular family spanning two generations. Alford (1918) examined a couple of male twins (1920, 35) and found 67% agreement in their color synesthesia, although Alford was not sure whether this agreement was supported by certain inaccuracies in his experimental methods.

Variants of synesthesia

The first case of synesthesia (Sachs 1812) offered four types: (1) letters-to-color, (2) musical tones-to-color, (3) numbers-to-color, and (4) days of the week-to-color. All are colored sequences, in that the trigger is an element that arises within an ordered list of letters, days, numbers etc. During the nineteenth century, more and more types of synesthesia were discovered (e.g., the first number-form-synesthesia; Hudson 1873). Later, Bleuer and Lehmann (1881, 3–4) reported six different variants of the condition: (1) ear to eye: "Schallphotisma" (sound photism); (2) eye to ear: "Lichtphonisma" (light phonism); (3) taste to color: "Geschmacksphotisma" (taste photism); (4) smell to color: "Geruchsphotisma" (smell photism); (5) pain/warmth/touch to color/form; (6) form to color. Flournoy (1893) differentiated three variants within visual-synesthesia: (1) photisms, when the color is combined with a stimulus; (2) schemata and diagrams, when the synesthesia takes the form of a spatial representation; (3) personification, when letters or other triggers are experienced in the form of persons e.g., number 3 might be a young boy, number 4 a busy mother etc.

The most detailed schema of the different types of synesthesia that had been discovered up until the 1910s, which is based on the different senses, was offered by Wheeler (1920, 32–33; précised in Wheeler and Cutsforth 1922, 4). It is ordered in such a way that the first element in each row represents the most common. Concerning VII.A, Wheeler added: "It is more likely, however, that associations play a very important role in the origin of this form of synaesthesis" (Wheeler 1920, 33):

I.   Of acoustic origin:
    A. colored hearing of 1. isolated tones, 2. noises, 3. music, 4. chords, 5. vowels, 6. consonants, 7. words a. names of people and other proper names, b. common parts of speech, c. days of the week, d. months of the year, e. seasons, f. epochs of history, g. virtues and other abstract terms, h. phases of human life, i. names of tastes, j. names of odors, 8. digits, 9. dates
    B. gustatory audition taste equivalents of words
    C. figured audition geometrical forms associated with words
    D. pain-audition toothache equivalents for tones of certain quality.
II. Of visual origin:
    A. colored lines: 1. serrated lines, 2. broken lines
    B. colored forms and figures: 1. geometrical forms, square, circle, rectangle, triangle etc., 2. colored angles, obtuse, acute, 3. colored signs and designs, swastika etc., 4. colored multiplication, division, addition, subtraction signs
    C. colored letters, digits, words etc.
III. Of gustatory origin:
    A. colored tastes
    B. colored taste and pressure complexes
    C. colored taste and odor complexes.
IV. Of olfactory origin:
    A. colored odors.
V.   Of tactual origin:
    A. colored pain
    B. colored pressure
    C. colored temperature sensations: 1. warm, 2. cold, 3. mixtures
    D. auditory pain
    E. auditory temperature sensations
    F. cutaneous or muscular taste.
VI. Of affective origin:
    A. colored pleasantness and unpleasantness
    B. colored emotional complexes.
VII. Of possible combined visual and auditory origin:
    A. personification and dramatization of letters, digits, days of the week.

Finally, Flournoy (1893, 9–11) arranged synesthetic sensations into four categories of intensity: objective, located, imagined, and thought.

Relation between stimulus and synesthesia

Bleuler and Lehmann 1881 examined the relation between the stimulus and the resultant synesthetic experience, and highlighted several features:

> 1. Bright photisms are aroused by high sound qualities, strong pain, distinct limited touch sensations, small forms, sharp forms; 2. High phonisms are aroused by bright light, distinct boundary, small forms, sharp forms. Low phonisms by the opposite; 3. Photisms with distinct limited forms, as well as small photisms, and sharp photisms are aroused by high sound sensations. [...] 5. There is no permanent agreement across different people. (1881, 71ff)

Bleuler and Lehmann also found out that the frequency of synesthesia amongst psychopathic people is the same as within unimpaired people.

During the nineteenth century, the most common and most studied type of synesthesia was triggered by acoustic stimuli and gave rise to color sensations, and this included letter-to-color synesthesia, whether the letter was spoken or thought. The famous psychologist Alfred Binet described the results as follows:

> In colored audition the impressions of color are almost exclusively provoked by speech; the sounds and noises of Nature producing the same effect only by a kind of analogy with the human voice. Speech gives him who hears it an impression of color only when the emission is full; a murmur has not the effect of the singing voice or of a reading in public; the height of the tone influences the shadings; barytone and bass voices excite dark sensations and high voices light ones. On a closer examination of the source of the phenomenon it is found that the color, while it may borrow a general tint from the timbre of the voice, and consequently from the individuality of the speaker, depends more especially upon the words that are pronounced; each word has its peculiar color, or we might rather say colors, for some words have five or six; pushing the analysis further, we perceive that the color of words depends on that of the component letters, and that it is therefore the alphabet which is colored; and, finally, that the consonants have only pale and washed-out tints, and the coloration of language is derived directly from the vowels. With a few exceptions this is true for all the subjects.
>
> By a curious complication produced by education, the appearance of colors takes place in some persons not only when they hear the word pronounced or when they think of it, but even when they see it written. There are also persons who do not perceive the color except while they are reading. Many facts, however, seem to prove that reading is generally of no effect except as a suggestion of the spoken word, and therefore constitutes a kind of audition. (Binet 1893a, 815)

Another connection between stimulus and synesthesia was described in Wheeler's overview (Wheeler 1920, 33). He suggested that every type of synesthesia has a different localization, but in general, that the secondary sensations are localized in the same place as if they were primary sensations. For example, in sound-to-color synesthesia, colors were located in the direction of the sound, sometimes on the brain or against the forehead. For letter/digit/word-to-color synesthesia, colors were located in space in front of the individual, or as backgrounds for the visualized stimulus, and in some rare cases the letters themselves are colored. For taste-to-color synesthesia, colors are localized in space in front of the individual, and for sound-to-taste synesthesia, they are localized in the mouth.

Prevalence

Sachs was certain that he was not the only one seeing colors (1812, 80). Wartmann (1850) wrote that synesthesia "is perhaps not very rare" and could report synesthesia in two of his students. One year later, Cornaz, for the first time in history, raised the question of sex differences. He wrote:

> Is this state found equally in men and women? Up to this point it has appeared only in men; but the number is too small for us to be able to draw any conclusions from this. One only has to remember how rare it is to find Daltonism *dyschromat-opsia* and *achromatopsia* in women. We know that [...] the "sense of color" is more developed in this sex than among us; but according to this hypothesis, shouldn't hyperchromatopsia be more common among women? It's a reasonable supposition. (1851a, 8)

This is the first time it had been articulated that synesthesia may be more common in women. Chabalier followed up Cornaz and remarked that although synesthesia had only been reported in men, Ellen Tucker Emerson was unknown "it must be far more common among women, for whom the imagination has a greater dominion" (1864, 101). Chabalier took this view because, for him, the phenomenon was a form of illusion and so would likely be found where imagination was greatest.

The first percentages for prevalence were given in 1881 in the UK and in Germany. Thereafter, a number of prevalence estimates were presented in a number of studies. Only some of them can be summarized here. I present these prevalence reports for their historical interest, and the modern reader should receive them only with caution in a scientific sense. These studies did not use independent tests for synesthesia, and instead, identified synesthetes only be their self-descriptions. Recent studies have shown this to be a flawed method, which tends to greatly over-estimate prevalence (see Simner et al. 2006). With this in mind, however, I present next a brief summary of their findings.

Galton reported a frequency of number form synesthesia of 1 in 30 men [= 3.3%], 1 in 15 women [= 6.7%], 1 in 21 school boys [= 4.8%] and "certainly higher in girls than in boys" (1883, 133). Patrick (1893) also examined number form synesthesia and reported about 4 cases within 75 students 18–25 years [= 5.3%], with equal parts men 2 and women 2. Peabody 1915 received 160 positive answers after sending out a questionnaire on form-synesthesia e.g., number forms, and he gave percentages for the direction and the char-acter of the lines straight or broken lines for numbers the most frequent was a straight line to east: 70/160 = 43.8%, hours circle, north-east-south-west: 59 = 36.9%, days straight line to east: 51 = 31.9%, months straight line to east: 39 = 24.4%, and the alphabet straight line to east: 81 = 50.6%.

Bleuler and Lehmann (1881) reported 76 synesthetes among 596 people [= 12.75%]. Within this number, music-to-color synesthesia was the most frequent of all 28%. Bleuler and Lehmann examined 383 [= 64.3%] male and 213 [= 35.7%] female persons. Within their 76 synesthetes as a basic, 45 [= 59.2%] of them were men, 31 [= 40.8%] women. The vowel *a* mostly was united with the color black, *e* with yellow, *i* with white, *o* with yellow, *u* with red.

Flournoy (1882, 1883) reported 370 synesthetes within 694 who answered questionnaires, of which he sent out 2,500 copies. Given that a large proportion of the 2,500 questionnaires was not returned, he could not give a reliable estimate of prevalence. However, within his 370 synesthetes, 180 [= 48.6%] were men, 190 [= 51.4%] women; 177/370 [= 47.8%] had a color-synesthesia, 74 [=20.0%] form-synesthesia, 119 [= 32.2%] had both. Concerning the colors of vowels, Flournoy describe the most frequent associations as: *a* = black, *e* = yellow, *i* = white, *o* = yellow, *u* = green, *ou* = brown. Also concerning the colors of vowels, Flournoy developed a law of brightness: in the majority of cases *i* and *e* are bright, *u* and *ou* are dark, *a* and *o* are fluctuating between bright and dark.

Calkins (1892) asked 543 people about colored hearing and number-forms. She found that 98 [= 18.0%] of them had one or both of these kinds of synesthesia, 32 [= 5.9%] of them had colored hearing, 78 [= 14.4%] number-forms, and 14 [= 2.6%] had both. One year later 1893 Calkins revised her study and concluded: 35/525 [= 6.7%] had colored hearing, 65 [= 12.4%] number-forms, 18 had both [= 3.4%]. Two years after that, in 1895, she resumed her earlier studies and added to them new material. Only some of her results can be presented here: Altogether Calkins examined 979 people, of whom 298 were synesthetes [= 30.4%]. Within form-synesthetes, Calkins differentiated between the most frequent being month-forms 141/510 = 27.7%, followed by number-forms 119 = 23.3%, day-of-week forms 105 = 20.6%, century-forms 49 = 9.6%, and other forms 96 = 18.8%. For color-synesthetes, the most frequent triggers were words 72/212 = 34.0%, followed by music 64 = 30.2%, letters 44 = 20.8%, numerals 14 = 6.6%, tastes 8 = 3.8%, touches 8 = 3.8%, odors 1 = 0.5%, and pain 1 = 0.5%. Within letters, Calkins differentiated between those being triggered by vowels only 10/44 = 22.8%, consonants only 4 = 9.1%, and both 30 = 68.2%. Only 12 of 92 [= 13.0%] regarded their color synesthesia as helpful, but 44 [= 47.8%] regarded it as pleasant. Only 31 of 92 [= 33.7%] gave their color synesthesia a definite form, but 64 [= 70.0%] gave a definite location. Thirteen of 92 [= 14.1%] were sure that their synesthesia rose to the level of hallucination, while 54 [= 58.7%] were sure that it did not. Finally, Calkins (1895, 93) also reported on a different study by Williams with approximately 250 pupils under 18, of whom about 10% were young men. Williams found 11 synesthetes in total, comprising colored hearing 5 = 2.0% and form-synesthetes 6 = 2.4%.

Within 112 pupils aged 12 to 14 years, Lemaître (1901) found 40 [= 35.7%] with color-synesthesia, 21 [= 18.7%] with form-synesthesia, and 2 [= 1.8%] with personifications. Rose (1909) examined 254 women, of whom 23 [= 9.1%] had a color-synesthesia, and Rose differentiated between those with synesthesia to a very striking degree [6 = 26.1%]

within the synesthetes, to a moderate degree [7 = 30.4%], and to a slight degree [10 = 43.5%]. As well as 23 color-synesthetes, Rose found 32 form-synesthetes [= 12.6%], with both groups together being 55/254 [= 21.7%]. Within form-synesthetes, the most frequent triggering stimulus was the year [27 = 84.4%] inside the form-synesthetes, followed by numbers from 1 to 10 [21 = 65.6%], then days of the week [16 = 50%], and then centuries [2 = 6.3%].

Concerning colored vowels, Millet (1892) examined 141 cases and the most frequent attributions were a = black, e = yellow, i = white, o = red, u = green. Claparède (reported in Binet 1892) gave a different list, based on around 100 people: a = black, e = blue, i = red, o = yellow, u = green. Dresslar (1903) analyzed one synesthete and found out that the colors of words were determined in several ways: by the colors of initial letters, by the accented syllable, by repeated letters or digits, or by a letter/digit whose color was unusually vivid or striking. Rose (1909) ordered the colors of 245 synesthetes according to their frequencies. The most frequent synesthetic color was brown, followed by yellow, gray, red, blue, green, pink, white, orange, violet, lavender. The colors appeared most often triggered by letters, followed by names of people, names of cities, and musical tones. Forty per cent of the letters which triggered colors were vowels. Since the numbers of consonants in the alphabet is about four times the number of vowels, there is a "decided preponderance of vowels in color associations" (Rose 1909, 447). The order of the most frequent vowels attributed with colors was o-a-e-i-u. Mercante (1908, 1909) tested 900 children aged 8 to 18 years. Amongst the girls, he found 80% were synesthetes, a little more than within boys. Lemaître (1910) examined adolescents and found 37 synesthetes giving reported a rate of 25%.

Consistency

Bleuler and Lehmann (1881) reported that synesthetic sensations remain constant over time, but they did not conduct a long-term study. The first test of consistency was done by Kaiser. He asked a synesthete to describe his synesthetic sensations 10 years after an initial interview and found a total match with the descriptions given 10 years earlier (Kaiser 1872, 1882). Galton found the same result with a single synesthete after a gap of 2 years (1883, 147). Holden, spurred on by Galton (1880b), examined his daughter several times over a period of 24 years starting when she was 7 years old and discovered only small shiftings of colors and small changes in brightness from 1885 to 1906. Calkins (1893) tested 252 synesthetes, and in most cases repeated this after 1 year, or occasionally after a few months: in 141/252 cases [= 56.0%], the synesthesia did not change; in 91 [= 36.1%] it varied slightly, and in 20 [= 7.9%] the results were unverified or differed. Dresslar (1903) examined an individual several times between 1895 and 1903 and found practically no changes in her synesthesia. Quincke described a "fading" (1890), 438 of photisms during the life span. Jordan (1917) examined his son across an interval of 5 years and only found minor changes in the colors of his alphabet. In contrast, Wheeler, summarizing the theories up to 1918 wrote: "It seems probable then, that many cases of synesthesis disappear when the subject reaches maturity" (1920, 32).

QUESTIONNAIRES

The development of questionnaires started with Nussbaumer (1873a, 1873b) and was followed by Fechner (1879; now lost, see Steinbrügge 1887), then Galton whose text is given in Burbridge (1984, table 1, 448–449); all questionnaires are preserved in the Special Collection at University College London, Galton Papers 152/1–7, compare Merrington and Golden (1978), and Burbridge (1994), then Claparède and Flournoy (1892), Gruber (1893), Calkins (1895), Laignel-Lavastine (1901; in German: Stelzner 1903), and Dresslar (1903). Finally, the most detailed questionnaire arose during the period of a "synesthesia euphoria" in 1925 to 1933 (Jewanski 1995b; 2002) written by Georg Anschütz, and this contained 156 questions developed in 1925, published, for example, in Anschütz (1929, 19–24).

BIBLIOGRAPHIES

The most extensive bibliography of the period up till 1810 is by Jewanski (1999), but this only concerns possible cases of music-to-color synesthesia. For the period between 1812 to 1873, the most extensive bibliography is found in Jewanski et al. (2011b). For the period between 1874 to 1899, this would be Mahling (1926). Placing the increasing bibliographies of the nineteenth century in an order of quantity, we would find Cornaz (1851a, 1851b, 5 titles), Perroud (1863, 5 titles), Lussana (1883, 11 titles), Baratoux (1887, 20 titles), Suarez de Mendoza (1890, 59 titles, not enlarged in the 1899 edition), Krohn (1892, 85 titles), and Clavière (1898, 131 titles), although these bibliographies since Suarez de Mendoza also include some novels, i.e., fiction about synesthesia. Huge bibliographies from the early twentieth century are by Lipmann (1911, containing 138 references, excluding novels and Wheeler (1920), containing 145 references, excluding popular literature, additional reviews and reprints. During the entire twentieth century, there were mainly four who discussed synesthesia in the nineteenth century—Wheeler (1920), Mahling (1926), Wellek (1928), and Marks (1975). The most comprehensive are by Wheeler and Mahling. For bibliographies written within the twenty-first century, the predominant historical bibliographies are by Jewanski and colleagues (Jewanski, Day, and Ward 2009, 2012; Jewanski et al. 2011b, 2012, 2013a, 2013b).

Finally, the largest bibliography on synesthesia in the nineteenth century is still that of Mahling (1926). This contains 245 titles (including appendix) up to 1899, and also includes certain novels and titles, which also belong to his section on color-tone association; his complete bibliography (1786–1926) includes 550 titles. Mahling's work including a later analysis by Mahling in 1929 was criticized, corrected, and enlarged by Wellek (1931) on the basis of Wheeler (1920), and the 466 titles in Argelander (1927), but predominantly with titles from the early twentieth century.

CONCLUSION

Knowledge today by the average scientist about synesthesia in the nineteenth century up to 1920 is almost non-existent. Reading about the discussions which took place within this period, we must ask ourselves what more we really know than those early scientists from the nineteenth century. Today, we can use new methods such as functional magnetic resonance imaging or newly developed behavioral tests, which offer us great detail, but many of the main questions about synesthesia were already raised, discussed, and answered to some extent during the nineteenth century. Current scientific studies compare their results with studies that are no older than two or three decades. What is missing is a comparison with the huge number of statistical studies from the late nineteenth and early twentieth century. Without this we cannot be sure that synesthesia research today is not reinventing the wheel.

REFERENCES

The references include only those articles that are mentioned in the text; for bibliographies see section "Bibliographies." The reference section has been divided into two parts, the first covering the historical period of interest in this chapter from 1812 to 1922 and the second covering additional literature after that point.

Literature 1812–1922

Alford, L. B. 1918. A report of two cases of synaesthesia. *Journal of abnormal psychology* 13 (1):1–16.

Anonymous. 1849a. [Review of Cornaz 1848]. *Zeitschrift für die gesammte Medicin* 14 (42/4):492–508.

——. 1849b. [Comment of the editorial board to Anonymous 1849a]. *Zeitschrift für die gesammte Medicin* 14 (42/4):507, annotation.

——. 1852a. [Review of Cornaz 1851b]. *Schweizerische Zeitschrift für Medizin, Chirurgie und Geburtshülfe*, 304.

——. 1882. [Review of Bleuler and Lehmann 1881]. *The Times*, 12 January: p. 5, col. 6.

Baratoux, Jean. 1887. De l'audition colorée. *Le progrès médical* 2/15/6 50:495–446, 515–517, 538–539.

Benedikt, Moritz. 1873. [Comment on Nussbaumer 1873a, 1873c]. In Nussbaumer (1873a, 60–61).

Benoist, Émilien. 1899. *Contribution à l'étude de l'audition colorée*. Paris: Maloine. (Reprint: Whitefish Montana 2010: Kessinger.)

Berti, Antonio. 1865. Della pseudocromestesia. *Archivo Italiano per la malattie nervose e più particolarmente per le alienazioni mentali Milano* 2:22–28.

Binet, Alfred. 1892. Le problème de l'audition colorée. *La revue des deux mondes* 113:586–614. [Translated into English: Binet (1893a); translated into German: Binet (1893b).]

——. 1893a. The problem of colored hearing. *The Popular Science Monthly* 43:812–823. [Translation of Binet 1892.]

——. 1893b. Das Problem des Farbengehörs. *Medizinisch-pädagogische Monatsschrift für die gesammte Sprachheilkunde* 3:5–15, 51–54, 353–367. [Translation of Binet 1892.]

Bleuler, Eugen. 1913. Zur Theorie der Sekundärempfindungen. *Zeitschrift für Psychologie und Physiologie der Sinnesorgane. I. Abteilung: Zeitschrift für Psychologie* 65:1–39.

Bleuler, Eugen, and Karl Lehmann. 1881. *Zwangsmässige Lichtempfindungen durch Schall und verwandte Erscheinungen auf dem Gebiete der andern Sinnesempfindungen.* Leipzig: Fues.

Brühl, Carl Bernard. 1872. [Letter of reference.] In Nussbaumer (1873b, 4–5, annotation).

Calkins. Mary W. 1892. Experimental psychology at Wellesley College. *The American Journal of Psychology* 5 (2):264–271. [Wrong pagination: 464–271.]

——. 1893. A statistical study of pseudo-chromesthesia and of mental-forms. *The American Journal of Psychology* 5 (4):439–464.

——. 1895. Synæsthesia. *The American Journal of Psychology* 71:90–107.

Chabalier. 1864. De la pseudochromesthésie. *Journal de médecine de Lyon* 1 (2):92–102.

Claparède, Edouard, and Flournoy, Théodore. 1892. Enquête sur l'audition colorée. *Archives des sciences physiques et naturelles* 28:505–508.

Clavière, Jean. 1898. L'audition colorée. *L'Année psychologique* 5 (1):161–178.

Cooper, William W. 1852. Vision. In *The Cyclopædia of Anatomy and Physiology, vol. 4/2,* ed. Robert B. Todd, 1436–1469. London: Longman.

Cornaz, Charles-Auguste-Édouard. 1848. *Des abnormités congéniales des yeux et de leurs annexes.* Lausanne: Bridel.

——. 1851a. De L'Hyperchromatopsie. *Annales d'oculistique* 25 5/1, 1–3: 3–9. [Identical with Cornaz 1851b.]

——. 1851b. *De L'Hyperchromatopsie.* Bruxelles 1851: Stapleaux. [Identical with Cornaz 1851a.]

Deichmann, Ludwig. 1889. *Erregung secundärer Empfindungen im Gebiete der Sinnesorgane.* Greifswald: Abel.

Dresslar, F. B. 1903. Are chromæsthesias variable? A study of an individual case. *The American Journal of Psychology* 14 (3–4):368–382.

Durand de Gros, Joseph-Pierre. 1866. *Essais de physiologie philosophique.* Paris: Germer Baillière.

Fechner, Gustav Theodor. 1876. *Vorschule der Aesthetik.* Leipzig: Breitkopf & Härtel.

Flournoy, Théodore. 1890. Note sur l'audition colorée. *Archives des sciences physiques et naturelles* 23:352–354.

——. 1892. [Les résultats d'une enquête sur l'*audition colorée*]. *Archives des sciences physiques et naturelles* 28:505–508.

——. 1893. *Des phénomènes de synopsie audition colorée. Photismes—schèmes visuels—person-nifications.* Paris: Alcan. [Several reprints.]

Galton, Francis. 1880a. Visualised numerals. *Nature* 21:252–256.

——. 1880b. Visualised numerals. Letter to the editor. *Nature* 21: 323.

——. 1880c. Visualised numerals. *Nature* 21:494–495.

——. 1880d. Statistics of mental imagery. *Mind. A Quarterly Review of Psychology and Philosophy* 5 (19):301–318.

——. 1880e. Mental imagery. *The Fortnightly Review* 28 (165):312–324. [Reprint: Galton 1880f.]

——. 1880f. Mental imagery. *The Popular Science Monthly* 18 November:64–76. [Reprint from Galton 1880e.]

——. 1880g. *Visualised numerals: a memoir read before the Anthropological Institute on March 9, 1880, with the remarks of various speakers thereon*. London: Harrison and Sons. [Reprint from Galton 1881a.]

——. 1881a. Visualised numerals. *Journal of the Anthropological Institute of Great Britain and Irland* 10:85–102. [Reprint: Galton 1880g.]

——. 1881b. The visions of sane persons. *The Fortnightly Review* 29 (174):729–740. [Reprint: Galton 1881c, 1881d.]

——. 1881c. The visions of sane persons. *Proceedings of the Royal Institution of Great Britain* 9:644–655. [Reprint with slight revisions from Galton 1881b.]

——. 1881d. The visions of sane persons. *The Popular Science Monthly* 19 August:519–531. [Reprint from Galton 1881b.]

——. 1883. *Inquiries into Human Faculty and its Development*. London: Macmillan. [Several editions and reprints.]

——. 1892. [Remarks to Gruber 1892]. In Gruber (1892, 20).

Green, John O. 1873. [Review of Nussbaumer 1873a]. *The Boston Medical and Surgical Journal* 89 (14):356–357.

Gruber [Grüber], Édouard. 1890. Audition colorée. *Congrès international de psychologie physiologie, première session, Paris 1889*, 157. Paris: Bureau des revues.

——. 1892. L'audition colorée et les phénomènes similaires [including remarks by Francis Galton = Galton 1892]. In *International congress of experimental psychology, second session, London 1892*, 1–20. London: Williams & Norgate.

——. 1893. Questionnaire psychologique sur l'audition colorée, figurée et illuminée. *Revue philosophique de la France* 18 (35):499–502.

Grützner, P. 1888. Ueber den Einfluss einer Sinneserregung auf die übrigen Sinnesempfindungen. *Deutsche Medicinische Wochenschrift* 14 (44):905–907.

Hennig, Richard. 1896. Entstehung und Bedeutung der Synopsien. *Zeitschrift für Psychologie und Physiologie der Sinnesorgane* 10:183–222.

Hilbert, Richard. 1897. *Die Pathologie des Farbensinnes*. Halle a.S.: Marhold.

Hock, Jakob. 1873. Ophthalmoskopische Untersuchung der Augen des Herrn Nussbaumer. In Nussbaumer (1873c, 62–63).

Holden, Edward S. 1885. Color and other associations. *Science* 6 (137):242–243.

——. 1888. Color and other associations. *Science* 11 (257):12.

——. 1891. Colour-associations with numerals, &c. *Nature* 44 (1132):223–224.

——. 1895. Color-associations with numerals, etc. third note. *Science* N.S. 1 (21):576.

——. 1906. Color-associations with numerals, etc. fourth note. 1882–1906. *Science* N.S. 23 (581):270.

Hudson, Hannah Reba. 1873. Idiosyncrasies. *The Atlantic monthly: A magazine of literature, art and politics* 31 (184):197–201.

Hug-Hellmuth, Hermine von. 1912. Über Farbenhören. Ein Versuch, das Phänomen auf Grund der psycho-analytischen Methode zu erklären. *Imago: Zeitschrift für Anwendung der Psychoanalyse auf die Geisteswissenschaften* 1:228–264.

Itelson, G. 1897. Über paradoxe Nebenvorstellungen sog. audition colorée. *Dritter Internationaler Congress für Psychologie München 1896*, 476. München: Lehmann.

Jordan, David S. 1917. The colors of letters. *Science* N.S. 46 (1187):311–312.

Kaiser, Heinrich. 1872. *Compendium der physiologischen Optik*. Wiesbaden: C. W. Kreidel's Verlag.

——. 1882. Association der Worte mit Farben. *Archiv für Augenheilkunde* 11:96.

Klinckowström, A. 1891. Trois cas d'audition colorée dans la même famille. *Biologiska Föreningens forhandlingar* Stockholm 3:117–118.

Kovalevskij, Nikolaj O. 1884. Towards the issue of co-sensations Mitempfindungen Medicine newsletter 23 (3):35–36, 52–53. [Ковалевский Николай Осипович. 1884. К вопросу о соощущениях Mitempfindungen. *Медицинский вестник* 23 (3):35–36, 52–53.]

Krohn, William O. 1892. Pseudo-chromesthesia, or the association of colors with words, letters and sounds. *The American Journal of Psychology* 5 (1):20–41.

Laignel-Lavastine. 1901. Audition colorée familiale. *Revue neurologique* 9 (23):1152–1162.

Laures, Henry. 1908. *Les synesthésies*. Paris: Bloud.

Lemaître, Auguste. 1901. *Audition colorée et phénomènes connexes observés chez les écoliers*. Paris: Alcan. [Reprint: Whitefish, Montana 2010: Kessinger.]

——. 1910. *La vie mentale de l'adolescent et ses anomalies*. Saint-Blaise: Foyer Solidariste.

Lipmann, Otto. 1911. Synästhesie. Bibliographisches. *Die Differentielle Psychologie in ihren methodischen Grundlagen*, ed. William Stern, 475–480. Leipzig: Barth.

Locke, John 1690: *An Essay Concerning Human Understanding*. London 1690: Basset. [Many editions, reprints, and translations.]

Lussana, Filippo. 1873. *Fisiologia dei colori*. Padone: Sacchetto.

——. 1883. Sur l'audition colorée. *Archives Italiennes de biologie* 2:289–291.

Martin, Lillien J. 1909. Über ästhetische Synästhesie. *Zeitschrift für Psychologie und Physiologie der Sinnesorgane. I. Abteilung: Zeitschrift für Psychologie* 53:1–60.

Mercante, Víctor. 1908. La audición coloreada en los escolares. *El Monitor de la Educación Común* Buenos Aires 28 (427/26):418–439.

——. 1909. El fotismo cromático de las palabras verbocromía. Contribución al estudio de las aptitudes expresivas. *Archivos de psiquiatria y criminologia, medicina legal* Buenos Aires 8:399–475.

——. 1910. *La verbocromía. Contribución al estudio de las facultadas expresivas*. Madrid: Jorro.

Millet, Jules. 1892. *Audition colorée*. Montpellier: Hamelin frères.

Müller, Johannes Peter. 1826. *Zur vergleichenden Physiologie des Gesichtssinnes des Menschen und der Thiere nebst einem Versuch ueber die Bewegungen der Augen und des menschlichen Blickes*. Leipzig: Cnobloch.

Nordau, Max. 1892. *Entartung, Vol. 1*. Berlin: Duncker.

Nussbaumer, Fidelis A. 1873a. Ueber subjektive 'Farben'empfindungen, die durch objektive,'Gehör'empfindungen erzeugt werden. Eine Mittheilung durch Beobachtungen an sich selbst. *Wiener Medizinische Wochenschrift* 1: 4–7, 2:28–31, 3:52–54. [Including Brühl 1872; identical with Nussbaumer 1873b and 1873e.]

——. 1873b. *Ueber subjektive 'Farben'empfindungen, die durch objektive,'Gehör'empfindungen erzeugt werden. Eine Mittheilung durch Beobachtungen an sich selbst*. Wien: Selbstverlag. [Identical with Nussbaumer 1873a and 1873e.]

——. 1873c. Ueber subjective Farben-Empfindungen, welche durch objective Gehör-Empfindungen erzeugt werden. *Mittheilungen des Aerztlichen Vereines in Wien* 2 5: 49–63. [Including Brühl 1872, Benedikt 1873, and Hock 1873; identical with Nussbaumer 1873d.]

——.1873d. *Ueber subjective Farben-Empfindungen, welche durch objective Gehör-Empfindungen erzeugt werden*. Wien: Finsterbeck. [Identical with Nussbaumer 1873c.]

———. 1873e. Ueber subjektive Farbenempfindungen, die durch objektive Gehörempfindungen erzeugt werden. *Medizinische Neuigkeiten für praktische Ärzte* 23 13: 102–104, 14: 108–110, 15: 114–116. [Identical with Nussbaumer 1873a/b, but excluding Brühl 1872.]

Patrick, G. T. W. 1893. Number forms. *The Popular Science Monthly* 42:504–514.

Peabody, Charles. 1915. Certain further experiments in synæsthesia. *American Anthropologist* 17 (1):143–155.

Pedrono. 1882a. De l'audition colorée. *Journal de médecine de l'ouest* 2/6/16:294–311. [Identical with Pedrono 1882b.]

———. 1882b. De l'audition colorée. *Annales d'oculistique* 88:224–237. [Identical with Pedrono 1882a.]

Perroud. 1863. De l'hyperchromatopsie. *Mémoires et compte-rendus de la société des sciences médicales de Lyon* 2:37–41.

Pfister, Oskar. 1912. Die Ursache der Farbenbegleitung bei akustischen Wahrnehmungen und das Wesen anderer Synästhesien. *Imago: Zeitschrift für Anwendung der Psychoanalyse auf die Geisteswissenschaften* 1:265–275.

Philippe, J. 1894. [Review on Flournoy 1893]. *Psychological Review* 1 (3):318–322.

Quincke, H. 1890. Ueber Mitempfindungen und verwandte Vorgänge. *Zeitschrift für klinische Medizin* 17 (5):429–451, and table II & III.

Ranke, Johannes. 1875. Beiträge zu der Lehre von den Uebergangs-Sinnesorganen. *Zeitschrift für wissenschaftliche Zoologie* 25:143–162.

Rose, K. B. 1909. Some statistics on synæsthesia. *The American Journal of Psychology* 20:447.

Ruths, Christoph. 1898. *Experimental-Untersuchungen über Musikphantome, Vol. 1*. Darmstadt: Schlapp.

Sachs, Georg Tobias Ludwig. 1812. *Historiae naturalis duorum leucaetiopum: Auctoris ipsius et sororis eius*. Erlangen.

———. 1814. Eine physiologisch-optische Beobachtung 1814, ed. Harles, *Deutsches Archiv für die Physiologie* 1 1, 1815:188–201.

Schenkl. 1881. Casuistischer Beitrag zur Association der Worte mit Farben. *Prager Medicinische Wochenschrift* 6 (48):473–474.

Schlegel, Julius Heinrich Gottlieb. 1824. *Ein Beitrag zur nähern Kenntniß der Albinos*. Meinigen: Keyßner. [Mainly a German translation of Sachs 1812.]

Schöler, H. 1873. [Review of Nussbaumer 1873a, 1873c]. *Centralblatt für die medicinischen Wissenschaften* 11 (20):313–315.

Schooling, William. 1895. Colour-music. The suggestion of a new art. *Nineteenth century* 38:125–134. [Submitted April 1893].

Steinbrügge, Hermann Johann Friedrich. 1887. *Über secundäre Sinnesempfindungen*. Wiesbaden: Bergmann.

Stelzner, Helene Friedrike. 1903. Ein Fall von akustisch-optischer Synästhesie. *Albrecht von Graefes archive for clinical and experimental ophthalmology* 55 (3):549–563.

Suarez de Mendoza, Ferdinand. 1890. *L'Audition colorée. Étude sur les fausses sensations secondaires physiologiques et particulièrement sur les pseudo-sensations de couleurs associées aux perceptions objectives des sons*. Paris: Octave Doin. [Second enlarged edition: Suarez de Mendoza 1899.]

———. 1899. [Second edition of Suarez de Mendoza 1890, enlarged only by *Préface* and *Avant-propos*]. Paris: Société d'edition scientifiques.

Thoreau, Henry D. 1848. Letter to Ralph Waldo Emerson January 12, 1848. In The Emerson-Thoreau correspondence, ed. Franklin Benjamin Sanborn. *The Atlantic Monthly* 69 416, 1892, 736–753, here: 744–745.

Urbantschitsch, Victor. 1888. Über den Einfluss einer Sinneserregung auf die übrigen Sinnesempfindungen. *Pflügers Archiv für die gesamte Psychologie* 42:154–182.

Varigny, Georges de et al. 1890. Audition colorée [discussion]. In *Congrès international de psychologie physiologie, première session, Paris 1889*, 94–96. Paris: Bureau des revues.

Wahlstedt, Axel J. G. 1891. Tvänne fall af "färghörsel" audition colorée. *Biologiska Föreningens forhandlingar* Stockholm 3:12–20.

Wartmann, Elié. 1849a. Deuxieme mémoire sur le daltonisme ou la dyschromatopsie. *Mémoires de la société de physique et d'histoire naturelle de Genève* 12:183–231.

———. 1849b. *Deuxieme mémoire sur le daltonisme ou la dyschromatopsie*. Geneva: Fick.

———. 1850. [Private letter, 28 September, to Édouard Cornaz]. In Cornaz (1851a, 5).

Wehofer, Friedrich. 1912. ,Farbenhören' (chromatische Phonopsien) bei Musik. Ein Beitrag zur Psychologie der Synästhesien auf Grund eigener Beobachtungen. *Zeitschrift für angewandte Psychologie und psychologische Sammelforschung* 7 1:1–54.

Wheeler, Raymond H. 1920. *The Synaesthesia of a Blind Subject*. Eugene, OR: University of Oregon Press.

Wheeler, Raymond H., and Thomas D. Cutsforth. 1922. *The Synaesthesia of a Blind Subject with Comparative Data from an Asynaesthetic Blind Subject*. Eugene, OR: University of Oregon Press.

Wundt, Wilhelm. 1874. *Grundzüge der physiologischen Psychologie*. Leipzig: Engelmann.

Literature since 1923

Anschütz, Georg. 1929. *Das Farbe-Ton-Problem im psychischen Gesamtbereich. Sonderphänomene komplexer optischer Synästhesien ,Sichtgebilde'*. Halle: Marhold.

Argelander, Annelies. 1927. *Das Farbenhören und der synästhetische Faktor der Wahrnehmung*. Jena: Fischer.

Behne, Klaus-Ernst. 1991. Am Rande der Musik: Synästhesien, Bilder, Farben,... *Jahrbuch der Deutschen Gesellschaft für Musikpsychologie* 8:94–120.

Burbridge, David. 1994. An exploration of Francis Galton's imagery studies. *The British journal for the history of science* 27 (4):443–463.

Cytowic, Richard E. 2013. Synesthesia in the twentieth century: Synesthesia's renaissance. In *Oxford Handbook of Synesthesia*, ed. Julia Simner and Edward M. Hubbard, 399–408. Oxford: Oxford University Press.

Dorso-Sidoroff, Anton V. 2012. La investigación de la sinestesia en Rusia: arte y ciencia. In *Sinestesia. Las fundamentos teóricos, artísticos y científicos*, ed. Maria José de Cordoba and Dina Riccò, 230–273. Granada: Fundación Internacional Artecittà.

Jewanski, Jörg. 1995a. Farbe-Ton-Beziehung. In *Die Musik in Geschichte und Gegenwart*, ed. Ludwig Finscher, Sachteil vol. 3, 345–371. Kassel: Bärenreiter.

———. 1995b. Die Institution—Albert Wellek und seine Bedeutung für die Erforschung der Synästhesie. *Musikpsychologie. Jahrbuch der Deutschen Gesellschaft für Musikpsychologie* 12:134–148.

———. 1999. *Ist C = Rot? Eine Kultur- und Wissenschaftsgeschichte zum Problem der wechselseitigen Beziehung zwischen Ton und Farbe. Von Aristoteles bis Goethe*. Sinzig: studio.

———. 2002. Die neue Synthese des Geistes. Zur Synästhesie-Euphorie der Jahre 1925–1933. *Synästhesie. Interferenz—Transfer—Synthese*, ed. Hans Adler and Ulrike Zeuch, 239–248. Würzburg: Königshausen & Neumann.

———. 2006. Von der Farbe-Ton-Beziehung zur Farblichtmusik. In *Farbe—Licht—Musik. Synästhesie und Farblichtmusik*, ed. Jörg Jewanski and Natalia Sidler, 131–209. Bern: Lang.

——. 2007. Color organs and their connection with synaesthesia. Three case studies: Castel—Rimington—László. In: *II Congreso Internacional de Sinestesia: Ciencia y Arte*, ed. Fundación Internacional Artecittà and Maria José de Córdoba, 527–535. Granada: CD-ROM.

——. 2010a. Color organs: From the clavecin oculaire to autonomous light kinetics. In *See this sound. Audiovisuology compendium. An interdisciplinary survey of audiovisual culture*, ed. Dieter Daniels and Sandra Naumann, 76–87. Cologne: König.

——. 2010b. Color-tone analogies: A systematic presentation of the principles of correspondence. In *See this sound. Audiovisuology compendium. An interdisciplinary survey of audiovisual culture*, ed. Dieter Daniels and Sandra Naumann, 338–347, Cologne: König.

Jewanski, Jörg, Sean A. Day, and Jamie Ward. 2009. A colorful albino: The first documented case of synaesthesia, reported by Georg Tobias Ludwig Sachs in 1812. *Journal of the History of the Neurosciences* 18:293–303. [Enlarged version: Jewanski, Day, and Ward 2012.]

——. 2010. The first detailed case of colour-hearing in history, reported by F. A. Nussbaumer in 1873. Unpublished lecture, given at the annual conference of the UK synaesthesia association in Brighton.

——. 2012. 1812: el año en que por primera vez se habla de Sinestesia. In *Sinestesia. Las fundamentos teóricos, artísticos y científicos*, ed. Maria José de Cordoba and Dina Riccò, 40–72. Granada: Fundacion Internacional Artecittà. [Short version: Jewanski et al. 2009.]

Jewanski, Jörg, and Hajo Düchting. 2009. *Musik und Bildende Kunst im 20. Jahrhundert. Begegnungen—Berührungen—Beeinflussungen*. Kassel: University Press.

Jewanski, Jörg, Julia Simner, Sean A. Day, and Jamie Ward. 2011a. 1849: Three new cases of synaesthesia? Unpublished lecture, given at the annual conference of the UK Synaesthesia Association in London.

——. 2011b. The development of a scientific understanding of synaesthesia from early case studies 1849–1873. *Journal of the History of the Neurosciences* 20:284–305.

——. 2012. The First Researcher on Synaesthesia: Édouard Cornaz 1825–1911. In *Actas IV Congreso Internacional de Sinestesia: Ciencia y Arte Alméria, Spain, 16 al 19 Febrero 2012*, ed. Fundación Internacional Artecittà and Maria José de Córdoba, 9. Granada: Artecittà CD-ROM.

——. 2013a. Édouard Cornaz (1825–1911) and his importance as founder of synaesthesia research. *Musik-, Tanz- und Kunsttherapie. Zeitschrift für künstlerische Therapien* [print in preparation].

——. 2013b. The beginning of research on synaesthesia with children. Searching for traces in the 19th century. In *Synaesthesia with children. Creativity and learning, Conference proceedings Ulm, Germany, 11/12 May 2012*, ed. Christine Söffing and Jasmin Sinha. Luxemburg: Synaisthesis.

Lovelace, Christopher T. 2013. Synesthesia in the twenty-first century: Synesthesia's ascent. In *The Oxford Handbook of Synesthesia*, ed. Julia Simner and Edward M. Hubbard, 409–439. Oxford: Oxford University Press.

Mahling, Friedrich. 1923. *Zur Geschichte des Problems wechselseitiger Beziehungen zwischen Ton und Farbe*. Manuscript dissertation, University Berlin.

——. 1926. Das Problem der 'Audition colorée.' Eine historisch-kritische Untersuchung. *Archiv für die gesamte Psychologie* 57:165–301. [Reprint: Mahling 1927.]

——. 1927. Das Problem der 'Audition colorée.' Eine historisch-kritische Untersuchung. In *Farbe-Ton-Forschungen*, Vol. 1, ed. Georg Anschütz, 295–431. Leipzig: Akademische Verlagsanstalt. [Reprint of Mahling 1926.]

———. 1929. Das Farbe-Ton-Problem und die selbständige Farbe-Ton-Forschung als Exponenten gegenwärtigen Geistesstrebens. In *Festschrift für Johannes Wolf zu seinem 60. Geburtstag*, ed. Walter Lott et al., 107–111. Berlin: Breslauer.

Marks, Lawrence E. 1975. On coloured-hearing synaesthesia: Cross-modal translations of sensory dimensions. *Psychological bulletin* 82 (3):303–331.

Merrington, Maxine, and Jacqueline Golden, eds. 1978. *A list of the papers and correspondence of Sir Francis Galton held in the Manuscripts Room, the Library, the University College London.* London: Galton Laboratory.

Julia Simner, Catherine Mulvenna, Noam Sagiv, Elias Tsakanikos, S. Athene Witherby, Christine Fraser, Kirsten Scott, and Jamie Ward. 2006. Synaesthesia: The prevalence of atypical cross-modal experiences. *Perception* 35:1024–1033.

Vanechkina, Irina Leonidovna, Bulat Mahmudovich Galeev, and Sunbul' Mahmudovna Galyavina. 2005. 'Color hearing': Kazan was the first here, too. In *History of philosophy and theory of knowledge. Verges of relationship collection of articles*, 43–52. Simbirsk-Ulyanovsk: Simbirsk Book. [Ванечкина Ирина Леонидовна, Булат Махмудович Галеев и Сунбуль Махмудовна Галявина. 2005. «Цветной слух»: Казань и здесь была первой. В *История философии и теория познания. Грани взаимодействия: Сб. статей*, 43–52. Симбирск-Ульяновск: Симбирская книга.]

Wellek, Albert. 1928. *Doppelempfinden und Programmusik. Beiträge zur Psychologie, Kritik und Geschichte der Sinnenentsprechung und Sinnensymbolik.* Manuscript dissertation, University Vienna.

———. 1931. Zur Geschichte und Kritik der Synästhesie-Forschung. *Archiv für die gesamte Psychologie* 79:325–384.

CHAPTER 20

SYNESTHESIA IN THE TWENTIETH CENTURY

Synesthesia's renaissance

RICHARD E. CYTOWIC

Synesthesia research underwent a renaissance in the twentieth century. But from what state did it arise and what constituted its rebirth? Rather than enumerate a chronological record of period events—its success, failures, and changes in thinking—I decided to tell the century's arc as a narrative. I decided also against merely cataloguing a stream of facts and percentages and instead to ask two fundamental questions: "Why the renaissance of interest in synesthesia?" and "What was its *meaning* at the end of the century?" That is, what did the phenomenon mean not only to individuals, but also more broadly to science and society? The facts are broadly known; only in retrospect can their significance be understood.

A hint with respect to synesthesia's meaning lies in the many letters I have received over more than three decades (and still do) from individuals realizing for the first time that others like them exist. One cannot minimize their astonishment and enthusiasm at the discovery nor their relief at being believed, having usually endured a lifetime of being told that they were "making it up." The experience is often cathartic, even tearful. Many say, "You saved my life." For a writer or a scientist few testimonials can be as gratifying.

I am certain it is gratifying to conquer epidemics and scourges, but illness befalls individuals as a matter of fate, and the afflicted are passive players in its drama. Synesthesia on the other hand speaks to the essence of who one is. An idiosyncratic, highly particularized way of seeing the world comprises one's singular core of identity. To "save" an individual from the vicissitudes of ignorance, prejudice, or misunderstanding is not just to restore a singular sense of self and self-worth, but also to celebrate the singularity of subjectivity itself. No other enterprise advances science the way synesthesia does while simultaneously moving the human heart.

One can ask why certain turns happened during the century while others did not. Historians of science if not scientists themselves point out that our discipline has fashions just as hemlines and tie widths do. Sometimes, it is not ready for something new. It is doubtful whether any one thing explains the periodic waxing and ebbing of interest in synesthesia over the years. One can at best question trends and the underappreciated factor of chance. For example, Larry Marks wrote a review paper on colored hearing (Marks 1975) and a follow-on book about cross-modal perception (Marks 1978) which should have sparked interest in the long-forgotten topic of synesthesia, but failed to attract attention sufficiently wide or deep. It was chance that prepared my own mind to respond when it first heard a synesthete's offhand comment about "points on the chicken" (a description of his synesthetic shape sensations triggered by the flavor of foods). I spoke out and published, but the zeitgeist challenged synesthesia's reality and frowned on it as a research topic. Funding was impossible. My neurology colleagues actually warned me to drop the pursuit of my index case of taste-shape synesthesia. "New Age nonsense," they warned. "It will ruin your career."

Two decades would pass before a younger crop of academics could safely take it up without threatening their reputations. Chance lastly factored in the way synesthetes themselves responded. Out of hundreds who read or heard media reports, only some self-selected to write or call, and make themselves available for research. Fewer still expended the effort required to organize enterprises like the American Synesthesia Association, the UK Synaesthesia Association, and various offshoots.

The renaissance I see looking back is a movement away from the clinical classification of synesthetic accounts (what medical science calls nosology) to a multilayered characterization of it. At the present the field is at work on a top-to-bottom science of synesthesia, its investigations ranging from DNA studies, early cognition, and brain imaging all the way up to whole-organism behavior that includes art and creativity. Any science would be pleased to have an ambit that spanned levels of magnitude the way synesthesia does.

Gradually the nineteenth century moved away from its fascination with synesthesia's loosey-goosey aspects, what Kevin Dann characterizes as "synesthesia euphoria" in *Bright Colors Falsely Seen* (Dann 1998). In 1900, séances and automatic writing were still in vogue, and synesthesia was sufficiently theatrical and spiritual to stir popular attention. Alexander Scriabin was one of several composers who wrote color music, but with deliberately contrived tone–color associations. His invented pairings were actually borrowed from Madame Blavatsky's Theosophist tract, *The Secret Doctrine* (Cytowic and Eagleman 2009, 190). Slowly synesthesia's study grew mainstream with the application of proper experiments that could be repeated and verified. Then in the mid twentieth century it hit a bump following the rise of behaviorism, which generally regarded mental states and subjective accounts as unreliable and unscientific. Any investigation of synesthesia as a topic became automatically suspicious, and there followed three or four decades of disbelief that it could even be "real." My own small role in synesthesia's renaissance is fairly well known. In brief, its contours are as follows.

I fortuitously knew the word "synesthesia" from having read *The Mind of a Mnemonist* (Luria 1968), a short work about a vast memory. The case described by Luria, that of the extraordinary S, had savant-like abilities with respect to recall. His many forms of synesthesia provided numerous hooks for whatever he was to remember. A decade later I'd revisit S's fivefold sensory coupling and synesthesia's relationship to elevated memory. Initially, however, I filed the word and its splendid etymology away in the back of my mind. It shares a root with *an-aesthesia*, meaning "no sensation," but reverses the prefix to *syn-aesthesia,* making the word mean 'joined sensation.' Thus primed, I found myself at a dinner party in 1980 where my new neighbor and host delayed our seating with the comment, "There aren't enough points on the chicken." Michael Watson, my index case, simultaneously felt taste and flavor as a physical touch on his face and in his hands. "With an intense flavor," he explained, "a feeling sweeps down my arm into my hands as if I'm actually grasping something I feel its weight, temperature, texture, and shape." I intended to be merely polite. "Oh, you have synesthesia," I said.

But Michael froze in astonishment. "You mean there's a name for this?" he said.

Michael had always been dismissed as making it up. Now it is recognized that an initial shock is a common reaction on learning that one's heretofore private world has a scientific-sounding name, and that others like you exist who have comingled senses.

Scientists, by contrast, were less enthusiastic and open-minded. My colleagues wanted to know where the lesion was on Michael's computed tomography (CT) scan, missing the point that he was outwardly normal and neurologically intact. He didn't have a hole in his head but an extra mental state. He fit the category of "elevated functions."

I went my own way and eventually published the first book about the topic in English, *Synesthesia: A Union of the Senses.* It covered synesthesia's history and detailed forty-two cases from a neurological perspective (Cytowic 1989, 2002). A popular account of Michael Watson and early research efforts followed later in *The Man Who Tasted Shapes* (Cytowic 1993, 2003). Later, David Eagleman and I included all types of synesthesia in *Wednesday is Indigo Blue: Discovering the Brain of Synesthesia,* which won the Hoffer Book Award's 2011 Montaigne Medal (Cytowic and Eagleman 2009). Over three short decades the attitude had traveled from leery to laudatory.

As luck would have it I came upon a second synesthete the same month that I chanced upon Michael Watson. She was a psychologist who experienced colored hearing and colored smell. I happened to be at a medical institution where I had access to the current technology, but was even more fortune to find an open-minded mentor who'd actually heard the word "synesthesia," and a psychophysics lab in which he encouraged me to probe these two individuals and see whether their synesthesia emulated the general population in any way or differed from it completely. Older literature existed—going back more than two centuries. It was interesting from an historical viewpoint—for instance, Sir Francis Galton's detailed description from a century earlier read very much like the opening section of a modern scientific paper (Galton 1880)—but it was unhelpful in suggesting how one might actually approach a contemporary synesthete.

Anyone who has taken up the topic will likely have experienced a sequence of events similar to mine with respect to snowballing attention. In my case I presented a paper at The International Neuropsychological Society in 1980. Attendees from the press swarmed. They generated considerable publicity thanks to synesthesia's offbeat hook. One of my own patients who tasted phonemes excitedly brought in a clipping from

The National Enquirer, a supermarket tabloid. It read, "Bizarre Medical Oddity Affects Millions, husband's name tastes like wood!" I was mortified, but she of course was thrilled. Two papers later (Cytowic and Wood 1982a, 1982b), unsolicited material was pouring in from the post. A librarian, for example, sent 25 single-spaced pages in an effort to explain the number forms she called "memory maps." It included dozens of meticulously rendered crayon drawings. In another instance a university teacher wrote, "I waved the *Psychology Today* article at my husband, shouting, 'Look! This is me! I'm not nuts!'" Other letters began, "All my life … " or "I thought I was the only one in the world who saw letters in color …"

Interest among laypersons grew rapidly. For example, a TV reporter from North Germany flew to Washington to interview me in 1994. He was overwhelmed with inquiries once the segment aired, and asked for help in where to direct them. I suggested he contact the local medical school in Hanover. The ear he reached happily belonged to Hinderk Emrich who turned Hanover into a synesthesia research centre and home to the delightful *Synesthesia Café*, a gathering place where synesthetes can meet in privacy without scientists or the press listening in. Synesthetes love to talk among themselves, so it is not surprising that the synesthesia renaissance has spread from continent to continent. The Arctic cannot be far behind, for surely there must be synesthetic Eskimos.

During the past 30 years people have asked, "Why you?" That is, with synesthesia relegated to oblivion at the start, why did I bother to take it up and persist in reintroducing it to a doubting scientific mainstream? Until now I have not fully addressed the question. In the past I have said that my upbringing inculcated a taste for the offbeat and unusual which made me less ready to dismiss synesthesia as weird. Time, however, has revealed another layer of explanation I had not previously appreciated, namely my being gay. It is hard to imagine today but at the age of 10 years I understood very well that the state considered me a criminal, the church immoral, and my father's medical profession sick (psychiatry's *Diagnostic and Statistical Manual of Mental Disorders* would not remove homosexuality as an illness until 1973). Society denied my existence by insisting that my thoughts and feelings "shouldn't be." It was akin to saying that *I* shouldn't be. Growing up with such a message how could I not have been fascinated by something like synesthesia which the establishment also said shouldn't exist? I knew exactly how synesthetes felt when no one would believe them and everyone called them freaks.

Subsequent researchers encountered resistance similar to mine. Even at the end of this century Ramachandran and Hubbard had to chronicle the prevailing efforts to explain synesthesia away (Ramachandran and Hubbard 2001). Such people were either: (1) crazy, the phenomenon being the result of an overactive imagination or a desire to call attention to oneself by claiming to be special; (2) merely remembering childhood memories from coloring books or refrigerator alphabet magnets and their associations were simply overlearned; (3) engaging in tangential, metaphorical speech as in "sharp cheese" (even though cheese is physically soft rather than sharp, which begs the question of why language uses tactile adjectives to describe taste sensations or taste terms to describe persons as in the phrase "she's really sweet"); (4) or else they were just burned-out potheads and junkies. Interestingly, the latter idea is not entirely meritless given that

LSD and psilocybin can cause synesthesia both during the high and afterwards. The fact that any drug could induce a perceptual state similar to that of naturally occurring synesthesia is a gripping puzzle, yet it failed to arouse interest.

Claiming that synesthetes were merely being metaphoric was to employ a type of circular reasoning because we didn't and still do not accurately understand how the brain represents metaphor. Instead, turning the argument on its head suggests that understanding synesthetic perception might help get a handle on the neurological basis of metaphor and creativity. Larry Marks had in fact written about metonymy and synesthetic metaphor, but it was largely overlooked. After a talk at the World Congress of Neurology I was told, with conviction, that synesthesia was just poetry. It is the nature of orthodoxy to dismiss what it cannot understand and deny what does not fit into its scheme.

The hostile atmosphere led me to avoid suggesting that elements of language might somehow mediate synesthetic associations. Despite having cases of colored words and first names that evoked tastes in subjects, I chose to emphasize synesthesia's concrete perceptual nature. I felt that the scientific community would more readily accept sound–sight linkages given the well-established associations between everyday domains in instances such as ventriloquism, lip reading, and the localizing of cinema voices to the screen rather than the surrounding speakers. Unfortunately, my avoidance delayed an understanding of linguistic and conceptual factors in synesthesia until Jamie Ward and Julia Simner showed language-mediated synesthesia to be rule-based (Ward and Simner 2003). It was a wonderful and welcome advance.

By century's end we had done away with Fodor's modularity, a paradigm that reigned for a while and claimed by design that language, sensory, and other cognitive modules did not interact early with one another (Fodor 1983). The idea that the five senses travel inward from their receptors along separate channels gave way to today's understanding that they are highly intertwined, and that the cerebrum is full of recurrent feedback and feedforward loops. The brain was multiplex rather than modular. Synesthesia also provided a fresh look at the interplay between nature and nurture given that for most varieties a genetically inherited trait needs to interact in childhood with culturally learned artifacts such as letters, numbers, words, food names, time, or music. Perception wasn't developmentally fixed as early thinking saw it. Perhaps the most remarkable thing about synesthesia is that a nucleotide mutation can alter one's way of perceiving the world—as if a single switch can revise the most complex object in the universe, the human brain.

One way to measure the zeitgeist with respect to synesthesia is to count the number of papers published per unit time. Figure 20.1 groups peer-reviewed papers by decade from 1850 to 2006. The method has shortcomings, but one can nonetheless see considerable interest at the turn of the century followed by a drop off during the decades that behaviorism held sway as a psychological paradigm (roughly 1920 to 1940).

This kind of metric misses an important point, though. It leaves a gap between what science belatedly woke up to and what the validation of synesthesia means to affected individuals. It raises the issue of first-person versus third-person framing. Just as my early peers wanted to

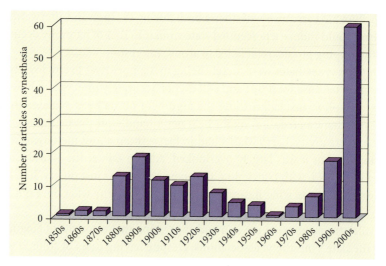

FIGURE 20.1 Peer-reviewed papers on synesthesia by decade from 1850 to 2006. There was considerable interest at the turn of the twentieth century, followed by a marked dropping off during the decades that behaviorism held sway as a dominant psychological paradigm. (Its height of popularity was between 1920 and 1940.) Increasing interest characterizes recent decades, indicating a second renaissance of synesthesia study.

know where the lesion was on Michael Watson's CT scan, critics even today demand third-person verification of what is essentially a first-person experience. Even though Michael Watson knew himself to be different all his life, he became frightened when our experiments exposed him to the latest brain-probing technology. He feared that an "objective" assessment of his claims would prove him to be crazy, or stoned as his friends had always suggested. Missing in this scenario was any iota given to his personal experience. That omission had been a constant shortcoming with synesthesia until the later decades.

It is curious how uncomfortable science has been with mental states during certain points in the twentieth century. A persistent question was whether synesthesia was real. The answer to such a presumptuous inquiry is, Real to whom—the questioner or the person who has it? Literature of the 1950s expressed considerable ambivalence about the role of the cerebral cortex in mental function. As late as the1970s my interest in aphasia (an inability to speak or comprehend language following brain injury) got me labeled as "philosophically minded" because language was considered outside the mainstream of neurology. Alzheimer's disease failed to excite the faculty, as did any aspect of human cognition. The experience of the preceding century seemed to have been forgotten.

For example, the polymath Gustav Fechner (1801–1887) meant to transcend physical absolutism. He articulated something that every physiologist once knew but became gradually lost in the twentieth-century's zeal to decipher the nervous system: namely, that a mental world exists. Then, as now, the question was how to do science in such an arena. Fechner's psychophysics, the relating of physical stimuli to perceived sensation, has no substitute. No amount of brain imaging or analyzing nerve impulses can

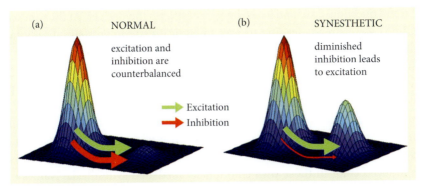

FIGURE 20.2 In this cartoon of neural connectivity, green represents excitatory connections and red represents inhibitory connections. (a) When inhibition functions normally, a bulge of activity in one area does not spread because the excitation and inhibition counterbalance each other. (b) When inhibition is diminished, activity in one area leads to activity in another.

substitute for an introspective report. Even today's craze of functional magnetic resonance imaging (fMRI) starts with the subject's state of mind, yet everyone's attention is quickly drawn to hot spots on the scans. In *Wednesday is Indigo Blue*, David Eagleman and I stressed that neuroimaging is misleading precisely because it emphasizes peak activations rather than capturing all of the entities that participate in the network underlying a given function (Figure 20.2).

At best scanning shows only a partial functional landscape and says nothing about entities that actively participate beneath the threshold of current fMRI technology. We doubt that synesthesia is located in any one place the way that Broca's aphasia defines Broca's area (that it, anatomically described as the third frontal convolution, whereas Wernicke's aphasia is defined functionally the way synesthesia is, making it impossible to point to a definitive locus). We prefer to think in terms of neural networks that connect several brain structures in concert, all of which contribute to the conscious synesthetic experience. Instead of being localized in the sense of classical neurology, David and I say that synesthesia exists as the dominant process in a distributed network at a given time (Cytowic and Eagleman 2009, 238–239). Other chapters in this handbook discuss localization. The point is that the normal brain is heavily subspecialized and that a constant cross talk among specialized and plastic areas permits them to collaborate. The difference between synesthetic and non-synesthetic brains is not whether cross talk exists, but rather its degree.

The desire for third-person technological verification dies hard, as does the belief that machine images of the brain are the only acceptable proof of reality. As recently as 2007 a newcomer spoke at an international conference. This neurosurgeon presented fMRI images and said, "This proves that synesthesia is real." He was uninterested in hearing that synesthesia's reality had long been established with paper and pencil, or about the use of standard techniques of sensory psychology—masking, visual crowding, priming, Stroop interference. His attitude was that nothing useful could be learned from the past, or by careful questioning of and listening to synesthetes themselves. At the time, clinical descriptions were already leading to psychophysical experiments specifically tailored to an individual that took advantage of the interplay between first-person and third-person accounts.

Take the example of emotionally-mediated synesthesia. The claim that certain people see colored auras around objects or individuals, and can "read" their moods is prima facie so outlandish as to induce eye rolling. Yet Jamie Ward probed such claims dispassionately and demonstrated that it is the valence of emotional connotation in the observer that determines the synesthetic colors that they see. For example, English first names induced color in those with emotionally mediated synesthesia. Names of people the subjects actually knew were more likely to induce color than names not among their acquaintance. Emotionally loaded words such as "love" and "anger" elicited color whereas color names did not. So explained, the phenomenon isn't spooky at all but fits in nicely with theory of mind and the ability to read other individuals.

At the beginning of the century, science labored under the notion of universals. That is, what applied to one logically applied to all. But by the century's end synesthesia had brilliantly resuscitated the single-case study and breathed new vigor into it. At first, practical reasons accounted for the situation because it was nearly impossible to round up more than one subject at a time. As the number of synesthetes making themselves available grew, however, researchers faced the opposite problem. How to group individuals whose idiosyncratic differences were great? There is a parallel here with earlier work begun in the late 1970s by George Ojemann. His electrical stimulation mapping of the cortex disclosed the need to revise traditional language models based on strict neuroanatomy. As measured by naming, reading, phoneme identification, oral praxis, and verbal memory, his studies confirmed that language was indeed discretely localized in any given individual, but highly variable in its location among individuals. As Ojemann said at the time, "The detailed functional anatomy of our brains may be as individualized as the detailed anatomy of our faces" (Ojemann and Whittaker 1978). Being functionally defined for now, the absolute coordinates for synesthesia's physical grounding in the brain likely varies from person to person. As noted earlier, being functionally defined may even mean that synesthesia can never be localized in the strict classical sense.

Work in this century speaks to the issue of subjectivity itself. Take the well-known example of differing eyewitness accounts. People who see the so-called exact same objective incident nonetheless give disparate accounts of it. For a long time science has labored under the notion of "objectivity" even though scientific theories are in part subjective and theory laden themselves, biasing them toward what a given researcher even finds interesting and worthy of study. Today's young researchers can explore widely and find niches that increasingly open up as each answered question raises many others. The "weird" quality of synesthesia—once a fatal flaw—now makes it easier to pursue other unusual phenomena that are not yet part of the standard cannon.

Around the year 2000 there seemed to be a point when things came together and synesthesia made sense. And then suddenly it didn't any more because more and more exceptions crept into the picture we had painted of how synesthesia worked. For example, well after childhood, but particularly around the time of puberty, the trait could appear or be lost. This contradicted the settled notion that the trait appears early in life and then becomes fixed. Then, one or two individuals appeared who seemed to have their colors actually determined by refrigerator magnets or coloring books. Still others showed that couplings *could* change over time, and that context *could* modify perceptions. Everything we knew suddenly didn't look so certain. Settled knowledge became unsettled once again. There were new questions to answer.

The late twentieth century focused on synesthesia's neural connectivity and functional landscape. We have not yet begun to fully explore individual differences, context, circadian variations, and volume transmission. Leveraging these might help discriminate exactly which brain areas are likely to be involved in which variety of synesthesia. Volume transmission in particular has never been addressed yet I believe is particularly challenging and proportionately fascinating. It is a way of transmitting information throughout both brain and body that relies on information transfer by small molecules such as hormones, peptides, and diffusible gasses. It operates over a wide range of distances and speeds. If one thinks of the traditional hardwiring of axons and synapses as a train traveling down a track, then volume transmission is the train leaving the track. This and understanding gene expression are but two of the challenges for the next hundred years.

REFERENCES

Cytowic, Richard E. 1989. *Synesthesia: A Union Of The Senses*. Springer Series in Neuropsychology. New York: Springer-Verlag.

———. 1993. *The Man who Tasted Shapes: A Bizarre Medical Mystery Offers Revolutionary Insights into Emotions, Reasoning and Consciousness*. New York: Putnam.

———. 2002. *Synesthesia: A Union of the Senses*. 2nd ed. Cambridge, MA: MIT Press.

———. 2003. *The Man Who Tasted Shapes, with a new afterword*. Cambridge, MA: MIT Press.

Cytowic, Richard E., and David M. Eagleman. 2009. *Wednesday is Indigo Blue: Discovering the Brain of Synesthesia*. Cambridge, MA: MIT Press.

Cytowic, Richard E., and Frank B. Wood. 1982a. Synesthesia. I. A review of major theories and their brain basis. *Brain and Cognition* 1 (1):23–35.

———. 1982b. Synesthesia. II. Psychophysical relations in the synesthesia of geometrically shaped taste and colored hearing. *Brain and Cognition* 1 (1):36–49.

Dann, Kevin. 1998. *Bright Colors, Falsely Seen: Synesthesia and the Search for Transcendental Knowledge*. New Haven, CT: Yale University Press.

Fodor, Jerry A. 1983. *The Modularity of Mind: An Essay on Faculty Psychology*. Cambridge, MA: MIT Press.

Galton, Francis. 1880. Visualized numerals. *Nature* 21:252–256.

Luria, Aleksandr R. 1968. *The Mind of a Mnemonist: A Little Book About a Vast Memory*. New York: Basic Books.

Marks, Lawrence E. 1975. On colored-hearing synesthesia. *Psychological Bulletin* 82:303–331.

———. 1978. *The Unity of the Senses: Interrelations among the Modalities*. New York: Academic Press.

Ojemann, George A., and Harry A. Whitaker. 1978. Language localization and variability. *Brain and Language* 1978; 6:239–260.

Ramachandran, Vilayanur S., and Edward M. Hubbard. 2001. Synaesthesisia – a window into perception, thought, and language. *Journal of Consciousness Studies* 8 (12):3–34.

Ward, Jamie, and Julia Simner. 2003. Lexical-gustatory synaesthesia: linguistic and conceptual factors. *Cognition* 89 (3):237–61.

CHAPTER 21

SYNESTHESIA IN THE
TWENTY-FIRST CENTURY

Synesthesia's ascent

CHRISTOPHER T. LOVELACE

INTRODUCTION

While interest in synesthesia among behavioral researchers has been growing since the mid twentieth century, the first decade of the twenty-first century has seen this interest grow into a steady flow of new data and ideas. While just a decade ago only a few scattered laboratories and investigators were actively interested in synesthesia, there are now over a dozen active laboratories around the world and about a half-dozen synesthesia associations, many of which hold annual meetings where researchers and synesthetes alike gather to share ideas and experiences.

Synesthesia has grown not only in the world of research, but also in the public consciousness. Print articles appear with some regularity in both science-oriented magazines such as *Scientific American* (Ramachandran and Hubbard 2003b) and *New Scientist* (Lehrer 2007; Motluk 2004) as well as newspapers and magazines (Bartlett 2002; Bhanoo 2011; Burne 2001; Conis 2007; Dayton 2012). Awareness of synesthesia is also increasing due in no small part to the ever-increasing amount of information available via the Internet, most notably a Wikipedia page regularly maintained and updated by synesthesia researchers (<http://en.wikipedia.org/wiki/Synesthesia>). One result, and facilitator, of this increase in awareness of synesthesia, as writer Pat Duffy has pointed out, is that there are increasing numbers of characters in works of fiction depicted as having synesthesia (Duffy and Simner 2010).

In this chapter, I will review the growth of interest in synesthesia over the first decade of the twenty-first century, with an overview of some of the significant trends in synesthesia research. The chapter begins with details on the methods used to locate publications on synesthesia. It continues with details on the frequency and types of publications on synesthesia appearing in the literature. The chapter concludes with two sections summarizing emerging trends in synesthesia research.

Literature Search Methodology

Since the present focus is on research, the literature reviewed here is drawn entirely from two large English-language databases that index publications relevant to medical and behavioral research: PubMed from the National Center for Biotechnology Information, US National Library of Medicine, and PsycINFO from the American Psychological Association.[1] While PubMed contains primarily articles from biomedical journals, PsycINFO is focused more closely on behavioral science, and includes primary-source articles (reports of original research), secondary-source articles (reviews of existing research), books, book chapters, dissertations, and book reviews.

Each of these databases was searched using the keywords "synesthe* OR synaesthe*" to capture both the US spelling (*synesthesia*) and the UK spelling (*synaesthesia*). The asterisk wildcard captures variants of each of these terms, such as *synesthete* (a person who experiences synesthesia), *synesthetic*, *synesthesiology* (the study of synesthesia), and *synesthesic* (infrequently used in place of *synesthetic*). Only articles published between 2001 and 2012 were included.[2] Entries for electronic, pre-publication versions of these articles may appear in these databases prior to their print publication; those articles were not included in the publication tallies, as their final publication year is as yet indeterminate.

One particular issue that arises in searching the literature on synesthesia is related to the term itself. As noted in the introductory chapters in two recent volumes on synesthesia (Cytowic and Eagleman 2009; Robertson and Sagiv 2005), the word *synesthesia* has over the last century and a half been used to refer to many different things. This remains true in the modern research literature. Some authors use the word to refer to artistic or literary metaphor (Cacciari 2008; Cazeaux 2002; Harris 2009). In the medical literature, *synesthesia* is used to generically refer to any abnormal "extra" sensation, often occurring across sense modality boundaries, and often as a result of things like hallucinogenic drug use (Babu, Mccurdy, and Boyer 2008; Luke 2011; Mcardle 2006; Smith 2005; Stuckey, Lawson, and Luna 2005), migraine (Alstadhaug and Benjaminsen 2010), or tissue damage (Beauchamp and Ro 2008; Brewis and Baguley 2007; Terzis, Dryer, and Bodner 2010; Thomas-Anterion et al. 2010).

The variety of synesthesia reviewed here is of the "developmental" type with early childhood onset, and automatic, consistent, and idiosyncratic *concurrents*—the "extra" sensations experienced by synesthetes—accompanying the appearance of specific *inducers*—the stimulus or cognition that initiates the appearance of the concurrent. The developmental synesthesias have a number of characteristics that distinguish them from metaphor or acquired synesthesias (Ramachandran and Hubbard 2001b). As noted by

---

[1] PubMed: <http://www.ncbi.nlm.nih.gov/pubmed>, PsycINFO: <http://www.apa.org/psycinfo>.
[2] As of 15 July 2012.

Ro et al. (2007), the experience of such acquired synesthesias may be fundamentally different from that of developmental synesthesia.

Additionally, a number of behavioral researchers use the word synesthesia to refer to the tendency to associate different sensory dimensions that is a part of normal perception. For example, Gallace and Spence (2006) investigated the relationship between auditory pitch and visual size in the general population, with lower pitches preferred as corresponding to larger images. While dimensions such as these can be reliably demonstrated to correspond to each other in influencing behavior, it is not the case that large images automatically elicit, in addition to the usual visual sensation, a conscious experience of a low-pitched sound for the average person. Instead, experiences such as these, termed "weak" synesthesia by Martino and Marks (2001), are simply multisensory correspondences experienced by most people. To focus the present discussion, I limit this review to studies of developmental—what Martino and Marks call "strong"—synesthesia, from this point forward simply referred to as synesthesia.[3]

Each of the articles returned from the literature searches was classified based on its relevance to research on developmental synesthesia.[4] Those with direct bearing on our understanding of developmental synesthesia ($N = 344$) are the focus of the current chapter. To fine-tune the present review, those that mention developmental synesthesia but focused on something else ($N = 69$) and those that used the term synesthesia to refer to something other than developmental synesthesia ($N = 75$) are not included here. I am in no way suggesting that these works are less important. Quite the contrary, they represent important intersections between synesthesia research and other areas of behavioral research.

Twenty-First-Century Publications in Synesthesia

Publication rates

These searches resulted in 488 unique hits representing many different approaches and research interests. Interestingly, a search (for "synesthe* OR synaesthe*") of the PsycINFO database resulted in 343 hits published between 1895 (the earliest date available) and 2000. The identical PsycINFO search for 2001 to 2012 returned 437 hits,

---

[3] In a recent article, Simner reviews and addresses the challenges that are present in defining synaesthesia (Simner 2012).

[4] Most hits were published in English (about 95%), and, due only to my own linguistic limitations, only those are included here.

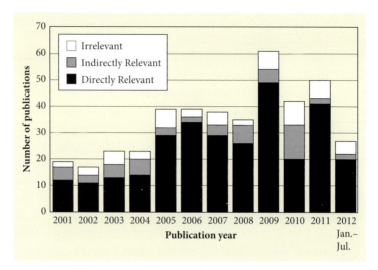

FIGURE 21.1 Number of hits from the combined PubMed/PsycINFO searches (for synesthe* OR synaesthe*) for the years 2001 to 2012, up to 15 July, shown separately based on relevance to developmental synesthesia (see text).

representing a more than tenfold increase in the per-decade publication rate from the previous century! Publication frequencies, separated by year of publication and relevance to developmental synesthesia, are shown in Figure 21.1.

Clearly, interest in synesthesia is on the rise. While there is a dip in publications in 2010, the publication rate recovered in 2011, and 2012 (shown up to July) is on track to exceed that number. Part of the reason for the dramatic increase in publications in 2005 was the inclusion of all 12 chapters from the book *Synesthesia: Perspectives From Cognitive Neuroscience* edited by Robertson and Sagiv (2005). This increase was sustained in the following year by the 2006 special issue of the journal *Cortex* on "Cognitive Neuroscience Perspectives on Synesthesia," with 22 articles. In 2009, that same journal included a special section with eight articles on "Synaesthetic Visuo-spatial Forms." The year 2011 saw a 12-article special issue of the *Journal of Neuropsychology*.

Publication types

While the late twentieth century saw the first modern books devoted to synesthesia (Baron-Cohen and Harrison 1997; Cytowic 1989, 1993; Dann 1998), the first decade of the twenty-first century has seen even more interest from publishers. In addition to re-printings of Cytowic's two earlier books (Cytowic 2002, 2003), there are also books suitable for the lay public (Duffy 2001; Harrison 2001; Ward 2008) as well as volumes intended for scientists (Cytowic and Eagleman 2009; Robertson and Sagiv 2005).

Especially encouraging with respect to the future of synesthesia research is the number of student dissertations specifically focusing on synesthesia. Of the 23 dissertations included in the PsycINFO results from 2001 to 2012, compared to 11 from 1966 to

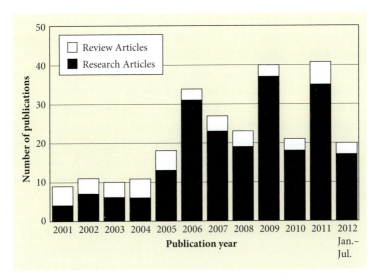

FIGURE 21.2 Number of research articles and review articles directly relevant to developmental synesthesia for the years 2001 to 2012, up to 15 July.

2000, 13 are directly relevant to developmental synesthesia (Berman 2011; Crane 2006; Esterman 2007; Gimmestad 2012; Gross 2009; Harris 2004; Hubbard 2005; Kim 2007; McCabe 2011; Ramos 2007; Sagiv 2004; Stephan 2005; Witthoft 2008).

Aside from books, book reviews, and dissertations, 216 of the 437 remaining publications are reports of original research with direct relevance to developmental synesthesia. As indicated in Figure 21.2, the yearly publication frequency of research studies mirrors that of the overall increases visible in Figure 21.1. There were additionally 48 published review articles, with the rate steady at about four per year (Figure 21.2). The research reports are the main focus of the remainder of this chapter.

TRENDS IN SYNESTHESIA RESEARCH

The following sections focus on emerging trends in research on synesthesia. These research studies have addressed a variety of questions with a diverse array of methods and participants. The next section describes the participants being included in modern synesthesia research studies. The section that follows describes some of the approaches being used to measure synesthesia. The final section goes into some of the questions currently being investigated by synesthesia researchers.

Research participants

Many of the early academic papers on synesthesia were descriptions of single cases. It is interesting to note that case studies are still very much a part of modern synesthesia research. Indeed, much of what we now know about synesthesia is based on thorough accounts of individual cases, such as Luria's "S" (Luria 1968) and Cytowic's "MW" (Cytowic 1993). Seventy-seven of these modern studies focused on presenting data from between one and six individual cases of synesthesia. Methods used in these case studies often took the form of descriptive case histories—12 studies used primarily this approach—or specific descriptions of a synesthete's inducer–concurrent mappings (e.g., the color that goes with each letter or number). These arc especially useful for defining new forms of synesthesia, establishing the consistency of mappings over time, and identifying factors that can modulate the experience of synesthesia. As we continue to tease apart the experiences that are or are not a part of synesthesia, and explore novel forms of synesthesia, interesting cases will continue to provide illustrative examples upon which we can build our understanding.

Of the research studies, 126 combined data across multiple synesthetes and usually included a comparison group of non-synesthetes as well. Synesthete group sizes ranged from two, especially for investigations of unusual forms (e.g., Cohen Kadosh et al. 2005), to upwards of 200, mostly in survey studies (Rich, Bradshaw, and Mattingley 2005). The proportion of group versus case studies has grown continuously during the first decade of the twenty-first century (Figure 21.3), possibly as a result of recruitment being facilitated by increased public awareness of synesthesia. As we further refine our understanding of synesthesia, it will be more important to study groups of synesthetes to improve the degree to which findings apply to synesthesia in general. For example, while there are cases of people with synesthesia displaying exceptional memory abilities (Baron-Cohen et al. 2007; Luria 1968), Rothen and Meier have argued that although synesthesia may

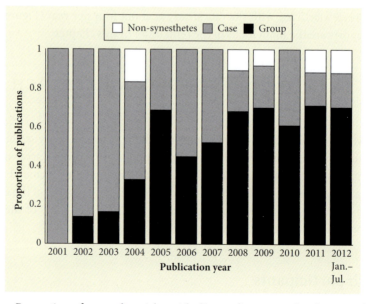

FIGURE 21.3 Proportion of research articles with direct relevance to developmental synesthesia using either groups or cases of synesthesia or non-synesthetes, by year.

yield limited, domain-specific memory advantages (Rothen and Meier 2010b), group studies are needed to reduce the impact of exceptional cases on our understanding of synesthesia in general (Rothen and Meier 2009).

Interestingly, while most of these studies used synesthetes as participants, a few included only non-synesthetes but collected data that directly spoke to some aspect of developmental synesthesia. A number of these studies investigated the developmental origins of synesthesia by examining synesthesia-like correspondences in children and adults (Mondloch and Maurer 2004; Spector and Maurer 2008, 2011; Wagner and Dobkins 2011). Ward investigated whether the inducer-concurrent mappings experienced by sound-color synesthetes might have aesthetic appeal to non-synesthetes (Ward, Moore, et al. 2008). Other investigators showed that it is possible to produce synesthete-like performance on some behavioral tasks via hypnosis (Cohen Kadosh et al. 2009) or learning (Meier and Rothen 2009; Rothen, Wantz, and Meier 2011).

Measurement of synesthesia

The following section summarizes the ways twenty-first-century researchers have measured synesthetic percepts. This is no mean feat considering that the concurrents are subjective—that is, like all perception, they happen entirely within the mind of the synesthete. Researchers have come up with clever ways to objectively measure such subjective experiences.

Behavioral measures

By far the most common dependent measure, used in 104 studies, involved some sort of structured behavioral test in which sensory stimuli were presented and behavioral or verbal responses recorded. Perhaps the most common behavioral measure is one that is intended to be diagnostic of developmental synesthesia: the Test of Genuineness (TOG). The TOG was initially developed by Baron-Cohen, Wyke, and Binnie (1987) as an assessment for word-color synesthesia, and simply has a synesthete verbally indicate the colors they experience for each of a set of inducers. Synesthetes, compared to non-synesthetes, are typically highly consistent in their color associations over months, years, and even decades (Simner and Logie 2007). Indeed, this consistency is taken as a hallmark of synesthesia. This measure was recently revised by Asher et al. (2006) to allow the putative synesthete to select physical color patches rather than verbally report concurrent colors. Online versions of the TOG similarly allow color selection using computerized color palettes (e.g., <http://synesthete.org/>; Eagleman et al. 2007). Measures of consistency such as the TOG are considered the "gold standard" with respect to confirming the presence of synesthesia.

Another hallmark of synesthesia is its automaticity; that is, the concurrents appear unbidden when an inducer is encountered (Mattingley et al. 2001; Spruyt et al. 2009). A novel behavioral task for synesthetic automaticity, the synesthetic Stroop task, was developed nearly 30 years ago (Wollen and Ruggiero 1983) and is still used to demonstrate the automatic nature and perceptual reality of synesthetic concurrents. This is a variant of the original Stroop task (Stroop 1935) in which one must name the print color of mismatching color words, for example the word "Red" printed in yellow ink. This takes much longer than naming the color of congruently colored words ("Red" printed in red ink) because the incongruent word meaning automatically primes an incorrect response ("red") that must be inhibited prior to making the correct response ("yellow"). In the synesthetic adaptation, a synesthete is presented with inducers along with mismatching representations of their associated concurrents. In the original synesthetic Stroop study (Wollen and Ruggiero 1983), a grapheme-color synesthete was asked to name the color of graphemes printed in a synesthetically incongruent color. So, if the letter "A" elicits a synesthetic concurrent of light green, then it would be printed in, say, orange. If the synesthete takes longer to name the physical color of the letter ("orange"), then this is taken as evidence that they had to first inhibit the incorrect response associated with the automatically-elicited concurrent ("light green") prior to making the correct response. That the concurrent is elicited automatically, and presumably cannot be inhibited to quickly produce the correct response in this task, is taken as objective evidence of the presence of synesthesia.

A more recent innovation is the use of visual search tasks in synesthesia. In a non-synesthetic visual search task, a visual target is presented among some number of distractors. If the target is unique in some basic feature, for example, it is a different physical color than the distractors, then focused spatial attention is not required to locate it. Instead, it "pops out" of the display, taking no longer to find as the number of distractors is increased. When the target and distractors contain the same features and differ only in their configuration, attention to individual items is required and adding distractors increases the time to find the target (Treisman 1982). Such would be the case for non-synesthetes looking for a letter "L" among a set of letter "Ts." However, for a grapheme-color synesthete who gets different concurrent colors for "L" and "T," the "L" might pop out and be detected quickly without the need for effortful search. This has, in fact, been shown to happen for at least some synesthetes (Palmeri et al. 2002; Smilek, Dixon, and Merikle 2003). While the visual search task typically involves a single target among some number of distractors, Hubbard and Ramachandran (2001a) used a texture segregation variant of this task with a pair of grapheme-color synesthetes. Using two different graphemes that each induced different concurrent colors, a set of one of the graphemes was arranged to form a shape (e.g., a triangle) within a randomly arranged set of the other grapheme. They showed that, at least for some synesthetes, the different concurrent color of the grapheme forming the shape made it easily detectable.

One other behavioral task that is coming into frequent usage is based on the Spatial Numerical Association of Response Codes (SNARC) task (Dehaene, Bossini, and Giraux 1993). This has been used as a way to quantitatively assess number-form synesthesia, where spatial locations are associated with numeric sequences (Piazza, Pinel, and Dehaene 2006). In non-synesthetes, responses based on numeric quantities can be influenced by an implicit number line, for example with smaller numbers to the left and larger numbers to the right. Responses to small numbers are therefore faster using left-hand button presses, while responses to larger numbers are faster with right-hand presses. In number-form synesthetes, performance corresponded not to this canonical number line but rather to their idiosyncratic spatial layout (Hubbard et al. 2009; Jarick, Dixon, Maxwell, et al. 2009).

Questionnaire-based measures

Eleven studies used questionnaires or structured interviews as their primary approach. These can be useful for examining more general aspects of synesthetic experience, such as relationships with other similar experiences (Burrack, Knoch, and Brugger 2006), and for evaluating large numbers of participants. For example, Rich, Bradshaw, and Mattingley (2005) surveyed 192 synesthetes using paper questionnaires to investigate the prevalence of synesthesia and some demographic characteristics of synesthetes. Use of the Internet has allowed other researchers to easily and efficiently recruit and survey large numbers of synesthetes to, for example, examine variability among synesthetic experiences (Niccolai, Jennes, et al. 2012; 63 synesthetes) or the relationship between synesthesia and creativity (Sitton and Pierce 2004; 210 synesthetes and non-synesthetes). Skelton, Ludwig, and Mohr (2009) developed a questionnaire approach to the assessment of projector versus associator synesthetes (see later).

Physiological measures

Another innovation in the measurement of synesthesia involves recording of physiological signals,[5] used by 54 of the studies included here. By far, the dominant technique in this area is functional magnetic resonance imaging (fMRI), used in 25 studies. This is a type of functional neuroimaging in which strong magnetic fields are used to record brain activity in an awake, behaving human participant. It has allowed twenty-first-century researchers to follow up on earlier studies that used brain imaging techniques with somewhat lower spatial and temporal resolution.

One of the goals of functional neuroimaging in synesthesia is similar to behavioral tests in that they aim to support the perceptual reality of the concurrents. If synesthesia were simply the result of an overactive imagination, one would not expect an inducer to robustly activate the low-level brain representation of its associated concurrent. A number of studies have followed up on earlier work (Paulesu et al. 1995) by using fMRI to examine brain activity related to synesthetic concurrents. A pair of early single-case fMRI studies found that acoustic inducers produced, in addition to the auditory brain activity one would expect, low-level visual activation interpreted to be related to the color concurrents (Aleman et al. 2001; Weiss et al. 2001). Nunn et al. (2002) confirmed these observations in a group of 12 synesthetes. For this study, the authors took the extra step of mapping the color-sensitive areas of each subject's brain for comparison to the synesthetic inducer (auditory word) related activation. They found color-area activation

---

[5] See Rouw, Scholte, and Colizoli (2011) for a recent review of this literature.

to spoken words in the synesthetes, but not in 27 non-synesthete controls. They even tried to elicit such activity in the controls by having them learn and practice word-color pairings, but this was insufficient to elicit color-related activity. Other imaging studies have confirmed the finding of color-area activation to colored concurrents in synesthetes (Specht and Laeng 2011; Sperling et al. 2006; Weiss, Zilles, and Fink 2005), and have found that this can be positively correlated with behavioral indices of synesthetic perception (Hubbard et al. 2005). One recent imaging study used a parametric approach in which color concurrents and real colors were varied systematically to reveal that the amount of activity in color-related brain areas in color synesthesia is related to the distance between color concurrents in color space (Laeng, Hugdahl, and Specht 2011). This further supports the idea that synesthetic concurrent colors may rely on the same brain mechanisms that are responsible for the perception of physical colors. However, this may not hold for all forms of synesthesia; Neufeld, Sinke, Dillo, et al. (2012) recently found no activity in color processing brain areas in synesthetes for whom musical sounds induce colors. Also, a repetition suppression fMRI study by van Leeuwen, Petersson, and Hagoort (2010) showed that synesthetic concurrent colors might not engage these areas the same way that physical colors do.

Several studies have used functional neuroimaging to examine unique cases of synesthesia. Often, such studies represent a researcher's access to only a single case of an unusual form of synesthesia. Examples include studies of chromatic-lexical synesthesia in which familiar names are associated with colors (Weiss et al. 2001) and lexical-gustatory synesthesia, where words induce tastes (Jones et al. 2011). Other case studies have examined things like synesthesia-related activity in visual brain areas in a color synesthete who had lost his vision in adulthood (Niccolai, van Leeuwen, et al. 2012; Steven, Hansen, and Blakemore 2006) and the neurophysiology of the synesthetic experiences of a savant synesthete with remarkable memory abilities (Bor, Billington, and Baron-Cohen 2007).

While many of these studies involved only language-color synesthetes, more recent studies are beginning to look at other forms of synesthesia, such as those involving spatial (Tang, Ward, and Butterworth 2008) or tactile (Blakemore et al. 2005) concurrents. Many authors have been able to recruit larger numbers of synesthetes to investigate the sources of individual differences in synesthesia, such as whether the concurrents are projected into space (Rouw and Scholte 2010; Van Leeuwen et al. 2010), or cases where the inducer-concurrent relationship is bidirectional (see later; Cohen Kadosh, Cohen Kadosh, and Henik 2007).

In a few cases, rather than focusing on synesthesia in and of itself, neuroimaging has been used to study synesthesia as special case of normal perception. For example, the Aleman et al. (2001) study cited earlier was framed with respect to evaluating synesthesia as a special case of especially intense visual mental imagery to address the question as to whether imagery relies on activity in early visual brain areas. Rich et al. (2006) also investigated something similar.

In addition to examining brain activity, a number of studies used brain imaging to investigate the *structure* of the synesthete brain, both in terms of the degree or pattern of interconnectivity between areas of the brain as well as the size or neural density of brain structures. Rouw and Scholte (2007) performed one of the first such studies. Using diffusion tensor imaging (DTI), they found differences in the inter-connections between disparate brain areas between grapheme-color synesthetes and non-synesthetes as well as between subtypes of synesthetes. Using a slightly different technique (fractional anisotropy), Jäncke et al. (2009) did not find the same differences in connectivity between synesthetes and non-synesthetes, though they did find other structural brain differences between these groups. Other studies have looked at functional, rather than structural, interconnections between brain areas in synesthetes, with somewhat conflicting results (Dovern et al. 2012; Hänggi, Wotruba, and Jäncke 2011; Neufeld, Sinke, Zedler, et al. 2012). It remains to be seen whether these differences are due to differences between measurement techniques or some characteristic of the synesthete participants themselves (e.g., Van Leeuwen, Den Ouden, and Hagoort 2011). Additionally, it remains to be seen whether the structural differences observed between synesthetes and non-synesthetes are either a cause or result of having synesthesia.

While imaging studies allow for accurate localization of brain activity, other approaches allow for a more fine-grained analysis of the time course of brain activity during experiences of synesthesia. These approaches include recording brain activity at the scalp either electrically with event-related brain potentials (ERPs; Beeli, Esslen, and Jäncke 2008; Brang et al. 2008; Brang et al. 2011; Cohen Kadosh et al. 2007; Gebuis, Nijboer, and Van Der Smagt 2009; Goller, Otten, and Ward 2009; Terhune, Cardeña, and Lindgren 2010; Teuscher et al. 2010) or magnetically with magnetoencephalography (MEG; Brang, Hubbard, et al. 2010). One additional line of investigation involves manipulating brain function using transcranial magnetic stimulation (TMS) in which a strong magnetic pulse is used to non-invasively stimulate the brain. Several studies have shown that application of TMS to an appropriate location can interfere with synesthetic percepts (Bien et al. 2012; Esterman et al. 2006; Muggleton et al. 2007; Rothen et al. 2010) and can also be used to investigate functional differences in the synesthete brain (Terhune et al. 2011).

Questions being addressed

Current research on synesthesia is engaging a wide variety of questions about synesthesia. Following are some of the more prominent issues currently under investigation.

Is synesthesia a perceptually real phenomenon?

One of the oldest questions addressed in synesthesia research is whether the concurrents can be perceptually real. Since the type of concurrent for most forms of synesthesia is linked to sensory experience, the most common being color, one might ask whether experiencing a concurrent is similar to the experience of actually seeing, say, a color. An alternative is that synesthetes are reporting an overlearned association. One approach to distinguishing between perceptual and learning accounts of synesthesia has been to use behavioral tasks that require perceptual judgments based on the type of concurrent under investigation (Palmeri et al. 2002). By showing that a synesthete's reported concurrents can affect performance on perceptual or cognitive tasks, synesthesia researchers have established that these concurrents are not the product of an overactive imagination or learned associations, but instead represent a very real part of the synesthete's perceptual and cognitive world.

Interference caused by concurrent colors as seen in the synesthetic Stroop task (described earlier) is often taken as evidence of the automaticity and perceptual reality of the synesthetic concurrents. Indeed, the synesthetic Stroop task is still often used in evaluating the presence of synesthesia in potential research participants. However, recent research has demonstrated that this may not necessarily be so. Elias et al. (2003) compared the performance of two participants on a synesthetic Stroop task. One was a grapheme-color synesthete, but the other was a non-synesthete who had spent eight years doing cross-stitch in which different colors of thread were indicated by numeric codes (e.g., the number 7 might indicate they should use a particular red thread). If this sort of overlearned semantic (i.e., non-perceptual) association could elicit a Stroop effect, then this would call into question the validity of the synesthetic Stroop task as an objective measure of the perceptual reality of synesthetic concurrents. Indeed, Elias et al. reported that both of these participants—but not a group of controls with no such associations—showed robust Stroop interference. These two participants also produced similar patterns of brain activation, as measured using fMRI, while performing this Stroop task. The authors take these behavioral and neurophysiological similarities as evidence that the synesthetic Stroop task, in synesthetes, engages primarily semantic-associative processes and, thus, does not provide a specific measure of the perceptual reality of the concurrent percepts themselves. Meier and Rothen (2009) demonstrated something similar, showing that only a week's training on a small set of letter–color pairs was sufficient to establish Stroop interference in non-synesthetes. However, these non-synesthetes failed to show the conditioned fear response previously demonstrated when synesthetes received conditioning trials based on induced concurrents. This observation has thus far been replicated and extended by this group (Rothen et al. 2011) and one other (Colizoli, Murre, and Rouw 2012). These results suggest that, while "synesthetic" Stroop interference can be seen in learned associations in non-synesthetes, there are still fundamental differences between genuine synesthesia and learned associations.

While the synesthetic Stroop task may not be as valid a measure of synesthesia as previously assumed, there are other tasks that demonstrate the perceptual reality of synesthetic concurrents in some cases, such as those that show that color concurrents can interfere with the perception of physical colors (Kim, Blake, and Palmeri 2006). Smilek et al. (2001) showed that for one synesthete, "C," it could be more difficult to perceive achromatic inducer graphemes that were shown on a background that was the same color as that grapheme's concurrent color compared to when the background was a different color. They also showed that, for this same synesthete, concurrent colors could facilitate perception of inducers, specifically by preventing object substitution masking (Wagar et al. 2002).

Is synesthesia common?

Estimates on the prevalence of synesthesia have varied widely. While those from the twentieth century were quite low—from 1 in 100,000 (Cytowic 1993) to 1 in 2,000 (Baron-Cohen et al. 1996)—more recent studies suggest that synesthesia may be far more common. In a study harkening back to Francis Galton's *anthropometric laboratory* at the 1884 International Health Exhibition in London (Hothersall 2004), Simner and her colleagues tested 1190 visitors to the London Science Museum, as well as 500 university students, for the presence of synesthesia (Simner et al. 2006). They found 11 of the museum visitors (1.1%) and 22 of the university students (4.4%) to be synesthetes. (The proportion within students was higher because these were tested for more forms of synesthesia.) Given that Simner et al. asked about only a discrete set of synesthetic forms, the actual number of individuals reporting *any* form of synesthesia would likely have been higher.

They found that, contrary to previous estimates, synesthesia might be present in up to 4% of the population. In spite of grapheme-color being the prototypical form of synesthesia, they found the most commonly reported form to be day-color, with grapheme-color synesthesia having only a prevalence of about 1%.

Where do the concurrents appear?

When color synesthetes are asked "where do you see the colors?" they often say that they appear in their mind's eye; that is, somewhere "inside my head." A few, however, will say that the colors appear in the external world, often projected onto the inducer. Although it had been mentioned before (Smilek et al. 2001), the first well-documented description of this distinction came from Dixon, Smilek, and Merikle (2004), who dubbed those who perceive the concurrents in the mind's eye as *associators* and those who perceive the concurrents externally as *projectors*. This distinction can be easily assessed (Skelton et al. 2009) and is an important source of individual differences between synesthetes, as it can account for differences in research results and can do much to inform theories of synesthesia (Ward et al. 2007) and thinking about the neural mechanisms that may give rise to synesthesia (Gebuis et al. 2009; Rouw and Scholte 2007, 2010; van Leeuwen et al. 2010).

Must an inducer be attended to produce a concurrent?

Given what we know about how inducer and concurrent dimensions work in the brain, it would be very useful indeed to know whether attention must be directed towards an inducer prior to its generating a concurrent. If not, then this would suggest a low-level connection between the inducer and concurrent dimensions. If attention is required, then this might suggest that higher-level input is required. The visual search task (described earlier) has been used extensively to demonstrate this. Because, for synesthetes, targets in these tasks often "pop out," it has been suggested that the concurrent colors may arise independent of attentional processing. However, as with the synesthetic Stroop effect, some recent research has called into question this interpretation of these data. In fact, several studies have failed to find this effect (Edquist et al. 2006; Gheri, Chopping, and Morgan 2008; Nijboer, Satris, and Van Der Stigchel 2011; Rothen and Meier 2009; Sagiv, Heer, and Robertson 2006). More recent work suggests that synesthetes can outperform non-synesthetes on this task, but either the pop-out effect only happens with appropriate stimulus parameters (Laeng 2009) or the search is not pre-attentive (Ward et al. 2010). Several other studies have also found attention to the inducer to be necessary to generate synesthetic concurrents (Mattingley, Payne, and Rich 2006; Nijboer and Van Der Stigchel 2009; Rich and Mattingley 2010). More research is needed to evaluate this effect, particularly with respect to the role of individual differences in synesthetic mechanisms and phenomenology, such as the *projector* versus *associator* distinction mentioned above. It may be the case that synesthetic concurrents arise quickly, albeit not pre-attentively (Spruyt et al. 2009).

Can a concurrent ever induce an inducer?

Synesthesia canon in the twentieth century held that, in addition to being automatic and consistent, synesthesia was unidirectional. That is, inducers induced concurrents, but not the other way around. For example, while in grapheme-color synesthesia the letter "A" might induce a sensation of light orange, seeing the color light orange would not automatically induce a sensation of the letter "A." Anecdotally, this conforms to the subjective reports of many synesthetes. However, a number of recent authors have been challenging this assumption of unidirectionality in synesthesia, suggesting that synesthesia can, at least in some cases, be *bidirectional*. Cohen Kadosh et al. (2005) adapted the size congruity paradigm used in studies of numerical cognition in which the magnitude of a number and the size of the printed digit can correspond such that people will tend to respond more efficiently to a large 9 and a small 2 than when the relative sizes are reversed. These authors reasoned that if, in number-color synesthetes, presenting a concurrent color can induce a sensation of numeric magnitude—the opposite of the usual inducer–concurrent relationship—then it should be possible to observe a similar effect. They presented two such synesthetes with digits printed in colors such that the colors were either inconsistent with the numeric magnitude of the digit, for example, 9 printed in the concurrent color for 2, or was the same as that digit's concurrent. They found that the synesthetes' responses were less efficient for the incongruently colored digits than the congruently colored digits. Thus, it seems that even though colors may not induce a conscious sensation of visual digits, they can induce a sensation of numeric magnitude.

Other studies have investigated the bidirectionality of number-color synesthesia using other tasks involving things like the association between numeric magnitude and an implicit left–right number line (the SNARC task, described earlier; Brugger et al. 2004), a Mental Dice Task (Knoch et al. 2005), line length estimation (Cohen Kadosh and Henik 2006), a variant of the synesthetic Stroop task (Johnson, Jepma, and De Jong 2007), and a mathematical multiplication verification task (Gevers et al. 2010). Several laboratories have also begun investigating the neurophysiology of bidirectional synesthesia (Cohen Kadosh et al. 2007; Gebuis et al. 2009; Rothen et al. 2010).

Even though most of these studies involve only a few synesthetes, they support the idea that, at least under some circumstances, synesthesia can be bidirectional. While most of this work has been done in digit-color synesthesia—likely because that is the form for which the first appropriate behavioral tests of bidirectionality were developed—others have shown bidirectionality in letter-color synesthetes (Meier and Rothen 2007; Weiss, Kalckert, and Fink 2009) and at least one lexical-gustatory synesthete (Richer, Beaufils, and Poirier 2011).

Is there a great deal of heterogeneity among synesthetes?

Part of the challenge of doing research in synesthesia is that there are many differences between synesthetes that can obscure the general principles that govern how synesthesia works (Dixon and Smilek 2005). Two sources of individual differences among synesthetes—where the concurrents appear (projectors versus associators) and bidirectionality—were discussed earlier. Another source of heterogeneity among synesthetes is the multiplicity of *forms* that synesthesia might take. The most often described form tends to be *grapheme-color synesthesia*, in which letter and number inducers elicit color concurrents. However there are many other forms as well (Day 2005). While most of these have been long known, some have only recently started to receive attention in the research literature. Most studies continue to study only grapheme-color synesthetes, possibly because they are the easiest to recruit, but there are many interesting case and small-group studies that are beginning to explore other forms.

Ever since Galton's early descriptions (Galton 1880), it has been known that spatial location is a common concurrent in synesthesia. Modern estimates put the prevalence of such forms at over 10–20% in general (Brang, Teuscher, et al. 2010) and perhaps up to 60% in color synesthetes (Sagiv et al. 2006). In spite of this, the spatial forms have, until recently, received little attention in the research literature. However, there has been an increase in interest, as evidenced by a 2009 special section of the journal *Cortex* on "Synaesthetic Visuo-spatial Forms." Two such spatial forms are *time-space synesthesia* and *number-form synesthesia*. In time-space synesthesia, spatial locations are associated with periods of time such as hours, days, months, or years (Jarick, Dixon, Stewart, et al. 2009; Smilek, Callejas, et al. 2007). This form has been shown to influence directed spatial attention (Diesendruck et al. 2010) and to be related to improved visuo-spatial cognition (Mann et al. 2009; Simner, Mayo, and Spiller 2009; Teuscher et al. 2010). In number-form synesthesia, spatial locations are associated with numeric sequences. Number-form synesthesia has been shown to impact mathematical calculations (Ward, Sagiv, and Butterworth 2009) and spatial attention (Jarick, Dixon, and Smilek 2011), and may interact with mental imagery (Price 2009a). Current work is geared towards learning the mechanisms that might underlie this variant of synesthesia (Makioka 2009; Price 2009b; Tang et al. 2008). It is notable that Eagleman (2009) has suggested a common

basis for these spatial forms in that the inducers tend to be overlearned sequences, referring to them collectively as *spatial sequence synesthesia.*

A known, but relatively overlooked, form involves the association of person-like
qualities (gender, personality, etc.) as concurrents with sequential inducers (letters,
numbers, months, etc.). Simner refers to this as *ordinal linguistic personification* (OLP)
and has investigated one such synesthete, "AP" (Simner and Holenstein 2007; Simner
and Hubbard 2006) along with a more recent group study with five such synesthetes
(Simner, Gärtner, and Taylor 2011). In what is perhaps a variation of this form, Smilek,
Malcolmson, et al. (2007) reported on one individual who associates personality characteristics with inanimate objects—not just ordinal sequences—in a form they refer to
as *object-personality synesthesia.*

One form that was well studied in the last decade is *lexical-gustatory synesthesia.*
Interest in this form started with descriptions of synesthete JIW, who experiences flavor concurrents to auditory words (Simner and Logie 2007; Ward and Simner 2003).
Researchers have gone on to examine this form in group studies by comparing such
experiences to the canonical grapheme-color synesthesia (Ward, Simner, and Auyeung
2005) and also by manipulating the inducing words to better characterize what exactly is
acting as the inducer in this form (Simner and Haywood 2009).

Another novel form of synesthesia that has received a great deal of recent attention
is that of *vision-touch synesthesia*—also called *mirror-touch synesthesia*—as reported
by Blakemore et al. (2005). People who experience this form will feel on their own
body touches observed one someone else's body. So, seeing someone else's cheek being
touched will elicit the tactile concurrent of a touch on the synesthete's own cheek. This
experience may be associated with hyperactivity in the brain's mirror neuron system
and could have implications for somatosensory perception in non-synesthetes (Serino,
Pizzoferrato, and Làdavas 2008). Researchers are just beginning to investigate the basic
function and phenomenology of this form (Banissy et al. 2009; Holle et al. 2011), and
research involving mirror-touch synesthesia may have important implications for our
understanding of things like empathy (Banissy and Ward 2007) and face recognition
(Banissy et al. 2011). Another similar, possibly related, phenomenon is synesthesia for
pain, in which one experiences a pain concurrent upon observing or imagining someone else's pain (Giummarra and Bradshaw 2009).

Several additional interesting forms of synesthesia have come to light in the last
decade. Jäncke and his collaborators (Beeli, Essen, and Jäncke 2005; Hänggi et al.
2008) have studied a musician with *tone-taste synesthesia* who reported experiencing different tastes and colors in response to different pitch intervals. Ramachandran
and Brang (2008) describe two people with *tactile-emotion synesthesia* for whom different tactile textures elicited different emotions. Saenz and Koch (2008) describe four
people with *hearing-motion synesthesia* for whom visual motion or flashes induced
sounds. Nikolić et al. (2011) described two experienced swimmers with *swimming-style
synesthesia* who associated swimming styles with distinct colors.

One additional source of variability among synesthetes, mentioned anecdotally
previously and investigated more systematically in recent years, is that synesthetes

with one form sometimes experience additional forms of synesthesia. Of 22 confirmed synesthetes identified in the prevalence study by Simner et al. (2006), eight reported experiencing multiple forms of synesthesia. In their study of OLP, Simner and Holenstein (2007) found that the OLP form of synesthesia may often co-occur with grapheme-color synesthesia. Sagiv et al. (2006) found that around 60% of their sample of 100 synesthetes with color concurrents also experienced numbers as having spatial location.

Is synesthesia heritable?

One of the newest lines of investigation in synesthesia research is directed towards evaluating the anecdotal observation that synesthesia can be inherited and may, thus, be genetically determined. Seven recent studies have examined this issue. Some studies have examined the plausibility of different modes of inheritance by looking at pairs of twins. Smilek and his collaborators (Smilek, Dixon, and Merikle 2005; Smilek, Moffatt, et al. 2002) have examined pairs of identical twins only one of whom was a synesthete, suggesting that if there is a genetic component to synesthesia, the mode of inheritance is more complex than simple genetic transmission. Hancock (2006) evaluated the consistency of inducer-concurrent mappings between a pair of identical twins both of whom were synesthetes. They experienced similar forms and inducer-concurrent mappings, however it is unclear whether their associations are indicative of genuine synesthesia or learned associations.

Perhaps a more complete picture of the genetics of synesthesia can be gained from large group studies. Given the rarity of synesthesia, the most feasible approach to such studies is to contact a large number of synesthetes, for example via telephone, and ask them about synesthetic relatives to look for patterns of inheritance. Three studies have used such an approach. These studies produced similar rates of positive responses: 36% (Rich, Bradshaw, and Mattingley 2005), 42% (Barnett et al. 2008), and 44% (Ward and Simner 2005), suggesting that synesthesia may, indeed, be heritable.

Because synesthesia is fairly rare, gathering genetic material from large numbers of synesthetes for a direct genetic analysis is a challenge. However, a few researchers have accepted this challenge. Two recent studies have reported results from such analyses. Asher et al. (2009) investigated auditory-visual synesthesia in 43 families, finding a complex mode of inheritance with involvement of multiple genes. However, Tomson et al. (2011), investigated individuals across five families with spatial sequence synesthesia involving color concurrents, finding involvement of only a single gene. They suggest that different forms of synesthesia may involve different patterns of genetic inheritance.

Is synesthesia associated with enhanced sensory or cognitive abilities?

Much anecdotal evidence exists to suggest that synesthetes may perform better than non-synesthetes in a variety of sensory and cognitive domains. Recent years have seen an upswing in research studies that are systematically addressing such questions.

Memory

Ever since Luria's description of synesthesia in the Russian mnemonist Shereshevskii (Luria 1968), it has been suggested that synesthesia can be accompanied by superior memory abilities. Smilek, Dixon, et al. (2002) suggested that, in at least one synesthete's case, synesthetic concurrents may be beneficial in supporting greater memory abilities. A few years later, Mills et al. (2006) reported another case of letter-color synesthesia with a superior memory for names. Authors of both studies noted only improved memory for verbal, inducer-relevant material, suggesting that the synesthetic concurrents may specifically play a role in improving memory. Baron-Cohen et al. (2007) described the extraordinary feats of savant and synesthete Daniel Tammet, and suggest the possibility that synesthesia and savantism may co-occur (see also Simner et al. 2009).

Rothen and Meier have suggested that synesthesia may, in fact, not be accompanied by overall improvements in memory, but rather by improvements only within a limited domain, and that previous results may be the result of selection bias based on a few unusual cases (Rothen and Meier 2009, 2010b). While synesthetes may overestimate their own memory abilities (Yaro and Ward 2007), and there are group studies that show synesthesia-related memory advantages, at least for some memory tasks and some forms of synesthesia (Brang, Teuscher, et al. 2010; Gross et al. 2011; Simner et al. 2009; Yaro and Ward 2007), the issue remains unresolved. Radvansky, Gibson, and McNerney (2011) have recently explored inconsistencies in the literature and discuss possible mechanisms.

Creativity

In addition to improved memory, it has also been suggested that synesthesia may accompany enhanced creativity (Domino 1989). While some studies have looked for increased incidence of synesthesia, for example, noting that synesthetes are more likely to be involved in creative pursuits (Rich, Bradshaw, and Mattingley 2005; Rothen and Meier 2010a), other research has assessed this question more directly. Sitton and Pierce (2004) showed a positive relationship between self-reported synesthesia and a measure of creativity in a sample of 210 individuals. Ward, Thompson-Lake, et al. (2008) showed that a large sample of 82 objectively defined synesthetes reported spending more time in creative pursuits than a group of 119 non-synesthetes, and also that the synesthetes scored higher on a particular test of creativity than the non-synesthetes. (See also Mulvenna 2007). Domingo et al. (2010) suggested that creativity may be more prevalent among projector synesthetes than associator synesthetes. It is important to note, however, that while synesthetes might be more creative than non-synesthetes, the reason for this difference—whether related to synesthesia or something else—has yet to be determined.

Sensory and cognitive abilities

There is other evidence that synesthesia may be related to improvements in perception (Banissy, Walsh, and Ward 2009), mental imagery (Barnett and Newell 2008; Brang and Ramachandran 2010), and visuo-spatial (Simner et al. 2009), temporal (Mann et al.

2009), and mathematical (Ward et al. 2009) cognitive abilities. For example, Banissy, Walsh, and Ward (2009) found that synesthetes who experienced color concurrents performed better than synesthetes without color concurrents and non-synesthetes on a color discrimination test. Ward, Sagiv, and Butterworth (2009) found that synesthetes who experienced numbers as having spatial location outperformed non-synesthetes on a test of simple arithmetic.

What brain mechanisms give rise to synesthesia?

There is still much debate as to the neural mechanisms that might produce synesthesia. Most ideas focus on ways in which activity in the brain areas that represent the inducer could result in additional activity in areas that represent the concurrent. That is, when a grapheme-color synesthete sees a letter of the alphabet, the brain areas responsible for recognizing the letter are active, as they are in non-synesthetes also. But somehow, the area that represents color is also activated, producing the concurrent color sensation. Although other ideas are coming out, there have thus been two dominant theories. The *crosstalk* theory, put forward by Ramachandran and Hubbard (2001a), posits that inducer and concurrent representations are connected by direct neural pathways, perhaps remnants from the normal neural pruning that occurs during development (Spector and Maurer 2009). This came partially from the observation that the neural representations of graphemes and colors in the brain lie next to each other. An alternative to this idea, the *disinhibited feedback* theory, was postulated by Grossenbacher and Lovelace (2001). They suggested that, rather than rely on unusual connections between brain areas, synesthesia might result from an unusual flow of information between brain areas along pathways that exist in everyone. That is, we know that there are brain areas that handle converging inputs from different kinds of representations, such as letters and colors. As with most brain areas, inputs to this area are also accompanied by feedbackward outputs, with information flowing from this area of convergence back to the specific representations. Whereas in most people this feedbackward flow of information is normally inhibited, it might be that, in synesthetes, input from the inducer representation to the convergence area activates the feedbackward connection from the convergence area to the concurrent representation, thus producing the experience of a concurrent. Part of the impetus for this idea comes from the observation that synesthesia-like experiences can be gotten from some hallucinogenic drugs (Siegel and Jarvik 1975) and, given the short time frame, must rely on existing connections in the brain. Note that both of these ideas posit that concurrents result from activity in the concurrent representation in the brain, and this is at least partially supported by the brain imaging research cited earlier. The difference is in how that representation is activated by an inducer: either directly (crosstalk) or via a third area (disinhibited feedback). There are studies that support both the crosstalk theory (reviewed by Hubbard, Brang, and Ramachandran 2011) as well as the disinhibited feedback theory (e.g., Cohen Kadosh et al. 2009; Gaschler-Markefski et al. 2011; Neufeld, Sinke, Dillo, et al. 2012; Neufeld, Sinke, Zedler, et al. 2012; Van Leeuwen et al. 2010; Ward, Huckstep, and Tsakanikos 2006).

These ideas continue to be tested and revised (e.g., Hubbard 2007). However, additional research is needed to further elucidate these theories as well as others that have been put forward, such as re-entrant processing (Smilek et al. 2001), cascaded cross-tuning (Brang, Hubbard, et al. 2010), or hyperbinding (Esterman et al. 2006; Mulvenna and Walsh 2006; Sagiv, Heer, and Robertson 2006).

Summary

Although awareness of, and interest in, synesthesia continues to rise, there is much yet to be done. Despite well over a century of interest in synesthesia, we are still just now learning the basic tenets of not only how synesthesia works but also what synesthesia is. One key will be to increase public awareness of synesthesia, both to facilitate recruitment of research participants and also to allay any remaining stigma that may be associated with experiencing synesthesia. Having a term defined in this way tends to imply that there is an association with some sort of disorder or psychopathology. In fact, little evidence exists to suggest that synesthesia may be consistently linked with any disorder or illness (although see Banissy et al. 2012). However, the popular press writers often use unfortunate headlines, such as "500,000 Children Suffer From Cross-sensory Condition" (DailyMail.co.uk 2008), or *The Illness That Confuses the Senses* (Garner 2001).

As Ramachandran and Hubbard (2003a) point out, only recently has synesthesia begun to take its place in the realm of science as a real phenomenon with testable theories as to its mechanism and with important implications for our understanding of human behavior. As we continue to pursue understanding of this fascinating trait, we will better understand not only synesthetes, but also us poor non-synesthetes for whom the world is not quite so colorful.

References

Aleman, André, Geert-Jan M. Rutten, Margriet M. Sitskoorn, Geraud Dautzenberg, and Nick F. Ramsey. 2001. Activation of striate cortex in the absence of visual stimulation: An fMRI study of synesthesia. *NeuroReport* 12:2827–2830.

Alstadhaug, Karl B., and Espen Benjaminsen. 2010. Synesthesia and migraine: Case report. *BMC Neurology* 10:121.

Asher, Julian E., Michael R. F. Aitken, Nasr Farooqi, Sameer Kurmani, and Simon Baron-Cohen. 2006. Diagnosing and phenotyping visual synaesthesia: a preliminary evaluation of the Revised Test of Genuineness (TOG-R). *Cortex* 42:137–146.

Asher, Julian E., Janine A. Lamb, Denise Brocklebank, Jean-Baptiste Cazier, Elena Maestrini, Laura Addis, Mallika Sen, Simon Baron-Cohen, and Anthony P. Monaco. 2009. A whole-genome scan and fine-mapping linkage study of auditory-visual synesthesia reveals evidence of linkage to chromosomes 2q24, 5q33, 6p12, and 12p12. *American Journal of Human Genetics* 84:279–285.

Babu, Kavita M., Christopher R. McCurdy, and Edward W. Boyer. 2008. Opioid receptors and legal highs: Salvia divinorum and kratom. *Clinical Toxicology* 46:146–152.

Banissy, Michael J., Josephine E. Cassell, Sian Fitzpatrick, Jamie Ward, Vincent X. Walsh, and Neil G. Muggleton. 2012. Increased positive and disorganised schizotypy in synaesthetes who experience colour from letters and tones. *Cortex* 48:1085–1087.

Banissy, Michael J., Roi Cohen Kadosh, Gerrit W. Maus, Vincent Walsh, and Jamie Ward. 2009. Prevalence, characteristics and a neurocognitive model of mirror-touch synaesthesia. *Experimental Brain Research* 198:261–272.

Banissy, Michael J, Lúcia Garrido, Flor Kusnir, Bradley Duchaine, Vincent Walsh, and Jamie Ward. 2011. Superior facial expression, but not identity recognition, in mirror-touch synesthesia. *Journal of Neuroscience* 31:1820–1824.

Banissy, Michael J., Vincent Walsh, and Jamie Ward. 2009. Enhanced sensory perception in synaesthesia. *Experimental Brain Research* 196:565–571.

Banissy, Michael J., and Jamie Ward. 2007. Mirror-touch synesthesia is linked with empathy. *Nature Neuroscience* 10:815–816.

Barnett, Kylie J., Ciara Finucane, Julian E. Asher, Gary Bargary, Aiden P. Corvin, Fiona N. Newell, and Kevin J. Mitchell. 2008. Familial patterns and the origins of individual differences in synaesthesia. *Cognition* 106:871–893.

Barnett, Kylie J., and Fiona N. Newell. 2008. Synaesthesia is associated with enhanced, self-rated visual imagery. *Consciousness and Cognition* 17:1032–1039.

Baron-Cohen, Simon, Daniel Bor, Jac Billington, Julian Asher, Sally Wheelwright, and Chris Ashwin. 2007. Savant memory in a man with colour form-number synaesthesia and Asperger syndrome. *Journal of Consciousness Studies* 14:237–251.

Baron-Cohen, Simon, Luch Burt, Fiona Smith-Laittan, John Harrison, and Patrick Bolton. 1996. Synaesthesia: Prevalence and familiality. *Perception* 25:1073–1079.

Baron-Cohen, Simon, and John E. Harrison, eds. 1997. *Synaesthesia: Classic and Contemporary Readings*. Oxford: Blackwell.

Baron-Cohen, Simon, Maria A. Wyke, and Colin Binnie. 1987. Hearing words and seeing colours: An experimental investigation of a case of synesthesia. *Perception* 16:761–767.

Bartlett, Allison H. 2002. An ear for color: Exploring the curious world of synesthesia, where senses merge in mysterious ways. *The Washington Post*, 22 January.

Beauchamp, Michael S., and Tony Ro. 2008. Neural substrates of sound-touch synesthesia after a thalamic lesion. *Journal of Neuroscience* 28:13696–13702.

Beeli, Gian, Michaela Esslen, and Lutz Jäncke. 2005. Synaesthesia: When coloured sounds taste sweet. *Nature* 434:38.

Beeli, Gian, Michaela Esslen, and Lutz Jäncke. 2008. Time course of neural activity correlated with colored-hearing synesthesia. *Cerebral Cortex* 18:379–385.

Berman, Brady A. 2011. Pseudochromesthesia and psychosis proneness. *Dissertation Abstracts International: Section B: The Sciences and Engineering* 71:6432.

Bhanoo, Sindya N. 2011. Getting a handle on why 4 equals green. *New York Times*, 22 November. <http://www.nytimes.com/2011/11/22/science/mapping-grapheme-color-synesthesia-in-the-brain.html>.

Bien, Nina, Sanne ten Oever, Rainer Goebel, and Alexander T Sack. 2012. The sound of size: Crossmodal binding in pitch-size synesthesia: A combined TMS, EEG and psychophysics study. *Neuroimage* 59:663–672.

Blakemore, S.-J., D. Bristow, G. Bird, C. Frith, and J. Ward. 2005. Somatosensory activations during the observation of touch and a case of vision-touch synaesthesia. *Brain* 128:1571–1583.

Bor, Daniel, Jac Billington, and Simon Baron-Cohen. 2007. Savant memory for digits in a case of synaesthesia and Asperger syndrome is related to hyperactivity in the lateral prefrontal cortex. *Neurocase* 13:311–319.

Brang, D., L. Edwards, V. S. Ramachandran, and S. Coulson. 2008. Is the sky 2? Contextual priming in grapheme-color synaesthesia. *Psychological Science* 19:421–428.

Brang, David, Edward M. Hubbard, Seana Coulson, Mingxiong Huang, and Vilayanur S. Ramachandran. 2010. Magnetoencephalography reveals early activation of V4 in grapheme-color synesthesia. *Neuroimage* 53:268–274.

Brang, David, Stanley Kanai, Vilayanur S. Ramachandran, and Seana Coulson. 2011. Contextual priming in grapheme-color synesthetes and yoked controls: 400 msec in the life of a synesthete. *Journal of Cognitive Neuroscience* 23:1681–1696.

Brang, David, and Vilayanur S. Ramachandran. 2010. Visual field heterogeneity, laterality, and eidetic imagery in synesthesia. *Neurocase* 16:169–174.

Brang, David, Ursina Teuscher, Vilayanur S. Ramachandran, and Seana Coulson. 2010. Temporal sequences, synesthetic mappings, and cultural biases: The geography of time. *Consciousness and Cognition* 19:311–320.

Brewis, S., and D. M. Baguley. 2007. Management of tinnitus induced by brainstem and cerebellar infarction associated with complications of cerebello-pontine angle surgery. *Journal of Laryngology & Otology* 121:393–394.

Brugger, Peter, Daria Knoch, Christine Mohr, and Lorena R. R. Gianotti. 2004. Is digit-color synaesthesia strictly unidirectional? Preliminary evidence for an implicitly colored number space in three synesthetes. *Acta Neuropsychologica* 2:252–258.

Burne, Jerome. 2001. Body and mind: Can you feel the guitar sound on your ankles? *Financial Times*, 6 January.

Burrack, Anna, Daria Knoch, and Peter Brugger. 2006. Mitempfindung in synaesthetes: Co-incidence or meaningful association? *Cortex* 42:151–154.

Cacciari, Cristina. 2008. Crossing the senses in metaphorical language. In *The Cambridge Handbook of Metaphor and Thought*, ed. Raymond W. Gibbs, Jr., 425–443. New York: Cambridge University Press.

Cazeaux, Clive. 2002. Metaphor and the categorization of the senses. *Metaphor and Symbol* 17:3–26.

Cohen Kadosh, Roi, Kathryn Cohen Kadosh, and Avishai Henik. 2007. The neuronal correlate of bidirectional synesthesia: A combined event-related potential and functional magnetic resonance imaging study. *Journal of Cognitive Neuroscience* 19:2050–2059.

Cohen Kadosh, Roi, and Avishai Henik. 2006. When a line is a number: Color yields magnitude information in a digit-color synesthete. *Neuroscience* 137:3–5.

Cohen Kadosh, Roi, Avishai Henik, Andres Catena, Vincent Walsh, and Luis J. Fuentes. 2009. Induced cross-modal synaesthetic experience without abnormal neuronal connections. *Psychological Science* 20:258–265.

Cohen Kadosh, Roi, Noam Sagiv, David E. J. Linden, Lynn C. Robertson, Gali Elinger, and Avishai Henik. 2005. When blue is larger than red: Colors influence numerical cognition in synesthesia. *Journal of Cognitive Neuroscience* 17:1766–1773.

Colizoli, Olympia, Jaap M. J. Murre, and Romke Rouw. 2012. Pseudo-synesthesia through reading books with colored letters. *PLoS ONE* 7:e39799.

Conis, Elena. 2007. Seeing music, tasting colors. *LA Times*, 23 July. <http://articles.latimes.com/2007/jul/23/health/he-esoterica23>.

Crane, Carol A. 2006. A neuropsychological and familial study of developmental synesthesia. *Dissertation Abstracts International: Section B: The Sciences and Engineering* 66:4477.

Cytowic, Richard E. 1989. *Synesthesia: A Union of the Senses*. 1st ed. New York: Springer Verlag.

——. 1993. *The Man Who Tasted Shapes*. 1st ed. New York: Putnam.

——. 2002. *Synesthesia: A Union of the Senses*. 2nd ed. Cambridge, MA: MIT Press.

——. 2003. *The Man Who Tasted Shapes*. 2nd ed. Cambridge, MA: MIT Press.

Cytowic, Richard E., and David M. Eagleman. 2009. *Wednesday is Indigo Blue: Discovering the Brain of Synaesthesia*. Cambridge, MA: MIT Press.

DailyMail.co.uk. 2008. 500,000 Children Suffer From Cross-Sensory Condition. *Daily Mail*, March 18. <http://www.dailymail.co.uk/health/article-538468/500-000-children-suffer-cross-sensory-condition.html>.

Dann, Kevin T. 1998. *Bright Colors Falsely Seen: Synaesthesia and the Search for Transcendental Knowledge*. New Haven, CT: Yale University Press.

Day, Sean A. 2005. Some demographic and socio-cultural aspects of synesthesia. In *Synesthesia: Perspectives From Cognitive Neuroscience*, ed. Lynn C Robertson and Noam Sagiv, 11–33. New York: Oxford University Press.

Dayton, Lily. 2012. The blended senses of synesthesia. *LA Times*, 20 February. <http://www.latimes.com/health/la-he-synesthesia-brain-20120220,0,6760571.story>.

Dehaene, Stanislas, Serge Bossini, and Pascal Giraux. 1993. The mental representation of parity and numerical magnitude. *Journal of Experimental Psychology: General* 122:371–396.

Diesendruck, Liana, Limor Gertner, Lior Botzer, Liat Goldfarb, Amir Karniel, and Avishai Henik. 2010. Months in space: Synaesthesia modulates attention and action. *Cognitive Neuropsychology* 27:665–679.

Dixon, Mike J., and Daniel Smilek. 2005. The importance of individual differences in grapheme-color synesthesia. *Neuron* 45:821–823.

Dixon, Mike J., Daniel Smilek, and Philip M. Merikle. 2004. Not all synaesthetes are created equal: Projector versus associator synaesthetes. *Cognitive, Affective, and Behavioral Neuroscience* 4:335–343.

Domingo, Samantha, Laxmi N. Lalwani, Leanne Boucher, and Jaime L. Tartar. 2010. Individuals with grapheme-color associations exhibit creativity. *Imagination, Cognition and Personality* 30:289–299.

Domino, G. 1989. Synesthesia and creativity in fine arts students: An empirical look. *Creativity Research Journal* 2:17–29.

Dovern, Anna, Gereon R. Fink, A. Christina B. Fromme, Afra M. Wohlschläger, Peter H. Weiss, and Valentin Riedl. 2012. Intrinsic network connectivity reflects consistency of synesthetic experiences. *Journal of Neuroscience* 32:7614–7621.

Duffy, Patricia L. 2001. *Blue Cats and Chartreuse Kittens: How Synesthetes Color Their World*. New York: W. H. Freeman.

Duffy, Patricia L., and Julia Simner. 2010. Synaesthesia in fiction. *Cortex* 46:277–278.

Eagleman, David M. 2009. The objectification of overlearned sequences: A new view of spatial sequence synesthesia. *Cortex* 45:1266–1277.

Eagleman, David M., Arielle D. Kagan, Stephanie S. Nelson, Deepak Sagaram, and Anand K. Sarma. 2007. A standardized test battery for the study of synesthesia. *Journal of Neuroscience Methods* 159:139–145.

Edquist, Jessica, Anina N. Rich, Cobie Brinkman, and Jason B. Mattingley. 2006. Do synaesthetic colours act as unique features in visual search? *Cortex* 42:222–231.

Elias, Lorin J., Deborah M. Saucier, Colleen Hardie, and Gordon E. Sarty. 2003. Dissociating semantic and perceptual components of synaesthesia: behavioural and functional neuroanatomical investigations. *Cognitive Brain Research* 16:232–237.

Esterman, Michael, Timothy Verstynen, Richard B. Ivry, and Lynn C. Robertson. 2006. Coming unbound: Disrupting automatic integration of synesthetic color and graphemes by transcranial magnetic stimulation of the right parietal lobe. *Journal of Cognitive Neuroscience* 18:1570–1576.

Esterman, Michael Scott. 2007. Cognitive and neural influences on the perceptual integration of color and shape. *Dissertation Abstracts International: Section B: The Sciences and Engineering* 68:1302.

Gallace, Alberto, and Charles Spence. 2006. Multisensory synesthetic interactions in the speeded classification of visual size. *Perception & Psychophysics* 68:1191–1203.

Galton, Francis. 1880. Visualised numerals. *Nature* 21:252–256.

Garner, Clare. 2001. The illness that confuses the senses. *Daily Mail* <http://www.dailymail.co.uk/health/article-38923/The-illness-confuses-senses.html>.

Gaschler-Markefski, Birgit, Gregor R. Szycik, Christopher Sinke, Janina Neufeld, Udo Schneider, Frank Baumgart, Oliver Dierks, *et al.* 2011. Anomalous auditory cortex activations in colored hearing synaesthetes: An fMRI-study. *Seeing and Perceiving* 24:391–405.

Gebuis, Titia, Tanja C. W. Nijboer, and Maarten J. Van der Smagt. 2009. Multiple dimensions in bi-directional synesthesia. *The European Journal of Neuroscience* 29:1703–1710.

Gevers, Wim, Ineke Imbo, Roi Cohen Kadosh, Wim Fias, and Robert J. Hartsuiker. 2010. Bidirectionality in synesthesia: Evidence from a multiplication verification task. *Experimental Psychology* 57:178–184.

Gheri, C., S. Chopping, and M. J. Morgan. 2008. Synaesthetic colours do not camouflage form in visual search. *Proceedings of the Royal Society of London B: Biological Sciences* 275:841–846.

Gimmestad, Katherine D. 2012. Assessment of transient negative affect in synesthesia. *Dissertation Abstracts International: Section B: The Sciences and Engineering* 72:7046.

Giummarra, Melita J., and John L. Bradshaw. 2009. Synaesthesia for pain: Feeling pain with another. In *Mirror Neuron Systems: The Role of Mirroring Processes in Social Cognition*, ed. Jaime A. Pineda, 287–307. Totowa, NJ: Humana Press.

Goller, Aviva I., Leun J. Otten, and Jamie Ward. 2009. Seeing sounds and hearing colors: An event-related potential study of auditory-visual synesthesia. *Journal of Cognitive Neuroscience* 21:1869–1881.

Gross, Veronica. 2009. Memory, Visual perception, and health in synesthesia. *Dissertation Abstracts International: Section B: The Sciences and Engineering* 69:5939.

Gross, Veronica C., Sandy Neargarder, Catherine L. Caldwell-Harris, and Alice Cronin-Golomb. 2011. Superior encoding enhances recall in color-graphemic synesthesia. *Perception* 40:196–208.

Grossenbacher, Peter G., and Christopher T. Lovelace. 2001. Mechanisms of synesthesia: Cognitive and physiological constraints. *Trends in Cognitive Sciences* 5:36–41.

Hancock, Peter. 2006. Monozygotic twins' colour-number association: A case study. *Cortex* 42:147–150.

Hänggi, Jürgen, Gian Beeli, Mathias S. Oechslin, and Lutz Jäncke. 2008. The multiple synaesthete E.S.: Neuroanatomical basis of interval-taste and tone-colour synaesthesia. *Neuroimage* 43:192–203.

Hänggi, Jürgen, Diana Wotruba, and Lutz Jäncke. 2011. Globally altered structural brain network topology in grapheme-color synesthesia. *Journal of Neuroscience* 31:5816–5828.

Harris, James C. 2009. The yellow cow. *Archives of General Psychiatry* 66:809–810.

Harris, Joseph E. 2004. Musique coloree: Synesthetic correspondence in the works of Olivier Messiaen (France). *Dissertation Abstracts International Section A: Humanities and Social Sciences* 65:1169.

Harrison, John. 2001. *Synaesthesia: The Strangest Thing.* New York: Oxford University Press.

Holle, Henning, Michael Banissy, Thomas Wright, Natalie Bowling, and Jamie Ward. 2011. "That's not a real body": Identifying stimulus qualities that modulate synaesthetic experiences of touch. *Consciousness and Cognition* 20:720–726.

Hothersall, David. 2004. *History of Psychology.* 4th ed. Boston, MA: McGraw-Hill.

Hubbard, Edward M. 2005. Psychophysical and neuroimaging investigations of synesthesia. *Dissertation Abstracts International: Section B: The Sciences and Engineering* 65:4862.

——. 2007. Neurophysiology of synesthesia. *Current Psychiatry Reports* 9:193–199.

Hubbard, Edward M., A. Cyrus Arman, Vilayanur S. Ramachandran, and Geoffrey M. Boynton. 2005. Individual differences among grapheme-color synesthetes: brain-behavior correlations. *Neuron* 45:975–985.

Hubbard, Edward M., David Brang, and Vilayanur S. Ramachandran. 2011. The cross-activation theory at 10. *Journal of Neuropsychology* 5:152–177.

Hubbard, Edward M., Mariagrazia Ranzini, Manuela Piazza, and Stanislas Dehaene. 2009. What information is critical to elicit interference in number-form synaesthesia? *Cortex* 45:1200–1216.

Jäncke, Lutz, Gian Beeli, Cornelia Eulig, and Jürgen Hänggi. 2009. The neuroanatomy of grapheme-color synesthesia. *The European Journal of Neuroscience* 29:1287–1293.

Jarick, Michelle, Michael J. Dixon, and Daniel Smilek. 2011. 9 is always on top: Assessing the automaticity of synaesthetic number-forms. *Brain and Cognition* 77:96–105.

Jarick, Michelle, Mike J. Dixon, Emily C. Maxwell, Michael E. R. Nicholls, and Daniel Smilek. 2009. The ups and downs (and lefts and rights) of synaesthetic number forms: Validation from spatial cueing and SNARC-type tasks. *Cortex* 45:1190–1199.

Jarick, Michelle, Mike J. Dixon, Mark T. Stewart, Emily C. Maxwell, and Daniel Smilek. 2009. A different outlook on time: Visual and auditory month names elicit different mental vantage points for a time-space synaesthete. *Cortex* 45:1217–1228.

Johnson, Addie, Marieke Jepma, and Ritske de Jong. 2007. Colours sometimes count: Awareness and bidirectionality in grapheme-colour synaesthesia. *Quarterly Journal of Experimental Psychology* 60:1406–1422.

Jones, C. L., M. A. Gray, L. Minati, J. Simner, H. D. Critchley, and J. Ward. 2011. The neural basis of illusory gustatory sensations: Two rare cases of lexical-gustatory synaesthesia. *Journal of Neuropsychology* 5:243–254.

Kim, Chai-Youn. 2007. Perceptual nature and neural mechanisms of color-graphemic synesthesia. *Dissertation Abstracts International: Section B: The Sciences and Engineering* 67:6088.

Kim, Chai-Youn, Randolph Blake, and Thomas J. Palmeri. 2006. Perceptual interaction between real and synesthetic colors. *Cortex* 42:195–203.

Knoch, Daria, Lorena R. R. Gianotti, Christine Mohr, and Peter Brugger. 2005. Synesthesia: When colors count. *Cognitive Brain Research* 25:372–374.

Laeng, Bruno. 2009. Searching through synaesthetic colors. *Attention, Perception & Psychophysics* 71:1461–1467.

Laeng, Bruno, Kenneth Hugdahl, and Karsten Specht. 2011. The neural correlate of colour distances revealed with competing synaesthetic and real colours. *Cortex* 47:320–331.

Lehrer, Jonah. 2007. Blue Monday, green Thursday. *New Scientist* 194:48–51.

Luke, David. 2011. Discarnate entities and dimethyltryptamine (DMT): Psychopharmacology, phenomenology and ontology. *Journal of the Society for Psychical Research* 75:26–42.

Luria, Aleksandr R. 1968. *The Mind of a Mnemonist: A Little Book About a Vast Memory*. New York: Basic Books.

Makioka, Shogo. 2009. A Self-organizing learning account of number-form synaesthesia. *Cognition* 112:397–414.

Mann, Heather, Jason Korzenko, Jonathan S. A. Carriere, and Mike J. Dixon. 2009. Time-space synaesthesia—a cognitive advantage? *Consciousness and Cognition* 18:619–627.

Martino, Gail, and Lawrence E. Marks. 2001. Synesthesia: Strong and weak. *Current Directions in Psychological Science* 10:61–65.

Mattingley, Jason B., Jonathan M. Payne, and Anina N. Rich. 2006. Attentional load attenuates synaesthetic priming effects in grapheme-colour synaesthesia. *Cortex* 42:213–221.

Mattingley, Jason B., Anina N. Rich, Greg Yelland, and John L. Bradshaw. 2001. Unconscious priming eliminates automatic binding of colour and alphanumeric form in synaesthesia. *Nature* 410:580–582.

McArdle, P. A. 2006. Cannabis use by children and young people. *Archives of Disease in Childhood* 91:692–695.

McCabe, Matthew Leonard. 2011. Color and sound: Synaesthesia at the crossroads of music and science. *Dissertation Abstracts International Section A: Humanities and Social Sciences* 71:2698.

Meier, Beat, and Nicolas Rothen. 2007. When conditioned responses "fire back": Bidirectional cross-activation creates learning opportunities in synesthesia. *Neuroscience* 147:569–572.

——. 2009. Training grapheme-colour associations produces a synaesthetic Stroop effect, but not a conditioned synaesthetic response. *Neuropsychologia* 47:1208–1211.

Mills, Carol B., Joanne Innis, Taryn Westendorf, Lauren Owsianiecki, and Angela McDonald. 2006. Effect of a synesthete's photisms on name recall. *Cortex* 42:155–163.

Mondloch, Catherine J., and Daphne Maurer. 2004. Do small white balls squeak? Pitch-object correspondences in young children. *Cognitive, Affective & Behavioral Neuroscience* 4:133–136.

Motluk, Alison. 2004. How minds play tricks with words and colours. *New Scientist* 2461:9.

Muggleton, Neil, Elias Tsakanikos, Vincent Walsh, and Jamie Ward. 2007. Disruption of synaesthesia following TMS of the right posterior parietal cortex. *Neuropsychologia* 45:1582–1585.

Mulvenna, Catherine M. 2007. Synaesthesia, the arts and creativity: A neurological connection. In *Neurological Disorders in Famous Artists—Part 2*, ed. J. Bogousslavsky and M. G Hennerici. 206–222. Basel: Karger.

Mulvenna, Catherine M., and Vincent Walsh. 2006. Synaesthesia: Supernormal integration? *Trends in Cognitive Sciences* 10:350–352.

Neufeld, Janina, Christopher Sinke, Markus Zedler, Wolfgang Dillo, Hinderk M. Emrich, Stefan Bleich, and Gregor R. Szycik. 2012. The neural correlates of coloured music: A functional MRI investigation of auditory-visual synaesthesia. *Neuropsychologia* 50:85–89.

Neufeld, J., C. Sinke, M. Zedler, W. Dillo, H. M. Emrich, S. Bleich, and G. R. Szycik. 2012. Disinhibited feedback as a cause of synesthesia: Evidence from a functional connectivity study on auditory-visual synesthetes. *Neuropsychologia* 50:1471–1477.

Niccolai, Valentia, Janina Jennes, Petra Stoerig, and Tessa M. van Leeuwen. 2012. Modality and variability of synesthetic experience. *American Journal of Psychology* 125:81–94.

Niccolai, Valentia, Tessa M. van Leeuwen, Colin Blakemore, and Petra Stoerig. 2012. Synaesthetic perception of colour and visual space in a blind subject: An fMRI case study. *Consciousness and Cognition* 21:889–899.

Nijboer, Tanja C. W., Gabriela Satris, and Stefan Van der Stigchel. 2011. The influence of synesthesia on eye movements: No synesthetic pop-out in an oculomotor target selection task. *Consciousness and Cognition* 20:1193–1200.

Nijboer, Tanja C. W., and Stefan Van der Stigchel. 2009. Is attention essential for inducing synesthetic colors? Evidence from oculomotor distractors. *Journal of Vision* 9:21.1–21.9.

Nikolić, Danko, Uta M. Jürgens, Nicolas Rothen, Beat Meier, and Aleksandra Mroczko. 2011. Swimming-style synesthesia. *Cortex* 47:874–879.

Nunn, J. A., L. J. Gregory, M. J. Brammer, S. C. R. Williams, D. M. Parslow, M. J. Morgan, R. G. Morris, E. T. Bullmore, S. Baron-Cohen, and J. A. Gray. 2002. Functional magnetic resonance imaging of synesthesia: Activation of V4/V8 by spoken words. *Nature Neuroscience* 5:371–375.

Palmeri, Thomas J., Randolph Blake, René Marois, Marci A. Flanery, and William Whetsell, Jr. 2002. The perceptual reality of synesthetic colors. *Proceedings of the National Academy of Sciences of the United States of America* 99:4127–4131.

Paulesu, E., J. Harrison, S. Baron-Cohen, J. D. G. Watson, L. Goldstein, J. Heather, R. S. J. Frackowiak, and C. D. Frith. 1995. The physiology of coloured hearing: A PET activation study of colour-word synaesthesia. *Brain* 118:661–676.

Piazza, M., P. Pinel, and S. Dehaene. 2006. Objective correlates of an unusual subjective experience: A single-case study of number-form synaesthesia. *Cognitive Neuropsychology* 23:1162–1173.

Price, Mark C. 2009a. Spatial forms and mental imagery. *Cortex* 45:1229–1245.

——. 2009b. What kind of mental images are spatial forms? *Cognitive Processing* 10:S276–S278.

Radvansky, Gabriel A., Bradley S. Gibson, and M. Windy McNerney. 2011. Synesthesia and memory: Color congruency, von Restorff, and false memory effects. *Journal of Experimental Psychology: Learning, Memory, and Cognition* 37:219–229.

Ramachandran, Vilayanur S., and David Brang. 2008. Tactile-emotion synesthesia. *Neurocase* 14:390–399.

Ramachandran, Vilayanur S., and Edward M. Hubbard. 2001a. Psychophysical investigations into the neural basis of synaesthesia. *Proceedings of the Royal Society of London B: Biological Sciences* 268:979–983.

——. 2001b. Synaesthesia: A window into perception, thought and language. *Journal of Consciousness Studies* 8:3–34.

——. 2003a. The phenomenology of synesthesia. *Journal of Consciousness Studies* 10:49–57.

——. 2003b. Hearing colors, tasting shapes. *Scientific American* 288:52–59.

Ramos, Amy L. 2007. Exploring the role of visual selective attention in synesthesia. *Dissertation Abstracts International: Section B: The Sciences and Engineering* 67:4735.

Rich, Anina N., John L. Bradshaw, and Jason B. Mattingley. 2005. A systematic, large-scale study of synaesthesia: Implications for the role of early experience in lexical-colour associations. *Cognition* 98:53–84.

Rich, Anina N., and Jason B. Mattingley. 2010. Out of sight, out of mind: The attentional blink can eliminate synaesthetic colours. *Cognition* 114:320–328.

Rich, Anina N., Mark A. Williams, Aina Puce, Ari Syngeniotis, Matthew A. Howard, Francis McGlone, and Jason B. Mattingley. 2006. Neural correlates of imagined and synaesthetic colours. *Neuropsychologia* 44:2918–2925.

Richer, François, Guillaume-Alexandre Beaufils, and Sophie Poirier. 2011. Bidirectional lexical-gustatory synesthesia. *Consciousness and Cognition* 20:1738–1743.

Ro, Tony, Alessandro Farnè, Ruth M. Johnson, Van Wedeen, Zili Chu, Zhiyue J Wang, Jill V. Hunter, and Michael S. Beauchamp. 2007. Feeling sounds after a thalamic lesion. *Annals of Neurology* 62:433–441.

Robertson, Lynn C., and Noam Sagiv, eds. 2005. *Synesthesia: Perspectives From Cognitive Neuroscience*. New York: Oxford University Press.

Rothen, Nicolas, and Beat Meier. 2009. Do synesthetes have a general advantage in visual search and episodic memory? A case for group studies. *PLoS ONE* 4:e5037.

——. 2010a. Higher prevalence of synaesthesia in art students. *Perception* 39:718–720.

——. 2010b. Grapheme-colour synaesthesia yields an ordinary rather than extraordinary memory advantage: Evidence from a group study. *Memory* 18:258–264.

Rothen, Nicolas, Thomas Nyffeler, Roman von Wartburg, René Müri, and Beat Meier. 2010. Parieto-occipital suppression eliminates implicit bidirectionality in grapheme-colour synaesthesia. *Neuropsychologia* 48:3482–3487.

Rothen, Nicolas, Andrea-Laura Wantz, and Beat Meier. 2011. Training synaesthesia. *Perception* 40:1248–1250.

Rouw, Romke, and H. Steven Scholte. 2007. Increased structural connectivity in grapheme-color synesthesia. *Nature Neuroscience* 10:792–797.

——. 2010. Neural basis of individual differences in synesthetic experiences. *Journal of Neuroscience* 30:6205–6213.

Rouw, Romke, H. Steven Scholte, and Olympia Colizoli. 2011. Brain areas involved in synaesthesia: A review. *Journal of Neuropsychology* 5:214–242.

Saenz, Melissa, and Christof Koch. 2008. The sound of change: Visually-induced auditory synesthesia. *Current Biology* 18:R650–R651.

Sagiv, Noam. 2004. Cognitive and neural bases of synesthesia. *Dissertation Abstracts International: Section B: The Sciences and Engineering* 65:1047.

Sagiv, Noam, Jeffrey Heer, and Lynn Robertson. 2006. Does binding of synesthetic color to the evoking grapheme require attention? *Cortex* 42:232–242.

Sagiv, Noam, Julia Simner, James Collins, Brian Butterworth, and Jamie Ward. 2006. What is the relationship between synaesthesia and visuo-spatial number forms? *Cognition* 101:114–128.

Serino, Andrea, Francesca Pizzoferrato, and Elisabetta Làdavas. 2008. Viewing a face (especially one's own face) being touched enhances tactile perception on the face. *Psychological Science* 19:434–438.

Siegel, Ronald K., and Murray E. Jarvik. 1975. Drug-induced hallucinations in animals and man. In *Hallucinations: Behavior, Experience, and Theory*, ed. Ronald K. Siegel, and Louis Jolyon West, 81–161. New York: John Wiley & Sons.

Simner, Julia. 2012. Defining synaesthesia. *British Journal of Psychology* 103:1–15.

Simner, Julia, Oliver Gärtner, and Michelle D. Taylor. 2011. Cross-modal personality attributions in synaesthetes and non-synaesthetes. *Journal of Neuropsychology* 5:283–301.

Simner, Julia, and Sarah L. Haywood. 2009. Tasty non-words and neighbours: The cognitive roots of lexical-gustatory synaesthesia. *Cognition* 110:171–181.

Simner, Julia, and Emma Holenstein. 2007. Ordinal linguistic personification as a variant of synesthesia. *Journal of Cognitive Neuroscience* 19:694–703.

Simner, Julia, and Edward M. Hubbard. 2006. Variants of synesthesia interact in cognitive tasks: Evidence for implicit associations and late connectivity in cross-talk theories. *Neuroscience* 143:805–814.

Simner, Julia, and Robert H. Logie. 2007. Synaesthetic consistency spans decades in a lexical-gustatory synaesthete. *Neurocase* 13:358–365.

Simner, Julia, Neil Mayo, and Mary-Jane Spiller. 2009. A foundation for savantism? visuo-spatial synaesthetes present with cognitive benefits. *Cortex* 45:1246–1260.

Simner, Julia, Catherine Mulvenna, Noam Sagiv, Elias Tsakanikos, Sarah A. Witherby, Christine Fraser, Kirsten Scott, and Jamie Ward. 2006. Synaesthesia: The prevalence of atypical cross-modal experiences. *Perception* 35:1024–1033.

Sitton, Sarah C., and Edward R. Pierce. 2004. Synesthesia, creativity and puns. *Psychological Reports* 95:577–580.

Skelton, Richard, Casimir Ludwig, and Christine Mohr. 2009. A novel, illustrated questionnaire to distinguish projector and associator synaesthetes. *Cortex* 45:721–729.

Smilek, D., B. A. Moffatt, J. Pasternak, B. N. White, M. J. Dixon, and P. M. Merikle. 2002. Synaesthesia: A case study of discordant monozygotic twins. *Neurocase* 8:338–342.

Smilek, Daniel, Alicia Callejas, Mike J. Dixon, and Philip M. Merikle. 2007. Ovals of time: Time-space associations in synaesthesia. *Consciousness and Cognition* 16:507–519.

Smilek, Daniel, Mike J. Dixon, Cera Cudahy, and Philip M. Merikle. 2001. Synaesthetic photisms influence visual perception. *Journal of Cognitive Neuroscience* 13:930–936.

——. 2002. Synesthetic color experiences influence memory. *Psychological Science* 13:548–552.

Smilek, Daniel, Mike J. Dixon, and Philip M. Merikle. 2003. Synaesthetic photisms guide attention. *Brain and Cognition* 53:364–367.

——. 2005. Synaesthesia: Discordant male monozygotic twins. *Neurocase* 11:363–370.

Smilek, Daniel, Kelly A. Malcolmson, Jonatha S. A. Carriere, Meghan Eller, Donna Kwan, and Michael Reynolds. 2007. When "3" is a jerk and "E" is a king: Personifying inanimate objects in synesthesia. *Journal of Cognitive Neuroscience* 19:981–992.

Smith, David E. 2005. LSD, spirituality and the creative process. *Journal of Psychoactive Drugs* 37:235–236.

Specht, Karsten, and Bruno Laeng. 2011. An independent component analysis of fMRI data of grapheme-colour synaesthesia. *Journal of Neuropsychology* 5:203–213.

Spector, Ferrine, and Daphne Maurer. 2008. The colour of Os: Naturally biased associations between shape and colour. *Perception* 37:841–847.

——. 2009. Synesthesia: A new approach to understanding the development of perception. *Developmental Psychology* 45:175–189.

——. 2011. The colors of the alphabet: Naturally-biased associations between shape and color. *Journal of Experimental Psychology: Human Perception and Performance* 37:484–495.

Sperling, Julia M., David Prvulovic, David E. J. Linden, Wolf Singer, and Aglaja Stirn. 2006. Neuronal correlates of colour-graphemic synaesthesia: A fMRI study. *Cortex* 42:295–303.

Spruyt, Adriaan, Johannes Koch, Heleen Vandromme, Dirk Hermans, and Paul Eelen. 2009. A time course analysis of the synesthetic colour priming effect. *Canadian Journal of Experimental Psychology* 63:211–215.

Stephan, Barbara B. 2005. Synesthesia and dyslexia: Implications for increased understanding. *Dissertation Abstracts International: Section B: The Sciences and Engineering* 65:6059.

Steven, Megan S., Peter C. Hansen, and Colin Blakemore. 2006. Activation of color-selective areas of the visual cortex in a blind synesthete. *Cortex* 42:304–308.

Stroop, John R. 1935. Studies of interference in serial verbal reactions. *Journal of Experimental Psychology* 18:643–662.

Stuckey, David E., Robert Lawson, and Luis Eduardo Luna. 2005. EEG gamma coherence and other correlates of subjective reports during ayahuasca experiences. *Journal of Psychoactive Drugs* 37:163–178.

Tang, Joey, Jamie Ward, and Brian Butterworth. 2008. Number forms in the brain. *Journal of Cognitive Neuroscience* 20:1547–1556.

Terhune, Devin Blair, Etzel Cardeña, and Magnus Lindgren. 2010. Disruption of synaesthesia by posthypnotic suggestion: An ERP study. *Neuropsychologia* 48:3360–3364.

Terhune, Devin Blair, Sarah Tai, Alan Cowey, Tudor Popescu, and Roi Cohen Kadosh. 2011. Enhanced cortical excitability in grapheme-color synesthesia and its modulation. *Current Biology* 21:2006–2009.

Terzis, Julia K., Marylou M. Dryer, and Bruce I. Bodner. 2010. Corneal neurotization: A Novel technique for the anesthetic cornea. *Cornea* 29:812–819.

Teuscher, Ursina, David Brang, Vilayanur S. Ramachandran, and Seana Coulson. 2010. Spatial cueing in time-space synesthetes: An event-related brain potential study. *Brain and Cognition* 74:35–46.

Thomas-Anterion, Catherine, Christelle Creac'h, Elsa Dionet, Céline Borg, Chantal Extier, Isabelle Faillenot, and Roland Peyron. 2010. De novo artistic activity following insular-SII ischemia. *Pain* 150:121–127.

Tomson, Steffie N., Nili Avidan, Kwanghyuk Lee, Anand K. Sarma, Rejnal Tushe, Dianna M. Milewicz, Molly Bray, Suzanne M. Leal, and David M. Eagleman. 2011. The genetics of colored sequence synesthesia: Suggestive evidence of linkage to 16q and genetic heterogeneity for the condition. *Behavioural Brain Research* 223:48–52.

Treisman, A. 1982. Perceptual grouping and attention in visual search for features and for objects. *Journal of Experimental Psychology: Human Perception and Performance* 8:194–214.

Van Leeuwen, Tessa M., Hanneke E. M. den Ouden, and Peter Hagoort. 2011. Effective connectivity determines the nature of subjective experience in grapheme-color synesthesia. *Journal of Neuroscience* 31:9879–9884.

Van Leeuwen, Tessa M., Karl Magnus Petersson, and Peter Hagoort. 2010. Synaesthetic colour in the brain: beyond colour areas. A functional magnetic resonance imaging study of synaesthetes and matched controls. *PLoS ONE* 5:e12074.

Wagar, B. M., M. J. Dixon, D. Smilek, and C. Cudahy. 2002. Colored photisms prevent object-substitution masking in digit-color synesthesia. *Brain and Cognition* 48:606–611.

Wagner, Katie, and Karen R. Dobkins. 2011. Synaesthetic associations decrease during infancy. *Psychological Science* 22:1067–1072.

Ward, Jamie. 2008. *The Frog Who Croaked Blue: Synesthesia and the Mixing of the Senses.* London: Routledge.

Ward, Jamie, Brett Huckstep, and Elias Tsakanikos. 2006. Sound-colour synaesthesia: To what extent does it use cross-modal mechanisms common to us all? *Cortex* 42:264–280.

Ward, Jamie, Clare Jonas, Zoltan Dienes, and Anil Seth. 2010. Grapheme-colour synaesthesia improves detection of embedded shapes, but without pre-attentive "pop-out" of synaesthetic colour. *Proceedings of the Royal Society of London B: Biological Sciences* 277:1021–1026.

Ward, Jamie, Ryan Li, Shireen Salih, and Noam Sagiv. 2007. Varieties of grapheme-colour synaesthesia: A new theory of phenomenological and behavioural differences. *Consciousness and Cognition* 16:913–931.

Ward, Jamie, Samantha Moore, Daisy Thompson-Lake, Shireen Salih, and Brianna Beck. 2008. The aesthetic appeal of auditory-visual synaesthetic perceptions in people without synaesthesia. *Perception* 37:1285–1296.

Ward, Jamie, Noam Sagiv, and Brian Butterworth. 2009. The impact of visuo-spatial number forms on simple arithmetic. *Cortex* 45:1261–1265.

Ward, Jamie, and Julia Simner. 2003. Lexical-gustatory synaesthesia: Linguistic and Conceptual factors. *Cognition* 89:237–261.

——. 2005. Is synaesthesia an X-linked dominant trait with lethality in males? *Perception* 34:611–623.

Ward, Jamie, Julia Simner, and Vivian Auyeung. 2005. A comparison of lexical-gustatory and grapheme-colour synaesthesia. *Cognitive Neuropsychology* 22:28–41.

Ward, Jamie, Daisy Thompson-Lake, Roxanne Ely, and Flora Kaminski. 2008. Synaesthesia, creativity and art: What is the link? *British Journal of Psychology* 99:127–141.

Weiss, Peter H., Andreas Kalckert, and Gereon R. Fink. 2009. Priming letters by colors: Evidence for the bidirectionality of grapheme-color synesthesia. *Journal of Cognitive Neuroscience* 21:2019–2026.

Weiss, Peter H., N. Jon Shah, Ivan Toni, Karl Zilles, and Gereon R. Fink. 2001. Associating colours with people: A case of chromatic-lexical synaesthesia. *Cortex* 37:750–753.

Weiss, Peter H., Karl Zilles, and Gereon R. Fink. 2005. When visual perception causes feeling: Enhanced cross-modal processing in grapheme-color synesthesia. *Neuroimage* 28:859–868.

Witthoft, Nathan. 2008. Experience and perception. *Dissertation Abstracts International: Section B: The Sciences and Engineering* 69:723.

Wollen, Keith A., and Frank T. Ruggiero. 1983. Colored-letter synesthesia. *Journal of Mental Imagery* 7:83–86.

Yaro, Caroline, and Jamie Ward. 2007. Searching for Shereshevskii: What is superior about the memory of synaesthetes? *Quarterly Journal of Experimental Psychology* 60:681–695.

CHAPTER 22

SYNESTHESIA IN SPACE VERSUS THE "MIND'S EYE"

How to ask the right questions

CHRISTINE MOHR

The etymology of synesthesia is derived from the Greek *syn* meaning "together" and *aesthesis* meaning "sensation"; literally translated as "a union of the senses" (Cytowic 2002). Accordingly, synesthesia is a phenomenon wherein a simultaneous dual perception arises from a single sensory input, with the additional percept belonging to either the same or a different sensory modality. The most prevalent form of synesthesia is grapheme-color synesthesia (Day 2005; Rich, Bradshaw, and Mattingley 2005; Simner et al. 2006) in which perceiving an achromatic grapheme (e.g., the letter "g") can trigger the percept of an idiosyncratic color experience (e.g., the color "blue") (Day 2005; Rich, Bradshaw, and Mattingley 2005), sometimes accompanied by texture, shape and movement qualities (Tyler 2005). Independent reports include for instance the simultaneous activation of smells, taste and color induced by pain, or when viewing words or shapes (Cytowic 2002; Tyler 2005; Ward and Simner 2003).

As a phenomenon, synesthesia has long been described (Flournoy 1892; Galton 1880; see also Jewanski, Day, and Ward 2009), but the continuity of scientific interest has been far from stable. One major research wave came around the turn of the last century (e.g., Alford 1918; Mahling 1926) before interest abated with the rise of behaviorism. This latter movement questioned the need to investigate purely cognitive functions, and by inference something as "spiritual" as the mind (Skinner 1938; Watson 1928). In this time period, researchers attempted to explain reports of synesthetic experiences as a type of learned behavior (Howells 1944) as suggested previously (Kaiser 1882). Ultimately, behaviorism was unable to explain every human behavior and experience through learning and reinforcement (e.g., Chomsky 1959), and its decline was met with a rise in a new school of thought, cognitive psychology, which gained recognition in the mid 1950s (Bechtel, Abrahamsen, and Graham 1998). With this approach came the study of the mind, including phenomena that are not readily available through observed behavior such as the experience of synesthesia (Marks 1975) or mental imagery (Shepard and

Metzler 1971). Using well-established, cleverly modulated cognitive paradigms (e.g., the Stroop paradigm, see later) as well as neuroimaging methods, researchers began to accumulate evidence for the genuineness of the idiosyncratic synesthetic experience (Rich and Mattingley 2002). Even more impressive, a number of these carefully prepared studies became published in highly prestigious journals, despite only a relative few number of cases being described (Beeli, Esslen, and Jäncke 2005; Dixon et al. 2000; Wagar et al. 2002).

In recent years, we have seen an increasing number of publications in which groups of synesthetes rather than individual cases or small samples have been reported (e.g., Barnett et al. 2008; Mattingley et al. 2001; Simner et al. 2009), and in which commonalities, differences, and associated abilities have been demonstrated (Barnett and Newell 2008; Dailey, Martindale, and Borkum 1997; Dixon and Smilek 2005; Hubbard et al. 2005; Mills et al. 2009; Rothen and Meier 2009; Yaro and Ward 2007). This research period has shown that individuals who report synesthetic experiences are probably not part of a homogenous group. On the contrary, ever more different forms of synesthesia have been described, and with them, their own associated cognitive functions and neuronal networks (e.g., Banissy et al. 2011; Brang et al. 2010; Callejas, Acosta, and Lupianez 2007; Fitzgibbon et al. 2010; Freund 2009; Giummarra et al. 2010; Jarick et al. 2009; Mann et al. 2009; Michael et al. 2010; Muggleton et al. 2007; Ramachandran and Brang 2008; Smilek et al. 2007).

The categorization of individuals into different groups reflecting their self-reported experiences is reminiscent of categorization procedures common in the mental health sector. Here, patients report psychiatric experiences (e.g., hallucinations, anxiety) that are subjective, experiences of the mind, and mostly inaccessible to the observer apart from through self-report. In order to be "diagnosed" with a particular mental health condition (a "syndrome"), individuals need to present with a collection of "symptoms" over a given period of time (American Psychiatric Association 1994). In most instances the causes for symptoms are unknown. Yet, categorizing individuals into different groups according to these self-reported "symptoms" allows the formulation of a priori assumptions that can be tested scientifically. For instance, if a patient reports auditory or visual hallucinations, we would expect to find (and this has indeed been found) neuronal correlates for these hallucinations within networks that are commonly involved in the processing of auditory (Chibbaro et al. 2005; Poulet et al. 2005) or visual (Josephson and Kirsch 2006; Oertel et al. 2007) information, respectively. Mapping this same reasoning onto the study of synesthesia, one could also expect (and again, it has been found) that brain areas that are commonly involved in the experience of a given sensory percept are also activated during the synesthetic experience (e.g., Beauchamp and Ro 2008; Hanggi et al. 2008; Laeng, Hugdahl, and Specht 2011; Sperling et al. 2006).

Despite my earlier comparison between synesthesia and psychiatric experiences, synesthesia research and neuroscientific analogies with other types of conditions have shown us that illusory sensory perceptions do not need to reflect a pathological condition (Ohayon 2000; Posey and Losch 1984). Furthermore, they can teach us important information about the brain's architecture and functioning. However, a reliable categorization of individuals into different groups of synesthetes is essential to enhancing our understanding in this research field. One categorization (projector and associator synesthetes; see later) will be the main focus for the remainder of this chapter. A thorough account on different sensory synesthetic experiences is available throughout this handbook, the proposed brain correlates in Part V, and ideas on the origins of synesthesia in the opening chapters.

ASSOCIATORS VERSUS PROJECTORS

The categorization of individuals into projector and associator synesthetes was introduced in the seminal work by Smilek et al. (2001) entitled "Synesthetic photisms influence visual perception." On page 930 of this paper, the authors write that "Some digit-color synesthetes also report a curious subjective phenomenon. When shown a digit, the color of the photism is not experienced "in the mind's eye," but rather it is experienced as though the color was "externally projected" onto the digit." These seemingly different synesthetic experiences, in particular the experienced overlap of the colored photism with the presented grapheme in projector synesthetes motivated the authors to run a visual experiment in which they elaborated on such subjective reports. In their study, they presented graphemes on a background that was either congruent or incongruent with the color that was experienced when seeing a particular grapheme. For example, if the synesthete experienced red from the letter A, the background would be either red (congruent) or, say, green (incongruent). The results confirmed the authors' expectation that a projector synesthete would find it harder to identify and decide upon this grapheme when it was presented in the congruent condition (where the synesthetic color of the grapheme matched the real-world background) as compared to the incongruent experimental condition.

After this seminal report, the distinction of projector and associator synesthetes became more widely established and tested for (see also Dixon and Smilek 2005; Dixon, Smilek, and Merikle 2004; Hubbard and Ramachandran 2005; Rouw and Scholte 2010; and see Duffy 2001; Tyler 2005, for synesthetes' perspectives). It was specified in later papers that projector synesthetes could perceive the synesthesic colors in external space (Dixon and Smilek 2005; Dixon, Smilek, and Merikle 2004; Ward, Huckstep, and Tsakanikos 2006), appearing as a transient mist, a transparent overlay or as saturating the printed letter (Cytowic 1993, 2005; Tyler 2005). In the latter case, this would involve a simultaneous perception of both the synesthetic and display color existing within the same proximate perceptual space, where these colors do not mix or occlude each other (Kim and Blake 2005), and can be perceived as perceptually "real" (Palmeri et al. 2002). In contrast, associators' synesthetic colors are experienced internally, in their "mind's eye" (Dixon and Smilek 2005; Dixon, Smilek, and Merikle 2004). According to Dixon, Smilek, and Merikle (2004), the synesthetic experience of associators:

> can be likened, at least in part, to that of a non-synesthete viewing a black-and-white picture of a stop sign. We "know" the stop sign is a highly specific shade of fire engine red and can readily form an image of this color in our mind's eye, but we do not project this color onto the picture. (226)

The key difference between synesthetes and non-synesthete here is the high automaticity with which this experience is triggered for the former; synesthetes cannot help but experience their idiosyncratic, and highly automatic synesthetic photisms. Moreover, while non-synesthetes might have strong color "experiences" viewing black and white objects that would otherwise have unambiguous real-world colors (e.g., bananas, fire engines), synesthetes have comparable experiences for other "objects" such as graphemes.

As already indicated by Smilek et al. (2001), the categorization of individuals into projector and associator synesthetes is not restricted to the phenomenological self-report level, but can be differentiated through cognitive performance as well (see also Dixon, Smilek, and Merikle 2004; Ward et al. 2007). In a subsequent study by Dixon, Smilek, and Merikle (2004), grapheme-color synesthetes performed a "synesthetic Stroop task." In a conventional Stroop task, non-synesthetes are slow to name the ink-color of "incongruent" color words (e.g., slow to name ink-color if the word "red" is written in green ink). In the synesthetic version of the Stroop task, stimuli (e.g., digits) are presented in colors which are either congruent or incongruent with the synesthetic color. Typically, synesthetes are slow to name the ink-color in the incongruent condition, where ink-color conflicts with their synesthesia (e.g., slow to name green ink-color for the printed number 5, if 5 happens to be synesthetically red). In such studies, including the paper by Dixon and colleagues, stimuli must be individually prepared, i.e., according to each individual's synesthesia. This is because the synesthetic color of digits and other triggers can differ vastly from synesthete to synesthete. In the Dixon et al. study, participants were instructed to name either the color of the digits, or the color of the synesthetic photism elicited by the grapheme. Supporting the experience of their phenomenological descriptions, self-reported projector synesthetes showed larger interference (i.e., were slower) when naming the ink-color as compared to naming the synesthetic color elicited by the grapheme. The opposite was observed for self-reported associator synesthetes.

Dissociations between projector and associator synesthetes have also been confirmed with brain imaging studies. In their recent functional magnetic resonance imaging study, Rouw and Scholte (2010) had projector synesthetes, associator synesthetes, and healthy controls perform a grapheme perception task. The task was personalized for each participant, in that individual stimuli were selected that elicited strong synesthetic colors, weak synesthetic colors, or no synesthetic color (the latter being true for all stimuli in control participants). Comparison of blood oxygen level responses yielded differences between conditions that supported differences in the nature of the synesthetic experience: in projectors, the outside-world synesthetic experience was related to brain areas that have been linked to perception and action within the outside world (e.g., visual cortex, motor cortex). In associators, the in-the-mind synesthetic experience was related to brain areas that have been linked to memory (e.g., hippocampus, parahippocampal gyrus). Given the interest in how projector-associator categorizations might differentially influence behavioral performance (Dixon and Smilek 2005; Dixon, Smilek, and Merikle 2004; Edquist et al. 2006; Hubbard et al. 2005; Ward et al. 2007) and brain activation patterns (Rouw and Scholte 2007, 2010), one might hope that researchers would apply a reliable measurement to distinguish between projector and associator synesthetes. Indeed, we might hope that the methodology would be as rigorous as that applied to separating synesthetes from non-synesthetes (e.g., Eagleman et al. 2007; Mattingley et al. 2001). Unfortunately (and this is probably not surprising given that we are facing a relatively new categorization or phenomenon) widely available self-report measures are scarce, or in other words, they need first be developed and evaluated. I next consider how the phenomenological differences between associators and projectors might be detected methodologically.

Studies that aimed to systematically differentiate between the subjective reports of associators and projectors have demonstrated that the true difference in experience across groups can be unhelpfully complex, and so not easily captured by a simple set of questions (Rouw and Scholte 2007; Ward et al. 2007). Moreover, experiences can typically be contradictory and unreliable upon retest (Edquist et al. 2006; Skelton, Ludwig, and Mohr 2009) in that synesthetes asked about their experiences using verbal questionnaires can describe them differently on different occasions. When exploring previous reports on groups of projector and associator synesthetes in more detail, the lack of a consistent assessment method becomes evident. In Dixon, Smilek, and Merikle (2004), the two groups were determined by self-report. The exact question, and the number of times the subjective experience was assessed, however, were not specified. Ward et al. (2007) determined groups through self-report by an extended interview, and gave details of inconsistencies which led the researchers to make additional distinctions among the groups (for details see later). Edquist et al. (2006) asked individuals to indicate which statement from a set of three options ("out there in space," "in my mind's eye," or "neither") was the best in describing how their synesthetic color appeared. Importantly, these authors provided an additional structured questionnaire to collect more detailed and systematic information on participants' synesthetic color experiences (reproduced in Table 22.1). Participants not only responded *yes* or *no* to the indicated questions, but responded on a 5-Likert scale ranging from 1 (strongly disagree) to 5 (strongly agree). The authors found that synesthetes responded inconsistently within and between sessions (9 of the 14 participants provided their responses twice 12 months apart). This inconsistency was considered severe enough to refrain from the application of a projector-associator categorization, and instead, to analyze the data for the whole group, and then individually. Finally, Rouw and Scholte (2007, 2010) used a

Table 22.1 Items from the structured interview used by Edquist et al. (2006) and Skelton, Ludwig, and Mohr (2009)

	Edquist et al. (2006)	Skelton, Ludwig, and Mohr (2009): D-SEQ
1	When I look at a letter or number I see a color	The color has the same shape as the letter or number
2	When I look at a letter or number I get a feeling of color	The color looks like it is on the page
3	The color has the same shape as the letter or number	You see a colored copy of it in your "mind's eye" and black and white on the page
4	The color is some other shape	The figure[a] is not colored, but you are aware that it has a specific associated color
5	The color looks like it is on the page	How would you best describe your synesthesic colors?
6	The color is not on the page, but it is out there in space	i) solid-transparent
7	The color is in my mind's eye	ii) over the letter—around the letter
8	When I imagine a letter or number the color is the same as when I look at the letter or number on the page	iii) on the page—in front of the page
9	When I imagine a familiar object (e.g. a banana) I see it out in space	
10	When I imagine a familiar object (e.g. a banana) I see it in my mind's eye	

[a] Please note that here, the term 'figure' was used to denote a letter or number.

24-item questionnaire (using a Likert scale) and nine open questions. For each individual, the authors calculated a score by subtracting the mean score on six "associator" questions (for example, "When I look at a particular letter/digit, the color appears only in my mind and not somewhere outside my head such as on the paper") from the mean score on six "projector" questions (for example, "the color seems to be projected on the letter/digit") (Rouw and Scholte 2007, 796). The authors considered individuals to be associators when they had a difference score below zero, and to be projectors when they had a difference score above zero (see end of chapter for a more detailed account on related problems in group allocation). Unfortunately, the authors did not provide their full questionnaire; moreover, the questionnaire was filled in only once (i.e., consistency was not further considered), and detailed results were not presented. Overall, it is apparent that different methods have been used to distinguish between projector and associator synesthetes across studies; furthermore, even within individuals using the same test, the categorizations produced with these methods can apparently change over time.

Confronted with the finding that projector/associator status is apparently inconsistent over time, one option would be to consider this variability as an accurate reflection of the psychological state of affairs: i.e., that synesthesic experiences are indeed changeable (Edquist et al. 2006). On the other hand, this conclusion would seem inconsistent with the fact that synesthetes describe their experiences as unchanging. An alternative interpretation is that synesthetes might be inconsistent in their responding because of the linguistic format of the assessment (i.e., oral in open interview, or written in questionnaires). This is especially important since the questions deal with what is a strictly visual experience, i.e., whether colors are projected or associated. An additional consideration to make about written questionnaires is that synesthesia research is not only performed in Western adult literate populations, but also in children of varying language and literacy skills (Green and Goswami 2008; Hunt 2005; Maurer and Mondloch 2006; Simner et al. 2009; Walker et al. 2010). It is also carried out in different cultures, which might require adequate translations, and again the assumption of literacy (Barnett et al. 2009; Day 2005; Hupka et al. 1997; Proios, Weniger, and Willmes 2002). Furthermore, although synesthesia research profits from not being dominated by the most studied population in psychology (undergraduate psychology students; see Henrich, Heine, and Norenzayan 2010) this raises the question of how varying education level might affect responses. As such, we might require a more widely applicable questionnaire because of potential difficulties in understanding questions or response formats (Bergh et al. 2011; Graesser et al. 2000). Given the issues highlighted here, it might be the case that the particular format of the question (verbal versus non-verbal/ pictorial) plays a crucial role in whether or not we obtain consistent results. Ward et al. (2007) interestingly noted that they:

> have observed that synesthetes struggle to find the words to describe their experiences, and the same terms are often used to denote different things. For example, many synaesthetes restrict the use of the term "mind's eye" to denote internalised space, but others may use it to describe synaesthetic perception regardless of spatial location. This can undoubtedly lead to inconsistencies in categorising synaesthetes whose experiences are nonetheless stable. (924)

If we would like to account for individual differences in the synesthetic experience, while factoring out developmental, cultural, and societal differences, it would be essential to create means that are independent of the language spoken, of general language abilities, and of educational backgrounds.

In a recent study, facing similar problems to those of Edquist et al. (2006) and Ward et al. (2007), we made an initial attempt to account for some of the problems described above (Skelton, Ludwig, and Mohr 2009). We contrasted two *Synesthesic Experience Questionnaires* (SEQs) that aimed to separate projector from associator synesthetes. Both questionnaires were assessed using the same population consisting of 12 grapheme-color synesthetes. In a first experiment, we provided participants with a self-report measure based on descriptive statements (henceforth called D-SEQ) thought to verbally describe the associator and projector experience (see Table 22.1 for the exact wording of our items). The first item aimed to test whether the synesthetic color seems like a "superimposed" colored percept of the grapheme. The second item aimed to test whether the color is perceived in external space, or might be perceived in the mind's eye. The third item tried to further verify the associator experience, i.e., that the percept in external space is indeed achromatic, and the color is perceived in the mind's eye. The fourth item aimed to test whether the color is perceived in the mind's eye, like an associated percept, and is not perceived as a sensory experience in external space. Finally, the fifth item asked for additional dimensions (i, ii, and iii in Table 22.1). These items were answered by synesthetes on a 5-point Likert scale in order to assess to what extent the statements reflected each individual's own synesthetic experiences when viewing letters or numbers (Edquist et al. 2006). We instructed participants in the following way "Please indicate how strongly these notions apply to you with 1 being the least applicable and 5 being the most applicable." After approximately 4 months, we invited participants to answer the D-SEQ again. None of the participants had been informed that a retest would take place. When comparing the responses within and between testing sessions, we did not find any indication that our synesthetes' experiences were stable over time (see also Edquist et al. 2006). The second item was the only one that showed sufficient test–retest reliability (participants answered similarly to this statement at both testing sessions).

Depending on the perspective one would like to take, it could be argued that the result of this first experiment was another confirmation that synesthetes' experiential reports are seemingly contradictory and unreliable, variably changing from "projected on the page" to "in their mind's eye," or vice versa upon retest (see also Edquist et al. 2006; Ward et al. 2007), and that this variability is simply part of the changeable synesthetic experience (Edquist et al. 2006). As mentioned before, such a conclusion would be inconsistent with synesthetes' explicit self-reports that their experiences are stable over extended periods of time. Our synesthetes also reported consistent colors/hues when performing a test of "genuineness" (Baron-Cohen et al. 1987, 1996; Mattingley et al. 2001), i.e., they selected highly similar colors at two separate testing sessions (the second session was again not forewarned), and this was not the case for a group of non-synesthetic controls (Skelton, Ludwig, and Mohr 2009). To find alternative explanations for the inconsistency in our associator/projector questionnaire, we asked our synesthetes about their experience of the questionnaire itself. This questioning indicated that response variation might be the result of our inaccurate portrayal of synesthetes' experiences, and the ambiguous nature of our questions. In other words, synesthetes flagged up the types of methodological challenges we reviewed earlier in this chapter (Ward and Mattingley 2006; Ward et al. 2007) and these are problems that might affect most research on individual differences in synesthesia (e.g., Dixon and Smilek, 2005; Dixon, Smilek, and Merikle 2004; Edquist et al. 2006; Sagiv et al. 2006). These considerations motivated us to create a different form of questionnaire, one that depended more heavily on illustrations (henceforth referred to as the I-SEQ) (Skelton, Ludwig, and Mohr 2009). In summary, our motivation to create what became the final format of the I-SEQ was based on: (1) synesthetes' comments (including those from the D-SEQ), (2) the observation that synesthetes were struggling to verbally explain their "visual" experiences, (3) previous descriptions of the projector and associator experience (e.g., Cytowic 1993, 2005; Dixon and Smilek 2005; Tyler 2005), (4) previous attempts to standardize the assessment of individual differences in synesthesia (e.g., Edquist et al. 2006), and finally (5) independent results showing that illustrations can clarify text comprehension (e.g., Brookshire et al. 2002; Larkin and Simon 1987; Trevena et al. 2006).

The final I-SEQ consisted of two illustrations reflecting projected synesthetic experiences and three illustrations reflecting associated synesthetic experiences (the original questionnaire can be found in Skelton, Ludwig, and Mohr 2009; please see Figure 22.1 for new examples that we have since revised based on this earlier test). We added verbal clarifications to our visual illustrations. As we did for the D-SEQ, we used a Likert scale in our I-SEQ so that individuals could portray both the direction and extent of individual differences in their synesthetic experience, and we again administered the questionnaire twice with testing sessions being approximately 1 month apart. The exact instruction of the I-SEQ read as follows:

> Please fill in the following as accurately as possible. This information is extremely valuable to this study. You may go back and change your answers at any time. Below are various illustrations of how synesthetes may experience their colors when viewing letters. Please rate how close the illustrations represent your experiences when viewing the letters presented below [example letters of S R T are provided, see Figure 22.1] (1 being the least accurate and 7 being the most accurate). There is additional space to provide details of how your experiences may differ from those illustrated.

Two examples of projected and associated experiences from the I-SEQ are exemplified in Figure 22.1 respectively. The full original questionnaire can be found in the Appendix of Skelton, Ludwig, and Mohr (2009).

In contrast to the D-SEQ, the results from the I-SEQ showed that synesthetes responded comparably at both testing sessions. When results from the D-SEQ and I-SEQ were contrasted, group-wise comparisons showed that the responses of synesthetes were statistically comparable between testing sessions for the I-SEQ (i.e., the illustrated questionnaire), but not for the D-SEQ (i.e., the verbal questionnaire). Moreover, correlation analyses indicated that responding in the D-SEQ was unrelated to responding in the I-SEQ, showing that the two questionnaires overall were unrelated (Skelton, Ludwig, and Mohr 2009). The test–retest reliability of the I-SEQ has been promising, but did not solve another problem inherent to questionnaires aimed at enabling categorization: how to interpret results from rating scales (continuous variable) given that we might wish for a categorical distinction between, on the one hand projectors, and on the other hand, associators. In the ideal case, questionnaires such as the I-SEQ (Skelton, Ludwig, and Mohr 2009) or any other version used previously (Edquist et al. 2006; Rouw and Scholte 2007, 2010), would be accompanied with some form of cut-off score(s) to reliably allocate individuals to either the associator or projector group. One "simple" solution would be to calculate a mean, sum, or median score across items with the respective scores ranging between a fixed minimum and maximum. For ease of explanation, let us imagine the case in which the mean would be a score of 0, the minimum would be a score of −1 and the maximum a score of +1. Even in this simple scenario, we would not really know how to continue with a binary categorization. For instance, we could decide that individuals with a score of 0 are "undecided" synesthetes, those with scores >0 are projector synesthetes and those with scores <0 are associator synesthetes (the direction would obviously depend on the formulation of the Likert scale; see e.g., Rouw and Scholte 2007, 2010). Taking such an approach has, however, obvious limitations. One criticism would be the procedural consequence that individuals with a score of 0.01 would be allocated to the same group as an individual with a score of 0.99. If we assume that each item is equally weighted, the former is certainly more similar to the "undecided" synesthete than the latter. Another possibility would be to classify synesthetes as "undecided" if they fell within a pre-determined range around the zero value (Skelton, Ludwig, and Mohr 2009). Any reason with which to apply one (e.g., beyond ± 0.10) but not another range (± 0.20) would seem arbitrary without prior testing (see later and Skelton, Ludwig, and Mohr 2009).

The problems raised here ask for answers on how we could decide where to place boundaries beyond which we would feel confident that we are dealing with "projector-ness" or "associator-ness." Answers would certainly involve the application of common experimental scientific standards, ideally based on the investigation of larger samples of synesthetes in which: (1) we assess the test-retest reliability of individual differences through standardized psychometric tools, (2) we aim to empirically determine a cut-off score beyond which individuals would be classified as projector or associator synesthetes (e.g., through the use of behavioral paradigms that have differentiated associators from projectors in the past, Dixon, Smilek, and Merikle 2004; Smilek et al. 2001; Ward et al. 2007), and (3) we consider what the group of "undecided" synesthetes might represent.

FIGURE 22.1 Examples similar to those presented in the I-SEQ (Skelton, Ludwig, and Mohr 2009) reflecting associator (a) and projector (b) experiences respectively. Participants are asked to specify on a 7-point Likert scale to what extend these illustrations reflect their own experience. Illustrations by Gabrielle Tschumi (<http://www.gabdessine.ch>).

While the problems associated with the first two points have been addressed earlier, the final point needs further comment.

For grapheme-color synesthetes, the failure to reliably categorize them as either associators or projectors has led some researchers to suggest alternative (or embedded) additional categorizations (Edquist et al. 2006; Ward et al. 2007). From a seemingly extended interview of their synesthetes, Ward et al. (2007) suggested several additional distinctions with one focusing particularly on the problems inherent in a projector-associator categorization. The authors noted that some projectors experienced colors on the surface of a page (which they labeled "surface-projectors") while others experienced colors in externalized near space (which they labeled "near-space projectors"). These researchers observed that in a previous behavioral task that distinguished associator and projector synesthetes (Dixon, Smilek, and Merikle 2004), the near space-projectors performed comparably to associator synesthetes. Ward et al. also suggested subdivisions within the category of associator synesthetes: the authors noted that some synesthetes reported seeing colors internally (which they labeled "see-associators"), while others reported simply knowing the colors (which they labeled "know-associators"). As far as we are aware, there is no additional empirical evidence that would help us to decide whether these additional subgroups should be maintained. Likewise, it could be the case that such subcategorizations emerged because synesthetes developed different strategies in responding to questions. For instance, if asked whether they "see" their colors, synesthetes might associate this description with a pathological condition (e.g., having a hallucination, being "mad") and deny it; this in turn would generate a "no" response bias when compared to the question of simply "knowing" colors (Ward et al. 2007). Thus, social and/or clinical implications mean different response strategies might emerge, and in turn could create different "synesthesia response types." Context-dependent response biases have been reported elsewhere, in, for example, personality questionnaires (Mohr and Leonards 2005), self-esteem questionnaires (Forsman 1993), addiction assessment measures (Carey 2002), and pain measures (Robinson et al. 1997).

Higher Versus Lower Synesthesia

The second distinction on individual differences in synesthesia considered by Ward et al. (2007) is for "higher" and "lower" synesthetes, as proposed in earlier literature (Hubbard and Ramachandran 2005; Ramachandran and Hubbard 2001). This categorization was motivated by the level or complexity of the synesthesia-inducing stimulus, or put differently, by the question of which processing stage the synesthesia is triggered at. In the case of lower synesthesia, the experience is triggered by lower perceptual processes (e.g., shape detection), and in the case of the higher synesthesia, by higher cognitive processes (e.g., linguistic processing of letters, words). While one can speculate whether the two distinctions (higher–lower; associator–projector) do or do not map onto each other, or whether they are actually orthogonal or randomly independent (Ward et al. 2007), the

higher–lower distinction of Ramachandran and Hubbard has only recently been investigated beyond phenomenological descriptions (Gebuis, Nijboer, and Van der Smagt
2009; Hochel and Milan 2008). What is required is some type of reliable empirical support, through the application of appropriate paradigms analogous to the ones introduced for the associator–projector distinction (e.g., Dixon, Smilek, and Merikle 2004;
Rouw and Scholte 2007, 2010; Ward et al. 2007) and those testing brain responses of
synesthetic experiences more directly (Gebuis, Nijboer, and Van der Smagt 2009).

Comparable to the attempts made for the associator–projector distinction, categorization into higher and lower synesthesia might be made possible through an appropriately
tested psychometric tool. Anybody wishing to develop and use such a measure would be
advised to publish the measurement tool, and its respective results in full (Edquist et al.
2006; Skelton, Ludwig, and Mohr 2009), ideally using illustrations (Skelton, Ludwig,
and Mohr 2009). Only too often are we left with incomplete descriptions as to how studies have been performed because we do not have access to the full material (questions,
stimuli, cut-off scores) and the respective comprehensive results. This tendency can be
observed in synesthesia research (Rouw and Scholte 2007, 2010; Ward et al. 2007), but
are pertinent to other domains as well (e.g., Fernandino, Iacoboni, and Zaidel 2007;
McCreery and Claridge 1995; Mohr, Rowe, and Crawford 2008).

In the present chapter, we have discussed methodological challenges and requirements
in the assessment of individual differences in synesthesia. Work on the distinction of synesthetes into projector and associator categories has so far focused on grapheme-color

FIGURE 22.2 Illustrations of two other possible forms of synesthesia for which we might find
a distinction of projector versus associator experiences. Depicted here are just the associator-
type versions, for taste-shape synesthesia (a) or smell-color synesthesia (b). Illustrations by
Gabrielle Tschumi (<http://www.gabdessine.ch>).

synesthetes. This might reflect a justified focus on one type of synesthesia perhaps because this distinction may only exist for grapheme-color synesthetes alone (although it can be at least imagined in other variants also; see Figure 22.2). Alternatively, it might be a less justified focus, simply because other forms of synesthesia are less prevalent and by consequence less well studied. We argue that it is worthwhile investigating whether this (or any other described) individual difference in synesthesia does exist beyond a certain variant. If the same individual difference were found reliably for other forms of synesthesia, this might then be a general marker of the "syndrome," irrespective of the sensory "symptoms." On the other hand, if this same individual difference turned out to be specific to one particular form of synesthesia only, we would have found a marker with which distinct forms of synesthesia could be separated. Finally, if certain individual differences were found to change over time, we would have discovered new measures with which to further our understanding of the developmental aspects of synesthesia (such as the observation that synesthesia seems to decline or weaken over time; Baron-Cohen et al. 1996; Riggs and Karwoski 1934).

CONCLUSIONS

In the present chapter, we introduced the concept of synesthesia, its heterogeneous phenomenology, and the individual difference of projector and associator experiences. The reliable categorization of individuals into different forms of synesthesia might help us to obtain a better picture as to which forms might exist, and which mechanisms might contribute to these and other individual differences. Yet, the literature lacks reliable methods to help categorize individuals into different groups. We here report on findings in which we tested the possibility that visual illustrations could allow a more reliable division of individuals into projector and associator synesthetes, compared to when mere verbal descriptors were used. By consequence, we suggest that visual illustrations could help to reduce the inconsistency and variability with which synesthetes report individual differences in their synesthetic experience. In particular, obtaining more reliable measures might indicate that it is not the synesthetic experience that varies over a relatively short period of time (weeks, months, several few years), but rather that the descriptors were inappropriate to capture individuals' experience at the time of testing. If we find better means, we also open new avenues in our understanding of individual differences in synesthesia. Before this can be achieved, researchers in the field would be advised to firstly design appropriate assessment tools (ideally using visual illustrations), reduce the use of verbal descriptions, assess these tools in large enough samples and gauge test–retest reliability, determine appropriate cut-off scores (the best case being if self-report is verified with behavioral performance), consider alternative categorizations of individual differences, and investigate whether reliable individual differences hold true across different forms of synesthesia. Obviously, attempting to account for all these open issues requires serious research efforts from the various groups and individuals working in the field. Expecting these efforts to be done seems justified, because the time to merely describe and "prove" the phenomenon (or phenomena) of synesthesia has passed to some extent, and by inference, it is now time to develop reliable and valid research tools with which experiences can be determined and classified. Scientific rigor has been introduced when synesthetes are appropriately classified, and the same should be expected where subgroups and individual differences are concerned.

ACKNOWLEDGEMENTS

My appreciation goes to Richard Skelton and Gabrielle Tschumi. Richard Skelton, a former University of Bristol master student, was the original driving force in the development of the I-SEQ. He has since left synesthesia research to pursue his professional aspirations in becoming an educational psychologist. Gabrielle Tschumi, who created the illustrations shown here, is a psychologist and artist living in Lausanne, Switzerland. Part of her artistic work can be seen at <http://www.gabdessine.ch>, where she can also be contacted for additional material. Finally, I would like to thank her for choosing to use me as the inspiration for her illustrations—this was a great source of pleasure for me!

REFERENCES

Alford, L. B. 1918. A report on two cases of synesthesia. *The Journal of Abnormal Psychology* 13:1–11.

American Psychiatric Association. 1994. *Diagnostic and Statistical Manual of Mental Disorders, Fourth Edition*. Washington, DC: American Psychiatric Association.

Banissy, Michael J., Lúcia Garrido, Flor Kusnir, Bradely Duchaine, Vincent Walsh, and Jamie Ward. 2011. Superior facial expression, but not identity recognition, in mirror-touch synesthesia. *Journal of Neuroscience* 31:1820–1824.

Barnett, Kylie J., Joanne Feeney, Michael Gormley, and Fiona N. Newell. 2009. An exploratory study of linguistic-colour associations across languages in multilingual synaesthetes. *Quarterly Journal of Experimental Psychology* 62:1343–1355.

Barnett, Kylie J., Ciara Finucane, Julian E. Asher, Gary Bargary, Aiden P. Corvin, Fiona N. Newell, and Kevin J. Mitchell. 2008. Familial patterns and the origins of individual differences in synaesthesia. *Cognition* 106:871–893.

Barnett, Kylie J., and Fiona N. Newell. 2008. Synaesthesia is associated with enhanced, self-rated visual imagery. *Consciousness and Cognition* 17:1032–1039.

Baron-Cohen, Simon, Lucy Burt, Fiona Smith-Laittan, John Harrison, and Patrick Bolton. 1996. Synaesthesia: Prevalence and familiarity. *Perception* 25:1073–1079.

Beauchamp, Michael S., and Tony Ro. 2008. Neural substrates of sound-touch synesthesia after a thalamic lesion. *Journal of Neuroscience* 28:13696–13702.

Bechtel, William, Adele A. Abrahamsen, and George Graham. 1998. The life of cognitive science. In *A Companion to Cognitive Science*, ed. William Bechtel and George Graham, 1–104. Oxford: Blackwell.

Beeli, Gian, Michaela Esslen, and Lutz Jäncke. 2005. Synaesthesia—when coloured sounds taste sweet. *Nature* 434:38–38.

Bergh, Irmelin, Ingelina Lundin Kvalem, Nina Aass, and Marianne Jensen Hjermstad. 2011. What does the answer mean? A qualitative study of how palliative cancer patients interpret and respond to the Edmonton Symptom Assessment System. *Palliative Medicine* 25:s716–s724.

Brang, David, Ursina Teuscher, Vilayanur S. Ramachandran, and Seana Coulson. 2010. Temporal sequences, synesthetic mappings, and cultural biases: The geography of time. *Consciousness and Cognition* 19:311–320.

Brookshire, Jamye, Lauren F. V. Scharff, and Laurie E. Moses. 2002. The influence of illustrations on children's book preferences and comprehension. *Reading Psychology* 23:323–339.

Callejas, Alicia, Alberto Acosta, and Juan Lupianez. 2007. Green love is ugly: Emotions elicited by synesthetic grapheme-color perceptions. *Brain Research* 1127:99–107.

Carey, Kate B. 2002. Clinically useful assessments: Substance use and comorbid psychiatric disorders. *Behaviour Research and Therapy* 40:1345–1361.

Chibbaro, Giorgio, Marco Daniele, Giovanna Alagona, Concetta Di Pasquale, Michele Cannavo, Vincenzo Rapisarda, Rita Bella, and Giovanni Pennisi. 2005. Repetitive transcranial magnetic stimulation in schizophrenic patients reporting auditory hallucinations. *Neuroscience Letters* 383:54–57.

Chomsky, Noam. 1959. A review of Skinner's verbal behavior. *Language* 35:26–58.

Cytowic, Richard E. 1993. *The Man Who Tasted Shapes*. New York: Putnam.

———. 2002. *Synesthesia: A Union of the Senses*. Cambridge, MA: MIT Press.

———. 2005. Synesthesia: Perspectives from cognitive neuroscience. *Journal of Consciousness Studies* 12:141–143.

Dailey, Aurdrey, Colin Martindale, and Jonathan Borkum. 1997. Creativity, synesthesia, and physiognomic perception. *Creativity Research Journal* 10:1–8.

Day, Sean A. 2005. Some demographic and socio-cultural aspects of synesthesia. In *Synesthesia: Perspectives from Cognitive Neuroscience*, ed. Lynn C. Robertson and Noam Sagiv,11–33. Oxford: Oxford University Press.

Dixon, Mike J., and Daniel Smilek. 2005. The importance of individual differences in grapheme-color synesthesia. *Neuron* 45:821–823.

Dixon, Mike J., Daniel Smilek, Cera Cudahy, and Philip M. Merikle. 2000. Five plus two equals yellow. *Nature* 406:365–365.

Dixon, Mike J., Daniel Smilek, and Philip M. Merikle. 2004. Not all synaesthetes are created equal: Projector versus associator synaesthetes. *Cognitive, Affective, & Behavioral Neuroscience* 4:335–343.

Duffy, Patricia L. 2001. *Blue Cats and Charteuse Kittens*. New York: Henry Holt & Company.

Eagleman, David M., Arielle D. Kagan, Stephanie S. Nelson, Deepak Sagaram, and Anand K. Sarma. 2007. A standardized test battery for the study of synesthesia. *Journal of Neuroscience Methods* 159:139–145.

Edquist, Jessica, Anina N. Rich, Cobie Brinkman, and Jason B. Mattingley. 2006. Do synaesthetic colours act as unique features in visual search? *Cortex* 42:222–231.

Fernandino, Leonardo, Marco Iacoboni, and Eran Zaidel. 2007. The effects of bilateral presentations on lateralized lexical decision. *Brain and Cognition* 64:60–67.

Fitzgibbon, Bernadette M., Melita J. Giummarra, Nellie Georgiou-Karistianis, Peter G. Enticott, and John L. Bradshaw. 2010. Shared pain: From empathy to synaesthesia. *Neuroscience and Biobehavioral Reviews* 34:500–512.

Flournoy, Théodore. 1892. L'audition colorée. *Archives des Sciences Physiques et Naturelles* 28:505–508.

Forsman, Lennart. 1993. Giving extreme responses to items in self-esteem scales: response set or personality trait? *European Journal of Psychological Assessment* 9:33–40.

Freund, Peter E. S. 2009. Social synaesthesia: Expressive bodies, embodied charisma. *Body & Society* 15:21–31.

Galton, Francis. 1880. Visualised numerals. *Nature* 22:494–495.

Gebuis, Titia, Tanja C. W. Nijboer, and Maarten J. Van der Smagt. 2009. Multiple dimensions in bi-directional synesthesia. *European Journal of Neuroscience* 29:1703–1710.

Giummarra, Melita J., Bernadette M. Fitzgibbon, Nellie Georgiou-Karistianis, Michael E. R. Nicholls, Stephen J. Gibson, and John L. Bradshaw. 2010. Ouch! My phantom leg jumps/hurts when you stab my virtual hand. *Perception* 39:1396–1407.

Graesser, Arthur C., Katja Wiemer-Hastings, Roger Kreuz, Peter Wiemer-Hastings, and Kent Marquis. 2000. Quaid: A questionnaire evaluation aid for survey methodologists. *Behavior Research Methods Instruments & Computers* 32:254–262.

Green, Jennifer A. K., and Usha Goswami. 2008. Synesthesia and number cognition in children. *Cognition* 106:463–473.

Hanggi, Juerge, Gian Beeli, Mathias S. Clechslin, and Lutz Jäncke. 2008. The multiple synaes-thete Es—neuroanatomical basis of interval-taste and tone-colour synaesthesia. *Neuroimage* 43:192–203.

Henrich, Joseph, Steven J. Heine, and Ara Norenzayan. 2010. The weirdest people in the world? *Behavioural Brain Sciences* 33:61–83; discussion 83–135.

Hochel, Matej, and Emilio G. Milan. 2008. Synaesthesia: The existing state of affairs. *Cognitive Neuropsychology* 25:93–117.

Howells, Thomas H. 1944. The experimental development of color-tone synesthesia. *Journal of Experimental Psychology* 34:87–103.

Hubbard, Edward M., A. Cyrus Arman, Vilayanur S. Ramachandran, and Geoffrey M. Boynton. 2005. Individual differences among grapheme-color synesthetes: brain-behavior correla-tions. *Neuron* 45:975–985.

Hubbard, Edward M., and Vilayanur S. Ramachandran. 2005. Neurocognitive mechanisms of synesthesia. *Neuron* 48:509–520.

Hunt, Harry T. 2005. Synaesthesia, metaphor and consciousness—a cognitive-developmental perspective. *Journal of Consciousness Studies* 12:26–45.

Hupka, Ralph B., Zbigniew Zaleski, Jurgen Otto, Lucy Reidl, and Nadia V. Tarabrina. 1997. The colors of anger, envy, fear, and jealousy—a cross-cultural study. *Journal of Cross-Cultural Psychology* 28:156–171.

Jarick, Michelle, Mike J. Dixon, Mark T. Stewart, Emily C. Maxwell, and Daniel Smilek. 2009. A different outlook on time: Visual and auditory month names elicit different mental vantage points for a time-space synaesthete. *Cortex* 45:1217–1228.

Jewanski, Jörg, Sean A. Day, and Jamie Ward. 2009. A colorful albino: The first documented case of synaesthesia, by Georg Tobias Ludwig Sachs in 1812. *Journal of the History of the Neurosciences* 18:293–303.

Josephson, S. Andrew, and Heidi E. Kirsch. 2006. Complex visual hallucinations as post-ictal cortical release phenomena. *Neurocase* 12:107–110.

Kaiser, Heinrich. 1882. Assoziation der Worte mit Farben. *Archiv für Augenheilkunde* 11:96.

Kim, Chai-Youn, and Randolph Blake. 2005. Last but not least – watercolor illusion induced by synesthetic colors. *Perception* 34:1501–1507.

Laeng, Bruno, Kenneth Hugdahl, and Karsten Specht. 2011. The neural correlate of colour distances revealed with competing synaesthetic and real colours. *Cortex* 47:320–331.

Larkin, Jill H., and Herbert A. Simon. 1987. Why a diagram is (sometimes) worth 10000 words. *Cognitive Science* 11:65–99.

Mahling, Friedrich. 1926. Das Problem der 'Audition colorée'. *Archiv für die gesamte Psychologie* 57:165–301.

Mann, Heather, Jason Korzenko, Jonathan S. A. Carriere, and Mike J. Dixon. 2009. Time-space synaesthesia – a cognitive advantage? *Consciousness and Cognition* 18:619–627.

Marks, Lawrence E. 1975. Colored-hearing synesthesia – cross-modal translations of sensory dimensions. *Psychological Bulletin* 82:303–331.

Mattingley, Jason B., Anina N. Rich, Greg Yelland, and John L. Bradshaw. 2001. Unconscious priming eliminates automatic binding of colour and alphanumeric form in synaesthesia. *Nature* 410:580–582.

Maurer, Daphne, and Charles J. Mondloch. 2006. The infant as synesthete? *Processes of Change in Brain and Cognitive Development: Attention and Performance* XXI:449–471.

McCreery, Charles, and Gordon Claridge. 1995. Out-of-the body experiences and personality. *Journal of the Society for Psychical Research* 60:129–148.

Michael, George A., Hélène Galich, Solveig Relland, and Sabine Prud'hon. 2010. Hot colors: The nature and specificity of color-induced nasal thermal sensations. *Behavioural Brain Research* 207:418–428.

Mills, Carol B., Shari R. Metzger, Catherine A. Foster, Malina N. Valentine-Gresko, and Stephanie Ricketts. 2009. Development of color-grapheme synesthesia and its effect on mathematical operations. *Perception* 38:591–605.

Mohr, Christine, and Ute Leonards. 2005. Does contextual information influence positive and negative schizotypy scores in healthy individuals? The answer is maybe. *Psychiatry Research* 136:135–141.

Mohr, Christine, Angela C. Rowe, and Matthew T. Crawford. 2008. Hemispheric differences in the processing of attachment words. *Journal of Clinical and Experimental Neuropsychology* 30:471–480.

Muggleton, Neil, Elias Tsakanikos, Vincent Walsh, and Jamie Ward. 2007. Disruption of synaesthesia following TMS of the right posterior parietal cortex. *Neuropsychologia* 45:1582–1585.

Oertel, Viola, Anna Rotarska-Jagiela, Vincent G. van de Ven, Corinna Haenschel, Konrad Maurer, and David E. J. Linden. 2007. Visual hallucinations in schizophrenia investigated with functional magnetic resonance imaging. *Psychiatry Research: Neuroimaging* 156:269–273.

Ohayon, Maurice M. 2000. Prevalence of hallucinations and their pathological associations in the general population. *Psychiatry Research* 97:153–164.

Palmeri, Thomas J., Randolph Blake, René Marois, Marci A. Flanery, and William Whetsell. 2002. The perceptual reality of synesthetic colors. *Proceedings of the National Academy of Sciences of the United States of America* 99:4127–4131.

Posey, Thomas B., and Mary E. Losch. 1984. Auditory hallucinations of hearing voices in 375 normal subjects. *Imagination, Cognition and Personality* 3:99–113.

Poulet, Emmanuel, Jérôme Brunelin, Benoit Bediou, Rémi Bation, Louis Forgeard, Jean Dalery, Thierry d'Amato, and Mohamed Saoud. 2005. Slow transcranial magnetic stimulation can rapidly reduce resistant auditory hallucinations in schizophrenia. 2005. *Biological Psychiatry* 57:188–191.

Proios, Hariklia, Dorothea Weniger, and Klaus Willmes. 2002. Number representation deficit: A bilingual case of failure to access written verbal numeral representations. *Neuropsychologia* 40:2341–2349.

Ramachandran, Vilayanur S., and David Brang. 2008. Tactile-emotion synesthesia. *Neurocase* 14:390–399.

Ramachandran, Vilayanur S., and Edward M. Hubbard. 2001. Psychophysical investigations into the neural basis of synaesthesia. *Proceedings of the Royal Society B: Biological Sciences* 268:979–983.

Rich, Anina N., John L. Bradshaw, and Jason B. Mattingley. 2005. A systematic, large-scale study of synaesthesia: Implications for the role of early experience in lexical-colour associations. *Cognition* 98:53–84.

Rich, Anina N., and Jason B. Mattingley. 2002. Anomalous perception in synaesthesia: A cognitive neuroscience perspective. *Nature Reviews Neuroscience* 3:43–52.

Riggs, Lorrin A., and Theodore Karwoski. 1934. Synaesthesia. *British Journal of Psychology* 25:29–41.

Robinson, Michael E., Cynthia D. Myers, Ian J. Sadler, Joseph L. Riley, 3rd, Steven A. Kvaal, and Michael E. Geisser. 1997. Bias effects in three common self-report pain assessment measures. *Clinical Journal of Pain* 13:74–81.

Rothen, Nicolas, and Beat Meier. 2009. Do synesthetes have a general advantage in visual search and episodic memory? A case for group studies. *PloS ONE* 4:e5037.

Rouw, Romke, and H. Steven Scholte. 2007. Increased structural connectivity in grapheme-color synesthesia. *Nature Neuroscience* 10:792–797.

——. 2010. Neural basis of individual differences in synesthetic experiences. *Journal of Neuroscience* 30:6205–6213.

Shepard, Roger N., and Jacqueline Metzler. 1971. Mental rotation of 3-dimensional objects. *Science* 171:701–703.

Simner, Julia, Jenny Harrold, Harriet Creed, Louise Monro, and Louise Foulkes. 2009. Early detection of markers for synaesthesia in childhood populations. *Brain* 132:57–64.

Simner, Julia, Catherine Mulvenna, Noam Sagiv, Elias Tsakanikos, Sarah A. Witherby, Christine Fraser, Kerstin Scott, and Jamie Ward. 2006. Synaesthesia: The prevalence of atypical cross-modal experiences. *Perception* 35:1024–1033.

Skelton, Richard, Casimir Ludwig, and Christine Mohr. 2009. A novel, illustrated questionnaire to distinguish projector and associator synaesthetes. *Cortex* 45:721–729.

Skinner, Burrhus F. 1938. *The Behavior of Organisms*. New York: Appleton-Century Crofts, 1938.

Smilek, Daniel, Mike J. Dixon, Cera Cudahy, and Philip M. Merikle. 2001. Synaesthetic photisms influence visual perception. *Journal of Cognitive Neuroscience* 13:930–936.

Smilek, Daniel, Kelly A. Malcolmson, Jonathan S. A. Carriere, Meghan Eller, Donna Kwan, and Michael Reynolds. 2007. When 3 is a jerk and T' is a king: Personifying inanimate objects in synesthesia. *Journal of Cognitive Neuroscience* 19:981–992.

Sperling, Julia M., David Prvulovic, David E. J. Linden, Wolf Singer, and Aglaja Stirn. 2006. Neuronal correlates of colour-graphemic synaesthesia: A fMRI study. *Cortex* 42:295–303.

Trevena, Lyndal J., Heather M. Davey, Alexandra Barratt, Phyllis Butow, and Patrina Caldwell. 2006. A systematic review on communicating with patients about evidence. *Journal of Evaluation in Clinical Practice* 12 (1):13–23.

Tyler, Christopher W. 2005. Varieties of synesthetic experience. In *Synesthesia: Perspectives from Cognitive Neuroscience*, ed. Lynn C. Robertson and Noam Sagiv, 34–46. New York: Oxford University Press.

Wagar, Brandon M., Mike J. Dixon, Daniel Smilek, and Cera Cudahy. 2002. Colored photisms prevent object-substitution masking in digit-color synesthesia. *Brain and Cognition* 48:606–611.

Walker, Peter, J. Gavin Bremner, Uschi Mason, Jo Spring, Karen Mattock, Allan Slater, and Scott P. Johnson. 2010. Preverbal infants' sensitivity to synaesthetic cross-modality correspondences. *Psychological Science* 21:21–25.

Ward, Jamie, Brett Huckstep, and Elias Tsakanikos. 2006. Sound-colour synaesthesia: To what extent does it use cross-modal mechanisms common to us all? *Cortex* 42:264–280.

Ward, Jamie, Ryan Li, Shireen Salih, and Noam Sagiv. 2007. Varieties of grapheme-colour synaesthesia: A new theory of phenomenological and behavioural differences. *Consciousness and Cognition* 16:913–931.

Ward, Jamie, and Jason B. Mattingley. 2006. Synaesthesia: An overview of contemporary findings and controversies. *Cortex* 42:129–136.

Ward, Jamie, and Julia Simner. 2003. Lexical-gustatory synaesthesia: Linguistic and conceptual factors. *Cognition* 89:237–261.

Watson, John D. 1928. *The Ways of Behaviourism*. New York: Harper and Brothers, 1928.

Yaro, Caroline, and Jamie Ward. 2007. Searching for Shereshevskii: What is superior about the memory of synaesthetes? *Quarterly Journal of Experimental Psychology* 60:681–695.

CHAPTER 23

SYNESTHESIA

A psychosocial approach

MARKUS ZEDLER AND MARIE REHME

INTRODUCTION

From the very beginning, when we first started inviting synesthetes to the *Hanover Synaesthesia Café* in the early 1990s, we began to wonder whether there was something special about their personalities. The Synaesthesia Café was founded by Professor Hinderk Emrich, and is an annual meeting of invited synesthetes held at the Hanover Medical School, usually on the first weekend of Advent. All synesthetes who get in contact with us are invited along, and we felt it was important to select out other interested parties such as members of the press and scientists. The Synaesthesia Café is therefore a place for synesthetes only—as well as for those of us who prepare their cakes, coffee, and tea (!), the latter being a particular favorite of our invited guests, despite Germany's more extensive coffee-drinking tradition. But before we get carried away and suggest that tea-drinking might be a special trait associated with synesthesia, we point out that the very experience of meeting synesthetes has nonetheless led to more serious investigations about their personality types. We began to ask whether anything in general could be inferred about these, and this is the focus of the current chapter.

The contact with synesthetes that is afforded by our yearly meetings is light-hearted and free of interactive stress. We have always appreciated our dealings with synesthetes and are glad to have the opportunity to meet them under these conditions. It is easy to see that synesthetes feel comfortable in an atmosphere of open conversation and interest, without us creating any sensation of voyeurism. Over the years these experiences with synesthetes of all types have led us to ask whether the pleasure in these meetings comes from a special personality type, the *synesthetic personality*. In this chapter we describe the features that might be encompassed within this personality type, although with one clear caveat. The synesthetes we are describing are those that have made the effort to contact us and attend our meetings. In this sense, they are a special group of synesthetes, who may or may not be reflective of their wider peer group. Nonetheless, these observations have been made by our psychiatrists here in Hanover, who are used to seeing a wide range of personality types, many of whom have also self-referred. To this extent, therefore, we hope we are able to describe what may be different about the very large numbers of synesthetes that we have encountered in the last decade. Furthermore, we hope that our observations might spark further research on perhaps more randomly selected cohorts of synesthetes. As such, our comments might be taken as hypotheses for further exploration.

In many discussions in the Café or in one-on-one consultations we have met strong "synesthetic" characters with low levels of anxiety, who seem to have a firm self-consciousness with very little appearance of any negative aspects (e.g., of narcissism or other negative traits). They seem to be mentally healthier than others who visit us. This might be no surprise given at least one neurophysiological model of the function of synesthesia, which suggests a role of the so-called limbic system (e.g., Cytowic 1989), responsible for emotional, motivational, and urge functions in the brain. This model assumes a hyperactivity of emotional brain functions in synesthetes, which may have some psychological implications for their personalities. As such, we might offer the tentative opinion that synesthesia could serve as a protection against certain mental illnesses, or even be some type of "opposite" to emotional disturbances such as schizophrenia. In any case, in the following section we discuss how certain personality traits, whether or not they are firmly associated with synesthesia, might come to interact with the state of being synesthetic, at least in those who have visited our labs, clinics, and café.

MENTAL PROTECTION BY SYNESTHESIA

Through our work on synesthesia we have been in contact with more than 500 synesthetes. They have written to us, called us with their anecdotes or problems, and asked many questions about their experiences. Many have also visited us, and some have come to our outpatient consultations. In response, we have asked them about their lives, their synesthesia, and their psychosocial outlooks. Our clinic also specializes in addiction, although to our knowledge there has not been one synesthete who suffered addiction, to either alcohol or drugs. Normally in Germany, around 10% of people experience alcohol-related problems to some extent. When talking with our synesthetic contacts about their mental health, the expected 50 subjects with any degree of problematic consumption of alcohol could not be found. Although this may only be true of those synesthetes within our selected sample, we nonetheless wondered, therefore, whether there is any protection against this factor for people with synesthesia.

Another unusual aspect has been found particularly in certain female synesthetes. When investigating whether any (or no) pathological symptom could be found in synesthetes, we paid special attention to the following. In several single cases, synesthetes described what can be referred to as "auto-aggressive behavior," and this came either with or without a post-traumatic stress disorder. Auto-aggressive behavior is behavior such as self-harm (e.g., cutting one's arms) and this was described to us by a very small group of synesthetes when they found themselves in emotionally overloaded situations. In every case, however, the behavior lasted only a very short period of time, and then stopped completely. After this auto-aggressive period ended, there was no evidence of any continued personality disorder (i.e., no borderline disease). In other words, synesthetes were showing symptoms which could be found in certain psychiatric disorders, but in the absence of those disorders themselves. In psychiatry, it is not unusual to find temporary psychopathological symptoms without any underlying pathological validity. In psychodynamics we learn that symptoms are often necessary mechanisms when dealing with conflicts or even when simply dealing with life. So there are two possible ways to explain these synesthetes' psychopathological symptoms, which nonetheless ended quickly. On the one hand, it may be that synesthetes used this auto-aggressive behavior to deal with their synesthesia and the fact that they are different to most people (at least in their perceptual life). Psychodynamic theory suggests that a strong processing of identity does indeed need "tools." However, because synesthetes are not, ultimately, mentally ill, these symptoms quickly terminated once they had served their purpose. On the other hand, it may be that synesthetes experience the same life efforts as other people, and may develop psychopathological symptoms such as self-harm from any psycho-reactive situation, just like anybody else. However, they may find it easier to extract themselves from depressive circuits, which would explain the early termination of these unwanted behaviors. In other words, the brain may heal itself and not become stuck in depression or addiction. It may even be the case that this propensity for recovery relates to the fact that synesthetes are known to have hyperconnected brains (Rouw and Scholte 2007). In any case, it seems to be that these synesthetes do not find themselves stuck in difficult situations, and that they go into problems with lower levels of anxiety and come out stronger. One synesthete told us: "When I recognized a conflict—maybe with my friend or with myself—I feel it very hard. It's there...I do not want to escape...My friend knows me and he knows that the outcome of my dealing with conflict is normally always positive." In this way, the synesthete seems to automatically follow the type of behavioral patterns that might be recommended by a psychologist. And this may not be the only piece of helpful behavior which synesthetes automatically employ. In the same way that depression and addiction are treated by numerous different but integrated techniques (such as psychotherapy, ergo therapy, physiotherapy, art therapy, music therapy, etc.) our synesthetes appeared to have a type of inbuilt pluralism in their response to problems.

When Synesthetes Meet with Psychiatrists

One possible dilemma for a synesthete could be if he comes to learn that his synesthesia is only very rarely associated with psychological problems. This might cause problems if he feels himself experiencing difficulties in daily life. His prior knowledge about the robustness of synesthetes might lead him to ask: "Am I so weak that I need help, even though I am a synesthete?" But of course, any person can get into a situation where psychological support would be helpful, and the same is true of synesthetes. In rare cases, synesthetes might experience depressive symptoms as a result of the process of searching for their identity, given that they are different from the average person, at least as far as their percepts are concerned. Synesthetes are sometimes misunderstood, and sometimes feel it is better not to tell others about their synesthesia. Indeed, the phenomenon of synesthesia is not so well known that all medicals practitioners and psychologists know of it. In at least one case, a synesthete had visited the doctor after recognizing that she had a perception which other people around her did not have. She reported feeling very frightened, wondering whether it could be some type of psychotic illness or disorder, related to foolishness or even the prospect of death, or at least to psychiatric hospital and to stigmatization. The doctor had never heard of the phenomenon, but he associated the synesthetic perception with hallucinations such as those found with schizophrenia and prescribed a neuroleptic drug. However, when synesthetes visit a psychiatrist, they normally come because of some problem *other* than an overload of the senses. In Germany, some therapists send their patients with special questions to our workgroup at the Hannover Medical School. In most of these cases, some brief support leads to a satisfactory outcome, in which the synesthete accepts that synesthesia is simply a normal but alternative variant of consciousness.

SYNESTHESIA AS AN ADVANTAGE

As well as questions about synesthesia as an emotional phenomenon we also receive many questions about how to use synesthesia to increase cognitive power, for example, from mathematicians, teachers, and even once from a Japanese television team. Published case reports tell us about mnemonists with synesthesia (Luria 1968), or about other special cognitive qualities of synesthetes. It has even been suggested that synesthesia might interact with autism spectrum disorders (ASD) to create individuals with extraordinary skills of "savantism" (e.g., Baron-Cohen et al. 2007). In summary, a number of studies have now shown a range of advantages associated with synesthesia, and these are reviewed elsewhere in this volume. In such cases, the focus of these researchers was on *cognitive* advantages, although we might also look for advantages in modes of consciousness, which might lead synesthetes to an enlightened emotional and social well-being, or at least to better approaches to understanding life.

Categorizing personalities comes with strong reservations, of course, especially in a group of people such as synesthetes, who are psychologically normal and not unwell. However, talking about how their personalities might confer advantages appears to trigger different comments from our synesthetes. They feel fully understood by the science community when they are considered totally "normal," but slightly misunderstood when they are investigated as being different neurobiologically (e.g., in brain imaging studies).

There are many missing elements in our knowledge about synesthetes, and so we may fail to understand them to the extent that any man or a woman would normally like to be understood. This seeking-to-be-understood has been a central problem in many of the accounts we have been told by synesthetes. Although synesthetes appear to have a great interest in the scientific and neurological basis of their abilities, neuroimaging and neurophysiologic measures alone do not represent a sufficient answer to their dialectic conflict of being both normal and in a way special.

Since synesthesia seems to be only one symptom of a hyperconnected brain (Hänggi, Wotruba, and Jäncke 2011), there may also be a kind of personality-type influenced by this particular way of experiencing the world. In other words, synesthesia, like creativity, emotional intelligence, intuition, and even special intelligence might predict certain specialties in personality. For this reason, we began to investigate synesthetes using psychometric methods, i.e., by psychological questionnaires as well as by interviews focusing on qualitative social investigation. After our tests, we pass our findings back to our synesthetes and discuss their meaning. We will give details of these results further later (see "Results of the personality study").

LONELINESS

The earliest experience of being a synesthete in the world often elicits a sense of being alone. Nobody appears to have the same perceptions as you, and you are apparently totally unique. Because of this, you may feel that nobody could know exactly what is it like to be you. This, in particular, may be one of the most difficult and intense experiences, and may be the key experience that synesthetes encounter when they are first shaken from their colorful world by learning that others do not share their sensations. But a second realization is that others may find life more difficult because they do *not* have synesthesia. When the synesthete first recognizes that others do not have an identical scale of perception, his or her identity may become formed around this fact (Emrich 2011). Hence, synesthetes may be first defined by a feeling of difference. Although certain regularities in synesthesia have been shown from synesthete to synesthete in the way that each colors his world (e.g., the letter A tends to be red for a significantly large group of synesthetes; Emrich, Schneider, and Zedler 2004), it is still the case that a synesthete will never find another person with *exactly* the same colors for *all* their letters. Furthermore, synesthetes can experience many different sensations (color, taste, touch, etc.) from many different triggers (letters, music, food), and one can even find individual differences even where synesthetes otherwise experience similar triggers and sensations (Rouw and Scholte 2010). Together, these combined experiences lead to a clear notion of individuality. Psychologically, humans seek to form part of a group in whichever way they can. To be within a group gives identity, and this is an important goal for any human being in a social environment. The sense of being "out-grouped" can therefore exert severe emotional pain.

Qualia are the subjective contents of experiences, which some have suggested cannot be measured by neuroscientific methods. You can investigate the mechanisms of how synesthesia works, but you cannot know what it *feels like* to perceive synesthetic sensations. Given these characteristics of qualia, nobody can feel exactly how it is to be another person. But in synesthesia this difference is overly reinforced. One way out of this conflict is to try to *explain* what it is like to be synesthetic. However, because of the difficulties in explaining this in everyday language, many synesthetes find a compulsion towards artistic creativity (e.g., art or music) where the limitations of language are removed. Another way of removing the conflict between the sense of individuality and the wish to be part of a group is by coming together at events such as the Synaesthesia Café in Hannover, or via any of the now-numerous Internet forums for synesthetes.

In establishing their personality and identity, synesthetes might experience typical highs and lows. There is the initial confrontation with the scientific label "synesthesia," for example. There are uplifting descriptions of the phenomenon as a special advantage in life, and there are suggestions that it might be better to be a synesthete in terms of intelligence, creativity, emotion, memory, and so on. But there are also notions about the rarity of the condition, which might (unnecessarily) worry synesthetes about their mental state. Finally, the condition could even evoke stigmatization if synesthetes discuss their experiences with non-synesthetes who are unfamiliar with the condition.

If synesthesia, per se, is only one symptom of a hyperconnected brain (Hänggi, Wotruba, and Jäncke 2011) we might consider the "qualia problem" (how to understand the internal life of another person) not only in regard to synesthetic perceptions themselves, but also in regard to any other collateral features that may accompany synesthesia. Overall, the synesthetes we have spoken with would like to be understood. Since some express strong beliefs in their intuition about others (see later), being understood themselves to the same degree could be their main challenge.

SYNESTHETES IN CONFLICTS

So-called emotionally-mediated synesthetes perceive their feelings in other sensory qualities (Ward 2004). For example, they might see angry, sad, happy, or any manner of emotions in particular colors. This leads to a very intense experience of emotions. Sometimes these accompanying colors might make it easier to identify emotions, and this might have its uses. In psychotherapy, for example, colors could be used in the process of identifying emotions in conditions where this would otherwise be difficult, such as post-traumatic stress disorder or borderline personality disorder. In any supportive or therapeutic situation, these colors might help resolve emotional conflicts, and may develop much faster than expected, but also be deeper or more extreme than usual. While having more than one percept associated with any given stimulus might have certain benefits (e.g., in memory functions, as reviewed elsewhere in this volume) it might also lead to a more intensive consciousness. Emotionally-mediated synesthetes in our group talk about having not only a combination of emotions and senses, but also about their use in problem solving or emotional conflicts, where they find that their colored emotions give more intense connections to other functions such as memory. As such, these colors can serve as an orientation system for them.

SOCIAL INTERACTIONS

We have been curious about whether the hyperconnectivity associated with synesthesia has any other implications for thinking. To address this, we asked synesthetes if they found any difference between talking with other synesthetes or talking with non-synesthetes. One answered: "Talking with non-synesthetes is sometime hard, because they are so slow to understand." His/her suggestion was that a speed of understanding comes not only when discussing synesthetic themes, but when discussing practically everything. Another synesthete said: "When I see that my boyfriend is having an inner conflict, I see it in colors; it's a kind of red and brown or even yellow, which appears in the air. For him it is really hard to see what happened. And it doesn't help his self-confidence to know I knew before him that something was wrong. Twice we've even thought about splitting up because of this, but thank God we didn't do that." These anecdotes suggest that synesthesia can act as a bond or a division between individuals. Social studies about the impact of synesthesia on living together are somewhat missing in synesthesia research, and many hints about how synesthesia might play out in social interactions can be seen any time that synesthetes meet, be it in consultations, at conferences, at the Synaesthesia Café, or when working together (e.g., when coming together to found the German Synaesthesia Association). Future studies might explore the nature of social interactions among synesthetes, examining their approach to problem solving or even studying how they spend their time in groups of synesthetes. Social interactions could be investigated either in behavioral tasks, or in neurobiological investigations via linked functional magnetic resonance imaging (Montague et al. 2002).

SYNESTHESIA UNDER STRESSFUL CONDITIONS

In our research projects, certain synesthetic subjects have told us about a feeling of inconvenience caused by synesthesia in stressful situations. In such situations (e.g., rapid problem solving) the hyperarousal associated with synesthesia often seems to exacerbate the stress of the situation. From these reports, it is important to understand why some synesthetes, in particular those with multiple synesthetic symptoms, suffer from this, being unable to concentrate for long periods of time when under stress. Those synesthetes who experience problems tell us that they try to avoid stressful settings altogether because they feel they are in some way "over-stimulated." It doesn't seem to matter what form the pressure takes, whether it is a pressure on the emotions, or simply from a task with a time limit. Synesthetes also report synesthesia-related pressures in daily life. When driving a car, for example, they can experience an overwhelming synesthetic perception from the different impressions of radio music, scenery, talking partner, or children in the back seat. We sought to examine the effects of pressure in more detail, with a possible alternative hypothesis that synesthesia might instead help the individuals to better manage a situation that causes pressure.

To assess this point we ran a short test with a healthy 25-year-old woman with multiple synesthetic symptoms. We explored the possible hyperarousal of the participant under a stressful (i.e., fast decision-making) situation, using an interview technique. In our task, the subject had to solve an easy Sudoku puzzle. The synesthete reported suffering from severe difficulties when attempting to solve the puzzle, and these included difficulty recognizing the numbers under the time pressure. This was exacerbated by a colorful confusion in front of her eyes, tied in with her synesthetic experiences. She suggested that this confusion limited her concentration and logical problem-solving abilities. She told us, furthermore, that she had had encountered similar situations in the past, whenever there were too many synesthetic impressions at all once. When this happened, she retreated into herself and tried to break down the synesthetic sensations to a reduced level. In our study, the participant tried to eliminate the overcrowded sense of synesthesia by stopping the experiment. The woman described being unable to think logically under stress from the puzzle in its timed situation. From this study, it seems as if synesthesia can therefore be a disturbing factor in problem solving.

Narcissism

To further investigate the synesthetic personality, we performed an investigation with the Narcissism Inventory (NI; Denecke and Hilgenstock 1989) and the Freiburg Personality Inventory (FPI; Messner 1968). Our study started with the hypothesis derived from our first-hand encounters with numerous synesthetes, that synesthetes may suffer less from narcissism and negative symptoms such as anxiety (i.e., that they may feel more content with their lives). One hundred and three synesthetes were investigated by use of questionnaires. Our findings were reported back to synesthetes themselves, and the results of the NI in particular led to great interest from our participants. In this test, related to the group as a whole, synesthesia correlated with a number of significantly high narcissism scores. In the subgroup of the test which deals with "the threatened self" there were significant findings of: a more helpless self, social and archaic retreat, and higher rates of depersonalization and de-realization. But on the other hand, synesthetes also showed a significantly highly basic potential of hope, which means they had strong confidence in their possibilities and power. In the subgroup of the test dealing with the classic narcissistic self, synesthetes showed a distinct sense of their own self-significance, which is a trait that might provide protection against critics and insults. Self-regulatory processes were identified in synesthetes by the strategy of Grounded Theory, a qualitative method for creating a theory by empirical data (Strauss and Corbin 1996). In particular, a higher score of narcissism is found in people who have initiated a strong process of identity (the searching for who you are), and this factor might play an important role in the relationship between synesthesia, personality, and mental health (Kaluza 2008).

We also tested these 103 synesthetes (86 women, 17 men) with the Revised Freiburg Personality Inventory and compared the results with a large normative group according to age, which has been shown to play a role in responses to this questionnaire. Our analyses provided interesting results for our question about a special synesthetic type (Plümer 2008). The test categorized individuals according to several signs of personality. Not all these signs showed significant differences for synesthetes compared to norms. However, the following listed categories showed interesting results for certain groups of synesthetes. In presenting these findings, however, we are clear to point out once again that our sample were self-selected synesthetes who had made an effort to come forward to meet us. As such, this fact alone may account for at least some portion of the personality traits shown by our synesthete group (e.g., the fact that they are more likely to be socially engaged and have a higher achievement orientation):

1. *Social engagement*: social engagement played an especially important role among synesthetic women. Significantly higher scores in social orientation were found in female synesthetes aged 25 to 44 years old, compared to norms. It seems to be that these synesthetes feel more socially responsible, and more ready to help others.

2. *Achievement orientation*: significance in this item was found in the group of 45- to 59-year-old female synesthetes with a similar trend in the younger group, also. They showed a significantly higher achievement orientation, were more ambitious, and more active. Synesthetic women liked to compete with others and gave a high priority to their professional careers.

3. *Excitability*: 25 to 44-year-old synesthetic women found it significantly easier to become excited, were more sensitive, and even sometimes more unrestrained.

4. *Somatic complaints*: we found significance only in the group of 45- to 59-year-old, and older, synesthetic women. They especially showed fewer somatic complaints than controls, a higher psycho-vegetative stability (i.e., stress factors don't irritate them too easily), and fewer psychosomatic complaints such as hand tremor or chest pain.

5. *Health concern*: synesthetic 45- to 59-year-old women were significantly less concerned about their health and robustness.

6. *Life satisfaction*: the hypothesis of a higher score in life satisfaction in synesthetes could not be shown after Bonferroni adjustment, although a trend was evident. The older group especially (45–59 years) showed more life satisfaction, were happier, and were more self-content. If given the option, they would not choose to change their past history.

7. *Self-assurance*: for the item of "inhibitedness" there was a trend in especially the younger and older synesthetes for being unconstrained and self-assured. These individuals like to contact others, and the younger synesthetes were also more extraverted, more impulsive, and more lively compared with norms. They like to act, and to tell others what to do. Older synesthetes showed a higher emotional stability, were more relaxed, and more self-confident. Men were not very well investigated, because there were far fewer men (17) in the sample than women (86), and they showed only a trend for higher social engagement.

Finally, when comparing our synesthetes to controls by age, another important fact was revealed. The older synesthetes sometimes showed signs of long-term suffering from a feeling of being "abnormal," without knowing that synesthesia is a normal variant of a healthy consciousness. In contrast, the young group showed no relicts of long-term anxiety or thoughts of being mentally ill. These younger participants learned about the quality of their special perceptions earlier in their life, which is one more piece of evidence for the importance of the growing public understanding about the condition of synesthesia.

Sexuality

We performed a study to investigate the sexuality of synesthetes because a number of our synesthetes report synesthetic perceptions during orgasm, and this type of experience has been reflected in other reports. Day (2005) found that 23 of 1147 synesthete subjects had orgasms as inducers for colored visions, making up 2% of that sample. Nineteen synesthetes participated in our investigation by filling out two questionnaires. One test was a general investigation of sexual health "Kurzfragebogen zur Erfassung sexueller Probleme" (KFSP), a short questionnaire for the evaluation of sexual problems, and one test investigated general forms of altered states of consciousness: OAVAV (questionnaire for "ozeanische Selbstentgrenzung, angstvolle Ich-Auflösung, visionäre Umstrukturierung, auditorische Wahrnehmungsveränderung und Vigilanzreduktion"). This test is a German version of the assessment of altered states of consciousness (ASCs; Dittrich 1998) and investigates the following three dimensions: "oceanic boundless" (falling deeper like in a kind of trance), "dread of ego dissolution," and "visionary restructuralization." Our results showed no signs of sexual problems or other deviations (e.g., in sexual appetite, arousal/lubrication, orgasm ability) in the diagnostic scale KFSP, and no higher score of general sexual satisfaction. However, we found significantly higher scores of "oceanic boundlessness" and "visionary restructuralization" in the group of synesthetes. In other words, it seems that synesthetic women do feel a deeper state of trance in sexuality. In general there were no signs of a higher satisfaction, but achieving a deeper trance and synesthetic colors in orgasms may lead female synesthetes to a deeper level of fulfillment.

EMPATHY AND LUCIDITY

According to the three-component-system hypothesis of perception (Emrich 2005), sensation is the bottom-up mechanism of information in the brain, constructivism is the top-down component, and a third component, censorship, is a type of "ratiomorphous" apparatus (i.e., a preconscious organizing centre, of the type Jung called the "Self"). It is the very strong top-down mechanism which seems to be the source of the firm belief in many synesthetes that they have unusual abilities in intuition, and also in abilities such as fortune-telling or death-foretelling. Our top-down process of constructivism helps us to know how to act in the world, comparing our daily perceptions with memories from the past and with our world model, in order to evoke an internal construct of fictional reality (Prinz 2006). The experiences we encounter in the world become "viable" by becoming categorized within our system of possibilities within the world model. Although in conditions such as schizophrenia, the top-down-processes seem to be disturbed, these appear to work exceptionally well in synesthesia.

Many synesthetes describe phenomena which could fall into the category of "synchronicity" (Jung 1993). Ask a group of them, as we have, and you get an unbelievably firm agreement in beliefs for the power of intuition (and a similar observation also made by Cytowic (1998)). Contributing to their firm belief is strong déjà vu processes and changes in the ascribing of memories to a period. This belief in the power of precognition may therefore be a particular feature of people with synesthesia. However, we should point out that Rich, Bradshaw, and Mattingley (2005) investigated this same issue. When they compared synesthetes' responses to those from the general population, it because clear that non-synesthetes, too, reported extremely high levels of these unusual experiences as well. As such, our synesthetes may be exhibiting nothing more than an "average" belief system, similar to others. It would therefore be useful for us to systematically compare their reported beliefs with those of a control group.

One particular form of synesthesia is synesthesia triggered by touch and pain, which could be from touch/pain in the synesthete himself but also for the touch/pain experienced by others. This latter is called mirror touch synesthesia, in which viewing another being touched causes a sensation of touch against the synesthete's own body (Banissy et al. 2011; Fitzgibbon et al. 2011). This condition has been linked with increased empathy in these synesthetes, and we might suppose that a stronger ability for empathy could change other components within the character of the synesthete. At the very least, the ability to identify pain in another person would be of clear value (Fitzgibbon et al. 2011). The possibility of shared emotions has not been yet investigated and may fit well with the assumed social competence of synesthetes, and may even contribute to the strong belief in certain synesthetes of having a sixth sense (Emrich, Schneider, and Zedler 2004).

Another often-reported phenomenon by synesthetes is lucid dreaming. This is a form of dreaming in which one is *aware* that one is dreaming and that the events in the dream are not reality. It is possible to influence these dreams and one may perform volitional actions such as flying from roof-tops, or other types of experiences which are only afforded while dreaming. Lucid dreaming is used in special forms of psychotherapy and appears to be a common phenomenon in sleeping synesthetes, according to those who attend our sessions. To investigate this special dreaming as a higher conscious, we tested 100 synesthetes with a specifically developed questionnaire (Zedler et al. 2003). Eighty-two per cent of the synesthetes described clearly the experiences of lucid dreaming. Since this is used in certain fields as a therapeutic device, we might ask whether synesthetes benefit from this higher lucidity. What does it tell us about their consciousness?

Conclusions and Future Directions

In this chapter we have described the characteristics reported by a group of synesthetes who attend our labs, clinics, and the Synaesthesia Café. We have aimed to provide a summary of the descriptions they offer, without firmly suggesting that these characteristics are true of all synesthetes. Instead, our aim has been to ask how synesthesia might interact with those qualities described, and whether we might see viable explanations for how synesthesia might have given rise to some of these qualities, at least in some individuals. In summarizing these qualities, we make it clear that from a psychiatric point of view, there is nothing "abnormal" about the synesthetic personality type, if such a thing exists. We have not found synesthesia to be associated with any psychiatric symptom or extreme personality trait. Indeed, quite the contrary, synesthesia might be considered something of the opposite to conditions such as schizophrenia, which, while also associated with visual disturbances, has visual symptoms that are, more properly, hallucinations (unlike synesthesia). Emotionally, synesthetes seem highly functioning, even perhaps something opposite to those experiencing ASD, since synesthetes show in many cases a type of brilliant emotional and social competence. When talking in confidence with synesthetes, one often hears descriptions of experiences which could come straight from C.G. Jung's writing on synchronicity, and this could perhaps be explained by top-down constructivism with firm belief.

If future studies confirm our hypothesis that synesthesia endows a protective quality for mental health, this may take synesthesia research into a new direction. We invite different disciplines to investigate synesthesia as a psychodynamic phenomenon. Genuine synesthesia seems to be a hereditary phenomenon. It cannot be learned, but it may exert an influence not only on the synesthetes himself, but on those with whom he or she interacts. This is true also for interactions with the scientist; scientists have to deal with both their fascination for the subject, and also their fascination for the participants themselves, for their way of life, and not at least (from an analytical point of view) for the psychodynamic processes involved when working together with synesthetes. Working with synesthetes and with other interdisciplinary synesthesia researchers provides fruitful exchanges between participants and scientists. Synesthesia conferences themselves are thrilling multidisciplinary events where synesthetes meet with scientists and artists, in a way that is fundamentally different from most academic conferences in any other field of study. Through these conferences and through scientific investigations, it is possible that future research might uncover new ways to study the fates and lives of those who live with synesthesia.

REFERENCES

Banissy, Michael J., Roi Cohen Kadosh, Gerrit W. Maus, Vincent Walsh, and Jamie Ward. 2011. Prevalence, characteristics and a neurocognitive model of mirror-touch synaesthesia. *Experimental Brain Research* 198 (2–3):261–272.

Baron-Cohen, Simon, Daniel Bor, Jac Billington, Julian Asher, Sally Wheelwright, and Chris Ashwin. 2007. Savant memory in a man with colour from number synaesthesia and Asperger syndrome. *Journal of Consciousness Studies* 14:237–251.

Cytowic, Richard E. 1989. *Synesthesia. A Union of the Senses.* New York: Springer Verlag.

Day, Sean. 2005. Some demographic and socio-cultural aspects of synesthesia. In *Synaesthesia: Perspectives from Cognitive Neuroscience,* ed. Lynn C. Robertson and Noam Sagiv, 11–33. New York: Oxford University Press.

Denecke, Friedrich-Wilhelm, and Burkhard Hilgenstock. 1989. *Das Narzissmusinventar.* Bern: Huber.

Dittrich, A. 1998. The standardized psychometric assessment of altered states of consciousness (ASCs) in humans. *Pharmacopsychiatry* 31:80–84.

Emrich, Hinderk M. 2005. Ego-experience, synaethesia and emotion. *Analytische Psychologie,* 34:243–250.

——. 2011. Synästhesie und Suchbewegungen des Geistes im kontextuellen Raum: Heilende Atmosphären? Presented at Atmosphären erleben. Dimensionen eines diffusen Phänomens, Karlsruhe, 4 June.

Emrich, Hinderk M., Udo Schneider, and Markus Zedler. 2004. *Welche Farbe hat der Montag? Synästhesie: Das Leben mit verknüpften Sinnen.* Stuttgart: Hirzel Verlag.

Fitzgibbon, Bernadette M., Melita J. Giummarra, Nellie Georgiou-Karistianis, Peter G. Enticott, and John L. Bradshaw. 2011. Shared pain: From empathy to synaesthesia. *Neuroscience and Biobehavioural Reviews* 34:500–512.

Hänggi, Jurgen, Diana Wotruba, and Lutz Jäncke. 2011. Globally altered structural brain network topology in grapheme-color synesthesia. *The Journal of Neuroscience* 31 (15):5816–5828.

Jung, Carl G. 1993. *Synchronicity: An Acausal Connecting Principle.* Bollingen: Bollingen Foundation.

Kaluza, D. 2008. "Ich bin Synästhetiker"—Zur Bedeutung des wissenschaftlich etikettierten Synästhesiephänomens für Synästhetiker. Thesis, Free University of Berlin.

Luria, Aleksandr R. 1968. *Mind of a Mnemonist.* London: Basic Books.

Messner, K. 1968. Documentation and statistics in the psychosomatic department of the University Clinic of Freiburg i. Br. *Zeitschrift für Psychosomatishe Medizin Psychoanalyse* 14(4):298–301.

Montague, P. Read., Gregory S. Berns, Jonathan D. Cohen, Samuel M. McClure, Guiseppe Pagnoni, Mukesh Dhamala, Michael C. Wiest, *et al.* 2002. Hyperscanning: Simultaneous fMRI during linked social interactions. *NeuroImage* 16 (4):1159–1164.

Plümer, Sara. 2008. *Ein evaluierender Vergleich von Persönlichkeitsmerkmalen bei Synästhetikern.* Dissertation, Hannover Medical School.

Prinz, Wolfgang. 2006. What re-enactment earns us. *Cortex* 42 (4):515–517.

Rich, Anina N., John L. Bradshaw, and Jason B. Mattingley. 2005. A systematic, large-scale study of synaesthesia: Implications for the role of early experience in lexical-colour associations. *Cognition* 98:53–84.

Rouw, Romke, and H. Steven Scholte. 2007. Increased structural connectivity in grapheme-color synesthesia. *Nature Neuroscience* 10:792–797.

——. 2010. Neural basis of individual differences in synesthetic experiences. *The Journal of Neuroscience* 30 (18):6205–6213.

Strauss, Anselm, and Juliet Corbin. 1996. *Grounded Theory: Grundlagen qualitativer Sozialforschung*. Weinheim: Beltz.

Ward, Jamie. 2004. Emotionally mediated synaesthesia. *Cognitive Neuropsychology* 21 (7):761–772.

Zedler, Markus, Udo Schneider, Mine Büyükoktay, G. Wegener, and Hinderk M. Emrich 2003. Synästhesie als "Hyperbinding"—ein Modell in der Bewusstseinsforschung. Untersuchungen zur Phänomenologie an einem deutschsprachigen Synästhetikerkollektiv. In *Experimentelle Psychologie—Abstracts der 45. Tagung experimentell arbeitender Psychologen*, ed. Jürgen Golz, Franz Faul, and Rainer Mausfeld, 43. Kiel: Christian-Albrechts-Universität zu Kiel.

PART V

NEUROLOGICAL BASIS OF SYNESTHESIA

CHAPTER 24

SYNESTHESIA AND FUNCTIONAL IMAGING

EDWARD M. HUBBARD

INTRODUCTION

Researchers have debated the neural mechanisms that give rise to synesthesia since the earliest days of synesthesia research (e.g., Flournoy 1893). However, it is only with the advent of sophisticated neuroimaging techniques like positron emission tomography (PET) and, more recently, functional magnetic resonance imaging (fMRI) that these questions could be empirically addressed by examining patterns of brain activation in synesthetes and non-synesthetes alike. Since the first attempt to measure brain activity related to synesthetic experiences over 25 years ago (Cytowic and Stump 1985), our understanding of brain functions and the sophistication of neuroimaging methods has increased dramatically.

These advances have led to a number of detailed neurophysiological models of synesthesia, and to a wealth of studies aimed at testing them. Here, I will not discuss studies using methods such as electroencephalography (Brang et al. 2011; Niccolai, Wascher, and Stoerig 2012) or magnetoencephalography (Brang et al. 2010) although in many cases the findings using these other methods converge with those from neuroimaging methods (for a review of studies using these other methods, see Hubbard et al. 2011; Jäncke, Chapter 28; Ramachandran and Brang, Chapter 48, this volume). Instead, I focus exclusively on functional neuroimaging studies of various forms of synesthesia (summarized in Table 24.1 at the end of this chapter), in which neural activity is inferred from bloodflow measures of metabolic activity.

Early studies of synesthesia focused primarily on synesthesia involving color, elicited either by auditory words and tones (word/tone-color synesthesia), or by letters and numbers (grapheme-color synesthesia) by contrasting brain responses to stimuli that either did or did not elicit synesthetic experiences. However, more recent studies have moved away from these simple task-based designs to explore functional connectivity in the synesthetic brain independent of whether participants are experiencing synesthesia or not. One advantage of these "resting state" studies is that they may be less affected by possible demand characteristics or motivational factors that may differ between synesthetes and non-synesthetes. Additionally, the models and methods that were originally developed to explore tone-color synesthesia and grapheme-color synesthesia are now being applied to the exploration of other forms of synesthesia. Here, I describe these studies both in an historical context and as they relate to different neurophysiological models of synesthesia.

MW: The First Neuroimaging Study of Synesthesia

Cytowic and Wood (1982a, 1982b) suggested that synesthesia was due to a *neural linkage* rather than *semantic mediation* based on the distinct, reliable percepts reported by two synesthetic participants, one who experienced taste-shape synesthesia (MW), and the other who experienced music-color synesthesia. Because other neural events including lysergic acid diethylamide (LSD)-induced hallucinations and epileptic seizures were known to induce synesthesia-like experiences, and because these events were associated with reduced cortical blood flow, Cytowic and Wood (1982a) hypothesized that synesthesia might result from cortical inhibition, and suggested that the limbic system might be the locus of synesthesia. Cytowic and Stump (1985) tested this hypothesis by asking MW to inhale radioactive Xenon (Xe^{133}) gas mixed with room air. With this methodology, cerebral blood flow (CBF) is then measured by detectors placed over the scalp that detect the emission of X-rays and gamma rays as a consequence of the decay of the unstable Xenon isotopes. Cytowic and Stump found that cortical blood flow decreased during MW's synesthetic experiences, consistent with their model, but because the Xe^{133} method does not provide spatial information and is insensitive to subcortical blood flow, they were unable to directly test their hypothesis that synesthesia depends on limbic structures.

Early Investigations of Auditory Word/Music-Color Synesthesia

After Cytowic and Wood's early investigations of MW's taste-shape synesthesia there were no other neuroimaging investigations of synesthesia for more than 10 years. In these intervening 10 years, another imaging method, PET, became a standard method for the emerging field of cognitive neuroscience through the combined efforts of cognitive psychologists and radiologists (Petersen et al. 1988). Like Xe[133], PET depends on the decay of short-lived radioactive isotopes. For example, radioactive oxygen (O[15]) or radioactively labeled glucose are injected into the bloodstream, and are then absorbed by active brain regions. When the radioisotope decays, it emits a positron, which travels a short distance before interacting with an electron. The annihilation of the positron and electron generates a pair of gamma rays that travel in opposite directions, which are then detected by sensors placed around the head. Because the gamma rays are detected at the sensors at slightly different times, the relative position along the axis of the sensors can be inferred, and by placing sensors at carefully calculated positions, multiple axes through the body can be measured simultaneously. In this way, PET yields "tomographic" images (slice pictures), and is able to provide detailed spatial information about differences in regional CBF (rCBF) unlike Xe[133], which provided only global measurements of cortical blood flow.

Earlier PET studies had demonstrated changes in rCBF in cortical regions when participants viewed colored versus black and white displays, and identified these regions as the "color center" in humans (Lueck et al. 1989). To test the hypothesis that these color selective areas of the cortex were also active during the experience of colors in word-color synesthesia, Paulesu et al. (1995) measured rCBF with PET while six auditory word-color synesthetes listened to words (which elicited synesthetic colors) versus tones (which did not). Also tested on the same task were six non-synesthete controls. Areas of the posterior inferior temporal cortex and parieto-occipital junction—but not early visual areas V1, V2, or V4—were activated during word listening more than during tone listening in synesthetic participants, but not in controls. However, despite being a tomographic technique, anatomical localization in PET is limited because of the distance positrons travel before interacting with electrons. In addition, the failure to find activity in early visual areas (e.g., V4) may also have been due to limited sensitivity, rather than a true absence of activity.

After this early study, there was again a substantial gap of 7 years before the next imaging study of synesthesia, and in these intervening 7 years, neuroimaging methods again improved, with the discovery of the blood oxygenation level-dependent (BOLD) fMRI signal in 1991 (for a review, see Huettel et al. 2004). Unlike Xe[133] and PET, which require the use of inhaled or injected radioactive tracers, the BOLD signal depends on the natural magnetic properties of the hemoglobin molecule in blood. Oxygen carrying hemoglobin (oxyhemoglobin) responds more strongly to the strong magnetic fields in MRI than does deoxyhemoglobin. When brain regions are active, the blood supply overcompensates so that the relative concentration of oxyhemoglobin increases, leading to changes in the fMRI signal, allowing researchers to infer the location of neural activity. Because fMRI does not use radioactivity, fMRI scanners do not need to be near cyclotrons which are necessary to create the radioactive isotopes, and is safe for repeated measurements. Although fMRI has relatively slow temporal resolution on the order of 4 to 6 seconds, due to the sluggish hemodynamic response, it has excellent spatial resolution, with typical functional scans being on the order of $3 \times 3 \times 3$ mm (compared with 4 to 8 mm for PET), and higher sensitivity than previous imaging methods.

Using fMRI, Nunn et al. (2002) tested six female, right-handed auditory word-color synesthetes and six matched non-synesthetes. Nunn et al. reported that regions of the brain involved in the processing of colors (including the color center V4 and/or V8) were more active when word-color synesthetes heard spoken words than when they heard tones, but not earlier visual areas such as V1 or V2. No such difference was observed in controls, even when they were extensively trained to imagine specific colors for specific words. Similarly, in a case study of a synesthete who experienced colors for people's names, Weiss et al. (2001) reported that hearing names that elicited synesthetic colors led to activity in left extra-striate cortex (near to V4), but not in V1. However, in another case study of an auditory word-color synesthete, Aleman et al. (2001) report activation of (anatomically defined) primary visual cortex but were unable to determine if area V4 was active in this single participant.

Grapheme-Color Synesthesia as A Model System

As neuroimaging investigations of word-color synesthesia were yielding striking insights into the neural mechanisms of this form of synesthesia in the early 2000s, behavioral studies were beginning to focus on grapheme-color synesthesia. For example, behavioral studies of grapheme- color synesthesia demonstrated that the synesthetic sensations were automatic using modified Stroop-interference paradigms (Dixon et al. 2000; Mattingley et al. 2001); others demonstrated the perceptual reality of synesthetic colors using a variety of visual search paradigms (Palmeri et al. 2002; Ramachandran and Hubbard 2001a; Smilek et al. 2001; for reviews see Rich and Mattingley, Chapter 14; Kim and Blake, Chapter 15, this volume).

As a model system, grapheme-color synesthesia has several advantages over other forms of synesthesia. First, understanding the perceptual, cognitive and neural mechanisms of reading and color perception has been the topic of substantial research efforts independent of the synesthesia research community. Second, from a methodological perspective, grapheme-color synesthesia is ideally suited to the constraints of MRI environments. These environments are typically very noisy, which complicates effective study of the neural mechanisms of auditory language processing, and because of the presence of the magnetic field all metallic objects should be kept out of the scanner, making it difficult, for example, to create mechanical devices to present tastes, smells, and even controlled tactile stimulation to participants in the scanner. On the other hand, visual presentation in MRI simply requires a computer projector placed outside the scanner environment, a screen, and a mirror to reflect the image into the participant's eyes while they lie on the scanner bed.

Building on this knowledge, when we began to search for a possible neural basis for grapheme-color synesthesia, we were struck by the fact that brain regions involved in letter and number processing (the "grapheme area" or the "visual word form area"; VWFA) lie adjacent to the V4 color processing area (Ramachandran and Hubbard 2001a, 2001b). Given that synesthesia was known to run in families (Baron-Cohen et al. 1996; Galton 1883; see Johnson, Allison, and Baron-Cohen, Chapter 1, this volume) we suggested that a genetic factor might cause a failure in the neuronal pruning processes that usually take place during childhood development; this failure could give rise to adjacent brain regions in the fusiform gyrus being unusually connected in adult synesthetes, thereby leading to "cross-activation" between these regions (Hubbard and Ramachandran 2003; Ramachandran and Hubbard 2001b). Although this theory shares certain key aspects with the neonatal synesthesia theory, which suggests that everyone is born a synesthete (Maurer 1997) and the breakdown in modularity theory (Baron-Cohen 1996; Baron-Cohen et al. 1993), our original proposal capitalized on our emerging understanding of the neural mechanisms of reading and color perception to go beyond these general notions of hyperconnectivity, and to suggest specific brain regions as the locus for a specific form of synesthesia.

In addition to the cross-activation theory (see Figure 24.1a), two other main classes of model have been proposed to explain synesthetic experiences: the disinhibited feedback model and the re-entrant processing model (for a thorough review of these issues, see Hubbard and Ramachandran 2005). The disinhibited feedback theory (Figure 24.1c) suggests that synesthesia may be due to disinhibited feedback from a "multisensory nexus" such as the temporo-parietal-occipital junction, and that synesthetic concurrents arise because of disinhibited feedback from higher-level visual areas in pathways common to synesthetes and non-synesthetes alike (Grossenbacher and Lovelace 2001).

The re-entrant processing (Figure 24.1b) model posits cross-talk between form and color processing areas in the fusiform (as in the cross activation model), but, as in the disinhibited feedback model, it also suggests that elicitation of synesthetic colors requires neural activity from higher level areas in the temporal lobe (e.g., the anterior inferior temporal lobe) to feed back to V4 (Smilek et al. 2001).

Recently, a fourth model of synesthesia has been proposed, the "hyperbinding" model (Esterman et al. 2006; Robertson 2003). Under normal circumstances, the brain must bind together information from color, form, motion, and so on into a coherent representation of the world (Treisman 1980) and this binding process depends on parietal mechanisms (Robertson 2003). The hyperbinding model suggests that synesthesia arises through an over-activation of these same parietal binding mechanisms (see Alvarez and Robertson, Chapter 16, this volume). While anomalous binding may play an important role in the full explanation of the synesthetic experiences, it is not sufficient to say that synesthesia is a result of anomalous binding, since binding must have features upon which to act. Thus, one of these described mechanisms for generating additional synesthetic experiences may act in concert with over-active binding mechanisms.

It is important to note that a single model may fail to capture the variability in synesthetic experiences. The neural mechanisms may have both a common factor, which is present in all synesthetes, and other variable factors, which influence the strength of the synesthetic experiences, leading to individual differences in their experiences (Dixon

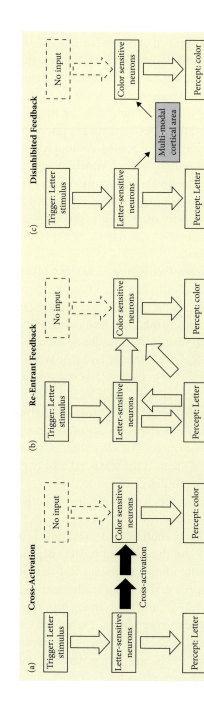

FIGURE 24.1 The main classes of neurophysiological theories of synesthesia. Arrows indicate the flow of information, and boxes indicate processing stages/areas. Solid lines indicate active regions/areas, while dotted lines indicate non-active regions and pathways. (a) The cross-activation model. Letter input leads to cross-activation of color areas (black arrows), which then leads to both the percept of letters and colors. (b) The re-entrant feedback model. Feedback from higher-order conceptual areas involved in the conscious percept of the letter feeds back both to physical form areas and to color areas, leading to the percept of a color. (c) The disinhibited feedback model. Information propagates up from letter processing to a multi-modal cortical area (gray box) before feeding back to color selective areas. Modified from *Trends in Cognitive Sciences*, 10 (8), Catherine M. Mulvenna and Vincent Walsh, Synaesthesia: supernormal integration?, pp. 350–352, Copyright (2006), with permission from Elsevier.

et al. 2004; Hubbard, Arman et al. 2005). In addition, the different models are not necessarily mutually exclusive. Indeed, as mentioned earlier, the hyperbinding account must work in concert with one of the other models to explain the genesis of the features that are bound if we are to explain synesthetic experiences.

It is also possible that different neural theories will account for different types of synesthesia, as the local cross-activation, re-entrant feedback, and hyperbinding theories have focused primarily on grapheme-color synesthesia, while feedback models have focused on word-color and tone-color synesthesia. While it is probable that at the architectural level, different forms of synesthesia will have different neural substrates, the fact that synesthetes within the same family may inherit different forms of synesthesia (Ward and Simner 2005) suggests that the neurophysiological mechanisms may be shared across different forms of synesthesia.

FUNCTIONAL NEUROIMAGING OF GRAPHEME-COLOR SYNESTHESIA

With the rise of grapheme-color synesthesia as a model system and improved methods for neuroimaging, the study of the neural mechanisms of synesthesia has truly exploded (for reviews, see Hubbard 2007a; Hubbard and Ramachandran 2005; Hubbard et al. 2011; Rouw et al. 2011). Early investigations focused primarily on the question of whether color selective brain regions were active, even to the extent of collecting functional brain imaging data only from specific regions that were hypothesized to be involved in the generation of synesthetic experiences. More recent investigations have moved beyond this singular focus on color selective regions to more thoroughly investigate network properties in synesthesia (see Rouw et al. 2011).

In an early study of grapheme-color synesthesia, we predicted that viewing black graphemes on a white background would lead to greater activity in color selective region V4. To test this theory, we compared fMRI responses to graphemes against non-grapheme stimuli matched for visual complexity in six synesthetes and six non-synesthetes (Hubbard, Arman, et al. 2005). Color and grapheme regions of interest (ROIs) were defined using a priori methods in a separate scan for each participant. We found greater modulation of V4 activity for graphemes versus non-graphemic stimuli in synesthetes than in non-synesthetes, consistent with our predictions (Figure 24.2a and 24.2b). Importantly, we did not observe differences in the responses to colors in the brains of synesthetes compared with non-synesthetes, and did not observe differences in the response to graphemes outside of V4, arguing against generalized differences in the synesthetes. Interestingly, we also found that performance on an independent perceptual task in which synesthetic colors conferred a behavioral advantage correlated with V4 activation in the synesthetes (Figure 24.2c), supporting the idea of a direct relationship between neural activity and perceptual experience (Hubbard, Arman, et al. 2005). This pattern of results has important implications for our understanding of the variability observed in behavioral studies (Dixon and Smilek 2005).

A number of subsequent neuroimaging studies of grapheme-color synesthesia have also examined whether color selective regions, including V4, were more active in synesthetes when viewing black-and-white graphemes. Like Hubbard, Arman et al. (2005), Sperling et al. (2006) measured fMRI BOLD response in four synesthetes in retinotopically defined V1 to V4 to graphemes that elicited synesthetic colors versus those that did not. Overall, they found greater activation in V4 when synesthetes were presented with graphemes that caused them to report seeing colors than when presented with graphemes that did not.

However, not all studies identified activity in the region of V4. Rich et al. (2006) used whole-brain fMRI and statistical parametric mapping (SPM) to analyse fMRI responses in a group of seven synesthetes and seven controls in three separate imaging paradigms. They first localized color selective ROIs using colored Mondrians versus grayscale images, which should selectively activate V4. They then measured fMRI responses within these ROIs in synesthetes and controls while these participants viewed either colored letters (which also induced synesthesia in the synesthetes) or grayscale letters, while monitoring for a brief disappearance of one of the letters. Rich et al. did not find greater activation of the V4 complex in synesthetes, but instead found activation of more anterior color areas, related to color naming and categorization. In addition, unlike in the previous Nunn et al. (2002) study, they found color imagery was capable of eliciting activation in the V4 complex in both synesthetes and non-synesthetes. Similarly, Weiss et al. (2005) examined fMRI signals in nine grapheme-color synesthetes, using a 2×2 factorial design. Subjects were presented with letters that either did or did not induce colors (many synesthetes report not having colors for all stimuli), with either colored or grayscale letters. Weiss et al. did not observe any significant activation in visual areas, but did observe a significant activation in the left intraparietal sulcus, consistent with the hyperbinding account of synesthesia.

The reasons for these differences in the strength of the findings are still unclear, but may be due to individual differences in the synesthetes tested across the studies (Hubbard, Arman, et al. 2005; Rouw and Scholte 2010). For example, one individual difference comes in the localization of synesthetic colors from synesthete to synesthete: *associator synesthetes* experience their colors internally (often described as being "in the mind's eye") while *projector synesthetes* experience their colors externally, for example, projected onto the written typeface (Dixon et al. 2004). Individual differences such as this might then be responsible for the different outcomes found in past imaging studies. For example, Rouw and Scholte (2010) measured fMRI responses (and voxel-based morphometry: VBM) in a group of 42 grapheme-color synesthetes (16 projectors and 26 associators) to identify: (1) brain regions that showed differences across all synesthetes compared with controls, (2) brain regions that showed differences between the two groups of synesthetes. Across all synesthetes compared with non-synesthetes, the authors found increased activation in a network of regions involved in perceptual binding including parietal and frontal regions, and the parieto-occipital sulcus near the precuneus. However, when they directly compared activation in the associators versus projectors, they found increased activation in hippocampal regions for the associators compared with the projectors. These results (and the corresponding VBM analyses) suggest that projector synesthesia may arise from more sensory mechanisms, while associator synesthesia may from more cognitive mechanisms including memory processes.

Another important aspect of evaluating these discrepant results is that until recently, most studies of synesthesia were statistically underpowered. Standard whole brain fMRI analyses using SPM and random effects analyses require a minimum of 20 participants in order to allow inferences about both positive and negative findings (Thirion et al. 2007). Analyses using restricted ROIs are less likely to be as severely underpowered, because the restricted number of voxels tested reduces the adverse statistical impact of the multiple comparisons problem. Techniques such as retinotopy which permit delineation of individual participant areas may similarly be less adversely affected because differences in brain anatomy are taken into consideration when examining patterns of activation. Given these considerations, positive findings should be given substantially more weight than negative ones when attempting to develop models of grapheme-color synesthesia.

Consistent with this, studies that examined larger numbers of synesthetic participants typically do find activation of color selective regions near the coordinates of V4 (Rouw and Scholte 2007; van Leeuwen et al. 2010). For example, as part of a larger study of anatomical connectivity (DTI) in synesthesia, Rouw and Scholte (2007) scanned a total of 18 synesthetes and 18 controls when they viewed graphemes that elicited strong, weak, or no synesthetic experiences. They found increased activation for strong and weak synesthetic experiences (compared with no synesthetic experience) across multiple brain regions including frontal regions, parietal regions and fusiform gyrus, near the coordinates of V4. Similarly, van Leeuwen et al (2010) scanned 19 synesthetes and 19 controls, and also found increased activation in a network of regions including superior parietal cortex and color-related areas. Consistent with the possibility that individual differences complicate the interpretation of group-level neuroimaging analyses, projectors showed greater activation in parietal cortex than did associators.

However, power and individual differences are unlikely to fully account for the discrepant results in the literature. In another recent study, Hupé et al. (2012) scanned ten grapheme-color synesthetes compared against 25 non-synesthetes. They used retinotopic mapping methods to define a priori visual ROIs, and also assessed individual differences across synesthetes. Even so, these authors did not find increased activation at a group level for synesthetes compared with non-synesthetes in visual areas related to color experience. Instead, they suggest that the neural mechanisms of grapheme-color synesthesia may be distributed, or may critically depend on brain regions outside the classical color areas. This conclusion is difficult to reconcile with the other studies reviewed here (and converging results from other methodologies) but given the methodological rigor in their study, any coherent model of grapheme-color synesthesia will have to account for these results (see Kim and Blake, Ch. 15, this volume for one possible explanation).

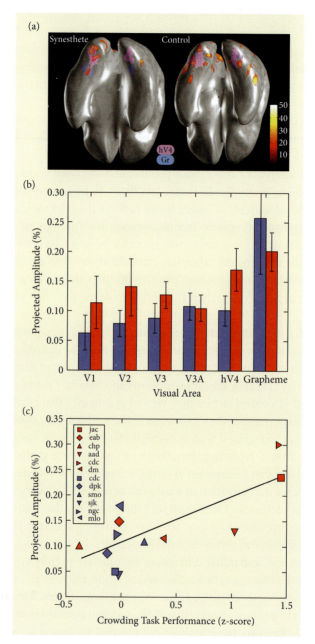

FIGURE 24.2 (a) Activation during grapheme viewing from a representative synesthete and control participant. Retinotopic region V4 is indicated in pink and grapheme responsive areas are indicated in blue. (b) Average projected amplitude for synesthetes and controls across early visual areas, showing significantly greater activation in synesthetes than in controls in area V4. (c) Correlation between activation in V4 during grapheme viewing and performance enhancement on an independent perceptual task. Data reprinted from *Neuron*, 45 (6), Edward M. Hubbard, A. Cyrus Arman, Vilayanur S. Ramachandran, and Geoffrey M. Boynton, Individual differences among grapheme-color synesthetes: Brain-behavior correlations, pp. 975–985 © 2005, Elsevier.

ALTERNATIVES TO BLOCK-DESIGNS IN THE STUDY OF GRAPHEME-COLOR SYNESTHESIA

These considerations have led a number of authors to move beyond the simple "block-design" methods used in the studies described earlier, in which blocks of synesthesia-inducing stimuli are contrasted with non-synesthesia inducing stimuli. Although these alternative designs still depend on measuring blood flow to infer neural activity, they permit stronger inferences about the pattern of neural activity across different conditions, and therefore shed additional light on the neural mechanisms of grapheme-color synesthesia.

For example, taking advantage of the fact that synesthetic Stroop-interference increases with increasing difference between the real text color and the synesthetic color (Nikolic et al. 2007), Laeng et al. (2011) measured parametric modulations of neural activity in response to graphemes that were presented in colors that were either more or less similar to those reported by two grapheme-color synesthetes. They found that activation increased as a function of the color distance between the real and synesthetic colors in both synesthetes, and that the location of this activation was quite close to the coordinates from other studies that examined both real and synesthetic color perception, including V4.

Another method for examining shared neural substrates for real color perception and synesthetic color is the fMRI-adaptation (fMRI-A) method, which takes advantage of the fact that repeated presentations of a stimulus lead to decreased neural responses (Miller et al. 1991) and corresponding decreases in the fMRI BOLD signal. Presentation of stimuli that depend on different populations of neurons leads to a "rebound" effect in which fMRI responses increase to baseline levels or beyond (Grill-Spector and Malach 2001; Naccache and Dehaene 2001).

Several recent studies have applied this logic to the study of grapheme-color synesthesia, but did not find significant adaptation or rebound effects. Van Leeuwen et al. (2010) presented graphemes which elicited synesthetic colors and real color patches, in which the color patches were either congruent with, incongruent with, or neutral with respect to synesthetic colors. The authors predicted decreased fMRI responses when the graphemes and color patches were congruent due to repetition suppression effects on these populations of neurons for those colors fatiguing. No such repetition suppression effect was observed, with fMRI responses being the same for the congruent and incongruent conditions, but lower for both conditions than for the neutral condition. As such, the authors suggest that synesthetic colors do not depend on the same neural mechanisms as real color perception in color selective areas (see also, Hupé et al. 2012).

However, the interpretation of fMRI adaption experiments is fraught with difficulties (Krekelberg et al. 2006). It is known that the BOLD signal includes both spiking and non-spiking activity, and therefore reflects mostly inputs to an area (Logothetis and Wandell 2004). Because adaptation occurs at multiple levels in the visual pathway from the retina to higher-order visual areas, and because adaptation at early stages of processing is "inherited" at subsequent stages of processing, this inherited adaptation complicates the interpretation of any fMRI adaptation paradigm. In the case of grapheme-color synesthesia, even if real colors and synesthetic colors eventually converge on the same neurons, the pathways would differ for real and synesthetic colors. Real color patches would activate, and therefore cause adaptation at the level of the retina, V1, V2, and eventually color selective areas like V4 while synesthetic colors might only lead to activation of color selective neurons in V4. As such, the absence of measured adaptation in this study might reflect differences in inherited adaptation, rather than a lack of a shared neural substrate for real and synesthetic colors (Krekelberg et al. 2006). As an example of these concerns, an fMRI-adaptation study of orientation tuning found no differences in adaptation in V1 for gratings of the same orientation versus different orientations (Boynton and Finney 2003). Orientation specific adaptation effects were present only in later areas like V2 and V4, despite the well-established fact that V1 neurons are orientation selective. Finally, it is known that adaptation is greater for expected stimuli than for unexpected stimuli (Summerfield et al. 2008). Since van Leeuwen et al. (2010) presented twice as many incongruent stimuli as congruent stimuli, it possible that increased adaptation to the congruent stimuli was countered by increased responses due to the greater novelty of the congruent stimuli. Because of its power to infer neural processes, fMRI-A is an important method, but these methodological issues are critical for designing effective fMRI-A studies.

LOCALIZED DIFFERENCES VERSUS NETWORK DIFFERENCES

A growing awareness of the importance of binding and parietal mechanisms led to the introduction of a "two-stage model" of grapheme-color synesthesia (Hubbard 2007a, 2007b). The cross-activation theory proposed that synesthetic experiences are generated via cross-activation in the fusiform gyrus, but assumed that parietal binding and attention mechanisms were similar in synesthetes and non-synesthetes. Conversely, the "hyperbinding" theory of grapheme-color synesthesia suggested that synesthetic experiences depend on increased binding between color and form (Esterman et al. 2006; Robertson 2003).

Although the evidence reviewed earlier clearly demonstrates a critical role for early color-selective visual areas in the genesis of synesthetic experiences, a number of studies have also demonstrated the importance of parietal regions involved in attention and binding. For example, intraparietal regions are consistently more active in synesthetes than in non-synesthetes (Nunn et al. 2002; Paulesu et al. 1995; van Leeuwen et al. 2010; Weiss et al. 2005). Taken together, these results suggest that, while the activation of color specific visual areas may be the origin of synesthetic experiences, these color experiences must still be bound by (possibly overactive) parietal mechanisms. While anomalous binding may play an important role in the full explanation of the synesthetic experiences, it is not sufficient to say that synesthesia is a result of anomalous binding, since binding must have features upon which to act. We thus suggest that synesthetic colors are first elicited in fusiform regions via cross-activation, but are then bound by parietal mechanisms in the same way as other visual features.

One particularly powerful way to examine these questions depends on the advent of methods to measure "functional connectivity" (FC), especially in the absence of a task (called resting state fMRI or rs-fMRI; Fox and Raichle 2007; Gusnard and Raichle 2001). FC is assessed by measuring the correlation between the time series of any two brain regions. The more strongly correlated the time series is, the more strongly activity in one brain area depends on brain activity in another area, and the more functionally connected those brain regions are. The analysis of correlations can be done either within a hypothesis-driven framework, in which ROIs are defined a priori, or in a data-driven framework, in which spatio-temporal networks are identified through the use of independent components analysis (ICA), or through a combination of both methods. In addition to measuring simple connectivity, by looking at time-lagged correlations it is also possible to infer which brain region is driving which, using modeling techniques like structural equation models (SEM), dynamic causal modeling (DCM), and Grainger causality.

Van Leeuwen et al. (2011) used DCM analyses to examine network connectivity between three regions thought to be involved in the generation of synesthetic experiences: fusiform regions involved in letter-shape analysis (which they refer to as the LSA), V4, and parietal cortex for associators and projectors. For projectors, the LSA directly drives V4 in a bottom-up manner, while for associators, the LSA drives parietal cortex, which in turn drives V4. Critically, they showed the degree to which synesthetes' reports of externally projected experiences was correlated with the degree to which the bottom-up versus top-down models fit the brain imaging data. This suggests that, even if V4 is activated in both groups of synesthetes, the pathways taken for this information may vary.

In another recent study, rs-fMRI and ICA were used to identify intrinsic connectivity networks (ICNs) in 12 grapheme-color synesthetes and 12 matched non-synesthetic controls (Dovern et al. 2012). The authors identified a set of seven "synesthesia-relevant" ICNs, including primary visual cortex, primary auditory cortex and parietal regions and a parieto-frontal network. FC was greater in the synesthetes both within and between these ICNs and FC strength was correlated with the behaviorally assessed consistency in synesthetes' reports. Synesthetes had three times more significant connections between the seven ICNs than did controls. Crucially, synesthetes had stronger connections between both visual networks and the right fronto-parietal network than controls, and color consistency in synesthetes was correlated with connectivity between visual networks and the auditory and right fronto-parietal networks.

Other recent studies have similarly demonstrated the importance of both visual areas and parietal networks in generating synesthetic experience (Sinke, Neufeld, et al. 2012;

Specht and Laeng 2011) and have generally supported the idea that visual and parietal networks are more strongly connected in synesthesia, consistent with a two-stage model of grapheme-color synesthesia (Hubbard 2007a, 2007b; Hubbard et al. 2011). Taken together, these results also demonstrate that increased connectivity between regions might be even more widespread than originally thought. For example, Sinke, Neufeld, et al. (2012) showed that FC was greater in synesthetes even in primary visual areas, suggesting even more widespread differences than predicted in previous models.

Less Studied Variants of Synesthesia

In the past few years, neuroimaging investigations have expanded well beyond grapheme-color synesthesia to include many other forms of synesthesia. Although these investigations are only beginning, we hope to spur future research into these questions, using neuroimaging methods similar to those used in the study of grapheme-color synesthesia. Although a great deal of data has been collected on grapheme-color synesthesia, for most other forms of synesthesia, a great deal more work is needed, and examination of some of these forms may require revising or even rejecting current models. Indeed, additional research may demonstrate that different mechanisms are important to explain different forms of synesthesia, and may even suggest that grapheme-color synesthesia is a non-representative model of how synesthesia works generally.

Sequence-space synesthesia

In another form of synesthesia, numbers and other ordinal sequences including months of the year and days of the week are associated with specific spatial locations (Galton 1880b, 1880a). This often co-occurs with grapheme-color synesthesia (Sagiv et al. 2006; Seron et al. 1992) and has been referred to as *spatial sequence synesthesia* (SSS; Eagleman 2009), although it is sometimes described with various other terms depending on the particular subvariants under discussion (e.g., described as *number form synesthesia* when triggered by numbers; Hubbard, Piazza, et al. 2005; or as *time-space synesthesia* when triggered by months etc. Smilek, Callejas, et al. 2007). Based on numerous patient and neuroimaging studies, parietal cortex is generally recognized as a key region for numerical and spatial processes (Dehaene et al. 2003; Hubbard, Piazza, et al. 2005; Simon et al. 2002) including processing of non-numerical ordinal sequences, such as letters (Fias et al. 2007) and months (Ischebeck et al. 2008). Building on these observations, we proposed that this form of synesthesia arises through cross-activation in parietal regions (Hubbard, Piazza, et al. 2005; Ramachandran and Hubbard 2001b), and furthermore, that non-conscious numerical-spatial interactions that are present in everyone (e.g., the SNARC effect Dehaene et al. 1993) are mediated by similar, albeit weaker connections in parietal cortex (Hubbard, Piazza, et al. 2005). An alternative model suggests that temporal regions, rather than parietal regions, are the locus of this form of synesthesia (Eagleman 2009) as sequences are "reified" and thought of as visual objects, which can then be operated on with normal visuo-spatial mechanisms of attention, including panning, zooming, and translating.

Preliminary support for the parietal model comes from fMRI data showing increased posterior parietal activation in number-form synesthetes when they performed a number task that focused on the ordinal position of the number in a sequence ("first" versus "fifth") compared against a task that focused on numerical magnitude ("one" versus "five"; Tang et al. 2008). This focus on numerical sequence is important, as it has been suggested that order and sequence is more important to explain SSS than numerical magnitude (Eagleman 2009; Hubbard et al. 2009; Sagiv et al. 2006). Consistent with this model, a patient who suffered a gunshot wound which entered near the right angular gyrus and lodged near the left temporal-parietal junction complained that his "number plan" for months of the year, days of the week and letters of the alphabet, was no longer distinct (Spalding and Zangwill 1950).

Steven et al. (2006) conducted a single-case study of a synesthetic participant, JF, who had become blind due to retinal degeneration 10 years before the fMRI session. Prior to becoming blind, JF reported both SSS and colors for "time words" (day and month names). Steven et al. showed that V4 could be activated by auditory presentation of time words versus frequency matched non-time words. Similar visual activations were not observed in a non-synesthetic late-blind participant or a non-synesthetic sighted participant, suggesting that the functional differences that lead to synesthesia persist even in the absence of visual input. In a follow-up study, Niccolai et al. (2012) sought to disentangle the effects of SSS and color synesthesia on JF's brain activation patterns. They presented time words that elicited both SSS and colors ("Monday," "February"), time words that elicited only SSS ("morning," "Easter"), and time words that elicit neither SSS nor colors ("season," "year"). Words that elicited SSS and colors led to greater activation of color selective areas near (anatomically defined) V4, while words that elicited only SSS led to greater activation of posterior/inferior parietal cortex, consistent with the parietal model.

Mirror-touch synesthesia

In mirror-touch synesthesia, observing touch to another person's body is felt as touch by the synesthete (Banissy and Ward 2007; Banissy et al. 2009; see Banissy, Chapter 30, this volume). One proposed mechanism for this form of synesthesia is enhanced responsiveness in the tactile mirror neuron system, which has been demonstrated to be active both when being touched and when observing others being touched. To date, there has been only one neuroimaging study of this form of synesthesia (Blakemore et al. 2005). Consistent with predictions, neuroimaging of a single mirror-touch synesthete, C, compared against 12 non-synesthetes showed enhanced activation in multiple regions of the tactile mirror system, including primary and secondary somatosensory regions. Investigation of the data from each participant demonstrated greater activation in C than in any of the 12 non-synesthetes. To date, there have been no follow-up neuroimaging studies of this form of synesthesia.

Ordinal linguistic personification

Ordinal linguistic personification (OLP) is another form of synesthesia, in which people associate letters and numbers with personalities (e.g., "A" may be thought of as female and "the boss," while "B" might be her toddler son). We suggested that this form of synesthesia depends on cross-activation between brain regions involved in sequence representations, such as the inferior parietal cortex and regions involved in personality attribution (Simner and Hubbard 2006) while other models have suggested numerous anatomical substrates in a "personification network" (Smilek, Malcolmson, et al. 2007) including the angular gyrus, but also including extra-striate and fusiform regions, the amygdala and medial frontal cortex. Recently, a single-case fMRI study examined the neural substrates of this form of synesthesia (Amin et al. 2011). Their participant, AA, reported personifying about half of the letters in the alphabet, but not the others. In this way, the authors were able to directly contrast activations when AA viewed letters she personified versus letters she did not. The authors found a single focus of activation in the precuneus, which leads them to suggest that "OLP may represent an aberration of self-reflection and/or mental imagery" (275), although the authors suggest caution in interpreting the absence of other activations, given the single-case design. Future studies will be needed to better understand the neural mechanisms of OLP in a larger number of participants.

Lexical-gustatory synesthesia

Finally, lexical-gustatory synesthesia involves tasting the flavors of food in response to heard, read, or thought words (Ward and Simner 2003; Ward et al. 2005). Given the role of insular cortex and its adjacency to auditory regions involved in the analysis of auditory words, it seems natural to speculate that lexical-gustatory synesthesia might arise through cross-activation of these regions. In the only neuroimaging study of this form of synesthesia to date, Jones et al. (2011) demonstrated increased activation in the insula and the precuneus in two lexical-gustatory synesthetes. Interestingly, insular activation was related to the emotional valence of the experienced taste (pleasant/unpleasant) while precuneus activation was related to the subjective intensity of the tastes. Whether these findings hold across all synesthetes, and how these different regions interact to yield the full-blown experience of lexical-gustatory synesthesia is still to be determined.

Future Directions

Although the past 25 years have seen great progress in our understanding of the neural basis of synesthesia, there is still much work to be done. First, many different types of evidence have been brought to bear on the neural basis of grapheme-color synesthesia, but similarly intensive studies have not yet been carried out on the other forms of synesthesia, and to date none of the studies demonstrating anatomical and functional differences in other forms of synesthesia have been replicated. Thus, greater efforts to apply the methods developed in the study of grapheme-color synesthesia to other forms of synesthesia will be critical. Indeed, systematic exploration of other forms of synesthesia may lead to the conclusion that different forms of synesthesia depend on different mechanisms, although much of the available evidence appears consistent with the cross-activation theory (Hubbard et al. 2011).

Second, there are no empirical studies of the neural development of synesthesia (but see Mitchell, Chapter 27, this volume, for a discussion). Methods for neuroimaging with children are becoming widespread, and have been applied to a number of questions in cognitive and perceptual development. Similar methods, combined with methods of identifying and tracking children who are synesthetic (e.g., Simner et al. 2009) or who are likely to become synesthetic (e.g., Green and Goswami 2008) will be critical to understanding the development of synesthesia, and how genes and experience interact. One recent proposal (Cohen Kadosh et al. 2009) suggests that both play a role, building on the interactive specialization framework (Johnson 2001, 2011).

However, interactive specialization is intended as a domain-general account of brain development, and as such does not distinguish between evolutionarily ancient systems and modern cultural systems. Why, for example, is grapheme-color synesthesia more common than face-color synesthesia if adjacency and brain wiring are the only factors that count? Perhaps the degree to which cortex must reorganize during learning is greater for novel culturally acquired systems like graphemes (Dehaene and Cohen 2007) and ordinal sequences (Cohen Kadosh et al. 2009) than for items that have a long evolutionary history, like faces or colors. This greater degree of cortical reorganization for novel cultural artifacts might provide greater opportunities for cross-activation in the cortical recycling process.

Finally, we must address the relative absence of neuroimaging data directly testing other neurophysiological models of synesthesia. For example, the evidence that synesthesia arises from altered neurotransmitter balance leading to disinhibition is largely anecdotal. Grossenbacher and Lovelace (2001) note that experiences similar to synesthesia can sometimes be elicited with psychedelics. However, systematic analysis demonstrates numerous important differences between these forms of synesthesia, and suggests that they arise from different neural mechanisms (Sinke, Halpern, et al. 2012).

Additionally, none of these pharmacological hypotheses of synesthesia have been tested with neuroimaging methods such as PET, single photon emission computed tomography (SPECT), or magnetic resonance spectroscopy (MRS). Future studies using these methods will help to identify whether there are any differences in neurotransmitter concentrations, receptor density or other alterations in synthesis or breakdown of specific neurotransmitters involved with cortical inhibition and excitation. Radioactive tracer molecules developed for use with PET and SPECT, called radioligands, show striking specificity, differentially binding to specific neurotransmitter receptors within specific brain regions. Based on the hypothesis that synesthesia results from differences in cortical excitability (Terhune et al. 2011), and in particular, from disinhibited feedback, we might also predict imbalances in the primary neurotransmitter systems involved in cortical excitation and inhibition, glutamate and GABA, respectively. MRS methods are ideally suited to measuring levels of these neurotransmitters, including GABA and glutamate/glutamine. MRS methods have shed considerable light on the processes of glutamate and GABA synthesis use and reuptake (for a review, see Petroff 2002) and could shed similar light on the relative role of these neurotransmitters, if any, in the increased cortical excitability thought to be associated with synesthesia. Future studies using these methods will be critical to evaluating the possibility that differences in neurotransmitter function underlie synesthesia.

Table 24.1 Neuroimaging studies of synesthesia

Study	Form of synesthesia	Method	Participants (syn. versus con.)
Cytowic and Stump 1985/Cytowic 1989/2002	Taste-shape	Xe^{133}	n = 1, within participants
Paulesu et al. 1995	Auditory-word color	PET	n = 6 vs 6
Aleman et al. 2001	Grapheme-color	fMRI	n = 1, within participants
Weiss et al. 2001	Colors for names of personally familiar people	fMRI	n = 1, within participants
Nunn et al. 2002	Auditory word-color	fMRI	n = 13 vs 27
Elias et al. 2002	Grapheme-color	fMRI	n = 1, within participants
Hubbard et al. 2005	Grapheme-color	fMRI with retinotopy	n = 6 vs 6
Blakemore et al. 2005	Mirror touch	fMRI	n = 1 vs 12
Weiss et al. 2005	Grapheme-color	fMRI	n = 9, within participants
Sperling et al. 2006	Grapheme-color	fMRI with retinotopy	n = 4

Table 24.1 *Continued*

Study	Form of synesthesia	Method	Participants (syn. versus con.)
Steven et al. 2006	Auditory-color time words vs non-time words	fMRI	n = 1 late blind vs n = 1 late blind control and n = 1 sighted
Gray et al. 2006	Grapheme-color ACE	fMRI	n = 8 with, n = 7 without, n = 7 controls
Rich et al. 2006	Grapheme-color	fMRI	n = 7 vs 7
Rouw and Scholte 2007	Grapheme-color	fMRI (+DTI)	n = 18 vs 18
Cohen Kadosh et al. 2007	Explicit bi-directional grapheme-color	fMRI	n = 1
Tang et al. 2008	Number forms (SSS)	fMRI	n = 10 vs 10
Beauchamp and Ro 2008	Acquired sound-touch	fMRI	n = 1 vs 9
Rouw and Scholte 2010	Grapheme-color	fMRI (+VBM)	n = 42, 16 projectors vs 26 associators vs 42
Van Leeuwen et al. 2010	Grapheme-color	fMRI + fMRI-A	n = 19 vs 19
Van Leeuwen et al. 2011	Grapheme-color	functional connectivity	n = 19 vs 19 (same participants as van Leeuwen et al., 2010)
Gaschler-Markefski et al. 2011	Auditory word-color	fMRI	n = 7 vs 7
Laeng et al. 2011	Grapheme-color	fMRI color distance	n = 2, within participants
Specht and Laeng 2011	Grapheme-color	fMRI, ICA	n = 2 vs 2 (same participants as Laeng et al., 2011)
Jones et al. 2011	Lexical-gustatory	fMRI	n = 2 vs 10
Amin et al. 2011	Personification	fMRI	n = 1, within participants
Hupé et al. 2012	Grapheme-color	fMRI + fMRI-A with retinotopy	10 vs 25
Neufeld et al. 2012	Auditory-visual	Functional connectivity	n = 14
Niccolai, van Leeuwen, et al. 2012	Blind SSS	fMRI	n = 1, within participants (same as Steven et al. 2006)
Dovern et al. 2012	Grapheme-color	Functional connectivity	n = 12 vs 12
Sinke, Neufeld, et al. 2012	Grapheme-color	Functional connectivity	n = 18 vs 18

REFERENCES

Aleman, André, Geert-Jan M. Rutten, Margriet M. Sitskoorn, Geraud Dautzenberg, and Nick F. Ramsay. 2001. Activation of striate cortex in the absence of visual stimulation: An fMRI study of synesthesia. *Neuroreport* 12 (13):2827–2830.

Alvarez, Bryan D., and Lynn C. Robertson. 2013. Synesthesia and binding. In *The Oxford Handbook of Synesthesia,* ed. Julia Simner and Edward M. Hubbard, 317–333 . Oxford: Oxford University Press.

Amin, Maina, Olufemi Olu-Lafe, Loes E. Claessen, Monika Sobczak-Edmans, Jamie Ward, Adrian L. Williams, and Noam Sagiv. Understanding grapheme personification: a social synaesthesia? *Journal of Neuropsychology* 5 (2):255–282.

Banissy, Michael J. 2013. Synesthesia, mirror-neurons, and mirror-touch. In *The Oxford Handbook of Synesthesia,* ed. Julia Simner and Edward M. Hubbard, 584–603. Oxford: Oxford University Press.

Banissy, Michael J., and Jamie Ward. 2007. Mirror-touch synesthesia is linked with empathy. *Nature Neuroscience* 10 (7):815–816.

Banissy, Michael J., Roi Cohen Kadosh, Gerrit W. Maus, Vincent Walsh, and Jamie Ward. 2009. Prevalence, characteristics and a neurocognitive model of mirror-touch synaesthesia. *Experimental Brain Research* 198 (2–3):261–272.

Baron-Cohen, Simon. 1996. Is there a normal phase of synaesthesia in development? *Psyche* 2 (27).

Baron-Cohen, Simon, Lucy Burt, Fiona Laittan-Smith, John E. Harrison, and Patrick Bolton. 1996. Synaesthesia: prevalence and familiality. *Perception* 25 (9):1073–1079.

Baron-Cohen, Simon, John Harrison, Laura H. Goldstein, and Maria Wyke. 1993. Coloured speech perception: Is synaesthesia what happens when modularity breaks down? *Perception* 22 (4):419–426.

Beauchamp, Michael S., and Tony Ro. 2008. Neural substrates of sound–touch synesthesia after a thalamic lesion. *The Journal of Neuroscience* 28 (50):13696–13702.

Blakemore, Sarah Jayne, Davina Bristow, Geoffrey Bird, Christopher Frith, and Jamie Ward. 2005. Somatosensory activations during the observation of touch and a case of vision-touch synaesthesia. *Brain* 128 (7):1571–1583.

Boynton, Geoffrey M., and Eva M. Finney. 2003. Orientation-specific adaptation in human visual cortex. *The Journal of Neuroscience* 23 (25):8781–8787.

Brang, David, Edward M. Hubbard, Seana Coulson, Minxiong Huang, and Vilayanur S. Ramachandran. 2010. Magnetoencephalography reveals early activation of V4 in grapheme-color synesthesia. *Neuroimage* 53 (1):268–274.

Brang, David, Stanley Kanai, Vilayanur S. Ramachandran, and Seana Coulson. 2011. Contextual priming in grapheme-color synesthetes and yoked controls: 400 msec in the life of a synesthete. *Journal of Cognitive Neuroscience* 23 (7):1681–1696.

Cohen Kadosh, Roi, Avishai Henik, and Vincent Walsh. 2009. Synaesthesia: learned or lost? *Developmental Science* 12 (3):484–491.

Cytowic, Richard E. 1989/2002. *Synesthesia: A union of the* senses. 2nd ed. Cambridge, MA: MIT Press.

Cytowic, Richard E., and David A. Stump. 1985. Reduced cortical blood flow in geometrically-shaped taste synesthesia. *International Neuropsychological Society.*

Cytowic, Richard E., and Frank B. Wood, 1982a. Synesthesia: I. A review of major theories and their brain basis. *Brain & Cognition* 1 (1):23–35.

——. 1982b. Synesthesia: II. Psychophysical relations in the synesthesia of geometrically shaped taste and colored hearing. *Brain & Cognition* 1 (1):36–49.

Dehaene, Stanislas, Serge Bossini, and Pascal Giraux. 1993. The mental representation of parity and numerical magnitude. *Journal of Experimental Psychology: General* 122:371–396.

Dehaene, Stanislas, and Laurent Cohen. 2007. Cultural recycling of cortical maps. *Neuron* 56 (2):384–398.

Dehaene, Stanislas, Manuela Piazza, Philippe Pinel, and Laurent Cohen. 2003. Three parietal circuits for number processing. *Cognitive Neuropsychology* 20 (3/4/5/6):487–506.

Dixon, Mike J., and Daniel Smilek. 2005. The importance of individual differences in grapheme-color synesthesia. *Neuron* 45 (6):821–823.

Dixon, Mike J., Daniel Smilek, Cera Cudahy, and Philip M. Merikle. 2000. Five plus two equals yellow: Mental arithmetic in people with synaesthesia is not coloured by visual experience. *Nature* 406 (6794):365.

Dixon, Mike J., Daniel Smilek, and Philip M. Merikle. 2004. Not all synaesthetes are created equal: projector versus associator synaesthetes. *Cognitive Affective and Behavioral Neuroscience* 4 (3):335–343.

Dovern, Anna, Gereon R. Fink, A. Christina B. Fromme, Afra M. Wohlschläger, Peter H. Weiss, and Valentin Riedl. 2012. Intrinsic network connectivity reflects consistency of synesthetic experiences. *The Journal of Neuroscience* 32 (22):7614–7621.

Eagleman, David M. 2009. The objectification of overlearned sequences: a new view of spatial sequence synesthesia. *Cortex* 45 (10):1266–1277.

Elias, Lorin J., Deborah M. Saucier, Colleen Hardie, and Gordon E. Sarty. 2003. Dissociating semantic and perceptual components of synaesthesia: behavioural and functional neuroanatomical investigations. *Cognitive Brain Research* 16 (2):232–237.

Esterman, Michael, Timothy Verstynen, Richard B. Ivry, and Lynn C. Robertson. 2006. Coming unbound: disrupting automatic integration of synesthetic color and graphemes by transcranial magnetic stimulation of the right parietal lobe. *Journal of Cognitive Neuroscience* 18 (9):1570–1576.

Fias, Wim, Jan Lammertyn, Bernie Caessens, and Guy A. Orban. 2007. Processing of abstract ordinal knowledge in the horizontal segment of the intraparietal sulcus. *The Journal of Neuroscience* 27 (33):8952–8956.

Flournoy, Théodore. 1893. *Des phénomènes de synopsie [On the phenomena of synopsia]*. Genève: Charles Eggimann & Co.

Fox, Michael D., and Marcus E. Raichle. 2007. Spontaneous fluctuations in brain activity observed with functional magnetic resonance imaging. *Nature Reviews Neuroscience* 8 (9):700–711.

Galton, Francis. 1880a. Visualised numerals. *Nature* 21 (533):252–256.

——. 1880b. Visualised numerals. *Nature* 21 (543):494–495.

——. 1883. *Inquiries into human faculty and its development*. London: Dent & Sons.

Gaschler-Markefski, Birgit, Gregor R. Szycik, Christopher Sinke, Janina Neufeld, Udo Schneider, Frank Baumgart, Oliver Dierks, *et al.* 2011. Anomalous auditory cortex activations in colored hearing synaesthetes: An fMRI-study. *Seeing and Perceiving* 24 (4):391–405.

Gray, Jeffrey A., David M. Parslow, Michael J. Brammer, Susan Chopping, Goparlen N. Vythelingum, and Dominic H. ffytche. 2006. Evidence against functionalism from neuroimaging of the alien colour effect in synaesthesia. *Cortex* 42 (2):309–318.

Green, Jennifer A. K., and Usha Goswami. 2008. Synesthesia and number cognition in children. *Cognition*, 106:463–473.

Grill-Spector, Kalinit, and Malach, Rafael 2001. fMR-adaptation: a tool for studying the functional properties of human cortical neurons. *Acta Psychologica (Amsterdam)* 107 (1–3):293–321.

Grossenbacher, Peter G., and Christopher T. Lovelace. 2001. Mechanisms of synesthesia: cognitive and physiological constraints. *Trends in Cognitive Sciences* 5 (1):36–41.

Gusnard, Debra A., and Marcus E. Raichle. 2001. Searching for a baseline: functional imaging and the resting human brain. *Nature Reviews Neuroscience* 2 (10):685–694.

Hubbard, Edward M. 2007a. Neurophysiology of synesthesia. *Current Psychiatry Reports* 9 (3):193–199.

——. 2007b. A real red-letter day. *Nature Neuroscience* 10 (6):671–672.

Hubbard, Edward M. and Ramachandran, Vilayanur S. 2003. Refining the experimental lever: A reply to Shannnon and Pribram. *Journal of Consciousness Studies* 10 (3):77–84.

——. 2005. Neurocognitive mechanisms of synesthesia. *Neuron* 48 (3):509–520.

Hubbard, Edward M., A. Cyrus Arman, Vilayanur S. Ramachandran, and Geoffrey M. Boynton. 2005. Individual differences among grapheme-color synesthetes: Brain-behavior correlations. *Neuron* 45 (6):975–985.

Hubbard, Edward M., David Brang, and Vilayanur S. Ramachandran. 2011. The cross-activation theory at 10. *Journal of Neuropsychology* 5 (2):152–177.

Hubbard, Edward M., Manuela Piazza, Philippe Pinel, and Stanislas Dehaene. 2005. Interactions between number and space in parietal cortex. *Nature Reviews Neuroscience* 6 (6):435–448.

Hubbard, Edward M., Mariagrazia Ranzini, Manuela Piazza, and Stanislas Dehaene. 2009. What information is critical to elicit interference in number-form synesthesia? *Cortex* 45 (10):1200–1216.

Huettel, Scott A., Allen W. S. Song, and Gregory McCarthy. 2004. *Functional Magnetic Resonance Imaging*. Sunderland, MA: Sinauer Associates.

Hupé, Jean-Michel, Cécile Bordier, and Michel Dojat. 2012. The neural bases of grapheme-color synesthesia are not localized in real color-sensitive areas. *Cerebral Cortex* 22 (7):1622–1633.

Ischebeck, Anja, Stefan Heim, Christian Siedentopf, Laura Zamarian, Michael Schocke, Christian Kremser, Karl Egger, Hans Strenge, Filip Scheperjans, and Margarete Delazer. 2008. Are numbers special? Comparing the generation of verbal materials from ordered categories (months) to numbers and other categories (animals) in an fMRI study. *Human Brain Mapping* 29 (8):894–909.

Johnson, Donielle, Carrie Allison, and Simon Baron-Cohen. 2013. The prevalence of synesthesia: The consistency revolution. In *The Oxford Handbook of Synesthesia*, ed. Julia Simner and Edward M. Hubbard, 3–22. Oxford: Oxford University Press.

Johnson, Mark H. 2001. Functional brain development in humans. *Nature Reviews Neuroscience* 2:475–483.

——. 2011. Interactive specialization: A domain-general framework for human functional brain development? *Developmental Cognitive Neuroscience* 1 (1):7–21.

Jones, C. L., M. A. Gray, L. Minati, J. Simner, H. D. Critchley, and J. Ward. 2011. The neural basis of illusory gustatory sensations: Two rare cases of lexical-gustatory synaesthesia. *Journal of Neuropsychology* 5 (2):243–254.

Kim, Chai-Youn, and Randolph Blake. 2013. Revisiting the perceptual reality of synesthetic colour. In *The Oxford Handbook of Synesthesia*, ed. Julia Simner and Edward M. Hubbard, 283–316 . Oxford: Oxford University Press.

Krekelberg, Bart, Geoffrey M. Boynton, and Richard J. A. van Wezel. 2006. Adaptation: from single cells to BOLD signals. *Trends in Neurosciences* 29 (5):250–256.

Laeng, Bruno, Kenneth Hugdahl, and Karsten Specht. 2011. The neural correlate of colour distances revealed with competing synaesthetic and real colours. *Cortex* 47 (3):320–331.

Logothetis, Nikos K., and Brian A. Wandell. 2004. Interpreting the BOLD signal. *Annual Review of Physiology* 66:735–769.

Lueck, Christian J., S. Zeki, K. J. Friston, M. P. Deiber, P. Cope, V. J. Cunningham, A. A. Lammertsma, C. Kennard, R. S. J. Frackowiak. 1989. The colour centre in the cerebral cortex of man. *Nature* 340 (6232):386–389.

Mattingley, Jason B., Anina N. Rich, Greg Yelland, and John L. Bradshaw. 2001. Unconscious priming eliminates automatic binding of colour and alphanumeric form in synaesthesia. *Nature* 410 (6828):580–582.

Maurer, Daphne. 1997. Neonatal synaesthesia: Implications for the processing of speech and faces. In *Synaesthesia: Classic and Contemporary Readings*, ed. Simon Baron-Cohen and John E. Harrison, 224–242. Malden, MA: Blackwell Publishers Inc.

Miller, Earl K., Lin Li, and Robert Desimone. 1991. A neural mechanism for working and recognition memory in inferior temporal cortex. *Science* 254 (5036):1377–1379.

Mitchell, Kevin J. 2013. Synesthesia and cortical connectivity: a neurodevelopmental perspective. In *The Oxford Handbook of Synesthesia*, ed. Julia Simner and Edward M. Hubbard, 530–557. Oxford: Oxford University Press.

Naccache, Lionel, and Stanislas Dehaene. 2001. The priming method: Imaging unconscious repetition priming reveals an abstract representation of number in the parietal lobes. *Cerebral Cortex* 11 (10):966–974.

Neufeld, Janina, Chris Sinke, Markus Zedler, Wolfgang Dillo, Hinderk M. Emrich, Stefan Bleich, and Gregor R. Szycik. 2012. Disinhibited feedback as a cause of synesthesia: Evidence from a functional connectivity study on auditory-visual synesthetes. *Neuropsychologia* 50 (7):1471–1477.

Niccolai, Valentina, Tessa M. van Leeuwen, Colin Blakemore, and Petra Stoerig. 2012. Synaesthetic perception of colour and visual space in a blind subject: an fMRI case study. *Consciousness and Cognition* 21 (2):889–899.

Niccolai, Valentina, Edmund Wascher, and Petra Stoerig. 2012. Distinct neural processes in grapheme-colour synaesthetes and semantic controls. *The European Journal of Neuroscience* 36 (11):3593–601.

Nikolic, Danko, Philipp Lichti, and Wolf Singer. 2007. Color opponency in synaesthetic experiences. *Psychological Science* 18 (6):481–486.

Nunn, Julia A., L. J. Gregory, M. J. Brammer, S. C. R. Williams, D. M. Parslow, M. J. Morgan, R. G. Morris, E. T. Bullmore, S. Baron-Cohen, and J. A. Gray. 2002. Functional magnetic resonance imaging of synesthesia: Activation of V4/V8 by spoken words. *Nature Neuroscience* 5 (4):371–375.

Palmeri, Thomas J., Randolph Blake, René Marois, Marci A. Flanery, and William Whetsell Jr. 2002. The perceptual reality of synesthetic color. *Proceedings of the National Academy of Sciences of the United States of America* 99:4127–4131.

Paulesu, E., J. Harrison, S. Baron-Cohen, J. D. G. Watson, L. Goldstein, J. Heather, R. S. J. Frackowiak, and C. D. Frith. 1995. The physiology of coloured hearing: A PET activation study of colour-word synaesthesia. *Brain* 118:661–676.

Petersen, Steven E., P. T. Fox, M. I. Posner, M. Mintum, and M. E. Raichle. 1988. Positron emission tomographic studies of the cortical anatomy of single-word processing. *Nature* 331 (6157):585–589.

Petroff, Ognen A. C. 2002. GABA and glutamate in the human brain. *The Neuroscientist* 8 (6):562–573.

Ramachandran, V. S., and David Brang. 2013. From molecules to metaphor: Outlooks on synesthesia research. In *The Oxford Handbook of Synesthesia*, ed. Julia Simner and Edward M. Hubbard, 999–1021. Oxford: Oxford University Press.

Ramachandran, Vilayanur S. and Hubbard, Edward M. 2001a. Psychophysical investigations into the neural basis of synaesthesia. *Proceedings of the Royal Society Biological Sciences Series B* 268 (1470):979–983.

———. 2001b. Synaesthesia: A window into perception, thought and language. *Journal of Consciousness Studies* 8 (12):3–34.

Rich, Anina N., and Jason B. Mattingley. 2013. The role of attention in synesthesia. In *The Oxford Handbook of Synesthesia*, ed. Julia Simner and Edward M. Hubbard, 265–282. Oxford: Oxford University Press.

Rich, Anina N., Mark A. Williams, Aina Puce, Ari Syngeniotis, Matthew A. Howard, Francic McGlone, and Jason B. Mattingley. 2006. Neural correlates of imagined and synaesthetic colours. *Neuropsychologia* 44 (14):2918–2925.

Robertson, Lynn C. 2003. Binding, spatial attention and perceptual awareness. *Nature Reviews Neuroscience* 4 (2):93–102.

Rouw, Romke and H. Stephen Scholte. 2007. Increased structural connectivity in grapheme-color synesthesia. *Nature Neuroscience* 10 (6):792–797.

———. 2010. Neural basis of individual differences in synesthetic experiences. *The Journal of Neuroscience* 30 (18):6205–6213.

Rouw, Romke, H. Stephen Scholte, and Olivia Colizoli. 2011. Brain areas involved in synaesthesia: a review. *Journal of Neuropsychology* 5 (2):214–242.

Sagiv, Noam, Julia Simner, James Collins, Brian Butterworth, and Jamie Ward. 2006. What is the relationship between synaesthesia and visuo-spatial number forms? *Cognition* 101 (1):114–128.

Seron, Xavier, Mauro Pesenti, Marie-Pascale Noel, Gérard Deloche and Jacques-André Cornet. 1992. Images of numbers: Or 'When 98 is upper left and 6 sky blue'. *Cognition* 44 (1–2):159–196.

Simner, Julia, Jennifer Harrold, Harriet Creed, Louise Monro, and Louise Foulkes. 2009. Early detection of markers for synaesthesia in childhood populations. *Brain*, 132:57–64.

Simner, Julia, and Edward M. Hubbard. 2006. Variants of synesthesia interact in cognitive tasks: Evidence for implicit associations and late connectivity in cross-talk theories. *Neuroscience* 143 (3):805–814.

Simon, Olivier, Jean-François Mangin, Laurent Cohen, Denis Le Bihan, and Stanislas Dehaene. 2002. Topographical layout of hand, eye, calculation, and language-related areas in the human parietal lobe. *Neuron* 33 (3):475–487.

Sinke, Christopher, Janina Neufeld, Hinderk M. Emrich, Wolfgang Dillo, Stefan Bleich, Markus Zedler, and Gregor R. Szycik. 2012. Inside a synesthete's head: A functional connectivity analysis with grapheme-color synesthetes. *Neuropsychologia* 50 (14):3363–3369.

Sinke, Christopher, John H. Halpern, Markus Zedler, Janina Neufeld, Hinderk M. Emrich, and Torsten Passie. 2012. Genuine and drug-induced synesthesia: A comparison. *Consciousness and Cognition* 21 (3):1419–1434.

Smilek, Daniel, Alicia Callejas, Mike J. Dixon, and Philip M. Merikle. 2007. Ovals of time: Time-space associations in synaesthesia. *Consciousness and Cognition* 16 (2):507–519.

Smilek, Daniel, Mike J. Dixon, Cera Cudahy, and Philip M. Merikle. 2001. Synaesthetic photisms influence visual perception. *Journal of Cognitive Neuroscience* 13 (7):930–936.

Smilek, Daniel, Kelly A. Malcolmson, Jonathan S. A. Carriere, Meghan Eller, Donna Kwan, and Michael Reynolds. 2007. When '3' is a jerk and 'E' is a king: Personifying inanimate objects in synesthesia. *Journal of Cognitive Neuroscience* 19 (6):981–992.

Spalding, John M. K., and Oliver Zangwill. 1950. Disturbance of number-form in a case of brain injury. *Journal of Neurology, Neurosurgery, and Psychiatry* 12:24–29.

Specht, Karsten, and Bruno Laeng. 2011. An independent component analysis of fMRI data of grapheme-colour synaesthesia. *Journal of Neuropsychology* 5 (2):203–213.

Sperling, Julia M., David Prvulovic, David E. J. Linden, Wolf Singer, and Aglaja Stirn. 2006. Neuronal correlates of graphemic colour synaesthesia: A fMRI study. *Cortex* 42 (2):295–303.

Steven, Megan S., Peter C. Hansen, and Colin Blakemore. 2006. Activation of color selective areas of visual cortex in a blind synesthete. *Cortex* 42 (2):304–308.

Summerfield, Christopher, Emily H. Trittschuh, Jim M. Monti, M.-Marsel Mesulam, and Tobias Egner. 2008. Neural repetition suppression reflects fulfilled perceptual expectations. *Nature Neuroscience* 11 (9):1004–1006.

Tang, Joey, Jamie Ward, and Brian Butterworth. 2008. Number forms in the brain. *Journal of Cognitive Neuroscience* 20 (9):1547–1556.

Terhune, Devin B., Sarah Tai, Alan Cowey, Tudor Popescu, and Roi Cohen Kadosh. 2011. Enhanced cortical excitability in grapheme-color synesthesia and its modulation. *Current Biology* 21 (23):2006–2009.

Thirion, Bertrand, Philippe Pinel, Sébastien Mériaux, Alexis Roche, Stanislas Dehaene, and Jean-Baptiste Poline 2007. Analysis of a large fMRI cohort: Statistical and methodological issues for group analyses. *Neuroimage* 35 (1):105–120.

Treisman, Anne M. 1980. A feature-integration theory of attention. *Cognitive Psychology* 12:97–136.

van Leeuwen, Tessa M., Hanneke E.M. den Ouden, and Peter Hagoort. 2011. Effective connectivity determines the nature of subjective experience in grapheme-color synesthesia. *The Journal of Neuroscience* 31 (27):9879–9884.

van Leeuwen, Tessa M., Karl M. Petersson, and Peter Hagoort. 2010. Synaesthetic colour in the brain: beyond colour areas. A functional magnetic resonance imaging study of synaesthetes and matched controls. *PLoS ONE* 5 (8):e12074.

Ward, Jamie, and Julia Simner. 2003. Lexical-gustatory synaesthesia: linguistic and conceptual factors. *Cognition* 89 (3):237–261.

——. 2005. Is synaesthesia an X-linked dominant trait with lethality in males? *Perception* 34 (5):611–623.

Ward, Jamie, Julia Simner, and Vivian Auyeung. 2005. A comparison of lexical-gustatory and grapheme-colour synaesthesia. *Cognitive Neuropsychology* 22 (1):28–41.

Weiss, Peter H., N. Jon Shah, Ivan Toni, Karl Zilles, and Gereon R. Fink. 2001. Associating colours with people: a case of chromatic-lexical synaesthesia. *Cortex* 37 (5):750–753.

Weiss, Peter H., Karl Zilles, and Gereon R. Fink. 2005. When visual perception causes feeling: Enhanced cross-modal processing in grapheme-color synesthesia. *Neuroimage* 28 (4):859–868.

....

CHAPTER 25

SYNESTHESIA, HYPERCONNECTIVITY, AND DIFFUSION TENSOR IMAGING

....

ROMKE ROUW

HYPERCONNECTIVITY AND SYNESTHESIA

....

For a synesthete, a music tone interval of "minor second" might obviously relate to the taste "sweet" (Hänggi, Wotruba, and Jäncke 2011). The core characteristic in synesthesia is that a particular sensation or experience will evoke another, seemingly unrelated, experience. The sensation or experience seems to be evoked with no particular effort, no "decision" or complex conscious thought, and no effortful recalling from memory about what the concurrent experience should be. Instead, one experience seems to "hitchhike" with another experience, in a fast and seemingly effortless way. Any model of synesthesia needs to explain the reason and nature of this connection between one experience and another. In a neurobiological model, it seems imperative that activation in one brain area (related to the inducer sensation) somehow evokes activation in another brain area (related to the concurrent sensation). The particular properties of this mechanism are, however, still much debated.

We will first discuss current theoretical models on the neurobiology of synesthesia. An intuitively logical explanation of the additional activation is that it is subserved by additional physical connections in the brain. Note that both initial growth of connections in infants and the pruning process in a young child can underlie early aberrant development of structural connectivity, as shown in children with autism spectrum disorder (Wolff et al. 2012). One developmental model of synesthesia proposed that all babies experience a mixing of senses (Maurer 1997), and only with age does modularity develop. In accordance, a recent study showed that 2- and 3-month-old babies prefer certain shape–color combinations over others, while no such preferences were obtained in 8-month-olds or adults (Wagner and Dobkins 2011). Perhaps in synesthetes, early hyperconnectivity continues to exist and facilitates the shaping of stable cross-modular associations. Ramachandran and Hubbard (2001a, 2001b) furthermore put forward the notion that the specific type of synesthesia relates to the specific location of additional connectivity in the brain. Certain types of synesthesia are more common than others, which can be explained by the fact that cross-connectivity is more likely developed in adjacently located brain areas. Indeed, grapheme-color synesthesia (colored letters and numbers) is one of the most common kinds of synesthesia, and a brain region specialized in recognizing word forms (Cohen et al. 2000) is adjacently located in the fusiform gyrus to a brain region known for its role in color perception (McKeefry and Zeki 1997). This model therefore predicts that grapheme-color synesthesia is related to increased connectivity near the fusiform gyrus. The model also provides a framework to explain how these deviant patterns of connectivity could come about: the genetic predisposition to develop synesthesia includes a tendency to early hyperconnectivity. Through these connections, direct "cross-activation" from inducer to concurrent brain areas is facilitated, leading to the synesthetic (concurrent) experience in response to the inducing experience. Thus, this model provides a framework for the neurobiological properties of synesthesia. Ten years after initial publications, the core assumptions of the model have received empirical support, while other empirical findings led to a revised version of the model (Hubbard, Brang, and Ramachandran 2011).

With little work yet done on the (development of) neurobiological characteristics of synesthesia, present theory-building is still in its early stages. Rather than increased connectivity, other researchers put forward that synesthesia is best understood by functional differences in the brain. The additional activation then occurs through abnormal feedback processing. Abnormal feedback can travel back within the sensory processing stream, such as from anterior fusiform gyrus back to posterior inferior temporal regions and V4 (Grossenbacher and Lovelace 2001) and Smilek et al. (2001) proposed that a "higher level" or association brain area mediates the additional activation. Through such a "multisensory nexus" (such as the superior temporal sulcus, regions in the parietal cortex, or the temporo-parietal occipital junction), disinhibited feedback flows back to lower-level sensory brain areas. One important issue in the debate is therefore whether the additional activation is caused by a difference in structural connectivity, or whether there are no structural differences and the increased activation is instead only caused by altered function. Of course, while the accent might be different, most researchers will agree that substantial functional brain differences are likely to cause structural brain differences (e.g., Draganski et al. 2004; Maguire et al. 2000) and vice versa. Therefore, an interaction between these two factors will most likely take place during the development of the synesthetic brain. Another issue in the debate is whether activation flows directly from the inducer to the concurrent, or whether it is mediated by a "higher-level" or associative brain area. In summary, while all researchers agree that some type of "hyperconnectivity" must exist in synesthesia to underlie the additional sensation, the nature of this hyperconnectivity is debated. Two issues are important to keep in mind when discussing properties of hyperconnectivity in one human subject group versus another.

First, a fundamental distinction should be made between different types of connectivity in the brain: structural connectivity, functional connectivity and effective connectivity (Friston 1994). These refer, respectively, to the physical properties of anatomical connections, statistical dependence in patterns of brain activation, and causal influences from one neural element to another (Sporns et al. 2004). Each of these types of connectivity has different methodology in terms of data collection and data analyses.

Second, anatomical connectivity from "one neural unit to another" can refer to exceedingly different spatial scales. Physical properties in the neural network range from the microscopic scale involving architectonics at the cellular level (such as different parts of a neuron) to the macroscopic scale involving regions of the cerebral cortex (such as a Brodmann area, a cerebral lobe, or a particular white matter tract). In turn, "connectivity" can refer to an individual (synaptic) connection at the microscale, to connections between neuronal populations at the mesoscale, or to white matter pathways between brain regions at the macroscale (Sporns et al. 2004). Currently, the properties of these different types of connectivity, and the relationships between these levels of analyses, are not yet mapped out for the human brain (Crick and Jones 1993). This is particularly the case for micro- and mesoscale levels, where research tends to focus on animal models of connectivity. It is however unclear how primate (or other animal) atlases translate to the human brain (e.g., Tootell, Tsao, and Vanduffel 2003). Using these animal models to make predictions about the human brain therefore remains problematic. In particular for the typically complex human mental processes involved in synesthesia, any neurobiological model needs to build on knowledge of the human brain. An important recent development to take on this issue is the construction of a connection matrix of the human brain (the human "connectome" project; Hagmann et al. 2008; Sporns, Tononi, and Kotter 2005).

The role of structural brain differences is an important topic of debate in synesthesia research. In this chapter, "synesthetic hyperconnectivity" will be discussed with a focus on the anatomical differences at the macroscale level of spatial resolution. One practical reason is that there is a technique available that allows *in vivo* non-invasive measurements at the macroscale in healthy human subjects. Most information currently available about hyperconnectivity in synesthesia is obtained by use of this technique. We will explicate this technique, which is based on diffusion estimates during magnetic resonance imaging (MRI), in the next paragraph. As explained before, no empirical evidence has so far been obtained about structural connectivity in synesthetes at a finer spatial scale. Alternatives to measures taken in animals are either *in vitro* studies of human tissue (such as dead tissue), or studies where humans have been operated on to allow recordings at finer spatial resolutions. These operations are done for clinical reasons and in certain patient groups (e.g., microelectrodes implanted in epileptic patients; Fried et al. 1999; Ojemann et al. 1988). None of these approaches is thus fit for studying connectivity patterns in healthy normal synesthetes. Another reason to focus on macroscale anatomical differences is of a theoretical nature: the most comprehensive synesthesia model currently available (Hubbard, Brang, and Ramachandran 2011) makes specific predications about structural differences at the level of network systems neuroscience. Indeed, the crossing-over between different types of experiences and the apparent loss of modularity in these cross-sensations (Baron-Cohen et al. 1993) do point at effects at the macroscale level from one functionally specialized brain region to another. In this chapter, after explaining the methodology used, I will present studies using this methodology to study synesthesia as well as their obtained results.

What Is Diffusion Tensor Imaging?

Imagine a large bowl of water. If we zoom in on a single water molecule in that bowl, we expect it to be moving in a random fashion. This random pattern of movement (Brownian motion) entails that over time, there is an approximate equal displacement in all directions. Now, let's take a handful of spaghetti and put it in the bowl. The diffusion of our water molecule is disrupted: it can still freely move in parallel to the spaghetti, but motion in the perpendicular direction is restricted. There is now more motion in certain directions than in other directions. Displacement with equally strong movement in all directions is called *isotropic* diffusion. The more directionally dependent the displacement becomes, the more *anisotropic* the diffusion pattern.

Water is the most common molecule in the human body. Rather than being like a large bowl of water, the human body is structured, with different structures having different local microstructural characteristics of water diffusion. Diffusion MRI utilizes the powerful concept that imaging these patterns of diffusion of water molecules allows us to reveal *in vivo* properties of human (brain) tissue at a microscopic scale. In the mid-eighties of the previous century, the method of diffusion-weighted magnetic resonance imaging (DWI) was realized. The basis of the method is adding diffusion-sensitizing gradients to an (magnetic resonance) imaging sequence (for a review see Basser 2009; Basser and Özarslan 2009). This creates a diffusion-weighted image, where each image voxel contains information about the diffusion at that location. The diffusion of water molecules is not influenced by the methodology of magnetic resonance (MR) measurements, such as the strong magnetic field.

As early as 1954, Carr and Purcell (1954) described how the echo magnitude in Hahn's spin-echo method (Hahn 1950) could be sensitized to the effects of the diffusion of water molecules. By applying a constant field gradient throughout the experiment, the homogeneity of the magnetic field is varied linearly. In this inhomogeneous field, diffusion of the molecules can be measured as relative signal loss. With the difference in the strength of the magnetic field, the protons precess at different rates depending on their location. The diffusion estimate is based on the phase dispersion of the magnetization. A larger diffusivity of the spin-labeled molecules will give larger attenuation of the observed magnitude signal. Stejskal and Tanner (1965) further improved the method by introducing two sequential diffusion gradient pulses of short duration. This allows one to exactly control the diffusion time (time between the two pulses), independently from the encoding time (pulse duration). Two gradient pulses are applied in the same direction but with opposite magnitude. The second pulse thus rephases the spin, unless the molecule has moved. If a particle has not moved, the net attenuation of the first pulse dephase and second pulse rephase is zero. Random diffusion of the molecules, in contrast, leads to a diverse field of incomplete cancellations. Incomplete cancellation, as explained before, results in phase dispersion that results in relative signal loss. This method allows one to calculate a more precise diffusion estimate.

Wesbey, Moseley, and Ehman (1984) reported the first *in vitro* measurement of molecular self-diffusion coefficients in a (0.35 Tesla) magnetic resonance imager. This added "apparent diffusion coefficients" (ADC) to the parameters measured by MRI. In the ADC image one scalar parameter is estimated per voxel, such as the main orientation or the mean rate of diffusion in that voxel. The DWI image thus shows properties of the underlying structure. For example, an infarct obstructs diffusion, which changes the local color compared with the surroundings. As only displacements along the direction of the gradient are visible, the direction of the gradient pulse is changed to observe variations in the diffusion measurement. In current research, different choices can be made in gradient application, which is reflected in the *b-value*. The b-value is a function of the strength, duration, and the temporal spacing of the diffusion sensitizing gradients. Higher b-values imply more influence of the gradients on the diffusion-weighted images. The most popular acquisition technique to obtain diffusion-weighted images is a single-shot diffusion-weighted, echo-planar (EPI) protocol (Turner et al. 1990).

In the 1990s, a mathematical model was developed to utilize more fully the truly three-dimensional information revealed by the diffusion patterns. Directionality is inherently part of the obtained information. Envisioning a mathematical estimate, or diffusion *tensor*, enriched the amount of information available per voxel (Basser, Mattiello, and Le Bihan 1994a; Basser, Mattiello, and Le Bihan 1994b; Basser and Pierpaoli 1996). While scalar parameters (such as apparent diffusivity) need intervoxel comparisons to learn about the spatial distribution of the chemical or physical state of tissue, the tensor inherently contains intravoxel structural information. By presenting a series of pulsed-gradient, spin-echo nuclear magnetic resonance (NMR) experiments, and using multivariate linear regression, Basser and Le Bihan (1992) presented a method to estimate Deff. Deff is the estimated effective diffusion tensor to characterize diffusion anisotropy within a voxel. It contains the direction (three orthotropic axes or Eigenvectors) and the mean diffusion distances in these directions (Eigenvalues). As we will see in the next paragraph, this opened the doorway to many new applications, such as *in vivo* tracking of white matter tracts in the human brain.

DWI has exceedingly increased our potential to obtain information about the structural properties of living tissue. Diffusion coefficients can be measured in various types of tissues (e.g., muscle, spinal court, or the human brain of a neonate; Cleveland, Chang, and Hazlewood 1976; Hajnal et al. 1991; Huang et al. 2006). This methodology can be used to infer the anatomical architecture of the human brain *in vivo*, as well as changes in this architecture within or across individuals in development or trauma. This has clinical implications, such as in the mapping of white matter (WM) prior to surgery (e.g., Witwer et al. 2002) and early detection of brain ischemia (Fisher et al. 1992;

Van Gelderen et al. 1994; Warach et al. 1992). It also has implications for research on neurological or psychiatric diseases such as schizophrenia (Kubicki et al. 2007; Lim et al. 1999). In terms of measuring brain properties in the healthy human brain, particular progress is made in mapping out the (directional) properties of white matter tracts.

About the Interpretation of Diffusion Tensor Imaging Results

In the current context, DTI methodology is of interest as both directional information and relative strength of each direction is provided per voxel. Furthermore, the non-invasive methodology allows the examining of properties of white matter tracts in normal healthy humans *in vivo*. Before turning to results obtained in DTI studies with synesthetes, I first discuss in this section the factors involved in the interpretation of DTI results.

From the DTI results different diffusion measurements can be calculated (Le Bihan et al. 2001). Mean diffusivity (MD) is an averaged measure characterizing overall displacement of molecules. The degree to which diffusion is anisotropic can also be expressed, in such indices as fractional anisotropy (FA) or relative anisotropy (RA) (Basser and Pierpaoli 1996; Conturo et al. 1996). Anisotropy relates to the degree of directionality, not to the strength of the diffusion (total displacement) itself. If we put broccoli rather than spaghetti in the bowl of water, diffusion is more anisotropic (more directionally dependent) at the location of the flower stem than at the location of the flower, even when the average disruption of diffusion does not differ between those two locations. In the human brain, more coherently orientated structures in white matter cause increased anisotropic diffusion in white matter as compared with the gray matter.

What exactly causes anisotropic diffusion in the white matter? While the myelin sheath is an obvious and important factor in anisotropic diffusion patterns, it is not the only factor. The directionality of the diffusion is influenced by several longitudinally oriented structures of the myelinated axon. Next to myelin, also the axonal membrane, microtubules and neurofilaments hinder water diffusion perpendicular to the length of the axon (Beaulieu 2002). These properties can even be sufficient for anisotropy: a normal non-myelinated nerve can result in obtained anisotropic diffusion (e.g., in the olfactory nerve of the garfish; Beaulieu and Allen 1994); in non-myelinated fibers in neonates, (Hüppi et al. 1998). In interpreting diffusion-dependent measurements obtained with DTI, it is thus important to keep in mind that several central nervous system (CNS) features give rise to anisotropy. Next to axonal membranes and non-myelinated fibers, cell membranes, vascular structures, cytoskeleton, and macromolecules can also influence diffusion patterns in the CNS. Within a tract of white matter, properties of the axons such as their radius, thickness of myelin, myelin permeability, and packing density influence the diffusion (an)isotropy. The size, shape, composition, and spacing between the obstructions all influence the way in which diffusion is hindered. Anisotropy indicates not only the presence of orientation-dependent structures, but also the coherence of these orientations.

Per image voxel, a parameter (tensor or scalar variable) is calculated. The parameter contains all the information of microstructural influences on the diffusion measurement. The outcome of this measurement is therefore a non-specific summation index of all structural information in the entire voxel. The size of a voxel is, however, typically a few millimeters cubed, which contains thousands of axons. This coarse spatial resolution of the measurement implies a problem in calculating specific aspects of the underlying structure. It is currently not possible to attribute one particular microstructural feature (e.g., packing density) to the obtained diffusion measurement.

In sum, while it is hard to decipher how each aspect of the underlying microstructure influences the diffusion parameter, increased anisotropy in a white-matter voxel mostly reflects axon-directional measurements (including myelin and other longitudinally oriented structures). Degree of anisotropy reflects both the strength and the coherence of these directions. More generally speaking, increased anisotropic diffusion in white matter reflects an overall increased "strength" and/or coherence of the white matter tracts.

So far, we have discussed inter-voxel calculations in DTI methodology. However, the coherence between these voxels provides information about entire pathways of white matter (Basser et al. 2000; Poupon et al. 2000; Wiegell, Larsson, and Wedeen 2000). MR diffusion tractography allows the mapping out of these pathways non-invasively and *in vivo* in the human brain. Fiber tracking algorithms provide a good estimation of fiber orientation and strength, measuring within or between-subjects effects. There are several different approaches to performing tractography. One way to reconstruct across-voxel white matter trajectories is to take one voxel as a start or "seed" location. Line propagation or streamline techniques use the principal eigenvector of the diffusion tensor, with the assumption that the main direction will correspond to the longitudinal axis of the white matter tract. This provides a good estimate of the location and orientation of the main white matter tracts. Traditional MR diffusion models do not however make good estimates at locations where two or more white matter tracts have unequal orientations (e.g., if fiber bundles intersect). Another limitation of tractography is that it cannot distinguish between anterograde and retrograde direction.

Recent developments hold great promise to counter problems that currently confound the interpretation of DTI data. One important issue is that if two or more white matter tracts cross within a voxel, this is traditionally treated by the diffusion tensor as "noise" (or general decreased anisotropy) in the measurement. Two or more fiber bundles present in the same voxel is known as intra-voxel orientational heterogeneity (IVOH; Tuch 2002; Tuch et al. 2002). This problem is particularly relevant in regions of complex fiber crossings, and when obtaining long-range white matter tracts with tractography. Recently, techniques have been developed to estimate more directions, and to extract more information from the diffusion-weighted signal (however, this procedure also significantly adds to the scanning time). High-angular resolution diffusion imaging (HARDI) applies a large number of independent diffusion-sensitized gradients (Tuch et al. 2002). The HARDI signal can be used to model which directions are related to maximum anisotropic diffusion measures. If there is only one major tract, there are only two maximum anisotropic diffusion measures (in opposite directions). Each additional tract (with another orientation) will add a pair of maxima into the model. As a graphic representation of this distinction, imagine a jellybean. Its orientation can indicate only one main direction (anterograde and retrograde). The shape of a gummy bear can, however, indicate the relative strength of several directions. Via traditional tensor math (adding more than one tensor per voxel), via more complex tensor analyses, or via a "model free" analysis, the set of directions can subsequently be modeled as fibers and fiber crossings. Model-independent approaches as q-space methods (Callaghan 1991; Callaghan, Eccles, and Xia 1988) or diffusion spectrum imaging (Tuch et al. 2002) avoid the assumption of a single direction. These promising developments make probabilistic modeling of more than one fiber tract feasible (e.g., Tournier et al. 2004; Tuch et al. 2003).

DIFFUSION TENSOR IMAGING AND SYNESTHESIA

The final section of this chapter will present studies that examined structural (hyper) connectivity in synesthesia and obtained their results using the DTI methodology. Currently only three studies have examined the structural properties of the brains of synesthetes versus non-synesthetes (Hänggi et al. 2008; Jäncke et al. 2009; Rouw and Scholte 2007). Two studies examined grapheme-color synesthesia and one study examined a subject with interval-taste and tone-color synesthesia (see later). These studies will be presented one by one below (for a table with all these FA results see Rouw, Scholte, and Colizoli 2011).

We studied structural connectivity in synesthetes by use of DTI (Rouw and Scholte 2007) by contrasting 18 synesthetes that experience colors with letters and numbers, with 18 matched controls without synesthesia. As explained in the previous section, acquisition of diffusion-weighted measurements by attenuation of the MR signal allows one to make an estimate of the degree of diffusion anisotropy per voxel per individual. For each subject, in each voxel the mean FA value was calculated. From these values, the mean FA skeleton was created representing the centers of all tracts common to the group. This is a procedure of the TBSS analysis (tract-based spatial statistics, Smith et al. 2004; Smith et al. 2006), which is part of FSL (Smith et al. 2004). The FA data of each subject is projected onto this skeleton, which allows comparisons between (groups of) subjects. The significance of the comparison between synesthetes and non-synesthetes was determined with voxel-wise cross-subject statistics (permutation testing). The threshold is at a t-value higher than 3, with a minimum clustersize set at 40 mm^3. This procedure obtained a clear pattern of results. Higher FA values for synesthetes as compared with control non-synesthete subjects were obtained in four different brain areas.

Of particular interest was increased anisotropy obtained in the white matter near to the fusiform gyrus. In the fusiform gyrus, a region specialized in the perception of colors (McKeefry and Zeki 1997) is located adjacent to an area specialized in the recognition of the (form of) graphemes (Cohen et al. 2000). The finding is thus in line with the model (see earlier) of direct "cross-activation" between inducer and concurrent areas, mediated by increased structural connectivity between these regions in the fusiform gyrus (Hubbard, Brang, and Ramachandran 2011; Ramachandran and Hubbard 2001, 2001) (see Figure 25.1). Tractography showed that this increased FA near the fusiform gyrus was obtained in a network of local corticocortical association fibers in the inferior temporal lobe. In addition to the cluster near the fusiform gyrus, increased FA values were obtained in left superior parietal cortex and bilaterally in frontal cortex beneath the central sulcus. Tractography in these regions indicated that the parietal cluster shows strongest connectivity within the parietal cortex, while the frontal clusters were part of tracts projecting medially toward the corpus callosum. There were no significantly lower FA values in the synesthetic group as compared with the control group. The results thus support the notion of anatomical hyperconnectivity in

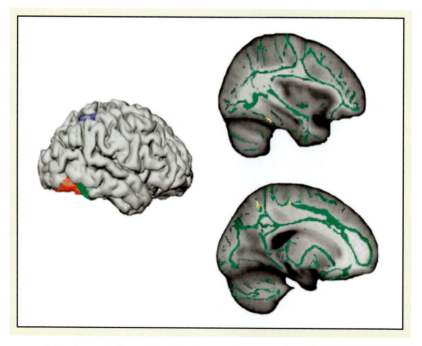

FIGURE 25.1 *Left*: theoretical model with increased connectivity between relevant inducer (green) and concurrent (red) brain area The blue area is proposed to be involved as a higher level, 'binding' area or 'hub' (in blue). Reprinted by permission from Macmillan Publishers Ltd: *Nature Neuroscience*, 10 (6), Hubbard, Edward M., A real red letter day, pp. 671–672, copyright (2007). *Right*: obtained increased structural connectivity as found with DTI (adapted from Rouw and Scholte 2007) in grapheme-color synesthetes compared with non-synesthetes (above: X = 36; below: X = −18).

grapheme-color synesthetes. Furthermore, findings show that a difference between synesthetes and non-synesthetes was obtained not only at the predicted location in the inferior temporal cortex. Other, "higher" and more associative brain regions were found to be related to synesthesia as well.

Our study additionally showed an effect of different types of synesthetic experiences on the obtained white matter measurements. We designed a "projector/associator (PA) questionnaire" (Rouw and Scholte 2007) to evaluate individual differences in the type of experience related to the synesthesia. Some synesthetes (termed "projector" synesthetes) report seeing the synesthetic color "in the outside world," while others (termed "associator" synesthetes) report the color "inside my mind" only (Dixon, Smilek, and Merikle 2004). The total PA score indicates the degree to which the synesthete is projector or associator (respectively higher or lower score). In the DTI study, a positive correlation was obtained between PA score and the mean FA value in the cluster in inferior temporal cortex. Thus, the "projector" type of synesthesia was related to higher FA values in this cluster near the fusiform gyrus. This correlation suggests a relationship between differences in neural substrate and differences in subjective synesthetic experiences. This suggestion was recently supported in a study showing structural brain differences between associator and projector synesthetes using voxel-based morphometry (VBM; Rouw and Scholte 2010). Projectors (as compared with associators) showed increased gray matter in sensory-specific cortex (including primary visual and auditory cortex), precentral (premotor) as well as in frontal cortex. In contrast, associator synesthetes (as compared with projector synesthetes) showed relative increased gray matter in angular gyrus and the hippocampus. Perhaps the nature of the synesthetic experience is related to functional properties of the mediating neural substrate. Projectors, who experience the synesthesia in the "outside world," showed effects in brain areas involved in sensing and acting in the outside world. In contrast, the "inside my mind" experience of associators was found to be related to the hippocampus, a brain region generally known for its role in memory functions.

Jäncke et al. (2009) examined different neuroanatomical correlates of (grapheme-color) synesthesia. The study particularly focused on the fusiform gyrus and adjacent brain regions in the ventral visual stream. Both surface-based morphometry (cortical thickness, cortical volume and cortical surface area) and FA analyses (WM coherence) were performed based on magnetic resonance images. Synesthetes showed, as compared with non-synesthetes, increased values of thickness, volume and surface area in the gray matter of the right and left fusiform gyrus and adjacent regions. This finding included increased gray matter volume roughly in the area of V4, and a correspondence between the location of peak difference in increased gray matter volume and the location of increased FA in our temporal cluster (Rouw and Scholte 2007). Several other areas in ventral visual cortex also showed synesthesia-related effects. Furthermore, non-predicted increases were obtained in brain regions outside this ventral region. In the diffusion-weighted images, structural connectivity was studied based on fractional anisotropy measures. In this analysis, 14 synesthetes were compared with 14 matched controls. The procedure of data analysis was similar to that of

Rouw and Scholte (2007), creating a mean FA skeleton (using TBSS scripts from FSL; Smith et al. 2004). The significance of the comparison between the two groups was calculated with voxelwise t-tests for independent comparisons (instead of the non-parametric tests). The authors focused on those regions with strong a priori hypotheses (in bilateral temporo-occipital regions). Using t-tests with a threshold set at $p < 0.01$ and a minimum clustersize of 30 voxels did not obtain significant differences in this region. Lowering the threshold to $p = 0.05$ did result in larger FA values in synesthetes as compared with non-synesthetes; again, increased FA values were found near the fusiform gyrus in grapheme-color synesthetes as compared with non-synesthetes.

There are no easy or clear-cut rules to determine correct thresholding in these whole-brain analyses (mainly because the multiple-comparison problem cannot readily be solved). In the current (hypothesis-testing) situation a threshold of $p < 0.05$ is not atypical; note also that this is a theoretically relevant finding in the predicted direction (increased in synesthetes as compared with non-synesthetes). The authors' conclusion that *no* differences in FA were detected in fusiform gyri between synesthetes and non-synesthetes therefore seems needlessly stringent. To what extent in this study the same cluster was obtained as in Rouw and Scholte (2007) is, however, not clear, the coordinates of the cluster were not provided. It is important to see if other studies will replicate this result of increased FA values near to the fusiform gyrus in synesthetes.

At a threshold of $p < 0.01$ increased FA values in synesthetes were obtained outside the ventral visual cortex; in the hippocampus, the inferior fronto-occipital fasciculus and in the splenium of the corpus callosum. The inverse contrast (decreased FA values in synesthetes) was not examined. As PA values were not measured, it is not clear whether the obtained differences are related to this individual difference in synesthetic experience. For example, it would be interesting to know if the differences obtained in hippocampus relate to associators in this particular sample of synesthetes. In conclusion, this study has enhanced our understanding of neuroanatomical correlates of grapheme-color synesthesia. The findings support local anatomical differences in gray and white matter characteristics in the ventral visual cortex, including regions near the V4 complex. Again, this is not the only brain region showing strong effects in the synesthete versus non-synesthete comparison.

This research group also examined white matter properties in a different type of synesthesia. Synesthete ES is a professional musician with absolute pitch perception. She experiences different types of taste when hearing particular musical tone intervals (Beeli, Esslen, and Jäncke 2005). Besides this unusual interval-taste synesthesia, she has tone-color synesthesia, where a particular tone evokes a specific color. Hänggi et al. (2008) used diffusion tensor analysis and T1-weighted magnetic resonance imaging to extract FA values as well as white and gray matter volumetric measurements. Interestingly, ES was compared with 17 professional female musicians as well as 20 normal control females. As in the two previously discussed studies, for each subject an FA map was created using FSL, and non-linear registration of all FA images were applied into standard space with TBSS (Smith et al. 2006). With SPM5

(<http://www.fil.ion.ucl.ac.uk/spm/>), a mean and standard deviation image was computed for the control group. Z-score maps for the synesthetes were computed by voxelwise subtracting the group FA mean image from the synesthete FA image and dividing it by the standard deviation image. These z-score maps were thresholded with a height threshold of z = 3.1 (p <0.001) and with an extent threshold of K = 50 (50 mm^3). As compared with professional musicians (comparison with the normal controls yielded similar results), increased FA in ES was found in the left planum temporale/Heschl's gyrus, in the right Heschl's gyrus/insula, and in the left and right lateral occipital cortex. These regions are functionally related to either inducer or concurrent in her types of synesthesia. Increased FA was also obtained in right middle temporal gyrus-temporo-occipital part, in right superior frontal gyrus/premotor cortex, and in left cerebellum. Decreased FA values in ES were found in the left internal capsule, left postcentral gyrus, right precentral gyrus, left corticospinal tract, left posterior thalamic radiation, both anterior intraparietal sulci, and in the right pallidum. Decreased FA was also found in right lateral occipital gyrus, left inferior frontal gyrus, and right frontal pole. Thus, ES showed structural differences in primary auditory cortex/Heschl's gyrus and planum temporale, which are functionally related to auditory perception and related to the inducer sensation of her types of synesthesia; hearing intervals or hearing musical tones. Differences were also obtained in areas related to the concurrent function; the insula is functionally important in taste perception, and color perception is based in occipital regions. As in the other studies, several brain regions were obtained in addition to the predicted brain regions.

Hänggi and colleagues also applied probabilistic fiber tractography to examine which areas are hyperconnected (Behrens et al. 2007). At each voxel, distributions of diffusion parameters were built that allow modeling crossing fibers within a voxel. The authors used a multiple ROIs (region of interest) approach where only tracts that pass through all these ROIs are retained. The ROIs were three neighboring areas in which large FA differences were obtained between synesthete ES and the control groups: the insula, Heschl's gyrus, and the planum temporale. The connectivity distribution of ES was compared with that of ten controls. Tractography revealed hyperconnectivity in ES, as compared with the musicians, in bilateral perisylvian-insular regions. In sum, this study examined a very interesting case of synesthesia and contrasted her with a carefully matched control group (professional musicians with perfect pitch perception). The FA analysis, probabilistic fiber tractography, and voxel-based morphometry showed significant effects in both inducer and concurrent brain areas. As in the other studies, effects were, however, obtained in other brain regions as well.

In sum, these studies showed hyperconnectivity in synesthetes as compared with non-synesthetes. At present it is difficult to draw strong conclusions about exact locations of hyperconnectivity, as so far there are only a small number of studies. Also, ideally a larger number of subjects would be included per study. The current evidence supports the notion of hyperconnectivity near to the brain region involved in inducer and the concurrent sensation (e.g., for grapheme-color synesthetes the color area and the word form area). Clearly, findings are not restricted to these regions.

FUNCTIONAL CONNECTIVITY AND SYNESTHESIA

As a final note, while in this chapter we focused on DTI/FA studies, recent years have seen remarkable progress in brain connectivity methodologies (Friston 2011; Sporns 2011). In the past 2 years, a handful of synesthesia studies have used these methodologies. These include a structural connectivity study; namely a network analyses of cortical thickness (Hänggi, Wotruba, and Jäncke 2011). There have also been functional connectivity studies, which are based on correlations between spatially remote neurophysiological events (Friston 1994), and which basically measure functional interactions. Neufeld and colleagues (Neufeld et al. 2012) analyzed functional MRI (fMRI) data obtained by presenting simple and complex sounds to auditory-visual synesthetes. Functional connectivity was also studied in so-called "resting-state" or task-free context, obtained with electroencephalography (Jäncke and Langer 2011) or with fMRI (Dovern et al. 2012). Next to structural and functional connectivity, the third type of connectivity is effective connectivity (Sporns 2011). Effective connectivity reflects the influence one neural system exerts over another. Van Leeuwen, den Ouden, and Hagoort (2011) studied effective connectivity in synesthesia with dynamic causal modeling of fMRI data.

What can be concluded from these studies? Again, at present there are only a small number. Moreover, the methods are substantially different from each other. It is currently not yet clear how one type of measurement (e.g., in functional connectivity) relates to another measurement (e.g., structural connectivity properties). Bearing this in mind (and therefore noting that these next conclusions should be regarded as preliminary) what follows is a short summary of these recent findings. While general connectivity patterns (e.g., obtained small-world network or obtained hubs) were similar between synesthetes and non-synesthetes, certain overall differences were also obtained in synesthetes as compared with non-synesthetes. These include increased clustering and increased global hyperconnectivity (Hänggi, Wotruba, and Jäncke 2011) or increased intranetwork functional connectivity (Dovern et al. 2012). Another relevant finding is that individual synesthetic experiences are reflected in the results. These include findings specifically related to the type of synesthesia. Neufeld et al. (2012) found in auditory-visual synesthetes stronger connectivity of the left inferior parietal cortex with the left primary auditory and right primary visual cortex, and Jäncke and Langer (2011) found in colored-hearing synesthetes a strong right-sided auditory cortex hub. Individual differences between synesthetes were also reflected in the network, such as in the strength of the synesthetic experiences (Dovern et al. 2012) or the projector-associator distinction (van Leeuwen, den Ouden, and Hagoort 2011). More specifically, color activation was mediated through the fusiform gyrus in projector synesthetes, but via the parietal lobe in associator synesthetes. Furthermore, in these connectivity studies several other (unexpected) brain regions were again obtained. Finally, while the parietal lobe is generally found to be important in network analyses, these studies point at a specific role for parietal lobe in synesthetic functioning (Jäncke and Langer 2011; Neufeld et al. 2012;

van Leeuwen, den Ouden, and Hagoort 2011). Thus, both the lower (modality specific) and higher (association) cortical areas were important in relation to synesthesia in these connectivity studies.

Conclusions

We now return to the two questions raised in the introduction. The first question is whether synesthesia entails structural brain differences or only altered brain function. The second is whether activation flows directly from the inducer to the concurrent, or is instead mediated by "higher-level" or associative brain areas. While so far only a few studies have appeared, consistencies across these studies allow for the first tentative conclusions. The most important finding obtained across these studies is that the brains of synesthetes show structural differences from the brains of matched non-synesthetes. DTI studies found synesthesia related to differences in white matter properties. These findings indicate structural hyperconnectivity in synesthetes as compared with non-synesthetes. As noted previously, this does not mean that there are structural differences *rather than* functional differences. Not only are structural differences likely to entail functional differences, but long-term functional differences can also cause structural brain differences (Bezzola et al. 2011; Loui et al. 2011; Mackey, Whitaker, and Bunge 2012).

Second, hyperconnectivity was obtained in inducer and concurrent brain areas. A role of "higher" or associative brain regions, particularly in parietal cortex, is supported as well. Some models suggest that both higher- and lower-level areas are incorporated in the synesthetic network (Jäncke and Langer 2011; Weiss and Fink 2009). Other models suggest instead that these findings reflect two subsets of synesthetes (for example, projector versus associator or "higher" versus "lower" synesthetes, one more depending on the "direct-connection" route and the other mediated by "associative brain areas"; Hubbard and Ramachandran 2005; Hubbard et al. 2005; Ramachandran and Hubbard 2001; van Leeuwen, den Ouden, and Hagoort 2011).

Increased connectivity is obtained in unexpected brain regions as well. One explanation is that these are only noise-like effects (e.g., individual variation that happens to be present in this particular subject/subject group, but is not specifically related to synesthesia). It is, however, also possible that these findings reflect aspects of synesthesia that still need to be unveiled (see also Rouw, Scholte, and Colizoli 2011).

Changes in brain structure might be the intermediating step between differences in genetic predisposition and additional activation in the non-stimulated "concurrent" brain areas. However, synesthesia will also be influenced by a child's environment and learning patterns (and vice versa), which in turn are likely to affect brain structure. Indeed, previous research have found both genetic (Asher et al. 2009; Tomson et al. 2011) and environmental (Simner et al. 2005; Witthoft and Winawer 2006) factors associated with synesthesia. If both environmental and genetic factors are involved, they will most likely shape the synesthetic brain in an interactive manner. An important topic that needs to be studied is therefore which developmental patterns lead to adult synesthesia. Currently, how these additional sensations are shaped over the years has only been theoretically described (e.g., see Bargary and Mitchell 2008). An important future direction of research is to study the particulars of the developmental pattern, including the development of hyperconnectivity, in synesthetic as compared with non-synesthetic children.

REFERENCES

Asher, Julian E., Janine Lamb, Denise Brocklebank, Jean-Baptiste Cazier, Elena Maestrini, Laura Addis, Mallika Sen, Simon Baron-Cohen, and Anthony P. Monaco. 2009. A whole-genome scan and fine-mapping linkage study of auditory-visual synesthesia reveals evidence of linkage to chromosomes 2q24, 5q33, 6p12, and 12p12. *The American Journal of Human Genetics* 84 (2):279–285.

Bargary, Gary, and Kevin J. Mitchell. 2008. Synaesthesia and cortical connectivity. *Trends in Neurosciences* 31 (7):335–342.

Baron-Cohen, Simon, John Harrison, Laura H. Goldstein, and Maria Wyke. 1993. Coloured speech perception: Is synaesthesia what happens when modularity breaks down? *Perception* 22 (4):419–426.

Basser, Peter J. 2009. Diffusion and diffusion tensor MR imaging: Fundamentals. In *Diffusion MRI: From quantitative measurement to in-vivo neuroanatomy*, ed. Heidi Johansen-Berg and Timothy E. J. Behrens. London: Elsevier.

Basser, Peter J., and Denis Le Bihan. 1992. Fiber orientation mapping in an an-isotropic medium with NMR diffusion spectroscopy. *Proceedings 11th Annual Meeting SMRM* 1 (1221).

Basser, Peter J., James Mattiello, and Denis Le Bihan. 1994a. Estimation of the effective self-diffusion tensor from the NMR spin-echo. *Journal of Magnetic Resonance Series B* 103 (3):247–254.

———. 1994b. MR diffusion tensor spectroscopy and imaging. *Biophysical Journal* 66 (1):259–267.

Basser, Peter J., and Evren Özarslan. 2009. Introduction to diffusion MRI. In *Diffusion MRI: From quantitative measurement to in-vivo neuroanatomy*, ed. Heidi Johansen-Berg and Timothy E. J. Behrens, 2–10. London: Elsevier.

Basser, Peter J., Sinisa Pajevic, Carlo Pierpaoli, Jeffrey Duda, and Akram Aldroubi. 2000. In vivo fiber tractography using DT-MRI data. *Magnetic Resonance in Medicine* 44 (4):625–632.

Basser, Peter J., and Carlo Pierpaoli. 1996. Microstructural and physiological features of tissues elucidated by quantitative-diffusion-tensor MRI. *Journal of magnetic Resonance* 213 (2):560–570.

Beaulieu, Christian. 2002. The basis of anisotropic water diffusion in the nervous system—a technical review. *NMR in Biomedicine* 15 (7–8):435–455.

Beaulieu, Christian, and Peter S. Allen. 1994. Determinants of anisotropic water diffusion in nerves. *Magnetic Resonance in Medicine* 31 (4):394–400.

Beeli, Gian, Michaela Esslen, and Lutz Jäncke. 2005. Synaesthesia: When coloured sounds taste sweet. *Nature* 434:38.

Behrens, T. E., H. J. Berg, S. Jbabdi, M. F. Rushworth, and M. W. Woolrich. 2007. Probabilistic diffusion tractography with multiple fibre orientations: What can we gain? *NeuroImage* 34 (1):144–155.

Bezzola, Ladina, Susan Mérillat, Christian Gaser, and Lutz Jäncke. 2011. Training-induced neural plasticity in golf novices. *The Journal of Neuroscience* 31 (35):12444–12448.

Callaghan, P. T., C. D. Eccles, and Y. Xia. 1988. NMR microscopy of dynamic displacements: k-space and q-space imaging. *Journal of Physics E: Scientific Instruments* 21:820–828.

Callaghan, Paul T. 1991. *Principles of Nuclear Magnetic Resonance Microscopy.* Oxford: Clarendon Press.

Carr, Herman Y., and Edward M. Purcell. 1954. Effects of diffusion on free precession in nuclear magnetic resonance experiments. *Physical Review* 94 (3):630–638.

Cleveland, Gordon G., Donald C. Chang, and Carlton F. Hazlewood. 1976. Nuclear magnetic resonance measurement of skeletal muscle: Anisotrophy of the diffusion coefficient of the intracellular water. *Biophysical Journal* 16:1043–1053.

Cohen, Laurent, Stanislas Dehaene, Lionel Naccache, Stephan Lehericy, Ghislaine Dehaene-Lambertz, Marie-Anne Henaff, and Francois Michel. 2000. The visual word form area—Spatial and temporal characterization of an initial stage of reading in normal subjects and posterior split-brain patients. *Brain* 123:291–307.

Conturo, Thomas E., Robert C. McKinstry, Erbil Akbudak, and Bruce H. Robinson. 1996. Encoding of anisotropic diffusion with tetrahedral gradients: A general mathematical diffusion formalism and experimental results. *Magnetic Resonance in Medicine* 35 (3):399–412.

Crick, Francis, and Edward Jones. 1993. Backwardness of human neuroanatomy. *Nature* 361 (6408):109–110.

Dixon, Mike J., Daniel Smilek, and Philip M. Merikle. 2004. Not all synaesthetes are created equal: Projector versus associator synaesthetes. *Cognitive, Affective & Behavioral Neuroscience* 4 (3):335–343.

Dovern, Anna, Gereon R. Fink, A. Christina B. Fromme, Afra M. Wohlschlager, Peter H. Weiss, and Valentin Riedl. 2012. Intrinsic network connectivity reflects consistency of synesthetic experiences. *The Journal of Neuroscience* 32 (22):7614–7621.

Draganski, Bogdan, Christian Gaser, Volker Busch, Gerhard Schuierer, Ulrich Bogdahn, and Arne May. 2004. Neuroplasticity: Changes in grey matter induced by training—newly honed juggling skills show up as a transient feature on a brain-imaging scan. *Nature* 427 (6972):311–312.

Fisher, Mark, Christopher H. Sotak, Kazuo Minematsu, and Limin Li. 1992. New magnetic resonance techniques for evaluating cerebrovascular disease. *Annals of Neurology* 32:115–122.

Fried, Itzhak, Charles L. Wilson, Nigel T. Maidment, Jerome Engel, Eric Behnke, Tony A. Fields, Katherine A. MacDonald, Jack W. Morrow, and Larry Ackerson. 1999. Cerebral microdialysis combined with single-neuron and electroencephalographic recording in neurosurgical patients—Technical note. *Journal of Neurosurgery* 91 (4):697–705.

Friston, Karl J. 1994. Functional and effective connectivity in neuroimaging: A synthesis. *Human Brain Mapping* 2:56–78.

——. 2011. Functional and effective connectivity in neuroimaging: A review. *Brain Connectivity* 1 (1):13–24.

Grossenbacher, Peter G., and Christopher T. Lovelace. 2001. Mechanisms of synesthesia: Cognitive and physiological constraints. *Trends in Cognitive Sciences* 5 (1):36–41.

Hagmann, Patric, Leila Cammoun, Xavier Gigandet, Reto Meuli, Christopher J. Honey, Van J. Wedeen, and Olaf Sporns. 2008. Mapping the structural core of human cerebral cortex. *PLoS Biology* 6 (7):1479–1493.

Hahn, Erwin L. 1950. Spin echoes. *Physical Review* 80 (4):580–594.

Hajnal, Joseph V., Mark Doran, Alisdair S. Hall, Alan G. Collins, Angela Oatridge, Jacqueline M. Pennock, Ian R. Young, and Graeme M. Bydder. 1991. MR imaging of anisotropically restricted diffusion of water in the nervous-system—technical, anatomic, and pathological considerations. *Journal of Computer Assisted Tomography* 15 (1):1–18.

Hänggi, Jürgen, Gian Beeli, Mathias S. Oechslin, and Lutz Jäncke. 2008. The multiple synaesthete ES—neuroanatomical basis of interval-taste and tone-colour synaesthesia. *NeuroImage* 43 (2):192–203.

Hänggi, Jürgen, Diana Wotruba, and Lutz Jäncke. 2011. Globally altered structural brain network topology in grapheme-color synesthesia. *The Journal of Neuroscience* 31 (15):5816–5828.

Huang, Hao, Jiangyang Zhang, Setsu Wakana, Weihong Zhang, Tianbo Ren, Linda J. Richards, Paul Yarowsky, *et al.* 2006. White and gray matter development in human fetal, newborn and pediatric brains. *NeuroImage* 33 (1):27–38.

Hubbard, Edward M., A. Cyrus Arman, Vilayanur S. Ramachandran, and Geoffrey M. Boynton. 2005. Individual differences among grapheme-color synesthetes: Brain-behavior correlations. *Neuron* 45 (6):975–985.

Hubbard, Edward M. 2007. A real red letter day. *Nature Neuroscience* 10 (6):671–672.

Hubbard, Edward M, David Brang, and Vilayanur S. Ramachandran. 2011. The cross-activation theory at ten. *Journal of Neuropsychology* 5:152–177.

Hubbard, Edward M., and Vilayanur S. Ramachandran. 2005. Neurocognitive mechanisms of synesthesia. *Neuron* 48 (3):509–520.

Hüppi, Petra S., Stephan E. Maier, Sharon Peled, Gary. P. Zientara, Patrick D. Barnes, Ferenc A. Jolesz, and Joseph J. Volpe. 1998. Microstructural development of human newborn cerebral white matter assessed in vivo by diffusion tensor magnetic resonance imaging. *Pediatric Research* 44 (4):584–590.

Jäncke, Lutz, and Nicolas Langer. 2011. A strong parietal hub in the small-world network of coloured-hearing synaesthetes during resting state EEG. *Journal of Neuropsychology* 5 (2):178–202.

Jäncke, Lutz, Gian Beeli, Cornelia Eulig, and Jürgen Hänggi. 2009. The neuroanatomy of grapheme-color synesthesia. *European Journal of Neuroscience* 29 (6):1287–1293.

Kubicki, Marek, Robert McCarley, Carl-Fredrik Westin, Hae-Jeong Park, Stephan Maier, Ron Kikinis, Ferenc A. Jolesz, and Martha E. Shenton. 2007. A review of diffusion tensor imaging studies in schizophrenia. *Journal of Psychiatric Research* 41 (1–2):15–30.

Le Bihan, Denis, Jean-Francois Mangin, Cyril Poupon, Chris A. Clark, Sabina Pappata, Nicolas Molko, and Hughes Chabriat. 2001. Diffusion tensor imaging: Concepts and applications. *Journal of Magnetic Resonance Imaging* 13 (4):534–546.

Lim, Kelvin O., Maj Hedehus, Michael Moseley, Alexander de Crespigny, Edith V. Sullivan, and Adolf Pfefferbaum. 1999. Compromised white matter tract integrity in schizophrenia inferred from diffusion tensor imaging. *Archives of General Psychiatry* 56 (4):367–374.

Loui, Psyche, Hui C. Charles Li, Anja Hohmann, and Gottfried Schlaug. 2011. Enhanced cortical connectivity in absolute pitch musicians: A model for local hyperconnectivity. *Journal of Cognitive Neuroscience* 23 (4):1015–1026.

Mackey, Allyson P., Kirsty J. Whitaker, and Silvia A. Bunge. 2012. Experience-dependent plasticity in white matter microstructure: reasoning training alters structural connectivity. *Frontiers in Neuroanatomy* 6:32.

Maguire, Eleanor A., David G. Gadian, Ingrid S. Johnsrude, Catriona D. Good, John Ashburner, Richard S. J. Frackowiak, and Christopher D. Frith. 2000. Navigation-related structural change in the hippocampi of taxi drivers. *Proceedings of the National Academy of Sciences of the United States of America* 97 (8):4398–4403.

Maurer, Daphne. 1997. Neonatal synaesthesia: Implications for the processing of speech and faces. In *Synaesthesia: Classic and Contemporary Readings*, ed. Simon Baron-Cohen and John E. Harrison, 224–242. Malden, MA: Blackwell Publishers Inc.

McKeefry, D. J., and S. Zeki. 1997. The position and topography of the human colour centre as revealed by functional magnetic resonance imaging. *Brain* 120:2229–2242.

Neufeld, Janina, Christopher Sinke, Markus Zedler, Wolfgang Dillo, Hinderk M. Emrich, Stefan Bleich, and Gregor R. Szycik. 2012. Disinhibited feedback as a cause of synesthesia: Evidence from a functional connectivity study on auditory-visual synesthetes. *Neuropsychologia* 50 (7):1471–1477.

Ojemann, George A., Otto Creutzfeldt, Ettore Lettich, and Michael M. Haglund. 1988. Neuronal-activity in human lateral temporal cortex related to short-term verbal memory, naming and reading. *Brain* 111:1383–1403.

Poupon, C., C. A. Clark, V. Frouin, J. Regis, I. Bloch, D. Le Bihan, and J. F. Mangin. 2000. Regularization of diffusion-based direction maps for the tracking of brain white matter fascicles. *NeuroImage* 12 (2):184–195.

Ramachandran, Vilayanur S., and Edward M. Hubbard. 2001a. Psychophysical investigations into the neural basis of synaesthesia. *Proceedings of the Royal Society B: Biological Sciences* 268 (1470):979–983.

——. 2001b. Synaesthesia: A window into perception, thought and language. *Journal of Consciousness Studies* 8 (12):3–34.

Rouw, Romke, and H. Steven Scholte. 2007. Increased structural connectivity in grapheme-color synesthesia. *Nature Neuroscience* 10 (6):792–797.

——. 2010. Neural basis of individual differences in synesthetic experiences. *The Journal of Neuroscience* 30 (18):6205–6213.

Rouw, Romke, H. Steven Scholte, and Olympia Colizoli. 2011. Brain areas involved in synaesthesia: A review. *Journal of Neuropsychology* 5 (2):214–242.

Simner, Julia, Jamie Ward, Monika Lanz, Ashok Jansari, Krist Noonan, Louise Glover, and David A. Oakley. 2005. Non-random associations of graphemes to colours in synaesthetic and non-synaesthetic populations. *Cognitive Neuropsychology* 22 (8):1069–1085.

Smilek, Daniel, Mike J. Dixon, Cera Cudahy, and Philip M. Merikle. 2001. Synaesthetic photisms influence visual perception. *Journal of Cognitive Neuroscience* 13 (7):930–936.

Smith, Stephen M., Mark Jenkinson, Mark W. Woolrich, Christian F. Beckmann, Timothy E. J. Behrens, Heidi Johansen-Berg, Peter R. Bannister, *et al.* 2004. Advances in functional and structural MR image analysis and implementation as FSL. *NeuroImage* 23:S208–S219.

Smith, Stephen M., Mark Jenkinson, Heidi Johansen-Berg, Daniel Rueckert, Thomas E. Nichols, Clare E. Mackay, Kate E. Watkins, *et al.* 2006. Tract-based spatial statistics: Voxelwise analysis of multi-subject diffusion data. *NeuroImage* 31 (4):1487–1505.

Sporns, Olaf, Dante R. Chialvo, Marcus Kaiser, and Claus C. Hilgetag. 2004. Organization, development and function of complex brain networks. *Trends in Cognitive Sciences* 8 (9):418–425.

Sporns, Olaf, Guilio Tononi, and Rolf Kotter. 2005. The human connectome: A structural description of the human brain. *PloS Computational Biology* 1 (4):245–251.

Sporns, Olaf. 2011. *Networks of the Brain*. Cambridge, MA: MIT Press.

Stejskal, E. O., and J. E. Tanner. 1965. Spin diffusion measurements: Spin echoes in the presence of a time-dependent field gradient. *The Journal of Chemical Physics* 42 (1):288–292.

Tomson, Steffie N., Nili Avidan, Kwanghyuk Lee, Anand K. Sarma, Rejnal Tushe, Dianna M. Milewicz, Molly Bray, Suzanne Leal, and David M. Eagleman. 2011. The genetics of colored sequence synesthesia: Suggestive evidence of linkage to 16q and genetic heterogeneity for the condition. *Behavioral Brain Research* 223 (1):48–52.

Tootell, Roger B. H., Doris Tsao, and Wim Vanduffel. 2003. Neuroimaging weighs in: Humans meet macaques in 'primate' visual cortex. *The Journal of Neuroscience* 23 (10):3981–3989.

Tournier, J. Donald, Fernando Calamante, David G. Gadian, and Alan Connelly. 2004. Direct estimation of the fiber orientation density function from diffusion-weighted MRI data using spherical deconvolution. *NeuroImage* 23 (3):1176–1185.

Tuch, D. S. 2002. *Diffusion MRI of complex tissue structure*. Cambridge, MA: Harvard University-Massachusetts Institute of Technology.

Tuch, D. S., T. G. Reese, M. R. Wiegell, N. Makris, J. W. Belliveau, and V. J. Wedeen. 2002. High angular resolution diffusion imaging reveals intravoxel white matter fiber heterogeneity. *Magnetic Resonance in Medicine* 48 (4):577–582.

Tuch, David S., Timothy G. Reese, Mette R. Wiegell, and Van J. Wedeen. 2003. Diffusion MRI of complex neural architecture. *Neuron* 40 (5):885–895.

Turner, R., D. Le Bihan, J. Maier, R. Vavrek, L. K. Hedges, and J. Pekar. 1990. Echo-planar imaging of intravoxel incoherent motion. *Radiology* 177:407–414.

van Gelderen, Peter, Marloes H. M. de Vleeschouwer, Daryl DesPres, James Pekar, Peter C. M. van Zil, and Chrit T. Moonen. 1994. Water diffusion in acute stroke. *Magnetic Resonance in Medicine* 31:154–163.

van Leeuwen, Tessa M., Hanneke E. M. den Ouden, and Peter Hagoort. 2011. Effective connectivity determines the nature of subjective experience in grapheme-color synesthesia. *The Journal of Neuroscience* 31 (27):9879–9884.

Wagner, Katie, and Karen R. Dobkins. 2011. Synaesthetic associations decrease during infancy. *Psychological Science* 22 (8):1067–1072.

Warach, S., D. Chien, W. Li, M. Ronthal, and R. R. Edelman. 1992. Fast magnetic-resonance diffusion-weighted imaging of acute human stroke. *Neurology* 42 (9):1717–1723.

Weiss, Peter H., and Gereon R. Fink. 2009. Grapheme-colour synaesthetes show increased grey matter volumes of parietal and fusiform cortex. *Brain* 132 (1):65–70.

Wesbey, George E., Michael E. Moseley, and Richard L. Ehman. 1984. Translational molecular self-diffusion in magnetc-resonance imaging. II. Measurement of the self-diffusion coefficient. *Investigative Radiology* 19 (6):491–498.

Wiegell, Mette R., Henrik B. W. Larsson, and Van J. Wedeen. 2000. Fiber crossing in human brain depicted with diffusion tensor MR imaging. *Radiology* 217 (3):897–903.

Witthoft, Nathan, and Jonathan Winawer. 2006. Synesthetic colors determined by having colored refrigerator magnets in childhood. *Cortex* 42 (2):175–183.

Witwer, Brian P., Roham Moftakhar, Khader M. Hasan, Praveen Deshmukh, Victor Haughton, Aaron Field, Konstantinos Arfanakis, *et al.* 2002. Diffusion-tensor imaging of white matter tracts in patients with cerebral neoplasm. *Journal of Neurosurgery* 97 (3):568–575.

Wolff, Jason J., Hongbin Gu, Guido Gerig, Jed T. Elison, Martin Styner, Sylvain Gouttard, Kelly N. Botteron, *et al.* 2012. Differences in white matter fiber tract development present from 6 to 24 months in infants with autism. *The American Journal of Psychiatry* 169 (6):589–600.

CHAPTER 26

CAN GRAY MATTER STUDIES INFORM THEORIES OF (GRAPHEME-COLOR) SYNESTHESIA?

PETER H. WEISS

INTRODUCTION

After *functional* imaging had already revolutionized the neurosciences, researchers realized that modern *structural* imaging (mainly based on magnetic resonance imaging (MRI)) could contribute to the understanding of the human brain to a similar extent. There is of course a longstanding tradition in (clinical) cognitive neurosciences of relating the location and extent of lesions in brain-damaged patients to their cognitive deficits (Rorden and Karnath 2004), but it was only recently that proper statistical methods, like voxel-based morphometry (VBM; Good et al. 2001) or voxel-based lesion symptom mapping (VLSM; Bates et al. 2003), were introduced to allow for a quantitative *in vivo* evaluation of structural brain differences in patients and healthy subjects. In healthy subjects, VBM-investigations of gray matter (GM) differences have been performed to elucidate the neural mechanisms underlying (extraordinary) cognitive abilities in, for example, musicality (Gaser and Schlaug 2003), bilingualism (Mechelli et al. 2004), but also literacy (Carreiras et al. 2009) and general intelligence (Haier et al. 2004). Thus, it is not surprising that these methods have also been applied to the research on the neural mechanisms of synesthesia, a condition in which stimulation of a sensory modality leads to additional (sensory) percepts either in the same modality (e.g., grapheme-color synesthesia; Weiss and Fink 2009) or another modality (e.g., tone-color synesthesia; Hänggi et al. 2008).

Structural neuroimaging studies in synesthesia were, at least in part, driven by the fact that evidence for structural brain differences in synesthetes would speak in favor of certain synesthesia theories but would be difficult to reconcile with others. Therefore, the current chapter reviews the published studies exploring GM differences in synesthesia and examines how these structural imaging results may inform current theories about the neural mechanisms of synesthesia. As large sample sizes are critical for the quantitative analysis of structural brain differences, many VBM-studies focused on grapheme-color synesthesia, one of the most common forms of synesthesia. Thus, the emphasis of this chapter will be on the current knowledge about GM differences in grapheme-color synesthesia. Furthermore, a critical discussion of the limitations of the approaches used to study synesthetic GM differences as well as future perspectives and challenges of structural neuroimaging research in synesthesia will be provided.

Studies of Gray Matter Differences in Grapheme-Color Synesthesia

Motivated by a diffusion tensor imaging (DTI) study in grapheme-color synesthesia showing increased structural connectivity in right temporal and left parietal cortex (but also in superior frontal cortex bilaterally; Rouw and Scholte 2007; see Rouw, Chapter 25, this volume for a description of this methodology and finding), we used VBM to examine whether this altered local connectivity in temporo-occipital and parietal areas was associated with GM changes (Weiss and Fink 2009). A region-of-interest (ROI) approach revealed specific increases of the GM volume in the left caudal intraparietal sulcus (IPS) and the right fusiform gyrus of 18 grapheme-color synesthetes when compared to 18 matched control subjects. Adopting the cyto-architectonically defined maximum probability maps (MPM; Eickhoff et al. 2005), the areas with increased GM volume in grapheme-color synesthesia could be localized to the human intraparietal area 3 (hIP3; Scheperjans et al. 2008) and the ventral visual area 4 (V4v; Rottschy et al. 2007; see Figure 26.1). These DTI and VBM findings were consistent with a two-stage model of grapheme-color synesthesia proposed by Hubbard (2007) which implies both cross-activation at the level of the fusiform gyrus and "hyperbinding" at the level of the parietal cortex.

In a large sample of grapheme-color synesthetes (n = 42), Rouw and Scholte used concurrent VBM and functional magnetic resonance imaging (fMRI) to explore the neural basis of individual differences in grapheme-color synesthesia (Rouw and Scholte 2010). They were particularly interested in whether the subjective quality of the synesthetic experience (i.e., whether synesthetic colors are perceived "in the mind" versus "in the outside world"; a distinction known as associator versus projector synesthesia), would have a differential neural basis. For projector synesthetes, increased GM volumes were found in the left visual (calcarine sulcus) and right auditory (Heschl's gyrus) cortices. In addition, the left precentral gyrus as part of the motor system, a large cluster in the medial frontal cortex, and bilateral precuneus showed increased GM volumes in projector synesthetes. The main finding for the associator synesthetes was a bilateral GM

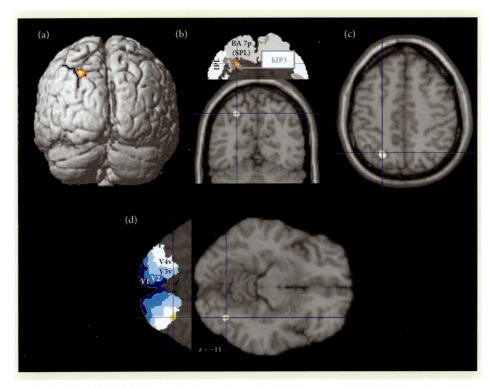

FIGURE 26.1 Voxel-based morphometry (VBM) findings in grapheme-color synesthesia. (a–c) Grapheme-color synesthetes show increased grey matter (GM) volume in the left caudal intraparietal sulcus (IPS, maximum at −24, −64, +47). The upper left panel (a) shows the caudal IPS region projected onto a three-dimensional surface rendering of a single-subject brain spatially normalized to the MNI space. The blue line indicates the intraparietal sulcus (IPS). The upper middle panel (b) shows the caudal IPS region superimposed on a coronal section of the normalized standard single-subject brain provided by SPM2 (lower part) to illustrate its location in the depth of the IPS (see crosshair). Furthermore, the upper part of (b) shows that the GM difference in the caudal IPS can be assigned to the maximum probability map of human intraparietal area 3 (hIP3, dark grey). Furthermore, the GM difference is located neither in the maximum probability map of Brodmann area (BA) 7p (posterior), which is part of the superior parietal lobe (SPL, light grey), nor in the areas comprising the inferior parietal lobe (IPL, white). The right upper panel (c) depicts the caudal IPS region (crosshair) superimposed on an axial section of the normalized standard single subject brain provided by SPM2. (d) Grapheme-color synesthetes show also increased GM volumes in the right fusiform gyrus (maximum at +34, −69, −11). The lower right panel shows this fusiform gyrus region superimposed on an axial slice of an individual brain normalized to MNI space. The lower left panel illustrates that this region is located within the maximum probability map of right ventral visual area 4 (V4v, white area) provided by the Anatomy tool box (Eickhoff et al. 2005). The dark blue, blue, and light blue areas indicate the maximum probability maps of V1, V2, and V3v, respectively. Reprinted from *Brain*, 132(1), Peter H. Weiss and Gereon R. Fink. Grapheme-colour synaesthetes show increased gray matter volumes of parietal and fusiform cortex, pp. 65–70, figure 1. Copyright (2009), with permission from Oxford University Press [http://brain.oxfordjournals.org/content/132/1/65.full]. For permission to reuse this material, please visit http://www.oup.co.uk/academic/rights/permissions.

increase in the (para-) hippocampal area and the angular gyrus. Interestingly, the para-hippocampal gyrus was found to be bilaterally activated in associator synesthetes during fMRI. In addition to these differential GM changes, Rouw and Scholte also found increased GM volumes in the left superior parietal cortex common to all synesthetes (projectors and associators combined) when compared to control subjects (Rouw and Scholte 2010). For the cingulate cortex, there was even a decrease of GM in the synesthetes compared to controls.

In summary, these imaging data from a large sample suggest that structural differences in the superior parietal cortex, an area involved in the integration of sensory information, are common in grapheme-color synesthesia. Consistent with their subjective color experiences, projector synesthetes show GM changes in areas involved in interacting with the outside world, while associator synesthetes exhibit GM changes in regions related to memory and imagery processes.

Rouw and Scholte had evaluated their synesthetes as projectors or associators using a multi-point questionnaire, and a scoring system referred to as "projector/associator (PA) score." Note that Weiss and Fink did not find significant correlations between PA scores and the individual GM values in the right fusiform gyrus and left caudal IPS in their sample of 18 grapheme-color synesthetes. On the other hand, in a similar sized sample of grapheme-color synesthetes, Rouw and Scholte (2007) found significant correlations between PA scores and the individual fractional anisotropy (FA) values in the right temporal cortex derived from DTI. Notably, PA scores did not correlate with FA values in the left (superior) parietal area (−17, −61, +55; Rouw and Scholte 2007), which was close to the left superior parietal cortex area (−11, −58, +61) common to all synesthetes as revealed by the VBM study (Rouw and Scholte 2010).

A recent fMRI study on grapheme-color synesthesia adopting dynamic causal modeling (DCM) revealed different effective connectivity patterns in projectors and associators (van Leeuwen, Ouden, and Hagoort 2011). The authors showed that V4 cross-activation during grapheme-color synesthesia was induced via a bottom-up pathway (within the fusiform gyrus) in projector synesthetes, but via a top-down pathway (via the parietal lobe) in associators. The PA difference score was significantly correlated with a better or worse fit of the respective effective connectivity model in the DCM analysis. Taken together, the findings by Rouw and Scholte (2007, 2010) and by van Leeuwen, Ouden, and Hagoort (2011) strongly suggest that the PA concept in grapheme-color synesthesia has a structural and functional imaging correlate and therefore underline the neurobiological validity of this concept.

The third study investigating GM differences in grapheme-color synesthesia adopted surface-based morphometric methods to examine cortical volume, cortical thickness, and cortical surface area in 24 synesthetes and 24 controls (Jäncke et al. 2009). The three parameters were different at the predicted locations, i.e., in ventral visual stream regions including right and left fusiform gyrus, right lingual gyrus, and right intra-calcarine cortex (primary (V1) and secondary (V2) visual cortex), all involved in either color, letter, or word processing. With respect to the GM differences in the (right) fusiform gyrus, this study replicated the findings of Weiss and Fink (2009). However, no changes for these surface-based parameters were found for the parietal cortex. Moreover, at the same statistical threshold, additional differences in cortical volume, thickness, and surface area were found in widespread brain regions for which the authors had no a priori hypothesis. Therefore, this structural imaging study stressed the importance of the fusiform gyrus in grapheme-color synesthesia, but—in contrast to the studies by Rouw and Scholte (2010) and Weiss and Fink (2009)—failed to support a significant parietal involvement in this form of synesthesia. Therefore, even when considering structural imaging studies only in grapheme-color synesthesia, there are both mutual findings, but also clear differences between studies. This pattern of results makes it unlikely that structural differences in the synesthetic brain alone can explain (grapheme-color) synesthesia. Instead, it rather suggests that additional functional brain differences (i.e., in effective connectivity (van Leeuwen, den Ouden, and Hagoort 2011) or in functional connectivity (Dovern et al. 2012) contribute to the phenomenology of synesthesia.

STUDIES OF GRAY MATTER DIFFERENCES IN OTHER FORMS OF SYNESTHESIA

In 2008, Hänggi and colleagues reported an extensive structural imaging investigation of the female synesthete ES (Hänggi et al. 2008). ES is a professional musician with absolute pitch perception who experiences two types of synesthesia: interval-taste synesthesia (hearing different tone intervals induces specific tastes; e.g., major third => sweet; Beeli, Esslen, and Jäncke 2005) and the more common tone-color synesthesia (a given tone induces the experience of a specific color; e.g., the musical note C => red). In addition to VBM, the authors performed DTI for the assessment of FA and probabilistic fiber tractography in ES and 17 professional musicians as well as 20 normal control subjects. Compared to both control groups, FA as well as GM and WM alterations were observed in the auditory, gustatory, and visual areas of ES's brain. Thus, ES showed neuroanatomical peculiarities in brain regions that process the inducing stimuli (auditory cortex) and the concurrent synesthetic experience (gustatory cortex for the interval-taste synesthesia and visual cortex for the tone-color synesthesia) providing a neuroanatomical basis for both types of synesthesia. Interestingly, these differences were mainly observed bilaterally. Furthermore, for the auditory areas (e.g., Heschl's gyrus, planum temporale) that process the inducer (i.e., the trigger) for both types of synesthesia, the authors found a decrease of GM volume in ES, when compared to the professional musicians, but not when compared to the non-musical controls. However, for the brain regions processing the synesthetic concurrents the pattern is heterogeneous as there is also a decrease in GM volume for the gustatory cortex (insula), but an increase of GM volume for the visual cortex. This is in contrast to the structural imaging studies in grapheme-color synesthesia which mostly consistently showed an *increase* of GM volume in synesthetes. Therefore, the relationship of the direction of GM volume differences (decrease versus increase) and synesthetic experiences does not seem to be straight forward. Moreover, it is often overlooked that many brain regions which are not directly related to synesthetic inducers or concurrents show up in structural imaging studies (cf. tables 1 and 2 of Hänggi et al. 2008, or table 3 of Jäncke et al. 2009). ROI approaches as in Weiss and Fink (2009) may circumvent this problem. However, this technique has its own limitations, especially when the synesthetic network consists of more brain regions than only those we have a clear hypothesis for.

CURRENT PROBLEMS

Most likely due to the recruitment strategies used it was initially assumed that (grapheme-color) synesthesia was far more prevalent in women than men (up to six times more prevalent in some studies). This assumption even influenced hypotheses about the mode of inheritance in synesthesia, e.g., single-gene, X-linked dominant mode of inheritance with a skewed female to male ratio (Baron-Cohen et al. 1996). More recent studies using innovative recruitment strategies could not find such large or even significant gender differences in the prevalence of synesthesia (Simner et al. 2006). Accordingly, current genetic studies did not reveal any significant linkage to the X chromosome, but rather favor a complex mode of inheritance involving different chromosomes—2q, 5q, 6p, and 12p (Asher et al. 2009) or 16q (Tomson et al. 2011). Thus, an "artificially inflated" gender bias has influenced the research on the genetic basis of synesthesia. Neuroanatomical gender differences have been observed in synesthesia-relevant brain regions, such as visual cortex (Amunts et al. 2007) and parietal lobe (Frederikse et al. 1999). Therefore, the findings of current studies investigating GM differences in synesthesia have to be viewed with caution as there is a clear gender bias in the examined populations. Of the 18 grapheme-color synesthetes examined by Weiss and Fink (2009) only two were men. Jäncke and colleagues (2009) examined 20 female and only four male grapheme-color synesthetes. There were only synesthetic women (n = 18 and n = 42) in the studies by Rouw and Scholte (2007, 2010). Finally, the multiple synesthete ES investigated by Hänggi and colleagues is a woman (Hänggi et al. 2008). In addition to properly controlling for gender in the examined synesthetic and control samples, structural imaging studies in male synesthetes are needed to exclude confounds by known neuroanatomical gender differences, and thereby validate the current knowledge about GM differences in synesthesia.

Taking into account the precision with which modern structural imaging techniques can pick up even subtle neuroanatomical differences, it is surprising to see that the results of these studies are dealt with in an imprecise manner. The synesthesia-relevant areas in the fusiform gyrus may serve as an example. The right fusiform gyrus region with increased anisotropy in the DTI study of Rouw and Scholte (2007) was located in the standard MNI (Montreal Neurological Institute) space at the coordinates +36, −40, −21. The area in the right fusiform gyrus that showed increased GM volumes in the

VBM-study by Weiss and Fink (2009) had the coordinates +34, −69, −11. Thus, especially for the anterior-posterior direction (y-coordinate) there is a difference of almost 3 cm (29 mm). With respect to the modular structure of the synesthesia-relevant visual (Rottschy et al. 2007) and parietal cortex (Grefkes and Fink 2005) such distances have a major functional significance. Using maximum probability maps (MPMs) provided by the Anatomy tool box (Eickhoff et al. 2005), Weiss and Fink were able to localize the fusiform gyrus region with increased GM volume in grapheme-color synesthetes to the ventral visual area 4 (V4v; see Figure 26.1). This cyto-architectonically defined area corresponds to the color-processing area in the human brain. Therefore, with neuroanatomical methods these authors were able to associate structural GM differences in synesthetes precisely to a functional area (here: color processing area V4v). Future structural imaging studies in synesthesia should aim for such a neuroanatomical precision by using state-of-the-art localization techniques as, for example, the Anatomy tool box. Unfortunately, the issue is even more complex when the role of areas, like the grapheme area/visual-word form area (VWFA), in (grapheme-color) synesthesia is investigated, as these areas are only functionally defined (Hubbard et al. 2005). In contrast to the color-processing area that also has a structural correlate (V4v; Nunn et al. 2002; Weiss and Fink 2009).

The issue of anatomical precision also has an impact on discussions about hemispheric asymmetries in synesthesia. TMS applied over the *right* parietal cortex (Esterman et al. 2006; Muggleton et al. 2007) interfered with synesthetic experiences (see Muggleton and Tsakanikos, Chapter 29, this volume), while functional and structural imaging with MRI revealed increased neural activity and increased structural connectivity as well as increased GM volume in the *left* parietal cortex of grapheme-color synesthetes (Rouw and Scholte 2007, 2010; Weiss and Fink 2009; Weiss, Zilles, and Fink 2005). In discussions about these apparently discrepant findings, it is often overlooked that in addition to differences in brain side there is also a significant distance between the brain sites. The ventral-dorsal position (z-coordinate) of the stimulation site in Muggleton et al. (2007) was +27, that of Esterman et al. (2006) was +32, while the z-coordinate of the IPS area (hIP3) with increased GM volumes in the study by Weiss and Fink (2009) was +47. Such a neuroanatomical distance of (about) 2 cm translates to the fact that structural GM differences have been observed in the caudal intra-*parietal* sulcus (IPS), while the TMS interference effects have been observed for the transverse *occipital* sulcus (TOS). Thus, these findings are not only inconsistent with respect to the hemisphere, but also the part of cortex (i.e., parietal versus occipital cortex) involved.

FUTURE PERSPECTIVES

The discussed studies clearly show that the modern techniques of structural imaging can reliably detect anatomical GM differences in synesthetes. However, these studies leave us with the important question of whether these anatomical differences are the cause or the consequence of synesthesia. Developmental studies of (grapheme-color) synesthesia (including longitudinal VBM-investigations) are needed to shed some light on the question of whether the observed structural GM differences in diverse brain regions, especially the fusiform gyrus and the parietal cortex, precede or result from lifelong synesthetic experiences (Green and Goswami 2008;Simner et al. 2008).

This question is even more pressing as VBM-studies in (non-synesthetic) adults have revealed (temporary) GM changes due to practice in the visual (Ilg et al. 2008) and the motor system (Draganski et al. 2004). Moreover, recent studies showed that by training of specific letter-color associations (Meier and Rothen 2009) or by posthypnotic suggestion (Cohen Kadosh et al. 2009) non-synesthetes can—at least in part—exhibit the behavioral consequences of (grapheme-color) synesthesia. Therefore, pre- and post-training/intervention VBM-studies may be used to investigate whether trained/induced synesthetic experiences of non-synesthetes have also a neuroanatomical correlate, e.g., whether they are associated with GM differences in certain brain regions as in genuine grapheme-color synesthesia. These studies are certainly easier to be accomplished than longitudinal VBM-studies in child populations with synesthesia.

Currently, structural imaging of clinical populations is used for statistical lesion mapping (e.g., voxel-based lesion symptom mapping, VLSM; Bates et al. 2003) to explore the neural basis of cognitive disorders after stroke, such as neglect (Verdon et al. 2010), apraxia (Dovern et al. 2011), or anosognosia (Vossel et al. 2012). Taking into account the frequency of synesthesia in the general population, e.g., grapheme-color synesthesia has a prevalence of 1% (Simner et al. 2006), one could consider structural imaging studies in neurological stroke patients that exhibit synesthesia. Such studies could use statistical lesion mapping methods to specifically look for brain regions that when (structurally) compromised by neurological disorders affect synesthetic experiences. This way, structural imaging research in synesthesia could not only reveal neuroanatomical correlations and associations of a given synesthesia type, but could also approach the question of which brain regions in the synesthesia network are essential for the generation and perception of synesthetic experiences. Thus, such research endeavors would complement the findings of studies using non-invasive neuromodulatory techniques (like transcranial magnetic stimulation; Esterman et al. 2006; Muggleton et al. 2007), and transcranial direct current stimulation (Terhune et al. 2011) to elucidate the neural basis of synesthesia.

References

Amunts, Katrin, Este Armstrong, Aleksandar Malikovic, Lars Hömke, Hartmut Mohlberg, Axel Schleicher, and Karl Zilles. 2007. Gender-specific left-right asymmetries in human visual cortex. *The Journal of Neuroscience* 27:1356–1364.

Asher, Julian E., Janine Lamb, Denise Brocklebank, Jean-Baptiste Cazier, Elena Maestrini, Laura Addis, Mallika Sen, *et al.* 2009. A whole-genome scan and fine-mapping linkage study of auditory-visual synesthesia reveals evidence of linkage to chromosomes 2q24, 5q33, 6p12, and 12p12. *The American Journal of Human Genetics* 84 (2):279–285.

Baron-Cohen, Simon, Lucy Burt, Fiona Laittan-Smith, John E. Harrison, and Patrick Bolton. 1996. Synaesthesia: Prevalence and familiarity. *Perception* 25:1073–1079.

Bates, Elizabeth, Stephen M. Wilson, Ayse Pinar Saygin, Frederic Dick, Martin I. Sereno, Robert T. Knight, and Nina F. Dronkers. 2003. Voxel-based lesion-symptom mapping. *Nature Neuroscience* 6:448–450.

Beeli, Gian, Michaela Esslen, and Lutz Jäncke. 2005. Synaesthesia: When coloured sounds taste sweet. *Nature* 434 (7029): 38–38.

Carreiras, Manual, Mohamed L. Seghier, Silvio Baquero, Adelina Estévez, Alfonso Lozano, Joseph T. Devlin, and Cathy J. Price. 2009. An anatomical signature for literacy. *Nature* 46:983–986.

Cohen Kadosh, Roi, Avishai Henik, Andres Catena, Vincent Walsh, and Luis J. Fuentes. 2009. Induced cross-modal synaesthetic experience without abnormal neuronal connections. *Psychological Science* 20 (2):258–265.

Dovern, Anna, Gereon R. Fink, A. Christina B. Fromme, Afra M. Wohlschläger, Peter H. Weiss, and Valentin Riedl. 2012. Intrinsic network connectivity reflects consistency of synesthetic experiences. *The Journal of Neuroscience* 32:7614–7621.

Dovern, Anna, Gereon R. Fink, Jochen Saliger, Hans Karbe, Iring Koch, and Peter H. Weiss. 2011. Apraxia impairs intentional retrieval of incidentally acquired motor knowledge. *The Journal of Neuroscience* 31:8102–8108.

Draganski, Bogdan, Christian Gaser, Volker Busch, Gerhard Schuierer, Ulrich Bogdahn, and Arne May. 2004. Changes in grey matter induced by training. *Nature* 427:311–312.

Eickhoff, Simon B., Klaas E. Stephan, Hartmut Mohlberg, Christian Grefkes, Gereon R. Fink, Katrin Amunts, and Karl Zilles. 2005. A new SPM toolbox for combining probabilistic cytoarchitectonic maps and functional imaging data. *NeuroImage* 25:1325–1335.

Esterman, Michael, Timothy Verstynen, Richard B. Ivry, and Lynn C. Robertson. 2006. Coming unbound: Disrupting automatic integratin of synaesthetic color and graphemes by transcranial magnetic stimulation of the right parietal lobe. *Journal of Cognitive Neuroscience* 18 (9):1570–1576.

Frederikse, Melissa E., Angela Lu, Elizabeth Aylward, Patrick Barta, and Godfrey Pearlson. 1999. Sex differences in the inferior parietal lobule. *Cerebral Cortex* 9:896–901.

Gaser, Christian, and Gottfried Schlaug. 2003. Brain structures differ between musicians and non-musicians. *The Journal of Neuroscience* 23:9240–9245.

Good, Catriona D., Ingrid S. Johnsrude, John Ashburner, Richard N. A. Henson, Karl J. Friston, and Richard S. J. Frackowiak. 2001. A voxel-based morphometric study of ageing in 465 normal adult human brains. *NeuroImage* 14:21–36.

Green, Jennifer A. K., and Usha Goswami. 2008. Synesthesia and number cognition in children. *Cognition* 106:463–473.

Grefkes, Christian, and Gereon R. Fink. 2005. The functional organization of the intraparietal sulcus in humans and monkeys. *Journal of Anatomy* 207:3–17.

Haier, Richard J., Rex E. Jung, Ronald A. Yeo, Kevin Head, and Michael T. Alkire. 2004. Structural brain variation and general intelligence. *NeuroImage* 23:425–433.

Hänggi, Jürgen, Gian Beeli, Mathias S. Oechslin, and Lutz Jäncke. 2008. The multiple synaesthete E.S. Neuroanatomical basis of interval-taste and tone-colour synaesthesia. *NeuroImage* 43 (2):192–203.

Hubbard, Edward M. 2007. Neurophysiology of synesthesia. *Current Psychiatry Reports* 9 (3):193–199.

Hubbard, Edward M., A. Cyrus Arman, Vilayanur S. Ramachandran, and Geoffrey M. Boynton. 2005. Individual differences among grapheme-color synesthetes: Brain-behavior correlations. *Neuron* 45 (6):975–985.

Ilg, Rudiger, Afra M. Wohlschläger, Christian Gaser, Yasmin Liebau, Ruth Dauner, Andreas Wöller, Claus Zimmer, Josef Zihl, and Marc Mühlau. 2008. Gray matter increase induced by practice correlates with task-specific activation: A combined functional and morphometric magnetic resonance imaging study. *The Journal of Neuroscience* 28:4210–4215.

Jäncke, Lutz, Gian Beeli, Cornelia Eulig, and Jürgen Hanggi. 2009. The neuroanatomy of grapheme-colour synesthesia. *European Journal of Neuroscience* 29 (6):1287–1293.

Mechelli, Andrea, Jenny T. Crinion, Uta Noppeney, John O'Doherty, John Ashburner, Richard S. Frackowiak, and Cathy J. Price. 2004. Structural plasticity in the bilingual brain. *Nature* 431:757–757.

Meier, Beat, and Nicolas Rothen. 2009. Training grapheme-colour associations produces a synaesthetic Stroop effect, but not a conditioned synaesthetic response. *Neuropsychologia* 47:1208–1211.

Muggleton, Neil, Elias Tsakanikos, Vincent Walsh, and Jamie Ward. 2007. Disruption of synaesthesia following TMS of the right posterior parietal cortex. *Neuropsychologia* 45 (7):1582–1585.

Nunn, J. A., L. J. Gregory, M. J. Brammer, S. C. R. Williams, D. M. Parslow, M. J. Morgan, R. G. Morris, E. T. Bullmore, Simon Baron-Cohen, and J. A. Gray. 2002. Functional magnetic resonance imaging of synaesthesia: Activation of V4/V8 by spoken words. *Nature Neuroscience* 5 (4):371–375.

Rorden, Chris, and Hans-Otto Karnath. 2004. Using human brain lesions to infer function: A relic from a past era in the fMRI age? *Nature Reviews Neuroscience* 5:813–819.

Rottschy, Claudia, Simon B. Eickhoff, Axel Schleicher, Hartmut Mohlberg, Milenko Kujovic, Karl Zilles, and Katrin Amunts. 2007. Ventral visual cortex in humans: Cytoarchitectonic mapping of two extrastriate areas. *Human Brain Mapping* 28:1045–1059.

Rouw, Romke, and H. Steven Scholte. 2007. Increased structural connectivity in grapheme-color synesthesia. *Nature Neuroscience* 10 (6):792–797.

——. 2010. Neural basis of individual differences in synesthetic experiences. *The Journal of Neuroscience* 30 (18):6205–6213.

Scheperjans, Filip, Klaudia Hermann, Simon B. Eickhoff, Katrin Amunts, Axel Schleicher, and Karl Zilles. 2008. Observer-independent cytoarchitectonic mapping of the human superior parietal cortex. *Cerebral Cortex* 18:846–867.

Simner, Julia, Jenny Harrold, Harriet Creed, Louise Monro, and Louise Foulkes. 2009. Early detection of markers for synaesthesia in childhood populations. *Brain* 132:57–64.

Simner, Julia, Catherine Mulvenna, Noam Sagiv, Elias Tsakanikos, Sarah A. Witherby, Christine Fraser, Kirsten Scott, and Jamie Ward. 2006. Synaesthesia: The prevalence of atypical cross-modal experiences. *Perception* 38:1024–1033. doi:10.1068/p5469.

Terhune, Devin B., Sarah Tai, Alan Cowey, Tudor Popescu, and Roi Cohen Kadosh. 2011. Enhanced cortical excitability in grapheme-color synesthesia and its modulation. *Current Biology* 21:2006–2009.

Tomson, Steffie N., Nili Avidan, Kwanghyuk Lee, Anand K. Sarma, Rejnal Tushe, Dianna M. Milewicz, Molly Bray, Suzanne M. Leal, and David M. Eagleman. 2011. The genetics of colored sequence synesthesia: Suggestive evidence of linkage to 16q and genetic heterogeneity for the condition. *Behavioral Brain Research* 223:48–52.

van Leeuwen, Tessa M., Hanneke E. M. den Ouden, and Peter Hagoort. 2011. Effective connectivity determines the nature of subjective experience in grapheme-colour synaesthesia. *The Journal of Neuroscience* 31:9879–9884.

Verdon, Vincent, Sophie Schwartz, Karl-Olof Lovblad, Claude-Alain Hauer, and Patrik Vuilleumier. 2010. Neuroanatomy of hemipstial neglect and its functional components: a study using voxel-based lesion-symptom mapping. *Brain* 133: 880–894.

Vossel, Simone, Peter H. Weiss, Philipp Eschenbeck, Jochen Saliger, Hans Karbe, and Gereon R. Fink. 2012. The neural basis of anosognosia for spatial neglect after stroke. *Stroke* 43:1954–1956.

Weiss, Peter H., and Gereon R. Fink. 2009. Grapheme-colour synaesthetes show increased gray matter volumes of parietal and fusiform cortex. *Brain* 132:65–70.

Weiss, Peter H., Karl Zilles, and Gereon R. Fink. 2005. When visual perception causes feeling: Enhanced crossmodal processing in grapheme-color synesthesia. *NeuroImage* 28:859–868.

CHAPTER 27

SYNESTHESIA AND CORTICAL CONNECTIVITY

A neurodevelopmental perspective

KEVIN J. MITCHELL

INTRODUCTION

The phenomenon of synesthesia provides a rich model to investigate many fundamental subjects in neuroscience, including the nature of conscious perception, the extent and origins of individual differences in perception, the binding problem, multisensory integration, attention, mechanisms of language, mathematical and musical skill acquisition, mental imagery, and many others. As a genetic condition thought to reflect hyperconnectivity between cortical areas, it also represents a unique model to investigate the developmental processes by which cortical areas become specialized for specific functions and incorporated into dedicated networks. I will argue that the converse is also true: that to truly understand the nature of this condition it is necessary to consider it from a developmental perspective.

THE DEVELOPMENTAL ORIGINS OF SYNESTHESIA

The most commonly discussed models to explain synesthesia posit either a structural or functional difference in the brain that somehow causes activity in one cortical area to cross-activate another (Bargary and Mitchell 2008). In the "structural" model, extra connections are posited from one cortical area to the other in synesthetes (Hubbard 2007; Hubbard and Ramachandran 2005). In the "functional" model(s), the connections are there in synesthetes and non-synesthetes alike but are somehow disinhibited in synesthetes so that they are capable of activating the second cortical area (Grossenbacher and Lovelace 2001; Smilek et al. 2001; Ward et al. 2006). This disinhibition could be either direct, of connections between the two areas, or indirect, of feedback connections from a mutual higher-order area. There are supporting arguments for each of these models and the available evidence has not yet distinguished between them.

However, these models all ignore an essential part of the phenomenology of synesthesia, namely that it is developmental in nature. Models considering only differences in the adult brain are too static in nature (Karmiloff-Smith 2011). Developmental lesions, either genetic or neurological, are not the same as adult alterations (Karmiloff-Smith 2006, 2007). For example, in considering the possible effects of a mutation affecting inhibitory neurotransmission—say in a GABA receptor—one should not expect these effects to be the same as those caused by acutely blocking this receptor in an adult. Similarly, simply positing extra connections between areas A and B as the cause of cross-activation from A to B, ignores the developmental consequences that would have arisen given the existence of such connections and the multiplicity of mechanisms by which they might arise.

As we will see, the development of the brain and especially of the cortex is highly contingent on earlier processes—changes to connectivity of one area at an early stage will affect the subsequent development of all interconnected, later-developing areas. To understand a phenotype, we must consider not just that something *is* different, but the combined effects of things *having been* different throughout the development and life of the individual. It is therefore crucial to consider the developmental processes and trajectories that may link mutations causing synesthesia with the ultimate phenotype(s).

In the following sections I consider synesthesia in the light of the known processes and principles of cortical specialization, from early, genetically programmed arealization and molecular specification of connectivity to later, experience-dependent development. These discussions will highlight the dual processes of integration and segregation that ultimately yield interconnected networks of cortical areas (Mitchell 2011a). As we are currently under-constrained by definitive data distinguishing between various possibilities, I speculate rather liberally on how synesthesia may fit into and inform this framework.

THE NATURE OF THE BEAST

Before considering models to explain the genesis of synesthesia it is important to define what it is exactly we are seeking to explain. The phenotype that brings synesthesia to the attention of researchers is, of course, the experience whereby a certain stimulus generates a specific and consistent additional percept or association in another modality or processing stream. This is the phenomenon that has stimulated models of cross-activation from one cortical area to another as underlying any of the multiple forms of synesthesia. There may be much more to the *condition* of synesthesia than the synesthetic *experience* itself, however.

Clues that this might be the case come from studies into the familiality of various forms of synesthesia. In considering models to explain these experiences, an obvious question is whether they are in fact related to each other. Does the mechanism that causes colored hearing have anything to do with what causes someone to taste words? There are conceptual similarities, to be sure, but do these reflect common biological origins? Do we need a single model to explain all types or distinct models for each type?

One way to address this problem is to ask whether these different forms typically arise together in individuals or are observed co-occurring within families. It is indeed well known that many synesthetes experience multiple forms (Cytowic and Eagleman 2009; Cytowic 1989, 2002; Simner and Holenstein 2007; Simner et al. 2006); a person with one form of synesthesia is statistically more likely to experience another form than a random person (Simner et al. 2006). Indeed, in some cases, synesthetes may, upon introspection, become aware of additional types of synesthetic associations that they experience implicitly (e.g., Tyler 2005). There is also one report of an additional form of synesthesia being brought to the level of conscious awareness by pharmacological treatment, specifically administration of melatonin (Brang and Ramachandran 2008). In a survey of synesthetes and their relatives in the Irish population, we found that a variety of forms of synesthesia can also co-occur within families, in different people (Barnett, Finucane, et al. 2008). These included grapheme-color or linguistic-color synesthesia, tastes to shapes, number forms, number personification, colored emotion, colored music, and others.

These findings imply that these different experiences are indeed related at a genetic level and share an underlying biological mechanism. However, recent genetic studies indicate something apparently contradictory, namely that there are different genetic mechanisms at play in different families.

Two genetic linkage studies have now been carried out for synesthesia, each of which combined multiple families, with multiple synesthetes in each family. Asher and colleagues analyzed 43 families with auditory-visual synesthesia (Asher et al. 2009), while Tomson et al. analyzed five families with grapheme-color synesthesia (Tomson et al. 2011). In both studies, the inheritance patterns within families were most consistent with dominant Mendelian inheritance with quite high penetrance, as observed previously (Barnett, Finucane, et al. 2008; Baron-Cohen et al. 1996; Cytowic 1989, 2002; Ward and Simner 2005). Nevertheless, no strong single linkage peak emerged in either study, which combined families in an effort to boost statistical power and resolution. If all cases of synesthesia were due to mutation in the same gene, these studies should have detected a strong signal at a particular location. These findings are thus most consistent with substantial genetic heterogeneity, i.e., the involvement of distinct genetic loci in different families.

This implies that whatever the underlying commonality in mechanism, it is not at the level of a specific gene. These findings can be reconciled by a model which proposes that: (1) what is inherited is a predisposition to manifest synesthesia in general, rather than a specific type, and (2) that this predisposition can be caused by mutations in any of an unknown number of genes. Note that such a situation, involving both genetic heterogeneity and variable phenotypic expression for each mutation, pertains for genes predisposing to a range of psychiatric disorders such as schizophrenia and autism (Mitchell 2011b).

Under such a model, the specific form of synesthesia that emerges in an individual who has inherited this general predisposition would be affected by additional factors, possibly including genetic background, developmental variation, and experience (Barnett, Finucane, et al. 2008; see later). We have proposed that this kind of situation could arise if the mutations leading to synesthesia result initially in quite widespread alterations in cortical wiring. These might then be resolved differently in individuals to generate the ultimate phenotype (Bargary and Mitchell 2008; Barnett, Finucane, et al. 2008). A variation on this idea is that a mutation may lead to increased *probability* of altered wiring across the brain, with the specific profile emerging affected by chance (see later). There is now an accumulation of convergent evidence supporting the model of more widespread altered connectivity in the brain of synesthetes.

EVIDENCE FOR BROAD ALTERATIONS IN CONNECTIVITY

A growing number of neuroimaging studies have been carried out to investigate the neural basis of synesthesia (Aleman et al. 2001; Barnett, Foxe, et al. 2008; Beeli et al. 2007; Brang et al. 2010; Goller, Otten, and Ward 2009; Gray et al. 2006; Hubbard et al. 2005; Nunn et al. 2002; Paulesu et al. 1995; Rich et al. 2006; Sperling et al. 2006; Steven et al. 2006; Weiss, Zilles, and Fink 2005). These have provided some insights while leaving several major questions unanswered. First, several functional magnetic resonance imaging (fMRI) studies of synesthetes with auditory-visual or grapheme-color synesthesia have found anomalous activation of visual areas in response to presentation of the "inducer"—either aurally presented sounds or visually presented achromatic graphemes. These studies have thus demonstrated the "reality" of synesthesia objectively—the brains of synesthetes really do respond differently to those of non-synesthetes, with greater activation in additional areas, as predicted from the descriptions of the subjective experiences.

However, in addition to this major conclusion, equally remarkable is the variability of findings from different studies. Several studies (Hubbard et al. 2005; Nunn et al. 2002; Sperling et al. 2006; Steven et al. 2006; van Leeuwen et al. 2010) have found extra activation in or around V4, for example—a region involved in color perception—but others have seen activation in other visual areas (primary, secondary, or higher-order) (Aleman et al. 2001; Rich et al. 2006; van Leeuwen et al. 2010) or non-visual areas, such as parietal or frontal cortex (Laeng et al. 2011; Nunn et al. 2002; Rouw and Scholte 2007; Sperling et al. 2006; Steven et al. 2006; Weiss, Zilles, and Fink 2005). Deactivation of certain areas in response to synesthesia-inducing stimuli has also been observed (Paulesu et al. 1995). Phenotypic heterogeneity, including between "projector" and "associator" synesthetes may explain some of the variation in these results (Hubbard et al. 2005; Rouw and Scholte 2010). Nevertheless, a simple model of excess cross-activation between highly restricted cortical areas seems too minimal to accommodate all these findings.

Neuroimaging studies have also identified structural differences in the brains of synesthetes compared to controls (Jäncke et al. 2009; Rouw and Scholte 2007, 2010; Weiss and Fink, 2009). In almost all cases, synesthetes showed greater volumes of areas of gray or white matter or greater fractional anisotropy within certain white matter tracts than controls. Some of these differences are in the general region of visual areas thought to be involved in the synesthetic experience but others are more widespread, in parietal or even frontal regions. A very recent study analyzed global connectivity patterns in the brains of synesthetes, using networks derived from correlations in cortical thickness (Hänggi, Wotruba, and Jäncke 2011). The global network topology was significantly different between synesthetes and controls, with synesthetes showing increased clustering, suggesting global hyperconnectivity. The differences driving these effects were widespread and not confined to areas hypothesized to be involved in the grapheme-color synesthetic experience itself.

Electrophysiological studies have also revealed additional phenotypes, most likely unrelated to the synesthetic experience itself. Synesthetes showed alterations in the amplitudes of visual evoked potentials in response to very simple visual stimuli, which do not induce a synesthetic experience (Barnett, Foxe, et al. 2008). The direction of this effect differed for different kinds of stimuli, arguing against indirect explanations, such as attentional differences. Synesthetes showed a reduced amplitude response to low-contrast stimuli designed to isolate the magnocellular visual pathway, while they showed increased amplitude responses to higher-contrast stimuli, which also recruited the parvocellular pathway. These differences, which were evident at very early time-points, suggest that structure or function of early visual circuits is altered in synesthetes. Differences in auditory evoked potentials have also been reported in synesthetes (Beeli et al. 2007; Goller, Otten, and Ward 2009). In these studies, the only stimuli used were sounds that did induce synesthesia, though the differences again occurred in the earliest components of the evoked potentials. This may be consistent with a basal difference in auditory processing, rather than reflecting the synesthetic experience itself, which is likely triggered at later stages of processing (Bargary et al. 2009).

These various findings are congruent with observations of differences in a range of psychological faculties or behavioral traits. Synesthetes have been shown to differ from controls in rates of *mitempfindung* (an experience of referred tactile sensation) (Burrack, Knoch, and Brugger 2006) and on scores of mental imagery (Barnett and Newell 2008), sensory sensitivity (Banissy, Walsh, and Ward 2009) and positive and negative schizotypy (Vincent Walsh, personal communication).

There is thus strong and convergent evidence from various sources in favor of the hypothesis of widespread differences in connectivity in the brain of synesthetes. In order to understand how such differences could arise, we must consider the processes by which cortical connectivity is normally determined.

CORTICAL CONNECTIVITY
AND SPECIALIZATION

The emergence of distinct areas of cortex, connected into networks more or less specialized for particular functions, involves a series of processes. These begin with the early patterning of the developing cortical sheet and the molecular specification of initial connectivity, followed by the experience-dependent remodeling of connectivity patterns in conjunction with ongoing brain maturation (Dehaene and Cohen 2007; Johnson 2010; Price et al. 2006; Sur and Rubenstein 2005). Genetic lesions affecting either initial connectivity or the biochemical processes associated with maturation and experience-dependent remodeling could thus explain an eventual difference in connectivity.

Primary connectivity

At very early stages, the developing telencephalon is patterned by the actions of diffusible proteins secreted from patterning centers, such as the anterior neural ridge or cortical hem (O'Leary et al. 2007). These proteins specify the positions of cells along the major axes of the telencephalon (rostral–caudal and medial–lateral). The concentrations of these signaling molecules at different points are eventually translated into a combinatorial code of gene expression. Their main targets are genes that encode transcription factors—proteins that in turn regulate the expression of many downstream genes. These transcription factors tend to be expressed in broad domains of the cortical sheet. While there are no genes known whose expression pattern uniquely defines a specific cortical area at this early stage, their overlapping patterns do coincide with the borders of primary sensory and motor areas (Dye, El Shawa, and Huffman 2010a, 2010b; Rash and Grove 2006). Of particular interest, the downstream genes that are controlled by these regulatory proteins will include those encoding surface molecules that subsequently act to specify connectivity (Figure 27.1).

Though the identities of such cues are not yet known, it is clear that they must exist, as the initial connections of cortical areas are quite precise. These include both thalamocortical and intracortical connections. In the case of thalamocortical projections, there was some evidence supporting a model whereby topographic sorting of axons from the dorsal thalamus en route to the cortex was sufficient to direct them to correct regions of the cortex, abrogating the need for cortical areal connectivity cues (Garel et al. 2002;

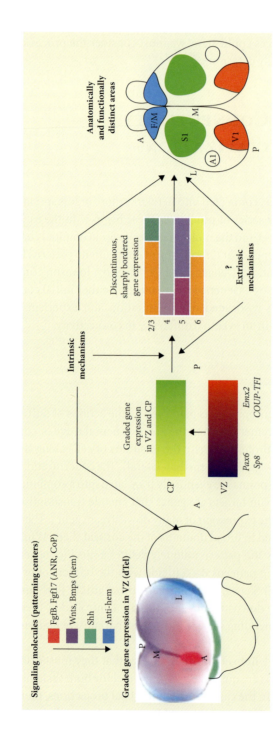

FIGURE 27.1 Mechanisms of specification and differentiation of cortical areas. The developing telencephalon is patterned by gradients of secreted signaling molecules released from distinct patterning centers, including the anterior neural ridge (ANR), commissural plate (CoP), and cortical hem. These are translated into graded and then discrete patterns of transcription factor expression within the ventricular zone (VZ), which are then imparted to their progeny in the cortical plate (CP). The CP also initially exhibits gradients of gene expression that are gradually converted to distinct patterns with sharp borders. Coincident with this process, distinct cortical layers (2–6), and the anatomically and functionally distinct areas seen in the adult (M1, S1, A1, V1), differentiate from the CP. Overlapping expression of largely unknown surface cues specifies the initial guidance and areal and laminar connectivity of incoming thalamic axons. These axons in turn reinforce the identity of the developing areas and influence its intracortical connectivity. Reprinted from *Neuron*, 56 (2), Dennis D.M. O'Leary, Shen-Ju Chou, and Setsuko Sahara, Area Patterning of the Mammalian Cortex, pp. 252–269, Copyright (2007), with permission from Elsevier.

Vanderhaeghen and Polleux 2004). However, it is now clear that such sorting is neither necessary nor sufficient to specify connectivity from specific thalamic nuclei to their cognate cortical areas—appropriate connections can form even when thalamic axons follow very aberrant routes to reach their final targets (Frappe, Gaillard, and Roger 2001; Little et al. 2009).

Initial patterns of intracortical connectivity are also quite precise from the outset, at least for primary sensory and motor areas. A recent, very comprehensive study has documented the emergence of such projections over prenatal and postnatal development in the mouse (Dye, El Shawa, and Huffman 2010a, 2010b). Several important findings emerge: first, the projections to and from primary visual area (V1) do not overlap with those to and from primary somatosensory (S1) or auditory (A1) areas. Indeed, the projection fields traced from V1 and S1 abut each other at a very tight boundary. Second, an effectively adult projection pattern of primary sensory areas is established by late embryogenesis. What follows over subsequent neonatal and postnatal development is the expansion of intervening association areas, which never receive inputs from or project to primary sensory areas. These findings complement those from grafting studies in the mouse (Frappe, Gaillard, and Roger 2001; Gaspard et al. 2008) and organotypic cultures of rat cortex (Bai et al. 2005), which show similar levels of specificity in thalamocortical and/or intracortical projections.

Studies in the monkey also show generally similar patterns of initial specificity in the hierarchical connectivity within the visual system (Barone et al. 1996; Coogan and Van Essen 1996). Feedforward projections were observed as being particularly specific from the outset, while feedback projections showed more extensive remodeling over development (Batardiere et al. 2002).

Observations in humans are generally congruent with this picture, though many details remain unknown. Thalamocortical projections arise early and reach the developing cortex by 13 to 14 postconceptual weeks (PCW) (Kostović and Judaš 2010). These projections are highly specific from the outset with respect to target cortical area (Kostović and Rakic 1984). As in other species, thalamocortical axons in humans have a "waiting period" in the subplate zone, where they make transient synaptic connections, prior to innervation of the cortical plate itself (which does not begin in humans until 24 PCW) (Kostović and Judaš 2010; Lopez-Bendito and Molnar 2003). Callosal projections begin to form by 15 PCW and exhibit considerable exuberance, with large numbers of axons being pruned at neonatal stages (Vasung et al. 2010). Similar exuberance is observed in other species, including cats and monkeys, though it is important to note that the initial projections are topographically organized from the outset, not randomly exuberant (Innocenti and Price 2005). Long-range intrahemispheric pathways (such as the longitudinal fasciculi) develop in late gestation, followed by short-range connections between nearby areas (Burkhalter 1993; Kostović and Jovanov-Milošević 2006; Vasung et al. 2010). Importantly, these are quite specific from the outset in terms of areal targeting, in humans (Burkhalter 1993), as observed in other animals.

These findings imply the existence of molecules that direct the axonal guidance and synaptic connectivity of thalamocortical and corticocortical projections. Some such molecules have been identified for thalamocortical pathfinding and connectivity. These include members of the ephrin and Eph-receptor families (Dufour et al. 2003), sema-phorins and their receptors (Leighton et al. 2001; Little et al. 2009; Wright et al. 2007), netrins (Bonnin et al. 2007; Powell et al. 2008), slits and Robos (Braisted, Ringstedt, and O'Leary 2009; Lopez-Bendito et al. 2007), cadherins (Poskanzer et al. 2003), neuro-trophins (Ma et al. 2002) and cell adhesion molecules of the L1 family (Demyanenko, Riday, et al. 2011; Demyanenko,Siesser, et al. 2011). Mutations in various members of these gene families result in aberrant thalamocortical pathfinding and connectivity (Vanderhaeghen and Polleux 2004).

In contrast, while some molecules are known that help determine connectivity of cortical neurons to contralateral (Chedotal and Richards 2010) or subcortical targets (Arlotta et al. 2005; Low et al. 2008; Torii and Levitt 2005), remarkably, no surface mol-ecules are yet known that specify interareal patterns of intrahemispheric connectivity (Price et al. 2006).

Hierarchical dependence of connectivity

While initial patterns of cortical connectivity are specified by a molecular program intrinsic to the cortex, the ultimate patterns of intracortical connectivity of the primary areas depend heavily on their receiving appropriate inputs from the thalamus.

In the first place, thalamic axons induce area-specific patterns of proliferation and cell migration that ultimately determine area-specific cytoarchitectonic characteristics, such as those distinguishing areas V1 and V2 (which include the number and packing of various cell types in different layers; Dehay and Kennedy 2007; Lukaszewicz et al. 2006). Thalamic inputs to primary areas are also essential for the emergence or maintenance of areal-specific patterns of gene expression at later stages (Gitton, Cohen-Tannoudji, and Wassef 1999; Paysan et al. 1997).

Alteration of thalamic input also dramatically affects corticocortical connectivity of the deprived area, including callosal and intrahemispheric connections. For example, removal of the eyes of prenatal macaques in early to mid-gestation results in a reduction of the size of area 17 (presumptive V1) and of area 18 (V2), based on cytoarchitecture, and the emergence of a cytoarchitectonically novel area, termed area X, in the interven-ing cortical region (Rakic et al. 1991). This manipulation also alters the connectivity of area 18, with significantly greater numbers of callosal connections than in normal ani-mals (Dehay et al. 1989), most probably reflecting a stabilization of normally transient callosal connections in this species (Innocenti and Price 2005; Price et al. 2006).

Even more dramatic alterations are observed in experiments on opossum. Due to its very precocious birth it is possible, by postnatal surgery, to remove visual inputs at an effectively earlier stage than was done in the macaque, prior to the arrival of dorsal lat-eral geniculate nucleus axons to the visual cortex. This results in the transformation of most of area 17 and apparently all of area 18 into an area X (Kahn and Krubitzer, 2002). It also dramatically alters patterns of intrahemispheric connectivity (Karlen et al. 2006). Dye-tracing from area 17 shows inappropriate connections from many non-visual areas of cortex, including somatosensory, auditory and frontal areas and occipital cortex in these animals becomes functionally responsive to somatosensory and/or auditory stimuli. Similar results have been observed after fetal visual thalamic ablations in the hamster (Kingsbury et al. 2002).

Altering patterns of electrical activity, rather than connections themselves also illustrates the dependent nature of cortical areal development on appropriate inputs. Incoming sensory information can be altered in ferrets by surgical manipulations that rewire retinal inputs into the medial geniculate nucleus (MGN), which normally receives auditory inputs and projects to primary auditory cortex (A1). In this situation, MGN axons still project normally to A1, which now becomes visually responsive (Sharma et al. 2000; von Melchner, Pallas, and Sur 2000). The intra-areal circuitry of A1 is dramatically altered to a pattern much more like that of normal V1, with, for example, local horizontal connections linking columns of similar orientation selectivity. As the emergence of such structures in normal visual cortex is known to be dependent on patterned electrical activity, the interpretation is that the altered activity into rewired A1 is sufficient to change its fate to that of V1 (Pallas 2001). The fact that occipital cortex in early-blind humans becomes responsive to auditory or somatosensory stimuli suggests that similar mechanisms are at play in humans (Bavelier and Neville 2002; Pascual-Leone et al. 2005).

The conclusions from these studies are that: (1) primary sensory areas require normal thalamic inputs and patterns of activity in order to develop characteristic cytoarchitecture and local and long-range patterns of cortical connectivity; and (2) secondary areas are also dramatically affected, presumably in an indirect fashion, as these areas do not receive inputs from the manipulated areas of thalamus. This suggests that, just as primary areas are dependent on inputs from the thalamus, secondary areas are dependent on inputs from appropriately differentiated primary areas and so on up the hierarchy (Bargary and Mitchell 2008).

Transient connections

Studies of developing cortex in monkeys, cats, ferrets, and other mammals have revealed the presence of some long-range intracortical projections that are transient in nature, notably in the corpus callosum, but also some from areas of one sensory modality to another (Dehay, Kennedy, and Bullier 1988; Innocenti and Clarke 1984; Price and Blakemore 1985; Webster et al. 1991). Under typical conditions, most such transient connections do not enter gray matter and do not form synaptic boutons (Innocenti and Price 2005). Whether such connections exist in humans is an open question.

Where transient projections have been reported, they are not randomly exuberant— they are quite precise and their regression follows a stereotyped timeframe. By analogy to the stereotyped pruning of transient subcortical projections, such as from visual cortex to the spinal cord, this regression may involve a specific molecular program that is normally activated at a particular developmental stage (Luo and O'Leary 2005; Vanderhaeghen and Cheng 2010).

Maturation timing and evolutionary novelty

The connectivity of primary areas thus involves early patterning and attraction of appropriate thalamic inputs, followed by instructive influences of those inputs, which help specify the later emerging connectivity with other cortical areas. One can speculate that a similar scheme applies to the development of connectivity of higher-order areas. In general, for any particular area, the connectivity that emerges with later-developing areas may thus be contingent on the patterns of afferent connectivity from earlier-maturing areas.

This interactive program follows the timeline of maturation of different brain regions and cortical areas. There is very strong and convergent evidence across multiple species, including humans, that primary areas mature earlier than secondary and tertiary sensory areas, which mature earlier than association areas (Bourne 2010; Guillery 2005). This evidence derives from histological studies of myelination, by Flechsig and others (reviewed in Guillery 2005), gene expression (Bourne and Rosa 2006), synapse number and density (Huttenlocher and Dabholkar 1997), dendritic spines (Petanjek et al. 2011) and other markers and from neuroimaging studies of white matter maturation (Paus et al. 2001), cortical thickness (Shaw et al. 2008; Toga et al. 2006) and thalamic connectivity (Fair et al. 2010), as well as from a multitude of studies on functional responsiveness (Dehaene and Cohen 2007; Kanwisher 2010).

These trends also reflect the evolutionary history of these areas. Over evolution, the territory taken up by such higher-order association areas has greatly expanded. Their delayed maturation means that their connectivity can develop in concert with experience, allowing more advanced organisms to adapt the functions of these areas in response to the environment in which they mature (Karlen and Krubitzer 2006; Krubitzer 2009). This flexible strategy reaches its peak in humans, where many areas become specialized for culturally specific stimuli in a manner requiring years of experience (Baker et al. 2007; Dehaene and Cohen 2007; Golarai et al. 2007; Kanwisher 2010).

Experience-dependent specialization and the emergence of cortical networks

The genetic program specifies cortical areas that are experience-expectant—wired to receive particular inputs and ready to respond to them by elaborating or specializing their local circuitry and refining their connectivity with other areas.

The model of "interactive specialization" (Johnson 2010) proposes that cortical areas become specialized in a competitive process of strengthening or weakening connections within a network. It argues, crucially, that regressive events are as important to this process as the formation or strengthening of connections. Loss of responsiveness of an area to a non-preferred category may reflect pruning of synapses carrying that information or, alternatively, the development of active inhibitory processes that mediate cross-category lateral inhibition (Adesnik and Scanziani 2010; Allison, Puce, and McCarthy 2002). As networks respond to statistical regularities and contingencies in sensory inputs, schemata will come to be represented as patterns of weighted synaptic connections within and between particular brain regions.

This general framework is supported by several recent developmental imaging studies, which also provide details of the processes that accompany specialization. Both progressive and regressive changes were observed in the network of areas responsive to faces across children of different ages, with increased tuning of some areas for faces and loss of responsiveness of other areas to faces (Joseph et al. 2010). Similarly, Cantlon et al. found areas that are somewhat selective for either faces or symbols (including letters and numbers) in the visual system of 4-year-old children (Cantlon et al. 2011). Importantly, greater behavioral category-specific recognition was associated not with higher responsiveness in these areas to the preferred category, but with lower responsiveness to the non-preferred category.

Both progressive and regressive changes are also observed in developmental studies of brain-wide functional connectivity (Fair et al. 2009; Supekar et al. 2009; Uddin et al. 2010). Using various measures, these have consistently found a steady transition from local to distributed brain networks over time as the strength of local connections decreases while that of longer-range connections increases. This leads to a greater functional segregation of distinct networks, which is paralleled by similar changes in measures of structural connectivity (Hagmann et al. 2010).

The definition of cortical areas and their specialization for specific functions thus depends on the molecular specification of early identity and wiring, followed by activity-dependent elaboration and refinement of connectivity and experience-dependent segregation and integration into interconnected cortical networks, through both progressive and regressive processes, in concert with the ongoing maturation of the brain.

DEVELOPMENT OF ABERRANT CORTICAL CONNECTIVITY IN SYNESTHESIA

Having considered the normal processes that determine cortical connectivity, are we any closer to discerning the mechanisms that could lead to altered structural connectivity in synesthesia? There are so many specific cellular processes involved in establishing intracortical connectivity that it is probably hubris to speculate which particular ones might be involved. However, one can imagine three broad classes of mutations that might result in altered connectivity. These are mutations in: (1) genes specifying early neurodevelopmental processes, such as cell migration, axon guidance, or synaptic target selection; (2) genes mediating axonal pruning or activity-dependent synaptic remodeling and refinement of connectivity, or (3) genes that determine the neurochemical balance of excitation and inhibition in various brain circuits.

A particularly attractive possibility, which is both plausible and parsimonious, is that connectivity is normal at the start but the processes of pruning are defective so that as learning proceeds, the normal regressive events do not occur. This would result in hyper-connectivity where extra parameters are incorporated into the schema of some type of object. This kind of hypergnosia would be effectively the opposite of models to explain disconnection syndromes such as dyslexia, prosopagnosia, and other associative agno-sias, where a failure to integrate distributed areas into a functional network may be to blame (Mitchell 2011a) (Figure 27.2).

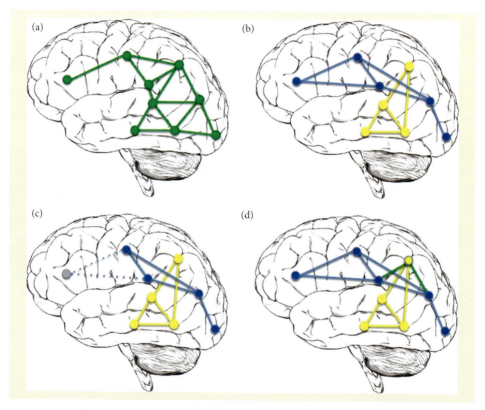

FIGURE 27.2 The emergence of specialized cortical networks. Panel (a) represents, in highly schematized fashion, cortical networks in a young child and shows areas broadly responsive to several stimuli, but not yet selective for a specific category. Functional connectivity is denoted by lines. In adults (b), these areas have segregated into two distinct networks (blue and yellow), through strengthening of some, mainly long-range connections and pruning of other, mainly local connections. (c) A disconnection syndrome, caused by a failure to form or strengthen long-range connections (dotted lines), resulting in an associative agnosia. (d) Local hyperconnectivity, caused by failure to prune connections (or to develop cross-in-hibitory systems, not illustrated here), results in cross-activation of an additional cortical area and could explain synesthesia. Reprinted from *Current Opinion in Genetics & Development*, 21 (3), Kevin J. Mitchell, Curiouser and curiouser: genetic disorders of cortical specialization, pp. 271–277, Copyright (2011), with permission from Elsevier.

Whatever the primary mechanism, there will be a strong and reiterative interplay between structure and function, so that it may be hard to determine which difference comes first simply from observing the outcome. Ultimately, a full understanding of the origins of synesthesia as a condition will most likely await identification of specific causative mutations and subsequent elucidation of the underlying biological mechanisms. However, even with such information in hand, we will have only a partial explanation of the origins of the particular synesthetic experience in each individual. To fully understand how this emerges will require consideration of additional factors.

Individual Differences and the Emergence of the Phenotype

If we propose that it is a predisposition to synesthesia in general that is inherited, then what determines the specific phenotype—the type and characteristics of synesthesia in each individual?

As with many neurodevelopmental disorders, the link from genotype to eventual phenotype may be quite indirect (Mitchell 2011b). The ultimate phenotype is likely to be affected by at least three additional sources of variation: (1) genetic background, (2) developmental variation, and (3) experience.

Genetic background and sex effects

Genetic background is certainly likely to play an important role in the expression of the synesthetic phenotype, as it does for essentially every other genetic condition. That is, even the most highly penetrant disease-causing mutations are affected by genetic modifiers that contribute to differences in phenotype in different carriers (Mitchell 2012). The most common variable factor in the genetic background, and certainly the easiest to identify, is the presence or absence of the Y chromosome. There has been considerable debate in the field as to whether synesthesia shows a sex difference in prevalence, in particular, whether it is more common in females.

Several population-based surveys have reported increased rates of female versus male synesthete respondents, ranging from 3:1 to 6:1 (Barnett, Finucane, et al. 2008; Baron-Cohen et al. 1996; Cytowic 1989, 2002; Rich et al. 2005). Family-based studies report a similar range (Barnett, Finucane, et al. 2008; Tomson et al. 2011). In contrast, Ward et al. found a female:male ratio of only 2:1 in a familial study (Ward and Simner 2005), while two cross-sectional sampling surveys found no difference in the numbers of male and female synesthetes (Simner et al. 2006; Simner et al. 2009). Overall, the consensus seems to be that the increase in females affected is likely real but probably not more than about 2:1 (Julia Simner, personal communication). If that is the case, then we can ask why that would be so and whether it is informative as to the underlying mechanisms.

There are a number of genetic explanations that could account for such a pattern. First, if the condition is caused by an X-linked dominant mutation, then this would occur about twice as often in females as in males (simply because they have two X chromosomes) and could account for an approximate 2:1 ratio. The lack of linkage findings on the X chromosome suggests that is unlikely to be the case. Second, if the condition were X-linked and dominant in females, but lethal in hemizygous males (like some mutations causing Rett syndrome), then this could generate a predominance of affected females. Several studies have ruled this possible mechanism out—synesthete females do not show the reduction in viable male offspring that would be predicted by this model (Barnett, Finucane, et al. 2008; Cytowic 1989, 2002; Ward and Simner 2005). This leaves the possibility that the interaction involves not the X chromosome, but the Y chromosome, i.e., that it reflects differences in how the male and female brains are wired generally, which affect the phenotypic outcome of mutations predisposing to synesthesia.

This provides an interesting contrast with many psychiatric or neurodevelopmental conditions, where there is an observed excess of cases among males, including autism, schizophrenia, and dyslexia, for example (Cahill 2006). This excess may reflect underlying differences in brain structure that affect vulnerability to the effects of mutations. For example, in a study of chromosomal deletions or duplications in patients with autism, these events tended to be much larger in affected females than in males (Levy et al. 2011). The lack of observed small events in female patients suggests that females are more resilient and males more vulnerable to the autism-associated effects of such mutations (Zhao et al. 2007).

This raises the possibility that the opposite situation may pertain with respect to mutations causing synesthesia—that females may be more susceptible to their effects. Though quite speculative, the known group differences between male and female brains are congruent with this idea, especially in the context of the proposed hyperconnectivity in synesthesia. Several recent imaging studies with very large numbers of subjects have found general sex differences in a number of parameters of network connectivity, either in specific brain regions or across the entire brain network. In a study based on diffusion-weighted imaging tractography, female brains showed, on average, greater overall connectivity and greater efficiency of network connectivity across the entire brain (Gong et al. 2009). Network connectivity defined by resting state fMRI correlations showed highly congruent differences between male and female brains, with females showing significantly higher local functional connectivity density, reflecting greater integration and less functional segregation in females (Tomasi and Volkow 2011). Another study using resting state correlations also found differences between male and female brains, though in this case some areas (mainly association and frontal areas) showed greater connectivity in females and others (mainly early sensory areas) showed greater connectivity in males (Biswal et al. 2010). One could thus certainly imagine that if synesthesia results from a mutation causing hyperconnectivity, that the effects of such a mutation might be greater in females than in males.

Whether the genetic background (including sex) really has important effects on the synesthetic phenotype remains unknown. What is known is that even monozygotic twins can differ substantially in whether they experience synesthesia or not (Smilek et al. 2002; Smilek et al. 2005) and in its precise nature (Barnett, Finucane, et al. 2008). Thus, there must be additional, non-inherited factors that influence the ultimate phenotype.

Intrinsic developmental variation

One of those factors is likely to be chance—stochastic events that are intrinsic to the developing brain (Mitchell 2007). The developmental program that specifies brain connectivity is less like a blueprint than a recipe (a recipe without a cook)—an incredibly complicated set of processes carried out by mindless biochemical algorithms mediated by local interactions between billions of individual components. As each of these processes is subject to some level of "noise" at the molecular level (Kaern et al. 2005), it is not surprising that the outcome of this process varies considerably, even between monozygotic twins.

This noise arises from random thermal fluctuations in molecular shape and movement that affect fundamental cellular processes like gene expression or cellular signaling. Normally, these fluctuations are buffered by intact molecular systems, which are adapted to deal with them and still produce the same outcome (Wagner 2007). But when some components are disrupted, this buffering can break down, making the outcome much more susceptible to noise. What often happens when mutations arise that affect one of the components of cellular developmental processes is that the phenotype does not change from always wild-type to always mutant—instead, phenotypic variability increases (Mitchell 2007).

The phenotype at a cellular level—say in the migration of a certain type of cell or the projection of a certain type of axon—is thus inherited in a probabilistic fashion, not deterministically. When played out independently many times across this brain, this probabilistic inheritance will generate a unique profile of phenotypic differences. Depending on where such anomalies arise, different brain systems may be impacted, resulting in a variable spectrum of phenotypes or clinical symptoms across people carrying a particular mutation (even identical twins). This fits with observations of variable phenotype in families where conditions like epilepsy or dyslexia and dyscalculia are segregating.

A recent twin study found that while risk of epilepsy in general was very highly heritable, the specific type emerging (e.g., generalized versus localization-related) was less so, and, among those with an identifiable focus, there was effectively no heritability for which brain region was affected (Corey et al. 2011). A similar idea has been proposed before for dyslexia (Ramus 2004), which may be associated in some cases with cellular ectopia—aggregations of neurons that have failed to migrate properly and instead are localized within the white matter (Galaburda et al. 2006). The idea is that these could disrupt communication between brain areas involved in processing or representing the visual shapes of letters and the sounds they make (or between the visual shapes of whole words and the concepts they represent). In this regard, it is interesting to note that dyscalculia (a specific difficulty with arithmetic) is often also found in families with dyslexia (Landerl and Moll 2010). This suggests that the hypothetical neurodevelopmental deficit may affect different brain systems depending on where in the brain it manifests most severely in development.

Experience

In addition to genetic background and intrinsic developmental variation, there is also likely a crucial role for experience in determining the eventual phenotype. This is particularly obvious in cases where the stimuli that induce synesthetic associations or percepts are members of learned categories, such as letters, numbers, days of the week, musical notes, words, etc. Even for inducing stimuli such as tastes, there is presumably an emergence of perceptual expertise with repeated experience, which allows categorical recognition of particular flavors.

The possible influence of experience can be approached from several angles—whether it affects the type of synesthesia that emerges in an individual, whether it affects the specific associations that arise and, more generally, whether it explains why some types of synesthesia are so much more common than others.

In the first case, there is little direct evidence that experience affects the type(s) of synesthesia that emerges in an individual. However, it certainly seems possible that the emergence of synesthetic associations for any particular category of objects may depend on the level of perceptual expertise that a person develops. For example, the development of synesthetic associations or concurrent percepts for musical notes, chords, keys, and other aspects of musical structure may depend on the attainment of musical expertise and the ability to recognize or at least perceptually distinguish such elements. More generally, synesthetic associations may emerge for any over-learned category, which may come to be processed by a dedicated cortical network. The gradual emergence of synesthetic associations to a second alphabet or second language may reflect such a process (Barnett et al. 2009; Mills et al. 2002).

In relation to the specific paired associations that arise in an individual, one may be struck by different aspects of the phenomenology. On the one hand, the generally arbitrary pairings may be seen as evidence for associations arising mainly from random map-to-map connectivity between cortical areas (Bargary and Mitchell 2008; Barnett, Finucane, et al. 2008). On the other, the trends in such pairings that are apparent across groups of synesthetes (Barnett, Finucane, et al. 2008; Simner 2007) may be taken as evidence for an instructive role for experience in dictating the associations (Rich et al. 2005). Indeed, it has been argued that the observation that such trends sometimes apply in non-synesthetes as well implies that synesthetic associations are an exaggeration of cross-modal mechanisms common to all people (Spector and Maurer 2011; Ward et al. 2006).

The observations of general arbitrariness with overlying trends may be reconciled by a model which supposes that (1) initial connections between cortical areas lead to broad and non-specific cross-activation, but that (2) in the process of development of perceptual expertise in the inducing area, subsets of connections to the concurrent area will be stabilized, and that (3) this stabilization is subject to semantic, cultural, or implicit influences which may substantially bias the outcome.

For example, in someone with the predisposition to grapheme-color synesthesia, if the neurons that are coming to represent the sound and shape of the letter Y are consistently co-activated (due to cultural influences) with those representing the color yellow, then connections between those particular respective ensembles may be favored (over connections to ensembles representing other colors). Similarly, if the simple line and circle shapes of the letters I and O are typically associated with black or white, then this bias may be cemented in the associations with the letters themselves in synesthetes (Spector and Maurer 2011).

This kind of cultural, top-down effect could also explain the influence in rare cases of colored toys, such as refrigerator magnets, on letter-color associations (Witthoft and Winawer 2006), the occurrence of clock face arrangements of the numbers 1 to 12 in many synesthetes' number forms (Galton 1883), or the association of words with particular tastes described by a word sharing a phonetic or semantic component (e.g., "Barbara" may taste of rhubarb; Ward and Simner, 2003).

GENERAL TRENDS ACROSS
TYPES OF SYNESTHESIA

The question of why certain types of synesthesia are more common than others is not satisfactorily answered by any models yet proposed. This seems to be an especially thorny problem for models invoking widespread connectivity differences. The answer may lie in how experience interacts with and resolves such connectivity differences during acquisition of expertise with particular categories of objects and concomitant cortical specialization.

Some general trends across different types of synesthesia may be quite informative in this regard. In many cases, the inducing stimuli are learned, categorical objects, rather than simple sensory stimuli. This is by no means exclusive, however—many cases of colored hearing involve responses to all kinds of sounds, for example. Over-generalizing from the cases that do involve learned stimuli is thus dangerous, but we can at least consider them as a subset and ask why they are so common. On the other side, the concurrent percepts or associations tend to be much simpler and more abstract—flashes of color, rather than visions of specific objects, for example. In many cases, they represent properties of an object, rather than an object itself.

From a developmental perspective, these differences are reflected in the timing of maturation of the relevant cortical areas, with implications for their hierarchical interdependence. The concurrents are typically represented by the activity of early-maturing areas, while the inducers are encoded by activity within areas that specialize late in response to experience (Grill-Spector, Golarai, and Gabrieli 2008; Kanwisher 2010). Earlier-maturing areas are believed to be less plastic than those which mature later; indeed, it could be said that plasticity—adapting to the regularities of incoming stimuli—is one of the major functions of the later-maturing ones (Bavelier and Neville 2002; Dehaene and Cohen 2007). The early-maturing areas are thus already dedicated to a specific function at the time that the later-maturing areas are specializing.

Thus, the activation of the early areas already *means something* and that meaning is fixed (Hurley and Noë 2003). (Presumably, that meaning is read out by higher-order areas that receive afferent connections from the early areas.) Cross-activation from a later-maturing area, as it comes to represent some specific category of objects, will not be able to alter the meaning of activation of the early area—it will instead lead to the incorporation of that meaning as an extra association into the schema of the objects it represents. In this sense, the synesthetic experience may be better thought of as *co-activation* of the concurrent area within a network representing all the attributes of a particular object, rather than *cross-activation* simply from an inducer area to a concurrent area (Mitchell 2011a). Support for this idea comes from a magnetoencephalography study of grapheme-color synesthesia, which found that the activation attributed to the color area V4 occurred effectively simultaneously with that of the grapheme area (Brang et al. 2010).

This kind of model, admittedly very speculative and probably naive, may also explain why synesthesia tends to be unidirectional. The extended cortical network representing the schema of an object may be activated by attributes that are sufficiently specific to that schema—such as the shape or sound of a letter, but not activated by attributes which are less specific—such as the synesthetic color (which will obviously also be associated with any number of other objects). Because the concurrents tend to be simple and abstract, they are less likely to be specific to any particular object.

CONCLUSION

The complex and dynamic interplay between form and function highlights the importance of a developmental perspective when thinking about the possible mechanisms underlying synesthesia. The development of inexpensive whole-genome sequencing methods (Ng et al. 2009; Shendure and Ji 2008) makes it quite likely that mutations predisposing to synesthesia will be identified in the near future. These may tell us what cellular processes are primarily affected—axon guidance, target selection, axonal pruning, synaptic refinement, particular neurochemical pathways, or something we have not even thought of yet. Such identification will be just the first step in elucidating the underlying biological mechanisms. The pathway from mutation to eventual phenotypic effect(s) is likely to be long and quite possibly indirect. The particular phenotype that arises in any individual will depend on the interplay between initial patterns of wiring and the processes by which experience sculpts emerging networks. As we attempt to disentangle these interactions, it will be important to keep in mind that the effects of any such mutation will be best interpreted as affecting not how various cortical areas *are* wired but how they *get* wired.

REFERENCES

Adesnik, Hillel, and Massimo Scanziani. 2010. Lateral competition for cortical space by layer-specific horizontal circuits. *Nature* 464:1155–1160.

Aleman, André, Geert-Jan M. Rutten, Margriet M. Sitskoorn, Geraud Dautzenberg, and Nick F. Ramsay. 2001. Activation of striate cortex in the absence of visual stimulation: an fMRI study of synesthesia. *Neuroreport* 12:2827–2830.

Allison, Truett, Aina Puce, and Gregory McCarthy. 2002. Category-sensitive excitatory and inhibitory processes in human extrastriate cortex. *Journal of Neurophysiology* 88:2864–2868.

Arlotta, Paolo, Bradley J. Molyneaux, Jinhui Chen, Jun Inoue, Ryo Kominami, and Jeffrey D. Macklis. 2005. Neuronal subtype-specific genes that control corticospinal motor neuron development in vivo. *Neuron* 45:207–221.

Asher, Julian E., Janine Lamb, Denise Brocklebank, Jean-Baptiste Cazier, Elena Maestrini, Laura Addis, Mallika Sen, Simon Baron-Cohen, and Anthony P. Monaco. 2009. A whole-genome scan and fine-mapping linkage study of auditory-visual synesthesia reveals evidence of linkage to chromosomes 2q24, 5q33, 6p12, and 12p12. *The American Journal of Human Genetics* 84:279–285.

Bai, Wanzhu, Mami Ishida, Masaru Okabe, and Yasoyoshi Arimatsu. 2005. Role of the protomap and target-derived signals in the development of intrahemispheric connections. *Cerebral Cortex* 16 (1):124–135.

Baker, Chris I., Jia Liu, Lawrence L. Wald, Kenneth K. Kwong, Thomas Benner, and Nancy Kanwisher. 2007. Visual word processing and experiential origins of functional selectivity in human extrastriate cortex. *Proceedings of the National Academy of Sciences of the United States of America* 104:9087–9092.

Banissy, Michael J., Vincent Walsh, and Jamie Ward. 2009. Enhanced sensory perception in synaesthesia. *Experimental Brain Research* 196:565–571.

Bargary, Gary, Kylie J. Barnett, Kevin J. Mitchell, and Fiona N. Newell. 2009. Colored-speech synaesthesia is triggered by multisensory, not unisensory, perception. *Psychological Science* 20:529–533.

Bargary, Gary, and Kevin J. Mitchell. 2008. Synaesthesia and cortical connectivity. *Trends in Neurosciences* 31:335–342.

Barnett Kylie J., Joanne Feeney, Michael Gormley, and Fiona N. Newell. 2009. An exploratory study of linguistic-colour associations across languages in multilingual synaesthetes. *The Quarterly Journal of Experimental Psychology* 62:1343–1354.

Barnett, Kylie J., Ciara Finucane, Julian E. Asher, Gary Bargary, Aiden P. Corvin, Fiona N. Newell, and Kevin J. Mitchell. 2008. Familial patterns and the origins of individual differences in synaesthesia. *Cognition* 106:871–893.

Barnett, Kylie J., John J. Foxe, Sophie Molholm, Simon P. Kelly, Shani Shalgi, Kevin J. Mitchell, and Fiona N. Newell. 2008. Differences in early sensory-perceptual processing in synesthesia: a visual evoked potential study. *NeuroImage* 43:605–613.

Barnett, Kylie J., and Fiona N. Newell. 2008. Synaesthesia is associated with enhanced, self-rated visual imagery. *Consciousness and Cognition* 17:1032–1039.

Baron-Cohen, Simon, Lucy Burt, Fiona Laittan-Smith, John E. Harrison, and Patrick Bolton. 1996. Synaesthesia: Prevalence and familiality. *Perception* 25:1073–1079.

Barone, P., C. Dehay, M. Berland, and H. Kennedy. 1996. Role of directed growth and target selection in the formation of cortical pathways: prenatal development of the projection of area V2 to area V4 in the monkey. *Journal of Comparative Neurology* 374:1–20.

Batardiere, Alexandre, Pascal Barone, Kenneth Knoblauch, Pascale Giroud, Michel Berland, Anne-Marie Dumas, and Henry Kennedy. 2002. Early specification of the hierarchical organization of visual cortical areas in the macaque monkey. *Cerebral Cortex* 12:453–465.

Bavelier, Daphne, and Helen J. Neville. 2002. Cross-modal plasticity: where and how? *Nature Reviews Neuroscience* 3:443–452.

Beeli, Gian, Michaela Esslen, and Lutz Jäncke. 2007. Time course of neural activity correlated with colored-hearing synesthesia. *Cerebral Cortex* 18 (2):379–385.

Biswal, Bharat, Maarten Mennes, Xi-Nian Zuo, Suril Gohel, Clare Kelly, Steve M. Smith, Christian F. Beckmann, et al. 2010. Toward discovery science of human brain function. *Proceedings of the National Academy of Sciences of the United States of America* 107:4734–4739.

Bonnin, Alexandre, Masaaki Torii, Lilly Wang, Pasko Rakic, and Pat Levitt. 2007. Serotonin modulates the response of embryonic thalamocortical axons to netrin-1. *Nature Neuroscience* 10:588–597.

Bourne, James A. 2010. Unravelling the development of the visual cortex: implications for plasticity and repair. *Journal of Anatomy* 217:449–468.

Bourne, James A., and Marcello G. P. Rosa. 2006. Hierarchical development of the primate visual cortex, as revealed by neurofilament immunoreactivity: Early maturation of the middle temporal area (MT). *Cerebral Cortex* 16:405–414.

Braisted, Janet E., Thomas Ringstedt, and Denis D. O'Leary. 2009. Slits are chemorepellents endogenous to hypothalamus and steer thalamocortical axons into ventral telencephalon. *Cerebral Cortex* 19 (Suppl 1):i144–151.

Brang, David, Edward M. Hubbard, Seana Coulson, Minxiong Huang, and Vilayanur S. Ramachandran. 2010. Magnetoencephalography reveals early activation of V4 in grapheme-color synesthesia. *NeuroImage* 53 (1):268–274.

Brang, David, and Vilayanur Ramachandrann. 2008. Psychopharmacology of synesthesia; the role of serotonin S2a receptor activation. *Medical Hypotheses* 70:903–904.

Burkhalter, A. 1993. Development of forward and feedback connections between areas V1 and V2 of human visual cortex. *Cerebral Cortex* 3:476–487.

Burrack, Anna, Daria Knoch, and Peter Brugger. 2006. Mitempfindung in synaesthetes: Co-incidence or meaningful association? *Cortex* 42:151–154.

Cahill, Larry. 2006. Why sex matters for neuroscience. *Nature Reviews Neuroscience* 7:477–484.

Cantlon, Jessica F., Philippe Pinel, Stanislas Dehaene, and Kevin A. Pelphrey. 2011. Cortical representations of symbols, objects, and faces are pruned back during early childhood. *Cerebral Cortex* 21(1):191–199.

Chedotal, Alaine, and Linda J. Richards. 2010. Wiring the brain: the biology of neuronal guidance. *Cold Spring Harbor Perspectives in Biology* 2:a001917.

Coogan, Thomas A. A., and David C. Van Essen. 1996. Development of connections within and between areas V1 and V2 of macaque monkeys. *Journal of Comparative Neurology* 372:327–342.

Corey, Linda A., John M. Pellock, Marianne J. Kjeldsen, and Karl Otto Nakken. 2011. Importance of genetic factors in the occurrence of epilepsy syndrome type: A twin study. *Epilepsy Research* 97:103–111.

Cytowic, Richard E. 1989. *Synaesthesia: A Union of the Senses*. 1st ed. New York: Springer-Verlag.

——. 2002. *Synesthesia: A Union of the Senses*. 2nd ed. Cambridge, MA: MIT Press.

Cytowic, Richard E., and David M. Eagleman. 2009. *Wednesday is Indigo Blue: Discovering the Brain of Synesthesia*. Cambridge, MA: MIT Press.

Dehaene, Stanislas, and Laurent Cohen. 2007. Cultural recycling of cortical maps. *Neuron* 56:384–398.

Dehay, Colette, Gwynn Horsburgh, Michel Berland, Herbert Killackey, and Henry Kennedy, H. 1989. Maturation and connectivity of the visual cortex in monkey is altered by prenatal removal of retinal input. *Nature* 337:265–267.

Dehay, Collette, and Henry Kennedy. 2007. Cell-cycle control and cortical development. *Nature Reviews Neuroscience* 8:438–450.

Dehay, Collette, Henry Kennedy, and Jean Bullier. 1988. Characterization of transient cortical projections from auditory, somatosensory, and motor cortices to visual areas 17, 18, and 19 in the kitten. *Journal of Comparative Neurology* 272:68–89.

Demyanenko, Galina P., Thorfinn T. Riday, Tracy S. Tran, Jasbir Dalal, Eli P. Darnell, Leann H. Brennaman, Takeshi Sakurai, *et al.* 2011. NrCAM deletion causes topographic mistargeting of thalamocortical axons to the visual cortex and disrupts visual acuity. *The Journal of Neuroscience* 31:1545–1558.

Demyanenko, Galina P., Priscila F. Siesser, Amanda G. Wright, Leann H. Brennaman, Udo Bartsch, Melitta Schachner, and Patricia F. Maness. 2011. L1 and CHL1 Cooperate in thalamo-cortical axon targeting. *Cerebral Cortex* 21:401–412.

Dufour, Audrey, Julie Seibt, Lara Passante, Vanessa Depaepe, Thomas Ciossek, Jonas Frisen, Klas J. Kullander, John G. Flanagan, Franck Polleux, and Pierre Vanderhaeghen. 2003. Area specificity and topography of thalamocortical projections are controlled by ephrin/Eph genes. *Neuron* 39:453–465.

Dye, Catherine A., Hani El Shawa, and Kelly J. Huffman. 2010a. A lifespan analysis of intraneo-cortical connections and gene expression in the mouse I. *Cerebral Cortex* 21 (6):1311–1330.

——. 2010b. A lifespan analysis of intraneocortical connections and gene expression in the mouse II. *Cerebral Cortex* 21 (6):1331–1350.

Fair, Damien A., Deepti Bathula, Kathryn L. Mills, Taciana G. Costa Dias, Michael S. Blythe, Dongyang Zhang, Abraham Z. Snyder, *et al.* 2010. Maturing thalamocortical functional connectivity across development. *Frontiers in System Neuroscience* 4 (10).

Fair, Damien A., Alexander L. Cohen, Jonathon D. Power, Nico U. F. Dosenbach, Jessica A. Church, Francis M. Miezin, Bradley L. Schlaggar, and Steven E. Petersen. 2009. Functional brain networks develop from a 'local to distributed' organization. *PLoS Computational Biology* 5:e1000381.

Frappe, Isabelle, Afsaneh Gaillard, and Michel Roger. 2001. Attraction exerted in vivo by grafts of embryonic neocortex on developing thalamic axons. *Experimental Neurology* 169 (2):264–275.

Galaburda, Albert M., Joseph LoTurco, Franck Ramus, R. Holly Fitch, and Glenn D. Rosen. 2006. From genes to behavior in developmental dyslexia. *Nature Neuroscience* 9:1213–1217.

Galton, Francis. 1883. *Enquiries into the Human Faculty and its Development.* London: Everyman.

Garel, Sorel, Kyuson Yun, Rudolf Grosschedl, and John L. Rubenstein. 2002. The early topography of thalamocortical projections is shifted in Ebf1 and Dlx1/2 mutant mice. *Development* 129:5621–5634.

Gaspard, Nicolas, Tristan Bouschet, Raphael Hourez, Jordane Dimidschstein, Gilles Naeije, Jelle van den Ameele, Ira Espuny-Camacho, *et al.* 2008. An intrinsic mechanism of corticogenesis from embryonic stem cells. *Nature* 45: 351–357.

Gitton, Yorick, Michel Cohen-Tannoudji, and Marion Wassef. 1999. Role of thalamic axons in the expression of H-2Z1, a mouse somatosensory cortex specific marker. *Cerebral Cortex* 9:611–620.

Golarai, Golijeh, Dara G. Ghahremani, S. Whitfield-Gabrieli, Allan Reiss, Jennifer L. Eberhardt, John D. E. Gabrieli, and Kalanit Grill-Spector. 2007. Differential development of high-level visual cortex correlates with category-specific recognition memory. *Nature Neuroscience* 10:512–522.

Goller, Aviva I., Leun Otten, and Jamie Ward. 2009. Seeing sounds and hearing colors: An event-related potential study of auditory–visual synesthesia. *Journal of Cognitive Neuroscience* 21 (10):1869–1881.

Gong, Goalang, Pedro Rosa-Neto, Felix Carbonell, Zhang J. Chen, Yong He, and Alan C. Evans. 2009. Age- and gender-related differences in the cortical anatomical network. *The Journal of Neuroscience* 29:15684–15693.

Gray, Jeffrey A., David M. Parslow, Michael J. Brammer, Susan Chopping, Goparlen N. Vythelingum, and Dominic H. Fytche. 2006. Evidence against functionalism from neuroimaging of the alien colour effect in synaesthesia. *Cortex* 42 (2):309–318.

Grill-Spector, Kalanit, Goalang Golarai, and John Gabrieli. 2008. Developmental neuroimaging of the human ventral visual cortex. *Trends in Cognitive Science* 12:152–162.

Grossenbacher, Peter G., and Christopher T. Lovelace. 2001. Mechanisms of synesthesia: Cognitive and physiological constraints. *Trends in Cognitive Science* 5 (1):36–41.

Guillery, R. W. 2005. Is postnatal neocortical maturation hierarchical? *Trends in Neuroscience* 28 (10):512–517.

Hagmann, P., O. Sporns, N. Madan, L. Cammoun, R. Pienaar, V. J. Wedeen, R. Meuli, J. P. Thiran, and P. E. Grant. 2010. White matter maturation reshapes structural connectivity in the late developing human brain. *Proceedings of the National Academy of Sciences of the United States of America* 107:19067–19072.

Hänggi, Jürgen, Diana Wotruba, and Lutz Jäncke. 2011. Globally altered structural brain network topology in grapheme-color synesthesia. *The Journal of Neuroscience* 31 (15):5816–5828.

Hubbard, Edward M. 2007. Neurophysiology of synesthesia. *Current Psychiatry Reports* 9 (3):193–199.

Hubbard, Edward M., A. Cyrus Arman, Vilayanur S. Ramachandran, and Geoffrey M. Boynton. 2005. Individual differences among grapheme-color synesthetes: Brain-behavior correlations. *Neuron* 45 (6):975–985.

Hubbard, Edward M., and Vilayanur S. Ramachandran. 2005. Neurocognitive mechanisms of synesthesia. *Neuron* 48:509–520.

Hurley, Susan, and Alva Noë. 2003. Neural plasticity and consciousness. *Biology and Philosophy* 18:131–168.

Huttenlocher, Peter R., and Arun S. Dabholkar. 1997. Regional differences in synaptogenesis in human cerebral cortex. *The Journal of Comparitive Neurology* 387 (2):167–178.

Innocenti, Giorgio M., and Stephanie Clarke. 1984. Bilateral transitory projection to visual areas from auditory cortex in kittens. *Developmental Brain Research* 14 (1):143–148.

Innocenti, Giorgio M., and David J. Price. 2005. Exuberance in the development of cortical networks. *Nature Reviews Neuroscience* 6:955–965.

Jäncke, Lutz, Gian Beeli, Cornelia Eulig, and Jürgen Hänggi. 2009. The neuroanatomy of grapheme-color synesthesia. *European Journal of Neuroscience* 29 (6):1287–1293.

Johnson, Mark H. 2010. Interactive specialization: A domain-general framework for human functional brain development? *Developmental Cognitive Neuroscience* 1 (1):7–21. doi:10.1016/j.dcn.2010.07.003.

Joseph, Jane E., Ann D. Gathers, and Ramesh S. Bhatt. 2010. Progressive and regressive developmental changes in neural substrates for face processing: Testing specific predictions of the interactive specialization account. *Developmental Science* 14(2):227–241. doi:10.1111/j.1467–7687.2010.00963.x.

Kaern, Mads, Timothy C. Elston, William J. Blake, and James J. Collins. 2005. Stochasticity in gene expression: from theories to phenotypes. *Nature Reviews Genetics* 6:451–464.

Kahn, Dianna M., and Leah Krubitzer. 2002. Massive cross-modal cortical plasticity and the emergence of a new cortical area in developmentally blind mammals. *Proceedings of the National Academy of Sciences of the United States of America* 99 (17):11429–11434.

Kanwisher, Nancy. 2010. Functional specificity in the human brain: a window into the functional architecture of the mind. *Proceedings of the National Academy of Sciences of the United States of America* 107 (25):11163–11170.

Karlen, Sarah J., Dianna M. Kahn, and Leah Krubitzer. 2006. Early blindness results in abnormal corticocortical and thalamocortical connections. *Neuroscience* 142:843–858.

Karlen, Sarah J., and Leah Krubitzer. 2006. The evolution of the neocortex in mammals: Intrinsic and extrinsic contributions to the cortical phenotype. *Novartis Foundation Symposium* 270:146–159; discussion 159–169.

Karmiloff-Smith, Annette. 2006. The tortuous route from genes to behavior: A neuroconstructivist approach. *Cognitive, Affective, & Behavioral Neuroscience* 6 (1):9–17.

——. 2007. Atypical epigenesis. *Developmental Science* 10:84–88.

——. 2011. Static snapshots versus dynamic approaches to genes, brain, cognition and behaviour in neurodevelopmental disabilities. In *International Review of Research on Developmental Disabilities*, ed. Deborah J. Fidler, 1–16. Amsterdam: Elsevier.

Kingsbury, Marcy A., Nadine A. Lettman, and Barbara L. Finlay. 2002. Reduction of early thalamic input alters adult corticocortical connectivity. *Developmental Brain Research* 138:35–43.

Kostović, Ivica, and Nataša Jovanov-Milošević . 2006. The development of cerebral connections during the first 20–45 weeks' gestation. *Seminars in Fetal & Neonatal Medicine* 11 (6):415–422.

Kostović, Ivica, and Miloš Judaš. 2010. The development of the subplate and thalamocortical connections in the human foetal brain. *Acta Paediatrica* 99:1119–1127.

Kostović, Ivica, and Pasko Rakic. 1984. Development of prestriate visual projections in the monkey and human fetal cerebrum revealed by transient cholinesterase staining. *The Journal of Neuroscience* 4 (1):25–42.

Krubitzer, Leah. 2009. In search of a unifying theory of complex brain evolution. *Annals of the New York Academy of Sciences* 1156:44–67.

Laeng, Bruno, Kenneth Hugdahl, and Karsten Specht. 2011. The neural correlate of colour distances revealed with competing synaesthetic and real colours. *Cortex* 47:320–331.

Landerl, Karin, and Kristina Moll. 2010. Comorbidity of learning disorders: prevalence and familial transmission. *The Journal of Child Psychology & Psychiatry* 51 (3):287–294.

Leighton, Philip A., Kevin J. Mitchell, Lisa V. Goodrich, Xiaowei Lu, Kathy Pinson, Paul Scherz, William C. Skarnes, and Marc Tessier-Lavigne. 2001. Defining brain wiring patterns and mechanisms through gene trapping in mice. *Nature* 410:174–179.

Levy, Dan, Michael Ronemus, Boris Yamrom, Yoon-Ha Lee, Anthony Leotta, Jude Kendall, Steven Marks, *et al.* 2011. Rare de novo and transmitted copy-number variation in autistic spectrum disorders. *Neuron* 70 (5):886–897.

Little, Graeme E., Guillermina Lopez-Bendito, Annette E. Rünker, Noelia Garcia, Maria C. Piñon, Alain Chédotal, Zoltán Molnár, and Kevin J. Mitchell. 2009. Specificity and plasticity of thalamocortical connections in Sema6A mutant mice. *PLoS Biology* 7 (4):e98.

Lopez-Bendito, Guillermina, Nuria Flames, Le Ma, Coralie Fouquet, Thomas Di Meglio, Alain Chedotal, Marc Tessier-Lavigne, and Oscar Marin. 2007. Robo1 and Robo2 cooperate to control the guidance of major axonal tracts in the mammalian forebrain. *The Journal of Neuroscience* 27:3395–3407.

Lopez-Bendito, Guillermina, and Zoltán Molnár. 2003. Specificity and plasticity of thalamo-cortical connections in Sema6A mutant mice. *Nature Reviews Neuroscience* 4:276–289.

Low, Laurence K., Xiao-Bo Liu, Regina L. Faulkner, Jeffrey Coble, and Hwai-Jong Cheng. 2008. Plexin signaling selectively regulates the stereotyped pruning of corticospinal axons from visual cortex. *Proceedings of the National Academy of Sciences of the United States of America* 105 (23):8136–8141.

Lukaszewicz, Agn è s, Véronique Cortay, Pascale Giroud, Michel Berland, Iain Smart, Henry Kennedy, and Colette Dehay. 2006. The concerted modulation of proliferation and migration contributes to the specification of the cytoarchitecture and dimensions of cortical areas. *Cerebral Cortex* 16 (Suppl 1):i26–i34.

Luo, Liqun, and Dennis D. M. O'Leary. 2005. Axon retraction and degeneration in development and disease. *Annual Review of Neuroscience* 28:127–156.

Ma, Long, Takayuki Harada, Chikako Harada, Mario Romero, Jean M. Hebert, Sisan K. McConnell, and Luis F. Parada. 2002. Neurotrophin-3 is required for appropriate establishment of thalamocortical connections. *Neuron* 36 (4):623–634.

Mills, Carol B., Meredith L. Viguers, Shari K. Edelson, Amanda T. Thomas, Stephanie L. Simon-Dack, and Joanne A. Innis. 2002. The color of two alphabets for a multilingual synesthete. *Perception* 31:1371–1394.

Mitchell, Kevin J. 2007. The genetics of brain wiring: From molecule to mind. *PLoS Biology* 5:e113.

——. 2011a. Curiouser and curiouser: Genetic disorders of cortical specialization. *Current Opinion in Genetics & Development* 21 (3):271–277.

——. 2011b. The genetics of neurodevelopmental disease. *Current Opinion in Neurobiology* 21:197–203.

——. 2012. What is complex about complex disorders? *Genome Biology* 13:237.

Ng, Sarah B., Emily H. Turner, Peggy D. Robertson, Steven D. Flygare, Abigail W. Bigham, Choli Lee, Tristan Shaffer, *et al.* 2009. Targeted capture and massively parallel sequencing of 12 human exomes. *Nature* 461:272–276.

Nunn, J. A., L. J. Gregory, M. J. Brammer, S. C. R. Williams, D. M. Parslow, M. J. Morgan, R. G. Morris, E. T. Bullmore, S. Baron-Cohen, and J. A. Gray. 2002. Functional magnetic resonance imaging of synesthesia: Activation of V4/V8 by spoken words. *Nature Neuroscience* 5 (4):371–375.

O'Leary, Dennis D. M., Shen-Ju Chou, and Setsuko Sahara. 2007. Area patterning of the mammalian cortex. *Neuron* 56:252–269.

Pallas, Sarah L. 2001. Intrinsic and extrinsic factors that shape neocortical specification. *Trends in Neuroscience* 24:417–423.

Pascual-Leone, Alvaro, Amir Amedi, Felipe Fregni, and Lotfi B. Merabet. 2005. The plastic human brain cortex. *Annual Review of Neuroscience* 28:377–401.

Paulesu, Eraldo, John Harrison, Simon Baron-Cohen, John D. G. Watson, Laura Goldstein, John Heather, Richard S. J. Frakowiak and Christopher D. Frith. 1995. The physiology of coloured hearing. A PET activation study of colour-word synaesthesia. *Brain* 118 (Pt 3):661–676.

Paus, T., D. L. Collins, A. C. Evans, G. Leonard, B. Pike, and A. Zijdenbos. 2001. Maturation of white matter in the human brain: A review of magnetic resonance studies. *Brain Research Bulletin* 54 (3):255–266.

Paysan, Jacques, Albrecht Kossel, Jürgen Bolz, and Jean-Marc Fritschy. 1997. Area-specific regulation of gamma-aminobutyric acid type A receptor subtypes by thalamic afferents in developing rat neocortex. *Proceedings of the National Academy of Sciences of the United States of America* 94:6995–7000.

Petanjek, Zdravko, Miloš Judaš, Goran Šimić, Mladan Roko Rasin, Harry B. M. Uylings, Pasko Rakic, and Ivica Kostović. 2011. Extraordinary neoteny of synaptic spines in the human prefrontal cortex. *Proceedings of the National Academy of Sciences of the United States of America* 108:13281–13286.

Poskanzer, Kira, Leigh A. Needleman, Ozlem Bozdagi, and George W. Huntley. 2003. N-cadherin regulates ingrowth and laminar targeting of thalamocortical axons. *The Journal of Neuroscience* 23:2294–2305.

Powell, Ashton W., Takyuki Sassa, Yongqin Wu, Marc Tessier-Lavigne, and Franck Polleux, F. 2008. Topography of thalamic projections requires attractive and repulsive functions of Netrin-1 in the ventral telencephalon. *PLoS Biology* 6:e116.

Price, David J., and Colin Blakemore. 1985. Regressive events in the postnatal development of association projections in the visual cortex. *Nature* 316:721–724.

Price, David J., Henry Kennedy, Colette Dehay, Libing Zhou, Marjorie Mercier, Yves Jossin, André M. Goffinet, Fadel Tissir, Daniel Blakey, and Zoltán Molnár. 2006. The development of cortical connections. *European Journal of Neuroscience* 23:910–920.

Rakic, Pasko, Ivan Suner, and Robert W. Williams. 1991. A novel cytoarchitectonic area induced experimentally within the primate visual cortex. *Proceedings of the National Academy of Sciences of the United States of America* 88:2083–2087.

Ramus, Franck. 2004. Neurobiology of dyslexia: A reinterpretation of the data. *Trends in Neuroscience* 27:720–726.

Rash, Brian G., and Elizabeth A. Grove. 2006. Area and layer patterning in the developing cerebral cortex. *Current Opinion in Neurobiology* 16 (1):25–34.

Rich, Anina N., John L. Bradshaw, and Jason B. Mattingley. 2005. A systematic, large-scale study of synaesthesia: implications for the role of early experience in lexical-colour associations. *Cognition* 98 (1):53–84.

Rich, Anina N., Mark A. Williams, Aina Puce, Ari Syngeniotis, Matthew A. Howard, Francis McGlone, and Jason B. Mattingley. 2006. Neural correlates of imagined and synaesthetic colours. *Neuropsychologia* 44 (14):2918–2925.

Rouw, Romke, and H. Steven Scholte. 2007. Increased structural connectivity in grapheme-color synesthesia. *Nature Neuroscience* 10 (6):792–797.

——. 2010. Neural basis of individual differences in synesthetic experiences. *The Journal of Neuroscience* 30 (18):6205–6213.

Sharma, Jitendra, Alessandra Angelucci, and Mriganka Sur. 2000. Induction of visual orientation modules in auditory cortex. *Nature* 404:841–847.

Shaw, Philip, Noor J. Kabani, Jason P. Lerch, Kristen Eckstrand, Rhoshel Lenroot, Nitin Gogtay, Deanna Greenstein, *et al.* 2008. Neurodevelopmental trajectories of the human cerebral cortex. *The Journal of Neuroscience* 28 (14):3586–3594.

Shendure, Jay, and Hanlee Ji. 2008. Next-generation DNA sequencing. *Nature Biotechnology* 26:1135–1145.

Simner, Julia. 2007. Beyond perception: Synaesthesia as a psycholinguistic phenomenon. *Trends in Cognitive Science* 11:23–29.

Simner, Julia, and Emma Holenstein. 2007. Ordinal linguistic personification as a variant of synesthesia. *Journal of Cognitive Neuroscience* 19 (4):694–703.

Simner Julia, Catherine Mulvenna, Noam Sagiv, Elias Tsakanikos, S. Athene Witherby, Christine Fraser, Kirsten Scott, and Jamie Ward. 2006. Synaesthesia: The prevalence of atypical cross-modal experiences. *Perception* 35:1024–1033.

Smilek, D., B. A. Moffatt, J. Pasternak, B. N. White, M. J. Dixon, and P. M. Merikle. 2002. Synaesthesia: A case study of discordant monozygotic twins. *Neurocase* 8 (4):338–342.

Smilek, Daniel, Michael J. Dixon, Cera Cudahy, and Philip M. Merikle. 2001. Synaesthetic photisms influence visual perception. *Journal of Cognitive Neuroscience* 13 (7):930–936.

Smilek, Daniel, Mike J. Dixon, and Philip M. Merikle. 2005. Synaesthesia: Discordant male monozygotic twins. *Neurocase* 11:363–370.

Spector, Ferrine and Daphne Maurer. 2011. The colors of the alphabet: naturally-biased associations between shape and color. *Journal of Experimental Psychology. Human Perception & Performance* 37:484–495.

Sperling, Julia M., David Prvulovic, David E. J. Linden, Wolf Singer, and Aglaja Stirn. 2006. Neuronal correlates of colour-graphemic synaesthesia: A fMRI study. *Cortex* 42:295–303.

Steven, Megan S., Peter C. Hansen, and Colin Blakemore. 2006. Activation of color-selective areas of the visual cortex in a blind synesthete. *Cortex* 42 (2):304–308.

Supekar, Kaustubh, Mark Musen, and Vinod Menon. 2009. Development of large-scale functional brain networks in children. *PLoS Biology* 7:e1000157.

Sur, Mriganka, and John L. R. Rubenstein. 2005. Patterning and plasticity of the cerebral cortex. *Science* 310:805–810.

Toga, Arthur W., Paul M. Thompson, and Elizabeth R. Sowell. 2006. Mapping brain maturation. *Trends in Neuroscience* 29:148–159.

Tomasi, Dardo, and Nora D. Volkow. 2011. Gender differences in brain functional connectivity density. *Human Brain Mapping* 33 (4):849–860.

Tomson, Steffie N., Nili Avidan, Kwanghyuk Lee, Anand K. Sarma, Rejnal Tushe, Dianna M. Milewicz, Molly Bray, Suzanne M. Leal, and David M. Eagleman. 2011. The genetics of colored sequence synesthesia: Suggestive evidence of linkage to 16q and genetic heterogeneity for the condition. *Behavioral Brain Research* 223 (1):48–52.

Torii, Masaaki, and Pat Levitt. 2005. Dissociation of corticothalamic and thalamocortical axon targeting by an EphA7-mediated mechanism. *Neuron* 48 (4):563–575.

Tyler, Christopher W. 2005. Varieties of synesthetic experience. In *Synesthesia: Perspectives from Cognitive Neuroscience,* ed. Lynn C. Robertson and Noam Sagiv, 34–46. New York: Oxford University Press.

Uddin, Lucina Q., Kaustubh Supekar, and Vinod Menon. 2010. Typical and atypical development of functional human brain networks: Insights from resting-state FMRI. *Frontiers in Systems Neuroscience* 4:21.

van Leeuwen Tessa M., Karl M. Petersson, and Peter Hagoort. 2010. Synaesthetic colour in the brain: Beyond colour areas. A functional magnetic resonance imaging study of synaesthetes and matched controls. *PLoS ONE* 5:e12074.

Vanderhaeghen, Pierre, and Hwai-Jong Cheng. 2010. Guidance molecules in axon pruning and cell death. *Cold Spring Harbor Perspectives in Biology* 2:a001859.

Vanderhaeghen, Pierre, and Franck Polleux. 2004. Developmental mechanisms patterning thalamocortical projections: Intrinsic, extrinsic and in between. *Trends in Neuroscience* 27 (7):384–391.

Vasung, Lana, Hao Huang, Nataša Jovanov-Milošević, Mihovil Pletikos, Susumu Mori, and Ivica Kostović . 2010. Development of axonal pathways in the human fetal fronto-limbic brain: Histochemical characterization and diffusion tensor imaging. *Journal of Anatomy* 21:400–417.

von Melchner, Lauri, Sarah L. Pallas, and Mriganka Sur. 2000. Visual behaviour mediated by retinal projections directed to the auditory pathway. *Nature* 404:871–876.

Wagner, Andreas. 2007. *Robustness and Evolvability in Living Systems*. Princeton, NJ: Princeton University Press.

Ward, Jamie, Brett Huckstep, and Elias Tsakanikos. 2006. Sound-colour synaesthesia: To what extent does it use cross-modal mechanisms common to us all? *Cortex* 42:264–280.

Ward, Jamie, and Julia Simner. 2003. Lexical-gustatory synaesthesia: Linguistic and conceptual factors. *Cognition* 89:237–261.

——. 2005. Is synaesthesia an X-linked dominant trait with lethality in males? *Perception* 34 (5):611–623.

Webster, Maree J., Leslie G. Ungerleider, and Jocelyne Bachevalier. 1991. Connections of inferior temporal areas TE and TEO with medial temporal-lobe structures in infant and adult monkeys. *The Journal of Neuroscience* 11:1095–1116.

Weiss, Peter H., and Gereon R. Fink. 2009. Grapheme-colour synaesthetes show increased grey matter volumes of parietal and fusiform cortex. *Brain* 132 (1):65–70.

Weiss, Peter H., Karl Zilles, and Gereon R. Fink. 2005. When visual perception causes feeling: Enhanced cross-modal processing in grapheme-color synesthesia. *NeuroImage* 28 (4):859–868.

Witthoft, Nathan, and Jonathan Winawer. 2006. Synesthetic colors determined by having colored refrigerator magnets in childhood. *Cortex* 42 (2):175–183.

Wright, Amanda G., Galina P. Demyanenko, Ashton Powell, Melitta Schachner, Lilian Enriquez-Barreto, Tracy S. Tran, Franck Polleux, and Patricia F. Maness. 2007. Close homolog of L1 and neuropilin 1 mediate guidance of thalamocortical axons at the ventral telencephalon. *The Journal of Neuroscience* 27 (50):13667–13679.

Zhao, Xiaoyue, Anthony Leotta, Vlad Kustanovich, Clara Lajonchere, Daniel H. Geschwind, Kiely Law, Paul Law, *et al.* 2007. A unified genetic theory for sporadic and inherited autism. *Proceedings of the National Academy of Sciences of the United States of America* 104 (31):12831–12836.

....

CHAPTER 28

THE TIMING OF NEUROPHYSIOLOGICAL EVENTS IN SYNESTHESIA

....

LUTZ JÄNCKE

INTRODUCTION

....

Synesthesia is a rare perceptual phenomenon in which actual sensory impressions resulting from an inducing stimulus in one modality elicit concurrent perceptions in another sensory modality. The term synesthesia was first used by the French neurophysiologist Vulpian (1866). But the Swiss psychiatrists Bleuler and Lehmann (1881) were the first to conduct sophisticated investigations of this particular phenomenon (see Jewanski, Chapter 19, this volume for a full historical review). Bleuler's interest in synesthesia was mainly driven by the goal of understanding hallucinatory experiences, especially in schizophrenia. A better understanding of the psychological, neurophysiological, and neuroanatomical underpinnings of synesthesia itself failed thereafter to attract research interest. But with the advent of modern brain imaging methods and techniques to measure the neurophysiological underpinnings of psychological phenomena, a growing community of neuroscientists is now engaged in the study of synesthesia. An important milestone was the first brain imaging study of Paulesu et al. (1995) who used positron emission tomography to measure hemodynamic responses in synesthetes during synesthetic experiences. Several other studies followed using functional magnetic resonance imaging (fMRI) to explore the hemodynamic responses in synesthetes (Elias et al. 2003; Hubbard et al. 2005; Nunn et al. 2002; van Leeuwen, Petersson, and Hagoort 2010; Weiss, Zilles, and Fink, 2005; Weiss et al. 2001). In general, these studies show that the concurrent synesthetic perception is associated with hemodynamic responses in brain areas that are normally involved in processing stimuli in the modality in which these concurrents are experienced. Thus, in colored hearing synesthetes a tone induces activations in the auditory cortex and in the fusiform color area.

Alongside these first brain imaging studies, event-related potentials (ERPs) were measured with electroencephalography (EEG) in synesthetes, allowing the delineation of the time course of neurophysiological activations associated with synesthetic experiences (Barnett et al. 2008; Beeli, Esslen, and Jäncke 2008; Brang et al. 2008; Brang et al. 2010; Brang et al. 2011; Cohen Kadosh, Cohen Kadosh, and Henik 2007; Gebuis, Nijboer, and Van der Smagt 2009; Goller, Otten, and Ward 2009; Niccolai et al. 2012; Sagiv et al. 2003; Schiltz et al. 1999; Teuscher et al. 2010; see Table 28.1 for a summary of these studies). Based on these experiments, the neurophysiological underpinnings of synesthesia may be described and discussed in terms of three basically different neurophysiological models: (1) the two-stage *cross-activation and hyperbinding model* (Hubbard 2007), (2) the *disinhibited feedback model* (Grossenbacher and Lovelace 2001), and (3) the *limbic-mediation model* (Cytowic and Wood 1982). I will briefly describe these models because they make different predictions about the time course of synesthetic experiences and the underlying neurophysiological processes.

NEUROPHYSIOLOGICAL MODELS

The cross-activation and hyperbinding model was proposed on the basis of fMRI studies in grapheme-color synesthetes (grapheme-color synesthetes experience colors from letters and/or digits; Hubbard 2007). According to this model, the grapheme area (posterior temporal grapheme area (PTGA)) and color processing brain area (V4) are thought to be aberrantly connected. A key idea behind this is that cross-activation between these brain areas occurs because of an abnormal excess of anatomical connections between these grapheme and color processing brain areas. This aberrant connectivity should result in strong co-activation of these areas during grapheme processing. Both perceptions are then bound together by parietal mechanisms, resulting in hyperbinding. This model has received some support, specifically for the experience of auditory-color synesthesia (e.g., Jäncke and Langer 2011).

The disinhibited feedback model is based on studies demonstrating specific forms of acquired and congenital synesthesias rather than on data from brain imaging studies (Grossenbacher and Lovelace, 2001). The disinhibited feedback model diverges from the cross-activation and hyperbinding model in that it posits normal connectivity patterns in synesthetes. It suggests also that synesthesia results from disinhibited feedback from higher-level cortical areas in the visual processing hierarchy. A hybrid model, the so-called re-entrant processing model, shares with the cross-activation model the notion of hyperconnectivity between form and color processing areas in the fusiform area, and suggests, like the disinhibited feedback model, that synesthetic colors require feedback of neural activity to V4 that originates in higher-level areas (e.g., anterior inferior temporal and posterior inferior temporal; Smilek et al. 2001).

The limbic mediation hypothesis, first proposed by Richard Cytowic and Frank Wood (1982), proposes that synesthesia is mediated by the limbic system and especially the

Table 28.1 Summary of studies on synesthesia employing ERP techniques in the context of EEG or MEG recordings

Study	Type of stimuli	Type of synesthetes	Type of response	General finding
Barnett et al. 2008	High and low spatial frequency gratings and luminance-contrast squares	Linguistic-color synesthetes n = 15	VEP	Larger C1 and P1 in synesthetes
Beeli et al. 2008	Auditory stimuli (words, digits)	Auditory-visual (colored-hearing) n = 16	AEP Inverse solution with LORETA	Differences in the early N1 and in the P2 Early responses in the color area starting at 100 ms and extending to 2000 ms after stimulus presentation in the color area; absent in non-synesthetes
Brang et al. 2008	Visually presented sentences, words, colors, and digits in a congruent or incongruent semantic context	Grapheme-color N = 8	VEP	Congruent graphemes elicited larger N1, smaller P2, and reduced N400 amplitudes in synesthetes but not age-matched naive control subjects
Brang et al. 2010	Graphemes and non-graphemic stimuli	Grapheme-color N = 4	VEO (from MEG) Inverse solution with L1-minimum-norm (VESTAL) approach	Early responses in the color area starting at 100 ms and extending to 370 ms after stimulus presentation in the color area; absent in non-synesthetes
Brang et al. 2011	Sentence final graphemes which are either congruent or incongruent with the semantic context	Grapheme-color N = 12	VEP	Congruent graphemes elicited larger N1, smaller P2, and reduced N400 amplitudes in synesthetes but not age-matched naive control subjects
Cohen Kadosh et al. 2007	Triangles and digits	Grapheme-color N = 1	VEP	Triangles comparison task: color congruency (i.e., larger triangle in the color of a larger vs smaller digit) modulated the N170; absent in non-synesthetes Numbers comparison task: color congruency (i.e., digits in own vs each other's colors) modulated the P300 amplitude; absent in non-synesthetes

(Continued)

Table 28.1 (*Continued*)

Study	Type of stimuli	Type of synesthetes	Type of response	General finding
Gebuis et al. 2009	Numbers primed by preceding colors Colors primed by preceding numbers	Grapheme-color N = 14	VEP	Synesthetes with a large behavioral priming effect revealed ERP modulation at frontal and parietal electrode sites Synesthetes with a small priming effect revealed a frontal effect only
Goller et al. 2009	Tones of different frequencies	Auditory-visual N=9	AEP	Differences in the early N1 and the later N2 A negative slow wave at 400–800 ms in synesthetes, which was absent in controls
Niccolai et al. in press	Graphemes and color patches	Grapheme-color N = 7	VEP	Synesthetes and trained non-synesthetes showed more negative going N300 and N400 ERP amplitudes Synesthetes also showed congruency-dependent modulation of the early N170
Sagiv et al. 2003	Letters	Grapheme-color N = ?[a]	VEP	Early negative modulation of the ERP component between 150 and 200 ms (i.e., N170)
Schiltz et al. 1999	Letters	Grapheme-color N = 17	VEP	Increased positivity at frontal and central scalp sites from 150 to 600 ms in synesthetes compared with non-synesthetes
Teuscher et al. 2010	Arrows, words, and month names	Time-space N = 12	VEP	P3b (370 ms) and positive slow wave (600–900 ms) after presentation of month names as probes are larger in synesthetes

AEP: auditory evoked potential; VEP: visual evoked potential
[a] This is an abstract of a conference presentation for which the printed version was not available to the author

hippocampus, on which multiple sensory signals converge. According to this hypothesis, synesthetes should have more connective fibers leading from the limbic system to the neocortex. Based on this limbic–neocortex hyperconnectivity, Cytowic and Wood propose that synesthetes are more aware or conscious of functional cross-modal couplings. Thus, the notion of a kind of enhanced cross-modal coupling is pivotal to this theory. Interestingly, this model does not make any assumptions about the time course of synesthetic experiences and the associated neurophysiological activations.

Different predictions can be drawn from these models about the timing of neural activations. As explicitly formulated in Brang et al. (2010), but not considered in the paper of Grossenbacher and Lovelace (2001), there should be a particular time lag between the processing of the inducing stimulus (the inducer) and the concurrent perception. In terms of neurophysiological activation, it is thus hypothesized that the neurophysiological activation of the brain areas associated with processing of the concurrent perception follows with a significant delay after the activation of the brain areas associated with the processing of the inducing stimulus. The cross-activation and hyperbinding model suggests increased local connectivity and predicts the activation of V4 during the initial sweep of activity in PTGA (Ramachandran and Hubbard, 2001). Activation of V4 and PTGA should therefore occur more or less simultaneously. The limbic mediation hypothesis does not make any assumptions about the timing of the neurophysiological processes. However, since the limbic system and the neocortex are strongly interconnected and the limbic system is involved in simple and complex cognitive and sensory processes, fast and slow processes are possible. Thus, even if hyperconnectivity between limbic and neocortical systems exists, activation time lags between the involved brain areas are possible but not necessary.

TIME COURSE OF ACTIVATION IN SYNESTHETES

The analysis of the time course of neurophysiological activations during synesthetic experience enables the preceding neurophysiological models of synesthesia to be tested. The same time course data also provides a useful means with which to test whether synesthetic experiences are driven by early perceptual (bottom-up) or later more cognitive processing steps (top-down), or even by an interaction of these earlier and later processes. Recent papers have proposed that both bottom-up and top-down processes might be involved in synesthesia.

Ramachandran and Hubbard (2001) posit the classification of synesthetes as "higher" or "lower": "higher" synesthetes are those for whom the grapheme "concept" is critical in triggering synesthesia, and "lower" synesthetes are those for whom the "percept" of the physical grapheme is necessary to elicit the synesthetic experience. "Lower" synesthetes would thus show greater neurophysiological modulation of early processing steps, while "higher" synesthetes would should greater neurophysiological modulation of late processing steps.

EEG and magnetoencephalographic (MEG) methods have been used to delineate the time course of neurophysiological activation during synesthetic perceptions because they allow the measurement of cortical activation on a millisecond basis. Two types of studies have thus far used these techniques in synesthesia research: the first used measures of evoked potentials time-locked to the inducing stimuli (Beeli, Esslen, and Jäncke

2008; Brang et al. 2008; Brang et al. 2010; Goller, Otten, and Ward 2009; Schiltz et al. 1999), which were either visual (e.g., graphemes for grapheme-color synesthetes) or auditory stimuli (tones or words for auditory-color graphemes), and the second type used priming techniques and measured higher-order cognitive processes in the context of synesthetic experience (Gebuis, Nijboer, and Van der Smagt 2009; Niccolai et al. 2012).

Most studies measuring ERPs to the inducing stimuli have shown modulations of the early components (N1, P2, and N2) in synesthetes. Using auditory stimuli in auditory-visual synesthetes, two studies found differences between synesthetes and controls for the early sensory components (of the auditory evoked potential (AEP)) which mostly reflect early activations of the auditory cortex occurring approximately 100–120 ms after onset of the auditory stimulus. In one study (Goller, Otten, and Ward 2009) the N1 and the later occurring N2 were significantly smaller in synesthetes compared with non-synesthetes (Goller, Otten, and Ward 2009). In the other study (Beeli, Esslen, and Jäncke 2008) the latencies of the N1 and P2 components were longer than in controls. Two further studies using visual inducers for grapheme-color synesthetes also identified modulations of the early ERP components in visual evoked potentials (VEPs) (N1, P2; Brang et al. 2008; Brang et al. 2010). The visual N1 occurs at approximately 120–200 ms after onset of the visual stimuli and reflects activity of the extrastriate cortex. The N1, with a lateral occipito-temporal scalp distribution, peaks at about 170 ms, with major generators located in the ventral visual stream, particularly in the lateral occipito-temporal areas. These studies thus imply that early processing steps are different in synesthetes. This interpretation finds some support in Barnett et al. (2008) who tested whether different visual stimuli that do not induce concurrent color perceptions in synesthetes modulate early processing steps. In fact, they identified very early processing differences in visual sensory processing commencing just 65–100 ms after stimulus presentation. These differences were found in the C1 and P1 reflecting activity in both primary and secondary visual cortex (Noesselt et al. 2002).

Taken together, the preceding data suggest that basic synesthetic experience is associated with specific early sensory processing steps and that specific bottom-up processes are operative in synesthesia. As previously mentioned by others (Shalgi and Foxe 2009), these early processing differences between synesthetes and non-synesthetes might reflect a basic difference in the wiring of the synesthetic brain, a difference that impacts very early sensory processing and implicates specific bottom-up processes in synesthesia. That synesthetes are different in the hard-wiring of the brain was demonstrated in recent neuroanatomical studies (Hanggi, Wotruba, and Jäncke 2011; Hänggi et al. 2008; Jäncke et al. 2009; Rouw and Scholte 2007, 2010).

In two of these studies the authors estimated the intracerebral sources of the electrical and magnetic topographical maps using modern mathematical methods to "solve" the inverse solution. Using LORETA (low-resolution electrical tomography), Beeli, Esslen, and Jäncke (2008) demonstrated in their study of auditory-color synesthetes that the N1 of the AEP is mainly associated with simultaneous activation in the auditory cortex and in the V4 area when their synesthetes listened to tones or words. Interestingly, this simultaneous activation remained stable for approximately 2 s. Using MEG, Brang et al. (2010) performed a similar experiment on four grapheme-color synesthetes and were able to demonstrate, by measuring magnetic VEPs, modulation of the N1 and the subsequent P2. By estimating the intracerebral sources of the scalp magnetic fields, they identified neurophysiological activation within the color and grapheme areas in synesthetes at N1 (which is 120 ms after presentation of the visual inducer). These findings are quite important in considering the preceding neurophysiological models because the studies did not identify time lags between activations in brain areas processing the inducer or the concurrent perceptions. These findings therefore lend weight to the cross-activation hyperbinding model.

The study of Schiltz et al. (1999) was one of the first EEG studies (most likely *the* first) on synesthetes. They tested 17 grapheme-color synesthetes who were presented with runs of visual letters and required to detect certain target letters (e.g., vowels). Measuring VEPs to the inducing visual stimuli, the authors reported an increased positivity at frontal and central scalp sites that emerged around 150 ms and was maintained until 600 ms compared with non-synesthetes. These results are different than those of the studies in the preceding section because the increased positivity occurred later and was reported only in the frontal and parietal brain areas. This most likely reflects therefore the effect of neural activity from association areas and not of the "lower" perceptual processing areas, and which pertain to slow potential shifts and not to clear-cut ERP components. The authors relate the stronger positivity at frontal leads in synesthetes to a kind of disinhibition of the frontal cortex, which in turn disinhibits concurrent perceptions. Although these results and the given interpretation do not entirely fit to the other studies and models reviewed here, this study does emphasize the idea that higher-order processes could also be involved in synesthesia.

Higher-order processes associated with synesthesia have been examined with studies in which more cognitively demanding experimental paradigms are used. A typical example of this study type is the experiment reported by Gebuis, Nijboer, and Van der Smagt (2009). They investigated the currently debated possible bi-directionality of synesthesia using ERPs. Synesthesia is mostly described as a uni-directional phenomenon, in which a particular inducer triggers a particular concurrent perception, but presenting the concurrent as a stimulus typically does not trigger the experience of its inducer. For example, in grapheme-color synesthesia, a particular grapheme (the inducer) might induce a particular color perception (the concurrent perception) but the color rarely induces the perception of its grapheme. However, several recent behavioral studies have emphasized that there are "back-and-forth" associations between inducer and concurrent, even if the color cannot induce the *perception* of a particular grapheme (Knoch et al. 2005; Meier and Rothen, 2007; Weiss, Kalckert, and Fink, 2009). One approach to explaining this bidirectional relationship is the assumption that synesthetes (or at least some synesthetes) do rely on a kind of higher-order concept of the triggering inducer, which might be activated from both directions (bottom-up and top-down). In the study of Gebuis, Nijboer, and Van der Smagt the authors measured VEPs to stimuli that served as inducers or evoked the "concurrent" perceptions directly. Here, they were interested in grapheme-color synesthetes and measured VEPs to numbers primed by preceding colors and VEPs to colors primed by numbers. Thus, they measured VEPs to both directions. The primes were stimuli that were congruent or incongruent with their synesthetic experience. Using this experimental technique, Gebuis and colleagues demonstrated that synesthetes are negatively impacted (have longer reaction times) when the number is primed by a color or when the color is primed by a number other than the respective number or color for which they have a specific color-number mapping (incongruent trials). Control subjects, on the other hand, are oblivious to this distinction. The electrophysiological responses are also interesting in that incongruent trials elicited larger frontal P3a amplitudes and longer parietal P3b latencies for the synesthetes (for a similar finding in one synesthete see also Cohen Kadosh, Cohen Kadosh, and Henik 2007). These effects did not differ between tasks, suggesting that the neurophysiological correlates underlying synesthesia are similar in both directions. However, the effects did differ between two types of synesthetes: those who had a small behavioral effect showed only the frontal modulation, while those who had a large behavioral effect showed both the frontal and the parietal modulations. These findings are interpreted as support for a distinction between "higher" and "lower" synesthetes (Hubbard et al. 2005). As noted earlier, Hubbard et al. proposed that "higher" synesthetes' perceptions are elicited by the concept of the trigger (top-down processes), whereas the experience of "lower" synesthetes is elicited by the percept of the trigger (bottom-up perceptual processes). This finding supports therefore the idea that synesthesia depends on two processes, an early bottom-up and a late top-down-process. It is possible that some synesthetes are dependent on one of the two processes or even on both. The earlier results of the Schlitz et al. study now make sense in the light of this hypothesis. Obviously, most of the synesthetes in the Schlitz et al. study were of the top-down type.

In order to focus more strongly on the top-down processes operative in synesthetes some recent studies used contextual priming tasks in grapheme-color synesthetes and VEP measurements. For example, Brang et al. (2008) used contextual priming in which sentences were used to invoke a particular color concept (e.g., "The sky is … ") and which ended with a grapheme (e.g., the number "8") that elicited a congruent or incongruent synesthetic color. Brang et al. identified a congruency effect for early ERP components (N1 and P2) consistent with the earlier-mentioned findings of early processing differences in synesthetes. They also uncovered a congruency-effect for the later occurring N400, which is known to be influenced by meaningful primes.

A late congruency effect was also observed in a variant of synesthesia, called time-space synesthesia. Subjects with this kind of synesthesia consistently and automatically associate time units such as months of the year with specific spatial locations (Teuscher et al. 2010). In this study, reaction times and ERPs were recorded in 12 time-space synesthetes and 12 control participants while they performed a peripheral target detection task. Three different types of cues were used in this task: arrows pointing left or right, direction words "left" or "right," and month names associated with either the left or the right side of the synesthete's mental calendar. These cues were followed by probes on the left or right side of the screen. The participants were required to respond to the probes with button presses and ERPs were calculated to these probes. Reaction times and ERP data suggested that month words functioned very effectively as cues to direct attention in space in synesthetes only. The ERPs to the probes cued by month names revealed effects of cue validity on the P3b component peaking 370 ms post-onset and on the subsequent positive slow wave (pSW) observed 600–900 ms post-onset (both larger for invalid probes). These data supplement the above findings in suggesting that cue validity influenced later cognitive processes in these time–space synesthetes also.

A very recent study examined the congruency between the color of a stimulus and the color of its concurrent, both in grapheme-color synesthetes and in non-synesthetes trained on grapheme-color associations (Niccolai et al. 2012). Niccolai et al. employed a priming task that included a prime (grapheme) followed by a target stimulus being either congruent or incongruent with the color induced by the prime. In this study they also examined non-synesthetes who were trained to associate particular colors with the primes. The ERPs recorded to the targets revealed that the late "cognitive" components (N300, N400, and P300) indexing semantic and working memory processes, were more negative going in synesthetes and non-synesthetes. The synesthetes also showed larger and faster early responses as indexed by the N170. Taken together, this study demonstrates that both early- and late-stage cognitive components are involved in synesthesia.

Summary and Conclusion

Exploiting the superior time resolution of EEG and MEG, the time course of neurophysiological activation during synesthetic experiences can now be traced with great precision. The EEG and MEG studies published so far can be separated in two categories: those which investigated the neurophysiological time course to the inducing stimuli, and those which explored the time course of neurophysiological activation during priming tasks. With the exception of one investigation, all studies examining the time course of neurophysiological activation evoked by the inducer demonstrate modulation of early ERP components (N1 and P2) in synesthetes. One study, which explored basic visual processing using visual stimuli that did not evoke synesthetic experiences, also uncovered different neurophysiological activations at very early processing stages. Those studies using experimental paradigms specifically designed to test higher order processes identified neurophysiological modulations in later occurring ERP components (300–600 ms), these results underscoring the idea that there are also higher-order cognitive processes involved in synesthesia. There are also data to suggest the existence of at least two types of synesthetes, that is, those who rely more strongly on different perceptual (or bottom-up processes) and those who rely more strongly on top-down-processes (following the distinction in "lower" and "higher" synesthetes). Still to be explicitly investigated is whether synesthetes are able to switch between different "low" and "high" synesthesia or whether these attributes are trait-like.

The findings relating to the time course of neurophysiological activations are also useful for testing the currently debated neurophysiological models of synesthesia. The first two studies that directly tested for time-lags between neural activations associated with the processing of the inducer and concurrent perception revealed similar results. These studies showed that there is no time lag between these activations. Thus, a critical assumption of the disinhibited feedback model is not supported by these data. These data rather support the cross-activation and hyperbinding model of synesthesia. However, this model does not allow an explanation of inter-individual differences in synesthesia (e.g., "high" versus "low" synesthetes, associators versus projectors, uni-directional versus bi-directional synesthetes etc.; for a review of these different types see van Leeuwen, Chapter 13, this volume). A further point, which needs to be examined in more detail in the future, is whether different kinds of synesthesia are associated with similar activation time courses or whether different synesthesias are characterized by specific time courses. In addition, further theoretical work is needed to describe the psychological and neurophysiological mechanisms underlying this interesting phenomenon.

REFERENCES

Barnett, Kylie J., John J. Foxe, Sophie Molholm, Simon P. Kelly, Shani Shalgi, Kevin J. Mitchell, and Fiona N. Newell. 2008. Differences in early sensory-perceptual processing in synesthesia: A visual evoked potential study. *NeuroImage* 43 (3):605–613.

Beeli, Gian, Michaela Esslen, and Lutz Jäncke. 2008. Time course of neural activity correlated with colored-hearing synesthesia. *Cerebral Cortex* 18 (2):379–385.

Bleuler, Eugen, and Karl Bernhard Lehmann. 1881. *Zwangsmässige Lichtempfindungen durch Schall und verwandte Erscheinungen auf dem Gebiete der andern Sinnesempfindungen.* Leipzig: Fues's Verlag.

Brang, David, L. Edwards, Vilayanur S. Ramachandran, and Seana Coulson. 2008. Is the sky 2? Contextual priming in grapheme-color synaesthesia. *Psychological Science* 19 (5):421–428.

Brang, David, Edward M. Hubbard, Seana Coulson, Minxiong Huang, and Vilayanur S. Ramachandran. 2010. Magnetoencephalography reveals early activation of V4 in grapheme-color synesthesia. *NeuroImage* 53 (1):268–274.

Brang, David, Stanley Kanai, Vilayanur S. Ramachandran, and Seana Coulson. 2011. Contextual priming in grapheme-color synesthetes and yoked controls: 400 ms in the life of a synesthete. *Journal of Cognitive Neuroscience* 23 (7):1681–1696.

Cohen Kadosh, Roi, Kathrin Cohen Kadosh, and Avishai Henik. 2007. The neuronal correlate of bidirectional synesthesia: A combined event-related potential and functional magnetic resonance imaging study. *Journal of Cognitive Neuroscience,* 19 (12):2050–2059.

Cytowic, Richard E., and Frank B. Wood. 1982. Synesthesia: I. A review of major theories and their brain basis. *Brain Cognition* 1 (1):23–35.

Elias, Lorin J., Deborah M. Saucier, Colleen Hardie, and Gordon E. Sarty. 2003. Dissociating semantic and perceptual components of synaesthesia: Behavioural and functional neuro-anatomical investigations. *Cognitive Brain Research* 16 (2):232–237.

Gebuis, Titia, Tanja C. W. Nijboer, and Maarten J. Van der Smagt. 2009. Multiple dimensions in bi-directional synesthesia. *European Journal of Neuroscience* 29 (8):1703–1710.

Goller, Aviva I., Leun J. Otten, and Jamie Ward. 2009. Seeing sounds and hearing colors: An event-related potential study of auditory-visual synesthesia. *Journal of Cognitive Neuroscience* 21(10):1869–1881.

Grossenbacher, Peter G., and Christopher T. Lovelace. 2001. Mechanisms of synesthesia: Cognitive and physiological constraints. *Trends in Cognitive Science* 5 (1):36–41.

Hänggi, Jürgen, Gian Beeli, Mathias S. Oechslin, and Lutz Jäncke. 2008. The multiple synaesthete E.S.: Neuroanatomical basis of interval-taste and tone-colour synaesthesia. *NeuroImage* 43 (2):192–203.

Hänggi, Jürgen, Diana Wotruba, and Lutz Jäncke. 2011. Globally altered structural brain network topology in grapheme-color synesthesia. *The Journal of Neuroscience*, 31 (15):5816–5828.

Hubbard, Edward M. 2007. Neurophysiology of synesthesia. *Current Psychiatry Reports* 9 (3):193–199.

Hubbard, Edward M., A. Cyrus Arman, Vilayanur S. Ramachandran, and Geoffrey M. Boynton. 2005. Individual differences among grapheme-color synesthetes: Brain-behavior correlations. *Neuron* 45 (6):975–985.

Jäncke, Lutz, Gian Beeli, Cornelia Eulig, and Jürgen Hanggi. 2009. The neuroanatomy of grapheme-color synesthesia. *European Journal of Neuroscience* 29 (6):1287–1293.

Jäncke, Lutz, and Nicolas Langer. 2011. A strong parietal hub in the small-world network of coloured-hearing synesthetes during resting state EEG. *Journal of Neuropsychology* 5 (2):178–202.

Jewanski, Jörg. 2013. Synesthesia in the nineteenth century: Scientific origins. In *The Oxford Handbook of Synesthesia*, ed. Julia Simner and Edward M. Hubbard, 369–398. Oxford: Oxford University Press.

Knoch, Daria, Lorena R. Gianotti, Christine Mohr, and Peter Brugger. 2005. Synesthesia: When colors count. *Cognitive Brain Research* 25 (1):372–374.

Meier, Beat, and Nicolas Rothen. 2007. When conditioned responses "fire back": Bidirectional cross-activation creates learning opportunities in synesthesia. *Neuroscience* 147 (3):569–572.

Niccolai, Valentina, Edmund Wascher, and Petra Stoerig. 2012. Distinct neural processes in grapheme-colour synaesthetes and semantic controls. *European Journal of Neuroscience* 36 (11):3593–3601.

Noesselt, Toemme, Steve A. Hillyard, Marty G. Woldorff, Ariel Schoenfeld, Tilman Hagner, Lutz Jäncke, Claus Templemann, Herman Hinrichs, and Hans-Jochen Heinze. 2002. Delayed striate cortical activation during spatial attention. *Neuron* 35 (3):575–587.

Nunn, J. A., L. J. Gregory, M. J. Brammer, S. C. R. Williams, D. M. Parslow, M. J. Morgan, R. G. Morris, E. T. Bullmore, S. Baron-Cohen, and J. A. Gray. 2002. Functional magnetic resonance imaging of synesthesia: Activation of V4/V8 by spoken words. *Nature Neuroscience* 5 (4):371–375.

Paulesu, Eraldo, John Harrison, Simon Baron-Cohen, John D. G. Watson, Laura Goldstein, John Heather, Richard S. J. Frakowiak, and Christopher D. Frith. 1995. The physiology of coloured hearing. A PET activation study of colour-word synaesthesia. *Brain*, 118 (Pt 3):661–676.

Ramachandran, Vilayanur S., and Edward M. Hubbard. 2001. Psychophysical investigations into the neural basis of synaesthesia. *Proceedings of the Royal Society B: Biological Sciences* 268 (1470):979–983.

Rouw, Romke, and H. Steven Scholte. 2007. Increased structural connectivity in grapheme-color synesthesia. *Nature Neuroscience* 10 (6):792–797.

——. 2010. Neural basis of individual differences in synesthetic experiences. *The Journal of Neuroscience* 30 (18):6205–6213.

Sagiv, Noam, Robert T. Knight, and Lynn C. Robertson. 2003. Electrophysiological markers of synesthesia. Paper presented at the 10th Annual Meeting of the Cognitive Neuroscience Society, New York, March.

Schiltz, Kolja, Karen Trocha, Bernardina M. Wieringa, Hinderk M. Emrich, Sönke Johannes, and Thomas F. Münte. 1999. Neurophysiological aspects of synesthetic experience. *Journal of Neuropsychiatry and Clinical Neurosciences* 11 (1):58–65.

Shalgi, Shani, and John J. Foxe. 2009. The neurophysiology of bi-directional synesthesia (Commentary on Gebuis et al.). *European Journal of Neuroscience* 29 (8):1701–1702.

Smilek, Daniel, Mike J. Dixon, Cera Cudahy, and Philip M. Merikle. 2001. Synaesthetic photisms influence visual perception. *Journal of Cognitive Neuroscience* 13 (7):930–936.

Teuscher, Ursina, David Brang, Vilanayur S. Ramachandran, and Seana Coulson. 2010. Spatial cueing in time–space synesthetes: An event-related brain potential study. *Brain and Cognition* 74 (1):35–46.

Van Leeuwen, Tessa M., Karl M. Petersson, and Peter Hagoort. 2010. Synaesthetic colour in the brain: Beyond colour areas. A functional magnetic resonance imaging study of synaesthetes and matched controls. *PLoS ONE* 5 (8):e12074.

Vulpian, E. F. Alfred. 1866. *Leçons sur la physiologie générale et comparée du système nerveux, faites en 1864 au Muséum d'histoire naturelle.* Paris: Gerner-Baillière.

van Leeuwen, Tessa M. 2013. Individual differences in synesthesia. In *The Oxford Handbook of Synesthesia*, ed. Julia Simner and Edward M. Hubbard, 241–264 . Oxford: Oxford University Press.

Weiss, Peter H., Andreas Kalckert, and Gereon R. Fink. 2009. Priming letters by colors: Evidence for the bidirectionality of grapheme-color synesthesia. *Journal of Cognitive Neuroscience* 21 (10):2019–2026.

Weiss, Peter H., N. Jon Shah, Ivan Toni, Karl Zilles, and Gereon R. Fink. 2001. Associating colours with people: A case of chromatic-lexical synaesthesia. *Cortex* 37 (5):750–753.

Weiss, Peter H., Karl Zilles, and Gereon R. Fink. 2005. When visual perception causes feeling: Enhanced cross-modal processing in grapheme-color synesthesia. *NeuroImage* 28 (4):859–868.

CHAPTER 29

THE USE OF TRANSCRANIAL MAGNETIC STIMULATION IN THE INVESTIGATION OF SYNESTHESIA

NEIL G. MUGGLETON AND ELIAS TSAKANIKOS

INTRODUCTION

Synesthesia is thought to occur in at least 4% of the population, with a female to male ratio of 1:1 (Simner et al. 2006; Ward and Simner 2005). It is, in principle, the perception of an extraordinary sensation, such as color or taste, being triggered by activities such as reading or listening to music (Simner 2012). These are sensations of which the synesthetes are aware and they typically occur in addition to the normal sensations. Ward and Mattingley (2006) offered three defining features for synesthesia: first that synesthetic experiences are percepts or percept-like experiences; second, that these are a consequence of attributes with which they are not normally associated; and third, that these percepts occur automatically. The percept induced by an attribute does not typically override the attribute which gives rise to it (Ward and Simner 2005).

There are both numerous combinations of associations that fall within the category of synesthesia, and a great deal of differences in individual experiences. These differences come not only in the modalities (visual, tactile, etc.) of the synesthetic experience and its triggers, but there are also notable differences in, for example, the nature of the elicited sensations even within the same perceptual domain. Again, color-grapheme synesthesia offers a convenient illustration of this. This type of synesthesia, in which colors are induced by letters, numbers, or other language-based stimuli seems to be one of the most frequently observed (e.g., Baron-Cohen et al. 1996; Simner et al. 2006).

The nature of the color induced by a specific grapheme may be "seen" on the letter in some individuals ("projector synesthetes"), whereas others report the phenomenon as in the mind's eye ("associator synesthetes"; Dixon et al. 2000). An additional distinction has been made by Ramachandran and Hubbard (2001). They subdivide synesthetes based on whether synesthesia is induced by the basic properties of an object or attribute, for example, the shape or texture of an item, termed "lower synesthesia," or by conceptual characteristics, termed "higher synesthesia." An example of the latter would be if a number induced a consistent color irrespective of whether it was represented as a digit, a word, or as roman numerals.

To date, a large proportion of the investigations of synesthesia have been concerned with establishing it as a real phenomenon and have involved behavioral characterization. Particularly rare types of synesthesia, such as synesthesia involving color for musical notation, have only recently been experimentally validated for the first time as "genuine" phenomena (Ward, Tsakanikos, and Bray 2006). This research activity, in combination with the diversity both between and within synesthetic types, means that the underlying neural mechanisms are an area in which a great degree of clarification remains possible.

There is also much to be done to extend investigation of synesthesia beyond behavioral characterization, using the techniques typically applied to clarifying the neural basis of normal and clinical behaviors in neural psychology. Both imaging techniques, such as functional magnetic resonance imaging (fMRI), diffusion tensor imagine (DTI), and electrophysiological recording, as well as interference techniques, such as transcranial magnetic stimulation (TMS; see later), are still mostly in their infancy in terms of application to the investigation of synesthesia. TMS is a non-invasive methodology with which researchers can stimulate relatively specific parts of the brain, and thereby infer their function (see Figure 29.1 for a typical TMS machine). Like the other techniques mentioned, TMS has been relatively underemployed in investigating synesthesia but the small number of studies that do exist will be discussed.

It remains for the potential of the application of this technique to be fully utilized however, and it may play a significant role in helping to clarify the nature and neural origins of synesthetic experiences. As with any good experimental approach, this is ideally done in the context of a theoretical framework so we will first briefly consider the current theoretical accounts of synesthesia followed by a description of the different methodological approaches that can be used with TMS (incorporating discussion of the studies already carried out where they exist) before considering the ways in which these methodologies may be able to contribute to a better understanding of synesthesia in the future.

SYNESTHESIA THEORIES

Not surprisingly, there is disagreement as to what may form the basis of synesthetic experiences, and it is this disagreement that forms the basis of much of the work to investigate the phenomenon. The first account suggests that elevated connections or communication between areas may be the cause of the effect. This view, suggested by Ramachandran and Hubbard (2001), argues that for color-grapheme synesthesia, for

FIGURE 29.1 A typical TMS machine consisting of the body component and a figure-of-eight-shaped coil via which stimulation is delivered.

example, there is hyperconnectivity between color and grapheme areas (at the level of the fusiform gyrus for lower synesthetes and at the level of the angular gyrus for higher synesthetes). They argue that this effectively results in cross activation of these areas and synesthetic experiences are the result (see Hubbard, Chapter 24, this volume for a full review).

An alternative suggestion is that rather than hyperconnectivity, synesthesia is a consequence of disinhibited feedback, but that this involves no difference in connectivity (Grossenbacher and Lovelace 2001). In this hypothesis, it is argued that the top-down feedback from points of convergence of multiple neural pathways in non-synesthetes is sufficiently inhibited to avoid synesthetic induction. In synesthetes, Grossenbacher and Lovelace suggest that less inhibition occurs and such signals may propagate with the consequence that abnormal, synesthetic sensations are experienced. Regardless of the nature of the underlying neural mechanism, experimental evidence indicates that certain types, such as sound-color synesthesia, seem to recruit some of the same mechanisms used in normal cross-modal perception rather than using synesthesia-specific direct, privileged pathways between auditory and visual areas (Ward, Huckstep and Tsakanikos 2006).

TRANSCRANIAL MAGNETIC STIMULATION

TMS is a technique remarkably well described by its name. It involves stimulation of cortical areas by application of a magnetic field near or on the scalp. The nature of such fields means that they are unimpeded by the intervening tissue, such that if the field is of sufficient strength then it is possible to be confident that the area underlying the point of application is being reached. Historically there were a number of attempts to magnetically stimulate the brain, using the fact that an electric current is always associated with a magnetic field. However, technical issues tended to mean that either the effects seen were a consequence of the electric currents used to generate the magnetic field causing stimulation themselves or that these precluded use in an experimental setting. Modern use of TMS, and the demonstration of the viability of its use as an experimental tool, began in 1985 when Barker et al. (1985) used cortical stimulation to elicit a motor response. By delivering TMS over the vertex they were able to produce hand movements as a consequence of stimulation of the hand motor area. The key to their ability to deliver TMS in this manner was being able to generate sufficiently large currents (in the order of kA) to produce a magnetic field of a large enough strength. Also key was their ability to induce this field sufficiently rapidly (in a couple of hundred microseconds) as the induced activity in the cortex is dependent on the rate of change of the magnetic field.

The effectiveness of magnetic stimulation arises from the fact that when a changing magnetic field is applied to a conductor, a current is induced. TMS therefore aims to disrupt or affect neural processing by the induction of electrical activity in neurons, typically described as inducing noise. Indeed, recent evidence directly supporting TMS acting by inducing noise into neural systems has been obtained by Schwarzkopf, Silvanto, and Rees (2011). They showed that either improvement in task performance (by stochastic resonance, whereby a weak signal can be strengthened by noise) or worsening of performance could be obtained on the same task by varying the level of TMS stimulation.

Using TMS in Behavioral Investigations

The majority of behavioral studies in which TMS is used employ what is usually termed a "virtual lesion" approach. In these studies, the aim is usually to determine whether a candidate brain area is necessary for performance on a task by disrupting the area during task performance. The first example of this, like many of the early TMS studies, involved investigation of the motor cortex. Day et al. (1989) stimulated the motor cortex while requiring subjects to make a wrist movement response. Delivery of TMS following the signal to make a movement resulted in significant elevation of response times. This design essentially forms the template of many of the recent and current TMS studies being carried out. Performance on a task is compared under conditions where stimulation is delivered over a candidate site of interest, no stimulation is delivered, and (ideally) stimulation is delivered over a second site, not thought to be involved in the task under investigation. As in the case of Day et al. (1989) the dependant measure is often response time on the task in question (e.g., Ashbridge, Walsh, and Cowey 1997), but by no means exclusively so. Depending on the task and the nature of the response required, it is equally feasible to obtain effects on accuracy measures (e.g., Juan and Walsh 2003; Muggleton et al. 2003).

Single pulses of TMS (of the type used in the motor studies described earlier) have high temporal accuracy, and have undoubted potential for application to the study of synesthesia. However, currently there is very little data of this type in the literature so we first address an alternative approach which has received more (although by no means extensive) application, which is the use of repetitive TMS (rTMS). We will describe the rTMS methodology in detail (and then return again to single-pulse possibilities later in this chapter). While many of the early studies employing TMS involved investigation of the motor system, Pascual-Leone et al. (1994) showed the first effects using rTMS outside of this domain. In many ways, rTMS simply involves using a train of pulses delivered for a short duration, so maintaining the ability to test whether an area is necessary for a task or function at the cost of temporal information regarding *when* it is necessary. In the case of Pascual-Leone et al. (1994), pulses were delivered at 25 Hz over occipital, parietal, and temporal cortex to investigate visual extinction (difficulty perceiving a visual stimulus in, for example, the left side of space when a stimulus is also present in the right side of space), a phenomenon commonly seen following parietal cortex damage. This study therefore used "virtual lesions" to produce "virtual patients."

Studies of Synesthesia Using rTMS

FMRI has offered several candidate areas, activation of which seems to be associated with synesthetic experience. TMS offers a way to test for the necessity and also, with an appropriate design, the specific role of these areas.

Esterman et al. (2006) conducted the first of the few studies employing rTMS in an investigation of color-grapheme synesthesia in two subjects, both of whom were classified as projector synesthetes. The study involved a synesthetic Stroop task, in which (in the absence of TMS stimulation) synesthetes are typically slower to name font colors if these conflict with synesthetic colors (e.g., slower to name the font color of a green A, if A is synesthetically red). This type of interference is taken as evidence that synesthetic colors are automatically triggered. Esterman and colleagues found that the level of synesthetic interference on a Stroop-type task was reduced when TMS was delivered over the right parieto-occipital cortex but not when it was delivered over the same site in the other hemisphere, nor when area V1 was stimulated. The region they investigated has been implicated in visual search for targets defined by color and form using fMRI (Donner et al. 2002). Lesions to the same area produce deficits such as neglect (e.g., Mort et al. 2003) and effects consistent with problems in color-form binding (Friedman-Hill, Robertson, and Treisman 1995).

Around a similar time Muggleton et al. (2007) also investigated color-grapheme synesthesia using rTMS. This study investigated the involvement of regions of the parietal cortex in synesthesia with the aim of both replicating and extending the findings of Esterman et al. (2006). There were several reasons for the selection of the sites investigated in this study. First was the fact that the sort of stimuli frequently associated with color synesthesia (e.g., color-grapheme synesthesia) such as numbers, letters, days, and months (Simner et al. 2006) have been linked with the left angular gyrus (Hubbard et al. 2005). Indeed, numerical and magnitude information have been suggested to be processed by a common magnitude system, of which the parietal cortex forms a part (Walsh 2003). The parietal lobe has also been suggested to play a role in the binding of the attributes of a stimulus, such as color and form (Friedman-Hill, Robertson, and Treisman 1995; Treisman 1996) and regions within the parietal lobe have also been linked to multisensory integration (Ashbridge, Walsh, and Cowey 1997; Friedman-Hill, Robertson, and Treisman 1995). Activation in the intraparietal sulcus has been seen in response to graphemes evoking synesthesia, irrespective of the congruency of the grapheme color to the synesthetic color (Weiss, Zilles, and Fink 2005). Similar effects have also been reported in response to colors evoked by tones (Nunn et al. 2002).

The first aim of this study was therefore to test whether the involvement of the occipito-parietal region stimulated by Esterman et al. (2006) was limited to only projector synesthetes and also to evaluate the involvement of a left parietal region implicated in synesthesia by imaging studies.

A color priming task was employed in which the font color of a grapheme had to be indicated by means of a key press. This color could be either congruent (expected to result in faster responses) or incongruent (expected to produce slower responses) with the synesthetic color elicited by the grapheme. TMS was delivered over different sites of interest in different blocks and the modulation of the synesthetic effects on the task (i.e., the difference between the response times for the incongruent and congruent conditions) evaluated. Any reduction in the difference between the two conditions would be indicative of a reduced synesthetic effect.

Of the sites tested, reliable disruption was seen only when TMS was delivered over the right parieto-occipital junction, similar to the site stimulated by Esterman and colleagues. Interestingly, this effect was found even though four of the five subjects tested were associators. Esterman et al. (2006) had suggested that projector synesthetes might show a greater parietal involvement than associator synesthetes, due to the parietal cortex performing binding of the synesthetic color to the location of the grapheme in these individuals. However, a more recent study by Ward et al. (2007) concluded that both types of synesthesia involved the spatial binding of graphemes and colors, implying that both may be examples of anomalous binding. The effects in the study by Muggleton et al. (2007) could be taken as evidence against the suggestion of Esterman et al. (2006) of greater parietal involvement for projector synesthetes, or, following the results obtained by Ward et al. (2007) may be in partial agreement with Esterman et al. in that the TMS effect is disruption of binding but that this is also necessary in associator synesthetes.

The absence of effects with stimulation of the left parietal lobe is of interest in that this seems to contradict the information obtained from imaging data (Nunn et al. 2002; Weiss, Zilles, and Fink 2005). It is possible that the activations seen are a consequence of synesthetic experiences but the role played by these areas is not necessary for the experience to arise in the first place. Alternatively the involvement of this area may be task dependent and is important, but not for the particular task we used (Cohen Kadosh, Cohen Kadosh, and Henik 2007).

Finally, and most recently, Rothen et al. (2010) made use of TMS in an investigation of color-grapheme synesthesia. Their study was concerned with the directionality of the synesthetic experience. While, for example, a particular grapheme may induce the sensation of a specific color, the reverse, induction of a grapheme by a specific color, was assumed to not occur in the same individuals. However, the discovery of an individual with such bidirectional synesthesia (Cohen Kadosh, Cohen Kadosh, and Henik 2007) and the fact that behavior can be influenced in a manner consistent with such bidirectionality, even in the absence of any explicit experience of this (e.g., Brang et al. 2008; Cohen Kadosh et al. 2005) led Rothen et al. (2010) to test the involvement of the parieto-occipital cortex in bidirectional effects in a group of synesthetes with no explicit bidirectional synesthetic experiences. Rothen et al. used a conditioning task to investigate the neural basis of bidirectionality. Subjects were presented with conditioning trials such that presentation of a color (conditioned stimulus (CS)) became associated with a startle response. Presentation of a grapheme which resulted in the synesthetic sensation of the same color would therefore be expected to also elicit a startle response if there was a bidirectionality to the synesthesia. By delivering TMS during the conditioning trials it was possible to test for the directionality of the synesthetic effect in a brain area. The researchers predicted that TMS would suppress the implicit activation of the grapheme during the conditioning trials, and that this would lead to an attenuated response when the grapheme itself was presented later.

Results obtained did support a role for the parieto-occipital site in implicit bidirectionality as well as confirming that cross-activation (i.e., that presentation of a synesthetic color is also associated with an implicit activation of the associated grapheme representation) occurs even in synesthetes without awareness of bidirectional synesthesia. Thus, this effect was seen despite the fact that all subjects subjectively reported only a unidirectional relationship between graphemes and evoked colors (see Meier and Rothen, Chapter 35, this volume, for more discussions of this finding). These results also seem to be consistent with the parieto-occipital cortex being involved in both explicit and implicit synesthetic binding. Unlike the previous two studies (Esterman et al. 2006; Muggleton et al. 2007) these effects were seen for both hemispheres. The findings are also argued to be consistent with synesthetic feature binding involving similar processes to normal feature binding (e.g., Corbetta et al. 1995; Robertson et al. 2003; see Alvarez and Robertson, Chapter 16, this volume, for more on synesthesia and binding).

POTENTIAL APPLICATIONS OF TMS TO THE INVESTIGATION OF SYNESTHESIA

There clearly remains a great deal of room for future work employing rTMS. Such studies could both investigate the necessity of candidate brain regions in synesthetic phenomena and potentially offer insight into underlying mechanisms by employing appropriate behavioral paradigms in combination with such a TMS approach. It is also clear that the studies mentioned here represent only the start of such work: only a few possible regions have been investigated, in a relatively small number of subjects to date (although Rothen et al. 2010 has a larger group of participants) and only in color-grapheme synesthesia. While the studies to date support a role for the parieto-occipital region in synesthetic experiences in the case of color-grapheme synesthesia, it remains to be tested whether the necessity of this region extends to other types of synesthetic experience. Even within this subset of synesthesia as a whole, differences between projector and associator synesthetes would benefit from further investigation, with similarities potentially offering insight into any commonalities in origin of the effect and differences potentially being relevant to the manifestation of the specific unusual sensation.

ALTERNATIVE rTMS APPROACHES

All of the TMS studies of synesthesia to date have employed rTMS in an "online" manner. That is, they have involved delivering TMS over a candidate site with the aim of disrupting it during the period of stimulation. There are also two other approaches which employ rTMS, but do so in an offline manner, i.e., TMS is delivered with the aim of producing disruption that persists beyond the time window of stimulation. The first of these is 1 Hz stimulation. As the name suggests, this involves stimulation over the area of interest at 1 Hz for a period of several minutes, resulting in a window of disruption following cessation of the stimulation. While this approach has been used successfully in a number of studies, including those assessing effects on behavior, a different, more recent offline approach may also prove useful in investigating synesthesia. By combining a high-frequency component (50 Hz for three pulses) with a lower-frequency element (5 Hz), it is possible to produce prolonged periods (10–15 minutes) of disruption following a brief period (20 s) of stimulation. This stimulation is termed theta burst TMS and was first demonstrated in the motor cortex (Huang et al. 2005) and it has subsequently been used successfully in behavioral paradigms (Vallesi, Shallice, and Walsh 2007). This approach is of possible interest in synesthesia not only because it offers another potential way to disrupt the functioning of cortical regions of interest, but it also seems to offer the possibility of indirect modulation of the color area, V4 (Kalla et al. 2009). In the study by Kalla et al. (2009) the primary interest was investigation of the role of dorsolateral prefrontal cortex in a search for a target defined by a combination of color and shape. Theta stimulation was used due to the discomfort associated with stimulation of this site being a potential confound. But, and more pertinently, the visual motion area MT/V5 was also stimulated as a control site and resulted in facilitation on the search task compared to pre-stimulation performance. These findings were consistent with results reported previously (Walsh et al. 1998) using rTMS. These findings are of interest to synesthesia research as they potentially represent facilitation as a consequence of reduced inhibition of the color processing area V4 by disruption of V5. Such a finding would be consistent with the nature of the connections between these two areas (Pascual-Leone and Walsh 2001; Walsh et al. 1998). The seemingly long time course of the facilitatory effect seen by Kalla et al. (2009) may therefore allow the effects of modulation of V4 in synesthesia involving colors to be further probed. This is particularly useful because as yet there are no TMS studies showing successful modulation of color processing.

Using the Temporal Accuracy of TMS to Investigate Synesthesia

Single-pulse TMS offers a way of investigating the timing of the involvement of an area in a process. Thus, whereas rTMS can inform as to the necessity of the involvement of a brain area in a process, both involvement and timing information can be obtained by using single pulses. So far all of the TMS studies in synesthesia research, like many of the ones investigating other cognitive processes, have been performed using rTMS. This generally reflects pragmatism. If you are uncertain that an area is involved in a task or process it is often preferable to test for its involvement with the relatively fewer number of conditions required for an rTMS study before requiring the potentially much larger number of trials necessary for a timing study (due to there being a set of trials for each site and each time interval, rather than one set per site). Timing studies also have associated issues relating to the number of pulses permissible in a test session; see Wassermann et al. 1998. There is also the potential for long testing blocks which sometimes tend to lead to degradation in data quality due to subject fatigue. However, once the necessity of an area in a process has been established it becomes much more reasonable to embark on a timing study. Additionally, there are ways to compromise between timing accuracy and the number of conditions required.

Examples of TMS Timing Studies

There are a number of studies in which the timing of the involvement of an area in a cognitive task has been performed so we have selected two, both investigating conjunction search tasks (where the target is defined by a combination of features such as color and shape), that serve as appropriate illustrations of the application of the methodology. This task involves the presentation of an array of elements in which a target may be present or absent. In conjunction search the target is defined by a combination of features such as color and shape and an example stimulus is shown in Figure 29.2.

In the first of these studies, single-pulse TMS was employed to investigate the involvement of posterior parietal cortex in visual conjunction searches. Ashbridge, Walsh, and Cowey (1997) applied single pulses of TMS over the posterior parietal cortex of subjects

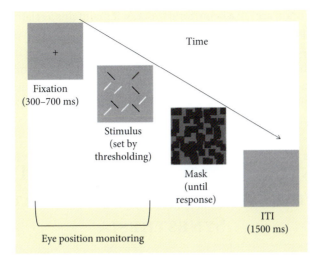

FIGURE 29.2 An example of a conjunction search array. A target present array is shown. Distractors are the white elements oriented bottom-left to top-right and the black elements oriented top-left to bottom-right. The target in this example is the black element oriented bottom-left to top-right and so shares a color with half of the distractors and orientation with the other half.

performing either feature or conjunction visual search tasks. As numerous subsequent studies have shown, there were no effects of TMS when a target was defined by a single attribute in the feature search task. However, disruption of conjunction search performance was seen for right parietal cortex stimulation, with elevation of response times when pulses were delivered 100 ms after the onset of a target present trial and similarly, when applied 160 ms after the onset of a target absent trial. Interestingly, this timing at which parietal cortex seemed to be critically involved in the task is consistent with data seen in monkey single-cell recording studies (e.g., Thompson and Schall 1999) and, while the nature of the role of parietal cortex in visual search is the subject of discussion, these findings are consistent with disruption of the binding of the attributes making up the stimuli in the conjunction search task.

In the second study a modified approach was employed, forming a compromise between the higher accuracy of single-pulse TMS and the lower accuracy associated with rTMS. O'Shea et al. (2004) used a double-pulse TMS approach, along the lines of that previously employed by Juan et al. (2003). In this, two pulses were delivered on each trial of the task in question to investigate the timing of the involvement of the frontal eye fields (an area that had previously been shown to be involved; Muggleton et al. 2003) in conjunction search performance. These pulses were delivered 40 ms apart and were used to provide a moving window of disruption. This means that pulses were delivered at 0 and 40 ms, 40 and 80ms, and so on, such that a readily manageable set of timings, each separated by 40 ms were investigated, compared to single pulses which can be separated by much smaller intervals leading to a potentially large number of trials. Thus, while this might be viewed as a compromise in terms of specifying the exact timing of the involvement of a brain area in a behavioral process, it maintains a relatively good level of accuracy in comparison to the expected time course of the involvement of brain areas, while still being reasonably convenient. A similar approach has been used in a range of further studies, including direct comparison of the involvement of two areas (frontal eye fields and posterior parietal cortex) in the same task (conjunction visual search; Kalla et al. 2008) as well as in other tasks, such as those investigating face processing (Pitcher et al. 2007).

POTENTIAL APPLICATION OF TMS TIMING METHODOLOGIES TO THE INVESTIGATION OF SYNESTHESIA

Given that synesthesia seems to involve the interplay of information from several areas and also that it has been suggested that the phenomenon may be a consequence of either abnormal connectivity (Hubbard and Ramachandran 2001), or altered feedback (Grossenbacher and Lovelace 2001), use of the temporal accuracy of disruption possible with TMS may prove beneficial in clarifying which (if either) of these proposed mechanisms offers the best account. For example, if synesthesia is a consequence of increased connectivity then, while the areas involved may show elevated activations, it would not be unreasonable to suspect that the timing of their involvement would be relatively consistent with that seen in non-synesthetic processing. In other words, the timing of disruption of a task involving the areas implicated in a task (perhaps a color judgment task in the case of color-grapheme synesthesia) would be similar for both synesthetes and control subjects. Similarly, if synesthesia were a consequence of altered feedback then there may be later involvement of the areas receiving altered feedback and so a different pattern of disruption may be seen.

This would be similar to the timing approach used with TMS to investigate the necessity of areas for visual perception (e.g., Silvanto et al. 2005) and the effects of interactions between areas on perception (e.g., Silvanto, Lavie, and Walsh 2006). Thus, with further clarification of the areas that are critical to give rise to synesthetic experiences, it should become feasible to test which of the current theories offers the best account of the mechanisms underlying synesthesia.

SUMMARY

TMS provides the ability to both test the necessity of the involvement of an area in behavior with a range of temporal accuracies from several minutes, down to milliseconds, while also allowing for the investigation of timing of area involvements and the interactions between areas. However, to date, the application of TMS to the investigation of synesthesia remains in its infancy. While there have been some studies applying TMS to the investigation of color-grapheme synesthesia, relatively few potential brain areas of interest have been investigated. There remains great potential for the exploitation of the strengths of TMS to clarify the underlying neural mechanisms of synesthesia both in terms of processes specific to each type that has been seen, as well as in the elucidation of any common underlying mechanisms that seem likely to exist.

References

Alvarez, Bryan D., and Lynn C. Robertson. 2013. Synesthesia and binding. In *The Oxford Handbook of Synesthesia,* ed. Julia Simner and Edward M. Hubbard, 317–333. Oxford: Oxford University Press.

Ashbridge, Elizabeth, Vincent Walsh, and Alan Cowey. 1997. Temporal aspects of visual search studied by transcranial magnetic stimulation. *Neuropsychologia* 35:1121–1131.

Barker, A.T., I. L. Freeston, R. Jalinous, P. A. Merton, and H. B. Morton. 1985. Magnetic stimulation of the human brain (abstract). *Journal of Physiology (London)* 369: 3P.

Baron-Cohen, Simon, Lucy Burt, Fiona Laittan-Smith, John E. Harrison, and Patrick Bolton. 1996. Synaesthesia: prevalence and familiality. *Perception* 25 (9):1073–1079.

Brang, David, L. Edwards, Vilayanur S. Ramachandran, and Seana Coulson. 2008. Is the sky 2? Con-textual priming in grapheme-color synaesthesia. *Psychological Science,* 19 (5):421–428.

Cohen Kadosh, Roi, and Avishai Henik. 2007. Can synaesthesia research inform cognitive science? *Trends in Cognitive Sciences* 11 (4):177–184.

Cohen Kadosh, Roi, Katrin Cohen Kadosh, and Avishai Henik. 2007. The neuronal correlate of bidirectional synesthesia: A combined event-related potential and functional magnetic resonance imaging study. *Journal of Cognitive Neuroscience* 19 (12):2050–2059.

Cohen Kadosh, Roi, Noam Sagiv, David E. J. Linden, Lynn C. Robertson, Gali Elinger, and Avishai Henik. 2005. When blue is larger than red: Colors influence numerical cognition in synesthesia. *Journal of Cognitive Neuroscience* 17 (11):1766–1773.

Corbetta, Maurizio, Gordon L. Shulman, Francis M. Miezin, and Steven E. Petersen. 1995. Superior parietal cortex activation during spatial attention shifts and visual feature conjunction. *Science* 270 (5237):802–805.

Day, B. L., J. C. Rothwell, P. D. Thompson, A. Maertens de Noordhout, K. Nakashima, K. Shannon, and C. D. Marsden. 1989. Delay in the execution of voluntary movement by electrical or magnetic brain stimulation in intact man. Evidence for the storage of motor programs in the brain. *Brain* 112:649–663.

Dixon, Mike J., Daniel Smilek, Cera Cudahy, and Philip M. Merikle. 2000. Five plus two equals yellow. *Nature* 406 (6794):365.

Donner, Tobias H., Andreas Kettermann, Eugen Diesch, Florian Ostendorf, Arno Villringer, and Stephan A. Brandt. 2002. Visual feature and conjunction searches of equal difficulty engage only partially overlapping frontoparietal networks. *NeuroImage* 15:16–25.

Easterman, Michael, Timothy Verstynen, Richard B. Ivry, and Lynn C. Robertson. 2006. Coming unbound: Disrupting automatic integration of synesthetic color and graphemes by transcranial magnetic stimulation of the right parietal lobe. *Journal of Cognitive Neuroscience* 18 (9):1570–1576.

Friedman-Hill, Stacia, Lynn C. Robertson, and Anne Treisman. 1995. Parietal contributions to visual feature binding: Evidence from a patient with bilateral lesions. *Science* 269:853–855.

Grossenbacher, Peter G., and Christopher T. Lovelace. 2001. Mechanisms of synaesthesia: Cognitive and physiological constraints. *Trends in Cognitive Sciences* 5 (1):36–41.

Huang, Ying Zu, Mark J. Edwards, Elisabeth Rounis, Kailash P. Bhatia, and John C. Rothwell. 2005. Theta burst stimulation of the human motor cortex. *Neuron* 45:201–206.

Hubbard, Edward M. 2013. Synesthesia and functional imaging. Synesthesia and binding. In *Oxford Handbook of Synaesthesia*, ed. Julia Simner and Edward M. Hubbard, 475–499. Oxford: Oxford University Press.

Hubbard, Edward M., A. Cyrus Arman, Vilayanur S. Ramachandran, and Geoffrey M. Boynton. 2005. Individual differences among grapheme-colour synaesthetes: Brain-behavior correlations. *Neuron* 45 (6):975–985.

Hubbard, Edward M., Manuela Piazza, Philippe Pinel, and Stanislas Dehaene. 2005. Interactions between numbers and space in parietal cortex. *Nature Reviews Neuroscience* 6:435–448.

Juan, Chi-Hung, and Vincent Walsh. 2003. Feedback to V1: A reverse hierarchy in vision. *Experimental Brain Research*. 150 (2):259–263.

Kalla, Roger, Neil G. Muggleton, Alan Cowey, and Vincent Walsh. 2009. Human dorsolateral prefrontal cortex is involved in visual search for conjunctions but not features: A theta TMS study. *Cortex* 45 (9):1085–1090.

Kalla, Roger, Neil G. Muggleton, Chi-Hung Juan, Alan Cowey, and Vincent Walsh. 2008. The timing of the involvement of the frontal eye fields and posterior parietal cortex in visual search. *Neuroreport* 19:1067–1071.

Meier, Beat, and Nicolas Rothen. 2013. Synesthesia and memory. In *The Oxford Handbook of Synesthesia*, ed. Julia Simner and Edward M. Hubbard, 692–706. Oxford: Oxford University Press.

Mort, Dominic J., Paresh Malhotra, Sabira K. Mannan, Chris Rorden, Alidz Pambajian, Chris Kennard, and Masud Husain. 2003. The anatomy of visual neglect. *Brain* 126:1986–1997.

Muggleton, Neil G., Chi-Hung Juan, Alan Cowey, and Vincent Walsh. 2003. Human frontal eye fields and visual search. *Journal of Neurophysiology* 89: 3340–3343.

Muggleton, Neil, Elias Tsakanikos, Vincent Walsh, and Jamie Ward. 2007. Disruption of synaesthesia following TMS of the right posterior parietal cortex. *Neuropsychologia* 45 (7):1582–1585.

Nunn, J. A., L. J. Gregory, M. Brammer, S. C. R. Williams, D. M. Parslow, and M. J. Morgan. 2002. Functional magnetic resonance imaging of synesthesia: Activation of V4/V8 by spoken words. *Nature Neuroscience* 5 (4):371–375.

O'Shea, Jacinta, Neil G. Muggleton, Alan Cowey, and Vincent Walsh. 2004. Timing of target discrimination in human frontal eye fields. *Journal of Cognitive Neuroscience* 16: 1060–1067.

Pascual-Leone, A., E. Gomez-Tortosa, J. Grafman, D. Always, P. Nichelli, and M. Hallett. 1994. Induction of visual extinction by rapid-rate transcranial magnetic stimulation of parietal lobe. *Neurology* 44 (3 Pt 1):494–498.

Pascual-Leone, Alvaro and Vincent Walsh. 2001. Fast backprojections from the motion to the primary visual area necessary for visual awareness. *Science* 292:510–512.

Pitcher, David, Vincent Walsh, Galit Yovel, and Bradley Duchaine. 2007. TMS evidence for the involvement of the right occipital face area in early face processing. *Current Biology* 17 (18):1568–1573.

Ramachandran, Vilayanur S., and Edward M. Hubbard. 2001. Synaesthesia: A window into perception, thought and language. *Journal of Consciousness Studies* 8 (12):3–34.

Robertson, Lynn C. 2003. Binding, spatial attention and perceptual awareness. *Nature Reviews Neuroscience* 4 (2):93–102.

Rothen, Nicolas, Thomas Nyffeler, Roman von Wartburg, René Müri, and Beat Meier. 2010. Parieto-occipital suppression eliminates implicit bidirectionality in grapheme-colour synaesthesia. *Neuropsychologia* 48:3482–3487.

Schwarzkopf, Dietrich S., Juha Silvanto, and Geraint Rees. 2011. Stochastic resonance effects reveal the neural mechanisms of transcranial magnetic stimulation. *The Journal of Neuroscience* 31 (9):3143–3147.

Silvanto, Juha, Alan Cowey, Nilli Lavie, and Vincent Walsh. 2005. Striate cortex (V1) activity gates awareness of motion. *Nature Neuroscience* 8 (2):143–144.

Silvanto, Juha, Nilli Lavie, and Vincent Walsh. 2006. Stimulation of the human frontal eye fields modulates sensitivity of extrastriate visual cortex. *Journal of Neurophysiology* 96 (2):941–945.

Simner, Julia. 2012. Defining synaesthesia. *British Journal of Psychology* 103:1–15.

Simner, Julia, Catherine Mulvenna, Noam Sagiv, Elias Tsakanikos, Sarah A. Witherby, Christine Fraser, Kirsten Scott, and Jamie Ward. 2006. Synaesthesia: The prevalence of atypical cross-modal experiences. *Perception* 35:1024–1033.

Thompson, Kirk G., and Jeffrey D. Schall. 1999. The detection of visual signals by macaque frontal eye field during masking. *Nature Neuroscience* 2:283–288.

Treisman, Anne. 1996. The binding problem. *Current Opinion in Neurobiology* 6 (2):171–178.

Vallesi, Antonino, Tim Shallice, and Vincent Walsh. 2007. Role of the prefrontal cortex in the foreperiod effect: TMS evidence for dual mechanisms in temporal preparation. *Cerebral Cortex* 17:466–474.

Walsh, Vincent. 2003. A theory of magnitude: Common cortical metrics of time, space and quantity. *Trends in Cognitive Science* 7 (11):483–488.

Walsh, Vincent, Amanda Ellison, Lorella Battelli, and Alan Cowey. 1998. Task-specific impairments and enhancements induced by magnetic stimulation of human visual area V5. *Proceedings of the Royal Society B: Biological Sciences* 265:537–543.

Ward, Jamie, Brett Huckstep, and Elias Tsakanikos. 2006. Sound-colour synaesthesia: To what extent does it use cross-modal mechanisms common to us all? *Cortex* 42 (2):264–280.

Ward, Jamie, Ryan Li, Shireen Salih, and Noam Sagiv. 2007. Varieties of grapheme-colour synaesthesia: A new theory of phenomenological and behavioural differences. *Consciousness and Cognition* 16 (4):913–931.

Ward, Jamie, and Jason B. Mattingley. 2006. Synaesthesia: An overview of contemporary findings and controversies. *Cortex* 42:129–136.

Ward, Jamie, and Julia Simner. 2005. Is synaesthesia an X-linked trait lethality in males? *Perception* 34 (5):611–623.

Ward, Jamie, Elias Tsakanikos, and Alice Bray. 2006. Synaesthesia for reading and playing musical notes. *Neurocase* 12:27–34.

Wassermann, Eric M. 1998. Risk and safety of repetitive transcranial magnetic stimulation: Report and suggested guidelines from the International Workshop on the safety of repetitive transcranial magnetic stimulation, June 5–7, 1996. *Electroencephalography and Clinical Neurophysiology* 108:1–16.

Weiss, Peter H., Karl Zilles, and Gereon R. Fink. 2005. When visual perception causes feelings: Enhanced cross-modal processing in grapheme-color synesthesia. *NeuroImage* 28:859–868.

CHAPTER 30

....

SYNESTHESIA, MIRROR NEURONS, AND MIRROR-TOUCH

....

MICHAEL J. BANISSY

INTRODUCTION

....

As noted elsewhere in this volume, synesthesia is a condition where a stimulus in one attribute (the inducer) triggers a conscious experience of another attribute (the concurrent) not typically associated with the inducer. For example, in grapheme-color synesthesia the letter "A" (or "B" or "C" and so on) may trigger synesthetic experiences of colors (Cohen Kadosh and Henik 2007; Rich and Mattingley 2002). A large body of synesthesia research has focused on synesthesia involving color, which is often reported as being the most common concurrent of the condition (Baron-Cohen et al. 1996; Rich, Bradshaw, and Mattingley 2005; Simner et al. 2006). More recently, however, a newly documented form of synesthesia has been described in which individuals experience tactile sensations on their own body when simply observing touch to another's body (Banissy and Ward 2007; Blakemore et al. 2005; Holle et al. 2011). This variant of synesthesia, known as mirror-touch synesthesia, is the focus of the present chapter and here I will describe the prevalence and characteristics of developmental mirror-touch synesthesia, the neurocognitive mechanisms that contribute to this variant, and the extent to which we can use this interpersonal variant of synesthesia to inform us about mechanisms of social perception more generally. I shall also discuss cases in which mirror-touch synesthesia has been reported to be acquired after injury, and I will consider them in relation to acquired synesthesia more generally.

Developmental Mirror-Touch Synesthesia: Prevalence and Characteristics

Synesthesia has been considered by some as having three defining characteristics: (1) concurrents are conscious perceptual or percept-like experiences; (2) experiences are induced by an attribute not typically associated with that conscious experience; (3) these experiences occur automatically (Ward and Mattingley 2006). This section describes evidence indicating how mirror-touch synesthesia matches onto these three criteria and also considers wider characteristics of this variant of synesthetic experience.

With regard to the automaticity of developmental mirror-touch synesthesia, the question is whether mirror-touch synesthetes experience their synesthetic touch sensations immediately/automatically, or whether they require some type of conscious effort (of a kind not normally associated with "synesthesia" proper). Banissy and Ward (2007) reported a behavioral study of ten developmental mirror-touch synesthetes in which they explored this aspect of mirror-touch synesthesia by developing a "visuo-tactile synesthetic Stroop experiment." In the task, synesthetes and matched non-synesthetic controls were asked to detect a site touched on their own facial cheeks while observing touch to another person's facial cheeks or to a corresponding object. Participants were asked to report the site of actual touch (left side of the body, right side of the body, or no touch at all) and to ignore observed touch (which was either on the left, right, or both sides). For synesthetes, but not controls, the synesthetic experience evoked by observed touch could either be congruent or incongruent with the site of actual touch.[1] For example, if observing touch to the left cheek evokes synesthetic touch on the right cheek then actual touch to the right cheek would be congruent with their synesthesia, but actual touch to the left cheek would be incongruent with their synesthesia (Figure 30.1). Synesthetes, but not control participants, were faster at detecting the location of actual touch during the congruent condition relative to the incongruent condition. Further, synesthetes produced a higher percentage of errors consistent with their synesthesia (e.g., reporting touch on trials involving no actual touch; hereafter referred to as "mirror-touch errors"). No significant differences were found when the observed stimuli (i.e., observing touch to another person's cheek) were replaced with a stimulus that did not evoke synesthetic experiences of touch (e.g., a flash of light on the cheek rather than a touch; Banissy et al. 2009). In other words, synesthetes had previously reported that observing a flash of light against another person's body did not cause touch sensations against their own body, and as a consequence, there were no "mirror-touch errors" found under these conditions. The

---

[1] It is of note that in other forms of synesthesia associative training in healthy subjects can induce this kind of Stroop interference effect (e.g., Elias et al. 2003; Meier and Rothen 2009).

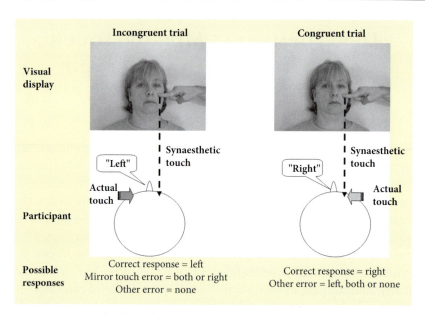

FIGURE 30.1 Summary of task used in Banissy and Ward (2007). Participants were required to report the site upon which they were actually touched (i.e. left cheek, right cheek, both cheeks, or no touch) while ignoring observed touch (and the synesthetic touch induced from it). Note that although the example given is for a specular mirror-touch synesthete, both specular and anatomical subtypes (see text and Figure 30.2) were tested and congruency was determined according to each synesthete's self-reports. Adapted from Banissy, Michael J., and Jamie Ward, Mirror-touch synaesthesia is linked with empathy. Nature Neuroscience 10 (7), pp. 815–816 © 2007, The Authors, with permission.

findings therefore provided evidence supporting the suggestion that mirror-touch synesthetes experience touch on their own body when observing bodily touch and imply that the synesthetic experience in mirror-touch synesthesia is percept-like.

Using the aforementioned "visuo-tactile congruity paradigm" as a measure for the authenticity of mirror-touch synesthesia, my colleagues and I (Banissy et al. 2009) examined the prevalence of developmental mirror-touch synesthesia among university undergraduates at University College London and the University of Sussex. Five hundred and sixty-seven participants were recruited for the study. All were undergraduate students recruited before/after classes being held at each university. Participants were given a description of synesthesia (including examples of what did and did not constitute synesthesia) and were then administered a questionnaire asking about different variants of synesthesia. They were not told that the study was a prevalence study, nor did they receive specific details about mirror-touch synesthesia (i.e., they received a general description of synesthesia rather than specific details about individual subtypes). One question on the questionnaire related to mirror-touch synesthesia, in which participants were asked to indicate the extent to which they agreed with the question "Do you experience touch sensations on your own body when you see them on another person's body?" All participants who gave positive responses to this question (approximately 10.8% of all subjects) were contacted and interviewed about their experiences. These participants were presented with a series of videos that showed another person, object, or cartoon face being touched, and asked to indicate the location (if any) in which they experienced a tactile stimulus themselves and the type of experience. Typical responses of potential mirror-touch synesthetes (approximately 2.5% of all subjects) included reports that observing touch elicits a tingling somatic sensation in the corresponding location on their own body, and that a more intense and qualitatively different sensation is felt for painful stimuli (e.g., videos of a pin pricking a hand rather than observed touch to the hand). Of these 14 subjects, nine showed a significantly different pattern of performance compared to matched non-synesthetic subjects on the visuo-tactile synesthetic Stroop experiment developed by Banissy and Ward (2007), indicating a prevalence rate of 1.6%. In comparison to previous prevalence estimates of other types of synesthesia this places mirror-touch synesthesia as one of the more common forms of synesthesia, along with grapheme-color synesthesia (1.4% prevalence) and day-color synesthesia (2.8% prevalence; Simner et al. 2006).

A study examining the perceptual characteristics of the inducer in mirror-touch synesthesia indicates a number of common factors that mediate the synesthetic experience in mirror-touch (Holle et al. 2011). In that study, a group of 14 previously verified mirror-touch synesthetes were presented with a series of film clips and asked to report the presence/absence of synesthetic experience, the location of experience, and the intensity of the experience. Films included painful stimulation (e.g., a person being prodded by a knife), thermal stimulation (e.g., a person being touched by a candle), and tactile stimulation (e.g., a person being touched by another person). The target of the stimulation (i.e., the person/thing touched) also differed insofar as whether we showed touch to another person, touch to an object, touch to a dummy body part, or touch shown only within a static photograph. The findings showed that observed touch to another person in a video evoked a significantly more intense synesthetic experience than observing similar touch in static photographs, and was also more intense than observing touch to either dummy body parts or objects in videos. This implies that visual recognition of bodies alone (in the case of dummy body parts) is not driving mirror-touch synesthesia. The intensity of synesthetic sensations did not differ by the body part observed (face, hand, arm, leg, etc.) or by the spatial orientation of the body part when observing touch to a real person (e.g., whether the hands of another person appeared as crossed or uncrossed when touched). Painful stimuli to a real face (e.g., a sharp object prodding the face) did, however, evoke a stronger experience than a non-painful tactile stimulus to the face (e.g., a feather stroking the face).

In addition to commonalities, some important individual differences have also been found across mirror-touch synesthetes (Banissy and Ward 2007; Banissy et al. 2009; White and Aimola Davies 2012). It appears that mirror-touch synesthetes can be divided into at least two subgroups based upon the spatial mapping between observed and felt (synesthetic) touch (Figure 30.2). Some synesthetes report that an observed touch to the left cheek is felt on their right cheek (as if the observed person is a mirror reflection of oneself—and this type of experience is hereafter referred to as the "specular"

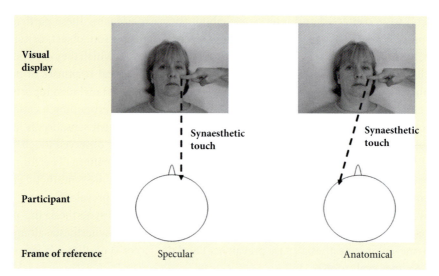

FIGURE 30.2 Specular and anatomical spatial mappings reported by mirror-touch synesthetes. Under a specular frame of reference, mirror-touch synesthetes report synesthetic touch as if looking in a mirror. Under an anatomical frame of reference synesthetic experience is as if self and other share the same anatomical body space.

subtype), whereas others report synesthetic touch on their left cheek when observing touch to another person's left cheek (as if self and other share the same anatomical body space—hereafter referred to as the "anatomical" subtype). Our own studies indicate that the specular subtype is the more common, with approximately 80% of cases studied to date reporting a specular spatial mapping (see Banissy et al. 2009). This bias towards a specular mapping in synesthetes is consistent with studies on imitation behavior indicating that both adults and children tend to imitate in a specular mode (Franz, Ford, and Werner 2007; Schofield 1976). The possibility that there may be at least two spatial frames of reference that could be adopted when observing another's tactile experiences is also consistent with neurophysiological findings in primates documenting anatomical and specular spatial frames of reference that mediate bimodal visual-tactile cells in the macaque parietal cortex. These cells respond when the monkey is touched and when the monkey observes touch to the same body part of someone else (Ishida et al. 2009).

In addition to differences in the spatial frame of reference adopted by mirror-touch synesthetes another intriguing characteristic shown by some but not all mirror-touch synesthetes, is the extent to which observing touch to *objects* can elicit synesthetic interactions. This type of experience has been reported as a consistent experience in approximately 18% of cases studied by our group (e.g., Banissy et al. 2009). For some of these "object-touch" synesthetes, this experience is reported to occur in the synesthete's fingertip that corresponds to the finger observed touching the objects, but for others, synesthetic touch is linked onto particular body locations that are thought to correspond to the object being touched (e.g., when looking directly at a monitor being touched by another, the synesthetic touch experience maps onto the face, but when standing in front of the monitor the experience maps onto the trunk).

One further feature where developmental mirror-touch synesthesia shares characteristics with more commonly studied variants of synesthesia is how consistent the sensations are over time. In grapheme-color synesthesia, for example, if "A" is red at time 1 then it will be at time 2, several weeks, months, years, or even decades later (Baron-Cohen, Wyke, and Binnie 1987; Simner and Logie 2007). The experiences of mirror-touch synesthetes are also enduring, and an individual's spatial subtype (i.e., whether they belong to the specular or anatomical category) is consistent both across time (Holle et al. 2011) and across different body parts (Banissy and Ward 2007). There are also additional characteristics that appear common to mirror-touch synesthesia and other variants of the condition. Mirror-touch synesthetes have been found to show an increased tactile sensitivity (Banissy, Walsh, and Ward 2009), which is in line with evidence of heightened perceptual processing of the synesthetic concurrent in other variants of synesthesia (e.g., increased color responsiveness in synesthetes who experience color (Yaro and Ward 2007) and increased color and tactile responsiveness in synesthetes who experience both touch and color (Banissy, Walsh, and Ward 2009)). It is also common for mirror-touch synesthetes to report an additional type of synesthesia (e.g., Banissy, Walsh, and Ward 2009; Banissy et al. 2009) and a similar trend is found in other types of the condition (Simner et al. 2006).

One aspect in which developmental mirror-touch may be considered to differ slightly from other more commonly studied variants of synesthesia is that the mappings in mirror-touch synesthesia appear to be non-arbitrary, insofar as somatotopy is typically preserved between observed and felt touch (e.g., observing touch to face will normally trigger an experience on the synesthetes' face). Indeed, when mirror-touch synesthesia was first documented there was some resistance (and arguably still is) to the notion that it was a variant of synesthesia because the experience was simply "too literal" to be synesthesia. On closer inspection this may not be such an apparent difference. While it was once believed that synesthetic experiences were consistent arbitrary associations, this view is no longer widely held and there is growing evidence of *non*-arbitrary associations in other variants of synesthesia: for example, between pitch and lightness in tone-color synesthesia (Ward, Huckstep, and Tsakanikos 2006); number and lightness in number-color synesthesia (Cohen Kadosh, Henik, and Walsh 2007); grapheme frequencies and color in grapheme-color synesthesia (Simner et al. 2005); and phonology and tastes in lexical gustatory synesthesia (Ward and Simner 2003). Direct links have also been reported: for example, in lexical-gustatory synesthesia food-words often taste of the denoted food (e.g., the word "sausage" tends to taste of sausage; Ward, Simner, and Auyeung 2005) and color words sometimes map onto the same colors in linguistic-color synesthesia (e.g., the word "red" is colored red; Gray et al. 2002; Rich, Bradhaw, and Mattingley 2005). In this regard, there is a growing consensus to view mirror-touch synesthesia being part of the "synesthesia family," as opposed to an unusual experience that is more common in and shares phenomenological similarities with synesthesia (e.g., mitempfindung; Burrack, Knoch, and Brugger 2006).

In sum, mirror-touch synesthesia describes an automatic percept-like tactile experience when simply observing touch to another person (or possibly to an object). Despite only recently being systematically investigated, it appears to be surprisingly common and shares some similarities with other more commonly studied variants of synesthesia (e.g., in terms of consistency over time and in relation to extended perceptual characteristics). There are, however, some important individual differences between mirror-touch synesthetes, including the frame of reference adopted when perceiving touch to another person (specular/anatomical distinction). These will be considered below in relation to potential neurocognitive mechanisms that may mediate the synesthetic experience in mirror-touch synesthesia.

DEVELOPMENTAL MIRROR-TOUCH SYNESTHESIA: NEUROCOGNITIVE MECHANISMS

In addition to describing the perceptual characteristics of mirror-touch synesthesia, another important question is what mechanisms evoke synesthetic experiences of touch in this variant of synesthesia. Several biasing principles have been suggested as mechanisms that mediate what forms of synesthesia will or will not be developed (e.g., Bargary and Mitchell 2008; Cohen Kadosh and Walsh 2008; Eagleman 2009; Hubbard and Ramachandran 2005; Ramachandran and Hubbard 2001; Sagiv and Ward 2006; Smilek et al. 2001). One common biasing principle that has been associated with accounts of synesthesia is the role of adjacency between neighboring brain regions (e.g., between adjacent visual grapheme and color processing areas in grapheme-color synesthesia; Ramachandran and Hubbard 2001). The principle of adjacency is less clear in developmental mirror-touch synesthesia because there are no apparent neighboring brain areas that may mediate visuo-tactile experiences. An alternative biasing principle that may be more relevant is the "normal" architecture for multisensory interactions (Sagiv and Ward 2006). Moreover, there is now good evidence for a network of brain regions that are recruited by non-synesthetes when observing touch to others (Blakemore et al. 2005; Ebisch et al. 2008; Keysers et al. 2004; McCabe et al. 2008) and mirror-touch synesthesia may reflect hyperactivity within this network (Blakemore et al. 2005). Here, this possibility is discussed and additional neurocognitive mechanisms that may mediate individual differences between mirror-touch synesthetes are described.

The observed touch network is comprised of the primary and secondary somatosensory cortices, premotor cortex, intraparietal sulcus, and the superior temporal sulcus (Blakemore et al. 2005; Ebisch et al. 2008; Keysers et al. 2004; McCabe et al. 2008). The overlap between brain areas that are involved in passively experiencing touch to oneself and observing touch to another person (i.e., primary somatosensory and secondary somatosensory cortices) has been interpreted as evidence of a mirror-touch system in which observed touch is matched to the observer's own sensorimotor representation of touch. This interpretation builds upon the findings of mirror neurons within the monkey premotor cortex and inferior parietal lobule (Gallese et al. 1996; Rizzolatti and Craighero 2004), which respond both when a monkey performs an action and when the monkey watches another person perform a similar action. In humans, indirect evidence of brain areas with similar mirroring properties has been found for action (Buccino et al. 2001), pain (Avenani et al. 2005; Singer et al. 2004), disgust (Wicker et al. 2003) and other emotions (Carr et al. 2003; Warren et al. 2006). Therefore, the overlap between the brain areas that become active when observing touch and experiencing touch are consistent with the notion of a mirror system for touch in the human brain.

Blakemore et al. (2005) examined the role of the mirror-touch system in non-synesthetes and a single mirror-touch synesthete named "C." C reports experiencing touch on her own body when observing another person being touched, but not when observing inanimate objects being touched. Her experiences mirror observed touch to another person, such that observing touch to another person's left facial cheek leads to a sensation of touch on her own right facial cheek (i.e., she adopts a specular frame of reference). Using functional magnetic resonance imaging Blakemore and colleagues investigated the neural systems underlying C's synesthetic experience by contrasting brain activity when watching videos of humans relative to objects being touched (the latter did not elicit synesthesia) in the synesthete and in 12 non-synesthetic control subjects. As expected, non-synesthetes activated a network of brain regions during the observation of touch to a human relative to an object (including primary and secondary somatosensory cortex, premotor regions, and the superior temporal sulcus). Similar brain regions were also activated during actual touch, indicating that observing touch to another person activates a similar neural circuit as actual tactile experience—the mirror-touch system. A comparison between synesthete C and non-synesthetic subjects indicated that the synesthete showed hyperactivity within a number of regions within this network (including primary somatosensory cortex) and additional activity in the anterior insula. This suggests that mirror-touch synesthesia is a consequence of increased neural activity in the same mirror-touch network that is evoked in non-synesthetic controls when observing touch to another person (Blakemore et al. 2005) and therefore may be mediated by the "normal" architecture for multisensory interactions.

The fact that additional bilateral anterior insula activation was observed in C, but not in non-synesthetes when observing touch is also of interest. Neural activity in the anterior insula has been related to self-awareness (Critchley et al. 2004) and processing one's awareness of others (Craig 2004; Lamm and Singer 2010). It is therefore thought to be involved in self-other distinctions (Fink et al. 1996; Kircher et al. 2001; Ruby and Decety 2001) and one possibility is that the additional activation of the insula in mirror-touch synesthesia reflects an error in the neural systems distinguishing between self and other, leading to the source of another person's tactile experience being mislocated onto the synesthete's own body (Banissy, Walsh, and Muggleton 2011). Moreover, one possibility is that mirror-touch synesthesia is linked to alterations in perceived body space (i.e., the boundaries of perceived body space between self and other may be more expansive in mirror-touch synesthesia; Aimola Davies and White 2013; Banissy, Walsh, and

Muggleton 2011; Banissy et al. 2009) and abnormal activity in the anterior insula is one candidate brain region that may mediate this process (see Banissy and Ward 2013).

In addition to general differences in mechanisms of self-other distinction (i.e., those that distinguish mirror-touch synesthetes from non-synesthetes), it is also likely that there are a number of factors mediating individual differences (e.g., specular/anatomical distinction) between mirror-touch synesthetes. While this has not yet been studied systematically at a neural level, my colleagues and I provided a neurocognitive model to account for these differences and suggested three key mechanisms that are important to mirror-touch synesthesia: (1) identifying the type of visual stimulus touched ("What" mechanism), (2) discriminating between self and other ("Who" mechanism), and (3) locating where on the body and in space observed touch occurs ("Where" mechanism) (Banissy et al. 2009).

The "What" mechanism is considered to be involved in several discriminations related to the nature of the inducer (e.g., "Is this a human or object?"). As noted earlier, one intriguing characteristic shown by some mirror-touch synesthetes is that observing touch to objects can elicit synesthetic interactions (e.g., Banissy and Ward 2007). One brain region of the observed-touch network (Blakemore et al. 2005) that may be central to this is the intraparietal sulcus (IPS). Recent findings indicate that visual object information is processed along the dorsal stream to areas along the medial bank of the intraparietal sulcus (IPS; including IPS1 and IPS2; Konen and Kaster 2008). For mirror-touch synesthetes, this pathway may be particularly important when considered in relationship to visual-tactile body maps within the intraparietal cortex. Single-cell recording in primates has identified bimodal neurons in the intraparietal cortex which fire in response to not only passive somatosensory stimulation, but also to a visual stimulus presented in close proximity to the touched body part (Duhamel, Colby, and Goldberg 1998). Intriguingly, the visual spatial reference frames of such bimodal neurons are dynamic and if the monkey is trained to use a tool the visual receptive field extends to incorporate the tool into the representation of the body (Iriki, Tanaka, and Iwamura 1996). Similar evidence of dynamic multisensory body representations in the parietal cortex has been reported in human subjects (Berlucchi and Aglioti 1997; Bremmer et al. 2001; Colby 1998; Maravita and Iriki 2002). Therefore, one possibility is that the degree to which observing touch to an object is able to elicit visual-tactile synesthetic interactions depends upon the extent to which the object is incorporated into visual-tactile representations of the body, potentially within the intraparietal cortex.

The key process instigated by the "Who" mechanism is to distinguish between the self and other. It has been suggested that mirror-touch synesthesia may reflect a breakdown in the mechanisms that normally distinguish between self and other, leading to altered boundaries of perceived body space and misrepresentations of another's body onto the synesthete's own body schema (e.g., Banissy, Walsh, and Muggleton 2011; Banissy et al. 2009; Aimola Davies and White, 2013). Some factors mediating this may include the perspective of the viewed body part and the similarity between the observers and observed. In relation to the later, if similarity is important in mediating activity within the mirror-touch system then one may predict that non-synesthetes should show some level of modulation when observing touch to themselves versus other people. In accordance with this, Serino, Pizzoferrato, and Làdavas (2008) report that, for non-synesthetes, there is an enhancement in tactile sensitivity when observing touch, which is maximized when observing touch to one's own face rather than another's face.

The final class of mechanism that also seems important in mediating individual differences between mirror-touch synesthetes involves linking visual representations of body with tactile representations based on spatial frames of reference (Banissy et al. 2009). One way to consider the differences in the spatial frame adopted by mirror-touch synesthetes is through the notion of embodied and disembodied representations of perspective taking (see Brugger 2002; Giummarra et al. 2008). Specular mirror-touch synesthetes appear to process the visual representation of the other body as if looking at their own reflection (i.e., in an embodied manner to oneself), while for the anatomical subtype the spatial mapping between self and other could be considered to be disembodied because the synesthete's own body appears to share the same bodily template as the others person (i.e., the synesthete is rotating their body into the perspective of the other person). This distinction may then be borne out at the neural level. For example, disembodied experiences have been suggested to arise from functional disintegration of low-level multisensory processing mechanisms (Blanke and Mohr 2005; Bünning and Blanke 2005) and abnormal activity at the temporal parietal junction (TPJ; Arzy et al. 2006; Blanke et al. 2002; Blanke et al. 2004), therefore one may suggest the anatomical, but not specular, subtype will be associated with these neurocognitive mechanisms.

Acquired Mirror-Touch/Mirror-Pain Synesthesia

So far the focus of this chapter has been on developmental cases of mirror-touch synesthesia. Recently, however, a number of studies have begun to describe cases of mirror-touch/mirror-pain synesthesia that have been acquired following sensory loss or brain injury. In this section, these studies are reviewed and considered in relationship to other acquired variants of synesthesia.

The first reported case of an acquired interpersonal synesthesia was related to observed pain rather than observed touch. This anecdotal report, given to clinicians posthumously by the patient's wife, describes a man who experienced observed pain to others as actual pain on his own body (Bradshaw and Mattingley 2001). The patient was known to have suffered widespread cancer, but as this case was reported post-mortem no information about the functional neural circuitry involved was available. As alluded to earlier, more recently, evidence for the interpersonal sharing of observed pain has been provided (Avenanti et al. 2005; Morrison et al. 2004; Singer et al. 2004). For example, observing pain to another person results in neural activity in similar brain regions as when we experience pain ourselves (Morrison et al. 2004; Singer et al. 2004) and leads to modulation of corticospinal motor representations in a somatotopic manner (e.g., observing pain to the first dorsal interosseous (FDI) muscle modulates the observer's own FDI muscle activity; Avenanti et al. 2005). These findings provide evidence for a mirror-pain resonance system in all people, in which observed pain is matched to the observer's own sensorimotor representation of pain, and may be important in both acquired and developmental cases of mirror-pain synesthesia (Fitzgibbon, Giummarra, et al. 2010).

In addition to the discussed case, other cases of acquired mirror-pain and/or mirror-touch synesthesia have been reported. These cases tend to be related to sensory loss following limb amputation. For example, Ramachandran and Brang (2009) report cases of acquired mirror-touch synesthesia following arm amputation. In that study, four patients with upper limb amputations who reported phantom limb sensations, and healthy controls, were shown videos of another person's hand being touched. Patients reported a consistent tactile experience in their phantom hand when simply observing touch to the intact hand of another person.

In fact, it appears that there might be a particularly high prevalence of mirror-touch/mirror-pain synesthesia in individuals that experience phantom limb sensations following amputation. For example, Fitzgibbon and colleagues (Fitzgibbon, Enticott, et al. 2010) report that 16.2% of self-referred amputees (n = 12 out of 74 amputees) experience sensations of phantom pain (i.e., pain in their phantom limb) when observing pain to others. Furthermore, Goller and colleagues (2013) report that almost a third of amputees (n = 8 out of 28 amputees) report tactile sensations on their phantom limb or stump when observing touch to another person. While these findings are based only on self-reports, and therefore may reflect some false positives, they are high levels when compared to the 10.8% of healthy adults who self-report developmental mirror-touch synesthesia (Banissy et al. 2009).

These acquired cases are in line with reports of developmental mirror-touch synesthesia, but there are some differences. In the case of amputees who report acquired mirror-touch, the most notable difference is the location of synesthetic experience. In developmental mirror-touch synesthesia, somatotopy is typically preserved such that observing touch to another person's face will evoke a synesthetic sensation on the synesthete's own face. In phantom limb amputees, synesthetic sensations tend to be evoked on the phantom limb or stump, irrespective of the body part seen (i.e., synesthetic experiences gravitate towards the stump; Goller et al. 2013; Figure 30.3). This difference is consistent with other variants of acquired synesthesia insofar as it is quite common for synesthesia following sensory loss to occur close to the location where stimulation is removed (e.g., Ro et al. 2007). The difference may also be informative about the neural mechanisms that are contributing to mirror-touch/pain in amputees. One possibility is that these experiences reflect a removal of neural signals from the amputated limb that would normally inhibit activity within the mirror-touch system in order to prevent observed touch/pain being experienced when viewing touch to others (Ramachandran and Brang 2009).

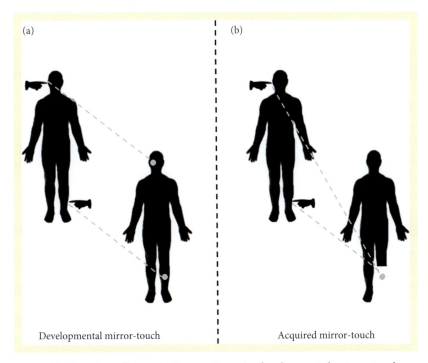

(a)

(b)

Developmental mirror-touch

Acquired mirror-touch

FIGURE 30.3 The location of synesthetic experience in developmental mirror-touch synesthesia and acquired mirror-touch synesthesia in amputees. For developmental mirror-touch synesthetes, synesthetic touch is evoked in the corresponding body part (e.g., touch to face evokes synesthetic touch on the face). For amputees, synesthetic touch gravitates towards the phantom limb or stump irrespective of where touch is observed. Gray dots indicate the location of synesthetic experience.

BEYOND MIRROR-TOUCH SYNESTHESIA: SENSORIMOTOR SIMULATION AND SOCIAL PERCEPTION

A further reason why mirror-touch synesthesia is of interest is in relation to what this variant of synesthesia can tell us about mechanisms of social perception and cognition in non-synesthetes. As noted earlier, functional brain imaging has linked mirror-touch synesthesia to heightened neural activity in a network of brain regions which are also activated in non-synesthetic control subjects when observing touch to others (the mirror-touch system; Blakemore et al. 2005). Therefore, it is reasonable to consider mirror-touch synesthesia as a consequence of over-activity within the typical system that is activated by us all when observing touch to others and to ask what secondary impact this has on other aspects of perception that the mirror-touch system is thought to be involved in.

One component of perception that the mirror-touch system has been associated with is as a candidate neural mechanism to aid social perception through sensorimotor simulation (Gallese and Goldman 1998; Keysers and Gazzola 2006; Oberman and Ramachandran 2007). Accounts of social perception involving sensorimotor simulation contend that in order to understand another's emotions and physical states, the perceiver must map the bodily state of the observer onto the same representations involved in experiencing the perceived state oneself (Adolphs 2002, 2003; Gallese and Goldman 1998; Gallese, Keysers, and Rizzolatti 2004; Goldman, and Sripada 2005; Keysers and Gazzola 2006; Oberman and Ramachandran 2007). This view is supported by evidence from electrophysiological, functional brain imaging, and psychophysical studies indicating an involvement of sensorimotor resources in aspects of social perception abilities. For example, responses in expression-relevant facial muscles are increased during subliminal exposure to emotional expressions (Dimberg, Thunberg, and Elmehed 2000) and preventing the activation of expression relevant muscles impairs expression recognition (Oberman, Winkielman, and Ramachandran 2007). Perceiving another's expressions and producing one's own also recruits similar cortical sensorimotor regions (e.g., Carr et al. 2003; van der Gaag, Minderaa, and Keysers 2007; Warren et al. 2006; Winston, O'Doherty, and Dolan 2003) and neuropsychological findings indicate that damage to right somatosensory cortices is associated with expression recognition deficits (Adolphs et al. 2000).

A complementary approach to the studies described previously is to consider whether facilitation of sensorimotor mechanisms in mirror-touch synesthesia promotes social perception abilities. For example, Banissy and Ward (2007) examined empathy (the capacity to share the thoughts and feelings of others) in developmental mirror-touch synesthesia in an attempt to determine the relationship between heightened activity in the mirror-touch system and this aspect of social perception. We compared the empathic abilities of mirror-touch synesthetes to non-synesthetic and synesthetic control subjects (i.e., individuals who experience synesthesia but not mirror-touch synesthesia) using the Empathy Quotient (a standardized self-report scale designed to empirically measure empathy; Baron-Cohen and Wheelwright 2004). Mirror-touch synesthetes were found to show significantly higher levels of emotionally reactive empathy compared to controls (e.g., affective components of empathy and instinctive empathic responses to others), but did not differ in their levels of cognitive empathy (e.g., mentalizing and cognitive perspective taking) or in their social skills level. Importantly, synesthetes without mirror-touch synesthesia did not differ from non-synesthetes in their levels of empathy, implying that heightened emotional empathy relates specifically to mirror-touch synesthesia (and the neural system which underpins this condition). In accordance with this, neuroimaging findings indicate that, in healthy adults, emotional empathy (i.e., experiencing an appropriate emotional response as a consequence of another's state) engages the cortical sensorimotor network (including the premotor cortex, primary somatosensory cortex and motor cortex) more than cognitive empathy (i.e., predicting and understanding another's mental state by using cognitive processes; Nummenmaa et al. 2008) and grey matter volume in the neural regions linked to sensorimotor resonance correlates with individual differences in emotional empathic abilities for healthy adults (Banissy et al. 2012). Further, neuropsychological findings have demonstrated a functional and anatomical double dissociation between deficits in cognitive empathy and emotional empathy, with emotional empathy being linked to lesions to the human mirror system and cognitive empathy being associated to lesions to the ventromedial prefrontal cortices (Shamay-Tsoory, Aharon-Peretz, and Perry 2009). This functional coupling between emotional and cognitive empathy suggests that emotional empathy may be linked more closely to sensorimotor simulation of another's state and the evidence that mirror-touch synesthetes only significantly differ from controls on levels of emotional reactivity is consistent with this.

It is not just developmental mirror-touch synesthetes who have been shown to differ in their levels of emotional reactive empathy. A recent study by Goller et al. (2013) indicates that acquired cases of mirror-touch synesthesia are also associated with increases in this aspect of social perception. In their study, the empathic abilities of amputees that reported mirror-touch synesthesia were compared to amputees who do not report mirror-touch synesthesia. As per Banissy and Ward (2007), the authors use the Empathy Quotient to examine empathic abilities and found that amputees who report mirror-touch synesthesia showed higher levels of emotional reactive empathy, but not cognitive empathy or social skills (Goller et al. 2013).

Developmental mirror-touch synesthetes have also been shown to differ in another aspect of social perception that is thought to utilize sensorimotor systems, namely expression processing. My colleagues and I compared mirror-touch synesthetes and non-synesthetic controls on facial expression recognition, identity recognition, and identity perception tasks (Banissy et al. 2011). Based on the hypothesis that mirror-touch synesthetes have heightened sensorimotor simulation mechanisms we predicted that synesthetes would show superior performance on expression recognition tasks but not on the facial identity control tasks that are less dependent on simulation. Consistent with these predictions, mirror-touch synesthetes were superior when recognizing the facial expressions, but not facial identities of others (Banissy et al. 2011). These findings are in accordance with transcranial magnetic stimulation, neuropsychological and functional brain imaging findings indicating the involvement of sensorimotor systems in expression processing but not identity processing (e.g., Banissy et al. 2010; Pitcher et al. 2008). They are therefore consistent with simulation accounts of expression recognition contending that one mechanism involved in expression, but not identity recognition, is an internal sensorimotor re-enactment of the perceived expression (Adolphs 2002; Gallese, Keysers, and Rizzolatti 2004; Goldman, and Sripada 2005; Keysers and Gazzola 2006). When combined with the evidence of heightened affective empathy in developmental and acquired mirror-touch synesthesia, they also help to demonstrate an interesting avenue in which mirror-touch synesthesia may be able to inform us about mechanisms of social perception in non-synesthetes.

CONCLUSIONS

In sum, this chapter has described the prevalence and characteristics of mirror-touch synesthesia; the neurocognitive mechanisms that contribute to this experience; and discussed the extent to which mirror-touch synesthesia can be used to inform us about mechanisms of social perception. While much has been learnt already, a number of key questions remain, including the mechanisms that mediate individual differences in mirror-touch synesthesia, the role of mechanisms of self-other distinction in mirror-touch synesthesia, and the extent to which mirror-touch synesthesia shares similarities/differences to other variants of synesthesia. These and other questions will provide interesting avenues for future studies into this variant of synesthetic experience.

REFERENCES

Adolphs, Ralph. 2002. Neural systems for recognizing emotion. *Current Opinion in Neurobiology* 12:169–177.

——. 2003. Cognitive neuroscience of human social behaviour. *Nature Reviews Neuroscience* 4:165–178.

Adolphs, Ralph, Hanna Damasio, Daniel Tranel, Greg Cooper, and Antonio R. Damasio. 2000. A role for somatosensory cortices in the visual recognition of emotion as revealed by three-dimensional lesion mapping. *The Journal of Neuroscience* 20 (7):2683–2690.

Aimola Davies, Anne M., and Rebekah C. White. 2013. A sensational illusion: vision-touch synaesthesia and the rubber hand paradigm. *Cortex* 49:806–818.

Arzy, Shahar, Gregor Thut, Christine Mohr, Christoph M. Michel, and Olaf Blanke. 2006. Neural basis of embodiment: Distinct contributions of the temporoparietal junction and the extrastriate body area. *The Journal of Neuroscience* 26:8074–8081.

Avenanti, Alessio, Domenica Bueti, Gaspare Galati, and Salvatore Aglioti. 2005. Transcranial magnetic stimulation highlights the sensorimotor side of empathy for pain. *Nature Neuroscience* 8:955–960.

Banissy, Michael J., Roi Cohen Kadosh, Gerrit W. Maus, Vincent Walsh, and Jamie Ward. 2009. Prevalence, characteristics, and a neurocognitive model of mirror-touch synaesthesia. *Experimental Brain Research* 198:261–272.

Banissy, Michael J., Lúcia Garrido, Flor Kusnir, Bradely Duchaine, Vincent Walsh, and Jamie Ward. 2011. Superior facial expression, but not identity recognition, in mirror-touch synaesthesia. *The Journal of Neuroscience* 31:1820–1824.

Banissy, Michael J., Ryota Kanai, Vincent Walsh, and Geraint Rees. 2012. Inter-individual differences in empathy are reflected in human brain structure. *NeuroImage* 62 (3):2034–2039.

Banissy, Michael J., Disa Anna Saute, Jamie Ward, Jane E. Warren, Vincent Walsh, and Sophie K. Scott. 2010. Suppressing sensorimotor activity modulates the discrimination of auditory emotions but not speaker identity. *The Journal of Neuroscience* 30 (4):13552–13557.

Banissy, Michael J., Vincent Walsh, and Neil G. Muggleton. 2011. Mirror-touch synaesthesia: A case of faulty self-modelling and insula abnormality. *Cognitive Neuroscience* 2 (2):114–115.

Banissy, Michael J., Vincent Walsh, and Jamie Ward. 2009b. Enhanced sensory perception in synaesthesia. Experimental Brain Research 196:565–571.

Banissy, Michael J., and Jamie Ward. 2007. Mirror-touch synaesthesia is linked with empathy. Nature Neuroscience 10:815–816.

———. 2013. Mechanisms of self-other representations and vicarious experiences of touch in mirror-touch synesthesia. Frontiers in Human Neuroscience 7:112. doi:10.3389/fnhum.2013.00112.

Bargary, Gary, and Kevin J. Mitchell. 2008. Synaesthesia and cortical connectivity. Trends in Neurosciences 31:335–342.

Baron-Cohen, Simon, Lucy Burt, Fiona Laittan-Smith, John E. Harrison, and Patrick Bolton. 1996. Synaesthesia: Prevalence and familiality. Perception 25:1073–1079.

Baron-Cohen, Simon, Maria A. Wyke, and Colin Binnie. 1987. Hearing words and seeing colours: An experimental investigation of synaesthesia. Perception 16: 761–767.

Baron-Cohen, Simon, and Sally Wheelwright. 2004. The empathy quotient: An investigation of adults with Asperger syndrome or high functioning autism, and normal sex differences. Journal of Autism and Development Disorders 34 (2):163–175.

Berlucchi, Giovanni, and Salvatore Aglioti. 1997. The body in the brain: Neural basis of corporeal awareness. Trends in Neuroscience 20:560–564.

Blakemore, Sarah-Jane, Davina Bristow, Geoffrey Bird, Christopher Frith, and Jamie Ward. 2005. Somatosensory activations during the observation of touch and a case of vision-touch synaesthesia. Brain 128:1571–1583.

Blanke, Olaf, Theodore Landis, Laurent Spinelli, and Margitta Seeck. 2004. Out-of-body experiences and autoscopy of neurological origin. Brain 127:243–258.

Blanke, Olaf, and Christine Mohr. 2005. Out-of-body experience, heautoscopy, and autoscopic hallucinations of neurological origin: Implications for neurocognitive mechanisms of corporeal awareness and self-consciousness. Brain Research Reviews 50:184–199.

Blanke, Olaf, Stéphanie Ortigue, Theodore Landis, and Margitta Seeck. 2002. Stimulating illusory own body perceptions. Nature 419:269–270.

Bradshaw, John L., and Jason B. Mattingley. 2001. Allodynia: A sensory analogue of motor mirror neurons in a hyperaesthetic patient reporting instantaneous discomfort to another's perceived sudden minor injury? Journal of Neurology, Neurosurgery and Psychiatry 70 (1):135–136.

Brugger, Peter. 2002. Reflective mirrors: Perspective-taking in autoscopic phenomena. Cognitive Neuropsychiatry 7 (3):179–194.

Bremmer, Frank, Anja Schlak, N. Jon Shah, Oliver Zafiris, Michael Kubishik, Klaus-Peter Hoffmann, Karl Zilles and Gereon R. Fink. 2001. Polymodal motion processing in posterior parietal and premotor cortex: A human fMRI study strongly implies equivalences between humans and monkeys. Neuron 29 (1):287–296.

Buccino, G., F. Binkofski, G. R. Fink, L. Fadiga, L. Fogassi, V. Gallese, V., R. J. Seitz, K. Zilles, G. Rizzolatti, and H. J. Freund. 2001. Action observation activates premotor and parietal areas in a somatotopic manner. European Journal of Neuroscience 13 (2):400–404.

Bünning, Silvia, and Olaf Blanke. 2005. The out-of body experience: Precipitating factors and neural correlates. Progress in Brain Research 150:331–350.

Burrack, Anna, Daria Knoch, and Peter Brugger. 2006. Mitempfindung in synaesthetes: Co-incidence or meaningful association? Cortex 42:151–154.

Carr, Laurie, Marco Iacoboni, Marie-Charlotte Dubeau, John C. Mazziotta, and Gian Luigi Lenzi. 2003. Neural mechanisms of empathy in humans: A relay from neural systems for imitation to limbic areas. Proceedings of the National Academy of Sciences of the United States of America 100 (9):5497–5502.

Cohen Kadosh, Roi, and Avashai Henik. 2007. Can synaesthesia research inform cognitive science? *Trends in Cognitive Sciences* 11:177–184.

Cohen Kadosh, Roi, Avashai Henik, and Vincent Walsh. 2007. Small is bright and big is dark in synaesthesia. *Current Biology* 17:R834–R835.

———. 2009. Synaesthesia: Learned or lost? *Developmental Science* 12:484–491.

Cohen Kadosh, Roi, and Vincent Walsh. 2008. Synaesthesia and cortical connections: Cause or correlation? *Trends in Neurosciences* 31:549–550.

Colby, Carol L. 1998. Action-orientated spatial reference frames in cortex. *Neuron* 20:15–24.

Craig, Bud. 2004. Human feelings: Why are some more aware than others? *Trends in Cognitive Science* 8:239–241.

Critchley, Hugo D., Stefan Diens, Pia Rotshtein, Arne Öhman and Raymond J. Dolan. 2004. Neural systems supporting introceptive awareness. *Nature Neuroscience* 7 (2):189–195.

Dimberg, Ulf, Monika Thunberg, and Kurt Elmehed. 2000. Unconscious facial reactions to emotional facial expressions. *Psychological Science* 11 (1):86–89.

Duhamel, Jean-Réne, Carol L. Colby, and Michael E. Goldberg. 1998. Ventral intraparietal area of the macaque: Congruent visual and somatic response properties. *Journal of Neurophysiology* 79 (1):126–136.

Eagleman, David M. 2009. The objectification of overlearned sequences: A new view of spatial sequence synesthesia. *Cortex* 45 (10):1266–1277.

Ebisch, Sjoerd J. H., Mauro G. Perucci, Antonio Ferretti, Cosimo Del Gratta, Gian Luca Romani, and Vittorio Gallese. 2008. The sense of touch: Embodied simulation in a visuo-tactile mirroring mechanism for observed animate or inanimate touch. *Journal of Cognitive Neuroscience* 20 (9):1611–1623.

Elias, Lorin J., Deborah M. Saucier, Colleen Hardie, and Gordon E. Sarty. 2003. Dissociating semantic and perceptual components of synaesthesia: Behavioural and functional neuro-anatomical investigations. *Cognitive Brain Research* 16:232–237.

Fink, Gereon R., Hans J. Markowitsch, Mechthild Reinkemeier, Thomas Bruckbauer, Josef Kessler, and Wolf-Dieter Heiss. 1996. Cerebral representations of one's own past: Neural networks involved in autobiographical memory. *The Journal of Neuroscience* 16 (13):4275–4282.

Fitzgibbon, Bernadette M., Peter G. Enticott, Anina N. Rich, Melita J. Giummarra, Nellie Georgiou-Karistianis, Jack W. Tsao, Sharon R. Weeks, and John L. Bradshaw. 2010. High incidence of 'synaesthesia for pain' in amputees. *Neuropsychologia* 48 (12):3675–3678.

Fitzgibbon, Bernadette M., Melita J. Giummarra, Nellie Georgiou-Karistianis, Peter G. Enticott, and John L. Bradshaw. 2010. Shared pain: From empathy to synaesthesia. *Neuroscience and Biobehavioral Reviews* 34 (4):500–512.

Franz, Elizabeth A., Shelley Ford, and Simon Werner. 2007. Brain and cognitive processes of imitation in bimanual situations: Making inference about mirror neuron systems. *Brain Research* 1145:138–149.

Gallese, Vittorio, Luciano Fadiga, Leonardo Fogassi, and Giacomo Rizzolatti. 1996. Action recognition in the premotor cortex. *Brain* 119:593–609.

Gallese, Vittorio, and Alvin Goldman. 1998. Mirror neurons and simulation theory of mind reading. *Trends in Cognitive Sciences* 2 (12):493–501.

Gallese, Vittorio, Christian Keysers, and Giacomo Rizzolatti. 2004. A unifying view of the basis of social cognition. *Trends in Cognitive Sciences* 8 (9):396–403.

Giummarra, Melita J., Stephen J. Gibson, Nellie Georgiou-Karistianis, and John L. Bradshaw. 2008. Mechanisms underlying embodiment, disembodiment and loss of embodiment. *Neuroscience and Biobehavioural Reviews* 32:143–160.

Goldman, Alvin, and Chandra S. Sripada. 2005. Simulationist models of face-based emotion recognition. *Cognition* 94:193–213.

Goller, Aviva I., Kerrie Richards, Steven Novak, and Jamie Ward. 2013. Mirror-touch synaesthesia in phantom limbs of amputees. *Cortex* 49:243–251.

Gray, J. A., Chopping, S., Nunn, J., Parslow, D., Gregory, L., Williams, S., M. J. Brammer and S. Baron Cohen. 2002. Implications of synaesthesia for functionalism. *Journal of Consciousness Studies* 9 (12):5–31.

Holle, Henning, Michael J. Banissy, Thomas Wright, Natalie Bowling, and Jamie Ward. 2011. 'That's not a real body': Identifying stimulus qualities that modulate synaesthetic experiences of touch. *Consciousness and Cognition* 20 (3):720–726.

Hubbard, Edward M., and Vilanayur S. Ramachandran. 2005. Neurocognitive mechanisms of synaesthesia. *Neuron* 48:509–520.

Iriki, Atsushi, Michio Tanaka, and Yoshiaki Iwamura. 1996. Coding of modified body schema during tool use by macaque postcentral neurones. *Neuroreport* 7 (14):2325–2330.

Ishida, Hiroaki, Katsumi Nakajima, Masahiko Inase, and Akira Murata. 2009. Shared mapping of own and others' bodies in visuotactile bimodal area of monkey parietal cortex. *Journal of Cognitive Neuroscience* 22 (1):83–96.

Keysers, Christian, and Vittorio Gazzola. 2006. Towards a unifying theory of social cognition. *Progress in Brain Research* 156:379–401.

Keysers, Christian, Bruno Wicker, Valeria Gazzola, Jean-Luc Anton, Leonardo Fogassi, and Vittorio Gallese. 2004. A touching sight: SII/PV activation during the observation and experience of touch. *Neuron* 42:335–346.

Kircher, Tilo T. J., Carl Senior, Mary L. Phillips, Sophia Rabe-Hesketh, Philip J. Benson, Edward T. Bullmore, Mick Brammer, Andrew Simmons, Mathias Bartels, and Anthony S. David. 2001. Recognizing one's own face. *Cognition* 78:B1–B15.

Konen, Christina S., and Sabine Kaster. 2008. Two hierarchically organized neural systems for object information in human visual cortex. *Nature Neuroscience* 11:224–231.

Lamm, Claus, and Tania Singer. 2010. The role of the anterior insula cortex in social emotions. *Brain Structure & Function* 214 (5–6):579–591.

Maravita, Angelo, and Atsushi Iriki. 2002. Tools for the body (schema). *Trends in Cognitive Sciences* 8 (2):79–86.

McCabe, Ciara, Edmund T. Rolls, Amy Bilderbeck, and Francis McGlone. 2008. Cognitive influences on the affective representations of touch and the sight of touch in the human brain. *Social Cognitive and Affective Neuroscience* 3 (2):97–108.

Meier, Beat, and Nicolas Rothen. 2009. Training grapheme-colour associations produces a synaesthetic Stroop effect, but not a conditioned synaesthetic response. *Neuropsychologia* 47:1208–1211.

Morrison, India, Donna Lloyd, Giuseppe di Pellegrino, and Neil Roberts. 2004. Vicarious responses to pain anterior cingulated cortex: Is empathy a multisensory issue? *Cognitive, Affective, & Behavioral Neuroscience* 4 (2):270–278.

Nummenmaa, Lauri, Jussi Hirvonen, Riitta Parkkola, and Jari K. Hietanen. 2008. Is emotional contagion special? An fMRI study on neural systems for affective and cognitive empathy. *NeuroImage* 43 (3):571–580.

Oberman, Lindsay M., and Vilanayur S. Ramachandran. 2007. The simulating social mind: The role of the mirror neuron system and simulation in the social and communicative deficits of autism spectrum disorders. *Psychological Bulletin* 133 (2):310–327.

Oberman, Lindsay M., Piotr Winkielman, and Vilayanur S. Ramachandran. 2007. Face to face: Blocking facial mimicry can selectively impair recognition of emotional expressions. *Social Neuroscience* 2 (3–4):167–178.

Pitcher, David, Lúcia Garrido, Vincent Walsh, and Bradley C. Duchaine. 2008. Transcranial magnetic stimulation disrupts the perception and embodiment of facial expressions. *The Journal of Neuroscience* 28 (36):8929–8933.

Ramachandran, Vilanayur S., and David Brang. 2009. Sensations evoked in patients with amputation from watching an individual whose corresponding intact limb is being touched. *Archives of Neurology* 66:1281–1284.

Ramachandran, Vilanayur S., and Edward M. Hubbard, E. 2001. Synaesthesia: A window into perception, thought and language. *Journal of Consciousness Studies* 8:3–34.

Rich, Anina N., John L. Bradshaw, and Jason B. Mattingley. 2005. A systematic large-scale study of synaesthesia: Implications for the role of early experience in lexical-colour associations. *Cognition* 98 (1):53–84.

Rich, Anina N., and Jason B. Mattingley. 2002. Anomalous perception in synaesthesia: A cognitive neuroscience. *Nature Reviews Neuroscience* 3:43–52.

Rizzolatti, Giacomo, and Laila Craighero. 2004. The mirror-neuron system. *Annual Review of Neuroscience* 27:169–192.

Ro, Tony, Alessandro Farnè, Ruth M. Johnson, Van Wedeen, Zili Chu, Zhiyue Wang, Jill V. Hunter, and Michael S. Beauchamp. 2007. Feeling sounds after a thalamic lesion. *Annals of Neurology* 62 (5):433–441.

Ruby, Perrine, and Jean Decety. 2001. Effect of subjective perspective taking during simulation of action: A PET investigation of agency. *Nature Neuroscience* 4:546–550.

Sagiv, Noam, and Jamie Ward. 2006. Cross-modal interactions: Lessons from Synaesthesia. *Progress in Brain Research* 155:259–271.

Schofield, W. N. 1976. Do children find movements which cross the body midline difficult? *Quarterly Journal of Experimental Psychology* 28:571–582.

Serino, Andrea, Francesca Pizzoferrato, and Elisabetta Làdavas. 2008. Viewing a face (especially one's own face) being touched enhances tactile perception on the face. *Psychological Science* 19 (5):434–438.

Shamay-Tsoory, Simone G., Judith Aharon-Peretz, and Daniella Perry. 2009. Two systems for empathy: A double dissociation between emotional and cognitive empathy in inferior frontal gyrus versus ventromedial prefrontal lesions. *Brain* 132:617–627.

Simner Julia and Roger H. Logie. 2007. Synaesthetic consistency spans decades in a lexical-gustatory synaesthete. *Neurocase* 13:358–365.

Simner, Julia, Catherine Mulvenna, Noam Sagiv, Elias Tsakanikos, Sarah A. Witherby, Christine Fraser, Kirsten Scott, and Jamie Ward. 2006. Synaesthesia: The prevalence of atypical cross-modal experiences. *Perception* 35:1024–1033.

Simner, Julia, Jamie Ward, Monika Lanz, Ashok Jansari, Krist Noonan, Louise Glover, and David A. Oakley. 2005. Non-random associations of graphemes and colour in the synaesthetic and normal populations. *Cognitive Neuropsychology* 22 (8):1069–1085.

Singer, Tania, Ben Seymour, John O'Doherty, Holger Kaube,, Raymond J. Dolan, and Chris D. Frith. 2004. Empathy for pain involves the affective but not sensory components of pain. *Science* 303:1157–1162.

Smilek, Daniel, Mike J. Dixon, Cera Cudahy, and Philip M. Merikle. 2001. Synaesthetic photisms influence visual perception. *Journal of Cognitive Neuroscience* 13 (7):930–936.

Van der Gaag, Christiaan, Ruud B. Minderaa, and Christian Keysers. 2007. Facial expressions: What the mirror neuron system can and cannot tell us. *Social Neuroscience* 2 (3–4):179–222.

Ward, Jamie, Brett Huckstep, and Elias Tsakanikos. 2006. Sound-colour synaesthesia: To what extent does it use cross-modal mechanisms common to us all. *Cortex* 42 (2):264–280.

Ward, Jamie, and Jason B. Mattingley. 2006. Synaesthesia: An overview of contemporary findings and controversies. *Cortex* 42:129–136.

Ward, Jamie, and Julia Simner. 2003. Lexical-gustatory synaesthesia: Linguistic and conceptual factors. *Cognition* 89 (3):237–261.

Ward, Jamie, Julia Simner, and Vivian Auyeung. 2005. A comparison of lexical-gustatory and grapheme-colour synaesthesia. *Cognitive Neuropsychology* 22 (1):28–41.

Warren, Jane E., Disa A. Sauter, Frank Eisner, Jade Wiland, M. Alexander Dresner, Richard J. S. Wise, Stuart Rosen, and Sophie K. Scott. 2006. Positive emotions preferentially engage an auditory-motor 'mirror' system. *The Journal of Neuroscience* 26:13067–13075.

White, Rebekah C., and Aimola Davies, Anne M. (2012). Specular vision-touch synaesthesia: two reference frames. *Perception* 41:871–874.

Wicker, Bruno, Christian Keysers, Jane Plailly, Jean-Pierre Royet, Vittorio Gallese, and Giacomo Rizzolatti. 2003. Both of us disgusted in my insula: The common neural basis of seeing and feeling disgust. *Neuron* 40:655–664.

Winston, J., O'Doherty, J., and Dolan, R. 2003. Common and distinct neural during direct and incidental processing of multiple facial emotions. *NeuroImage* 20 (1):84–97.

Yaro, Caroline, and Jamie Ward. 2007. Searching for Shereshevski: What is superior about the memory of synaesthetes? *Quarterly Journal of Experimental Psychology* 60 (5):681–695.

PART VI

COSTS AND BENEFITS: CREATIVITY, MEMORY, AND IMAGERY

CHAPTER 31

....

SYNESTHESIA AND CREATIVITY

....

CATHERINE M. MULVENNA

INTRODUCTION

In the late 1800s, a Frenchman by the name of Alfred Binet, described as a loner and a self-taught psychologist, embarked on a career that had a profound and long-term impact on our understanding of the human mind. His forward-thinking contributions included the idea that human intelligence can be measured (leading to the IQ test), and that even unusual human preferences can be categorized and explained (even taboo preferences such as "erotic fetishism," a term he coined). In the midst of Binet's writings is a text that talks of synesthetes. In particular, Binet makes the simple observation that synesthetes possess a lively imagination (Binet 1893; see Baron-Cohen et al. 1987), thus making him possibly the first to highlight a longstanding and notoriously debated link between synesthesia and creativity. Over a century later, the literature on synesthesia and creativity continues to raise many questions: are synesthetes exceptionally creative? Is there any evidence for this or does media reporting of synesthetic artists simply drive this idea? Could synesthesia itself be a form of creativity? Furthermore, since creativity comes in a plethora of different forms—from painting to brainstorming—might synesthetes' apparent "lively imaginations" serve them in *all* domains, or just in some of them?

These questions and others are dealt with in the chapter that follows. To this end, some related topics need to be covered in a little detail, such as what exactly creativity is and how it can be measured—a lofty topic, but one that is approachable within the confines of psychological testing. The present chapter is deliberately thorough in its account of creativity testing and the methodological idiosyncrasies that this requires. Thus, this review may serve as a tool to help future investigators contribute to the growing literature on this topic as much as it can provide an overview of previous works. In parallel with the account of experimental creativity tests in the field, the literature that concentrates on testing creativity specifically in synesthetes is also presented. The chapter then moves on to consider the broader questions that have fascinated artists, scientists, and layman alike for decades, such as how and why synesthetes may have increased artistry or creative thinking skills, and what this means for our understanding of creativity in the neural mechanisms of synesthesia. For what we learn about creativity in synesthetes, indeed in any population that excels in creativity, can be used to shed light on the basis of creativity in all of us.

The Investigation of Individual Differences in Synesthesia

The question of creativity in synesthetes relates not only to the characteristics of this relatively rare population, but holds a greater relevance beyond the field of synesthesia. This broader relevance concerns the question of how attributes relate to, and are generated by, the tens of billions of neurons in the human brain. It is highly attractive to neuropsychologists and neuroscientists to potentially relate an individual's capacity for generating novel ideas or generating fine pieces of art to discrete differences in patterns of neural activation or structure. Furthermore, it offers positive methodological sensibilities: the synesthete population is relatively accessible and straightforward to investigate. Within the field of neuropsychology, we use atypical cognition to make inferences about typical brain function (Gazzaniga and Miller 1989). Historically, the field has tended to focus on impaired brains, as for example, in lesion studies, which can reveal the cognitive function(s) typically performed by what have become damaged cortical areas on a case-by-case basis in impaired patients (Farah and Feinberg 2000). Such methods provide valuable insights into normal neurocognitive function. However, due to the nature of these methods, the information gained is typically (and understandably) compromised by the interferences of medication, rehabilitation and variance in location and severity of damage (Farah and Feinberg 2000). By contrast, synesthetes present with atypical cortical function and structure (e.g., Nunn et al. 2002; Rouw and Scholte 2007), and atypical perception and cognition (e.g., Marks 1978; Rich and Mattingley 2001), but are a healthy, high-functioning, non-medicated group (see Cytowic 1995; Ramachandran and Hubbard 2001). Furthermore, synesthetes have relatively *systematic*, stable, and spatially localized differences in neurophysiology (e.g., Nunn et al. 2002; Rouw and Scholte 2007, and their perceptual and cognitive differences examined thus far are stable (e.g., Marks 1978; Rich and Mattingley 2001). Thus, the synesthete population offers several benefits that make them an attractive and valuable population for future investigation of the neural basis of cognitive and perceptual functions in the human brain. The present chapter focuses on creativity, and later will describe how the study of synesthesia can inform about the neural underpinnings of creative thinking and bring us closer to answering the question of what it takes for the human brain to generate a novel idea.

The Beginnings—Creativity in the art World

Before it became a topic for the science community, the question of creativity in synesthetes had its beginnings in the art world. Both synesthetes and non-synesthetes alike have drawn upon the idea of synesthesia to produce artistic pieces, and some of the world's most celebrated creative individuals appear to have been synesthetes, including painters David Hockney Joan Mitchell and Vincent Van Gough, composers Oliver Messaien and Leonard Bernstein, drummer Elvin Jones, writer Vladimir Nabokov (see Box 31.1).

Box 31.1 Highly creative individuals over the last 100 years have been describing cross-sensory experiences highly indicative of synesthesia

"Colors are very important to me because I have a gift—it's not my fault, it's just how I am—whenever I hear music or even if I read music, I see colors." He claimed peculiarities like "the lower range of C-sharp was 'copper with gold highlights,' D flat was 'orange with stripes of pale yellow, red and gold.'" (Duffy 2001 and Cytowic 2002)

French composer *Olivier Messiaen*

There are pale blue spots on the yellow glare. Only my eyes saw the pale blue spots. They did my eyes good. Why didn't anyone else? (Kandinsky 1981)

Russian painter *Vasily Kandinsky*

Sounds are clothed in colors and colors in music. (Baudelaire 1971)

French symbolist poet *Charles Baudelaire*

"B" has the tone called burnt sienna by painters...dull green, combined somehow with violet is the best I can do for "W." (Nalokov 1947)

Russian novelist *Vladimir Nabokov*

The letter G is black with glints of yellow in it. I can't figure out why the yellow glints are there; it's just the way G looks. (Duffy 2001)

American writer *Patricia Lynne Duffy* (living classified synesthete)

I listened to *Dieu Parmi Nous* (God amongst us) and I thought it was wonderful...I could see dark blue's/orange and numerous complementary colours playing against each other. (Mark Rowan-Hull personal communication)

English Painter *Mark Rowan-Hull* (living classified synesthete)

When I see equations, I see the letters in colours—I don't know why. As I'm talking, I see...light-tan j's, slightly violet-blueish n's and dark brown x's flying around. And I wonder what the hell it must look like to students. (Feynman 1988)

American Nobel Prize-winning physicist *Richard Feynman*

Over and above impacting particular individuals, synesthesia may have fundamentally changed the trajectory of art over the last century. Take, for example, Wassily Kandinsky, who is believed to have experienced complex audio-visual synesthesia (Mulvenna 2012); i.e., images of moving, colored shapes triggered by music. It is said that the paintings in which he depicted his rich and wild synesthetic images gave birth to the revolutionary doctrine of Abstraction[1] (Brougher et al. 2005). Whether or not this is accurate, synesthesia was undoubtedly a popular idea in early art symbolism. From that era onwards a strong link between synesthesia and the arts was forged and reinforced, and this continues among artists today (for discussion, see Berman, Steen, and Maurer 2008; Mulvenna 2003; van Campen 1997; see also, Steen and Berman, Chapter 34; van Campen, Chapter 32, this volume). This connection raised both excitement that synesthesia could possibly be "causing" creativity, and cynicism that the link was nothing more than an over-reporting of synesthetic artists in the media (see Kay and Mulvenna 2006). For some time, what was understood about art and synesthesia was derived from a body of literature that was rich in anecdotal example but low on direct, empirical evidence. What needed to be established was whether the synesthete population as a whole exhibits a set of creative abilities that exceeds those of their non-synesthetic counterparts. Thus began scientific investigations into creativity and synesthesia.

WHAT IS CREATIVITY?[2]

Creativity is a complex construct to define, almost to the point of infamy within fields of systematic investigation (see Folley 2006). However, a surprisingly tangible model emerges when one looks solely to state-of-the-art investigations: creativity occurs when a process or a product is considered both *novel* and *appropriate* for the task situation (Abraham and Windmann 2007; Amabile 1996; Andreasen 1978; Csikszentmihalyi 1998; Feist 1993; Guilford 1967; MacKinnon 1970; Martindale 1999; Rothenberg 1976; Runco and Charles 1993; Simonton 1988; Sternberg 1988; Sternberg and Lubart 1995). Nonetheless, there are different types of creativity and I turn to this next.

---

[1] In the arts, abstraction typically refers to works that are not a literal depiction of experience. In the case of synesthetic art, the works often are the literal depiction of *synesthetic* experience. It is interesting to consider whether this type of synesthetic art will remain under the umbrella of abstraction in its classic sense, whether it moves into realism, or whether it is 'idio-realism' in that it depicts the idiosyncratic reality of the artist, but can still be appreciated as an abstract representation by other observers.

[2] Since creativity is conceptually complex (see Folley 2006), consideration has been taken to systematically and comprehensively review the relevant aspects of the field as much as possible, while remaining within the space constraints of the present chapter. The exploration of what creativity means to society outside of science and across different cultures extends beyond the scope of the current chapter.

Types of Creativity: the Distinction between Creative Cognition and Creative Output

Despite a range of creativity domains (the visual arts, performance art, brainstorming, etc.), the number of creativity tests in psychological research is relatively modest. These tests fall into two categories—those for *creative output* (e.g., Amabile 1983, 1996) and those for *creative cognition* (Finke, Ward, and Smith 1992; Smith, Ward, and Fink 1995). Creative output (e.g., a painting or a performance) requires, at least, a particular skill set that is physical, perceptual and/or verbal. However, creative cognition (e.g., the *ideas* behind a painting or performance, such as whether to use a novel paint-dripping technique) requires, at least, a particular skill set of associative and emergent thinking. Individuals whom we peg as creative might excel in either creative output or creative cognition or both. The question we will ask later is whether synesthetes as a group excel in creative output or in creative cognition, or both, or indeed, as some researchers on the extreme of the debate may still argue, none of these at all.

Measurement of creative output

Creative output concerns the presentation of an idea in a secondary medium (Baer 1993, 1998; Baer and Kaufman 2008; Kaufman and Baer 2004; Plucker 1998; Plucker and Beghetto 2004) and includes the categories of visual arts, performing arts, arts and crafts, and culinary arts. It is considered the most complex form of creativity to measure (see Getzels and Csikszentmihalyi 1976). In contrast to creative cognition, where the aim can be described as solution-finding to a prescribed problem (see later), creative output typically has the aim of self-expression and subjective aesthetics. Since the aim of creative output in everyday life is more ambiguous, what exactly to measure in the laboratory is more ambiguous too.

An additional complexity in the measurement of creative output is the secondary medium itself. The individual who produces creative output requires not just an idea, but also production skills (the motor skills to paint, the auditory skills for memory and differentiation between sounds, etc.), domain-relevant knowledge (to know what is novel and appropriate in this domain), and the intrinsic motivation to communicate through secondary media (Amabile 1983; Csikszentmihalyi 1996; Heilman et al. 2003). The experimenter is faced with the challenge of how to compare creative outputs from different media, for example, from the painting to the poem. Additionally, the likelihood of an individual generating creative output is strongly influenced by factors such as socioeconomic status and cultural environment, so between-group matching is highly advisable (and I return to this later). Three main approaches to the measurement of creative output are described in the following section, along with their relative methodological challenges.

Measurement of creative output: self-report

One approach to measuring an individual's creative output is to have them self-report their creative achievements, which has been used by several synesthesia studies (Rich, Bradshaw, and Mattingley 2005; Sitton and Pierce 2004; Ward et al. 2008). Self-report questionnaires can be used on large numbers of participants and have the additional, crucial benefit of allowing responders to refer to different creative media, therefore allowing these to be directly compared. Tests of creative product can have a test–retest reliability of r = 0.81 (Creative Achievement Questionnaire; Folley 2006) but rely on accurate subjective reporting, and so can be affected by personal interpretations of what should be reported as an achievement, and also by memory, age, and socioeconomic factors. To counteract the latter issues, strict demographic matching between groups is important because some groups suffer response biases more than others; women choose significantly more extreme responses than men (i.e., the 7s and 1s in a 7-point scale more than the 4s; Crandall 1973; Newcomb, Huba, and Bentler 1986). Age correlates negatively with working memory, which can affect the amount of information reported. Education and culture also impact moderate versus extreme biases in responding (Hui and Traindis 1989). The self-report method is especially vulnerable to response biases (e.g., Harrison et al. 1996; Lanyon and Goodstein 1997); including one particular bias known as the *social desirability bias*. This is the tendency for participants to represent themselves in a favorable light, either consciously or unconsciously (e.g., Crowne and Marlowe 1964; Edwards 1953). This means that self-referred synesthetes, for example, may describe themselves as more creative than they really are. They may also do this simply from knowing that synesthesia is often associated with art.

In the case of response biases, future experiments could keep participants blind to their synesthete classification, or (mis)lead all groups to believe they have been selected because of high creativity (thus balancing any possible skew in the response bias of synesthetes). One can also collect information from participants that reveal their individual likelihood of susceptibility to a social desirability bias, which can then be considered at the analysis stage. Examples of techniques include: (1) incorporating social desirability or "lie scales" into the self-report material (e.g., the *Marlowe-Crowne Social Desirability Scale*; Crowne and Marlowe 1960; and the *Lie scale of the Eysenck Personality Inventory*; Eysenck and Eysenck 1964) or (2) collecting additional reports from other individuals who know or observe the participant (e.g., Conway and Huffcutt 1997; Furnham and Stringfield 1994; Harris and Schaubroeck 1988; Reid, King, and Wickwire 1959; Yamamoto 1964).

Several studies have used self-report questionnaires to gather information about creative output in synesthetes (Rich, Bradshaw, and Mattingley 2005; Sitton and Pierce

2004; Ward et al. 2008) and they all show that synesthetes engage in creative activities (professions, hobbies, etc.) more than non-synesthetes. For instance, in one particularly fruitful investigation, Rich, Bradshaw, and Mattingley (2005) used advertisements in a newspaper to recruit individuals who believed they had synesthesia in Australia. With an eventual testing sample of 192 synesthetes (and non-synesthetes recruited with a different method), a comprehensive set of structured questionnaires found that synesthetes (24%) were over ten times more likely to engage in artistic pursuits in or outside work than a group of non-synesthetes (1–2%). Ward et al. (2008) showed that the tendency for synesthetes to engage in creative arts was, at least in part, dependent on their particular type of synesthesia (e.g., those with music-triggered synesthesia were more likely to play an instrument than other synesthetes). Collectively, studies of this kind indicate that synesthetes do pursue the arts more than non-synesthetes. Future studies may ask whether this significant relationship withstands tests that are not as sensitive to response biases and self-selection (which I return to later in this chapter).

Measurement of creative output: the consensual assessment technique

A second common measure of creative output is the *Consensual Assessment Technique* (CAT; Amabile 1982; see Baer and McKool 2009 for review). This approach tries to overcome the challenge of comparing between creative media by setting a task that involves only one medium (Getzels and Csikszentmihalyi 1976). In this experiment, a product is asked for, such as a collage, a painting, or a story. The determining factor of whether an individual's output is creative is the consensus of three or more independent judges, preselected based on their positions as experts in the field. This creativity measurement is therefore unusual—and hailed as advantageous—because there is no predetermined scoring system for the creative product; i.e., it does not depend on any one theory of creativity. Another advantage is that the results are not based on self-report. Furthermore, it is less susceptible to biases from socioeconomic status and familial attitude to the arts because it ignores past creative output and focuses solely on the creative expression during the experiment. The inter-rater reliability of the separate judge's scoring is reported in each experiment, thus revealing the weight of the "consensus."

The CAT is reported to have high internal and external validity (see Amabile 1996; Baer 1993, 1998; Baer and McKool 2009; Carson 2006) but has not yet been applied to the study of creativity in synesthetes. One question about artistic synesthetes concerns whether they are being creative per se, or if they are merely depicting their synesthetic experience, e.g., producing a painting of their visual experiences in audio-visual synesthesia. The question is whether (1) there is an act of creativity if there is no symbolism involved and (2) whether works that do not depict synesthetic experiences by the same artist would be judged as creative. The CAT would be ideal in addressing these issues, since the prescribed task would be independent of synesthetic experiences.

Measurement of creative output: tests of figural creativity

A third approach is to test the ability to translate a creative idea through a secondary medium. The *Torrance Test of Creative Thinking—Figural Form* (TTCTf) asks participants to generate multiple different ideas and translate them through simple figures/drawings that are akin to doodles (Torrance and Ball 1984). The responses are not scored for artistic aesthetics, but rather, are intricately scored on three main measures of creativity: *fluency* (the number of relevant ideas produced), *originality* (the statistical rarity of each partial response; i.e., whether they are ideas away from the obvious and established), and *flexibility* (the variance of categories covered in each response; and I return to this feature later). This approach uniformly assesses the non-verbal ability of an individual to generate and express ideas creatively, and requires no artistic quality to receive a high score (Chase 1985). The figural Torrance Test has been used in one investigation of creativity in 13 objectively classified grapheme-color synesthetes, who scored no differently to non-synesthete controls (Mulvenna 2012), and I discuss the implications of this in a later section.

The collective results of investigations of creative output in synesthetes indicate that synesthetes pursue the arts more than non-synesthetes but that they are not more proficient at communicating creative ideas through secondary media. Several scenarios could explain this apparent oxymoron, such as the difference between different subtypes of synesthesias (only grapheme-color synesthetes were tested for figural creativity, but multiple subtypes of synesthetes gave self-reports of artistic pursuits) or the different methodologies (e.g., self-report measures of creative pursuit, and psychometric tests of creative translation). However, another explanation for these two seemingly incongruent conclusions is that synesthesia may have two almost parallel relationships with creativity. I discuss this later in the chapter (see "A dual model of creativity and art in synesthetes") but now turn to the second type of creativity, creative cognition.

CREATIVE COGNITION

Creative cognition is the process of generating *ideas* that are both novel and appropriate (Finke et al. 1992; Smith et al. 1995). It is commonly referred to as *problem-solving*, or *abstract*, or *divergent*, or *lateral thinking*, or *analogical reasoning* (Green et al. 2006; Holyoak and Thagard 1997) and can be applied to a wide variety of goals that transcend aesthetics or artistic creation (Edelman 2006), from "... [hypothesizing] the structure of the atom, to laying out a garden" (Cattel and Butcher 1968, 279).

The importance of understanding the mechanisms of creative cognition has long been recognized due to its role in innovation and progression (Holyoak and Thagard 1995; Mayer 1999; Sternberg 1977). Thus, if synesthetes were found to excel in creative cognition they could be considered a population of innovators and so may be particularly desirable in any situation that called for problem-solvers. With regards to research into the mechanisms of creativity, one could target synesthetes in particular, and I return to this later in the chapter. Next I review three main approaches to the measurement of creative cognition—self-report questionnaires, divergent thinking tasks, and convergent thinking tasks.

Measurement of creative cognition: self-report

The first method is the use of self-report questionnaires (Domino 1994; Myers 1945; Runco, Plucker, and Lim 2001). For instance, the *Runco Ideational Behavior Scale* uses an individual's subjective accounts of his or her own thinking style, or adjectives they would use to describe themselves, to generate a numerical score that enables direct, quantitative comparison between individuals or groups (Runco et al. 2001). One study (Domino 1989) showed that synesthetes generated higher scores than non-synesthete controls on this type of self-report creativity questionnaire. However, the advantages and disadvantages of self-report methodologies have already been described earlier in the chapter, and they apply equally to this type of self-report questionnaire in creative cognition. Furthermore, Domino recruited what we will later term "self-reported synesthetes," and this causes additional problems in interpreting his results (see "Classification of groups: a caution about self-reported synesthetes").

Measurement of creative cognition: divergent thinking tasks

In psychometric tests of divergent thinking, participants are presented with open-ended problems/questions and asked to generate multiple alternative responses. For example, participants may be asked how life on earth would change if all we could see of people were their feet (in the Torrance Test of Creative Thinking, see next paragraph). Every alternative response the participant generates receives an individual creativity score. The questions are designed so that there can be seemingly infinite alternative responses. Answers are not correct or incorrect, but rather, are high or low in originality and/or flexibility, typically with a systematic approach to scoring originality (Binet and Henri 1895; Guilford 1950, 1959, 1967).

The main test of divergent thinking is the *Torrance Test of Creative Thinking* (TTCTv; Torrance 1966, 1974, updated 1998) which contains six creative cognition questions to be answered with pen and paper within prescribed 5- and 10-minute time limits. Every response made by a participant, who can produce up to 40 or more in the time limit, is again given individual scores for fluency, originality, and flexibility (see earlier). The inclusion of flexibility (i.e., the ability to produce a variety of kinds of ideas; e.g., alternative uses of a cardboard box might not just be as a container, but also as clothing, furniture, a toy, something to throw, etc.) is important because flexibility has long been recognized as central to the creative process, being referred to as *associative hierarchies* (Mednick 1962), or *defocused attention* (Mendelsohn 1976). High mental flexibility is associated with co-activation and communication between regions of the brain that ordinarily are not strongly associated (Heilman, Nadeau, and Beversdorf 2003) and incidentally, this is a description that is also given to neural activity in synesthetes (for review see Bargary and Mitchell 2008, and Part V of this volume).

Domino (1989) was the first synesthesia investigator to use divergent thinking tasks (e.g., *The Similes Test*; Schaefer 1969). He compared an impressively large sample of 61 synesthetes to 61 non-synesthetes, finding that synesthetes out-performed their controls. However, since the investigation occurred before an objective measure of synesthesia was widely used, such as consistency testing,[3] the classification method for synesthetes was solely self-report, and this raises possible problems for internal validity (see later, also Mulvenna 2003, 2007; van Campen 1997; Ward et al. 2008). Later investigations did use objective measures to verify synesthesia: Mulvenna (2003, 2012) found that overall scores in the TTCTv, plus its scores for fluency flexibility and originality individually, were significantly higher for synesthetes compared to non-synesthetes. Thus far, only one of the most common subtypes of synesthesia has been tested with the TTCTv; namely grapheme-color synesthesia (occurring in approximately 1% of the general population; Simner et al 2006). Future investigations can clarify whether this relationship extends to all forms of synesthesia.

One of the six questions in the TTCTv is an *Alternate Uses Task* (Guilford, Christensen, Merrifield and Wilson 1978; Wallach and Kogan 1965), and this can also be used as a stand-alone measurement. In one recent amended version of the Alternate Uses Task without the standard scoring for originality, Ward et al. (2008) found no difference between a large sample of synesthetes and non-synesthetes in their fluency scores. With regards to divergent thinking and creativity, the omission of the standard originality scoring of Guilford's Alternate Uses Task (Binet and Henri 1895; Guilford 1950, 1956, 1959, 1967; for discussion see Abraham and Windmann 2007) makes it difficult to draw a comparison to standard investigations of creativity. However, with regards to the broader quest to understand the idiosyncrasies of the synesthete population as a whole, this task was useful in indicating that synesthetes perform no differently from non-synesthetes in their ability to generate multiple responses (i.e., in their verbal fluency).

Measurement of creative cognition: convergent thinking tasks

A third common measure of creative cognition is a convergent thinking task. *Convergent thinking* is a term applied to creative questions for which there is only one correct answer,

---

[3] In a standard synesthetic consistency test, suspected synesthetes describe their synesthetic associations for a list of stimuli (e.g., they provide their colors for a list of letters). They are later recalled without warning to repeat the test and their consistency across tests is assessed. Synesthetes tend to be highly consistent over time and they can be compared to controls, who are instructed to invent analogous associations, but are significantly less consistent in recalling them. See Johnson, Allison, and Baron-Cohen (Chapter 1, this volume) for more details on this test, and how it has been used in synesthesia research.

with the assumption that feats of mental flexibility and broad association are necessary to arrive at that answer. Convergent thinking questions therefore differ from divergent thinking questions, which have infinite possible responses. In the *Remote Associates Test* (RAT) (Mednick 1962), the classic convergent thinking task, every question involves the presentation of three words. The participant is asked to report another word that connects all three presented words (e.g., "boot," "summer," "ground" = "camp"). This task—like divergent thinking—generates an objective numerical score of one type of creativity which can be compared across individuals. However it involves word generation (as a model for idea generation), and therefore relies heavily on language ability and education level. When the RAT was carried out by a large sample of self-selected synesthetes (see later for a discussion on this method of recruitment), they scored significantly higher than non-synesthetes, which suggests that synesthetes excel in the convergent thinking form of creative cognition (Ward et al. 2008).

CREATIVE PERCEPTION

Thus far we have talked about measurements of creative cognition and creative outputs. However, many have claimed that central to any individual's creative ability is also an elevated propensity for, and appreciation of, visual imagery (e.g., Shepard 1978), termed *the creative eye*, or *creative perception*. This type of creativity does not rely on any previous creative experience or verbal fluency skills, and is therefore free of the environmental constraints on most other creative domains. The *Barron–Welsh Revised Art Scale* (BWRAS; Barron 1963) is "a non-verbal predictor of…openness to experience and associative richness associated with the creative temperament." In this, participants must indicate whether they "like" or "dislike" each of a set of black line drawings and their responses are compared with those of a comparison population of artists (whose preferences for these pictures were significantly different to non-artist controls). Like the CAT, the TTCTf and divergent thinking tasks (and in contrast to self-report measures of creative cognition or creative output) a participant can have no previous experience in, or exposure to, the arts and still achieve a high score in the creative perception test.

If the relation between synesthesia and creativity were driven solely by synesthetic experiences, one might expect visual synesthetes (e.g., grapheme-color synesthetes) to excel in this test of (visual) creative perception and not in other forms of creativity. However, one investigation of creative perception in synesthetes (Mulvenna 2012) found quite the opposite pattern: grapheme-color synesthetes scored no differently to highly matched non-synesthetes in creative perception (but see Domino 1989), but scored significantly higher in creative cognition (Mulvenna, 2012, described earlier). This unexpected finding will be discussed with the other findings at the end of this chapter. Before then, I describe several important methodological considerations in the testing of creativity in synesthetes.

QUASI-EXPERIMENTS IN THE INVESTIGATION OF CREATIVITY IN SYNESTHETES

Experiments that compare the creativity of synesthetes to non-synesthetes fall under the category of "quasi-experiment" because individuals are assigned to groups based on a dependant variable that is already present (or has already occurred). In such studies there is a risk of pre-existing confounding variable(s) and therefore, care must be taken in: (1) the classification of groups and (2) the matching across groups; these issues shall be touched upon here.

Classification of groups: a caution about self-reported synesthetes

Standard synesthesia classification indicates that 4% of all individuals are synesthetes (Simner et al. 2006), but between 20% and 80% of individuals *claim* to be synesthetes (Kay and Mulvenna 2006; Mulvenna 2003; Simner et al. 2006). The classifications of the "synesthete group" in creativity studies may therefore be confounded by this high rate of false-positives, if classification relies on self-report only. This is the case for several early studies, which were either conducted before the standard test for objective synesthesia classification was widely established (Domino 1989), or where the researchers elected not to use it (Sitton and Pierce 2004). Taken alone, it would have been difficult to distinguish whether the studies identified factors that were significantly related to synesthetes, or factors that were significantly related to individuals who self-report experiences of synesthesia (and who may be, for example, simply suggestible non-synesthetes). Particularly important is that false-positives in self-reporting synesthesia very often come from artists, who mistake "synesthesia" for a heightened appreciation of color (Simner 2012; Simner et al. 2006). This, of course, could have catastrophic consequences for any investigation of creativity in synesthetes. Fortunately, the main finding from both Domino (1989) and Sitton and Pierce (2004)—that synesthetes have increased creative cognition—was replicated in investigations that used objective, robust means to classify synesthetes (e.g., Mulvenna 2012; Ward et al 2008). One finding, however, (a significant advantage for synesthetes in creative perception; Domino 1989) was *not* replicated when synesthetes were objectively verified and self-report biases were removed (Mulvenna 2012). Future studies are therefore encouraged to continue to exploit the now-well-known objective measures to identify synesthetes (e.g., consistency over time) if their creativity is under investigation.

Matching across groups: a caution about demographics and recruitment

I noted earlier that demographic factors correlate directly and strongly with creativity and should be adequately controlled for. The main factors in question are: gender (e.g., Kaufman and Baer 2008, age (e.g., Feist and Runco 1993), intelligence/education (e.g., Eysenck 1995), and also certain personality traits. Two personality factors that are correlated with creative ability in multiple domains are *openness to experience* (Gelade 2002; King and Broyles 1997; King and Pope 1999) and *extraversion* (King and Broyles 1997; Martindale and Dailey 1996) and so group matching should be particularly mindful of these two traits.

Steps should also be taken to recruit synesthetes and non-synesthetes in the same way. Synesthesia's rarity has led to the use of a recruitment method that is termed "self-selection":[4] the individual proactively selects/refers him or herself for study, often after experimenters disseminate posters, flyers, newspaper articles, and so on, asking individuals who believe they have synesthesia to contact the researcher. This method is an efficient way to recruit. However, even assuming all participants are then objectively verified as genuine synesthetes, this method of recruitment can still lead to differences across synesthetes and controls that compromise investigations of creativity, in four ways (Campbell and Stanley 1966; Isaac and Michael 1971).

First, self-selecters may not be typical synesthetes, but rather a subsection who experience the most vivid and/or extreme cases of synesthesia. Second, the very act of self-selecting favors individuals who are open to experience, a trait that correlates highly with creativity (see earlier in chapter). Third, since self-selectors are, by definition, aware of the research topic, they may have a better idea of what is required and be more susceptible to implicit cues from the experimenter "demanding" particular reactions (e.g., Barber and Silver 1968; Rosenthal and Fode 1963). Finally, synesthetes are often drawn from outside the university population (with recruitment via general media) while controls tend to be students, and this brings its own set of individual differences to the task.

The use of self-selecting synesthetes (and not a self-selecting control group) occurred in some previous creativity studies (Domino 1989; Rich, Bradshaw, and Mattingley 2005; Sitton and Pierce 2004; Ward et al. 2008) but not in all (Dailey et al 1997; Mulvenna 2003, 2012). Therefore, replications with non-self-selecting samples are recommended before strong conclusions are drawn. How, then, can synesthetes be recruited without self-selection? One population-screening approach from Mulvenna (2012) is represented in Figure 31.1.

---

[4] An alternative to a self-selected synesthete is one who agrees to take part in research before the topic of synesthesia is disclosed.

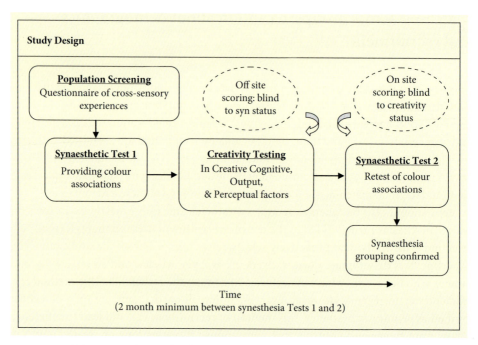

Study Design

Population Screening
Questionnaire of cross-sensory experiences

Off site
scoring: blind
to syn status

On site
scoring: blind
to creativity
status

Synaesthetic Test 1
Providing colour associations

Creativity Testing
In Creative Cognitive,
Output,
& Perceptual factors

Synaesthetic Test 2
Retest of colour associations

Synaesthesia
grouping confirmed

Time
(2 month minimum between synesthesia Tests 1 and 2)

FIGURE 31.1 Schematic of a study design to minimize confounding variables. "Syn status" = synesthetic status. Thirteen grapheme-color synesthetes were identified by screening 1486 individuals using a standard synesthesia questionnaire (see Jones 1976; Mulvenna 2003, 2005, 2012; Simner et al. 2006) which asked participants to describe any unusual cross-sensory experiences. To minimize recruitment biases (see text) participation was confirmed before individuals received questionnaires, and individuals who attempted to self-select for participation were declined. Participants reporting experiences suggestive of grapheme-color synesthesia then provided their synesthetic colors for a list of grapheme stimuli in a subsequent interview. Controls were selected from the same large (n = 1486) population based on their negative responses to these synesthesia tests, and by careful demographic matching for any trait that might relate to creative ability. Participants then completed the creativity battery, and then potential synesthetes again provided their synesthetic colors for a test of consistency (to verify their status as synesthete or non-synesthete). Hence, formal classification of synesthesia/non-synesthesia was not confirmed until after creativity testing to further minimize response bias and/or experimenter bias. Participants were not alerted to their group allocation and creativity scoring was carried out by blind, off-site scorers at the Scholastic Testing Service Inc.

In conclusion, it is difficult to avoid the pitfalls of the quasi-experiment in the investigation of synesthesia, but population-screening approaches such as that of Mulvenna (2012) can minimize the range of possible confounds.

WHAT IS THE SOURCE OF CREATIVITY IN SYNESTHETES?

Synesthesia as creativity

In previous sections I have reviewed the methodologies used to test creativity in synesthetes. These have shown that synesthetes excel in the generation of creative ideas, and follow artistic pursuits more than non-synesthetes but that their artwork may not be judged as "more creative." In this section, I consider the mechanisms that underlie their enhanced cognitive creativity by first considering two useful questions about the creativity-synesthesia link: are synesthetes merely being imaginative in their reports of synesthesia? And, is the experience of synesthesia a creative act in itself?

The question of whether synesthesia is nothing more than imagination or metaphor is perhaps the oldest question in the scientific literature on synesthesia: are synesthetes simply describing everyday experiences in a more poetic way? This idea was quashed some time ago: empirical evidence (reviewed in Parts I, III, and V of this handbook) shows that synesthetes have differences in their perceptual and neurophysiological make-up (e.g., Bargary and Mitchel 2008; Nunn et al. 2002) and that these appear to be automatic and lifelong (e.g., Simner et al 2009). Therefore the synesthetic experience is not imagined or merely fanciful, and therefore the link to creativity cannot be explained in this way.

The question of whether (perceptual, neurophysiological) synesthesia is itself an act of creativity can also be dismissed in the context of our contemporary understanding of creativity. By the standards described in this chapter, properties of synesthesia do not characterize creativity, for the following reasons:

(1) Since synesthesia occurs involuntarily, synesthetes are not purposefully generating a novel idea (i.e., it is not creative cognition).
(2) A synesthete is not generating a new product with the association (i.e., it is not creative output; unless they communicate it through different media such as painting, in which case it would be the communication, not the synesthesia that was creative).
(3) A synesthete is not interpreting features (of, say, the letter Q as "mossy green") that could be shared by others, as in the case of visual abstraction and symbolism (i.e., it is not creative perception). In fact, synesthetes are often at a loss as to why one feature would be connected to the other.

Thus, the experience of synesthesia does not meet any of the contemporary parameters of creative cognition, output, or perception and so the synesthesia-creativity link cannot be reduced to mere experience of synesthesia. Let us then consider other ways to trace the source of synesthetic creativity.

The creative brain

Although no firm conclusions have yet been reached regarding the neural mechanisms that underlie synesthesia, particularly in regard to structural systems or functional processes, there is growing evidence that one important source of synesthesia may be found in a propensity for neural co-activation of disparate regions of the brain, in the presence of enhanced structural or functional neural connectivity (for review see Bargary and Mitchell 2008, and Part V of this handbook). Might, then, neural connectivity be a significant common denominator to synesthesia and creativity?

Investigations of neural connectivity have identified particular patterns with regard to creativity. For instance, the generation of novel ideas is heavily based in the ability to make remote associations (e.g., Eysenck 1995) and the ability to generate remote associations is positively associated with increased functional connectivity (i.e., lower modularity; Folley 2006). Investigations using methods such as electroencephalography (EEG; i.e., recording electrical activity along the scalp) show that the production of creative ideas is supported by synchronous connectivity of diverse and distal cortical areas (Bhattacharya and Petsche 2002; Folley 2006; Molle et al. 1996; Molle et al. 1997; Petsche et al. 1997). Production of creative ideas is also supported by recruitment of more information within the dynamic workspace (Carlsson et al. 2000; Geake and Hansen 2010) and is indicative of the broader activation that accompanies looser attentional control (Molle et al. 1996. Furthermore, investigations of psychosis-proneness also show links between creativity and increased synaptic connectivity and functional integration (Crow 1995; Horrobin 1998).

From the earlier mentioned links between creativity and neural connectivity, and from demonstrations of increased connectivity in color-grapheme synesthesia (Rouw and Scholte 2007) there is an argument for neural mechanisms related to connectivity being a possible mediator of enhanced creativity in synesthetes. Future directions for this topic could investigate whether synesthetes draw on a "more dynamic workspace" both during creativity tasks and during tasks of cognitive systems that are understood to contribute to creative cognition (cognitive control, working memory, verbal fluency, etc.). This would help us understand whether synesthetes show more cortical activation overall, and/or whether they show activation across more disparate regions of the cortex. If so, this greater dynamic workspace could be a mediator for synesthetes' greater cognitive creativity, and not be limited to the connectivity of their synesthetic experiences.

A dual model of creativity and art in synesthetes

The presence of synesthesia is associated with a significant advantage in creative thinking (Domino 1989; Mulvenna 2003, 2012; Ward et al. 2008), but not, as far as the evidence at hand shows, an advantage in communicating creativity through secondary media or in artistic ability (Mulvenna 2003, 2012). Thus it would appear that while creativity and

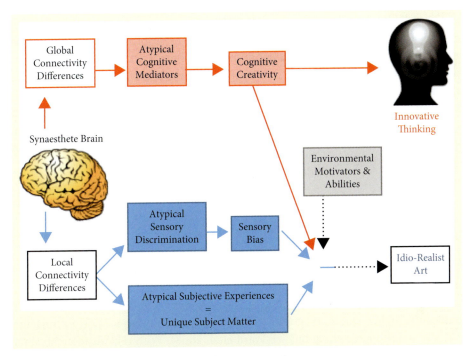

FIGURE 31.2 Dual model of creativity and art in synesthetes.

art are related to each other, synesthesia relates differently to each of them. A new dual model is proposed to account for these links and is shown in Figure 31.2.

Essentially, this model suggests there could be a divergence in the chain of factors that contribute to artistic output and to creative cognition in synesthetes. The chain of factors that could lead to increased creative cognition is shown in the upper red section. This depicts how neurocognitive difference in synesthetes that occur over and above those necessary for synesthetic experiences (see Rouw and Scholte 2007), may also be the underlying support for enhanced creative abilities in synesthetes, mediated by atypical cognition. The chain of factors that could lead to artistic output is shown in the lower blue section. This shows that the neuro-perceptual differences related directly to the synesthetic experience contribute toward a synesthete pursuing creative output. This motivation comes both from the synesthetic experiences per se ("Atypical subjective experiences") which provide a unique subject matter but also from superior abilities in perception ("Atypical sensory discrimination"; see, e.g., Banissy, Walsh, and Ward 2009). It may also be fed by heightened abilities in cognitive creativity (in red in Figure 31.2) which may aid in decisions about subject matter or technique. Critically, an additional, external factor is also required in order for synesthetic art to be generated ("Environmental motivators and abilities"). This factor is by no means incidental; artistic output involves the communication of an idea or stimulus through a secondary medium (Baer 1993, 1998;; Plucker and Beghetto 2004), through artistic production skills, through environmental accommodations in background and current situation, and through the motivation to pursue art (see Getzels and Csikszentmihalyi 1976; Heilman et al. 2003). All these factors could contibute to the production of idio-realistic synesthetic art (see footnote 1 for a definition of this term). In short, synesthetes have neuro-perceptual differences that can contribute towards elevated pursuit of artistry, but only when also accompanied by environmental factors and abilities that would also be needed by others (non-synesthetes) to excel in the arts. One final implication of this model is the idea that synesthesia could be an external marker for a broader set of neurocognitive differences that have various consequences on the perceptual and cognitive makeup of the individual.

CONCLUSIONS: CREATIVITY IN SYNESTHETES

I have discussed issues related to measuring creativity in synesthetes and it is useful to summarize what those investigations have shown. With regards to psychological tests of creative thinking—spanning divergent and convergent thinking—synesthetes score significantly higher than non-synesthetes (Dailey 1997; Domino 1989; Mulvenna 2003, 2012; Sitton and Pierce 2004; but see Ward et al. 2008). With regards to creative pursuits in the arts (professions and/or hobbies), synesthetes report engaging significantly more than non-synesthetes (Rich, Bradley, and Mattingley, 2005; Rothen and Meier 2010; Sitton and Pierce 2004; Ward et al 2008). However, with regard to translating ideas through drawn figures, synesthetes' creativity scores were no different from non-synesthetes (Mulvenna 2003, 2012) and they did not show superior creative perception in their judgments of art (Mulvenna, 2012).

Taken together, these conclusions suggest that synesthetes excel in the generation of creative ideas, and pursue artistic endeavors more than non-synesthetes but, curiously, that the artwork they produce may not be judged as "more creative" per se than artwork from non-synesthetes. This unexpected complexity is interesting for several reasons. First, it suggests that the original impression of a higher presence of synesthetes in the art world was accurate. Second, it suggests that the translational ability—to translate an idea through another media—does not carry this creativity with it. This finding indicates that synesthetic art would not in itself be judged as significantly more novel than art produced by a non-synesthete. This theory may be tested directly in future experiments that might adopt the *Consensual Assessment Technique* (CAT; Amabile 1982). This technique, detailed earlier in the chapter, has creative outputs (such as paintings, poems) assessed by a group of independent experts in the field.

Overall, the picture that emerges is one of synesthetes as creative thinkers. While synesthetes pursue the arts more than others, the link to the arts is secondary to the robust and reliable relationship synesthesia has with creative cognition. Thus, for synesthetes, the distinction from non-synesthetes lies not in the creativity of their art, but in the creativity of their *thoughts*.

REFERENCES

Abraham, Anna, and Sabine Windmann. 2007. Creative cognition: the diverse operations and the prospect of applying a cognitive neuroscience perspective. *Methods* 42:38–48.

Amabile, Teresa, M. 1982. Social psychology of creativity: A consensual assessment technique. *Journal of Personality and Social Psychology* 43:997–1013.

——. 1983. *The Social Psychology of Creativity*. New York: Springer-Verlag.

——. 1996. *Creativity in Context: Update to the Social Psychology Of Creativity*. Boulder, CO: Westview Press.

Andreasen, Nancy, C. 1978. Creativity and psychiatric illness. *Psychiatric Annals* 8 (3): 23–45.

Baer, John. 1993. *Creativity and Divergent Thinking: A Task-Specific Approach*. Hillsdale, NJ: Erlbaum.

——. 1998. The case for domain specificity in creativity. *Creativity Research Journal* 11:173–177.

Baer, John, and James C. Kaufman. 2008. Gender differences in creativity. *Journal of Creative Behavior* 42:75–106.

Baer, John, and Sharon S. McKool. 2009. Assessing creativity using the consensual assessment technique. In *Handbook of Research on Assessment Technologies, Methods, and Applications in Higher Education,* ed. John Baer, and Sharon S. McKool, 65–77. Hershey, PA: IGI Global.

Banissy, Michael J., Vincent Walsh, and Jamie Ward. 2009. Enhanced sensory perception in synaesthesia. *Experimental Brain Research* 196:565–571.

Barber, Theodore X., and Maurice J. Silver. 1968. Fact, fiction, and the experimenter bias effect. *Psychological Bulletin Monograph Supplement* 70:1–29.

Bargary, Gary, and Kevin J. Mitchell. 2008. Synaesthesia and cortical connectivity. *Trends in Neurosciences* 31:335–342.

Baron-Cohen, Simon, Maria A. Wyke, and Colin Binnie. 1987. Hearing words and seeing colours: An experimental investigation of a case of synaesthesia. *Perception* 16:761–767.

Barron, Frank. 1963. *Barron-Welsh Art Scale, A Portion of the Welsh Figure Preference Test*. Palo Alto, CA: Consulting Psychologists Press.

Berman, Greta, Carol Steen, and Daphne Maurer. 2008. *Synesthesia: Art and the Mind*. Hamilton, ON: McMaster Museum of Art/ABC Art Books.

Bhattacharya, Joydeep, and Helmuth Petsche. 2002. Shadow of artistry: Cortical synchrony during perception and imagery of visual art. *Cognitive Brain Research* 13:179–186.

Binet, Alfred. 1893. L'application de la psychometrie a l'etude de l'audition coloree. *Revue Philosophique* 36:334–336.

Binet, Alfred, and Victor Henri. 1895. La psychologie individuelle. *Annee psychologique* 2:411–465.

Brougher, Kerry, Jeremy Strick, Ari Wiseman, and Judith Zilczer. 2005. *Visual Music: Synaesthesia in Art and Music Since 1900*. London: Thames & Hudson.

Carlsson, Ingegard, Peter E. Wendt, and Jarl Risberg. 2000. On the neurobiology of creativity. Differences in frontal activity between high and low creative subjects. *Neuropsychologia* 38:873–885.

Carson, Shelley. 2006. Creativity and Mental Illness. Invitational Panel Discussion hosted by Yale's Mind Matters Consortium, New Haven, CT.

Cattel, Raymond B., and Harold J. Butcher. 1968. *The Prediction of Achievement and Creativity*. New York: Bobbs-Merrill.

Chase, C. I. 1985. Review of the Torrance Test of Creative Thinking. In *The Ninth Mental Measurements Yearbook*, ed. James V. Mitchell, 1631–1632. Lincoln, NE: University of Nebraska.

Conway, James M., and Alan I. Huffcutt. 1997. Psychometric properties of multi-source per-
    formance ratings: A meta-analysis of subordinate, supervisor, peer, and self-ratings. *Human
    Performance* 10:331–360

Crandall, Rick. 1973. The measurement of self-esteem and related constructs. In *Measures of
    Social Psychological Attitudes*, ed. John P. Robinson and Phillip R. Shaver, 45–168. Ann Arbor,
    MI: Institute for Social Research.

Crow, Timothy J. 1995. A theory of evolutionary origins of psychosis. *European
    Neuropsychopharmacology* 5:59–63.

Crowne, Douglas P., and David Marlowe. 1964. *The Approval Motive*. New York: Wiley.

Csikszentmihalyi, Mihaly. 1998. Creativity and genius: A system perspective. In *Genius and
    Mind: Studies of Creativity and Temperament*, ed. Andrew Steptoe, 39–66. Oxford: Oxford
    University Press.

Cytowic, Richard E. 1995. Synesthesia, phenomonelogy and neuropsychology: A review of cur-
    rent knowledge. *Psyche* 2 (10).

Dailey, Audrey, Colin Martindale, and Jonathan Borkum. 1997. Creativity, synaesthesia, and
    physiognomic perception. *Creativity Research Journal* 10 (1):1–8.

Domino, George. 1989. Synaesthesia and creativity in fine arts students: An empirical look.
    Creativity Research Journal 2:17–29.

———. 1994. Assessment of creativity with the ACL: An empirical comparison of four scales.
    Creativity Research Journal 7:21–33.

Edelman, Gerald. 2006. *Second Nature: Brain Science and Human Nature*. New Haven, CT: Yale
    University Press.

Edwards, Allen L. 1953. The relationship between the judged desirability of a trait and the prob-
    ability that the trait will be endorsed. *Journal of Applied Psychology* 37:90–93.

Eysenck, Hans J. 1995. Can we study intelligence using the experimental method? *Intelligence*
    20:217–228.

Farah, Martha J., and Todd E. Feinberg. 2000. Disorders of perception and awareness. In *Patient-
    based Approaches to Cognitive Neuroscience: Issues in Clinical and Cognitive Neuropsychology*,
    ed. Farah, Matha J. and Todd. E. Feinberg, Cambridge, 143–154. Cambridge, MA: MIT
    Press.

Feist, Gregory J., and Mark A. Runco. 1993. Trends in the creativity literature: An analy-
    sis of research in the Journal of Creative Behavior 1967–1989. *Creativity Research Journal*
    6:271–286.

Finke, Ronald A., Thomas B. Ward, and Steven M. Smith. 1992. *Creative Cognition: Theory,
    Research and applications*. Cambridge, MA: MIT Press.

Folley, Bradley S. 2006. The cognitive neuroscience of creativity in schizophrenia spectrum.
    PhD Thesis, Vanderbilt University.

Furnham, Adrian, and Paul Stringfield. 1994. Congruence of self and subordinate ratings
    of managerial practices as a correlate of superior evaluation. *Journal of Occupational and
    Organizational Psychology* 67:57–67.

Gazzaniga, Michael S., and George A. Miller. 1989. The recognition of antonymy by a language-
    enriched right hemisphere. *Journal of Cognitive Neuroscience* 1 (2):187–193.

Geake John G., and Peter C. Hansen. 2010. Functional neural correlates of fluid and crystallized
    analogizing. *NeuroImage* 49:3489–3497.

Gelade, Gary A. 2002. Creative style, personality, and artistic endeavor. *Genetic, Social, and
    General Psychology Monographs* 128 (3):213–234.

Getzels, Jacob W., and Mahily Csikszentmihalyi. 1976. *The Creative Vision*. New York: Wiley.

Green, Adam E., Jonathan A. Fugelsang, and Keven N. Dunbar. 2006. Automatic activation of categorical and abstract analogical relations in analogical reasoning. *Memory and Cognition* 34:1414–1421.

Guilford, Joy P. 1950. Creativity. *American Psychologist* 5 (9):444–454.

——. 1959. Traits of creativity. In *Creativity and its Cultivation*, ed. Harold H. Anderson, 142–161. New York: Harper and Row.

——. 1967. *The Nature of Human Intelligence*. New York: McGraw Hill.

Guilford, Joy, P., Paul R. Christensen, Philip R. Merrifield, and Robert C. Wilson. 1978. *Alternate Uses: Manual of Instructions and Interpretation*. Orange, CA: Sheridan Psychological Services.

Harris, Michael M., and John Schaubroeck. 1988. A meta-analysis of self-supervisor, self-peer, and peer-supervisor ratings. *Personnel Psychology* 41:43–62.

Harrison, David A., Mary E. McLaughlin, and Terry M. Coalter. 1996. Context, cognition and common method variance: Psychometric and verbal protocol evidence. *Organizational Behavior and Human Decision Processes* 68:246–261.

Heilman, Kevin M., Stephen E. Nadeau, and David O. Beversdorf. 2003. Creative innovation: Possible brain mechanisms. *Neurocase* 9 (5):369–379.

Holyoak, Keith J., and Paul Thagard. 1997. The analogical mind. *American Psychologist* 52:35–44.

——. 1995. *Mental Leaps: Analogy in Creative Thought*. Cambridge, MA: MIT Press.

Horrobin, D. F. 1998. Schizophrenia: The illness that made us human. *Medical Hypotheses* 50:269–288.

Hui, C. Harry, and Harry C. Traindis. 1989. Effects of culture and response format on extreme response style. *Journal of Cross Cultural Psychology* 20:296–309.

Johnson, Donielle, Carrie Allison, and Simon Baron-Cohen. 2013. The prevalence of synesthesia: The consistency revolution. In *The Oxford Handbook of Synesthesia*, ed. Julia Simner and Edward M. Hubbard, 3–22 . Oxford: Oxford University Press.

Jones, H. J. 1976. *Synesthesia and its role in memory*. Doctoral dissertation, University of Texas at Austin.

Kaufman, James C, and John Baer. 2004. Sure I'm creative—but not in math!: Self-reported creativity in diverse domains. *Empirical Studies of the Arts* 22:143–155.

Kay, Christian J., and Catherine M. Mulvenna. 2006. Synaesthesia, neurology and language. In *Progress in Colour Studies 2: Psychological Aspects,* ed. Nicola Pitchford, and Carole P. Biggam, 203–224. Amsterdam: John Benjamins.

King, Laura A., and Sheri J. Broyles. 1997. Wishes, gender, personality, and well-being. *Journal of Personality* 65 (1):49–76.

King, Brenda J., and Brian Pope. 1999. Creativity as a factor in psychological assessment and healthy psychological functioning. *Journal of Personality Assessment* 72:200–207.

Lanyon, Richard I., and Leonard D. Goodstein. 1997. *Personality Assessment*. 3rd ed. New York: Wiley.

MacKinnon, Donald W. 1970. Creativity: A multi-faceted phenomenon. In *Creativiy: A Discussion at the Nobel Conference*, ed. John D. Roslansky, 17–32. Amsterdam: North Holland.

Marks, Lawrence E. 1978. *The Unity of the Senses: Interrelations Among the Modalities*. New York: Academic Press.

Martindale, Colin. 1999. Biological bases of creativity. In *Handbook of Creativity*, ed. Robert J. Sternberg, 137–152. New York: Cambridge University Press.

Martindale, Colin, and Audrey Dailey. 1996. Creativity, primary process cognition and personality. *Personality and Individual Differences* 20:409–414.

Mayer, Richard E. 1999. Problem solving. In *Encyclopedia of Creativity*, ed. Mark A. Runco and Steven R. Pritzker, 437–448. San Diego, CA: Academic.

Mednick, Sarnoff. 1962. The associative basis of the creative process. *Psychological Review* 69 (3):220

Mendelsohn, Gerald A. 1976. Associative and attentional processes in creative performance. *Journal of Personality* 44:341–369.

Molle, Matthias, Lisa Marshall, Werner Lutzenberger, Reinhard Pietrowsky, Horst L. Fehm, and Jan Born. 1996. Enhanced dynamic complexity in the human EEG during creative thinking. *Neuroscience Letters* 208:61–64.

Molle, Matthias, Reinhard Pietrowsky, Horst L. Fehm, and Jan Born. 1997. Regulation of human thought by neuropeptide ACTH 4–10: an analysis of the EEG's dimensional complexity. *Neuroreport* 8:2715–2720.

Mulvenna, Catherine M. 2003. The relationship between synaesthesia and creativity. BA dissertation, Glasgow University.

———. 2007. Synaesthesia, arts and creativity: A neurological connection. *Frontiers of Neurology and Neuroscience* 22:206–222

———. 2012. On creativity in synaesthetes: Roles of neural connectivity, cognitive control and perceptual correspondence. PhD thesis, University College London.

Myers, Isabel B. 1945. *Type as the Index to Personality*. Swarthmore, PA.

Newcomb, Michael D., George J. Huba, and Peter M. Bentler. 1986. Life change evens among adolescents: An empirical consideration of some methodological issues. *Journal of Nervous and Menial Disease* 774:280–289.

Nunn, J., L. J. Gregory, M. Brammer, S. C. R. Williams, D. M. Parslow, M. J. Morgan, R. G. Morris, E. T. Bullmore, S. Baron-Cohen, and J. A. Gray. 2002. Functional magnetic resonance imaging of synesthesia: activation of V4/V8 by spoken words. *Nature Neuroscience* 5 (4):371–375.

Petsche, H., S. Kaplan, A. Von Stein, and O. Filz. 1997. The possible meaning of the upper and lower alpha frequency ranges for cognitive and creative tasks. *International Journal of Psychophysiology* 26:77–97.

Plucker, Jonathan A. 1998. Beware of simple conclusions: The case for the content generality of creativity. *Creativity Research Journal* 11:179–182.

Plucker, Jonathan A., and Robert A. Beghetto. 2004. Why creativity is domain general, why it looks domain specific, and why the distinction doesn't matter. In *Creativity: From Potential to Realization*, ed. Robert J. Sternberg, Elena L. Grigorenko, and Jerome L. Singer, 153–167. Washington, DC: American Psychological Association.

Ramachandran, Vilayanur S., and Edward M. Hubbard. 2001. Psychophysical investigations into the neural basis of synaesthesia. *Proceedings of the Royal Society B: Biological Sciences* 268 (1470): 979–983.

Reid, J. B., F. J. King, and P. Wickwire. 1959. Cognitive and other personality characteristics of creative children. *Psychological Reports* 5:729–737.

Rich, Anina N., John L. Bradshaw, and Jason B. Mattingley. 2005. A systematic, large-scale study of synaesthesia: Implications for the role of early experience in lexical-colour associations. *Cognition* 98 (1):53–84.

Rich, Anina N., Jason B. Mattingley, and Jonathan M. Payne. 2001. The role of attention in colour-graphemic synaesthesia. *Australian Journal of Psychology* 53:199–199.

Rosenthal, Robert, and Kermit L. Fode. 1963. The effect of experimenter bias on the performance of the albino rat. *Behavioral Science* 8:183–189.

Rothen, Nicolas, and Beat Meier. 2010. Higher prevalence of synaesthesia in art students.
Perception 39 (5):718.

Rothenberg, Albert. 1976. Homospatial thinking in creativity. *Archives of General Psychiatry* 33
(1):17–26.

Rouw, Romke, and H. Steven Scholte. 2007. Increased structural connectivity in grapheme-
color synesthesia. *Nature Neuroscience* 10 (6):792–797.

Runco, Mark A., and Robyn E. Charles. 1993. Judgements of originality and appropriateness as
predictors of creativity. *Personality and Individual Differences* 15:346–537.

Runco, Mark A., Jonathan A. Plucker, and Woong Lim. 2001. Development and psychometric
integrity of a measure of ideational behavior. *Creativity Research Journal* 13:393–400.

Schaefer, C. E. (1969). *Similes Manual*. New York: Center for Urban Education.

Shepard, Roger N. 1978. Externalization of mental images and the age of creation. In *Visual
learning, Thinking, and Communication*, ed. Bikkar A. Randhawa and W. Coffman, 133–190.
New York: Academic Process.

Simner, Julia. 2012. Defining synaesthesia. *British Journal of Psychology* 103:1–15.

Simner, Julia, Jenny Harrold, Harriet Creed, Louise Monro, and Louise Foulkes. 2009. Early
detection of markers for synaesthesia in childhood populations. *Brain* 132 (1):57–64.

Simner, Julia, Catherine M. Mulvenna, Noam Sagiv, Elias Tsakanikos, Sarah A. Witherby,
Christine Fraser, Kirsten Scott, and Jamie Ward. 2006. Synaesthesia: The prevalence of atypical cross-modal experiences. *Perception* 35 (8): 1024–1033.

Simonton, Dean K. 1988. Creativity, leadership, and chance. In *The Nature of Creativity:
Contemporary Psychological Perspectives*, ed. Robert J. Sternberg, 11–38. New York: Cambridge
University Press.

Sitton, Sarah C., and Edward R. Pierce. 2004. Synesthesia, creativity and puns. *Psychological
Reports* 95 (2):577–580.

Smith, Steven M., Thomas B. Ward, and Ronald A. Fink. 1995. *The Creative Cognition Approach.*
Cambridge, MA: MIT Press.

Sternberg, Robert J. 1988. *The Nature of Creativity: Contemporary Psychological Perspectives.*
New York: Cambridge University Press.

Sternberg, Robert J., and Todd I. Lubart. 1995. Defying the crowd: Cultivating creativity in a
culture of conformity. *Personality and Individual Differences* 21:143–153.

Torrance, E. Paul. 1966. *Torrance Tests of Creative Thinking*. Princeton, NJ: Personnel Press.

——. 1974. *The Torrance Tests of Creative Thinking-Norms-Technical Manual Research
Edition-Verbal Tests, Forms A and B- Figural Tests, Forms A and B.* Princeton, NJ:
Personnel Press.

——. 1998. *The Torrance tests of creative thinking norms—technical manual figural streamlined)
forms A and B.* Bensenville, IL: Scholastic Testing Service, Inc.

Torrance, E. Paul., and Ball, O. E. 1984. *Torrance tests of creative thinking. Streamlined.*
Bensenville, IL: Scholastic Testing Service.

Van Campen, Crétien. 1997. Synesthesia and artistic experimentation. *Psyche* 3:6.

——. 2013. Synesthesia in the visual arts. In *The Oxford Handbook of Synesthesia*, ed. Julia
Simner and Edward M. Hubbard, 631–646 . Oxford: Oxford University Press.

Wallach, Michael A., and Nathan Kogan. 1965. *Modes of Thinking in Young Children: A Study of
the Creativity—Intelligence Distinction.* New York: Holt, Rinehart and Winston.

Ward, Jamie, Samantha Moore, Daisy Thompson-Lake, Shireen Salih, and Brianna Beck. 2008. The aesthetic appeal of auditory-visual synaesthetic perceptions in people without synaesthesia. *Perception* 37 (8):1285–1296.

Yamamoto, Kaoru. 1964. *Experimental Scoring Manuals for Minnesota Tests of Creative Thinking and Writing*. Kent, OH: Kent State University.

CHAPTER 32

....

SYNESTHESIA IN
THE VISUAL ARTS

....

CRETIEN VAN CAMPEN

Experiments with synesthesia in the visual arts date back several centuries further in time than scientific research into the subject. Since the seventeenth century, artists have been working on the relationships between different sensory modalities. The Italian artist Arcimboldo, for instance, experimented at the court of Rudoph II in Prague by accompanying the hearing of music from a harpsichord with the sight of corresponding images of strips of colored paper (Gage 1993). At the end of the nineteenth century, these artistic experiments in audiovisual correspondences had developed into performances for large audiences. Artists played classical music by Beethoven, Chopin, and other composers in combination with colored light projections on the stage (Peacock 1998). A decade later, the Russian composer Alexander Scriabin even added parts for a light projector to his musical score for orchestra (Galeyev and Vanechkina 2001; Peacock 1985). At the end of the nineteenth century, scientific investigations into *audition colorée* (color hearing) started to become a substantial area of psychological research.[1] Before that time, artists, including painters, dramatists, and composers, had already established a body of knowledge about how to use correspondences between the senses (Campen 2007; Mahling 1926).

The focus on synesthesia has changed the visual arts across the last few centuries. The interest of artists in synesthetic phenomena and interactions between aesthetic stimuli from different sense modalities has formed the seeds for new art movements. For instance, ideas about sensory correspondences representing a higher reality by the French poet Charles Baudelaire had a substantial impact on the mystical paintings of the Symbolists. Ideas about *Gesamtkunstwerke* (works of art which integrate music, image, dance, and other disciplines) by the German composer Richard Wagner encouraged artists like Wassily Kandinsky and Piet Mondrian, who became key advocates of abstraction in painting (Düchting 1996; Gage 1999; Maur 1999). In more modern times,

---

[1] Prior to that was an early single study by the physician Sachs in 1812 (Jewanski, Day, and Ward 2009).

the contemporary digital arts are indebted to synesthetic experiments into audiovisual perception on early computers in the fifties and sixties, by artists like Edgar Varèse in France and James Whitney in the US (Brougher et al. 2005; Daniels, Naumann, and Thoben 2010).

Since no instruments were available to show synesthetic phenomena to audiences (painters had their palette and musicians their musical instruments) these early pioneers of synesthetic art were often inventors too. A fine example is the colossal color light organ that Alexander Rimmington built at the end of the nineteenth century (Jewanski and Sidler 2006; Peacock 1988). As a result of this type of engineering, synesthetic experiments in the visual arts have not only contributed ideas but also concrete instruments to Western culture. Scientific research has built on these artistic tools in direct and indirect ways. The construction of digital algorithms to translate music into images seems to have inspired scientific experimental research. Later these algorithms found their way into popular culture by their implementations in personal computers and on the Internet (e.g., in the video application of music players).

In this chapter I would like to show what kind of insights and tools the visual arts have contributed to our understanding of the intriguing phenomenon of synesthetic perceptions. It is sometimes thought that artists can only illustrate what science has devised. I think it has often been the reverse: much research into perception has been inspired by artistic experiments. Artistic investigations have revealed aspects of synesthesia that scientists have scrutinized more vigorously, and I will illustrate this with examples later in the chapter. I should clarify that this chapter provides no historical or systematic complete list of artistic experiments with synesthesia. My aim is rather to offer a broad picture of the investigations, and uses and meanings of synesthesia in various visual art forms. I shall restrict myself to a subset of fields in the contemporary visual arts: painting, film and animation, installations, art educational projects, product design, and urban architecture. I have picked a number of projects and will reflect upon them. The following questions guided my review: what can we learn about synesthesia from art projects? What do they teach us about perception and cognition? Have they made the general public more aware of synesthetic perceptions?

I begin by asking what is regarded as synesthesia in the arts? Artists use less strict definitions of synesthesia than scientists. Scientists use several definitions and lists of criteria for synesthetic perceptions (which can be found elsewhere in this volume). Researchers have a different goal than artists. Researchers need to be able to measure synesthesia, while this need is not so much felt by artists who primarily want to show synesthetic phenomena. As such, the question "What is synesthesia?" plays a lesser role in the arts. Synesthesia is considered by many artists as an interesting but normal component of human perception since they tend to focus on the intuitive cross-sensory experiences of all people (cf. Part VII of this book). In contrast, most scientists are interested in synesthesia as a deviation from normal perception (also known as "neurological synesthesia"). Hence, artists more often explore synesthesia as an integral part of daily perception and not as an isolated neurological phenomenon in itself, as do in scientific studies. I elaborate on this, because for an understanding of the artistic projects that I will discuss it is important to understand how artists deal with synesthesia and that this is generally differently from how scientists do this (cf. Campen 2011).

For this review I consider synesthesia as a Gestalt perception, an integrated perception consisting of different sense elements that normally do not go together, e.g., colored sounds. Scientists who adhere to a neurological definition of synesthesia may find this fuzzy and overlapping with other related fields of scientific study, e.g., cross-modal perception. A last remark from a cultural anthropological angle is that artistic and scientific definitions and conceptualizations of synesthesia in the Western world are based on typical notions of divisions of the human experience into separate senses (sight, hearing, taste, smell, and touch; Howes 2011). In non-Western cultures the classification of the senses sometimes is different and as a consequence ideas on cross-modal and synesthetic perceptions differ or do not exist. Therefore I will limit my review to Western art of the last few centuries.

PAINTING

From a historical perspective, one finds most artistic experiments with synesthesia in the field of painting. Many painters have tried to render music in pictures. Although references to music and musical instruments in paintings date back to antiquity, from the end of the nineteenth century artists started to try to visualize music itself.[2]

Artistic attempts at painting music went hand in hand with a development of abstraction in the history of artistic painting. Many modern painters have been guided by the abstract character of music. Fine examples can be found in a range of different art movements such as Symbolism (e.g., Redon), Impressionism (e.g., Monet), Neo-Impressionism (e.g., Seurat) and the early non-figurative movements like Der Blaue Reiter (e.g., Kandinsky) and De Stijl (e.g., Mondrian). In works by these artists one can find many non-figurative color compositions that suggest a sense of music and movement. In fact this is pure illusion since a two-dimensional static painting contains no sound, music, or movement at all. However, artists have understood that abstract pictorial elements like color and composition offer opportunities to render and recall music in paintings. Even without musical accompaniment, paintings could evoke musical sensations. Let us consider Mondrian's *Victory Boogie-woogie* painting (Figure 32.1). Mondrian wanted to evoke a feeling of the Jazz of Manhattan—take note of the street pattern as another motif in the painting—simply by color and composition. Even the art historian Ernst Gombrich who was not especially fond of abstract art admitted: "I don't know exactly what boogie-woogie is, but Mondrian's painting explains it to me" (Gombrich 1960).

---

[2] The composer Bach appears to be strikingly popular to painters of music, which we can infer from the selection by art historian Karin von Maur (1999) in the catalogue *The Sound of Images* of twentieth-century musical paintings.

FIGURE 32.1 Piet Mondrian, *Victory Boogie-Woogie*, 1942–1944. Gemeentemuseum, The Hague, The Netherlands.

The artist who has made the general public most broadly aware that paintings can evoke musical sensations is Wassily Kandinsky. Kandinsky made clear that as one paints more abstract figures, the beholder is less distracted by figurative meanings (of trees, persons, chairs, etc.) and the musical quality of the pictorial composition itself comes to the fore (Kandinsky 1911/2001). At the Bauhaus academy in Germany, Kandinsky and his colleagues experimented with the integration of different sense modalities by collaborating with artists from different disciplines like dancers, musicians, theatre makers, and painters (Hahl-Koch 1985; Ione 2004). This multisensory or intermedial approach is still present in contemporary visual works by David Hockney, Carol Steen (e.g., Steen and Berman, Chapter 34, this volume), Marcia Smilack, Ans Salz, and many others, who explore their own synesthetic perceptions.[3] Next I discuss the work of one contemporary younger artist with strong synesthetic perceptions.

Timothy Layden is a London-based American artist and musician who paints and draws "shapes of sound" as he names his works. *Tres elementos* (Figure 32.2) is a typical work that emerged from his personal synesthetic musical and sound experiences. The synesthetic elements are clearly visible in this work. Laden explains them as follows:

> One morning while I played guitar, a group of friends, a family, interacted with me…Sounds like rain give off a white glow in the background. Popping and

---

[3] More references to artists who explore synesthetic perceptions can be found in the Leonardo online bibliography *Synesthesia in Art and Science*: <http://www.leonardo.info/isast/spec.projects/synesthesiabib.html>.

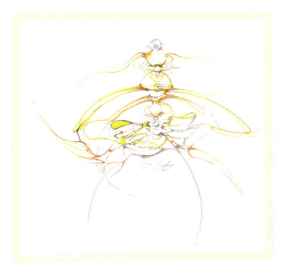

FIGURE 32.2 Timothy B. Layden. *Tres Elementos*. Ink on paper, 2008. © Timothy Blayden, 2013. Reproduced with permission.

dragging, little shards of color come out of a fog. Guitar sounds bounce off of a rounded tapping, breaking into multi coloured liquid beads. A slow bass like the bodies of snakes tangles and bends with changing tones. A baby's laughter snaps and splashes, breaking apart the snaking tubes. Voices colour the beading guitar; blue yellow, red. Shapes clasp hold of each other, fuse and become one before they unwrap with long strings and are broken apart by various sounds like footsteps, hands moving objects, zipping and rattling keys. A continued repeating rhythm of related sounds creates spiralling eddies from where a white light slowly pulsates while objects project outwards in a shower from behind the scene. (Layden 2010)

Because Layden is a synesthete, sounds have distinct shapes for him, as his sketches clarify. The sketch of the sound of a slammed coin drawer (Figure 32.3a) shows planes and beads. Layden explains that it is "a rolling sound that breaks and spreads like shattering beads." Another example of a low sound is the sketch of a hip hop bass rhythm (Figure 32.3b) that Layden perceives as "stacking stones" (Layden 2010).

These are just a few examples of a synesthetic influence from the large production of musical paintings and drawings in the last centuries. It is obvious that there is a large audience for this art form. In other words, many people, not just those who are diagnosed with neurological synesthesia, can understand and appreciate synesthetic correspondences between sound and images. This is corroborated by many scientific experiments in which non-synesthetes, too, consistently match sensory stimuli from different modalities (cf. reviews by Marks, 1978, 2004; see also Part VII in this handbook). It is an interesting area where art and science meet and interact in the exploration of aspects of synesthetic perception.

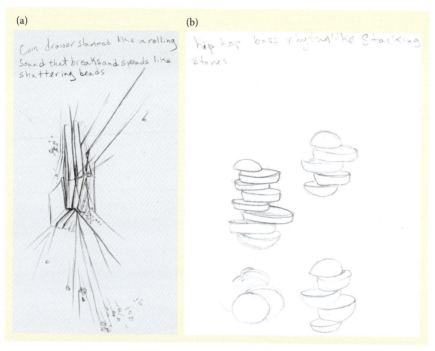

FIGURE 32.3 Timothy B. Layden, sound sketches on paper, 2010. © Timothy Blayden, 2013. Reproduced with permission.

FILM AND ANIMATION

Abstract paintings have constraints in rendering music. They are fixed in time and the space is limited to the two-dimensional plane. The collaboration of artists from different disciplines at the Bauhaus and other academies soon led to explorations in the field of abstract film and animation in the beginning of the twentieth century. One of these pioneers was Oskar Fischinger, who worked in his home country of Germany and later at the Disney studios in the US (Moritz 2004). His animation movies, which were mostly non-figurative, were the time-consuming result of drawing one film frame after another. These show that such moving non-figurative images were perhaps better suited to evoke the illusion of music.[4]

In the history of artistic film, as in the history of artistic painting, artists often appear to look for non-figurative pictorial elements to evoke musical responses in their audience. This is especially true of animation, which perhaps succeeded better than painting in evoking these responses. In the hands of Walt Disney, it became a very popular tool, and this can be seen in his most challenging Disney work *Fantasia* of 1940, in which he

[4] His films are archived at the Oskar Fishinger Trust: <http://www.oskarfischinger.org>.

aimed to transmit "difficult" classical music to a large audience by combining the music with animation. Although it has non-figurative patterns within it, *Fantasia* is mostly a figurative piece, starring well-known characters like Mickey Mouse. Nowadays, music videos of popular music are still mainly figurative, starring the band members and actors. Contemporary animation films that explore synesthetic perceptions are mainly non-figurative in character.[5] The same might be argued of their sound. Classical tunes have been replaced by often gravelly and noisy sounds, leaving the beholder with something barely recognizable. The reason for this I will explain later. I point out here that the 2-yearly conferences of the Arte Citta in Spain are a showcase of synesthetic animation projects (cf. Cordoba et al. 2009).

An interesting collaboration of visual artist Samantha Moore and neuropsychologist Jamie Ward showed scientific evidence for the appreciation of synesthetic correspondences in audiovisual animations by the general public. In collaboration with synesthetes, they derived animated audiovisual clips of synesthetic experiences and added a number of control audiovisual clips in which the original synesthetic stimulus was distorted by altering the color or orientation. The synesthetic audiovisual animations were generally preferred over the control animations by the general audience (Ward et al. 2008).

Immersive Art, Interactive Art, and Installations

In addition to the perception of images and movements, the perception of space is a third essential element in establishing a meaningful correspondence between hearing and seeing. Already by the 1920s the Danish-American artist Thomas Wilfred was creating light spaces on stage in order to evoke musical experiences in the audience. No musical instruments or sounds were involved. The movement of colors projected in space by his self-constructed device, the Clavilux, were even in silence strong elicitors of musical sensations in the minds of the listeners (Brougher et al. 2005; Jewanski and Sidler 2006).

From the 1950s, new digital techniques and the introduction of computers accelerated the development of this art form. Light projectors were changed for computer generated images and sounds. The American James Whitney composed computer-generated patterns, and most known to a wider audience are his images for Stanley Kubrick's film *Space Odyssey* in 1968 (Brougher et al. 2005). Though Kubrick placed romantic music by Joseph Strauss under Whitney's abstract patterns, a more successful combination was with music by the contemporary Hungarian composer György Ligeti. The latter had a

---

[5] Cf. the collection of the Center for Visual Music: <http://www.centerforvisualmusic.org>.

good sense for abstract audiovisual correspondences, since he had strong synesthetic perceptions himself. In an interview he said about his perceptions of sounds:

> The involuntary translation of optical and tactical impressions in acoustical ones happens to me frequently. Colour, form, and substance almost always evoke sounds, just as in the opposite direction, every acoustic sensation evokes form, colour, and material qualities. Even abstract concepts like quantity, relationship, cohesion, and event appear to me in sensual form and have a location in an imaginary space. (Cited in Campen 2007, 22)

Nowadays, a number of artists work simultaneously in the field of electronic music and digital animation, supported by powerful computers. A contemporary device that is reminiscent of the synesthetic explorations of Wilfred's Clavilux, is the *Capsule* by the Italian artist Tez. Tez designed a capsule that surrounds the human head in 360 degrees (Figure 32.4). On the inside of the capsule, images are shown and music is heard in a surround mode. Tez explores the correspondences of sound and image and uses the essential element of space in human perception. The beholder is not just looking at images and listening to sounds, the beholder is "immersed in" audiovisual sense impressions, which makes the experience more vivid and intense.[6] Just as synesthetes report on their personal impressions of, for instance, colored hearing, experiences within the Capsule (almost) cannot be detached from the body of the beholder, and can feel like a very natural part of their daily way of perceiving and acting.

Another example of immersive art that explores synesthetic perceptions is a work by the German artist Kurt Henschläger, entitled *ZEE*. The visitor enters a large tent that is filled with mist as well as by stroboscopic colored light patterns and hard noise. The experience is so intense and disorienting that every visitor has to sign a health declaration before entering the tent. But inside the tent the visitor can almost experience how the brain makes perception from scratch. Being completely disoriented at the start, one begins to find patterns in the sea (*zee* in Dutch) of sensorial stimuli. For some people synesthetic patterns may arise, since in this state, sounds, vision, proprioception, movement, smells, and other sense impressions are difficult to distinguish.[7] Visiting *ZEE*, it reminded me of the idea of a "primordial sensory soup" newborns might live in (Campen 2007; Maurer and Maurer 1998) which might in turn be the origins of synesthetic perceptions (Maurer and Mondloch 2004; cf. Maurer, Gibson, and Spector, Chapter 3, this volume). And when I slowly started to find meaningful patterns and got a better hold of my environment, I was thinking of the hypothesis that this newborn sensory soup is pruned into meaningful sense perceptions during development (Maurer and Mondloch 2004). However I do not want to suggest that the installation is an ultimate test of theories of the development of synesthesia. My point is that the installation can show to a larger audience how uncommon intersensory experiences (i.e., synesthetic perceptions)

---

[6] A video of the *Capsule* can be seen online at: <http://vimeo.com/12597280>.

[7] A very limited impression of *ZEE*, which is not immersive at all, can be viewed online: <http://vimeo.com/4104503>.

FIGURE 32.4 The *Capsule* by TeZ, exterior and image still from inside, 2008. © 2012, TeZ/
Maurizio Martinucci.

can develop. It can make the public aware that our daily way of sensorial living is not the
only option.

Immersive art is a rather new art form, which nonetheless has already revealed interesting dynamics of perception that seem to be related to synesthetic perception. What is
hardly studied in scientific experiments with synesthesia and might open new perspectives
are bodily experiences in a sensorial environment. The artistic experiments above show, at
least to the visitors, that the experience of being a body in a "sensorial sea" is elementary
in the development of synesthetic perceptions. In scientific studies of synesthesia, the role
of the subjective body has mainly been theoretical so far (cf. Merleau-Ponty 1945/2002;
Sinha 2009). Though not scientifically tested and controlled, artists have, in my opinion,
explored empirical tools to investigate this subject. For the public, these immersive installations may have made the idea of "developmental synesthesia" a sensible one.

ART EDUCATION

The science of synesthesia has not yet produced practical applications.[8] Research
is mainly fundamental in character. In contrast, in the field of the arts a number of

---

[8] One successful exception is *The vOICe*, an application that helps blind people navigate through
their surroundings by translating images they 'could' see into sounds they can hear (cf. <http://www.
seeingwithsound.com> and Ward and Meijer 2010; see also Renier and De Volder, Chapter 42, this volume).

(a) (b)

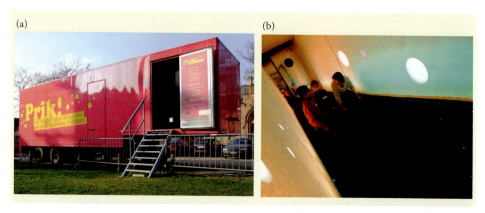

FIGURE 32.5 The interior and exterior of the Belgian educational program Prik! © 2008, Danny Van Rumste. Reproduced with permission.

applications have been developed that appeal to synesthetic perceptions and the awareness of the interrelatedness of the human senses. I will discuss a few successful examples in the field of art education, industrial design, and urban architecture.

In Germany, Christine Söffing has organized workshops on color and synesthesia for children and teachers for many years now.[9] In a school project, they have made, for instance, a synesthetic sensual city map of two districts of Ulm, Germany. The participants in the school projects work with materials (paint, sculptures, musical instruments, and fragrances) that stimulate different sense modalities; not only color and sound, but also touch and smell. The effect is that teachers and children become aware of synesthetic aspects of perception and the interrelatedness of the senses. Söffing often starts with simple questions to the children, asking, for instance, if they can hear colors, if they can taste music, or if they can feel smells. This represents the beginning of an exploring odyssey through the senses and the children return with synesthetic experiences that are new to most of them.

In Belgium, the national institute for art education RASA[10] invited a visual artist, a sound designer, and a fragrances expert to construct a synesthetic space for children in primary school. *Prik!* (*Stimulate!*) is an installation built in a candy pink painted trailer (Figure 32.5). The children enter the space on a moving ground covered with a long-haired dark carpet; left and right they are surrounded by gauze curtains where from time to time moving objects bump into them. The action is accompanied by fragrances and soft musical sounds. The children are excited by this multisensory playground, and sometimes over-awed, so it was decided to let them walk the space in pairs and hand in hand to feel safe in this new environment. The learning aim of the project, which travels in a trailer by truck through Belgium and visits many schools and educational centers, is to make children aware of their senses and their interrelations.

[9] More information on the projects is available online: <http://www.synesthesiewerkstatt.de>.
[10] More information on RASA is available online: <http://www.rasa.be>.

INDUSTRIAL DESIGN

On the crossroad between artistic explorations of intersensory correspondences, and scientific research into synesthesia, is the field of industrial design, which shows some interesting applications. For instance, the design of the form and color of bottles that contain perfumes has been using the results of studies into synesthetic correspondences between odors and images. In laboratory experiments participants had to match colors and fragrances. The results showed that pastel color distinguished better between odors than highly saturated colors (Schifferstein and Tanudjaja 2004). The design package of products is related to its contents and it appears from these studies that knowledge from synesthesia research is being applied. Another example comes from the area of car design. There has been a long tradition of the expression of character and image in the visual design of cars. Nowadays also the sound environment inside the car is subject to engineering and a relatively new field of sound design is emerging. This has brought the question of how to pleasantly integrate the different sense impressions of car-driving (Ho and Spence 2008). Hence, synesthesia has been studied as one of the sources for car design (Haverkamp 2012).

URBAN ARCHITECTURE

Synesthesia findings have also been introduced in the design of living environment by architects and urban planners. For instance, the Dutch architecture office K2 consulted a synesthete who perceived music in color for their design of a pattern of colored plates on the facades of a housing block in the Jacob Obrechtlaan (a lane named after the fifteenth-century Dutch composer Jacob Obrecht) in Schiedam, The Netherlands. The synesthete translated a number of bars by this composer into a sequence of colors and the architects integrated these colors into their design of the facades (Tan 2011) (Figure 32.6).

In several cities local projects in urban design have started with multisensory design, touching upon synesthetic perception. A first example is the interactive color installation *Moodwall* in Amsterdam designed by media architecture collective Urban Alliance. The 24-metre long interactive *Moodwall* consists of 2,500 LEDs placed behind a corrugated semi-transparent wall lining a pedestrian underpass in a somewhat volatile neighborhood in Amsterdam (Figure 32.7). The wall "greets" passers-by—via an integrated sensor system—with colored lights or moving images. In the current theme, movements of passing pedestrians and cyclists (the underpass is car-free) are translated into abstract patterns that, as it were, accompany the passers-by during their passage. The *Moodwall* provides visual stimuli, mostly color, and this subconsciously affects proprioception, the sense of the inner body. Passing cyclists and pedestrians are influenced without being aware of it. They feel more at ease and are perhaps amused by the funny color patterns

FIGURE 32.6 Colors in a building block in the Jacob Obrechtlaan, Schiedam, The Netherlands, which are based on perceptions of a synesthete (2007). Photo: Christian Richters. Reproduced with permission.

FIGURE 32.7 The *Moodwall* in Amsterdam is an interactive public installation that uses movement-image correspondences and algorithms (2009). Photo: Jasper Klinkhamer. Reproduced with permission.

that walk or bike along with them. The designers and municipal authorities expect that it will enhance the general sense of security and community.[11]

A different project is the D-tower in Doetinchem, a provincial town in the east of the Netherlands. This project doesn't translate into color the residents' movements, but rather their moods. Every day the D-tower computer measures which of four emotions features most prominently in residents' responses to an Internet survey. Nightly at 8pm, the D-tower takes on a color for the next 24 hours: yellow for fear, green for hate, red

[11] A video impression of the *Moodwall* is available online: <http://www.illuminate.nl/outdoor-media/projects/16/moodwall-bijlmerdreef-amsterdam-zuidoost.asp>.

(a)   (b)

FIGURE 32.8 The D-tower (Doetinchem, The Netherlands) is based on correspondences of color and emotion. © NOX/Lars Spuybroek. Reproduced with permission.

for love, and blue for happiness (Figure 32.8). The D-tower project explores a type of color-emotional synesthesia. Visible from afar like a lighthouse, the illuminated tower indicates the residents' mood. Visitors approaching the city thus know what they're "in for." The tower is a collaborative effort between Dutch artist Q.S. Serafijn, architect Lars Spuybroek and the inhabitants of Doetinchem.[12]

A similar international project is called Emotional Cities. At <http://www.emotionalcities.com>, people from all countries can evaluate their daily emotional state by completing an online questionnaire. The emotional states are represented by a color code. The database of the site continuously calculates the average values of cities and countries. Besides showing the results online using graphs, light installations have been set up in numerous places around the world that reflect the local results in color, for instance, in Oslo.

CONCLUDING REMARKS

The long history of artistic experimentation with synesthesia, of which I have discussed just a few examples in this chapter, has shown many possible uses of synesthesia.

[12] More information on the D-tower project is available online: <http://www.d-toren.nl/site>.

The visual arts, often in collaboration with other disciplines, have been successful in a number of ways. Artists have made the public more aware of how synesthesia feels. Scientific journalists and books by scholars have informed the public about synesthesia. Where scientists "tell" what synesthesia is, artists "show" what synesthesia is. The latter function is indispensable in explaining synesthesia to larger audiences than the comparably small group of synesthetes. Visitors of art projects can experience themselves how the senses are inter-related and how a person with strong synesthesia might perceive the world. To people unaware of synesthesia this is often as convincing as hard scientific evidence from researchers (which the public often also finds too technical).

Artists have explored new territories in human perception. Scientific research into synesthesia is, to my regret, mainly focused on a few types, i.e., the perception of colored letters and numbers, while over 60 types have been reported by synesthetes (Day 2011). The few art projects that I have discussed in this chapter have explored aspects of synesthetic experiences that have had little attention from scientific studies into synesthesia: e.g., the role of timing, movement, the subjective body, total environment, and emotions. In the same way as artists and scientists have already interacted in the field of audiovisual correspondences, there are yet more subjects I think artists and scientists might collaborate on, thereby acknowledging that research takes time and that artists and scientists often work in different worlds.

Art projects also help people to explore their own synesthetic sensibilities. As genetic research suggests, some people are more prone than other to have, synesthetic experiences. However it is the environment which transforms the genotype into the phenotype of actually having synesthetic perceptions. A child that participates in synesthetic workshops or is exposed to audiovisual art might have a higher chance of developing his or her synesthetic abilities than a child that is raised in a less diverse sensory environment. Art can also help synesthetes to share their experiences with non-synesthetes. Synesthetes often find it difficult to communicate their uncommon perceptions to other people. Sometimes they are not taken seriously for that reason. Artists have tools and skills to communicate complex sensorial phenomena to a larger audience. Moreover, artists are often more liberal in the face of unusual experiences and have shown interest in collaborating with synesthetes, at least as far as my observations are concerned.

Ultimately, art can contribute to the well-being of people by offering new meaningful sensations. Sensory awareness and pleasure have proven to be a main predictor of emotional well-being (Lyubomirsky 2008). Many synesthetes report that they enjoy their synesthetic perceptions, these being a meaningful part of their life. It is something they do not want to miss, as this would reduce their quality of life. With special regard to the majority of non-synesthetes in the public, one might suggest that art which reveals synesthetic sensations, including new ways of perceiving the world, will sustainably contribute to the well-being of the beholders.

REFERENCES

Brougher, Kerry, Jeremy Strick, Ari Wiseman, and Judith Zilczer, eds. 2005. *Visual Music: Synaesthesia in Art and Music Since 1900*. London: Thames and Hudson.

Campen, Cretien van. 2007. *The Hidden Sense: Synesthesia in Art and Science*. Cambridge: MIT Press.

——. 2011. Visual Music and musical paintings: The quest for synaesthesia in the arts. In *Art and the Senses*, ed. Francesca Bacci and David Melcher, 495–512. Oxford: Oxford University Press.

Cordoba M. José de, Edward M. Hubbard, Dina Riccò, and Sean A. Day 2009. *Actas del II Congresi Internacional de sinestesia, cienca y arte*. Granada: Arte Citta <http://www.artecitta.es>.

Daniels, Dieter, Sandra Naumann, and Jan Thoben. 2010. *See this Sound. Audiovisualogy. Compendium of an Interdisciplinary Survey of Audiovisual Culture*. Vienna: Ludwig Boltzmann.

Day, Sean A. 2011. Types of synesthesia. <http://www.daysyn.com/Types-of-Syn.html>.

Düchting, Hajo. 1996. *Farbe am Bauhaus. Synthese und Synästhesie*. Berlin: Gebr. Mann.

Gage, John. 1993. *Colour and Culture. Practice and Meaning from Antiquity to Abstraction*. London: Thames and Hudson.

——. 1999. Making sense of colour: The synaesthetic dimension. In *Colour and Meaning: Art, Science and Symbolism*, 261–268. Oxford: Thames and Hudson.

Galeyev, Bulat, and Irina L. Vanechkina. 2001. Was Scriabin a synesthete? *Leonardo* 34(4): 357–361.

Gombrich, Ernst H. 1960. *Art and Illusion: A Study in the Psychology of Pictorial Representation*. Oxford: Phaidon Press.

Hahl-Koch, Jelena. 1985. Kandinsky, Schönberg und der 'Blaue Reiter'. In *Vom Klang der Bilder*, ed. Karin von Maur, 354–359. Munich: Prestel.

Haverkamp, Michael. 2012. *Synesthetic Design. Handbook for a Multi-Sensory Approach*. Basel: Birkhäuser.

Ho, Cristy, and Charles Spence. 2008. *The Multisensory Driver: Implications for Ergonomic Car Interface Design*. Aldershot: Ashgate.

Howes, David. 2011. Hearing scents, tasting sights: Toward a cross-cultural multi-modal theory of aesthetics. In *Art and the Senses*, ed. Francesca Bacci and David Melcher, 161–182. Oxford: Oxford University Press.

Ione, Amy. 2004. Kandinsky and Klee: Chromatic Chords, Polyphonic Painting and Synesthesia. *Journal of Consciousness Studies* 11 (3–4):148–158.

Jewanski Jörg, Sean A. Day, and Jamie Ward J. 2009. A colorful albino: the first documented case of synaesthesia, by Georg Tobias Ludwig Sachs in 1812. *Journal of the History of the Neurosciences* 18 (3):293–303.

Jewanski, Jörg and Natalia Sidler, eds. 2006. *Farbe—Licht—Musik. Synästhesie und Farblichtmusik*. Bern: Peter Lang.

Kandinsky, Wassily. 2001. *Concerning the Spiritual in Art*. New York: MFA. (Originally published in 1911: Ueber das Geistige in der Kunst.)

Layden, Timothy B. 2010. The shape of sounds. <http://www.tblayden.com>.

Lyubomirsky, Sonja. 2008. *The How of Happiness: A Scientific Approach to Getting the Life You Want*. New York: Penguin Press.

Mahling, Friedrich. 1926. Das Problem der 'Audition colorée': Eine historisch-kritische Untersuchung. *Archiv für die gesamte Psychologie* 57: 165–301.

Marks, Lawrence E. 1978. *The Unity of the Senses Interrelationships Among the Modalities*. New York: Academic Press.

———. 2004. Cross-modal interactions in speeded classification. In *Handbook of Multisensory Processes*, ed. Gemma Calvert, Charles Spence, and Barry E. Stein, 85–106. Cambridge, MA: MIT Press.

Maur, Karin von. 1999. *The Sound of Painting: Music in Modern Art*. Munich: Prestel.

Maurer, Daphne, Laura C. Gibson, and Ferrinne Spector. 2013. Synesthesia in infants and very young children. In *The Oxford Handbook of Synesthesia*, ed. Julia Simner and Edward M. Hubbard, 46–63 . Oxford: Oxford University Press.

Maurer, Daphne and Charles Maurer. 1988. *The World of the Newborn*. New York: Basic Books.

Maurer, Daphne, and Catherine J. Mondloch. 2004. Neonatal aynesthesia: A ee-evaluation. In *Synesthesia: Perspectives from Neuroscience*, eds. Lynn C. Robertson and Noam Sagiv, 193–213. New York: Oxford University Press.

Merleau-Ponty, Maurice. 2002. *Phenomenology of Perception*. London: Routledge. (Originally published in 1945.)

Moritz, William. 2004. *Optical Poetry. The Life and Work of Oskar Fischinger*. Bloomington, In: Indiana University Press.

Peacock, Kenneth. 1985. Alexander Scriabin's color hearing. *Music Perception* 2(4): 483–506.

———. 1998. Instruments to perform color-music: Two centuries of technological experimentation. *Leonardo* 21(4): 397–406.

Renier, Laurent, and Anne G. De Volder. 2013. Sensory substitution devices: Creating "artificial synesthesias". In *The Oxford Handbook of Synesthesia*, ed. Julia Simner and Edward M. Hubbard, 853–868 . Oxford: Oxford University Press.

Schifferstein, Hendrik N.J. and Inge Tanudjaja. 2004. Visualising fragrances through colours: the mediating role of emotions. *Perception* 33:1249–1266.

Sinha, Jasmin R., ed. 2009. *Synästhesie der Gefühle. Tagungsband zur Tagung 'Die fröhliche Sieben—Synästhesie, Personifikation und Identifikation'*. Luxemburg: Synaisthesis.

Steen, Carol, and Greta Berman. 2013. Synesthesia and the artistic process. In *The Oxford Handbook of Synesthesia*, ed. Julia Simner and Edward M. Hubbard, 671–691 . Oxford: Oxford University Press.

Tan, Jeanne. 2011. Vibrant notes. In *Colour hunting. How colour influences what we buy, make and feel*, ed. Hanneke Kamphuis and Hedwig van Onna, 128–131. Amsterdam: Frame Publishers.

Ward, Jamie, and Peter Meijer. 2010. Visual experiences in the blind induced by an auditory sensory substitution device. *Consciousness and Cognition* 19 (1):492–500.

Ward, Jamie, Samantha Moore, Daisy Thompson-Lake, Shireen Salih, and Brianna Beck. 2008. The aesthetic appeal of auditory—visual synaesthetic perceptions in people without synaesthesia. *Perception* 37 (8):1285–1296.

CHAPTER 33

....

SYNESTHESIA IN LITERATURE

....

PATRICIA LYNNE DUFFY

INTRODUCTION

....

In F. Scott Fitzgerald's novel, *The Great Gatsby* (1925/1995), the author describes the "yellow cocktail music" at the character Jay Gatsby's lavish Long Island parties. By putting together the sight word, "yellow" with the sound word, "music," the author evokes the parties' ambiance by letting readers both hear and "see" the pervasive music. When we think of the subject of "synesthesia and literature," this may bring to mind just such literary uses of synesthetic or cross-sensory metaphor, where perceptions from two different sensory modalities are blended together, for effect.

Literature around the world is full of cross-sensory metaphors, and this has been explored in numerous studies both scientific and literary, including such influential works as George Laker's (1980) classic *Metaphors We Live By*, Lawrence Marks' *Synaesthesia: the Unity of the Senses*, and Glenn O'Malley's *Shelley and Synaesthesia*. In both everyday language and literature, metaphor allows us to bring to light different aspects of the thing perceived, heightening the experience of it. But what of the people whose everyday perceptions of the world appear to resemble those cross-sensory metaphors in an automatic, real-life, *perceptual* sense—who in some ways appear to experience, literally, what the metaphor tries to express figuratively? What of the people who literally "see" the color yellow upon hearing the cocktail music? In other words, what of those with the neurological condition of synesthesia? The daily experience of such individuals (whom we can describe as "neurological synesthetes") involves a dual or multisensory response to stimuli that would produce only a unisensory response for most people. For example, synesthetes can experience music or even noise as both sound *and* color, as something both heard *and* seen.

While the field of synesthesia and literature covers a broad area, this chapter focuses on a particular "place" in that vast territory: how the experience of neurological synesthesia has been portrayed in literary works, with a special focus on twentieth- and twenty-first-century writings, particularly in English.[1] It also focuses on the roots of these portrayals in nineteenth-century European literature.

The term, "neurological synesthesia" can be used to describe those individuals with "developmental" or "congenital" synesthesia (i.e., those who have experienced synesthetic perceptions since infancy/childhood) and also "acquired synesthesia" (i.e., those who have acquired the perception as a result of drug use, head injury, or other trauma in later life). Neurological synesthetes have long been an object of curiosity and the "meaning" of their perceptions has elicited different theories, some exalting and some denigrating the "condition." The nineteenth-century Romantics glorified synesthetic perception. As Kevin Dann writes in his historical account of synesthesia, *Bright Colors Falsely Seen*:

> To many observers, synaesthetes…have been permitted a view of something that seems to hold more truth than their own non-synaesthetic…imagery. (Dann 1998, 15)

Other thinkers, however, have not viewed strong synesthetic experiences in this lofty way. Instead, some have viewed neurological synesthesia as an unwholesome, unnatural, even pathological fusion and "confusion" of different sensory perceptions—compared to the "normal" perceptions of "healthy" persons (i.e., "normalcy" is equated with "health"). This chapter will focus on the various "meanings" ascribed to the experience of neurological synesthesia in fictional portrayals of synesthetes.

We can find occasional synesthete-characters in fictional works of past centuries; however, in recent years, with renewed interest in synesthesia research, the appearance of synesthete-characters in fiction has multiplied, almost constituting a new literary genre and introducing a new literary type. This has been fed by a resurgence of scientific and artistic research into synesthesia in recent decades, with information subsequently filtering from the research community into popular media. It has led a range of artists, including fiction writers (some synesthetes themselves, some not) to portray neurological synesthetes as characters in their creative works. The nature of the different portrayals can be indicative of our developing general understanding of synesthesia and those who experience it. These fictional portrayals may or may not always be "accurate," i.e., they may or may not correspond to reports of actual "real-life" synesthetes. Not surprisingly, some of the most realistic depictions of synesthetic experience tend to come from

---

[1] As described further later in the chapter, my particular focus on recent English-language fiction is dictated by the disproportionately larger number of works written within this category. Public awareness of synesthesia has risen dramatically within the last 50 years, and along with this, the number of synesthetes appearing as characters in fiction has risen accordingly, compared to earlier times. Moreover, most of these recent sources appear to be written in English, perhaps reflecting the relative abundance of science writings in this language. Prior to this, another era of heightened interest in synesthesia was the nineteenth century, and particularly dominant in the French Symbolist movement. The two époques (nineteenth century, and late twentieth/early twenty-first century) are the central focus of this chapter. This is not to say that interesting sources do not exist in other eras and other languages—they do—although they fall outside the focus of the current work.

synesthete authors themselves (e.g., Vladimir Nabokov, Jane Yardley; see later in this chapter). Elsewhere, an author might simply see a dramatic or symbolic possibility in attributing the trait of synesthesia to a character. By doing so, the author may be more interested in producing a desired literary effect than in producing a portrayal faithful to the scientific data on synesthetes. Nevertheless, the different portrayals tell us something about how the human imagination has approached and tried to understand the phenomenon of neurological synesthesia and of those who are hosts to it.

We shall see in this chapter that synesthetic perception also takes on symbolic meaning, representing either a human capacity to transcend familiar perceptual boundaries or a degeneration of sorts to an earlier, "primitive" form of perception. While research shows that neurological synesthesia can take many forms, the types in literary depictions are mostly "word-color," "music-color," "taste-color," and "word-taste" (i.e., synesthetes who experience colors from words, music, or taste, and those who experience taste from words). Our exploration of the different fictional representations of synesthetes and synesthesia will also move through some nineteenth-, twentieth-, and twenty-first-century works by a range of writers, both "popular" and "literary," who have depicted the experience of synesthesia. We will see how later American and European literary portrayals of synesthetes had their roots in earlier depictions, particularly those by nineteenth-century poets Charles Baudelaire and Arthur Rimbaud, along with an influential work of Joris-Karl Huysmans—and the responses to those portrayals by admirers and critics alike.

The purpose of this chapter is not to judge the literary merits of the works discussed, but rather to go across the literary spectrum and consider the images of synesthetes that emerge from a range of fictional genres: from Romantic, to avant-garde, to naturalist, to realist, to magic-realist, to science-fiction, to mystery, to those in comic book/graphic novels. I begin by describing some of the literary roots of synesthesia, stemming from the Symbolist movement in nineteenth-century French poetry. I then more generally review fictional portrayals of synesthesia and synesthetes. In doing so, I show that they appear to fall into one of five categories (which become the subsequent sections of this chapter): (1) synesthesia as Romantic ideal, (2) synesthesia as Romantic pathology, (3) synesthesia as pathology, (4) synesthesia as emotional completeness, and (5) synesthesia as accepted anomaly.

The Roots of Portrayals of Synesthetes and Synesthesia

A prominent early appearance of synesthesia in literary works came at the end of the nineteenth century. At that time, the circle of French Symbolist poets were particularly captivated by "colored hearing" or "chromosthesia" (colored sensation). The nineteenth-century French poet Arthur Rimbaud, author of the famous poem, "Vowels" (originally,

"Voyelles") about the perception of colored vowel sounds, first came across "audition colorée" (colored hearing) while combing through medical journals for scientific accounts of visionary experience[2] (and perhaps for understanding some of the drug-related hallucinations he had experienced). As John Harrison wrote in his *Synaesthesia: The Strangest Thing*:

> Rimbaud had been fascinated with the idea of sensory fusion and spent much of his time searching French medical literature for descriptions of visionary experience. (Harrison 2001, 13)

And, as Kevin Dann writes in his historical account of synesthesia, *Bright Colors Falsely Seen*, Rimbaud connected visionary experience with the ability to "hear colors":

> Rimbaud linked synaesthesia with mystical visions not out of his own experience... but because he was following his sources, the early nineteenth century medical literature. An inveterate reader of encyclopedias and dictionaries, he searched those texts... and came upon descriptions of audition colorée ...... the critic Felix Feneon had suggested that Rimbaud's poem "Voyelles" was inspired by the medical literature on audition colorée... a suggestion later echoed by Rimbaud's friend Ernest Delehaye in his biography of the poet. (Dann 1978, 23, 25)

Rimbaud's fascination with "colored hearing" (later called synesthesia) led him to write the poem, "Vowels" in 1871 (later published in 1883). This comprised four stanzas of surreal associations, starting with descriptions of colored vowel sounds:

> A black, E white, I red, U green, O blue: vowels,
> I shall tell, one day, of your mysterious origins:
> A, black velvety jacket of brilliant flies
> which buzz around cruel smells,
> Gulfs of shadow; E, whiteness of vapours and of tents,
> Lances of proud glaciers, white kings, shivers of cow-parsley;
> I, purples, spat blood, smile of beautiful lips
> in anger or in the raptures of penitence;
> U, waves, divine shudderings of viridian seas,
> the peace of pastures dotted with animals, the peace of the furrows
> which alchemy prints on broad studious foreheads;
> O, sublime Trumpet full of strange piercing sounds,
> Silences crossed by words and by angels:
> –O the Omega! the violet beam of His Eyes!
>
> (Rimbaud in Bernard (translator) 1962, 171)

Rimbaud and the other Symbolists believed that synesthetic perceptions were an indication that the "ordinary" things of this world were charged with an aesthetic and

---

[2] Dann suggests Emile Littre's single-volume *Dictionnaire de médicine, de chirurgie, de pharmacie, des sciences, accessoires et de l'art vétérinaire* as one likely source consulted by Rimbaud.

spiritual intensity which only a few "sensitives" or "seers" were able to apprehend. In the Symbolists' view, the true function of poets was to transmit to others this heightened vision of "the ordinary" through the language of their poetic works—and synesthetic perception was exalted as a manifestation of such heightened vision. Indeed, in the final stanza of Rimbaud's "Voyelles," the synesthete-speaker's exploration of his vision culminates in reaching a mystical state, "crossed by worlds and by angels." However, it seems that Rimbaud, himself, may never have experienced the congenital, neurological variety of synesthesia that he and his fellow poets so admired. As the poet wrote, "I invented the colors of the vowels!" (Rimbaud 1873/1937, 285). In other words, writing the poem, "Voyelles" was perhaps a way for Rimbaud to imaginatively project himself into the synesthetic form of perception that he'd read about and which intrigued him (although Rimbaud possibly *had* experienced synesthetic perceptions as a result of the drug experimentation popular among his Symbolist circle) (Baron-Cohen and Harrison 1997, 9).

The Symbolist circle linked synesthesia and other non-ordinary perceptual states with the ability to glimpse the Romantic "sublime," the ultimate truth and beauty the Romantics viewed as a source of artistic and mystical vision. Some believed that non-ordinary perceptual states like synesthesia were indicative of a future development of human consciousness. This view had descended from earlier Romantic poets such as Charles Baudelaire, who believed that "sensitives" and "seers" were able to perceive the mysterious subterranean connections among what appeared as discrete sensory experiences. In his poem, "Correspondences," Baudelaire describes the faint "echoes" of synesthetic merging into a single unity, described as the "one low shadowy note"—the harmonious union of things heard, smelled, and seen, where "sound calls to fragrance, color calls to sound":

> Like echoes long that from afar rebound,
> merged till one deep low shadowy note is born,
> vast as the night or as the fires of morn,
> sound calls to fragrance, colour calls to sound.
>
> (Baudelaire in Shanks (translator) 1931)

Baudelaire, and later Rimbaud's circle, believed this hidden unity was directly accessible only to the true poet—and to the synesthete—and Baudelaire returned to it in his later book, *Artificial Paradises*, where he describes his experience of sensory unity while under the influence of hashish:

> Sound holds color, color holds music. Musical notes become numbers. (Baudelaire in Diamond (translator) 1996, 19)

This "unity" was also described almost 100 years later by neuroscientist Lawrence Marks in his now classic work on the nature of metaphor, *Synaesthesia: the Unity of the Senses*, and by Kevin Dann, in *Bright Colors Falsely Seen*, his historical account of synesthesia:

> To comprehend...that there are correspondences between dimensions of auditory and visual experience...is to discern, however dimly or remotely, that amidst the diversity of sensory perceptions, there is unity. (Marks 1978, 2)

One can understand synaesthesia as a natural metaphor that is easily transferred to other topics because it is so expressive of the concepts of unity and harmony; because these things are in turn linked with our idea of the divine...when physicians and psychologists of the nineteenth century began to describe cases of chromosthetes...poets understood these individuals as gifted visionaries, like themselves. (Dann 1998, 42)

Like others of his circle, Rimbaud believed the way for the "poet-voyant" ("seer-poet") to attain such vision was by experimenting with sensory experience, or by imagining new combinations of sensory possibilities, even if the latter took a form considered "unnatural" and led to psychological torment. As Rimbaud wrote in his 1871 "Letter to Paul Demeny," better known as "La Lettre du Voyant" ("Letter of a Seer"):

I say one must be a seer, make oneself a seer.
The Poet makes himself a seer by a long, gigantic and rational *derangement of all the senses*. All forms of love, suffering and madness...He exhausts all poisons in himself and keeps only their quintessences. Unspeakable torture where he needs all his faith, all his superhuman strength, where he becomes among all men the one accursed and the supreme Scholar! Because he reaches the *unknown!* (Rimbaud in Fowlie (translator), 2005, 377)

The result of exploring such visions would lead to a future universal poetic language:

The time of universal language will come...This language will be for the soul, containing everything, smells, sounds, colors, thought holding on to thought and pulling...These poets will exist. (Rimbaud in Fowlie (translator), 2005, 379)

Not only poets, but also scientists became intrigued by perceptions of "smells, colors, and sounds" corresponding, and by the late nineteenth century, the time was ripe for a reinvigorated study of synesthesia. "Voyelles" had an impact not only on the circle of 1880's Symbolist poets and their admirers, but also on scientists of the day. In fact, in a reflection between art and science, the year after "Voyelles" was published, 16 scientific papers on audition colorée were also published (prior to "Voyelles," the average was about three per year). At the 1889 International Conference on Physiological Psychology in Paris, the talks on audition colorée drew the most attention. As Kevin Dann writes:

In the mid-1880's, the two topics talked about in nearly every Paris and Berlin salon were Wagner and the unconscious; audition colorée, especially Rimbaud's poetic treatment of the subject. (Dann 1998, 25)

The discussion was furthered by poet and arts essayist, Rene Ghil's book, *Traité du Verbe*. In his book, Ghil, also at the forefront of the Symbolist movement, wrote of "audition colorée" as pointing to an evolving higher consciousness marked by a sensory and artistic fusion:

Indéniablement maintenant, voire de la Science autopsié, peint ses gammes le fait de l'Audition Colorée miraculeusement montée qu'avec humilité nous souhaitons, ou tous les Arts, inconsciemment impiés reviendront se perdre en la totale Communion: la Musique l'épouvante qui intronise la Divinité seule, Poésie ....A moi, de m'enquérer de la cause: une phase, sans doute, d'une evolution progressive de nos sens elevés. (Ghil, 1886, 25) [translation: Now, undeniably, scientific review gives validity to the miraculous fact of colored hearing, which points to that distant time we humbly await, where all the Arts, in their unconscious irreverence, will return and lose themselves in a total Communion: that terrifying Music that will enthrone the only Divinity, Poetry...In my estimation, this is most certainly a phase in the evolution of our higher senses.]

While the circle of Symbolist poets and their followers represented synesthesia as a glimpse into the Sublime (i.e., a glimpse into more refined and mystical realms of reality; a step forward in human evolution) others took a far dimmer view of the phenomenon. A debate ensued. Literary critics such as Max Nordau asserted that views expressed by Symbolists Baudelaire and Rimbaud were decadent, "exert[ing] a disturbing and corrupting influence on a whole generation" (Nordau, 1895, preface, viii). Nordau viewed the blended perceptions of synesthetes as a degenerate, "diseased state of mind." For Nordau, the idea of even accepting, let alone celebrating synesthetes' "confused" perceptions (as he termed them) was dangerous to human advancement. In his 1895 book, *Degeneration* (originally published in German, 1892 as *Ertartung*), Nordau described the blended perceptions of synesthesia as "a descent from the height of human perfection to the low level of the mollusk" (Nordau 1895, 142).

Other critics and scientists of a more rational and less Romantic turn of mind supported Nordau's view, but not all. Romanian scientist Eduourd Gruber exalted, in fact, the sound-color perceptions of the synesthetes he studied as "an echo of the mathematical structure of the Cosmos" (Dann 1998, 32). By the 1890s, it became clear that those interested in synesthesia fell into two camps—those who glorified the perception and those who denigrated it. Swiss psychologist Theodore Flournoy tried to mediate between the two extreme views, calling for a more objective view of colored hearing. As Flournoy said, synesthesia deserved "Ni cet excès d'honneur, ni cette indignité" (Flournoy 1893, 250), or "Neither excess of honor nor indignity." Such a moderate view, he felt, would be the best way to further research in the field. Until the trait of synesthesia was better understood, no conclusion about its value (or lack thereof) could be reached.

In looking at later fictional representations of synesthetes and their experiences, it is not Flournoy's more objective view that is expressed, but rather the extreme views, even in the fictional portrayals of today. In literary portrayals of synesthetes that have appeared over the decades, we find examples of synesthetic perceptions either lifting their hosts to transcendent realms (e.g., extolling the primacy of individual imagination) or plunging them into pathological symptoms of sensory overload, such as headaches, seizures, isolation, or an unwholesome "unraveling" and distorting of the senses. An example of the former is the Romantic view we find in Vladimir Nabokov's novel *The Gift* (1963/1991) and an example of the latter is the pathological Colonel Kachhwah in Salman Rushdie's *Shalimar the Clown* (both discussed later in this chapter). In some cases, we see a combination of these extremes: though the synesthetic perceptions may overwhelm their synesthete-hosts with various forms of suffering, they are also a source of artistic and mystical vision, allowing them to experience life on a "higher" or "deeper" plane. Such a view is expressed in the portrayal of the composer, Milan, in Holly Payne's The *Sound of Blue*, and of the nun, Sister John, in Mark Salzman's *Lying Awake* (discussed later).

Only in a few very recent works of fiction do we find synesthetes possessing an anomalous trait deserving "neither excess of honor not indignity," but which is simply a feature of the way they perceive the world. We find such views in portrayals, discussed below, of the character Darlene Sable in T.J. Parker's detective novel, *The Fallen*, in Jane Yardley's *Painting Ruby Tuesday*, and in Monique Truong's *Bitter in the Mouth*. However, even these more objective portrayals contain hints of the extreme parallel views, so strong is the nineteenth-century influence represented by Nordau, Rimbaud, and Baudelaire. In the following sections I classify five different functions of synesthesia within fiction, primarily from twentieth- and twenty-first-century sources.

SYNESTHESIA AS ROMANTIC IDEAL

As noted earlier, the Romantic ideal extols the primacy and beauty of individual imagination and presents an expanded vision of reality. This ideal is found to a great extent in synesthete characters penned by Nabokov, such as the character Fyodor in Nabokov's work, *The Gift*. Fyodor is a young, gifted émigré poet living in Berlin, who experiences words as having vivid colors. The portrayal of Fyodor's synesthetic perceptions evokes a vision of transcendent beauty, and as such, synesthetic perception gets a Romantic treatment (minus any decadent edge) in this character. At the start of *The Gift*, Fyodor says,

> The various numerous "a"s of the four languages which I speak differ for me in tinge, going from lacquered-black to splintery-gray like different sorts of wood. I recommend to you my pink flannel "m" .... If I had some paints handy I would mix burnt sienna and sepia for you as to match the color of a..."ch" sound...and you would appreciate my radiant "s" if I could pour into your cupped hands some of those luminous sapphires that I touched as a child. (Nabokov 1963/1991, 75)

For the character Fyodor, the perception of language as a landscape of shimmering, luminous colors and textures is a gift which allows the poet to express the transcendent beauty of words. It also harkens back to a romanticized view of the "pure perceptions" of childhood, which we also find in nineteenth-century early Romantic poets like Wordsworth (e.g., in his "Ode: Intimations of Immortality from Recollections of Early Childhood"; 1804). From the Romantic view, it is the poet's task to restore the glory of childhood perceptions, and to let others see the beauty of the Sublime

The author Nabokov was himself a literary artist and a synesthete, very much like his main character Fyodor. Given this, one wonders if Nabokov is putting some of his own feelings about his synesthesia into the mouth of his protagonist. In his 1951 autobiography, *Speak Memory*, author Nabokov tells us he, himself "presents a fine case of colored hearing." An excerpt follows from the author's now famous description of his colored (and textured) alphabet:

> A French a evokes polished ebony. The black group [of letters] also includes hard g (vulcanized rubber) and y (a sooty rag being ripped). Oatmeal n, noodle-limp l, and the ivory-backed hand mirror of o take care of the whites...Passing on to the blue group, there is steely x, thundercloud z, and huckleberry k...I hasten to complete my list before I am interrupted. In the green group, there are alder-leaf f, the unique apple of p, and pistachio r. Dull green somehow combined with violet, is the best I can do for w...Finally, among the reds, b has the tone called burnt sienna by painters, m is a fold of pink flannel, and today I have at last perfectly matched v with "Rose Quartz" in Maerz and Paul's Dictionary of Color. (Nabokov 1989b, 34–35)

Nabokov also portrays a synesthete-character, Cincinnatus in his 1959 experimental novel, *Invitation to a Beheading*. Cincinnatus is a prisoner, jailed for an incomprehensible crime called "gnostical turpitude." His crime appears to be insisting on the validity of his own personal heightened synesthetic perception in a society where citizens dare not go against the "officially sanctioned" version of reality. Even his name, Cincinnatus suggests a kind of double "sinning at us." Cincinnatus takes a defiant pride in his unique form of perception, which he feels results from senses more acute and more alive than most. Reminiscent of Rimbaud's view of the poet and his special gift of perception, the character says,

> I am not an ordinary—I am the one among you who is alive—not only are my eyes different and my hearing and my sense of taste—not only is my sense of smell like a deer's, my sense of touch like a bat's—but most important, I have the capacity to conjoin all of this in one point. (Nabokov 1951/1989b, 52)

Interestingly, in a novel by Brent Kernan called *The Synaesthete* (written nearly half a century later, in 2002), the main character, Carly Jackson, recalls the character Cincinnatus. Like Cincinnatus, Carly is a synesthete who hears colors and sees flavors. As Cincinnatus is accused of "gnostical turpitude," Carly is accused of a similarly mysterious crime of "moral turpitude," also a crime of differing perception stemming from her synesthesia. Like Cincinnatus, Carly is society's prisoner: in her case, a prisoner of the military, who wants to use her synesthesia for its own purposes. (Carly's character will be further explored in this chapter's next section, "Synesthesia as Romantic pathology.")

If the characters Cincinnatus and Carly Jackson show us individual perception suppressed, then the character Synaesthesia Jackson in the 2000 *Top Ten* graphic-novel/comic book series, shows synesthetic perception unchained and liberated. Synaesthesia Jackson is a detective on the "Top Ten Police Force" in Neopolous, a city populated exclusively by super-heroes, each with a different superpower. Detective Synaesthesia Jackson's superpower lies in her synesthesia. Here liberated, synesthetic perception (suppressed or controlled in characters Cincinnatus and Carly) has the power to fuse disparate clues into a single solution to a crime. For example, this super-hero describes how her synesthesia led to her certainty of a suspect's guilt:

> It was her perfume I smelled on Graczik's body, but I translated it into music. She was Graczik's off-world drug customer. (Ha and Moore 2002, n.p.)

While Synaesthesia Jackson's experiences may not guide her to Rimbaud's realm of mystical truth, her unusual lens brings her to a "place" where disparate perceptions converge to show another kind of "truth"—that of a person's guilt or innocence. The depiction of the character's synesthetic perception descends from the romantic notion of synesthesia as heightened perception—and in this work, it is a superpower, no less!

Detective Jackson's language of synesthesia enables her to synesthesize information and solve crimes; it does not, however, escape the skepticism of the other super-heroes on the Top Ten force who are not synesthetes. Her fellow super-heroes wonder if Detective Synaesthesia could have solved the mysteries even without the synesthetic perceptions, which make no sense to them. Was it really necessary to translate the perfume into music to know it was a valid clue? Was the synesthetic response superfluous? Would just smelling the perfume on the victim's body have been enough? Despite the poking of fun, the *Top Ten* series nevertheless represents Synaesthesia Jackson's "language of synesthetic clues" as a superpower (whose only "down side" is the doubt of others), and so we place her story in the category of "synesthesia as Romantic ideal," albeit with a modern whiff of skepticism.

SYNESTHESIA AS ROMANTIC PATHOLOGY

In the nineteenth century, the advent of the industrial revolution and the rise of science made many question the tenets of long-held conventional religious belief and traditional values about what constituted the "proper place" of things. Further, artists felt that the increasing acceptance of an objective, scientific world view put the validity of individual imagination and spiritual vision under attack. Artists felt the need to break through to a new vision by rejecting received truths and experimenting with the unknown, even if that meant cultivating experiences deemed forbidden. For example, Baudelaire's poem "Correspondences" expresses the idea of finding the soul through the pursuit of heightened sensory experience, even those experiences that might "corrupt." It is this element of corruption that we might consider a Romantic pathology.

The ambiance of Baudelaire's poem also pervades J.-K. Huysmans' 1884 novel, *Against Nature* (original French title: *A Rebours*). The novel's very title suggests a kind of corruption, a going against the natural order of things. The portrayal of the main character, Des Esseintes, is emblematic of modern sensibility at that time, as he can believe in neither received truths about God nor the goodness of nature. Instead, Des Esseintes looks within himself, to the landscape of his own idiosyncrasies, and pursues personal

obsessions and exotic sensations. Synesthetic blendings become emblematic of the decadent delights in which the character revels. In the following passage, probably the most-
oft quoted one from *Against Nature*, the character perceives the taste of a given liquor as
corresponding to the sound of a particular musical instrument—so that he succeeds in
"transferring different pieces of music to his palate":

> Indeed, each and every liquor, in his opinion, corresponded in taste with the sound
> of a particular instrument. Dry curucao, for instance, was like the clarinet with its
> piercing, velvety note; kummel like the oboe with its sonorous, nasal timbre; crème
> de menthe and anisette like the flute, at once sweet and tart, soft and shrill...He
> even succeeded in transferring specific pieces of music to his palate...by mixing or
> contrasting related liquors. (Huysmans in Baldick (translator), 1959, 58–59)

This notion of transferring music to one's palate and playing symphonies in one's mouth
was a shocking one; to many, it crossed forbidden boundaries and degraded the ethe-
real beauty of music. Huysmans' novel was condemned as hostile to religion by Catholic
reviewers of his time, and even the great novelist Emile Zola, who, as leader of the school
of Naturalism (the faithful rendering in fiction of "things as they are" without prettifying
or romanticizing them) felt *Against Nature* went "too far," saying Huysmans' work dealt
a "terrible blow" to the movement.

Others like George Moore and Oscar Wilde greatly admired the novel's "naturalist"
depiction of sensations previously unexplored in literature. As Wilde described *Against
Nature*, "the heavy odour of incense seemed to cling about its pages and to trouble
the brain" (Baldick 1959, 11). The view of synesthesia as Romantic pathology also carried over into twentieth- and even twenty-first-century novels, as we shall see later in
this chapter. Even in the 1964 book, *Shelley and Synaesthesia*, author Glenn O'Malley
describes the dim view of synesthetic imagery taken by earlier critics and even many of
his own contemporaries,

> Such transfers among vocabularies (e.g., "strident color") are still regarded as
> eccentric or even abnormal in origin so that a writer's frequent or otherwise
> extraordinary use of them may invite special notice along psychological lines.
> (O'Malley 1964, 3)

Synesthesia can also be viewed as Romantic pathology in later fictional works. If
the 2000 *Top Ten* character, Synaesthesia Jackson shows synesthetic vision liberated,
the 2002 novel *The Synaesthete*, shows main character Carly Jackson's synesthetic
vision held hostage (by military, cyber, and social forces). As mentioned earlier in
this chapter, synesthete Carly is accused of the crime of "moral turpitude"—a crime
of differing perception which apparently threatens the status quo. As Kernan's novel
is written in a higher-tech age than was, say, Nabokov's, the imaginative possibilities
of a character's synesthesia have expanded. In the futuristic world in which Carly
moves, the military view her synesthesia as a pathology, although they also see synesthetic perception's vast potential if properly controlled and exploited for their

purposes (which is to create a new computer source code). As her former commanding officer says of Carly:

> The specialist came to us with a disease of the mind. It's called synaesthesia…but it becomes useful because her mind reduces sensory perception down to mathematics, to symbolic representations of what she perceives. I'll give you a simple example. Mathematics and music are integrally related. A pitch can be heard, but it can also be represented by the rate of vibrations traveling through a medium…all mathematical relationships can be reduced to music…any computer program can be played on a piano…Source code which is written out as language is infinitely inferior to source code that can be expressed or understood through the senses because only then can the true simultaneity of events be expressed. (Kernan 2002, 79–80)

Carly is compelled to put her synesthesia in the service of the military. Later in the novel, she uses her synesthetic abilities to escape from military control and becomes a "cyber-outlaw." However, her synesthetic gifts and the expanded potential they bring, come with a price: if not properly channeled, her synesthesia can cause Carly to suffer overwhelming headaches and hallucinations that she is unable to distinguish from reality. In this way, the portrayal of Carly's synesthesia fits neatly under "synesthesia as Romantic pathology." Her outlaw activities in the cyber-world give her an almost super-hero status, but this is tempered by the sensory confusion she must contend with.

Similarly, in T.J. Parker's 2007 novel *The Fallen* (which reached *The New York Times'* best-seller list), the synesthetic abilities of the main character, Detective Robbie Brownlaw help him to solve crimes for the city of San Diego. Detective Brownlaw is not a congenital synesthete, but rather gains synesthetic abilities after a fall from a ten-story-building causes a neural abnormality. Following his fall and the onset of his acquired synesthesia, Detective Brownlaw begins to perceive people's words as colors and shapes coming from their mouths. The particular colors and shapes let him know the emotional state of the person—and most importantly, whether s/he is telling the truth. The character describes his newly-acquired experience of synesthesia as follows:

> My life was ordinary until three years ago when I was thrown out of a downtown hotel window. No one knows it except my wife, but I now have synaesthesia, a neurological condition where your senses get mixed up. Sometimes when people talk to me, I see their voices as colored shapes. It happens when they get emotional… [The shapes] linger in mid-air between the speaker and me. (Parker 2007, 5)

Detective Brownlaw's synesthetic signals help him when he investigates a murder, uncovering related corruption, and a prostitution ring called "Squeaky Cleans":

> "You can tell us what you know about Squeaky Cleans," I said.
>   "Squeaky Cleans?" he asked. "I'm not sure what you mean."
>   The red squares of the lie spilled from his mouth. (Parker 2007, 173)

Although the Detective's synesthesia offers an advantage for his job, it also creates a problem in his personal life:

> The condition is hard for me to talk about, even with [my wife] Gina . . . it annoys her that even her white lies announce themselves to me as bright red squares. (Parker 2007, 6)

After his marriage breaks up, Brownlaw explores synesthesia research and associations on the web and discovers a department at the University of California, San Diego dedicated to the study of synesthesia (a fact). He then attends a meeting of the San Diego "Synesthesia Society." The evening's speaker was Darlene Sable, (fictional) author of *Red Sax and Lemon Cymbals*,[3] which gives a description of her growing up synesthetic. After the meeting, some members go out for coffee, and Detective Brownlaw is asked to describe his synesthesia to the group:

> "I see blue triangles from a happy speaker. Red squares come from liars. Envy comes out in green trapezoids, so "green with envy" is literally true for me. Aggression shows up as small black ovals."
>
> "That's not synaesthesia," said Bart. "I've read every word ever written about the subject, and no one has ever established that a speaker's emotions can be visualized . . . What do you see coming from my mouth right now?"
>
> "Little black ovals. Quite a few of them." [answered the detective.] (Parker 2007, 279–280)

This exchange gives us a bit of satire on disputes among synesthetes, which sometimes occur, while at the same time showing us how Detective Brownlaw's synesthesia functions.

As news of scientific research has filtered into mainstream society, a number of authors have been inspired to create detective-characters with synesthesia, almost leading to a whole genre of synesthete-detective novels (mentioned in a list of "Further reading" at the end of this chapter). In *The Fallen* and others, the detective-character acquires the synesthetic perception as a result of a near-fatal accident. The resulting synesthesia is depicted as giving the character an extra-sensory advantage, i.e., an ability to view a normally hidden layer of reality, thus putting this type of portrayal in the category of synesthesia as Romantic pathology.

Synesthetic colors are put to a very different use—and in a very different setting—in Holly Payne's 2005 novel, *The Sound of Blue*, which is mostly set in a refugee camp during the Balkan War. The character, Milan is a Serbian composer who experiences music as having color. His synesthetic experiences, though beautiful, trigger epileptic episodes. The luminous colors of music the composer experiences share more with the

---

[3] Author T.J. Parker confirms that the book on synaesthesia, *Blue Cats and Chartreuse Kittens* (Duffy 2001) inspired the parody-title *Red Sax and Lemon Cymbals* in his book, *The Fallen*.

transcendent beauty experienced by Nabokov's Fyodor, but with an added Romantic pathology. As the novel tells us of Milan, the composer,

> Color had ordered the composer's hand. Without color, he heard nothing. He filled notebooks with the sound of yellow and red. Purple. Green. Pink...Like Liszt and Stravinsky, Kandinsky and Rimbaud, Milan shared the multisensory perception of synaesthetes, and unfortunately the seizures that about 4 per cent of them endured...Milan's epilepsy resulted from his multi-sensory experiences...The hallucinations, when triggered repeated themselves involuntarily and could drive him to the brink of madness with their vividness. (Payne 2005, 90–91)

Milan suffers for his musical visions with headaches and seizures, which reaches back to Rimbaud's notion of artists as a "seers" who must suffer for their sublime visions. For Milan, the product of these visions is a refuge—and a source of meaning in his life:

> He felt secure in the music and sheltered from the torment of seizures within the shades and shadows of blue. (Payne 2005, 91)

Here the character's synesthesia is presented as a "blessed" pathology: one that, despite the pain it produces allows a peak into a sublime realm. The vision taken from this realm is incorporated into works of art, which have a stirring, and also a healing effect on others as well. Milan's compositions have a deeply moving and soothing effect on fellow-residents of the Balkans refugee camp:

> Sara, too, turned toward the sound...the coupling of notes was unlike any she had ever heard...The sounds pierced and jabbed her heart...the notes gathered in circles, releasing halos of sound that floated up for each of them to hold. (Payne 2005, 48)

The idea that synesthetic perception can take one beyond the boundaries of ordinary consciousness, leading to the creation of works of art that give others a taste of sublime realms is also expressed in Mark Salzman's 2000 novel, *Lying Awake*. Here, too, the novel's main character, Sister John, is able to inspire others with the beauty of her synesthesia-inspired art and visions. Sister John is both a poet and nun, and her synesthetic perceptions of colored and textured hearing are components of the exquisite poetry she writes and the mystical states she experiences.

> When he [the priest] began chanting Mass...his voice was a rich sienna, the color of reassurance...Sister John heard each of her sister's voices as if they were chanting alone: Sister Christine sounded as if her throat were lined with mother-of-pearl, while Sister Anne's voice had more texture, like a bowed instrument...Mother Mary Joseph's voice was mostly breath, forming a kind of white sound that helped blend the others. (Salzman 2000, 134)

However, as in *The Sound of Blue* and other works in this category, suffering is concomitant to the synesthetic experience. Sister John's ecstatic experiences are preceded by debilitating migraine headaches and followed by seizures that cause her to need medical treatment

> Hearing the voices together, she perceived them as all woven together to form a tapestry...
> The tapestry lit up.
> Fractures and other imperfections—including her epilepsy—became irrelevant; a much deeper beauty revealed itself now. (Saltzman 2000, 135)

The view of synesthesia expressed here is also in the category of Romantic pathology— however with a modern edge. When a CT scan reveals that the nun's non-ordinary states of consciousness are caused by a form of epilepsy, Sister John must face the question: are her experiences genuine encounters with the Divine—or mere symptoms of a neural pathology?

SYNESTHESIA AS INDICATIVE OF PATHOLOGY

Yet another group of novels present synesthetic perception as pathology, but minus the bonus of contact with the mystical, the Sublime, or the super-human. For example, in Salman Rushdie's 2005 novel, *Shalimar the Clown*, the character's synesthesia has no redeeming power and is shown as symptomatic of a dark psychological pathology caused by repression of his own humanity. The synesthete-character is Colonel (later General) Kachhwah, a commanding officer in the Indian army, stationed in 1959 Kashmir. His synesthesia is a complex multifaceted type, at times causing an unbearable feeling of sensory overload. As the novel describes Colonel Kachhwah's condition:

> He barely had words to describe...these blurrings. He saw sounds nowadays. He heard colors. He tasted feelings. He had to control himself in conversation, lest he ask, "What is that red noise?" (Rushdie 2005, 100)

We see Colonel Kachhwaha's synesthesia results from his suppressing an impulse toward beauty and poetry:

> His senses were changing into one another... What was hearing? What was taste? He hardly knew. He was in command of twenty thousand men and he thought the color gold sounded like a bass trombone. He needed poetry. A poet could explain him to himself, but he was a soldier...If he spoke of his need for poetry, his men would think him weak. (Rushdie 2005, 100)

In his inner world, Colonel Kachhwah's synesthetic perceptions also serve to distort and disguise the horror of his actions

> The confusion of his senses grew ever more extreme. The idea of violence had a velvet softness now...Bullets entered flesh like music, the pounding of clubs was the rhythm of life, and then there was...the demoralization of the population through the violation of its women. In that dimension every color was bright and tasted good. (Rushdie 2005, 291)

Here synesthesia is symptomatic of a kind of decadence (in this case a "decaying" of the Colonel's humanity). But it is a decadence unredeemed by spiritual longing or the pursuit of poetical vision of ultimate truth or beauty.

While Colonel Kachhwah's synesthesia manifests as a psychological pathology, in Julia Glass' 2006 novel, *The Whole World Over*, the character Saga's synesthesia manifests as a physical one. Saga is a 34-year-old woman whose colored-word synesthesia results from a head injury. She suffers memory loss. Since her injury, words have taken on colors for her. Saga's synesthesia is portrayed as symptomatic of her injury and also her resulting isolation from the flow of life around her:

> The word would fill her mind for a few minutes with a single color: not an unpleasant sensation but still an intrusion. (Glass 2006, 116)

At the same time, Saga's experience of colored words strikes the reader as poetic. It is typical of synesthetic descriptions, in its attempt to evoke the perception's colors with great precision:

> There was the house. House: a word as big and gray as a summer storm cloud, but flat, solid, quiet. House. Ramekin. Boyfriend (china blue, Yale blue). Baby (white as the innards of a milkweed pod): Four delicious words. (Glass 2006, 256)

The story, which is set mainly in Manhattan, New York—ends with the tragedy of 9/11. Saga's colored words also becomes emblematic of a larger social pathology

> She avoided the paper along with radio and TV. Too much busy noise. Sometimes a swath of current events...dropped into her consciousness like a comet—that's how she knew that she'd once known about Bosnia and Romanian orphans. *Herzogovina*...The word a deep blue lavender, the color of Uncle Marsden's favorite hyacinths. (Glass 2006, 444)

If Saga's synesthesia is symptomatic of pathology, her colorful words also hold the components of the life story she has lost along with her memory. The vivid words she now experiences are the building blocks of the story she will eventually recover, bit by bit. In this way, Saga's synesthesia is not just a symptom of her pathology but also a key to healing it. I further examine this healing quality of synesthesia in the next section.

SYNESTHESIA AS EMOTIONAL COMPLETENESS

The notion of synesthetic colors as having healing power is expressed in the acclaimed 1994 magic-realist novel, *Saudade*. One can imagine the possibilities of presenting synesthetic perception in a magic-realist context, and the author, Katherine Vaz, realizes them beautifully here. In *Saudade*, the main character, Clara, is born deaf to a family in a fishing community in the Azores Islands of Portugal. Clara's synesthesia is not depicted as pathological, but rather, as a quirkily beautiful compensation or coping-mechanism for her congenital deafness. She develops a visual language of words as colored shapes, which helps her learn to read. In the course of the novel, a tragedy occurs: Clara's child dies; this emotional trauma causes her to lose her relationship to language and her ability to read (an ability she very much prizes). It is during this painful period of her life that Clara meets Helio, who becomes her lover. Helio is intrigued by Clara's secret world of color and wants to share it, while also wanting to help Clara overcome her trauma. He re-teaches her to read, realizing the key is employing her personal, synesthetic colors:

> To recapture her lost ability of reading, he chose 26 tints for each letter of the alphabet and set about copying books for her. "Clara, what do you think?" he asked.
> "Well, fine," said Clara. "But why don't you make words into their own color-shapes instead of spelling them out?" (Vaz 1994, 217)

Helio encourages Clara to explore her perceptions more deeply. In doing so, she discovers that the colors of words can be transposed to form the colors of music

> Colors could guide her not only to producing sounds on an instrument, they had sound themselves! It meant that words could be reborn as colors but also as actual music…"I can play books directly on the piano!," Clara tells Helio excitedly. (Vaz 1994, 228)

Clara and Helio collaborate on synesthetic art—the rest of the town rejoices and is exhilarated, even liberated by it:

> When he wrote a painting in tribute…and Clara converted it to music, the caged birds throughout town chewed their iron bars, desperate to fly toward the rejoicing, and the people of Lodi begged Clara for a concert. (Vaz 1994, 229)

In this way, in *Saudade*, the synesthetic vision comes to represent wholeness, health, and a healing that can be shared with others through art.

Synesthetic colors can therefore represent health and wholeness for the character who possesses them. This view of synesthesia reaches back to Rimbaud and Baudelaire's belief in the transformative power of personal perception and its promise of taking those who pursue it to a place of truth and greater vision. In *Saudade*, that vision includes physical and psychological health and wholeness.

Similarly, in the 2003 pre-teen book, *A Mango-Shaped Space*, the 13-year-old Mia loses her synesthesia when her beloved cat, Mango dies. Mia regains the perception only after resolving the trauma of her loss.[4] The following is an exchange between Mia and her psychologist:

> "If I'm so strong, then why are my colors gone?"
> He doesn't answer right away. "When did this happen?"
> "Right after Mango...after he...after he died."
> "How do you feel about it?"
> "Empty," I tell him honestly. "Flat."
> ..."Your colors will return, Mia. I promise. And you'll feel three-dimensional again."
>
> (Mass 2005 255)

Equating the presence of synesthetic perception with well-being, wholeness and completeness is also represented in Jane Yardley's novel, *Painting Ruby Tuesday*. The main character, Annie is a songwriter who perceives music and language in color. The novel shows flashbacks to her childhood, where she copes with the death of a synesthete-friend. We see how her synesthetic experience provides an aid in solving the mystery of her friend's death. Here we have the idea of synesthesia as a special way of seeing/thinking that may offer advantages—but the perception is not viewed as "mystical" or "super-human." Rather it is identified more with the idea of completeness, originality, and artistic vision possessed by a unique few. In one of the novel's scenes, Annie and another synesthete-musician explore their musical perceptions to a piece of Boogie-Woogie. They are both exhilarated by the synesthetic landscape they share:

> "What colors do you hear there?"....
> "It sounds green to me" I said...
> "Ok, let's see if I can modulate it to bring you some others."
> Her Broadway boogie-woogie slid bluely into the relative minor key. "Now?" she asked.
> "Bluer!," I laughed back at her. "It's going blue!"
> "Magic!," cried Mrs. Clitheroe, her hands dancing on the keyboard.
> "Knock knock," said a man's voice. "Are we interrupting something?"
> It was Horace and Doris Frobisher from Sunday School.
> I wanted to holler at them. I wanted to scream,
> "Get out! Leave us alone!"
>
> (Yardley 2003, 79–80)

---

[4] A non-fictional first-hand account of the loss of synesthesia following trauma is given by Day, Chapter 44, this volume.

Here, a hole of sorts is punctured in the soaring spirits and synesthetic visions of the two friends by the presence of the uncomprehending Sunday school couple, whose more conventional, prosaic vision deflates the synesthetes' expanding one.

SYNESTHESIA AS ACCEPTED ANOMALY

In this final section we might consider how synesthesia can be represented in fiction as an accepted anomaly: it is taken as an everyday facet of life for the synesthete. An example is found in Parker's *The Fallen*. The synesthetic perceptions of the novel's protagonists are ultimately viewed as an ordinary fact about the character's way of perceiving the world. They might yet bring their host a layer of aesthetic delight and a sense of well-being, but only so long as they are simply accepted as a unique way of perceiving. The character, Darlene Sable writes a book to explain her journey as a synesthete:

> From early childhood she remembered "seeing music"…the saxophone was of course, red, and cymbals lemon yellow; violins were lime green, guitars magenta, and so on. By the time she was five, she knew that not everyone saw music like she did…though it never interfered with her life in any way. (Parker 2007, 278)

Here, synesthesia is not represented as a debilitating, painful pathology, but simply as a way the character happens to perceive the world. Her synesthesia still offers an aesthetic advantage, allowing her to appreciate a beautiful visual dimension to the music:

> As an adult, she had become a piano instructor and nothing pleased her as much as sitting next to a young student and seeing the swells of crimson music flowing out of the instrument. (Parker 2007, 279)

I described earlier a tone of satire found in *The Fallen*, which again shows how hard it is for most to fathom the synesthete's experience or the seriousness synesthetes can attach to it. Despite the satire, however, the view of congenital synesthesia in *The Fallen* comes close to Flournoy's idea of synesthesia as deserving "neither excess of honor nor indignity." Darlene's only real problem vis-à-vis her synesthetic perception is feeling it misunderstood by the majority who does not share it. When Darlene learns to accept her synesthesia, she gives herself over to the enjoyment of this fact of her inner life.

Similarly, in the 2007 short piece, *Phone Home*, author Natasha Lvovich, herself a synesthete, presents her Russian-émigré's character's synesthesia merely as a fact of her inner life. The character is conscious of the visual quality, the "look" of her inner panic; its synesthetic elements form the building blocks of her awareness. In the following excerpt, we find a striking description of feeling taking form, as the character experiences the tragedy of 9/11:

> First, in complete silence, the yellow wall in my room cracks, spreading its spider web threads as fast and as slowly as is only possible in a dream. Chill is crawling down my spine; hot puffs throb into my head. This is panic, fear, terror—a preverbal pre-Russian sensation that has yet no name. I am regressing into pre-consciousness, into pure physiology: the adrenaline, the serotonin, the chemical reactions in my brain, until I start to discern first colors then words: thin scarlet and gluey yellow—*koshmar* (horror, literally meaning nightmare), then chestnut brown *remont*. (Lvovich 2010)

In the category of "synesthesia as accepted anomaly," we also have a strong sense of a character's "meta-perception," i.e., his or her ability to observe herself perceiving. Similarly, in Monique Truong's (2010) *Bitter in the Mouth*, both the main character's synesthetic word-taste perceptions—as well as her own hyper-awareness of them—are presented. The main character's word-taste synesthesia is shown as a fact of her inner life—one that comes with distracting discomforts, but also pleasures. This character, Linda/Linh-Dao, is of Vietnamese origin, adopted as a baby by well-to-do white parents in the southern town of Boiling Springs, North Carolina. Linda/Linh-Dao must contend with both the inner and outer anomalies of her identity—the aspect that is visible and obvious to others (the fact of her Asian heritage and the discrimination she faces in her all-white, small, southern town) and the one that is known only to herself (her experience of flavored words):

> When my teacher asked, "Linda, where did the English first settle in North Carolina?" the question would come to me as, "Linda*mint*, where did the English*maraschinocherry* first *Pepto-Bismol* settle in North Carolina*cannedpeas*?"
> Many of the words that I heard or had to say aloud brought with them a taste—unique, consistent, and most often unrelated to the meaning of the word that had sent the taste rolling into my mouth. (Truong 2010, 21)

Linda shares her secret "word-tastes" only with her best friend, Kelly. The two friends communicate in letters to minimize the overwhelming barrage of tastes brought on by spoken words in a conversation (reading written words does not bring the character the "taste-reaction"):

> I had shared my secret sense with Kelly in letter #26. After she read that her name tasted of canned peaches, she wrote back and asked "Packed in heavy syrup or in its own juice?" (Truong 2010, 21)

In response, Kelly helps Linda devise ways to overcome the distraction of incoming flavored words, by offering her different foods (chewing gum, mints, and even dipping tobacco) to overwhelm the synesthetic tastes. With the help and acceptance of her friend

Kelly, Linda/Linh-Dao finds effective coping mechanisms for her stream of incoming word-flavors. She becomes an "A" student, and follows in the family tradition of going to Yale University and becoming a lawyer. While her synesthetic sensory load must be managed, she never wishes to be rid of it. Her flavored words can bring her pleasure too. She describes her happy experience hearing the name of her beloved uncle, also known as "Baby Harper":

> Baby*honey* Harper*celery*.
>   The honey, a percolating bubble full of flowers and citrus, bursts wide open when the sea of celery—the only vegetable I know that comes pre-salted—washes in. An unexpectedly pleasurable combination of flavors that made me wobbly in the knees. (Truong 2010, 43)

Toward the end of the book, Linda/Linh-Dao learns that her "condition" is part of a known phenomenon. After watching and reading the transcript of a PBS television program on synesthesia, Linda is relieved to find others with similarly anomalous perceptions. She develops a strong desire to understand and connect with the community of synesthetes, but is disappointed when the program's producer is hesitant to give her their contact details. She feels an immediate link with them as they tell their stories. Her research continues into the lives of famous and deceased synesthetes, such as Nabokov, Kandinsky, Messiaen, and Scriabin.

The book also makes a plea for all those non-artists—the baker, the lawyer—who are part of the community of synesthetes. It is interesting to note that despite the distracting element of her synesthesia, Linda/Linh-dao never expresses a desire to be rid of it. Nor does it prevent her from becoming a top student and excelling academically. Instead, the character accepts her own synesthesia as the anomaly that it is, enjoying its pleasures and coping with its down-sides. Synesthesia is portrayed, not as pathology, but rather as a unique form of perception linking its host to a vivid history and community. Linda/Linh-Dao comes to understand, accept, and even respect her synesthesia without glorifying or romanticizing it. As such, the portrayal of synesthesia is in line with Flournoy's recommendation to bestow "neither excess of honor nor indignity."

CONCLUSION

Synesthesia, that quirky perception, difficult to fathom, mysterious to most, ruffles long-held notions about what perception is and how it works. It shakes up the usual belief systems about what is "real" and gives birth to a range of interpretations. Synesthetes will continue to intrigue, to frustrate, to infuriate, and to find their way into literature. And these days, more of them are making it to the center of the story.

It has long been a task of literature to bring once marginal characters to the story's center, where their voices become louder. Modern fiction has brought us a diversity of world views, as once minor or unrepresented characters move to center stage. And now, more and more, such emerging characters are those with neurological anomalies like synesthesia. New worlds are opened by synesthete characters, who allow readers to see life through their eyes, ears, and taste buds. New understandings are also provided by the various interpretations of them viewed through lenses of different philosophical and literary traditions. Whether Romantic, Naturalist, or Positivist, such lenses can be sign-posts that guide us on the road of our developing understanding of the diversity of worlds within the "one world" we share.

It is hoped that research into the vast, wide-open area of synesthesia and literature will continue beyond the particular territory of this chapter. As an early reviewer of this chapter pointed out, a much-needed area of study is how synesthesia is represented by authors in different literary genres, in different decades, and in different languages.

As both mirror and window, creative literature can reflect the state of our evolving knowledge, while also pointing it in new directions. The literary portrayals of synesthetes (discussed earlier in the context of the five categories of literary portrayals), whether descending from Rimbaud, Nordau, or Flournoy, show our developing understanding of synesthetes, their ways of apprehending the world, and the implications these may have for the human need to reach beyond the accepted "known." What connects all the diverse views of synesthesia and synesthetes in these various fictional works is well-expressed by Kevin Dann in *Bright Colors Falsely Seen*:

> Synaesthetic perception, which is forever inventing the world anew, militates against conventionalism. (Dann 1998, 122)

Whether in real or symbolic ways, synesthesia has come to represent wider possibilities of the nature of perception and of the reality we perceive—which, perhaps touches on the human desire to break beyond what is familiar to a vision of the new.

REFERENCES

Baron-Cohen, Simon and John Harrison, eds. 1997. *Synaesthesia: Classic and Contemporary Essays*. Oxford: Blackwell Publishers.

Bernard, Oliver, ed. and trans. 1962. *Arthur Rimbaud: Collected Poems*. London: Penguin Classics. (Originally published in 1883.)

Dann, Kevin T. 1998. *Bright Colors Falsely Seen: Synaesthesia and the Search for Transcendental Knowledge*. New Haven, CT: Yale University Press.

Diamond, Stacy. 1996. *Artificial Paradises. 'Of Wine and Hashish'*. Translated from the French ['Du Vin et du Haschich' by Charles Baudelaire] by Stacy Diamond. New York: Citadel Press. (Originally published in 1851.)

Duffy, Patricia L. 2001. *Blue Cats and Chartreuse Kittens: How Synaesthetes Color their World*. New York: Times Books, Henry Holt and Company.

Fitzgerald, F. Scott. 1995. *The Great Gatsby*. New York: Scribner. (Originally published in 1925.)

Flournoy, Théodore. 1893. *Des phénomènes de synopsie (audition colorée)*. Paris: Alcan.

Fowlie, Wallace, ed. 1966. *Rimbaud Complete Works, Selected Letters*. Poem, 'Vowels'. Translated from the French ['Voyelles' by Arthur Rimbaud] by Wallace Fowlie. Chicago, IL: University of Chicago Press. (Originally published in 1883.)

——, trans. 2005. 'Letter to Paul Demeny'. In *A. Rimbaud, Complete Works, Selected Letters, A Bilingual Edition*, Chicago, IL: University of Chicago Press. (Originally published in 1871.)

Ghil, Rene. 1886. *Traité du Verbe*. Paris: Chez Giraud.

Glass, Julia. 2006. *The Whole World Over*. New York: Pantheon Books, Random House

Ha, Gene and Alan Moore. 2002. *Top Ten Book Two*. La Jolla, CA: America's Best Comics, LLC.

Harrison, John. 2001. *Synaesthesia: The Strangest Thing*. Oxford: Oxford University Press.

Huysmans, Joris-Karl. 1959. *Against Nature*. Translated from the French [*A Rebours*] by Robert Baldick. London: Penguin Books. (Originally published in 1884.)

Kernan, Brent. 2002. *The Synaesthete*. Lincoln, NE: iUniverse,

Laker, George. 1980. *Metaphors to Live By*. Chicago, IL: University of Chicago Press.

Lvovich, Natasha. 2010. Phone home. *Paradigm Journal* 4. <http://www.paradigmjournal.com>.

Mass, Wendy. 2005. *A Mango-Shaped Space*. New York: Little, Brown, & Company.

Nabokov, Vladimir. 1989a. *Invitation to a Beheading*. New York: Vintage Books, Random House, (Original printing G.P. Putnam's Sons, 1959.)

——. 1989b. *Speak Memory*. New York: Vintage Books, Random House, (Originally published Harper & Bros., 1951.)

——. 1991. *The Gift*. Translated from the Russian [*Dar*] by Michael Scammell with the collaboration of the author. New York: Vintage Books, Random House. (Original printing G.P. Putnam's Sons, 1963).

Nordau, Max. 1895. *Degeneration*. Translated from the German [*Entartung*]. New York: D. Appleton & Company. (Originally published in German 1892.)

O'Malley, Glenn. 1964. *Shelley and Synaesthesia*. Chicago, IL: Northwestern University.

Marks, Lawrence E. 1978. *Synaesthesia: The Unity of the Senses*. New York: Academic Press.

Parker, T. Jefferson. 2007. *The Fallen*. New York: HarperCollins.

Payne, Holly. 2005. *The Sound of Blue*. New York: Plume, Penguin Group.

Rimbaud, Arthur. 1937. '*Alchimie du Verbe*.' *Une Saison en Enfer, Oeuvres de Arthur Rimbaud*. Paris: Mercure de France (Originally published in 1873.)

Rushdie, Salman. 2005. *Shalimar the Clown*. New York: Random House.

Salzman, Mark. 2000. *Lying Awake*. New York: Alfred A. Knopf.

Shanks, Lewis Piaget. 1931. Translated from the French "Correspondance" by Charles Baudelaire, 1854 in *The Flowers of Evil*. New York: Ives Washburn.

Truong, Monique. 2010. *Bitter in the Mouth*. New York: Random House.

Vaz, Katherine. 1994. *Saudade*. New York: Wyatt Books, St. Martin's Press.

Yardley, Jane. 2003. *Painting Ruby Tuesday*. London: Doubleday.

FURTHER READING

Other recommended works with characters who describe synaesthetic experiences:*Timbuktu* by Paul Auster (main character—a dog—experiences of "symphony of smells").

Miracle Myx by Dave Diotalevi (main character is a synaesthete-detective).

Still Waters by Nigel McCreery (main character is a synaesthete-detective).

Astonishing Splashes of Colour by Clare Morall (main character is a young woman who experiences coloured auras around people.

Ada, by Vladimir Nabokov (character Van remembers in terms of color).

In Search of Lost Time, by Marcel Proust (character, Marcel describes music and words in terms of colour).

Christopher by Richard Pryce (an early 1911 novel with a synaesthete-character).

Foam of the Daze, by Boris Vian (character makes a "pianococktail" in which he matches a food taste of texture to each musical note).

....

CHAPTER 34

SYNESTHESIA AND THE ARTISTIC PROCESS

....

CAROL STEEN AND GRETA BERMAN

INTRODUCTION
(ON THE NATURE OF PERCEPTION)

....

The study of the processes used by synesthetic artists is not only fascinating but vitally important if we hope to achieve an understanding of artistic procedure in general, as well as a greater awareness of the presence of synesthesia in art. To begin to explore these issues, we need to delve into some universal questions about perception and consciousness as they relate to artists and the world in which they work. Indeed, this focused investigation will start by exploring expectations held by both the "art world" and art audiences. These two domains have often exerted a powerful effect on the traditional education and practices of artists, in terms of their thinking, their use of tools, their common working techniques, and their materials; in short, on the creation of their art. Some of the issues underlying these assumptions apply to the work of all artists, non-synesthetic as well as synesthetic. We want to examine some of the ways these ideas have influenced artists who have had to deal with their synesthesia, especially if they knew their perceptions were different from others. This in turn raises questions about the intent of the artist. How is he or she interested in communicating a specific message? How does this affect the artist's output?

In general, artists whose works have gained acceptance from their peers and from their audiences have been expected to stay within the styles of their time. Their oeuvre falls within certain prescribed parameters; their creative output meets the prevailing standards of working practices, subject matter, and technical prowess. However, history is full of stories of artists who went against the usual expectations. Artists, like Vincent van Gogh, who could not conform, suffered accordingly; the appreciation of their works had to wait until the times changed and a different aesthetic was accepted. In our chapter we expand on ideas first formulated in Berman et al. (2008), in exploring how the approach of the synesthetic artist may differ from that of other artists, as well as considering from where artists' visions or conceptions arise. This chapter deals mainly with painting. Artists in other disciplines, including music, animation, sculpture, and environmental work also use synesthesia to create their pieces. This chapter is exploratory and we hope it will lead to additional studies on the use of synesthesia in art.

Visual artists traditionally might begin to work from their awareness of the "real," visible world which usually means that they draw from direct observations of actual landscapes, objects in nature, living people and creatures, or from specifically composed or stylized still lifes. Another accepted way of creating art derives from the use of images arising out of the artist's imagination, the unconscious, dreams, or "automatism," as is found in Surrealism. Imagery also can develop as an extension of motor activity, such as scribbling or the broad sweeping gestures of Abstract Expressionists like Franz Kline, Mark Rothko, Willem de Kooning, and Jackson Pollock. It can even spring from the imitation of others, or the conscious manipulation of images to explore concepts that characterize art movements such as Cubism and Futurism. But whatever the artists' subject matter, they usually felt that they (and others) were aware of their intention, style, imagery, and the message they were trying to convey.

WHAT IS DIFFERENT ABOUT SYNESTHETIC ARTISTS?

For synesthetic artists (i.e., those artists with the neurological trait of synesthesia), their source of imagery can also be called "realistic," although it is a very special, idiosyncratic reality, being one that only they can observe.[1] Like realist artists, synesthetes can choose to paint, sculpt, photograph, or animate what they see. However, they are able to see their specific synesthetic visions (or *photisms* as the scientists call them) by paying attention not only to what they observe through their eyes, but also to visual experiences triggered from other senses (e.g., colors triggered by heard sounds, or by smells, feeling, tastes—or any combination of these and other senses). Synesthetic perceptions may also arise from non-sensory triggers, such as graphemes (i.e., letters, numbers) and other ordinal sequences (e.g., days, months, and other time units). Furthermore, a synesthete's emotional responses to experiences or personalities can also produce specific shapes and colors for them.

We need to correct, from the start, the misconception that synesthetic artists work from only a few synesthetic triggers, given that some types of synesthesia are far more

---

[1] These synesthetic correspondences in art can still be understood by people who are non-synesthetic. This was demonstrated by Jamie Ward, Samantha Moore, and colleagues, who showed in their experiment that audiovisual animations were appreciated more by a non-synesthetic audience if those displays were exactly representing the experiences of sound-color synesthetes, compared to if they were marginally altered (by rotating the visual image 90°; Ward et al. 2008).

well-known than others. The sound-to-color trigger is usually thought to be the most common synesthetic form that artists explore (e.g., painting music), but it may also be that this one just happens to produce strong moving photisms that are especially inspirational to an artist. Nonetheless, it must be remembered that this is only one type of synesthesia exploited by artists—albeit an important one—and that there are others that produce similarly observed lines, shapes, and forms which may be equally integral to the synesthete's artist process.

One fact that must be made clear from the start is that synesthetes do not necessarily slavishly copy what they see any more than traditional landscape artists paint every leaf and blade of grass or grain of sand. The first author of this chapter, Carol Steen, who has colored graphemes, colored sound, colored touch, colored pain, and colored smells (as well as shapes accompanying those colors), can assert that her synesthetic photisms come too quickly for this—there are too many of them to capture even if she wanted to, which she clearly does not. Instead, she picks and chooses, according to which aspects of an experience she wants to explore, opting not to work from unpleasant sensations, for example, if she feels that they might muddy her color palette or disturb her sense of synesthetic balance or timing.

Given that the synesthetic artist must filter her experiences to generate the final artistic product, the issue for the artist becomes one of analyzing and working from her sense of inherent aesthetic "rightness" (which may at times be very hard to articulate). She must make informed decisions about the usage or portrayal of her visions, and this requires a type of self-observation. Moreover, the ability to self-observe might rely on certain types of knowledge: that synesthesia exists, that it is shared by some but not most others, and that it is "normal" and not harmful, and so on. In addition to this, there is a need to ask questions about how synesthetic artists create with their unusual perceptions, whether they are aware of doing so, and how their work differs from, or resembles that of non-synesthetes. We are also interested in exploring in this chapter probable commonalities of imagery or method that occur from synesthetic artist to synesthetic artist (i.e., what different synesthetes might have in common in their perceptions, and in how these perceptions come to be expressed). These are all questions that relate to the synesthetic consciousness.

WHAT IS SYNESTHETIC CONSCIOUSNESS?

A first issue of importance concerns the degree to which artists are conscious of their synesthetic abilities, and the role their knowledge and experiences play in their art. While most synesthetes are well aware of their perceptions, they may not recognize that all people do not see the kinds of things that *they* can. (In fact, the reverse is sometimes also true; some synesthetes may not realize that any other synesthetes exist in the world.) Synesthetic artists may also not be aware that "families" of lines, shapes, and forms have been identified as being commonly seen by fellow synesthetes. In the 1920s, Heinrich

Klüver studied the synesthetic perceptions of people who had taken hallucinogenic drugs (which may resemble, to some extent, the perceptions of people with congenital synesthesia). He listened to their oral descriptions, and wondered whether they all saw the same things to some extent. He asked his subjects to be as specific as possible, and noticed that "basic patterns of perception existed" (Cytowic 1993, 124–125). In his linear and skeletal drawings, Klüver noted that individuals who experienced synesthesia shared a number of common perceptions. He created a taxonomy of these forms and named these visual depictions "form constants" (see Figure 34.1).

As Cytowic (1993) suggests, Klüver believed that these form constants were elementary features that the brain was hardwired to readily perceive. As such, artworks from different synesthetes might display similar themes in terms of the basic shapes they represent. Hence, these shapes might be seen as a source of inspiration for some synesthetic artists. Indeed, Cytowic writes that the synesthetic artist Kandinsky "described these "Form Constants" during a feverish delirium: Pictures, microscopic preparations, or ornamental figures were drawn on the dark ground of the visual field" (Wassily Kandinsky, as cited in Cytowic 1993, 126).

As noted earlier, synesthetes may or may not recognize that some of the shapes (or "form constants") on which they build their art may be shared by other synesthetes. Equally, they may or may not realize that synesthesia is not experienced by all people, or even that other synesthetes do nonetheless exist. The first author can tell a story recognizable to many synesthetes about how she discovered that her perceptions were different from those of others, and this story is repeated here in the first person:

> When I was seven years old, as a friend and I walked home from school one warm fall afternoon in Detroit, Michigan, I made the mistake of telling her that the letter "a" was the prettiest pink I had ever seen. I thought she would agree, but I was very surprised when she suddenly stopped walking, turned to face me, wrinkled up her face, and pronounced, "You're weird." I had mixed feelings about her blunt comment; one was to tell her that I had made the color up, the other was to deny her the knowledge of what "b" or "c" or another letter or number looked like. Instead, I said nothing and we resumed our now silent walk home. This brief exchange had two immediate and powerful effects on me: I stopped talking about my colored letters and I also ignored my other joined sense perceptions. I went into denial, not knowing if admitting my joined sensations to myself would be a good idea or not. This was not the only time I'd ignored the truths of my colored, moving, invisible-to-others, multi-sensory, real world. And I didn't mention my synesthesia again until I was twenty.

As an adult, the first author Carol Steen became an artist, and much later, subsequently learned about Klüver's form constants. One day, while searching in her painting storage area for a piece to send to an exhibition, she came across one of her earlier works, a delicate, lightweight, tar covered, wooden comma-shaped sculpture, 30 inches long and 2 inches high, that she had created when she was in her 40s (see Figure 34.2).

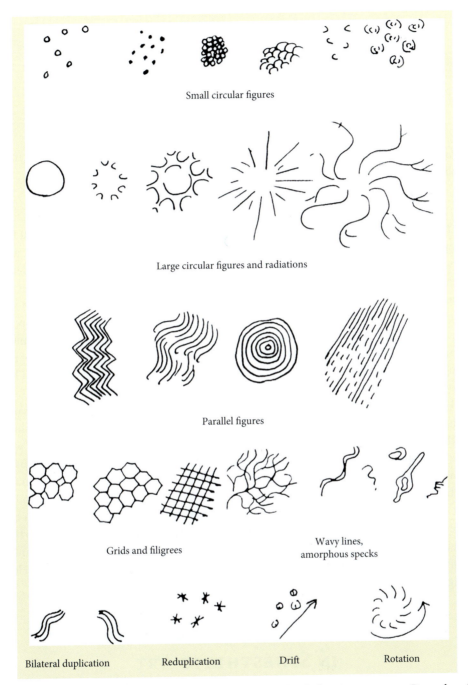

Small circular figures

Large circular figures and radiations

Parallel figures

Grids and filigrees

Wavy lines,
amorphous specks

Bilateral duplication   Reduplication   Drift   Rotation

FIGURE 34.1 Heinrich Klüver's *Form Constants*, pen and ink drawing on paper. Reproduced from Horowitz, M. *Image Formation and Cognition*, p. 216, figure 6 © 1970, Appleton Century Crofts, with permission.

FIGURE 34.2 Carol Steen, *Black Comma*, 1980, Tar covered wood, 2 × 30 × 2 inches. Collection of the artist.

This was a revelatory moment for the artist. There was something familiar about the shape of the piece she was holding in her hands. She checked her reference books, and among Klüver's illustrations, done over 90 years earlier, was a simple comma shaped line that looked exactly like the shape of this sculpture. Indeed, Steen discovered Klüverian examples throughout her works, everywhere she looked. She now understands that she had always worked with her synesthetic perceptions, though unaware of doing so. In fact, her in-depth understanding of the importance of this discovery would take many years. It was not until she was nearly 50 that she became fully aware of the extent of her synesthetic abilities, and conscious of all the instances when she had used them in her artwork.

Finding *Black Comma* that day changed Carol Steen's work as an artist, and the same might be true of other synesthetic artists who learn about associations they may share with other synesthetes. The artist might go from having no clear understanding of why she preferred to work in certain ways with specific lines, shapes, textures, and forms to now making deliberate artistic explorations—using the forms that come so naturally to her. In other words, the synesthete's knowledge of the presence of synesthesia in her art might fundamentally change her approach to art, and *knowledge of synesthesia* can become a key component of the journey taken by a synesthetic artist. Synesthetic artists therefore might have an urge to understand whether aspects of their art have connections with the works of other artists. Who else uses synesthesia in their works? How might this manifest itself?

FINDING "FORM CONSTANTS" IN SYNESTHETIC ART

We saw earlier that it might be possible to analyze synesthetic art for similarities from artist to artist, and indeed, for instances of form constants within those different works. Klüver's taxonomy of form constants were itemized by Richard Cytowic, and it was possible to compare these directly with the themes from the first author's own art, as a case in point. This type of comparison might include not only the forms that Klüver had described, but additional themes we have observed in the works of other artists whom we believe are likely to have been synesthetic. Some of these forms include circular figures and figures that are wavy or parallel, as well as those that radiate, drift and appear to move. Anyone looking at paintings by Van Gogh, Charles Burchfield, Wassily Kandinsky, and David Hockney, for example, will surely observe these form constants repeatedly. Movement is also apparent in works by Heinrich Hein and Max Gehlsen, for example, who often attempted to make their static figures move. There are numerous ways to simulate movement on a flat surface—ways that will be discussed in later sections—but technology has made many more of these possible. In fact, by using Adobe's *After Effects®*, Steen recently made several short animations of some of Klüver's form constants (which are only skeletal drawings, not what synesthetes see).

Movement in Synesthetic Art

Some forms of synesthetic perceptions move; others do not, although not enough information has yet been gathered to identify all the moving and static forms. Certain types of movement are represented not only in Klüver's form constants (from descriptions given by Cytowic 1993) but are also suggested by certain combinations of shapes in synesthetes' artwork. From Klüver's constants, we have the following types of movement: shapes can radiate, rotate, morph, kaleidoscope, drift, spiral, and reduplicate. Shapes experienced by synesthetes also show movement and can appear suddenly, permutate, magnify, repeat, dart quickly, and change colors abruptly and (seemingly) arbitrarily. In addition, both shapes and colors can disappear without warning. In trying to understand what synesthetes actually see, we might formulate some questions: when do the shapes appear, change, or vanish? Were they solid, transparent or opaque? How long were they seen? Where did they go when they moved? What was the timing of their movements?

The answers to some of these questions are immediate to any synesthete from even brief introspection. When shapes disappear, they can do so in any number of ways: they can change shape or color, fade gradually, stop, morph into another shape, move to the top, sides or bottom of a (usually) black background, or stay where they are and vanish. And once they disappear, they're gone—at least for the first author of this chapter. And of course, moving photisms can be affected by their trigger. With music, the tempo affects the timing of the photisms' movements. In the case of the first author, for example, synesthetic perceptions can move something like the aurora borealis, or like combinations of fireworks or solar flares. For example, imagine a simple, single firework that is beautiful by itself but when it's joined by numerous others with changing shapes and colors the whole vision becomes something far more amazing. It is equally interesting to examine what synesthetes do *not* see. In her synesthetic photisms, the first author, for example, has never seen visions of anything that could be described as being representational, or figurative. She does not see people, animals, vegetation, landscapes, anything living, water, structures, or anything man-made. This seems to be typical of many synesthetes' reports, in that their shapes are abstract rather than literal/concrete. This is perhaps why synesthetic artwork can look so abstract to the observer (even if it is a literal "realist" depiction of the perceptions of the synesthete).

One of the readily observed aspects of a moving photism is that what is seen changes in shape, color, and position. And while we do not yet know exactly which forms of synesthesia move, not all of them do. This lack of information has not stopped artists from trying to use what they see, and there are a number of ways in which synesthetic artists might aim to capture the movements of their synesthetic forms. One of the limiting factors for painters wishing to capture movement is that they usually work on a single, static surface. When this is the case, they have two main choices: they must either use a method such as morphing or permutation to show a sequence; or place shapes one on top of another, so that parts of the previously painted shapes show through, like pentimenti (where a painting has been altered from its original by the artist, as evidenced by traces of previous work underneath). The artists can divide the surface to be painted into sections like a cartoon strip or storyboard, showing images with gradual changes from one section to another. Or they can show shapes changing sequentially on the same broad canvas. These configurations can either be fairly consistent, or morph in an irregular manner. By repeating similar colors and/or shapes, the artist can demonstrate shared origins of these shapes; this repetition, in turn, will serve to convey a sense of movement.

Some examples of these processes can be seen in the work of two German synesthetic artists, who had sound-color synesthesia. These were Heinrich Hein (exact dates unknown) and Max Gehlsen, (1881–1960) who, during the 1920s, created paintings that attempted to depict movement. In creating their works, Hein and Gehlsen would listen to German Folk songs, and also to Wagner, and try to illustrate what they saw. Hein and Gehlsen created movement in different ways, as can be seen for example in two of their drawings that are reproduced in plates XXIII and III of Georg Anschütz's *Farbe-Ton-Forschungen, Vol. 1* (Anschütz 1927). In these, Hein painted movement by creating a series of painted shapes which change sequentially like a cartoon strip, as in the first method we mentioned. In contrast Max Gehlsen painted movement using only one undivided surface, and his image in this particular drawing is of a repeating pattern of thin yellow lines which retreat into the distance (see Anschütz 1927).

Like Gehlsen and Hein, the American artist, Charles Burchfield (1893–1967) appears to have had sound-color synesthesia, among several other forms (although he did not comment directly on this). Among these other forms he may have possessed were personifications (where letters, numbers, and other sequences take on genders and personalities), colored smell and time-space synesthesia (where time is "seen" projected onto a spatial time-line). These synesthesias may have caused him to produce certain shapes and placements of objects in his paintings. He even created shapes that he identified as drawings of highly specific emotions, often using them in his paintings like a private symbolic code. Also, like Gehlsen, he chose not to divide his paintings into regular sections. In his extensive journals, he often described his desire to translate into paint phenomena like the sounds of insects, birds, and telephone wires, or the smells of a favorite spring flower. But he may have lacked *knowledge* of synesthesia, as well as methods of portraying movement that modern technology might provide.

In more recent times, there has been an established history of synesthetic experiments in visual music and animation, dating back perhaps first to Oscar Fishinger in the 1930s (see, for example, discussions in Brougher et al. 2005; Campen 2007). The development of technologies (e.g., recent advances in computer animation) has allowed synesthetes to capture not only the essence of movement, but also the particular qualities of color that accompany a synesthetic sensation (see later for more on color). Hence, Steen, Hockney, and Smilack have all turned their attention to technology (e.g., computer simulation) when working accurately with the colors of light, colors they can now show to others. This technology also enables them to demonstrate other aspects of synesthesia, such as movement. Steen is working with animation; Smilack is planning to work with neon; and Hockney is producing innovative and original pieces using an iPad. In this way, these artists are continuing a long tradition in using new technologies to explore synesthetic perceptions (Campen 2007).

Given that these animation possibilities were not exploited by Burchfield, one might question the extent to which he succeeded in painting his observations (moving or otherwise) as accurately as he may have seen them. Perhaps earlier artists were limited by the fact that they had to paint their myriad of sensations on just one surface. In fact, Burchfield may have attempted to overcome this by actually using several pieces of paper joined together in many of his works, a method specific to him. In any case, the extent to which Burchfield achieved movement in his pieces can be seen in his work *The Insect Chorus* (see Figure 34.3) where this sense of movement also elicits specific feelings of emotions, discussed further later in this chapter.

How Does the Artistic Process Differ between Synesthetic and Non-Synesthetic Artists?

Crucial to our observation of synesthetic artists is the fact that they may feel an enormous compulsion to capture and reproduce what they see. One could say that many visual artists do the same, but synesthetes may feel a particular compulsion simply because their internal world is so different from what is generally visible to others. After seeing a particularly stimulating vision, synesthetes may feel the necessity to record what they have seen immediately—their urgency to paint must be expressed. In addition, the multidimensional/multisensory nature of synesthetic perceptions might compel artists to seek idiosyncratic methods with which to portray them, and this usually means

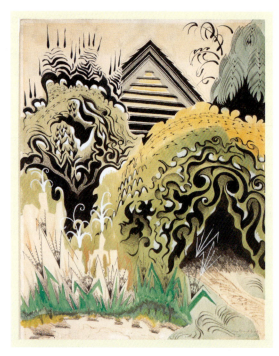

FIGURE 34.3 Charles Burchfield, *The Insect Chorus*, 5 September 1917, opaque and transparent watercolor with ink, graphite, and crayon on off-white paper, 20 × 15⅛ inches. Munson-Williams-Proctor Arts Institute, Museum of Art, Utica, New York, Edward W. Root Bequest, 1957. Reproduced with permission from the Charles E. Burchfield Foundation.

abandoning some of the traditional ways of creating a painting, composing a photograph, or making a sculpture. In other words, in order to capture what they see, synesthetic artists may need to break some long-standing rules (a characteristic of modern art in general), and this presents some challenges.

One problem for a synesthetic artist, then, is how to deal with the fact that their colors can be extraordinarily bright, the colors of light rather than pigment. For some synesthetes, their colors might be seen as similar to sunlight streaming through a stained glass window. For this reason, traditional techniques of oil painting cannot be satisfactory. The question is, how can one make pigment look as bright as colored light? In order to achieve this, painters often work with pure, unmixed oil paint or watercolor taken directly from the tube, or use color combinations designed to intensify their brightness. The first author, for example, likes to work with oils from the tube applied directly to the canvas. If any color mixing occurs, she uses the speed of the paint's application to blend the wet colors directly on the canvas. She also likes to work on a black textured background because this increases the brilliance of the colors. This background is also true to how she sees her colored photisms, as these appear against a gently moving black background that has a texture as soft and rich as silk velvet.

Burchfield, on the other hand, preferred to work with watercolors. Interestingly, water-color colors are rarely mixed. If one looks at the number of prepared colors available in the types of paint painters use, such as oil, gouache, or acrylic, watercolor colors have the largest selection precisely because they are meant to be used unmixed. Burchfield said that he chose to use watercolor because he found that he could work more rapidly that way, since oil paints slowed him down. It is possible that he might have also preferred the inherent brightness of unmixed colors he found in this medium. As mentioned earlier, he often pasted his watercolors together, to make larger and more expansive work.

Related to this is the concern of getting the visuals onto canvas as quickly as they are seen, because synesthetic visions remain visible for such short durations. In this regard, and for some synesthetes at least, the memory of what is experienced is never as com-plete or bright as what is seen in the actual moment. Because photisms appear, move, and disappear so rapidly, synesthetic artists often need to work with extreme speed. Indeed, the first author does this by foregoing brushes, and using her gloved hands and fingers to "get things down" as fast as possible. In general, synesthetes painting music must paint in the moment, or replay the music at another time if they wish to add something to the painting. The necessity for speed can also depend on the nature of the synesthetic experiences, since some are longer- or shorter-lasting than others. For example, when the first author works from touch, like the instantaneous visions seen during a tetanus injection, she notes that these are of such brief duration that she has to hurry back to her studio and paint as quickly as possible, before they are forgotten. She feels that the over-whelming beauty of what she has seen compelled her to paint. Unfortunately, since the complexity of her vision prevents her from recalling more than a fraction of it, she must consolidate the images and movements into a kind of shorthand that remains true (see Figure 34.4).

As a consequence, Steen's paintings from touch tend to be much smaller than those created from recorded sound, because with sound she can more easily replay the music as often as desired. In other words, with colored music, memory is no longer an issue since a particular passage can simply be reheard. However, if the synesthete forgets what song she was listening to, the unfinished painting may remain unresolved, and this is because synesthetic sensations are almost always unidirectional (e.g., sounds might trigger colors, but those same colors do not trigger the auditory experience of sound). For this reason, the artist cannot necessarily "read back" the content of the picture from the visual elements it is composed of.

One exception to the more common type of unidirectional synesthete is Marcia Smilack, a photographic artist with multimodal synesthesia (e.g., sound-to-color, sight-to-texture, personifications and so on) some of which are bidirectional (sound-to-color, color-to-sound). Smilack employs a camera to "catch" the reflections she sees, hears, and feels on water. She works looking into her camera, sees her images upside-down, and captures the reflections on the water of the "right-side-up" world on the shore. She describes the role of synesthesia in her work as follows: "if I experience a sensation of texture, motion or taste, I take the picture... It works like this: I watch the surface of the sea until I experience one of my synesthetic responses. When I do, I trust it to be

FIGURE 34.4 Carol Steen, *Blue Streak*, 2003, oil on paper, 3 × 5 inches, Collection of the artist.

FIGURE 34.5 Marcia Smilack, *Weekends are Taller than Weekdays*, 2002, Giclee on watercolor paper, 48 × 60 inches. Reproduced with permission from the artist.

a reliable signal that tells me it is the right time to take the picture, so I click the shutter" (Smilack 2012). Smilack has said that she considers herself a "fisherman for images," who uses the wind on water as an artist would use brushes against canvas. An example of this is seen in Figure 34.5, where the hazy "right-side up" buildings are in fact inverted reflections cast onto water.

We saw earlier that synesthetic artists might feel the need to work especially quickly and may struggle with the qualities of available paints when attempting to depict the luminance of synesthetic sensations. One other concern is how to depict colored photisms that suddenly disappear, thereby leaving behind "visual holes" through which the background shows. Previously, we pointed out that synesthetic artists sometimes re-expose themselves to the trigger stimulus (e.g., they may replay the music they are painting). Alternatively, they may depict this sudden absence of image by leaving the background exposed. In other words, paintings of colored moving shapes sometimes include these empty "traces" of where shapes had once been. This is certainly true for the first author of this chapter, and a similar observation might be made in other synesthetic artists, since we have noticed these holes occurring along the edges of the paper or canvas of other (likely) synesthetic artists' works; in fact, they can occur anywhere inside the composition of the painting. These can easily be seen in the works of Smilack, Joan Mitchell, August Strindberg, Steen, and Burchfield, and indeed, many synesthetic artists appear to be absorbed with visual "holes." One example of visual holes or the background showing through in Joan Mitchell's works can be seen in her painting, *Wind* (1990–1991) (see Figure 34.6). Mitchell had several forms of synesthesia including sound-to-color, personality-to-color, emotion-to-color, and colored graphemes (Albers 2011).

Equally, synesthetic artist Burchfield also felt the importance of "holes" through which a background could be perceived. He wrote about his painting *Orion and the Moon* (1917; Figure 34.7) "The other night I lay awake...; outside the sky was blanketed with...luminous clouds, in which now and then appeared ragged holes through which glowed the deep indigo sky" (in Moore and Sessions 2010).

We have also observed these "holes" in the landscape paintings of playwright and artist, August Strindberg, whom we also suspect to have been a synesthete. Strindberg, who used colors unmixed, straight out of the tube, is known to have been fascinated

FIGURE 34.6 Joan Mitchell, *Wind*, 1990–1991, oil on canvas (diptych), 102 1/4 × 157 1/2 inches. Courtesy of the Joan Mitchell Foundation, © Estate of Joan Mitchell.

FIGURE 34.7 Charles Burchfield, *Orion and the Moon*, 1917, watercolor and crayon on paper, 23⅜ × 34 ¾ inches, Courtesy D.C. Moore Gallery, NYC. Reproduced with permission from the Charles E. Burchfield Foundation.

by the correspondence between music and visual art. About this painting, *Wonderland* (also called *Magic Cave*; shown in Figure 34.8), Strindberg wrote: "a thick interior of the woods. In the middle there is a hole which opens up to an ideal landscape, where sunlight of all colors comes in…" He added that there was another, more esoteric meaning too: "The wonderland, light's struggle against darkness…" (Strindberg, cited by Berman 1975, 116).

This awareness of "background" is also found in works by the first author, Carol Steen, who lets the background become as much a part of the painting as the foreground in her work *Clouds Rise Up* (2004–2005) (see Figure 34.9). In this, the energetic linear marks of orange and red are two actual sounds produced by a single note played on a shakuhatchi flute, whereas the background is the color of the flute itself, a metallic forest green.

Another characteristic of synesthetic art, which is likely to be true for many synesthetic artists, is the necessity to be extremely precise about color hues and intensities. This reflects the huge importance placed by synesthetes in general on clearly specifying the colors of their sensations, as has been noted elsewhere (Simner et al. 2005). Indeed, synesthetes even use significantly more color terms than non-synesthetes when verbally describing cross-sensory associations (Simner et al. 2005). Likewise, a similar attention to color hues can also be found in synesthetic art. We have observed that David Hockney, for example, who has sound-color synesthesia (Cytowic 2002), as well as Carol Steen, and Marcia Smilack, paint (or in Smilack's case, photograph) using very carefully chosen hues. Van Gogh, who is thought to have had colored sounds and colored emotions, also refers to very precise colors. In his voluminous letters, he frequently describes and enumerates these. One specific reference to colored sound appears in a letter of 17 June 1890 to Gauguin: "It is greens of different quality, of the same value, in such a way as to form a green whole which would by its vibration make one think of the soft sound

FIGURE 34.8 August Strindberg, *Wonderland*, 1894, Oil on cardboard, 28½ × 20½ inches. Photo ©Erik Cornelius, Nationalmuseum, Stockholm.

of the ears swaying in the breeze. It's not at all easy as a color scheme" (Van Gogh, Letter 643 Auvers-sur-Oise, *c*.17 June 1890 [An unfinished letter found among his papers], in Brooks 2012).

In terms of other color schemes, Smilack tends to speak and photograph using certain color chords. *Yellow and Pink Chord* is a sunset scene over the harbor in Menemsha (*c*.1988). *Yellow Boat Minor Chord* was a reflection of a sunset mixed in with the sailboats, "pretending to be the real thing" (Smilack 2012). *Singing Arches* is also pink against yellow. This appears to be a favorite color/musical combination for the artist, one she often sees synesthetically. However, she is also very sensitive to gradations of hues. In fact, she has said "my response to the slightest tonal changes—so small as to almost be unseen by most people—is part of the trigger for my synesthesia, and why it is a constantly occurring phenomenon: because by its very nature, light is always changing and therefore tonal changes are always occurring in real time" (Marcia Smilack, personal communication). We know that synesthetic artists do not see all colors in their photisms. Perhaps, because synesthetes see some colors and color combinations more frequently than others, they often tend to use these colors in their works. Shades of yellow and blue are particularly noticeable in the works of both Van Gogh and Smilack. These color choices, of course, vary from artist to artist. Interestingly, Hockney's Autumn 2010

FIGURE 34.9 Carol Steen, *Clouds Rise Up*, 2004–2005, Oil on canvas-covered masonite, 25 × 20½ inches. Collection of the artist.

show at the Pace Wildenstein Galleries in New York City had a highly specific palette. Could the reason for this be that this is what the trigger showed to him?

An important issue in synesthetic art—as in all forms of art—is how the artist chooses to filter the experience. Consider, for example, a synesthetic artist who paints a piece of music. If asked whether she sees exactly the same things upon replaying the music, she might respond yes, although it's a question of what she wants to pay attention to. A piece of orchestrated music is very complicated; many instruments are heard and therefore seen. One can watch the drums, or the violins, or the clarinets, and see certain colored moving shapes, but listening to the same music again, now paying attention to, say, the bass and the flutes, the colored moving shapes may be different. In this way, although the synesthetic artwork might be considered realistic in its accurate portrayal of a perceived experience, it might also be filtered via the particular focus (or "message") of the artist.

Synesthetic painters may also have a specific message in mind when they use a particular shape or color. They may, in fact, be creating with their own codes. As leading Burchfield scholar Nancy Weekly noted in the introduction to her presentation at McMaster Museum of Art:

> American watercolor master Charles E. Burchfield called 1917 his "Golden Year" as it was his most prolific and inventive. A radical stylistic shift occurred when he created a personal, visual language of symbols that would provide forms he adapted for

use throughout his career. He made sound visible in patterns for insects and he gave human characteristics to inanimate objects. (Weekly 2008)

Weekly further elaborated on these ideas in addressing the painting *The Insect Chorus* (see Figure 34.3):

> His abstract motifs in insect fantasies transform one sense impression in terms of another...Huge black swirls of Fear suggest a giant cicada's head hidden in shrubbery...a shaded triangular alcove signifies the end of summer as Melancholy/Meditation/Memory of pleasant things that are gone forever. In the foreground, a "high shrill pinpoint cricket chorus" dominates the lawn...Each distinctive sound has a coordinating audio-cryptogram, with patterns repeated to represent a segment of time or the number of active insects. (Weekly 2008)

In other words, the emotions and sounds of the scene are translated into particular shapes and colors, which the artist uses to convey his particular message.

Nancy Weekly has also described the personification or anthropomorphism in Burchfield's art, and this is reflected more generally in the work of other synesthetic artists. In Burchfield's case, Weekly suggests this was because "anthropomorphism made it possible for Burchfield to express emotions and observations in a truly experimental way" (Weekly 2008). In other words, Burchfield had a specific emotional code, in that he expressed emotion by personifying inanimate subjects. It may also have been a direct, literal representation of his synesthesia, since it's thought that one variant he experienced was synesthetic personifications (where letters, numbers, and other sequences take on genders and personalities). Synesthetic personifications can sometimes extend to inanimate objects (Smilek et al. 2007), and this may have been the case with Burchfield. Burchfield even labeled drawings and doodles with different emotional states. A similar emergence of personifications within synesthetic art comes from Marcia Smilack, who frequently expresses this, both in her photos and in words. Here is what she has to say about personification: "All of the houses I photograph are people. Windows are eyes, bridges are mouths, arches are voices, lights are dancers. Faster than thought can censor feeling, I see them first as animate and can use them as markers for my changing states of consciousness" (Smilack 2012).

Synesthetic artists may also differ to some degree from other artists and the general population in that they usually do not distinguish between "real" and "abstract." Synesthetic visions are all very real to the synesthete. However, these visions often depict images that could be considered dreamlike, as opposed to images from the world experienced by the average person when awake. Unlike that waking world, which can be shared, photographed, and dissected, the synesthetes' internal world cannot. An excellent example of this can be seen in the exchange of letters between Van Gogh, Gauguin, and Emile Bernard in 1889. Van Gogh insists that he can show Christ in the Garden of Olives without literally portraying the characters. In a letter he says, "So at present am working in the olive trees, seeking the different effects of a grey sky against yellow earth, with dark green note of the foliage; another time the earth and foliage all purplish against yellow sky, then red ochre earth and pink and green sky. See, that interests me more than the so-called abstractions" (Van Gogh, Letter 822 Arles, *c.*26 November 1889, in Brooks 2012). In this way, the artist appears to flip between impressions that are life-like and external, on the one hand, and dream-like and internal on the other. (Note that these internal abstractions may or may not be the result of synesthetic impressions of emotion; the point here, rather, is the collapsing of "real" and "internal.")

A final feature of particular note in synesthetic art is how the artist chooses to express time. Time is a particularly strong trigger for synesthetic experiences (Simner 2009) as, for example, in *time-space synesthesia*, where time is "seen" projected into space (e.g., as columns rising up towards the body) or *day-color synesthesia*, where particular colors and/or shapes are linked with each day or the week. Burchfield frequently depicts cyclical features of time in nature, especially changes of seasons. As Weekly has pointed out (Weekly 2007, 14) "Often Burchfield's seasonal transitions used perspective to convey the duration of time, with the present being in the foreground and the future off into the distance." She also points out a "skewed" chronological viewpoint in *Early Spring, c.*1966–1967; here Winter seems to hide inside the trees, while dandelions representing Spring appear in the foreground. This focus on time also brings to mind Marcia Smilack's photograph entitled *Weekends are taller than Weekdays*—in particular, this alludes to the synesthetic trait in which people envisage days, weeks, and seasons as shapes, or with specific locations in space (see Figure 34.5). Smilack describes how for her in this photo Sunday is represented by one tall building on the left, Saturday by another tall tower on the right, and Monday through Friday by a squat white structure reflected in the middle. It would be interesting to observe how other time-related elements appear in the works of other synesthetic artists, and the extent to which these might differ, or be similar to, the approaches taken for representing time by non-synesthetes.

CONCLUSION

Artwork, of course, varies from synesthete to synesthete, but a series of similarities in method, conception, and output can be found if one takes the time to look closely. For example, one might possibly notice a greater prevalence in their works of what might be called Klüverian form constants. Hence, it may be possible to see in the works of Burchfield, Hockney, Steen, Van Gogh, Smilack, and Strindberg, the same soft-edged shapes, crescents, zigzags, streaks, and numerous lines that Klüver described. Some of their lines are thin, others thick, some parallel each other in waves, or radiate from a central point. Synesthetic perceptions may include flashes, bursts, and sharp pinpricks of light that often explode into vast diaphanous shapes (as has been noted previously by Steen 2001).

Other similarities can be seen in the approach to color and texture. As differently as Steen and Smilack work (Steen paints and sculpts; Smilack photographs), they share many characteristics in common. There is no question that they "speak the same language," and both resonate to the images of Burchfield and to Van Gogh. Both Steen and Smilack have separately, in descriptions of their process, referred to the texture of forms. Steen writes about seeing shapes that are "velvety soft" and "chiffon-like." Smilack reports that she has snapped the shutter when she felt a satiny texture against her skin. Van Gogh's use of thick textures of oil paint may simulate the tactile quality he felt in things. He also had a proclivity to use unmixed, thick paints squeezed right out of the tube, and this direct approach to unmixed paints can be seen too in the output of the first author here, Carol Steen.

In summary, in looking for signs of synesthesia in the works of painters, we might search out evidence that the colors are fresh, bright, and straight from the tube, applied with speed, and are soft at their edges. In many paintings by synesthetes, colors do not go all the way to the edges, leaving "holes," and frequently their creators have made them in a furor of energy. They often use unexpected colors or color combinations. Some synesthetes do not see all the colors in their visions and so may have a restricted palette. Steen, for example, never uses violet because she rarely sees it in a photism, and finds working with it to be unfamiliar. The keen representation of movement is also a recurring theme. Hence, layers of colored shapes painted one on top of the others, or the use of morphing and permutation to suggest movement and change in location of shapes, also serve as synesthetic evidence. One quickly seen shape is often replaced by another shape or color, and synesthetic painters commonly use layering, though they are aware that painting on top of something will partially obscure whatever colors or images were put down originally.

We might also recognize synesthesia in the "process." Though Smilack may think about what she wants to photograph for a long time, searching for images then experiencing and re-experiencing the synesthetic trigger, she eventually will capture her visions when the sensation is right, with the feeling of touch against the skin and the click of the shutter. Mitchell would paint a few brushstrokes, and then back up to look at what she had done. Steen takes her iPod with her to the art store, listening to songs she wants to paint; while there, she uncaps the tubes of paint to see if the paint inside matches the colors of the songs. Then she paints while playing that music. She often goes for acupuncture treatments, seeking inspirational visions, and then runs home to paint what she saw. Burchfield, Van Gogh, Hockney, Mitchell, and Smilack would all go back to look at, and work with the same landscape over and over. All might pay attention to their synesthetic triggers, hoping to ensnare the visions before they're gone. However, in addition of course, synesthetic artists are not limited only to those abilities, they also use their extensive formal training in their compositions and color choices. Together these provide a wholly specialized approach to method for the synesthetic artist, which might give rise to commonalities across synesthetes in general, but can also show differences according to the particular nuances afforded by each variant of synesthesia experienced by the artist. We end this chapter by listing, for each artist discussed in our chapter, those synesthetic variants which we know, or believe them to (have) possess (ed). This list, shown in Table 34.1, has both an empirical and speculative basis. We have marked with asterisks those cases where we have independent corroboration (either from direct

Table 34.1 Artists and their synesthetic variants, where, by convention, the trigger is listed before the synesthetic sensation (e.g., "sound–color" means that hearing sounds triggers synesthetic sensations of color). Asterisks show cases with independent corroboration, and the sources for these are given in column 3

Artist	Years	Source	Variants
Charles Burchfield*	1893–1967	Weekly 2010	Sound-color/shapes, shape-emotion, Smell-color/shape, time-space
Max Gehlsen*	1881–1960	Anschutz 1927	Sound-color/shape
Heinrich Hein*	Unknown	Anschutz 1927	Sound-color/shape
David Hockney*	1937–	Cytowic 2002	Sound-color, personification
Wassily Kandinsky*	1866–1944	Cytowic 1993	Sound-color, color-sound
Joan Mitchell*	1925–1992	Albers 2011	Sound-color, personality-color, emotion-color, grapheme-color
Marcia Smilack*	1949–	Smilack, personal communication	Sound-shape/color, shape/color-sound, emotion-shape/color, shape-emotion, personification, vision-texture, time-space, word-shape
August Strindberg	1849–1912		Personification, emotion-color
Carol Steen*	1943–	Steen, self-report	Grapheme-color, word-color, sound-color, smell-color, touch-color, pain-color/shape
Vincent van Gogh	1853–1890		Sound-color, personification, emotion-color

knowledge as in the case of the author, from personal communication with the artist, or from a published verifiable source). Those remaining, more speculative cases, we have based on our interpretation of what artists have said, written down, or painted, and we look forward to future research examining these suppositions in more detail.

REFERENCES

Albers, Patricia. 2011. *Joan Mitchell, Lady Painter. A Life.* New York: Alfred A. Knopf.

Anschütz, Georg. ed. 1927. *Farbe-Ton-Forschungen, Vol. 1.* Leipzig: Germany: Akademische Verlagsgesellschaft.

Berman, Greta. 1975. Strindberg, painter, critic, modernist. *Gazette des Beaux-Arts* October:113–122.

Berman, Greta, and Carol Steen (eds). 2008. *Synesthesia: Art and the Mind.* Hamilton, ON: McMaster Museum of Art.

Brooks, David. 2012. Vincent van Gogh. The letters. <http://vggallery.com/letters/others.htm>.

Brougher, Kerry, Jeremy Strick, Art Wiseman, Judith Zilcer, and Olivia Mattis. 2005. *Visual Music: Synaesthesia in Art and Music Since 1900.* New York: Thames & Hudson.

Campen, Cretien van. 2007. *The Hidden Sense: Synesthesia in Art and Science.* Cambridge, MA: MIT Press.

Cytowic, Richard E. 1993. *The Man Who Tasted Shapes*. New York: Jeremy P. Tarcher/Putnam.

———. 2002. *Synaesthesia: A Union of the Senses*. 2nd ed. Cambridge, MA: MIT Press.

Moore, Bridget, and Ralph Sessions. 2010. *Charles Burchfield: Fifty Years as a Painter / Texts by Charles Burchfield*. New York: DC Moore Gallery/Distributed Art Publishers.

Horowitz, Mardi J. 1970. *Image Formation and Cognition*. New York: Appleton Century Crofts.

Simner, Julia. 2009. Synaesthetic visuo-spatial forms: Viewing sequences in space. *Cortex* 45:1138–1147.

Simner, Julia, Jamie Ward, Monika Lanz, Ashok Jansari, Krist Noonan, Louise Glover, and David A. Oakley. 2005. Non-random associations of graphemes to colours in synaesthetic and non-synaesthetic populations. *Cognitive Neuropsychology* 22:1069–1085.

Smilack, Marcia. 2012. *Marcia Smilack, Reflectionist*. <http://www.marciasmilack.com>.

Smilek, Daniel, Kelly A. Malcolmson, Jonathan S. A. Carriere, Meghan Eller, Donna Kwan, and Michael Reynolds. 2007. When '3' is a jerk and 'E' is a king: Personifying inanimate objects in synaesthesia. *Journal of Cognitive Neuroscience* 19:981–992.

Steen, Carol. 2001. Visions shared: A firsthand look into synaesthesia and art. *Leonardo* 34(3):203–208.

Ward, Jamie, Samantha Moore, Daisy Thompson-Lake, Shireen Salih, and Brianna Beck. 2008. The aesthetic appeal of auditory-visual synaesthetic perceptions in people without synaesthesia. *Perception* 37(8):1285–1296.

Weekly, Nancy. 2007. *Ecstatic light*. New York: D C Moore Gallery.

———. 2008. Invitational Workshop, McMaster Museum of Art, Hamilton, ON, Canada, 25 September.

———. 2010. Colour and sound: Charles E. Burchfield and the question of synaesthesia. In *Sensory Crossovers: Synaesthesia in American art*, ed. Sharyn R. Udall. Alburquerque, NM: The Albuquerque Museum.

CHAPTER 35

SYNESTHESIA AND MEMORY

BEAT MEIER AND NICOLAS ROTHEN

INTRODUCTION

Synesthesia provides for a richer world of experience than normal. Thus, synesthesia may lead to additional retrieval cues and, as a consequence, to an advantage in memory tasks. Evidence in favor of this hypothesis originally came from single-case studies. A case of a synesthete with particularly extraordinary memory ability was Shereshevsky (S), a Russian journalist and mnemonist, described by Luria (1968). S had multiple synesthesias, a very detailed memory for real-life events, and in experimental memory tasks he was able to encode complex materials within a short period of time and recall them accurately even after several years. One of the questions that arose from observations like these was whether synesthesia causes an extra-ordinary memory in general—or simply an advantage for the retrieval from memory. The latter advantage has been suggested repeatedly in the literature, as well as by synesthetes themselves (cf. Cytowic 1993, 2002; Rothen and Meier 2010; Yaro and Ward 2007). However, as self-reports are disputable, controlled experiments are required to resolve this question. Several group studies have addressed this issue. Some have indeed found a performance benefit, at least for some memory tests (e.g., Gross et al. 2011; Radvansky, Gibson, and McNerney 2011; Rothen and Meier 2010; Yaro and Ward 2007). However the memory advantage was not as pronounced as would have been expected from single-case studies. Moreover, a performance advantage for synesthetes could not be confirmed for the digit matrix task in which single cases demonstrated extra-ordinary abilities (see later; Rothen and Meier 2010; Yaro and Ward 2007).

Thus, one major question is to find out under what particular circumstances synesthetes might show a memory performance advantage. Another question is what exactly causes the potential memory advantage. Theoretically, it may be that synesthesia leads to a richer world of experiences and thus to additional retrieval cues in general (cf. Rothen, Meier, and Ward 2012). Accordingly, a general advantage would be expected across a large variety of materials and memory tests. However, it is also possible that the performance benefit for synesthetes is more specific and directly related to inducers, that is, to those materials which trigger the synesthesia (e.g., graphemes for grapheme-color synesthetes). This explanation is related to a dual-coding theory of cognition (cf. Paivio 1969). According to this theory the ability to encode a stimulus in two different ways increases the chance of remembering it compared to a stimulus that was only coded one way. Thus, in synesthesia, the additional memory code triggered by the inducer (i.e., the synesthetic concurrent, e.g., color) would result in a stronger representation and accordingly to a performance advantage compared to non-synesthetes. A third possibility is that the memory advantage of synesthetes is domain-specific. According to this account, the benefit is not restricted to the inducer, but extends to the concurrent (e.g., grapheme-color synesthetes would not only show a performance benefit for graphemes, but also for colors). This theoretical position is compatible with the observation that implicit associations also exist from the concurrent to the inducer (cf. Brugger et al. 2004; Cohen Kadosh et al. 2005; Meier and Rothen 2007; Rothen et al. 2010). Although at the level of conscious experience, the occurrence is typically unidirectional (i.e., a grapheme triggers a color experience, but a color does not trigger a grapheme experience).

In this chapter, we will present a review of the available empirical findings, case reports, and groups studies. The focus is mainly on grapheme-color synesthesia because most of the studies have addressed this form of synesthesia. Table 35.1 provides an overview of these studies and their main findings. We will evaluate the findings according to the three explanations just outlined, that is, whether synesthesia provides for a general, an inducer-specific, or a domain-specific advantage. The review is complemented with an integration of these findings with links to the neural basis of synesthesia and memory.

Memory in Grapheme Color Synesthesia

Case studies

Luria (1968) documented the extraordinary memory of S across a period of almost 30 years, beginning in the early 1930s. It all began when the editor of the newspaper for which S worked as a journalist noted with surprise that S never took any notes, but nevertheless remembered all kinds of information with astonishing accuracy. He sent him to Luria to have his memory investigated. Luria conducted a number of experiments in which S demonstrated his enormous capacity to remember. In one of the tasks he was asked to learn a matrix which consisted of 50 digits, arranged in rows and columns. S needed about 3 minutes for study, and after that he was able to recall the numbers in succession. He was also able to recall a particular column, even in reverse order, or to "read off" the numbers which formed the diagonals. Moreover, he was able to accurately recall such matrices even years later. It turned out that synesthesia was the key to S's extraordinary memory. For digits and letters he experienced colors, movements, and/or forms (e.g., "3 is a pointed segment which rotates"; Luria 1968, 26), words elicited "puffs

Table 35.1 Overview of studies on memory in synesthesia ordered by support for an inducer-specific, domain-specific (inducer and concurrent) and/or more general advantage

Study type	Author	N	Inducer	Domain	General	Memory test
Case studies						
	Luria (1968)	S	+	+	+	Digit Recall
	Baron-Cohen et al. (2007)	DT	+	nt	nt	Digit Recall
	Smilek et al. (2001)	C	+	nt	nt	Digit Recall
	Mills et al. (2006)	MLS	+	nt	nt	Name Recall, BVRT, RAVLT, RCFT
	Brang and Ramachandran (2010)	JS	nt	nt	+	Hidden Objects, Change Detection
Group studies						
	Yaro and Ward (2007)	16	+/–	+	–	Digit Recall, RAVLT, RCFT, Color Recognition
	Rothen and Meier (2009)	13	–	nt	nt	Digit Recall
	Rothen and Meier (2010)	44	+	+	+	Wechsler Memory Scale (WMS)
	Gross et al. (2011)	≤ 9	+	+	+	WMS, RCFT, CVLT, Recognition Memory
	Radvansky, Gibson, and McNerney (2011)	10	+	nt	nt	Wordlist Recall
	Meier and Rothen (2007)	13	+	nt	nt	Synesthetic Conditioning Task
	Rothen et al. (2010)	36	+	+	nt	Synesthetic Conditioning Task & TMS
	Simner, Mayo, and Spiller (2009)	≤ 10	+	+	nt	Event Memory, Spatial Abilities

+ = support, nt = not tested, – no support. Abbreviations of memory tasks see text.

of steam" and splashes, tones triggered colors, sounds triggered tastes, and visual and auditory stimuli also elicited sensations of taste and touch. Luria suggested that these synesthetic experiences created "a background for each recollection, furnishing him with additional "extra" information that would guarantee accurate recall" (Luria 1968, 28). Although the overall characterization of the case of S would seem to support the hypothesis of a general memory advantage, the presence of the various kinds of synesthesia may also indicate that his extraordinary memory was directly related, and therefore limited, to the different domains of his synesthesia. Moreover, S refined his already extraordinary memory ability with mnemonics such as the method of loci and visual imagery which may have been a further and distinguishable source of his extraordinary memory. However, his pronounced use of imagery combined with his synesthetic experiences resulted not only in an excellent memory, it also made it difficult for him to think clearly or to read, because images "kept rising to the surface in his mind" (Luria 1968, 113). Luria characterized him as a dreamer who had difficulties distinguishing between his internally generated thoughts and images, and external reality.

More recently, it has been suggested that S may have suffered from autism which together with his synesthesia may have been the basis for his exceptional memory (Baron-Cohen et al. 2007; Bor, Billington, and Baron-Cohen 2007). Baron-Cohen et al. (2007) presented a similar case, Daniel Tammet (DT), at that time a 26-year-old language genius who was diagnosed as having Asperger's syndrome. Similar to S, DT came to the attention of the researchers because of his extraordinary memory. He was European champion for reciting Pi to over 22,000 decimal places from memory in 2004, and in addition, he published a book in which he described his synesthesia (Tammet 2006). For him, each integer up to 10,000 had its own unique shape, color, texture and feel, and as a consequence, a list of numbers created the experience of a complex landscape. He could intuitively "see" results of calculations in the synesthetic landscape without using conscious mental effort and he was able to "sense" whether a number was a prime or a composite. When his memory was tested in the laboratory (Baron-Cohen et al. 2007), he showed a digit span of 11.5 compared to 6.5 in controls. However, in a face recognition test with a retention interval of about an hour his accuracy was only slightly above chance. Baron-Cohen et al. (2007) concluded that his number memory was superior while his face memory was impaired. Thus, this study provides evidence for a selective memory advantage which seems to be restricted to the realm of the inducer.

However, it is important to note that the presence of Asperger's syndrome or a similar mental condition is not a precondition for extraordinary memory in synesthesia. For example, (Smilek et al. 2002) reported the case of an inconspicuous student (C). After a classroom demonstration on the limits of human memory in which students were presented with four lists of nine digits, she baffled the instructor by recalling each of the lists almost perfectly. In more formal testing, C was tested with three matrices of 50 digits, similar to those used by Luria (1968). One matrix consisted of black digits, another of digits colored congruently with C's synesthetic colors, and a third of digits incongruent with her synesthetic colors. When tested immediately after learning, C showed excellent performance for the black and the congruent matrix. However, her recall for the incongruent matrix was very poor. When tested again after 48 hours with the black matrix, there was no decline in performance. In the control group there was no performance difference between the black, the congruent, and the incongruent matrices and the control group showed a significant decrease when tested again after 48 hours. Smilek et al. (2002) suggested that synesthetic colors provided additional memory cues and therefore played an essential role in C's memory abilities. While these results clearly indicate a memory advantage for the materials that triggered the synesthesia (i.e., digits), it is not clear whether C would have shown a more general memory advantage if she had been tested with different materials.

Similar findings were reported from Mills et al. (2006). They tested the case of a 48-year-old language professor, MLS, who reported that synesthesia helped her to remember names. In one experiment, MLS and two different control groups (one consisting of language professors, the other of visual art professors) were presented with a list of 30 fictitious first and last names followed by a free recall test. Three successive study–test cycles were administered. From the second cycle on, the results showed the expected benefit for MLS which persisted through to a second session 6 months later. In another experiment, MLS was given three standardized tests, two visual tests, the Benton Visual Retention Test (BVRT-R) and the Rey Complex Figure Test (RCFT), and one verbal test, the Rey Auditory Verbal Learning Test (RAVLT). The BVRT consists of ten stimulus cards which contain geometrical shapes. Each is presented for 10 s and must be recalled immediately by drawing the figure from memory. The RCFT consists of the study of a single complex figure with an immediate copy trial and a delayed free recall trial. The RAVLT consists of the presentation of a 15-word list with an immediate recall. This study-test cycle is repeated five times. Then a second 15-word list is presented for immediate recall. After 20 minutes a delayed recall trial of the first list is administered.

Compared to age- and education-matched norm scores, MLS performed numerically, but not statistically higher in the BVRT-R. A similar result was found for the delayed recall of the RCFT. In contrast, MLS showed a clear advantage on the RAVLT. MLS's performance was already close to ceiling after the third study-test cycle. These results again support the notion that synesthesia gives rise to a memory advantage that is specific to the particular inducer. That is, MLS was able to use her synesthesia to remember verbal materials, but she did not show a general memory performance benefit.

A somewhat different result was found in a case study by Brang and Ramachandran (2010). They tested the case of a 25-year-old university student (JS) who experienced (explicit) bidirectional grapheme-color synesthesia. That is, for him graphemes elicited colors and in addition, he also experienced that colors elicited the corresponding graphemes. Moreover, he reported that he would retain a vivid mental picture of even complex scenes for a relatively long period. Brang and Ramachandran (2010) tested this supposed eidetic memory with a hidden object test and a change detection task. In the hidden objects test, JS and a control group were shown three complex visual scenes which contained several target items. Each scene was presented for 30 s and then replaced by a white sheet. A list of target items was read to the participants with the instruction to mark the previous location of each item on the white sheet. In the change detection task, pairs of complex visual images were presented in succession with small changes between the two images. The task was to spot the difference. In both tasks, JS outperformed all participants of the control group, a result that was replicated 6 months later. Importantly, JS did not experience colors for the displays and thus, these results would indicate that, at least for some synesthetes the memory advantage goes beyond the domain of the synesthesia. However, one could also argue that this result is rather due to enhanced imagery in synesthesia—a feature that was also evident in the case of S and is supported by self-report studies on the vividness of imagery in synesthesia (cf. Barnett and Newell 2008; Price 2009).

Altogether the single-case studies illustrate the large individual differences that occur within synesthesia. Some of the cases demonstrated exceptional memory performance and some of them showed a more moderate performance advantage. Unfortunately, testing was restricted to the realm of the inducer of the synesthesia, that is, to verbal and/or numerical materials in most of the cases and thus it seems that the advantage was inducer-specific. Only the results from JS who showed enhanced retention of complex scenes with materials that did not elicit synesthesia can challenge this conclusion (Brang and Ramachandran 2010). Similarly to S, as described by Luria, JS also showed very vivid imagery and it is an open question how imagery may contribute to the memory advantage in synesthesia. Moreover, from the single-case studies it is not clear whether a memory advantage is specific to some individuals or whether it is a fundamental feature of synesthesia, that is, one cannot make generalizations about the memory benefit (see Rothen and Meier 2009). Several group studies have been conducted to test the generality, the magnitude, and the extent of the potential memory benefit in synesthetes. These are reviewed in the next section.

Group studies

Yaro and Ward (2007) recruited a sample of 46 grapheme-color synesthetes and asked them to rate their memory ability. Overall, they reported better than average memory and more frequent use of visual strategies to aid memory. In a second experiment, objective memory performance was tested in a subgroup of 16 synesthetes. As in the study by Mills et al. (2006), the RAVLT and the RCFT were used. In addition, digit matrices with 27 numbers were constructed and presented either in a 3×9 or in a 9×3 array. The matrices were composed individually for each synesthete such that the digits were printed in colors that were either congruent or incongruent with their synesthetic experiences. In addition, a third matrix of colored squares was used in order to test whether synesthetes may have superior memory for color. Moreover, to test whether synesthetes may have an advantage in processing color information, the Farnsworth–Munsell Color Perception test was used in its original and a modified form. In the original form four trays of colored caps must be sorted to form a regular color series transforming from one hue to another (e.g., from red to yellow). In the modified form five color targets were selected from each of the trays and each was presented for 5 s with the instruction to memorize the specific shade of color. Subsequently, these color targets were presented again, together with two similar caps with a slightly different hue and participants had to select the target color.

The results showed a significant performance advantage for the RAVLT (i.e., memory for auditorily presented words), but not for the RCFT (i.e., memory for a complex visual figure), thus replicating the findings of Mills et al. (2006) in a group study. In the digit matrix recall task, Yaro and Ward (2007) found neither a memory advantage for synesthetes nor a differential effect for the congruent versus incongruent matrices. However, for the color matrix task, they found an advantage for the synesthetes in the delayed recall test, suggesting a performance benefit in the domain of the concurrent. A similar result was found for the Farnsworth–Munsell Color Perception tests. Synesthetes outperformed the controls, both in the color perception test and in the color recognition memory test. Therefore, this study provides evidence that synesthetes may have a performance advantage not only for inducers that trigger synesthesia, but also for concurrents, or, even more generally, for the modality in which the concurrents are elicited (i.e., color in general for grapheme-color synesthetes, not only synesthetic colors). Yaro and Ward (2007) concluded that the dual-coding theory cannot account for these results.

A somewhat surprising finding from the study of Yaro and Ward (2007) was the failure to replicate the performance benefit of synesthetes in the digit matrix recall task and the failure to replicate the effect of (in)congruency on memory performance. However, Rothen and Meier (2009) found a similar pattern of results when they compared a group of 13 grapheme-color synesthetes and a control group. Participants were tested with two matrices, one consisting of 50 black digits and one consisting of 50 incongruently colored digits (i.e., colored in a way that did not match their synesthetic color). The latter matrix was composed individually for each synesthete such that the digits were incongruent with each synesthete's own synesthetic concurrents. Memory was tested immediately after learning, after a delay of 30 minutes, and after a delay of 2 to 3 weeks. The results showed no performance benefit for the group of synesthetes compared to the controls, either in immediate or in delayed recall. In addition, there was no disadvantage for memorizing the matrix with incongruently colored digits compared to the black digits. The results suggest that synesthesia per se may not lead to a memory performance advantage, at least not when tested with that particular method.

In a further study, Rothen and Meier (2010) used a standardized memory test, the Wechsler Memory Scale (WMS-R). The specific research question was whether synesthesia would lead to extra-ordinary memory—which was defined as a score of more than one standard deviation above the norm. This was based on the consideration that about two-thirds (i.e., 68.2%) of the observations lay within one standard deviation (SD) above/below the mean and thus only about 16% of the normal population have scores higher than one SD above the mean, that is "extra-ordinary" memory. The WMS-R consists of several subtests: *Digit Span Forward* involves the presentation and immediate recall of a digit-string of increasing length in forward order. *Digit Span Backward* involves the presentation and immediate recall of a digit-string of increasing length in backward order. In *Visual Memory Span Forward*, the experimenter produces sequences of increasing length by touching little blocks which are positioned on a grid. After each sequence, the participant has to reproduce the sequences in forward order. In *Visual Memory Span Backward*, the same procedure is administered but the participant has to reproduce the sequence in backward order. *Figural Memory* examines the ability to remember complex geometrical figures and to recognize them amongst others in an immediate recognition test. *Logical Memory* examines the ability to recall the ideas from two short stories which are presented orally. It is tested immediately and again after a delay. *Visual Paired Associate Learning* involves making a total of six associations between a specific color and a meaningless line drawing. Cued recall of the color is tested after each presentation of the six color-drawing pairs and again after a delay. *Verbal Paired Associate Learning* consists of the oral presentation of six word pairs. Cued recall of the second word is tested when probed with the first one after each presentation of the six pairs and after a delay. *Visual Reproduction* consists of the presentation of geometrical shapes and the immediate and delayed pencil and paper reproduction. Between the *immediate* and the *delayed recall* of *Logical Memory*, *Visual Paired Associate Learning*, *Verbal Paired Associate Learning*, and *Visual Reproduction*, there was a filled retention interval of about 30 minutes.

As this study used a fairly large sample size (i.e., 44 grapheme-color synesthetes), the results are presented in Figure 35.1. Individual test scores were standardized using the corresponding normed reference data. While there was no advantage in the short-term memory tasks, there was a consistent advantage for both verbal and visual memory subtests (within one standard deviation above the norm mean, depicted in green color in Figure 35.1). However, only for immediate visual paired associate learning was this advantage beyond one standard deviation, that is, in an "extraordinary" range (depicted in red color in Figure 35.1). When additional indices for visual and for verbal memory subtests were calculated according to the WMS manual, the synesthetes showed a particular benefit for visual over the verbal memory index. Thus, this study also supports the argument that the memory advantage is not restricted to the inducers. Rather, it seems that "synesthetes [also] profit from the experiences in the domain of the synesthetic concurrent, that is, the visual modality for grapheme-color synesthesia" (Rothen and Meier 2010, 262). As mentioned earlier, this advantage in the visual domain might be related to the enhanced imagery abilities typically reported by synesthetes and, in general, the greater reliance on visual strategies for information processing (cf. Barnett and Newell 2008; Yaro and Ward 2007).

Gross et al. (2011) followed up on the question as to whether the memory advantage of synesthetes is specific to verbal tasks or whether it might extend to visuo-spatial tests. They recruited a total of nine synesthetes who were notably younger on average than the group tested by Rothen and Meier (2010). In the short-term memory test of the WMS (i.e., Digit Span and Visual Span) they found no performance advantage for the synesthetes. In the verbal paired associates WMS subtest they found an advantage for synesthetes, at least for the first trial (on later trials performance was at ceiling). Thus, these results replicate the findings by Rothen and Meier (2010). In order to avoid the presence of color, they devised a modified version of the visual paired associate WMS subtest. Rather than using associations between colors and meaningless line drawings as learning materials, the associations consisted of common shapes and meaningless line drawings. No advantage for synesthetes was found. However, performance was at ceiling after two trials. In addition to these WMS subscales, two modified versions of the Warrington Recognition Memory Test were used. One involved words, the other involved faces. During the study phase, participants were required to rate each item as pleasant or unpleasant, and in a later test phase, 25 old and 25 new items were presented with the instruction to decide whether the item had been presented before or not. Synesthetes performed better than controls with words, but not with the faces. As a

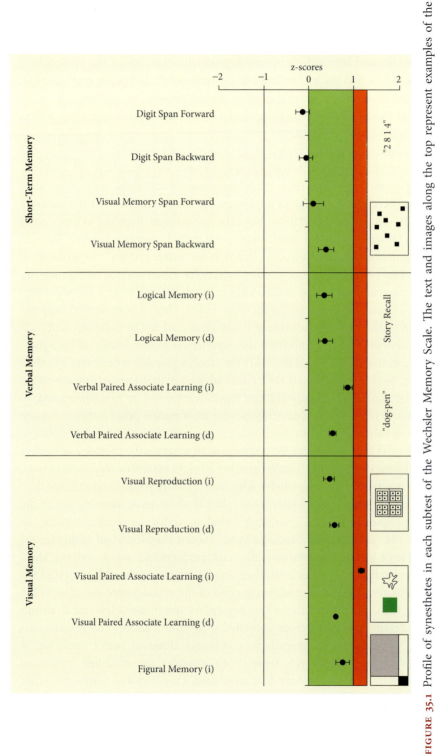

FIGURE 35.1 Profile of synesthetes in each subtest of the Wechsler Memory Scale. The text and images along the top represent examples of the stimulus materials for each sub-test. Values represent mean z-scores, error bars represent standard errors. (i) = immediate test, (d) = delayed test. Adapted from Grapheme–colour synaesthesia yields an ordinary rather than extraordinary memory advantage: Evidence from a group study, Nicolas Rothen and Beat Meier, *Memory*, 18 (3), pp. 258–264 © 2010, Taylor and Francis reprinted by permission of the publisher (Taylor & Francis Ltd, <http://www.tandf.co.uk/journals>).

further measure of verbal memory, the California Verbal Learning Test (CVLT) which has a similar structure as the RAVLT was used. Synesthetes performed better than the control group in the delayed recall but not in the immediate recall conditions. Finally, the RCFT was also used and while Gross et al. (2011) did not find an overall performance difference, they found better performance for synesthetes in the immediate copy subtest, and using a qualitative scoring method they also found higher configural accuracy, that is, higher accuracy for the overall shape of the figure. Together, these results replicate an advantage for synesthetes with verbal materials, and again they suggest that a more general advantage may be present which can extend to the visual domain.

Given that the performance benefit for synesthesia-inducing materials is well-established, an open question is what processes are driving this advantage. One possibility is that the experience of synesthetic colors favors item-specific against relational processing. That is, the synesthetic color experience may increase item-specific processing at the letter and word level separate from semantic meaning, and as a result a decrease in relational processing can occur. This possibility was addressed specifically for word list recall by Radvansky, Gibson, and McNerney (2011). They tested a sample of ten grapheme-color synesthetes in four separate experiments. In the first experiment, they manipulated the print color of the words. In one condition the colors matched the synesthetic color (i.e., congruent condition), in another condition the words were printed in a different color (i.e., incongruent condition) and in a control condition the words were presented in black. Each list consisted of 12 words and each word was presented for 1 s and after each list the participants had to recall the words by typing them into the computer. The results showed a performance advantage for the synesthetes compared to the control group in each condition. Moreover, the synesthetes recalled slightly fewer words in the incongruent than in both the congruent and the control condition while no such difference was found for the control group. In the second experiment, different word lists were used and only one word in each list was presented in color (i.e., in red) in order to test the von Restorff isolation effect (von Restorff 1933). This effect refers to the phenomenon that when one item of a different kind is presented within a list of homogeneous items, memory for this item is enhanced. Compared to the control group, the synesthetes showed a performance advantage for the black words, but no von Restorff effect for the colored word. In contrast the control group showed a performance improvement for the colored words such that their performance nearly reached the level of the synesthetes. Thus, for synesthetes the additional color did not add to performance, presumably because they already experienced colors for all of the words. In a third experiment, Radvansky, Gibson, and McNerney (2011) manipulated distinctiveness semantically and again the synesthetes showed an overall advantage in list recall, but no von Restoff effect. Radvansky and colleagues suggested that the additional color experiences of the synesthetes are based on the physical form of the words (i.e., the letters that make them up) and this results in a shift in emphasis of processing on the lexical surface form of the words at the expense of the word meanings, thereby both increasing item-specific processing and decreasing relational processing. In the fourth experiment, the critical manipulation was that all of the words within a list were strongly related to an unmentioned critical word—a manipulation that typically leads to enhanced false memory for the latter (i.e., the Deese–Roediger–McDermott false memory effect; Deese 1959; Roediger and McDermott 1995). Specifically, when studying a list consisting of words that are associated with "bread" (i.e., butter, food, eat, sandwich, rye, jam, etc.) false recall of "bread" is more likely than when studying a more heterogeneous word list. Once again the results showed a list recall advantage for synesthetes. In addition they showed fewer intrusions (i.e., fewer false memories for the implied but absent words) than the control group. Radvansky, Gibson, and McNerney (2011) took these results as support for the hypothesis that when learning word lists, synesthetes rely more on item-specific processing and less on relational processing. Overall, the results replicate the finding that grapheme-color synesthetes have an advantage for recalling information from the realm of the inducer (i.e., for verbal materials). However, they do not speak against the possibility that synesthesia may yield a more general memory advantage. However, this was not tested.

The main focus of all the previous studies was on declarative explicit memory and on short-term memory, that is, on tasks that required the deliberate recollection of previously encountered information. So far, only one study was designed to test the impact of synesthesia on non-declarative memory. Meier and Rothen (2007) tested a group of 13 grapheme-color synesthetes with a classical conditioning task. Participants were presented with colored squares and occasionally a specific grapheme was presented in black on a white background. The grapheme was selected such that it elicited a particular color experience (e.g., blue). During the conditioning phase, this particular color (i.e., the conditioned stimulus) was followed immediately by a loud startling noise which served as an unconditioned stimulus. All participants showed a startle reaction as indicated by an increase in skin conductance response (SCR) for the unconditioned stimulus. After conditioning, for the synesthetes, but not for the controls, there was also a startle response when a grapheme was presented—although a grapheme was never coupled with the startling sound. Thus, a synesthetic conditioned response occurred. In a further study, it was tested whether this effect can be suppressed by applying transcranial magnetic stimulation (TMS; Rothen et al. 2010). With TMS the functionality of a specific brain area can be temporarily affected by inducing a strong magnetic field. Specifically, TMS was applied over the parieto-occipital cortex during the presentation of the conditioned color stimulus that was followed by the startling sound. The results showed that this eliminated the conditioned response. Thus, implicit activation of the synesthetic inducer during conditioning must be at the core of the synesthetic conditioning effect. To sum up, these results add evidence that synesthesia creates learning opportunities which are not present in non-synesthetes.

Memory in Other Forms of Synesthesia

So far, most of the work has focused on memory in grapheme-color synesthesia. However, similar principles may apply to other forms of synesthesia as well. It is important to note that any form of synesthesia potentially enriches the world of experiences compared to normal and thus, at least for inducers, specific memory advantages might be expected in any form of synesthesia.

Simner, Mayo, and Spiller (2009) recruited a group of ten time-space synesthetes, that is, individuals who see ordered sequences (such as weeks, months, years) in particular spatial arrays. Their goal was to test whether the synesthetes have an advantage in remembering public and autobiographical events, that is, information from the realm of the inducer, and whether they have an advantage in visuo-spatial abilities such as mental rotation and visual memory. A memory test of public events consisted of assigning a correct year to a given event from three different domains (international political events, films, songs). An autobiographical memory test was to list as many facts as possible for 9 different years from their life (the 9 different years were determined individually for each participant; they represented equi-distant years starting from when the participant was 5 years old and ending 3 years prior to taking the test). The results showed that synesthetes were more accurate in dating the public events in each of the three domains and they also recalled more autobiographical events. To test for visuo-spatial abilities, the Benton's test of three-dimensional (3D) praxis, the Progressive Silhouttes subtest from the Visual Object and Space Perception (VOSP) battery, the Visual Patterns Test (VSP), and the California Mental Rotation Test (CMRT) were used. The Benton Test assesses the ability to manipulate objects in 3D space, the VOSP assesses the ability to recognize a 3D object from an unusual two-dimensional (2D) angle, the VSP assesses memory for patterns of black and white squares in grids of varying sizes, and the CMRT assesses the ability to mentally manipulate 2D drawings of 3D objects. In brief, the results revealed that synesthetes outperformed controls (or the respective norm groups) in all of these tests. Thus, this study provides further evidence for the generality of a performance advantage for synesthetes that goes beyond the realm of the inducer and involves the domain of the concurrent as well.

The Benefits and Costs of Synesthesia: A Preliminary Summary

Research on memory in synesthesia is still in its infancy. However, the studies reviewed here allow for several tentative conclusions (see Table 35.1). First, there is consistent evidence that a memory advantage can occur in grapheme-color synesthesia, in particular for recalling lists of words and lists of digits. As these materials trigger the synesthetic experience, this supports the hypothesis that the memory advantage is directly linked to the realm of the inducer—at least. It is noteworthy that learning lists of single items provokes an item-specific processing style and it is possible, that this particular benefit of synesthetes may be reduced when words are used in context as in the Logical Memory subscale of the Wechsler Memory Scale.

Importantly, potential costs of synesthesia for memory performance can also be identified at this level. When incongruently colored stimuli were used as the to-be-remembered materials, memory performance was impaired, at least in some studies. However, rather than at the level of memory retrieval, this cost is probably due to weaker encoding (i.e., the physical color does not match the synesthetic color) and probably also on a motivational level ("this is ugly"). However, it is possible that inconsistent results regarding incongruently colored stimuli are also due to individual differences between different types of synesthetes. Possibly, projectors who experience the color "out in the world" may be more affected than associators who experience color "in their mind's eye" (cf. Dixon, Smilek, and Merikle 2004).

Second, in those studies which addressed the question as to whether a memory advantage would extend to the domain of the concurrent, a consistent advantage was found. These results indicate that a simple dual-coding account is not sufficient, because this account would not have predicted a performance advantage for the domain of the concurrent (i.e., the concurrent does not provide for an explicit additional memory code). Rather, a possible explanation is that these results are due to implicit information activation from the concurrent to the inducer. An alternative explanation, which is compatible with the former, is that synesthetes have a more elaborate processing capacity for colors. This idea is plausible given that synesthetes have a very precise representation of the specific color tone of their synesthetic color experiences. Moreover, there is empirical evidence that synesthetes have enhanced sensory perception in the domain of their synesthesia (Banissy, Walsh, and Ward 2009).

Third, at least some studies have reported a benefit for synesthetes for materials that are related neither to the inducer nor the concurrent. One possibility is that these are simply random results. However, given the rather small sample size in most of the studies in which null results were found and the numerical advantage in some of these studies, it is more likely that these results are indeed real (cf. Table 35.1). This would be consistent with the idea that some aspects of the information processing system of synesthetes work fundamentally differently (see Rothen, Meier, and Ward 2012). In fact there is evidence from electroencephalography that synesthetes differ from controls in early visual processing (Barnett et al. 2008). Notably this was found for materials which are not at all related to synesthesia (i.e., high-spatial-frequency patches and high-contrast check pattern). Moreover, results from structural imaging studies also provide evidence that there are altered brain networks in synesthetes (Jäncke et al. 2009; Rouw and Scholte 2007, 2010; Weiss and Fink 2009). It is possible that these differences are directly related to cognitive processes and memory capabilities. Testing this hypothesis will be an attractive avenue for further research.

A further avenue for future research concerns the investigation of other types of synesthesia. So far, most studies have investigated memory in grapheme-color synesthesia, and only one study has tested sequence-space synesthesia. It will be important to replicate and extend the findings from sequence-space synesthesia. However, there are many other forms of synesthesia and it will be important to investigate whether these synesthetes also show enhanced memory performance. Moreover, it will also be important to test whether the presence of multiple synesthesias can additionally boost memory performance.

References

Banissy, Michael J., Vincent Walsh, and Jamie Ward. 2009. Enhanced sensory perception in synaesthesia. *Experimental Brain Research* 196:565–571.

Barnett, Kylie J., John J. Foxe, Sophie Molholm, Simon P. Kelly, Shani Shalgi, Kevin J. Mitchell, and Fiona N. Newell. 2008. Differences in early sensory-perceptual processing in synesthesia: A visual evoked potential study. *NeuroImage* 43:605–613.

Barnett, Kylie J., and Fiona N. Newell. 2008. Synaesthesia is associated with enhanced, self-rated visual imagery. *Consciousness and Cognition* 17:1032–1039.

Baron-Cohen, Simon, Daniel Bor, Jac Billington, Julian E. Asher, Sally Wheelwright, and Chris Ashwin. 2007. Savant memory in a man with colour form-number synaesthesia and Asperger syndrome. *Journal of Consciousness Studies* 14:237–251.

Bor, Daniel, Jac Billington, and Simon Baron-Cohen. 2007. Savant memory for digits in a case of synaesthesia and Asperger syndrome is related to hyperactivity in the lateral prefrontal cortex. *Neurocase* 13:311–319.

Brang, David, and Vilayanur S. Ramachandran. 2010. Visual field heterogeneity, laterality, and eidetic imagery in synesthesia. *Neurocase* 16:169–174.

Brugger, Peter, Daria Knoch, Christine Mohr, and Lorena R. R. Gianotti. 2004. Is digit-color synaesthesia strictly unidirectional? Preliminary evidence for an implicitly colored number space in three synaesthetes. *Acta Neuropsychologica* 2:252–258.

Cohen Kadosh, Roi, Noam Sagiv, David E. J. Linden, Lynn C. Robertson, Gali Elinger, and Avishai Henik. 2005. When blue is larger than red: Colors influence numerical cognition in synesthesia. *Journal of Cognitive Neuroscience* 17:1766–1773.

Cytowic, Richard E. 1993. *The Man Who Tasted Shapes*. London: Abacus.

———. 2002. *Synesthesia: A Union of the Senses*. 2nd ed. Cambridge, MA: MIT Press.

Deese, James. 1959. On the prediction of occurrence of particular verbal intrusions in immediate recall. *Journal of Experimental Psychology* 58:17–22.

Dixon, Mike J., Daniel Smilek, and Philip M. Merikle. 2004. Not all synaesthetes are created equal: Projector versus associator synaesthetes. *Cognitive, Affective, & Behavioral Neuroscience* 4:335–343.

Gross, Veronica C., Sandy Neargarder, Catherine L. Caldwell-Harris, and Alice Cronin-Golomb. 2011. Superior encoding enhances recall in color-graphemic synesthesia. *Perception* 40:196–208.

Jäncke, Lutz, Gian Beeli, Cornelia Eulig, and Jürgen Hänggi. 2009. The neuroanatomy of grapheme-color synesthesia. *European Journal of Neuroscience* 29:1287–1293.

Luria, Aleksandr R. 1968. *The Mind of a Mnemonist: A Little Book About a Vast Memory*. Cambridge, MA: Harvard University Press.

Meier, Beat, and Nicolas Rothen. 2007. When conditioned responses 'fire back': Bidirectional cross-activation creates learning opportunities in synesthesia. *Neuroscience* 147:569–572.

Mills, Carol Bergfeld, Joanne Innis, Taryn Westendorf, Lauren Owsianiecki, and Angela McDonald. 2006. Effect of a synesthete's photisms on name recall. *Cortex* 42:155–163.

Paivio, Allan. 1969. Mental imagery in associative learning and memory. *Psychological Review* 76:241–263.

Price, Mark C. 2009. Spatial forms and mental imagery. *Cortex* 45:1229–1245.

Radvansky, Gabriel A., Bradley S. Gibson, and M. Windy McNerney. 2011. Synesthesia and memory: Color congruency, von Restorff, and false memory effects. *Journal of Experimental Psychology: Learning, Memory, and Cognition* 37:219–229.

Roediger, Henry L., and Kathleen B. McDermott. 1995. Creating false memories: Remembering words not presented in lists. *Journal of Experimental Psychology: Learning, Memory, and Cognition* 21:803–814.

Rothen, Nicolas, and Beat Meier. 2009. Do synesthetes have a general advantage in visual search and episodic memory? A case for group studies. *PLoS ONE* 4:e5037

——. 2010. Grapheme–colour synaesthesia yields an ordinary rather than extraordinary memory advantage: Evidence from a group study. *Memory* 18:258–264.

Rothen, Nicolas, Beat Meier, and Jamie Ward. 2012. Enhanced memory ability: Insights from synaesthesia. *Neuroscience & Biobehavioral Reviews* 36:1952–1963.

Rothen, Nicolas, Thomas Nyffeler, Roman von Wartburg, René Müri, and Beat Meier. 2010. Parieto-occipital suppression eliminates implicit bidirectionality in grapheme-colour synaesthesia. *Neuropsychologia* 48:3482–3487.

Rouw, Romke, and H. Steven Scholte. 2007. Increased structural connectivity in grapheme-color synesthesia. *Nature Neuroscience* 10:792–797.

——. 2010. Neural basis of individual differences in synesthetic experiences. *The Journal of Neuroscience* 30:6205–6213.

Simner, Julia, Neil Mayo, and Mary-Jane Spiller. 2009. A foundation for savantism? Visuo-spatial synaesthetes present with cognitive benefits. *Cortex* 45:1246–1260.

Smilek, Daniel, Mike J. Dixon, Cera Cudahy, and Philip M. Merikle. 2002. Synesthetic color experiences influence memory. *Psychological Science* 13:548–552.

Tammet, Daniel. 2006. *Born on a Blue Day*. London: Hodder & Stoughton.

von Restorff, Hedwig. 1933. Über die Wirkung von Bereichsbildungen im Spurenfeld [The effects of field formation in the trace field]. *Psychologische Forschung* 18:299–342.

Weiss, Peter H., and Gereon R. Fink. 2009. Grapheme-colour synaesthetes show increased grey matter volumes of parietal and fusiform cortex. *Brain* 132:65–70.

Yaro, Caroline, and Jamie Ward. 2007. Searching for Shereshevskii: What is superior about the memory of synaesthetes? *The Quarterly Journal of Experimental Psychology* 60:681–695.

....

CHAPTER 36

SYNESTHESIA AND
SAVANTISM

....

MARY JANE SPILLER AND ASHOK S. JANSARI

INTRODUCTION

....

Studies have suggested that synesthetes show superior memories in areas related to their synesthesia (e.g., Simner, Mayo, and Spiller 2009). An important question that such studies beg is whether there is a causal link between these two abilities (good memory for a class of information and synesthetic experience for it), or whether this is an illusory link, or indeed whether both of these two abilities are themselves caused by another factor. Unrelated to synesthesia, a group of individuals, known as "savants" (see later) show extraordinary abilities in some very restricted domains (e.g., memory). Furthermore these individuals show these abilities in the context of profound impairments in other cognitive, communicational, or emotional realms. If individuals with these extraordinary abilities in particular domains, and impairments in others, are also synesthetes, then this may provide a window into addressing whether synesthesia contributes to enhanced cognitive abilities.

This chapter addresses the earlier-posed question by looking at the issues of savantism and a related condition known as Asperger syndrome. The chapter will primarily focus on two synesthetes who have been described in recent literature as displaying savant-like abilities in particular domains, and also restricted interests and/or obsessional behavioral traits typical of Asperger syndrome. The reason for the focus on two individuals is that as shown elsewhere in this volume, synesthesia itself is only experienced by a small subset of the whole population. Given that savantism is an even rarer condition, currently, the ability to locate individuals that show both conditions is very difficult. Therefore, as is the methodology in cognitive neuropsychology for the study of rare syndromes (and indeed the way that the early research on synesthesia proceeded), the need for detailed case studies to infer general mechanisms is necessary (Jansari 2005). A related issue that will also emerge is that in the early stages of exploring a new area, research can only be as good as the methods, but also the definitions and categorization, that are used. As a richer understanding of a phenomenon is unveiled, our categorization becomes more precise which in turn allows for a deeper exploration of the issues. Our hope is that as the fields of synesthesia, savantism, and Asperger syndrome move forward, the involvement of synesthesia in the development of savantism will be further clarified.

What is Savant Syndrome?

Individuals with savant syndrome typically have extraordinary skills in a particular area, despite having some level of intellectual impairment. For example, Kim Peek (the inspiration for the 1988 film *Rain Man*) had a remarkable memory and reading speed despite having a developmental disorder and an IQ of 87 (although it is thought that this probably did not fully reflect his true abilities as he scored in the "superior" range for some of the subtests; Peek 1996; Treffert and Christensen 2005). In his fifties, he had memorized more than 9,000 books, from which he could recite large passages. He could accurately recall details of compositions he may have heard only once, sometimes more than 40 years ago. He also knew all the telephone area codes and postal zip codes in the US and could provide detailed travel directions between or within any of the major US cities. All of these exceptional memory skills were in stark contrast to other areas of his life. Kim could not button his shirt, deal with abstract thought, or manage everyday tasks (Treffert and Christensen 2005). Other examples include calendar-calculating twins (Horwitz et al. 1965; Sacks 1985) who are able to calculate any day of the week for any date in a 40,000 year time-span, and a blind, autistic musical savant with exceptional time-keeping skills and precise spatial location abilities (see Treffert 1989 for further descriptions).

Savant syndrome has been written about for over 200 years, but the first specific description and use of the term was in the late nineteenth century. Down (1887) used the phrase "idiot savant" to describe individuals with "special faculties" such as remarkable drawing skills, arithmetical genius, or precise time-keeping skills, despite having prevailing developmental disorders. The more commonly used phrase now is "savant" or "savant syndrome." Miller (1998) suggests that we should use the term savant to describe individuals who show a superior performance in an area compared to other people, and also who show a discrepancy between their performance in that area and their general functioning level. It has also been suggested that savants can be further described as either "talented savants," who show an outstanding skill in comparison to their own level of general functioning, and "prodigious savants" who have an outstanding skill in relation to both their own general level of function and to the wider population (Treffert 1989). Overall, the important aspect seems to be the discrepancy between an exceptional skill in one area that contrasts to impairments in other areas of functioning.

Treffert (2009) describes how savant skills can be divided into five general categories; music, art, calendar calculating, mathematics, and mechanical or spatial skills. Musical skills include the ability to replay complex musical sequences sometimes after just one hearing. Artistic savants often have the skill of producing complex scenes with accurate detail following a single brief viewing of a scene. Calendar calculating is the ability to work out the day of the week of any given date, and mathematics abilities include lightening calculations and the ability to identify prime numbers. Mechanical or spatial skills often include the ability to build complex models with an intricate level of detail, and being able to accurately estimate distances without the assistance of measuring devices. There is disagreement in the literature about which of the skills are most common, with some studies suggesting calendrical skills to be most common (Howlin et al. 2009; Saloviita et al. 2000) and others suggesting that it is musical ability (Rimbrand 1978). Across all of these abilities, it has been suggested all individuals with savant syndrome have a remarkable memory (Treffert 2009). It also seems that individuals with savant syndrome have higher than average IQs compared to individuals with intellectual or developmental disabilities who do not have savant syndrome. For example, in their large-scale study, Howlin et al. (2009) found that no individual with a non-verbal IQ below 50 met the criteria for a savant skill.

One of the developmental disabilities that frequently co-occur with savant syndrome is autism, or autistic spectrum disorders (ASD). Autism affects how someone communicates with and relates to other people, and the way that someone perceives the world (National Autistic Society 2011). There is a spectrum of autistic disorders, with differing degrees of social, communication, and imagination impairment. This means that some people with a diagnosis of ASD need specialist support throughout their lives whiles other can live independently. Earlier studies estimated that 10% of people with ASD have some kind of savant skill (Rimland 1978), but more recently the estimate has been as high as 30% (Howlin et al. 2009). However, it is important to note that savant syndrome does not always co-occur with ASD. It is thought that around 50% of individuals with savant syndrome have ASD, while the other 50% have either other developmental or intellectual disabilities, or neurological damage (Treffert 2009). Whereas savant syndrome is thought to be found in between 10% and 30% of the ASD population, it has been estimated that savant skills are found in between 0.6% and 0.1% of other intellectual or developmental disabilities (Hill 1977; Saloviita et al. 2000). In addition, savant skills have also been documented in individuals diagnosed with, for example, manic-depressive illness (DeLong and Aldershof 1988), Tourette's syndrome (Moriarty, Ring, and Robertson 1993; Nelson and Pribor 1993) and frontotemporal dementia (Miller et al. 1996). It has been noted, however, that disorders which are associated with savant skills have some similar traits to ASD (Heaton and Wallace 2004). For example, cognitive features and behavioral traits characteristic of ASD, such as restricted interests, obsessive–compulsive behaviors/tendencies and a similar feature-biased information processing style, are common features of these disorders which have been found to co-occur with savant syndrome (O'Connor and Hermelin 1991).

It has therefore been proposed that for people with intellectual or developmental disabilities, the presence of traits which predispose these individuals towards obsessions and restricted interest may help to develop the savant skills. Heaton and Wallace (2004) outlined three areas of evidence to support this idea. First, the majority of individuals with savant syndrome have been diagnosed with ASD, and by definition people with autism show obsessive and restricted interests (American Psychiatric Association 1994). Second, when savant skills are found in people without ASD diagnosis, they often have developmental/acquired disorders which include obsessional behaviors/restricted interests (as described earlier). The third area of evidence comes from studies of "neurotypical" individuals which have found that talented people are likely to show some autistic features. A study of musicians with absolute pitch, for example, found they showed evidence of having autism-related language, personality, and cognition compared to musicians without absolute pitch (Brown et al. 2003). Heaton and Wallace (2004) therefore conclude that there is converging evidence showing the importance of obsessive and restrictive interests in the development of savant skills, for individuals with and without a diagnosis of ASD. Further support for this idea comes from a recent population based twin study, which found that parents' reports of children with savant-like skills were more likely to show ASD-like traits than children without savant-like skills. Specifically, the children reported to have savant-like skills showed restricted and repetitive behaviors and interests (Happe and Vital 2009). The explanation given by these authors is that a detail-focused cognitive style, typical of, but not restricted to, someone with ASD, allows the development of savant talents.

In summary, savant skills can therefore be thought of as exceptional skills in a narrow area, contrasted with deficits in other areas of functioning. These talents are sometimes referred to as "islands of genius" (Treffert 2009). Savant syndrome is often found in people with ASD, but a diagnosis of ASD is not always present. However it seems that a particular cognitive and behavioral style, characteristic of ASD is always present, and this may help in the development of the extraordinary abilities. It has been noted in the literature that these exceptional abilities can also be related to excellent sensory discrimination, with synesthesia sometimes being listed as a "skill" (Treffert 2009). The prevalence of synesthesia co-occurring with savant skills is unknown. At chance level we would expect around 4% of people with savant skills to also have synesthesia. If this rate was found to be higher than chance, then we would need to consider some type of meaningful relationship between synesthesia and savantism as has been suggested by some (see later). With the recent resurgence of scientific interest in synesthesia, some interesting cases have come to light of synesthetes who have savant-like skills, raising questions about the nature of the relationship between synesthesia and savantism.

DT and Digits

Introducing DT

DT is a savant who has been diagnosed with Asperger syndrome, a form of autism that typically has fewer problems with language than some forms of ASD and average or above average IQ (National Autistic Society 2011). Interestingly, DT also has synesthesia; for DT, numbers have personalities, shapes, colors, and textures, and some words have colors. Many of DT's savant skills relate to numbers, such as his amazing numerical memory and mathematical calculation skills. After achieving the European record for reciting pi to 22,514 digits in 2004, DT has been the focus of various television programs about his exceptional abilities. He has since published his memoirs describing his life and the effect he feels synesthesia and Asperger syndrome have had on his way of perceiving and understanding the world (Tammet 2006). He has also taken part in numerous scientific studies that have aimed to document his unique mind to help to expand our understanding of the way both synesthesia and Asperger syndrome may contribute towards the savant skills DT possesses. In order to explore this, it is important to first present details of DT's synesthesia, his diagnosis of Asperger syndrome, and then to consider how these may contribute to his exceptional memory for numerical information.

DT and synesthesia

In his memoirs DT states that "numbers are my friends and they are always around me" (Tammet 2006, 2). He goes on to describe how each number is unique and has its own personality (which is often referred to as ordinal-linguistic personality synesthesia). For example, the number four is both shy and quiet, and is his favorite number. He suggests this might be because it reminds him of himself. Numbers also have shapes and sizes, and he describes how nines are as tall as skyscrapers. Numbers also have colors, textures, and motions (referred to as grapheme-color synesthesia). Additionally, some words have colors, and days of the week have colors and emotions: "Tuesdays are warm while Thursdays are fuzzy" (Tammet 2006, 9). Like other synesthetes, DT reports that he has always had these synesthetic experiences, as far back as he can remember.

DT describes how he has used his synesthesia since a young age to handle and calculate huge numbers without any conscious effort. DT has never needed to write things down when doing complex calculations as he has always found it easier to mentally visualize the answer using his synesthetic shapes. He particularly enjoys doing complex calculations. His favorite type is power multiplication, seeing the results of power multiplications as distinctive visual patterns in his mind's eye, the mental shapes and colors growing more complex as the sums and results grow. For example 37 to the power of 5 ($37 \times 37 \times 37 \times 37 \times 37 = 69{,}343{,}957$) looks like "a large circle composed of smaller circles running clockwise from the top round" (Tammet 2006, 5).

DT's synesthesia has been verified by two different groups of researchers. Baron-Cohen et al. (2007) tested his synesthesia with the *Test of Genuineness* (Asher et al. 2006). The test requires participants to describe the synesthetic experience they have for a series of inducers (the stimuli which induce the synesthesia), such as numbers, words, and non-words. Then without prior warning the participants are asked to retake the test, usually several months later, and their responses at the two time points are compared for similarity. For DT the results showed that he was 90% consistent in his responses, which is a typical level for synesthetes. In comparison, when non-synesthetes take the test, and are given the retest after only a 2-week interval, and with prior warning, their typical consistency rates are between 35% to 38% (Baron-Cohen et al. 1993; Simner et al. 2005).

The consistency of DT's shapes for digits has also been tested with a less descriptive and more "hands-on" method. Azoulai, Hubbard, and Ramachandran (2005) asked DT to form three-dimensional representations of 20 different number shapes in play dough. Azoulai and colleagues noted that the shapes DT formed for each number were unique from each other, with a high level of detail, including textural details and color. They tested the consistency of his "numerical landscapes" across time, by giving him a surprise retest 24 hours later, to assess the consistency of the shapes. The shapes DT created in the surprise retest were found to be almost identical to the original shapes, with the same level of detail. This therefore provides further objective evidence to support his subjective descriptions of his synesthesia.

DT and Asperger syndrome

In his memoirs DT describes how he has always had an almost obsessive need for order and routine in every aspect of his life. He likes to have the same breakfast every day (weighed to the exact gram), cups of tea at the same time each day, and needs to count the number of items of clothing he is wearing before he leaves the house. He reports feeling anxious and stressed if he is not able to do any of this, and uses counting to calm himself and return his breathing to normal. He also finds emotions hard to understand. Interestingly he has learnt to use numbers to help him understand how other people are feeling. For example, the number six is his least favorite number as it is small and does not have a distinctive shape or texture. He can understand a friend's description of feeling sad by imagining himself sitting next to a number six. Or if he wants to understand how someone feels if they say they feel intimidated by something, he imagines standing next to a number nine, which towers over him. Both the obsessive need for order and the problems understanding emotions show evidence of ASD-like tendencies. They also illustrate nicely how DT uses numbers and the synesthetic percepts these induce, to help him function successfully on a day-to-day basis.

When DT was at school in the 1980s and 1990s, Asperger syndrome had not yet been formally recognized as part of the autism spectrum. For someone to be diagnosed as having Asperger syndrome they need to meet the criteria for autism but have no history of language or cognitive delay (World Health Organization 1994). Due to his good language skills and lack of cognitive delay DT would not have been tested for autism at school. His own descriptions of his extreme need for order and routine, and problems understanding other people's emotions suggested that a diagnosis of Asperger syndrome was a potential explanation for aspects of his cognitive and behavioral profile.

In order to screen DT for a possible diagnosis of ASD, Baron-Cohen et al. (2007) initially tested DT with the *Autism Spectrum Quotient* (AQ) (Baron-Cohen et al. 2001) and the *Empathy Quotient* (EQ) (Baron-Cohen and Wheelwright 2004). The AQ measures the presence of autistic traits in an individual by asking them to say how much they agree with a series of statements relating to certain behaviors and characteristics. The EQ is also a self-report measure, which measures how well someone feels they can relate to other people's feelings and emotions. People with ASD typically score much lower on this than people without ASD. On both of these scales DT scored in the clinical range suggesting likely Asperger syndrome. Follow-up testing with the *Adult Asperger's Assessment* (AAA) (Baron-Cohen et al. 2005) showed that the combination of his social difficulties and obsessional interests were the basis for a diagnosis of Asperger syndrome. The AAA has been designed specifically for assessing adults for Asperger syndrome, and involves interviewing a parent or carer about aspects of the individual's childhood development that relate to a diagnosis of Asperger syndrome. For a child a diagnosis of Asperger syndrome can be useful to ensure they receive the necessary support throughout their education, whereas it could be argued that for a well-adjusted adult it is not of as much use. However, Baron-Cohen et al. report that DT decided that the diagnosis helped him to understand his own development.

How good is DT's memory?

It was DT's extraordinary numerical memory that first brought him to the attention of scientists, as well as to the media. In 2004 DT set the European record for reciting pi, having recited 22, 514 digits of pi without error in 5 hours and 9 minutes. He did it to raise money for an epilepsy charity, and took just 3 months to learn the digits. DT used his numerical landscapes to memorize the digits, visualizing each of the decimal places as if it was a real landscape in his mind's eye. For example, for DT the Feynman point of pi, 999,999 (named after Richard Feynman, between the 762nd and 767th decimal place of pi) looks beautiful as a "deep thick rim of dark blue light" (Tammet 2006, 226).

In order to see if DT's exceptional memory skills can be seen in other aspects of his memory, and how his memory compares to other people, DT's memory has also been tested with standardized memory tests (Baron-Cohen et al. 2007). He was tested with the visual digit-span test, which assesses short-term memory for digit-sequences. While the average for the adult population is 6.5, DT's span is an incredible 11.5. He was also tested on the spatial span task, which assesses short-term memory for spatial sequences and so is not related to numbers. On this he scored in a similar range as controls (6.5 compared to 5.3) suggesting that his general short-term memory for non-numerical information is average. Finally he was shown a set of 82 faces and was given a surprise memory recognition test. His performance on this was quite poor, with an accuracy rate close to chance level that was comparable to the performance of an 8-year-old (DT was 26 years old at the time of testing).

Therefore, despite his exceptional memory for numerical information, DT's performance on the standard tests show that other areas of his memory are either average (visuo-spatial short-term memory) or impaired (memory for faces). This pattern of an individual with extraordinary skills alongside areas of impairment is one of the defining features of savant syndrome (Miller 1998; Treffert 1989). DT's exceptional skill, in comparison to his general level of performance in other areas, and also in relation to the general population, is his numerical memory. Researchers have since gone on to try and unravel whether this exceptional skill was linked in any way to his synesthesia and/or Asperger syndrome, or whether their co-occurrence within the same individual was simply coincidental.

Does synesthesia contribute to DT's savant skills?

DT's subjective descriptions illustrate how he feels his synesthesia helps him to remember numbers. He makes use of the numerical landscapes that he visualizes when thinking of the numbers. He describes how when he needs to memorize a long sequence of numbers, he breaks the numbers into segments, with the size of segments varying according to how the digits look "synesthetically" together in his mind. When he then needs to recall the entire sequence of digits, he recalls it segment by segment, remembering each digit within each segment by "looking" at the pattern in his mind. In this DT is using the "method of loci" that was used by Greek orators to remember large amounts of information by "placing" it in specific physical locations in their minds' eye (Yates 1966). However, whereas most people would spend a long time perfecting these abilities to remember a large amount of information, it seems that for DT, his synesthesia makes this task much easier and allows him to remember an exceptional amount of information with very little effort.

One way in which the contribution of synesthesia to DT's savant skills has been explored is to compare DT's memory for digits when they are visually presented in different sizes. For DT numbers have very precise synesthetic sizes, for example, with 9 being very, very tall like a skyscraper, and 6 being very small. If these sizes are important for DT's memory of numbers then he should be less able to remember digits when they are incorrectly sized. Azoulai et al. (2005) tested this prediction by showing DT matrices of 100 random numbers and asking him to memorize them. There were three different number conditions. In the first the numbers were all shown as the same size ("normal size"). In the second condition the number sizes matched DT's own synesthetic sizes for numbers ("congruent size"), so 6 was presented as very small and 9 was very tall. The third number condition displayed numbers which did not match the sizes of DT's number landscape ("incongruent size"). It was predicted that DT would perform worst in this "incongruent" condition, as having the numbers displayed in the incorrect sizes would make it more difficult to memorize. He was given 3 minutes to memorize each of the matrices. After viewing each matrix there was a 5-minute delay, during which he was prevented from rehearsing the digits in a verbal loop, and subsequently he was asked to recall as many of the numbers as he could, in order. Two surprise retests were also given at 24- and 72-hour intervals. A group of control non-synesthete participants were also tested to act as a comparison group.

The results showed that DT performed best in the "normal size" condition, recalling 68% of the digits at all three times of testing. This compares to just 8% for the control participants after the short delay, and 4% after 24 hours. DT therefore has superior memory compared to the controls, as shown by Baron-Cohen et al. (2007) with the standardized memory tests. Additionally these results show that whereas the controls show clear memory decay with time, DT does not, as he remains consistently accurate. In terms of DT's performance across the different conditions, as predicted DT performed worst in the "incongruent size" condition, with 16% accuracy after the short delay (although better than the controls at 6%), and then dropped to 4% and 0% over the subsequent tests. In comparison in the "congruent size" condition DT had a 50% accuracy rate across all three testing points which surprisingly is less than for the "normal size" condition. The authors have suggested that a possible explanation for DT not performing best in the congruent condition is that the number sizes were not exactly the same as he experiences in his synesthetic number landscape. The number 9, for example, is really tall while 6 is very small, and so it would not be feasible to get the proportions precisely right for presentation on a standard computer screen. Overall, the authors conclude that these results show that DT is not relying on mere rote rehearsal, as the incongruent condition clearly impaired his performance, highlighting the role his synesthetic numerical landscape can play in his extraordinary memory.

The contribution of synesthesia to DT's savant skills has also been explored by looking at the way he breaks number sequences into segments or chunks. Research with "neurotypical" individuals has shown that this chunking technique can be very beneficial to memorizing number sequences (Ericsson, Chase, and Falloon 1980). Furthermore, the superior encoding of mathematically structured sequences of digits (such as 24,689,753), compared to the recall of random digit sequences has been found to be associated with increased activation of an area of the brain referred to as the lateral prefrontal cortex (LPFC; Bor and Owen 2007). The question that arises is whether DT would show the same advantage for sequences with a mathematical structure, and whether the same pattern of activity would be found in his brain. As DT reports using his synesthetic number landscape to encode numerical sequences, Bor, Billington, and Baron-Cohen (2007) predicted that the presence or absence of a mathematical structure to a sequence would not make a difference to his ability to recall the sequence. They also predicted that the presence or absence of a mathematical structure would not make a difference to the pattern of the neural processing associated with the encoding of each sequence. For example, the sequence "24689753" has a mathematical structure and typically would be easier to encode and recall than a random sequence. However, for DT the mathematical structure will not necessarily be of benefit, as with both types of sequence he would be expected to use his synesthetic numerical landscape. To test this Bor, Billington, and Baron-Cohen (2007) carried out a neuroimaging and neuropsychological experiment to compare DT to a group of matched controls who did not have synesthesia, savantism, or Asperger syndrome. Whilst in a functional magnetic resonance imaging (fMRI) scanner, DT and the controls were aurally presented with a series of eight-digit sequences, and after a short delay of variable length, the participants were asked to verbally recall each sequence.

As predicted, DT was found to perform equally well on each type of sequence (98% and 99% accurate on the structured and unstructured trials respectively). A comparison control group was found to do significantly better with the structured sequences than unstructured (88% versus 81%), but overall there was no significant difference between the performance of the controls and DT. The mathematical structure therefore made no difference to DT's performance and Bor and colleagues suggest that this provides support for the idea that DT uses his synesthetic number landscape to process numbers. Furthermore it is reported that after testing he claimed to have not noticed the difference between the two types of sequence, whereas the vast majority of the controls noticed that some sequences had structure and some did not. The neuroimaging data also support this idea because whereas the controls showed a clear difference in levels of activation of the LPFC when processing the two types of sequence, DT did not. Overall this study shows how DT processes number sequences in a different way to "neurotypicals." As shown by Azoulai et al. (2005), it appears that his synesthetic numerical landscape allows him to use a different approach to encoding and recalling numbers, and so his synesthesia may play an important role in his savant skills. However, it is also important to consider the impact his diagnosis of Asperger syndrome may have, as the different cognitive processing style typical of individuals with an ASD could also be an important factor.

Does Asperger syndrome contribute to DT's savant skills?

Individuals with Asperger syndrome, and ASD in general, are thought to have a specific cognitive style, characteristic of ASD. There is a debate in the literature about the exact nature of this (e.g., compare the Weak Central Coherence Theory (Happe 1996) to the Hyper-Systemiser Theory (Baron-Cohen and Belmonte 2005)). However, an idea common to these theories is that with the cognitive style characteristic of ASD, attention is typically focused on local detail, rather than at the global level as found with the general population. This therefore allows people with ASD to ignore any distracters found at the global level (Ring et al. 1999). It has been suggested that this cognitive style may help develop savant skills (as outlined in the earlier section; Happe and Vital 2009). In order to show that DT's savant skills are at least in part due to this style of processing it is therefore necessary to measure his preference for local level processing and ability to ignore global level interference.

In order to explore DT's cognitive processing style, Bor et al. (2007) conducted a study that made use of the Navon task (Navon 1977). This task involves visually presenting a large individual letter, which is constructed with lots of smaller letters. For example, it could be a large A constructed with many small Hs. The larger or "global" letter can either match or not match the smaller or "local" level letters. The task is to name the target letter, which can be either at the global or local level, depending on task instructions. Typically, compared to when the local level and global level are congruent (e.g., a large H made up of small Hs) when the local level and global level letters are incongruent with each other (e.g., a large A made with small Hs) when attempting to identify the smaller letter, people show interference from the global level. It is as if the larger letter is difficult to ignore, and acts as a distractor from identifying the smaller letters. However, studies with individuals with ASD show an ability to ignore the global level distractor, in comparison to "neurotypical" controls. Due to DT's diagnosis of Asperger syndrome, Bor, Billington, and Baron-Cohen (2007) therefore expected him to show this ability to ignore the global level distracters and focus on the local level detail.

In order to test this prediction, Bor, Billington, and Baron-Cohen (2007) showed DT and a group of neurotypical controls a series of Navon-type figures. The participants had to view each stimulus and indicate each time they saw a specific target letter, either at the global or local level. The results showed that DT had a bias for local processing, and although DT and the controls showed some level of global level interference, for DT this was significantly smaller. Additionally, the controls showed significantly less local level interference than DT when the target letter was shown at the global level. Therefore, as predicted based on his Asperger syndrome diagnosis, DT showed a preference for local level processing that is typical of ASD. This provides further support for the idea that the cognitive style typical of ASD may be important for the development of savant-like skills.

Overview of DT's savant skills and the contribution of synesthesia and Asperger syndrome

DT's extraordinary numerical memory, and potentially his mathematical abilities, are well documented. Like other savants, DT has exceptional abilities in a narrow area of expertise. In comparison to these savant abilities, he is found to be impaired in other areas. However, it should be noted that these comparisons have not been fully explored, and future studies may need to use a broader range of standard tests to fully document his cognitive profile. As predicted, his cognitive processing style has been found to be typical of individuals with ASD, having a preference for processing local details rather than global level details. Furthermore, his memory for numbers has been shown to be based on his synesthetic number landscape, as his ability to encode and recall numbers is disrupted if the numbers are presented in the "incorrect" size, synesthetically speaking. His processing of numerical sequences has also been shown to be atypical, as rather than benefiting from mathematical structure when encoding numerical sequences, he seemingly processed mathematically structured and unstructured sequences in the same way (presumably using his synesthetic numerical landscape). This was shown in terms of accuracy rates and with associated neural activity.

The evidence presented therefore suggests that both synesthesia and Asperger syndrome contribute to DT's savant skill. Like other documented savants, his pre-occupation and restricted interest in numbers and his cognitive style help him to focus on particular areas. However, in DT's case he has a uniquely detailed number landscape to both "enjoy" and utilize, as a direct result of his synesthesia. Baron-Cohen et al. (2007)

have speculated that this unusual combination of synesthesia and Asperger syndrome may increase the likelihood of having a savant memory. Of course much more research is needed to test this idea, as so far this has been based on a single-case study, but they have hypothesized that synesthesia provides the basis of the unusual skill or ability, and that ASD, or similar traits, gives the obsessive focus to polish these skills to savant level. As will be discussed in more detail later in this chapter, importantly Simner, Mayo, and Spiller (2009) have gone on to provide empirical evidence that synesthesia is associated with skills within the same domain as the type of synesthesia, although not to savant level of expertise in the absence of the ASD-like traits.

AJ and Dates

Introducing AJ

In relation to time, DT states that "Thinking of calendars always makes me feel good, all those numbers and patterns in one place" (Tammet, 2006, 9). DT describes how he enjoys the fact that numbers in calendars are predictable (for example, the 13th day of the month is always 2 days before the day the first of the month falls on), and some months always have the same patterns as others (for example, 1 January always falls on the same day of the week as 1 October). For DT, therefore, it seems that his like for calendars comes from his enjoyment of numbers. For another synesthete things are very different. Parker, Cahill, and McGaugh (2006) report the intriguing case of AJ, a 41-year-old woman, who is a visual-spatial synesthete: she sees time in spatial patterns. What makes her seemingly unique is her savant-like skill when it comes to her auto-biographical memory. AJ has an extraordinary memory for dates and personal events. Importantly, AJ has *not* been diagnosed with ASD, although she does have another condition associated with obsessive traits (see later). It is therefore interesting to examine her cognitive and behavioral profile to see which aspects contribute to her unique savant-like skill, and to see if it is associated with other aspects typically found with savant syndrome. It is also interesting to consider the contribution synesthesia makes to her savant-like skill.

AJ reports that she enjoys dates, dating events, and going over dates in her mind. Her detailed memory for dates starts when she was 8 years old in 1974, but it is strongest from when she was 14 in 1980 until the present time. Helpfully, she kept diaries from the age of 10 to 34, thus providing a resource for verification of her recollections. AJ describes her memories as vivid, like a film, and says they are full of emotion. She says it is automatic and she is not in control. When someone tells AJ a date she immediately knows the day of the week it fell on and something she did either on that day, or a day either side. The memories she recalls relate to her own personal history, as even when given dates of public events she will relate them to her own personal experience. Memories also trigger further memories, in an automatic sequence, spontaneously cueing the next memory.

This constant cascade of memories and dates can be a burden, and at times overpowering. Importantly, AJ has not trained herself to remember dates, or deliberately created mnemonics to encode and retrieve the detailed memories, the technique used by others with superior memories (Ericsson et al. 2004).

AJ and synesthesia

When thinking of time, AJ describes seeing a mental calendar. Therefore, as first noted by Simner, Mayo, and Spiller (2009), AJ has time-space synesthesia (sometimes known as visuo-spatial synesthesia). When given a date in her calendar she says she can see it, reporting "I don't see the whole day at one time. I get to a portion of the day so I can see what day it was and whatever sticks out in my mind" (Parker, Cahill, and McGaugh 2006, 41). AJ has a spatial calendar for years and another for months of the year. Her calendar for years goes from left to right until 1970 when it changes direction and goes from top to bottom. Her calendar for months is described as having January at the 11 o'clock position, with the other months going in a counter-clockwise order. The counter-clockwise and presumably circle-like shape of her month calendar is commonly reported by other time-space synesthetes (Eagleman 2009; Smilek et al. 2007). For both the monthly and yearly calendars she states that she does not know why she sees time in this way, but that it is just the way she has always seen it ever since she can remember. Again, this is very similar to other time-space synesthetes' reports (Eagleman 2009). Parker, Cahill, and McGaugh asked AJ to draw her yearly and monthly calendars on four separate occasions, and each time she drew very similar forms. Essentially, this is equivalent to the Test of Genuineness Baron-Cohen et al. (2007) used to assess DT, and so this repeated testing of AJ provides important verification of her visuo-spatial synesthesia. Unfortunately, Parker, Cahill, and McGaugh do not mention if AJ has been tested for, or if she reports, any other type of synesthesia.

AJ and her memory

AJ reports having an extraordinary memory for personal dates and events. This can be demonstrated by giving her dates between 1980 and the present time to which she will say the day of the week the day fell on that year and provide details of events that happened that day. These are then verified either with her personal diaries or through speaking with a relative. To assess her memory for dates more objectively Parker, Cahill, and McGaugh asked AJ to write the dates that Easter Sunday fell on between 1980 and 2003. This is not an easy task as Easter Sunday can fall anywhere between 22 March and 25 April due to it following the pattern of the Paschal full moon. Within 10 minutes of being asked, AJ had produced the list of dates, including details of her own personal entries for the dates. She was found to be accurate for 23 of the 24 dates, and the incorrect response was only 2 days out. It is worth noting that AJ is Jewish and therefore has no personal interest in knowing anything about Easter Sunday. Parker, Cahill, and McGaugh retested AJ 2 years later, and found this time she was 100% accurate, with the same notes about her personal entries. This provides clear support for AJ's claims of having an exceptional autobiographical memory.

Subjectively, AJ reports that her memory for things other than autobiographical events is not good. This includes rote learning of historical dates. Interestingly, AJ says she did not do particularly well at school, despite her remarkable memory. She says that she did not enjoy school, and that she needs to enjoy something and be interested in it in order to remember it. Furthermore, when asked to recall aspects of her meeting with Parker and colleagues 2 months previously, she was unable to recall or recognize aspects, even when prompted with a video tape. This suggests that AJ may only have strengths in her autobiographical memory, and may even have deficits in some aspects of memory. If support is found for this, it would mean that her psychological profile is similar to a savant such as DT, with exceptional abilities in a relatively narrow area of expertise and impairments in functioning in other aspects of cognition.

In order to assess for this possibility, Parker, Cahill, and McGaugh tested AJ's memory and other aspects of her cognition with a number of standardized tests such as the Wechsler Adult Intelligence Scale-Revised (WAIS-R), the Wechsler Memory Scale-Revised (WMS-R), the Autobiographical Memory Test (AMT), the Warrington Word Recognition and Face Recognition Tests, the California Verbal Learning Test, as well as other tests of cognitive ability not directly related to memory. These tests highlighted areas in which she did indeed have some strengths, showing well above average performance in a number of different areas. The area she showed strengths in mainly related to aspects of memory, in particular her episodic memory. Not surprisingly she had a perfect score on the AMT. Other memory tests she did well on, often scoring perfect or near ceiling scores, were generally tests that involved structured materials at the encoding and retrieval stages (including the WMS-R visual paired associates test and the Warrington Word Recognition Test). AJ also showed strong attention skills with her performance on the digit span and attention/concentration index of the WMS-R.

Importantly, however, the tests also showed many areas where she had weaknesses, showing impaired performance. AJ's poor performance on some tests of executive function (such as the Wisconsin Card Sorting Test) suggest that she has a tendency towards perseveration, meaning that she often repeats the same response, and finds it difficult to switch responses when required. The tests also showed that she has problems with abstraction and analogical reasoning (with the Halstead Reasoning Test and the Similarities subtest on the WAIS-R). In comparison, her performance on tests of executive function which require less abstraction, such as the Stroop test, was in the normal range. AJ showed deficits on memory tests that required her to organize the material in both the visual and verbal domain, such as the California Verbal Learning Test and Complex Figure Test (but it should be noted that this was not due to problems with visual memory per se as she did well in other visual memory tests that did not require organization of materials). Furthermore AJ's poor performance on the Warrington Face

Recognition Test showed that she has problems with her memory for faces, which is similar to DT's performance on a face memory test conducted by Baron-Cohen et al. (2007). In contrast to her impaired memory for faces, AJ showed a good ability to visually discriminate between different faces on the Benton Face Perception Test. This therefore suggests that her poor performance on the Warrington Face Recognition Test was not due to problems with processing faces per se, and was due to a memory deficit. Overall therefore it seems that AJ's cognitive profile can be seen to be similar to that of someone with savant syndrome, with strengths in particular restricted areas, which in this case is autobiographical memory, and some particular weaknesses in others, such a memory for faces, and the capacity for abstraction and self-organizing materials to be remembered.

AJ and savant syndrome?

Parker, Cahill, and McGaugh (2006) refer to AJ's autobiographical memory syndrome as *hyperthymestic syndrome*, from the Greek words hyper meaning "more than normal" and thymesis meaning "remembering" (more recently they have referred to this as highly superior autobiographical memory (HSAM); LePort et al. 2012). They propose two defining features; first the amount of time the individual spends thinking about their own personal past is abnormally large, and second the individual's ability to recall specific events from their past is exceptional. Parker, Cahill, and McGaugh (2006) clearly state that AJ does not have calendrical calculating savant skills, although it can be argued that her skills are savant-like. They do, however, comment on some of the similarities between AJ's unusual autobiographical memory and savant syndrome.

   These similarities include the fact that AJ's interest in dates started at an early age, and there is evidence of atypical development and obsessive–compulsive tendencies before she started to write her diaries at age 10. For example, she describes how she has always needed order in her life, saying that she was "traumatized" by a family move from the east to west coast of the USA when she was 10 years old. As a child she did not like things to be moved in her bedroom and she kept her doll collection in a very precise and complex order. Furthermore, she has a history of anxiety. It is suggested by Parker, Cahill, and McGaugh that AJ has a variant of a neurodevelopmental fronto-striatal disorder. As described earlier, her exceptional autobiographical memory is also contrasted with deficits in other areas of cognitive function, as found in savantism. It would therefore seem that as suggested by Heaton and Wallace (2004), the development of her savant-like skills could be associated with her restricted and obsessional interests/behaviors. Crucially her cognitive/behavioral profile is similar to that of someone with a diagnosis of ASD. And furthermore, like DT, AJ's synesthesia provides an atypical perceptual schema that can be seen to potentially contribute to her savant-like skill. The suggestion that synesthesia, in collaboration with other factors, could be a possible foundation for savant syndrome or savant talents needs to be considered.

SYNESTHESIA AS A FOUNDATION FOR SAVANTISM?

The cases of DT and AJ show two examples of synesthesia making a significant contribution to extraordinary memories. For DT, the spatial form of his numerical landscape helps him to recall strings of digits of incredible length, while AJ's visual-spatial calendar for months and years allows her to "see" her past from day to day, and she recalls an amazing level of detail. However, in neither case should it be argued that it is the synesthesia *alone* which produces these astounding feats. Both DT and AJ can be seen to have atypical cognitive and behavioral profiles which may inevitably have played an important role.

In addition to his synesthesia, DT has a diagnosis of Asperger syndrome. Consequently, DT shows clear evidence of the restricted and obsessional interests, and feature-biased information processing style that have been suggested to be characteristic of savant syndrome (Happe and Vital 2009; Heaton and Wallace 2004). Importantly, it has been suggest that DT's savantism is a possible result of the combination of Asperger syndrome and synesthesia; the synesthesia provides an individual with the cognitive advantages in a particular domain, and the ASD or similar ASD-like traits, cause obsessive over-rehearsal of those skills to savant level (Baron-Cohen et al. 2007; Simner, Mayo and Spiller 2009). Baron-Cohen et al. (2007) propose that future studies need to explore whether having both ASD and synesthesia increase the likelihood of savantism, by comparing the rates of savantism found in individuals with no diagnosis of ASD and no synesthesia, to individuals with ASD but not synesthesia, and those with both ASD and synesthesia. As they point out, this is an area of the literature that has not received much attention to date. Although work is ongoing, little is known about the prevalence of synesthesia in individuals with a diagnosis of ASD.

Unlike DT, AJ does not have a diagnosis of ASD and has not been formally identified as having savant syndrome by Parker, Cahill, and McGaugh (2006). However, as suggested by Simner, Mayo, and Spiller (2009), she clearly has a savant-like skill; her exceptional autobiographical memory certainly shows superior performance to that of other people, and the results of the standardized tests suggest she has a discrepancy between her excellent performance on structured memory tests and poor performance on memory tests for faces, and tests measuring aspects of executive function. Other visuo-spatial synesthetes have been shown to have superior performance on tests of visual memory recall, spatial processing, and memory for events in time (Simner, Mayo, and Spiller 2009), showing how the additional experiences that synesthetes have can shape their cognitive abilities. In contrast to AJ, visuo-spatial synesthetes tested by Simner, Mayo, and Spiller did not show the restricted interest and obsessional behaviors that Parker, Cahill, and McGaugh (2006) have described AJ to have, or the cognitive profile with traits characteristic of ASD. Furthermore, although the synesthetes showed above average memory for events in time, it was not exceptional. Simner, Mayo, and Spiller (2009) in their discussion of AJ, have stated that she appears to demonstrate the necessary components of having savant syndrome. Drawing similar conclusions to Baron-Cohen et al. (2007), Simner, Mayo, and Spiller speculate that for some individuals these visuo-spatial forms could be "the foundation upon which the repetitive and obsessive tendencies operate to create savant ability for dates and events in time" (2009, 258). The theory proposed by Baron-Cohen et al. is that synesthesia can provide a skill in a particular domain, related to the specific form of synesthesia, and the co-occurrence of synesthesia with ASD-like obsessive tenancies results in obsessive over-rehearsal of this skill, producing savant abilities. Initial support for this theory has been provided by Simner, Mayo, and Spiller (2009), who found that that synesthesia is associated with enhanced cognitive abilities in the domain related to the individual's form of synesthesia.

When considering the contribution synesthesia may make to savantism, it is important to consider Sacks' (1985) description of the calendrical calculating twins, noted in the earlier part of this chapter. Sacks describes how the twins, when given a date, as they work out what day of the week it fell on "their eyes move and fix in a peculiar way...as if they were unrolling, or scrutinizing, an inner landscape, a mental calendar" (1985, 187). The twins are unable to do simple calculations, or understand what is meant by multiplication or division but yet they can produce ten-digit prime numbers spontaneously, and work out the date of Easter Sunday 40,000 years either side of the current time. Like DT, they have a remarkable memory for digits, repeating 300-digit sequences without any mistakes or seemingly any effort. They also have extraordinary memories for events from their own lives, like AJ, recalling the details of any given date, even to the extent of the weather for the day, from the age of 4 years onwards. Sacks describes how when asked how they manage this, the twins simply state that they "see it." Sacks goes on the compare their ability to "see" their memory to S, a synesthete and savant studied by Luria (1968). He says that although the twins may "lack the rich synesthesia and conscious organization" of S's memory, he is in no doubt that they have what he refers to as "a prodigious panorama, a sort of landscape or physiognomy" (Sacks 1985, 189) of everything they have experienced from which they can accurately recall details of their lives. Sacks suggests that for the twins numbers are like real objects, which they enjoy spending time with, which we might relate back to DT's comments about number being his friends.

Synesthesia-like "number landscapes" may therefore make an important contribution to savant skills such as those displayed by the calendrical calculating twins. Sacks (1985) suggests that the twins are not using calculations to work out the dates of Easter over an 80,000-year period, but rather they are inspecting their "prodigious panorama" with their mind's eye, and "seeing" the numbers involved. Future research with individuals with savant skills therefore needs to consider that there may be some form of synesthesia present, which arguably could be difficult with individuals who have limited language abilities. However, in order to more fully understand the cognitive profile of savant syndrome this seems an essential area for exploration. In addition to the restricted and obsessional interests, and feature-biased information processing style that have been suggested to be characteristic of savant syndrome (Happe and Vital 2009;

Heaton and Wallace 2004), in some cases the contribution of synesthesia may also need to be considered.

A recent study attempted to use fMRI to unpick the issue of whether savants use calculations when answering date-related questions. Cowan and Frith (2009) were able to scan two people who had calendrical calculating savant skills, and ASD. Whilst in the scanner the participants were asked to solve a series of date problems and to do some mental arithmetic, to test the prediction that if they are using calculations to answer the date problems there will be similar patterns of neural activation for both types of task. Cowan and Frith report that, as predicted, there was similar activation when solving date problems as when they solved mental arithmetic problems. Furthermore, there was increased activation in this area when the date problems involved more remote dates. The authors therefore concluded that the calendrical skills could be due to intensive practice with the same type of calculations used in solving mental arithmetic problems, for at least some individuals with savant syndrome. It should be kept in mind, however, that the neural activation in question was in the parietal cortex, an area that has previously been implicated in spatial coordinate systems, as well as the generation of synesthetic experiences (Hubbard et al. 2005; Tang, Ward, and Butterworth 2008). Therefore, the idea remains that calendrical calculators may be using a synesthetic number form or spatial sequence to aid their calculations.

In summary, the current chapter has considered how synesthesia may contribute towards some individuals' exceptional cognitive skills. It is not being argued that synesthesia alone is the basis for savantism, but rather that future research needs to explore the possibility that synesthesia, in addition to the ASD-like behavioral and cognitive characteristics, could be the focus of the restricted and obsessive tendencies (Simner, Mayo, and Spiller 2009), and synesthesia when accompanied by a diagnosis of ASD could increase the likelihood of the development of savant skills (Baron-Cohen et al. 2007). At present there are only a handful of studies relating to synesthesia and savantism, and so a substantial amount of research needs to be done in this area to address these possibilities. Our understanding of synesthesia is continuing to grow, as shown throughout this volume, while at the same time ongoing research continues to shape our understanding of savant syndrome and savant-like skills. Within the synesthesia research community there is a need to develop methods for assessing synesthesia in a non-verbal population, and for people with intellectual disabilities. This will allow a greater understanding of the prevalence of synesthesia in individuals with ASD and other developmental and intellectual deficits. Further case studies of individuals with savant syndrome and synesthesia are also needed, as the current chapter has only explored savant skills relating to numbers and time. Case studies of synesthesia contributing to artistic or musical savant skills are currently lacking from the literature. Overall, from the two case studies presented here, synesthesia can be seen to be making a contribution to individuals' savant-like skills. With such a small evidence base, however, it is very difficult to make any strong conclusions about the role synesthesia may play in the development of savant syndrome. It is clear that we are very much at the beginning of our journey towards understanding whether synesthesia could be considered a foundation for savantism.

REFERENCES

American Psychiatric Association. 1994. *Diagnostic and Statistical Manual of Mental Disorders. Fourth Edition.* Arlington, VA: American Psychiatric Publishing Inc.

Asher, Julian, Michael R. F. Aitken, Nasr Farooqi, Sameer Kurmani, and Simon Baron-Cohen. 2006. Diagnosing and phenotyping visual synaesthesia—a preliminary evaluation of the revised test of genuineness (TOG-R). *Cortex* 42 (2):137–146.

Azoulai, Shai, Edward M. Hubbard, and Vilayanur S. Ramachandran. 2005. Does synaesthesia contribute to mathematical savant skills? *Journal of Cognitive Neuroscience* 69 (Suppl):B173.

Baron-Cohen, Simon, and Matthew K. Belmonte. 2005. Autism: A window onto the development of the social and the analytic brain. *Annual Reviews of Neuroscience* 28:109–126.

Baron-Cohen, Simon, Daniel Bor, Jac Billington, Julian Asher, Sally Wheelwright, and Chris Ashwin. 2007. Savant memory in a man with colour form-number synaesthesia and Asperger syndrome. *Journal of Consciousness Studies* 14 (9–10):237–251.

Baron-Cohen, Simon, John Harrison, Laura H. Goldstein, and Maria Wyke. 1993. Coloured speech perception: Is synaesthesia what happens when modularity breaks down? *Perception* 22(4):419–426.

Baron-Cohen, Simon, and Sally Wheelwright. 2004. The Empathy Quotient (EQ): An investigation of adults with Asperger's syndrome or high functioning autism and normal sex differences. *Journal of Autism and Developmental Disorders* 34:163–175.

Baron-Cohen, Simon, Sally Wheelwright, Janine Robinson, and Marc Woodbury-Smith. 2005. The Adult Asperger's Assessment (AAA): a diagnostic method. *Journal of Autism and Developmental Disorders* 35:809–819.

Baron-Cohen, Simon, Sally Wheelwright, Richard Skinner, Joanne Martin, and Emma Clubley. 2001. The Autism Spectrum Quotient (AQ): Evidence from Asperger's syndrome, high functioning autism, males and females, scientists and mathematicians. *Journal of Autism and Developmental Disorders* 31:5–17.

Bor, Daniel, Jac Billington, and Simon Baron-Cohen. 2007. Savant memory for digits in a case of synaesthesia and Asperger syndrome is related to hyperactivity in the lateral prefrontal cortex. *Neurocase* 13:311–319.

Bor, Daniel, and Adrian M. Owen. 2007. A common prefrontal-parietal network for mnemonic and mathematical recoding strategies within working memory. *Cerebral Cortex* 17:778–786.

Brown, Walter A., Karen Cammuso, Henry Sachs, Brian Winklosky, Julie Mullane, Raphael Bernier, Sarah Svenson, Deborah Arin, Beth Rosen-Sheidley, and Susan E. Folstein. 2003. Autism related language, personality and cognition in people with absolute pitch: Results of a preliminary study. *Journal of Autism and Developmental Disorders* 33:163–167.

Cowan, Richard, and Chris Frith. 2009. Do calendrical savants use calculation to answer date questions? A functional magnetic resonance imaging study. *Philosophical Transactions of the Royal Society B: Biological Sciences* 364:1417–1424.

DeLong, G. Robert, and Ann L. Aldershof. 1988. An association of special abilities with juvenile manic-depressive illness. In *The Exceptional Brain: Neuropsychology of Talent and Special Abilities,* ed. Loraine K. Obler and Deborah Fein, 387–395. New York: Guildford.

Down, John L. 1887. *On Some of the Mental Affections of Childhood and Youth.* London: Churchill

Eagleman, David. 2009. The objectification of overlearned sequences: A new view of spatial sequence synaesthesia. *Cortex* 45:1266–1277.

Ericsson, K. A., W. G. Chase, and S. Falloon. 1980. Acquisition of a memory skill. *Science* 208:1181–1182.

Ericsson, K. Anders, Peter F. Delaney, George Weaver, and Rajan Mahadevan. 2004. Uncovering the structure of a memorists superior 'basic' memory capacity. *Cognitive Psychology* 49:191–237.

Happe, F. 1996. Studying weak central coherence at low levels: Children with autism do not succumb to visual illusions. A research note. *Journal of Child Psychology Psychiatry* 37:873–877.

Happe, F., and Vital, P. 2009. What aspects of autism predispose to talent? *Philosophical Transactions of the Royal Society B; Biological Sciences* 364:1369–1375.

Heaton P., and Wallace G. 2004. Annotation: the savant syndrome, *Journal of Child Psychology & Psychiatry* 45:899–911.

Hill, A. Lewis. 1977. Idiot savants: A categorization of abilities. *Mental Retardation* 12:12–13.

Horwitz, William A., Clarice Kesterbaum, Ethel Person, and Lissy Jarvik. 1965. Identical twin 'idiot savants' calendar calculators. *American Journal of Psychiatry* 121:1075–1079.

Howlin, Patricia, Susan Goode, Jane Hutton, and Michael Rutter. 2009. Savant skills in autism: psychometric approaches and parental reports. *Philosophical Transactions of The Royal Society B: Biological Sciences* 364:1359–1367.

Hubbard, Edward M., Manuela Piazza, Philippe Pinel, and Stanislas Dehaene. 2005. Interactions between number and space in the parietal cortex. *Nature Reviews Neuroscience* 6:435–448.

Jansari, Ashok. 2005. Cognitive neuropsychology. In *Cognitive Psychology: A Methods Companion*, ed Nick Braisby, 139–181. Oxford: Oxford University Press

LePort, Aurora K. R, Aaron T. Mattfeld, Heather Dickinson-Anson, James H. Fallon, Craig E. L. Stark, Frithjof Kruggel, Larry Cahill, and James L. McGaugh. 2012. Behavioral and neuroanatomical investigation of highly superior autobiographical memory (HSAM). *Neurobiology of Learning and Memory* 98:78–92.

Luria, Aleksandr R. 1968. *The Mind of a Mnemonist*. New York: Basic Books.

Miller, Bruce L., Marcel Ponton, D. Frank Benson, J. L. Cummings, and I. Mena. 1996. Enhanced artistic creativity with temporal lobe degeneration. *Lancet* 348:1744–1755.

Miller, Leon K. 1998. Defining the savant syndrome. *Journal of Developmental and Physical Disabilities* 10:73–85.

Moriarty, J. H., A. Ring, and M. M. Robertson. 1993. An idiot savant calendrical calculator with Gilles de la Tourette syndrome: Implications for an understanding of the savant syndrome. *Psychological Medicine* 23:1019–1021.

National Autistic Society. Autism and Asperger's Syndrome: An introduction. <http://www.autism.org.uk/en-gb/about-autism/autism-and-asperger-syndrome-an-introduction.aspx>.

Navon, DAVID. 1977. Forest before trees: The precedence of global features in visual perception. *Cognitive Psychology* 9:353–383.

Nelson, E. C., and E. F. Pribor. 1993. A calander savant with autism and Tourette Syndrome: Response to treatment and thoughts on the interrelationship of these conditions. *Annals of Clinical Psychiatry* 5:135–140.

O'Connor, Neil, and Beate Hermelin. 1991. Talents and preoccupations in idiot-savants. *Psychological Medicine* 21:959–964.

Parker, Elizabeth S., Larry Cahill, and James L. McGaugh. 2006. A case of unusual autobiographical remembering. *Neurocase* 12:35–49.

Peek, Fran. 1996. *The Real Rain Man*. Salt Lake City, UT: Harkness Publishing Consultants.

Rimland, B. 1978. Savant capabilities of autistic children and their cognitive implications. In *Cognitive Development of Mental Illness*, ed G. Serban, 43–65. New York: Brummer/Mazel.

Ring, Howard A., Simon Baron-Cohen, Sally Wheelwright, Steve C. R. Williams, Mick Brammer, Chris Andrew, and Edward T. Bullmore. 1999. Cerebral correlates of preserved cognitive skills in autism; A functional MRI study of embedded figures task performance. *Brain* 122:1305–1315.

Sacks, Oliver. 1985. *The Man Who Mistook His Wife for a Hat*. London: Picador.

Saloviita, Timo, Liisa Ruusila, and Unto Ruusila. 2000. Incidence of savant syndrome in Finland. *Perceptual and Motor Skills* 91:120–122.

Simner, Julia, Neil Mayo, and Mary J. Spiller. 2009. A foundation for savantism? Visuo-spatial synaesthetes present with cognitive benefits. *Cortex* 45:1246–1260.

Simner, Julia, Jamie Ward, Monika Lanz, Ashok Jansari, Krist Noonan, Louise Glover, and David A. Oakley. 2005. Non-random associations of graphemes to colours in synaesthetic and non-synaesthetic populations. *Cognitive Neuropsychology* 22 (8):1069–1085.

Smilek, Daniel, Alicia Callejas, Mike J. Dixon, and Philip M. Merikle. 2007. Ovals of time: time-space associations in synaesthesia. *Psychological Science* 13:548–552.

Tammet, Daniel. 2006. *Born on a Blue Day: A Memoir of Asperger's and an Extraordinary Mind*. London: Hodder & Staughton Ltd.

Tang, Joey, Jamie Ward, Brian Butterworth. 2008. Number forms in the brain. *Journal of Cognitive Neuroscience* 20:1547–1556.

Treffert, Darold. 1989. *Extraordinary People: Understanding 'Idiot Savants.'* New York: Harper & Row.

——. 2009. The savant syndrome: an extraordinary condition. A synopsis: past, present and future. *Philosophical Transactions of the Royal Society B: Biological Sciences* 364:1351–1357.

Treffert, Darold, and Daniel D. Christensen. 2005. Inside the mind of a savant. *Scientific American* 293:108–111.

World Health Organization. 1994. *International Classification of Diseases*. 10th ed. Geneva: World Health Organization.

Yates, Frances. 1966. *The Art of Memory*. Chicago, IL: University of Chicago.

CHAPTER 37

SYNESTHESIA, IMAGERY, AND PERFORMANCE

MARK C. PRICE

INTRODUCTION

Most people experience some degree of mental imagery—for example, the ability to imagine the visual appearance of objects, people, or events in their "mind's eye." We might also imagine the sound of music, the smell of a flower, or a sensation of touch. These types of experience have long been known to range from people who report that rich imagery pervades most of their thoughts to people who profess to have no imagery experience at all (Galton 1883; Reisberg, Pearson, and Kosslyn 2003). Historically, some of the first scientists to study synesthesia, such as Galton (1880b), considered that synesthetic experiences just constitute one end of this wide natural gradation of mental imagery experience. Indeed synesthesia, in some of its forms, continues to be often described as a variety of mental imagery, although of a more involuntary and especially salient kind.

In research on conventional mental imagery, it is increasingly argued that imagery experiences are at least partly mediated by neural activation in parts of our cortex which also serve to process the perceptual information coming from the outside world via our sensory receptors (Borst and Kosslyn 2008; Kosslyn 1994; Thompson et al. 2009). For example, in the influential tradition of imagery research represented by the work of Kosslyn (e.g., Kosslyn 2005), a conscious image arises when information from long-term memory is loaded "top-down" into a functional system referred to as the sensory buffer, which is neurally implemented as activation in early (and topographically organized) sensory areas of the cortex. The study of mental imagery is also central to the parallel tradition of research on working memory, which refers to our crucial ability to hold and manipulate new or recalled information in an active and available state during ongoing cognitive tasks. In this tradition (e.g., Pearson 2001), various working memory subsystems such as some kind of sensory buffer, or a central executive system, are proposed as the substrate for conscious mental imagery of visuo-spatial information—i.e., what things look like, or more abstract spatial information such as the spatial relations of objects or object parts.

Like conventional mental imagery, certain synesthetic experiences can also be considered as an individual variation in conscious sensory experience, whose immediate cause is internally triggered sensory activation rather than direct external activation via standard sensory pathways. Scientific parsimony suggests that the expression of synesthetic associations as conscious sensory imagery might at least partly involve standard imagery mechanisms. This would reflect the increasing emphasis on the continuity between synesthetic processes and normal cognition (Sagiv and Ward 2006; Ward et al. 2007). Furthermore when synesthetes deliberately introspect their synesthetic sensations, or even transform them in some in some manner (e.g., in the context of a memorization task), then image manipulation might plausibly be mediated in similar ways to standard imagery.

Studying the relationship of synesthesia to standard imagery may therefore help to explain why synesthesia is experienced, and to explain how synesthetic sensations can help or impair performance in laboratory or real-world tasks. In the following sections I summarize the small but growing body of research that has so far been conducted on this relationship, and suggest areas in which our knowledge could be usefully expanded. I will focus specifically on the relation between visuo-spatial imagery, which is the most studied variety of mental imagery, and two of the most common varieties of synesthesia (Sagiv et al. 2006; Simner et al. 2006), both of which have salient visuo-spatial properties. These are (1) grapheme-color synesthesia, in which letters and numerals elicit color sensations, and (2) sequence-space synesthesia, in which ordered time units such as weekdays, calendar months or years, and/or other sequence members such as numerals, alphabet letters or even shoe sizes, are felt to occupy precise locations in imaginal space or in space around the body (peripersonal space) that are in turn part of a larger visuo-spatial pattern or *spatial form* (see Jonas and Jarick, Chapter 7, this volume; Simner 2009).

First I consider evidence that these varieties of synesthesia are associated with individual variation in standard visuo-spatial imagery. Second, I discuss some potential implications of this association for how experiments are conducted and for theories of synesthesia. Next I consider various possibilities for the nature of any causal relationships between synesthetic and standard imagery. Fourth, I speculatively discuss how individual variation in synesthetic experience may be explained by what we already know about different varieties of visuo-spatial imagery, including distinctions between visual and spatial imagery, and between different reference frames. I also raise the possibility that individual differences in the way that we can transform images in various ways may be related to some of the dynamic properties of some types of synesthesia, for example, sequence-space synesthesia. Fifth, I consider evidence that imagery is not only an aspect of synesthetic concurrents (i.e., the triggered experience), but can also play the role of synesthetic inducer (i.e., the triggering percept or thought). Lastly I summarize some warnings about our ability to metacognitively evaluate our own imagery that are relevant to synesthesia research.

SYNESTHESIA IS ASSOCIATED WITH STRONG MENTAL IMAGERY

As already mentioned, it is well documented that people differ in their subjective experience of mental imagery. Likewise, they also vary in their objective performance on behavioral tasks that are taken to reflect the ability to generate, inspect, or transform mental images. This raises the question of how synesthetes and non synesthetes compare in the strength of their standard non-synesthetic imagery. If synesthetic imagery at least partly taps the mechanisms of normal imagery, then we might predict normal imagery to be reasonably well developed among synesthetes.

There is certainly qualitative evidence that many synesthetes report the experience of rich general mental imagery in their daily life. For example, one grapheme-color synesthete who experiences Thursday to be colored blue, and also experiences vivid sequence-space synesthesia, reports in her autobiographical book (Duffy 2001) that:

> I might meet the friend I'm going to meet on, say, the blue Thursday square and glide over to it as if we were already there together. If I have to take the subway to meet the friend on Thursday, the blue square where I see us standing will open up into the Manhattan cityscape with the subway entrance's green neo bulbs atop its blackish-green poles signalling the downward flight of cement steps. (149)

More formal self-report measures have supported that some varieties of synesthesia are indeed associated with above-average visual imagery experience. Barnett and Newell (2008) found that 38 synesthetes, mostly females with some form of linguistic-color (e.g., grapheme-color) synesthesia, on average reported more vivid visual imagery than 38 age-matched controls. The self-report instrument in this study was the Vividness of Visual Imagery Questionnaire (VVIQ; Marks 1973; 1977) in which participants rate the vividness of images that they are asked to create. Although there has been controversy over the reliability of the VVIQ, and its relation to objective imagery skills, meta-analysis has supported its validity as a test of individual differences in the vividness of visual imagery (McKelvie 1995). Vividness is in turn argued to reflect the subjective similarity between perceiving the external world and experiencing a mental image of the same percept (Reisberg et al. 2003).

Similarly, Price (2009) compared the visual imagery experience of 12 female sequence-space synesthetes against 24 non-synesthetes. The synesthetes all experienced spatial forms for months and weekdays in the shape of lines, ribbons, or sections of space running either in a simple circle or in a more irregular three-dimensional (3D) trajectory. Some also experienced a spatial form for numbers. Instead of measuring the vividness of visual imagery, two different self-report scales were used to measure the prevalence of spontaneous visual imagery in daily life. One scale was the 12-item Subjective Use of Imagery Scale (SUIS, Reisberg et al. 2003), and the other was a 15-item visual imagery subscale of the Object–Spatial Imagery Questionnaire (OSIQ, Blajenkova,

Kozhevnikov, and Motes 2006). Both these scales are known to be correlated to VVIQ scores (Blajenkova, Kozhevnikov, and Motes 2006; Reisberg et al. 2003) and also to each other (Price 2009). Price found that the synesthetes scored significantly higher than controls on both scales (see also Rizza and Price (2012) for replication of this trend with the OSIQ). For the SUIS, the above-average scores of the synesthetes were also confirmed against a further control group of 182 females. Additionally, a survey of 252 non-self-selected university students revealed a highly significant positive correlation between SUIS scores and the graded tendency to report experiencing spatial layouts for calendar and number sequences (Price, Solberg, and Blakstad 2009).

One of the controversies in the imagery literature has been over whether subjective imagery experience is epiphenomenal or is related to performance in behavioral measures of imagery. However, if the self-report measure is matched carefully to the type of imagery one is interested in, correlations do seem to be found (Dean and Morris 2003). For example various behavioral data suggest that the experience of vivid images is functionally related to working memory activation (Reisberg et al. 2003). Additionally, the construct validity of the OSIQ self-report scales is supported by behavioral data (Blajenkova, Kozhevnikov, and Motes 2006). Convergent with this, there is now some data to suggest that the strong subjective imagery of both grapheme-color and sequence-space synesthetes is mirrored by strong objective imagery performance.

Comparing six grapheme-color synesthetes each against ten matched controls, Spiller and Jansari (2008) found that the synesthetes were faster on a task that required generating and inspecting a visual image. The task, which has been used previously in research on visual imagery (e.g., Mast and Kosslyn 2002), involved forming a visual image of an aurally-presented letter inside a drawn circle and judging whether most of the letter fell inside or outside a designated area of the circle. Similarly Simner, Mayo, and Spiller (2009) assessed a group of between four and eight sequence-space synesthetes with 3D spatial forms on four different tests of visuo-spatial skills. The tests were a constructional praxis task, a 3D mental rotation task, a visual silhouette recognition task, and a test of short-term visual memory for a checkerboard matrix. Compared to controls or to established population norms, the synesthetes showed above-average performance on all tasks.

These data therefore support the idea that two of the most common varieties of synesthesia seem to be correlated with strong imagery at both subjective and objective levels. The objective evidence is important because it provides behavioral validation of the subjective reports and suggests that the subjective experience of imagery reflects a skill with practical consequences. The subjective evidence is important because it suggests that the imagery advantage is unlikely to just be a skill inherited from practice in inspecting or manipulating synesthetic imagery such as spatial forms, but is a pervasive individual difference in the intensity and/or frequency of everyday visual imagery.

It is important to stress that none of the studies summarized so far have claimed that synesthetes have *exceptional* everyday imagery. Rather, the synesthetes are just above average. In the study by Price (2009) which compared self-reported imagery experience in sequence-space synesthetes against non synesthetes, the plotted distributions of individual scores indicated that the group difference was largely mediated by the absence of low scorers in the synesthete group. This correlational pattern is consistent with the plausible suggestion that a certain level of imagery ability is required if synesthetic associations are to manifest themselves as explicit visuo-spatial images.

It is also important to bear in mind that that these data on the relationship of normal and synesthetic imagery are mostly based on small groups of synesthetes. Especially given the concerns that motivation and experimental demand characteristics may contaminate comparisons between synesthete and control participants (Gheri, Chopping, and Morgan 2008), the findings require replication in larger samples. Indeed, Rizza and Price (2012) recently replicated higher self-reported visual imagery scores for sequence-space synesthetes in a sample of 12 synesthetes and 12 controls (see also Spiller et al. 2012), but found no difference between these groups in their performance on a mental rotation task. This fails to replicate the aforementioned findings of Simner, Mayo, and Spiller (2009). On the other hand, evidence presented in the next section supports the idea of superior imagery skill among synesthetes. It is possible that some of these apparent contradictions may be explained by individual differences between participants. For example, Simner (2009) pointed out that the synesthetes sampled by Simner et al. (2009) had unusually high levels of IQ and education (not matched in the study by Rizza and Price 2012) and suggested that the benefit of synesthesia on task performance may be mediated by intelligence. Participants in Simner et al. (2009) may also have had a particularly large number of forms (on average five for time units alone). This variable was not examined in Rizza and Price (2012), but number of forms might reflect the strength of synesthesia which could contribute to differences in performance across studies. Other kinds of individual differences between synesthetes that might explain contradicting behavioral results are also discussed in the later section entitled "Distinctions between varieties of mental imagery can help to explain individual differences in synesthetic experience and performance."

Some Methodological Implications of Synesthetes' Strong General Imagery Skill

The suggested non-equivalence of general imagery skills in synesthete versus non-synesthete groups would, if upheld, present a potential methodological confound for behavioral comparisons of these groups (Barnett and Newell 2008; Price 2009). This is especially important for tasks which directly tap some aspect of imagery or visuo-spatial working memory skill beyond those already discussed, or for any tasks where imagery strategies could at least facilitate or impair performance. In practice this extends at least to tasks which involve generating, maintaining, inspecting or transforming visuo-spatial stimuli (note in addition that these various skills are not unitary, a point to which I return further later).

One task that has played a central role in synesthesia research is consistency testing of synesthetes' inducer-concurrent associations. And for sequence-space synesthesia especially, consistency testing is a good example of a task that directly taps components of imagery. Studies of sequence-space synesthetes often compare synesthete and non synesthetes in their ability to reproduce consistent spatial layouts for sequences such as numbers, months or weekdays. Typically, these layouts are expressed using mouse clicks on a two-dimensional (2D) computer monitor (Brang et al. 2010; Hubbard et al. 2009; Piazza, Pinel, and Dehaene 2006; Smilek et al. 2007; Teuscher et al. 2010) although 3D spatial forms have also been tested using a laser pointer to express spatial location (Jarick, Dixon, Stewart, et al. 2009; Smilek et al. 2007). Price (2009) speculated that this kind of test could be sensitive to individual differences in the ability to generate, maintain, or inspect visuo-spatial images, questioning whether consistency data can be taken as a pure measure of pre-existing visuo-spatial forms stored in long-term memory. The problem is compounded when consistency testing takes place within experimental sessions, in which case they essentially become tests of visuo-spatial short term memory. In support of this speculation, Brang et al. (2010) recently reported that for within-session computerized consistency testing, 11 synesthetes with circular spatial forms for months were better than 48 yoked control participants at reproducing not just their own spatial forms, but also the layout of spatial forms that belonged to *other* synesthetes. Therefore a large component of the consistency advantage for this type of synesthesia may be attributable to a general superiority in imagery skills.

If synesthetes are more likely than others to generate strong stable visuo-spatial imagery, their tendency to employ this kind of representation may manifest during laboratory experiments, even when imagery is not specifically demanded. This may again influence the relative performance of synesthete versus control participants.

For example, Yaro and Ward (2007) reported that grapheme-color synesthetes who were asked to memorize phone numbers were more likely than controls to report using strategies based on visual imagery. In combination with their life-long practice in visualizing graphemes, this tendency may benefit performance in any task where grapheme-based imagery is relevant. There are also examples of tasks where the tendency to employ visuo-spatial imagery strategies can impair performance. Ward, Sagiv, and Butterworth (2009) compared control participants with synesthetes who had spatial forms for numbers during simple mental maths calculations. The synesthetes turned out to be relatively slower than controls on single-digit multiplication. This type of maths operation is usually associated with more verbal strategies but it seemed that unusual reliance on a more visuo-spatial strategy was slowing their mental calculation times. This performance cost could have been directly linked to the synesthetic imagery of the participants' number forms. However, since we now know that people with spatial forms may be better and more prevalent imagers, it could have also been linked to the adoption of a general imagery strategy in the task.

The potential influence of imagery on performance is obviously important when behavioral differences between synesthete and non synesthete groups are used as the basis for arguing that the mental processes of synesthetes show real differences from controls. Price (2009) has argued that two of the behavioral paradigms most often used to behaviorally verify the reality and claimed automaticity of spatial forms may again be sensitive to the influence of general imagery strategies.

One of these paradigms involves using the written label of sequence members (e.g., numerals, month names, weekday names) as centrally-presented cues that appear to shift the spotlight of visuo-spatial attention to areas of space that the synesthete reports associating with the sequence member (e.g.. May is experienced on the right hand side of a month circle or month line). The shift of attention is measured in terms of better target detection in the cued than uncued area of space, even though non-predictive cues are used. Several studies have reported cueing effects of this kind which differ from those found for control participants and reflect the approximate location of the sequence members in the synesthetes' reported number lines (Hubbard et al. 2009; Jarick, Dixon, and Smilek 2011; Jarick, Dixon, Maxwell, et al. 2009; Jarick, Dixon, Stewart, et al. 2009; Jarick et al. 2011; Jonas et al. 2011; Smilek et al. 2007; Teuscher et al. 2010). These cueing effects are usually interpreted as reflecting involuntary shifts of visuo-spatial attention, triggered by automatized associations between sequence members and locations in space. However Price (2009; see also Price and Mattingley, 2013) warned that these spatial cueing effects could be influenced or even entirely mediated by synesthetes' intentional imagery strategies. In support of this proposal, there is ample evidence that spatial cueing effects of this kind in non synesthetes can be modulated by mental imagery instructions (Galfano, Rusconi, and Umiltà 2006; Ristic, Wright, and Kingstone 2006).

The other paradigm involves synesthete participants making simple binary response time decisions (using left-hand key presses versus right-hand key presses) about sequence members whose written label is again presented at central visual fixation—for example, the task might be deciding whether a numeral is larger or smaller than a reference number. This is a variation of the classic SNARC effect (spatial–numerical association of response codes; Dehaene, Bossini, and Giraux 1993). Several studies have found that response times are faster when they are made with the hand that is on the same side of space that a sequence member occupies in a synesthetes' spatial form (e.g., If May is experienced on the right, responses would be faster for this month when the right hand key press is used than a left hand key press; Hubbard et al. 2009; Jarick, Dixon, Maxwell, et al. 2009; Price and Mentzoni 2008). These SNARC-like spatial congruity effects between the spatial layout of response keys and synesthetes' spatial forms have even been found when the decision task is a variety of parity task (e.g., "Is the presented numeral or calendar month an odd or even numbered sequence member?"; Jarick, Dixon, Maxwell, et al. 2009; Price and Mentzoni 2008). Because a left–right spatial and categorical dichotomization of an ordinal sequence is usually assumed to be irrelevant for parity judgment, the continued effect of response hand has been interpreted as evidence for the automaticity of synesthetes' spatial associations. However, as for spatial cueing tasks, it is known that SNARC effects are influenced by intentional visuo-spatial strategies (Bächtold et al. 1998) and it has been suggested that they may largely reflect short-term, task-specific strategies rather than persistent automatized associations

(Caessens et al. 2005; Fischer 2006; Proctor and Vu 2002). Price (2009) therefore suggested that the unusual SNARC-like effects found in sequence-space synesthetes might be related to their elevated tendency to experience normal intentional imagery and use it to help task performance.

To test the plausibility of this idea, Price (2009) instructed normal non-synesthete participants to visually image the months of the year in various spatial layouts before participating in the same tests that synesthetes with month forms had taken part in. This simple manipulation of voluntary imagery was sufficient to elicit month-SNARC effects that were congruent with the spatial layout of the instructed images (e.g., instructing participants to imagine a month circle with May on the right would result in faster right-hand than left-hand responses). Moreover the effects were similar in magnitude to the month-SNARC effects that Price and Mentzoni (2008) had previously been obtained for sequence-space participants. This was even the case when the experimental task was parity judgment, refuting the assumption that SNARC effects obtained with parity judgment reflect only automatic spatial associations. These data therefore support the plausibility that intentional imagery could account for observed SNARC-like effects in sequence-form synesthetes, and they challenge one source of evidence that the behavior of sequence-space synesthetes needs to be attributed to fundamentally different processes than those found in control participants.

In conclusion, the above-average strength of standard visuo-spatial imagery among at least some groups of synesthetes, and their possibly elevated tendency to use visuo-spatial strategies, present a potentially confounding factor for many behavioral comparisons between synesthete and control groups. Just as researchers take care to match control participants for characteristics like age or gender, so future studies should take care to consider standard imagery as a covariate in any tests of behavior where imagery could be plausibly related to performance advantages or disadvantages. Barnett and Newell (2008) have extended this methodological recommendation to neuroimaging paradigms as well as behavioral ones, and suggested that differences in the vividness of mental imagery might account for inconsistent findings regarding the neural correlates of real versus imagined versus synesthetic colors. It should also be noted that although data so far only extends to visuo-spatial imagery, imagery in other modalities such as auditory, tactile and olfactory senses may play a role in studies of synesthetes with these modalities of current experience.

POSSIBLE CAUSAL RELATIONSHIPS BETWEEN STANDARD AND SYNESTHETIC IMAGERY

The fact that an association is observed between the experience of standard and synesthetic imagery begs a closer analysis of their causal relationship. Various potential options are considered next.

Synesthesia might cause better imagery

One possibility is that the frequent experience of synesthetic imagery generally improves people's visuo-spatial imagery skills. For example, Simner, Mayo, and Spiller (2009) suggested this might apply to sequence-space synesthetes, whose everyday practice in inspecting and transforming their synesthetic spatial forms could explain why their study observed synesthetes to have better than average performance on visuo-spatial tasks. However, if grapheme-color synesthetes can be reliably shown to have above-average visuo-spatial skills, it would be more difficult to explain how the experience of colored letters (which appears to be a less dynamic and a spatially simpler experience than spatial forms) translates into a generalized imagery skill. For both types of synesthesia, it is also unclear why the experience of synesthetic imagery would translate into an increased subjective vividness and frequency of normal visual mental imagery throughout daily life.

Synesthesia and imagery might be causally unrelated

A second possibility that also seems unlikely is that synesthetic and standard imagery are not causally interrelated at all, despite being correlated. As was argued earlier, a strong ability to experience conscious sensory imagery in the absence of usual external stimulation seems a plausible prerequisite for having any conscious synesthetic experience.

Imagery might be necessary for synesthesia

A third possibility is therefore that imagery skill is at least a *necessary* condition for some types of synesthetic experience. This would not preclude the possibility that the synesthetic sensory associations are mediated by (1) the type of cortical cross-connectivity that has been the main focus of research on the neural correlates of synesthesia, and (2) perhaps also by parietal lobe binding processes that have been suggested as a second component in the construction of synesthetic experience (Hubbard 2007). However, it seems parsimonious to suggest that the conscious experience of these associations is instantiated by the activation of topographically mapped sensory cortex which has also been argued to mediate standard conscious imagery (Kosslyn 2005).

For standard imagery, neuroimaging data already provides correlational support for the role of sensory cortex in mediating the subjective salience of imagery. Cui et al. (2007) reported that activation in occipital cortex is associated with the self-reported vividness of participants' visual imagery as expressed by their VVIQ scores. Olivetti Belardinelli et al. (2009) have extended this type of finding to imagery in other sensory modalities. They found that the reported vividness of gustatory imagery, kinesthetic imagery, tactile imagery and somatic imagery all correlated with greater activation of the corresponding (modality specific) cortical area that is specialized for preliminary processing of perceptual signals for each of these different senses. This suggests that modality-specific early sensory cortex should be an important region of interest for neuroimaging studies of synesthetic experience in all sensory domains.

Preliminary data that grapheme-color synesthetes differ from controls in the response properties of early visual cortex have in fact been reported. Barnett et al. (2008) found group differences in the amplitude of scalp recorded electrical signals (evoked potentials) to external visual stimuli, even though these stimuli were not ones that induced synesthetic experiences. Additionally, functional magnetic resonance imaging (fMRI) has revealed greater cortical activity in the early retinotopic visual areas of grapheme-color synesthetes than controls during behavioral tasks in which synesthetic experiences are induced and where grapheme-color synesthetes show behavioral advantages (Hubbard, Arman, et al. 2005). At a group level this activity was correlated with synesthetic performance, although considerable individual variation was observed. For example, significantly greater activation of cortical area V1 to graphemes than non-linguistic symbols was found for some but not all synesthetes, and Hubbard et al. stressed that individual differences between synesthetes may account for conflicting results in the literature over observed brain activation patterns. However in a notable failure to replicate, Hupé, Bordier, and Dojat (2012) recently found no evidence that the experience of synesthetic color (as assessed by objective measures of the strength of grapheme-color associations) was related to greater neural activation in any retinotopic visual areas of the cortex.

Individual differences might also account for conflicting data over whether synesthetic color imagery involves activation of cortical visual area V4, which is known to be involved in both color perception and in normal color imagery. Using grapheme-color synesthetes, Rich et al. (2006) observed fMRI activation in V4 during voluntary imagery of colors but not during synesthetic color experiences. Instead they found that synesthetic color imagery was associated with activation in cortical areas (left medial lingual gyrus) that are thought to be involved in retrieval of higher-level conceptual knowledge about color. Synesthetic color may therefore have been experienced by these participants as an overlearned association rather than as vivid color imagery. However, some neuroimaging studies have claimed that cortical area V4 is indeed activated during the experience of grapheme-color synesthesia (for overviews see, e.g., Barnett and Newell 2008; Hupé, Bordier, and Dojat 2012), supporting similarities with routine color imagery. One possibility is that the extent to which synesthesia involves routine imagery processes may therefore vary between individuals; I return to the issue of individual differences further later. Another possibility, suggested by Hupé, Bordier, and Dojat (2012) who failed to find evidence for synesthetic activation of V4 activation in their own study, is that previous claims are contaminated by procedural confounds.

This distinction I am proposing between mechanisms of synesthetic association and their expression in a conscious image is explicit in at least one model of how synesthetic associations may arise. Makioka (2009) described a two-layer connectionist neural network model that generated self-organizing patterns of spatial correspondences for numerals, although it was argued that the principles of the model can be applied to other synesthetic correspondences. The model was able to simulate many (although not all) varieties of the contorted and idiosyncratic number lines that are reported by sequence-space synesthetes. The main focus of this model was the mapping from number magnitude to spatial location, but Makioka speculated that the generation of actual mental images of the number lines might occur via further feedback connections between representations of number magnitude, representation of spatial location, and representation of the visual appearance of numerals. While the details of image generation appear oversimplified in this account, the conceptual separation of synesthetic association and image generation led Makioka to the intriguing but testable speculation that some non-synesthetes might have spatial forms but not be consciously aware of them. This view has continuity with the long-held view that implicit spatial representation of number magnitude is a routine aspect of numerical cognition even in non synesthetes (Hubbard, Piazza, et al. 2005), although implicit number lines are usually much simpler than those expressed by sequence-space synesthetes.

Imagery might be necessary and sufficient for some varieties of synesthesia

A fourth possible causal relationship between synesthetic and standard imagery is that normal imagery processes are both *necessary and sufficient* to mediate synesthetic imagery. Under the strongest version of this position, no special synesthetic mechanism would be needed to establish or maintain idiosyncratic sensory associations in long-term memory and, at least for some synesthetes, these associations could manifest as sensory imagery. A weaker version of the causal relationship would be that special synesthetic processes are involved, but only in developmentally establishing long-term synesthetic associations in the first place. Obviously these suggestions would have the attraction of parsimony if they were able to account adequately for the observed neural, behavioral, experiential and even genetic correlates of synesthesia.

Although classic varieties of synesthesia such as grapheme-color synesthesia are generally portrayed to be firmly established as a life-long, hereditary, automatic, low-level perceptual phenomenon based on unusual patterns of cortical activity, it may be premature to reject this fourth type of causal relationship. Even if reported differences in the neural circuitry of synesthetes can be robustly replicated, these could derive from lifelong experience with certain types of sensory association rather than cause them. Hereditary aspects of synesthesia could relate to the varieties and subsystems of mental imagery. There have also been challenges to both the automaticity of grapheme-color synesthetic experience and the extent to which it is equivalent to bottom-up activation of low-level perceptual representations (Gheri, Chopping, and Morgan 2008; Hupé, Bordier, and Dojat 2012; Mattingley 2009; Nijboer, Satris, and Stigchel 2011; van Leeuwen, Petersson, and Hagoort 2010; Treisman 2005). Convergent with these challenges, it has even been shown that the conscious experience of synesthesia can be disrupted by posthypnotic suggestion (Terhune, Cardeña, and Lindgren 2010). In a review of grapheme-color synesthesia, Mattingley (2009, 145) concluded that "it is not yet clear that any test yet devised can unambiguously determine whether synesthesia is experienced as a sensory event, an overlearned association, or a vivid mental image."

Sequence-space synesthesia might be particularly related to imagery

The plausibility that normal imagery processes are necessary and perhaps even sufficient for synesthetic experience may of course vary between varieties of synesthesia. However, potential parallels between normal imagery processes and synesthetic experience may be greatest for one of the commonest synesthetic varieties, namely sequence-space synesthesia.

It has been popular to speculate that synesthetic spatial forms derive from unusual degrees of cross activation, either between spatial representation and number/magnitude representation in parietal cortex (Hubbard, Brang, and Ramachandran 2011; Hubbard, Piazza, et al. 2005; Tang, Ward, and Butterworth 2008) or between representation of ordinal categories in right middle temporal gyrus and depictive representations of visual form in adjoining inferior temporal lobe (Eagleman 2009). There is as yet little direct evidence for these proposals, although neuroimaging data has revealed parietal activity associated with synesthetic number lines, reflecting the role of parietal cortex in mediating spatial representations (Tang, Ward, and Butterworth 2008) or perhaps in directing spatial attention (Eagleman 2009; Makioka 2009). An alternative explanatory starting point has been that spatial forms may originate from visuo-spatial strategies used to learn abstract verbal sequences during childhood (Galton 1881; Price 2009; Sagiv et al. 2006; Seron et al. 1992). Under this view, it remains an open question whether the development of spatial forms requires anything more than (1) a predisposition for explicit visuo-spatial coding, (2) the ability to consciously experience vivid visuo-spatial mental imagery, and (3) some explanation for the various and sometimes irregular linear trajectory taken by spatial forms.

In fact many characteristics of spatial forms conform more with the creative, dynamic, representational properties of intentional visuo-spatial imagery than with the simple, one to one, unelaborated and unchanging sensory associations that are taken as synesthetic hallmarks:

(1) Spatial forms are often reported to be dynamic. In addition to reports that forms are imaged from an external, static, egocentric point of view, people can report that their image of the form rotates in relation to their viewpoint, or that they feel they move within their form. It is also common for people to report that they can "zoom into" parts of their spatial forms, reflecting a shift of their attentional window that is characteristic of normal visuo-spatial imagery (Kosslyn, Shephard, and Thompson 2007).

(2) The basic spatial associations of sequence members are sometimes elaborated when the trajectory of the form is felt to have the character of a ribbon or a

tube, when the form includes a background, when it contains visual imagery of the written label of sequence members or even contains complex scenes. Additional imagery of this type is also sometimes reported to be under voluntary control.

(3) The internal shape of forms is not always consistent, but may change depending on which part of a sequence is being attended. For example the reported relative spatial position of 2 months or 2 letters of the alphabet can sometimes vary according to which months or letters are the focus of attention (personal observation).

(4) Spatial forms have been reported to increase in complexity from childhood to adulthood, and may sometimes continue to evolve during adulthood (Phillips 1897). For example it is common for people who experience spatial time-lines for the years of their life to report that these forms grow as new years are incorporated. Completely new forms can arise in adulthood, such as for university exam marking grades. It is also not uncommon for people to report specific learning experiences, perhaps at school, which triggered the construction of one of their spatial forms.

(5) A minority of sequence-form synesthetes report a vast number of different forms (e.g., Hubbard et al. 2009), suggesting that visuo-spatial encoding has developed into a cognitive strategy. Some of these forms are very suggestive of memorization strategies, for example, a form for the Lord's Prayer (Phillips 1897).

(6) Furthermore, arguments that spatial forms are involuntary experiences mediated by automatic mental processes have been challenged. Price and Mattingley (2013) suggest that existing empirical evidence cannot rule out the possibility that spatial forms are more intentionally activated.

(7) Even if spatial forms *are* experienced as highly involuntary, and even if they appear to be quite invariant over time, this would not in any case be at odds with them being primarily a variety of mental image. Consistent and automatized imagery can occur in flashback imagery, sometimes associated with clinical conditions such as post-traumatic stress disorder. It can also arise from intense practice as in the mnemonics that are constructed by people who take part in memory sport.

(8) It has long been noted (Phillips 1897) that the experience of spatial forms is not all or none but runs in a graded spectrum. At one end of this spectrum we find simple implicit associations between sequence positions and space, such as the well documented tendency for many people to associate smaller numbers with the left side of space and larger numbers with the right side of space (Hubbard, Piazza, et al. 2005). At the other end of the spectrum we find the more exotic cases of spatial forms which are vividly experienced as 3D patterns and which may appear highly irregular. These tend to be the type of spatial form targeted by single-case studies. In between these extremes are people with vague conscious impressions of spatial layouts (e.g., the months arranged in a regular 2D circle) that feel more under voluntary control.

(9) Even the more complex types of spatial form may often be accounted for in terms of rational visuo-spatial strategies. As pointed out by Makioka (2009), the neural connectivity that establishes idiosyncratic synesthetic associations between sequence positions and space is constrained by the need to preserve ordinal sequence as well as to reflect various conceptual constraints on spatial layout. For example, January and December may be placed close together in space since they are temporally adjacent, leading to circular or other closed patterns for month forms. Superimposed on this kind of constraint we then see a tendency to express conceptually or personally salient information as an apparent spatial irregularity. For example, a number line may bend at decade breaks (especially between 10 and 11), a month calendar form may distend at months that have positive associations (e.g., childhood summer holidays) or distort to represent an important event (e.g., the synesthete's birthday). In this respect spatial forms are personal stories with partly and sometimes wholly forgotten origins, expressed in a visuo-spatial format and superimposed by a certain degree of randomness.

As described further earlier, it is has been shown that some behavioral correlates of sequence-space synesthesia can be mimicked by instructing non-synesthetes to employ imagery strategies, and there is data suggesting that superior performance of sequence-space synesthetes in consistency tests can at least partly be accounted for by their above-average visuo-spatial skills. When this behavioral data is taken together with the experiential continuity of spatial forms and normal visuo-spatial imagery, which has been stressed since the early days of research on spatial forms (Galton 1880a; Phillips 1897), a strong case can be made that the processes of normal mental imagery are involved in sequence-space synesthesia and perhaps even sufficient for it. If one goal of synesthesia research is to account for synesthetic experience as far as possible in terms of normal cognitive processes (e.g., Ward et al. 2007) then, for at least some varieties of synesthesia, mental imagery is a good candidate for this explanatory continuity.

DISTINCTIONS BETWEEN VARIETIES OF MENTAL IMAGERY CAN HELP TO EXPLAIN INDIVIDUAL DIFFERENCES IN SYNESTHETIC EXPERIENCE AND PERFORMANCE

Even within specific varieties of synesthetic inducer-concurrent pairing, it has been observed that there is considerable individual variation in both synesthetic experience and behavioral performance, leading to calls in synesthesia research for close attention to individual differences (e.g., Hubbard, Arman, et al. 2005). For example, one well-known individual difference in synesthesia has been the distinction between grapheme-color synesthetes who claim that colors induced by printed text are projected into space outside their body—so-called *projector* synesthetes—and those who report that colors reside in their mind's eye—so-called *associator* synesthetes (Dixon, Smilek, and Merikle 2004). Despite some controversy (Edquist et al. 2006), this distinction continues to be upheld both by more refined self-report data and by neural differences or performance differences in classic behavioral measures of synesthesia (Hubbard, Arman, et al. 2005; Rouw and Scholte 2007; Skelton, Ludwig, and Mohr 2009; Ward et al. 2007).

   Like most mental functions studied by cognitive neuroscience, mental imagery is not a unitary process (Thompson et al. 2009). To the extent that mental imagery is a component of synesthetic experience, individual differences in synesthesia may therefore partly reflect the many separable types of representation and process which are known to contribute to normal mental imagery and which are also known to differ between individuals. Because the majority of synesthetic experiences have a spatial component (Ward et al. 2007), and because some of the most common types of synesthesia have a visual component, an analysis of the known subcomponents of visuo-spatial imagery is particularly pertinent. Next I summarize some relevant aspects of what is known about (1) the types of spatial reference frame involved in visuo-spatial imagery, (2) different operations that can be applied to images and (3) the distinction between visual and spatial imagery.

Types of reference frame

Ward et al. (2007) argued that the difference between projector and associator synesthetes is a reflection of the type of spatial reference frame that is evoked when the synesthetes view text, and that the behavioral correlates of the projector-associator distinction can be explained in terms of whether a given task requires attention to be moved between reference frames. Specifically, a distinction can be made between external space and so-called imaginal space which are known from studies of spatial neglect to be doubly dissociated (e.g., Bartolomeo 2002). Refining the dichotomous projector-associator distinction, Ward et al. distinguished between two types of projector and two types of associator. In *surface-projectors*, grapheme color is experienced on the surface of a viewed page of text since the color is imaged in a frame of reference that is external to the body and is object-centered on the physical grapheme in question. In *near-space projectors*, color is again experienced external to the body but is now located in free space relative to the viewer's body. On the other hand, *see-associators* have an impression of color in imaginal space—i.e., in an abstract internal spatial reference frame. Ward et al. suggest this is the frame of reference in which normal visual imagery mostly occurs, although this issue does not appear to have been much addressed in the literature on normal imagery. Finally, for *know-associators*, color is not linked to any spatial reference frame and is just known rather than experienced as any kind of image. This might correspond to the kind of participant for whom Rich et al. (2006) found no activation of

V4 when viewing graphemes, but instead found evidence of activation related to color knowledge.

It should be noted that grapheme-color see-associators usually claim to experience that their color imagery is not free floating but bound to images of the inducing graphemes in imaginal space (Ward et al. 2007). This emphasizes that the imagery experienced in grapheme-color synesthesia is more complex than just color sensation, even when the imagery is not projected. The broader character of this imagery is another issue that seems to have received sparse attention so far in the research literature.

The nature of spatial reference frames are at least as important in shaping varieties of synesthesia in which concurrent sensations are more spatially complex or distended. For example, grapheme-color synesthetes sometimes report that when they hear or think of words, they experience the colored letters of the words as if the words are presented in front of (or running past) their eyes like subtitles. This so-called *ticker-tape* experience, which has received very little attention in the literature so far, is also found in people with no grapheme-color experience who experience vivid imagery of uncolored words flowing past them. Similarly, in a variety of auditory-visual synesthesia, sounds elicit colored geometric objects in specific spatial locations (Chiou, Stelter, and Rich, in press). In as much as it appears to involve visuo-spatial imagery of object-like entities in spatial locations, this phenomenon would seem to have much in common with sequence-space synesthesia. The relative frequency with which these tickertape or geometric object experiences are projected or viewed in imaginal space remains largely unexplored.

Spatial forms, for which spatial extension is a core property, appear to be reported variously as either projections or internal images (Ward et al. 2007). Although the large survey of number forms by Phillips (1897) reported these to be mostly projected, Sagiv et al. (2006) reported a fairly even split between projectors and associators. (This raises the possibility that recruitment biases may contaminate estimates of the relative frequency of projector versus associator synesthetes in some studies.) In a small group of grapheme-color synesthetes surveyed by Ward et al. (2007), most participants also experienced spatial forms but, although the sample contained a mixture of projectors and associators for both types of synesthesia, there did not appear to be any systematic relationship between whether grapheme colors were projected and whether spatial forms were projected. Unlike grapheme-color synesthesia, there is still no behavioral data that distinguishes spatial form projectors from associators, so verbal self-report data on this distinction should be taken with caution. This is especially important given warnings from studies of grapheme-color synesthesia that simple verbal self-report is unreliable in this domain (Edquist et al. 2006; Skelton, Ludwig, and Mohr 2009). It is possible, for example, that people are more likely to rate their spatial forms as projections if the imagery is more vivid. On the other hand, there may be a real difference in spatial reference frames (even though these may turn out to be independent from the reference frames adopted in any other visuo-spatial synesthesia that people experience). If so, certain predictions for behavioral performance may follow. In spatial cueing experiments with sequence-space synesthetes for example (see earlier), the cueing induced by numerals or other sequence members may be stronger when the spatial form, like the cued targets, is situated in space around the synesthete's body.

In summary, the particular spatial reference frame in which synesthetic imagery is represented may constrain experience and perhaps also performance. Future research should therefore explore and refine the types of distinction outlined previously. For example, Ward et al. (2007) list other relevant subclassifications of the location in space that may be represented by a reference frame. These include the distinction between *near* and *far* external space (Halligan and Marshall 1991; Vuilleumier et al. 1998) which is reflected by spatial forms that occur close to the body versus those that occur further away, such as a month form experienced just out of reach above a person's head (Phillips 1897). In addition to making a basic distinction between reference frames that are *object-based* (i.e., define their reference origin relative to an external object) or *ego-centric* (i.e., are defined relative to the body), it should also be noted that ego-centric reference frames can code location relative to the position and orientation of different body parts such as the trunk, the head, the foveal fixation point of the eye, or an effector such as the hand (Zacks and Michelon 2005). These distinctions appear to have received little attention so far in studies of either synesthetic or normal imagery.

It should also be noted that information can be simultaneously represented in more than one spatial reference frame at once (Zacks and Michelon 2005). For example, it is possible that some individuals can maintain two coexisting images of grapheme colors, one of which is a projection and one of which is an association in imaginal space (Skelton, Ludwig, and Mohr 2009). Furthermore, simultaneous spatial representations need not always correspond to each other (Zacks and Michelon 2005) so, for example, conflicting simultaneous representations of spatial forms might in principle be possible.

Image transformation

In addition to distinguishing between different spatial reference frames, we also need to consider the manner in which we can interact with and transform visuo-spatial images. The relevance to synesthesia is that some visuo-spatial synesthetic imagery, such as tickertape synesthesia and sequence-space synesthesia, can have highly dynamic properties.

It is well known that studies of visual imagery in non synesthetes find that the ability to construct detailed visual images is a separable skill from the ability to either inspect images or to transform images, with different cortical areas being involved in the different tasks (e.g., Kosslyn et al. 2004). More recently, neuroimaging has also identified separable cortical networks for the ability to visualize detailed spatial location and the ability to transform images via mental rotation (Thompson et al. 2009). This suggests, for example, that the visual or spatial detail of synesthetic spatial forms might vary independently from people's ability to inspect or transform their image of the form.

Further distinctions have been made between different varieties of image transformation. Zacks and Michelon (2005) provided a detailed overview of the evidence that two

different ways of updating spatial reference frames, including imagined spatial transformations, rely on distinct neural processing resources across parietal, occipital, and
temporal cortex, and that people's ability to conduct these different transformations are
partly independent. One type of transformation is object-based, and involves movement
of an object-centered reference frame relative to the egocentric frames of the observer
and relative to the environment. This is the most studied type of transformation and
includes mental rotation or positional translation of objects. The other type of transformation is egocentric, and involves imagined movement of an observer's egocentric reference frames relative to object-centered and environment-centered reference frames.
This includes perspective transformation where an observer imagines themself rotating
around an object, or rotating in the middle of an object, or imagines translational movement across an environment.

Although it has received little comment so far in the literature, sequence-space synesthetes' reports of the ways in which they experience dynamic transformation of their
spatial forms include both object-centered and egocentric transformations. For example, an observer might feel that an object-centered spatial model of the calendar months
rotates around or in front of them as the months go by (object-centered transformation). Or they might feel they navigate through, or around, an object-centered spatial
model of the calendar months (egocentric transformation). This raises the question of
whether people's preferred mode of transformation is related to individual differences in
transformation skill which can in turn be measured by visuo-spatial psychometric tests.
It also raises the question of whether the known properties of object-centered versus
egocentric transformations are reflected in the characteristics of people's spatial forms.
For example, Zacks and Michelon (2005) speculate that environmental constraints may
optimize perspective transformations for transformations in the horizontal plane, and
object-based transformations may be optimized for objects that are small enough to be
physically manipulated. A testable prediction is therefore that people might be more
likely to navigate through their spatial forms in the horizontal plane, and that forms
which move relative to the observer are more common for forms that distend over a
small area of space. For people who are able to deliberately transform their images of
spatial forms, other predictions also follow from known properties of different transformations. These include the relative ease of different types of spatial judgment after
a transformation has been implemented, and the time course of deliberate rotational
transformations (Zacks and Michelon 2005).

Visual imagery versus spatial imagery

The term *visuo-spatial imagery* is a useful one because representations of spatial relationships usually have some degree of visual content, and because visual images (like
visual percepts) have a strong spatial component. However it is now well established
that visual and spatial components of mental imagery are partly separable in terms of
their neural substrates, the kinds of behavioral task for which they are most important

and by which they can be measured, and individual differences in imagery skill and phenomenology (Kosslyn, Shephard, and Thompson 2007).

Our understanding of the functional distinction between the two types of imagery remains incomplete (Hegarty 2010). However spatial imagery is considered to be an explicit representation of the relative spatial positions of objects arranged in space, or of parts of one object (Hegarty 2010). *Spatial imagery* is multimodal—i.e., receives input from many different sensory modalities in addition to vision, and does not need to include visual details (e.g., a conscious feeling of the relative location of two points in space). In spatial images it is relatively easier to simulate or analyze spatial relationships in a piecemeal manner (Hegarty 2010). *Visual imagery* is more depictive of visual appearance. It represents what are sometimes known as *object properties* such as overall shape and surface characteristics as defined for example by contour, texture, brightness or color. It is considered to be a more holistic or *unitized* representation than spatial imagery (Hegarty 2010; Kosslyn 2005) and has been claimed to be more associated with image vividness than is the case for spatial images (Reisberg, Pearson, and Kosslyn 2003).

Both types of imagery appear to involve overlapping activation of the cortical occipito-temporal ventral stream pathway for visual object recognition, and of the occipito-parietal dorsal stream pathway which is more concerned with space representation and in coding visual input so it can be used to guide spatially directed action. However some components of parietal activation are more strongly related to spatial imagery, and some parts of the ventral pathway are specifically engaged by visual imagery (Kosslyn 2005; Mazard et al. 2004).

Although the two types of imagery system will normally be interacting strongly with each other to support our visuo-spatial images, it has also been claimed that there is a tendency across the normal population for people to favor either a more visual style of imagery or a more spatial style (Kozhevnikov, Blazenkova, and Becker 2010; Kozhevnikov, Kosslyn, and Shephard 2005). These traits are revealed by self-report scales which correlate with performance on different behavioral tests (Blajenkova, Kozhevnikov, and Motes 2006). A negative association between the tendency to strongly experience the two types of imagery (i.e., the stronger one's visual imagery, the weaker one's spatial imagery) is convergent with neuroimaging data that only visual imagery appears to activate early visual cortex, while spatial imagery is associated with *deactivation* of these areas (Mazard et al. 2004).

In terms of performance, people with good visual imagery (referred to as *object visualizers*) are faster and more accurate in visual memory tasks, maybe since complex images can be activated more quickly if they are encoded in a holistic spatial manner (Kozhevnikov, Kosslyn, and Shephard 2005). People with good spatial imagery (sometimes confusingly referred to as *spatial visualizers*) are good at dynamic image transformations due to their ability to analyze the explicit spatial structure of their spatial representation in a part by part manner (Kozhevnikov, Kosslyn, and Shephard 2005). That people vary in spatial skill is acknowledged not only in the mental imagery literature, but also in research on spatial navigation (Aginsky et al. 1997) and working memory (Gyselinck et al. 2007).

The distinctions between these two types of imagery are clearly relevant to synesthetic imagery where the importance of spatial representation has been stressed (Ward et al. 2007) and which often includes visual components. The type of imagery which dominates in synesthetic experience should have implications for the quality of that experience and for the ways in which the imagery could be used as a cognitive tool. This is especially the case given that the experience and skill with standard imagery may, as was described earlier, be stronger in some groups of synesthetes than in non-synesthetes.

Interestingly the type of imagery which has been claimed to be stronger in grapheme-color synesthetes, both experientially and behaviorally, is visual rather than spatial (Barnett and Newell 2008; Spiller and Jansari 2008). If the relationship between visual and spatial imagery in non-synesthetes extends to grapheme-color synesthetes, their spatial imagery might therefore be predicted to be normal or even poorer than normal. It would also suggest that the synesthetic imagery experienced by associators in their imaginal space is likely to be a holistic depiction of the perceptual properties of a colored grapheme. This may correspond well to what is already known about the phenomenology of associators.

It seems initially more curious that strong visual imagery experience is associated with sequence-space synesthesia (Price 2009; see earlier section "Synesthesia is associated with strong mental imagery") because "spatial" forms are defined and usually characterized as inherently spatial in nature. If the normative relationship between visual and spatial imagery holds for sequence-space synesthetes, their strong visual imagery might again predict that spatial imagery should not be exceptional in this synesthete group. In fact Price (2009) did directly compare the same sequence-space synesthetes to control participants on self-reported spatial imagery, using the 15-item spatial subscale of the Object–Spatial Imagery Questionnaire. The subscale has recently been confirmed as a measure of spatial imagery per se and not merely a measure of behavioral skill in spatial transformation (Borst and Kosslyn 2010). On this measure of imagery experience there was no indication of a group difference, contrasting with the difference found for visual imagery. The absence of a synesthete advantage in self-reported spatial imagery has now also been replicated by Rizza and Price (2012). These findings are convergent with the behavioral data showing that sequence-space synesthetes are objectively better than controls on some visual imagery and visual memory tasks (Simner, Mayo, and Spiller 2009). However, they seem inconsistent with reports (ibid.) that the synesthetes are also better at mental rotation, which is usually considered to be a spatial imagery task and has been shown to correlate with self-reported spatial imagery but not self-reported visual imagery (Blajenkova, Kozhevnikov, and Motes 2006). This anomaly is not readily explained (see Simner 2009) but, as mentioned earlier (in the section entitled "Synesthesia is associated with strong mental imagery") the mental rotation finding has not been replicated.

Parsimony suggests that if sequence-space synesthetes tend to be visual imagers, then their spatial forms should be more visual than spatial in character. In other words the spatial forms may be holistic visual depictions of the overall shape of the spatial layout, and be associated with activity in the ventral stream pathway for object recognition, perhaps including activation of early visual cortex. As argued by Price (2009), this would still be compatible with the ability to zoom into, inspect, and transform one's imagery of a spatial form since these are standard properties of visual imagery. In addition, the vividness and rapid activation of spatial forms are particularly resonant with them being visual images (Price 2009). The proposal that spatial forms are more visual than spatial has also been put forward by Eagleman (2009) although his explanation is centered on connectivity between the ventral stream pathway and potential sequence processing areas rather than on the mechanisms of standard visual imagery.

Another possibility is that sequence-space synesthetes can, after all, sometimes be spatial imagers rather than visual imagers. In the small experimental samples studied so far it would be possible for the majority of participants to have fallen into one or other of these groups. Supposing some sequence-space synesthetes do have a dominantly spatial style of imagery, we would expect this to be reflected in the character of their spatial form. Informal observation indeed suggests that while some forms are experienced as unitary depictive images with visual properties, other forms are after all more spatial in nature. This applies especially to forms in which people report that they are dynamically immersed. The character of spatial forms may therefore vary as a reflection of individual differences on the visual-spatial imagery dimension. If sequence-space synesthetes or other varieties of synesthetes vary in terms of this dimension as well as in terms of the projector-associator dimension, an obvious question is whether these dimensions are orthogonal or interrelated. For example, might visual imagers be more likely to experience their spatial forms in imaginal space, and spatial imagers be more likely to project their forms?

A second question concerns the relationship between the possible benefits of spatial forms in daily life (or in laboratory experiments) and the type of imagery that dominates. It has already been shown that spatial forms are associated with unusually good date recall for personal and historical events (Simner, Mayo, and Spiller 2009), and also with faster mental scanning through the calendar sequence (Mann et al. 2009). Future studies should attempt to devise tasks that could distinguish between the advantages or costs of representing sequences as holistic visual images versus explicit spatial maps which can be more easily and flexibly inspected.

Individual differences pose further problems for consistency tests

The previous discussions raise yet further reasons why it may be difficult to devise appropriate consistency tests for sequence-space synesthetes. As mentioned earlier, the most popular technique to measure the spatial location of sequence members has been (for reasons of convenience) to ask participants to indicate the locations of sequence members on a computer screen. However, individual differences in how spatial forms are experienced—which in turn may reflect individual differences in standard imagery processes—will often make it difficult for people to accurately represent their spatial forms on a small two-dimensional surface. This is likely to be the case when spatial forms extend over a wide visual angle or are experienced as three-dimensional. It is also likely to be the case when people feel they are located within their spatial form, or when they routinely zoom into the part of the spatial form they are attending to, or when a spatial form moves relative to the person's viewpoint depending on which sequence member is attended. Additionally, reporting the positions of sequence members in external space may be more natural for projected forms than forms in imaginal space, and may in any case be an unnatural task if the forms are visual images rather than spatial maps. This may explain why no study to date has convincingly shown that sequence-space participants are statistical outliers in these consistency tests when compared to control participants. Instead, the more modest advantages that are found may, as argued previously, reflect group differences in general imagery skills.

IMAGERY AS AN INDUCER OF SYNESTHESIA

I have focused so far on the involvement of mental imagery in people's induced synesthetic experiences—i.e., in their synesthetic *concurrents*. However one study has also examined whether imagery can act as the initial trigger, or *inducer*, of synesthetic experience.

It is already known that some synesthetes experience their concurrent sensation (e.g., a color) even when they just *think* about the usual perceptual inducer of the experience (e.g., a printed grapheme). It is also known that some (but not all) synesthetes claim to experience their concurrent if they try to deliberately generate a mental image of the usual inducer (Grossenbacher and Lovelace 2001). To test this more formally, Spiller and Jansari (2008) asked whether grapheme-color synesthetes would show any interference between (1) colors that they might synesthetically experience when imagining a letter and (2) real colored surfaces in their visual environment.

The synesthetes were asked to generate a visual mental image of a letter over a real colored background, and to then inspect the spatial relationship between the image and the background. The background was either congruent with the potential synesthetic color of the imaged letter (e.g., a red background for a letter that is usually perceived to be synesthetically red) or was incongruent (e.g., a green background for a "red" letter). Results varied between participants. Some showed no influence of the relationship between synesthetic and real color. Some showed slower image inspection times when the background color was different from the synesthetic color of the imaged letter. And some showed slower inspection times when the background color was the same as the supposed color of the imaged letter, perhaps because the letter did not stand out so well against the background. These intriguing individual differences did not appear to be related to self-reported vividness of normal imagery, or to overall skill in image generation and inspection, or to the projector–associator distinction. They perhaps arose from differences in the extent to which a synesthetic color was induced, or in the way this color interacted with the real background during image inspection, or in different ways of grouping and attending the composite sensation of image and background. They may also have been related to individual differences in normal or synesthetic imagery that were either unmeasured or inaccurately reflected by self-report scales.

In any case these data are a reminder that we still have a very incomplete understanding of individual differences and of interactions between normal and synesthetic imagery.

A WARNING ON INTROSPECTING OUR IMAGERY

In the earlier discussion of how imagery processes can be subdivided and related to various individual differences, I have emphasized how these distinctions may help to clarify the experiential nature of synesthetic imagery. However our ability to accurately introspect the nature of mental imagery may be limited in certain ways. A short summary of these limitations, as already described for normal imagery by Schooler and Schreiber (2004), may therefore provide a useful caution for future studies of synesthetic imagery.

Schooler and Schreiber outlined three broad reasons why people's ability to meta-cognitively represent and verbally report their conscious experiences, including experiences of mental imagery, cannot always be relied on.

First, people's meta-consciousness of imagery experiences can diverge from their first order experience of imagery because their expectancies and motivations color their attempts to retrieve memories of what they originally experienced. This is referred to as the problem of *substitution* and is a well-known limitation of introspective methods.

Second, there may a problem of *detection* of the more subtle aspects of experience. Schooler and Schreiber argued this may explain why people fail to notice that certain details are missing from a mental image, or are sometimes bad at noticing how their images are built up. For example, Kosslyn et al. (1988) reported behavioral data showing that visual images involving letters were built up in a piecemeal manner, even though participants thought they imaged everything simultaneously. Reporting subtle distinctions such as the difference between visual and spatial images are likely to suffer from this problem.

Third, metacognitive distortion of experience may be driven by *translation* problems when people attempt to decompose holistic experiences for the purposes of report. This distortion appears to be especially likely when experiences such as percepts are decomposed and translated into words, a problem which is referred to as *verbal overshadowing*. For example when people verbally describe a face they have just seen, subsequent recognition of the face is impaired, although mentally imaging the face does not have this effect (Schooler and Engstler-Schooler 1990). This may be why Skelton, Ludwig, and Mohr (2009) found that self-report measures of the projector-associator distinction are more reliable when they are based on ratings of illustrations rather than purely verbal statements. Verbal overshadowing would also be predicted to distort people's description of their synesthetic spatial forms if, as argued, these are often experienced as predominantly visual images. Since verbal overshadowing has been replicated for various types of visual and spatial stimuli, as well as stimuli in other modalities such as audition and taste (Schooler and Schreiber 2004), it is likely to be relevant to many types of synesthetic experience.

What people report about the sensations involved in synesthetic experience may therefore diverge from the actual characteristics of the experiences. This emphasizes the importance of behavioral measures of experiential distinctions, and demands that the design of self-report measures should be sensitive to the problems outlined by Schooler and Schreiber (2004).

CONCLUSION

There is growing evidence that normal visuo-spatial imagery is related to the image-like experiences reported by people with two of the most common varieties of synesthesia, namely grapheme-color and sequence-space synesthesia. I have argued that the study of this relationship can both inform our understanding of synesthesia and help us to refine our methods for investigating this phenomenon.

At least some synesthesias seem to be associated with elevated intensity or prevalence of everyday visual imagery at a subjective level, and with a raised tendency to adopt visuo-spatial strategies. There are also indications that some synesthesias may be associated with better than average visuo-spatial skills in behavioral tasks, although this claim has to be qualified by recent replication failures. From a methodological perspective, this has important potential implications when comparing synesthetes with controls in consistency tests or any other behavioral measures that could reflect an influence of imagery processes. It suggests that measures of imagery may be a crucial covariate to include in future research on synesthesia, perhaps at least as important as the usually controlled variables such as age and gender. From a theoretical perspective it is parsimonious to consider that standard imagery processes may be necessary for synesthetic experience to emerge. For certain varieties of synesthesia, a case can even be made that standard imagery processes might be both necessary and sufficient for synesthetic experience. This argument applies at least to sequence-space synesthesia where the use of imagery by control participants has already been shown to mimic some aspects of synesthetic performance, and where the character of synesthetic experience is so convergent with non-synesthetic visuo-spatial imagery. However, some degree of involvement of imagery processes seems likely in other synesthesias with visuo-spatial concurrents such as color (e.g., grapheme-color synesthesia), visualized text (tickertape synesthesia) or colored geometric objects. Similar arguments may apply to concurrents in other modalities although this is even less explored.

Imagery is an aspect of our mental life that can help to explain some of the continuities between normal and synesthetic cognition. For example, our understanding of the precise nature of the synesthetic experience and its behavioral correlates can be usefully informed by our knowledge of the many sub-processes that underlie standard imagery. These include distinctions between different spatial frames of reference, between visual and spatial imagery, between representation and transformation of images, and between different types of image transformation. Since these dissociable variables are related to individual differences in imagery style and imagery skill, they can help us to account for why synesthetic concurrents should express themselves in different ways in different individuals. Imagery is therefore very relevant to the emerging consensus that individual differences are a crucial aspect of synesthesia research, and distinguishing the subcomponents of imagery should be an important consideration when developing behavioral, self-report or neural measures of synesthesia.

We still have much to learn about the relation of standard imagery and synesthetic experience, for example, about the manner in which various aspects of individual differences are orthogonal or interrelated. The analysis of the relation between imagery and synesthesia also needs to be expanded beyond the realm of visuo-spatial experience. Finally, the vivid and stable imagery of synesthetes may provide a useful platform to challenge and refine our current understanding of mental imagery in general.

REFERENCES

Aginsky, Vlada, Catherine Harris, Ronald Rensink, and Jack Beusmans. 1997. Two strategies for learning a route in a driving simulator. *Journal of Environmental Psychology* 17:317–331.

Barnett, Kylie J., John J. Foxe, Sophie Molholm, Simon P. Kelly, Shani Shalgi, Kevin J. Mitchell, and Fiona N. Newell,2008. Differences in early sensory-perceptual processing in synaesthesia: A visual evoked potential study. *NeuroImage* 43:605–613.

Barnett, Kylie J., and Fiona N. Newell. 2008. Synaesthesia is associated with enhanced, self-rated visual imagery. *Consciousness and Cognition* 17:1032–1039.

Bartolomeo, Paolo. 2002. The relationship between visual perception and visual mental imagery: A reappraisal of the neuropsychological evidence. *Cortex* 38:357–378.

Bächtold, Daniel, Martin Baumüller, and Peter Brugger. 1998. Stimulus response compatibility in representational space. *Neuropsychologia* 36:731–735.

Blajenkova, Olessia, Maria Kozhevnikov, and Michael A. Motes. 2006. Object–spatial imagery: A new self-report imagery questionnaire. *Applied Cognitive Psychology* 20:239–263.

Borst, Gregoire, and Stephen M. Kosslyn. 2008. Visual mental imagery and visual perception: Structural equivalence revealed by scanning processes. *Memory and Cognition* 36(4):849–862.

——. 2010. Individual differences in spatial mental imagery. *The Quarterly Journal of Experimental Psychology* 63(10):2031–2050.

Brang, David, Ursina Teuscher, Vilayanur S. Ramachandra, and Seana Coulson. 2010. Temporal sequences, synesthetic mappings, and cultural biases: The geography of time. *Consciousness and Cognition* 19:11–320.

Caessens, B., W. Notebaert, B. Burle, and E. Soetens. 2005. Voluntary and involuntary control over automatic processing in spatial congruency tasks. *European Journal of Cognitive Psychology* 17:577–589.

Chiou, Rocco, Marleen Stelter, M., and Anina N. Rich. In press. Beyond colour perception: Auditory-visual synaesthesia induces experiences of geometric objects in specific locations. *Cortex*.

Cui, Xu, Cameron B. Jeter, Dongni Yang, P. Read Montague, and David M. Eagleman. 2007. Vividness of mental imagery: Individual variability can be measured objectively. *Vision Research* 47:474–478.

Dean, Graham M., and Peter E. Morris. 2003. The relationship between self-reports of imagery and spatial ability. *British Journal of Psychology* 94(2):245–273.

Dehaene, Stanislas, Serge Bossini, and Pascal Giraux. 1993. The mental representation of parity and number magnitude. *Journal of Experimental Psychology: General* 122:371–396.

Dixon, Mike J., Daniel Smilek, and Philip M. Merikle. 2004. Not all synaesthetes are created equal: Projector versus associator synaesthetes. *Cognitive, Affective and Behavioral Neuroscience* 4:335–343.

Duffy, Patricia L. 2001. *Blue Cats and Chartreuse Kittens. How Synaesthetes Colour Their Worlds*. New York: Holt.

Eagleman, David M. 2009. The objectification of overlearned sequences: A new view of spatial sequence synaesthesia. *Cortex* 45:1266–1267.

Edquist, Jessica, Anina N. Rich, Cobie Brinkman, and Jason B. Mattingley. 2006. Do synaesthetic colours act as unique features in visual search? *Cortex* 42:222–231.

Fischer, Martin H. 2006. The future for SNARC could be stark. *Cortex* 42:1061–1142.

Galton, Francis. 1880a. Statistics on mental imagery. *Mind* 5:301–318.

———. 1880b. Visualised numerals. *Nature* 21:494–495.

———. 1881. Visualised numerals. *The Journal of the Anthropological Institute of Great Britain and Ireland* 10:85–102.

———. 1883. *Inquiries into Human Faculty*. London: Dent.

Galfano, G., E. Rusconi, and C. Umiltà. 2006. Number magnitude orients attention, but not against one's will. *Psychonomic Bulletin and Review* 13:869–874.

Gheri, Carolina, S. Chopping, and Michael J. Morgan. 2008. Synaesthetic colours do not camouflage form in visual search. *Proceedings of the Royal Society B: Biological Sciences* 275:841–846.

Grossenbacher, Peter G., and Christopher T. Lovelace. 2001. Mechanisms of synaesthesia: Cognitive and physiological constraints. *Trends in Cognitive Sciences* 5:36–41.

Gyselinck, Valérie, Rossana De Beni, Francesca Pazzaglia, Chiara Meneghetti, and Amandine Mondoloni. 2007. Working memory components and imagery instructions in the elaboration of a spatial mental model. *Psychological Research* 71:373–382.

Halligan, Peter W., and John C. Marshall. 1991. Left neglect for near but not far space. *Nature* 350:498–500.

Hegarty, Mary. 2010. Mechanical reasoning by mental simulation. *Trends in Cognitive Sciences* 86:280–285.

Hubbard, Edward M. 2007. Neurophysiology of synaesthesia. *Current Psychiatry Reports* 9:193–199.

Hubbard, Edward M., A. Cyrus Arman, Vilayanur S. Ramachandran, and Geoffrey M. Boynton. 2005. Individual differences among grapheme-color synesthetes: Brain-behavior correlations. *Neuron* 45:975–985.

Hubbard, Edward M. David Brang, and Vilayanur S. Ramachandran. 2011. The cross-activation theory at 10. *Journal of Neuropsychology* 5:152–177.

Hubbard, Edward M., Manuela Piazza, Philippe Pinel, and Stanislas Dehaene. 2005. Interactions between number and space in parietal cortex. *Nature Reviews, Neuroscience* 6:435–448.

Hubbard, Edward M., Mariagrazia Ranzini, Manuela Piazza, and Stanislas Dehaene. 2009. What information is critical to elicit interference in number-form synesthesia? *Cortex* 45(10):1200–1216.

Hupé, Jean-Michael, Cécile Bordier, and Michel Dojat. 2012. The neural bases of grapheme-color synesthesia are not localized in real color-sensitive areas. *Cerebral Cortex* 22:1622–1633.

Jarick, Michelle, Mike J. Dixon, Emily C. Maxwell, Mike E. R. Nicholls, and Daniel Smilek. 2009. The ups and downs and lefts and rights of synaesthetic number forms: Validation from spatial cueing and SNARC–type tasks. *Cortex* 45(10):1190–1199.

Jarick, Michelle, Michael J. Dixon, and Daniel Smilek. 2011. 9 is always on top: Assessing the automaticity of synaesthetic number-forms. *Brain and Cognition* 77 (1):96–105.

Jarick, Michelle, Mike J. Dixon, Mark T. Stewart, Emily C. Maxwell, and Daniel Smilek. 2009. A Different outlook on time: Visual and auditory month names elicit different mental vantage points for a time–space synaesthete. *Cortex* 45(10):1217–1228.

Jarick, Michelle, Candice Jensen, Michael J. Dixon, and Daniel Smilek. 2011. The automaticity of vantage point shifts within a synaesthetes' spatial calendar. *Journal of Neuropsychology* 5:333–352.

Jonas, Clare, and Michelle Jarick. 2013. Synesthesia, sequences, and space. In *The Oxford Handbook of Synesthesia*, ed. Julia Simner and Edward M. Hubbard, 123–148. Oxford: Oxford University Press.

Jonas, Clare N., Alisdair J. G. Taylor, Sam Hutton, Peter H. Weiss, and Jamie Ward. 2011. Visuospatial representations of the alphabet in synaesthetes and non-synaesthetes. *Journal of Neuropsychology* 5:302–322

Kosslyn, Stephen M. 1994. *Image and Brain: The Resolution of the Imagery Debate*. Cambridge, MA: MIT Press.

———. 2005. Mental images and the brain. *Cognitive Neuropsychology* 22:333–347.

Kosslyn, Stephen M., Carolyn B. Cave, David A. Provost, and Susanne M. von Gierke. 1988. Sequential processes in image generation. *Cognitive Psychology* 20:319–343.

Kosslyn, Stephen M., Jennifer Shephard, and William Thompson. 2007. Spatial processing during mental imagery: A neurofunctional theory. In *Spatial Processing in Navigation, Imagery and Perception*, ed. Fred Mast and Lutz Jäncke, 1–16. New York: Springer.

Kosslyn, Stephen M., William Thompson, Jennifer Shephard, Giorgio Ganis, Deborah Bell, Judith Danovitch, Leah Wittenber, and Nathaniel Alpert. 2004. Brain rCBF and performance in visual imagery tasks: Common and distinct processes. *European Journal of Cognitive Psychology* 165:696–716.

Kozhevnikov, Maria, Olesya Blazhenkova, and Michael Becker. 2010. Trade-off in object versus spatial visualization abilities: Restriction in the development of visual-processing resources. *Psychonomic Bulletin and Review* 17(1):29–35.

Kozhevnikov, Maria, Stephen Kosslyn, and Jennifer Shephard. 2005. Spatial versus object visualizers: A new characterization of visual cognitive style. *Memory and Cognition* 33:710–726.

Makioka, Shogo. 2009. A self-organizing learning account of number–form synaesthesia. *Cognition* 112:397–414.

Mann, Heather, Jason Korzenko, Jonathan S. A. Carriere, and Mike J. Dixon. 2009. Time-space synaesthesia—A cognitive advantage? *Consciousness and Cognition* 18:619–627.

Marks, D. F. 1973. Visual imagery differences in the recall of pictures. *British Journal of Psychology* 64:7–24.

———. 1977. Imagery and consciousness: A theoretical review from an individual differences perspective. *Journal of Mental Imagery* 12:275–290.

Mast, Fred W., and Stephen M. Kosslyn. 2002. Visual mental images can be ambiguous: Insights from individual differences in spatial transformation abilities. *Cognition* 86(1):57–70.

Mattingley, Jason B. 2009. Attention, automaticity, and awareness in synaesthesia. The Year in Cognitive Neuroscience 2009. *Annals of the New York Academy of Sciences* 1156:141–167.

Mazard, Angélique, Nathalie TzourioⱮazoyer, Fabrice Crivello, Bernard Mazoyer, and Emmanuel Mellet. 2004. A PET meta–analysis of object and spatial mental imagery. *Journal of Cognitive Psychology* 165:673–695.

McKelvie, Stuart J. 1995. The VVIQ as a psychometric test of individual differences in visual imagery vividness: a critical quantitative review and plea for direction. *Journal of Mental Imagery* 19:1–106.

Nijboer, Tanja C. W., Gabriela Satris, and Stefan Van der Stigchel. 2011. The influence of synesthesia on eye movements: No synesthetic pop-out in an oculomotor target selection task. *Consciousness and Cognition* 20(4):1193–1200.

Olivetti Belardinelli, M., M. Palmiero, C. Sestieri, D. Nardo, R. Di Matteo, A. Londei, A. D'Ausilio, A. Ferretti, C. Del Gratta, and G. L. Romani. 2009. An fMRI investigation on image generation in different sensory modalities: The influence of vividness. *Acta Psychologica* 132:190–200.

Pearson, David G. 2001. Imagery and the visuo-spatial sketchpad. In *Working Memory in Perspective*, ed. Jackie Andrade, 33–59. New York: Psychology Press.

Piazza, A., P. Pinel, and S. Dehaene. 2006. Objective correlates of an unusual subjective experience: A single-case study of number-form synaesthesia. *Cognitive Neuropsychology* 23:1162–1173.

Phillips, D. E. 1897. Genesis of number-forms. *American Journal of Psychology* 8:506–527.

Price, Mark C. 2009. Spatial forms and mental imagery. *Cortex* 45(10):1229–1245.

Price, Mark C., and Jason B. Mattingley. (2013). Automaticity in sequence-space synaesthesia: A critical appraisal of the evidence. *Cortex* 49:1165–1186.

Price, Mark C., and Rune A. Mentzoni. 2008. Where is January? The month-SNARC effect in sequence-form synaesthetes. *Cortex* 44(7):890–907.

Price, Mark C., Tormod Elias Solberg, and Oskar Blakstad. 2009. Measures of synaesthetic *spatial forms* in the general population. Poster presented at the 16th conference of the European Society for Cognitive Psychology (ESCOP), Krakow, 2–5 September.

Proctor, Robert W., and Kim-Phuong L. 2002. Eliminating, magnifying, and reversing spatial compatibility effects with mixed location–relevant and irrelevant trials. In *Common Mechanisms in Perception and Action: Attention and Performance XIX*, ed. Wolfgang Prinz and Bernard Hommel, 443–473. Oxford: Oxford University Press.

Reisberg, Daniel, David G. Pearson, and Stephen M. Kosslyn. 2003. Intuitions and introspections about imagery: The role of imagery experience in shaping an investigator's theoretical views. *Applied Cognitive Psychology* 17:147–160.

Rich, Anina N., Mark A. Williams, Aina Puce, Ari Syngeniotis, Matthew A. Howard, Francic McGlone, and Jason B. Mattingley. 2006. Neural correlates of imagined and synaesthetic colours. *Neuropsychologia* 44:2918–2925.

Ristic, Jelena, Alissa Wright, and Alan Kingstone. 2006. The number line effect reflects top–down control. *Psychonomic Bulletin and Review* 135:862–868.

Rizza, Aurora, and Mark C. Price. 2012. Do sequence-space synaesthetes have better spatial imagery skills? Maybe not. *Cognitive Processing* 13 (1):299–303.

Rouw, Romke, and H. Steven Scholte. 2007. Increased structural connectivity in grapheme-color synaesthesia. *Nature Neuroscience* 10:792–797.

Sagiv, Noam, Julia Simner, James Collins, Brian Butterworth, and Jamie Ward. 2006. What is the relationship between synaesthesia and visuo–spatial number forms? *Cognition* 101:114–128.

Sagiv, Noam, and Jamie Ward. 2006. Crossmodal interactions: lessons from synesthesia. *Progress in Brain Research* 155:259–271.

Schooler, Jonathan W., and Tonya Y. Engstler-Schooler. 1990. Verbal overshadowing of visual memories: Some things are better left unsaid. *Cognitive Psychology* 17:36–71.

Schooler, Jonathan W., and Charles A. Schreiber. 2004. Experience, meta-consciousness, and the paradox of introspection. *Journal of Consciousness Studies* 117(8):17–39.

Seron, Xavier, Mauro Pesenti, Marie-Pascale Noel, Gérard Deloche, and Jacques-André Cornet. 1992. Images of numbers, or 'When 98 is upper left and 6 sky blue'. *Cognition* 44:159–196.

Simner, Julia. 2009. Synaesthetic visuo-spatial forms: Viewing sequences in space. *Cortex* 45(10):1138–1147.

Simner, Julia, Neil Mayo, and Mary-Jane Spiller. 2009. A foundation for savantism? Visuo-spatial synaesthetes present with cognitive benefits. *Cortex* 45(10):1246–1260.

Simner, Julia, Catherine Mulvenna, Noam Sagiv, Elias Tsakanikos, S. Athene Witherby, Christine Fraser, Kirsten Scott, and Jamie Ward. 2006. Synaesthesia: The prevalence of atypical cross-modal experiences. *Perception* 35:1024–1033.

Skelton, Richard, Casimir Ludwig, and Christine Mohr. 2009. A novel, illustrated questionnaire to distinguish projector and associator synaesthetes. *Cortex* 45(6):721–729.

Smilek, Daniel, Alicia Callejas, Mike J. Dixon, and Philip M. Merikle. 2007. Ovals of time: Time–space associations in synaesthesia. *Consciousness and Cognition* 16:507–519.

Spiller, Mary J., and Ashok S. Jansari. 2008. Mental imagery and synaesthesia: Is synaesthesia from internally–generated stimuli possible? *Cognition* 109:143–151.

Spiller, Mary J., Clare Jonas, Julia Simner, and Ashok S. Jansari. 2012. Exploring synaesthetes' mental imagery abilities across multiple sensory modalities. Paper presented at the UK Synaesthesia Association Annual Conference, Oxford University, April.

Tang, Joey, Jamie Ward, and Brian Butterworth. 2008. Number forms in the brain. *Journal of Cognitive Neuroscience* 209:1547–1556.

Terhune, Devin B., Etzel Cardeña, and Magnus Lindgren. 2010. Disruption of synaesthesia by posthypnotic suggestion: An ERP study. *Neuropsychologia* 48(11):3360–3364.

Teuscher, Ursina, David Brang, Vilayanur S. Ramachandran, and Seana Coulson. 2010. Spatial cueing in time–space synesthetes: An event–related brain potential study. *Brain and Cognition* 74:35–46.

Thompson, W. L., Slotnick, S.D., Burrage, M. S., and Kosslyn, S. M. 2009. Two forms of spatial imagery: Neuroimaging evidence. *Psychological Science* 20(10):1245–1253.

Treisman, Anne. 2005. Synaesthesia: Implications for attention, binding, and consciousness—a commentary. In *Synaesthesia. Perspectives from Cognitive Neurocience*, ed. Lynn C. Robertson and Noam Sagiv, 239–254. New York: Oxford University Press.

van Leeuwen, Tessa M., Karl M. Petersson, and Peter Hagoort. 2010. Synaesthetic colour in the brain: Beyond colour areas. A functional magnetic resonance imaging study of synaesthetes and matched controls. *PLoS One* 5(8):e12074.

Vuilleumier, P., N. Valenza, E. Mayer, A., Reverdin, and T. Landis. 1998. Near and far visual space in unilateral neglect. *Annals of Neurology* 43:406–410.

Ward, Jamie, Brett Huckstep, and Elias Tsakanikos. 2006. Sound-colour synaesthesia: To what extent does it use cross–modal mechanisms common to us all? *Cortex* 42(2):264–280.

Ward, Jamie, Ryan Li, Shireen Salih, and Noam Sagiv. 2007. Varieties of grapheme-colour synaesthesia: A new theory of phenomenological and behavioural differences. *Consciousness and Cognition* 16:913–931.

Ward, Jamie, Noam Sagiv, and Brian Butterworth. 2009. The impact of visuo-spatial number forms on simple arithmetic. *Cortex* 45(10):1261–1265.

Yaro, C., and Ward, J. 2007. Searching for Shereshevskii: What is superior about the memory of synaesthetes? *Quarterly Journal of Experimental Psychology* 605:681–695.

Zacks, Jeffery M., and Pascale Michelon. 2005. Transformations of visuospatial images. *Behavioral and Cognitive Neuroscience Reviews* 4:96–118.

PART VII

CROSS-MODALITY
IN THE GENERAL
POPULATION

CHAPTER 38

WEAK SYNESTHESIA IN PERCEPTION AND LANGUAGE

LAWRENCE E. MARKS

In "Decline of the American Songbird," the poet Colin Cheney (2010) declares that: "If a sound casts a shadow, the suburbs /sound like overcast sky" (40). These lines, perhaps intended as an allusion to T.S. Eliot's "evening . . . spread out against the sky/Like a patient etherized upon a table" ("The Love Song of J. Alfred Prufrock," 2–3), provide a useful example of cross-modal or synesthetic metaphor, one of the protean forms that weak synesthesia can assume. Weak synesthesia refers to cross-sensory (and other) correspondences that are readily apprehended by the general population, as contrasted with strong synesthesia, in which the correspondences are actually evoked and experienced, but only by a small minority of people. Thus, to a person with strong synesthesia, a man's voice may evoke the darkness of a shadow. Cheney's metaphor is useful in the present context because it makes explicit an undercurrent of conditionality that is implicit in weak synesthesia, an "as-if" quality that contrasts sharply with the unconditional quality of strong synesthetic experiences, reminiscent of the contrast between "knowing about" and "knowing."

A famous example in the history of "knowing about" synesthesia appears in John Locke's (1690) *Essay Concerning Human Understanding*:

> A studious blind Man, who had mightily beat his Head about visible Objects, and made use of the explication of his Books and Friends, to understand those names of Light, and Colours which often came in his way; bragged one day, That he now understood what Scarlet signified. Upon which his Friend demanding, What scarlet was? the blind Man answered, It was like the Sound of a Trumpet. (Locke 1690, 199)

As Locke recognized, the blind man did not experience scarlet when he heard a trumpet, but instead came to "know about" scarlet—as the color that a trumpet's sound would have if the trumpet's sound had a color. The passage continues: "Just such an Understanding of the name of any other simple idea will he have, who hopes to get it only from a Definition, or other Words made use of to explain it" (199).

Where a person who experiences strong synesthesia may describe, for example, how a note played on a trumpet evokes a visual sensation or quality of scarlet, or how the distant rumble of thunder evokes a shadowy color that resembles an overcast sky, those of us who lack strong synesthesia by definition do not have these kinds of auxiliary experiences. In the present chapter, *synesthetes* refer to individuals who experience strong synesthesia and *non-synesthetes* to those who do not. Nevertheless, many non-synesthetes in the general population, while lacking strong synesthesia, nevertheless recognize the similarity between dim colors and soft sounds, and between bright colors and loud sounds. This is evident both in the ways that non-synesthetes judge the similarity of sounds and lights (Marks 1989) and in the ways that non-synesthetes judge words such as "soft" and "murmur" to *mean* dim, "loud" and "shout" to *mean* bright (Marks 1982a).

Weak Synesthesia Versus Strong Synesthesia

Relying on terminology used a quarter-century earlier (Marks 1975), Martino and Marks (2001) distinguished weak synesthesia from strong synesthesia as follows: "Strong synaesthesia is characterized by a vivid image in one sensory modality in response to stimulation in another one. Weak synaesthesia is characterized by cross-sensory correspondences expressed through language, perceptual similarity, and perceptual interactions during information processing" (61). Both characterizations are overly narrow, in that they restrict the terms strong and weak synesthesia to cross-modal instances. Even so, the characterizations provide a convenient springboard for the present review.

In a sense, the term "weak synesthesia" may be a misnomer—to the extent that it suggests that weak synesthesia is necessarily experienced, phenomenally, as a ghost or simulacrum of strong synesthesia—akin to the distinction that David Hume (1739) made between impressions and ideas, whose difference, Hume claimed: "consists in the degrees of force and liveliness, with which they strike upon the mind, and make their way into our thought or consciousness" (11–12). But weak synesthesia typically does not involve the evocation of an explicit phenomenal experience in another domain (see Spence 2011). A person may imagine a color or shape when she hears a musical passage, but weak synesthesia need not entail such perceptual imagery. On the other side of this coin, strong synesthesia itself is hardly uniform: Some synesthetes, for example, project their induced colors externally, seeing them "out there," whereas other synesthetes see the colors "in the mind's eye" (Dixon, Smilek, and Merikle 2004). The precise relation between weak synesthesia and strong synesthesia remains unclear, a situation that is exacerbated by the difficulties entailed in characterizing the domain of strong synesthesia itself. These difficulties inspired a recent suggestion that strong synesthesia may itself comprise several distinct categories (dubbed "synesthetic pluralism"), only some of which may be prototypical (see Marks 2011). But these issues fall outside the scope of the present chapter.

What is central to weak synesthesia is a perceptual or conceptual recognition of similarity between sensory, cognitive, or affective attributes in different domains. Often, especially when the domains comprise perceptual experiences in different sense modalities, the similarities have analogs in strong cross-modal synesthesia. As Martino and Marks (2001) pointed out, weak synesthesia can also have implicit correlates—for example, in cross-dimensional congruence effects observed in various information-processing tasks. But from the present perspective, these implicit measures are not definitional: just as strong synesthesia is characterized, first and foremost, by its phenomenology, so too is weak synesthesia. In strong synesthesia, phenomenal experience in one domain evokes phenomenal experience in another; in weak synesthesia, phenomenal experience in one domain evokes the perception or conception of similarity to phenomenal experience in another. Assessing cross-modal or cross-dimensional interactions in information-processing tasks may turn out, of course, to be critical to understanding the mechanisms underlying both weak and strong synesthesia (see Marks 2004; Spence 2011). The present perspective is compatible with recent neurophysiological and genetic findings (Asher et al. 2009; Barnett et al. 2008), implying that (strong) synesthesia derives from a neurophysiological condition, or set of neurophysiological conditions, having a substantial genetic component.

An alternative view does not distinguish so sharply between strong and weak synesthesia. The substantial evidence indicating that weak synesthesia is virtually universal has led some investigators to suggest that synesthesia, broadly construed, may be universal, or nearly so, that everyone may be "at least slightly synesthetic." Thus, Ramachandran (2011) recently wrote: "even in those of us who are nonsynesthetes a great deal of what goes on in our mind depends on entirely normal cross-modal interactions that are not arbitrary. So there is a sense in which at some level we are all 'synesthetes'" (108). Under this interpretation, synesthesia could constitute a more-or-less continuous attribute of personality or mode of consciousness, with no sharp boundary necessarily separating weak synesthesia from strong (e.g., Glicksohn, Salinger, and Roychman 1992; Hunt 2005). By this view, weak synesthesia and strong synesthesia would presumably mark distinct poles or regions of phenomenal experience, an alternative to strict separation between weak and strong synesthesia, and to the hypothesis of "synesthetic pluralism" (Marks 2011), mentioned earlier.

WEAK CROSS-MODAL SYNESTHESIA

Although weak synesthesia, like strong synesthesia, can involve diverse domains of perception, cognition, and affect, both within modalities and across them, the present chapter focuses on weak cross-modal synesthesia. As a consequence, the chapter will not review findings on, for example, forms of weak synesthesia that may occur within modalities (as reported, e.g., by Simner et al. 2005, regarding associations between graphemes and colors). Nor will the chapter consider weak perceptual or linguistic personification, the strong form of which appears wedded to synesthesia (e.g., Calkins 1893; Galton 1880; Simner and Holenstein 2007; Smilek et al. 2007). Finally, the chapter will not review evidence of implicit cross-modal correspondences as revealed, for instance, through interactions measured in discriminative response times (for reviews, see Marks 2004; Spence 2011; Parise and Spence, Chapter 39, this volume). Instead, the chapter centers on two realms in which weak synesthesia reveals itself: in the perception of similarities or correspondences across different sensory modalities, and in the expression and recognition of cross-sense similarities in language. The latter realm has been dubbed *synesthetic metaphor* and often, within the realm of poetry and fiction, as *literary synesthesia*.

WEAK CROSS-MODAL SYNESTHESIA IN PERCEPTION: TASTE, SMELL, AND SOMATIC SENSATIONS

Like strong cross-modal synesthesia, weak cross-modal synesthesia can involve any of the senses—the so-called "lower" senses of taste, smell, pain, touch, temperature, and kinesthesia-proprioception, as well as the "higher" senses of hearing and sight. Among the weak synesthesias involving these lower senses, two are especially widespread and well known: The first is the perception of colors having different degrees of heaviness (Bullough 1907), with darker and more saturated colors being judged as heavier than light, unsaturated colors (Alexander and Shansky 1976). The second is the perception of colors having thermal qualities—for instance, blue and green being perceived as "cool" or "cold," red and yellow as "warm" or "hot" (Morgan, Goodson, and Jones 1975; Newhall 1941). Also widespread, although perhaps less well known, is the perception of olfactory stimuli as "tasting" sweet (a gustatory quality) when taken in the mouth (e.g., Frank and Byram 1988). Both the warmth/coolness of colors and the sweet "tastes" of odors have been attributed by some investigators to associative learning (e.g., Morgan, Goodson, and Jones 1975; Stevenson, Boakes, and Prescott 1998). Stevenson and colleagues even dubbed the acquisition of taste qualities by odors as "learned synesthesia."

Through experience we learn about those properties of objects and events that produce systematically correlated information, both within and between sense modalities. As discussed later, the greater the size of an object, the greater its mass, *ceteris paribus*, and so also the lower its natural resonance frequency. As a result, when objects fall to the ground, large ones "thud" whereas small ones "ping"—perhaps a source of the weak synesthetic association between smaller visual size and higher auditory pitch (e.g., Osgood, Suci, and Tannenbaum 1957). And many children hear the story of the three bears recited with the large papa bear speaking in a deep, loud voice, the little baby bear in a higher, softer one. So too do we learn associations among the olfactory, visual, and gustatory attributes of foods: that strawberries have a distinct odor and flavor (olfactory), a red color (vision), and a sweet taste (gustatory), and that red and white wines have distinctive odors (Ballester et al. 2009) and flavors (Morrot, Brochet, and Dubourdieu 2001). Crisinel and Spence (2010) found evidence of correspondences between high-pitched sounds and sour tastes and between low-pitched sounds and bitter and umami (savory) tastes, and Spence and Gallace (2011) found consistent matches between food tastes and both words and shapes.

Other instances of weak cross-modal synesthesia involving the so-called lower senses are not so easily attributed to experience, however, as in the complex relation between color intensity and perceived odor intensity (Zellner and Whitten 1999) and in the consistent attribution of specific colors to fragrances used in perfumes (Gilbert, Martin, and Kemp 1996; Schifferstein and Tanudjaja 2004; see also Demattè, Sanabria, and Spence 2006; Zellner et al. 2008). Nor is it evident how experience might account for the similarity between increasing odor intensity and increasing lightness of colors (Kemp and Gilbert 1997), or for the similarity of specific odors to lower-pitched and higher-pitched sounds (Belkin et al. 1997).

Weak synesthesia is characterized in terms of similarity, where one quality is perceived or conceived as being like another. Weak synesthesia could originate in learned associations, so that long-wavelength light is perceived as warm as well as red, or the olfactory flavorant amyl acetate is perceived as sweet as well as banana-like. But weak synesthesia may sometimes rest on intrinsic resemblances: The color orange appears more similar to red than to green, presumably because neurons in the brain that signal "redness" also signal "orangeness" but not "greenness." By analogy, a melody played on a flute may be perceived as bright as well as high in pitch or register, compared to the same melody played on an English horn, perhaps because there are neurons or neural circuits responsive to both high pitch and high brightness (see Marks and Bornstein 1987). As discussed later in this chapter, Békésy (1957, 1959) reported how auditory (and vibrotactile) stimuli produce perceptions of size that vary inversely with the signal frequency, and the related auditory and vibrotactile size to underlying mechanisms of neural processing. This model provides an alternative explanation of correspondence between auditory pitch and visual size. Instead of having to learn the association through the resonance properties of materials, Békésy's model suggests that perceptual similarity mirrors intrinsic neurally-based similarity.

Weak synesthesia may arise, therefore, either from associations based in contiguity or from resemblance—these being two central and long-standing principles of psychological explanation in a variety of realms, including learning, memory, perception, and language (e.g., Köhler 1941; Robinson 1927). Further, these two psychological principles, association by contiguity and association by resemblance, have analogs in rhetoric: in the linguistic tropes known, respectively, as metonymy and metaphor (see Wellek and Warren 1956). Given this psychological-linguistic parallel, one may be tempted to label Joseph Auslander's "silver needle-note of a fife" (*Steel*, 138) as a synesthetic metaphor, but, following Ullmann (1945), to label Byron's "odorous purple of a new-born rose"

(*Childe Harold's Pilgrimage*, CIV, xxviii, 8) as a synesthetic metonymy. The analogy is taken up later, after considering the most extensively studied forms of weak cross-modal synesthesia, namely, those involving hearing and vision.

WEAK AUDITORY-VISUAL SYNESTHESIA IN PERCEPTION

Evidence of auditory-visual correspondences appeared already in the first half of the twentieth century, one of the best known examples being the pair of abstract figures created by Wolfgang Köhler (1947): the rounded, lobular figure he called "maluma" (originally, "baluma"; Köhler 1929), and the straight-edged, acutely angled figure he called "takete." Köhler reported that subjects readily identified which name matched which figure—a finding subsequently confirmed in non-Western as well as Western cultures and in children as well as adults (e.g., Davis 1961; Holland and Wertheimer 1964; but see Rogers and Ross 1975 for possible limitations). In a more recent demonstration, Ramachandran and Hubbard (2001) reported that most subjects matched the names "bouba" and "kiki" to rounded and angular figures, respectively, that were constructed as analogs to Köhler's maluma and takete figures. Maurer, Pathman, and Mondloch (2006) similarly interpreted the results of their study in young children and adults, which tested rounded and angular figures, including bouba and kiki.

It has generally been assumed that these cross-modal matches arise from correspondences between the auditory attributes of the words and the visual features of the figures, that is, from correspondences between the low-pitched, temporally extended vowel sounds of maluma/bouba and the softly rounded figures, and between the high-pitched, brief vowel sounds of takete/kiki and the angular figures (e.g., Marks 1978; Ramachandran and Hubbard 2001; see also O'Boyle and Tarte 1980). But sound may be only part of the story, as Ramachandran and Hubbard point out the potentially important role of phoneme-specific motor acts in the oral cavity and their concomitant kinesthetic signals. Perhaps the cross-modal equivalences between the words and visual figures are strongly embedded in, and largely mediated through, the implicit or explicit motor activity and kinesthetic feedback associated with speaking the words. Along these lines, Vladimir Nabokov (1949) made a pertinent observation with regard to his own strong letter-color synesthesia: "On top of all this, I present a fine case of 'colored hearing.' Perhaps 'hearing' is not quite accurate, since the color sensation seems to be produced by the physiological act of my orally forming a given letter while I imagine its outline" (33). The possible roles of motor activity and kinesthesia are considered later (see also Cacciari 2008; Cytowic 2002).

More than half a century ago, Karwoski and his colleagues carried out a series of experimental studies of both strong and weak synesthesia (Karwoski and Odbert 1938; Karwoski, Odbert, and Osgood 1942; Odbert, Karwoski, and Eckerson 1942; Riggs and

Karwoski 1934) in which these investigators made several important observations. The three experiments reported by Karwoski, Odbert, and Osgood (1942) are noteworthy. The first experiment asked subjects, pre-selected by the authors as evidencing strong synesthesia or strong visual imagery, to draw the visual images seen in response to brief, simple melodies. The second experiment asked subjects who lacked strong synesthesia or visual imagery nevertheless to draw whatever came to mind in response to the same melodies. The third experiment used results of the earlier experiments, together with those of Odbert, Karwoski, and Eckerson (1942), to create pairs of bipolar visual adjectives for randomly chosen (hence presumably mostly non-synesthetic) subjects to match to pairs of bipolar auditory and emotional adjectives. The upshot of the three experiments was the conclusion that, to use present terminology, weak cross-modal synesthesia and its representations within weak verbal synesthesia have much in common with each other and with strong perceptual synesthesia: although weak and strong auditory-visual synesthesia and are not identical, both involve correspondences or links between dimensions of perceptual experience, indeed, between perceptual "meanings," across different senses. These cross-modal correspondences, Karwoski, Odbert, and Osgood concluded, are as much cognitive as perceptual.

Like strong synesthesia, weak auditory-visual synesthesia involves the alignment of dimensions such that greater visual brightness corresponds to higher pitch and tempo in hearing, smaller size corresponds to higher pitch, and larger size corresponds to greater loudness (Karwoski, Odbert, and Osgood 1942). Similar correspondences between auditory and visual dimensions are evident in results of Willmann (1944), who asked composition students and composers to create musical pieces for each of several visual themes. (The findings raise interesting and important issues about the role of weak synesthesia in music and visual art, a topic that regrettably falls outside the scope of this chapter; but see Day, Chapter 44; Steen and Berman, Chapter 34; and van Campen, Chapter 32, this volume.) Presumably, in non-synesthetes, auditory-visual resemblances can reveal themselves in both perception and language, much as they do, albeit more automatically, in the perceptual experience of strong synesthetes (see also Cacciari 2008; Marks 1975, 1978; Ward, Huckstep, and Tsakanikos 2006). In this spirit, Ward, Huckstep, and Tsakanikos (2006) concluded that sound-color synesthesia "recruits normal mechanisms of cross-modal perception and attention and can therefore be used to speak to theories of normal cognition" (279).

One significant observation of Karwoski, Odbert, and Osgood (1942) was that weak auditory-visual synesthesia (like strong synesthesia) can be multidimensional: for instance, both auditory pitch and auditory tempo align with visual size. Pitch and tempo also both align with visual shape. A quantitative study that illustrates this point was reported nearly a half century later (Marks 1989). In one experiment, the subjects were presented single pure tones that varied in both frequency and intensity, together with a dim light and a bright light, and asked which of the two lights was more similar to each tone. In another experiment, subjects compared the degree of similarity between pairs of tones, pairs of lights, and pairs comprising a tone and a light. The results of both experiments converged in showing how both pitch and loudness jointly contribute to perceived auditory-visual similarity (subjects judged bright lights most similar to loud and high-pitched tones, but judged dim lights most similar to soft and low-pitched tones).

Previously, Wicker (1968) had reported evidence of pitch-lightness similarity—lightness being a perceptual attribute of illuminated surfaces, brightness being an attribute of self-luminous objects. Lightness varies (in achromatic stimuli) from black through gray to white, whereas brightness varies from dim to bright. The distinction is important, as increasing pitch is associated with both increasing brightness and increasing lightness, whereas increasing loudness is associated only with increasing brightness, but not with increasing lightness (Marks, 1974). Using surfaces viewed against a midgray background as visual stimuli, Wicker's study revealed two sets of auditory-visual associations: between pitch and lightness and between loudness and lightness contrast. Recently, Mulvenna (2012) reported evidence of pitch-lightness correspondence in the Himba of Namibia, pre-literate, semi-nomadic tribes people having virtually no contact with Western civilization.

The findings of Marks (1989) in particular show clearly how greater brightness corresponds to both greater loudness and higher pitch. In this regard, a couple of points are noteworthy. First, a sensory attribute of brightness is often applied to experiences in various sensory modalities, including hearing (see Nafe 1924; in hearing, brightness is sometimes also called auditory density: Guirao and Stevens 1964); and second, results of early psychoacoustic studies suggested that brightness in hearing reflects both pitch and loudness (Boring and Stevens 1936; Guirao and Stevens 1964), as Marks's results imply. These findings are compatible with the long-standing claim that brightness—a composite of intensity, spatial acuteness or sharpness, rapid onset, and so forth—may constitute a "universal" feature of phenomenal experience (Hornbostel 1925/1927, 1934; Hartshorne 1934), and by implication that brightness can mediate weak cross-modal synesthesia.

The existence of a weak synesthetic correspondence between loudness and brightness is hardly surprising. Both attributes characterize perceived intensity in their respective sense modalities, and intensity or magnitude has long been noted as a central vehicle for cross-modal resemblance (e.g., Hartshorne 1934; Hornbostel 1925/1927, 1934; Marks 1978), revealing itself early in infancy (Lewkowicz and Turkewitz 1980). The existence of a universal attribute, intensity, has served as the basis for traditional psychophysical research on cross-modality intensity matching (e.g., Stevens, Mack, and Stevens 1960; Stevens and Marks 1965). Note, however, that traditional cross-modality matching experiments instruct subjects how to match perceived intensities in different modalities, specifically, to match greater loudness with greater brightness. Studies of weak synesthesia, however, are much more open-ended, not defining for the subjects the direction, if any, of the cross-modal correspondence, but instructing them to choose or generate the best match. Smith and Sera (1992) have examined how a general conception of magnitude develops in young children and, more recently, Walsh (2003) has described a theory of magnitude whose components reflect quantitative metrics of space, time, and quantity (see also Walsh, Chapter 41, this volume).

Parallels to weak synesthesia can also be found in the literature on sound symbolism and phonetic symbolism—the attribution of meanings to sounds, especially to speech sounds. To start, note that many studies of sound and phonetic symbolism show the presence of associations, parallel to those discussed earlier, between the auditory attribute of pitch and the visual attributes of brightness and size (Bentley and Varon 1933; Czurda 1953; Hevner 1937b; Koriat and Levy 1977; McMurray 1960; Newman 1933; Sapir 1929; Wissemann 1954; see also Ultan 1978, for a multilanguage analysis, but Taylor 1963; Taylor and Taylor 1965 for possible limitations). The vowels /e/ and /i/ are generally perceived as relatively high in pitch compared to /a/, /o/, and u/—pitch being closely associated with the frequency of the vowel's second formant (Delattre et al. 1952)—and consequently are perceived also as darker and larger. As Werner (1957) wrote: "A four-year-old girl says: 'Father talks just like Santa Claus…boom, boom, boom! As dark as night…! But we talk light, like the daytime…bim, bim, bim!'" (262). Tsur (2006) proposed that these auditory-visual associations arise early in perceptual processing, before the speech sounds are categorized phonetically.

A second point of note is the overlap, but not identity, between sound symbolism and phonetic symbolism. Sound symbolism is a broader term in that it applies to meanings associated with non-speech as well as speech sounds. But phonetic symbolism is broad too, in that it applies to meanings associated with non-acoustic properties of speech, and in particular, with motor speech acts. As noted earlier, the associations reported by Köhler (1947) between maluma and a rounded shape and between takete and an angular shape may depend on either the sounds of these pseudowords or the motor acts involved in pronouncing them. Grammont (1930) pointed out how meanings may be mediated by kinesthetic or proprioceptive stimuli associated with speech production—for example, how the initial consonant combination /sp/ indicates extrusion. For more extensive reviews of sound symbolism and phonetic symbolism, see Marks (1978), Ultan (1978), Nuckolls (1999), Hinton, Nichols, and Ohala (1994) and Cuskley and Kirby (Chapter 43, this volume).

WEAK AUDITORY-VISUAL SYNESTHESIA IN CHILDHOOD

The evidence of cross-modal equivalence, in children, of words such as bouba and kiki with, respectively, rounded and angular visual shapes (Maurer, Pathman, and Mondloch 2006) suggests, not surprisingly, that children too reveal weak synesthesia. Simpson, Quinn, and Ausubel (1956) asked nearly 1000 3rd to 6th grade children to name the colors suggested by each of a set of various pure tones varying widely in sound frequency. As sound frequency increased, the number of "blue" and "violet" color responses declined, while the number of "yellow" and "green" responses increased. Both adults (Marks 1982a) and children (Marks, Hammeal, and Bornstein 1987) judge "yellow" to be a light color—there are no dark yellows, dark yellow being called "tan" or "brown"—so the results of Simpson, Quinn, and Ausubel likely represent a pitch-brightness similarity (see Marks 1996; Spence 2011). Perhaps children come to recognize the variations in lightness of different colors from their crayons—yellow crayons being light, blue and violet crayons often dark.

A systematic study of weak perceptual synesthesia in both children between 4 and 13 years and adults showed widespread uniformity in the recognition of auditory-visual similarity (Marks, Hammeal, and Bornstein 1987). Already by age 4, most children matched both the louder of two tones and the higher pitched of two tones to the brighter of two lights, as most adults readily did, with pitch-brightness correspondence appearing to be even more consistent than loudness-brightness correspondence—despite the central role that magnitude can play in mediating weak synesthetic correspondences. In addition, young children in this study did not uniformly match the higher pitched of two sounds to the smaller of two visual objects; only children older than 9 years did.

The last outcome may have reflected Marks, Hammeal, and Bornstein's use of overly simple stimuli—auditory tones and simple visual circles. It is worth noting that Marks and colleagues also had the children rate the literal and synesthetically metaphorical meanings of words describing auditory and visual stimuli. On this verbal task, even 9-year-olds rated some of the words denoting high-pitched sounds, such as "squeak," as smaller than words denoting low-pitched sounds, such as "thunder," and words denoting relatively small objects, such as "puddle," as higher in pitch than words denoting large objects, such as "ocean"—although overall on the verbal task, 9-year-olds did not clearly evidence systematic pitch-size correspondence. Even so, results from the verbal task suggest possible limitations imposed on the perceptual task by the choice of stimuli.

In support of this interpretation, Mondloch and Maurer (2004) later showed that 30- to 36-month-old children not only match the higher-pitched sound to the brighter of two objects when the objects are bouncing balls, but also tend to match the higher-pitched sound to the smaller of two balls. As Mondloch and Maurer pointed out, the correspondence between higher auditory pitch and smaller size could be learned from the acoustic resonance properties of objects, for instance, from the higher fundamental voice frequencies of children versus adults (see also Marks, Hammeal, and Bornstein 1987; Osgood et al. 1957).

But the association between pitch and size could have another source. Békésy (1957, 1959) noted that vibratory stimuli presented to the skin (mechanical) or ear (sound) both produce sensations that themselves vary in phenomenal size: As the frequency of a sinusoidal stimulus increases, its perceived auditory or tactile size declines in roughly direct proportion. From this observation, Békésy inferred that perceived size is neurally encoded both in hearing and in touch in inverse relation to stimulus frequency, hence inversely with pitch. Along similar lines, Stevens (1934a, 1934b) noted that, apparently without the use of visual imagery, a blind subject was able to make judgments of auditory volume (size) similar to those made by sighted subjects: the volume or size of a sound increases with intensity (loudness) but decreases with frequency (pitch). Békésy's and Stevens's observations are consistent with the hypothesis that the cross-modal correspondence, in both weak and strong synesthesia, between pitch and size—like the correspondences between loudness and brightness and between pitch and brightness—might reflect common aspects of intrinsic neural codes for size (as for intensity and brightness) in the auditory and visual systems (see Marks 1978; Marks and Bornstein 1987).

Several findings suggest the presence of auditory-visual similarities early in infancy. Using an habituation paradigm, Lewkowicz and Turkewitz (1980) reported perceptual equivalence between loudness and brightness in 1-month-old infants, and Smith and Sera (1992) later showed how comparative judgments given by children reveal, by age 4, an implicit conception of common magnitude or "moreness"—for example, greater size in vision, greater loudness in hearing. There is also evidence of cross-modal similarity in infancy involving attributes other than intensity. Using a preferential-looking paradigm, Walker et al. (2010) found evidence in 3- to 4-month-olds of equivalence between high versus low pitch and high versus low visual spatial position, and between high versus low pitch and angular versus rounded visual shapes (similar to takete/kiki versus maluma/bouba). Braaten (1993) reported some evidence of correspondence between high versus low pitch and high versus low visual position in 6-month-old infants. Finally, Wagner et al. (1981) found evidence of associations in 1-year-old infants between, for example, arrows pointing up or down (arrowheads located high or low) and tones ascending or descending in frequency. Maurer has speculated on the ways that early intersensory organization may constrain the development of strong and, by implication, weak synesthesia (Maurer 1993; Maurer and Mondloch 1996, 2005; Spector and Maurer 2009). In sum, the evidence at hand, although not overwhelming, is nevertheless consistent with the view that several examples of weak cross-modal synesthesia are evident early in infancy. Even though one cannot rule out the possibility that these examples of weak cross-modal synesthesia arise from associations that are learned very early on, the examples are also consistent with the view that they are "hard-wired" through intrinsic mechanisms of sensory coding (see Cacciari 2008; Marks 1978, 1996; Marks and Bornstein 1987).

Weak Auditory-Visual Synesthesia in Language

Weak synesthesia reveals itself in language, as cross-modal or synesthetic metaphors—a topic of increasing interest (see, for example, the recent volume edited by Forceville and Urios-Aparisi 2009). When we speak of a voice as rough or smooth, we imply that the voice has a "temporal texture," with large or small moment-to-moment excursions in acoustic features such as intensity or frequency. And we commonly do this with relative ease, consistent with the view that the cognitive processes involved in producing and comprehending metaphors largely overlap those involved in producing and understanding literal statements (e.g., Gibbs 1984; Glucksberg and Keysar 1990), a notion that fits comfortably with the hypothesis that weak cross-modal synesthesia in language follows from weak cross-modal synesthesia in perception.

Early research on weak synesthesia in language followed on the heels of analogous research in perception. As discussed earlier, Karwoski, Odbert, and Osgood (1942) observed similar cross-modal relations in responses to perceptual stimuli, presented to both synesthetes and non-synesthetes, and in responses on verbal scales made by mostly non-synesthetic subjects. These findings suggest that weak synesthesia, the ability to recognize similarities between perceptual attributes in different domains, is available to and through language. Just as bright lights are perceived to be more similar to loud and high-pitched sounds than to soft and low-pitched ones, words that refer to bright visual experiences should be associated with words that refer to high-pitched and loud experiences. Metaphorically, the word "bright" may in part *mean* "high in pitch" and "loud." Instead of asking subjects to match sounds and lights, one can also ask them to match appropriately selected words.

One way to test this prediction is to present subjects with words or phrases that refer to auditory and visual experiences and ask the subjects to rate the meanings on two kinds of scales: literal scales, a scale of pitch or loudness with auditory words or a scale of brightness with visual words; and metaphorical scales, a scale of brightness with auditory words or a scale of pitch or loudness with visual words. Marks (1982a) conducted a study along these lines, and the results were clear-cut: Words that mean "soft" or "low pitched" also mean "dim," whereas words that mean "loud" or "high pitched" also mean "bright" (and vice versa). "Brown" and "black" are dark colors, and consequently low pitched, whereas "yellow" and "white" are bright colors, and high pitched. A "cough" is low in pitch, hence dark; a "sneeze" high in pitch, hence bright. "Loud sunlight" is brighter than "soft sunlight," whereas plain "sunlight" falls between; similar relations hold for "soft moonlight" and "loud moonlight," which are rated as less bright and less loud than, respectively, "soft sunlight" and "loud sunlight."

Weak cross-modal synesthesia appears to be part and parcel of verbal understanding. Presumably, weak synesthesia makes possible the ready comprehension of metaphors of sound and light such as those found in the works of the poet Swinburne, to wit, in "Bright sound of battle along the Grecian waves, /Loud light of thunder above the Median graves" (*Birthday Ode*, 61–62). In an experimental test of the ways that people interpret the metaphorical meanings of synesthetic expressions in poetry, Marks (1982b) presented subjects with 15 short phrases, one at a time, and asked the subjects to adjust the luminance of a light and the amplitude of a tone so that the light's brightness and the tone's loudness matched the values implied by each poetic phrase. The resulting settings showed a linear relation between log luminance of the light and decibels sound pressure level, with the slope of the line virtually identical to the slope obtained when subjects match loudness and brightness directly (Stevens and Marks 1965). The difference, of course, is that in direct cross-modality matching, subjects are explicitly instructed to set loudness and brightness levels to match each other. In Marks's experiment with synesthetic metaphors, the subjects were instructed to match loudness and brightness to the literal or metaphorical meanings of the poetic excerpts. So the results suggest that, in interpreting auditory-visual metaphors, people use implicit knowledge of loudness-brightness equivalence and, further, that they do it in a way that mimics, quantitatively, the relation seen in direct perceptual matches.

Like adults, children too are able to use their implicit knowledge of auditory-visual (and other) equivalences to produce and understand metaphors. In teaching poetry to children, the poet Kenneth Koch (1970) recounted that:

> In giving the Color Poem, for instance, I asked [the children] to close their eyes; then clapped my hands and asked them what color that was. Almost everyone raised his hand: "Red!" "Green!" "White" I asked them what color Paris was; London; Rome; Los Angeles. I told them to close their eyes again and I said certain words and certain numbers, asking them what color those were. (30)

Children as young as 3 to 4 years are able to make metaphorical matches (Gardner 1974), and children as young as 6 are able to interpret synesthetic metaphorical expressions, "loud sunlight" being brighter, for instance, than "soft sunlight" and "loud moonlight" brighter than "soft moonlight" (Marks, Hammeal, and Bornstein 1987). Marks and colleagues obtained semantic ratings from 4- to 13-year-old children and adults, the same subjects who provided cross-modal matches, as discussed in the previous section. The subjects made literal ratings, such as the loudness of "whisper" and the brightness of "sunlight," metaphorical ratings, such as the brightness of "whisper" and the loudness of "sunlight," and ratings of metaphors, such as the loudness or brightness of "sunlight roars" and "moonlight whispers." Many of the words and phrases tested in the study were identical to those tested by Marks (1982a) in the much more elaborate study of cross-modal similarity in adults.

Several findings of Marks, Hammeal, and Bornstein (1987) are noteworthy. Most important was the clear connection between children's performance on the verbal task, where they rated metaphorical (auditory-visual) meanings, and their performance on the perceptual task, where they made pair-wise auditory-visual matches. At a given age, performance on the verbal rating task with each cross-modal similarity relation—pitch-brightness, loudness-brightness, pitch-size—tended to lag slightly behind performance on the corresponding perceptual task. For example, nearly 90% of 4-year-olds matched the higher-pitched of two tones to the brighter of two lights (perceptual task). Four-year-olds rated the word "bright" to be not only literally brighter than the word "dim," but also metaphorically higher in pitch, and they rated "high pitch" to be both higher in pitch and brighter than "low pitch." On the other hand, while children of all ages, like adults, rated "sunlight" to be brighter than "moonlight," only children of age 9 and older, like adults, rated "sunlight" to be higher in pitch.

Findings of Smith and Sera (1992) suggest complex interactions between perception and language in the development of cross-modal understanding. Along related lines, the verbal ratings and perceptual match obtained by Marks, Hammeal, and Bornstein

(1987) suggest different developmental trajectories in the three main cross-modal associations. In both the children's understanding of synesthetic metaphors and their perceptual matches, the association between pitch and brightness appeared earliest, the association between pitch and size latest. To simplify the comparison of performance on the verbal and perceptual tasks, at each age, the ratings obtained from each subject in the verbal task could be averaged for each cross-modal pairing and scored as a match or mismatch, making it possible to compare the resulting binary scores to the binary results of perceptual matching (Marks 2000). Especially with the pitch-brightness and loudness-brightness association, the youngest children showed greater consistency on the perceptual task compared to the verbal task. The differences between perceptual and verbal performance could simply reflect the verbal task's greater difficulty. Alternatively, the differences could reflect developmental lags in mapping perceptually comprehended weak synesthetic relations into language.

But even if this view is correct, it does not mean that weak cross-modal synesthesia, even when observed in perceptual tasks, always relies exclusively on perceptual mechanisms. Once cross-modal relations are assimilated into cognitive and linguistic processes, the cognitive processes may operate more or less autonomously of perception. On the other hand, it is also possible that perceptual processes may influence linguistic ones. Cacciari, Massironi, and Corradini (2004) found evidence of interactions of perceptual and linguistic processes in affective reactions, produced when the subjects were presented with narratives, colors, and color words. These results imply that perceptual processes of weak synesthesia may operate even within contexts dominated by linguistic information (see also Kaden, Wapner, and Werner 1955).

Several studies have aimed to sort out perceptual and cognitive interactions by measuring response times in tasks of rapid stimulus classification, allowing assessment of implicit cross-modal correspondences. This topic falls outside the scope of the present chapter (for a thorough review, see Spence 2011; Parise and Spence, Chapter 39, this volume). Suffice it so say here that although substantial interactions may occur primarily at a semantic level (e.g., Melara and Marks 1990), it is likely that both perceptual and cognitive mechanisms cooperate in weak cross-modal synesthesia (Cacciari, Massironi, and Corradini 2004).

Marks, Hammeal, and Bornstein (1987) noted an interesting asymmetry in children's cross-modal interpretations of verbal expression: in several instances, words describing auditory experiences were interpreted metaphorically in visual terms more readily than words describing visual experiences were interpreted metaphorically in auditory terms. For example, from age 8 on, children rated "sneeze" and "squeak" as not only higher pitched than "cough" and "thunder," but also as nearly as much brighter. By comparison, the children rated "sunlight" as considerably brighter than "moonlight," but only modestly higher in pitch. Similarly, children readily judged a "puddle" to be literally much smaller than an "ocean," but not metaphorically as much higher in pitch. The observations of asymmetry in the interpretation of several of the metaphors is of special interest in that it parallels observations made in the domain of synesthetic metaphors in literary language, especially poetry.

SYNESTHETIC METAPHOR IN LITERARY LANGUAGE

Everyday discourse is replete with synesthetic (cross-modal) expressions, as when we call a pattern of bright, saturated colors "loud" or a melody "sweet." So too is much literary language, where the multisensory metaphors may be much more elaborate, to wit, in Shelley's lines: "this is the mystic shell;/See the pale azure fading into silver/Lining it with a soft yet glowing light;/Looks it not like lulled music sleeping there?" (*Prometheus Unbound*, III, iii, 70–73). In one of the earliest studies of synesthetic language in poetry, subjects showed little general agreement between affective and esthetic responses to synesthetic passages taken from poetry, a notable exception being the abovementioned lines from Shelley, which were reported to be both affectively and esthetically pleasing (Downey 1912). Downey also used her study as a vehicle for assessing whether the poets that she examined, Poe, Swinburne, Keats, and Blake as well as Shelley, were themselves synesthetic, concluding that there was little evidence suggesting they were. Nevertheless, investigations of synesthesia in literature sometimes still try to answer this question (e.g., Scullion and Treby 2010).

Inspiration for the question apparently began in the nineteenth century, with Charles Baudelaire's poem *Correspondances* [*Correspondences*], in which "Les parfums, les couleurs et les sons se répondent" ["Perfumes, colors, sounds correspond"], and, more importantly, with Arthur Rimbaud's famous sonnet on "Voyelles" ["Vowels"], which begins, "A noir, E blanc, I rouge, U vert, O bleu: voyelles, /Je dirai quelque jour vos naissances latentes" ["A black, E white, I red, U green, O blue: vowels, /Some day shall I speak of your secret birth"]. A half century later, Héraut (1934) identified a possible source of Rimbaud's colored vowels: the spelling book that the poet had used as a child, in which the vowels appeared in just these colors—a finding that leaves open the question whether Rimbaud simply remembered the colors of the letters, or whether they might have been the associative source for strong synesthesia, given evidence that specific environmental stimuli may serve as the source of strong grapheme-color synesthesia (Witthoft and Winawer 2006; see also Simner et al. 2009).

As Erhardt-Siebold (1932) remarked:

> Not with every sound does the poet really see a distinct color, but the impressions evocated by the sound or sounds reminds the poet of a similar impression called forth by color. He does not see but he thinks colors. In life, impressions are not confined to one of our senses, but generally crowd in upon several senses and are blended. Memory then cannot differentiate...a perfume can recall an optic impression, the touch of the soft spring wind...a recollection of sweet spring-scents. (581)

Erhardt-Siebold is speaking here about contiguity as much as resemblance, suggesting, as noted earlier, that synesthetic metaphors may combine sensations that previously arose contiguously (see also Ullmann 1942b).

As noted earlier, contiguity and resemblance are long-standing psychological principles of association, and these principles parallel the rhetorical categories of metonymy
and metaphor (Wellek and Warren 1956). Little has been written of cross-modal metonymy, although Ullmann (1957) has interpreted poetic lines that seem synesthetically
metaphorical as being metonymic. Given the mounting evidence for the role of experience in general and for associative learning in particular in the development of strong
synesthesia (in, e.g., grapheme-color synesthesia and word-flavor synesthesia; Simner
and Haywood 2009; Simner et al. 2009), it is plausible to hypothesize that strong synesthesia and weak synesthesia both reflect, each in its own way, the outcome of processes
that combine associations arising from contiguity with associations based in intrinsic
resemblances. Simner and Haywood's (2009) studies of the associative basis for strong
word-flavor synesthesia, for example, imply a metonymic structure.

In a series of seminal studies, Ullmann (1942a 1943, 1945, 1957) examined the use of
synesthetic metaphors in several English, American, French, and Hungarian poets,
including Keats, Byron, Gautier, and Longfellow, focusing on an exhaustive statistical
analysis of the transfers of meanings from one sense modality to another. One outcome
of Ullmann's analyses was a marked asymmetry in the relative frequencies of auditory-
visual metaphors: metaphors in which sound events take on visual meanings greatly
outnumber metaphors in which visual events take on auditory meanings. A reader of
the poetry of Longfellow, for example, is much more likely to come across metaphors
such as "A voice fell, like a falling star" (*Excelsior*) or "Your name is ever green in Alcalá"
(*The Spanish Student*), than metaphors such as "Like the swell of some sweet tune, /
Morning rises into noon" (*Maidenhood*). These examples come from Ullmann (1942a,
224). Similar statistical results appear in Day's (1996) tabulations of synesthetic metaphors in various English texts.

Although poetry contains many notable auditory-visual metaphors, the statistical analyses show these to be in the minority. Indeed, Ullmann (1945, 1957) concluded
that, within the realm of synesthetic metaphors in nineteenth-century poetry, tactile
qualities are most likely to be applied to other modalities, and hearing is most likely to
receive non-auditory qualities—hence the most commonly found metaphoric transfers
are from touch to hearing. Inspired to seek broad laws of semantics, laws that are panchronistic, like those of physics, Ullmann (1945) suggested a directional law of synesthetic metaphorical transfer, whereby "the majority of transfers are directed from lower
towards higher levels of the sensorium" (813), with touch, taste, and smell designated
lower, vision and hearing higher. Because vision appears at the top of the hierarchy,
however, the greater frequency of vision-to-hearing metaphors compared to hearing-
to-vision metaphors is anomalous—an outcome that Ullmann (1957) attributes to the
relative paucity of terms that are available to describe sounds, compared to the relative
abundance of terms for vision.

Closely related to Ullmann's panchronistic principle is the directional scheme that
Williams (1976) developed on the basis of his diachronic (historical) analysis of the
ways that the meanings of English-language adjectives changed over the past millen-
nium. In Williams's scheme, most changes in meaning went upward—from touch to

taste, color, and sound; from taste to smell and sound; and from sound to color and color to sound. Williams noted the rough resemblance of his principle to Ullmann's. The findings of both Williams and Ullmann bear on the issue of polysemy, the multiple meanings that many words develop. Williams notes that "bitter derives from [the Anglo-Saxon] *bitan*, 'to bite,' a tactile-associated word" (1976, 475), its meaning transferring later to taste. The original somatosensory meanings of "bitter," as sharp and intense, are especially appropriate, therefore, to expressions such as "bitter cold," perhaps not originally a synesthetic expression at all; it dates from the Elizabethan era, when Shakespeare's "freeze, freeze though bitter sky" (*As You Like It*, II: vii) was surely fresh and original. Bitter is both biting and unpleasant, and both qualities are doubtless pertinent, for example, to understanding expressions such as the "great and exceedingly bitter cry" of *Exodus* (27: 34).

The statistical tendencies first described by Ullmann were subsequently reported also in poetry in Hungarian (Dombi Erzsébet 1974), Chinese (Yu 1992), Hebrew (Shen and Cohen 1998), and Indonesian (Shen and Gil 2008), and in contemporary Chinese fiction (Yu 2003) (for a partial dissent, see Bretones-Callejas 2001 and, for detailed and thoughtful analyses, see Cacciari 1998, 2008). As Cacciari wrote:

> The sense directionality proposed by the taxonomic approach basically reflects the differential relevance and reliability that most of the western culture has attributed to the knowledge obtained from the sense organs. Unsurprisingly, it almost perfectly mirrors the senses hierarchy of Aristotle that ordered the intellectual relevance of the senses starting from sight, followed by hearing, olfaction, taste, and touch. (2008, 428)

Ullmann (e.g., 1943, 1957) sought to characterize his putative semantic laws and principles as ones that pertain to linguistics, without reducing these to principles of psychology. On the other hand, it is obvious that language—which is to say, human verbal behavior—is the outcome of processes that may be described at various mechanistic levels, including those of neurophysiology and cognition, making it plausible to ask whether and how cognitive processes, for example, might account for Ullmann's generalizations, to the extent that they are accurate.

Shen and his colleagues have sought to account for the directionality reported by Ullmann and others in the mapping of cross-modal metaphors within poetry (Shen 1995; Shen and Aisenman 2008; Shen and Cohen 1998; Shen and Gil 2008). Arguing that the directionality is virtually universal across languages, cultures, and historical genres, Shen proposes that the metaphorical transfers from lower to higher sense modalities reflect the mappings of more accessible concepts onto less accessible ones—a view that Shen grounds in Gestalt notions of figural "goodness." According to Gestalt theory, stimuli that are simple and regular (e.g., symmetric) are relatively easy to perceive; in Shen's adaptation of the argument, metaphors can illuminate concepts that are otherwise difficult or inaccessible through concepts that are simpler and more accessible. Shen takes as support for this contention his experimental results indicating that comprehension increases when conceptual structures are used more often (Shen and Cohen 1998) and that lower-to-higher structures are judged to be more natural than the reverse, are easier to recall, and are easier to contextualize (Shen and Aisenman 2008). Shen's approach seems plausible enough, although it calls for more thorough analysis of the underlying cognitive processes.

By implication, Shen's theory treats synesthetic metaphor as part and parcel of ordinary mechanisms of cognition, an approach at the heart of Yu's (1995, 2003, 2004) theory of conceptual metaphor. In Yu view, poetic metaphors, although often elaborate and uncommon, nevertheless rely on the same mechanisms that underlie the construction and understanding of metaphors found in everyday discourse. Thus, for example, Yu (2003) analyzed the unusual synesthetic metaphors of the contemporary Chinese fiction writer Mo Yan and found that they largely conformed to Ullmann's and Williams's pattern of directionality. Although Yu does not describe in detail the processes that underlie directionality, his broad approach relies heavily on the notion, discussed later, that characterizes meaning and metaphor in general, and synesthetic metaphor in particular, in terms of embodiment (see also Cacciari 2008). The basic point was made by Lakoff and Johnson (1980): that meanings derive importantly from bodily experiences. This notion is central to research on embodied cognition, which sees mind as inextricably related to body, with cognition, including metaphor, being to a great extent concrete and based on physical interactions with the world (see Gibbs 2006; Gibbs, Lima, and Francozo 2004).

WEAK SYNESTHESIA: EMBODIMENT AND EMOTION

Current theories of embodied cognition (e.g., Clark 1997; Wilson 2002) may provide a fruitful framework for understanding metaphor in general (Gibbs 2006; Gibbs, Lima, and Francozo 2004) and synesthetic metaphor and weak synesthesia more explicitly (Yu 1995, 2003; see also Cytowic 2002; Modell, 1997). As noted earlier, these theories treat mind as embedded in body, making the body an indispensable component when considering how mental life emerges from action and interaction with the environment. As Lakoff and Johnson (1980) noted, many common metaphors use body states as their vehicles, as in "weighed down by responsibilities." Recall Nabokov's (1949) observation that his letter-color synesthesia seemed to arise from motor acts involved in producing the spoken letters. In a related vein, Mesz, Trevisan, and Sigman (2011) asked trained musicians to improvise on the basis of the taste words "sweet," "sour," "salty," and "bitter," finding consistent patterns in the improvisations ("bitter" associated with low pitch and legato, "salty" with staccato, "sour" with high pitch and dissonance ones, and "sweet" with consonance). Gibbs, Lima, and Francozo (2004) recount the ways that people use hunger as a vehicle for thinking about and reporting desires, as in various expressions about the "hunger" for love and lust, and Gibbs (2006) describes the role that simulated bodily activity may play in conceptualizing metaphors, as in "grasping" an idea. Further, body states and reactions are central to emotion. If cognition is rooted substantially in bodily activity, then it would be plausible to look for the ways that weak synesthesia may emerge from a nexus of affective and motor as well as perceptual responses to sensory stimulation. Many of these processes are incorporated within Seitz's (2005) theory, which proposes four fundamental types of metaphor, involving mappings that are perceptual–perceptual, cross-modal, movement–movement, and perceptual–affective.

Affect is often a notable characteristic of both weak and strong synesthesia. In this regard, Ward (2004) reports a case study of an individual in whom emotions produced strong synesthetic colors. Both weak synesthesia and strong synesthesia have long been associated with affective states. As William Butler Yeats remarked:

> All sounds, all colours, all forms, either because of their preordained energies or because of long association, evoke indefinable and yet precise emotions, or, as I prefer to think, call down among us certain disembodied powers, whose footsteps over our hearts we call emotions; and when sound, and colour, and form are in a musical relation, a beautiful relation to one another, they become as it were one sound, one colour, one form, and evoke an emotion that is made out of their distinct evocations and yet is one emotion. (1903, 243)

When asked to match moods and colors to short orchestral excerpts, people associate tender and more leisurely music with lighter colors and more solemn and sad musical excerpts with darker colors (Odbert, Karwoski, and Eckerson 1942; see also Lehman 1972). Light, saturated colors are judged happier (and "showier") than darker, less saturated colors (Wright and Rainwater 1962; see also D'Andrade and Egan 1974). Barbiere, Vidal, and Zellner (2007) found that songs judged as "happy" and "sad" were generally assigned bright and gray colors, respectively, leading the authors to infer that emotional responses underlie music-color correspondence. Tones are judged happier and brighter when they are high in pitch rather than low, played in an ascending rather than descending series, and played at a fast tempo rather than slow (Collier and Hubbard 2001a, 2001b; see also Hevner 1936, 1937a; Horstmann 2010).

A possible link between emotion and synesthesia may come through what Werner (1957) called *physiognomic perception*, the relatively undifferentiated affective and expressive qualities of perceptual experience, as when we see a willow tree as "sad" (see Schlessinger 1980). Results of Lindauer (1990) show, for example, that Köhler's (1947) takete shape is physiognomically more aggressive and tense as well as synesthetically brighter and smaller than the maluma shape.

Three-quarters of a century ago, Börnstein (1936) proposed that stimulation in all sense modalities leads to general physiological responses that include changes in muscle tonicity. Equivalent motor excitation in different modalities might serve as a source of cross-sensory correspondence. Börnstein's hypothesis found its home in the work of Heinz Werner, who pointed to the significance of physiognomic perception as he developed his sensory-tonic theory of perception (Werner and Wapner 1949, 1952). In a series of experiments, Werner, Wapner, and colleagues catalogued a wide range of multisensory interactions involving muscular tone, muscular activity, and body orientation. For example, in darkness, a loud sound presented to one ear or electrical stimulation to one side of the neck has an effect on perceived verticality that is equivalent to the effect produced by shifting the orientation of a visible rod from the vertical (Wapner, Werner, and Chandler 1951). This finding suggests a functional equivalence in bodily responses to visual, auditory, and proprioceptive stimulation.

Finally in this regard, there is the intriguing evidence offered by Clynes (1973, 1975), who reported that when people are instructed to express an emotion, such as love or grief, by pressing a finger on a response key, they create a regular and reliable pattern of pressure that is characteristic of each emotion—which Clynes called an *essential* or *sentic form*. He further argued that emotions constitute the underlying spatiotemporal patterns of activity manifested in the central nervous system, and therefore also realizable through patterned stimulation in various modalities, especially hearing (e.g., Clynes and Nettheim 1982).

Despite reports of failures to replicate some of Clynes's findings (Nettelbeck, Henderson, and Willson 1989; Trussoni, O'Malley, and Barton 1988), a more recent line of investigation provides new evidence that specific patterns of tactile stimulation can characterize specific emotions. Hertenstein and his colleagues have shown in several studies that emotions can be recognized by being touched on the arm by another person or by watching one person being touched by another (e.g., Hertenstein et al. 2006, 2009). For example, sympathy is associated with stroking and patting, disgust with pushing—although the process of communication can depend on the genders of the dyadic pair (Hertenstein and Keltner 2011). These observations speak to a possible role for *empathy* in some forms of weak synesthesia, as suggested by empathy's role in other reported examples of secondary sensory experiences—in mirror-touch synesthesia (e.g., Banissy and Ward 2007), in empathic pain (e.g., Jackson, Meltzoff, and Decety 2005), and in the couvade syndrome, where partners report experiencing the symptoms of pregnant women (e.g., Lipkin and Lamb 1982) (see Marks 2011).

CONCLUSION

The sources of weak synesthesia are manifold: some forms of weak synesthesia appear to be unlearned, others learned. When learned, some are learned more or less universally, others culturally or idiosyncratically. A constellation of sensory, motor, perceptual, emotional, and cognitive processes can contribute to weak synesthesia, which pervades both perception and language. Weak synesthesia reveals itself most notably through cross-modal resemblances and their expression through language—in the perception of cross-modal similarities and in the production and understanding of cross-modal (synesthetic) metaphors. It is likely that many, perhaps most, cross-modal similarities originate in perception proper—whether intrinsic to sensory coding or learned through associated experiences—and subsequently become available to linguistic processes, although, to be sure, it is possible that, in the spirit of Locke's blind man coming to know about the color scarlet, one could learn about cross-modal correspondences through language.

Weak synesthesia in language reveals itself in and through synesthetic metaphors. Often conventional, especially those of everyday speech, synesthetic metaphors can be familiar and overwrought, though rarely overcast or etherized. The evidence that pre-school-aged children can perceive similarities across sensory domains and comprehend some synesthetic metaphors suggests that weak (or even strong) synesthesia may play a central role in the development of metaphor comprehension and metaphor creation more generally—as several investigators have suggested or implied (e.g., Cytowic 2002; Marks 1978; Ramachandran and Hubbard 2001; see also Cacciari 2008; Ramachandran and Brang, Chapter 48, this volume). Metaphors can extend and expand meanings, and extensions of meaning are fundamental to thinking (Langer 1967). "The proliferation of resemblances extends an object," wrote Wallace Stevens (1951, 78). Young children find cross-sensory metaphors relatively easy to understand and to create, as though early in life they have discovered a metaphorical imperative, seeking out ways of interacting with the world and comprehending it. Synesthetic meanings are dynamic, again in the poet Stevens's words, "desiring the exhilarations of changes . . . / The motive for metaphor . . . / The A B C of being" (*The Motive for Metaphor*, 13–16). Driven largely through cross-modal perceptual resemblances, synesthetic metaphors are noteworthy for their succinctness, which makes them potent and cogent, enabling them to serve as a cognitively dense shorthand, a system of tweets that pre-dates Twitter, exposing resemblances and begetting them.

REFERENCES

Alexander, Kenneth R., and Michael S. Shansky. 1976. Influence of hue, value, and chroma on the perceived heaviness of colors. *Perception & Psychophysics* 19:72–74.

Asher, Julian E., Janine A. Lamb, Denise Brocklebank, Jean-Baptiste Cazier, Elena Maestrini, Laura Addis, Mallika Sen, Simon Baron-Cohen, and Anthony P. Monaco. 2009. A whole-genome scan and fine-mapping linkage study of auditory-visual synesthesia reveals evidence of linkage to chromosomes 2q24, 5q33, 6p12, and 12p12. *American Journal of Human Genetics* 84:279–285.

Ballester, Jordi, Hervé Abdi, Jennifer Langlois, Dominique Peyron, and Dominique Valentin. 2009. The odor of colors: Can wine experts distinguish the odors of white, red, and rosé wines? *Chemosensory Perception* 2:203–213.

Banissy, Michael J., and Jamie Ward. 2007. Mirror-touch synesthesia is linked with empathy. *Nature Neuroscience* 10:815–817.

Barbiere, J. Michael, Ana Vidal, and Debra A. Zellner. 2007. The color of music: Correspondence through emotion. *Empirical Studies of the Arts* 25:193–208.

Barnett, Kylie J., Ciara Finucane, Julien E. Asher, Gary Bargary, Aiden P. Corvin, Fiona N. Newell, and Kevin J. Mitchell. 2008. Familial patterns and the origins of individual differences in synaesthesia. *Cognition* 106:871–893.

Békésy, Georg von. 1957. Neural volleys and the similarity between some sensations produced by tones and by skin vibration. *Journal of the Acoustical Society of America* 29:1059–1069.

———. 1959. Similarities between hearing and the skin senses. *Psychological Review* 66:1–22.

Belkin, Kira, Robyn Martin, Sarah E. Kemp, and Avery N. Gilbert. 1997. Auditory pitch as a perceptual analogue to odor quality. *Psychological Science* 8:340–342.

Bentley, Madison, and Edith J. Varon. 1933. An accessory study of 'phonetic symbolism.' *American Journal of Psychology* 45:76–86.

Börnstein, Walter. 1936. On the functional relations of the sense organs to one another and to the organism as a whole. *Journal of General Psychology* 15:117–131.

Boring, E. G., and Stevens, S. S. 1936. The nature of tonal brightness. *Proceedings of the National Academy of Sciences of the United States of America* 22:514–521.

Braaten, Richard F. 1993. Synesthetic correspondence between visual location and auditory pitch in infants. Paper presented at the Thirty-Fourth Annual Meeting of the Psychonomic Society, Washington, DC, November.

Bretones-Callejas, Carmen M. 2001. Synaesthetic metaphors in English. *ICSI Technical Report*, 8. <http://www.icsi.berkeley.edu/techreports>.

Bullough, E. 1907. On the apparent heaviness of colours. *British Journal of Psychology* 2:111–152.

Cacciari, Cristina. 1998. Why do we speak metaphorically? Reflections on the functions of metaphor in discourse and reasoning. In *Figurative Language and Thought*, ed. Albert N. Katz, Cristina Cacciari, Raymond W. Gibbs, Jr., and Mark Turner, 119–157. Oxford: Oxford University Press.

——. 2008. Crossing the senses in metaphoric language. *The Cambridge Handbook of Metaphor and Thought*, ed. Raymond W. Gibbs, Jr., 425–443. Cambridge: Cambridge University Press.

Cacciari, Cristina, Manfredo Massironi, and Paola Corradini. 2004. When color names are used metaphorically: The role of linguistic and chromatic information. *Metaphor and Symbol* 19:169–190.

Calkins, Mary W. 1893. A statistical study of pseudo-chromesthesia and mental-forms. *American Journal of Psychology* 5:439–464.

Cheney, Colin. 2010. Decline of the North American songbird. *Here Be Monsters*, 39–40. Athens, GA: University of Georgia Press.

Clark, Andy. 1997. *Being There: Putting Brain, Body, and World Together Again*. Cambridge, MA: MIT Press.

Clynes, Manfred. 1973. Sentography: Dynamic forms of communication of emotion and qualities. *Computers in Biology and Medicine* 3:119–130.

——. 1975. Communication and generation of emotion through essentic form. In *Emotions: Their Parameters and Measurement*, ed. Lennart Levi, 561–602. New York: Raven Press.

Clynes, Manfred, and Nigel Nettheim. 1982. The living quality of music: Neurobiologic patterns of communicating feeling. In *Music, Mind and Brain: The Neuropsychology of Music*, ed. Manfred Clynes, 47–82. New York: Plenum.

Collier, William G., and Timothy L. Hubbard. 2001a. Judgments of happiness, brightness, speed and tempo change of auditory stimuli varying in pitch and tempo. *Psychomusicology* 17:36–55.

——. 2001b. Musical scales and happiness/awkwardness evaluations: Effects of pitch, direction, and scale mode. *American Journal of Psychology* 114:355–375.

Crisinel, Anne-Sylvie, and Charles Spence. 2010. As bitter as a trombone: Synesthetic correspondences in nonsynesthetes between tastes/flavors and musical notes. *Attention, Perception, & Psychophysics* 72:1994–2002.

Cuskley, Christine, and Simon Kirby. Synaesthesia, cross-modality & language evolution. In *Oxford Handbook of Synesthesia*, ed. Julia Simner and Edward M. Hubbard, 869–899. Oxford : Oxford University Press.

Cytowic, Richard E. 2002. *Synesthesia: A Union of the Senses*. 2nd ed. Cambridge, MA: MIT Press.

Czurda, Margarete. 1953. Beziehungen zwischen Lautcharakter und Sinneseindrucken [Relations between sound characteristics and sensory impressions]. *Wiener Archiv für Psychologie, Psychiatrie, und Neurologie* 3:73–84.

D'Andrade, R., and Egan, M. 1974. The colors of emotions. *American Ethnologist* 1:49–63.

Davis, R. 1961. The fitness of names to drawings: A cross-cultural study in Tanganyika. *British Journal of Psychology* 52:259–268.

Day, Sean A.. 1996. Synaesthesia and synaesthetic metaphors. *Psyche* 2(32). <http://www.the-assc.org/files/assc/2358.pdf>.

———. 2013. Synesthesia: A first-person perspective. In *The Oxford Handbook of Synesthesia*, ed. Julia Simner and Edward M. Hubbard, 903–923. Oxford: Oxford University Press.

Delattre, Pierre, Alvin M. Liberman, Franklin S. Cooper, and Louis J. Gerstman. 1952. An experimental study of the acoustic determinants of vowel color: Observations on one- and two-formant vowels synthesized from spectrographic patterns. *Word* 8:195–210.

Demattè, M. Luisa, Daniel Sanabria, and Charles Spence. 2006. Cross-modal associations between odors and colors. *Chemical Senses* 31:531–538.

Dixon, Mike J., Daniel Smilek, and Philip M. Merikle. 2004. Not all synaesthetes are created equal: Distinguishing between projector and associator synaesthetes. *Cognitive, Affective, & Behavioral Neuroscience* 4:335–343.

Dombi Erzsébet, P. 1974. Synaesthesia and poetry. *Poetics* 3(3):23–44.

Downey, June E. 1912. Literary synesthesia. *Journal of Philosophy, Psychology and Scientific Methods* 9:490–498.

Erhardt-Siebold, Erika von. 1932. Harmony of the senses in English, German, and French Romanticism. *Publications of the Modern Language Association* 47:577–592.

Forceville, Charles J., and Eduardo Urios-Aparisi, eds. 2009. *Multimodal Metaphor*. Berlin: Mouton de Gruyter.

Frank, Robert A., and Jennifer Byram. 1988. Taste-smell interactions are tastant and odorant dependent. *Chemical Senses* 13:445–455.

Galton, Francis. 1880. Visualised numerals. *Nature* 21:252–256, 494–495.

Gardner, Howard. 1974. Metaphors and modalities: How children project polar adjectives onto diverse domains. *Child Development* 45:84–91.

Gibbs, Raymond W. Jr. 1984. Literal meaning and psychological theory. *Cognitive Science* 8:275–304.

———. 2006. Metaphor interpretation as embodied simulation. *Mind and Language* 21:434–458.

Gibbs, Raymond W. Jr., Paula Lenz Costa Lima, and Edson Francozo. 2004. Metaphor is grounded in embodied experience. *Journal of Pragmatics* 36:1189–1210.

Gilbert, Avery N., Robyn Martin, and Sarah E. Kemp. 1996. Cross-modal correspondence between vision and olfaction: The color of smells. *American Journal of Psychology* 109:335–351.

Glicksohn, Joseph, Orna Salinger, and Anat Roychman. 1992. An exploratory study of syncretic experience: Eidetics, synaesthesia and absorption. *Perception* 21:637–642.

Glucksberg, Sam, and Boaz Keysar. 1990. Understanding metaphorical comparisons: Beyond similarity. *Psychological Review* 97:3–18.

Grammont, Maurice. 1930. La psychologie et la phonétique [Psychology and phonetics]. *Journal de Psychologie Normal et Pathologique* 27:544–613.

Guirao, Miguelina, and S. S. Stevens. 1964. Measurement of auditory density. *Journal of the Acoustical Society of America* 36:1176–1182.

Hartshorne, Charles. 1934. *The Philosophy and Psychology of Sensation*. Chicago, IL: University of Chicago Press.

Héraut, Henri. 1934. Du nouveau sur Rimbaud: La solution de l'énigme des 'Voyelles' [New on Rimbaud: The solution to the mystery of the sonnet of the 'Vowels']. *Nouvelle Revue Française* 43:602–608.

Hertenstein, Matthew J., Rachel Holmes, Margaret McCullough, and Dacher Keltner. 2009. The communication of emotion via touch. *Emotion* 9:566–573.

Hertenstein, Matthew J., and Dacher Keltner. 2011. Gender and the communication of emotion via touch. *Sex Roles* 64:70–80.

Hertenstein, Matthew J., Dacher Keltner, Betsy App, Brittany A. Bulleit, and Ariany R. Jaskolka. 2006. Touch communicates distinct emotions. *Emotion* 6:528–533.

Hevner, Kate. 1936. Experimental studies of the elements of expression in music. *American Journal of Psychology* 47:246–268.

———. 1937a. The affective value of pitch and tempo in music. *American Journal of Psychology* 49:621–630.

———. 1937b. An experimental study of the affective value of sounds in poetry. *American Journal of Psychology* 49:419–434.

Hinton, Leanne, Johanna Nichols, and John J. Ohala, eds. 1994. *Sound Symbolism*. Cambridge: Cambridge University Press.

Holland, Morris K., and Michael Wertheimer. 1964. Some physiognomic aspects of naming, or, maluma and takete revisited. *Perceptual and Motor Skills* 119:111–117.

Hornbostel, Erich M. von. 1925. Die Einheit der Sinne. *Melos, Zeitschrift für Musik*, 4:290–297. (English translation: 1927.The unity of the senses. *Psyche* 7:83–89).

———. 1934. Über Geruchshelligkeit [On odor brightness]. *Pflügers Archiv für die Gesamte Physiognomie der Menschen und der Tiere* 227:517–538.

Horstmann, Gernot. 2010. Tone-affect compatibility with affective stimuli and affective responses. *Quarterly Journal of Experimental Psychology* 63:2239–2250.

Hume, David. 1739. *A Treatise of Human Nature: Being an Attempt to Introduce the Experimental Method into Moral Subjects, Vol. I. Of the Understanding*. London: John Noon.

Hunt, Harry T. 2005. Synaesthesia, metaphor and consciousness. *Journal of Consciousness Studies* 12:6–45.

Jackson, Philip L., Andrew N. Meltzoff, and Jean Decety. 2005. How do we perceive the pain of others? A window into the neural processes involved in empathy. *NeuroImage* 24:771–779.

Kaden, Stanley E., Seymour Wapner, and Heinz Werner. 1955. Studies in physiognomic perception: II. Effect of directional dynamics of pictured objects and of words on the position of the apparent horizon. *Journal of Psychology* 39:61–70.

Karwoski, Theodore F., and Henry S. Odbert. 1938. Color-music. *Psychological Monographs* 50 (2, Serial No. 222).

Karwoski, Theodore F., Henry S. Odbert, and Charles E. Osgood. 1942. Studies in synesthetic thinking. II. The role of form in visual responses to music. *Journal of General Psychology* 26:199–222.

Kemp, Sarah E., and Avery N. Gilbert. 1997. Odor intensity and color lightness are correlated sensory dimensions. *American Journal of Psychology* 110:35–46.

Koch, Kenneth. 1970. *Wishes, Lies, Dreams: Teaching Children to Write Poetry*. New York: Random House.

Köhler, Wolfgang. 1929. *Gestalt Psychology*. New York: Liveright.

———. 1941. On the nature of associations. *Proceedings of the American Philosophical Society* 84:489–502.

———. 1947. *Gestalt Psychology*. 2nd ed. New York: Liveright.

Koriat, Asher, and Ilia Levy. 1977. The symbolic implications of vowels and of their orthographic representations in two natural languages. *Journal of Psycholinguistic Research* 6:93–103.

Lakoff, George, and Mark Johnson 1980. *Metaphors We Live By*. Chicago, IL: University of Chicago Press.

Langer, Susanne K. 1967. *Mind: An Essay on Human Feeling*. Baltimore, MD: Johns Hopkins Press.

Lehman, Richard S. 1972. A multivariate model of synesthesia. *Multivariate Behavioral Research* 7:403–439.

Lewkowicz, David J., and Gerald Turkewitz. 1980. Cross-modal equivalence in early infancy: Auditory-visual intensity matching. *Developmental Psychology* 16:597–607.

Lindauer, Martin S. 1990. The meanings of the physiognomic stimuli taketa and maluma. *Bulletin of the Psychonomic Society* 28:47–50.

Lipkin, Mack Jr., and Gerri S. Lamb. 1982. The couvade syndrome: An epidemiologic study. *Archives of Internal Medicine* 96:509–511.

Locke, John. 1690. *An Essay Concerning Humane Understanding*. London: Thos. Bassett.

Marks, Lawrence E. 1974. On associations of light and sound: The mediation of pitch, loudness, and brightness. *American Journal of Psychology* 87:173–188.

———. 1975. On colored-hearing synesthesia: Cross-modal translations of sensory dimensions. *Psychological Bulletin* 82:303–331.

———. 1978. *The Unity of the Senses: Interrelations Among the Modalities*. New York: Academic Press.

———. 1982a. Bright sneezes and dark coughs, loud sunlight and soft moonlight. *Journal of Experimental Psychology: Human Perception and Performance* 8:177–193.

———. 1982b. Synesthetic perception and poetic metaphor. *Journal of Experimental Psychology: Human Perception and Performance* 8:15–23.

———. 1989. On cross-modal similarity: The perceptual structure of pitch, loudness, and brightness. *Journal of Experimental Psychology: Human Perception and Performance* 15:586–602.

———. 1996. On perceptual metaphors. *Metaphor and Symbolic Activity* 11:39–66.

———. 2000. Synesthesia. In *Varieties of Anomalous Experience: Phenomenological and Scientific Foundations*, ed. Etzel Cardeña, Steven Jay Lynn, and Stanley Krippner, 121–149. Washington, DC: American Psychological Association.

———. 2004. Cross-modal interactions in speeded classification. In *The Handbook of Multisensory Processes*, ed. Gemma Calvert, Charles Spence, and Barry E. Stein, 85–106. Cambridge, MA: MIT Press.

———. 2011. Synesthesia: Then and now. *Intellectica* 55:47–80.

Marks, Lawrence E., and Marc H. Bornstein. 1987. Sensory similarities: Classes, characteristics, and cognitive consequences. In *Cognition and Symbolic Structures: The Psychology of Metaphoric Transformation*, ed. Robert E. Haskell, 49–65. Norwood, NJ: Ablex.

Marks, Lawrence E., Robin J. Hammeal, and Marc H. Bornstein. 1987. Perceiving similarity and comprehending metaphor. *Monographs of the Society for Research in Child Development* 52 (Whole No. 215).

Martino, Gail, and Lawrence E. Marks. 2001. Synesthesia: Strong and weak. *Current Directions in Psychological Science* 10:61–65.

Maurer, Daphne. 1993. Neonatal synaesthesia: Implications for the processing of speech and faces. In *Developmental Neurocognition: Speech and Face Processing in the First Year of Life*, ed. Bénédict de Boysson-Bardies, Scania de Schonen, Peter Jusczyk, Peter McNeilage, and John Morton, 109–124. Dordrecht: Kluwer.

Maurer, Daphne, and Catherine J. Mondloch. 1996. Synesthesia: A stage of normal infancy? In *Fechner Day 96: Proceedings of the 12th meeting of the International Society for Psychophysics*, ed. Sergio C. Masin, 107–112. Padua: ISP.

———. 2005. Neonatal synesthesia: A reevaluation. In *Synesthesia: Perspectives from Cognitive Neuroscience*, ed. Lynn C. Robertson and Noam Sagiv, 193–213. New York: Oxford University Press.

Maurer, Daphne, Thanujeni Pathman, and Catherine J. Mondloch. 2006. The shape of boubas: Sound-shape correspondences in toddlers and adults. *Developmental Science* 9:316–322.

McMurray, Gordon A. 1960. Meaning associated with the phonetic structure of unfamiliar foreign words. *Canadian Journal of Psychology* 14:166–174.

Melara, Robert D., and Lawrence E. Marks. 1990. Processes underlying dimensional interactions: Correspondences between linguistic and nonlinguistic dimensions. *Memory and Cognition* 18:477–495.

Mesz, Bruno, Marcos A. Trevisan, and Mariano Sigman. 2011. The taste of music. *Perception* 40:209–219.

Modell, Arnold H. 1997. The synergy of memory, affects, and metaphor. *Journal of Analytical Psychology* 42:105–117.

Mondloch, Catherine J., and Daphne Maurer. 2004. Do small white balls squeak? Pitch-object correspondences in young children. *Cognitive, Affective, & Behavioral Neuroscience* 4:133–136.

Morgan, George A., Felix E. Goodson, and Thomas Jones. 1975. Age differences in the associations between felt temperatures and color choices. *American Journal of Psychology* 88:125–130.

Morrot, Gil, Frédéric Brochet, and Denis Dubourdieu. 2001. The color of odors. *Brain and Language* 79:309–320.

Mulvenna, Catherine M. 2012. On creativity in synaesthetes: Roles of neural connectivity, cognitive control, and perceptual correspondence. Doctoral dissertation, University College London.

Nabokov, Vladimir. 1949. Portrait of my mother. *New Yorker* 27(7):33–37.

Nafe, John P. 1924. An experimental study of the affective qualities. *American Journal of Psychology* 35:507–544.

Nettelbeck, T., C. Henderson, and R. Willson. 1989. Communicating emotion through sound: An evaluation of Clynes' theory of sentics. *Australian Journal of Psychology* 41:25–36.

Newhall, S. M. 1941. Warmth and coolness of colors. *Psychological Record* 4:198–212.

Newman, Stanley S. 1933. Further experiments in phonetic symbolism. *American Journal of Psychology* 45:53–75.

Nuckolls, Janis B. 1999. The case for sound symbolism. *Annual Review of Anthropology* 28:225–252.

O'Boyle, Michael W., and Robert D. Tarte. 1980. Implications for phonetic symbolism: The relationship between pure tones and geometric figures. *Journal of Psycholinguistic Research* 9:535–544.

Odbert, H. S., T. F. Karwoski, and A. B. Eckerson. 1942. Studies synesthetic thinking: I. Musical and verbal associations of color and mood. *Journal of General Psychology* 26:153–173.

Parise, Cesare, and Charles Spence. Audiovisual cross-modal correspondances in the general population. In *The Oxford Handbook of Synesthesia* , ed. Julia Simner and Edward M. Hubbard, 790–815. Oxford : Oxford University Press.

Parise, Cesare, and Charles Spence. Magnitudes, Metaphors and Modalities: A Theory of Magnitude revisited. In *The Oxford Handbook of Synesthesia*, ed. Julia Simner and Edward M. Hubbard, 837–852. Oxford : Oxford University Press.

From Molecules to Metaphor: Outlooks on Synesthesia Research. In *The Oxford Handbook of Synesthesia*, ed. Julia Simner and Edward M. Hubbard, 999–1021. Oxford : Oxford University Press.

Osgood, Charles E., George J. Suci, and Percy H. Tannenbaum. 1957. *The Measurement of Meaning*. Urbana, IL: University of Illinois Press.

Ramachandran, Vilayanur S. (2011). *The Tell-Tale Brain: A Neuroscientist's Quest for What Makes Us Human.* New York: Norton.

Ramachandran, Vilayanur S., and Edward M. Hubbard. 2001. Synaesthesia—a window into perception, thought and language. *Journal of Consciousness Studies* 8:3–34.

Riggs, Lorrin A., and Theodore Karwoski. 1934. Synaesthesia. *British Journal of Psychology* 25:29–41.

Robinson, Edward S. 1927. The similarity factor in 'retroaction'. *American Journal of Psychology* 39:297–312.

Rogers, Susan K., and Abraham S. Ross. 1975. A cross-cultural test of the Maluma-Takete phenomenon. *Perception* 4:105–108.

Sapir, Edward. 1929. A study of phonetic symbolism. *Journal of Experimental Psychology* 12:225–239.

Schifferstein, Hendrik N. J., and Inge Tanudjaja. 2004. Visualising fragrances through colours: The mediating role of emotions. *Perception* 33:1249–1266.

Schlessinger, Louis B. 1980. Physiognomic perception: Empirical and theoretical perspectives. *Genetic Psychology Monographs* 101:71–97.

Scullion, Val, and Marion Treby. 2010. Creative synaesthesia in E. T. A. Hoffmann's *Ritter Gluck*. *European Review* 18:239–262.

Seitz, Jay A. 2005. The neural, evolutionary, developmental, and bodily basis of metaphor. *New Ideas in Psychology* 23:74–95.

Shen, Yeshayahu. 1995. Cognitive constraints on directionality in the semantic structure of poetic vs. non-poetic metaphors. *Poetics* 23:255–274.

Shen, Yeshayahu, and Ravid Aisenman. 2008. 'Heard melodies are sweet, but those unheard are sweeter': Synaesthetic metaphors and cognition. *Language and Literature* 17:107–121.

Shen, Yeshayahu, and Michal Cohen. 1998. How come silence is sweet but sweetness is not silent: A cognitive account of directionality in poetic synaesthesia. *Language and Literature* 7:123–140.

Shen, Yeshayahu, and David Gil. 2008. Sweet fragrances from Indonesia: A universal principle governing directionality in synaesthetic metaphors. In *New Beginnings in Literary Studies*, ed. Jan Auracher and Willie van Peer, 49–71. Cambridge: Cambridge Scholars Publishing.

Simner, Julia, Jenny Harrold, Harriet Creed, Louise Monro, and Louise Foulkes. 2009. Early detection of markers for synaesthesia in childhood populations. *Brain* 132:57–64.

Simner, Julia, and Sarah L. Haywood. 2009. Tasty non-words and neighbours: The cognitive roots of lexical-gustatory synaesthesia. *Cognition* 110:171–181.

Simner, Julia, and Emma Holenstein. 2007. Ordinal linguistic personification as a variant of synesthesia. *Journal of Cognitive Neuroscience* 19:694–703.

Simner, Julia, Jamie Ward, Monika Lanz, Ashok Jansari, Krist Noonan, Louise Glover, and David A. Oakley. 2005. Non-random associations of graphemes to colours in synaesthetic and non-synaesthetic populations. *Cognitive Neuropsychology* 22:1069–1085.

Simpson, Ray H., Marian Quinn, and David P. Ausubel. 1956. Synesthesia in children: Association of colors with pure tone frequencies. *Journal of Genetic Psychology* 89:95–103.

Smilek, Daniel, Kelly A. Malcolmson, Jonathan S. A. Carriere. Meghan Eller, Donna Kwan, and Michael Reynolds. 2007. When '3' is a jerk and 'E' is a king: Personifying inanimate objects in synaesthesia. *Journal of Cognitive Neuroscience* 19:981–992.

Smith, Linda B., and Maria D. Sera. 1992. A developmental analysis of the polar structure of dimensions. *Cognitive Psychology* 24:99–142.

Spector, Ferrine, and Daphne Maurer. 2009. Synesthesia: A new approach to understanding the development of perception. *Developmental Psychology* 45:175–189.

Spence, Charles. 2011. Cross-modal correspondences: A tutorial review. *Attention, Perception, & Psychophysics* 73:971–995.

Spence, Charles, and Alberto Gallace. 2011. Tasting shapes and words. *Food Quality and Preference* 22:290–295.

Steen, Carol, and Greta Berman. 2013. Synesthesia and the artistic process. In *The Oxford Handbook of Synesthesia*, ed. Julia Simner and Edward M. Hubbard, 671–691. Oxford: Oxford University Press.

Stevens, Joseph C., Joel D. Mack, and S. S. Stevens. 1960. Growth of sensation on seven continua as measured by force of handgrip. *Journal of Experimental Psychology* 59:60–67.

Stevens, Joseph C., and Lawrence E. Marks. 1965. Cross-modality matching of brightness and loudness. *Proceedings of the National Academy of Sciences of the United States of America* 54:407–411.

Stevens, S. S. 1934a. Are tones spatial? *American Journal of Psychology* 46:145–147.

——. 1934b. The volume and intensity of tones. *American Journal of Psychology* 46:397–408.

Stevens, Wallace. 1951. *The Necessary Angel*. New York: Knopf.

Stevenson, Richard J., Robert A. Boakes, and John Prescott. 1998. Changes in odor sweetness resulting from implicit learning of a simultaneous odor-sweetness association: An example of learned synesthesia. *Learning and Motivation* 29:113–132.

Taylor, Insup Kim. 1963. Phonetic symbolism re-examined. *Psychological Bulletin* 60:200–209.

Taylor, Insup Kim, and Maurice M. Taylor. 1965. Another look at phonetic symbolism. *Psychological Bulletin* 64:413–427.

Trussoni, Steven J., Anthony O'Malley, and Anthony Barton. 1988. Human emotive communication by touch: A modified replication of an experiment by Manfred Clynes. *Perceptual and Motor Skills* 66:419–424.

Tsur, Reuven. 2006. Size-sound symbolism revisited. *Journal of Pragmatics* 38:905–924.

Ullmann, Stephen. 1942a. Metaphors in Longfellow's poetry. *Review of English Studies* 18:219–228.

——. 1942b. The range and mechanism of changes of meaning. *Journal of English and Germanic Philology* 41:46–52.

——. 1943. Laws of language and laws of nature. *Modern Language Review* 38:328–338.

——. 1945. Romanticism and synaesthesia: A comparative study of sense transfer in Keats and Byron. *Publications of the Modern Language Association* 60:811–827.

——. 1957. *The Principles of Semantics*. 2nd ed. Glasgow: Jackson.

Ultan, Russell. 1978. Sound-size symbolism. In *Universals of Human Language. Vol. 2. Phonology*, ed. Joseph H. Greenberg, 525–568. Stanford, CA: Stanford University Press.

Van Campen, Cretien. 2013. Synesthesia in the visual arts. In *The Oxford Handbook of Synesthesia*, ed. Julia Simner and Edward M. Hubbard, 631–646. Oxford: Oxford University Press.

Wagner, Sheldon, Ellen Winner, Dante Ciccetti, and Howard Gardner. 1981. Metaphorical mapping in human infants. *Child Development* 52:728–731.

Walker, Peter, J. Gavin Bremner, Uschi Mason, Jo Spring, Karen Mattock, Alan Slater, and Scott P. Johnson. 2010. Preverbal infants' sensitivity to synaesthetic cross-modality correspondences. *Psychological Science* 21:21–25.

Walsh, Vincent. 2003. A theory of magnitude: Common cortical metrics of time, space, and quantity. *Trends in Cognitive Science* 7:483–488.

Wapner, Seymour, Heinz Werner, and Kenneth A. Chandler. 1951. Experiments on sensory-tonic field theory of perception. I. Effect of extraneous stimulation on the visual perception of verticality. *Journal of Experimental Psychology* 42:341–345.

Ward, Jamie. 2004. Emotionally mediated synaesthesia. *Cognitive Neuropsychology* 21:761–772.

Ward, Jamie, Brett Huckstep, and Elias Tsakanikos. 2006. Sound-colour synaesthesia: To what extent does it use cross-modal mechanisms common to us all? *Cognition* 42:264–280.

Wellek, Rene, and Austin Warren. 1956. *Theory of Literature*. 2nd ed. New York: Harcourt, Brace, and World.

Werner, Heinz. 1957. *Comparative Psychology of Mental Development*. Rev. ed. New York: International Universities Press.

Werner, Heinz, and Seymour Wapner. 1949. Sensory-tonic field theory of perception. *Journal of Personality* 18:88–107.

——. 1952. Toward a general theory of perception. *Psychological Review* 59:324–338.

Wicker, Frank W. 1968. Mapping the intersensory regions of perceptual space. *American Journal of Psychology* 81:178–188.

Williams, Joseph M. 1976. Synaesthetic adjectives: A possible law of semantic change. *Language* 52:461–478.

Willmann, Rudolph R. 1944. An experimental investigation of the creative process in music: The transposability of visual design stimuli to musical themes. *Psychological Monographs* 57 (261):1–76.

Wilson, Margaret. 2002. Six views of embodied cognition. *Psychonomic Bulletin & Review* 9:625–636.

Wissemann, Heinz. 1954. *Untersuchungen zur Onomatopoiie* [Investigations on Onomatopoeia]. Heidelberg: Winter.

Witthoft, Nathan, and Jonathan Winawer. 2006. Synesthetic colors determined by having colored refrigerator magnets in childhood. *Cortex* 42:175–183.

Wright, Benjamin, and Lee Rainwater. 1962. The meanings of colors. *Journal of General Psychology* 67:89–99.

Yeats, W. B. 1903. The symbolism of poetry. *Ideas of Good and Evil*, 237–256. London: A. H. Bullen.

Yu, Ning. 1992. A possible semantic law in synesthetic transfer: Evidence from Chinese. *The Southeastern Conference on Linguistics [SECOL] Review* 16:20–40.

——. 1995. Metaphorical expressions of anger and happiness in English and Chinese. *Metaphor and Symbolic Activity* 10:59–92.

——. 2003. Synesthetic metaphor: A cognitive perspective. *Journal of Literary Semantics* 32:19–34.

——. 2004. The eyes for sight and mind. *Journal of Pragmatics* 36:663–686.

Zellner, Debra A., Amy McGarry, Rachel Mattern-McClory, and Diana Abreu. 2008. Masculinity/femininity of fine fragrances affects color-odor correspondences: A case for cognitions influencing cross-modal correspondences. *Chemical Senses* 33:211–222.

Zellner, Debra A., and Lori A. Whitten. 1999. The effect of color intensity and appropriateness on color-induced odor enhancement. *American Journal of Psychology* 112:585–604.

CHAPTER 39

··

AUDIOVISUAL CROSS-MODAL CORRESPONDENCES IN THE GENERAL POPULATION

··

CESARE PARISE AND CHARLES SPENCE

INTRODUCTION

··

Humans and other animals are equipped with multiple sensory channels with which to perceive the environment that surrounds them. Multiple sources of information concerning the external world and our body can provide us with richer, more robust, and more precise information, ultimately allowing for more adaptive behavior. Think of a dog barking nervously behind a picket fence. Visual and auditory cues both provide useful information about *where* the dog is located *when* it barks. The spatial and temporal properties of the environment (and of the events taking place within it) can be redundantly sensed, though with different levels of precision, via multiple sensory channels, and hence are typically considered as being *amodal* stimulus properties (i.e., non-modality-specific properties, a concept dating back to Aristotle's *sensus communis*). Redundant cues therefore refer to sensory information, often perceived through different sensory channels (though not necessarily through all of them), that refers to the very same property of the physical world. This is the case for the size or the shape of an object, which can be redundantly sensed by vision and touch. Multiple senses, however, also provide complementary (i.e., non-redundant) information. The color of the barking dog in this example can only be perceived visually, while the pitch of the dog's growl can only be sensed auditorily. Being the perceptual correlates of different stimulus properties, color and pitch can therefore be considered as complementary cues (see Green and Angelaki 2010).

Over the course of the last decade or so, there has been a resurgence of research interest in studying the mechanisms by which our brains integrate redundant cues from multiple sensory channels (e.g., see Murray and Wallace 2011; Stein 2012), such as the seen and felt size of an object (Ernst and Banks 2002; Rock and Victor 1964). A growing body of empirical research now demonstrates that the integration of redundant cues about the same physical properties allows humans and other animals to generate more precise and robust combined sensory estimates (Ernst and Bülthoff 2004; Trommershäuser, Landy, and Körding 2011). On the other hand, having multiple complementary cues tuned to different properties of the environment provides non-redundant information about the external environment, and undoubtedly accounts for some of the richness of our sensory experiences.

For more than a century now, scientists have acknowledged the existence of seemingly arbitrary compatibility effects between cross-modal complementary cues even in non-synesthetes (Külpe 1893; Stumpf 1883; for revews, see Marks, Chapter 38, this volume; Spence 2011). Most people, for example, readily associate large objects with low-pitched sounds, while considering it less natural to match them with shrill sounds (Gallace and Spence 2006; P. Walker and Smith 1985; R. Walker 1987). Such observations have led some researchers to hypothesize that all humans are, at least to a certain extent, synesthetic[1] (e.g., Martino and Marks 2001; Mulvenna and Walsh 2006; Rudmin and Cappelli 1983; Simpson, Quinn, and Ausubel 1956; Ward, Huckstep, and Tsakanikos 2006). That said, it is typically asserted by the proponents of such claims that the "strength" of the synesthetic experiences might vary dramatically between individuals. It is, however, important to note that complementary cues are often correlated in the real world. Hence, it might well be argued that rather than constituting a form of "weak" synesthesia, such cross-modal correspondences simply reflect the learnt associations between the features of naturally-occurring multisensory stimuli: Let us now return to our original example, if the nervous dog barking behind the fence happens to be a small Chihuahua, it is very unlikely that his (or her) growls will be deep (i.e., low-pitched)!

We will argue throughout this chapter (and additional views are given elsewhere; e.g., see Simner, Chapter 8, this volume) that there is still in our view *no* convincing evidence to link the phenomena of cross-modal congruency with full-blown cross-modal forms of synesthesia (see also Deroy and Spence, 2013; Spence 2011). We will suggest, for example, that the notion of the inducer and concurrent (respectively, the triggering and the triggered stimuli in synesthetic experiences), so central to any discussion of the phenomenon of sensory synesthesia, does not apply when thinking about the correspondences that affect the perception and performance of non-synesthetes. That is, as yet, there is *no* evidence that cross-modal correspondences have any necessary additional sensory qualia associated with them, as in the case of the consciously-experienced concurrent that is a core part of any definition of sensory synesthesia (see Grossenbacher and

---

[1] Synesthesia, in which stimulation in one sensory modality leads to experience(s) in a second unstimulated sensory modality, mostly involve *modal* properties (Ward 2010). This is the case, for example, with colored-hearing synesthesia, whereby the mere presentation of a sound automatically induces the concurrent conscious perception of a colorful patch of light (Day 2005; Walsh 1996). The fact, therefore, that flavours are sometimes reported as either inducers or concurrents might be taken to suggest that flavour should be considered as a separate sensory modality in addition to taste and smell (both retronasal and orthonasal).

Lovelace 2001; Ward, Chapter 49, this volume; though see Cohen Kadosh and Terhune 2012; Eagleman 2012; Simner 2012, for recent definitions of synesthesia that do not only involve sensory/perceptual concurrent). Moreover, while the cross-modal interactions experienced by synesthetes are idiosyncratic, cross-modal correspondences tend to be common within the population (given that often they simply reflect the statistics of the environment). We therefore prefer to avoid terms like "synesthetic correspondences" (or associations) when talking about cross-modal correspondences, as they explicitly (one might say pejoratively) suggest a link between full-blown synesthesia and cross-modal congruency in the normal population (see Spence 2011, on this point).

In the present chapter, we analyze the role of cross-modal correspondences between complementary cues (henceforth referred to simply as cross-modal correspondences) in multisensory perception. In particular, we will focus on those correspondences that exist between auditory and visual stimuli, since this is the modality pairing that has attracted the majority of research interest to date. First, we provide a general introduction to the topic of cross-modal correspondences. Next, we scrutinize their role in the processing of cross-modal signals and their modulatory effects on multisensory integration. Finally, a Bayesian framework is proposed in order to account for the consequences of cross-modal correspondences for multisensory integration and hence multisensory perception.

CROSS-MODAL CORRESPONDENCES

Cross-modal correspondences can be defined as the mapping that observers expect to exist between two or more features or dimensions from different sensory modalities (such as lightness and loudness), that induce congruency effects in performance and often, but not always, also a phenomenological experience of similarity between such features. In the simplest case of redundant cues, when two or more sensory channels are simultaneously sampling the same physical property, each modality should provide virtually the same estimate. That is, it is sufficient to sample a physical property (e.g., spatial location) of a distal stimulus via one sensory modality (e.g., audition) in order to know what to expect if the same physical property was to be sampled with another sensory modality (e.g., vision; Alais and Burr 2004). However, when multiple senses provide complementary information, the mapping between multiple sensory estimates is highly uncertain, and it is almost impossible, given a particular sensory estimate in one modality, to infer a complementary property in another. For example, the luminance and stiffness of an object, which are two complementary pieces of sensory information, are normally uncorrelated, hence knowing the luminance of an object does not provide any information about its stiffness. Nevertheless, even in the case of complementary cues, the mapping is often not completely uncertain, and it is often possible to observe *relative* compatibility effects. This is the case for auditory pitch and the size of seen or felt objects: although it is impossible, given a sound with a particular pitch, to map it to a specific size of resonating object, it is a reasonable assumption, given two sounds having different pitches and two visual stimuli with different sizes, that the sound with the higher-pitch would likely be mapped to the smaller object and the lower sound to the larger one.

In the remainder of this chapter, we will focus on those cross-modal correspondences that have been documented between complementary *polar* features (see later) of stimuli presented in different sensory modalities that are shared by most (if not all) individuals. Three criteria will therefore constitute the core of the cross-modal correspondences under discussion: complementarity, polarity, and universality, and these are defined in turn. As mentioned earlier, cross-modal correspondences often involve *complementary* (i.e., non-redundant) stimulus features such as pitch and elevation, pitch and size, lightness and loudness, etc. Such features may themselves be either modal or amodal (i.e., modality dependent or modality independent, such as color, pitch, and timbre, versus spatial and temporal features, respectively). Cross-modal congruency between redundant cues, whereby multiple senses provide independent estimates regarding the same physical properties in a common metric system (e.g., visual and haptic estimation of size, see Ernst and Banks 2002) will not be discussed here.

Polar dimensions, are those sensory dimensions along which stimuli can be experienced as one being "more than" or "less than" another (e.g., loudness, lightness, saturation, pitch, elevation, duration, size, mass, temperature). In the case of cross-modal correspondences between complementary polar dimensions, a pole of the first dimension is compatible with one pole of the second dimension and incompatible with the other. This is, for example, the case of the earlier-mentioned cross-modal correspondence between pitch and elevation, where high pitch is compatible with high elevation (Bernstein and Edelstein 1971; Cabrera and Morimoto 2007; Roffler and Butler 1968; Rusconi et al. 2006; Stumpf 1883).

Far from being idiosyncratic, many congruency effects are *universal* and most, if not all, individuals share the same patterns of cross-modal correspondence. A number of researchers have conducted cross-cultural studies in order to investigate the universality of cross-modal correspondences between the sound of spoken words and meaningless visual stimuli, a phenomenon known as sound symbolism, and often found little difference between cultures (Bremner et al. 2013; Davis 1961; Gebels 1969; Osgood 1960; Rogers and Ross 1968; Taylor and Taylor 1962; see Hinton, Nichols, and Ohala 1994, for a review). Moreover, recently, it has been demonstrated that Westerners can readily interpret non-Western metaphors used to describe the elevation of auditory pitch (Eitan and Timmers 2010). Nevertheless, not all cross-modal correspondences satisfy the universality criterion: Although most cultures match the pitch of a tone to the elevation of a visual stimulus, this was not true (that is, there was no mapping) for certain Native American populations studied by R. Walker (1987; see also Antovic, 2009). However, it should be noted that R. Walker's (1987) observations were based on an explicit task; hence it is still an open question as to whether indirect methods would converge on similar conclusions. Moreover, Marks (1974) has demonstrated that even within a given population, while the majority of participants matched increasing loudness to increasing brightness, a small proportion consistently matched increasing loudness to increasing darkness.

Having restricted the focus of the present discussion, the next step is to draw a taxonomy accounting for the commonalities and differences that exist between the various types of cross-modal correspondences that have been documented to date. Based on their putative underlying cause, we hereby identify three types of cross-modal correspondence between complementary polar cues (which, as we have argued earlier, are generally also universal).

A Taxonomy of Polar Cross-Modal Correspondences

Structural correspondences

These arise from the features of the nervous system. This idea dates back to S. S. Stevens (1957), who pointed to the fact that stimulus intensity is coded in the firing rate of neurons: the more intense the stimulus, the higher the rate of neuronal firing. Critically, this appears to hold true for every sensory modality, and hence the cross-modal correspondence between stimulus intensity in different modalities might simply reflect a common response of the brain to stimulus intensity. Such a structural hypothesis for cross-modal correspondences advocates the principle of neural economy (see Anderson 2010), whereby the brain adopts similar mechanisms to process a number of different features from different sensory modalities, which, as a consequence, might end up being associated. Being a by-product of the anatomo-functional features of the human nervous system, such structurally-based dimensional interactions are obviously likely to be universal.

Another form of structural correspondence can be postulated on the basis of Walsh's (2003) proposal that there exists a multipurpose system coding for magnitude in the inferior parietal cortex in humans (see also Walsh, Chapter 41, this volume). It has been argued that this system encodes the magnitude of spatial, temporal, and quantitative features of sensory inputs in a common metric irrespective of their modality of input. According to this view, cross-modal correspondences might reflect the outcome of such a system encoding multiple estimates of magnitude within a common pool of neurons. There are, however, also other means by which the structural features of our nervous system might underlie cross-modal correspondences. Indeed, multiple sensory dimensions might be associated as a consequence of their being processed in neighboring (see Ramachandran and Hubbard 2001) or interconnected brain areas (see Rouw and Scholte 2007). In this case, reciprocal connections and interactions between brain areas processing different sensory attributes might give rise to cross-modal correspondences. While this hypothesis provides an account for the existence of interactions between the processing of given sets of sensory attributes, it should be noted that it does not make specific predictions with regard to what will count as congruent or incongruent. In other words, dimensional interactions resulting from the processing of sensory information in adjacent/interconnected brain areas might easily give rise to what is known as Garner interference (Garner 1974), but not necessarily to Stroop-like interference (Stroop 1935).[2]

Statistical correspondences

The physical properties of the distal stimuli activating our senses are often correlated in nature. As a result of repeated exposure, sensory systems acquire information concerning the statistical regularities of the environment and hence the correlations between multiple sensory cues (Adams, Graf, and Ernst 2004; Stocker and Simoncelli 2006; Weiss, Simoncelli, and Adelson 2002). This information can then be used in order to decide which stimuli normally go together, and should therefore be integrated, and which to keep separate (Ernst 2007). A paradigmatic example of such statistical regularity is the relation between the size of physical bodies and their resonance frequencies: *ceteris paribus*, the resonance frequency is inversely proportional to the size of the resonator. That is, keeping density, tension, temperature, etc. constant, large bodies resonate at lower frequencies than smaller bodies. It would obviously be adaptive for the brain to learn this relation between pitch (the perceptual correlate of a sound's frequency) and size and then to exploit this knowledge in order to better process/predict audiovisual information.

The literature on multisensory perception contains numerous other cases of compatibility effects between cross-modal stimulus features that might plausibly involve similar learnt stimulus correlations (Bernstein and Edelstein 1971; Gallace and Spence 2006; Marks 1987a, 1987b, 1989, 2004; Martino and Marks 2000; Melara and O'Brien, 1987). Reflecting the properties of the environment (and hence also the laws of physics), most statistical correspondences are again likely to be universal. It might be argued that the probability that two cross-modal dimensions are associated by participants depends on the correlation between those two dimensions in the environment. Nevertheless, it is also possible for researchers to artificially introduce correlations between cross-modal features and train observers until their perceptual systems learn such correlations. Experimentally-induced cross-modal correspondences of this kind (Baier, Kleinschmidt, and Müller 2006; Ernst 2007; Zangenehpour and Zatorre 2010) would certainly also qualify as statistical correspondences, though obviously they fail to meet the universality criterion. It is worth noting that the natural statistics

---

[2] Garner interference refers to the modulation of performance in a speeded classification task due to the *random variation* of a stimulus feature which is irrelevant for the experimental task. Stroop interference refers to the modulation of performance in a speeded classification task due to the *(in)congruency* between the properties of task relevant and task irrelevant features. In other words, Garner interference refers to the effects due to the *presence* of a change in a task irrelevant feature, while in Stroop interference what matters is the *direction* of such changes.

of the environment might provide the basis for a number of the cross-modal associations between sensory dimensions that have been documented in the literature to date. This is, for example, the case for the association between color and taste/flavor (such as the cross-modal correspondence between redness and sweetness; e.g., see Levitan et al. 2008; Spence et al. 2010).

Semantically (or linguistically) mediated correspondences

This kind of correspondence originates from the use of a common lexicon to describe multiple perceptual properties (Gallace and Spence 2006; Long 1977; Martino and Marks 1999; Melara 1989; P. Walker and Smith 1984). So, for example, many languages around the world use cross-modal metaphors to describe sensory attributes (e.g., "warm colors" and "dark sounds"; Martino and Marks 2001). Some cross-modal correspondences might, therefore, result from the common linguistic labels used to describe various perceptual dimensions that eventually come to be associated. Of course, the very existence of such widespread linguistically-mediated correspondences begs the question of why so many languages "just so happen" to use the same words to describe distinct perceptual properties from different senses. It might even be argued that linguistically-mediated correspondences build on structural or statistical correspondences that, in the long run, might shape the languages' lexicons (see Cuskley and Kirby, Chapter 43, this volume).

Irrespective of lexical labels, however, semantic information can underlie cross-modal correspondences because associated items show similar semantic profiles. For example, Bozzi and Flores D'Arcais (1967) studied the correspondences between invented words and simple shapes. They found that compatible word-figure pairs also shared similar semantic associations (see later; see also Osgood, Suci, and Tannenbaum 1957, for similar findings). That said, it is ambiguous whether a common semantic profile or lexical label was the cause of the cross-modal correspondences documented in this study, or whether instead cross-modal correspondences were the underlying cause for similar semantic profiles and common linguistic coding. In Bozzi and Flores D'Arcais's study, for example, the pseudo-word "kirite" and a spiky figure were considered by participants to be phenomenologically similar with both being judged as "hard" rather than "soft." However, it is not clear whether they were considered as being congruent and hence having the same semantic associations, or whether instead they had the same semantic associations, and because of that, they were found to be congruent.

It is important to note that the taxonomy of cross-modal correspondences outlined here is by no means unequivocally defined nor should it necessarily be taken to be exhaustive.[3] In fact, a given cross-modal correspondence can often be classified in

---

[3] A fourth type of cross-modal correspondence might result from the similarities of the internal responses that different kinds of perceptual stimuli generate (Seo et al. 2010). The sight of a green landscape and a piece of music, for example, can both be relaxing. Hence, that piece of music and landscape end-up being associated (see also Cowles 1935; Karwoski, Odbert, and Osgood 1942).

terms of more than one category. This is the case for the mapping between lightness and loudness, which are both similarly coded in the rate of neural spikes (Stevens 1957), are both associated in nature (i.e., they both depend on the energy involved in the triggering physical event), and are often described by the same words (e.g., strong, soft). It could even be argued that most (perhaps all) cross-modal correspondences originate in the statistical regularities of the environment: in a relatively short time-scale, statistical regularities might shape the lexicon so that features that are commonly associated in the world come to be described using the same words (this might even be thought of as an example of lexical, rather than neural, economy; cf. Anderson 2010). Then, in a longer time-scale, the brain might come through evolution to develop similar strategies to process associated features (hence internalizing them as common neural coding principles, or co-locating them in adjacent, or well-connected brain regions), which, as a consequence, end-up giving rise to structural correspondences. However, in order to further substantiate any claims about the grounding of cross-modal correspondences on the natural statistics of the environment, researchers will, in the future, need to directly measure the physical properties of the environment and the natural correlations that exist between the multiple physical dimensions that we humans are sensitive to.

Cross-Modal Correspondences: Early Studies

Research on the topic of cross-modal correspondences has a long history in the field of experimental psychology. Linguistic and semantic correspondences were investigated first, and the history of research on this topic is intimately connected with that of sound symbolism. The first mention of a natural association between vocal stimuli and their meaning dates back to Plato's Cratylus, where the eminent philosopher discusses the arbitrariness of language and the symbolic properties of vocal sounds. The idea that a simple vocal sound might convey some meaning, which is essentially the notion of sound symbolism, saw a surge of interest in the twentieth century, primarily due to the work of Edgar Sapir (1929) and Wolfgang Köhler (1929).

In an attempt to investigate the symbolic values of vowels, Sapir (1929) gave participants two meaningless words, Mil and Mal, and told them that they both meant "table," but that one referred to a small table while the other word referred to a large table. Remarkably, when Sapir asked his participants to match those words to the sizes of the tables in the most natural way, he found that the majority associated the word Mil with the small table while associating Mal with the large table. Sapir interpreted this result by claiming "that vocalic and consonantal contrasts tended with many, indeed with most, individuals to have a definite symbolic feeling-significance that seemed to have little relation to the associative values of actual words" (228). In the same year, Köhler (1929) documented what is now possibly the most famous example of sound symbolism.

He gave participants two made-up words, Takete and Maluma (or Baluma), and two abstract shapes, a spiky and a rounded one, and told them that those two words were the names of the two shapes, but which was which? Most participants agreed that Maluma was the rounded figure, while Takete was the spiky one.

In the wake of Sapir (1929) and Köhler's (1929) early research, a number of scientists went on to further investigate the topic of sound symbolism, providing additional support for the notion of there being a non-arbitrary link between vocal sounds and meaning. Notably, cross-cultural studies found little difference in the magnitude or type of sound symbolic effects between different cultures (Davis 1961; though see also Diffloth 1994, Bremner *et al* 2012), thus pointing to the existence of a universal mapping between meaning and at least certain speech sounds.

Another line of research on cross-modal correspondences developed in parallel with that on sound symbolism and focused instead on the associations between elementary features of non-linguistic cross-modal stimuli. One of the first such cross-modal correspondences to capture the attention of psychophysicists was the association between auditory loudness and visual brightness (Cohen 1934; Hornbostel 1938; Külpe 1893), whereby both adults and children readily match loud sounds with light patches and vice versa (Bond and Stevens 1969; Root and Ross 1965; J. C. Stevens and Marks 1965).

The major scientific contribution of these pioneering studies was the discovery of a variety of cross-modal correspondences that were present in the normal (i.e., non-synesthetic) population. In the following years, researchers started to investigate the function of cross-modal correspondences and the focus of research interest rapidly shifted to studying the effects of such cross-modal phenomena on human perception and information processing (see Marks 2004; also Marks, Chapter 38, this volume). Typically, researchers studied the interactions between corresponding cross-modal dimensions on the *speed* of information processing. Often the participants in these studies would have to classify—as rapidly as possible—stimuli presented in a given modality along a target dimension, while trying to ignore irrelevant stimuli presented in another sensory modality. If the dimensions in the two modalities are not processed independently (i.e., if the dimensions are not orthogonal), reaction times (RTs) to the target stimuli should be modulated by variations of the stimuli in the irrelevant modality (Garner 1974). Moreover, if certain dimensions of the target and irrelevant stimuli happen to correspond cross-modally, participants should respond more rapidly when the stimuli in the two modalities are congruent as compared to when they are incongruent (Bernstein and Edelstein 1971).

Congruency effects have been documented between many of the cross-modal correspondences highlighted in previous studies (see Spence 2011, for a review) but, notably, only when compatible and incompatible stimulus pairs varied in a random fashion on a trial-by-trial basis (Bernstein and Edelstein 1971; Gallace and Spence 2006). These findings have led certain researchers to propose an interpretation of such dimensional interactions in terms of information accrual (Martino and Marks 1999). The idea here is that in order to select a response, the human information processing system accumulates information simultaneously in the two channels, and only when the evidence reaches a certain threshold is a response initiated. If the two channels provide congruent information, the evidence accumulated in one modality interacts with the information provided by the other sensory modality and hence information accrual is speeded-up. Conversely, when the information provided by the two channels is incompatible, the irrelevant modality slows down information accrual. More recently, congruency effects elicited by cross-modal correspondences have been interpreted in terms of a failure of selective attention (see Marks 2004), the claim being that even if participants are instructed to attend exclusively to a single modality, they simply cannot ignore whatever stimulus happens to be presented in the other (irrelevant) modality.

Most RT studies of cross-modal correspondences have investigated the effects of stimulus congruency in tasks in which the participants always had to pay attention to the stimuli presented within a single modality, while the stimuli presented in the other modality provided congruent or incongruent task-irrelevant information. This paradigm, however, seems to tackle an observer's ability to ignore irrelevant information rather than investigating how multiple sources of sensory information jointly contribute to determining a participant's responses. In order to investigate whether stimulus congruency speeds-up human information processing, Miller (1991) tested whether the cross-modal correspondence between auditory pitch and elevation (specified visually) could give rise to the redundant-targets effect (RTE). Miller's participants had to respond as quickly as possible to target stimuli. It is well known that the simultaneous presentation of multiple targets can speed-up observers' responses as compared to when single targets are presented due simply to statistical facilitation. According to the race model, when multiple stimuli are processed independently and the response is initiated by the faster process, it is more likely to provide faster responses as compared to single target conditions just as a result of probability summation (Raab 1962). Conversely, if multiple targets jointly co-activate a response, participants should exhibit an additional facilitation and respond faster than is predicted by the race model, an effect termed the RTE (Miller 1982, Otto and Mamassian, 2012).

In a "go/no-go experiment," Miller (1991) instructed his participants to respond as rapidly as possible to visual stimuli presented above or below fixation, and to high- and low-pitched auditory stimuli, while refraining from responding in the presence of visual stimuli presented at fixation or to auditory stimuli having an intermediate pitch. Unimodal or bimodal stimuli were presented pseudo-randomly on each trial. In line with the results of previous studies, participants responded more rapidly to congruent pitch–elevation combinations (e.g., high pitch, high elevation) as compared to incongruent combinations (e.g., high pitch, low elevation) on the bimodal trials. Furthermore, the RT to congruent bimodal stimuli systematically violated the race-model, thus providing evidence that congruent information about pitch and elevation is jointly processed, and concurrently activates an observer's *responses*, hence leading to a significant RTE. While such a paradigm allows for the detection of cross-modal congruency effects on human information processing, it is important to note that the results fail to provide any information about the processing level at which such effects take place. Indeed, dimensional interactions can arise on a *perceptual* level, thus leading to systematic distortions of perceptual experiences or at a subsequent stage of information processing (e.g., at the stage of *response selection*).

Cross-Modal Correspondences and Multisensory Integration

In order to determine whether cross-modal correspondences between complementary cues can operate at a perceptual level,[4] and to investigate their role in multisensory integration, researchers have adopted psychophysical techniques based on offline (i.e., unspeeded) responding instead. To explore this point, Parise and Spence (2008) investigated the effects of pitch-size congruency on the well-known temporal ventriloquism effect (Morein-Zamir, Soto-Faraco, and Kingstone 2003). Previous research has demonstrated that people find it easier to judge the temporal order in which two visual stimuli have been presented if one tone is presented before the first visual stimulus and a second tone is presented after the second visual stimulus. This enhancement of visual temporal sensitivity has been attributed to the temporal "capture" of the visual stimuli by the temporally proximate sounds, resulting in an expansion of the perceived interval between the two visual events (Bertelson and Aschersleben 2003; Fendrich and Corballis 2001; Morein-Zamir et al. 2003).

In their study, Parise and Spence (2008) sought to demonstrate whether the cross-modal congruency between pitch and size would modulate the magnitude of this effect: In particular, they hypothesized that the auditory capture of vision should be larger for pairs of congruent auditory and visual stimuli than for pairs of incongruent stimuli, as reflected by participants' sensitivity to the relative timing of the visual stimuli. On each trial, two visual stimuli were presented in rapid succession, with a variable time-lag (i.e., a variable *stimulus onset asynchrony* (SOA)) between them. The observers had to report the relative order of appearance of the stimuli (see Figure 39.1a). An auditory stimulus preceded the first and followed the second visual stimulus by 150 ms. On congruent trials, the first auditory stimulus was congruent with the first visual stimulus (e.g., a high-pitched tone and a small visual stimulus) and the second visual stimulus was congruent with the second auditory stimulus (e.g., a low-pitched tone and a large visual stimulus). Conversely, on incongruent trials, the first auditory stimulus was incongruent with the first visual stimulus (e.g., low-pitched tone and small visual stimulus) and the second visual stimulus was incongruent with the second auditory stimulus (e.g., a high-pitched tone and a large visual stimulus). Note that neither the size of the visual stimuli, nor the pitch of the auditory stimuli provided any task-relevant information to participants.

---

[4] Here perceptual is meant in terms of having an effect on perception of component features, not in terms of there being a sensory concurrent.

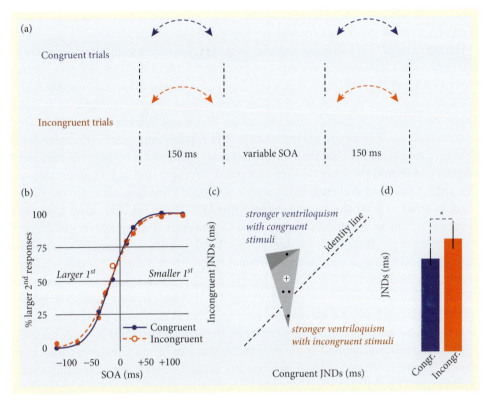

FIGURE 39.1 Pitch-size congruency modulates the temporal ventriloquist effect. (a) Schematic illustration of the events presented on each trial in a study by Parise and Spence (2008). Arrows represents the compatibility relation between visual and auditory stimuli. The SOA between the two visual stimuli was experimentally varied using the method of constant stimuli. (b) Psychometric function describing participants' temporal order judgment (TOJ) performance in the congruent (blue) and incongruent (red) trials. (c) Scatter and bagplot of participants' JNDs in congruent versus incongruent trials. The cross at the centre of the bagplot represent the centre of mass of the bivariate distribution of empirical data (i.e., the halfspace depth), the dark gray area (i.e., the bag) includes the 50% of the data with the largest depth, the light gray polygon contains all the non-outliers data points, and the stars represent the outliers. (d) Mean JNDs on congruent and incongruent trials. Error bars indicate the standard error of the mean, asterisks indicate statistical differences (p <0.05). Reprinted from *Neuroscience Letters*, 442 (3), Cesare Parise and Charles Spence, Synesthetic congruency modulates the temporal ventriloquism effect, pp. 257–261, Copyright (2008), with permission from Elsevier.

As predicted, the cross-modal congruency between auditory and visual stimuli modulated temporal sensitivity, with higher temporal resolution being measured for congruent than for incongruent conditions (see Figure 39.1b–d). This result provided the first empirical evidence that varying the cross-modal congruency of pairs of auditory and visual stimuli can modulate the temporal capture of vision by audition. More generally, these results demonstrate that cross-modal congruency can induce systematic distortions of *perceptual* experience (though see Keetels and Vroomen 2011).

Having demonstrated that cross-modal congruency systematically alters our perceptual experiences, researchers started to investigate the role of cross-modal correspondences in solving the "correspondence problem" (aka "causal inference," see Ernst and Bülthoff 2004; Körding et al. 2007; Parise, Spence, and Ernst 2012; Parise et al. 2013; Shams and Beierholm 2010; Spence et al. 2010; Welch and Warren 1980). When faced with multiple sensory inputs, the brain has to infer which stimuli refer to the same distal objects or events, and should therefore be integrated, and which of them have different origins, and should therefore be kept segregated. Previous studies have demonstrated that spatial and temporal cues, along with semantic information are exploited by the brain in order to solve the correspondence problem (Bresciani et al. 2005; Chen and Spence 2010; Doehrmann and Naumer 2008; Gepshtein et al. 2005; Körding et al. 2007; Parise, Spence, and Ernst 2012; Parise et al. 2013; Vatakis and Spence 2007). Cross-modal correspondences might operate as additional cues to help solve the correspondence problem by biasing the brain toward integrating congruent stimuli and segregating incongruent ones. In other words, auditory and visual stimuli are more likely to originate from a single event when their features are congruent along two or more dimensions. This should be especially valid for what we earlier termed statistical correspondences, where congruency is defined as the probability that two or more features co-occur in nature: If sensory systems exploit such statistical regularities when integrating multisensory signals, congruent stimuli should be more strongly integrated than incongruent ones (Ernst 2007).

Previous research has demonstrated that when conflicting multisensory signals are integrated, observers may lose sensitivity to such conflict (Ernst 2007; Hillis et al. 2002). Notably, the loss of sensitivity is proportional to the strength of the coupling between the unisensory signals: The stronger the coupling, the lower the sensitivity to intersensory conflict (Bresciani, Dammeier, and Ernst 2006; Ernst 2005, 2007). To test for the effects of pitch-size cross-modal correspondences in the temporal integration of audiovisual signals, Parise and Spence's (2009) observers were presented with slightly asynchronous auditory and visual stimuli and had to report their relative order of occurrence. If congruency promotes multisensory integration, hence reducing sensitivity to intersensory conflicts, one would expect lower sensitivity (i.e., higher just noticeable differences (JND)) to the temporal order of appearance of congruent than of incongruent audiovisual stimuli (Vatakis, Ghazanfar, and Spence 2008; Vatakis and Spence 2007, 2008). Interestingly, pitch-size congruency significantly affected participants' temporal order judgment (TOJ) performance and, as hypothesized, sensitivity was lower for congruent than for incongruent audiovisual pairings (see Figure 39.2).

In order to test for the generalizability of their results, Parise and Spence (2009) replicated their TOJ study exploiting the cross-modal correspondences between auditory pitch and waveform with the spikiness of simple visual figures. Their results indicated that audiovisual congruency promotes multisensory integration in the temporal domain.

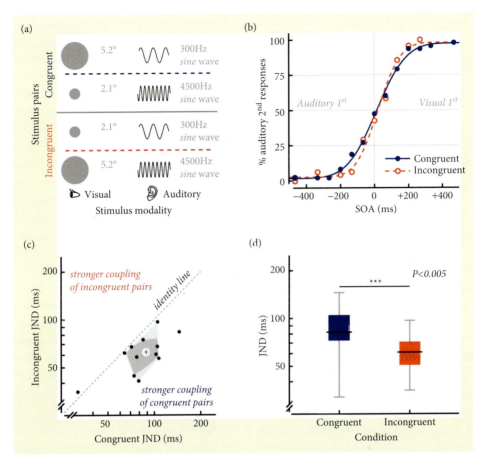

FIGURE 39.2 Pitch-size congruency modulates sensitivity to temporal conflicts. (a) Pairs of auditory and visual stimuli presented in congruent and incongruent trials of an experiment reported by Parise and Spence (2009). (b) Psychometric functions describing performance on congruent (blue line) and incongruent (red line) conditions. (c) Bagplot of participants' sensitivity (JNDs) on congruent versus incongruent trials. (d) Participants' sensitivity (JNDs), on congruent and incongruent trials. Reproduced from Parise Cesare, and Charles Spence, When birds of a feather flock together: Synesthetic correspondences modulate audiovisual integration in non-synesthetes. *PLoS ONE*, 4, e5664, 2009, PLOS.

Following the same logic as in the previous experiments, Parise and Spence (2009) went on to demonstrate that congruent audiovisual stimuli are also more strongly integrated in the spatial domain (see Alais and Burr 2004). Participants were presented with simultaneous visual and auditory stimuli coming from different locations along the horizontal axis and reported the left/right location of the auditory stimulus with respect to the visual one (see Figure 39.3). In some trials, the size of the visual stimuli and the pitch of the auditory stimuli were congruent, in others they were incongruent. Again, if stronger integration takes place between congruent stimuli, one would expect to find lower sensitivity (higher

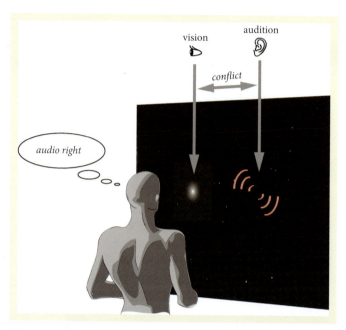

FIGURE 39.3 Schematic illustration of the participant and experimental apparatus from a study reported by Parise and Spence (2009). Visual stimuli (blobs) were projected onto a white sound-transparent screen placed in front of an array of eight loudspeakers. This apparatus allowed for the introduction of physical conflicts between the spatial location of the visual and auditory stimuli. Reproduced from Parise Cesare, and Charles Spence, When birds of a feather flock together: Synesthetic correspondences modulate audiovisual integration in non-synesthetes. *PLoS ONE*, 4, e5664, 2009, PLOS.

JNDs) on congruent trials than on incongruent trials. In keeping with this hypothesis, participants were less sensitive to spatial conflicts between visual and auditory stimuli when the stimuli were congruent than when they were incongruent (see Figure 39.4). These results extend the finding of the previous research and show that pitch-size compatibility promotes the spatial integration of audiovisual signals.

An influential Bayesian model of multisensory integration (Ernst 2005) provides an elegant framework in which to interpret Parise and Spence's (2009) results. According to this model, humans are optimal integrators, combining multiple sensory signals and prior knowledge together in order to derive more precise combined estimates (Ernst and Bülthoff 2004). Statistical correlations between multisensory signals learnt by the observer can be modeled as Bayesian priors describing the expected (a priori) joint probability distribution of those signals (Ernst 2007; see further discussion of this topic later in the chapter).

The reduced sensitivity to spatial and temporal conflicts between congruent audiovisual stimuli suggests that observers have learnt the natural mapping between pitch and size and exploit this information (i.e., a Bayesian prior) in order to integrate audiovisual signals. That is, whenever they hear a high-pitched sound, observers should (implicitly)

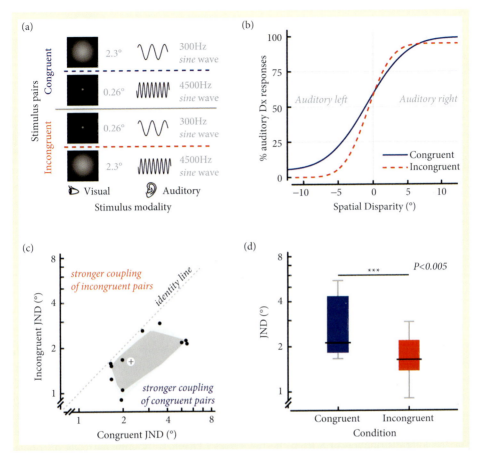

FIGURE 39.4 Pitch-size congruency modulates sensitivity to spatial conflict. (a) Pairs of auditory and visual stimuli presented on congruent and incongruent trials. (b) Psychometric functions describing performance in the congruent (blue line) and incongruent (red line) conditions. (c) Bagplot of participants' sensitivity (JNDs) on congruent versus incongruent trials. (d) Participants' sensitivity (JNDs), on congruent and incongruent trials. Reproduced from Parise Cesare, and Charles Spence, When birds of a feather flock together: Synesthetic correspondences modulate audiovisual integration in non-synesthetes. *PLoS ONE*, 4, e5664, 2009, PLOS.

expect a small object to have produced it, and eventually integrate the two sources of information into a coherent multisensory representation of a single event involving a small object resonating at high frequency. In other words, when the size of an object and the pitch of a sound are congruent, observers should expect such stimuli to be involved in the same event, hence their spatial location and temporal occurrence should coincide. Conversely, when cross-modal stimuli are incongruent, participants might consider those signals to be independent, with no need to postulate either the spatial or temporal co-occurrence of the constituent unisensory signals. It should be noted that although this Bayesian account seems most naturally attuned to what we termed

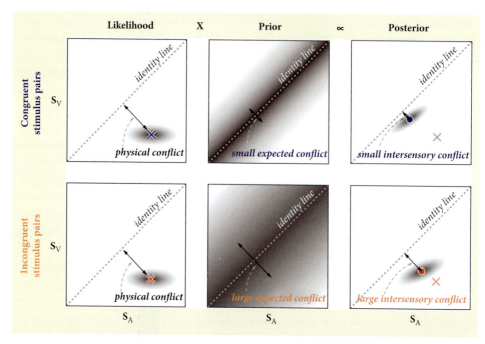

FIGURE 39.5 Cross-modal congruency promotes multisensory integration by acting on the coupling prior distribution. Multisensory integration results from the combination of sensory inputs (likelihood distribution) and prior knowledge (prior distribution) through Bayes' rule (i.e., likelihood*prior∝posterior). The likelihood distribution (left panels) represents the distribution of physical stimuli inducing a given sensory response. The axes represent a property S (e.g., spatial location) of visual and auditory stimuli. The prior (central panels) represents the expected joint distribution of S from the two sensory channels. A prior narrowly distributed along the identity line indicates that observes have a strong expectation that the two cues are identical and conflict free. In contrast, a flat prior indicates complete uncertainty about the mapping between the two cues (i.e., large and small cross-modal conflicts are equally likely). The integrated percept (the posterior, right panels) is the product of the prior and the likelihood distributions. A prior narrowly distributed along the identity line will bias the percept toward the identity line thus silencing cross-modal conflict (see upper panels). Conversely, a shallower prior would leave access to intersensory conflicts (see lower panels). (Note: all the distributions are assumed by the model to be bivariate Gaussian probability density functions.) Adapted from Ernst Marc O., A Bayesian view on multimodal cue integration, In Gunther Knoblich, Ian Thornton, Marc Grosejan, and Maggie Shiffrar (Eds.), Perception of the human body from the inside out, pp. 105–131, © 2005, Oxford University Press, with permission http://ukcatalogue.oup.com/]. For permission to reuse this material, please visit http://www.oup.co.uk/academic/rights/permissions.

statistical correspondences, this explanation might also apply to other kinds of cross-modal correspondence.

In purely statistical terms, the expected probability of a large conflict (either spatial or temporal) between congruent stimuli should be lower than for incongruent stimuli (see Figure 39.5). Therefore, combining this prior probability ("the coupling prior") with conflicting multisensory input (i.e., "the likelihood function") according to Bayes' rule, should lead to different results depending on the congruency between the signals: When they are congruent, the conflict is largely cancelled, whereas when they are incongruent the conflict would still be accessible (see also Bresciani et al. 2006; Ernst 2007). This prediction is largely supported by Parise and Spence's (2009) results.

Conclusion

In this chapter, we have presented evidence documenting the existence of cross-modal correspondences between complementary polar auditory and visual cues. From the early studies, mainly concerned with providing evidence for the existence of compatibility effects between apparently unrelated multisensory dimensions, researchers moved on to investigate the facilitatory effects of cross-modal correspondences on the rate of sensory information processing. The latest evidence indicates that cross-modal correspondences might promote multisensory integration by helping to solve the cross-modal correspondence problem (i.e., the problem of knowing which of many cues/stimuli detected by an organism should be bound together) and informing the system as to whether or not multiple sensory signals should be integrated. In a Bayesian framework cross-modal correspondence can therefore be represented on the coupling prior distribution, encoding expected mapping between multisensory stimuli.

Previous studies of multisensory integration have demonstrated that infants are not optimal integrators (Gori et al. 2008; Nardini et al. 2008). That is, they do not appear to combine multisensory information according to a maximum likely estimation strategy, whereby the final percept is a weighted average of the individual unimodal cues. This finding has been interpreted as a lack of knowledge in infants about which stimuli should be coupled (Ernst 2008). Considering that cross-modal correspondences may play a role in solving the correspondence problem (Parise and Spence 2009), it is somewhat surprising to find that a number of studies have also demonstrated the existence of cross-modal correspondences in infants (Maurer, Pathman, and Mondloch 2006; Mondloch and Maurer 2004; Smith and Sera 1992; Walker et al. 2010; for a review, see also Spector and Maurer 2009; Maurer, Gibson, and Spector, Chapter 3, this volume). It should, however, be noted that those studies did not directly investigate multisensory cue integration: rather their main aim was to highlight the existence of cross-modal correspondences in infants. That is, although the paradigms used in those studies were well-suited to measuring compatibility effects between cross-modal stimuli, they did not allow one to measure the effects of such compatibility on multisensory integration. It might be argued that infants recognize cross-modal congruency without necessarily using this information to solve the correspondence problem. This apparent inconsistency between the lack of optimal integration in infants and their ability to recognize cross-modal correspondences parallels the inconsistency between those studies that have shown that infants have quite developed multisensory abilities

Table 39.1 Differences between cross-modal correspondences and full-blown synesthesia

Cross-modal correspondences	Synesthesia
Universal	Rare
Shared correspondences	Idiosyncratic correspondences
No concurrent experiences	Concurrent sensory experiences
Can be learnt following training	Cannot normally be acquired by training

(Lewkowicz 2000; Lewkowicz, Leo, and Simion 2010) and those reporting that there is no optimal integration (Gori et al. 2008; Nardini et al. 2008). It will be a challenge for future research to investigate the developmental trajectory of cross-modal correspondences in terms of their role as cues that help a rapidly-developing infant to solve the correspondence problem. In this regard, if it is true that cross-modal correspondences are encoded in the coupling prior distribution (i.e., the probability distribution describing the expected joint distribution of the signals), and that what infants are missing is the knowledge about the mapping between multisensory signals (which is also represented in the coupling prior), we hypothesize that the effects of cross-modal correspondence in multisensory integration should not appear before optimal integration.

A final open question concerns the relation between cross-modal correspondences and synesthesia (see Table 39.1). As mentioned already, cross-modal correspondences have often been linked to full-blown synesthesia (see Martino and Marks 2001; Maurer 1997), and a number of authors have actually chosen to refer to what are here called "cross-modal correspondences" as "synesthetic correspondences" (e.g., Martino and Marks 2000, 2001; Parise and Spence 2008, 2009; P. Walker et al. 2010). Although, at first sight, it might be tempting to connect the two phenomena, as both involve multisensory perception and congruency effects, there are, in our view, a number of major differences between them that deserve further consideration.

First of all, to the best of our knowledge, the literature on cross-modal correspondences in the general population has never reported the presence of a synesthetic-like concurrent experience of a congruent stimulus in an unstimulated modality as a result of the presentation of an inducing stimulus in another modality. It should, however, be noted that recent studies have demonstrated that in those cases in which synesthesia is apparently unidirectional (i.e., when stimulation in one modality elicits a concurrent sensation in another modality but not the other way round), synesthesia sometime also occurs in the opposite direction albeit most often below the level of awareness (see Cohen Kadosh, Cohen Kadosh, and Henik 2007; Cohen Kadosh and Henik 2007; Cohen Kadosh, Henik, and Walsh 2007; Johnson, Jepma, and De Jong 2007; Meier and Rothen 2007). This latter phenomenon (i.e., synesthesia below the level of awareness) then starts to resemble the cross-modal correspondences documented in the non-synesthetic population more closely.

Second, while novel cross-modal correspondences can be experimentally induced after a relatively short (<1 hour) exposure to correlated cross-modal stimuli (see Ernst 2007), the conscious perception of synesthetic concurrents cannot be elicited in non-synesthetes even after many tens of thousands of presentations of arbitrary cross-modal stimulus pairings (e.g., Howells 1944; Kelly 1934; though see Cohen-Kadosh et al. 2009, for a case of hypnotic-induced synesthesia). That is, while it seems clear that perceptual learning plays a key role in the acquisition of cross-modal correspondences, it can hardly account for the development of most cases of full-blown synesthesia in which there is a perceptual concurrent (though one might postulate the existence of critical periods after which synesthesia cannot be induced anymore).

Moreover, cross-modal correspondences between polar dimensions appear to be largely *relative* phenomena, often occurring only after pairs of stimuli have been experienced as one being "more" than the other (though see Guzmann-Martinez et al. 2012; Roffler and Butler, 1968), whereas proper synesthetic experiences involve an absolute mapping between the inducer and the concurrent stimulus. In this regard, it is remarkable that the effects of cross-modal correspondences between complementary polar cues only occur when two stimuli can be clearly identified as one being "more" and the other being "less" along a given sensory dimension, but not when congruent and incongruent stimulus pairs are presented in different blocks of trials (Bernstein and Edelstein 1971; Gallace and Spence 2006). Nevertheless one might argue that the relative nature of the effects reported in many laboratory experiments may have resulted from the relatively small difference in the features under consideration.

With this in mind, we argue that in spite of their superficial similarities, synesthesia and cross-modal correspondences might well constitute two different, and possibly entirely unrelated, perceptual phenomena. That said, we are the first to admit that the question is not yet fully resolved. More studies will clearly be needed in order to investigate the precise nature of the relationship between these two empirical phenomena. In this regard, it would be interesting to compare the effects of cross-modal correspondences on normal and synesthetic populations on both the speed of information processing and multisensory integration (see Spence 2011). Moreover, the application of functional neuroimaging techniques to investigate the neural substrates underlying synesthesia and cross-modal correspondences might also provide valuable insights to help decide whether the two phenomena constitute instances of a single continuum or not.

ACKNOWLEDGMENTS

We would like to thank Irene Senna for her many helpful comments on an earlier draft of this manuscript.

References

Adams, Wendy J., Erich W. Graf, and Marc O. Ernst. 2004. Experience can change the 'light-from-above' prior. *Nature Neuroscience* 7:1057–1058.

Alais, David, and David Burr. 2004. The ventriloquist effect results from near-optimal bimodal integration. *Current Biology* 14:257–262.

Anderson, Michael L. 2010. Neural reuse: A fundamental organizational principle of the brain. *Behavioral and Brain Sciences* 33:245–266; discussion 266–313.

Antovic, Mihailo. 2009. Musical metaphors in Serbian and Romani children: An empirical study. *Metaphor and Symbol* 24:184–202.

Baier, Bernhard, Andreas Kleinschmidt, and Notger G. Müller. 2006. Cross-modal processing in early visual and auditory cortices depends on expected statistical relationship of multisensory information. *Journal of Neuroscience* 26:12260–12265.

Bernstein, Ira H., and Barry A. Edelstein. 1971. Effects of some variations in auditory input upon visual choice reaction time. *Journal of Experimental Psychology* 87:241–247.

Bertelson, Paul, and Gisa Aschersleben. 2003. Temporal ventriloquism: Crossmodal interaction on the time dimension: 1. Evidence from auditory-visual temporal order judgment. *International Journal of Psychophysiology* 50:147–155.

Bond, Barbara, and Stanley S. Stevens. 1969. Cross-modality matching of brightness to loudness by 5-year-olds. *Attention, Perception, and Psychophysics* 6:337–339.

Bozzi, Paolo, and Giovanni B. Flores D'Arcais. 1967. Experimental research on the intermodal relationships between expressive qualities. *Archivio di Psicologia, Neurologia e Psichiatria* 28:377–420.

Bremner Andrew, Serge Caparos, Jules Davidoff, Jan de Fockert, Karina J. Linnell, and Charles Spence (2012) "Bouba" and "Kiki" in Namibia? A remote culture make similar shape–sound matches, but different shape–taste matches to Westerners. Cognition, 126:165–172

Bremner, Andrew J., Sergio Caparos, Jules Davidoff, Jan de Fockert, Karina Linnell, and Charles Spence. 2013. Bouba and Kiki in Namibia? Western shape-symbolism does not extend to taste in a remote population. *Cognition* 126:165–172.

Bresciani, Jean-Pierre, Franziska Dammeier, and Marc O. Ernst. 2006. Vision and touch are automatically integrated for the perception of sequences of events. *Journal of Vision* 6:554–564.

Bresciani, Jean-Pierre, Marc O. Ernst, Knut Drewing, Guillaume Bouyer, Vincent Maury, and Abderrahmane Kheddar. 2005. Feeling what you hear: Auditory signals can modulate tactile tap perception. *Experimental Brain Research* 162:172–180.

Cabrera, Densil, and Masayuki Morimoto. 2007. Influence of fundamental frequency and source elevation on the vertical localization of complex tones and complex tone pairs. *Journal of the Acoustical Society of America* 122:478.

Chen, Yi-Chuan, and Charles Spence. 2010. When hearing the bark helps to identify the dog: Semantically-congruent sounds modulate the identification of masked pictures. *Cognition* 114:389–404.

Cohen, Nathan H. 1934. Equivalence of brightness across modalities. *American Journal of Psychology* 46:117–119.

Cohen Kadosh, Roi, Kathrin Cohen Kadosh, and Avishai Henik. 2007. The neuronal correlate of bidirectional synesthesia: A combined event-related potential and functional magnetic resonance imaging study. *Journal of Cognitive Neuroscience* 19:2050–2059.

Cohen Kadosh, Roi, and Avishai Henik. 2007. Can synaesthesia research inform cognitive science? *Trends in Cognitive Sciences* 11:177–184.

Cohen Kadosh, Roi, Avishai Henik, Andres Catena, Vincent Walsh, and Luis J. Fuentes. 2009. Induced cross-modal synaesthetic experience without abnormal neural connections. *Psychological Science* 20:258–265.

Cohen Kadosh, Roi, Avishai Henik, and Vincent Walsh. 2007. Small is bright and big is dark in synaesthesia. *Current Biology* 17:R834–R835.

Cohen Kadosh, Roi, and Devin Terhune. 2012. Redefining synaesthesia? *British Journal of Psychology* 103:20–23.

Cowles, John T. 1935. An experimental study of the pairing of certain auditory and visual stimuli. *Journal of Experimental Psychology* 18:461–469.

Cuskley, Christine, and Simon Kirby. 2013. Synesthesia, cross-modality, and language evolution. In *The Oxford Handbook of Synesthesia*, ed. Julia Simner and Edward M. Hubbard, 869–899. Oxford: Oxford University Press.

Davis, R. 1961. The fitness of names to drawings: A cross-cultural study in Tanganyika. *British Journal of Psychology* 52:259–268.

Day, Sean. 2005. Some demographic and socio-cultural aspects of synesthesia. In *Synesthesia: Perspectives from Cognitive Neuroscience,* ed. Lynn C. Robertson and Noam Sagiv, 11–33. New York: Oxford University Press.

Deroy, Ophelia, and Charles Spence. 2013. Why we are not all synesthetes (not even weakly so). *Psychonomic bulletin & review,* 1–22.

Diffloth, Gerald. 1994. i: *big*, a: *small*. In *Sound symbolism*, ed. Leanne Hinton, Johanna Nichols, and John J. Ohala, 107–114. Cambridge: Cambridge University Press.

Doehrmann, Oliver, and Marcus J. Naumer. 2008. Semantics and the multisensory brain: How meaning modulates processes of audio-visual integration. *Brain Research* 1242:136–150.

Eagleman, David. 2012. Synaesthesia in its protean guises. *British Journal of Psychology* 103:16–19.

Eitan, Zohar, and Renee Timmers. 2010. Beethoven's last piano sonata and those who follow crocodiles: Cross-domain mappings of auditory pitch in a musical context. *Cognition* 114:405–422.

Ernst, Marc O. 2005. A Bayesian view on multimodal cue integration. In *Perception of the Human Body From the Inside Out*, ed. Gunther Knoblich, Ian Thornton, Marc Grosejan, and Maggie Shiffrar, 105–131. New York: Oxford University Press.

——. 2007. Learning to integrate arbitrary signals from vision and touch. *Journal of Vision* 7:1–14.

——. 2008. Multisensory integration: A late bloomer. *Current Biology* 18:R519–R521.

Ernst, Marc O., and Martin S. Banks. 2002. Humans integrate visual and haptic information in a statistically optimal fashion. *Nature* 415:429–433.

Ernst, Marc O., and Heinrich H. Bülthoff. 2004. Merging the senses into a robust percept. *Trends in Cognitive Sciences* 8:162–169.

Fendrich, Robert, and Paul M. Corballis. 2001. The temporal cross-capture of audition and vision. *Perception and Psychophysics* 63:719–725.

Gallace, Alberto, and Charles Spence. 2006. Multisensory synesthetic interactions in the speeded classification of visual size. *Perception and Psychophysics* 68:1191–1203.

Garner, Wendell R. 1974. *The Processing of Information and Structure*. Potomac, MD: Lawrence Erlbaum Associates.

Gebels, Gustav. 1969. An investigation of phonetic symbolism in different cultures. *Journal of Verbal Learning and Verbal Behavior* 8:310–312.

Gepshtein, Sergei, Burge Johannes, Ernst Marc O., and Martin S. Banks. 2005. The combination of vision and touch depends on spatial proximity. *Journal of Vision* 5:1013–1023.

Gori, Monica, Del Viva Michela, Sandini Giulio, and David C. Burr. 2008. Young children do not integrate visual and haptic form information. *Current Biology* 18:694–698.

Green, Andrea M., and Dora E. Angelaki. 2010. Multisensory integration: Resolving sensory ambiguities to build novel representations. *Current Opinion in Neurobiology* 20:353–360.

Grossenbacher, Peter G., and Christopher T. Lovelace. 2001. Mechanisms of synesthesia: Cognitive and physiological constraints. *Trends in Cognitive Sciences* 5:36–41.

Guzman-Martinez, Emmanuel, Laura Ortega, Marcia Grabowecky, Julia Mossbridge, and Satoru Suzuki. 2012. Interactive coding of visual spatial frequency and auditory amplitude-modulation rate. *Current Biology* 22:383–388.

Hillis, James, Marc O. Ernst, Martin Banks, and Michael Landy. 2002. Combining sensory information: Mandatory fusion within, but not between, senses. *Science* 298:1627–1630.

Hinton, Leanne, Johanna Nichols, and John J. Ohala, eds. 1994. *Sound Symbolism*. Cambridge: Cambridge University Press.

Hornbostel, Erich. 1938. The unity of the senses. In *A Source Book of Gestalt Psychology*, ed. Willis D. Ellis, 210–216. New York: The Gestalt Journal Press.

Howells, T. 1944. The experimental development of color-tone synesthesia. *Journal of Experimental Psychology* 34:87–103.

Johnson, Addie, Marieke Jepma, and Ritske De Jong. 2007. Colours sometimes count: Awareness and bidirectionality in grapheme-colour synaesthesia. *Quarterly Journal of Experimental Psychology* 60:1406–1422.

Karwoski, Theodore, Odbert Henry, and Charles E. Osgood. 1942. Studies in synesthetic thinking: II. The role of form in visual responses to music. *Journal of General Psychology* 26:199–222.

Keetels, Mirjam, and Jean Vroomen. 2011. No effect of synesthetic congruency on temporal ventriloquism. *Attention, Perception, and Psychophysics* 73:1–10.

Kelly, E. Lowell. 1934. An experimental attempt to produce artificial chromaesthesia by the technique of the conditioned response. *Journal of Experimental Psychology*, 17:315–341.

Köhler, Wolfgang. 1929. *Gestalt Psychology*: New York: Liveright.

Körding, Konrad P., Ulrich Beierholm, Wei J. Ma, Steven Quartz, Joshua B. Tenenbaum, and Ladan Shams. 2007. Causal inference in multisensory perception. *PLoS ONE* 2:943.

Külpe, Oswald. 1893. *Grundriss der Psychologie: Auf experimenteller Grundlage* [Outline of Psychology: On an experimental basis]. Leipzig: W. Engelmann.

Levitan, Carmel, Massimiliano Zampini, Ryan Li, and Charles Spence. 2008. Assessing the role of color cues and people's beliefs about color-flavor associations on the discrimination of the flavor of sugar-coated chocolates. *Chemical Senses* 33:415–423.

Lewkowicz, David J. 2000. The development of intersensory temporal perception: An epigenetic systems/limitations view. *Psychological Bulletin* 126:281–308.

Lewkowicz, David J., Irene Leo, and Francesca Simion. 2010. Intersensory perception at birth: Newborns match non-human primate faces and voices. *Infancy* 15:46–60.

Long, John. 1977. Contextual assimilation and its effect on the division of attention between nonverbal signals. *Quarterly Journal of Experimental Psychology* 29:397–414.

Marks, Lawrence E. 1974. On associations of light and sound: The mediation of brightness, pitch, and loudness. *American Journal of Psychology* 87:173–188.

——. 1987a. On cross-modal similarity: Auditory-visual interactions in speeded discrimination. *Journal of Experimental Psychology: Human Perception and Performance* 13:384–394.

——. 1987b. On cross-modal similarity: Perceiving temporal patterns by hearing, touch, and vision. *Perception and Psychophysics* 42:250–256.

——. 1989. On cross-modal similarity: The perceptual structure of pitch, loudness, and brightness. *Journal of Experimental Psychology: Human Perception and Performance* 15:586–602.

———. 2004. Cross-modal interactions in speeded classification. In *The Handbook of Mutisensory Processes,* ed. Gemma A. Calvert, Charles Spence and Barry E. Stein, 85–106. Cambridge, MA: MIT Press.

———. 2013. Weak synesthesia in perception and language. In *The Oxford Handbook of Synesthesia,* ed. Julia Simner and Edward M. Hubbard, 761–789. Oxford: Oxford University Press.

Martino, Gail, and Lawrence E. Marks. 1999. Perceptual and linguistic interactions in speeded classification: Tests of the semantic coding hypothesis. *Perception* 28:903–924.

———. 2000. Cross-modal interaction between vision and touch: The role of synesthetic correspondence. *Perception* 29:745–754.

———. 2001. Synesthesia: Strong and weak. *Current Directions in Psychological Science* 10:61–65.

Maurer, Daphne. 1997. Neonatal synesthesia: Implications for the processing of speech and faces. In *Synaesthesia: Classic and Contemporary Readings,* ed. Simon Baron-Cohen, and John E. Harrison, 224–242. Malden, MA: Blackwell Publishing.

Maurer, Daphne, Laura C. Gibson, and Ferrinne Spector. 2013. Synesthesia in infants and very young children. In *The Oxford Handbook of Synesthesia,* ed. Julia Simner and Edward M. Hubbard, 46–63. Oxford: Oxford University Press.

Maurer, Daphne, Thanujeni Pathman, and Catherine Mondloch. 2006. The shape of boubas: Sound-shape correspondences in toddlers and adults. *Developmental Science* 9:316–322.

Meier, Beat, and Nicolas Rothen. 2007. When conditioned responses 'fire back': Bidirectional cross-activation creates learning opportunities in synesthesia. *Neuroscience* 147:569–572.

Melara, Robert D. 1989. Similarity relations among synesthetic stimuli and their attributes. *Journal of Experimental Psychology: Human Perception and Performance* 15:212–231.

Melara, Robert D., and Thomas P. O'Brien. 1987. Interaction between synesthetically corresponding dimensions. *Journal of Experimental Psychology: General* 116:323–336.

Miller, Jeff. 1982. Divided attention: Evidence for coactivation with redundant signals. *Cognitive Psychology* 14:247–279.

———. 1991. Channel interaction and the redundant-targets effect in bimodal divided attention. *Journal of Experimental Psychology: Human Perception and Performance* 17:160–169.

Mondloch, Catherine J., and Daphne Maurer. 2004. Do small white balls squeak? Pitch–object correspondences in young children. *Cognitive, Affective, and Behavioral Neuroscience* 4:133–136.

Morein-Zamir, Sharon, Salvador Soto-Faraco, and Alan Kingstone. 2003. Auditory capture of vision: Examining temporal ventriloquism. *Cognitive Brain Research* 17:154–163.

Mulvenna, Catherine M., and Vincent Walsh. 2006. Synaesthesia: Supernormal integration? *Trends in Cognitive Sciences* 10:350–352.

Murray, Michah M., and Mark T. Wallace, eds. 2011. *The Neural Bases of Multisensory Processes.* Boca Raton, FL: CRC Press.

Nardini, Marko, Peter Jones, Rachael Bedford, and Oliver Braddick. 2008. Development of cue integration in human navigation. *Current Biology* 18:689–693.

Osgood, Charles E. 1960. The cross-cultural generality of visual–verbal synesthetic tendencies. *Behavioral Science* 5:146–169.

Osgood, Charles E., George Suci, and Percy Tannenbaum. 1957. *The Measurement of Meaning.* Urbana, IL: University of Illinois Press.

Otto, Thomas U., and Pascal Mamassian. 2012. Noise and correlations in parallel perceptual decision making. Current Biology 22: 1391–1396

Parise, Cesare, and Charles Spence. 2008. Synesthetic congruency modulates the temporal ventriloquism effect. *Neuroscience Letters* 442:257–261.

———. 2009. When birds of a feather flock together: Synesthetic correspondences modulate audiovisual integration in non-synesthetes. *PLoS ONE* 4:e5664.

Parise, Cesare V., Vanessa Harrar, Marc O. Ernst, and Charles Spence. 2013. Cross-correlation between auditory and visual signals promotes multisensory integration. *Multisensory Research*. doi:10.1163/22134808–00002417.

Parise, Cesare V., Charles Spence, and Marc O. Ernst. 2012. When correlation implies causation in multisensory integration. *Current Biology* 22:46–49

Raab, David H. 1962. Statistical facilitation of simple reaction times. *Transactions of the New York Academy of Sciences* 24:574–590.

Ramachandran, Vilayanur, and Edward Hubbard. 2001. Synaesthesia: A window into perception, thought and language. *Journal of Consciousness Studies* 8:3–34.

Rock, Irvin, and Jack Victor. 1964. Vision and touch: An experimentally created conflict between the two senses. *Science* 143:594–596.

Roffler, Suzanne H., and Robert A. Butler. 1968. Localization of tonal stimuli in the vertical plane. *Journal of the Acoustical Society of America* 43:1269–1266

Rogers, Susan K., and Abraham S. Ross. 1968. A cross-cultural test of the Maluma-Takete phenomenon. *Perception* 4:105–106.

Root, R., and Sherman Ross. 1965. Further validation of subjective scales for loudness and brightness by means of cross-modality matching. *American Journal of Psychology* 78:285–289.

Rouw, Romke, and Steven H. Scholte. 2007. Increased structural connectivity in grapheme-color synesthesia. *Nature Neuroscience* 10:792–797.

——. 2010. Neural basis of individual differences in synesthetic experiences. *Journal of Neuroscience* 30:6205–6213.

Rudmin, Floyd, and Mark Cappelli. 1983. Tone-taste synesthesia: A replication. *Perceptual and Motor Skills* 56:118.

Rusconi, Elena, Bonnie Kwan, Bruno L. Giordano, Carlo Umilta, and Brian Butterworth. 2006. Spatial representation of pitch height: The SMARC effect. *Cognition* 99:113–129.

Sapir, Edward. 1929. A study in phonetic symbolism. *Journal of Experimental Psychology* 12:225–239.

Seo, Han-Seok, Artin Arshamian, Kerstin Schemmer, Ingeborg Scheer, Thorsten Sander, Guido Ritter, and Thomas Hummel. 2010. Cross-modal integration between odors and abstract symbols. *Neuroscience Letters* 478:175–178.

Shams, Ladan, and Ulrich R. Beierholm. 2010. Causal inference in perception. *Trends in Cognitive Sciences* 14:425–432.

Simner, Julia. 2012. Defining synaesthesia. *British Journal of Psychology* 103:1–15.

——. 2013. The "rules" of synesthesia. In *The Oxford Handbook of Synesthesia*, ed. Julia Simner and Edward M. Hubbard, 149–164. Oxford: Oxford University Press.

Simpson, Ray H., Marian Quinn, and David P. Ausubel. 1956. Synesthesia in children: Association of colors with pure tone frequencies. *Journal of Genetic Psychology: Research and Theory on Human Development* 89:95–103.

Smith, Linda B., and Maria D. Sera. 1992. A developmental analysis of the polar structure of dimensions. *Cognitive Psychology* 24:99–142.

Spector, Ferrine, and Daphne Maurer. 2009. Synesthesia: A new approach to understanding the development of perception. *Perception* 45:175–189.

Spence, Charles. 2011. Crossmodal correspondences: A tutorial review. *Attention, Perception, and Psychophysics*, 73:971–995.

Spence, Charles, Carmel A. Levitan, Maya U. Shankar, and Massimiliano Zampini. 2010. Does food color influence taste and flavour perception in humans? *Chemosensory Perception* 3:68–84.

Spence, Charles, Mary Ngo, Ju-Hwan Lee, and Hong Tan. 2010. Solving the correspondence problem in haptic/multisensory interface design. In *Advances in Haptics*, ed. Mehrdad H. Zadeh, 47–74. Vukovar, Croatia: In-Teh Publishers.

Stein, Barry E., ed. 2012. *The New Handbook of Multisensory Processing*. Cambridge, MA: MIT Press.

Stevens, Joseph C., and Lawrence E. Marks. 1965. Cross-modality matching of brightness and loudness. *Proceedings of the National Academy of Sciences of the United States of America* 54, 407–411.

Stevens, Stanley S. 1957. On the psychophysical law. *Psychological Review* 64:153–181.

——. 1975. *Psychophysics*. New York: Wiley-Interscience.

Stocker, Alan A., and Eero P. Simoncelli. 2006. Noise characteristics and prior expectations in human visual speed perception. *Nature Neuroscience* 9:578–585.

Stroop, John R. 1935. Studies of interference in serial verbal reactions. *Journal of Experimental Psychology* 18:643–662.

Stumpf, Karl. 1883. *Tonpsychologie* [Psychology of tones]. Leipzig: S. Hirzel.

Taylor, Iinsup K., and Maurice M. Taylor. 1962. Phonetic symbolism in four unrelated languages. *Canadian Journal of Psychology* 16:344–356.

Trommershäuser, Julia, Michael Landy, and Konrad Körding, eds. 2011. *Sensory Cue Integration*. New York: Oxford University Press.

Vatakis, Argiro, Asif A. Ghazanfar, and Charles Spence. 2008. Facilitation of multisensory integration by the 'unity effect' reveals that speech is special. *Journal of Vision* 8:1–11.

Vatakis, Argiro, and Charles Spence. 2007. Crossmodal binding: Evaluating the 'unity assumption' using audiovisual speech stimuli. *Perception and Psychophysics* 69:744–756.

——. 2008. Evaluating the influence of the 'unity assumption' on the temporal perception of realistic audiovisual stimuli. *Acta Psychologica* 127:12–23.

Walker, Peter, Gavin Bremner, Uschi Mason, Jo Spring, Karen Mattock, Alan Slater, and Scott Johnson. 2010. Preverbal infants' sensitivity to synaesthetic cross-modality correspondences. *Psychological Science* 21:21–25.

Walker, Peter, and Sylvia Smith. 1984. Stroop interference based on the synaesthetic qualities of auditory pitch. *Perception* 13:75–81.

——. 1985. Stroop interference based on the multimodal correlates of haptic size and auditory pitch. *Perception* 14:729–736.

Walker, Robert. 1987. The effects of culture, environment, age, and musical training on choices of visual metaphors for sound. *Attention, Perception, and Psychophysics* 42:491–502.

Walsh, Vincent. 1996. Perception: The seeing ear. *Current Biology* 6:389–391.

——. 2003. A theory of magnitude: Common cortical metrics of time, space and quantity. *Trends in Cognitive Sciences* 7:483–488.

Walsh, Vincent E. 2013. Magnitudes, metaphors, and modalities: A theory of magnitude revisited. In *The Oxford Handbook of Synesthesia*, ed. Julia Simner and Edward M. Hubbard, 837–852. Oxford: Oxford University Press.

Ward, Jamie. 2013. Synesthesia: Where have we been? Where are we going? In *The Oxford Handbook of Synesthesia*, ed. Julia Simner and Edward M. Hubbard, 1022–1039. Oxford: Oxford University Press.

Ward, Jamie, Brett Huckstep, and Elias Tsakanikos. 2006. Sound-colour synaesthesia: To what extent does it use cross-modal mechanisms common to us all? *Cortex* 42:264–280.

Weiss, Yair, Eero P. Simoncelli, and Edward H. Adelson. 2002. Motion illusions as optimal percepts. *Nature Neuroscience* 5:598–604.

Welch, Robert, and David Warren. 1980. Immediate perceptual response to intersensory discrepancy. *Psychological Bulletin* 88:638–667.

Zangenehpour, Shahin, and Robert J. Zatorre. 2010. Crossmodal recruitment of primary visual cortex following brief exposure to bimodal audiovisual stimuli. *Neuropsychologia* 48:591–600.

CHAPTER 40

CROSS-MODALITY IN SPEECH PROCESSING

ARGIRO VATAKIS

INTRODUCTION

Speech has been considered to be an exclusively auditory event (e.g., McClelland and Elman 1986). One, however, wonders how can this be true given that speech is a highly complex and multisensory phenomenon (e.g., Bernstein and Benoit 1996). Research in multisensory perception has shown that other sensory modalities (e.g., visual, somatosensory) also contribute to the successful perception of speech. The multisensory nature of speech is evidenced, for example, through research on the well-known McGurk effect (i.e., the influence of visual lip-reading cues on the perception of audiovisual speech;[1] McGurk and MacDonald 1976) as well as on the use of touch for speech perception by individuals suffering from hearing loss (e.g., Gault 1924), and on how visual information can enhance the perception of speech against a noisy background (e.g., Sumby and Pollack 1954). Psychophysical evidence has recently been coupled with functional brain imaging studies supporting the multimodality of speech by identifying specific brain regions that show integrative processing, when the visual- and auditory-speech signals are presented simultaneously (e.g., Calvert and Campbell 2003; Calvert, Campbell, and Brammer 2000).

New research continues to demonstrate the multimodality of speech as can be read in the recently published study by Gick and Derrick (2009), where naturalistic tactile information was shown to be integrated during auditory speech perception. Specifically, the authors manipulated the production of aspiration bursts in some English speech sounds (e.g., the burst of air released after the /p/ in *pin* but not after the /p/ in *stop*) by applying inaudible air bursts on the participants' skin. Participants were more likely to hear

---

[1] 'Audiovisual speech' comprises both visual information from observing the movement of the mouth and facial muscles, and auditory information from hearing the speech stream.

aspirated speech sounds in the presence of the airbursts (e.g., hear /p/ instead of /b/) as compared to the absence of airbursts, thus demonstrating robust audiotactile speech integration. The earlier-mentioned examples of the multimodal nature of speech lead to the natural inquiry of how exactly integration of the different modalities takes place in order to create a unified multisensory speech signal. This inquiry will be explored in the next section.

MULTISENSORY INTEGRATION

Our daily experiences are structured by multiple inputs from the same and/or different sensory modalities. We are constantly bombarded with huge amounts of information in the form of visual, auditory, tactile (and so on) stimuli from the surrounding environment. Combining these sensory inputs in the right way allows us to clearly localize, discriminate, and respond to a particular environmental event (e.g., Calvert, Spence, and Stein 2004). How does one, however, know how to combine the various sensory inputs that are attributed to any particular event? Research to date has shown that the "binding" (i.e., combining) of multiple sensory inputs about the same event depends on both temporal and spatial factors (e.g., Parise and Spence 2009; Slutsky and Recanzone 2001). Specifically, *spatial coincidence* (i.e., multiple sensory inputs originating from the same location in space; e.g., Soto-Faraco et al. 2002; Spence and Squire 2003; although see, for example, Fujisaki and Nishida 2005) and *temporal synchrony* (i.e., various sensory inputs occurring at approximately the same time) of multiple sensory inputs comprise two of the key factors that determine whether or not multisensory integration will take place in order to yield a unified percept of a given event (e.g., Stein and Meredith 1993). The integration of different sensory inputs is also governed by the *law of inverse effectiveness*, where multisensory integration is most effective when the individual sensory components are relatively weak in salience or strength (e.g., presentation of audiovisual speech in noise; e.g., Meredith and Stein 1983). This type of enhancement of multisensory integration in the presence of a degraded auditory- and/or visual-speech signal has been demonstrated in psychophysical (e.g., Breeuwer and Plomp 1986; McGrath and Summerfield 1985; Sumby and Pollack 1954) and, more recently, in imaging studies (e.g., Calvert, Campbell, and Brammer 2000; Stevenson and James 2009; but see Ross et al. 2007). Finally, another factor that is increasingly being recognized as critical for multisensory integration is the *semantic congruency* of the sensory stimuli presented (e.g., the presentation of a red square and a "red" speech sound; e.g., Chen and Spence 2010; Doehrmann and Naumer 2008; Hein et al. 2007; Laurienti et al. 2004). Multisensory integration is a very current topic in cognitive sciences and all the just mentioned rules or factors modulating integration (i.e., spatial coincidence, temporal synchrony, law of inverse effectiveness, semantic congruency) are being heavily investigated. In the present chapter, however, the focus will solely be on the temporal synchrony of multisensory integration (and the reader can refer to Calvert, Spence, and Stein (2004) for other topics not covered here).

TEMPORAL PERCEPTION: A TIME-WINDOW FOR MULTISENSORY INTEGRATION

Every day we partake in conversations where we listen to and watch an individual talking. Is this interaction problematic? Most of the time the answer is "No," the interaction is flawless and sometimes enjoyable! Although we experience synchrony in the multisensory speech events we are exposed to (i.e., all the information presented appears to us as a coherent whole), the generation of this percept is not an easy task. The complexity originates from neuronal and non-neuronal factors (see Vatakis and Spence 2010 for a detailed description of these factors) that influence the arrival and processing time of two or more sensory signals to the brain, even though those signals may or may not have emanated simultaneously from a given source (e.g., King 2005; Spence and Squire 2003).

Many studies have now shown that even though multisensory integration is frequently enhanced by simultaneously presented sensory signals (e.g., see Calvert et al. 2004; de Gelder and Bertelson 2003), precise temporal coincidence is not mandatory for a unified, multisensory representation of an event (e.g., Sugita and Suzuki 2003). This has been shown in studies utilizing both simple (e.g., light flashes, sound bursts) and complex stimuli (e.g., speech, or object-actions such as crashing a soda can with a hammer[2]). For example, it has been shown that the intelligibility of audiovisual speech remains high even when temporal asynchronies of as much as 250 ms are introduced between the visual and auditory signals (e.g., Dixon and Spitz 1980; Munhall et al. 1996). Similarly, the illusion of the ventriloquist effect (whereby the auditory signal appears to come from the location of the visual signal) can persist for temporal auditory- and visual-signal differences of approximately 300 ms (e.g., Bertelson and Aschersleben 1998; Caclin et al. 2002; Jones and Jarick 2006). The McGurk effect continues to be experienced even when the visual signal leads the auditory by up to 300 ms, or lags by up to 80 ms (e.g., Munhall et al. 1996).

The psychophysical research that has been conducted to date has shown that the ability of the human perceptual system to compensate for the typical temporal discrepancies associated with the processing of incoming sensory signals may be accounted

---

[2] Note that complex stimuli are defined here as stimuli of higher information content and a continuously changing audiovisual temporal profile.

for by the existence of a *temporal window of multisensory integration*. The existence of a temporal window does not imply an active process, rather it refers to the interval in which no signal discrepancy is perceived; anything beyond this interval will normally be perceived as being desynchronized. This temporal window has been shown to be relatively wide and flexible, allowing large temporal discrepancies to be tolerated and thus making the individual insensitive to the possible arrival and processing differences needed for each sensory signal (e.g., one does not perceived the faster arrival and processing of an auditory stream as compared to the visual stream of an audiovisual event; see Spence and Squire 2003; Vatakis and Spence 2010, for more details).

The temporal window of multisensory integration can be measured through the use of the *temporal order judgment* (TOJ) task (see Vatakis and Spence 2010, for the description of other related tasks). In a TOJ task, the participants are presented with a pair of stimuli (e.g., auditory, visual) at various stimulus onset asynchronies (i.e., with varying time-gaps between the onset of one stimulus and the subsequent onset of a second stimulus). Participants are asked to make a judgment as to the order of the stimulus presentation (e.g., Bald et al. 1942; Hirsh and Sherrick 1961). The data obtained from a TOJ task allows the calculation of two measures, the *just noticeable difference* (JND; a standardized measure of the sensitivity with which participants can judge the temporal order of the two stimuli presented) and the *point of subjective simultaneity* (PSS; an estimate of the time interval by which the stimulus in one sensory modality has to lead the stimulus in the other modality in order for synchrony to be perceived). The temporal window is calculated around the PSS, by the value of the JND measure (i.e., PSS ± JND). The following sections will discuss the way in which these measures have provided an understanding about the temporal processing of multisensory speech.

MULTISENSORY SPEECH PERCEPTION AND SYNCHRONY

Early studies on the topic of multisensory temporal perception focused on the use of simple stimuli (e.g., light flashes, sound bursts). These studies showed that discrete pairs of auditory- and visual-stimuli needed to be separated by approximately 60–70 ms in order for participants to judge accurately which modality was presented first (e.g., Zampini et al. 2003). In recent years, researchers investigated these temporal constraints under more realistic conditions by using more ecologically-valid stimuli (e.g., speech, musical, or object-action stimuli; e.g., Vatakis and Spence 2006a). Given the ubiquity of speech in our daily life, research has primarily focused on the perception of synchrony for audiovisual speech stimuli rather than music or object-actions (e.g., Dixon and Spitz 1980; Grant and Greenberg 2001; Steinmetz 1996; but see Vatakis and Spence 2010).

Temporal perception for continuous speech and non-speech events

Dixon and Spitz (1980) were the first to investigate the perception of synchrony for speech and non-speech stimuli. The participants in Dixon and Spitz's study had to monitor continuous videos consisting of audiovisual speech or object-action stimuli (a hammer repeatedly hitting a peg) and were instructed to respond as soon as they noticed the asynchrony. The videos started off in synchrony and were then gradually desynchronized at a constant rate of 51 ms/s up to a maximum asynchrony of 500 ms. Participant responses showed that in the case of speech, the auditory stream had to lag by 258 ms or else to lead by 131 ms before any temporal discrepancy was detected (see also Conrey and Pisoni 2006). While in the object-action event, an auditory lag of only 188 ms or a lead of 75 ms was sufficient for participants to detect the asynchrony. Thus, demonstrating significantly higher participant sensitivity to the asynchrony present in the object-action than in the speech event.

The results of Dixon and Spitz's (1980) seminal study, however, may not provide an accurate estimate of people's sensitivity to asynchrony for audiovisual stimuli due to some confounding factors. First, a spatial discrepancy (auditory streams were presented over headphones while the visual streams were presented from directly in front of the participants) could have impaired multisensory integration (e.g., Soto-Faraco et al. 2002; Spence and Driver 1997; though see Zampini et al. 2003). Second, subtle auditory pitch-shifting cues due to the gradual desynchronization of the auditory- and visual-streams could also have facilitated performance (Reeves and Voelker 1993). Third, the magnitude of the asynchrony was always proportional to the length of time for which the video had been presented, thus potentially confounding asynchrony with viewing duration. Fourth, the absence of catch trials does not allow the assessment of the influence of criterion shifts on performance (cf. Spence and Driver 1997). These potential confounds therefore imply that people's ability to discriminate the temporal order of audiovisual events may actually be much different than Dixon and Spitz's results suggest.

More recently, Hollier and Rimell (1998) also examined people's sensitivity to synchrony utilizing continuous speech and non-speech stimuli. Specifically, they presented two different impact events (a pen being dropped on a hard surface and an axe hitting a piece of wood) and a speech video. The delays introduced between the auditory- and visual-streams were +200, +300, ±150, ±100, ±50, and 0 ms (a "−" sign indicates that the auditory stream was presented first) and the participants were asked to report ("yes/no" vocal response in the presence of the experimenter) the moment at which they perceived an asynchrony. The results showed that for both speech and non-speech stimuli, participants detected the asynchrony at auditory leads of more than 100 ms and lags of 175 ms. The authors observed only that their participants were more sensitive to the video asynchrony in the case where the auditory stream was leading the visual stream in the speech stimulus.

Miner and Caudell (1998) also set out to investigate people's asynchrony detection thresholds by presenting a series of audiovisual stimuli: speech, three single impact events (a hammer striking a block, two drumsticks colliding, and two wine glasses colliding), and one repeated impact event (two silver balls colliding 12 times). The participants had to make a vocal yes/no response concerning whether the auditory- and visual-streams of the stimulus presented were synchronous or not (the delays utilized were not reported). The results showed that the average detection threshold was the lowest for the repetitive impact event (auditory/visual delays of 172 ms) and highest for the speech event (auditory/visual delays of 203 ms). It should be noted that the same spatial confound found in previous studies was also present here.

Temporal perception for continuous and brief speech events

Based on the studies reported in the previous section, it would appear that people are more sensitive to temporal asynchrony in object-action events as compared with speech events. As pointed out earlier, however, these early studies had some shortcomings that, as yet, have not been addressed. Further investigations of the temporal perception of synchrony focused on the use of audiovisual speech as their sole stimulus. In particular, these studies focused on the use of continuous and brief audiovisual speech stimuli, as well as McGurk speech tokens. In one such study, Rihs (1995) measured the influence of a continuous desynchronization of an audiovisual speech signal on people's perception of scenes presented in a television program. Participants, in this study, were presented with 50 s segments from a talk show with a fixed audiovisual delay (not reported) and had to report their perception of decreased video quality on a 5-point impairment scale (a decrease of ½-point on this scale was defined as the detectability threshold). According to the participants' reports, an auditory lead of about 40 ms and a lag of 120 ms constituted the interval needed for a scene impairment to be experienced. Rihs also measured the participants' acceptability thresholds (which were defined by a quality decrease of 1.5 points on the 5-point scale) finding that participants were willing to tolerate an auditory lead of as much as 90 ms and a lag of as much as 180 ms. The values reported by Rihs were much lower than those observed in Dixon and Spitz's (1980) study. In addition, the fixed delay used could have inadvertently promoted temporal adaptation effects (e.g., Navarra et al. 2005), thus rendering the results reported confounded.

Steinmetz (1996) conducted another study focusing on the effect of audiovisual stream delays on the temporal perception of continuous speech segments. In this study, video segments of television news reports were presented at three different viewing angles (head, shoulder, and body view). The auditory- and visual-speech streams were desynchronized in steps of 40 ms, resulting in ±120, ±80, ±40, and 0 ms audiovisual stream delays. At the end of each video, the participants had to complete a video-quality questionnaire and report which of the two streams they had perceived as leading/lagging. Steinmetz reported that the participants exhibited lower sensitivity to the desynchronization of speech events occurring far away (i.e., body view) than for events occurring proximal to the observer (i.e., head- and shoulder-view). Overall, the breakdown of the perception of synchrony for the news report videos was found to occur at intervals exceeding ± 80 ms auditory/visual lag. Even though this study hinted at the importance of the type of stimulus utilized or the manner of stimulus presentation on temporal perception, Steinmetz did not provide a detailed account of the experimental design, so that one cannot critically compare his results to those of other studies.

More recently, a series of studies has focused on the use of single sentences in looking at the audiovisual temporal perception for speech. For instance, Grant et al. (2004) reported that participants only noticed the asynchrony in a continuous stream of audiovisual speech when the auditory speech led the visual lip movements by at least 50 ms or else lagged by 220 ms or more.[3] Meanwhile, McGrath and Summerfield (1985) reported a study in which the intelligibility of audiovisual sentences in auditory white noise deteriorated at much lower visual leads (160 ms; see also Pandey, Kunov, and Abel 1986) than those observed in the studies of both Dixon and Spitz (1980) and Grant and colleagues.

Audiovisual synchrony perception has also been evaluated for brief speech tokens using the McGurk effect. For instance, Massaro, Cohen, and Smeele (1996) evaluated the temporal perception of synthetic and natural syllables dubbed onto congruent and incongruent synthetic animated facial point-light displays. In this study, two groups of participants were tested on their ability to identify the audiovisual speech tokens that had been presented. The first group was tested with videos of 67, 167, and 267 ms auditory- and visual-stream delays, while the second group was tested with delays of ±133, ±267, and ±500 ms. Results showed that congruent audiovisual identification was overall less affected by stream delays than the identification performance for incongruent speech pairs. Massaro and colleagues proposed that the boundary of audiovisual integration occurs at auditory and visual leads or lags of about ±250 ms (see also Massaro and Cohen 1993).

Munhall and colleagues (1996), however, described results that were quite different from those observed by Massaro, Cohen, and Smeele (1996). Specifically, Munhall et al. reported a series of experiments looking at the effect of asynchrony and vowel context in the McGurk effect. Their stimuli consisted of the auditory utterances of /aba/ and /ibi/ dubbed onto a video of an individual's face whose lip-movements were articulating /aga/. The range of auditory- and visual-stream asynchronies spanned from ±360 ms in steps of 60 ms and the participants had to complete an identification task. Overall, the results showed that responses driven by the auditory stream dominated for the majority of the asynchronies presented, while responses that were driven by the visual stream presented (i.e., /g/) predominated for auditory leads of 60 ms to lags of 240

---

[3] Note that spatial confounds were also present in this study (see also Grant and Greenberg 2001; Grant and Seitz 1998).

ms. Subsequently, van Wassenhove, Grant, and Poeppel's (2007) extension of Munhall et al.'s study (by testing more asynchronies under two different experimental conditions) revealed temporal windows of maximal audiovisual integration having a width of about 200 ms (e.g., van Wassenhove, Grant, and Poeppel 2003, 2005). Thus, Munhall et al.'s findings were replicated and extended by sampling a greater range of asynchronies, using smaller temporal step sizes, and determining the boundaries for subjective audiovisual simultaneity.

Infant temporal perception for continuous speech events

Apart from the research on healthy adults, empirical findings from a number of studies indicate that, beginning as early as the second month of life, human infants can integrate concurrent auditory- and visual-speech inputs on the basis of their temporal synchrony (Lewkowicz 1986, 1992; Spelke, Born, and Chu 1983). For example, Dodd (1979) has reported that infants spend longer looking at synchronized, continuous audiovisual speech stimuli than for the same speech stimuli when desynchronized. In the case of brief speech stimuli, Lewkowicz (2000) has demonstrated that the presentation of syllables with their auditory- and visual-streams delayed by 666 ms resulted in 6- and 8-month-old infants exhibiting sensitivity to the temporal delay as compared to the lack of sensitivity exhibited by the 4-month-old infants, while Dodd (1979) has shown that continuous audiovisual speech stimuli with a constant delay of 400 ms promoted sensitivity in 3-month-old infants. These studies therefore indicate that infants can discriminate synchronous from asynchronous audiovisual speech events at an early age (Lewkowicz 1992), thus implying that multisensory synchrony is a critical component in human development. Lewkowicz (1992, 1994) has proposed that the size of the temporal window for audiovisual synchrony perception is probably larger in infants as compared to adults due to experience (i.e., infants are inexperienced with temporal discrepancies) and the maturation levels of the nervous system (i.e., the rate of neural transmission in the nervous system of the infant is slower due to low levels of maturation of the neural processes).

Factors modulating temporal perception for speech stimuli

On the whole, the results of previous studies concerning the temporal perception of audiovisual speech have shown that the intelligibility of speech signals remains high over a wide range of audiovisual temporal asynchronies. Despite the differences in the type of stimuli, response tasks, and statistical procedures used in previous studies, three characteristics of the audiovisual temporal window are relatively consistent across the majority of the previous studies using complex stimuli. First, the temporal window for synchrony perception for audiovisual stimuli has a width in the order of several hundred milliseconds. Second, the temporal window of synchrony is asymmetrical (shifted towards vision) with participants facing higher difficulty in asynchrony detection when the visual signal leads as compared to cases where the auditory signal leads. Thirdly, the width of the temporal window exhibits great variability across individuals, experimental set-ups, and stimuli (Stone et al. 2001). Given the importance of understanding human temporal perception, the rest of the chapter will focus on the investigation of the factors that affect audiovisual temporal perception for speech alone or in comparison to non-speech stimuli.

The effect of stimulus type on temporal perception

A series of experiments were conducted in order to define the temporal limits for complex audiovisual stimuli more accurately, while eliminating the confounds identified in previous studies (Vatakis and Spence 2006a, 2006c). In particular, the experiments conducted utilized speech (i.e., continuous and brief speech tokens; sentences, words, and syllables) and non-speech stimuli (i.e., object-actions and musical stimuli; e.g., single impact events, such as smashing a block of ice with a hammer and playing musical pieces and single/double notes) in a TOJ task. The results of these experiments were similar to those reported by Dixon and Spitz (1980). More specifically, people found it easier to detect the temporal asynchrony present in desynchronized audiovisual object-action events than to detect the asynchrony in speech events. However, the overall pattern of results demonstrated that participants were generally more sensitive when reporting the temporal order of an audiovisual event than had been suggested by Dixon and Spitz's previous research.

The results of the experiments also demonstrated, for the first time, that people are less sensitive to the asynchrony present in musical events than in either speech or object-action events. Most importantly, however, the results showed that the temporal window of integration is modulated by the properties and complexity of a given stimulus as well as by the level of familiarity that a participant has with that particular stimulus. Specifically, the results showed that stimuli of shorter duration and of less complexity (i.e., where the stimulus properties remain relatively constant) led to a higher sensitivity to temporal order as compared to stimuli that were longer in duration and/or of higher complexity (e.g., the temporal window for a sentence as opposed to that for a syllable).

The effect of the physical characteristics of speech on temporal perception

Having a clearer picture of the actual limits of temporal perception for speech and non-speech stimuli, a new line of experiments was conducted on the perception of speech stimuli and how physical differences present in the articulation of various speech tokens affect people's temporal sensitivity. Specifically, the experiments were designed to investigate the possible effects that physical changes occurring during the articulation of different consonants (i.e., varying as a function of the place and manner of articulation and voicing[4]) and vowels (i.e., varying as a function of the height and backness of the tongue and roundedness of the lips; see Kent 1997) may have on the temporal window of audiovisual integration for speech stimuli (Vatakis and Spence 2007c.). The results of the experiments showed that visual speech had to lead auditory speech in order for the PSS to be attained (except in the case of vowels). These visual speech leads were generally larger for lower saliency visual speech signals (e.g., alveolar tokens such as /d/) as compared to the smaller visual leads observed for speech signals that were higher in visibility (such as bilabial tokens; e.g., /b/). These findings replicated previous research showing that the visual speech signal typically precedes the onset of the auditory speech signal in the perception of audiovisual speech (e.g., Munhall et al. 1996). More importantly, this investigation extended previous research by using multiple speakers and by demonstrating that the precedence of the visual speech signal changes as a function of the physical characteristics in the articulation of the particular speech signal that is uttered. In other words, highly-visible visual speech signals require less of a lead over the corresponding auditory signals than visual speech signals that are less visible (Vatakis et al. 2012).

The effects of visual signal manipulation on temporal perception

Audiovisual temporal perception can be modulated by the inherent differences in the properties of an audiovisual stimulus (e.g., physical differences due to the articulation of a speech sound). However, in an otherwise constant (i.e., in properties) stimulus, changes in the orientation of that stimulus (such as shifts in the orientation of a speaker's head during conversation) may also result in changes in sensitivity in the temporal perception of the stimulus. In order to test this possibility, dynamic speech and non-speech stimuli were presented in an upright or inverted orientation (Vatakis and Spence 2008b). The findings of these experiments showed that inversion of the speech stimulus resulted in the visual stream having to lead the auditory stream by a greater interval in order for the PSS to be reached. This result agrees with findings of previous studies on the face inversion effect. That is, that the inversion of a visual display leads to the loss of configural information and to the recruitment of additional processes for the processing of a face but not for the processing of non-speech events (see also Bentin et al. 1996).

---

[4] The place of articulation refers to the articulators involved in the production of a particular speech sound; the manner of articulation refers to how the sound is produced and the way in which the airstream is modified as it passes through the vocal tract; voicing refers to whether the vocal folds are vibrating during the production of consonants.

The effects of stimulus quality on audiovisual temporal perception

This inquiry focuses on how video quality affects the perception of synchrony for multisensory events by manipulating the frame rate of a given stimulus (Vatakis and Spence 2006b). When investigating audiovisual temporal perception and the factors affecting it, aside from the type of stimulus presented and the specific properties of that particular stimulus, one also has to take into account the medium by which that stimulus is presented to the observer. Researchers' attempts to move from the presentation of simple stimuli towards the presentation of dynamic, naturalistic stimuli have typically been achieved through the use of video. However, one of the problems associated with video presentation is the loss of frames during transmission. Thus, it seemed important to look at how video quality (in terms of variations of the frame rate) might affect temporal perception. We conducted research on audiovisual speech videos that were presented at various different frame rates in a TOJ task. The findings demonstrated that modulating the quality of speech videos by using high (i.e., 24 or 30 fps) versus low (i.e., 6 or 12 fps) frame rate videos influenced the modality leads/lags required for the PSS to be attained. Specifically, at lower frame rates, larger visual leads were required for the PSS to be reached, while at higher frame rates smaller visual leads were needed. These findings raise the important issue of the quality of the videos that have been used in previous research on audiovisual temporal perception, and also suggest that the estimate of the temporal window as defined by the broadcasting industry (e.g., a constant auditory signal should not lead by more than 45 ms or else lag by more than 125 ms; ITU-R BT.1359–1 1998) might not always be appropriate.

THE UNITY EFFECT IN AUDIOVISUAL SPEECH

When presented with an auditory and a visual stimulus, an observer can either perceive them as referring to the same unitary audiovisual event or else as referring to two separate unimodal events. The binding versus segregation of these unimodal stimuli depends on both low-level (i.e., stimulus-driven) factors, such as the spatial and temporal co-occurrence of the stimuli (e.g., Welch 1999), as well as on higher-level (i.e., cognitive) factors (e.g., Spence 2007), such as whether or not the participant assumes that the stimuli ought to "go together"—the so-called "unity effect" (i.e., the assumption that a perceiver has as to whether he/she is observing a single multisensory event versus multiple separate unimodal events; Welch and Warren 1980). It has been argued that whenever two or more sensory inputs are perceived as being highly consistent, observers will be more likely to treat them as referring to a single multisensory event (Jackson 1953; Welch and Warren 1980) and assume common spatiotemporal origin, and hence they will be more likely to bind them into a single multisensory perceptual event (see Bedford 2001).

The presentation of "informationally-rich" stimuli (i.e., events that have a greater internal temporal coherence and temporally-varying structure) may promote enhanced multisensory integration as compared to stimuli of "low" informational content (e.g., light flashes and sound bursts, where the only time-varying information consists of the onset and offset transitions). The possibility that "informationally-rich" stimuli may give rise to enhanced multisensory integration has been supported by Warren et al. (1981). In their study of spatial ventriloquism, the dynamic face of a speaker or a static visual stimulus (piece of tape placed at the location of the speaker's mouth) was presented together with an auditory speech signal under various degrees of spatial discrepancy. Warren et al. reported that the visual bias of perceived localization of the auditory stimulus was significantly larger when the visual stimulus consisted of the dynamic face associated with the speaker's voice than when it consisted of the simple static visual stimulus. Warren et al. argued that the "informationally-richer" auditory- and visual-signals had a higher degree of "compellingness" and, thus, more audiovisual integration was observed. It is, however, possible that Warren et al.'s findings reflect nothing more than a temporal coherence difference that was present in the particular conditions utilized.

In order to investigate the impact that the unity effect has on the temporal perception of audiovisual stimuli, matching and mismatching auditory- and visual-streams of speech (syllables and words) and non-speech (object-actions, music, and monkey calls) events were presented in a series of TOJ experiments (Vatakis and Spence 2007a, 2007b, 2008a, 2008d; see Figure 40.1). The results of 11 experiments provided the first psychophysical evidence that the unity effect can modulate the cross-modal binding of multisensory information at a perceptual level of information processing. This modulation was shown to be robust in the case of audiovisual speech events, while no such effect was reported for audiovisual non-speech or animal call events. Specifically, the results of the experiments showed that people were significantly more sensitive to the temporal order of the auditory- and visual-speech streams when they were mismatched (e.g., when the female voice was paired with a male face, or vice versa) than when they were matched. No such matching effect was found for audiovisual non-speech and animal call stimuli, where no sensitivity differences between matched and mismatched conditions were observed (see Figure 40.1).

Moreover, it was shown that this modulatory effect was not present for all human vocalizations (e.g., for humans imitating the "coo" call of a monkey) but that it was specific either to the integration of the auditory- and visual-speech signals, or perhaps to the presence of the auditory speech signal itself. What's more, the response bias account that has confounded the interpretation of all previous research in this area (see Bertelson and de Gelder 2004, for a review), cannot account for these findings. That is, any response bias to assume that the auditory- and visual-speech signals either were or were not matched should not have influenced whether the participants made either a "sound first" or a "visual first" response.

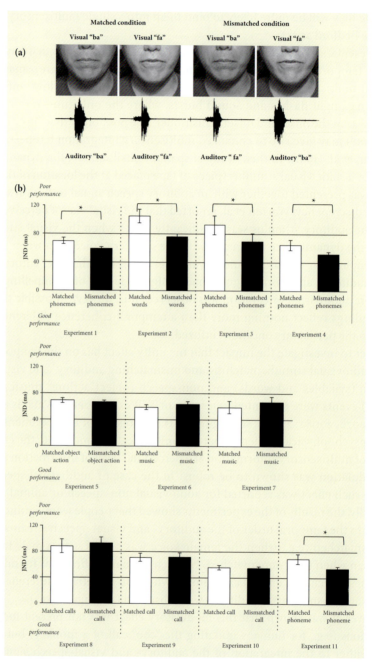

FIGURE 40.1 (a) Sample still frames taken from the matching and mismatching audiovisual /fa/ and /ba/ video clips. The frames highlight the most visible visual speech feature and the bottom panel shows a waveform of the speech signal. (b) Mean JNDs for the matched and mismatched audiovisual stimuli speech (experiments 1–4, 11), object-action (experiments 5–7), and non-speech calls (experiments 8–10). The error bars represent the standard errors of the means. Significant differences (p <0.05) are highlighted by an asterisk (experiments 8–11 from Vatakis et al. 2008; experiments 1–4 and 5–7 from Vatakis and Spence 2007b, 2008b, respectively).

CONCLUSIONS

To date, research on audiovisual temporal perception has shown that the temporal window of audiovisual synchrony perception is highly variable, has a width in the order of several hundred milliseconds, and is asymmetrical, being larger when the visual stimulus leads than when it lags. Through a series of experiments we have sought to identify the factors driving the variability noted in the previously published research on temporal perception for both speech and non-speech stimuli. Taken together, the empirical research outlined here has demonstrated that the temporal window of integration for audiovisual speech is modulated by the type, complexity, and properties of the particular stimulus used, the degree of unity of the auditory- and visual-speech streams (see also Parise and Spence 2009, for the case of non-speech stimuli), the orientation of the visual stimulus (Vatakis and Spence 2008a), and the medium used to present the experimental stimuli (Vatakis and Spence 2006b). Taken together, these findings provide a better estimation of the temporal window of integration for speech and non-speech stimuli, as well as the factors that can modulate this window and thus explain possible differences in experimental results and the differential participant sensitivity observed in temporal order tasks.

Theories of audiovisual speech integration

Speech perception represents the result of the synergistic contribution of both the auditory- and visual-inputs of a speech stimulus. The mechanisms by which the human perceptual system integrates the auditory- and visual-inputs in order to create the unified speech percepts still stand for further research. One of the most prominent theories of the mechanisms governing the integration of audiovisual speech is the "analysis-by-synthesis" model. This model is a fairly recent theory that postulates that visual speech inputs typically precede auditory speech inputs, thus producing an abstract speech representation (Halle 2002; van Wassenhove et al. 2005). The perceptual outcome of this representation depends on the saliency of the visual speech inputs and the redundancy between the visual- and auditory-speech inputs of a given speech signal. A given speech representation is updated as more visual speech information becomes available and the incoming auditory speech input is evaluated against the predicted representation. If the incoming auditory speech input is highly correlated with the given prediction of the speech representation then successful perception of the speech signal is attained. Thus, if a predictor is highly salient, this will lead to faster and more efficient auditory speech signal processing.

Although the research reported in this chapter was not designed for the evaluation of the existing theories of the audiovisual integration of speech perception, it is appropriate to point out some links between the data reported and the "analysis-by-synthesis" model. The investigations related to the effects of physical differences in the articulation of speech on temporal perception, showed that for the majority of speech tokens, the visual speech signal had to precede the corresponding auditory speech signal for synchrony to be perceived. Additionally, these results have shown that salient visual speech signals require less of a lead over auditory speech signals than visual speech signals that are less salient. These results appear to be consistent with the "analysis-by-synthesis" model and it would be worthwhile to further investigate the specific properties that define the saliency of a signal and the possible exceptions (e.g., vowels; salient visual onset but ambiguous offset) that the model cannot describe.

Audiovisual speech integration in the clinical setting

Multisensory interactions between auditory- and visual-speech inputs have primarily been investigated in healthy participants with only a limited number of case studies identifying patients who have reported a disruption of audiovisual perception as a consequence of other neurological deficits (e.g., Böhning, Campbell, and Karmiloff-Smith 2002; Campbell et al. 1997). Disruption, however, of one's ability to integrate auditory- and visual-inputs in isolation of any other neurological deficit has not been a common phenomenon. For example, Campbell et al. (1990) have described two cases of patients with left and right hemispheric lesions who did not exhibit any susceptibility to the McGurk effect. This phenomenon, however, could have been attributed to the fact that the patients also suffered from aphasia (acquired disorder that impairs one's ability to process language), alexia (acquired disorder characterized by the complete loss of reading ability), and prosopagnosia (neurological disorder where the individual is unable to recognize faces) which could also presumably have accounted for their inability to process and integrate auditory- and visual-speech signals. Meanwhile, in another study, Campbell and her colleagues reported the case of a patient with bilateral lesions in V5/MT who failed to correlate the visual lip-movement signal with the corresponding auditory speech signals of a speaker. This failure, however, could have been the result of akinetopsia (syndrome where a person loses the ability to perceive visual motion), which is associated with lesions in V5/MT (Campbell et al. 1997). Finally, Williams syndrome (a genetic disorder characterized by cardiovascular disease, developmental delay, and learning disability) patients have also been shown to exhibit a disrupted ability to integrate auditory- and visual-speech signals, but this is probably due to the impaired visuo-spatial processing that is characteristic of these patients (Böhning et al. 2002).

A specific disruption of the ability to integrate audiovisual speech has, in fact, never been reported until the recent case study by Hamilton and colleagues (2006). Hamilton et al. described a patient (AWF) who reported experiencing a temporal mismatch between the auditory- and visual-streams of a speech signal in the absence of any language or sensory impairment (a similar case, RW, experienced speech asynchrony, including for singing, for three years but psychophysical testing did not show deviation from normal temporal perception; Vatakis 2010). AWF reported a difficulty in understanding face-to-face speech and compared his experience to "watching a movie with the audio out of sync." Imaging data from this patient revealed a biparietal hypoperfusion with prominence in the right region of the brain. In order to evaluate the deficit objectively, AWF was subjected to various behavioral tasks (e.g., word-to-picture matching with auditory words paired together with congruent or incongruent facial movements, or no face images) and a McGurk effect task. AWF exhibited a substantial impairment on a variety of these tasks, with the greatest impairment observed under conditions where multiple sensory inputs were presented. Thus, AWF appeared unable to efficiently bind the auditory- and visual-inputs relating to a given event. The authors suggested that AWF's parietal cortical injury may have caused the apparent deficit in integrating audiovisual information. According to these and other studies, it would be interesting to explore how clinical cases with major deficits process temporal information of multisensory speech and non-speech stimuli. Such investigations should help to provide further insights as to the specific brain areas involved in temporal perception.

The accurate perception of temporal changes in events occurring in the environment is of critical importance to almost every behavior we engage in, from neural computation to driving a car, and from communicating to playing music. The findings reviewed here provide empirical evidence regarding some of the factors that modulate human audiovisual temporal perception for speech stimuli. It is, however, hoped that this chapter marks the start of a continuing investigation into the other possible factors that may also affect human temporal perception, which will allow us to better understand both temporal and speech perception and open up the path for more applied research (e.g., in timing and social signal processing).

Acknowledgments

This work has been supported by the European project COST ISCH Action TD0904 "Time In MEntaL activitY: theoretical, behavioral, bioimaging and clinical perspectives" (TIMELY; <http://www.timely-cost.eu>).

References

Bald, L., F. K. Berrien, J. B. Price, and R. O. Sprague. 1942. Errors in perceiving the temporal order of auditory and visual stimuli. *Journal of Applied Psychology* 26:382–388.

Bedford, Felice L. 2001. Towards a general law of numerical/object identity. *Current Psychology of Cognition* 20:113–175.

Bentin, Shlomo, Truett Allison, Aina Puce, Erik Perez, and Gregory McCarthy. 1996. Electrophysiological studies of face perception in humans. *Journal of Cognitive Neuroscience* 8:551–565.

Bernstein, Lynne E., and Christian Benoit. 1996. For speech perception by humans or machines, three senses are better than one. *ICSLP* 1477–1480.

Bertelson, Paul, and Gisa Aschersleben. 1998. Automatic visual bias of perceived auditory location. *Psychonomic Bulletin and Review* 5:482–489.

Bertelson, Paul, and Beatrice de Gelder. 2004. The psychology of multimodal perception. In *Crossmodal Space and Crossmodal Attention*, ed. C. Spence and J. Driver, 141–177. Oxford: Oxford University Press.

Böhning, M., R. Campbell, and A. Karmilov-Smith. 2002. Audiovisual speech perception in Williams syndrome. *Neuropsychologia* 40:1396–1406.

Breeuwer, M., and R. Plomp. 1986. Speechreading supplemented with auditorily presented speech parameters. *Journal of the Acoustical Society of America* 79:481–499.

Caclin, Anne, Salvador Soto-Faraco, Alan Kingstone, and Charles Spence. 2002. Tactile 'capture' of audition. *Perception and Psychophysics* 64:616–630.

Calvert, Gemma A., and Ruth Campbell. 2003. Reading speech from still and moving faces: The neural substrates of visible speech. *Journal of Cognitive Neuroscience* 15:57–70.

Calvert, Gemma A., Ruth Campbell, and Michael J. Brammer. 2000. Evidence from functional magnetic resonance imaging of crossmodal binding in the human heteromodal cortex. *Current Biology* 1011:649–657.

Calvert, Gemma A., Charles Spence, and Barry E. Stein. 2004. *The Handbook of Multisensory Processing*. Cambridge, MA: MIT Press.

Campbell, Ruth, Jeanette Garwood, Sue Franklin, David Howard, Theodore Landis, and Marianne Regard. 1990. Neuropsychological studies of auditory–visual fusion illusions. Four case studies and their implications. *Neuropsychologia* 28:787–802.

Campbell, Ruth, J. Zihl, Dominic W. Massaro, Kevin Munhall, and Michael M. Cohen. 1997. Speechreading in the akinetopsic patient (LM). *Brain* 120:1793–1803.

Chen, Yi-Chuan, and Charles Spence. 2010. When hearing the bark helps to identify the dog: Semantically-congruent sounds modulate the identification of masked pictures. *Cognition* 114:389–404.

Conrey, Brianna L., and David B. Pisoni. 2006. Auditory-visual speech perception and synchrony detection for speech and nonspeech signals. *Journal of the Acoustical Society of America* 119:4065–4073.

De Gelder, Beatrice, and Paul Bertelson. 2003. Multisensory integration, perception and ecological validity. *Trends in Cognitive Sciences* 7:460–467.

Dixon, Norman F., and Lydia Spitz. 1980. The detection of auditory visual desynchrony. *Perception* 9:719–721.

Dodd, Barbara. 1979. Lipreading in infants: Attention to speech presented in- and out-of-synchrony. *Cognitive Psychology* 11:478–484.

Doehrmann, Oliver, and Marcus J. Naumer. 2008. Semantics and the multisensory brain: How meaning modulates processes of audio-visual integration. *Brain Research* 1242:136–150.

Fujisaki, Waka, and Shin'ya Nishida. 2005. Temporal frequency characteristics of synchrony-asynchrony discrimination of audio-visual signals. *Experimental Brain Research* 166:455–464.

Gault, Robert H. 1924. Progress in experiments on tactual interpretation of oral speech. *Journal of Abnormal Psychology and Social Psychology* 19:155–159.

Gick, Bryan, and Donald Derrick. 2009. Aero-tactile integration in speech perception. *Nature* 463:502–504.

Grant, Ken W., and Steven Greenberg. 2001. Speech intelligibility derived from asynchronous processing of auditory-visual speech information. *Proceedings of the Workshop on Audio Visual Speech Processing*, 132–137, Scheelsminde, Denmark, 7–9 September.

Grant, Ken W., and Philip F. Seitz. 1998. The use of visible speech cues (speechreading) for directing auditory attention: Reducing temporal and spectral uncertainty in auditory detection of spoken sentences. In *Proceedings of the 16th International Congress on Acoustics and the 135th Meeting of the Acoustical Society of America*, eds. P. K. Kuhl and L. A. Crum, 3, 2335–2336. New York: ASA.

Grant, Ken W., Virginie van Wassenhove, and David Poeppel. 2004. Detection of auditory (cross-spectral) and auditory-visual (cross-modal) synchrony. *Speech Communication* 44:43–53.

Halle, Morris. 2002. *From Memory to Speech and Back*. Berlin: Mouton de Gruyter.

Hamilton, Roy H., Jeffrey T. Shenton, and H. Branch-Coslett. 2006. An acquired deficit of audiovisual speech processing. *Brain and Language* 98:66–73.

Hein, Grit, Oliver Doehrmann, Notger G. Müller, Jochen Kaiser, Lars Muckli, and Marcus J. Naumer. 2007 Object familiarity and semantic congruency modulate responses in cortical audiovisual integration areas. *Journal of Neuroscience* 27:7881–7887.

Hirsh, Ira J., and Carl E. Jr. Sherrick. 1961. Perceived order in different sense modalities. *Journal of Experimental Psychology* 62:424–432.

Hollier, Michael P., and Andrew N. Rimell. 1998. An experimental investigation into multi-modal synchronisation sensitivity for perceptual model development. *105th AES Convention*, Preprint No. 4790.

ITU-R BT.1359-1. 1998. *Relative timing of sound and vision for broadcasting* (Question ITU-R 35/11).

Jackson, C. V. 1953. Visual factors in auditory localization. *Quarterly Journal of Experimental Psychology* 5:52–65.

Jones, Jeffrey A., and Michelle Jarick. 2006. Multisensory integration of speech signals: The relationship between space and time. *Experimental Brain Research* 174:588–594.

Kent, Raymond D. 1997. *The Speech Sciences*. San Diego, CA: Singular.

King, Andrew J. 2005. Multisensory integration: Strategies for synchronization. *Current Biology* 15:R339–R341.

Laurienti, P. J., Kraft, R. A., Maldjian, J. A., Burdette, J. H., and Wallace, M. T. 2004. Semantic congruence is a critical factor in multisensory behavioral performance. *Experimental Brain Research* 158:405–414.

Lewkowicz, David J. 1986. Developmental changes in infants' bisensory response to synchronous durations. *Infant Behavior and Development* 9:335–353.

——. 1992. Infants' response to temporally-based intersensory equivalence: The effect of synchronous sounds on visual preferences for moving stimuli. *Infant Behavior and Development* 15:297–324.

——. 1994. Reflections on infants' response to temporally based intersensory equivalence: Response to Spelke. *Infant Behavior and Development* 17:287–290.

——. 2000. The development of intersensory temporal perception: An epigenetic systems/limitations view. *Psychological Bulletin* 126:281–308.

Massaro, Dominic W., and Michael M. Cohen. 1993. Perceiving asynchronous bimodal speech in consonant-vowel and vowel syllables. *Speech Communication* 13:127–134.

Massaro, Dominic W., Michael M. Cohen, and Paula M. T. Smeele. 1996. Perception of asynchronous and conflicting visual and auditory speech. *Journal of the Acoustical Society of America* 100:1777–1786.

McClelland, James L., and Jeffrey L. Elman. 1986. The TRACE model of speech perception. *Cognitive Psychology* 18:1–86.

McGrath, Matthew, and Quentin Summerfield. 1985. Intermodal timing relations and audiovisual speech recognition by normal hearing adults. *Journal of the Acoustical Society of America* 77:678–685.

McGurk, Harry, and John MacDonald. 1976. Hearing lips and seeing voices. *Nature* 264:746–748.

Meredith, M. Alex, and Barry E. Stein. 1983. Interactions among converging sensory inputs in the superior colliculus. *Science* 221:389–391.

Miner, Nadine, and Thomas Caudell. 1998. Computational requirements and synchronization issues of virtual acoustic displays. *Presence: Teleoperators and Virtual Environments* 7:396–409.

Munhall, Kevin G., P. Gribble, L. Sacco, and M. Ward. 1996. Temporal constraints on the McGurk effect. *Perception and Psychophysics* 58:351–362.

Navarra, Jordi, Argiro Vatakis, Massimiliano Zampini, Salvador Soto-Faraco, William Humphreys, and Charles Spence. 2005. Exposure to asynchronous audiovisual speech extends the temporal window for audiovisual integration. *Cognitive Brain Research* 25:499–507.

Pandey, C. Prem, Hans Kunov, and Sharon M. Abel. 1986. Disruptive effects of auditory signal delay on speech perception with lip-reading. *Journal of Auditory Research* 26:27–41.

Parise, Cesare, and Charles Spence. 2009. 'When birds of a feather flock together': Synesthetic correspondences modulate audiovisual integration in non-synesthetes. *PLoS ONE* 4:5664.

Reeves, Byron, and David Voelker. 1993. *Effects of Audio-Video Asynchrony on Viewer's Memory, Evaluation of Content and Detection Ability*. Research report prepared for Pixel Instruments. Los Gatos, California.

Rihs, S. 1995. The influence of audio on perceived picture quality and subjective audio-visual delay tolerance. In *Proceedings of the MOSAIC workshop: Advanced Methods for the Evaluation of Television Picture Quality*, eds. R. Hamberg and H. de Ridder, 133–137. Eindhoven: Institute for Perception Research.

Ross, Lars A., Dave Saint-Amour, Victoria M. Leavitt, Daniel C. Javitt, and John J. Foxe. 2007. Do you see what I am saying? Exploring visual enhancement of speech comprehension in noisy environments. *Cerebral Cortex* 17:1147–1153.

Slutsky, Daniel A., and Recanzone, Gregg H. 2001. Temporal and spatial dependency of the ventriloquism effect. *Neuroreport* 12:7–10.

Soto-Faraco, Salvador, Jessica Lyons, Michael Gazzaniga, Charles Spence, and Alan Kingstone. 2002. The ventriloquist in motion: Illusory capture of dynamic information across sensory modalities. *Cognitive Brain Research* 14:139–146.

Spelke, Elizabeth S., Wendy S. Born, and Flora Chu. 1983. Perception of moving, sounding objects by four-month-old infants. *Perception* 12:719–732.

Spence, Charles. 2007. Audiovisual multisensory integration. *Journal of the Acoustical Society of Japan: Acoustical Science and Technology* 28:61–70.

Spence, Charles, and Jon Driver. 1997. On measuring selective attention to a specific sensory modality. *Perception and Psychophysics* 59:389–403.

Spence, Charles, and Sarah B. Squire. 2003. Multisensory integration: Maintaining the perception of synchrony. *Current Biology* 13:R519–R521.

Stein, Barry E., and Alex M. Meredith. 1993. *The Merging of the Senses*. Cambridge, MA: MIT Press.

Steinmetz, Ralf. 1996. Human perception of jitter and media synchronization. *IEEE Journal on Selected Areas in Communications* 14:61–72.

Stevenson, Ryan A., and Thomas W. James. 2009. Audiovisual integration in human superior temporal sulcus: Inverse effectiveness and the neural processing of speech and object recognition. *Neuroimage* 44:1210–1223.

Stone, J. V., N. M. Hunkin, J. Porrill, R. Wood, V. Keeler, M. Beanland, M. Port, and N. R. Porter. 2001. When is now? Perception of simultaneity. *Proceedings of the Royal Society of London B: Biological Sciences* 268:31–38.

Sugita, Yoichi, and Yoiti Suzuki. 2003. Implicit estimation of sound-arrival time. *Nature* 421:911.

Sumby, W. H., and Irwin Pollack. 1954. Visual contribution to speech intelligibility in noise. *Journal of the Acoustical Society of America* 26:212–215.

Van Wassenhove, Virginie, Ken W. Grant, and David Poeppel. 2003. Electrophysiology of auditory-visual speech integration. In *International Conference on Auditory-Visual Speech Processing (AVSP)*, 31–35, St. Jorioz, France.

——. 2005. Visual speech speeds up the neural processing of auditory speech. *Proceedings of the National Academy of Sciences of the United States of America* 102:1181–1186.

——. 2007. Temporal window of integration in auditory-visual speech perception. *Neuropsychologia* 45:598–607.

Vatakis, Argiro. 2010. Audiovisual temporal perception and integration: Acquired deficits in audiovisual temporal perception for complex stimuli. Talk presented at the 'Time and Cognition: From behavioral studies to brain imaging' Symposium at the International Neuropsychological Society (INS), Krakow, Poland, 30 June–3 July.

Vatakis, Argiro, Asif A. Ghazanfar, and Charles Spence. 2008. Facilitation of multisensory integration by the 'unity effect' reveals that speech is special. *Journal of Vision* 8:1–11.

Vatakis, Argiro, Jordi Navarra, Salvador Soto-Faraco, and Charles Spence. 2007. Temporal recalibration during asynchronous audiovisual speech perception. *Experimental Brain Research* 181:173–181.

Vatakis, Argiro, and Charles Spence. 2006a. Audiovisual synchrony perception for music, speech, and object actions. *Brain Research* 1111:134–142.

——. 2006b. Evaluating the influence of frame rate on the temporal aspects of audiovisual speech perception. *Neuroscience Letters* 405:132–136.

——. 2006c. Audiovisual synchrony perception for speech and music using a temporal order judgment task. *Neuroscience Letters* 393:40–44.

——. 2007a. How 'special' is the human face? Evidence from an audiovisual temporal order judgment task. *Neuroreport* 18:1807–1811.

——. 2007b. Crossmodal binding: Evaluating the 'unity assumption' using audiovisual speech stimuli. *Perception and Psychophysics* 69:744–756.

——. 2007c. An assessment of the effect of physical differences in the articulation of consonants and vowels on audiovisual temporal perception. Poster presented at the 'One-day meeting for young speech researchers', University College London, London, UK.

——. 2008a. Investigating the effects of inversion on configural processing using an audio-visual temporal order judgment task. *Perception* 37:143–160.

——. 2008b. Evaluating the influence of the 'unity assumption' on the temporal perception of realistic audiovisual stimuli. *Acta Psychologica* 127:12–23.

——. 2010. Audiovisual temporal integration for complex speech, object-action, animal call, and musical stimuli. In *Multisensory Object Perception in the Primate Brain*, eds. Marcus J. Naumer and Jochen Kaiser, 95–121. New York: Springer.

Vatakis, A., Maragos, P., Rodomagoulakis, I., & Spence, C. 2012. Assessing the effect of physical differences in the articulation of consonants and vowels on audiovisual temporal perception. *Frontiers of Integrative Neuroscience* 6 (71):1–18.

Warren, David H., Robert B. Welch, and Timothy J. McCarthy. 1981. The role of visual-auditory 'compellingness' in the ventriloquism effect: Implications for transitivity among the spatial senses. *Perception and Psychophysics* 30:557–564.

Welch, Robert B. 1999. Meaning, attention, and the 'unity assumption' in the intersensory bias of spatial and temporal perceptions. In *Cognitive Contributions to the Perception of Spatial and Temporal Events*, eds. Gisa Aschersleben, Talis Bachmann, and Jochen Müsseler, 371–387. Amsterdam: Elsevier Science, B.V.

Welch, Robert B., and David H. Warren. 1980. Immediate perceptual response to intersensory discrepancy. *Psychological Bulletin* 88:638–667.

Zampini, Massimiliano, David I. Shore, and Charles Spence. 2003. Multisensory temporal order judgments: The role of hemispheric redundancy. *International Journal of Psychophysiology* 50:165–180.

....

CHAPTER 41

MAGNITUDES, METAPHORS, AND MODALITIES

A theory of magnitude revisited

....

VINCENT E. WALSH

INTRODUCTION

....

One might ask what a chapter on a theory of magnitude (ATOM) is doing in a book about synesthesia. One might very well ask that again having reached the end of this chapter, but I hope by then you'll be able to answer the question.[1] ATOM (Walsh 2003a) was proposed to address the problem of what a smart thing like number is doing in the parietal lobe in a region of the human cortex associated with automatic and motoric processing of which we are seldom aware, while all the other smart things we do and are aware of, such as language, faces, episodic memory, and object recognition, are associated with regions of the temporal lobe. In doing so, ATOM had to consider what other functions were associated with the intraparietal sulcus and surrounding cortex and I noted that, although the historical accidents of psychology and physiology had segregated time, space, and number into entirely separate functions and domains of study, the brain itself had taken no notice of psychology textbooks and single-unit recording papers. It was clear that these three functions were at the very least related, quite possibly anatomically overlapping, and may even share the same basic spatiotemporal metrics upon which numerical understanding is built.

One of the reasons that ATOM is relevant to synesthesia is that, like synesthesia, it presents a challenge to simplistic views of modularity in human perception and

---

[1] The answer for the reader who only has time to read one page is that I believe that magnitude processing and synesthesia are varieties of the same problem. They bridge development, sensory processing, integration, matching/scaling, and higher cognition (e.g., metaphor and language). Explanations for both require a new conceptual approach that takes into account all these elements and principles of cortical organization.

cognition. Our discipline is replete with examples of modularization that underpin and severely limit our conceptualization of the language of the brain. Sometimes we use the terminology as shorthand, and in my own work, for example, I sometimes write of "the visual motion area." Others write about "the face area," "the color area," "the body area," "the locus of attention," "the location of episodic memory," "the number area," "time neurons," "space neurons," "number neurons." At best these formulations are useful shorthand, but they are also over simplified and at worst misleading or even hideaways of willful ignorance.

By embracing these designations of modularity we close the door to new discoveries and new ways of thinking. Indeed we sometimes undergo "retrothink" in order to make interpretations fit what we know to be true. The clearest example of this is in the attention and brain imaging literature wherein activations in the parietal or prefrontal cortex are often considered de facto evidence of attentional processing even in the absence of attention being manipulated in the experiment. It is difficult to develop a new idea based on the premise that the old one *must* be right and this is perhaps why the field of attention, rather than advancing conceptually, seems to be in a phase of saying the same thing and changing only the name of the technique and the modality being studied.

What synesthesia teaches us, and what underlies ATOM, is that whenever we look hard at a problem, simplistic views of modularity break down. And to understand the development of relative specialization, and our ability to display modular-like behavior, we need to understand the ontogeny of the apparent modules and our experience of categories. If we consider early vision, the textbooks still teach a relative segregation of color, motion, and form—and it is useful as shorthand. But it doesn't survive inspection even at the level of the retina or V1. Although we emphasize modularity, many cells display double duty or even triple duty responses. Higher up the system, if one considers area V4, the so-called color area (as strong a candidate for a module as any visual area), even here we see responses to color, wavelength, orientation, contrast, and even motion (Van Essen and Maunsell 1983).

One of the reasons we cling to simple modularity is that it is difficult to study too many things—mastering the psychophysics of color is hard enough—and disciplines therefore emerge as psychologists and physiologists specialize.[2] It is also hard to examine a neuron for all its possible response properties and single-unit studies usually have a target stimulus in which they are interested. These are all fair reasons to limit experimentation, but they do not change the fact that when we examine sensory cortex we usually do so from a perspective based on the somewhat accidental subdisciplines of psychology and physiology and on the exigency of getting any data at all.

What is true for the sensory cortex is true for association cortex too. It is no more than an historical accident that time, space, and number have been studied for a century as three separate subjects. And the difficulties of examining responses of cells in the

---

[2] *We are undoubtedly modular in our specializations, but we should remember that the brain has a right to ignore us*

parietal lobe for more than one stimulus group are just as great as in the sensory cortices (and one can always hand wave about attentional modulation, so why work hard?).

A Recap: What Atom Did and Didn't Predict

The contention of ATOM is that to understand why the parietal cortex is organized as it is and to understand why number-related processes occur in it, we may need to consider numerical processing and development in the context of sensorimotor integration and action. The basis of this contention is that the parietal cortex surrounding the intraparietal sulcus is a major hub for these functions (see Bueti and Walsh 2009). The principles of cortical organization seem to suggest that nearby areas will not differ markedly in their functions. And even when they do they seem not to differ markedly in their organization or the way they perform their functions (Shamma 2001; Sur and Leamey 2001). I think this is a better starting point than trying to shoehorn the anomaly of number in the parietal cortex into some vague existing framework simply because it is the framework we have. For example, it has been suggested that because we spatially attend to number, that number therefore needs to be represented in or close to the areas associated with spatial attention. However, one also spatially attends to faces, cars, text, sound, memories, color, and a whole host of other objects and attributes that are not primarily represented in the same areas. Indeed if everything we attended to spatially had to be represented in the parietal cortex, it would be difficult to imagine what the occipital and temporal lobes might be for.

ATOM made several specific predictions. Based on some transcranial magnetic stimulation studies, behavioral data, and reinterpretations of imaging and single-unit studies, it was suggested that our experience of time, space, number, weight, and other prothetic[3] magnitudes originate from a single metric early in child development: the basis of ATOM is pre-linguistic. This is a strength, because it constrains the idea; and a weakness, because an understanding of magnitudes that doesn't take into account language and metaphor is somewhat local. ATOM also suggests that we learn about these

---

[3] Prothetic dimensions are those that can be "more than" or "less than." For example, we can have more or less light, noise, heat, stuff. Time, space, and number fall into this category because you can have more or less of them too. Speed is also in this category because things can move more or less fast. Pitch is not in this category because we don't say that a frequency is more or less than, we identify it as a different category of sound, say a C instead of a D (but pitch differences may be associated with finger movements of different sizes and there are differences between identification and discrimination—cf. Schwenzer and Mathiak 2011). Color is a troublesome one: something can be more or less red but at some point these differences cross categorical boundaries and we have pink, red, and scarlet. The category of stuff that changes identity with changes in "amount of stuff" in this way is termed *metathetic*. The distinction doesn't always work but it is a useful guide (Stevens 1957).

dimensions (time, space, etc.) through motor interaction with the environment. Because of this, the development of magnitude processing is therefore closely linked with motor reaching, grasping, and manipulating of objects. It was further suggested that the emergence of our ability to manipulate discrete quantities evolved from our abilities with continuous quantities.

Among the predictions made were that different magnitudes should show interference and priming effects (e.g., Cohen Kadosh, Cohen Kadosh, and Henik 2008; Droit-Volet 2010; Herrera et al. 2008; Vicario 2011; Xuan et al. 2007; see also Bueti and Walsh 2009). Another prediction was that other brain areas associated with magnitude processing (such as V5 for motion processing) should also display some evidence of involvement in other magnitudes (in the case of V5, time; see Bueti, Bahrami, and Walsh, 2008; Bueti et al. 2008). A third prediction was that the SNARC effect (spatial–numerical association of response code), in which small number judgments are associated with response codes in left space and large numbers with response codes in right space, should prove to be a generalized spatial quantity association of response code (SQUARC) effect, in which any spatially or action-coded magnitude will yield a relationship between magnitude and space (cf. Ishihara et al. 2008; Notebaert et al. 2006). All of these predictions have been confirmed to date. For example, temporal judgments are susceptible to spatial–numerical association of response code SNARC-like effects, consistent with the generalized spatial quantity association predicted in Walsh (2003a, 2003b) (see Brugger 2008; Ishihara et al. 2008; Müller and Schwarz 2008). There are several other interference studies relevant to the common cortical processing of magnitudes: number can influence spatial orientation (Fischer et al. 2003; Salillas et al. 2009) and so on.

An over-simplistic view of a generalized magnitude system might expect all interference effects to be symmetrical—that temporal cues, number, space, luminance, and action cues would all impinge on each other equally (an impression ATOM seems to have given unintentionally and one for which the picture is complicated by development—see later in this chapter). This is clearly not the case. Brown (1997), for example, found that number interfered with time but not vice versa, and Dormal and Pesenti (2007), for example, found that in a modified Stroop paradigm, spatial cues interfered with number processing but number did not interfere with spatial processing. Hurewitz et al. (2006) suggested a possible hierarchy of magnitudes from continuous to discrete variables following their finding that amount of stuff interfered with numerosity judgments more than numerosity interfered with "stuff." Whether these findings are evidence of constant asymmetries or are task dependent remains to be established (cf. Göbel et al. 2006). From the point of view of cortical loci, it is clear that some activation sites for time, space, and number overlap and a few do not. This should not be surprising: the architecture activated in any given experiment is highly dependent on the task and one should therefore not expect a single locus to account for all instances of magnitude processing (Cohen Kadosh and Walsh 2009).

There are some things that ATOM did not predict. The two most important misconceptions are: (1) that ATOM proposes that all prothetic dimensions are created equal: they are not and (2) that prothetic magnitudes will always interfere with each other.

During development the dimensions will not require equal effort to master, they will be associated with different levels of awareness and will receive different amounts and types of feedback. Different magnitudes will also be differently affected by the onset of language. If one considers time versus size, for example, we learn about timing relatively implicitly by interacting with moving objects or playing expectation games such as peek-a-boo. We don't receive much feedback from eager parents about the face appearing half a second before we expected it. But size is emphasized in language, and in games (big Ted, little Ted) and it is made explicit when dealing with food, toys, brothers and sisters, etc. It should be no surprise that time is often the weaker stimulus in interference experiments. Similarly, number is learned explicitly through language and we need to consider this in experiments. Where stimuli can be coded linguistically, number will be likely to dominate other magnitudes. So, ATOM is consistent with asymmetrical interactions and interactions are a function of the history of the dimensions and the tasks being used to test interactions.

NUMBER AND ACTION

One of ATOM's counter-intuitive predictions is that numerical information should influence action. A number–action link is not as well established as the number–space link, of which there are many examples. Fias et al. (2001) carried out a series of experiments in which subjects performed a judgment on a stimulus attribute that was more (orientation) or less (color and shape) associated with parietal cortex processes.

The stimuli were presented along with digits that were irrelevant to the task. The orientation judgments, but not the color or shape judgments, were influenced by the irrelevant number. A less intuitive interference study, but an important one in the context of our suggestion that discrete number evolved on the back of an analogue quantity system necessary for computing the metrics of action, was conducted by Andres et al. (2004), who required subjects to perform either a grip opening or closing movement to digit stimuli. Closure was initiated more quickly for small digits and opening more quickly for large digits. Andres et al. (2008) later established that as the hand neared the object, the interaction between digit magnitude and grip aperture decreased, and so they therefore concluded that magnitude influences action at the planning or programming stage of grasping movements (see also Badets and Pesenti 2010; Badets et al. 2007; Ishihara et al. 2006). Both Lindemann et al. (2007) and Moretto and di Pellegrino (2008) found evidence that mere exposure to magnitude information automatically primes grasping actions. Subjects were presented with numerical stimuli to which they made grip responses according to the semantic (parity) or surface (color) properties of the stimulus. Although the value of the digit was irrelevant, lower numerical values facilitated precision grip responses (associated with grasping smaller objects) and larger numerical values facilitated power grip responses associated with grasping larger objects. Lindemann et al. (2007) additionally found that larger numbers were associated with a larger initial power grip. These studies show that magnitude information influences the selection of action type, but at least one study (Fischer and Miller 2008) suggested that the influence of magnitude information does not extend to the dynamics of action such as force (see also Taylor-Cooke et al. 2006). One other study places the origin of interactions between space and number earlier in the chain of processing. Stoianov et al. (2008) conducted a spatial–numerical priming experiment in which they assessed forward and backward priming with verbal responses. They observed greater effects when the spatial prime followed a number target both for number comparisons and parity judgments, and concluded that the effects could not be ascribed to spatial–numerical response codes. It is a hypothesis and experiment that deserves further exploration.

SPACE AND TIME

One of the predictions of ATOM was that time perception should change as a function of the distance of the events being judged. Spatial judgments are affected as a function of being made in "near space" or "far space" (e.g., Bjoertomt et al. 2002). Another way of conceptualizing near and far space is as being in or outside of "action space." If magnitude systems originate in the need to compute space, time, and size for action, they should behave differently towards stimuli that are within or out with action space. Zach and Brugger (2008) tested this by requiring subjects to make duration estimates of clock movement imagined at two distances. Subjects reported time to run faster for the near clock than for the far clock. There is a possibility, however, that this experiment tested the relationship between size and time rather than distance and time.

DEVELOPMENT OF MAGNITUDE PROCESSING

One prediction from ATOM is that there should be some monotonic mapping of quantities: bigger, faster, brighter, further in one domain should correlate with bigger, faster, brighter, further in another. This kind of intuitive "more A–more B" mapping has been noted in developmental contexts and described in some detail by Stavy and Tirosh (2000) who give many examples of such mapping and reinterpreted several classical findings from developmental psychology (also cf. Kaufmann and Nuerk 2006; Rousselle and Noel 2007, 2008). Stavy and Tirosh suggested that children will often base magnitude judgments on irrelevant dimensions. One of their studies demonstrating this showed children two trains running along a track. The children were given all the information necessary to know that the trains ran at the same rate. When the trains differed in size, however, the subjects stated that the larger train was faster. In this case, size is affecting a judgment (speed) in which time is implicit, but children make the same class of error when making explicit temporal judgments. Levin (1977, 1979, 1982) asked children in kindergarten to judge which of two lights was presented for the longest time. The lights differed in brightness and size and the children consistently judged the larger or brighter stimuli to have persisted for more time.

A more pressing issue is how magnitudes develop pre-linguistically, and this is best left until I have discussed ATOM in the context of metaphorical theories of time and space.

ATOM AND METAPHORICAL THEORIES

The territory of ATOM was well defined:

> In the context of this article, then, the "important decision variables" are short "action-time" durations in the millisecond-to-seconds range, spatial information used for action, and co-ordinate transformations for action or predictions about the immediate sensorimotor consequences of action. (Walsh 2003a, 483)

So, there is no necessary prediction that ATOM should extend to episodic memory, planning, higher mathematical operations, or allocentric spatial tasks such as navigation. The proposal is that we learn about space and time through action, and that associations between space, time, and magnitudes relevant for action (such as size, speed, and, under some conditions, luminance and contrast) will be made through action. When we later learn about number, the neurons with capacity to represent quantity are those that have information about the continuous variables learned about motorically. Thus, the neuronal scaling mechanisms used for dimensions with action-relevant magnitude information will be co-opted in development for the scaling of number. Psychophysically, this has been shown to be the case (Burr and Ross 2008); the relevant neurons are found, as predicted, in the parietal cortex and dual-task experiments show interference between number and action (see earlier). The single unit recording literature erroneously emphasizes neurons specialized for time (cf. Walsh 2003a, 2003b), space, or number, but I suggest that this is a consequence of the immature state of the field. Similar overemphasis of specializations in the visual system led to concentrating on such things as "the color area," "the form area," or "the motion area," but it is now clear that many neurons at every level of visual analysis are double or even triple duty for form, motion, and chromatic content. Given the similarity of rules observed by sensory processing within and between modalities (Shamma 2001; Sur and Leamey 2001), we predict that similar multiduty neurons will be reported in the magnitude scaling system in due course.

However, one line of work has made us consider whether ATOM is itself too modular and narrow. Work on metaphorical representations of time and quantity offers challenges and extensions (Boroditsky 2000; Casasanto 2008; Casasanto and Boroditsky

2008). The issue of asymmetry of magnitudes was addressed by Casasanto et al. (2010). They investigated the relationship between space and time in children by showing children movies of animals travelling for different distances or different times. The children were between 4 and 10 years old and they were asked to judge whether one of two animals stopped in the same place, whether one travelled further than the other, whether the animals stopped at the same time, and whether one animal move for more time. In all conditions there was some effect of interactions between time and space judgments but temporal judgments were disproportionately affected by space information (and space relatively lightly disrupted by temporal information). These results were not caused by the space task being easier than the time tasks. So, in line with Brown (1997), Dormal and Pesenti (2007), and Hurewitz (2006) we see that all magnitudes are not created equal.

There is a challenge to be met here. I do not think there is any conflict between metaphorical theories and ATOM, they represent different levels of analysis, ATOM being pre-linguistic and motoric, metaphorical theories addressing linguistic and conceptual representation. The challenge is how we get from one level to the next. So, my question for the Casasanto et al. experiment would be, is there a way of testing these potential asymmetries in pre-linguistic children? Laurenco et al. (2010) trained 9-month-old infants to associate patterns with magnitudes of time, size and numerosity. When transferred between magnitudes, the preference for patterns associated with larger/smaller amounts of time, size, and numerosity transferred bidirectionally between magnitudes. And the transfer was symmetrical. This is an important study because it establishes pre-linguistic associations between magnitudes and it also, together with the work of Casasanto et al., sets the trajectory any explanation has to follow: from pre-linguistic and symmetrical to linguistic and asymmetrical. Another study also emphasizes that the division is not between ATOM and metaphor but between pre-linguistic and linguistic processes. Merrit et al. (2010) tested for interference between space and time and found that adults showed the asymmetry of space affecting time more than vice versa while rhesus monkeys, like Laurenco et al.'s (2010) children, showed symmetrical interference. There are many open questions. When does the asymmetry begin? It is perhaps best to track the decline (if that is the right word) of time. Does it become the "weaker" dimension because, unlike space and size, it is abstract and not made explicit in every interaction? What is the frequency of time and space words used with children? Can the asymmetries be reversed? How does the acquisition of explicit quantities affect the (a) symmetry of magnitudes?

The work of Laurenco et al. and Casasanto et al. provide a developmental line between infancy and adulthood. The ATOM hypothesis provides a way of testing the links directly to describe where our experience of magnitudes in the worlds shifts from equality to, perhaps, hierarchy. One goal of ATOM was to ask "Why is the parietal cortex organized as it is?" These studies generate the question "How does the parietal cortex change over development?"

ATOM AND SYNESTHESIA

So far I've concentrated on ATOM but some fundamental issues resonate with synesthesia and lead to questions deeper than matters of magnitude or synesthesia themselves. The challenge, then, is that of finding a framework within which we can describe the developmental trajectories of sensory development, describe interactions between the modalities in the adult brain, and describe the experience and expression of those modalities in language and higher cognition. This sentence could refer to magnitude processing or it could refer to sensory processing. It actually refers to both because both fields are doomed to incompleteness unless we embrace the challenge of a general explanation. We can tweak away for ever and generate another thousand attentional manipulations because a parameter can always be modified, but we will not sneak up on new conceptual approaches by adding more and more data points in a cognitive vacuum. I think it is worth considering whether magnitude processing and synesthesia share common principles and if they do how these principles can guide us.

The first common problem is that of modularity. Both ATOM and synesthesia are fatal blows to simple views of modularity. We never see "pure" color or "pure" motion. They and other attributes exist for us only in the context of other attributes. Similarly, we never experience pure time (whatever that might be), space, or quantity. There is always a context, a number of something, time since or time to, and a space in which we act. It is true that some brain areas show specialization for color more than motion, motion more than color, etc., but as I noted in the introduction, these are descriptions of the limits of single-unit recording as much as they are descriptions of the brain. The brain would have three possible strategies for integrating these relative specializations: (1) the putative specializations might not be as great as we imagine and, notwithstanding the sampling bias of single units and the analysis bias of brain imaging experiments, there may be many more double or even triple duty cells in so called specialized areas; (2) the relatively specialized areas integrate by direct cortico-cortical connections; (3) the relatively specialized areas are under the control of a master integration area, usually the parietal cortex.

The second common problem is that of symmetry/directionality. In synesthesia the experience is mostly unidirectional (so for a given synesthete, numbers might trigger color but not vice versa), but as Cohen Kadosh and others have shown, it can be bidirectional (see Cohen Kadosh and Henik, Chapter 6, this volume). In the magnitude domain, time is usually the poor relation of the magnitudes, at least after language acquisition. In both cases more effort is needed to establish the conditions of directionality and also the development of directionality. The answer may well address principles of development that extend beyond magnitudes or synesthesia.

The third common problem is that of mapping/integration. How much space is "7"? How much time is 30 inches? If magnitudes share a common metric then we need to know how that metric is developed and how it changes from task to task. In the synesthesia domain we need to ask how green is mapped on to the sound of 440 Hz, how jaggedy is the word "eleven," and how "9" maps on to red. One could wave these questions away and argue that they are random associations that stick in memory, but the cortex does not map randomly. Even when the visual cortex reorganizes in the blind the new map preserves the topography of the attribute being remapped (Kupers et al. 2006). As Cohen Kadosh et al. (2010) have shown, the mappings of size and luminance are not random, for example. I think it would even be worth stretching the idea to ask whether the rules for attribute mapping in synesthesia (see Simner, Chapter 8, this volume) are the same cortical rules as used for magnitude matching à la ATOM and remapping following acquired blindness (see the sixth common problem, in a later paragraph).

The fourth common problem is that of the shift from pre-linguistic to linguistic associations. As Laurenco et al.'s and Casasanto et al.'s findings suggest, the co-registration of attributes or magnitudes may differ as a function of language. And why wouldn't they? My prediction would be that pre-linguistic patterns will be preserved for some functions (rapid motor responses, for example) and that these might prevail in the kinds of experiments published by Andres (2004, 2008) and Lindemann (2007). If we avoid pursuing a dichotomy between the two they may prove useful in explaining when language matters for magnitudes or for synesthesia.

The fifth common problem is that of sensory versus metaphorical processing. One of the reasons that synesthesia has had such a hard time gaining its credibility badges is that, well, it is just upsetting to psychophysicists who have spent their lives asking people (actually usually themselves, one colleague, and one naïve subject) for yes/no, same/different answers, to have to consider people's impressions of "a kind of blue that is in front of the object."[4] But if synesthesia breaks the rules or hearts of psychophysicists then we need new rules (hearts mend with time). It may be that every sensation triggers a number of other sensations. The real question might be, not why do synesthetes see/hear/feel these things, but rather, how the brain manages to keep all the secondary associations out of awareness. Both synesthesia and our magnitude estimations are subject to language at some point. The question is how. Casasanto (2010) in his essay "Who's Afraid of the Big Bad Whorf" (don't you wish you thought of that title first?) reminds us that whether we think in language and whether language shapes thought are two very different questions. There is no doubt about the latter. Language shapes thought (Boroditsky 2000, 2001; Boroditsky and Ramscar 2002). I would not want to try to morph ATOM to include these influences but I would like to know how language shapes the representations underlying thought. What happens to the columnar representations of vision, the topographic maps of sight, the somatotopy of touch and the tonotopy of sound when languages reshapes our experience of them? This may be a more interesting avenue by which to study consciousness[5] than pitting seen versus unseen stimulus representations in binocular rivalry experiments.

---

[4] The author would like to say that some of his best friends and scientific heroes are psychophysicists.
[5] But please count me out of that one.

The sixth commonality is that both synesthesia and magnitude processing raise questions about the functions of the parietal cortex. Indeed one of the initial motivations behind ATOM was to ask why the parietal cortex is organized as it is. The role of the parietal lobe in magnitude processing is indisputable and I have made several predictions about functions there based on ATOM (see earlier). Interference with parietal function clearly impairs synesthesia (see Muggleton and Tsakanikos, Chapter 29, this volume) and the usual explanations are attentional or based on the role of the parietal cortex in sensory integration. Another possibility is that in order to scale some degree of redness to 7 or 440Hz to something jaggedy one needs to access a metric for 7 and for jaggedness. In other words synesthesia is the result of referring two outputs to a metric for scaling. The problem for this idea is that some of the synesthesias do not involve prothetic variables.

The seventh commonality is that both synesthesia and ATOM raise similar questions for development. When does language begin to influence our sensory experience and of course how? Understanding the transition between pre-linguistic and linguistic thought and experience may reveal common rules. Which brings me to the most important commonality.

The principles of cortical organization are often ignored in our domain specific view of cortical specialization but it seems to be a principle of brain mechanisms that when one solution to a problem is found, that solution is recycled over and over again. Perhaps "solution to a problem" is too active and it might be better to say that neurons have only a limited way of doing stuff, and that what we get out of them is determined by a few strategies. The most important example for this essay is that of cortical mapping. We have somatotopy, tonotopy, and retinotopy and which area represents touch, sound, and vision is not due to any intrinsic properties of the somatosensory, auditory, or visual cortex. It is determined by the inputs. The visual cortex could just as well map sound or touch as the auditory and somatosensory cortex could represent vision, as we have seen in animal rewiring studies and studies of short and long-term cortical reorganization in the blind (Kupers et al. 2006; Shamma 2001; Sur and Leamey 2001). What this means is that there should be common rules underlying different modalities of perception—spatiotopic representation, relational coding (e.g., Weber's law), adaptation effects, for example). The principles of wiring between areas also seem to be universal (most connections are with the next nearest neighbor and the further one travels from the source, the smaller the number of connections; Barone et al. 2000). So when we see two apparently different areas of research which both show the weaknesses of a modular view of our experience of the world, it is worth asking whether they are pointing us towards common principles. It is because of these cortical rules (and even metaphors need the cortex) that we think modularity, directional symmetry, mapping and integration, differences between pre-linguistic and linguistic thinking, sensory and metaphorical approaches to experience and the functions of the parietal cortex are likely to yield to a small number of rules across synesthesia and magnitudes.

Conclusions, Future Directions (and a Final Warning About Your Favorite Module)

Many challenges remain but some tough questions have already been faced. Making the link between action and metaphor (linking Laurenco to Casasanto; linking ATOM to metaphor) is perhaps one especially difficult enterprise. Sell et al. (2011) suggest some link between the two but Srinisivan and Carey (2010) posit a break between "lower" and metaphoric processing and in doing so suggest a "general purpose" spatial mechanism. Oliveri et al. (2009) remind us that the parietal cortex is not everything. By interfering with cerebellar function they selectively disrupted the mapping of time related words for the past in left space and for the future in right space. Yamakawa et al. (2009) extend the issue to social space. We have "close" friends, "distant," relatives and people who are "out of reach," people of "high" status, "low" profile, and a host of social relationships expressed in spatial metaphor. Yamakawa et al. reported overlapping regions of parietal activation when subjects were asked to judge social compatibility and physical distance. What does this tell us about magnitude processing and modularity? I think there are two things we can take from the work and ideas I have reviewed in this chapter. First, the brain is an addictive comparator. "More than" and "less than" are the foundations of our understanding of almost everything. I would not propose a single mechanism for all comparisons but we need to ask where this learning begins. My suggestion was, and still is, that it begins with motor development: Action is the beginning of all cognition. The second message to be taken away is that whatever is your favorite module, it is less of a module than you think. Synesthesia is a good example of this violation of modules, as is our continual use of shared maps between time, space, number, and other magnitudes.

Acknowledgments

Vincent Walsh is supported by a Royal Society Wolfson Award.

References

Andres, Michael, Marco Davare, Mauro Pesenti, Etienne Olivier, and Xavier Seron. 2004. Number magnitude and grip aperture interaction. *NeuroReport* 15:2773–2777.

Andres, Michael, David J. Ostry, Florence Nicol, and Tomas Paus. 2008. Time course of number magnitude interference during grasping. *Cortex* 44:414–419. doi:10.1016/j.cortex.2007.08.007.

Badets, Arnaud, Michael Andres, Samuel Di Luca, and Mauro Pesenti. 2007. Number magnitude potentiates action judgements. *Experimental Brain Research* 180:525–534. doi:10.1007/s00221-007-0870-y.

Badets, Arnaud, and Mauro Pesenti, M. 2010. Creating number semantics through finger movement perception. *Cognition* 115:46–53.

Barone, Pascal, Alexandre Batardiere, Kenneth Knoblauch, and Henry Kennedy. 2000. Laminar distribution of neurons in extrastriate areas projecting to visual areas V1 and V4 correlates with the hierarchical rank and indicates the operation of a distance rule. *The Journal of Neuroscience* 20 (9):3263–3281.

Bjoertomt, Otto, Alan Cowey, and Vincent Walsh. 2002. Spatial neglect in near and far space investigated by repetitive transcranial magnetic stimulation. *Brain* 125:2012–2022. doi:10.1093/brain/awf211.

Boroditsky, Lera. 2000. Metaphoric restructuring: Understanding time through spatial metaphors. *Cognition* 75:1–28.

———. 2001. Does language shape thought: Mandarin and English speakers' conceptions of time. *Cognitive Psychology* 43:1–22.

Boroditsky, Lera, and Michael Ramscar. 2002. The roles of body and mind in abstract thought. *Psychological Science* 13:185–189.

Brown, Scott W. 1997. Attentional resources in timing: interference effects in concurrent temporal and non-temporal working memory tasks. *Perception & Psychophysics* 5:1118–1140.

Brugger, Peter. 2008. SNARC, SCARC, SMARC and SPARC. Are there non spatial magnitudes? *Zeitschrift fur Neuropsychologie* 19:271–274.

Bueti, Domenica, Bahador Bahrami, and Vincent Walsh. 2008. Sensory and association cortex in time perception. *Journal of Cognitive Neuroscience* 20:1054–1062. doi:10.1162/jocn.2008.20060.

Bueti, Domenica, and Vincent Walsh. 2009. The parietal cortex and the representation of time, space, number and other magnitudes. *Philosophical Transactions of the Royal Society B: Biological Sciences* 364:1831–1840.

Bueti, Domenica, Vincent Walsh, Chris Frith, and Geraint Rees. 2008. Different brain circuits underlie time processing for action and perception. *Journal of Cognitive Neuroscience* 20:204–214. doi:10.1162/jocn.2008.20017.

Burr, David C. and John Ross. 2008. A visual sense of number. *Current Biology* 18:425–428. doi:10.1016/j.cub.2008.02.052.

Casasanto, Daniel. 2008. Who's afraid of the big bad Whorf?: Crosslinguistic differences in temporal language and thought. *Language Learning* 58:63–79.

Casasanto, Daniel, and Lera Boroditsky. 2008. Time in the mind: Using space to think about time. *Cognition* 106:579–593.

Casasanto, Daniel, Olga Fotakoupoulou, and Lera Boroditsky. 2010. Space and time in the child's mind: Evidence for a cross-dimensional asymmetry. *Cognitive Science* 34:387–405.

Cohen Kadosh, Roi, and Avishai Henik. 2013. Numbers, synesthesia, and directionality. In *Oxford Handbook of Synesthesia*, ed. Julia Simner and Edward M. Hubbard, 103–122. Oxford: Oxford University Press.

Cohen Kadosh, Roi, Avishai Henik, and Vincent Walsh. 2007. Small is bright and big is dark in synaesthesia. *Current Biology* 17:R834–R835. doi:10.1016/j.cub.2007.07.048.

———. 2009. Synaesthesia: Learned or lost? *Developmental Science* 12:484–491.

Cohen Kadosh, Roi, and Vincent Walsh. 2009. Numerical representation in the parietal cortex. Abstract or not abstract? *Behavioural and Brain Sciences* 32:313–328.

Cohen Kadosh, Roi, Neil Muggelton, Juha Silvanto, and Vincent Walsh. 2010. Double dissociation of format-dependent and number-specific neurons in human parietal cortex. *Cerebral Cortex* 20:2166–2171.

Cohen Kadosh, Roi, Kathrin Cohen Kadosh, and Avishai Henik. 2008. When brightness counts: the neuronal correlate of numerical-luminance interference. *Cerebral Cortex* 18:337–343. doi:10.1093/cercor/bhm058.

Dormal, Valérie, and Mauro Pesenti. 2007. Numerosity-length interference—a Stroop experiment. *Experimental Psychology* 54:289–297. doi:10.1027/1618-3169.54.4.289.

Droit-Volet, Sylvie. 2010. Speeding up a master clock common to time, number and length? *Behavioural Processes* 85:126–134.

Fias, Wim, Johan Lauwereyns, and Jan Lammertyn. 2001. Irrelevant digits affect feature-based attention depending on the overlap of neural circuits. *Cognitive Brain Research* 12:415–423. doi:10.1016/S0926-6410(01)00078-7.

Fischer, Rico, and Jeff Miller. 2008. Does the semantic activation of quantity representations influence motor parameters? *Experimental Brain Research* 189:379–391. doi:10.1007/s00221-008-1434-5.

Fischer, Martin H., Alan D. Castel, Michael D. Dodd, and Jay Pratt. 2003. Perceiving numbers causes spatial shifts of attention. *Nature Neuroscience* 6:555–556. doi:10.1038/nn1066.

Göbel, S. M., M. F. S. Rushworth, and V. Walsh. 2006. Inferior parietal rTMS affects performance in an addition task. *Cortex* 42:774–781. doi:10.1016/S0010-9452(08)70416-7.

Herrera, Amparo, Pedro Macizo, and Carlo Semenza. 2008. The role of working memory in the association between number magnitude and space. *Acta Psychologica* 128:225–237. doi:10.1016/j.actpsy.2008.01.002.

Hurewitz, Felicia, Rochel Gelman, and Brian Schnitzer. 2006 Sometimes area counts more than number. *Proceedings of the National Academy of Sciences of the United States of America* 103 (19):599–19 604. doi:10.1073/pnas.0609485103.

Ishihara, Masami, Peter E. Keller, Yves Rossetti, and Wolfgang Prinz. 2008. Horizontal spatial representations of time: evidence for the STEARC effect. *Cortex* 44:454–461. doi:10.1016/j.cortex.2007.08.010.

Ishihara, Masami, Sophie Jacquin-Courtois, Vasantha Flory, Romeo Salemmea, Kuniyasu Imanaka, and Yves Rossetti. 2006. Interaction between space and number representations during motor preparation in manual aiming. *Neuropsychologia* 44:1009–1016.

Kaufmann, Lian, and Hans-Christoph Nuerk. 2006. Interference effects in a numerical Stroop paradigm in 9–12 year old children with ADHD-C. *Child Neuropsychology* 12:223–243.

Kupers, Ron, Arnaud Fumal, Alain Maertens de Noordhout, Albert Gjedde, Jean Schoenen, and Maurice Ptito. 2006. Transcranial magnetic stimulation of the visual cortex induces somatotopically organized qualia in blind subjects. *Proceedings of the National Academy of Sciences of the United States of America* 103:13256–13260.

Levin, Iris. 1977. The development of time concepts in young children. Reasoning about duration. *Child Development* 48:435–444. doi:10.2307/1128636.

——. 1979. Interference of time related and unrelated cues with duration comparisons of young children: analysis of Piaget's formulation of the relation of time and speed. *Child Development* 50:469–477. doi:10.2307/1129425.

——. 1982 The nature and development of time concepts in children. The effects of interfering cues. In *The Developmental Psychology of Time*, ed. W. J. Friedman, 47–85. New York: Academic Press.

Laurenco, Stella F., and Matthew R. Longo. 2010 General magnitude representation in human infants. *Psychological Science* 21:873–881.

Lindemann, Oliver, Juan M. Abolafia, Giovanna Girardi, and Harold Bekkering. 2007. Getting a grip on numbers: numerical magnitude priming in object grasping. *Journal of Experimental Psychology. Human Perception and Performance* 33:1400–1409. doi:10.1037/0096-1523.33.6.1400.

Merrit, Dustin J., Daniel Casasanto, and Elizabeth Brannon. 2010. Do monkeys think in metaphors? Representations of space and time in monkeys and humans. *Cognition* 117:191–202.

Moretto, Giovanna, and Giuseppe di Pellegrino. 2008. Grasping numbers. *Experimental Brain Research* 188:505–515. doi:10.1007/s00221-008-1386-9.

Müller, Dana, and Wolfgang Schwarz. 2008. '1-2-3': is there a temporal number line? Evidence from a serial comparison task. *Experimental Psychology* 55:143–150. doi:10.1027/1618-3169.55.3.143.

Muggleton, Neil G., and Elias Tsakanikos. 2013. The use of transcranial magnetic stimulation in the investigation of synesthesia. In *The Oxford Handbook of Synesthesia*, ed. Julia Simner and Edward M. Hubbard, 570–583. Oxford: Oxford University Press.

Notebaert, Wim, Wim Gevers, Tom Verguts, and Wim Fias. 2006. Shared spatial reorientation for numbers and space: the reversal of the SNARC and Simon effects. *Journal of Experimental Psychology. Human Perception and Performance* 32:1197–1207.

Oliveri, Massimiliano, Sonia Bonni, Patrizia Turriziani, Giacomo Koch, Emanuele Lo Gerfo, Sara Torriero, Carmelo Mario Vicario, and Laura Petrosini. 2009. Motor and linguistic linking of space and time in the cerebellum. *PloS ONE* 4 (11):e7933.

Rousselle, Laurence, and Marie-Pascale. 2007. Basic numerical skills in children with mathematics learning disabilities: a comparison of symbolic vs non-symbolic number magnitude processing. *Cognition* 102:361–395. doi:10.1016/j.cognition.2006.01.005.

——. 2008. The development of automatic numerosity processing in preschoolers: evidence for numerosity-perceptual interference. *Developmental Psychology* 44:544–560. doi:10.1037/0012-1649.44.2.544.

Salillas, Elena, Demis Basso, Maurizia Baldi, Carlo Semenza, and Tomaso Vecchi. 2009. Motion on numbers. Trancranial magnetic stimulation on the ventral intraparietal sulcus alters both numerical and motion processes. *Journal of Cognitive Neuroscience* 21:2129–2138.

Schwenzer, M., and Mathiak, K. 2011. Numeric aspects in pitch identification: an fMRI study. *BMC Neuroscience* 12:26.

Sell, Andrea J., and Michael P. Kaschack. 2011. Processing time shift affects the execution of motor responses. *Brain and Language* 117:39–44.

Shamma, Shihab. 2001. On the role of space and time in auditory processing. *Trends in Cognitive Sciences* 5:340–348. doi:10.1016/S1364-6613(00)01704-6.

Simner, Julia. 2013. The "rules" of synesthesia. In *The Oxford Handbook of Synesthesia*, ed. Julia Simner and Edward M. Hubbard, 149–164. Oxford: Oxford University Press.

Srinisivan, Mahesh, and Susan Carey. 2010. The long and short of it: On the nature and origin of functional overlap of representations of space and time. *Cognition* 116:217–241.

Stavy, Ruth, and Dinah Tirosh. 2000. *How Students (Mis-) Understand Science, Mathematics: Intuitive Rules*. New York: Teachers College Press, Columbia University.

Stevens, S. S. 1957. On the psychophysical law. *Psychological Review* 64:153–181.

Stoianov, Ivilin, Peter Kramer, Carlo Umilta, and Marco Zorzi. 2008. Visuospatial priming of the mental number line. *Cognition* 106:770–779. doi:10.1016/j.cognition.2007.04.013.

Sur, Mriganka, and Catherine A. Leamey. 2001. Development, plasticity of cortical areas and networks. *Nature Reviews Neuroscience* 2:251–262. doi:10.1038/35067562.

Taylor-Cooke, P. A., R. Ricci, J. H. Baños, X. Zhou, A. J. Woods, and M. S. Mennemeier. 2006. Perception of motor strength and stimulus magnitude are correlated in stroke patients. *Neurology* 66:1444–1456.

Van Essen David C., and John H. R. Maunsell. 1983. Hierarchical organization and functional streams in the visual-cortex. *Trends in Neurosciences* 6:370-375.

Vicario, Carmelo M. 2011. Perceiving numbers affects the subjective temporal midpoint. *Perception* 40:23–29.

Walsh, Vincent. 2003a. A theory of magnitude: common cortical metrics of time, space and quantity. *Trends in Cognitive Sciences* 7:483–488. doi:10.1016/j.tics.2003.09.002.

——. 2003b. Time: The back-door of perception. *Trends in Cognitive Sciences* 7:335–338. doi:10.1016/S1364-6613(03) 00166-9.

Xuan, Bin, Daren Zhang, Sheng He, and Xiangchuan Chen. 2007. Larger stimuli are judged to last longer. *Journal of Vision* 7:1–5. doi:10. 1167/7.10.2.

Yamakawa, Yoshinori, Ryota Kanai, Michikazu Matsumura, and Eiichi Naito. 2009. Social distance evaluation in human parietal cortex. *PloS One* 4:e3460.

Zach, Peter, and Peter Brugger. 2008. Subjective time in near and far representational space. *Cognitive and Behavioral Neurology* 21:8–13. doi:10.1097/WNN.0b013e31815f237c.

CHAPTER 42

....

SENSORY SUBSTITUTION DEVICES

Creating "artificial synesthesias"

....

LAURENT RENIER AND ANNE G. DE VOLDER

INTRODUCTION

....

The term "sensory substitution" was introduced at the end of the 1960s to indicate the use of one sensory modality to supply environmental information normally gathered by another sense (e.g., the use of sound to provide information about visual scenes; Bach-y-Rita et al. 1969). Following the first attempts to create tools to compensate for the loss of sight (e.g., the long cane to assist blind people in their movements), Paul Bach-y-Rita and his collaborators developed the first sensory substitution device that was specifically dedicated to the scientific investigation of brain plasticity in early blind people (Bach-y-Rita and Kercel 2003; Bach-y-Rita et al. 1969). Since this pioneering work, the increasing interest for sensory substitution has given rise both to the development of various sensory substitution devices and to numerous studies in the cognitive neuroscience sphere (Renier and De Volder 2005). Sensory substitution has now become a vast field of study and constitutes both a research topic and a means to investigate other domains such as human perception (including what we might think of as "synthetic" or "artificial synesthesia") and brain plasticity. The purpose of this chapter is to provide an overview of some sensory substitution devices, to summarize the main questions explored over the last decades in this research area, to demonstrate how sensory substitution contributes to the study of brain function and human cognition, and to evaluate the rehabilitation potentialities of available systems.

Sensory Substitution Devices

While virtually every sense can be replaced by another one using human–machine interfaces, most sensory substitution devices were developed for vision substitution and there have been very few attempts to develop devices to substitute the olfactory and gustatory modalities. Vision is the predominant sense in sighted humans (Rock et al. 1999) and the most investigated one. The visual sense plays a central role in how we represent and interact with the world around us. The primacy of vision is structurally imbedded in cortical organization since about one-third of the cortical surface in primates is involved in visual processes (Kupers et al. 2011). Therefore, it is not surprising that the visual sense is also the most frequently substituted via sensory substitution devices (either via auditory or tactile modalities). Besides vision, however, there have been some attempts to replace hearing and the vestibular function by the tactile modality, and we describe a number of these approaches in the following sections.

Vision substitution

Historically, the first efficient sensory substitution instrument developed to replace vision was the long cane. This very simple instrument was used to assist blind people in their displacements (Hoover 1950). At the beginning of the nineteenth century, Louis Braille, who suffered blindness himself at the age of 3 years, invented one of the first sensory substitution system which used an arbitrary code (Mellor 2008; but for previous systems see also the Ecriture Nocturne of Charles Barbier de la Serre and the Embossed Alphabet of Valentin Haüy, e.g., Monnier 1989). Braille was further developed into a successful reading and writing system using a tactile code. The cane and Braille are still used today all around the world by blind people in their everyday lives.

Following these first successful steps, electronic versions of the long cane (e.g., laser cane and other obstacle detectors) were intended to improve orientation and mobility by providing spatial information (Farmer 1978; Kay 1961). Later, these sonar aids evolved into head-mounted versions, such as the well-known Sonicguide (Kay 1974; see also <http://www.batforblind.co.nz/index.php>) which used pitch and binaural balance, i.e., difference in the stimulation intensity between the ears. Those devices provided the user with information about obstacle location and distance. Other approaches such as the "SeeHear" chip from Caltech (Nielson, Mahowald, and Mead 1989) use binaural directional cues, much as natural human echolocation does. Human echolocation, initially described as "facial vision" (Supa, Cotzin, and Dallenbach 1944) is the ability of humans to detect objects in their environment by actively creating sounds (e.g., by tapping their canes, stomping their foot or making clicking noises with their mouths) and sensing echoes from those objects (Thaler, Arnott, and Goodale 2011).

In the same period as that of the Sonicguide, Bach-y-Rita and his collaborators (Bach-y-Rita et al. 1969) developed the Tactile Vision Substitution System (TVSS), offering the possibility of both localizing *and* recognizing objects. Currently, two main classes of vision sensory substitution devices exist, tactile and auditory. In other words, what would usually be visual information is fed to the senses in the form of touch or sound. These "modern" vision sensory substitution systems consist of a video camera coupled with a human–machine interface. The human–machine interface transmits the information to the brain either through tactile sense or the auditory modality, the so-called "sensory substitution channel" (Bach-y-Rita and Kercel 2003).

The TVSS and visual-to-tactile substitution devices

The original TVSS mapped black-and-white images from a video camera to a vibrotactile belt worn on the abdomen at a resolution of 20×20 pixels in the tactile array. This "new generation" of devices opened the way to the scientific study of sensory substitution. The TVSS in its pneumatic-, electric- or vibrotactile variants (Kaczmareck et al. 1991; Zappe et al. 2004) uses various skin areas of the body as the peripheral sense organ for input: the abdomen, the back, the thigh, or the forehead, as well as the tongue may be used for this purpose. Of these, the tongue which is a very sensitive organ seems more suitable than other body parts, as demonstrated by studies using a substitution device known as the Tongue Display Unit (TDU, Bach-y-Rita et al. 1998). The TDU transmits visual information via the tongue using electro-tactile stimulations; it reproduces "visual patterns" on a 144-pixel square matrix applied on the tongue. These sensory substitution systems provide analogue encoding of visual information (i.e., the spatial arrangement of the elements in a perceived scene is transposed onto the skin by a matrix of "tactors" that stimulates the somatosensory receptors in a defined skin area). Other devices using wearable vibrotactile belts (Haptic Belt; McDaniel et al. 2008) or gloves (VibroGlove; Krishna et al. 2010) enable people who are blind to perceive social situational information. Both technologies use miniature cameras that are mounted on a pair of glasses worn by the user who is blind. The Haptic Belt provides vibrations that convey the direction and distance at which a person is standing in front of a user, while the VibroGlove uses spatio-temporal mapping of vibration patterns to convey facial expressions of the interaction partner.

Visual-to-auditory substitution devices

Alternatives to the tactile systems include auditory devices such as: the vOICe (Meijer 1992), the prosthesis substituting vision with audition (PSVA; Capelle et al. 1998); the Cronly-Dillon algorithm (Cronly-Dillon, Persaud, and Gregory 1999), and the versatile vision-to-audition sensory substitution device (VIBE; Hanneton, Auvray, and Durette 2010). These allow online translation of visual patterns into sounds that the subject hears through headphones. We describe these in the following sections.

The vOICe

The vOICe (with the three capital letters referring to "Oh I see") converts live camera views from a video camera into "soundscapes" (Meijer 1992). A "soundscape" is an auditory signal that represents the components of the visual scene. The vOICe system uses general video-to-audio mapping by associating height with pitch, and brightness with loudness, in a left-to-right scan of any video frame. In other words, if the visual scene contains an object at height, which is also bright, the corresponding sound will be high in pitch and loud. The left-to-right scanning means that objects in the left-hand visual field are "sounded" before objects in the right. Views are typically refreshed about once per second with a typical image resolution of up to 60×60 pixels as can be proven by spectrographic analysis. More information about the vOICe device can be found at <http://www.seeingwithsound.com>.

The PSVA

The prosthesis substituting vision with audition (PSVA) translates real-time mono-chrome images from a miniature head-mounted video camera (frame rate: 12.5 Hz) into sounds using a pixel–frequency relationship (Capelle et al. 1998). The camera image is pixelated according to a simplified dual resolution model of the human retina. This arti-ficial retina consists of a square matrix of 8×8 large pixels with the four central ones replaced by 8×8 smaller pixels representing the fovea. Therefore, the fovea has four times the resolution of the periphery. A single sinusoidal tone is assigned to each pixel of the artificial retina with frequencies increasing from left to right and from bottom to top; frequencies range between 50 and 12,526 Hz. The grey scale level of each pixel modulates the amplitude of its corresponding sine wave. The final auditory output of the PSVA is the real-time weighted sum of all 124 sine waves. With head movements, visual frames are grabbed in real-time and then transformed into a set of corresponding com-plex sounds enabling the wearer to ultimately recognize the scene. A demonstration of the sound produced by a single pixel or a bar when detected by the system is available at <http://www.perceptionweb.com/perco899/arno.html>.

The VIBE

With the versatile vision-to-audition sensory substitution device (VIBE), the sound produced by this software is also a mixture of sinusoidal sounds produced by the "trans-lation" of an image into sounds. The visual scene is divided into sections or "receptive fields" that are each translated into a sine wave of a specific frequency according to its location (Hanneton et al. 2010). Each receptive field is a set of localized pixels. The sound's amplitude is determined by the mean luminosity of the pixels of the correspond-ing receptive field. In other words, brighter objects are translated into louder sounds. The frequency and the stimulation intensity in each individual ear (interaural disparity) are determined by the location of the object in the receptive fields of the system.

In contrast to tactile displays, devices that substitute audio for vision usually use an arbitrary code to translate images into sounds, though some of the key characteris-tics are quite intuitive and can be understood with little or no prior explanations (e.g., stimulation intensity difference between ear codes for the location of the object in the perceptual field; the left part of the perceptual field renders sounds mainly in the left ear). Despite this difference, both types of vision substitution systems (i.e., auditory and tactile displays) offer similar perceptual possibilities such as shape recognition (Amedi et al. 2007; Arno, De Volder, et al. 2001; Ptito et al. 2005), object localization and distance estimation (Auvray, Hanneton, and O'Regan 2007; Chebat et al. 2011; Proulx et al. 2008; Renier and De Volder 2010) or depth perception (Renier et al. 2005a; Segond, Weiss, and Sampaio 2005). It is worth noting that these modern sensory substitution devices generate elaborated perception that shares close similarities with vision (O'Regan and Noë 2001; Renier and De Volder 2010). For instance, distance estimation using a system with a video camera is based on visual pictorial (or monocular) cues such as the relative size, the height in the perceptual field, occlusion effects, or linear perspective (Renier and De Volder 2006; Renier,Laloyaux, et al. 2005) and they recruit specialized visual brain areas (Amedi et al. 2007; Renier, Collignon, et al. 2005). O'Regan and Noë (2001) put also a lot of emphasis on the fact that head movements, which are usually linked to visual changes in normal conditions, become artificially associated with equivalent changes in the auditory or tactile modality when using a vision sensory substitution system.

Hearing substitution

While there is no tactile–auditory substitution system currently available (i.e., no system that replaces environmental sound by touch signals), recent experiments show that vibrotactile stimuli can be used to facilitate hearing in normal and hearing-impaired people and may activate the auditory cortex (Schurmann et al. 2006). Schurmann and his collaborators tested subjects while stimulating their fingers and palms with vibration bursts and their fingertips with tactile pressure. They found that tactile stimulation of the fingers lead to activation of the auditory cortex, which suggests that there is a relationship between audition and touch. It makes sense to investigate the likelihood of a tactile–auditory sensory substitution system in the future.

Vestibular system substitution

Some people with balance disorders or adverse reactions to antibiotics suffer from bilateral vestibular damage. They experience difficulty with standing and in maintaining posture. Tyler et al. (2003) investigated the restitution of postural control through a tactile-for-vestibular sensory substitution. Using a head-mounted accelerometer (i.e., an instrument for measuring acceleration) and a brain-machine interface that employs electrotactile stimulation on the tongue, information about head-body orientation is relayed to the patient so that a new source of data is available to orient himself and maintain good posture (Tyler et al. 2003). The original version of the vestibular substitution system used the tongue display unit (TDU, Bach-y-Rita et al. 1998) and a miniature two-axis accelerometer that was mounted on a hat. Anterior–posterior and medial–lateral angular displacement data (derived by double integration of the acceleration data) were fed to TDU, which generated a patterned stimulus on a 144-point electrotactile array

(12×12 matrix) held against the superior, anterior surface of the tongue. Studies demonstrated that providing an open-loop human control system allowed rapid and significant improvements in all tested patients; after 3 to 5 days of training with the device, the head-body postural coordination was restored by means of vestibular substitution (Bach-y-Rita et al. 2005). Moreover, postural stability remained for a couple of days after removing the vestibular substitution, at which point the open-loop instability reappeared.

Processes Underlying Sensory Substitution

One of the main questions raised by sensory substitution concerns the exact nature of the related perceptions. What exactly *are* perceptions, and how can they be defined given that sensory substitution devices serve to separate the modality of the stimulus and the modality of the derived sensory experience? And what is that sensory experience *like*? From a general perspective, this problem asks what are the actual determinants of the nature of a perception? (A similar question is addressed in the chapter by Keeley, Chapter 46, this volume.) Is it the sensory organ used to receive the information? Or the pathway over which the sensory information is carried (Müller 1835; Norrsell, Finger, and Lajonchere 1999)? Is it the sensory modality of the original stimulus? Is it the nature of the information conveyed? For instance, distance and spatiality are thought to be more specifically related to vision than to any other sense in human beings. Is it the character of the cognitive and/or brain processing that determines its nature? According to Bach-y-Rita, perception is created within the brain and is relatively independent from the sensory modality of the stimulus, or the sense organ that receives it (Bach-y-Rita 1972). Several researchers have proposed that perception based on vision substitution by another sense (e.g., touch/sound signals) was visual since subjects using this type of device generally report visual rather than tactual or auditory sensations, and perceive objects as externally localized rather than on the skin, say (Auvray et al. 2005; Epstein et al. 1986; Ward and Meijer 2010). Supporting this viewpoint, Morgan (1977) underlined the fact that both vision and its sensory substitution provide access to the same kind of information and give rise to similar behavioral responses. It is worth noting that perception by means of sensory substitution of vision fits quite well with most of the definitions of visual perception. For instance, Rock, Gallant and Kube (1999, 5) defined visual perception as the "process of acquiring knowledge about environmental objects and events by extracting information from the light they emit or reflect." The earlier referenced "modern" vision substitution devices were developed to acquire environmental information in a similar way, namely, the extraction of information conveyed by the light, but providing this information to the user through another sense. O'Regan and Noë (2001) further pointed out the similarities regarding some sensory-motor contingencies of vision and those of sensory substitution devices that used a head-mounted camera. According to these authors, the nature of perception is mainly determined by the relationship between motor actions (e.g., reaching to touch an object) and their sensory consequences (the resultant tactile sensation), the so-called sensory-motor contingencies. They concluded that provided the sensation changes related to head movements occur in the auditory or tactile modality instead of the visual modality, the users of such sensory substitution devices should have visual experiences. Moreover, there are additional arguments that do account for the cognitive aspects of visual perception, in which visual information is interpreted beyond solely the available information in the visual receptive field (e.g., as in optical illusions). For instance, Renier and colleagues (Renier, Laloyaux, et al. 2005; Renier et al. 2006) demonstrated the possibility of perceiving pure visual phenomena using the PSVA (the Prosthesis Substituting Vision with Audition; a visual-to-auditory substitution device described earlier). Sighted subjects using the PSVA while blindfolded were sensitive to the Ponzo illusion (Renier et al. 2005) and the vertical-horizontal illusion (Renier and De Volder 2006) and were able to interpret visual depth cues when using the PSVA to estimate the distance to an object (Renier et al. 2010). This illustrates the top-down influences of visual processes in full accordance with theoretical models of visual perception (Gregory 1997). It clearly indicates the existence of a visual-like processing of sensory information gathered by the PSVA. In addition, previous visual experience was demonstrated to influence perception with the PSVA, since early blind subjects were not sensitive to visual illusions or to visual perspective (Renier, Laloyaux, et al. 2005). In addition to subjective reports and observed behavioral performance, results from brain imaging studies highlighted other similarities between vision, and perception by sensory substitution of vision. Several brain imaging studies demonstrated a recruitment of visual brain areas in sighted but blindfolded subjects who used a tactile (Ptito et al. 2005) or an auditory (Amedi et al. 2007; Arno, Vanlierde, et al. 2001; Reich et al. 2011; Striem-Amit et al. 2012) vision sensory substitution device to recognize two-dimensional figures. Furthermore, modulation of some of these brain activation foci according to what was perceived (i.e., two- versus three-dimensional scene), was also observed with the PSVA, as in vision (Renier, Collignon, et al. 2005).

Another theoretical question raised by sensory substitution concerns the cognitive processes involved in its use and the required learning to use such a device. Although experimental data indicate that sensory substitution shares cognitive processes with vision, little is known of their exact nature. One may expect that mental imagery and visual working memory play a crucial role in perception with a sensory substitution device, yet these points require further investigation. Although only some devices use an arbitrary code as in the vOICe or the PSVA, a training phase seems to be required in all sensory substitution systems (Bach-y-Rita 1972), including the analogue ones (e.g., the TVSS or the TDU transpose the spatial arrangement of the elements captured by the video camera onto a tactile matrix array; what is reproduced on the tactile matrix is a mirror of the image captured by the camera). Few of the learning mechanisms involved in the mastering of these devices have been studied, but the learning characteristics do fit quite well with the description of procedural learning (Poirier et al 2006a). Like procedural learning, sensory substitution involves the acquisition of perceptive-motor and/or cognitive skills. Performance increases with practice (e.g., Arno et al. 1999; Sampaio et al. 2001) and what is learned cannot be verbally explained. Auvray et al. (2007) described five different stages involved in the learning of the vOICe: "contact," "exteriorization," "spatialization," "comprehension of the information," and "immersion." We describe these next.

The step of "contact" involves the learning of sensorimotor regularities needed to stabilize and maintain contact with the perceived object (or the sensory stimulation). The "exteriorization" occurs when the user become aware that his or her sensations are due to the perception of an external and distal object (i.e., distal attribution). The "spatialization" corresponds to the understanding of the relationship between object location/shape and its perception according to different viewpoints; it allows users to locate objects and events in the environment relative to the viewer. The step of "comprehension of the information" is defined as the feeling of being in a perceptual open space. It involves a new automatic sensorimotor coupling which allows the user to feel entirely aware of his or her surrounding environment. The "immersion" involves an access to a meaningful perceptual experience arising from the sensations.

This description of the learning phase as evolving towards more automatic and rapid processing corresponds well to the description of the acquisition of procedural learning (Fitts 1954). The acquired ability is generally indicated by the fact that its use can be transferred from one motor system to another (e.g., switching the control of the camera from the head to the arm; Bach-y-Rita et al. 1969; Renier, Collignon, et al. 2005). The skin surface of the body receiving the information with the TVSS may also be changed (e.g., from the back to the abdomen), without the loss of perceptual capabilities (Bach-y-Rita et al. 1969). In the same way, Kim and Zatorre (2008, see also Arno et al. 1999) provided an additional demonstration of the degree to which learning using the vOICe generalizes to new (untrained) stimuli. Such generalization could provide a basis for the substitution in a constantly changing visual environment.

DOES SENSORY SUBSTITUTION PROVIDE ARTIFICIAL (SYNTHETIC) SYNESTHESIA?

Sensory substitution artificially extends the natural cross-modal perception possibilities of normal subjects by allowing them to process information normally related to one sense by another one (e.g., "hearing" object shapes). This new type of cross-modal perception fundamentally changed the classical distinction between senses making their natural boundaries vanish. However gaining access to environmental information is still different than feeling or experiencing sensations related to another modality. For instance, are blind users able to experience visual sensations (what philosophers call visual qualia) when they use a vision-to-hearing substitution device? Or do they just "hear" it? Ward and Meijer (2010) recently reported that through extensive use of the vOICe, some blind users described having experienced specifically *visual* sensations. Therefore, using a sensory substitution device to perceive objects would not only be a matter of conveying information in a general sense, but would also generate the corresponding subjective experience inherent to the substituted modality. In addition, after a period of training, some of these proficient blind users reported starting to experience visual sensations in response to environmental sounds while they were *not* using the vOICe. This leads to the suggestion that the blind users had acquired synesthesia after having used a vision substitution device based on sounds (Ward and Meijer 2010; see also Proulx 2010). This observation is in line with previous observations made by other researchers (Auvray et al. 2005; Bach-y-Rita 1972; Epstein et al. 1986; Morgan 1977; O'Regan and Noë 2001): the perception provided to the user is regarded by the proficient user as "real," and often outside the body, instead of imagined in the mind's eye. Its reality and vividness are what makes this perception so new, and the related artificial synesthesia so interesting in its violation of conventional notions of perception. In this way, this type of "artificial synesthesia" is a deliberately evoked or induced sensory fusion in which the real information of one sense is accompanied by a perception in another sense through the use of a cross-modal mapping device. This phenomenon is also known as "virtual synesthesia" or "synthetic synesthesia." However, it is the use of a *device* to map one type of sensory information stream into an information stream for another sensory modality which clearly distinguishes artificial synesthesia from spontaneous synesthesia or developmental synesthesia as well as from cross-modal associations in non-synesthetes for normal sensory inputs (see <http://www.seeingwithsound.com/asynesth.htm>). In other words, we are dealing with a form of learned synesthesia (acquired synesthesia) that might result from machine-generated cross-modal mappings, and this might be particularly relevant in studying the feasibility of developing useful artificial auditory (or tactile)-to-visual synesthesia for blind people. In contrast to "natural" synesthetes who usually report relatively simple or non-generic visual percepts of color, textures or shapes in association with certain sounds, and where different synesthetes report different percepts (Ward and Meijer 2010), here we are faced with the fascinating perspective of being able to promote virtually all kinds of learned auditory-induced or tactile-induced visual percepts, and thereby provide a form of synesthetic experience in each and everybody.

SENSORY SUBSTITUTION AND CROSS-MODAL PLASTICITY IN SENSORY IMPAIRED SUBJECTS

Studying sensory substitution in blindness (or in deafness) presents a unique opportunity for understanding how the brain adapts itself when it processes visual-like (or auditory-like) information after an extended period of sensory deprivation, or the complete absence of such since birth. Therefore, it is not surprising that brain plasticity rapidly became the most studied topic using sensory substitution devices (e.g., Arno, De Volder, et al. 2001). Early visual deprivation gives rise to a reorganization of the visual cortex (e.g., Bavelier and Neville 2002; Pascual-Leone et al. 2005; Rauschecker 1995), and to the emergence of compensatory mechanisms that make early blind people more efficient at achieving certain perceptual tasks, including sensory substitution (Arno, Vanlierde, et al. 2001; Lessard et al. 1998; Pascual-Leone and Torres 1993; Röder et al. 1999). Using functional imaging of the brain in congenitally blind subjects, a cross-modal recruitment of the occipital cortex was observed during speech processing and verbal memory (Amedi et al. 2003; Bedny et al. 2011; Reich et al. 2011; Röder et al. 2002), mental imagery tasks (De Volder et al. 2001), Braille reading (Büchel et al. 1998; Burton, Sinclair, and Agato 2012; Sadato et al. 1996), tactile perception (Pietrini et al. 2004), and sound localization (Gougoux et al. 2005; Kujala et al. 1992; Weeks et al. 2000). The functional specialization of the ventral, temporo-occipital and dorsal, parieto-occipital stream seems well preserved and developed in early blind subjects, as demonstrated by studies on mental imagery (De Volder et al. 2001; Vanlierde et al. 2003), working memory (Bonino et al. 2008), and auditory and tactile perception (Poirier et al. 2006b; Renier et al. 2010; Saenz et al. 2008). The main contribution of sensory substitution studies was the demonstration of a recruitment of the occipital cortex in early blind subjects, during the processing of auditory or tactile encoded visual information (Arno, De Volder, et al. 2001; Ptito et al. 2005). This functional role of the occipital cortex of blind subjects in non-visual tasks was also shown using transcranial magnetic stimulation to induce virtual lesions in the brain that interfered with Braille reading (Cohen et al. 1997), speech processing (Amedi et al. 2004), sound lateralization, and sensory substitution (Collignon et al. 2007; Merabet et al. 2009). Interestingly, Kupers et al. (2006) showed that transcranial magnetic stimulation applied on the occipital pole induced tactile sensations referred to the tongue in blind subjects who were trained to use the TDU, demonstrating further the cross-modal plasticity mechanisms that take place after a relatively short learning phase. More recently, we demonstrated that early blind subjects could learn visual perspectives while using the PSVA (Renier and De Volder 2010). One may hypothesize that the occipital cortex of blind people is the neural substrate of the compensatory perceptual mechanisms and that it contributes to the subjective visual phenomenology experienced by them.

Sensory Substitution and Vision Rehabilitation

The very first vision substitution methods, i.e., the long cane and Braille, were developed exclusively in a rehabilitation context. These assistive systems have given birth to electronic versions (e.g., Kay 1961) which are currently used all around the world by blind people. In contrast to Braille or the long cane, which aimed to restore only one function of vision (reading or obstacle detection), sensory substitution systems are intended to simultaneously restore several functions of vision (e.g., spatial localization and shape recognition, Bach-y-Rita 1972). As mentioned earlier, sensory substitution appeared gradually in basic research, but the idea of creating devices to assist blind people in their everyday life is one of recent interest (e.g., Bach-y-Rita et al. 2003; Veraart et al. 2004). Sensory substitution devices are quite adapted to different uses and situations and seem able to respond to most of the needs of blind people for object localization and recognition outside the proximal space. These characteristics can potentially facilitate their mobility and improve the quality of their interactions with the environment in general. Sensory substitution has significant advantages over visual prostheses, such as retinal implants and the other implanted electrodes that stimulate electrically the optic nerve or the visual cortex (Brelén et al. 2005; Brindley et al. 1968; Dobelle et al. 1979; Humayun et al. 1996). Sensory substitution systems are completely non-invasive (avoiding all the potential problems associated with implanted electrodes). They are suitable even for people with optic nerve damage and hypothetically also appropriate when sensory loss is a consequence of a cortical lesion. Another advantage is that they can be used after a very short training phase (i.e., a few hours). However, despite these qualities, very few sensory substitution devices are currently used by blind people in their daily life, though some of them such as the vOICe are available for free on the Internet and do not necessitate a lot of equipment to use them. One reason for this limited use of these devices by blind people may still be the relatively poor information conveyed to users by these devices as compared to vision. Nevertheless, sensory substitution is still a promising alternative to the traditional aids for blind people, such as implanted visual prostheses and other assistive technologies.

CONCLUSIONS

Although many technological hurdles remain before those devices can be used in daily life, sensory substitution is demonstrably suitable for many tasks such as spatial localization, distance estimation, and shape recognition. Examples would be applying these devices for mobility and object grasping tasks. However, despite these very encouraging aspects for rehabilitation, the main interest of sensory substitution still remains in basic research. Throughout the years, by demonstrating valuable practical possibilities to replace some of the key functions of vision, sensory substitution has become a vast and attractive research field in cognitive neuroscience. Although many issues remain yet to be investigated and better understood, studies on sensory substitution have demonstrated valuable contributions in the understanding of human perception, sensory interactions and integration, natural versus artificial synesthesia and brain plasticity.

References

Amedi, Amir, Noa Raz, Pazit Pianka, Rafael Malach, and Ehud Zohary. 2003. Early 'visual' cortex activation correlates with superior verbal memory performance in the blind. *Nature Neuroscience* 6: 758–766.

Amedi, Amir, William M. Stern, Joan A. Camprodon, Felix Bermpohl, Lotfi Merabet, Stephen Rotman, Christopher Hemond, Peter Meijer, and Alvaro Pascual-Leone. 2007. Shape conveyed by visual-to-auditory sensory substitution activates the lateral occipital complex. *Nature Neuroscience* 10(6):687–689.

Arno, Patricia, Christian Capelle, Marie-Chantale Wanet-Defalque, Mitzi Catalan-Ahumada, and Claude Veraart. 1999. Auditory coding of visual patterns for the blind. *Perception* 28:1013–1029.

Arno, Patricia, Anne G. De Volder, Annick Vanlierde, Marie-Chantal Wanet-Defalque, Emmanuel Streel, Annie Robert, Sandra Sanabria-Bohorquez, and Claude Veraart. 2001. Occipital activation by pattern recognition in the early blind using auditory substitution of vision. *NeuroImage* 13:632–645.

Arno, Patricia, Annick Vanlierde, Emmanuel Streel, Marie-Chantal Wanet-Defalque, Sandra Sanabria-Bohorquez, and Claude Veraart. 2001. Auditory substitution of vision: Pattern recognition by the blind. *Applied Cognitive Psychology* 15:509–519.

Auvray, Malika, Sylvain Hanneton, Charles Lenay, and Kevin O'Regan. 2005. There is something out there: distal attribution in sensory substitution, twenty years later. *Journal of Integrative Neuroscience* 4(4):505–521

Auvray, Malika, Sylvain Hanneton, and Kevin O'Regan. 2007. Learning to perceive with a visuo-auditory substitution system: localisation and object recognition with 'the vOICe'. *Perception* 36(3): 416–430.

Bach-y-Rita, Paul. 1972. *Brain Mechanisms in Sensory Substitution*. San Diego, CA: Academic Press.

Bach-y-Rita, Paul, Carter C. Collins, Frank Saunders, Benjamin White, and Lawrence Scadden. 1969. Vision substitution by tactile image projection. *Nature* 221:963–964.

Bach-y-Rita, Paul, Yuri P. Danilov, Mitchell E. Tyler, and Robert J. Grimm. 2005. Late human brain plasticity: Vestibular substitution with a tongue BrainPort human-machine interface. *Journal of Intellectica* 40: 115–122.

Bach-y-Rita, Paul, Kurt A. Kaczmarek, Mitchell E. Tyler, and Jorge Garcia-Lara. 1998. Form perception with a 49-point electrotactile stimulus array on the tongue: A technical note. *Journal of Rehabilitation Research and Development* 35:427–430.

Bach-y-Rita, Paul, and Stephen W. Kercel. 2003. Sensory substitution and the human-machine interface. *Trends in Cognitive Neurosciences* 7:541–546.

Bavelier, Daphne, and Helen J. Neville. 2002. Cross-modal plasticity: Where and how? *Nature Reviews Neuroscience* 3(6): 443–452.

Bedny, Marina, Alvaro Pascual-Leone, David Dodell-Feder, Evelina Fedorenko, and Rebecca Saxe. 2011. Language processing in the occipital cortex of congenitally blind adults. *Proceedings of the National Academy of Sciences of the United States of America* 108 (11):4429–4434.

Bonino, Daniela, Emiliano Ricciardi, Lorenzo Sani, Claudio Gentili, Nicola Vanello, Mario Guazzelli, Tomaso Vecchi, and Pietro Pietrini. 2008. Tactile spatial working memory activates the dorsal extrastriate cortical pathway in congenitally blind individuals. *Archives Italiennes de Biologie* 146(3–4):133–146.

Brelén, Marten E., Florence Duret, Benoît Gérard, Jean Delbeke, and Claude Veraart. 2005. Creating a meaningful visual perception in blind volunteers by optic nerve stimulation. *Journal of Neural Engineering* 2(1):S22–S28.

Brindley, Giles S., W. S. Lewin. 1968. The sensations produced by electrical stimulation of the visual cortex, *Journal of Physiology* 96:479–493.

Büchel, Christian, Cathy Price, Richard S. J. Frackowiak, and Karl Friston. 1998. Different activation patterns in the visual cortex of late and congenitally blind subjects. *Brain* 121:409–419.

Burton, Harold, Robert J. Sinclair, and Alvin Agato. 2012. Recognition memory for Braille or spoken words: an fMRI study in early blind. *Brain Research* 1438:22–34.

Capelle, Christian, Charles Trullemans, Patricia Arno, and Claude Veraart. 1998. Real time experimental prototype for enhancement of vision rehabilitation using auditory substitution. *IEEE Transactions on Biomedical Engineering* 45:1279–1293.

Chebat, Daniel R., Fabien C. Schneider, Ron Kupers, and Maurice Ptito. 2011. Navigation without vision: Detection and avoidance of obstacles using sensory substitution device. *Neuroreport* 22(7):342–347.

Cohen, Leonardo G., Pablo Celnik, Alvaro Pascual-Leone, Brian Corwell, Lala Faiz, James Dambrosia, Manabu Honda, *et al.* 1997. Functional relevance of cross-modal plasticity in blind humans. *Nature* 389 (6647):180–183.

Collignon, Olivier, Maryse Lassonde, Franco Lepore, Danielle Bastien, and Claude Veraart. 2007. Functional cerebral reorganization for auditory spatial processing and auditory substitution of vision in early blind subjects. *Cerebral Cortex* 17 (2):457–465.

Cronly-Dillon, John, Krishna Persaud, and Richard P. Gregory. 1999. The perception of visual images encoded in musical form: a study in crossmodality information transfer. *Proceedings of the Royal Society London B: Biological Sciences* 266:2427–2433.

De Volder, Anne G., Hinako Toyama, Yuichi Kimura, Motohiro Kiyosawa, Hideki Nakano, Annick Vanlierde, Marie-Chantal Wanet-Defalque, Masahiro Mishina, Keiichi Oda, Kiichi Ishiwata, and Michio Senda. 2001. Auditory triggered mental imagery of shape involves visual association areas in early blind humans. *NeuroImage* 14:129–139.

Dobelle, W. H., J. Turkel, D. C. Henderson, and J. R. Evans. 1979. Mapping the representation of the visual-field by electrical-stimulation of human visual cortex. *American Journal of Ophthalmology* 88:727–735.

Epstein, William, Barry Hugues, Sandra Schneider, and Paul Bach-y-Rita. 1986. Is there anything out there? A study of distal attribution in response to vibro-tactile stimulation. *Perception* 15:275–284.

Farmer, Leicester W. 1978. Mobility devices, *Bulletin of Prosthetic Research* 14:47–118.

Fitts, Paul M. 1954. The information capacity of the human motor system in controlling the amplitude of movement. *Journal of Experimental Psychology* 47:381–391

Gougoux, Frédéric, Robert J. Zatorre, Maryse Lassonde, Patrice Voss, and Franco Lepore. 2005. A functional neuroimaging study of sound localization: visual cortex activity predicts performance in early-blind individuals. *PLoS Biology* 3(2):e27.

Gregory, Richard L. 1997. *Eye and Brain: The Psychology of Seeing.* 5th ed. Princeton, NJ: Princeton University Press.

Hanneton, Sylvain, Malika Auvray, and Barthélémy Durette. 2010. The Vibe: a versatile vision-to-audition sensory substitution device. *Applied Bionics and Biomechanics* 7 (4):269–276.

Hoover, R. E. 1950. The cane as a travel aid. In *Blindness*, ed. P. A. Zahl, 353–365. Princeton, NJ: Princeton University Press.

Humayun, Mark S., Eugene de Juan, Gislin Dagnelie, Robert J. Greenburg, Roy H. Propst, and Howaerd Phillips. 1996. Visual perception elicited by electrical stimulation of retina in blind humans. *Archives of Ophthalmology* 114:40–46.

Kaczmareck, Kurt A., John G. Webster, Paul Bach-y-Rita, and Willis J. Tompkins. 1991. Electrotactile and vibrotactile displays for sensory substitution systems. *IEEE Transactions on Biomedical Engineering* 38:1–16.

Kay, Leslie. 1961. Orientation of bats and men by ultrasonic echo-location. *British Communications and Electronics* 8:582–586.

——. 1974. A sonar aid to enhance spatial perception of the blind: Engineering design and evaluation. *Radio and Electronic Engineer* 44:605–627.

Keeley, Brian L. 2013. What exactly is a sense? In *The Oxford Handbook of Synesthesia*, ed. Julia Simner and Edward M. Hubbard, 941-958. Oxford: Oxford University Press.

Kim, Jung-Kyong, and Robert J. Zatorre, 2008. Generalized learning of visual-to-auditory substitution in sighted individuals. *Brain Research* 1242:263–275.

Krishna, S., S. Bala, T. McDaniel, S. McGuire, and S. Panchanathan. 2010. VibroGlove: an assistive technology aid for conveying facial expressions. In *Proceedings of the 28th of the international conference extended abstracts on Human factors in computing systems*, 3637–3642. Atlanta, GA: ACM.

Kujala Teija, Kimmo Alho, Petri Paavilainen, Heikki Summala, and Risto Näätänen. 1992. Neural plasticity in processing of sound location by the early blind: an event-related potential study. *Electroencephalography and Clinical Neurophysiology* 84(5):469–472.

Kupers, Ron, Arnaud Fumal, Alain Maertens de Noordhout, Albert Gjedde, Jean Schoenen, and Maurice Ptito. 2006. Transcranial magnetic stimulation of the visual cortex induces somatotopically organized qualia in blind subjects. *Proceedings of the National Academy of Sciences of the United States of America* 103 (35):13256–13260.

Kupers, Ron, Pietro Pietrini, Emiliano Ricciardi, and Maurice Ptito. 2011. The nature of consciousness in the visually deprived brain. *Frontiers in Psychology* 2:19.

Lessard, Nadia, M. Pare, Franco Lepore, and Maryse Lassonde. 1998. Early-blind human subjects localize sound sources better than sighted subjects, *Nature* 395:278–280.

McDaniel, T., S. Krishna, V. Balasubramanian, D. Colbry, and S. Panchanathan. 2008. Using a haptic belt to convey non-verbal communication cues during social interactions to individuals who are blind. Presented at IEEE International Workshop on Haptic, Audio and Visual Environments and Games, 2008. HAVE, 13–18 October.

Meijer, Peter B. L. 1992. An experimental system for auditory image representations, *IEEE Transactions on Biomedical Engineering* 39:112–121.

Mellor, C. Michael. 2008. *Louis Braille: Le génie au bout des doigts*. Paris: Éditions du Patrimoine.

Merabet, Lotfi, Lorella Battelli, Souzana Obretenova, Sara Maguire, Peter Meijer, and Alvaro Pascual-Leone. 2009. Functional recruitment of visual cortex for sound encoded object identification in the blind. *Neuroreport* 20 (2):132–138.

Monnier, Raymonde. 1989. Haüy Valentin. In *Dictionnaire historique de la Révolution française*, ed. Albert Soboul, S. 536. Paris: Presses universitaires de France. (Reprinted 2005, Quadrige.)

Morgan, Michael J. 1977. *Molyneux's Question*. Cambridge: Cambridge University Press.

Müller, Johannes P. 1835. *Handbuch der Physiologie des Menschen für Vorlesungen*. 2nd. corr. ed. Koblenz: J. Hölscher.

Nielson, L., M., Mahowald, and C. Mead. 1989. SeeHear. In *Analog VLSI and Neural Systems*, ed. C. Mead, 207–227. Reading, MA: Addison-Wesley.

Norrsell, Ulf, Stanley Finger, and Clara Lajonchere. 1999. Cutaneous sensory spots and the 'law of specific nerve energies': History and development of ideas. *Brain Research Bulletin* 48 (5):457–465.

O'Regan, J. Kevin, AND Alva Noë. 2001. A sensorimotor account of vision and visual consciousness, *Behavioral and Brain Sciences* 24:939–1011.

Pascual-Leone, Alvaro, and Fernando Torres. 1993. Plasticity of the sensorimotor cortex representation of the reading finger in Braille readers. *Brain* 116 (Pt 1):39–52.

Pascual-Leone, Alvaro, Amir Amedi, Felipe Fregni, and Lotfi B. Merabet. 2005. The plastic human brain cortex. *Annual Review of Neuroscience* 28:377–401.

Pietrini, Pietro, Maura L. Furey, Emiliano Ricciardi, M. Ida Gobbini, W.-H. Carolyn Wu, Leonardo Cohen, Mario Guazzelli, and James V. Haxby. 2004. Beyond sensory images: Object-based representation in the human ventral pathway. *Proceedings of the National Academy of Sciences of the United States of America* 101:5658–5663.

Poirier, Colline, Anne G. De Volder, Dai Tranduy, and Christian Scheiber. 2006. Neural changes in the ventral and dorsal visual streams during pattern recognition learning. *Neurobiology of Learning and Memory* 85(1):36–43.

Poirier, Colline, Olivier Collignon, Christian Scheiber, Laurent Renier, Annick Vanlierde, Dai Tranduy, Claude Veraart, and Anne G. De Volder. 2006. Auditory motion perception activates visual motion areas in early blind subjects. *NeuroImage* 31(1):279–285.

Proulx, Michael J. 2010. Synthetic synaesthesia and sensory substitution. *Consciousness and Cognition* 19(1):501–503.

Proulx, Michael J., Petra Stoerig, Eva Ludowig, and Inna Knoll. 2008. Seeing 'where' through the ears: effects of learning-by-doing and long-term sensory deprivation on localization based on image-to-sound substitution. *PLoS ONE* 3(3):e1840.

Ptito, Maurice, Solvej M. Moesgaard, Albert Gjedde, and Ron Kupers. 2005. Cross-modal plasticity revealed by electrotactile stimulation of the tongue in the congenitally blind. *Brain* 128:606–614.

Rauschecker, Josef P. 1995. Compensatory plasticity and sensory substitution in the cerebral cortex. *Trends in Neurosciences* 18:36–43.

Reich, Lior, Marcin Szwed, Laurent Cohen, and Amir Amedi. 2011. A ventral visual stream reading center independent of visual experience. *Current Biology* 21(5):363–368.

Renier, Laurent, Raymond Bruyer, and Anne G. De Volder. 2006. Vertical-horizontal illusion present for sighted but not early blind humans using auditory substitution of vision. *Perception & Psychophysics* 68(4):535–542.

Renier, Laurent, Olivier Collignon, Colline Poirier, Dai Tranduy, Annick Vanlierde, Anne Bol, Claude Veraart, and Anne G De Volder. 2005. Cross-modal activation of visual cortex during depth perception using auditory substitution of vision. *NeuroImage* 26:573–580.

Renier, Laurent, and Anne G. De Volder. 2005. Cognitive and brain mechanisms in sensory substitution of vision: A contribution to the study of human perception. *Journal of Integrative Neuroscience* 4(4):489–503.

——. 2010. Vision substitution and depth perception: early blind subjects experience visual perspective through their ears. *Disability and Rehabilitation: Assistive Technology* 5(3):175–183.

Renier, Laurent, Cédric Laloyaux, Olivier Collignon, Dai Tranduy, Annick Vanlierde, Raymond Bruyer, and Anne G. De Volder. 2005. The Ponzo illusion with auditory substitution of vision in sighted and early blind subjects. *Perception* 34:851–867.

Rock, Irvin, Jack Gallant, and Paul Kube. (1999). An introduction to vision science. In Vision Science, ed. Stephen E Palmer, 3–44. Cambridge MA: MIT Press.

Röder, Brigitte, Olivier Stock, Siegfried Bien, Helen Neville, and Frank Rösler. 2002. Speech processing activates visual cortex in congenitally blind humans. *European Journal of Neuroscience* 16:930–936.

Röder, Brigitte, Wolfgang Teder-Salejarvi, Anette Sterr, Frank Rösler, Steven A. Hillyard, and Helen G. Neville. 1999. Improved auditory spatial tuning in blind humans. *Nature* 400:162–166.

Sadato, Nohiro, Alvaro Pascual-Leone, Jordan Grafman, Vincente Ibanez, Marie-Pierre Deiber, George Dold, and Mark Hallett. 1996. Activation of the primary visual cortex by Braille reading in blind subjects. *Nature* 380:526–528.

Saenz, Melissa, Lindsay B. Lewis, Alexander G. Huth, Ione Fine, and Christof Koch. 2008. Visual motion area MT+/V5 responds to auditory motion in human sight-recovery subjects. *The Journal of Neuroscience* 28(20):5141–5148.

Sampaio, Eliana, Stephane Maris, and Paul Bach-y-Rita. 2001. Brain plasticity: 'Visual' acuity of blind persons via the tongue. *Brain Research* 908:204–207.

Segond, Hervé, Déborah Weiss, and Eliana Sampaio. 2005. Human spatial navigation via a visuo-tactile sensory substitution system. *Perception* 34(10):1231–1249.

Schurmann, Martin, Gina Caetano, Yevhen Hlushchuk, Veikko Jousmaki, and Rita Hari. 2006. Touch activates human auditory cortex. *NeuroImage* 30:1325–1331.

Striem-Amit Ella, Ornella Dakwar, Lior Reich, and Amir Amedi. 2012. The large-scale organization of 'visual' streams emerges without visual experience. *Cerebral Cortex* 22(7):1698–1709.

Supa, Michael, Milton Cotzin, and Karl M. Dallenbach. 1944. 'Facial vision': The perception of obstacles by the blind. *The American Journal of Psychology* 57: 133–183.

Thaler, Lore, Stephen R. Arnott, and Melvyn A. Goodale. 2011. Neural correlates of natural human echolocation in early and late blind echolocation experts. *PLoS ONE* 6: e20162. doi:10.1371/journal.pone.0020162.

Tyler, Mitchell, Yuri Danilov, and Paul Bach-y-Rita. 2003. Closing an open-loop control system: vestibular substitution through the tongue. *Journal of Integrative Neuroscience* 2:159–164.

Vanlierde, Annick, Anne G. De Volder, Marie-Chantal Wanet-Defalque, and Claude Veraart. 2003. Occipito-parietal cortex activation during visuo-spatial imagery in early blind humans. *Neuroimage* 19:698–709.

Veraart, Claude, Florence Duret, Marten Brelen, Medhi Oozeer, and Jean Delbeke. 2004. Vision rehabilitation in case of blindness. *Expert Reviews in Medical Development* 1:139–153.

Ward, Jamie, and Peter Meijer. 2010. Visual experiences in the blind induced by an auditory sensory substitution device. *Consciousness and Cognition* 19(1):492–500.

Weeks, Robert, Barry Horwitz, Ali Aziz-Sultan, Biao Tian, C. Mark Wessinger, Leonardo G. Cohen, Mark Hallett, and Josef P. Rauschecker. 2000. A positron emission tomographic study of auditory localization in the congenitally blind. *The Journal of Neuroscience* 20:2664–2672.

Zappe, Anne-Catherin, Thorsten Maucher, Karlheinz Meier, and Christian Scheiber. 2004. Evaluation of a pneumatically driven stimulator device for vision substitution during fMRI studies. *Magnetic Resonance in Medicine* 51:828–834.

CHAPTER 43

SYNESTHESIA, CROSS-MODALITY, AND LANGUAGE EVOLUTION

CHRISTINE CUSKLEY AND SIMON KIRBY

INTRODUCTION

A central question for language evolution concerns the origin of linguistic symbols. Our species appears to be unique in possessing a learned system of arbitrary reference. Put differently, linguistic forms (words) are traditionally connected to their meanings only through convention, rather than by any goodness-of-fit; a rose, by another name, would still smell as sweet. The French word *pomme* expresses the concept "apple" equally as well as the Italian term *mela*. How can we explain the emergence of a system wherein the forms have no apparent connection to their meanings? This question is perhaps best framed by Harnad (1990) as the "symbol grounding problem." Harnad uses the example of a Chinese dictionary (Searle 1980): if an English speaker searches for the meanings of Chinese words, but where each word is defined only by other Chinese words, the English speaker cannot access any meanings. A symbol grounded only within a system of other symbols has no clear origin. How did this web of symbols begin?

In this chapter we will suggest a solution to the symbol grounding problem. Although words may be arbitrary in modern languages, we present a theory that words did indeed evolve, at least to some extent, based on a cross-modal goodness-of-fit: that is, in the origin of language, the sounds of words evoked the direct meaning of referents. Drawing on evidence from natural language systems as well as cross-modal associations, we will show that language users make implicit cross-modal associations between the sound quality of words and other sensory properties of the objects they denote. The primary evidence for this theory will draw on both natural language and experimental evidence, showing the potential for sound-to-meaning goodness-of-fit in language. Experimental evidence will focus specifically on the fact that humans have certain cross-sensory preferences for relating linguistic sound to other sensory dimensions possible (e.g., taste, shape), and that these a priori preferences may have guided the choice of word forms in language evolution. To this end, we will turn first to exactly how cross-modality can provide the basis for the emergence of such a system.

What cross-modality gives us

The lexicons on which languages are built are essentially systems of symbols. Symbol manipulation has been identified as a uniquely human faculty (Deacon 1997), as well as an essential feature of language, but there is no clear account of how our cognition came to support a symbol system that is seemingly disembodied: forms have no connections to their meanings. We will propose that shared sensory biases in the general population provided a basis for grounding language in our perceptual system and served to bootstrap a small lexicon which was initially less arbitrary than its evolutionarily later forms.

Cross-modal biases have been demonstrated experimentally across a range of modalities, including between taste and touch (Christensen 1980), pitch, and vowel quality (Crisinel and Spence 2009; Simner, Cuskley, and Kirby 2010), and touch and color (Simner and Ludwig 2009), among many others (see Part VII of this volume, as well as Calvert, Spence, and Stein 2004, for a review). The pervasiveness of cross-modal associations would suggest this might have been an important utility in an evolutionary sense. Connections between visual and motor areas, for example, would have allowed for complex motor actions guided by vision, such as seeing a branch in the visual field and preparing an appropriate grasp action in order to swing to it (Ramachandran 2004).

This view, of cross-modality as part of the normal cognitive suite, puts synesthesia at one end of a spectrum of cross-modal abilities.[1] Synesthetes, like all people, make cross-modal connections, although these are active for synesthetes at a very different level. In other words, where non-synesthetes might make an intuitive cross-modal association between certain sounds and certain shapes, synesthetes would have a fundamentally different experience of actually "seeing" these colors in the literal perceptual sense. Moreover, the associations of synesthetes are stronger and more temporally stable than run-of-the-mill cross-modal associations. Although particular synesthetic perceptions are considered unique to any particular synesthete, there are definite observable trends, most notably in grapheme-color synesthetes. For example, the letter *A* is likely across synesthetes to be red above all other colors (Simner et al. 2005), and similar letter shapes evokes similar colors for grapheme-color synesthetes (Brang et al. 2011). Trends among synesthetes are also echoed by trends in cross-modality in the general population for grapheme-color associations (Simner et al. 2005), pitch-lightness associations (Ward, Huckstep, and Tsakanikos 2006), and touch-vision associations (Simner and Ludwig 2009). From this perspective, synesthetes can be viewed as super cross-modal associators, with unusually strong, stable, and specific cross-modal biases.

---

[1] This chapter will not go into detail regarding the nature of synesthesia and its various varieties, as this is well covered in the remainder of the volume.

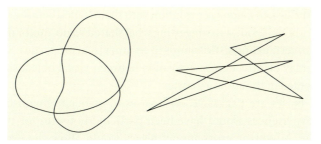

FIGURE 43.1 Maluma and takete shapes. Reproduced from Köhler, Wolfgang, *Gestalt Psychology*. 1e ©1929, Liveright.)

The idea that language may have non-arbitrary origins is not a particularly new one, although the notion of cross-modality as the basis for such a system is a newer idea. So-called "bow-wow" theories of language origins are some of the earliest on record, suggesting that language was built on direct imitations of sounds (see Atchison 2000 for a review). However, such theories have typically not been taken seriously by the field of linguistics, which emphasizes the fundamental arbitrariness of the sign (Saussure 1959), thus rejecting any natural connection between linguistic signs and their denotations in the world. Hockett's (1960) influential *Design Features of Natural Language*, particularly the feature of arbitrariness, further solidified this view. Any evolutionary perspectives eschewing arbitrariness—now considered a central and essential feature of language— were hardly going to be popular.

Despite this, Gestalt psychologists began experiments in motivated naming: exploring the possibility that certain names may better fit certain referents. The best known of these experiments was reported by Köhler (1929, 1947). In a simple forced choice task, subjects were given two nonsense words, *takete* and *maluma*, and two abstract shapes (shown in Figure 43.1), and asked to match the words to the shapes. Similar experiments have since been performed with children (Irwin and Newland 1940; Maurer, Pathman, and Mondloch 2006), as well as cross-culturally (Davis 1961) and with varying stimuli (Ramachandran and Hubbard 2001). The results of all of these experiments were rather striking: there appeared to be a strong and quantifiable bias in naming. In the vast majority of cases,[2] people assigned *maluma* to the curved figure and *takete* to the angular one, demonstrating a preference to map certain names to certain visual forms.

These experiments demonstrated that linguistic sounds have the potential for a "natural" connection to their referents. This connection is not limited to the uni-modal (i.e., within only the auditory modality) "bow-wow" variety of sound imitation, but holds for cross-sensory connections as well: the Köhler task demonstrated a common cross-sensory association between visual form and linguistic sound. Several authors hinted that this naming bias might be important in language (Köhler 1929, 1947; Werner 1957; Werner and Wapner 1952). Ramachandran and Hubbard (2001) were the first to

---

[2] One notable exception, Rogers and Ross (1975), will be discussed in further detail later.

explicitly relate the task to language evolution with their "synesthetic bootstrapping theory of language origins" (2001, 15), suggesting what shared visuo-motor mappings linked the articulation of certain linguistic sounds to certain visual properties. Specifically, they suggested there may be direct cross-activation between visual object shape and sound contours represented in the auditory cortex.

Cross-modal biases are pervasive, and biases to associate linguistic sounds with other sensory experiences would have been particularly useful for the evolution of spoken language. Linguistic cross-modal biases would allow the expression of our perceptions and experiences in any sensory domain through a single linguistic channel. Thus, we can expand upon antiquated "bow-wow" theories of language evolution, with a theory which allows both direct auditory imitation and cross-sensory imitation. Languages still use sounds to express concepts whose characteristics are auditory (e.g., *hiss* or *buzz*), but this also extends more widely to referents whose characteristics are not auditory. We can express various sensory experiences through a linguistic channel, and the fact that cross-modal biases are shared across all people would allow for the mutual understanding of an utterance formed on their basis (see Figure 43.2 which gives a schematic representation of how shared cross-sensory biases might have facilitated mutual comprehension in language evolution). In addition to this, recent research suggests that speech is not the only tool available to us in language. Language is a dual system, in which gestures play an integral role (Brown 2010; McNeill 2005; Tomasello 2008). Cross-modal biases, combined with a dual channel speech-gesture system, would have provided ample opportunity for an iconic system grounded in perception. In the emergence of language, we propose that these biases provided a perceptual grounding for a small lexicon, or *protolanguage* (see Arbib 2005; Bickerton 1990; Tallerman 2007; Wray 1998), which matured and expanded into the complex arbitrary systems we see today.

In the next section, we will review evidence for this theory as found in natural language systems, looking to modern languages for evidence of a connection between form and meaning.

Non-Arbitrariness in Modern Natural Language

Our theory generates a set of testable expectations. Firstly, we should expect to find some evidence of motivated forms in modern natural language—i.e., words that sound as if they fit what they denote, in a cross-sensory sense. But we quickly run up against the central tenet of linguistics discussed in the previous section: that word–meaning relationships are apparently arbitrary. However, a theory of sensory protolanguage— and the expectation that motivated forms should be present in modern language—does not wholly contradict the otherwise obvious arbitrariness of language. The majority

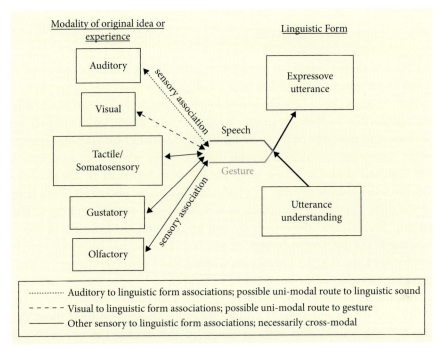

FIGURE 43.2 Figure shows what cross-modality affords us in theories of language evolution. Linguistic symbols as grounded in perceptual experiences, represented on the left (auditory, visual, tactile/somatosensory, gustatory, and olfactory). Shared cross-modal biases allow for common sensory associations between modalities, making the expression and understanding of varied aspects of experience possible through linguistic form. Shared associations are leveraged in the formation of an utterance as well as in utterance interpretation. Linguistic form is realized through a dual modality speech-gesture system; a view particularly relevant to language evolution, which likely occurred primarily in the context of face-to-face interactions. This dual system allows some ideas or events to be expressed through unimodal associations; most notably, gestures afford iconicity for visual events, and speech affords iconicity for auditory events.

of atomic elements in natural language (words or parts of words that cannot be further divided) remain arbitrary. However, there is also a subset of language which is not arbitrary, but sound symbolic, wherein sound actually encodes meaning in some way. Though sound symbolic aspects of language have been historically acknowledged, they have often been considered a peripheral phenomenon too rare to be functional (Hinton, Nichols, and Ohala 1994; Nuckolls 1999). Recently, however, as language typology expands beyond a more traditional focus on Indo-European languages to Austronesian and African language families as well as sign languages, non-arbitrariness has emerged as a universal in its own right (Perniss, Thompson, and Vigliocco 2010). Next, we will define the exact nature of the non-arbitrariness in question, and provide evidence of its pervasive presence in natural language, particularly in the form of sound symbolism.

Levels of non-arbitrariness

Arbitrariness is simply defined as a random relationship between the sound form of a word and its meaning, these holding only through convention among speakers. Thus, non-arbitrariness occurs where the sound forms of words do have an observable and regular relationship to their meanings. To understand where we can expect to find arbitrariness and non-arbitrariness, we have to understand how language systems are organized. Language operates on several distinct levels, which also form interacting areas of linguistic study (and these levels are shown in Figure 43.3). The phonological level involves the sounds relevant to a particular language: phonemes. Each language contains a finite number of phonemes, or sounds which contrast resulting in changes in meaning. For example, the sounds /p/ and /b/ are considered distinct phonemes in English, due to the different meanings for words such as *pat* and *bat* (/pæt/ and /bæt/). *Pat* and *bat* are known as a minimal pair, where a slight phonetic change (in this case, voicing—the vibration of the vocal cords is markedly delayed in the voiceless /p/, and more immediately present in the voiced /b/) results in an entirely different meaning.

Yet, /p/ and /b/ do not actually encode meaning; there is nothing about /b/ that denotes a flying rodent, and nothing about /p/ that evokes the action of patting. Meaning truly enters the picture at the morphological level. Morphology is concerned with the smallest units of meaning in a language; while phonemes can provide a *contrast* in meaning, morphemes encode meaning itself. Not all morphemes are words, and many words contain multiple morphemes. For example, the word *bat* is a single morpheme that is also a word. The word *re-establishment,* however, contains three distinct morphemes: *re-* (to do again), *establish* (to erect or begin), and *-ment* (which carries information about the word's category: noun). The morphemes *re-* and *-ment* are

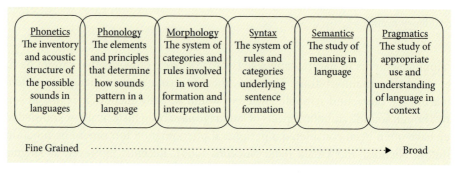

FIGURE 43.3 Figure shows the levels of language, forming interacting areas of linguistic study. Areas become more broad from left to right; with phonetics involving acoustic description well below the word level and pragmatics encompassing entire interactions. Meaning in a language traditionally enters at the morphological level. Definitions adapted from William O'Grady, Michael Dobrovolsky, and Francis Katamba, *Contemporary Linguistics: An Introduction* © 1996, Pearson Education Limited.

not considered words, as they cannot stand alone like *establish* or *bat,* but can be re-used by attaching to other words.

Non-arbitrariness above the morpheme level is uncontroversial. The meaning of the word *re-establishment* is not arbitrary with respect to its form; it is composed of the meaning of its morphemic subparts. Wherever we find the morpheme *re-,* we find the meaning "to do again." While words are composed of the meanings of their morphemic subparts, morphemes are not composed of the meanings of their phonemic subparts; phonemes do not encode meaning. A finite set of phonemes carrying no meaning can be recombined in a variety of ways to create meaningful morphemes. This feature of language is part of what provides its capacity to express a virtually unlimited array of concepts.

One of the major questions in language evolution is how we came to combine meaningful subparts (such as morphemes) to create larger meaningful words and sentences. However, underlying this question is the mystery of how meaningful subparts emerged at all; the ability to create words from meaningful morphemes requires the emergence of meaningful morphemes as a pre-requisite. A sensory theory of protolanguage seeks to answer how we came to have meaningful morphemes at all, considering the subparts of those morphemes are theoretically meaningless. Our theory suggests that at some basic psychological level, certain phonemes *can* have a natural connection to meaning. This being the case, we would expect to see sound-meaning correspondences below the morpheme level in natural languages. The next section will discuss instances of sound symbolism, where we do in fact observe sound-meaning correspondences.

Sound symbolism

Hinton, Nichols, and Ohaha (1994) identify four distinct types of sound symbolism. *Corporeal sound symbolism* includes coughs, hiccups, and other "natural" noises which give information about the state of a speaker; largely extra-linguistic, these are not relevant for the current discussion. *Conventional sound symbolism* includes cases where phonemes are associated with features of meaning non-arbitrarily (more on this later). *Imitative sound symbolism* includes conventionalized onomatopoeia (*hiss, buzz*) as well as more directly imitative sounds (*ssss, zzzz*). *Synesthetic*[3] *sound symbolism* includes sounds designed to cross-modally imitate other sensory phenomena; as the sound of the word *takete* might be taken to "imitate" an angular form. Of most interest to a sensory theory of protolanguage is imitative and synesthetic sound symbolism. We will consider these together using a new term: *sensory sound symbolism.* Imitative sound symbolic forms are certainly more straightforward than their synesthetic counterparts because they represent an association within the auditory modality alone, rather than one that crosses sensory boundaries (e.g., a visual experience expressed as a linguistic sound).

---

[3] Hinton and colleagues (1994) use the term synesthetic here in a slightly unconventional manner: they do not suggest these forms are confined to synesthetes or derive from their unique associations, but simply that there are shared cross-modal associations underlying some sound symbolic forms.

However, the two types of sound symbolism are unified, since linguistic symbols can be considered sensorily grounded in both cases (see Figure 43.2). More specifically, sensory sound symbolism constitutes a psychologically and linguistically natural connection, wherein form is motivated by meaning. It has been demonstrated using *cross-linguistic experiments*, in particular among a class of words called *ideophones* (which we define and describe in detail later).

Finally, sensory sound symbolism can be separated from what we might call *conventional sound symbolism*. Conventional sound symbolism is found in language in two forms: as significant *statistical correspondences* between form and meaning within the lexicon, and as *phonesthemes* (both defined and described in detail later). The following section will discuss both types of conventional and sensory sound symbolism in detail.

Conventional Sound Symbolism

Statistical correspondences

Where sound is somehow motivated by meaning below the morpheme level, we should expect measures of sound in a language system to correlate with measures of meaning. Put differently, words which sound similar should also share a significant similarity in meaning. Shillcock et al. (2001) examined the most frequent monomorphemic words in the British National Corpus (a large collection of spoken and written samples of English; 2001). Each word was compared to every other word on two measures: how similar the words were in terms of their sounds (phonologically), and how similar the words were in terms of their meanings (semantically). Shillcock and colleagues found a significant correlation between phonological and semantic similarity, indicating that words which sounded similar were more likely than chance to have similar meanings. Tamariz (2005) carried out a similar study with monomorphemic words in Spanish, likewise finding that phonologically close words were significantly more likely than chance to also be semantically close.

While this demonstrates that linguistic sound is somehow related to meaning below the morpheme level (since only monomorphemic words were considered), such a broad cross-lexical measure does not give any information about which particular sounds correspond to particular features of meaning, and why. These correspondences demonstrate a non-arbitrary relationship between form and meaning, but they do not reveal the basis of this relationship. They only fall out of the *system* writ large; a wide net must be cast in order to capture significant correspondences. Indeed, even though the correlation is highly significant, it accounts for a miniscule amount of the variance. This is as we would expect, given that any cross-lexical non-arbitrariness is far from obvious, and certainly not at the level of conscious awareness for most speakers of a language. Hence although sound and meaning correspondences are present and have significant strength, there is not sufficient evidence to suggest the exact nature of the correspondences, let alone whether they are motivated by cross-sensory associations.[4] Tamariz (2005) discusses the various pressures on a language system, suggesting that form-meaning correspondences may contribute to the overall systematicity in a language. This systematicity is useful for language learners; studies show that random systems are considerably more difficult for learners (Kirby, Cornish, and Smith 2008).

Monaghan, Christiansen, and Chater (2007) have taken a slightly different approach, and considered the matter cross-linguistically, specifically from the perspective of child language learners in English, Dutch, French, and Japanese. Rather than meaning distance per se, Monaghan and colleagues examined grammatical category information, contrasting open and closed class words[5] and nouns and verbs. In other words, they asked if open class words share more sound features with other open class words than with closed class words, performing similar analyses with nouns and verbs. Monaghan and colleagues found that words which shared class and grammatical categories shared phonological similarities in all four languages. Not all of these shared features were truly cross-linguistic; for example, while the presence of plosives (e.g., *p, d*) was a good cue for open classed words in English, the same did not necessarily hold for the other languages. However, some cues *were* shared across languages: overall length in phonemes was a good predictor of open class membership, the presence of bilabial phonemes (sounds produced using both lips; e.g., *m, b*) was a good predictor of nouns, and the presence of velar phonemes (sounds produced with the back of the tongue against the velum; e.g., *k, g*) was a good predictor of verbs (see also Farmer, Christiansen, and Monaghan 2006; Monaghan, Chater, and Christiansen 2005).

The cross-linguistic nature of these results is compelling, but the meaning metric used, though arguably more fine grained than Tamariz (2005) or Shillcock et al. (2001), is as much syntactic as it is semantic. Hence, correspondences observed between form and "meaning" appear to be driven by syntactic category rather than the individual lexical semantics themselves. Though these categories do have semantic features (nouns are more likely to be objects whereas verbs are more likely to be actions), they are still rather broad swathes demonstrating correspondences at the level of the system as a whole, rather than the lower phono-semantic level. Nonetheless, studies of statistical correspondences among monomorphemic words do demonstrate that there is non-arbitrariness in language, despite the historical view in linguistics that language is arbitrary. While these correspondences may represent sound symbolism

---

[4] For example, we could imagine a fictional lexicon where all round objects have the /e/ vowel present in the word *takete*. This language would be non-arbitrary, since there is a regular relationship between a particular vowel and roundedness—but it would not be naturally motivated. Instead, we know from Köhler's naming experiments that the word *takete* fits better with angular objects than round ones. But non-arbitrariness can still logically be present even if it contradicts the natural motivatedness evident from Köhler's experiment.

[5] Open class words, or content words, form a category of words which can be readily added to, and includes all nouns and verbs. Closed class words, also known as function words, form a category to which new items are rarely added, including things like prepositions (e.g., *in, of, at*), determiners (e.g., *the, a, this*) and conjunctions (e.g., *and, but*).

that is more sensory than conventional, there is no definitive evidence to suggest this is the case.

Phonesthemes

Phonesthemes are a more specific sound-meaning correspondence directly observable in individual monomorphemic words. Phonesthemes are operationally defined as monomorphemic words sharing correspondences in sound and meaning beyond the level that would be predicted by chance alone (Bergen 2004). For example, a group of words in English beginning with *gl-* all have meanings denoting visual lightness (e.g., *glint, glimmer;* also see Figure 43.4). While the consonant cluster *gl-* is not considered a morpheme, it appears to have a non-arbitrary relationship to this visual meaning-feature. Phonesthemes have been identified in a diverse array of languages, including Austronesian languages (Blust 1988), Ojibwa (Rhodes 1981), and Swedish (Abelin 1999).

Phonesthemes are compelling candidates for meaning-motivating-form at the phonemic level, but they may be problematic. First, phonesthemes are often identified

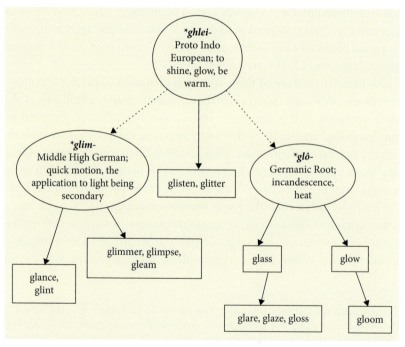

FIGURE 43.4 Figure shows the possible historical relationship among *gl-* phonesthemes identified by Bergen (2004). Solid lines indicate an attested historical relationship documented in the *Oxford English Dictionary* (2011); dotted lines indicate a possible relationship between Proto Indo European and later Germanic forms. Although these reconstructions are not uncontroversial, we contend they are at least as likely or possible as "natural motivatedness" between the form *gl-* and the meaning "having to do with vision or light."

by researchers through intuition, and are not objectively or independently verified (Drellishak 2007; Hutchins 1998). Where objective methods are used, results are mixed and confined to a small number of phonesthemes. Drellishak (2007) used three separate statistical approaches to the English lexicon, and uncovered only four phonesthemes in English: *sn-* (nose; snobbish), *st-* (firm; upright; linear), *-ing* (e.g., *bing, ting* for sounds), and *spr-* (to radiate out; elongated).[6] Bergen (2004) looked to the Brown Corpus (Kucera and Francis 1967) specifically for *gl-*, *sn-*, *sm-* and *fl-* phonesthemes. He found that all four clusters were more likely than chance to be used in the corpus with their phonesthetic meanings: for example, *gl-* was four times as likely to relate to vision as *sn-*.

In contrast, Hutchins (1998) compiled an exhaustive list of phonesthemes identified through intuition in the literature, resulting in over 145 phonestheme types. Using a subset of these, Hutchins tested whether nonsense words containing phonesthetic clusters were more likely to be associated with their phonesthetic meanings, rather than other meanings. Subjects chose the expected meaning well above chance levels, demonstrating a strong psychological basis for phonesthemes. In a study designed to examine online processing of phonesthemes, Bergen (2004) used a primed lexical decision task: subjects see a prime word followed by either a word or a non-word target, and are tasked with pressing a key indicating whether the target is a word or not. In such a task, the goal is to discern what effect the relationship between the prime and target has on decision times. In Bergen's (2004) task, primes were either unrelated to targets (e.g., prime: *frill*, target: *barn*), related only phonologically (e.g., prime: *drip*, target: *drab*), related only semantically (e.g., prime: *cord*, target: *rope*), related pseudo-phonesthetically (sharing features of sound and meaning which do not occur significantly often in English, e.g., prime: *crony*, target: *crook*), or related fully phonesthetically (e.g., prime: *glitter*, target: *glimmer*). Phonesthetic primes resulted in the most significant facilitation to reaction times when paired with a phonesthetic target. These data demonstrate a psychological basis of phonesthemes even below the conscious level demonstrated by Hutchins (1998). Using Hutchins' exhaustive list of phonesthemes, Otis and Sagi (2008) returned to a corpus approach. Using the Project Gutenberg corpus (Lebert 2005) and latent semantic analysis (LSA; Landauer and Dumais 1997) to provide meaning distance, they found that ten word-initial phonestheme clusters shared significant semantic properties, including *gl-*, *sn-*, and *spr-* (Otis and Sagi 2008).

While phonesthemes demonstrate a strong form meaning relationship (i.e., a psychological bias as well as a statistical reality in some cases) there remains major doubt as to whether phonesthemes are naturally "motivated," in the sense of deriving from some shared cross-modal rule. Similar phonesthemes have not been demonstrated cross-linguistically, and thus could be the result of historical idiosyncrasies in a particular language. Put differently, although present in a variety of unrelated languages, phonesthemes do not necessarily manifest similarly across languages (e.g., *gl-* does not

---

[6] Drellishak (2007) did not confine his search to monomorphemic words or even content words, which may have adversely affected his results.

indicate light in most other languages with phonesthemes). In fact, many *gl-* phonesthemes identified by Bergen (2004)[7] share etymologies (e.g., both English and Swedish share this phonestheme and both are Germanic). In other words, rather than the form being cross-modally motivated by the meaning, at least in the case of *gl-*, the observed relationship may be the result of a particularly productive branch of words that goes back as far as Proto Indo-European (see Figure 43.4 for a possible depiction of the shared historic roots of *gl-*).

It is still possible that some phonesthemes are naturally motivated. However, historical relationships are at least as plausible, and must be definitively ruled out before declaring phonesthemes to be sensory sound symbolic. Even so, the problem is still not straightforward: the fact that certain sets of words deriving from the same proto-form survive in a language may be the result of a cross-modal goodness of phonological and semantic fit. Put differently, a natural goodness-of-fit between form and meaning may lead to that particular pairing of form and meaning being especially productive. Phonesthemes remain an interesting case of non-arbitrariness in language, but without further evidence, must be classed as conventional rather than sensory sound symbolism.

Sensory Sound Symbolism

Ideophones

Sensory sound symbolism is exemplified by an intriguing category of words known as *ideophones*. Also termed *expressives* (Diffloth 1994; Tufvesson, 2011) or *mimetics* (Imai et al. 2008), ideophones are sometimes grouped with phonesthemes (Nuckolls 1999), but are quite distinct in that native speakers consciously report ideophones as being linguistic forms sensorily motivated by their meaning. Dingemanse (2009) defines ideophones as "marked words which vividly depict sensory events." Onomatopoeia in English is an excellent example; *hiss* actually directly depicts the sound made by a snake. Though ideophones encompass onomatopoeia, they also go beyond it, depicting not only auditory events, but visual, emotional, and tactile events, among others. For example, in the Togo region of Ghana, *giligili* evokes circular shape, and *wúrúfúú* a fluffy texture for speakers of Siwu (Dingemanse 2011). Since the very form of ideophones evokes sensory experience for language users, they appear to be an instance of cross-modal goodness-of-fit underlying modern natural language. Ideophones have fascinated many linguists, with Frankis (1991) going so far as to refer to them as "the lunatic fringe of language" (17).

In some instances, ideophones occur in a strange kind of minimal pair. These minimal pairs are different from the usual *pat/bat* type discussed earlier; here, a change in sound is accompanied by a *specific* change in meaning; phonemes are directly encoding

---

[7] Only monomorphemic roots are considered here; types identified by Bergen such as *glistening* and *glimmering* were considered instances of *glisten* and *glimmer* respectively.

meaning, such that changes in phonemes evoke a systematic meaning change. For example, in Japanese, *kirakira* means "to glitter or sparkle," where *giragira* means "to glare or dazzle." The voicing distinction, in this case between /k/ and /g/, is changing the meaning in terms of magnitude; a small to an overwhelming amount of reflected light. The voicing distinctions present in Japanese ideophones are also trends in Siwu (Dingemanse 2011), demonstrating an interesting cross-linguistic effect between two genetically distant languages. In other ideophonic languages, vowel quality distinctions have a similar effect, as in Bahnar, where a change in vowel height (e.g., /i/ versus /a/) indicates a difference in size (Diffloth 1994). These cross-linguistic trends make for testable predictions. Common ideophonic features occurring between genetically distinct and geographically disparate languages would point to an overall cognitive bias, eliminating the historical explanations possible for phonesthemes. If ideophones truly depict sensory events, we should expect people who do not speak Japanese, for example, to have some insight into the meanings of Japanese ideophones. Recent experiments show that ideophones do provide clues to meaning even for naïve listeners.

Experiments with natural language

Iwasaki, Vinson, and Vigliocco (2007a) compared Japanese and English speakers' intuitions regarding Japanese ideophones for motion and laughing (e.g., *bura-bura*: strolling, *kusu-kusu*: giggle). Despite no knowledge of Japanese, the English speakers rated the meanings of Japanese ideophones similarly to the Japanese speakers. For the motion ideophones, voicing was identified as indicative of large size in both groups (e.g., *b* is larger than *p*). Similar judgments between Japanese and English speakers were also found for Japanese pain ideophones (Iwasaki, Vinson, and Vigliocco 2007b). Another approach to the cognitive bias underlying ideophones examines learnability. If ideophones are forms motivated by their meanings, the natural connection between form and meaning should make them more easy to learn than forms with no natural relationship to their meaning. Imai et al. (2008) found that 3-year-old children were able to more effectively learn the meaning of novel verbs when they were ideophonic. Nygaard, Cook, and Namy (2009) found similar results with English speaking adults; subjects learned the definitions of Japanese ideophones significantly quicker when they were paired with their actual meaning (*hayai*: fast), as opposed to the opposite meaning (*hayai*: slow) or a completely arbitrary meaning (*hayai*: blunt)

These studies show that people with no knowledge of a language genetically distant from their own are able to access the meanings of its words based solely on their form. Surprisingly, this is also true for non-ideophones. Tsuru and Fries (1933; as cited in Brown, Black, and Horowitz 1955) first investigated this with English speakers and Japanese words. Though Japanese has an extensive system of ideophones, Tsuru and Fries intentionally used description words that were not ideophonic in character. Their prediction was that although ideophones appear to be a special case of particularly evocative words, that there is information in all word forms—even those in non-ideophonic languages—about meaning. In Tsuru and Fries' (1933) initial study, subjects were provided with pairs of English words and their Japanese equivalents, for example *bird* and *worm* with *tori* and *mushi*, or *white* and *black* with *shire* and *kuro* (the pairs were presented in random order). With no prior knowledge of Japanese, subjects chose the correct Japanese equivalent of the English words significantly above chance levels (*tori* means BIRD and *shire* means WHITE). Similar results have been found for English speakers with a diverse array of languages, including Hungarian (Klank, Huang, and Johnson 1971), Polish, Chinese, and Czech (Brown, Black, and Horowitz 1955), Croatian (Maltzman, Morisett, and Brooks 1956), Hebrew (Brackbill and Little 1957), Hindi (Brown and Nuttall 1959), and Thai, Karnese, and Yoruba (Slobin 1968). While some of the languages (e.g., Japanese and Yoruba) have ideophone systems, many lack ideophones (e.g., Czech, Croatian, Polish). More recently, Berlin (1994) has run a similar experiment with English speakers and Huambisa, a Jivorian language spoken in Peru. Using bird and fish names, Berlin had subjects classify which member of a pair was a bird and which a fish. Over a list of 50 animal names, subjects have 58% accuracy at guessing the correct category, a statistically significant finding. Moreover, Berlin found that accuracy with some pairs was extremely high, up to 98%.

Tasks of this type can only be possible if English speakers are detecting features in the forms of the foreign words which encode meaning, even outside ideophonic systems. Quite independently, Berlin (2006) and Westermann (1927) have made suggestions regarding the nature of these specific sound-meaning connections, based on corpus research (see Table 43.1which shows their collection of sound symbolic items proposed in the literature). In the case of Huambisa, Berlin (1994) suggests that specific vowel and consonant contrasts play an important role, with high vowels (like /i/) being associated with the quick movement of birds, while lower vowels like /a/ are associated with the slower flowing movement of fish.[8] As a follow-up, Berlin (1994) examined a comprehensive corpus of bird and fish names in Huambisa, finding a preference for high vowels in bird names and low vowels in fish names.

Based on Jesperson's (1933) informal examination of several languages, finding that high vowels are often associated with not only with speed but small size (as in English *teeny, little*; Nuckolls, 1999; see also Ohala, 1984[9]), Berlin (2006) also examined several other South American languages for patterns of size sound symbolism. This time using only bird names, species were divided into those over 10 inches and those under. As expected, the names of smaller birds were significantly more likely to contain higher vowels. Berlin performed a similar analysis on words for *squirrel* and *tapir* in 25 languages, finding /i/ significantly more frequently in words for *squirrel* and /a/ more frequently in words for *tapir*. Berlin (2006) suggests that ethnozoological nomenclature is

---

[8] Vowel height distinctions are now well documented in many ideophone systems (Dingemanse 2011).

[9] Despite these examples, English appears to be an exception to these trends. Newman (1933) and Brown (1958) both failed to find a significant correlation among English words denoting size and vowel quality.

Table 43.1 Features of sound and their associated meanings in the sound symbolism literature. Adapted from Westerman (1927) as reported in Fox (1935) and Berlin (2006)

Sound	Associated Meanings
Front vowels, high tone, short vowels, voiceless consonants	Bright, quick, sharp, pleasant taste, pleasant smell, intensive color, energetic, fresh, exact, rapid, abrupt, short, agile, long, straight, hagged, skinny, sharp, thin, slender, angular, small
Back vowels, low tone, long vowels, voiced consonants	Large, voluminous, heavy, soft, dull, slow, tasteless, unpleasant smell, heavy, blunt, chaotic, slow, sluggish, flowing, awkward, smooth, spherical, short, stocky, fat, hefty, squat, rotund

Reproduced from D. Westerman. Laut, Ton und Sinn in westafrinaische Sudansprachen. In *Festschrift Meinhof*, 315–328 © 1927, Kommissionsverlag von L. Friedgerichsen & Co.

of special interest, as it often involves conscious creation of labels, and thus is a subset of language where sensory sound symbolism is likely particularly strong.

In another corpus approach, Ultan (1978) examined 136 languages, searching specifically for phonemes which indicated size contrasts. While only a about a third of the languages surveyed contained such relevant contrasts, of those that did over 85% exhibited the pattern predicted by Jesperson and confirmed by Berlin, with the high vowel denoting smaller size.[10] Woodworth (1991) extended a similar method to words denoting physical distance, examining deictics (e.g., *this*, *that*) and finding that higher vowels were present for proximal pronouns for 70% of the 26 languages surveyed. Traunmuller (1996) confirmed these results even more specifically, connecting the observed trends directly with the frequency of the second formant (an acoustic correlate of vowel quality).

Even in the absence of a formal ideophonic system, many languages contain clues to meaning at the phonemic level. Trends among specific vocabulary elements, be they animal names or deictic pronouns, demonstrate this well at a linguistic level: a given language system takes advantage of sound-meaning patterns below the morphological level. Experimentally, even naive subjects seem to be able to pick up on these correspondences in completely foreign and unrelated languages, suggesting not only a psychological reality, but a universality of certain sound symbolic patterns.

LINGUISTIC CROSS-MODALITY

Sensory sound symbolic patterns found in natural language can provide the basis for a different approach to finding evidence for natural goodness-of-fit between linguistic

---

[10] See Diffloth (1994) and Bauer (1996) for a discussion of languages that do not conform to this pattern.

sound and meaning. Sound symbolic patterns found in natural language can be used to create novel linguistic stimuli testable against controlled perceptual stimuli, joining approaches from cross-modality more generally with the interest in linguistic sound symbolism. Various experiments have shown that people make common cross-modal associations between linguistic sounds and properties such as size (Newman 1933; Sapir 1929; Thompson and Estes, 2011), angularity (Maurer, Pathman, and Mondloch 2006; Ramachandran and Hubbard, 2001), and taste (Simner, Cuskley, and Kirby 2010). The following section reviews such studies.

Magnitude

Size vowel symbolism, the notion that some vowels are "smaller" than others, is of particular interest in studies of linguistic cross-modality. In fact, Jesperson's (1933) informal investigation into sound symbolism in natural language was inspired by experimental work done by Sapir (1929). Sapir used sets of simple non-words, such as *mil* and *mal*, which contrasted only vowel quality. Subjects were asked to match these words with a large or small object. Sapir found that 80% of over 400 subjects matched /a/ with large objects and /i/ with small objects. Newman (1933) extended Sapir's findings, showing that not only the absolute height of the vowels /i/ and /a/ affected judgments of size, but relative vowel height had a similar effect (see also Johnson 1967; Huang, Pratoomraj, and Johnson 1969).

More recently, Thompson and Estes (2011) used a different method incorporating consonants and improving Sapir's traditional forced choice paradigm. Instead, a single abstract object was presented in the context of a known object, such as a cow, to indicate size, alongside a list of five nonsense words to choose from. The nonsense words were designed using the vowel qualities identified by Sapir (1929) combined with voiced and voiceless consonants, the latter (voiceless consonants) predicted to correlate to smaller size. Thompson and Estes (2011) found that subjects were significantly more likely to choose words containing "large" phonemes (e.g., /a/, /m/, /w/) for the large abstract objects, and conversely, more likely to pair "small" phonemes (/i/, /k/, /t/) with small objects.

Ohala (1994) has suggested a plausible mediation for magnitude sound symbolism called "the frequency code hypothesis." Initially applying this to overall voice pitch (i.e., the *fundamental frequency* of the speech signal, known as Fo), Ohala points out that in the natural world, smaller animals produce high pitched sounds while larger animals emit low pitched sounds, thus, we could conclude that the pitch of the speech signal underlies size sound symbolism. However, incidental variations in pitch in human speech are not a reliable indicator of speaker size (Fitch 2000). Intentional variations in pitch play a phonemic role in some languages in the form of tone (e.g., in Mandarin), but the use of tone is not pervasive, making the explanatory power of fundamental frequency as the underlying mechanism for size sound symbolism limited.

However, all languages do make use of vowel quality: the difference between vowels such as /i/, /a/ and /o/.[11] Vowel quality is acoustically determined by the relationship between resonant frequencies of Fo known as the first, second, and third *formants*. Not only does the relationship between formants underlie vowel quality, but the overall value of the formants (as long as their relative distance is maintained) is also an honest signal of speaker size in humans (Fitch 2000). Fisher-Jorgensen (1978) found that this relationship could be captured by subtracting the value of the first formant from the second. This gives a frequency representing the vowel contrasts relevant in magnitude sound symbolism: the larger the difference between second and first formant, the smaller the size (Ohala 1994). For example, there is a large difference between the second and first formant in the vowel /i/, which is more likely to be associated with small objects (as in /mil/ vs. /mal/). The frequency code can also be extended to consonants: voiceless consonants have higher frequencies than voiced consonants, and dental, alveolar, palatal and front velars have higher frequency than labials and back velars (Ohala 1994). Physical size can also be extended to other magnitude dimensions, including light and dark (Newman 1933), as well as the many other sensory dimensions (detailed in Table 43.1). In summary, the frequency code gives a mechanism for explaining a multitude of common associations made between magnitude and vowel quality.

Visual angularity

Parallel to the work on magnitude sound symbolism, there has also been a large body of work examining visual angularity and linguistic sound, after Köhler's (1929, 1947) *takete/maluma* experiment (in which most people pair the word *takete* with an angular shape, and *maluma* with a rounded shape). The paradigm has been extended to include a variety of non-words, including *takete/uloomoo* (Davis 1961), *kiki/bouba* (Ramachandran and Hubbard 2001), and *teetay/goga* (Maurer, Pathman, and Mondloch 2006), as well as varying visual stimuli.

Köhler's (1947) report of the phenomenon was directly inspired by Usnadze (1924) and Fischer's (1922) accounts of similar experiments. Rather than using a forced choice paradigm, Fischer had subjects rate the goodness-of-fit of non-words to shapes, finding that certain names were rated as fitting certain shapes exceptionally well across subjects. Usnadze (1924) used a more qualitative method, focusing on what caused reported goodness-of-fit between a name and a figure. Subjects either matched a name with a figure using an associative strategy, based on existing lexical knowledge (e.g., choosing the word *jage* for the jagged shape), or an intrinsic strategy, matching specific qualities of sound (e.g., vowel) to visual qualities of the shape (e.g., size). Interestingly, Usnadze reported that after a short time interval, subjects were more

---

[11] Note that vowel quality is independent of voice pitch. For example, the word *teeny* can be sung in a high or low pitch.

likely to make the same or similar sound-shape associations as their own previous trials if they had used an intrinsic rather than associative strategy on the initial trial. In a more extensive follow-up, however, Fox (1935) found that associative choices resulted in better recall.

Given the limited number of subjects in early studies, subsequent attempts focused on extending the developmental and cultural spread to examine both the innateness of naming biases as well as their cultural universality. Irwin and Newland (1940) were the first to examine shape-name biases with children and adults. Using a paradigm modeled after Köhler's, subjects from age 4 years to adults were asked to label shapes with aurally presented non-words designed by the experimenters to "fit" the test shapes. Irwin and Newland found that adults performed as expected, but this weakened as the age of subjects decreased, and responses did not differ from chance for 4- to 8-year-olds. Davis (1961) undertook the first cross-linguistic examination of the effect, with the goal of discerning whether the effect may be confined to speakers of Germanic languages. Davis tested both English schoolchildren as well as children in Tanganyika (found in modern Tanzania) who spoke Swahili (a Niger-Congo language) and Kitongwe (a Bantu language). Using Köhler's original visual stimuli and replacing the word *maluma* with *uloomu* (due to an apparent lexical confound in Kitongwe), Davis found the effect was robust for both the English and Tanganyika populations. However, Rogers and Ross (1975) subsequently reported random responses when testing the effect with the Songe in Papua New Guinea.

More recently, Ramachandran and Hubbard (2001, 2005) have anecdotally reported the experiment using the words *bouba* and *kiki*, reviving interest in the paradigm, especially with respect to language evolution. Maurer and colleagues examined the effect among 3-year-old children and adults, using a set of four pairs of shapes (with an angular and rounded shape within each pair) and four pairs of carefully designed non-words. Unlike previous manipulations, the non-words were purposefully designed rather than intuitively chosen to differ only in terms of vowel roundedness (e.g., the vowel in *bow* is rounded, and the vowel in *bay* is unrounded), with the prediction that rounded vowels would match with rounded shapes. Maurer, Pathman, and Mondloch (2006) found the effect among both children and adults, contrary to Irwin and Newland's (1940) earlier findings. Connecting their results directly to Ramachandran and Hubbard's (2001) synesthetic bootstrapping theory, Maurer and colleagues suggest an articulatory mediation for their findings, wherein the rounding of the lips imitates the rounding of the shape.

Recent studies have increasingly moved towards more controlled stimuli from both linguistic and visual perspectives. Ahlner and Zlatev (2010) set out to use a larger set of non-words, using systematic combinations of front (e.g., /i/) and back (e.g., /u/) vowels with voiced sonorants (e.g., m, l) and voiceless obstruents (e.g., p, t). They found that adult Swedish speakers paired non-words with front vowels or voiceless obstruents with an angular shape, and this effect was particularly strong in non-words containing front vowels *and* voiceless obstruents together. Neilsen and Rendall (2011) also approached possible sound contrasts in terms of both vowel and consonant quality, as well as creating systematically varied round and angular shapes, finding that the quality of consonants was primarily responsible for non-word/angularity cross-modal associations.

Other recent approaches have deviated slightly from Köhler's original paradigm, choosing more implicit measures of associations. Westbury (2005) hypothesized that consonant articulation, in the form of stops (e.g., p, d, k) versus continuants (e.g., m, l, z), drives linguistic cross-modal associations involving visual angularity. Using a lexical decision task, both words and non-words were presented inside curved or angular frames. Westbury found that correct classification of non-words containing continuants was facilitated by curved frames, and correct classification of non-words containing stops was facilitated by angular frames. This was the first evidence of implicit sound symbolism for angularity, and the first study to show that a specific sound property (the continuant property of consonants) was related to angularity.

Another approach to angularity and linguistic sound looks at the learnability of sound-meaning mappings. Kovic and colleagues trained subjects on non-word-to-shape category associations, and then tested them using a timed categorization task (Kovic, Plunkett, and Westermann 2010). Subjects were trained to categorize figures with non-word labels that were either "sharp sounding" (e.g., /rɪf/) or "round sounding" (e.g., /mɔt/), in either a congruent (angular figures were *rifs*) or incongruent (angular figures were *mots*) condition. In the test phase, subjects heard the label followed by the presentation of an angular or curved figure and responded by pressing a "match" or "mismatch" button based on their training trials. Subjects who were trained in the congruent condition had significantly faster reaction times for both match and mismatch items.

Nielsen and Rendall (2012) used a similar paradigm, however, they approached the design of the non-words with the stop/continuant distinction established by Westbury (2005) in mind. Subjects were trained on form-meaning pairs which were either congruent (stop non-words were paired with angular shapes) or incongruent (stop non-words were paired with rounded shapes), and were then tested on these learned associations. Those who learned the incongruent vocabulary performed no different from chance, but subjects trained on the congruent condition performed significantly better than chance and significantly better than the incongruent group. This examination of learnability not only provides an implicit demonstration of cross-modal associations between linguistic form and angularity, but demonstrates that these biases might function to increase the learnability of a vocabulary system for language users.

Monaghan, Mattock, and Walker (2012) approached the learnability from a different angle, using the *cross-situational learning paradigm* (Monaghan and Mattock 2009; Yu and Smith 2007). In cross-situational learning, rather than training subjects on form-meaning pairs explicitly, a single word appears with multiple meanings over many training presentations—in this case, a single non-word appeared with multiple shapes. Subjects learned form-meaning pairs over successive trials by inference: for example, if the word *takete* appears with an angular shape over and over (even though another shape is always co-present), the form-meaning pair of *takete* + angular shape will be internalized. In other words, the non-word *takete* does not appear with the angular shape in isolation, but the angular shape reliably co-ocurrs with the word *takete* nonetheless. Monaghan and colleagues designed their non-word items carefully, utilizing the stop/continuant distinction as well as contrasting vowel quality (e.g., front /i/ or back /u/) in a separate condition. They found that form-meaning pairs were easier to learn where stops or front vowels were paired with angular items, and continuants or back vowels were paired with rounded items. These findings echo those of Neilsen and Rendall (2012), finding that sound symbolism facilitates learning even when more implicit strategies are necessary, as in cross-situational learning (see also Monaghan, Christiansen, and Fitneva 2011; Parault and Schwanenflugel 2006; Parault and Parkinson 2008).

Although the psychological evidence for sound symbolism regarding visual angularity is compelling, the mechanisms underlying the biases are unclear. The angularity of figures in all experiments is well controlled, but the linguistic stimuli vary, making it unclear what may be driving the effect from a linguistic perspective. Many investigations designed linguistic stimuli almost entirely based on intuition regarding goodness-of-fit with visual stimuli, making the effect rather circular (e.g., Davis 1961; Fox 1935; Irwin and Newland 1940; Kovic, Plunkett, and Westermann 2010; for further discussion see Westbury 2005). Some more recent investigations have chosen specific linguistic motivations for non-word stimuli, including vowel rounding (Maurer, Pathman, and Mondloch 2006) and manner of consonant articulation (Westbury 2005). However, neither of these studies held other phonetic factors in their linguistic stimuli constant, unlike Sapir's (1929) classic investigation, wherein *only* the vowel was changed to form an artificial minimal pair (e.g., *mil* versus *mal*). For example, in addition to manipulating vowel rounding, all of Maurer and colleagues' word pairs also alternate consonant voicing (e.g., *goga* contains voiced consonants and *teetay* voiceless). Though Westbury's (2005) consonants were for the most part carefully controlled, voicing varied systematically along with manner of consonant articulation, and vowel quality was not considered at all.

Linguistic cross-modality and taste

Most studies in linguistic cross-modality, even those directly examining natural language, have focused on the visual modality (e.g., size, angularity, lightness). Given the dominance of our visual system, and the excellent vision which defines primates (Jacobs 2009), the visual modality is a natural starting point. However, language encodes much more than the visual; if cross-modality were important in the evolution of language, we should expect it to connect linguistic sound not only to vision, but to all our sensory systems (as shown in Figure 43.2). Another reason to look beyond visual linguistic cross-modality is that the neurological condition of synesthesia is extremely varied, extending to taste in many cases (Day 2005). This is particularly relevant since cross-modal associations in synesthetes tend to mirror those in the general population.

Cross-modality and taste has been extensively studied, as the experience of eating is considered to be truly multi-modal, involving integration of smell, vision and sound (see Auvray and Spence 2008 for a review). A strawberry odor can amplify sweetness (Stevenson, Prescott, and Boakes 1999), and conversely, a sweeter solution will be rated as smelling fruitier (Verhagen and Engelen 2006). Discrimination between flavors is negatively affected when the color of a liquid does not match its taste (e.g., identifying a lime flavor in a red solution; Zampini et al. 2007), manipulating the sound produced when eating crisps can enhance perceived crunchiness (Zampini and Spence 2004), and color and label information can affect flavor perception (Shankar et al. 2009). However, the connection between taste and more abstract sensory experiences is less well studied.

Crisinel and Spence (2009) made the first empirical examination of taste and sound, asking subjects to categorize different bitter or sour tastes according to high or low pitch. Tastes were represented by names of foods associated with a particular taste quality, for example, coffee or tonic water for bitter and lime or vinegar for sour. Crisinel and Spence found that categorization accuracy was higher and response latency lower when high pitch was paired with sour items and low pitch with bitter items, demonstrating an apparent association between pitch and taste. A follow-up study (Crisinel and Spence 2010) confirmed these findings using additional implicit methods. However, these results may have been unduly influenced by the use of linguistic terms to mediate the experience of taste (i.e., cross-sensory mappings may have been based in part on the visual form of the words; see Simner, Cuskley, and Kirby 2010 for further detail). More recently, Gallace, Bochin, and Spence (2011) examined associations between linguistic sound and taste in greater depth. Rather than examining pitch, non-words derived from Kohler's classic *takete/maluma* task were rated for goodness-of-fit with common food items. Each non-word pair (*takete/maluma, kiki/bouba,* and *ruki/lula*) provided the anchors for two ends of a scale, and food items were rated along each scale between the words. Brie, chocolate mousse, and blueberry jam were rated positively with the words *bouba* and *lula*, while cheddar cheese, mint chocolate, and crisps were rated positively with the words *takete* and *ruki* (see also Spence and Gallace 2011).

Simner, Cuskley, and Kirby (2010) aimed to examine how phonological features, rather than pitch or particular non-words, were associated with pure tastants. Pure tastants were chosen instead of linguistic taste terms such as *sweet, sour,* and, *bitter,* since the graphemic or phonological properties of lexical items may influence responses (see earlier). The use of specific linguistic sounds makes this study highly relevant for a sensory theory of protolanguage. Rather than examining implicit associations using a timed categorization task, or having subjects rate goodness-of-fit using an external scale, Simner and colleagues measured associations by having subjects respond to tastes (sweet, salty, bitter and sour, each at low and high concentrations) by choosing a sound directly. The sounds were presented in the form of four continua reflecting various qualities of speech salient in the sound symbolism literature: F1 vowel quality (roughly corresponding to vowel height), F2 vowel quality (roughly corresponding to vowel rounding), voicing continuity,[12] and overall spectral frequency.[13]

With this method, Simner, Cuskley, and Kirby found that subjects rated higher concentrations as being significantly lower vowels (e.g., /a/), more fronted vowels, and with higher spectral balance. These findings agree in part with previous notions regarding magnitude sound symbolism in particular (e.g., the frequency code hypothesis, Table 43.1): for example, low vowels indicate larger magnitude and also mapped to higher taste concentrations. Front vowels, however, are usually associated with small size, but were found in Simner and colleagues' study to map to high concentrations. This simply underscores the fact that there may not be a single rule governing linguistic cross-modal associations across all sensory systems. While the frequency code hypothesis might explain many of the magnitude associations underlying visual linguistic cross-modality, such an ethological explanation may not apply to taste.

Systematic associations were found not only for concentration, but also for taste quality. Sweet was a lower, more continuous vowel than salt, bitter and sour, and was significantly lower than sour in particular on the spectral balance scale. Interestingly, the sweet taste was involved in all of the significant differences regarding taste quality. From an evolutionary perspective, sweet was the only taste examined which always indicates a viable or attractive food source (along with umami; see Zhao et al. 2003) and would therefore greatly benefit from a naming convention that systematically derived from some shared cross-modal basis. Taken together, these results provide compelling evidence that linguistic cross-modality goes beyond the visual domain, increasing its explanatory power in terms of the evolution of language.

CONCLUSIONS: A SENSORY THEORY OF PROTOLANGUAGE EMERGENCE

Many authors have debated the nature of protolanguage as being primarily gestural or musical (Arbib 2005; Mithen 2005); holistic or synthetic (e.g., Tallerman 2007; Wray 1998). Regardless of its nature, a detailed mechanism for the *emergence* of protolanguage remains a mystery, although many authors have argued that we should begin by looking to animal communication systems (e.g., see Fitch 2010). Few authors have proposed

---

[12] At one end of this scale, subjects heard a continuous vowel sound; as the value of the scale increased, periods of silence interrupted the continuous vowel resulting in pockets of voicing, mimicking words like kiki or takete.

[13] This was effected by changing all the formants of filtered white noise simultaneously from 0 to 5000 Hz, resulting in a scale from low-pitched white noise to high-pitched white noise.

solutions which offer a way to ground protolanguage, and thus language itself, in systems predating the emergence of language. Our account of protolanguage places our sensory system firmly at the root of our linguistic system, providing embodiment for an otherwise disassociated network of symbols. The use of sensory sound symbolism would have allowed us to express and understand a variety of elementary concepts, from sharing the visual details of our surroundings to valuable information about food sources. While a sensory protolanguage may solve the issue of grounding our symbol system, it leaves many questions in language evolution unanswered. What gave us the impetus to share information at all? How did we get from a small iconic system to a virtually infinite arbitrary one, and why?

The first question remains one of the major mysteries not only of language evolution, but of human culture and cognition more generally. Many authors have considered in detail how and why we may have acquired such an impetus to share (see Dunbar 2003; Tomasello et al. 2005). Tomasello et al. (2005) point out that it would have required some degree of a theory of mind: the ability to represent others' states of belief and desires. Interestingly, a lack of theory of mind appears to correlate with an inability to perform common cross-modal associations (Ramachandran and Oberman 2006), perhaps indicating that the perspective-taking involved in theory of mind is also crucial for sharing cross-modal associations. Whatever the origins of this drive to share or its reasons for persisting, we would assume it predates the emergence of protolanguage. Given that the sort of information relevant for sharing would have to be mediated by our perceptual system, grounding our hopeful utterances in shared sensory experience would have been a reasonable starting point.

How and why might an iconic protolanguage have become arbitrary? Pressures on an expanding language system—a small protolanguage shifting to a full-fledged lexicon—would have resulted in the leap from iconic to arbitrary. There are two related advantages to an iconic system: increased learnability and decreased processing demands. The first, increased learnability, has been demonstrated most powerfully with ideophones (e.g., Imai et al. 2008; Nygaard, Cook, and Namy 2009) for both Japanese and English speakers; Yoshida and Smith (2006) have also shown that ideophonic words are used more frequently with children, when word learning is at its peak. Learnability is not trivial; in fact, it is considered a core property of human language (Hockett 1960)—a language must be learnable by its users in order to be useful. Iconic forms are easier to learn precisely because they are grounded in existing perceptual and cognitive systems, rather than symbols defined only by convention and essentially requiring rote memorization. This leads onto the second advantage: an iconic system requires less processing power. Having been more easily stored, the retrieval of an iconic form is more straightforward than retrieval of an arbitrary form. Iconicity adds a natural strength in the bond between form and meaning, making the retrieval of a meaning with only the form, or vice versa, more automatic. As a simplified example, if all forms denoting small objects contained an /i/, the task of trying to retrieve the meaning of a form such as *mil* is constrained to meanings involving small objects. In an arbitrary system, however—where *mil* might denote any type of object—the task of retrieving its meaning remains largely unrestrained, and the search for the meaning of a given form must be exhaustive.

Given these advantages, why would language ever become an arbitrary system? Gasser (2004) has examined the advantages of iconicity in a set of simulations using a simple feedforward network. The network learns iconic languages with much lower error; however, this advantage only persists while the iconic language is small. Arbitrariness is a response to pressure for a language to convey more meanings. Monaghan, Christiansen, and Fitneva (2010) have suggested this may be why some non-arbitrary form-meaning relationships hold between the relatively small number of categories in a system (e.g., nouns and verbs as per Monaghan, Christiansen, and Chater's 2007 finding), but are not as apparent at finer levels of the lexicon (see also Tamariz 2005).

Finally, in order for a complete account of protolanguage emergence, there must be some attempt to demonstrate relevant continuity with our evolutionary relatives: other primates. Although complex tasks involving cross-modal association such as the *takete/maluma* task have not been tested with other primates, there is recent evidence that at least Chimpanzees engage in some cross-modal associations. Ludwig, Adachi, and Matsuzawa (2011) have shown that chimpanzees map high luminance to high pitch, a mapping well-documented in humans (Marks 1974). Chimpanzees have also shown impressive memory of numerical symbols in particular (Matsuzawa 2009), and Humphrey (2012) has suggested their success in symbolic memory tasks may be due to grapheme-color synesthesia, well-known to enhance the memory of human synesthetes (e.g., Yaro and Ward 2007). This would mean the cross-modal continuum mentioned earlier was likely present in our last common ancestor with chimpanzees, allowing it to be leveraged for language evolution in hominids.

Another, perhaps less abstract, cross-modal ability known as *cross-modal transfer* is found in both other primates and very young children. Cross-modal transfer provides an accurate expectation of an object's properties in one modality having only experienced it in another. For example, we have expectations about what an object may feel like (e.g., sharp) based on how it looks (e.g., angular). This has obvious survival value; one can make effective decisions regarding multisensory interaction with novel objects via input from a single modality. Cross-modal transfer has been found in infants as young as 6 months old (Rose, Gottfried, and Bridger 1981), as well as in chimpanzees (Davenport, Rogers, and Russell 1973) rhesus monkeys (Cowey and Weiskrantz 1975), and even bushbabies (Ward, Yehle, and Doerflein 1970). Savage-Rumbaugh and colleagues have found more robust cross-modal transfer in language trained chimpanzees, including tasks that involve "not only cross-modal associations, but also the transformation of information from symbolic to representational modes" (Savage-Rumbaugh, Sevcik, and Hopkins 1988, 617). This finding would suggest not only a continuity of cross-modal abilities between humans and chimpanzees, but also that the availability of a small lexicon may enhance abilities in cross-modal association. In the course of protolanguage emergence, cross-modal abilities such as cross-modal transfer may have been the genesis of an iconic system. Learning and use of such a system may have expanded cross-modal transfer to cross-modal association, allowing for the more abstract associations commonly found among humans.

Of course, this theory leaves many questions regarding language evolution unanswered, and there are still gaps even regarding protolanguage emergence. The emergence of theory of mind is an evolutionary problem requiring continued interdisciplinary study. Although we can outline clear stages in the emergence of protolanguage and the move to a larger lexicon, an exact timeline remains difficult to pin down. Written records of modern language go back at least 6,000 years, and estimates of the emergence of language range from tens of thousands to hundreds of thousands of years ago. Lastly, while a theory based on sensory associations offers a comprehensive answer to the symbol grounding problem, there are many important aspects of language evolution it cannot hope to explain, such as the emergence of syntax. However, we hope to have shown that a consideration of cross-modal associations evident in both synesthesia and the general population more widely can shed light on how our species moved from a state with no symbolic communication to one which laid the foundations of language as we know it today.

References

Abelin, Åsa. 1999. Studies in sound symbolism. Doctoral dissertation, Göteborg University.

Ahlner, Felix, and Jordan Zlatev. 2010. Cross-modal iconicity: A cognitive semiotic approach to sound symbolism. *Sign Systems Studies* 38:298–348.

Arbib, Michael A. 2005. From monkey-like action recognition to human language: An evolutionary framework for neurolinguistics. *Behavioral and Brain Sciences* 28:105–167.

Atchison, Jean. 2000. *The Seeds of Speech: Language Origin and Evolution*. Cambridge: Cambridge University Press.

Auvray, Malika, and Charles Spence. 2008. The multisensory perception of flavor. *Consciousness and Cognition* 17:1016–1031.

Bauer, L. 1996. No phonetic inventory in evaluative morphology. *Studia Linguistica* 50(2):189–206.

Bergen, Benjamin K. 2004. The psychological reality of phonaesthemes. *Language* 80:290–311.

Berlin, Brent. 1994. Evidence for pervasive synesthetic sound symbolism in ethnozoological nomenclature. In *Sound Symbolism*, ed. Leanne Hinton, Johanna Nichols, and John J. Ohala, 76–93. Cambridge: Cambridge University Press.

——. 2006. The first congress of ethnozoological nomenclature. *Journal of the Royal Anthropological Institute* 12:S23–S44.

Blust, Robert. 1988. *Austronesian Root Theory: An essay on the Limits of Morphology*. Amsterdam: John Benjamins.

Brackbill, Yvonne, and Kenneth B. Little. 1957. Factors determining the guessing of meanings of foreign words. *Journal of Abnormal and Social Psychology* 54:312–318.

Brang, David, Romke Rouw, Vilyanur S. Ramachandran, and Seana Coulson. 2011. Similarly shaped letters evoke similar colors in grapheme-color synaesthesia. *Neuropsychologia* 49:1355–1358.

British National Corpus, version 2 (BNC World). 2001. Distributed by Oxford University Computing Services on behalf of the BNC Consortium: <http://www.natcorp.ox.ac.uk/>.

Brown, J. Erin. 2010. Coordinated multi-modal expression and embodied meaning in the emergence of symbolic communication. In *The Evolution of Language: Proceedings of the 8th International Conference*, ed. Andrew D. M. Smith, Marieke Schouwstra, Bart de Boer, and Kenny Smith, 375–376. London: World Scientific.

Brown, Roger W. 1958. *Words and things*. Glencoe, IL: The Free Press.

Brown, Roger W., Abraham H. Black, and Arnold E. Horowitz. 1955. Phonetic symbolism in natural languages. *Journal of Abnormal and Social Psychology* 50:388–393.

Brown, Roger W., and Ronald Nuttall. 1959. Methods in phonetic symbolism experiments. *Journal of Abnormal and Social Psychology* 59:441–445.

Calvert, Gemma A., Charles Spence, and Barry E. Stein, eds. 2004. *The Handbook of Multisensory Processes*. Boston, MA: MIT Press.

Christensen, Carol M. 1980. Effects of taste quality and intensity on oral perception viscosity. *Perception and Psychophysics* 28:315–320.

Cowey, Alan, and Lawrence Weiskrantz. 1975. Demonstration of cross-modal matching in rhesus monkeys. *Macaca mulatta. Neuropsychologia* 13(1):117–120.

Crisinel, Anne-Sylvie, and Charles Spence. 2009. Implicit associations between basic tastes and pitch. *Neuroscience Letters* 464:39–42.

——. 2010. A sweet sound? Exploring implicit associations between basic tastes and pitch. *Perception* 39:417–425.

Davenport, R. K., C. M. Rogers, and I. Steele Russell. 1973. Cross-modal perception in apes. *Neuropsychologia* 11 (1):21–28.

Davis, R. 1961. The fitness of names to drawings: a cross-cultural study in Tanganyika. *British Journal of Psychology* 52:259–268.

Day, Sean A. 2005. Some demographic and socio-cultural aspects of synesthesia. In *Synesthesia: Perspectives from Cognitive Neuroscience*, ed. Lynn C. Robertson and Noam Sagiv, 11–33. Oxford: Oxford University Press.

Deacon, Terrence. 1997. *The Symbolic Species: The Co-evolution of Language and the Brain*. New York: W.W. Norton and Company.

Diffloth, Gérard. 1994. i: *big*, a: *small*. In *Sound Symbolism*, ed. Leanna Hinton, Johanna Nichols, and John J. Ohala, 107–114. Cambridge: Cambridge University Press.

Dingemanse, Mark. 2009. Ideophones in unexpected places. In *Proceedings of Conference on Language Documentation and Linguistic Theory 2*, ed. P. K. Austin, O. Bond, M. Charette, D. Nathan, and P. Sells, 83–97. London: SOAS.

——. 2011. Ideophones and the aesthetics of everyday language in a West-African society. *Senses and Society* 6(1):77–85.

Drellishak, Scott. 2007. Statistical techniques for detecting and validating phonesthemes. Paper presented at the Linguistics Society of America Annual Meeting, Anaheim, CA, January.

Dunbar, Robin. 2003. The social brain: mind, language and society in evolutionary perspective. *Annual Review of Anthropology* 32:163–181.

Farmer, Thomas A., Morten H. Christiansen, and Padraic Monaghan. 2006. Phonological typicality influences on-line sentence comprehension. *Proceedings of the National Academy of Sciences of the United States of America* 103:12203–12208.

Fischer, S. 1922. Über das Entstehen und Verstehen von Namen. *Archiv für die gesamte Psychologie* 42:335–368.

Fisher-Jørgensen, Eli. 1978. On the universal character of phonetic symbolism with special reference to vowels. *Studia Linguistica* 32:80–90.

Fitch, W. Tecumseh. 2000. The evolution of speech: A comparative review. *Trends in Cognitive Sciences* 4(7):258–267.

———. 2010. *The Evolution of Language*. Cambridge: Cambridge University Press.

Fox, Charles W. 1935. An experimental study of naming. *American Journal of Psychology* 47:545–579.

Frankis, J. 1991. Middle English ideophones and the evidence of manuscript variants: Explorations in the lunatic fringe of language. In *Language Usage and Description: Studies Presented to N.E. Osselto on the Occasion of his Retirement*, ed. I. T. van Ostade, 17–25. Amsterdam: Rodopi.

Gallace, Alberto, Erica Bochin, and Charles Spence. 2011. On the taste of 'Bouba' and 'Kiki': An exploration of word-food associations in neurologically normal participants. *Cognitive Neuroscience* 2 (1):34–46.

Gasser, Michael. 2004. The origins of arbitrariness in language. In *Proceedings of the Cognitive Science Society Conference*, 434–439. Hillsdale, NJ: LEA.

Harnad, Steven. 1990. The symbol grounding problem. *Physica D* 42:325–336.

Hinton, Leanne, Johanna Nichols, and John J. Ohala. 1994. Introduction: Sound symbolic processes. In *Sound Symbolism,* ed. Leanne Hinton, Johanna Nichols, and John J. Ohala, 1–14. Cambridge: Cambridge University Press.

Huang, Yan-Huang, Sawat Pratoomraj, and Ronald C. Johnson. 1969. Universal magnitude symbolism. *Journal of Verbal Learning and Behavior* 8:155–156.

Humphrey, Nicholas. 2012. 'This chimp will kick your ass at memory games—but how the hell does he do it?' *Trends in Cognitive Science* 16 (7):353–355.

Hutchins, Sharon S. 1998. The psychological reality, variability, and compositionality of English phonesthemes. Doctoral dissertation, Emory University.

Hockett, Charles F. 1960. The origin of speech. *Scientific American* 203:88–96.

Imai, Mutsumi, Sotaro Kita, Miho Nagumo, and Hiroyuki Okada. 2008. Sound symbolism facilitates early verb learning. *Cognition* 109(1):54–65.

Irwin, Francis W., and Elizabeth Newland. 1940. A genetic study of the naming of visual figures. *Journal of Psychology* 9:3–16.

Iwasaki, Noriko, David P. Vinson, and Gabriella Vigliocco. 2007a. What do English speakers know about gera-gera and yota-yota? A cross-linguistic investigation of mimetic words for laughing and walking. *Japanese Language Education Around the Globe* 17:53–78.

———. 2007b. How does it hurt, 'kiri-kiri' or 'siku-siku'? Japanese mimetic words of pain perceived by Japanese speakers and English speakers. In *Applying theory and research to learning Japanese as a foreign language*, ed. Masahiko Minimai, 2–19. Newcastle: Cambridge Scholars.

Jacobs, Gerald H. 2009. Evolution of color vision in mammals. *Philosophical Transactions of the Royal Society B: Biological Sciences* 364(1531):2957–2967.

Jesperson, Otto. 1933. Symbolic value of the vowel 'i'. In *Linguistica: Selected papers of O. Jesperson in English, French and German*, 283–303. Copenhagen, Denmark: Levin and Munksgaard.

Johnson, Ronald C. 1967. Magnitude symbolism of English words. *Journal of Verbal Learning and Verbal Behavior* 6 (4):508–511.

Kirby, Simon, Hannah Cornish, and Kenny Smith. 2008. Cumulative cultural evolution in the laboratory: An experimental approach to the origins of structure in human language. *Proceedings of the National Academy of Sciences of the United States of America* 105 (31):10681–10686.

Klank, Linda J., Yan-Huang Huang, and Ronald C. Johnson. 1971. Determinants of success in matching word pairs in tests of phonetic symbolism. *Journal of Verbal Learning and Verbal Behavior* 10:140–148.

Köhler, Wolfgang. 1929. *Gestalt Psychology*. 1st ed. New York, NY: Liveright.

———. 1947. *Gestalt Psychology*. 2nd ed. New York, NY: Liveright.

Kovic, Vanja, Kim Plunkett, and Gert Westermann. 2010. The shape of words in the brain. *Cognition* 114:19–28.

Kucera, H., and W. N. Francis. 1967. *Computational Analysis of Present-day American English*. Providence, RI: Brown University Press.

Landauer, Thomas K., and Susan T. Dumais, 1997. A solution to Plato's problem: The Latent Semantic Analysis theory of the acquisition, induction, and representation of knowledge. *Psychological Review* 104:211–240.

Lebert, Marie. 2005. Project Gutenburg, from 1971 to 2005. <http://www.etudes-francaises.net/dossiers/gutenberg_Eng.htm>.

Ludwig, Vera U., Ikuma Adachi, and Tetsuro Matsuzawa. 2011. Visuoauditory mappings between high luminance and high pitch are shared by chimpanzees (*Pan troglodytes*) and humans, *Proceedings of the National Academy of Sciences of the United States of America* 108:20661–20665.

Maltzman, Irving, Lloyd Morisett, and Lloyd O. Brooks. 1956. An investigation of phonetic symbolism. *Journal of Abnormal and Social Psychology* 53:249–251.

Matsuzawa, Tetsuro. 2009. Symbolic representation of number in chimpanzees. *Current Opinion in Neurobiology* 19:1–7.

Maurer, Daphne, Thanujeni Pathman, and Catherine J. Mondloch. 2006. The shape of boubas: Sound shape correspondences in toddlers and adults. *Developmental Science* 9:316–322.

McNeill, David. 2005. *Gesture and Thought*. Cambridge: Cambridge University Press.

Mithen, Steven. 2005. *The Singing Neanderthals: The Origins of Music, Language, Mind and Body*. London: Weidenfeld & Nicolson.

Monaghan, Padraic, Nick Chater, and Morten H. Christiansen. 2005. The differential contribution of phonological and distributional cues in grammatical categorisation. *Cognition* 96:143–182.

Monaghan, Padraic, Morten H. Christiansen, and Nick Chater. 2007. The phonological-distributional coherence hypothesis: Cross-linguistic evidence in language acquisition. *Cognitive Psychology* 55:259–305.

Monaghan, Padraic, Morten H. Christiansen, and Stanka A. Fitneva. 2010. Balancing arbitrariness and systematicity in language evolution. In: A.D.M. Smith, M. Schouwstra, B. de Boer, and K. Smith (Eds.), *The Evolution of Language: Proceedings of the 8th International Conference* (pp. 465–466). London: World Scientific.

———. 2011. The arbitrariness of the sign: Learning advantages from the structure of the vocabulary. *Journal of Experimental Psychology: General* 140:325–347.

Monaghan, Padraic, and Karen Mattock. 2009. Cross-situational language learning: The effects of grammatical categories as constraints on referential labelling. *Proceedings of the 31st Cognitive Science Society Conference*, 2226–2231. Mahwah, NJ: Lawrence Erlbaum.

Monaghan, Padriac, Karen Mattock, and Peter Walker. 2012. The role of sound symbolism in word learning. *Journal of Experimental Psychology: Learning, Memory and Cognition* 38 (5):1152–1164.

Neilsen, Alan, and Drew Rendall. 2011. The sound of round: Evaluating the role of consonants in the classic takete-maluma phenomenon. *Canadian Journal of Experimental Psychology* 65:115–124.

——. 2012. The source and magnitude of sound-symbolic biases in processing artificial word material and their implications for language learning and transmission. *Language and Cognition* 4 (2):115–125.

Newman, Stanley S. 1933. Further experiments in phonetic symbolism. *American Journal of Psychology* 45:53–75.

Nuckolls, Janis B. 1999. The case for sound symbolism. *Annual Review of Anthropology* 28:225–252.

Nygaard, Lynn C., Alison E. Cook, and Laura L. Namy. 2009. Sound to meaning correspondences facilitate word learning. *Cognition* 112(1):181–186.

Ohala, John J. 1984. An ethological perspective on common cross-language utilization of Fo of voice. *Phonetica* 41:1–16

——. 1994. The frequency code underlies the sound-symbolic use of voice pitch. In *Sound Symbolism*, ed. Leanne Hinton, Johanna Nichols, and John J. Ohala, 325–347. Cambridge: Cambridge University Press.

O'Grady, William, Michael Dobrovolsky, and Francis Katamba. 1996. *Contemporary Linguistics: An Introduction*. Essex: Pearson Education Limited.

Otis, Katya, and Eyal Sagi. 2008. Phonoaesthemes: A corpora-based analysis. In *Proceedings of the 30th Annual Meeting of the Cognitive Science Society*, ed. B. C. Love, K. McRae, and V. M. Sloutsky, 65–70. Austin, TX: Cognitive Science Society.

Oxford English Dictionary. 2011. Oxford: Oxford University Press. <http://oed.com>.

Parault, Susan J., and Paula J. Schwanenflugel. 2006. Sound-symbolism: A piece in the puzzle of word learning. *Journal of Psycholinguistic Research* 35:329–351.

Parault, Susan J., and M. Parkinson. 2008. Sound symbolic word learning in the middle grades. *Contemporary Educational Psychology* 33:647–671.

Perniss, Robin L. Thompson, and Gabriella Vigliocco. 2010. Iconicity as a general property of language: Evidence from spoken and signed languages. *Frontiers in Psychology* 1:1–15.

Ramachandran, Vilayanur S. (2004). *A brief tour of human consciousness.* New York: Pi Press.

Ramachandran, Vilayanur S. and Edward M. Hubbard. 2001. Synaesthesia: A window into perception, thought and language. *Journal of Consciousness Studies* 8 (1):3–34.

——. 2005. Synaesthesia: A window into the hard problem of consciousness. In *Synaesthesia: Perspectives from Cognitive Neuroscience* ed. Lynn C. Robertson and Noam Sagiv, 127–189. New York: Oxford University Press.

Ramachandran, Vilayanur S., and Lindsay M. Oberman. 2006. Broken mirrors: a theory of autism. *Scientific American* 295:62–69.

Rhodes, R. 1981. On the semantics of Ojibwa verbs of breaking. In *Papers of the twelfth Algonquian conference,* ed. W. Cowan, 47–56. Ottawa, Canada: Carleton University Press.

Rogers, Susan K., and Abraham S. Ross. 1975. A cross-cultural test of the maluma-takete phenomenon. *Perception* 5(2):105–106.

Rose, Susan A., Allen W. Gottfried, and Wagner H. Bridger. 1981. Cross-modal transfer in 6-month-old infants. *Developmental Psychology* 17(5):661–669.

Sapir, Edward. 1929. A study in phonetic symbolism. *Journal of Experimental Psychology* 12:239–255.

Saussure, Ferdinand. 1959. *Course in general linguistics.* New York: Philosophical Library.

Savage-Rumbaugh, Sue, Rose A. Sevcik, and William D. Hopkins. 1988. Symbolic cross-modal transfer in two species of chimpanzees. *Child Development* 59 (3):617–625.

Searle, John R. 1980. Minds, brains, and programs. *Behavioral and Brain Sciences* 3 (3):417:457.

Shankar, Maya U., Carmel A. Levitan, John Prescott, and Charles Spence. 2009. The influence of color and label information on flavor perception. *Chemosensory Perception* 2:53:58.

Shillcock, Richard, Simon Kirby, Scott McDonald, and Chris Brew. 2001. Filled pauses and their status in the mental lexicon. In *Disfluency in Spontaneous Speech (DiSS '01)*, 53–56. <http://www.isca-speech.org/archive_open/diss_01/dis1_053.html>.

Simner, Julia, Christine Cuskley, and Simon Kirby. 2010. What sound does that taste? Cross-modal mappings across gustation and audition. *Perception* 39:553–569.

Simner, Julia, Jamie Ward, Monika Lanz, Ashok Jansari, Krist Noonan, Louise Glover, and David Oakley. 2005. Non-random associations of graphemes to colours in synaesthetic and normal populations. *Cognitive Neuropsychology* 2:2069–1085.

Simner, Julia, and Vera Ludwig. 2009. What colour does that feel? Cross-modal correspondences from touch to colour. Paper presented at the Third International Conference of Synaesthesia and Art, Granada, Spain, April.

Slobin, Dan I. 1968. Antonymic phonetic symbolism in three natural languages. *Journal of Personality and Social Psychology* 10(3):301–305.

Spence, Charles, and Alberto Gallace. 2011. Tasting shapes and words. *Food Quality and Preference* 22(3):290–295.

Stevenson, Richard J., John Prescott, and Robert A. Boakes. 1999. Confusing tastes and smells: How odours can influence the perception of sweet and sour tastes. *Chemical Senses* 24:627–635.

Tallerman, Maggie. 2007. Did our ancestors speak a holistic protolanuage? *Lingua* 117 (3):579–604.

Tamariz, Monica. 2005. Configuring the phonological organization of the mental lexicon using syntactic and semantic information. In *Proceedings of the 27th Annual Conference of the Cognitive Science Society,* ed. Bruno G. Bara, Lawrence Barsalou, and Monica Bucciarelli, 2145–2150. Mahwah, NJ: Earlbaum.

Thompson, Patrick D., and Zachary Estes. 2011. Sound symbolic naming of novel objects is a graded function. *Quarterly Journal of Experimental Psychology* 64 (12):2392–2404

Tomasello, Michael. 2008. *Origins of Human Communication*. Boston, MA: MIT Press.

Tomasello, Michael, Malinda Carpenter, Josep Call, Tanya Behne, and Henrike Moll. 2005. Understanding and sharing intentions: The origins of cultural cognition. *Behavioral and Brain Sciences* 28:675–691.

Traunmuller, Hartmut. 1996. Sound symbolism in deictic words. Paper presented at Fonetik 96, Swedish Phonetics Conference, Nässlingen, Sweden, May.

Tufvesson, Sylvia. 2011. Analogy-making in the Semai sensory world. *Senses and Society* 6(1):86–95.

Ultan, Russell. 1978. Size-sound symbolism. In *Universals of Human Language, Volume 2*, ed. Joseph H. Greenberg, Charles R. Ferguson, and Edith Moravcsik, 527–568. Stanford, CA: Stanford University Press.

Usnadze, D. 1924. Ein experimenteller Beitrag zum Problem der psychologischen Grundlagen der Namengebung. *Psychologische Forschung* 5:24–43.

Verhagen, Justus V., and Lina Engelen. 2006. The neurocognitive bases of human multimodal food perception: Sensory integration. *Neuroscience and Biobehavioral Reviews* 30:613:650.

Ward, Jamie, Brett Huckstep, and Elias Tsakanikos. 2006. Sound-colour synaesthesia: To what extent does it use cross-modal mechanisms common to us all? *Cortex* 42:264–280.

Ward, Jeanette P., Arthur L. Yehle, and R. Stephen Doerflein. 1970. Cross-modal transfer of a specific discrimination in the bushbaby (*Galago senegalensis*). *Journal of Comparative and Physiological Psychology* 73(1):74–77.

Werner, Heinz, and Seymour Wapner. 1952. Toward a general theory of perception. *Psychological Review* 59:324–338.

Werner, Heinz. 1957. *Comparative Psychology of Mental Development*. New York: International University Press.

Westbury, Chris. 2005. Implicit sound symbolism in lexical access: Evidence from an interference task. *Brain and Language* 93(1):10–19.

Westermann, D. 1927. Laut, Ton und Sinn in westafrikanische Sudansprachen. In *Festschrift Meinhof*, ed. F. Boas, O. Dempwolff, G. Panconelli-Calzia, A. Werner, and D. Westermann, 315–328. Hamburg: Kommissionsverlag von L. Friederichsen & Co.

Woodworth, Nancy L. 1991. Sound symbolism in proximal and distal forms. *Linguistics* 29:273–299.

Wray, Alison. 1998. Protolanguage as a holistic system for social interaction. *Language and Communication* 18:47–67.

Yaro, Caroline, and Jamie Ward. 2007. Searching for Shereshevskii: What is superior about the memory of synaesthetes? *Quarterly Journal of Experimental Psychology* 60:681:695.

Yoshida, H., and L. Smith. 2006. Dynamic properties of form and meaning and children's learning of verbs. Paper presented at the 15th International Conference of Infant Studies, Kyoto, Japan, June.

Yu, Chen, and Linda B. Smith. 2007. Rapid word learning under uncertainty via cross-situational statistics. *Psychological Science* 18:414–420.

Zampini, Massimiliano, and Charles Spence. 2004. The role of auditory cues in modulating the perceived crispness and staleness of potato chips. *Journal of Sensory Studies* 19:347–363.

Zampini, Massimilliano, Daniel Sanabria, Nicola Phillips, and Charles Spence. 2007. The multisensory perception of flavor: Assessing the influence of color cues on flavor discrimination responses. *Food Quality and Preference* 18:975–984.

Zhao, Grace Q, Yifeng Zhang, Mark A. Hoon, Jayaram Chandrashekar, Isolde Erlenbach, Nicholas J. P. Ryba, and Charles S. Zuker. 2003. The receptors for mammalian sweet and umami taste. *Cell* 115:255–266.

PART VIII

PERSPECTIVES ON SYNESTHESIA

CHAPTER 44

....

SYNESTHESIA

A first-person perspective

....

SEAN A. DAY

INTRODUCTION: EARLY YEARS, FAMILY BACKGROUND

I am a congenital multiple synesthete, male, born January 30, 1962. By congenital synesthete, I mean that I experience a type of "merging of the senses," which has been with me for as long as I can remember, and which was endowed sometime before, at, or shortly after birth, rather than from any external event, such as head trauma or disease in later life. I have the following three types of synesthesias: "musical timbre to visual/spatial" (i.e., I see shapes, movements, and colors when I hear music, induced by the timbre); "flavor to visual/spatial" (I see shapes, movements, and colors when I taste food); and "odor to visual/spatial" (I see shapes, movements, and colors when I smell odors). My father does not have any type of synesthesia. My mother has "grapheme to color" synesthesia (i.e., colors from letters and numbers), but only for a few letters in the Roman alphabet and a few Arabic numerals; she also has "aura" synesthesia for famous faces, in which the faces of famous people are associated with colors, and "musical genre to color," in which, for example, ballet music might be pale blue and Doo Wop lime green. My eldest sister, 4 years older than myself, has two of the same types of synesthesia as my mother, lacking the music genre type, with her "grapheme to color" synesthesia also being limited. Both my mother and my eldest sister are "associator" synesthetes, in that their synesthetic colors are seen in their "minds' eyes"; I am a "projector" synesthete for all three of my types, in that my colors are "seen" projected out into space around my body. I also have a brother, 6 years older than myself, a sister 2 years older, and a sister 3 years younger; apparently, none of these siblings has any type of synesthesia.

I have no recollection of my first synesthetic experience, but I was definitely aware of my "timbre to visual/spatial" synesthesia by the age of 5 or 6 years, as, at that age, I was deliberately seeking out recordings to listen to in order to see the colors. The

"Cloudburst" movement of Ferde Grofé's *Grand Canyon Suite* was a particularly colorful piece which scared the hell out of me, with the timpani and other percussion sending forth rolling clouds of dark gray smoke, and the brass "stings" producing flares of bright red fire. It was very much like an image of Hell, much more frightening that Disney's classic portrayal of Modest Mussorgsky's *Night on Bald Mountain*, from *Fantasia*, which I had also seen in my pre-teen years.

Through my almost 20 years of operating the Synesthesia List, an online Internet forum which brings together synesthetes from around the world, I am very much aware that people sometimes keep their synesthetic experiences secret from others and so are, in some sense, "in the closet" (see, e.g., Day 2005; Duffy 2001; Mass 2003). I feel quite fortunate that I grew up in a household where I really did not have to worry at all about relating my synesthetic perceptions, nor fear that perhaps I might have some "problem" such as progressing insanity. My family was very well-read, especially in the sciences; by the time I was 9 or 10 years old, I was fully aware that I had a rare, genetically-based neurological trait which influenced my perception of music, that it was harmless, and that others around me did not necessarily have it. My family was also very musical, and interacted with many other musicians; so, by the age of 13 or 14 years, I had encountered a couple of other synesthete musicians, plus many other musicians who knew of, or had friends who were synesthetes. I did not, however, encounter the term "synesthesia" until I was 21 years old. Many synesthetes talk in terms similar to those of homosexual and transgender communities, about "coming out of the closet" to family, friends, and then the greater community regarding their synesthesia (see Day 2005; Cytowic, Chapter 20, this volume). My more relaxed situation was perhaps quite atypical in the late 1960s and early 1970s but is hopefully becoming more common: I was already basically "out" to anybody and everybody who might care before the age of 11 or 12.

My family was very bizarre and abnormal in any case. In a very conservative neighborhood in the very conservative town of East Jackson, Michigan, we lived in a bright lavender painted house, were visible members of a quite atypical religion for that area, had radical politics, had long hair and dressed in tie-dyed shirts with love beads, frequently attended science fiction conventions, recited Lewis Carroll, and so on. We relished and took great pride in our "weirdness." So, my synesthesia was quite trivial compared to other things about me as I was growing up. I should point out, however, that my extensive exposure to thousands of people with synesthesia has taught me that "eccentricity" is in no way a necessary or defining feature of synesthetes. I have met a whole range of different personality types with synesthesia, from the outlandish to the extremely conservative. All I can do here, however, is recount my own personal case.

I saw my having synesthesia as similar to if I was a speaker of Japanese while living in the US Midwest: speaking Japanese is not "abnormal" in and of itself. However, relatively few other people around you in the Midwest speak Japanese, so why bother to consistently try starting a conversation there with it? Yet, every once in a while, you might encounter someone who does speak Japanese; then, instead of just chatting in English, you can chat in your other language. And, if you do a little searching, you can find Japanese families and even communities to interact with.

Like most children in Michigan back in the 1960s, I started my education in performing on a musical instrument by learning how to play a plastic recorder in a junior high school band. Fortunately, the experience was not that bad, since the recorder synesthetically produced a mediocre blue colored thin, water-based "paint"; that was okay and not disturbing. In the basement of our sometime lavender house, we also had a broken-down, slightly out-of-tune piano, which I also started to plunk away on. For either Christmas or my birthday, I also acquired a toy single-keyboard organ; it had perhaps two and a half octaves, plus chord buttons (similar to an accordion), and could produce about four or five slightly different timbres.

By 7th grade, in junior high school (thus, when I was 12 years old), I was in the school's band. It was originally suggested that I should play the clarinet or saxophone. I tried the clarinet for a week or two, but could not tolerate the feel of a wooden reed on my tongue (I still can't—although it's unrelated to my synesthesia). I wanted to play keyboards, but the only thing that band class offered was to be in the percussion section, where, on rare occasions, one might play the xylophone or marimba. So I joined the percussion section, and learned how to drum. This really was not too bad, because, without exception, everyone else in percussion was there because they wanted to bang on drums exclusively, and had no interest in learning how to read music beyond deciphering rhythm. That left the glockenspiel, xylophone, marimba, tympanis, and any other pitched percussion instruments—with all their different colors—exclusively for me.

Sometime around when I was 12 or 13, after my repeated begging, my parents finally bought a small, spinet-sized electric organ; two keyboards, plus an octave and a half of foot pedals, with around 25 different timbre stops. This organ synesthetically produced a myriad of different colors; mainly, though, what I most often saw was like a huge sheet of highly burnished gold, reflecting back colors such as one would see in mother-of-pearl: pale pastel pinks, greens, blues, and purples. This organ, and the synesthetic colors it produced, were a focal point and defined my synesthesia during my teen years.

During my "tween" and earlier teenage years (that is, roughly, the 1970s), my family became involved in what was then the popular trend of Transcendental Meditation. I was given a mantra (long ago forgotten) and tried meditating a handful of times. It quickly disinterested me; I found no benefit in it. And, meditation had no effect whatsoever on my synesthesias. In my later teens and early twenties, (i.e., late 1970s and early 1980s), I tried self-hypnosis a handful of times. I was always quite successful in putting myself into a deep state after about 15 to 20 minutes. While I did indeed find great benefit in self-hypnotism being able to relax me—sometimes to a great extent, relieving stress—I also found being in a deep state of hypnosis exceedingly boring. Self-hypnotism also did nothing at all to my synesthesia.

As explained elsewhere throughout this volume, those whose synesthetic perceptions are visual can be grouped into two categories: projectors and associators. For all three of my types of synesthesia, I "project" my colored shapes into space. Since my timbre to visual/spatial synesthesia involves an inducer which can be outside of the body, this raises the question of where my synesthetic projections appear in relation to the sound source. We can start with perhaps the simplest example: a sound

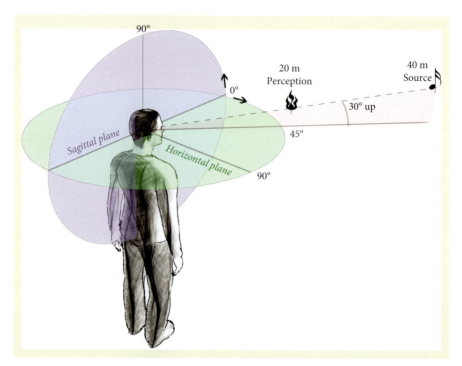

FIGURE 44.1 Graphical representation of the location of my synesthetic perception to music, given a music source 40 meters in front of my body, at 45° to my right, and at 30° above the horizon: my synesthetic perception would be in front of me, somewhere around 20 meters away, at 45° to my right and 30° above the horizon. © 2012, Joy A. Day.

source directly before me, at eye-level. My synesthetic perception will be roughly half the distance between the sound source and myself. "Roughly" because my perceptions for music are dynamic, rather than static, moving in three dimensions as the music progresses through time. So, for example, if the sound source is 50 meters away, my synesthetic perceptions would fall most likely in a range of about 20 to 30 meters away.

The situation for sounds behind me is more complicated so let me explain by setting up a system of Cartesian coordinates; we can then consider location on horizontal and vertical axes. Let us place the horizontal plane's zero point at eye level, with 0° on the circle being directly before me and 90° at my direct right. The vertical plane is sagittal, usually more so to my torso than to my head (but this is explained further in the following); let us place 0° for this circle directly before me, with 90° directly above me (see Figures 44.1 and 44.2). A simple explanation can then follow: let's say I am listening to a music source 40 meters away in front of my body, at 45° to my right and 30° above the horizon: my synesthetic perception would be somewhere around 20 meters away in front of my body, at 45° to my right and 30° above the horizon (see Figure 44.1). However, things change slightly

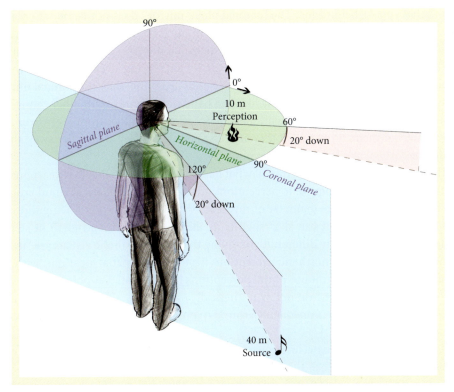

FIGURE 44.2 Graphical representation of the location of my synesthetic perception to music, given a music source 40 meters behind me, at 120° to my right, and at 20° below the horizon: my synesthetic perception would be in front of me, somewhere around 10 meters away, at 60° to my right and 20° below the horizon. © 2012, Joy A. Day.

if the sound is behind me and it is as if I have a mirror at my coronal plane, a vertical plane dividing my body's front and back sides. If the sound source is behind my coronal plane, my synesthetic projection gets mirrored to a corresponding location before me—but at about only a *quarter* of the distance between me and the source (see Figure 44.2). So, if the sound source is behind me, 40 meters away, at 120° to my right, and at 20° below the horizon, my synesthetic perception would appear before me, at 60° to my right, 20° below the horizon, at a distance of about 10 meters (see Figure 44.2).

SYNESTHESIA AND MAKING MUSIC

In the previous section I described hearing music from a source around me. However, I am also a musician. So, what if I myself am producing the music? In such cases, I am immersed within the synesthetic perception—which includes, rather intriguingly, colors that appear behind me. The "coronal plane mirror" does not come into play if the sound source is within about 1.5 meters from me (volume of the instrument does play a factor here). So, if I am playing an acoustic guitar or piano, I am immersed within the field of resulting synesthetic color. However, if I am playing an electric guitar whose sound is coming from an amplifier a distance away from me, then the coronal mirror factor *will* come into play. If I am playing in a band or orchestra, with other musicians around me, then not only do the synesthetic perceptions I produce from my instrument engulf me, but theirs do as well, if they are close enough; if they are further away, then, again, the coronal mirror factor comes into play.

This then also raises the question of what happens if I listen to music via earphones. With earphones, the synesthetic perceptions are located in a spherical cloud around my head, about twice the diameter of my head, with the centre-point being more or less between my ears—it can shift slightly as things slide back and forth in stereo. Note that this is distinctly different than saying that the synesthetic visuals are "in the mind's eye." Here, the synesthetic perceptions have specific spatial locations, with the focal point and a good amount of the perceptions being located at points internal to my skull. Also, note that I do not synesthetically "see" what is internal, only what is external to my head and immediately around it; only the external synesthetic perceptions are visual.

An awareness of the spatial location of things, such as the focal point, is separate from the synesthetic "seeing" aspect. This becomes very apparent as I also note what still seems to me an unusual aspect about how my synesthesias work: if I close my eyes, I do not synesthetically "see" anything while experiencing the inducer, whether it is music, flavors, or odors; however, I still experience synesthetic perceptions in that I know precisely where the visual perceptions would/will be spatially. For some reason, my mind apparently links my synesthetic "seeing" with normal ocular vision: I cannot "see" with my eyes closed.

My "flavors to visual/spatial" and "odors to visual/spatial" synesthetic perceptions are static, always before me at about eye-level, and never touch me—although many are close enough so that I can immerse my hands into them. If I do stick a hand into such a synesthetic perception, I do not synesthetically feel anything; but, if I move my hand around in the visual perception, I can swirl it, altering it and making the otherwise static perception dynamic for a moment.

My perceptions for music are translucent, see-through, similar to tinted glass or cellophane; my perceptions for flavors and odors, on the other hand, are solids which I cannot see past while they endure. However, while my synesthetic perceptions for music last as long as I am hearing music, my perceptions for flavors and odors only last for about 4 seconds after first tasting or smelling an item; then they dissipate in the course of a couple of seconds. One of my favorite things to do is to take long-distance cross-country drives on the highway, listening to music; it is like having a constantly changing tinted windshield; however, I never eat or drink when I am driving, and will pull to the side of the road if I encounter an odor (such as a skunk) which is too powerful to "see though."

ATTENTION AND SYNESTHETIC EXPERIENCE

The matter of my driving while experiencing synesthesia brings us to the issue of attention in regard to synesthesia, which is currently being explored by others (see, e.g., Ward et al. 2009). I have been asked many times by interviewers whether such moving synesthetic perceptions would be distracting, and make driving dangerous. As mentioned, my perceptions for music are transparent; I can see the traffic beyond. However, if I need to concentrate on the traffic, I can just "push" the synesthetic perceptions to my peripheral vision, clearing my main field of vision while the colors flicker on the borders. This happens quite frequently and automatically when I am driving. However, if traffic is really heavy, or weather or other factors make driving conditions really bad, then I do indeed have to turn off the music, to stop the flickering colors at the periphery from bothering me.

I started composing music, making up songs, when I was around 11 or 12 years old. I had hundreds of musical influences during my teen years, being very eclectic in my tastes. However, if I were to pick the top four, they would be the Beatles, J.S. Bach, Tchaikovsky, and, above all else, Duke Ellington. It was not until my 40s that I found out Ellington just happened to have had the same kind of "musical timbre to color and texture" synesthesia as I had, and that he based some of his orchestration choices upon it (such as composing pieces around a solo by Johnny Hodges' alto saxophone so that he could see his favorite color/texture, a light blue satin; see George 1981).

When I started composing music in my teens, I immediately thought of incorporating my synesthesia, in terms of choosing my orchestration for pieces by what colors I wanted to see. However, unfortunately, I quickly moved to going wholly overboard with this, moving instead towards trying to "paint pictures" via orchestration. This was fine for my own personal investigations and amusements. However, as I entered into university, majoring in music composition, it proved quite detrimental. I focused far too much on my synesthetic colors, ignoring what I was learning about balancing orchestration, even though I was studying such classics as Rimsky-Korsakov (1922). My products sometimes bordered on the ludicrous, tantamount to combining mandolins with bagpipes, and were somewhat equivalent to those of P.D.Q. Bach (a fictitious composer invented by musical satirist Peter Schickele, whose works use "instruments" such as foghorns, kazoos, and bicycles; Schickele 1976).

Moving from one university to another in 1982, I switched majors from music composition to anthropology for many other reasons than this. Still, this focus on my synesthetic colors hindered my music composition for at least 15 more years—basically, until I became aware that Duke Ellington had the same type of synesthesia as myself, and I looked at how he used his in orchestrating. While all musical instruments also produced synesthetic colors for Ellington, he did not focus on the combination of all the colors. Rather, if he bothered at all in regard to his synesthesia, he just focused on one instrument, the featured solo instrument, and built a piece toward portraying the characteristics of that color. Thus, for example, ignoring the colors produced by the trumpets or trombones, he would write a piece such that Johnny Hodges would create a specific shade and texture of light blue satin with his alto saxophone, that single thing being the focal point of the entire piece. Since about 1997—that is, since I was about 35 years old—this has also become my approach to orchestration: either just ignore my synesthesia altogether, or, if the piece calls for a solo or focal instrument, concentrate only on that one color and texture, without trying to combine it with those of other instruments.

However, that is just me. "Colored music" synesthesia does not necessarily have to be based upon timbre. It could, instead, be based upon the musical notes, or the key or tonality of the music, or the genre, or the overall structure. Thus, while famous musicians such as Duke Ellington and Leonard Bernstein had synesthesia based upon the timbres of musical instruments, György Ligeti's colored music was also an extrapolation of his grapheme-based synesthesia:

> I am inclined to synesthetic perception. I associate sounds with colours and shapes. [...] I feel that all letters have a colour.
> Major chords are red or pink, minor chords are somewhere between green and brown. I do not have perfect pitch, so when I say that C minor has a rusty red-brown colour and D minor is brown this does not come from the pitch but from the letters C and D. I think it must go back to my childhood. I find, for instance, that numbers also have colours; 1 is steely grey, 2 is orange, 5 is green. At some point these associations must have got fixed, perhaps I saw the green number 5 on a stamp or on a shop sign. But there must be some collective associations too. For most people the sound of a trumpet is probably yellow although I find it red because of its shrillness. (Ligeti 1983, 58)

Composer and pianist Amy Beach, on the other hand, had a "music-to-colors" synesthesia based not upon graphemes but upon her having "perfect pitch" and how this played into her recognizing musical keys:

> Amy's mother encouraged her to relate melodies to the colors blue, pink, or purple, but before long Amy had a wider range of colors, which she associated with certain major keys. Thus C was white, F-sharp black, E yellow, G red, A green, A-flat blue, D-flat violet or purple, and E-flat pink. Until the end of her life she associated these colors with those keys. (From an interview with Beach by George Y. Loveridge, in the *Providence Journal*, 4 December 1937, p. 5; quoted in Jenkins 1994, 5–6)

French pianist Hélène Grimaud appears to also have "colored music" for musical keys, although, here, it is more difficult to discern just what the fundamental inducers are:

> It was when I was eleven, and working on the F sharp major Prelude from the first book of Bach's Well-tempered Clavier—I perceived something that was very bright, between red and orange, very warm and vivid: an almost shapeless stain, rather like what you would see in the recording control-room if the image of sound were

projected on a screen. But as numbers had always had colours for me—two was yellow, four was red, five was green—and as I have always found music evocative, I didn't regard this as unusual. It was more the idea of colour than colour itself. Certain pieces always project me into a particular colour-world. Sometimes it's a result of the tonality—C minor is black, and D minor, the key that has always been closest to me, being the most dramatic and poignant, is blue, (Credo n.d.)

Then we have musicians such as Billy Joel (see Seaberg 2011) and Lady Gaga (Stefani Germanotta), for whom the musical piece as a whole has one or more particular colors. Lady Gaga stated in an interview, "When I write songs, I hear melodies and I hear lyrics, but I also see color. I see sound like a—like a wall of color. And, like for example, 'Poker Face' is a deep amber color" (jayohenjee 2010).

A question regarding music-induced synesthesia which I encounter often is its relationship to perfect pitch or relative pitch recognition. Most synesthetes with music-related synesthesia do not have perfect pitch; perfect pitch is a separate phenomenon, and quite rare. Relative pitch, on the other hand, is something one can improve with training, and many synesthetes with pitch-related synesthesia use the colors (or other synesthetic perception they have, such as flavor or touch) to improve their pitch recognition abilities.

Regarding perfect pitch, however, a subscriber to the Synesthesia List wrote:

I guess I have what I call "synesthesia-induced perfect pitch," because I recognize pitches based on the colors that I see, but this is strongest with piano and voice, I suppose because those are the primary instruments I use. With other instruments, I usually just get one overall color for the entire instrument. When I began playing guitar, slowly I began to gain colors for each pitch instead of the overall tan I had been seeing; so I guess that's changeable for me. While I can recognize pitches by the colors I see for them, I usually see a whole recording of a song as a few different colors that don't really relate to the key or the pitches, which has always confused me.

This example also serves to point out that an individual can have more than one type of music-related synesthesia.

One of my favorite examples of the differences in music-induced synesthesia emerged via the Synesthesia List and my interactions there with Scottish classical pianist Joseph Long. Long subscribed to the list group in 2001 or 2002, and we have been good friends ever since. We immediately picked up on the fact that we both had music-induced synesthesia. However, for Long, it is based upon the pitch of the tone not the timbre; thus, for Long, the piano produces a vibrant rainbow of colors.

Joseph and I had fun trading little anecdotes back and forth, being amused at our differences. But then I hit upon an idea for an experiment, to place before the whole Synesthesia List community: Joseph and I decided to take Alexander Scriabin's *Piano Sonata #5*, and Maurice Ravel's *Bolero*, listen to both, and note down our synesthetic responses. For Joseph Long, Scriabin's *Piano Sonata #5*, which he himself sometimes performs in concert, is a wild rainbow of colors, as it moves all over the keyboard, with very atypical tonal sequences and chord progressions. For me, the sonata is mono-chromatic throughout its entirety; a cyan color like anything else played on the piano. Contrariwise, for Long, Ravel's *Bolero* is visually tedious, as it presents the same small sequence of colors over and over again; for me, on the other hand, *Bolero* is a wonderful exploration of colors, as each reiteration of the theme changes orchestration, and more colors are added as more instrumental timbres are added towards the fantastically complex multicolored climax.

Over the last 35 years that I have pursued talking to musicians, I have seen that most jazz and rock synesthete musicians are fairly willing to talk about their perceptions; their surrounding environment is usually more accepting of such "eccentricities." Classical musicians, in general, to me, seemed far less willing to talk. However, still, each case is a little bit different. When jazz guitarist Tony DeCaprio confided in me about his colored music, back in 2000, he was nevertheless still very unwilling to talk to medical doctors or psychologists about it, for fear that they might declare him crazy, or want to test, observe, and attempt to treat him. I finally persuaded DeCaprio to give a formal talk about his synesthesia at an international conference in Granada, Spain, in 2007. As he began his presentation, DeCaprio was extremely nervous: he had performed on stage for decades; but he had never given a talk to doctors and professors—or, for that matter, anybody—about his synesthesia. By the end of his talk, the relief of "coming out" and discussing it with others was written all over his face. DeCaprio now writes articles (see DeCaprio 2012), where he directly talks about his synesthesia, and uses it as a basis for teaching improvisation to his students.

So, while we have synesthete musicians such as Lady Gaga and Pharrell Williams, who (at least now) have no reluctance to talk about their synesthesia, and others, such as Billy Joel and Itzhak Perlman, who have finally "come out of the closet" after decades (see Seaberg 2011), I feel it is sad that I nevertheless still encounter many synesthete musicians, artists, and writers who hold the position that the composer Jean Sibelius adopted:

> For him there existed a strange, mysterious connection between sound and color, between the most secret perceptions of the eye and ear. Everything he saw produced a corresponding impression on his ear—every impression of sound was transferred and fixed as color on the retina of his eye and thence to his memory. And this he thought as natural, with as good reason as those who did not possess this faculty called him crazy or affectedly original.
>
> For this reason he only spoke of this in the strictest confidence and under a pledge of silence. "For otherwise they will make fun of me!" (Adolf Paul 1890; quoted in Ekman 1938, 41–42)

FLAVORS, IN COLOR

Now, instead, when it comes to building things via my synesthetic perceptions, my focus is on creating new cuisine by combining the colors I perceive for different flavors.

I have done this in two different styles: Either by doing "exercises in subtleties," combining foods whose synesthetic colors are almost—but not quite—the same shade, such as chicken, oranges, vanilla, ice cream, and red wine (all shades of cyan), or raspberries, grilled squid, and almonds (all shades of bright orange). Alternatively, I've done this by creating sharp, bright contrasts, such as raspberries (bright orange) with raw spinach leaves (dark purple; see Day 2011). As of yet, I really have not created any dish which is "original" (chicken ice cream, for example, has been around for quite a while in Japanese and Californian restaurants). Yet, as I continue to experiment and explore new foods, I hope to eventually do so.

Until the age of 21, I was only aware that there was one general kind of synesthesia: music producing synesthetic colors, which could come about either congenitally or via drugs. Even though I was experiencing "flavor to visual/spatial" and "odor to visual/spatial" synesthesia since at least age 5, I was not overly aware that I was doing so until I was 21. As a teenager, in searching for synesthetes, the only type I was aware of to look for were others who might also see colors for music. Towards this, I did try to interact with other musicians as much as possible; but basically about all I could do was to keep my ears open and hope I might hear someone drop a hint now and then. This did, however, prove successful on more than a few instances, mainly just because of the volume of musicians I was encountering. By the time I was 20, I had encountered and talked with about ten other "music to color" synesthetes, and had heard stories about another 25 or so. While not necessarily "frustrated" by the low volume of synesthetes I had encountered, I desperately wanted to meet more—it was always such great fun to be able to talk about the colors of music with someone who could relate, even if the colors were different and worked differently for him or her! Probably one of my most cherished memories of this time was from a moment in the mid-1970s, when I was amongst a small, intimate group in a room, listening to Dizzy Gillespie ramble on, in person, about playing jazz with others he knew. I will not venture to say that Gillespie himself was a synesthete, but he was definitely and obviously familiar with music-related synesthesia amongst jazz musicians. Another would be from around 1981, working as a stage hand and chatting with members of the Count Basie Orchestra about synesthetes they knew.

As I've said, I was not fully aware of my "flavor to visual/spatial" and "odor to visual/spatial" synesthesia until age 21, when the flavor-based synesthesia was brought sharply to my attention as I sipped an extremely strong brew of espresso coffee and synesthetically saw before me a large pool of oily dark green liquid. Having consciously experienced "timbre to visual/spatial" synesthesia for at least 15 years prior to this, I immediately recognized the experience as a synesthetic perception, but was quite pleasantly startled to also realize that it resulted from tasting rather than hearing. Upon reflection after this event, though, I realized that I had actually been operating upon my "flavor to visual/spatial" (and, to a much lesser extent, my "odor to visual/spatial") synesthesia for years, since at least age 6 or 7 in my conscious memory and probably before, basing my food preferences and selections upon it.

Unlike with "grapheme to color" synesthesia, in which, for example, the word "red" might induce a synesthetic perception of green, a phenomenon known as the "alien color effect" (Gray et al. 2002), this type of "mismatching" sensation is less often found in taste-linked variants, such as lexical-gustatory (i.e., word to flavor) synesthesia. In this latter, food-words tend to taste of the denoted food (e.g., the word "sausage" tends to taste of sausage, rather than, say, licorice; e.g., Ward, Simner, and Auyeung 2005). My own "flavor to visual/spatial" synesthesia is rather different again, in that I cannot think of a particular instance which does *not* display the alien color effect! For example, the color of milk should be white, but it is synesthetically blue. Indeed, there is no correspondence even when the *name* of the food in English is a color word; for example, both "white sauce" and "brown sauce" produce shades of grayish puce and lavender; egg "whites" do not produce any color; "white" and "red" wines both make (different) shades of blue; spinach and other salad "greens" create shades of purple; and "oranges" produce synesthetic shades of blue. But blue cheese *is* a purplish-blue color; however, that is because cheeses, and dairy products in general, are usually blue. The particular flavor of blue cheese itself actually pushes my resulting synesthetic color towards purple.

It is possible to speculate that there might be direct chemical-to-color connections in my flavor-to-color synesthesia. However, I have only been able to deduce perhaps three instances where this might be the case: it is likely that citric acid produces the sky blue color I see for all citrus fruits, although the intensity of color correlates with the intensity of the taste itself. I have been clinically tested regarding this, with citric acid diluted in water, which produced the same base synesthetic color and visual appearance of other citrus fruits (closest to what I see for tart lemons, in fact) but its intensity was diminished as the solution became weaker. The second probable direct chemical connection is with table salt (sodium chloride) synesthetically producing a very soft gray color, with a texture like lint or an old, worn out woolen blanket; again, this one is consistent in tests with basic salt in water solutions. A third instance, although more speculative, is that lactic acid is responsible for making me see the watery shades of blue with dairy products. Then, there are also the shades of orange I see for most fish and sea-foods, and the shades of purples I see for most green, leafy vegetables (e.g., spinach and Brussels sprouts); these, however, have proven far too complex for me to break down to single components on my own. The orange for fish and sea-food might have more cultural rather than chemical causes for me, perhaps connected with a particular brand name's packaging color seen in my childhood. Yet, I am now beginning to think that the pink and purple shades I see for cucurbits might be chemically based, rather than, say, connected with the pink flesh of watermelons, as I am still unable to deduce any type of culture-based connection from my past that would tie together such items as cucumbers and pumpkins, yet I still experience the distinct purple-pink shades even when I am initially unaware that the food I am eating contains some form of cucurbit (e.g., a undisclosed ingredient hidden inside a pastry shell).

I also note that other synesthetes seem to have culture-based associations in their own taste synesthesias. James Wannerton is the current president of the UK Synaesthesia Association, and he experiences lexical-gustatory synesthesia (described earlier, in which hearing, reading, or saying words triggers sensations of flavor in the mouth). James Wannerton's synesthetic flavors appear to relate to his experience and culture in that they tend to be food flavors from his UK childhood (e.g., certain candy and choco-late brands). They are also related to his language experience since they are tied to spe-cific phonemes (speech sounds). So, for example, he experiences the synesthetic flavor of apple not only in the word "apple" but also specifically in certain other words that also contain the same /p/ sound (e.g., "parent"; see Ward and Simner 2003; Ward, Simner, and Auyeung 2005). Note that James Wannerton's synesthesia operates here a bit differ-ently than my own. For Wannerton, and others with lexical-gustatory synesthesia, all or most of the correspondences were shaped during childhood. While new words are, of course, encountered, they tend not to elicit tastes. For me, on the other hand, with my "flavor to visual/spatial" synesthesia, even now at my age, I encounter new flavors, and, with them, new, unique synesthetic color combinations.

My "flavor to visual/spatial" synesthesia has some influence on my food shopping habits. For example, dairy products produce shades of blue for me. Different grocery stores where I live each have their own set of different colored labels and caps for differ-ent types of milk. I tend to most commonly buy "2%" milk. At one store, this comes in blue-labeled cartons; at another, 2% has a green label, and it is skimmed milk which has the blue label. Thus, at this second store, I often find myself grabbing the blue carton, only to then stop, put it back, and take a green one instead. I have examined my line of thinking, asking myself whether it is simply the case that I'm used to the blue label and if that is my focus. But no; that's not how it works. It is not initially a matter of the label at all. Rather, it is "milk is blue," so I am looking for blue milk, and anything blue will draw me to it. Likewise, I will tend to grab containers of sour cream, any type of cheese, or ice cream in blue containers, regardless of the brand or whether it is a flavor I really want. I am more likely to consider coffee if it is in dark green packaging; more likely to take beef that is in dark blue packaging, chicken if it is in sky blue, spinach if it is in purple. However, I do notice that I don't look for beer or wines, nor for orange juice, with blue labels or packaging.

THE THREE-NOTE RULE

My music-based synesthesia quite definitely works on a "higher" level of recognition since it requires the trigger sound to be categorized as the timbre of a "musical instru-ment," as opposed to any environmental sounds. In my 20s, while attending an aca-demic conference in Montreal, I was made suddenly aware that, for me, this synesthesia operates on what I now call "the three-note rule": I need to hear the timbre produce three distinct pitches of a musical scale which I recognize (this extends beyond the "Western" even-tempered chromatic scale to also include various musical scales from India, China, and elsewhere), all within a given time (this is roughly based upon the note's endurance, but is somewhere around 25 seconds). With the third musical note, my synesthesia will be triggered as I recognize the sounds as producing "music" and thus as being a "musical timbre."

This was brought to my attention while riding on the Montréal Métro system. As trains pulled in, the brakes made three—but just three—squeals exactly the same pitches as the opening three notes of Aaron Copland's *Fanfare for the Common Man*. Upon the third squeal, my synesthesia would produce a quick flare of color (a dark gray with a silvery sheen) while the sound faded away. Further elucidation, however, occurred when I picked up a copy, one pre-Christmas season, of The Jingle Cats' *Meowy Christmas* (1993), which contains musical pieces made from the digitized recordings of cats meowing. A single sound, such as a car horn bleating just one pitch, or a cat producing "meow," produces no synesthetic perceptions for me. However, if cat meows are recorded, selected for musical pitch, spliced and sequenced, and then played back, as with the Jingle Cats, then, upon the third musically pitched (chromatic scale) meow, I will begin synesthetically seeing things (in the case of the Jingle Cats, a rain of very tiny, cut emeralds and blue sapphires).

While I have synesthesia for the timbres of musical instruments, I do not have synesthesia for speaking voices. Until I was 25 years old, I used to think that I also did not have synesthesia for voices when they sang. However, it was brought vividly to my attention that I indeed do synesthetically see things for singing voices when I first heard "A new machine, Part 1," by Pink Floyd (1987). The distortion of the voice in this recording altered what I normally see for singing voices enough for me to notice: for normal voices, what I synesthetically see is almost like totally clear water or glass, with just the faintest of rippled distortions producing pale sheens of pinks, blues, purples and greens. After hearing the Pink Floyd recording, I went back to listen to other distorted voices, such as Peter Frampton's voice on "Do You Feel Like We Do?" and Joe Walsh on "Rocky Mountain Way"; in both cases, I noticed my faint synesthesia for singing voice there, too. From this, I then turned to non-distorted choral voices, such as in Ravel's *Daphnis et Chloé* and Orff's "O Fortuna." With non-distorted voices, my synesthesia is far more difficult to see; I usually need to listen to the music in a very darkened room in order to see any synesthetic perceptions for these specific sounds. I do not, however, see my own voice when I sing.

SYNESTHESIA, DREAMS, DRUGS

I do experience synesthesia in my dreams. I do not often have dreams with music; but, when I do, the synesthetic colors are also there, the same as when I am awake. However, during dreams, my synesthesia for music works like that of an "associator" rather than a "projector." There are no spatial projections, nor any specific coordinates I could point to; just automatic, instantaneous connections between the timbres and their normal, typical colors. I even more rarely dream of eating foods; but again, when I do so, my synesthesia works like an associator. I have had the experience, on more than one occasion, of smelling (separately) gasoline and a skunk from an actually occurring external source near my sleeping body, and incorporating the smell into a dream. On these occasions,

I also had my typical corresponding synesthetic colors for the odors, but again without projecting the perception spatially. So, note here that, from this, we see that it is not wise to assume that "projector" or "associator" synesthetes are exclusively one or the other—instead, they may switch modality under different conditions.

Being a congenital synesthete myself, and content with my synesthesias as they are, I have had little interest in trying to induce synesthetic perceptions for myself via hallucinogens such as LSD (lysergic acid diethylamide), ayahuasca, or peyote. I have never really had any interest in using any type of drug (illegal or otherwise), beyond alcohol, for "recreational purposes." Over the years, however, I have noticed how various prescription medicines and other common drugs affect me. Acetaminophen tends to attenuate my synesthesia, as does aspirin. Ibuprofen tends to give me bad headaches, rather than relieving them, so I do not take it; the bad headaches from ibuprofen "gray out" or remove virtually all synesthetic perceptions. Naproxen sodium and codeine, on the other hand, tend to slightly enhance my synesthesia. A small bit of alcohol (i.e., moderate drinking) will significantly enhance my synesthesia; however, as may be predicted, beyond that certain amount, there is a crash in which my synesthesia is greatly reduced. Caffeine attenuates my synesthesia to a significant degree if I am "wired" and jittery from coffee. I have never smoked cigarettes or marijuana, but second-hand smoke significantly attenuates my synesthesia. Nitrous oxide ("laughing gas") greatly increases my synesthetic perceptions. Heavy doses of penicillin (taken orally or via injection) greatly increase my synesthesias, but also alter them significantly, changing colors, dynamics, and the appearance of textures.

LOSS OF SYNESTHESIA

It is common for synesthesia researchers to occasionally bring up the topic of losing one's synesthesia (see, e.g., Cytowic and Eagleman 2009; Dittmar 2009; Seaberg, 2011). Oliver Sacks (1995) writes of the loss of synesthesia due to injury, in the case of "Mr I" ("the color-blind painter"), who suffered a concussion in an automobile accident. Before the accident, Mr I experienced visual synesthesia to music stimuli (colored musical notes); after the accident, the synesthesia was deadened. Mr I suffered achromatopsia (inability to see colors in the world) and temporary alexia (inability to read) as well. Unfortunately, the location of the brain damage in Mr I remains unknown.

My own loss of synesthesia happened as follows: At 1:47 a.m., on the morning of September 21, 1999, Chichi, in Nantou, Taiwan, R.O.C., was hit with an earthquake which registered 7.3 on the Richter scale. At that time, I was living about 130 kilometers (about 80 miles) north-north-east, in Chungli. My apartment was on the 17th floor—the top floor—of my building. As the building shook and cracks ran across our ceilings and down our walls, my wife and I, having jumped out of bed, sat on the floor in our dining area, both petrified with fear. The earthquake, and the subsequent aftershocks, resulted in 2,416 deaths, 11,443 severely wounded, and 44,338 houses completely destroyed.

This earthquake, and the subsequent epidemics of cholera and hepatitis, left me with post-traumatic stress disorder. During the next 4 months, I was completely without any of my synesthesias. I was immediately aware of the loss, but was wholly unconcerned—I was simply too stressed out and had too many other concerns on my mind to care about my synesthesias being gone. About 2 months after the earthquake, though, I did start missing my synesthesias, albeit only now and then and just a little. I tried to produce some by listening to music; but I was still too stressed out, and music was still unenjoyable and provided no comfort. I also tried with foods, but all foods were bland and tasteless, producing no colors. I didn't really start becoming concerned about whether my synesthesias would return or not until about 4 months after the earthquake. However, within the same few days that I started to worry, my synesthesias began to return, very slowly, starting off very faintly and "all washed out." It took yet another 3 or more months before my synesthesias had returned to the full level they had prior to the earthquake. During those 4 months after the earthquake, I didn't really become depressed or anguished about my loss of synesthesia, and, actually, really didn't miss it much at all. It was of little concern. It was only once my synesthesia started coming back that I cared and realized how much I had missed my colored music, flavors, and smells.

Repetitive transcranial magnetic stimulation (TMS) to the right posterior parietal lobe can temporarily attenuate "grapheme to color" synesthesia (Esterman et al. 2006). TMS is a psychological research tool, which uses induced weak electric currents by a rapidly changing magnetic field. When the TMS device is held close to the head, this can cause activity in specific parts of the brain with minimal discomfort, and it allows researchers to study the functioning of the brain, by "knocking out" certain regions for short periods of time. This method has been used on synesthetes, and can cause the synesthesia to be lost temporarily. However, we should keep in mind that certain types of synesthesias can be temporarily lost in other ways. In the same way that synesthetes and non-synesthetes alike frequently "lose" one of their senses (e.g., when we have a cold and lose our sense of smell or ability to taste), colds and other temporary sensory interferences can affect synesthetic sensations. I get colds fairly frequently, almost always with severe nasal congestion, and am very use to the resulting significant reduction or total loss of two of my three types of synesthesia, those triggered by flavors and odors (actually, my "music to color" synesthesia takes a hit during a cold, too, as my general run-down feeling is reflected in my colors for music being all grayed out). Yet I know that the loss of my synesthesias is caused by the nasal congestion, and, once that is gone, my synesthesias will return.

So, not all such situations of loss of synesthesia(e) are "traumatic" to the synesthete. Once again, we need to keep in consideration which specific types of synesthesias, sensations and perceptions we are talking about, as well as the reason for the loss, the (short-term and long-term) importance of the loss, and the consequences of the loss. Losing one's "music to color" synesthesia permanently subsequent to a stroke is quite different than losing one's "flavor to color" synesthesia yet once again for a week due to another routine cold.

Are Synesthetic Experiences Ineffable?

Synesthesia is often described as being "ineffable," in that it is difficult to describe in words to a non-synesthete (see, e.g., Cytowic 2002; Cytowic and Eagleman 2009; Seaberg 2011). Many have claimed that it will always be impossible for a synesthete to convey to others precisely what exactly it is that he or she experiences. However, this is by no means always the case. For example, I can quite readily demonstrate to people—and produce upon request—what it is that I see synesthetically to the timbre of a tuba: dark, purplish-gray smoke (around RGB 48, 40, 50 in color). Likewise, trumpets typically produce reddish-orange flames such as are commonly seen in a household fireplace. Beef steak is no problem: a cube of blue (RGB 0, 0, 255) candle wax, about a third of a meter on a side. Grilled squid, a huge three-dimensional "cloud" (at least a meter for each axis) of shaving cream, colored bright orange (c.RGB 255, 165, 0). A theremin, a huge (again, at least a meter for each axis) cloud of pink candy floss (but of very thin density, such that it is wispy and see-through). No problem!

Similarly, other synesthetic perceptions I have are not ineffable, but are either extremely difficult or impossible to recreate physically. For example, an electric guitar produces, for me, a floating sphere (ranging in size, but usually less than a half-meter in diameter) of red plasma (ionized particles); this could be reproduced for demonstration, but it might take some fancy, expensive equipment, such as to produce a magnetic containment field. The Jingle Cats, described previously, would be a rain of extremely small, fine-cut emeralds and blue sapphires; extremely expensive, perhaps, but possible. Saxophones, on the other hand, make me see a floating sphere of hundreds of foot-long snakes—a "snake ball," such as with garter snakes when they mate; however, the "snakes" are glass tubings, lit up purple with glowing neon gas. That is, these purple neon glass tubes are alive and roiling in a ball like garter snakes, with the ball floating in space at eye level, usually about at arm's length. This is not "ineffable"; just physically impossible to recreate for demonstration to others.

Likewise, some things are only ineffable because the synesthete has not yet run across a matching representation. For example, I spent over 7 years actively searching for something that was the precise color and sheen of what I see synesthetically to the flavor of espresso coffee. I couldn't find it. Until McIlhenny Co. came out with their green Tabasco® sauce. Then, there it was. No problem; that's it. But then, some things still remain currently indescribable. What I see for the sound of a Franklin-style glass armonica, for example: the color is no problem to describe (a lavender color; RGB 135, 120, 170), and what I see is light reflected off of a surface; however, I have not yet encountered the correct type of surface that produces such a reflection—it could be a type of glass or a type of metal but is definitely not stone or plastic.

This raises the topic of whether many if not most non-synesthetes assume that synesthesia must, perforce, always be a highly emotional, moving, spiritual experience; to the extent that, for example, any (and every) time I hear music, it must make me spontaneously exclaim "OH, WOW!" and have high euphoric thrills. Such is not the case. Most congenital synesthesias, such as my own, being "every day," are quite "everyday" and mundane. Again, consider that, if synesthetic perceptions are basically invariable, such that I have been seeing the same sky blue mist for pianos and the same dark green oil for coffee for over 30 years, then it is very much "been there; done that." I have a fairly extensive musical background, including university courses; there are few musical instruments I have not encountered (here, of course, excluding all the various timbres produced electronically via synthesizers). At my age, "OH, WOW!" experiences regarding musical synesthesia, where I encounter something new and unexpected, are becoming quite rare, with my last one being more than 3 years ago now (that being my first time hearing an electronically modified Franklin-style glass armonica). "OH, WOW!" experiences for food flavors are becoming increasingly rare, too, leading me, in the past 3 or 4 years, to develop my current hobby of deliberately, intentionally hunting down foods I have never tried before. However, this is becoming quite difficult, too, with most such items now acquired via mail order, at expensive specialty shops, or when I travel overseas.

The Synesthesia List

I noted earlier that I have operated an e-mail listserv since 1992 called the Synesthesia List, for synesthetes and researchers. Before I was even 10 years old, I set out, determined to find as many others like me as I could, who also saw colors with music. I still don't really know why, except perhaps that I just wanted someone to talk with about it who could "speak the language"; someone "inside," who could share the jokes. The list group has brought me many experiences I never would have expected when I was a 10-year-old! Now, 40 years later, I have corresponded with literally thousands of synesthetes, from more than 46 different countries around the world, on six different continents—for a brief period, we even had a group member posting from Antarctica! I have encountered over 65 different types of synesthesia, and have discovered that my types are by no means the most common.

The Synesthesia List allows subscribers to join under a pseudonym, if desired. Over its 20 years, the list group has had some world-famous subscribers, including scientists, actors, and musicians, lurking under aliases. A number of renowned figures have also been described in other sources (e.g., Vladimir V. Nabokov had colored letters, as did Sir Robert Cailliau, co-developer of the World Wide Web; see and Nabokov 1966, and Seaberg 2011 respectively). Within the Synesthesia List itself, I've had many different discussion "threads" that were my "favorite." One of these occurred in the summer of 2011, on the topic of the "most shocking thing" subscribers realized as they learned about synesthesia. In particular, expressed disbelief about the experiences of non-synesthetes. One subscriber wrote:

I was extremely surprised that other people didn't see the colors and textures. I had just presumed it was the regular way to think. To this day, I can't figure out what other people actually do see in their minds, especially how do they figure out the centuries and any other number systems? Apparently, from what I gather, they just don't see anything. If that were the case for me, I don't truly know how I would function! I believe I would be totally lost.

Another wrote:

What I found most shocking is that other people can navigate through the world, and remember ANYTHING without either making a mental map or associating pictures, sounds or smells with things! What goes on in their heads to make them remember? Maybe they all do but just can't focus enough on their own process to recognize what's happening. I have spatial-sequence synesthesia and I would be mentally lost without my mental maps.

And yet another wrote:

I find it shocking that people can remember anything at all without having colors attached to them. I asked my mother how she remembers things like telephone numbers; does she visualize anything at all? She said no, she didn't, but that she remembers the numbers audibly. Instead, she stresses certain syllables to make them more memorable. It seems nearly impossible to me that absolutely no visualization of the numbers takes place in her memorization process. I would be completely lost if I suddenly lost my colors and internal ticker tape screen.

This volume is primarily written for non-synesthetes (the majority of humans) to better understand the world of synesthetes, as non-synesthetes often find this world to be so unusual and different. I still constantly find it amusing that synesthetes are likewise sometimes just as intrigued and baffled by the world of those who do not share their type of synesthesia.

I have also had many other "favorite" postings, over the years. However, even more than a decade later, one that I find the most touching was not from a synesthete, but from her non-synesthete husband. In May of 1998, Adrei Stefanescu wrote the following, regarding his wife, Lena, who has "sound to color," "flavor to color," "sound to odor," and "sound to flavor" synesthesias:

Lena is using my e-mail account, so for some time I have been following the discussions in this group, too. I am not a synesthete, and let me add, unfortunately. So, first I would like to ask you all to forgive me for peeping. But it has given me many insights into who Lena is, and has been key to a whole new understanding of her. So, secondly, thank you all for your openness.

That afternoon in August last year was a memorable day for both of us. I was preparing my things for the journey to a new job, and she quietly showed me an article in the German issue of the *Scientific American*. It was a review of Cytowic's book. Lena was too shaken to be able to say anything, so I read it without much comprehension. That evening, after overcoming the first emotional shock, she explained to me that she always had thought she was on the verge of madness, that she never dared to admit to anyone, let alone explain in what ways she was different. Lena then introduced me to the basics of her perception, to the mechanisms that allowed her to make associations which sometimes are astounding, her fantastic memory, and the importance of sounds in her life. She was crying out of happiness, and I was discovering a new person. I could hardly think of anything else during the next few days; somehow, I managed to get my new job started.

I now share her "secret," and it has enriched my life. It is one of the many good things that happened to us during the last year and a half or so, and I think it is one of the best.

Many synesthetes, such as Lena, when they first come across articles on synesthesia, researchers' webpages, the Synesthesia List, or academic books on the topic such as this one, feel an overwhelming sense of "validation"; a relief that they are not mad or deceiving themselves, that their experiences are real, documented elsewhere, have an established, scientific name, and not only are there people out there researching the topic, but also other people out there who share the same experiences. For myself, on the other hand, when I started my journey at the age of 10, I was not seeking validation regarding my synesthesias. I was already fairly confident in my synesthesias, although desperate to learn more. But now, these many years later, it is obvious to me I was definitely seeking something else: a reason and purpose for contacting other synesthetes, talking with them and sharing stories and information. Letters such as Andrei Stefanescu's are what grant me validation.

Running the Synesthesia List for 20 years, and pursuing everything I can on the topic of synesthesia, has been comforting, irritating, fascinating, aggravating, confusing, enlightening, intriguing, disconcerting, … Yet I'm still not satiated. But now my reasons for seeking out synesthetes have proliferated. Among other things, I want to make it far, far easier for future generations of 10-year-olds to have someone—such as myself—to talk to. To quote Jerry Garcia—a good choice for psychedelic visuals with music—"What a long strange trip it's been." And I've only just begun. So, more amazing foods (*pavo en mole poblano con helado,* anyone?) and more great music (bring on the Frank Zappa), then down and around the next bend in the road!

References

Credo. n.d.. Hélène Grimaud interviewed by Michael Church. <http://www.deutschegrammophon.com/special/insighttext.htms?ID=grimaud-credo&DETAIL=1>.
Cytowic, Richard E. 2002. *Synesthesia.* 2nd ed. Cambridge, MA: MIT Press.
——. 2013. Synesthesia in the twentieth century: Synesthesia's renaissance. In *The Oxford Handbook of Synesthesia*, ed. Julia Simner and Edward M. Hubbard, 399–408. Oxford: Oxford University Press.
Cytowic, Richard E., and David M. Eagleman. 2009. *Wednesday is Indigo Blue: Discovering the Brain of Synaesthesia.* Cambridge, MA: MIT Press.

Day, Sean. 2011. The human sensoria and a synesthetic approach to cooking. With contributions courtesy of James Wannerton. *Collapse* VII:378–409.

———. 2005. Some demographic and socio-cultural aspects of synaesthesia. In *Synaesthesia: Perspectives from Cognitive Neuroscience*, ed. Lynn C. Robertson, and Noam Sagiv, 11–33. New York: Oxford University Press.

DeCaprio, Tony. 2012. Super symmetry. <http://www.tonydecaprio.com/supersymmetry.htm>.

Dittmar, Alexandra, ed. 2009. *Synaesthesia: A 'Golden Thread' Through Life?* Essen, Germany: Die Blaue Eule.

Duffy, Patricia L. 2001. *Blue Cats and Chartreuse Kittens: How Synesthetes Color Their Worlds.* New York: Henry Holt.

Ekman, Karl. 1938. *Jean Sibelius: His Life and Personality.* Translated from the Finnish by Edward Birse. New York: Alfred A. Knopf.

Esterman, Michael, Tomothy Verstynen, Richard B. Ivry, and Lynn C. Robertson. 2006. Coming unbound: disrupting automatic integration of synesthetic color and graphemes by transcranial magnetic stimulation of the right parietal lobe. *Journal of Cognitive Neuroscience* 18 (9):1570–1576.

George, Don. 1981. *Sweet Man: The Real Duke Ellington.* New York: G.P. Putnam's Sons.

Gray, J., S. Chopping, J. Nunn, D. Parslow, L. Gregory, S. Williams, S., M. J. Brammer, and S. Baron-Cohen. 2002. Implications of synaesthesia for functionalism. *Journal of Consciousness Studies*, 9:5–31.

jayohenjee. 2010. Lady GaGa's interview in Singapore. <http://www.youtube.com/watch?v=SOynqo6e_CQ&feature=results_main&playnext=1&list=PL780B4CB0F5884F7A>.

Jenkins, Walter S. 1994. *The Remarkable Mrs. Beach, American composer.* Warren, MI: Harmonie Park Press.

Jingle Cats. 1993. *Meowy Christmas.* Hollywood, CA: Jingle Cats Music.

Ligeti, György. 1983. *Ligeti in Conversation.* London: Eulenburg Books.

Mass, Wendy. 2003. *A Mango-shaped Space.* New York: Little, Brown and Company.

Nabokov, Vladimir V. 1966. *Speak, Memory.* New York: Putnam.

Pink Floyd. 1987. 'A new machine, Part 1.' On *A momentary Lapse of Reason.* New York: CBS Inc.

Rimsky-Korsakov, N. (1922). *Principles of Orchestration*, ed. Michael Steinberg, and trans. Edward Agate. New York: Dover Publications, Inc.

Sacks, Oliver. 1995. *An Anthropologist on Mars.* New York: Vintage Books.

Schickele, Peter. 1976. *The Definitive Biography of P.D.Q. Bach.* New York: Random House.

Seaberg, Maureen. 2011. *Tasting the Universe.* Pompton Plains, NJ: New Pages Books.

Ward, Jamie, Clare Jonas, Zoltan Dienes, and Anil Seth. 2009. Grapheme-colour synaesthesia improves detection of embedded shapes, but without pre-attentive 'pop-out' of synaesthetic colour. *Proceedings of the Royal Society B: Biological Sciences* 277 (1684):1021–1026.

Ward, Jamie, and Julia Simner. 2003. Lexical-gustatory synaesthesia: Linguistic and conceptual factors. *Cognition*, 89:237–261.

Ward, Jamie, Julia Simner, and Vivian Auyeung. 2005. A comparison of lexical-gustatory and grapheme-colour synaesthesia. *Cognitive Neuropsychology*, 22 (1):28–41.

CHAPTER 45

....

SYNESTHESIA AND CONSCIOUSNESS

....

NOAM SAGIV AND CHRIS D. FRITH

INTRODUCTION

....

We have learnt much from studying selective deficits in neurological patients and what they tell us about normal brain function. This neuropsychological approach has been useful in the study of perception, attention, memory, and thought. However, interest in positive symptoms or phenomena such as synesthesia, hallucinations, and phantom limbs can be equally instructive.[1] Like deficits, positive symptoms could provide some useful clues concerning likely components and organization of the underlying cognitive or neural mechanisms and therefore facilitate the generation of new hypotheses. Additionally, they provide test cases for established theories of cognition. A good theory should be able to predict both negative and positive deviations from normal function when certain parameters are changed. Indeed, scientists are becoming increasingly convinced that there is much we could learn from synesthesia about normal function. While early synesthesia research focused primarily on documenting the phenomenon and verifying the genuineness of the subjective reports, current synesthesia research goes beyond this. Today, we are concerned with explaining the extraordinary perceptual experiences of synesthetes and considering what synesthesia may reveal about perception and cognition more generally (e.g. Cohen Kadosh, Gertner, and Terhune 2012; Sagiv and Ward 2006). In this chapter we will make the case for considering synesthesia as a model problem in the scientific study of consciousness and highlight some of the promising directions such a project could take.

---

[1] In neuropsychology, positive symptoms are characterized not by losing some ability or function but rather by adding or altering perception or cognitive processes in some way. For example, perceiving a stimulus in the wrong visual field (allesthesia), perceiving something that is not really there (e.g., hallucinations) or remembering something that did not really happen (e.g., déjà vu). This may or may not be accompanied by negative symptoms (i.e., deficits of perception, memory, etc.).

Consciousness

The problem of consciousness is one of the most challenging ones scientists are facing. It is usually divided into two major components—awareness and arousal (Zeman 2005). We will focus here on the problem of awareness or contents of consciousness (rather than levels or states of consciousness)—understanding our subjective, private experiences and how they emerge. This includes our thoughts, feelings, intentions, what we perceive, and the sense of authorship of our own actions.[2] The scientific study of consciousness examines the relationship between these subjective experiences and behavior, cognitive processes, brain structure and function, the course of development, as well as genetic, environmental, and cultural constraints. Scientists trying to understand consciousness are faced with many questions and problems. These include, for example, what distinguishes conscious from unconscious processing? How might we understand intentions, agency, free will, thought, and the relationship between attention and awareness? What determines the nature of our experiences, and what is the relationship between perception and reality? The study of consciousness is therefore an interdisciplinary endeavor and touches on many aspects of human cognition and brain function. It is not our intention to provide here a thorough introduction to the scientific study of consciousness (for an introduction, see Blackmore 2010; Revonsuo 2010; Zeman 2002).

Trying to understand consciousness follows a long tradition of attempts to address the mind-body problem. Chalmers' (1995) formulation of the problem—why should brain activity give rise to subjective experience in the first place?—has generated extensive debates (for a brief outline of the early debates, see Searle 1997). Such "why" questions are notoriously hard to answer[3] and scientists have always been better at describing *what*, *when*, and *how* things happen instead. Indeed considerable progress has been made understanding a number of key problems in the scientific study of consciousness: Identifying the neural correlates of consciousness (e.g., Frith, Perry, and Lumer 1999; Rees and Frith 2007), understanding the role of attention (e.g., Koch and Tsuchiya 2007; Lavie 2007), or how information is accessed (e.g., Block 2011) or integrated (e.g. Robertson 2003; Tononi 2007). Here we will focus on insights generated by empirical research.

Given the elusive nature of consciousness and the difficulty of providing a definition that encapsulates all aspects of consciousness, many studies have focused on specific,

---

[2] Following Searle (2000), we do not provide a precise, analytical definition of consciousness at the outset, and settle for this commonsense working definition for now.

[3] Richard Feynman (1983) once noted that explaining *why* something happens leads to an infinite series of questions (Why does A happen? Because of B; why is B true? Because of C; what explains C then? And so on). Therefore, we cannot usually give a full and comprehensive answer to "why" questions unless we do so within a framework in which some things are taken to be true (BBC2, 15 July 1983; *Fun to Imagine 2: Stretching, Pulling and Pushing*; <http://www.bbc.co.uk/archive/feynman/>).

circumscribed aspects of consciousness. Considerable progress has been made through the fractionation of consciousness into well-defined features or functions (such as visual awareness, bodily awareness, or the feeling of willing). It is sensible to start with a modest project—trying to understand how a single uni-modal perceptual experience arises. The problem of seeing the color red, for example, has been a particular favorite in philosophical debates on consciousness. Once we can provide an account of seeing red, we can try to extend our explanation to more complicated visual experiences and to other domains of human experience. We might then ask ourselves what synesthesia can bring to this debate, or indeed, how a general notion of consciousness might inform us about the nature of synesthesia.

SYNESTHESIA AS A MODEL PROBLEM FOR UNDERSTANDING EXPERIENCE

Seeing red may be a pure form of awareness, but focusing on this simple problem may come at a price. There may be features of perceptual awareness that are more readily noticed when looking beyond simple color vision. For example, active exploration of the environment, thought to be crucial in perceptual awareness, is more easily appreciated when considering tactile perception rather than visual perception (Noë 2004). Similarly, we can understand better the role of attention in consciousness within more natural settings, when varying perceptual load or manipulating the focus of attention (Kuhn, Amlani, and Rensink 2008).

We argue that synesthesia can serve a useful function in the scientific study of consciousness, since it could provide a new perspective on the problem and is a test-case for current theories. It is not immediately apparent why a relatively uncommon perceptual phenomenon should be useful at all in understanding perception or more broadly—consciousness. So let us try to clarify this. First, synesthesia is phenomenologically-defined. It is characterized by an atypical perceptual experience and like any other type of experience it can be compared with instances in which it does not arise (while the subjective reports of participants' conscious experience serve as a dependent variable; Baars 2003). The perceptual experiences of synesthetes (i.e., those who experience synesthesia) may be unusual, but its existence raises the same general problems: How do such experiences arise? What is their neural basis? How does attention modulate synesthetic experience? A second feature that makes synesthesia a particularly useful case study is the impressive variety of types of synesthesia, involving different combinations of sensory modalities and different types of experience. This provides us with a large number of observations and many opportunities to test our theories of brain function and the associated mental states. It also presents an opportunity to open up the debate on individual differences in subjective experience of the world around us. The third, practical reason that makes synesthesia valuable is that synesthetes are usually healthy and cooperative research participants and that synesthesia is more common than previously thought. This makes the condition easier to study than, for example, studying the perceptual anomalies in certain neurological or neuropsychiatric patients.

This chapter outlines why consciousness scientists and scholars should be interested in synesthesia, and why synesthesia researchers should be interested in consciousness. It delineates some the areas where synesthesia research is likely to contribute to our understanding of consciousness.

APPROACHES TO STUDYING SYNESTHESIA

Contemporary synesthesia studies are concerned with explaining how the phenomenon arises and exploring what it tells about perception and cognition more generally. Essentially, we are taking the neuropsychological approach. In neuropsychology, study of the deficits associated with circumscribed brain damage tells us something more generally about the relationship between cognition and brain function. In the same way one can study the deviations from the norm in healthy individuals with synesthesia (or in those who have acquired synesthesia). Cases of synesthesia are radically different than what we are used to, and so force us to reconsider our ideas about perception. New observations from such cases may help us generate new hypotheses about normal cognition and expose implicit assumptions. What we take for granted may not always be true. Indeed if there is anything that we have learned about consciousness it is that appearance and intuitions can be misleading.

One challenge in the study of synesthesia is assessing and quantifying the subjective reports of synesthetes. This has become somewhat easier in recent years as more cases of synesthesia have come to light. Prevalence estimates using different methodologies had varied widely. Recent studies taking into account both participants' self-reports and objective indices such as high consistency in their descriptions over time (e.g., the correspondences between specific letters and colors tend to be very stable) have typically lead to conservative estimates. After eliminating some of the sampling confounds that plagued earlier reports, Simner et al. (2006) were able to show that the prevalence of grapheme-color synesthesia (i.e., colored letters or digits) is close to 1.4%, and more than 4% of the population reported one of several common variants of synesthesia. One limiting factor in estimating the prevalence of synesthesia is the lack of agreement on a precise definition.[4] There is a growing consensus that better understanding of the underlying neurobiological mechanisms could inform the way in which we categorize synesthesia variants (Sagiv, Ilbeigi, and Ben-Tal 2011; Simner 2012) in addition to the phenomenological and behavioral characteristics. Patterns of inheritance of different variants as well as their co-morbidity may also prove useful in assessing the relationship

---

[4] For a discussion of the problem of defining synesthesia, please see Simner (2012), Eagleman (2012), Cohen-Kadosh and Terhune (2012), McPherson (2007), and Sagiv, Ilbeigi, and Ben-Tal (2011).

between different forms of synesthesia (e.g., Novich, Cheng, and Eagleman 2011). We will discuss here a number of synesthesia variants and related phenomena, highlighting their relevance for the study of consciousness (regardless of whether or not all these variants will end up being classified as types of synesthesia in their own right, as, for example, in the case of grapheme personification; see later and Amin et al. 2011). One of the principal factors that make defining synesthesia so difficult is our growing appreciation of the sheer variety of different ways in which synesthetes—and indeed all of us—might experience the world around us. This brings us to our first issue—individual differences.

INDIVIDUAL DIFFERENCE IN THE WAY WE PERCEIVE THE WORLD

The possibility that we literally see things differently from one another has intrigued scholars at least since John Locke's (1690/1979) discussion of the "inverted spectrum" argument. Is it possible that while we agree on the names of colors, we experience them differently? Behavioral measures can helps us rule out some possible transformations of individuals' color space (Palmer 1999a), but in general comparing experiences remains very challenging because we simply cannot get into other people's heads. Nevertheless, we can still say with confidence that some people do experience the world differently. Some notable examples can be traced back to the neurophysiology of sensory systems. Color blindness is one such example (e.g., Palmer 1999b). Dichromats—individuals missing one of the three types of cone photoreceptors—cannot discriminate between certain colors that the rest of us experience as very different. Conversely, a minority of women endowed with four types of cone photoreceptors seem to have a richer color experience (Jameson, Highnote, and Wasserman 2001). Similarly, genetic variations in taste receptors influence the sensitivity to bitter tastes (e.g., Des Gachons, Beauchamp, and Breslin 2009).

Variability in subjective experience of visual stimuli has also been recently linked to variability in the cerebral cortex. Schwarzkopf, Song, and Rees (2011) showed that V1 size negatively correlates with the subjective experience of object size, as indicated by the magnitude of two visual illusions. Anomalous functional organization of the cerebral cortex also underlies conditions such as congenital prosopagnosia (Behrmann et al. 2007). Individuals who are unable to tell the difference between two or more faces that look radically different to most of us, will not only score lower on behavioral face recognition tests, but obviously, will also have a very different experience in many everyday situations looking at faces. The examples described here are all concerned with differences in the *intensity* or magnitude of perceptual experience (or inability to detect a stimulus difference, at the extreme low end of the spectrum). Indeed, some progress has been made in quantifying individual difference in the intensity of stimuli (Bartoshuk et al. 2004). However, evidence concerning possible individual differences in the *quality* of experiences (not merely the intensity) has been rather limited.

Synesthesia provides us with one example of qualitatively different experiences. Synesthetes don't only perceive more than the rest of us, but they also differ among themselves on the quality of that additional experience. For example, for AD (a synesthete)—the letter C is yellow, and P is blue, while for CP (another synesthete)—the opposite is true—she perceives the letter C in blue while P is yellow (Sagiv and Robertson 2005). Synesthetes are living examples of a mixed-up spectrum of sorts. Their experience of colored surfaces (e.g., a red pepper) may be similar, but there are certain other sets of stimuli (e.g., black and white graphemes) that induce different color experiences for these individuals.[5] Thus, different colored-grapheme synesthetes have a different correspondence between colors and common objects (which are shared with the rest of the population) and between colors and graphemes (which are not). We know this because (a) they can report how their synesthetic color experience compares with color experiences we are all familiar with, and (b) because we have objective measures corroborating the self-reports. Demonstrations of the perceptual reality of synesthetic colors include, for example, the finding that colored-grapheme synesthetes can perform better than non-synesthetes on some visual search tasks by utilizing their synesthetic colors (Palmeri et al. 2002; Ramachandran and Hubbard 2001a). Such superior performance is difficult to fake, increasing our confidence in the reality of their experience. Furthermore, the advantage certain synesthetes gain in some behavioral tasks involving graphemes (namely texture segregation and crowding experiments), correlates with the degree to which the synesthetic colors engage early visual areas in different synesthetes (Hubbard et al. 2005). This heterogeneity is also present in the variability of the spatial reference frames within which different synesthetes perceive their synesthetic colors, i.e., projected externally in the synesthete's peri-personal space or perceived in the synesthete's mind's eye (Dixon, Smilek, and Merikle 2004; Ward et al. 2007). These differences affect the saliency of synesthetic colors.

In many types of synesthesia the correspondence between trigger for the synesthetic experience (inducer) and the synesthetic experience itself (concurrent) are idiosyncratic to the individual,[6] for example, recall the cases of AD and CP who have opposite colors for the letters C and P. Each of those correspondences provides us with a further

---

[5] At the very least we can say that the *relational structure* of the experiences they report differs, if one is forced to make the argument without any reference to the quality of experience whatsoever (c.f. Dennett 1991, 1999).

[6] Mirror touch synesthesia (Blakemore et al. 2005) presents an exception to this rule. There, the synesthetic experiences are more predictable: An individual *seeing* another individual receiving *tactile* stimulation to their hand, will experience a corresponding tactile experience on their own hand (not in a seemingly random, different body part). However, even mirror-touch synesthetes show a difference in the way they map the right and left sides of the observed body onto their own (Banissy and Ward 2007; Banissy et al. 2009). Some synesthetes consistently experiencing a specular mapping (left mapped to right—resembling a mirror reflection) while others map anatomically (the left is mapped to the left) as if adopting the other person's perspective or reference frame.

demonstration of qualitatively different subjective experiences when comparing two synesthetes with the same type of synesthesia, be it colored graphemes, lexical-gustatory synesthesia (i.e., words trigger tastes; Jones et al. 2011; Ward and Simner 2003), colored touch (Ludwig and Simner, 2013), colored music (e.g., Ward, Huckstep, and Tsakanikos 2006), or the visualization of spatial patterns induced by letters (Jonas et al. 2011), numbers (e.g., Sagiv et al, 2006; Tang, Ward, and Butterworth, 2009), or time units (Brang et al. 2011; Jarick et al. 2011; Smilek et al. 2007). Hence even among synesthetes there are individual differences. Indeed, one thing that synesthesia teaches us about our conscious experience is that we cannot take it for granted that others see the world in the same way. Such individual differences have implications for philosophical frameworks for understanding consciousness. Experience appears to vary independently of the stimulus and associated behavior in synesthesia. This has led some to claim that a purely behavioral functionalist framework may not be sufficient to account for synesthesia (Gray 2002, 2003; c.f. Noë and Hurley 2003). Indeed for a complete understanding we would have to take into consideration, not only a very detailed history of the stimuli to which individual synesthetes have been exposed, but also neurobiological constraints (Sagiv, Ilbeigi, and Ben-Tal 2011). As we fine tune our understanding of the neural basis of conscious perception in general and synesthesia in particular, we may be able to predict with greater accuracy how synesthetes' experiences might be different from those of non-synesthetes.

THE NEURAL CORRELATES OF CONSCIOUSNESS AND SYNESTHESIA

Now that scientists have established that synesthesia is not confabulatory in origin, attention has turned to trying to understand how such experiences arise in some individuals but not in others, and what these experiences have in common with other forms of ordinary and extraordinary forms of perception. One key project concerns the neural basis of synesthesia. In particular, studying the neural correlates of synesthetic experience seems to be a special case of the general quest for the neural correlates of consciousness (NCC)—identifying the minimal sets of neural mechanisms, activation of which is sufficient to give rise to a subjective experience of one sort or another. We will comment on this body of work here. It is not our intention to provide here a comprehensive review of neuroimaging studies of synesthesia (for a review see Rouw, Scholte, and Colizoli 2011, and other dedicated chapters in this volume), but rather to comment on the associated methodological issues, highlight a number of lines of research with implications for understanding consciousness, and identify directions for future research.

From a methodological point of view, the same advice concerning the NCC in general applies to the study of neural correlates of synesthetic experiences in particular (for a review see Frith, Perry, and Lumer 1999; Rees and Frith 2007). First we must be careful to distinguish between brain activations associated with processing of the stimuli, activations associated with the associated behaviors, and the NCC. For example, stimuli may be processed to some degree and affect behavior in the absence of any awareness. Hence it is important to establish both necessity and sufficiency for particular activations to be associated with conscious experience (for a review, see also Kanwisher 2001). Paradigms particularly suited to identifying the NCC require a change in subjective experience while the stimulus remains constant. We must also keep in mind different aspects of candidate NCCs, including, not only the location where activation is observed, but also the time-course and patterns of activity, as well as interactions between different areas. Caution must be applied in establishing causality in the absence of direct evidence (e.g., from brain stimulation or lesion studies).

However, studying the neural correlates of conscious synesthetic experience entails one more unique problem. We must also distinguish between the neural correlates of the *synesthetic experience* and the neural correlates of awareness of the *inducing stimulus*. This is challenging to achieve using within-subject designs since, when the evoking stimulus is unattended, the synesthetic experience is unlikely to arise (Sagiv, Heer, and Robertson 2006). Between-subject designs provide a relatively straightforward means for keeping the stimulus exactly the same, while comparing groups with and without synesthetic experiences. However, caution must also be applied in classifying and grouping synesthetes. Some synesthesia variants now have widely-used accepted labels; these may give us a false sense of confidence that we are dealing with a relatively uniform well-understood sort of experience. Time and again, we have discovered that there could be distinct sub-types within such groups. Researchers would be wise to first interview and listen carefully to what synesthetes have to say before classifying their experiences based on questionnaires that may sometimes contain terms that researchers and participants interpret in different ways (e.g., "the mind's eye"). Finally, researchers should keep in mind that brain activations associated with the type of synesthesia of interest may be "contaminated" by those associated with other variants of synesthesia also present in the same individual. Indeed, it is not uncommon for synesthetes to have multiple variants (e.g., Simner et al. 2006).

One common finding is that synesthetic experiences are associated with activations in sensory cortices thought to be necessary for processing and awareness of the stimuli normally associated with such experiences. For example, synesthetic taste experiences activate, among other areas, the primary gustatory cortex (Jones et al. 2011) located in the insula (Small 2010). Reassuringly, such activity is also observed during gustatory hallucination (Henkin, Levy, and Lin 2000). Similarly, synesthetic color is associated with the activations of V4/V8 (e.g., Nunn et al. 2002)—the brain's color center (Zeki and Bartels 1999). This may seem like a straightforward finding but in fact it carries significance for understanding the idea of "essential nodes" supporting conscious experience—areas that are necessary for such experiences (and may or may not have other functions). For example, we have long suspected that V4 is necessary for color vision (e.g., Zeki 1990), but in order to demonstrate it is necessary for color consciousness, we will need to show that there could be no color experience without V4. If we could find an example of color experience without V4 activation, this could be potential evidence against necessity. Evidence from patients with Charles Bonnet syndrome suggests that they too show V4 activation while hallucinating colors (ffytche et al. 1998). Studies of synesthetic color experience show a similar pattern of V4 activation (Hubbard et al. 2005; Nunn et al. 2002), providing further converging evidence to support the idea that V4 is indeed necessary for supporting the subjective experience of seeing color.

However, the picture is more complicated than this. Not all synesthesia studies have replicated this finding. Rouw et al. (2011) attribute this to lack of power in some cases (Aleman et al. 2001; Paulesu et al. 1995) or to the different experimental paradigm and analyses used by others (Weiss, Zilles, and Fink 2005; Rich et al. 2006). These inconsistencies may also be due to phenomenological heterogeneity and possible clustering of different subtypes of synesthetes (see our discussion of individual differences) that may have led to averaging out of some effects (Dixon and Smilek 2005). In any case, this merits further investigation and may lead to new insights into individual differences in synesthesia and functional organization of the sensory cortex in synesthetes.[7]

Is synesthetic color experience associated with additional activations outside the primary sensory cortices? Involvement of posterior parietal regions is a relatively consistent finding in the neuroimaging literature of colored-grapheme synesthesia (Rouw, Scholte, and Colizoli 2011). Authors of these studies propose that such activations reflect binding and attentional processes. This is consistent with behavioral studies showing that attention to the evoking stimulus is indeed required for awareness and binding of the synesthetic colors associated with graphemes. Indeed Sagiv, Heer, and Robertson (2006) predicted that this would be necessary for synesthesia to arise. However, using TMS to the parietal lobule, Esterman et al. (2006) were only able to reduce the magnitude of the synesthetic Stroop effect (where synesthetes struggle to process graphemes presented in colors that conflict with their synesthesia) but not to knock out synesthetic color experience altogether. Further research will be necessary in order to determine whether parietal involvement is essential for the experience of a synesthetic color at all, or at least for the experience of the synesthetic color as bound to the surface of the inducing stimulus (see also, Robertson 2003; Treisman 2005).

Does the experience of synesthesia depend on structural anatomical brain features present in synesthetes but not in non-synesthetes? Let us turn our attention next to brain connectivity. For more than a century, scientists have suspected that synesthesia is the consequence of a neural short circuit—that somehow parts of the brain were communicating in an atypical way (Marks 1975). Both Pedrono (1882) and de Rochas (1885) suggested a form of cross-activation in sensory brain areas. The idea has been

---

[7] Note that there is an implicit assumption in most discussions of the neural basis of synesthesia that, apart from the linkage between inducer and concurrent experience, the functional organization of the cerebral cortex is otherwise very similar. While we find this parsimonious and quite likely, it is worth noting that it is possible that the same factors that have led to the development of synesthesia have also resulted in slight differences in the functional organization (e.g., greater involvement of areas normally supporting imagery in perception of external stimuli).

revived and elaborated in the modern synesthesia literature (e.g. Hubbard, Brang, and Ramachandran 2011; Ramachandran and Hubbard 2001b). In 2007, Rouw and Scholte provided the first direct observation of localized cortical hyperconnectivity in developmental synesthetes using diffusion tensor imaging (DTI) to image white matter. However, Hänggi, Wotruba, and Jäncke (2011) argue that connectivity may be globally-altered.[8] Although substantial progress has been made in mapping the functions of different cortical areas in the past two decades, the effects of various patterns of cortical connectivity on cognition, brain function, and consciousness are not as well understood (but see, e.g., Hasenkamp and Barsalou 2012). Synesthesia provides us with an opportunity to examine this issue from a different angle, especially given the growing interest in connectivity in developmental conditions (e.g., Rippon et al. 2007; Stevens 2009).

Finally, synesthesia has considerable untapped potential to tell us more about the relationship between brain function, plasticity and conscious experience. Some additional areas of particular interest include, for example, plasticity and rehabilitation after brain damage (e.g., Ro et al. 2007) and acquiring new experience via sensory substitution devices, e.g., providing input from electronic visual sensors via an array of tactile stimulators or complex auditory signal instead, (e.g., Kupers et al. 2006; Proulx 2010; Ward and Wright, in press). This is sometimes described as a synthetic form of synesthesia.

REPRESENTATION AND CONSTRUCTION OF THE PERCEIVED WORLD AND THE SOCIAL WORLD

Information coming from different sensory modalities is combined in order to make sense of the world around us. However, this process often goes beyond sensory integration; quite often processing in one sensory channel can influence the processing in another. For example, in the cinema, we perceive the sound of actors' voices as coming from the actors' lips on the screen even though the loudspeakers may be elsewhere in the room (i.e., visual input can influence sound localization; for a review, see Macaluso and Driver 2005). More puzzling is the observation that sensory interactions could happen when only one sensory modality is stimulated—as is the case in synesthesia.[9] Indeed, synesthesia exemplifies well

---

[8] Note, however, that while a certain degree of (anatomical) hyperconnectivity between sensory areas may be sufficient to enable individuals to experience synesthesia, it is probably not necessary. Cohen Kadosh et al. (2009) have been able to induce synesthesia using post-hypnotic suggestion within a time-course that is simply too short to allow any new axons to grow. It is an open question whether the procedure has increased functional connectivity, or facilitated the experience of synesthetic color via an entirely different route. Synesthesia can also be induced by fast-acting hallucinogenic drugs (Hartman and Hollister 1963) or anesthetics (Gregory 1988, 203).

[9] It should be pointed out that this is not unique to synesthesia. Behavioral as well as neuroimaging studies have demonstrated this in the general population. For example, Conrad (1964) showed that in a letter recall task, participants' errors and confusions reflected the letters' acoustic similarities, even

the conclusions that we construct our perceived world, that our representations of the perceived world are not mere copies of the external world, and that the visual system does not operate like a simple camera. In fact, we could go as far as to say that perception is a fantasy that happens to coincide with reality much of our waking time (Frith 2007). In other words, perception is an inferential process. We make inferences about what is out there in the world based on the best-available input and prior experience, but these inferences can sometimes be wrong, resulting in perceptual illusions (Gregory 1980).

It seems that perception in synesthetes is perhaps even less constrained by the physical world. Note, however, that because synesthetic correspondences are usually consistent over time, synesthetes can utilize these additional percepts in order to make sense of the world around them (Sagiv, Ilbeigi, and Ben-Tal 2011). For example, when trying to identify the voice of a speaker, they could be aided by the visual impression that it evokes, in additional to the auditory experience of the voice itself. Like the rest of us, synesthetes explore the world with their senses; however, their perceptual experiences seem to be richer. There may be other ways in which perception and mental imagery vary in the general population and it is important to keep in mind that we may not all construct the perceived world in a similar manner.

Studying synesthesia may also yield insights into the construction of our social reality. In order to navigate in this social world—to understand others and predict their behavior—we must infer their mental states—their thoughts, feelings, intentions (e.g., Frith and Frith 2007), i.e., we must engage in "mentalizing." Amin et al. (2011) recently proposed that grapheme personification (thinking about letters and numbers as if they had gender, personality, and even mental states), may represent a case of benign hypermentalizing, and tentatively suggested that this may be a form of "social synesthesia." Whether one accepts this as a type of synesthesia in its own right (Simner and Holenstein 2007) or not, is less important than the interesting opportunity to look at social cognition and second-person approaches to understanding consciousness from a new angle. It raises fascinating questions about the role of the self in understanding others, not only by mirroring, but also via self-projection (for a discussion, see Sobczak-Edmans and Sagiv, Chapter 12, this volume).

Additionally, synesthesia can also raise interesting questions concerning agency and thought processes. For example, Dronkers et al. (2004) described a case of "ticker-tape" synesthete, who visualizes every word she hears. These letters and words don't have colors, but they are printed in a very particular font in front of her, like subtitles. Intriguingly, she also visualizes her own thoughts in a similar manner and describes the experience of reading her own thoughts as if she was a passive observer. She only knows what her thoughts are, after reading them. Observations of such benign, yet anomalous

---

though those letters were visually-presented. Calvert et al. (1997) showed that silent lip reading—a purely visual stimulus—activates primary auditory areas. Furthermore, Blakemore et al. (2005) found that some of the somatosensory activations found in synesthetes when they saw someone else being touched, are also present in the non-synesthete control group although they did not report any tactile experiences. Nevertheless, in synesthesia such cross-modal interactions are common.

forms of self-knowledge are rare. Indeed pathological failure to recognize one's own thoughts provided in a written format are even rarer (ffytche, Lappin, and Philpot 2004 describe a case of visual command hallucinations in a patient with pure alexia). Both cases, however, offer us an opportunity to re-examine the problems of sense of subjectivity and authorship of our own thoughts (Frith and Gallagher 2002)

CONCLUSION AND FUTURE DIRECTIONS

We reviewed here the case for looking at synesthesia as a model problem for the scientific study of consciousness. We have described some of the areas in which synesthesia could inform our understanding of consciousness, for example, looking for the latter's neural correlates. There are two areas in which synesthesia's contribution could be transformative. One is the appreciation and study of individual differences in conscious experience. The second is the course of development of conscious perception. Contemporary discussions on consciousness largely focus on the common experience of adults and for the most part ignore individual differences and the experiences of infants and children. We must take development seriously if we are to understand consciousness. Understanding the role of learning and the environment in the development of the different cognitive/perceptual styles seen in synesthetes may well inform general as well as remedial educational strategies (Simner and Hubbard, Chapter 4, this volume), as we understand the strengths as well as weaknesses associated with different types of synesthesia (e.g., Ward, Sagiv, and Butterworth 2009). Finally, understanding whether we could cultivate, enhance, or generate synesthesia may offer a way of opening the doors of perception to everyone.

ACKNOWLEDGMENTS

We thank Julia Simner for helpful comments on an earlier version of this manuscript.

REFERENCES

Aleman, André, Geert-Jan M. Rutten, Margriet M. Sitskoorn, Geraud Dautzenberg, and Nick F. Ramsey. 2001. Activation of striate cortex in the absence of visual stimulation: An fMRI study of synesthesia. *Neuroreport* 12 (13):2827–2830.

Amin, Maina, Olufemi Olu-Lafe, Loes E. Claessen, Monika Sobczak-Edmans, Jamie Ward, Adrian L. Williams, and Noam Sagiv. 2011. Understanding grapheme personification: A social synaesthesia? *Journal of Neuropsychology* 5 (2):255–282.

Baars, Bernard J. 2003. Treating consciousness as a variable: The fading taboo. In *Essential Sources in the Scientific Study of Consciousness*, ed. Bernard J. Baars, William P. Banks, and James B. Newman, 1–10. Cambridge, MA: MIT Press.

Banissy, Michael, Roi Cohen Kadosh, Gerrit Maus, Vincent Walsh, and Jamie Ward. 2009. Prevalence, characteristics and a neurocognitive model of mirror-touch synaesthesia. *Experimental Brain Research* 198:261–272.

Banissy, Michael J. and Jamie Ward. 2007. Mirror-touch synesthesia is linked with empathy. *Nature Neuroscience* 10 (7):815–816.

Bartoshuk, Linda M., Valerie B. Duffy, Barry G. Green, Howard J. Hoffman, Chia-Wen Ko, Laurie A. Lucchina, Lawrence E. Marks, Derek J. Snyder, and James M. Weiffenbach. 2004. Valid across-group comparisons with labeled scales: The gLMS versus magnitude matching. *Physiology & Behavior* 82 (1):109–114.

Behrmann, Marlene, Galia Avidan, Fuqiang Gao, and Sandra Black. 2007. Structural imaging reveals anatomical alterations in inferotemporal cortex in congenital prosopagnosia. *Cerebral Cortex* 17 (10):2354–2363.

Blackmore, Susan J. 2010. *Consciousness: An Introduction.* 2nd ed. London: Hodder Education.

Blakemore, Sarah-Jayne, Davina Bristow, Geoffrey Bird, Chris Frith, and Jamie Ward. July 2005. Somatosensory activations during the observation of touch and a case of vision–touch synaesthesia. *Brain* 128 (7):1571–1583.

Block, Ned. 2011. Perceptual consciousness overflows cognitive access. *Trends in Cognitive Sciences* 15 (12):567–575.

Brang, David, Ursina Teuscher, Luke E. Miller, Vilayanur S. Ramachandran, and Seana Coulson. 2011. Handedness and calendar orientations in time-space synaesthesia. *Journal of Neuropsychology* 5 (2):323–332.

Calvert, Gemma A., Edward T. Bullmore, Michael J. Brammer, Ruth Campbell, Steven C. R. Williams, Philip K. McGuire, Peter W. R. Woodruff, Susan D. Iversen, and Anthony S. David. 1997. Activation of auditory cortex during silent lipreading. *Science* 276 (5312):593–596.

Chalmers, David J. 1995. Facing up the problem of consciousness. *Journal of Consciousness Studies* 2 (3):200–219.

Cohen Kadosh, Roi, Limor Gertner, and Devin B. Terhune. 2012. Exceptional abilities in the spatial representation of numbers and time: Insights from synesthesia. *The Neuroscientist: A Review Journal Bringing Neurobiology, Neurology and Psychiatry* 18 (3):208–215.

Cohen Kadosh, Roi, Avishai Henik, Andres Catena, Vincent Walsh, and Luis J. Fuentes. 2009. Induced cross-modal synaesthetic experience without abnormal neuronal connections. *Psychological Science* 20 (2):258–265.

Cohen Kadosh, Roi and Devin B. Terhune. 2012. Redefining synaesthesia? *British Journal of Psychology* 103 (1):20–23.

Conrad, R. 1964. Acoustic confusion in immediate memory. *British Journal of Psychology* 55 (1):75–84.

de Rochas, A. 1885. L'Audition Colorée. *La Nature.* Pt. 1, 306–307, 406–408; Pt. 2, 274–275.

Dennett, Daniel C. 1991. *Consciousness Explained.* London: Penguin.

———. 1999. Intrinsic changes in experience: Swift and enormous. *Behavioral and Brain Sciences* 22 (06):951.

Des Gachons, Catherine Peyrot, Gary K. Beauchamp, and Paul A. S. Breslin. 2009. The genetics of bitterness and pungency detection and its impact on phytonutrient evaluation. *Annals of the New York Academy of Sciences* 1170 (1):140–144.

Dixon, Mike J. and Daniel Smilek. 2005. The importance of individual differences in grapheme-color synesthesia. *Neuron* 45 (6):821–823.

Dixon, Mike, Daniel Smilek, and Philip Merikle. 2004. Not all synaesthetes are created equal: Projector versus associator synaesthetes. *Cognitive, Affective, & Behavioral Neuroscience* 4(3):335–343.

Dronkers, Nina F., Rachel Edelson, Jenny Ogar, David Wilkins, and Joseph T. Elder. 2004. Letteral invision: A speech-to-text form of synesthesia. Paper presented at the 4th American Synesthesia Association Meeting, University of California, Berkeley, USA, 5–7 November.

Eagleman, David M. 2012. Synaesthesia in its protean guises. *British Journal of Psychology* 103 (1):16–19.

Esterman, Michael, Timothy Verstynen, Richard B. Ivry, and Lynn C. Robertson. 2006. Coming unbound: Disrupting automatic integration of synesthetic color and graphemes by transcranial magnetic stimulation of the right parietal lobe. *Journal of Cognitive Neuroscience* 18 (9):1570–1576.

ffytche, Dominic H., Robert J. Howard, Michael J. Brammer, Anthony David, Peter Woodruff, and Steven Williams. 1998. The anatomy of conscious vision: An fMRI study of visual hallucinations. *Nature Neuroscience* 1 (8):738–742.

ffytche, Dominic H., Julia M. Lappin, and Michael Philpot. 2004. Visual command hallucinations in a patient with pure alexia. *Journal of Neurology, Neurosurgery & Psychiatry* 75 (1):80–86.

Frith, Chris D. 2007. *Making Up the Mind: How the Brain Creates our Mental World.* Oxford: Blackwell.

Frith, Chris D. and Uta Frith. 2007. Social cognition in humans. *Current Biology* 17 (16):R724–32.

Frith, Christoper, and Shaun Gallagher. 2002. Models of the pathological mind. *Journal of Consciousness Studies* 9:57-80.

Frith, Chris, Richard Perry, and Erik Lumer. 1999. The neural correlates of conscious experience: An experimental framework. *Trends in Cognitive Sciences* 3 (3):105–114.

Gray, Jeffrey. 2003. How are qualia coupled to functions? *Trends in Cognitive Sciences* 7 (5):192–194.

Gray, Jeffrey A., Susan Chopping, Julia Nunn, David Parslow, Lloyd Gregory, Steve Williams, Michael J. Brammer, and Simon Baron-Cohen. 2002. Implications of synaesthesia for functionalism: Theory and experiments. *Journal of Consciousness Studies* 9 (12):5–31.

Gregory, Richard L. 1980. Perceptions as hypotheses. *Philosophical Transactions of the Royal Society of London B: Biological Sciences* 290 (1038):181–197.

——. 1988. *Odd Perceptions.* New York: Routledge.

Hänggi, Jürgen, Diana Wotruba, and Lutz Jäncke. 2011. Globally altered structural brain network topology in grapheme-color synesthesia. *The Journal of Neuroscience* 31 (15):5816–5828.

Hartman, Alan M. and Leo E. Hollister. 1963. Effect of mescaline, lysergic acid diethylamide and psilocybin on color perception. *Psychopharmacologia* 4:441–451.

Hasenkamp, Wendy and Lawrence W. Barsalou. 2012. Effects of meditation experience on functional connectivity of distributed brain networks. *Frontiers in Human Neuroscience* 6:38.

Henkin, Robert I., Lucien M. Levy, and Chin S. Lin. 2000. Taste and smell phantoms revealed by brain functional MRI (fMRI). *Journal of Computer Assisted Tomography* 24 (1):106–123.

Hubbard, Edward M., A. Cyrus Arman, Vilayanur S. Ramachandran, and Geoffrey M. Boynton. 2005. Individual differences among grapheme-color synesthetes: brain-behavior correlations. *Neuron* 45 (6):975–985.

Hubbard, Edward M., David Brang, and Vilayanur S. Ramachandran. 2011. The cross-activation theory at 10. *Journal of Neuropsychology* 5 (2):152–177.

Jameson, Kimberly A., Susan M. Highnote, and Linda M. Wasserman. 2001. Richer color experience in observers with multiple photopigment opsin genes. *Psychonomic Bulletin & Review* 8 (2):244–261.

Jarick, Michelle, Candice Jensen, Michael J. Dixon, and Daniel Smilek. 2011. The automaticity of vantage point shifts within a synaesthetes? Spatial calendar. *Journal of Neuropsychology* 5 (2):333–352.

Jones, Catherine L., Marcus A. Gray, Ludovico Minati, Julia Simner, Hugo D. Critchley, and Jamie Ward. 2011. The neural basis of illusory gustatory sensations: Two rare cases of lexical-gustatory synaesthesia. *Journal of Neuropsychology* 5 (2):243–254.

Jonas, Clare N., Alisdair J. G. Taylor, Sam Hutton, Peter H. Weiss, and Jamie Ward. 2011. Visuo-spatial representations of the alphabet in synaesthetes and non-synaesthetes. *Journal of Neuropsychology* 5 (2):302–322.

Kanwisher, Nancy. 2001. Neural events and perceptual awareness. *Cognition* 79 (1–2):89–113.

Koch, Christof and Naotsugu Tsuchiya. 2007. Attention and consciousness: Two distinct brain processes. *Trends in Cognitive Sciences* 11 (1):16–22.

Kuhn, Gustav, Alym A. Amlani, and Ronald A. Rensink. 2008. Towards a science of magic. *Trends in Cognitive Sciences* 12 (9):349–354.

Kupers, Ron, Arnaud Fumal, Alain Maertens de Noordhout, Albert Gjedde, Jean Schoenen, and Maurice Ptito. 2006. Transcranial magnetic stimulation of the visual cortex induces somatotopically organized qualia in blind subjects. *Proceedings of the National Academy of Sciences of the United States of America* 103 (35):13256–13260.

Lavie, Nilli. 2007. Attention and consciousness. In *The Blackwell Companion to Consciousness*, ed. Max Velmans and Susan Schneider, 485–503. Malden, MA, USA: Blackwell Publishing.

Locke, John. 1979. *An Essay Concerning Human Understanding*. Oxford: Clarendon Press. (Originally published 1690.)

Ludwig, Vera U. and Julia Simner. 2013. What colour does that feel? Tactile–visual mapping and the development of cross-modality. *Cortex* 49: 1089–1099.

Macaluso, Emiliano and Jon Driver. 2005. Multisensory spatial interactions: A Window onto functional integration in the human brain. *Trends in Neurosciences* 28 (5):264–271.

Marks, Lawrence E. 1975. On colored-hearing synesthesia: Cross-modal translations of sensory dimensions. *Psychological Bulletin* 82 (3):303–331.

Noë, Alva. 2004. *Action in Perception. Representation and Mind*. Cambridge, MA: MIT Press.

Noë, Alva, and Susan Hurley. 2003. The deferential brain in action: Response to Jeffrey Gray. *Trends in Cognitive Sciences* 7 (5):195–196.

Novich, Scott, Sherry Cheng, and David M. Eagleman. 2011. Is synaesthesia one condition or many? A large-scale analysis reveals subgroups. *Journal of Neuropsychology* 5 (2):353–371.

Nunn, Julia A., Lloyd J. Gregory, Michael J. Brammer, Steven C. Williams, David M. Parslow, Michael J. Morgan, Robin G. Morris, Edward T. Bullmore, Simon Baron-Cohen, and Jeffrey A. Gray. 2002. Functional magnetic resonance imaging of synesthesia: Activation of V4/V8 by spoken words. *Nature Neuroscience* 5 (4):371–375.

Palmer, Stephen E. 1999a. Color, consciousness, and the isomorphism constraint. *The Behavioral and Brain Sciences* 22 (6):923–43.

——. 1999b. *Vision Science: Photons to Phenomenology*. Cambridge, MA: MIT Press.

Palmeri, Thomas J., Randolph Blake, René Marois, Marci A. Flanery, and William Whetsell. 2002. The perceptual reality of synesthetic colors. *Proceedings of the National Academy of Sciences of the United States of America* 99 (6):4127–4131.

Paulesu, Eraldo, John Harrison, Simon Baron-Cohen, John D. Watson, Laura Goldstein, Jon Heather, Richard S. J. Frackowiak, and Chris D. Frith. 1995. The physiology of coloured hearing A PET activation study of colour-word synaesthesia. *Brain* 118 (3):661–676.

Pedrono. 1882. De l'Audition Colorée. *Annales d'Oculistique* 88:224–237.

Proulx, Michael J. 2010. Synthetic synaesthesia and sensory substitution. *Consciousness and Cognition* 19 (1):501–503.

Ramachandran, Vilayanur S. and Edward M. Hubbard. 2001a. Psychophysical investigations into the neural basis of synaesthesia. *Proceedings.Biological Sciences/the Royal Society* 268 (1470):979–983.

———. 2001b. Synaesthesia—a window into perception, thought and language. *Journal of Consciousness Studies* 8:3–34.

Rees, Geraint and Chris Frith. 2007. Methodologies for identifying the neural correlates of consciousness. In *The Blackwell Companion to Consciousness*, ed. Max Velmans and Susan Schneider, 553–566. Malden, MA: Blackwell Publishing.

Revonsuo, Antti. 2010. *Consciousness: The Science of Subjectivity*. Hove: Psychology Press.

Rich, Anina N., Mark A. Williams, Aina Puce, Ari Syngeniotis, Matthew A. Howard, Francis McGlone, and Jason B. Mattingley. 2006. Neural correlates of imagined and synaesthetic colours. *Neuropsychologia* 44 (14):2918–2925.

Rippon, Gina, Jon Brock, Caroline Brown, and Jill Boucher. 2007. Disordered connectivity in the autistic brain: Challenges for the 'new psychophysiology'. *International Journal of Psychophysiology* 63 (2):164–172.

Ro, Tony, Alessandro Farnè, Ruth M. Johnson, Van Wedeen, Zili Chu, Zhiyue J. Wang, Jill V. Hunter, and Michael S. Beauchamp. 2007. Feeling sounds after a thalamic lesion. *Annals of Neurology* 62 (5):433–441.

Robertson, Lynn C. 2003. Colour my i's blue. *Nature* 410:533–534.

Rouw, Romke, H. Steven Scholte, and Olympia Colizoli. 2011. Brain areas involved in synaesthesia: A review. *Journal of Neuropsychology* 5 (2):214–242.

Sagiv, Noam, Jeffrey Heer, and Lynn Robertson. 2006. Does binding of synesthetic color to the evoking grapheme require attention? *Cortex* 42 (2):232–242.

Sagiv, Noam, Alireza Ilbeigi, and Oded Ben-Tal. 2011. Reflections on synesthesia, perception, and cognition. *Intellectica* 55 (1):81–94.

Sagiv, Noam and Lynn C. Robertson. 2005. Synesthesia and the binding problem. In *Synesthesia: Perspectives from Cognitive Neuroscience*, ed. Lynn C. Robertson and Noam Sagiv, 90–107. New York: Oxford University Press.

Sagiv, Noam, Julia Simner, James Collins, Brian Butterworth, and Jamie Ward. 2006. What is the relationship between synaesthesia and visuo-spatial number forms? *Cognition* 101 (1):114–128.

Sagiv, Noam and Jamie Ward. 2006. Crossmodal interactions: Lessons from synesthesia. *Progress in Brain Research* 155:259–271.

Schwarzkopf, D. Samuel, Chen Song, and Geraint Rees. 2011. The surface area of human v1 predicts the subjective experience of object size. *Nature Neuroscience* 14 (1):28–30.

Searle, John R. 2000. Consciousness. *Annual Review of Neuroscience* 23:557–578.

———. 1997. *The Mystery of Consciousness*. New York: New York Review of Books.

Simner, Julia. 2012. Defining synaesthesia: A response to two excellent commentaries. *British Journal of Psychology* 103 (1):24–27.

Simner, Julia and Emma Holenstein. 2007. Ordinal linguistic personification as a variant of synesthesia. *Journal of Cognitive Neuroscience* 19 (4):694–703.

Simner, Julia and Edward M. Hubbard. 2013. Synesthesia in school-aged children. In *The Oxford Handbook of Synesthesia,* ed. Julia Simner and Edward M. Hubbard, 64–82. Oxford: Oxford University Press.

Simner, Julia, Catherine Mulvenna, Noam Sagiv, Elias Tsakanikos, Sarah A. Witherby, Christine Fraser, Kirsten Scott, and Jamie Ward. 2006. Synaesthesia: The prevalence of atypical cross-modal experiences. *Perception* 35 (8):1024–1033.

Small, Dana M. 2010. Taste representation in the human insula. *Brain Structure and Function* 214 (5):551–561.

Smilek, Daniel, Alicia Callejas, Mike J. Dixon, and Philip M. Merikle. 2007. Ovals of time: Time-space associations in synaesthesia. *Consciousness and Cognition* 16 (2):507–519.

Sobczak-Edmans, Monika and Noam Sagiv. 2013. Synesthetic personification: The social world of graphemes. In *The Oxford Handbook of Synesthesia,* ed. Julia Simner and Edward M. Hubbard, 222–238. Oxford: Oxford University Press.

Stevens, Michael C. 2009. The developmental cognitive neuroscience of functional connectivity. *Brain and Cognition* 70 (1):1–12.

Tang, Joey, Jamie Ward, and Brian Butterworth. 2008. Number forms in the brain. *Journal of Cognitive Neuroscience* 20 (9):1547–1556.

Tononi, Giulio. 2007. The information integration theory of consciousness. In *The Blackwell Companion to Consciousness*, ed. Max Velmans and Susan Schneider, 287–299. Malden, MA: Blackwell Publishing.

Treisman, Anne. 2005. Synesthesia: Implications for attention, binding, and consciousness—a commentary. In *Synesthesia: Perspectives from Cognitive Neuroscience*, ed. Lynn C. Robertson and Noam Sagiv, 239–254. New York: Oxford University Press.

Ward, Jamie, Brett Huckstep, and Elias Tsakanikos. 2006. Sound-colour synaesthesia: To what extent does it use cross-modal mechanisms common to us all? *Cortex* 42 (2):264–280.

Ward, Jamie, Ryan Li, Shireen Salih, and Noam Sagiv. 2007. Varieties of grapheme-colour synaesthesia: A new theory of phenomenological and behavioural differences. *Consciousness and Cognition* 16 (4):913–931.

Ward, Jamie and Noam Sagiv. 2007. Synaesthesia for finger counting and dice patterns: A case of higher synaesthesia? *Neurocase* 13 (2):86–93.

Ward, Jamie, Noam Sagiv, and Brian Butterworth. 2009. The impact of visuo-spatial number forms on simple arithmetic. *Cortex* 45 (10):1261–1265.

Ward, Jamie and Julia Simner. 2003. Lexical-gustatory synaesthesia: linguistic and conceptual factors. *Cognition* 89 (3):237–261.

Ward, Jamie and Thomas Wright. In press. Sensory substitution as an artificially acquired synaesthesia. *Neuroscience and Biobehavioral Reviews*.

Weiss, Peter H., Karl Zilles, and Gereon R. Fink. 2005. When visual perception causes feeling: Enhanced cross-modal processing in grapheme-color synesthesia. *NeuroImage* 28 (4):859–868.

Zeki, Semir. 1990. A century of cerebral achromatopsia. *Brain* 113 (6):1721–1777.

Zeki, Semir, and Andreas Bartels. 1999. Toward a theory of visual consciousness. *Consciousness and Cognition* 8 (2):225–259.

Zeman, Adam. 2002. *Consciousness: A User's Guide*. New Haven, CT: Yale University Press.

———. 2005. What in the world is consciousness? *Progress in Brain Research* 150:1–10.

....

CHAPTER 46

WHAT EXACTLY IS A SENSE?

....

BRIAN L. KEELEY

INTRODUCTION

....

Our most basic understanding of the sensory modalities derives from an almost unreflective, casual introspection of our perceptual engagement with the world: our perceptions of the world seem to come in different categories or classes. These categories—modalities—of perceptual experience appear to us as falling into largely distinct groupings and, further, are associated with different bodily organs. For example, when perceptually interacting with a rose, some of our experiences are of a red appearance, a subtle flowery odor, and a soft, velvety texture. Further, these experiences are presented to us in association with our eyes, nose, and fingertips, respectively; if I close my eyes, the experience of the redness of the rose changes, but not the velvety texture. Manipulating the petals of the rose in my fingers is accompanied by more noticeable changes in the appearance of its texture than in its odor. In addition, some take it as given that we find natural continuities and discontinuities among these perceptual experiences that coincide with their groupings with respect to the organs, viz. that the redness of the rose petals and the greenness of the rose stem are closely related to one another (both are colors) in a way that neither shares with the smell of the rose.

This extremely basic starting point begins to generate some of the deeper philosophical questions about the sensory modalities: to what degree are qualities experienced genuinely different from one another; just how different is our experience of the felt texture of a rose from its smell? In virtue of what is our sensory experience divided into separate modalities? (These more philosophical questions are different from more empirical questions: e.g., to what degree are different sensory experiences related to the activity of specific sensory organs? That is, the former asks a question about the nature of the experiences themselves whereas the latter asks about the genesis of those experiences.) In exploring questions regarding the nature of the sensory modalities, we are asking questions about the nature of quality, in that differences between the senses seem to be intimately tied to fundamental qualitative properties: color, pitch, size, texture, etc.

These descriptions are those of a neurotypical; that is, it describes the perceptual world met with by somebody with a relatively species-typical set of sensory mechanisms. However, there are those whose nervous systems are not organized in the normal fashion. One class of these individuals experience synesthesia, the topic of this volume.

I feel I should not continue without confessing that I'm no expert on the phenomenon of synesthesia. As far as I can tell, my perceptual experiences fall within the species-typical normal range. I have had the pleasure of meeting and talking to people who experience synesthesia and I have read my share of work about it; scientific (e.g., Baron-Cohen and Harrison 1997; Cytowic 1993, 2002), as well as personal memoir (e.g., Nabokov 1966; Prince-Hughes 2002). That said, I recognize that the phenomenon defies intuitions. One should be careful when applying common sense to uncommon situations.

My interest in synesthesia derives from an interest in sensory differentiation—an interest in the question of how we should count the number of senses possessed by a given organism. In the case of humans, the time-honored Western answer, which is traditionally attributed to Aristotle, is that we have five senses. In a series of papers over the last decade (2002, 2009a, 2009b), I've been exploring this question, primarily arguing for an approach to the question derived from the neurosciences.

While Aristotle's answer that we have five senses is taken by many to be common-sense—so much so that it is commonplace to speak of any additional proposed sensory ability as a "sixth sense" (Howes 2009)—there are reasons to think that Aristotle undercounted. For one, even Aristotle had difficulties taxonomizing the sense of touch. On the one hand, it involves a single organ (the skin), which makes it seem like a single sense. On the other hand, we sense many different-seeming things through touch: pressure and texture, temperature, pain. This suggests that touch should be Balkanized into separate senses.[1]

Another reason to think Aristotle undercounted are a number of additional candidate senses with varying degrees of evidence in their favor. Some historians of science argue that a sense of balance and a sense of the position of our own body (proprioception) were well-established by scientists during the nineteenth century (Wade 2003). These new senses fall under the rubric Charles Sherrington proposed at the end of that century: *interoception*, as opposed to *exteroception*; the latter of which captures Aristotle's five. With interoception comes the possibility of a sense of thirst and hunger and other bodily senses. In my 2002 paper, I discuss the possibility of a human pheromone sense that parallels similar senses in nonhuman animals (although see Keeley 2009b; Noë 2004, for further discussion). However, when we explore the possibility of such senses in addition to Aristotle's five, we find disagreement, which in turn, I believe points to the fact that we do not have a consensus on what we mean when we talk of the senses. But, we'll return to that issue later.

When giving talks on the topic of the senses and what differentiates them, easily the most common question I get during the Q&A session is: "So, what about synesthesia?" Often, the question is not any deeper than that, just that synesthesia "mixes up the

---

[1] See Ratcliffe (2012) and Fulkerson (2011) for some recent discussion of the unity of touch.

senses," so it ought to have some connection to the question of counting the senses. My stock answer has always been that although it might be surprising to hear this, synesthesia does not have much to tell us about differentiating the senses, because before we can talk about how the senses are "mixed" we need a prior account of what the senses are such that they are mixed.

However, that answer is facile. Reflecting on the relationship between synesthesia and the senses *does* lead in some interesting directions. Also, it is important to note that synesthesia can be interesting here in two different ways: it can tell us something interesting (or not) (1) about the senses themselves or (2) about our different theories or explanations of the senses. Here, I will be targeting the second notion more than the first. In this chapter, I will review a number of different proposals concerning the nature of the senses and what distinguishes them from one another. The interaction between findings on synesthesia and these different philosophical accounts reveals some of the deeper differences between these different theories of the senses. That is important because it underlines that these differences are real and not merely semantic or trivial. Perhaps surprisingly, it looks like on all of these different accounts of the senses, the story at the end of the day is the same; the phenomenon of synesthesia does not show that one of them is false, nor do the different accounts point to a difference in the number of senses when confronted with the fact of synesthesia. (These negative conclusions are the source of my original, facile, response to earlier questions.) However, *how* the different accounts come to these conclusions are significantly different. Further, the confidence we should have in those conclusions differs, especially in light of how much we still have to learn about synesthesia. Finally, I believe that synesthetic theories might find some useful ideas from this process as well; each account of the senses prioritizes different aspects of the perceptual process, and as such, they call into sharper focus different aspects of synesthesia.[2]

DIFFERENT ACCOUNTS OF THE SENSES

So, what exactly is a sense? The short answer to that question is that we don't know or, more to the point, we don't agree. There is no broad-based, contemporary consensus on

---

[2] One related and highly interesting topic that I just do not have the space here to discuss is the growing literature on multisensory integration, that is, how stimulation—even in neurotypical individuals—in one sensory modality affects one's experience in another. The most famous example of this is the McGurk effect, in which the visual cue one gets from watching the lips of another can cause one to experience a different auditory phoneme than the one uttered. That is, hearing one phoneme, while watching the lips of a face articulate a second phoneme can cause you to experience a *third* phoneme, as opposed to the presented auditory stimulus. Multisensory effects such as the McGurk effect would seem to bear some relation to synesthesia, although it is also clearly different. Please look at the contributions to this volume on this topic by Lawrence E. Marks (Chapter 38); Cesare Parise and Charles Spence (Chapter 39); and Argiro Vatakis (Chapter 40).

the defining features of the senses, although there are a number of competing accounts, all with current adherents. That said, there may be some degree of agreement within particular traditions as to what a sense is but—across disciplines—the situation is far less settled.

The senses as given in common sense

One response to the question "What are the senses?" is to answer that we already know quite a lot about the senses, as well as how many there are. Setting aside the more or less controversial candidate senses discussed briefly earlier, we might decide to agree with Aristotle's simple, initial discussion. The senses are a key category in our common-sense psychology; what philosophers refer to as our "folk psychology." We have, on this account, exactly five senses—vision, audition, olfaction, gustation, and touch. Each of these (in the normal, non-synesthetic case) has its own characteristic experiential "feel" and is associated with an obvious kind of organ—eyes, ears, nose, tongue, and skin, respectively.

At this point, there are two different ways this approach can go, depending on what one sees as the relationship between this commonsense view of the senses and our scientific understanding of same. These two directions are embodied in two different answers one can give to the question whether the commonsense account of the senses should be understood as offering a scientific (or perhaps a "proto-scientific") account of our capacity for perception, as implied by the reference to *folk psychology*, mentioned earlier. One response is that such a commonsense account is not intended nor should it be understood in such scientific terms. On this account, talk of the senses is not being offered as an "explanation." So, philosopher Matthew Nudds—the most prominent current proponent of such an approach—when addressing challenges to the common sense idea that there are five (and only five) senses says,

> [In response] we can either say that the distinction, as we actually make it, between five senses is mistaken and embrace a kind of eliminativism or revisionism about the senses (we might say that there are no senses as common-sense understands them, or that there are many more than common-sense recognizes); or we can reject the claim that the senses are sense-organs. The eliminativist or revisionist view is only plausible if it can be shown that common-sense embodies the kind of proto-scientific understanding of the senses which is *liable* to revision or replacement. I've not come across a good argument that it does. (2004, 34–35, emphasis in original)

What Nudds is proposing here is that the commonsense understanding of the senses is not an explanation of anything (an "explanans," in the language of philosophy of science); rather, it is that which stands in need of an explanation (an "explanandum"). We posit the senses not to explain—scientifically, proto-scientifically or otherwise—something else; what stands in need of explanation is why we commonsensically believe that there are five senses. In essence, Nudds believes we need an explanation why we (and Aristotle) commonly believe that there are five senses at all.

There are a number of difficulties with taking this approach, not the least of which is that it is far from clear just how "common" is this commonsense claim that we have exactly five senses.[3] But we do not really need to get into those problems here, because I feel I can justifiably assume that in the current context of discussing synesthesia (in a scientific handbook) we are discussing the senses in a scientific context.

This brings us to the second response to the question concerning the commonsense view of the senses: that this commonsense understanding represents some kind of basic scientific understanding of the senses—it is indeed a folk *theory*. As such, talk of the senses is part of our everyday means of understanding and predicting the behavior of others.[4] I yell out to a friend walking down the path in front of me and have the reasonable expectation that she will turn around. Why? Well, first, I expect her to respond at all because she should hear somebody call her name and, second, she will turn in the direction of my voice because normal humans, in normal circumstances, can be expected to orient themselves in order to "make visual contact" with somebody hailing them as I am hailing her. But imagine that I call her name and she does not turn around. I might be momentarily puzzled, jog to catch up with her, and then touch her shoulder. Again, I expect her to respond by turning towards me, this time because she feels my hand touch her shoulder. If she pauses to remove the earbuds attached to her portable music player, I have the answer to my earlier puzzlement: she didn't turn around when I called because she didn't hear me call to her; she was listening to music.

There's nothing exceptional about this scenario, but my point is to remind you about the role that positing senses plays in our everyday understanding of the behavior of our fellow humans (and many animals, as well). We understand that people have different senses, that their capacity to sense involves the operation of sensory organs, that they have different experiences associated with those senses. Further, we pay attention to what people sense as a means of understanding why they do what they do and in order to allow us to successfully interact with them.

What of synesthesia? Prima facie, we might see an immediate disconnect between the phenomenon of synesthesia and our folk psychology of perception. After all, synesthesia is fascinating, in large part, exactly because it is so unexpected. It seems reasonable to observe that our folk psychology leads us to expect the presentation of colored lights to

---

[3] In addition to the concerns raised in the previous section, the relatively new field of sensory anthropology has given us some of our first, good data on the question of what the folk of the world commonly think about our senses. Although Nudds reads the results differently, I see this work as undermining the claim that humans universally posit five (or fewer) senses (see Geurts 2002; Howes 1991, 2009; Young 2005).

[4] To be fair, Nudds would agree with this sentence, but he would deny that this practice of everyday understanding is *scientific* or *protoscientific*, if that implies that it is open to revision, as I believe it does imply.

a person to result in her responding by using visual color words to describe her experiences and not to respond by speaking of what those lights taste or sound like.

Cytowic, in the opening of his *The Man Who Tasted Shapes*, recounts his first encounter with a particular synesthete, "Michael," his dinner host one evening:

> I sat nearby while [Michael] whisked the sauce he had made for the roast chicken. "Oh, dear," he said, slurping a spoonful, "there aren't enough points on the chicken."
> "Aren't enough what?" I asked.
> He froze and turned red, betraying a realization that his first impression had been as awkward as that of a debutante falling down the stairs. "Oh, you're going to think I'm crazy," he stammered, slapping the spoon down. "I hope no one else heard," he said, quickly glancing at the guests in the far corner.
> "Why not?" I asked.
> "Sometimes I blurt these things out," he whispered, leaning toward me. "You're a neurologist, maybe it will make sense to you. I know it sounds crazy, but I have this thing, see, where I taste by shape." He looked away. "How can I explain?" he asked himself.
> "Flavors have shape," he started, frowning into the depths of the roasting pan. "I wanted the taste of this chicken to be a pointed shape, but it came out all round." He looked up at me, still blushing. "Well, I mean it's nearly spherical," he emphasized, trying to keep the volume down. "I can't serve this if it doesn't have points." (Cytowic 1993, 3–4)

To help keep them straight, we need different terms for the two kinds of perceptual experiences a synesthete has. I will use the term, "neurotypical sensation" to refer to the non-synesthetic sensations produced by the sense organs in a species-typical manner. I will refer to the atypical additional sensory experiences that a synesthete experiences a "synesthetic sensation."[5] For example, in the case of Michael, we will understand him to experience neurotypical sensations when an object of a particular shape is placed into his hand. His synesthesia manifests itself when he additionally has synesthetic sensations of shapes in response to food placed into his mouth, mixed with neurotypical gustatory sensations.

Thankfully, as Michael hoped, his report did make sense to Cytowic—as a trained neurologist, Cytowic was familiar with synesthesia. However, Michael's trepidation in confessing his perceptual experiences to Cytowic testifies to the typical response he gets. He goes on to explain that people, "think I'm on drugs or that I'm making it up. That's why I never intentionally tell people about my shapes. Only when it slips out" (Cytowic 1993, 4).

Surely, this shows that folk psychology fails in its explanatory project when it comes to synesthetic individuals. The vignette illustrates how synesthesia stands as a counter example to the commonsense way of dividing up the senses. People are surprised that another, otherwise apparently normal, human being can experience flavors as shapes. Flavors belong to one modality; shapes to another. But our being surprised is not the

---

[5] Other contributors to this volume use the term "concurrent" for this distinction. In this terminology, the stimulus triggering the concurrent is known as the "inducer."

same as our folk psychology failing in any robust sense of the term. "Failure" would only be appropriate here if the existence of synesthesia could not be incorporated into our folk psychology at all (or could not be incorporated without significant conceptual overhaul).

I would like to argue that synesthesia does not pose such a challenge. Consider the related case of individuals with diminished sensory capacity. Normal perceptual expectations are violated by a person who is, say, profoundly deaf, but who is a skilled lipreader. If I am unaware of her precise abilities and disabilities, I may form some false expectations and jump to the wrong conclusions about why she behaves as she does, such as if it were her that I hailed from behind in my earlier example. But, once I learn how to interact with her, I can deploy my folk psychology quite easily—I just need to make sure she can see my lips when I speak.

In a similar fashion, I can learn to adjust my folk psychology to interact with a person who has red-green colorblindness. It does not take a large conceptual change to my commonsense understanding of perception to understand that some people perceptually engage with the world in different ways. Synesthesia, therefore, can be slotted into this discussion as just another unusual, but not incomprehensible, way of perceiving the world.[6] Indeed, in some ways, it can be seen as the counterpart of colorblindness: whereas we can understand that a colorblind person will have diminished perceptual experiences of color stimuli relative to a normally-sighted person, we can understand a visual synesthete to have some kind of enhanced experience in response to the same stimuli. (Perhaps they experience a particular sound upon seeing red, say.) As it happens, this interpretation of synesthesia as a kind of complement to colorblindness was one of the earliest scientific views about these two phenomena; John Dalton first described colorblindness in 1798 and the earliest case of synesthesia was described in 1812. For more on this fascinating early scientific history, see Jörg Jewanski's contribution to this volume (Chapter 14). (Jewanski writes concerning one of the early theorists: "For Cornaz (1848), synesthesia was ... the opposite of Daltonism (color-blindness).")

Further, while synesthesia has some unusual features (and we will return to these later), notice that it does not obviously call on us to count the number of senses differently. It does not make sense to talk of synesthetes as having fewer senses than normal. Neither, the phenomenon does not fit the description of an additional sense; synesthesia is not a "sixth sense" (Howes 2009; Wade 2003). As the etymology of the term suggests, it is a merging or mixing of the senses, not in itself a novel one.

Our commonsense understanding of the senses informs our more scientific ones. Indeed, the folk psychological concept is sometimes pulled in very different ways, because it includes a number of different elements. One reason for the lack of agreement about how to think of a sense of balance, or proprioception, or a human pheromone

---

[6] As Richard Gray has noted to me in a comment on a draft of this chapter, it is not obvious that once ordinary people learn the details of synesthesia that they would naturally choose to class it as a form of *perception*. They might think of it more in terms of hallucination or an illusion. See Gray (2001), but also the discussion in Auvray and Deroy (forthcoming).

sense, say, is that such senses agree with the folk notion of a sense in some ways, but fail to agree in others. What's interesting, I think, about synesthesia is how it brings out the often obscured differences between our different understandings of the senses. In the next three sections, I will turn to three different contemporary scientific understandings of the senses that are derived from our commonsense understanding and explore how they address the phenomenon of synesthesia.

The senses as organs

A key component of the commonsense approach to understanding the senses is that talk of a sense requires the identification of an organ. In the case of the classic five senses, each clearly has an associated organ that appears to be necessary for the normal operation of the sense. If your eyes are sufficiently damaged, then you are blind; that is, you lack the sense of vision as we normally understand it. This notion of defining the senses in terms of their organs has a long history. During the Medieval period of Western Europe, a common metaphor for the senses was the gated avenues of a walled city; just as of any traveler you find in a city, one can ask "By which avenue did he enter?"; of any bit of empirical knowledge in the traveler's mind, one can ask "By which sensory organ did it enter?"

Earlier still, in Aristotle's *De Anima* (Aristotle 1931, 424a16–24), he makes the "organ of sense" central to his account, defining it as the thing in which is seated the power to be changed by the quality of a substance. He likens it to the process by which warm wax takes on the shape of a signet ring pressed into it. What's more, he noted that each organ had some degree of specificity in terms of what qualities could be impressed upon it. Only the eyes can receive color. Only the tongue can receive tastes.[7]

Aristotle's account of sense organs is, unsurprisingly, couched in the science of his day. However, much of his basic idea about the sense organs still survives in the general framework of sensory neurophysiology, to which I now turn in an attempt to make more precise the concept of a sense organ. First, a sensory organ has the property of being an end organ; that is, it lies at the outer edge of the nervous system, where the nervous system contacts the world, as it were. The nervous system is a highly interconnected network of cells and the vast majority of neurons are connected to other neurons. A relatively small set of neurons lie at the outer edge of this network. Some of these are effector neurons that project their axons onto muscles or glands; these are means by which the brain has an effect upon the world. Others of these are components of sensory organs; that is, their dendritic processes are connected to tissues that have the property of reacting to the presence, absence or change in some energetic property in the tissue or world.[8]

---

[7] For more on Aristotle's account of the senses, see Johansen (1998), Keeley (2009b), and Sorabji (1971).

[8] One exception to this rule is that some pain receptors take the form of bare dendritic nerve endings embedded in the tissue of the body, such as the skin. Such nociceptors become active if the tissue is cut or torn or otherwise damaged. In a sense, in this case, we can think of the innervated tissue itself as the sense organ. Regardless, the principle that sensory neurons lie at the outer edge of the neural network remains.

This capacity of sensory organs to convert specific types of energy into neural signals is their second defining feature; they contain specific transducers. For example, the retina of the eye has special cells—rods and cones—that have the capacity to react to the presence or absence of photonic energy. In fact, retinal cells have the capacity to respond to several different kinds of stimulation, e.g., mechanical distortion (think of pressing a finger to the lid-covered eyeball) or electrical stimulation. Therefore, part of the story of which modality to associate with a given organ must involve reference to the evolutionary or developmental history of an organism.[9] This connects the biological, sense organ account of the senses with the evolution of sensory systems more generally.

It should not come as a surprise that the kind of account being described here is one that appeals to neurobiology. When identifying and characterizing senses in nonhuman animals, neurobiology places a great deal of emphasis on the ability to discover the sensory organs involved, typically refraining from positing a sense in an organism until the organ can be found.[10]

It is an open question how far inward into the nervous system it is reasonable to extend the boundaries of a sensory organ. To the extent that the lateral geniculate nucleus of the human thalamus or primary visual cortex (V1) receive most of their neural input (ultimately) from the eye, it seems to make as much sense to include them as part of the visual sense organ as the rods, cones, and primary sensory neurons of the retina. Indeed, one might go as far as adding those motor systems that actively participate in the operation of the senses, as argued for by recent proponents of sensorimotor accounts of perception (Noë 2004; Varela, Thompson, and Rosch 1991). Minimally, this would include the neural systems controlling the musculature responsible for moving the eyeballs in their sockets or for squinting and opening the eyes. Although, to take such an account seriously, we would have to include much of the bodily musculature. (Consider the motor systems involved in my earlier example of hailing my friend and what she does to orient her visual system in response to my entreaties.)

Characterizing the senses as organs has only minimal involvement with synesthesia. Synesthetes have the same sensory organs as neurotypicals. They have no organs capable of responding to some unusual or unique type of physical energy. This is part of why it does not seem appropriate to characterize the phenomenon as a kind of sixth sense. They may, however, differ from neurotypicals in terms of how their organs are "wired up" to the rest of the nervous system. For example, part of the explanation for Michael's synesthesia might involve an atypical neural innervation of his somatosensory cortex by neurons ultimately tracing their origins to the taste buds and olfactory epithelium.

---

[9] For more, see Keeley (1999).

[10] For examples of such discoveries of new senses and the important role that organs play in the process, see Keeley (1999) and Wade (2003).

The senses as providers of sensory objects

There is another common way of differentiating the senses. Instead of doing so in terms of the organs, we could choose to pay attention to what the senses reveal to us about the world as sensed. Thanks to our senses, we become aware of a world of colors, sounds, smells and the like.

Aristotle also made use of this in his account of the senses. He calls the many things that we come to know via our senses—colors, odors, shapes—*objects of sense*. He then observes that these objects can be divided naturally into different classes. First, consider that some of these objects can be obtained through the activity of more than one sense. Take shape, for example; we can both see shape with our eyes and feel shape with our hands. These objects, which also include movement, rest, number, and magnitude, Aristotle calls the "common objects" of sense, perhaps because they are held in common between multiple senses.[11]

It is a second class of objects that is of most interest to us here. Aristotle notes that among the objects of sense, there are those that are uniquely and exclusively connected to a single sense. We come to know red and other colors only via the eyes (vision). Aristotle calls these singular properties "proper" (or "special") "objects" of the senses. As Aristotle scholar Richard Sorabji puts it, the proper objects are the things to which the very being of each sense is naturally related (1992, 56). The existence of these proper objects provides a theoretical basis on which to differentiate the senses from one another, in that they provide a principle for the attribution of a sense: if there is some object of knowledge that can only be acquired by the activity of a single organ, then we have grounds for speaking of a specific sense in that case.

This is now known as an intentionalist account within the philosophy of psychology (due to its use of a representational or "aboutness" feature within its framework; a property of mental states Brentano called "intentionality"; Brentano 1874). Vision, then, is understood by reference to the class of uniquely "visual qualities" (e.g., spectral and reflectance properties of light found in the world) to which the sense gives us access.[12]

---

[11] Aristotle's idea of the 'common sense'—the place where our various senses come together—eventually evolved into our modern notion of the introspective center of cognition—the locus of our sense of self, as well as into our current use of the term as meaning a capacity for sound judgment. For a fascinating history of this development, see Heller-Roazen (2009).

[12] Typically, humans are given access to the visual quality space by the operation of our eyes. However, some intentionalists argue that this is merely accidental, and that it is possible to do so by other means. For example, as part of his sensorimotor account of the senses, Alva Noë (2004) argues that we should consider sensory substitution systems, such as Bach-y-Rita's 'Tactile-Visual Sensory Substitution' (TVSS) as a form of vision (Bach-y-Rita 1972; Bach-y-Rita and Kercel 2003). In this system, blind individuals are equipped with a digital video camera attached to a two-dimensional array of vibrating pins placed against the back, allowing them to respond to visual features of the world. Because the TVSS system gives them access to the visual quality space, Noë believes we should say they have vision (or "quasi-vision," at least). For some alternative considerations of Noë's account, see Keeley (2009b).

An intentionalist account can be applied to the case of synesthesia, where it will have much the same outcome as when the same approach is taken to the neurotypical case. This is because the difference between synesthetes and neurotypicals is not due to any difference in the objects of perception. While, in synesthesia, we find atypical conscious responses to proper objects, what causes those responses (and, hence, what those atypical responses are "directed towards") are the typical set of proper objects. That is, in the case of Michael, what his synesthetic sensations are telling him about are the gustatory properties of the world; part of his conscious experience of flavors comes to him in the form of shape sensations. Nonetheless, the spikiness or roundness of shapes he feels are about the flavor of the chicken he is sampling in his mouth.

Just as Michael uses these shape experiences to assess flavors, the same can be said of other synesthetic pairings. For example, consider somebody with grapheme-color synesthesia. This is somebody who experiences consistent synesthetic color sensations in response to letters and number. Even when those characters are printed in a black ink, synesthetes might experience "E" as blue, say, and "3" as green. This, in turn, might give the synesthete an ability to experience a visual pop-out effect when attempting to find a single instance of a "3" in a large field of "E" distractors. A pop-out effect occurs in neurotypicals when a perceptual feature is so salient that it can be detected without inspecting each item in turn as part of a linear search, so a "3" printed in green ink embedded in a large number of "E"s printed in blue ink is found more quickly, on average than when all the characters are presented in the same color. The reasonable enough proposal here is that because the synesthetic color sensation produced by graphemes in color-grapheme synesthesia carries letter-shape information, it would allow the synesthetic individual to more quickly find the "3."

However plausible such a proposal might sound, apparently it is empirically controversial. On the one hand, some researchers have reported finding such pop-out effects in color-grapheme synesthetes (e.g. Palmeri et al. 2002; Ramachandran and Hubbard 2001). On the other hand, subsequent findings disagree with this conclusion or call an easy interpretation of these findings into question (Edquist et al. 2006; Nijboer, Satris, and Stigchel 2011; Sagiv, Heer, and Robertson 2006; Smilek, Dixon and Merikle 2001; Ward et al. 2010). It is not clear why, but Edquist et al. propose that this is because that while color does consciously inform the grapheme-color synesthete about the letter shape, it does not do so early enough in visual processing to generate a pop-out effect. The synesthetic sensation here is apparently being generated sufficiently downstream from the eye itself that this information is not available to the relatively low-level perceptual processes that produce the attention-grabbing abilities of neurotypical color sensations.

Concerning this pop-out muddle, if in the end something like Ramachandran and Hubbard's findings turn out to be supported, that would mean that in such cases, the synesthetic experience is tracking a property of the neurotypical stimulus. Hence, on

Also see Renier and De Volder (Chapter 42, this volume) for more on the relationship between synesthesia and sensory substitution.

the account discussed in this section, the number of senses would be divided up identically in the neurotypical and synesthetic cases. If something like what is proposed by Edquist and colleagues turns out to be correct, it suggests that whatever is going on in synesthesia, it seems to be neither here nor there on the question of the intentional objects of perception (because it does not figure into perceptual processing in a way that facilitates it). Either way there's not much to work out here when this account of the senses runs into synesthesia. However, unlike with the organ account, arriving at this conclusion is not nearly as obvious. (And given all that remains left to be learned about synesthesia, we should not conclude prematurely that this conclusion will hold up indefinitely.)

To take stock so far, I have argued that the facts of synesthesia do not cause conceptual difficulties when faced with accounts that place their emphasis on the organ or perceptual object elements of our commonsense account of the senses, nor do these accounts call for numbering the senses differently in synesthetes as versus neurotypical individuals. Perhaps this should not be too surprising because these accounts do not focus on precisely what seems to be most striking in the case of synesthesia: the reported conscious experiences of synesthetic individuals. That is what the final account of the senses does, to which I now turn.

The senses as providers of characteristic experiences

The final account of the senses we will consider is that which differentiates the senses from one another is that they each provide their own class of characteristic conscious experiences. As philosopher H. Paul Grice put it:

> It might be suggested that two senses, for example, seeing and smelling, are to be distinguished by the special introspectible character of the experience of seeing and smelling; that is, disregarding the differences between the characteristics we learn about by sight and smell, we are entitled to say that seeing is itself different in character from smelling. (1962/1989, 250)

In other words, seeing red is just experienced differently than seeing blue and seeing is experienced differently than hearing. Further, these differences are experienced in a way that we can report on them (in the terminology of philosophy, the differences are said to be "introspectible" by the subject).

The science that documents these introspectible differences is the science of psychophysics. Further, it has been argued that we can use the data of psychophysics to differentiate the senses. This way of characterizing the senses could be put in terms of the "quality spaces" they allow us to perceive and reason about.[13] This approach is based on

---

[13] In the philosophical literature, the proposal was originally made by Nelson Goodman (1951, 1977). For a more recent, detailed account making full contact with the psychophysics literature, see Clark (1993, 79–84). For more specifically on the notion of a "quality space" and its connection to the

the concept of "matching": the relation between two stimuli that differ physically but are nonetheless perceptually indiscriminable from one another. For example, two color patches might reflect slightly different wavelengths of light, but differ so minutely that any human subject would report the patches to be perceptually identical. Perhaps surprisingly, it turns out that the matching relation is not transitive: stimulus A may match stimulus B, and stimulus B match stimulus C, but stimulus A need not match stimulus C. Using this relationship, one can construct "matching spans" of stimuli in which each stimulus matches its immediate neighbors, but the ends of the spans are easily discriminable. For example, we can construct such matching spans for color, creating a series of stimuli that vary infinitesimally by wavelength from red to green, say. A given observer, when presented with any two adjacent elements from this series, will be unable to discriminate them, even though the subject can clearly distinguish red from green (the ends of the matching span).

Austen Clark explains how this concept of matching can be used to divide up the senses:

> Facts about matching can individuate modalities. Sensations in a given modality are connected by the matching relation. From any sensation in the given modality, it is possible to reach any other by a sufficiently long series of matching steps. Distinct modalities are not so connected. One can get from red to green by a long series of intermediaries, each matching its neighbors; but no such route links red to C-sharp. (1993, 140–141)

In other words, generate a sensory "map" of matching spans by probing a subject's judgments of introspectible identities and differences, note the discontinuities in the map, and you will have a way of determining the differences between the various sensory modalities in that subject. All the visual stimuli would be clumped together in one large set of matching spans, and all the auditory stimuli would be similarly clumped together. Further there would be no matching span connecting the two clumps.

While this approach might work in the non-synesthetic case, things are not so clear with synesthesia. After all, the hallmark of synesthesia is that these subjects have introspectible experiences characteristic (in non-synesthetes) of more than one sensory modality. For example, when Michael is presented with gustatory stimuli he experiences not only gustatory sensations, but also tactile ones (in the forms of shapes felt in his hands or on his face). This would seem to imply that the matching spans of synesthetes

senses, see Ross (2008). I add one note about putting psychophysics in this section, as opposed to the previous one. There is an ambiguity in what it is that psychophysics takes itself to be doing and how to understand what these quality spaces are. On the reading I am pursuing here, these quality spaces are the structure of our perceptual experiences, as revealed by subject reports. However, there are a number of philosophers, including Ross but also Michael Tye, who believe that the structure of our perceptual experience maps directly onto the structure of the intentional objects of perception. For one who takes that stand, one might argue that psychophysics primarily tells us about the intentional objects of experience and only secondarily about the character of experience. I do not believe this complication effects anything I say here.

are importantly different from those of neurotypicals.[14] Shouldn't we say that Michael has matching spans that run from the (typically) gustatory to the (typically) tactile? While it is tempting to answer "yes," I believe that the correct answer is "no" and I explain this as follows.

The experiential situation in synesthesia is somewhat more complicated than the neurotypical case, but it may be likely that they will end up with the same set of senses as neurotypicals. Consider that the creation of matching spans is based on comparison judgments of perceptible differences. When a flavor-tactile synesthete receives a flavor stimulation, he will experience both a flavor and a tactile percept. Change the chemical make-up of that stimulation to some infinitesimal degree, and he will (presumably) report the same pair of flavor and shape experiences—the two experiences match. Continue to change it a little more and when one (or both) of the experiences changes enough to be noticed introspectively by the subject, he will report that difference. This would be the first steps in creating matching spans for this subject. So far, so good. But notice that in order to extend that matching span from flavor (or flavor-tactile), we would need to find a stimulus that produced a tactile experience indistinguishable to the subject from that produced by some gustatory stimulus.

While it can be imagined that synesthetes could experience confusion, my understanding of the reports of synesthetes is that they do not ordinarily mistake their synesthetic sensations for their neurotypical ones. My understanding is that Michael, say, would not confuse the pointed feeling he may get from tasting a sauce with the related sensory experience he has holding any pointed object in his hand. The two experiences would never match in the sense required for this matching span account to work.

Further, there is yet another difference in the introspectible character of neurotypical and synesthetic sensations: the synesthetic ones are mixed in a way that the neurotypical ones are not. In synesthesia, it is not the case that the neurotypical sensations are replaced or eclipsed by the synesthetic ones; instead they are experienced in a conjoint fashion, perhaps akin to the way that shape and color are normally co-experienced in neurotypical vision. This mixture is one of the features of synesthetic experiences that makes them both unique and discriminable.[15]

It is interesting to compare synesthetic sensations with other characteristic experiences that sometimes accompany neurotypical sensations. Sometimes our neurotypical sensations are accompanied by other distinct experiences, as when one experiences

[14] This is true at least in those sensory pairs for which a given synesthete experiences synesthesia. The visual and auditory psychophysics of a gustatory-tactile synesthete such as Michael, say, might be within the neurotypical range.

[15] See Auvray and Deroy (forthcoming) for an interesting discussion of how to understand the relationship between what I am calling the synesthetic and neurotypical sensations here. They reject the 'dualistic' pairing that terms such as 'conjoint' imply. I am sympathetic to their line of analysis despite this choice of words on my part. I also recommend their paper as a good review of recent work in the philosophy of synesthesia.

déjà vu, a sensation invokes a strong feeling of surprise or recognition, or is experienced as pleasurable (or not). At other times, we may experience additional conscious experiences due to our own participation, as when we find ourselves making a significant effort to hear something clearly.[16]

Like synesthetic sensations, these other characteristics come together with neurotypical sensations. However, unlike synesthetic sensations, they are not so reliably associated with neurotypical sensations. This reliable association of the synesthetic sensations with neurotypical ones (synesthetes typically experience their synesthetic sensations conjointly with their modality specific ones) is one main reason why it is appropriate to think of synesthesia in sensory terms. Another is that the sensations felt are experienced as closely similar (but not identical) to neurotypical ones.

We can then see how synesthetic sensations are situated between neurotypical sensations and these other experiences. Like neurotypical sensations, they are consistently produced by the activity of sensory organs, but as the pop-out (or lack thereof) findings suggest, they are different from their related neurotypical sensations. This is borne out also by the first-person reports of synesthetes and the observation that they do not confuse their synesthetic and neurotypical sensations. In these ways and by their characteristic experiential profile, they are similar to other experiences we have in conjunction with neurotypical sensations, albeit less clearly so.

Conclusion

In this paper, I have discussed three different contemporary accounts of the senses, all deriving in different ways from the commonsense approach. The first, associated most closely with neurobiology, stresses the importance of the sensory organ. The second, favored by at least some philosophers, places the most emphasis on the information about the world to which the senses give us access. The third, derived from the science of psychophysics, concentrates on reports of the conscious experiences invoked by sensory stimulation. While these three different accounts do not always agree, they do represent different aspects of what we commonly think about the senses.

If this is the correct way of thinking about things, then synesthesia does not tell us anything special about how to divide up the senses. However, that does not make synesthesia any less fascinating. Further, the discussion has demonstrated that thinking about the question of how the senses are differentiated helps us pinpoint exactly where

---

[16] As I have described elsewhere (2009a), such experiences of effort, pleasure, etc. are the sorts of experiences to which the term "qualia" once referred. These days, a *quale* typically refers to a (neurotypical) sensation, such as the experience of red. However, until 1930 or so, experiences such as red were referred to as "sensations," and the term "quale" was reserved for these more ineffable, non-sensory experiences. In this older sense of the term, I would propose that synesthetic sensations would be considered qualia, not sensations. Neurotypical sensations are the "sensations" on this reading.

the interesting aspects of the phenomenon lie. What is interesting about synesthesia is not its relation to sensory organs, or concerning what synesthetes learn about the world; what is striking about synesthesia concerns the characteristic experiences that it involves.

Acknowledgments

I should express my appreciation to Richard Gray, who read and gave me useful feedback on the entire chapter, as did the editors and an anonymous reviewer of this volume. I also had useful discussions of this chapter with several members of the *Champalimaud Centre for the Unknown*, Lisbon—including, but not limited to, Susana Lima, Scott Rennie, Sam Meyler, and Gonçalo Lopes—where I was in residence for much of the writing and editing process. My apologies to anybody I have overlooked. Any remaining errors and infelicities are mine.

References

Aristotle. 1931. *De anima. The works of Aristotle*, Vol. III, ed. W. D. Ross. Oxford: Clarendon Press.

Auvray, Malika and Ophelia Deroy. Forthcoming. Synesthesia. In *Oxford Handbook of Philosophy of Perception*, ed. Mohan Matthen. Oxford: Oxford University Press.

Bach-y-Rita, Paul. 1972. *Brain Mechanisms in Sensory Substitution*. New York: Academic Press.

Bach-y-Rita, Paul, and Stephen W. Kercel. 2003. Sensory-'motor' coupling by observed and imagined movement. *Intellectica* 35:287–297.

Baron-Cohen, Simon, and John E. Harrison, eds. 1997. *Synaesthesthesia: Classic and Contemporary Readings*. Oxford: Blackwell Publishers.

Brentano, Franz. 1874. *Psychology from an Empirical Standpoint*. New York: Routledge.

Clark, Andy 1993. *Sensory Qualities*. Oxford: Oxford University Press.

Cytowic, Richard E. 1993. *The Man who Tasted Shapes*. New York: G.P. Putnam's Sons.

——, ed. 2002. *Synesthesia: A Union of the Senses*. Cambridge, MA: The MIT Press.

Edquist, Jessica, Anina N. Rich, Cobie Brinkman, and Jason B. Mattingley. 2006. Do synaesthetic colours act as unique features in visual search? *Cortex* 42(2):222–231.

Fulkerson, Matthew. 2011. The unity of haptic touch. *Philosophical Psychology* 24 (4): 493–516.

Geurts, Kathryn Linn 2002. *Culture and the Senses: Bodily Ways of Knowing in an African Community*. Berkeley, CA: University of California Press.

Goodman, Nelson. 1951. *The Structure of Appearance*, 1st ed. Cambridge, MA: Harvard University Press.

——. 1977. *The Structure of Appearance*, 3rd ed. Boston, MA: Dordrecht Reidel.

Gray, Richard. 2001. Synesthesia and misrepresentation: A reply to Wager. *Philosophical Psychology* 14 (3):339–346.

Grice, H. Paul. 1962. Some remarks about the senses. *Analytical philosophy*, series I, ed. R. J. Butler. Oxford: Oxford University Press. (Reprinted in *Studies in the way of words*, Paul Grice, 1989, 248–268. Cambridge, MA: Harvard University Press.)

Heller-Roazen, Daniel. 2009. *The Inner Touch: Archaeology of a Sensation*. New York: Zone Books.

Howes, David, ed. 1991. *The Varieties of Sensory Experience: A Sourcebook in the Anthropology of the senses*. Toronto, ON: University of Toronto Press.

——, ed. 2009. *The Sixth Sense Reader*. Sensory formations. Oxford: Berg.

Johansen, T. K. 1998. *Aristotle on the Sense-Organs*. New York: Cambridge University Press.

Keeley, Brian L. 1999. Fixing content and function in neurobiological systems: The neuroethology of electroreception. *Biology & Philosophy* 14:395–430.

——. 2002. Making sense of the senses: Individuating modalities in humans and other animals. *The Journal of Philosophy* 99(1):5–28. (Reprinted in *The Senses: Classic and Contemporary Philosophical Perspectives*, ed. Fiona Macpherson, 2011, 220–240. Oxford: Oxford University Press.)

——. 2009a. The early history of the quale and its relation to the senses. In *Routledge Companion to Philosophy of Psychology*, ed. J. Symons and P. Calvo, 71–89. London: Routledge.

——. 2009b. The role of neurobiology in differentiating the senses. In *Oxford Handbook of Philosophy and Neuroscience*, ed. J. Bickle, 226–250. Oxford University Press.

Nabokov, Vladimir. 1966. *Speak, Memory; An Autobiography Revisited*, Rev. ed. New York: Putnam.

Nijboer, T. C., G. Satris, and S. V. Stigchel. 2011. The influence of synesthesia on eye movements: No synesthetic pop-out in an oculomotor target selection task. *Consciousness and Cognition* 20 (4):1193–1200.

Noë, Alva. 2004. *Action in Perception*. Cambridge, MA: The MIT Press.

Nudds, Matthew. 2004. The significance of the senses. *Proceedings of the Aristotelian Society* CIV (1):31–51.

Palmeri, T. J., R. Blake, R. Marois, M. A. Flanery and W. Whetsell, Jr. 2002. The perceptual reality of synesthetic colors. *Proceedings of the National Academy of Sciences of the United States of America* 6:4127.

Prince-Hughes, Dawn, ed. 2002. *Aquamarine Blue 5: Personal Stories of College Students with Autism*. Athens, OH: Swallow Press/Ohio University Press.

Ramachandran, Vilayanur S., and E.M. Hubbard. 2001. Psychophysical investigations into the neural basis of synaesthesia. *Proceedings: Biological Sciences* 1470:979–983.

Ratcliffe, Matthew. 2012. What is touch? *Australasian Journal of Philosophy* 90 (3): 413–432.

Renier, Laurent, and Anne G. De Volder. 2013. Sensory substitution devices: Creating "artificial synesthesias." In *The Oxford Handbook of Synesthesia*, ed. Julia Simner and Edward M. Hubbard, 853–868 . Oxford: Oxford University Press.

Ross, Peter W. 2008. Common sense about qualities and senses. *Philosophical Studies* 138 (3):299–316.

Sagiv, Noam, Jeffrey Heer, and Lynn C. Robertson. 2006. Does binding of synesthetic color to the evoking grapheme require attention? *Cortex* 42(2):232–242.

Smilek, Daniel, Mike J. Dixon and Philip M. Merikle. 2001. Synaesthetic photisms guide attention. *Brain and Cognition* 53(2):364–367.

Sorabji, Richard. 1971. Aristotle on demarcating the five senses. *Philosophical Review* 80:55–79. Reprinted in *The Senses: Classic and contemporary philosophical perspectives*, ed. Fiona Macpherson. 2011. Oxford: Oxford University Press.

Sorabji, Richard. 1992. Intentionality and physiological processes: Aristotle's theory of sense-perception. In *Essays on Aristotle's De anima*, ed. M. C. Nussbaum and A. O. Rorty, 195–225. Oxford: Clarendon Press.

Varela, Francisco J., Evan Thompson, and Eleanor Rosch. 1991. *The Embodied Mind*. Cambridge, MA: The MIT Press.

Wade, Nicholas J. 2003. The search for a sixth sense: The cases for vestibular, muscle, and temperature senses. *Journal of the History of the Neurosciences* 12(2):175–202. (Reprinted in *The sixth sense reader,* ed. David Howes, 2009, 55–86. Oxford: Berg.)

Ward, Jamie, Clare Jonas, Zoltan Dienes, and Anil Seth. 2010, Grapheme-colour synaesthesia improves detection of embedded shapes, but without pre-attentive 'pop-out' of synaesthetic colour. *Proceedings of the Royal Society B: Biological Sciences* 277(16):1021–1026.

Young, Diana. 2005. The smell of greenness: Cultural synaesthesia in the western desert. *Etnofoor* 18(1):61–77.

CHAPTER 47

WHAT SYNESTHESIA ISN'T

MARY-ELLEN LYNALL AND COLIN BLAKEMORE

Synesthesia is a condition in which a particular sensory stimulus (or even the thought of that stimulus)—the *inducer*—reliably elicits not only the normal perceptual experience but also some additional, inappropriate sensation—the *concurrent*. In the earliest known reference to this phenomenon, John Locke (1690) described a blind man who, when asked to describe the color scarlet, replied that it is "like the sound of a trumpet." Indeed, the commonest forms of synesthesia involve seeing colors when listening to sounds or words, or reading letters or numbers. Like schizophrenia and dementia, synesthesia is often described as a singular phenotype. The implication is that this extraordinary condition is a well-defined "pathological" form of perception with a distinct neurological basis. However, like schizophrenia and dementia, convenient terminology and minimal definition might hide a variety of conditions, with different etiologies and manifestations. In this chapter we question the definition of synesthesia, its proposed causes and neurological underpinnings; whether it takes one or many forms, and whether it is a highly aberrant condition or merely the extreme end of a continuum of perceptual function. Despite the flurry of research on synesthesia in the past 20 years, aided by the advent of neuroimaging, many of these fundamental issues remain unresolved. We are left with more certainty about what synesthesia is not, than about what it is.

PROBLEMS WITH THE DEFINITION OF SYNESTHESIA

Any serious study of an unusual phenotype depends on the clarity of its description: but there is still ambivalence and debate about the essential criteria that define synesthesia. Early descriptions of the phenomenon, which was then usually called "hyperchromatopsia" ("hyperchromatopsie" in French), emphasized the vivid nature of the concurrent experiences, which were often described as illusions or hallucinations (see Jewanski et al. 2011). It was not until the late nineteenth century that Heinrich Kaiser (1872) described the first test of the stability of these sensory associations. He asked a synesthete with colored graphemes and colored words to describe his colors and "after one year, he again chose the same colors for the requested words. He also did not err on a single one" (cited by Jewanski et al. 2011, 295). Indeed, Kaiser found that this man's choices were essentially identical 10 years later. In subsequent descriptions, the emphasis remained on the unusual and explicit (i.e., consciously experienced) nature of synesthetic concurrents. They belong to the "raw" class of experience that Block (1998) calls phenomenal consciousness.

By the criterion that the concurrent sensation is spontaneous, inappropriate, and vividly experienced, synesthetes appear to be an absolutely distinct group. Either you have these strange extra "qualia," as some philosophers call the elements of phenomenal experience (Lewis 1929), or you don't. However, such a definition is encumbered with all the uncertainty of any report of subjectivity: it cannot be objectively confirmed (the so-called "other minds" problem). The decline of interest in synesthesia in the first half of the last century is often attributed to its presumed similarity to hallucinations and delusions. Synesthetes' reports of their essentially private experiences were commonly not taken seriously, or were dismissed as drug-induced or a form of hysteria (see Ramachandran and Hubbard 2001a).

Formalization of Kaiser's (1872) measure of reliability as the now-standard "Test of Genuineness" (TOG) by Baron-Cohen and his colleagues (Baron-Cohen, Wyke, and Binnie 1987; Baron-Cohen et al. 1993; Baron-Cohen et al. 1996) transformed this field (for review see Johnson, Allison, and Baron-Cohen, Chapter 1, this volume). It provided an objective measure of the reliability of the reports of concurrent sensations. The TOG involves recording the inducer–concurrent associations initially reported by individuals and comparing them with those described in a further test, usually performed at least some weeks later, and without prior warning. The TOG—considered by many to be the behavioral gold-standard for establishing synesthesia—legitimized research in this field, and it is now routinely employed to define cohorts of subjects in studies of synesthesia. However, it might have inadvertently distorted our definition of the phenomenon, our measures of its prevalence, and our understanding of its biological basis. The problem is that the TOG has shifted the definition of synesthesia towards the reliability of the inducer–concurrent association, rather than the spontaneity and subjectivity of the unusual concurrent experience. All that the test measures is the robustness of the association, not the precise form, nor the existence of a conscious experience. Moreover, there is no universally accepted definition of a level of performance that constitutes "genuineness." Typically, true synesthetes are said to have consistency of 80% to 100% across such tests (e.g., Simner and Logie 2007; Ward et al. 2007). But the nature of the test and the criteria adopted for true synesthesia have varied considerably. For instance, in an enormous study, Novich, Cheng, and Eagleman (2011) used a battery of "draconian" criteria, including performance on tests of reliability within 1 standard deviation (SD) of the mean scores, to select 12,127 "highly consistent synesthetes" (Eagleman 2012, 17) out of 19,133 individuals who claimed to be synesthetic. In another large survey, Simner et al. (2006) identified "verified synesthetes" as those who performed on a test of consistency better than 2 SD above the mean score of "control" synesthetes (as low as 53% consistency), even with immediate recall. In Simner et al.'s study, those people whose scores fell within this very liberal definition of synesthetic levels of reliability were "more likely" to report subjective synesthetic experiences in a questionnaire (p <0.01). The implication is that the reliability of some who claimed to have vivid concurrent sensations was worse than that of the average non-synesthetic population in other studies (see Figure 47.2 later in chapter); and that some who denied having conscious concurrent experiences were well within the range of consistency of "verified synesthetes."

If the *sine qua non* of synesthesia is that extraneous sensory associations are spontaneous and consciously experienced, the TOG does not test its genuineness. It is merely a "*test of consistency*" and should always be called such. There would be no problem in using reproducibility as a surrogate for subjectivity if the two characteristics were perfectly correlated. But they are not (see later).

Simner's valuable recent review (2012) raises the problem of circularity inherent in the use of consistency of association as the cardinal characteristic of synesthesia. If synesthetes are defined only in terms of a certain high level of performance on a test of consistency, they will include some who deny any phenomenal experience of their concurrent associations. If the definition is restricted to those who adamantly assert that they are consciously aware of their concurrents, some of these "synesthetes" will not have very consistent associations (even when malingerers or those who initially misunderstand the experimenter's questions are excluded). And if non-sensory subjective impressions (including emotions, imagery, memories and attributions of gender or personality) were permitted in the definition, virtually everyone would be a "synesthete." This dilemma has not been resolved.

In most studies of synesthesia, a group of "definite" synesthetes (who report conscious synesthetic experiences and perform well on a test of consistency) is usually contrasted with controls (who do not satisfy all these criteria). While there is a statistically significant link between consistency and subjective experience of synesthesia (Simner et al. 2006), consistency is neither necessary nor sufficient for such experiences to be reported. The tendency to exclude from studies individuals who claim to have synesthesia but who perform relatively badly on recall of their associations artificially constrains the definition of synesthesia (Cohen Kadosh, and Terhune 2012; Eagleman 2012; Simner 2012). Why should there not be individuals with vivid synesthesia whose associations change over time, just as there are undoubtedly many people with robust sensory associations who never experience them consciously. Only by teasing apart consistency and conscious synesthetic experience can we hope to find the true neurobiological and psychophysical correlates of synesthesia. For example, a neuroimaging study comparing those who report conscious synesthetic percepts, participants who do not but have similar scores on tests of consistency, and controls who have neither conscious associations nor good recall, would be enlightening. Such a study could reveal specifically the neural correlates of the conscious experience of synesthesia and of the basis of implicit associations.

Day (2005, 2009) recognized more than 60 sorts of inducer–concurrent associations, and Eagleman (2012) put the number as high as 150. Concurrent sensations as varied as tastes, smells, shapes, and colors can be triggered by such experiences as hearing particular words or music, touching objects, seeing familiar people, having orgasms, or pains, or eating certain foods (or even by thinking about these experiences). Depending on how liberally synesthesia is defined, it can include the attribution of animate qualities such as gender and personality to such inducing stimuli as graphemes and days of the week (Simner and Holenstein 2007; Simner and Hubbard 2006). But if such non-sensory qualities can be counted as concurrents, why should the emotions felt by most people when they listen to particular styles of music and when they view particularly evocative images not also count as synesthetic (see later)?

In their comprehensive survey of thousands of synesthetes, defined on the basis of a battery of questionnaires and a test of reliability, Novich, Cheng, and Eagleman (2011) found that synesthetic associations fall into five distinct groups, defined statistically on the basis that individuals are much more likely to have two or more forms of synesthetic association within a single group than across different groups. For example, a colored-digit synesthete is much more likely to have colored concurrents for other learned sequences (e.g., colored weekdays) than a completely different kind of synesthesia, such as tastes elicited by sound. The five groups are: colored sequence synesthesias (colors produced by graphemes and time-words); colored music synesthesias; non-visual sequelae synesthesias (smells, sounds, touches, and tastes elicited by visual or auditory stimuli), spatial sequence synesthesias (spatially distributed photisms produced by hearing or imagining ordered sequences such as numbers or days of the week: see Figure 47.1), and colored sensation synesthesias (color elicited by touch, temperature, pain, emotions, personalities, orgasms, smells or tastes). This clustering of types is likely to be valuable in studies of the organic basis of synesthesia and the possible genetic origin of at least some types of synesthesia.

Extraneous Sensory Association is Universal

While large surveys, such as those of Simner et al. (2006) and Novich, Cheng, and Eagleman (2011), help to constrain the definition of synesthesia and to identify distinct subpopulations of synesthetes, the exclusion criteria for such classifications might impose artificially sharp boundaries between synesthetes and the rest of the population. Indeed, the vast majority of people who deny having synesthetic experiences will, if encouraged, happily report an "association" between real stimuli and other, apparently irrelevant categories of sensory experience. In many cases, these associations are remarkably similar across the population and reproducible over time. For instance, although only a tiny fraction of people have true colored-sound synesthesia, most

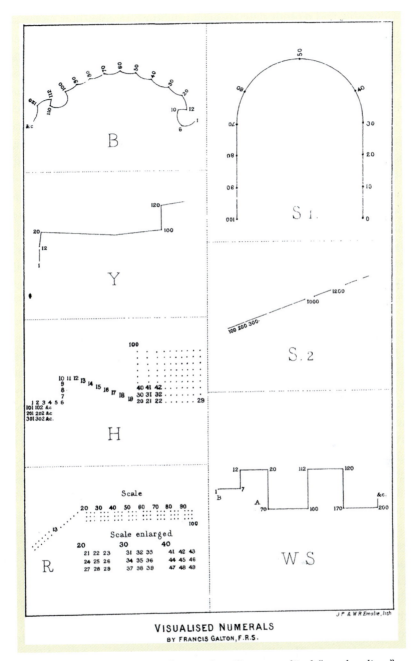

VISUALISED NUMERALS
BY FRANCIS GALTON, F.R.S.

FIGURE 47.1 Francis Galton was the first to describe externalized "number lines" or visuo-spatial number forms (a variant of spatial sequence synesthesia; see Sagiv et al. 2006). These illustrations of the spatial distribution of visualized numbers were drawn by six synesthetes. Reproduced from Galton, Francis, Visualised numerals, *The Journal of the Anthropological Institute of Great Britain and Ireland* 10 pp. 85–102, plate VII © 1881. For further examples see also Figure 7.1, Jonas and Jarick, Chapter 7, this volume.

people will readily and reproducibly say what brightness or color they "associate" with a particular pitch and loudness of sound (Marks 1987; Rich and Mattingley 2002; Ward, Huckstep, and Tsakanikos 2006). These associations are automatic (not dependent on deliberate training) and can influence the reaction time and accuracy of cross-modal responses. For example, most people associate low-pitched tones with darkness and high-pitched with brightness; and they respond faster to dark stimuli when accompanied by low-pitch rather than high-pitch tones (Marks 1987; see also Marks, Chapter 38, this volume). It is often suggested that the particular concurrent sensations experienced by a synesthete are usually both idiosyncratic (varying between individuals) and bizarre (in that they bear no relation to "normal" perceptual experience). However, the implicit sensory associations reported by non-synesthetes are often similar to the explicit concurrent experiences of synesthetes with the same inducing stimulus (this is reviewed by Simner, Chapter 8, this volume). Moreover, they can be as consistent over time as the associations of synesthetes. For instance, in Ward, Huckstep, and Tsakanikos' (2006) study, with a 2-month retest interval, two of ten colored-sound synesthetes fell within the range of consistency of the associations reported by "normal" people. (We use the adjective "normal" advisedly for individuals who do not enjoy explicit concurrent sensations. This is not to imply that synesthetes are "abnormal" or "subnormal": indeed we argue later in the chapter that they are likely, in some respects, to be super-normal.)

Most people will readily match a color to a passage of music. Haack called these kinds of color impressions "associative" or "forced" synesthesia (Haack 1980, 143). Cutietta and Haggerty (1987) documented such color associations for 30-second passages of music by Holst, Moussorgsky, and Handel in 1,256 volunteers, from 3 to 78 years of age. Not only were the colors reported by individuals highly consistent (typically >90% correlation in reports 1 week apart) but they were remarkably similar across subjects. Even for very young children, the reports were generally significantly correlated; and above 9 years of age, about 80% of people reported associations in the same segment of the spectrum (red for the Holst, blue for the Moussorgsky, and yellow for the Handel). Similarly, most non-synesthetes readily associate a particular brightness or color with the texture of a surface or a shape felt with the hands. Moreover, when questioned about the "certainty" of such associations, some non-synesthetes studied by Simner and Ludwig (2012) were more confident than a genuine colored-touch synesthete, and some were more reliable in a test of consistency! The only clear distinction between the synesthete and the "normal" subjects was the fact that the synesthete's concurrent associations were spontaneous (rather than evoked by questioning) and subjectively experienced.

The robustness of such cross-modal associations makes them reminiscent of true synesthesia. However, the fact that they are so common and consistent across the population is rather different from archetypal synesthesia. While there is a tendency for patterns of grapheme-color association to be similar across individual synesthetes (and also in non-synesthetes—Simner et al. 2005; Spector and Maurer 2011), a striking feature of most synesthetic associations is how different they can be from person to person (Baron-Cohen et al. 1993). Even within a single family of synesthetes, the particular associations and even the forms of synesthesia can vary enormously (Barnett, Finucane, et al. 2008).

WHAT COUNTS AS A CONCURRENT EXPERIENCE?

If the only firm definition of synesthesia rests on the concurrent associations being consciously experienced, what should we make of the *emotions* that most people experience, reliably and consistently, when they listen to particular pieces of music? As every film producer knows, music can evoke strong feelings of sadness, happiness, pride, love, fear, and so on. Equally, non-musical sounds, works of art, beautiful or ugly scenery, other people's faces, the sight of blood—all can elicit strong emotions. Such virtually universal and highly consistent associations are spontaneous and subjectively experienced. Even textured surfaces felt with the hands reliably elicit particular emotions in non-synesthetes (Suk et al. 2009). Tastes and smells can have rich emotional overtones (generating every feeling from disgust to ecstasy) and colors themselves provoke distinctive emotions. Is it not inconsistent that we count as synesthetes people who see colors when they have particular emotions (e.g., Novich, Cheng, and Eagleman 2011) but not the rest of us, who reliably experience emotions when we see particular colors?

Why do we not consider, say, Samuel Barber's *Adagio for Strings* as the inducer for a synesthetic concurrent experience of sadness, or the sight of one's national flag as the inducer for a concurrent of pride? It could be said that emotions don't count in this discussion because they are not conventional *sensory* experiences: they are not directly related to the form of the stimulus. That, in turn, raises almost metaphysical questions about the relationship between the physical nature of stimuli, the signals from sensory receptors and the qualia of perceptual experience. It is significant that most discussion of this issue centers on *visual* experience, where the correspondence between qualia (the perceived shape, position, brightness, and color of each object) and the physical characteristics of the object superficially seems straightforward. But the relationship between the vibrations that constitute sound stimuli and the perception of noise, music, speech etc. is complex and not so obviously a simple translation from physics to subjectivity. A particular chord in a passage of music is experienced in terms of its component tones, their loudness, the timbre of each, and the positions in space of the instruments, but the music will also evoke an aesthetic experience, and probably a particular emotion or emotions—not to mention the possibility of a flood of personal memories associated with it. Some members of this set of mental states can be directly and uniquely attributed to the physical stimulus, but many extrapolations and additions of subjective experience are equally automatic and consistent components of the experience of the sound, but very difficult to account for in terms of simple stimulus-perception connections. Does the word synesthesia come to mind?

Some of the qualia that can occur in response to a sound can also be evoked by a visual stimulus—the sense of a position in space, emotions, aesthetic feelings and memories. So, subjective impressions are not uniquely associated with one particular sensory modality. Moreover, one sensory stimulus can dramatically change the perceptual experience evoked by another. In the well-known McGurk effect (McGurk and MacDonald 1976), one's auditory perception of a spoken word or phoneme is dramatically altered by simultaneously viewing a video of someone's lips articulating a different word or phoneme (see Vatakis, Chapter 40, this volume, for a review of audio-visual speech integration).

Consider too the subjective experience of eating. The visual appearance of a platter of food undoubtedly influences the overall experience: try eating in total darkness. This effect extends not just to the aesthetics of the presentation. It is well known that if a familiar ingredient is stained to become a very different color (e.g., blue carrots), it utterly changes the experience of eating. Even what we loosely call "taste" is dependent on a complex interplay of true gustatory information from the tongue (usually a very minor component of the experience), smell, the kinesthetics and "mouth-feel" of the food, the size of the morsels and their temperature. And what if the food is so spicy that it is actually painful to eat? That pain becomes part of the qualia describing the foodstuff in your mouth, and it certainly modifies other aspects of the experience. But pain can also be part of the subjective experience of other sensory inputs—a cut or burn on the skin, a deep injury, or an arthritic knee; even a bright flash of light, or an excruciatingly loud noise. Pain is a promiscuous quale, which readily attaches itself to the perception of all kinds of stimuli.

Each real-world sensory stimulus—often involving more than one receptor system—leads to a perceptual experience consisting of many forms of qualia, some tightly and uniquely linked to the stimulus but others more generic. The different sensory components of the stimulus will modify each other's perceptual interpretation. And the experience might also contain a flood of looser associations, some consciously experienced, some implicit but reliable in nature. In these terms, should we be surprised to discover that qualia normally intrinsic to vision can also become associated with other forms of sensory stimulation, sometimes even consciously? If a snatch of music by Handel can be tonal, loud, straight in front of you, rich, bright, pleasant, and joyful, why shouldn't it also be yellow? What qualia *are*—indeed what consciousness *is*—remains a mystery. But it seems reasonable to imagine that some neural processes (perhaps largely innate but partly acquired) generate the elements of perceptual experience as a result of particular features of the information streaming in from the sense organs. The fact that localized damage in parts of the cerebral cortex devoted to visual analysis leads to selective blindness for certain visual qualia (e.g., color or movement) argues for the existence of distinct, even anatomically separate neural processes underlying particular qualia.

PROBLEMS IN DEFINING THE PREVALENCE AND GENETIC BASIS OF SYNESTHESIA

Synesthesia seems so unusual—apparently so different from normal perception—that it was traditionally thought of as a highly abnormal, even pathological phenomenon (see Ramachandran and Hubbard 2001a). If synesthesia were a distinct, reliably "diagnosable" condition, its prevalence in the population should be easy to assess. Similar rates of occurrence in separated human populations and higher incidence in certain families (as for schizophrenia), might point to a genetic basis. However, estimates of prevalence have varied enormously. Baron-Cohen et al. (1996) suggested a figure of 1 in 2,000, but the same group later reported a range of estimates from 0.05% to 1% of the population (Asher et al. 2009). The lower figures, with high female to male ratios, came from voluntary responses to newspaper-based surveys in which the number of people replying with evidence of synesthesia was compared with total circulation figures for the newspaper. More reliable estimates of prevalence come from Simner et al.'s (2006) dual-pronged study of 500 subjects recruited at Edinburgh and Glasgow Universities and 1,190 visitors to the London Science Museum. In the university population, 4.4% were judged to have some type of genuine synesthesia, 1.4% having colored-graphemes. In the Science Museum study, which was restricted to colored-grapheme synesthesia, a similar portion of the population (1.1%) was found to have this condition. Interestingly, in both samples, the female:male ratio was close to 1:1.

Francis Galton (1883) was the first to point out that synesthesia often runs in families. He suggested that it is a distinct, inherited condition and emphasized its aberrant nature. Over a century later, Simon Baron-Cohen and his colleagues (1996) reported the first rigorous evidence for a genetic basis. They reported that one-third of synesthetes can identify a close family member with the condition and they concluded from the patterns of familiality and the apparently greater prevalence in females (reported to be six times higher than in males) that the trait might be transferred through an X-linked gene. However, Baron-Cohen's laboratory (Asher et al. 2009) subsequently discovered instances of male-to-male transmission, which is incompatible with X-linkage. Their whole-genome scan in 43 families with colored hearing, based on 410 microsatellite markers, suggested linkage to a region of chromosome 2, with weaker evidence of involvement of chromosomes 5, 6, and 12. More recently, Tomson et al. (2011) used single nucleotide polymorphism (SNP) analysis in five families with colored-sequence synesthesia (colors induced by viewing graphemes or time-words) and identified linkage to a 25 MB region on chromosome 16, but only for two of the families. Hence, although the partial heritability of synesthesia is well established (see Asher et al. 2009), the genetic studies point to locus heterogeneity and possible polygenic interactions, rather than to a consistent genetic abnormality with Mendelian inheritance.

The prevalence of synesthesia within "synesthetic families" is probably only about 16% (Ward and Simner 2005). If all synesthesia were familial and roughly 5% of the whole population exhibits some form of synesthesia (Simner et al. 2006), almost one in three of all families might carry a genetic disposition to synesthesia. However, only a minority of synesthetes are aware of close relatives with the condition (about one-third according to Baron-Cohen et al. 1996; 42%, according to Barnett, Finucane, et al. 2008). There might, then, be significant incidence of "sporadic" (non-congenital) synesthesia. The possibility of "acquired" synesthesia was first raised by Perroud (1863). He described a 30-year-old who said that he had experienced colored graphemes for only the past 12 to 15 years. Perroud contrasted this with previously described cases, which he assumed to be inherited because the subjects said that they had had concurrent sensations for as long as they could remember. But acquisition of colored sequence synesthesia and spatial sequence synesthesia must depend on an ability to discriminate the inducing stimuli and to recognize them as members of the category. It would not have been unusual (in the mid nineteenth century) if Perroud's subject had not learned to read until his teens. So it might have been only the learning that was late, not the predisposition to synesthesia. Late onset of symptoms is not evidence against a genetic origin.

On the other hand, the possibility that a substantial fraction of cases of synesthesia is sporadic must be taken into account (but generally has not been) in any consideration of the neural basis of the condition. For instance, synesthetes are thought to have widespread abnormalities in structural and functional connectivity in the cerebral hemispheres (see later, and Part V of this volume). If synesthesia were always genetic, such differences in brain organization might be caused by anomalies in early development. But if putative sporadic cases can be identified (on the basis of a total lack of any familial pattern and the absence of any known genetic markers) it will be important to see whether they have similar unusual cortical connectivity and, if so, to consider whether and how it might have been acquired.

PROBLEMS WITH THE CLASSIFICATION OF COLORED-GRAPHEME SYNESTHETES

The majority of synesthetes describe their concurrent sensations as being part of their inner mental world (but more vivid and spontaneous than conventional imagery or memory). The colored-grapheme synesthete studied by Perroud (1863) said of his experiences: "A reminds me of the idea of yellow-orange, E the color blueish-gray or pearl-gray, I carmine red, O canary yellow, U dark brown" (translation from Jewanski et al. 2011, 291). Perroud (1863) wrote: "he cannot bring these letters to mind without bringing to mind at the same time the color he associates with each one" (a clear description of internalized synesthetic experience produced by merely imagining the inducing stimulus). When synesthetes report such internalized concurrent sensations they often describe them as being in "my mind," "my mind's eye," or "my head."

On the other hand, synesthetes sometimes report concurrent qualia as being in the external perceptual world. Some colored-grapheme synesthetes see their colors superimposed on the letters or digits as tightly as if they were printed or displayed in true color. Similarly, some colored-sequence and spatial-sequence synesthetes visualize an array of blobs (colored or achromatic) floating in two-dimensional or, more usually, three-dimensional space, corresponding to sequences such as digits or time-words (see Sagiv et al. 2006; Seron et al. 1992). Francis Galton was the first to describe what he called "visualized numerals" (Galton 1881—see Figure 47.1). Interestingly, for different subjects, such externalized "photisms" are clearly localized in either head-centered or egocentric spatial coordinates (e.g., Steven and Blakemore 2004), implying that externalized synesthetic visual qualia can be generated at various points within processing networks responsible for representation of external space.

Dixon, Smilek, and Merikle (2004) proposed the terms "associator" and "projector" for individuals who report internalized or externalized visual concurrents, respectively, and this nomenclature has been widely adopted. They initially classified 12 colored-grapheme synesthetes unequivocally as five projectors and seven associators, on the basis of their responses to three simple questions. But they provided independent support for the dichotomy through an objective test involving color interference. The subjects were shown colored letters and were asked to name either the true color or the synesthetic color for each letter. The projector synesthetes were faster at naming their concurrent colors than the actual colors, while the associators were quicker at naming the true colors. They suggested that this might mean that the concurrent colors of projectors are generated earlier and more quickly in the visual networks than those of associators. They did, however, point out that associators might be slower in reporting the concurrent color because it is not at the spatial location of the letter to which they are attending.

For several reasons, the projector–associator distinction is problematical. Most importantly, we argue that any such distinction should strictly be applied to the synesthetic experience rather than to the individual synesthete. The dogma that synesthetes fall neatly, unequivocally and permanently into one of these two categories is not supported by full consideration of the evidence. When more extensive questionnaires are used to generate quantitative measures of the tendency to one or other form of synesthesia, the scores of groups of synesthetes form a continuous distribution (e.g., Brang et al. 2001; Eagleman 2012; Rouw and Scholte 2007, 2010). Rouw and Scholte (2010) emphasized the bimodal distribution of scores along the projector-associator continuum, with a roughly 3:1 ratio of "associators" to "projectors." However, many colored-grapheme synesthetes have intermediate scores. In addition, the evaluation of individuals has often been restricted to one form of synesthesia (most frequently colored graphemes) and has not considered other forms of synesthesia that the subjects might have had. Questionnaires might be biased in a way that polarizes the judgments of participants (Eagleman 2012). And however comprehensive and neutral the questioning, synesthetes sometimes have difficulty in describing the location of their concurrent experiences (Ward et al. 2007).

Indeed, more open-ended questioning and retesting reveals synesthetes who externalize some concurrents but experience others in their minds, or who shift in their reports from one test to another. When Edquist et al. (2006) asked 14 colored-grapheme synesthetes basic questions similar to those of Dixon, Smilek, and Merikle (2004) about the perceived location of colored concurrents ("out in space," "in my mind's eye," or "neither"), two reported "neither." Answers on a comprehensive questionnaire contained so many inconsistencies that Edquist et al. (2006) felt that they could not justify classification into projectors and associators. Moreover, of the nine who were retested on the basic questions a month later, three changed their replies from "out in space" to "in my mind's eye" or vice versa. Skelton, Ludwig, and Mohr (2009) reported similar results from an extensive cartoon-based questionnaire. Some subjects shifted from one type of report to another over as little as a month. Half of those tested reported that the nature of their synesthetic experiences had changed considerably during their life, typically becoming progressively less intense and more internalized. Some explicitly said that their experiences are now associator-like but were previously projected externally. Most significantly, some had both internalized and externalized concurrent experiences simultaneously, for a single inducer! Clearly, even the simplest questionnaire to assess externalization/internalization ought to include the option "both" as well as "neither" (for review see Mohr, Chapter 22, this volume).

Ward et al. (2007), who studied 14 colored-grapheme synesthetes, were quite confident in classifying seven as projectors and seven as associators, purely on the basis of the description of their experiences while reading text. Now, most of them also experienced spatial forms for spoken letters, numbers and time-words but there was no obvious correlation between externalization for written text and for spatial forms. Half of those classified as "associators" when viewing text saw external spatial forms for heard time-words (Ward et al. 2007, table 1). Clearly the tendency of any individual to project concurrent experiences into external space is not consistent across all forms of synesthesia.

Two of the seven people whom Ward et al. (2007) initially classified as associators nevertheless saw colors externally as they read, although not bound to the text. For one of them, the "external screen" on which she saw the colors was outside her normal visual field (Ward et al. 2007, 917). The latter group's performance on the color interference task of Dixon, Smilek, and Merikle (2004) was similar to that of "in-the-mind" associators. But this should not be taken to imply that they belong to the same category: a more plausible interpretation is that performance on that task depends on whether the concurrent and the inducer share the same spatial location. On the basis of these two individuals, Ward et al. (2007) proposed a new taxonomy in which such colored-grapheme synesthetes are called "near-space projectors," while conventional projectors who see color tightly bound to the graphemes are called "surface projectors."

While many colored-grapheme synesthetes have a strong tendency to internalize their concurrent experiences for seen text and others usually externalize them, the sum of present evidence suggests that the projection-association distinction applies unambiguously only to the nature of synesthetic *experiences*, not to individual *synesthetes*. Classifying the forms of experience does not, of course, preclude the possibility that some individuals have only one form, but the growing tendency to assume that there are distinctly separate populations of synesthetes is not justified and is potentially misleading. In their work on structural differences in the brains of colored-grapheme synesthetes, Rouw and Scholte (2010) were careful to illustrate their results as correlations between variation in brain structure and variation in projector-associator scores from a questionnaire (see also Rouw, Chapter 25, this volume). There were clear trends, but no categorical distinctions. Nevertheless, their results are often summarized as if there were unambiguous populations with distinctly different brain organization. Projector synesthetes are said to have thicker gray matter in areas involved in early analysis for most of the senses—around the calcarine sulcus (vision), Heschl's gyrus (hearing), parietal operculum (somatic sensation) and the insula (taste)—and this has been related to the possibility of externalized experience in all the senses. But synesthesia for other senses was not reported for these subjects, and the results of Ward et al. (2007) show that the tendency to externalize or internalize is not even consistent for all visual concurrents.

Rouw and Scholte (2010) reported that their associators had thicker gray matter in and around the hippocampus (thought to be involved in episodic and spatial memory). However, the degree of variation in anatomy was distributed continuously across the population. And compared with controls, all the synesthetes had thicker gray matter and increased white matter volume in the left superior parietal region, and relatively thinner gray matter around the medial cingulate sulcus. It would be useful if future studies that attempt to correlate forms of synesthesia with biological variables, including brain structure and organization or genetic variation, could incorporate some numerical indication of the subjects' tendency to externalize, and should pay special attention to individuals whose concurrent experiences varies with the inducer, or change over time.

We believe that this situation urgently needs clarification, with revised terminology applied to the perceptual experiences rather than to individual synesthetes. Ward et al.'s (2007) distinction between "surface" and "near-space projection" is very interesting but we wonder whether the term "near-space" is appropriate for all projected photisms, since free-floating photisms can appear to be at a considerable distance (as in many instances of color-sequence synesthesia and spatial-sequence synesthesia). The terms "bound" (in the sense of being attached to the actual inducing stimulus) and "unbound" might be more appropriate. So, we suggest that three forms of synesthetic experience should be recognized:

- Internalized
- Externalized (unbound)
- Externalized (bound).

The terms "internal" and "external" have already been widely employed in discussions of the projection/association spectrum (e.g., Rouw, and Scholte 2010; Ward et al. 2007). Although the concept of internalization/externalization has been extensively explored only for colored-grapheme synesthesia, Ward et al. (2007) discuss examples that suggest that similar variations exist for other forms of synesthesia. The terminology we propose might then be appropriate for a wide range of synesthesias.

A good reason for avoiding the term "associator" or "association" in any definition of synesthesia is to avoid confusion with the many forms of extraneous association reported by individuals who would not normally be thought of as synesthetes. As described earlier, many such implicit associations are highly correlated across "normal" individuals and quite robust over time, but not synesthetic in the sense that they are not consciously experienced. Now, Ward et al. (2007) reported that two of the seven initially classified as "associators" did not actually consciously experience colors for written text, but simply had the feeling that they knew what color belonged to each grapheme. One might ask why these people were counted as synesthetes, but this was presumably because both of them saw synesthetic spatial forms for time-words. In a test of consistency for the verbal description of colors that they felt to be associated with graphemes they were remarkably reliable (96% and 100%). There have been similar descriptions of strong and robust grapheme-color associations without any perceptual awareness of the color (e.g., Hancock 2006). Ward et al. (2007) suggested that people who do not actually experience concurrents but are both consistent and confident in their presumed associations between graphemes and colors should be classed as synesthetes and they called them "know associators." While it was perfectly reasonable for Ward et al. (2007) to count their two such individuals as synesthetes on the basis of their explicit spatial forms for time-words, we question whether it was then justified to describe them as colored-grapheme synesthetes when they had no conscious experience of color while viewing (or listening to) graphemes. Given the virtually universal ability of "normal" people consistently to describe associations to other senses for a wide variety of real stimuli (described earlier), the invention of a category of genuine synesthesia for one form of reliable sensory association feels like a slippery slope into synesthesia for everyone!

Even for the apparently bizarre relationship between color and graphemes, a fraction of people who vehemently deny having any form of explicit synesthesia have quite reliable associations of which they are (until tested) unaware. For instance, Steven (2004) gave a test of consistency to 29 individuals without synesthesia for comparison with 13 colored-grapheme synesthetes. All of them were simply asked to describe the colors that *first came to mind* as they heard letters or numbers in pseudo-random order. One month later, they were given an unannounced retest (Figure 47.2b) and consistency was ranked by an independent assessor. The "true" synesthetes yielded highly consistent color naming (average 97%, SD 1.2) and the majority of the control subjects (21 out of 29) were much less consistent (mean 17.69%, SD 6.44). However, an apparently distinct group of eight of the "normal" subjects (28%) was surprisingly reliable (mean 69.56%, SD 4.31). Steven (2004) called this group "implicit synesthetes," although all of them denied conscious perception of their associated colors. Five were even unaware that they had consistently associated letter and colors, and were surprised by the results. The other three did realize that they had such associations, and said such things as "letters have always been associated with colors" and "A is just red." Such verbal descriptions are strikingly similar to those of real synesthetes, and, following Ward et al.'s taxonomy, they would be "know associators." But, in the absence of any claim of explicit synesthetic concurrents by such people, we question whether it is wise to call them synesthetes. Among Steven's "implicit synesthetes," the five who were initially unaware of their consistent grapheme-color association are now aware, because they were informed of their performance. Have they now been transformed into genuine synesthetes on the basis of that knowledge? To avoid "creeping synesthesia" and to preserve explicit subjectivity of the concurrent experience as the cardinal feature of synesthesia, we suggest that this and other forms of robust association without phenomenal consciousness, whether or not the individuals are initially aware that they have such associations, would be more appropriately called *implicit sensory association*.

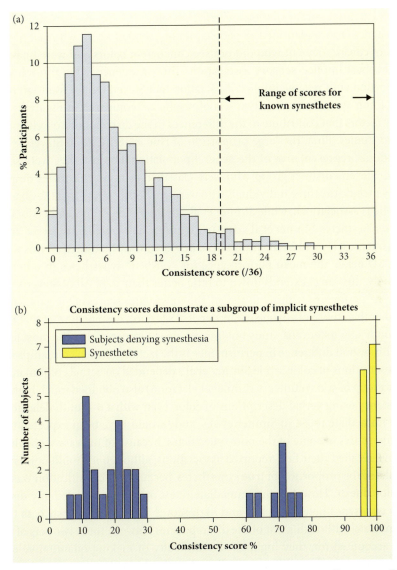

FIGURE 47.2 Distribution of reliability of grapheme-colour associations. Simner et al.'s (2006) results (a) are for 1,029 people (including 13 classified as real synesthetes, on the basis of reports of awareness of concurrent colors), with immediate retest. Reprinted from *Perception*, 35, Synaesthesia: the prevalence of atypical cross-modal experiences, Simner Julia, Catherine Mulvenna, Noam Sagiv, Elias Tsakanikos, and S. Athene Witherby, pp. 1024–1033 © 2006, Pion Ltd, London (<http://www.pion.co.uk> and <http://www.envplan.com>) with permission. Steven's (2004) results (b) are for 29 people (blue bars) who firmly denied having synesthetic experiences, tested for the colors that they associated with graphemes (spoken in the test), with a gap of 1 month between first and second tests. The yellow bars indicate results for 13 "true" colored-grapheme synesthetes, recruited separately, for comparison. The distinct group of eight non-synesthetes with very reliable associations included three who were already aware that they associated colors with graphemes ("know associators" in the terminology of Ward et al. 2007). Data for (b) were kindly provided by Megan Steven.

In their extensive survey of the prevalence of colored-grapheme synesthesia, Simner and colleagues (2006) identified 28 people (out of a total of 1,029) who had high scores on a test of consistency but who did not see concurrent colors and were unaware that they had robust implicit sensory association. This prevalence is ten times lower than the proportion with reliable implicit association that Steven (2004) found in her small sample of non-synesthetes. The two sets of results are compared in Figure 47.2. There are many factors that contribute to the differences in the distributions of reliability from these two studies. First, the large proportion of true synesthetes in Steven's sample is not, of course, representative of the general population, because they were separately recruited. Steven's distinct group who were classified as non-synesthetes despite high reliability include the three individuals who were previously aware that they had reliable (but implicit) associations, while Simner et al. counted such "know associators" among their true synesthetes. Simner et al.'s data in Figure 47.2a do not identify these "true" synesthetes, but most lay within the "range of scores for known synesthetes." This was specified as 2 SD below the mean performance for "verified" synesthetes in other studies. Surprisingly, this range extends down to little better than 50%. All of Steven's "implicit synesthetes" performed within this range! The consistency scores of Steven's synesthetes were higher than those of anyone in Simner et al.'s (2006), despite the fact that the retest was a month later in Stevens' study but immediate in Simner et al.'s. The most likely reason for this overall difference in performance is the fact that Steven's test employed only verbal descriptions of color, while Simner et al.'s depended on actual color matching. In a further group of 500 volunteers, Simner et al. (2006) also obtained much higher levels of consistency using verbal descriptions of color, even with a 6-month delay for retesting. The immediate retest in Simner et al.'s study would have been expected to inflate the relative scores of some of the non-synesthetes, because of the ease with which they could have recalled their first-reported associations, although it should not have artificially inflated the proportion of true synesthetes, because this classification was verified by additional tests. However, the immediate retest might have eroded any distinction between non-synesthetes with low and high scores for consistency, such as that seen in Steven's data. Although most of the discrepancies between these two sets of data can then be accounted for, they highlight the difficulty of making quantitative comparisons between results from different studies when there is no broad agreement about the appropriate battery of tests and the exact form in which quantitative results should be gathered and expressed.

While great interest has focused on the nature of concurrent experiences, it is important for any consideration of the neural basis of synesthesia to take account of the level of processing of the inducing stimulus from which the synesthetic association is triggered. There has been particular interest in the possibility that colored graphemes might result from "stray" connections between immediately adjacent cortical areas (see later). In some individuals, induction of the concurrent seems to depend on basic features of the shape of the grapheme: Ramachandran and Hubbard (2001a) called such people "lower synesthetes" and suggested that they might have excessive connectivity between areas in the fusiform gyrus (discussed later). However, the inducing stimulus for other color-grapheme synesthetes seems to be at a more advanced stage in cognitive processing. For such people, whom Ramachandran and Hubbard (2001a) called "higher synesthetes," colors are triggered by the broader concept of the grapheme. For instance, a color might be elicited not only by a particular digit but also by the equivalent Roman numeral or an array of that number of dots. Ramachandran and Hubbard (2001a) suggested that local connections within the angular gyrus might be responsible for this kind of synesthesia.

Other forms of synesthesia are also linked to different levels of cognitive processing of the inducing stimulus. Steven and Blakemore (2004) described the rich variety of inducing stimuli for a group of blind synesthetes who experience visual concurrents. One of them (JF) has "lower-level" tactile colored Braille: he "sees" an externalized array of colored dots ("like an LED display") as he touches each Braille character but not when he feels a dot array in the shape of a conventional grapheme. Now, a single Braille array can represent a letter, a digit, or a musical note, depending on the context; but for JF, the particular color is determined only by the geometry of the array, and does not vary with its contextual interpretation. By comparison, another subject (DH) did not have tactile colored Braille but saw colored dots in the pattern of the Braille array when she listened to spoken graphemes. However, in her case, the cognitive level of the inducing stimulus was "higher": the color of her dots for any particular Braille array depended on whether it was triggered by a spoken letter, digit or musical note. The processing level of the inducer also varied dramatically for different types of synesthesia in individual subjects. JF, for example, also has colored sequence synesthesia for time-words and in this case the colors are triggered at a level of analysis "higher" than phonological representation. Time-words (e.g., *Thursday*) induce colors, but phonologically very similar words (e.g., *thirsty*) do not. Even the semantic context influences whether a particular word generates its usual concurrent: the spoken word *March* provokes a color for JF in the sentence "This is the month of March" but not in the sentence "The soldiers are going on a march." These and many other examples in the literature demonstrate that, as for the projector/associator dichotomy, the higher/lower distinction of Ramachandran and Hubbard (2001a) applies not to individual synesthetes but to each form of synesthetic association. We suggest, then, that this distinction should be defined in terms of the nature of the inducer, with revised terminology:

- Lower-level inducer
- Higher-level inducer.

Ramachandran and Hubbard's (2001a) hypothesis of local stray connectivity, in either the fusiform gyrus or the angular gyrus, as the basis of synesthesia has led to the view that there is a relationship between the level of processing of the inducer and the nature of the concurrent experience. However, Ward et al. (2007) found no correlation between the lower/higher distinction and the tendency to externalize the concurrent color in a group of 14 colored-grapheme synesthetes. Each synesthetic association is defined in terms of both the level of processing of the inducer and the nature of the concurrent. This idiosyncratic variation is a serious complication in any attempt to study the neural basis of synesthesia, especially since neuroimaging studies usually involve the pooling of data from many subjects. It is also a challenge to the notion that synesthesia is caused by minor aberrations in local connectivity in the cortex.

EXPLANATIONS OF THE ETIOLOGY OF SYNESTHESIA MUST ACCOUNT FOR THE OVERWHELMING PREVALENCE OF COLORED CONCURRENTS

Clues to the etiology of synesthesia might lie in the nature of synesthetic experiences. Is there anything distinctive about concurrent percepts? In Simner et al.'s (2006) large, relatively unbiased study of synesthesia, it is striking that, of the nine types of concurrents included in their questionnaire (colors, shapes/patterns, tastes, smells, pains/touches, noises, flashes, music, movements), the vast majority of synesthetic percepts reported were visual: indeed 95% of all examples of synesthetic association involved color. In this study, synesthetes were allowed to specify their own concurrents if they differed from the suggestions on the questionnaire, so this outcome bias did not emerge from the methodology of testing.

It is surely significant that, except in highly artificial situations, color belongs to objects rather than being a sensory feature in its own right. Many easily recognizable objects can exist in a variety of colors (e.g., cars, cups, books, flowers, clothing). Black-and-white photographs are visually informative as well as aesthetically pleasing. Color is an optional extra in perception. Among mammals, only primates appear to have cortical areas specialized (at least in part) for the analysis of color (Gegenfurtner 2003) and primates might be special in the extent to which color plays an important part in behavior. The color of an object can help to segregate it from its background (e.g., spotting fruit on a tree) and can provide important information about its identity. However, chromatic information alone turns out to be a poor cue for identifying the boundaries of objects and their exact spatial location: isoluminant patterns (consisting of areas of color that do not differ in brightness) are difficult to segregate perceptually and they do not support stereoscopic vision (binocular depth perception). Perhaps the cortical analysis of color is a late development in mammalian evolution, and consequently the mechanisms for the attachment of colors to the neural representations of objects are less robust than other forms of natural sensory unification.

Another unusual aspect of color vision is that, in normal viewing conditions, the actual perceived color of an isolated surface cannot be computed unequivocally from the spectral composition of light reflected from it, because this depends on the wavelength content of the source of illumination. For example, a green apple still appears green when taken indoors, even though the switch to artificial lighting means it is reflecting relatively more long-wavelength light into the observer's eye than it was out-doors. The neural computation of surface color must be continuously updated on the basis of integrated information about the wavelength content of light reflected from other surfaces in the scene—a process called color constancy. Perhaps synesthetic color association results from some aberration of the mechanisms for the assignment of color values to objects.

Even among the rarer forms of synesthesia, the concurrents tend to be similar, "secondary" sensory characteristics, such as tastes, smells, noises and pain. Tastes and smells are normally perceptually assigned to particular foods. Noises come from noisy objects. Pains belong to wounds or parts of the body. "Primary" concurrents, such as the feeling of a shape in the mouth in association with particular food, are extremely rare (Simner et al. 2006). It must be said, however, that spatial sequence synesthesia seems different in this respect: the arrays of colored or colorless "photisms" elicited by hearing or thinking about numbers, days of the week, etc., often do have the "primary" characteristics of shape and size as well as position in space.

In some circumstances, synesthetes are affected by their illusory experiences in much the same way that "normal" observers, without explicit synesthesia, can be affected by over-learned sensory associations (and by the kinds of prevalent unconscious natural associations described earlier). For instance, "normal" observers take longer to report the font color of a printed word when the word itself describes a different color (e.g., RED printed in green)—the Stroop effect. Colored-grapheme synesthetes also have increased reaction time to report the true color of a letter if that color is different from the synesthetically-induced hue (about 160–200 ms longer for externalized ("projector") synesthesia, and 30–40 ms longer for internalized ("associator") synesthesia; see Meier and Rothen 2009). However a number of studies have shown that a period of simple associative training in non-synesthetes, linking letters and colors, also leads to delayed reaction time for the identification of the colors of letters when those colors conflict with the learned associations (Elias et al. 2003; Hancock 2006; Meier and Rothen 2009). Moreover, the delay in reaction time reported in these studies was 23–38 ms, which is similar to that for internalized synesthesia.

Berteletti, Hubbard, and Zorzi (2009) reported that a colored-digit synesthete was slower to recognize the font color of a small number of dots if this color clashed with the synesthetic color of the equivalent digit. This Stroop effect occurred despite the fact that the dot arrays did not explicitly evoke that color for this subject: presumably it was induced by some internal, unconscious representation of the color associated with the dot number. Interestingly, the mean prolongation of reaction time for irregularly arranged dot patterns was 38–58 ms—similar to the magnitude of the Stroop effect for internalized synesthesia and for learned associations in non-synesthetes. It would be interesting to know whether people with implicit grapheme-color association (those who deny conscious synesthetic experiences but perform well on the test of reliability—see Figure 47.2) also demonstrate Stroop-like effects on the basis of their associations, without further training, and, if so, whether the effect on reaction time is of similar magnitude to that for learned associations in true non-synesthetes.

Is Synesthesia an Exaggerated Form of Normal Binding?

A crucial task in perception of the world is to "bind" the various sensory qualities that contribute to each object. In particular, for every object that is seen, the neural representation of its color has to be perceptually linked to its defining characteristics, particularly its shape, size and position in space. This demands either a huge portfolio of hard-wired "detectors," representing all the common combinations of features, or a versatile associative mechanism that can register and store, temporarily, the unpredictable sensory conjunctions that occur in the constantly changing environment. Perhaps synesthesia is due to the formation of robust and persistent "detectors" for certain combinations of sensory characteristics. Many researchers (e.g., Cohen Kadosh and Walsh 2008) have compared synesthesia with the normal perceptual task of binding. Could a synesthete's green letter "T," say, be due to the stabilization of a binding process that normally happens only temporarily to encode the concept of a "green T"? The classical work on binding by Treisman and Gelade (1980) suggests that various aspects of a visual stimulus are separately analyzed and stored in working memory, and that their conjunction in perception and memory depends on active attention. Indeed, if attention is compromised during the brief presentation of a set of colored shapes, the stimuli recalled include "illusory conjunctions," in which colors are attached to the wrong shapes (Treisman and Schmidt 1982).

Treisman and Gelade (1980) found that the time taken to recognize particular *combinations* of sensory features (e.g., a green "T") depends on the number of distractors (red "T"s and green "X"s) in the display. This contrasts with trials where subjects simply have to detect, say, a sole blue letter or a sole letter "S" (i.e., a single sensory feature) in an array of others. Here, the time taken to recognize the odd symbol does not depend on the size of the array and the feature appears to "pop out"—a process called parallel search. The sensory conjunction of a green "T," however, cannot be achieved "pre-attentively" and hence it does not "pop out" from an array of other green letters. Detecting conjunctions requires directed attention and serial search—a process that takes longer as the array size is increased (see Figure 47.3). Treisman and her colleagues asked whether prolonged practice could lead to "unitization"—the formation of a bound neural representation so robust that the combined features could act as a unique stimulus and be detected pre-attentively in pop-out tasks:

> We had been interested in seeing whether practice could lead to unitization, in the sense of developing a special detector for the conjunction of green and "T," which could allow a change to parallel search...The present experiment, however suggests that unitization of color and shape is difficult and may be impossible to achieve. There may be built-in neural constraints on which dimensions can be unitized in this way (Treisman and Gelade 1980, 107)

FIGURE 47.3 Attention-dependent search and pre-attentive pop-out. These two panels consist of identical arrays of "distractors" with a single different "target" grapheme. On the left the graphemes are all the same color and the target can be found only by searching the array. Typically the reaction time for serial search is more than 1 s and it increases with the number of distractors and the size of the array. On the right, the distractors and target differ in color and the target pops out without directed attention. Reaction time for parallel detection of a target differing in color is typically about 250 ms and is independent of the number of distractors and the size of the display.

While unitization sufficient to produce stable binding is difficult to produce by practice in adult subjects, life-long habitual experience of conjoined shapes and colors (e.g., orange carrot-shapes and yellow banana-shapes) does seem to establish a small repertoire of such conjunction detection (Treisman 1986). Might the essential feature of synesthesia be an enhanced capacity to form such conjunction detectors? There are arguments against this interpretation. First, what real experiences could drive the establishment of conjunctions between, say, Thursday and yellow, or words and tastes? Why should any particular conjunction be favored rather than any other? Even if the synesthete's brain does contain unusual conjunction detectors, why should one element of the pair (the letter "N," say) induce the explicit, illusory perception of the other (an associated color), but not the reverse? And why should the concurrent be consciously experienced, any more than the outline of a banana induces an actual sensation of yellow? The body of work on binding and the rare unitization of sensory features in "normal" people does not support the idea that synesthesia is simply an exaggerated, rapid and florid form of unitization. Synesthetes never have a vast repertoire of extraneous sensory associations, which one might expect from a rampant unitization mechanism. Synesthetic associations are idiosyncratic; occur for a specific, small set of inducing stimuli; do not usually relate to features commonly associated in the environment; and are generally remarkably robust.

However, it is intriguing that, within the necessarily versatile process of feature combination, a small repertoire of stable associations (e.g., yellow and banana-shape) can be established in non-synesthetes. It is conceivable that the unitization process responsible for such rare normal associations is abnormally rapid yet highly idiosyncratic in synesthetes. But why should it be limited to very particular stimulus combinations, which might never have actually been experienced together? And, crucially, why should unitization lead to conscious experience of concurrents in the presence of the inducer alone in synesthetes but not in other individuals? Through several ingenious experiments, Sagiv, Heer, and Robertson (2006) explored the relationship between attention-dependent sensory binding and synesthesia. They showed that the emergence of colored concurrents in colored-grapheme synesthetes depends on attention, and they proposed "that the mechanisms giving rise to this type of synesthesia appear to follow at least some principles of normal binding, and even synesthetic binding seems to require attention" (Sagiv, Heer, and Robertson 2006, 232).

There remains the question of whether the various kinds of unusual sensory association (bound and unbound externalized synesthesia, internalized synesthesia and implicit sensory association) are really distinct characteristics. While explicit, conscious synesthetic experiences are unusual and surprising, perhaps they are the extreme of a tendency to form apparently irrelevant sensory associations, an aberration of some normal, functional process of multisensory association. Indeed, they might be merely "noise" in whatever process underpins the assignment of perceptual qualia to sensory stimuli. Despite doubts about a simple relationship between synesthesia and normal binding, it would certainly be interesting to explore whether synesthetes display aberrations in feature integration, for example, a higher susceptibility to illusory conjunctions (Treisman and Schmidt 1982) or greater ease in forming unitized conjunction detectors through associative learning. The answers to such questions could help elucidate the relationship between synesthesia and normal perceptual integration (see Alvarez and Robertson, Chapter 16, this volume, for a review of synesthesia and binding).

WHEN AND HOW ARE SYNESTHETIC ASSOCIATIONS FORMED?

The prevailing (but possibly erroneous) view that synesthesia is usually an inherited condition has frequently been taken to correlate with the prevailing (but possibly erroneous) view that inducer-concurrent associations are always established very early in life. Indeed, as mentioned earlier, when Perroud (1863) discovered an adult colored-grapheme synesthete who claimed to have had this condition for only 12 to 15 years, he assumed that it must have been a rare "acquired" case, because it had already become assumed that synesthesia is inherited and the associations are established very early. But inherited characteristics can express themselves long after normal development. For instance, some genetic neurological conditions (such as the rare familial forms of Alzheimer's and Parkinson's disease, and even the autosomal dominant condition Huntington's disease) become manifest only later in life. Even if a disposition towards synesthesia is inherited (perhaps in the form of unusual aspects of cortical connectivity—see later), highly specific associations with inducers that can be learned about only through individual experience (e.g., graphemes, days of the week, passages of music, the sight of particular friends) are likely to depend in some way on personal exposure. Indeed, Galton (1881) described a man who saw dates as colored and claimed that his associations were determined by the colored lettering in a history book from which he had studied as a child. This led to the view that synesthetic associations result from specific stimulus combinations experienced repetitively, very early in life. But there have been challenges to this simple idea.

Maurer (1997) suggested that all babies might be synesthetic and that this perceptual characteristic is lost in most children as a result of the "pruning" of connections in the cerebral cortex during maturation. Recently Wagner and Dobkins (2011) have produced some evidence that shapes superimposed on colored patches slightly affect the preferences of 2- to 3-month-olds in ways that are lost by 8 months. However, Simner et al. (2009) suggested that colored-grapheme synesthesia is acquired with the onset of literacy. While learning how to distinguish between graphemes might seem to be a prerequisite for the establishment of such associations, the basis of the particular inducer-concurrent relationships acquired by individual synesthetes remains mysterious. Treisman's rare "unitization" of particular combinations of shapes and colors depends on the habitual experience of pairs of features (e.g., banana shapes and yellow). While there are exceptional cases in which synesthetic associations clearly relate to common conjoint experiences early in life (Witthoft and Winawer 2013), it is inconceivable that the bizarre, distinctive inducer-concurrent relations of some synesthetes (e.g., words and tastes) could correspond to frequent early experience of equivalent real stimuli.

For grapheme-color associations, which have been most extensively studied, there is some degree of statistical regularity across synesthetes. For instance, Simner et al. (2005) reported that letters that are more commonly used in language tend to elicit more frequently experienced colors, and so there are some biases in grapheme-color associations across synesthetes (e.g., A is quite often red, C yellow). In their review of this topic, Spector and Maurer (2009) identified a number of associations that not only are fairly common among synesthetes but also occur quite often in the "forced" associations of non-synesthetic subjects. Some of these biases seem to relate to color names (G = green; Y = yellow) and this is also true to a small but significant extent in synesthetes (Simner et al. 2005). On the other hand, other slight biases, which seem (inexplicably) linked to the shape of the letters (X and Z = black; O and I = white), are even seen in the preferences of pre-literate toddlers (see Spector and Maurer 2009). On the basis of an analysis of the incidence of grapheme color associations in infants and children, Spector and Maurer (2011) proposed that certain colors tend to be "bound" to some specific shapes very early in life, but learning to read can induce additional associations. Brang et al. (2011) reported a modest tendency for similarly shaped letters to elicit similar colors within (but not necessarily between) synesthetes, this effect being somewhat more striking in those with strongly externalized synesthesia. Beeli, Esslen, and Jäncke (2007) found a correlation between the frequency of occurrence of letters in language and the saturation of the concurrent color, but they did not see a clear relationship between letter frequency and hue.

Letter-color associations that clearly relate to the name of the color might be explained by some sort of associative learning based on frequent repetition. But what of the not-uncommon, idiosyncratic letter-color associations that are peculiar to individual synesthetes? Witthoft and Winawer (2013) recently described 11 synesthetes whose concurrent colors corresponded closely to those of a set of refrigerator magnets in the form of letters that they had played with when children. Interestingly, Hancock (2006) described a pair of monozygotic twins who did not have explicit synesthesia but who shared reliable digit-color associations from a very early age: they would actually name digits with the associated color name at the age of 3. These associations were traced to the colors of digits in a jigsaw that they played with. When tested at later ages, they had extended their color associations to letters, but with less correlation between the two of them. It is tempting to think that such associations can be learned through repeated exposure when very young and that they progress to full-blown synesthesia in children with a disposition to this condition. These cases, though striking, are exceptional. Others have failed to discover a clear correlation between early experience of colored graphemes and individual grapheme-color associations (see Rich, Bradshaw, and Mattingley 2005 for a large-scale study).

Although most synesthetes say that they have had their particular concurrent experiences for as long as they can remember, there are indications that associations can be acquired later in childhood, and even as an adult. Perhaps the clearest evidence comes from individuals with late onset-blindness who nevertheless experience visual concurrents—see Steven and Blakemore (2004), Steven, Hansen, and Blakemore (2006), and Niccolai et al. (2012). In particular, some such individuals have colored Braille synesthesia and obviously this must have developed only after they started to learn Braille. The extensively-studied blind synesthete JF, who sees vivid, externalized patterns of colored dots when he touches Braille characters (discussed earlier) did not start to learn Braille until he was 5 years old. Even though he learned the conventional letters of the alphabet while he could still see, he does not recall ever having had colored grapheme synesthesia, so his colored Braille is unlikely to have resulted from transfer from pre-existing colored graphemes. Indeed, although he can touch-read patterns of dots arranged to represent conventional graphemes, these do not provoke colors but trigger uncolored externalized spatial sequences, which also developed after he became blind. JF also has spatial sequence synesthesia for a variety of categorical classifications. He experiences spatially organized, colored photisms when he hears or thinks about time-words, some of which he remembers seeing before he became blind. But he subsequently acquired equally clear visual patterns (some colored) for many other categories: for school classes, when he was in primary school; for instruments of the orchestra, in his early teens; for military groupings (platoons, companies, regiments, etc.) and for pay scales at work, as an adult.

Our conclusion is that, discounting synesthetic-like experiences induced in non-synesthetes by recreational drug use, brain damage, or post-hypnotic suggestion (Cohen Kadosh et al. 2009), some genuine synesthetes can acquire additional inducer-concurrents after their early years. Given the difficulty of performing detailed psychophysical and neuroimaging studies in very young babies, studies of the acquisition of new associations in adult synesthetes might be a more productive way of analyzing the ways in which such associations are established.

No Simple Link between Cortical Hyperconnectivity and Synesthetic Percepts

Methods for imaging the structure and activity of the human brain have energized the study of synesthesia and fuelled the prevailing view that synesthesia is due to excess "cross-talk" between different sensory modalities. Tomson and colleagues (2011, 51) noted that: "The difference between the synesthetic and non-synesthetic brain, therefore, appears to be not whether there is crosstalk, but rather how much there is." The implication is that the wiring of a synesthetic brain differs in degree, rather than specific form, from that in a non-synesthete. The commonest interpretation of "excessive cross-talk" is that the sensory areas in the cortex of synesthetes are over-connected (i.e., having extra axons and synapses linking them) and that the origin of this hyperconnectivity is some deviation from normal development. The density of synapses in the human cerebral cortex increases over the early years of life, followed by partial elimination of connections, often called "pruning." Perhaps the cortex of a synesthete remains over-connected compared with non-synesthetes, conceivably because of a genetic difference in the pruning process.

Speculations about over-connectivity in synesthetes were stimulated by anatomical evidence of widespread "exuberant" cortical connections in young animals, which gradually regress through the withdrawal of inappropriate axons. The most impressive evidence came from kittens, where there is substantial early over-connection between the two hemispheres and between different sensory areas (see Dehay, Kennedy, and Bullier 1988). Cortico-cortical projections are generally much less exuberant in baby monkeys, although, intriguingly, there is excessive early input to the color area V4 from the auditory cortex (Kennedy et al. 1997). Using electroencephalographic (EEG) recording, Neville (1995) found that when young human babies listen to spoken language there is activity not only in the auditory cortex but also over visual areas, and that the latter activity disappears by about the age of 3.

Cohen-Kadosh and Walsh have offered an alternative account in which increased cross-talk is caused by inappropriate disinhibition of sensory areas: a particular sensory input causes activity in inappropriate sensory areas because normally ineffective inputs are "released" by a reduction in cortical inhibition. They suggest that, rather than a failure of pruning, "imbalances in inhibitory circuits…can lead to long-lasting structural rewiring" (Cohen Kadosh and Walsh 2008, 549).

A number of neuroimaging studies using functional magnetic resonance imaging (fMRI) have described activation of the putative color area, V4, in the cortex of synesthetes when they are experiencing colored concurrents (e.g., Niccolai et al. 2012; Nunn et al. 2002; Steven, Hansen, and Blakemore 2006). However, several other fMRI studies have failed to detect V4 activation (e.g., Hupé, Bordier, and Dojat 2012; Rich et al. 2006; Steven 2004) and these differences in results are unexplained. Ramachandran and Hubbard pointed out that a region of the posterior temporal cortex implicated in the processing of graphemes or "word-form" is adjacent to the putative color area, V4, and they proposed that colored-grapheme synesthesia is due to "stray" connections between these two areas (Ramachandran and Hubbard 2001a, 2001b). Indeed Brang et al. (2010) reported that in synesthetes, but not controls, graphemes elicited responses (detected by magnetoencephalography) in V4 as well as the grapheme area. Moreover, activity in the grapheme area preceded that in V4 by only 5 ms. This result supports the idea of direct and immediate cross-activation of V4 through local connections, rather than the alternative hypothesis of disinhibited feedback from higher centers, which would necessarily take longer. However, the cortical over-connectivity that has been described in synesthetes (see later) is very widespread and not restricted to the posterior temporal lobe. And many other forms of synesthesia (e.g., colors induced by Braille, time-words or music; tastes evoked by words) seem to involve widely separated cortical areas.

The most compelling evidence for the over-connection hypothesis comes from structural imaging studies of the cerebral hemispheres of synesthetes and non-synesthetes. Diffusion tensor imaging (DTI) captures the integrity of white matter tracts in a measure called fractional anisotropy (FA). (See Rouw, Chapter 25, this volume, for a comprehensive overview of this methodology.) A DTI study of colored-grapheme synesthetes (Rouw and Scholte 2007), found differences in FA between synesthetes and non-synesthetes in the fusiform and inferior temporal cortex (parts of high-level visual cortex). However, there were also structural differences in frontal and parietal areas, which are less easily accounted for. In another DTI study of colored-grapheme synesthesia, Steven (2004) also detected a large region of increased FA (compared to controls) in the supramarginal gyrus of the left parietal lobe in synesthetes, and a smaller region in the right middle frontal region. The differences in white matter in the supramarginal gyrus are not surprising, since this region is connected to gray matter in the superior temporal sulcus/angular gyrus, where fMRI revealed unusual activity in the same cohort (Steven 2004) and in other synesthetes (Niccolai et al. 2012; Nunn et al. 2002; Rouw and Scholte 2010). Perhaps these supramarginal fibre tracts mediate unusual cortico-cortical connectivity underlying synesthetic percepts. However, as with the Rouw and Scholte study, the meaning of the structural differences found in frontal regions is less clear.

More explicit evidence for brain-wide hyperconnectivity comes from a recent study (Hänggi, Wotruba, and Jäncke 2011) of the topology of structural brain networks in

24 colored-grapheme synesthetes and 24 non-synesthetes. The authors used voxel-based morphometry (VBM) from structural MRI to measure cortical gray-matter thickness and took correlations between different cortical regions as an indirect indicator of connectivity, which enabled them to construct topological "graphs" of the structural brain networks of each participant. The architecture of these graphs was then characterized using graph-theoretic metrics, which capture general properties of the network, such as the "clustering coefficient." This coefficient, which provides information about the level of local connectedness within a network, was globally increased in synesthetes, pointing to cortex-wide local hyperconnectivity (see Figure 47.4).

The correlation between cortical over-connection and extraneous sensory experiences is seductively compelling. Extra connections between areas responsible for processing the inducer and generating the concurrent sensation could mediate the cross-talk proposed to underpin synesthesia. But there are unconvincing features of this hypothesis. Most notably, hyperconnectivity appears to be widespread throughout the cerebral hemispheres, rather than being restricted to the highly specific linkages needed to explain the synesthetic experiences of each individual. Also, the detection of such differences between small numbers of synesthetes and non-synesthetes with the relatively low-resolution techniques of VBM and DTI implies that the anatomical abnormalities are substantial—far exceeding what would seem to be expected to generate a limited repertoire of highly specific concurrent percepts. The mechanistic abnormalities that are posited as responsible for synesthesia seem irreconcilably general. Synaptic pruning and the development of inhibitory circuits, postulated to be aberrant in synesthesia, are surely crucial for all aspects of cognitive processing. Widespread defective pruning or imbalanced inhibitory circuits would be expected to produce greater and more generalized behavioral differences than those that characterize synesthesia.

What, then, is the origin of these diffuse structural differences? It is conceivable that they result from abnormal sensory activation during development, rather than causing it, just as the normal regression of some exuberant connectivity in the kitten cortex is regulated by sensory experience (Innocenti and Price 2005). Alternatively, the type of excessive connectivity that is necessary for synesthesia could be a generalized developmental error, which might then lead to other and more universal alterations in functional performance. There may be far more to the "synesthetic brain" than the experience of certain idiosyncratic synesthetic concurrents. Documenting the performance of a large cohort of synesthetes in a wide range of psychophysical and cognitive tasks, compared with non-synesthetes, would add considerably to this discussion.

Presumably, the structural differences seen in the cerebral hemispheres of synesthetes are the substrate of abnormalities in functional connectivity. Characterization of brain network organization in synesthesia could thus help us to understand the link between structural changes and synesthetic percepts. At present, however, there are few studies of functional connectivity or functional network organization in synesthesia (Dovern et al. 2012; Jäncke and Langer 2011; van Leeuwen et al. 2011). This is a crucial area for further research. Jäncke and Langer (2011) used resting-state EEG data to construct "graphs" (networks with nodes and connections) of the brain architecture of

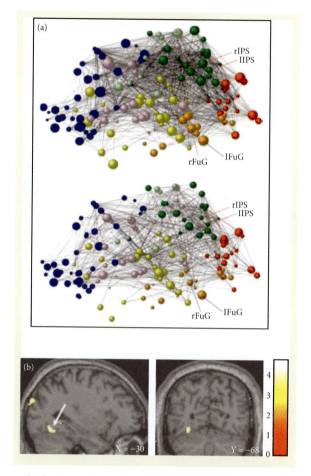

FIGURE 47.4 The cerebral cortex of synesthetes is characterized by global hyperconnectivity, yet highly localized aberrant functional activation. (a) Analysis of connectivity for 154 locations in the cerebral cortex (nodes), based on MRI gray-matter morphometry and graph-theoretical network analyses in 24 colored-grapheme synesthetes (top) and 24 non-synesthetes (bottom). Weighted degree centrality (a measure of the capability of each node to catch whatever is flowing through the network) is indicated by the size of the spheres. Both connectivity and degree centrality are greater in the synesthetes, across all lobes of the hemispheres (blue, frontal; pink, limbic; yellow, temporal; orange, temporo-occipital; red, occipital; green, parietal; light green, parieto-frontal). lFuG, rFuG = left and right fusiform gyrus; lIPS, rIPS = left and right intraparietal sulcus. (b) Sagittal (left) and coronal (right) views of the brain of a late-blind colored-time-word synesthete, showing fMRI activation (yellow voxels) in the putative color-processing area V4 of the left hemisphere (indicated by the white arrow in the sagittal view) when he heard time-words (days of the week, months of the year), contrasted with words that also referred to time units (e.g. "second," "season," "year") but did not elicit synesthetic colors. (a) Reproduced from Hänggi, J., Wotruba, D., and Jäncke, L., Globally Altered Structural Brain Network Topology in Grapheme-Color Synesthesia. *The Journal of Neuroscience*, 31(15), pp. 5816–5828, figure 4 © 2011, Society for Neuroscience, with permission. (b) Reproduced from Niccolai, V., van Leeuwen, T. M., Blakemore, C., and Stoerig, P., Synaesthetic perception of colour and visual space in a blind subject: An fMRI case study. *Consciousness and Cognition*, 21, pp. 889–899, figure 3.

colored-hearing synesthetes and non-synesthetes. The network properties of each of these subject-specific graphs were analyzed, and the graph-theoretic metrics generated were compared between the two groups. One measure calculated was "degree," which quantifies the interconnectedness of a particular region of interest with the rest of the brain. Of the 84 designated regions, those with a high degree were designated "hubs." The authors' hypothesis of increased degree in parietal hubs in synesthetes was borne out, and thought to reflect the role of the parietal area in binding synesthetic percepts to their inducer. Notably, however, synesthetes were found to have increased degree (or higher interconnectedness) in other hub regions (prefrontal, extra-striate and hippocampal). Of interest is the fact that disruption of neural activity by transcranial magnetic stimulation (TMS) of the parietal cortex in colored-grapheme synesthetes can reduce the interfering effect of synesthetic colors in a Stroop-like detection task (Muggleton et al. 2007). However this was true only for TMS over the right parietal area rather than the left, whereas several neuroimaging studies have implicated the left hemisphere, and especially regions around the angular gyrus, in synesthesia.

Another recent study (Dovern et al. 2012) characterized the functional connectivity of 12 colored-grapheme synesthetes, compared with 12 non-synesthetic controls, with data from resting-state fMRI. The authors used independent component analysis, informed by results from previous neuroimaging studies of synesthesia, to derive seven synesthesia-relevant brain networks involving visual, auditory, parietal and fronto-parietal regions. The synesthetic participants showed greater functional connectivity both within and between these networks, compared to controls. These two functional connectivity studies used different neuroimaging procedures, and focused on different forms of synesthesia, but both demonstrated widespread alterations in brain network properties that were present at rest, when synesthetic concurrents were not being experienced. This provides further hints that the "synesthetic brain" differs in more ways than simply the generation of synesthetic percepts. Indeed, there is evidence from other sources that sensory processing in synesthetes is more generally unusual. For example, Barnett, Foxe, et al. (2008) showed that there are differences between synesthetes and controls in the early sensory components of the visual evoked potential measured using EEG for simple stimuli that do not elicit synesthetic percepts.

The idea that individual synesthetic associations are local perturbations, reaching the threshold of consciousness, against a more generalized background of hyperconnectivity, is somewhat supported by family studies of synesthesia. Barnett and colleagues (Barnett, Finucane, et al. 2008) found that closely-related members of the same family can exhibit very different kinds of synesthesia. This might suggest that what is inherited is a generalized propensity towards hyperconnectivity, which, through stochastic processes or specific environmental interactions, produces different phenotypes in different individuals. However, some families do transmit subtypes of synesthesia quite reliably. Tomson et al. (2011) found evidence for a specific genetic linkage in families with colored sequence synesthesia (although in only two of the five families studied). Further work on the familial transmission of the five broad categories of synesthesia identified by Novich, Cheng, and Eagleman (2011), ultimately linked to neuroimaging studies of connectivity and functional activity, could give valuable clues to the genetic-developmental mechanisms underlying synesthesia, and indeed to the possible genetic regulation of local connectivity during normal development.

In the past decade, there has been an explosion in studies of functional connectivity, particularly in psychiatry. Many psychiatric conditions are characterized by brain-wide abnormalities in functional connectivity, as measured by neuroimaging techniques, such as correlation analysis of resting-state blood oxygenation level-dependent (BOLD) signals in fMRI (e.g., Lynall et al. 2010). Unfortunately, the widespread abnormalities, the unknown nature of putative underlying "dysconnectivity" and our lack of knowledge of the neural activity represented by correlations in the timescale of blood flow, make it difficult to draw conclusions about the neurobiology underlying such abnormalities. The nature of the perceptual phenomena in synesthesia, on the other hand, leads to strong predictions of increased but precise functional connectivity between very specific areas, suggested by the nature of the inducer and concurrent. As discussed earlier, the level of sensory or cognitive processing at which a particular stimulus triggers a synesthetic concurrent varies enormously between people and even for different forms of synesthesia in any individual. And the nature of the concurrent experience, whether externalized or internalized and the spatial coordinates within which is appears, can also vary within and between subjects. Varying the stimulus presented while functional connectivity is analyzed in synesthetes with different levels of inducer and different types of concurrent experience might enable study of the relationship between connectivity and synesthetic association in a controllable way.

No Clear Evidence That Synesthesia Provides an Advantage in Perception

The high prevalence of synesthesia and the likelihood that it is at least partly heritable raise questions about the possible adaptive value of this phenomenon, which might conceivably have stabilized its occurrence in human populations, despite the apparent disadvantage of perception of the world different from that of others.

Discussion of this question is dominated by results of Ramachandran and Hubbard (2001b) suggesting that concurrent colors can speed up the detection of the inducing features in situations in which the features alone (without the illusory color) would be much harder to detect. In normal vision, a "target" shape of one color, hidden in an array of similar shapes, uncolored or of a different color ("distractors"), is immediately recognized "pre-attentively." It "pops out" without systematic search of the array (see earlier), and the reaction time to detect it is typically only about 250 ms, independent of the total number of elements in the array. On the other hand, an achromatic grapheme (say an "H") amongst an array of other, different letters (say "F"s or "P"s) does not pop out and has to be found by serial search. The reaction time for detection is significantly longer (a second or more) and increases as the array is made larger. See Figure 47.3.

Ramachandran and Hubbard (2001b) presented displays consisting of a small number of identical graphemes (say "H"s) arranged to form one of four familiar shapes (rectangle, triangle etc.), set against a background array of distractors (say "F"s and "P"s). After a 1 s exposure, the subject had to name the shape. They argued that colored-grapheme synesthetes might have an advantage if different concurrent colors were evoked by the target and distractor graphemes, hence transforming the task from slow serial search to rapid, pre-attentive pop-out. Two colored-grapheme subjects performed better than 40 control subjects on this task (but only at a marginal level of significance—p <0.05—and without consideration of the small sample size). Ramachandran and Hubbard (2001b, 981) concluded that synesthesia is "genuinely perceptual and not confabulatory." But, at face value, this result implies much more—that the mechanism for attaching color to graphemes operates before the grapheme itself has been explicitly recognized. Indeed, Ramachandran and Hubbard (2001a) suggested that synesthetic association is pre-attentive and supports parallel, "pop-out" detection. This points to a possible adaptive value of synesthetic colors: the concurrent percepts might allow the rapid detection of unusual features that would not be so obvious to non-synesthetes.

Despite its widespread influence, Ramachandran and Hubbard's study and its interpretation have been criticized. The idea that colors can rapidly attach to target graphemes without them being distinguished from the distractor graphemes on the basis of their form (a task that itself requires serial search) seems implausible. There is a slight tendency for certain letters (X, Z, O, and I) to trigger particular concurrents (but black or white, not colored), apparently on the basis of elementary features of their shape (see Spector and Maurer 2009) and there is a very loose relationship between categories of grapheme shape and categories of concurrent color for individual synesthetes (Brang et al. 2011). But Ramachandran and Hubbard deliberately chose target and distractor graphemes of similar shape, so as not to support pop-out detection on the basis of differences in grapheme shape alone, yet inducing distinctly different colors.

The experiment has also been criticized because of the long exposure (1 s—long enough for visual search); the fact that the number of trials was not reported; that there were only two synesthetes; that they were told the identity of the target grapheme in advance; that the control subjects performed far above chance; that the significance of the difference between synesthetes and controls was only marginal on a parametric test (t-test), with no consideration of the small sample; and that there was no test of increasing the array size.

Some subsequent studies aimed at replicating the result and relating it specifically to "pop-out" have used the same unorthodox design (e.g., Hubbard et al. 2005). But the hypothesis that synesthetes can apply colors to graphemes that they have not recognized attentively is also apparently supported by an observation of Smilek et al. (2001). They claimed that one exceptional colored-grapheme synesthete could not recognize gray letters if the color of background on which they were briefly presented was the same as the concurrent color of the letter, implying that the letter, though not "seen," must have induced its own color and therefore been masked by the background. However, the design and analysis of this study were criticized by Sagiv, Heer, and Robertson (2006), who could not replicate this finding or the "pop-out" result of Ramachandran and Hubbard (2001b).

Palmeri et al. (2002) more conventionally measured reaction time (rather than percentage of successful trials) for detection of a single target grapheme hidden in an array of different graphemes and they varied the size of the array, in an effort to discriminate between pop-out and visual search. The one synesthete they studied actually commented on the way in which the concurrent color of the target grapheme stood out from the distractors if they had a different concurrent color, but not if they shared the same color. However, there was no statistical difference in performance under these two conditions for displays with up to 25 elements, nor between the performance of the synesthete and controls. Moreover, the fastest reaction times recorded were more than 1 s, far more than the usual 250 ms for normal pre-attentive color pop-out. Reaction time increased with the largest array size, although the increase was slightly less pronounced in the synesthete (with target and distractors of different concurrent color). Palmeri et al. (2002, 4130) concluded that the synesthete did not have pre-attentive pop-out, but that "as attention is allocated to a part of the visual field (a single digit or a small cluster of digits), synesthetic color seems to be bound to a visual form as that form is being recognized." In other words, attention to the region of the target enabled it to be recognized and only then did the concurrent color become clear.

Laeng, Svartdal, and Oelmann (2004) presented very similar results for a single synesthete, again with reaction times of more than 1 s but a shallow increase of reaction time with set size. They came to the same conclusion—that performance depends on whether the target grapheme lies close enough to fixation to be readily attended. A number of other large studies have failed to find a pop-out effect (Edquist et al. 2006; Rothen and Meier 2009; Sagiv, Heer, and Robertson 2006; Steven 2004; Ward, Jonas, and Seth 2009; for review see Rich and Mattingley, Chapter 14, this volume). Of the 36 synesthetes tested by Ward, Jonas, and Seth (2009) for accuracy on a visual search task with a 1 s exposure, some reported that they experienced synesthetic colors during some of the 56 trials while 17 never saw them. However, performance on the detection task was not correlated with the presence or absence of concurrent colors.

The present conclusion is that there is little if any evidence that automatic, pre-attentive generation of concurrent colors in colored-grapheme synesthetes is sufficient to support parallel, pop-out detection. Interestingly, those studies that have convincingly demonstrated a small advantage in the speed of search for large arrays have all employed distractors that generate their own concurrent color. Palmeri et al. (2002) and Sagiv, Heer, and Robertson (2006) both showed that any marginal advantage in searching large arrays disappeared when the distractors had no concurrent color. Perhaps, as Sagiv et al. (2006) suggest, distractors that have been attended to adequately to appear colored can be more easily ignored in the continuing search. Paradoxically, it might be the synesthetic characteristics of the background array that sometimes confer a slight advantage in search, rather than that of the target. At present, the actual experience of synesthetic concurrents cannot be said to be associated with any obvious improvements in perception that are clearly adaptive.

In the search for cognitive advantage in synesthesia, it is not surprising that efforts have focused on the potential value of the concurrent sensations. However, the generalized abnormalities in neural circuitry described in the brains of synesthetes, which might facilitate the establishment of synesthetic associations, could lead to other cognitive phenotypes that are genuinely advantageous: perhaps increased creativity or heightened mental imagery—attributes that would then correlate with synesthesia, as some studies have suggested (Barnett and Newell 2008; Ward et al. 2008). Interestingly, Banissy, Walsh, and Ward (2009) have provided evidence that normal color perception is generally enhanced in synesthetes.

Here we can liken work on synesthesia to the study of schizophrenia, where research was initially driven by the florid manifestations of hallucinations and delusions, but which is increasingly focusing on the more generalized cognitive deficits in, for example, working memory. Equally, much research on schizophrenia is directed at defining unusual features of close relatives of patients, who would be expected to share some of the characteristics important in the etiology, but have not suffered the full-blown condition. We are not, of course, suggesting that synesthesia is a "disease," but a similar approach could prove fruitful. This is another reason to focus on the more general characteristics of the "synesthetic brain."

Conclusions

We lack a clear understanding of what synesthesia *is*, at either the psychophysical or the neurobiological level. The tendency to form apparently irrelevant, often highly consistent sensory associations is not restricted to synesthetes: what is most distinctive about synesthetic associations is that they are consciously experienced. There is growing evidence for morphological and functional differences between synesthetic and non-synesthetic brains, but, paradoxically, these characteristics seem too generalized to provide a crisp explanation of the small repertoire of unusual concurrents experienced by most synesthetes. We hypothesize that the "synesthetic brain" might have a yet-to-be-discovered, broader and potentially adaptive cognitive phenotype.

If we cannot say what synesthesia is, can we say what it isn't? The evidence presented in this review, leads us, tentatively, to suggest the following:

(1) Synesthesia cannot be defined purely by the stability of the concurrent sensation. The "Test of Genuineness" does not test the genuineness of synesthesia: it is only a "test of consistency." Future experiments should tease apart the differential correlates of consistency and subjectivity of percepts.

(2) Normal perceptual experience often includes aspects (especially emotional) that are not directly attributable to the physical stimulus. Moreover, extraneous

sensory association is not unique to synesthetes: it is universal. The *sine qua non* of synesthesia is the explicit conscious experience of concurrents. We recommend referring to reproducible associations that do not elicit conscious concurrents as "implicit sensory association"; and we argue against the classification of people who know that they have reliable associations but do not actually experience concurrents ("know associators") as synesthetes.

(3) Synesthesia is neither rare nor simply inherited. "Sporadic" (non-familial) synesthesia, which might be quite common, deserves particular attention.

(4) Labeling individual synesthetes as "projectors" or "associators" is inappropriate. Although three forms of concurrent experience can be distinguished (we suggest the names "internalized," "bound externalized," and "unbound externalized"), individuals can exhibit more than one class or different classes for different sensory modalities, and may change over time.

(5) The level of analysis at which an inducer triggers a concurrent sensation can differ from one synesthetic association to another, even within an individual. Therefore it is not synesthetes but particular synesthetic inducers that are "higher" or "lower."

(6) There is no simple relationship between the level of analysis of the inducer and the tendency to externalize the concurrent. This compromises any attempt to explain all synesthetic associations in terms of local connectivity in the cortex.

(7) Synesthetic associations are not equally common in all modalities. Explanations of synesthesia must account for the apparently idiosyncratic but overwhelming incidence of colored concurrents.

(8) Although synesthetic associations bear a striking resemblance to the rare examples of "unitization" of features in normal vision (e.g., yellow banana shapes), synesthesia cannot be viewed simply as an exaggerated form of binding. However, the relationship between synesthesia and unitization deserves further attention.

(9) The widespread structural and functional hyperconnectivity in the cortex of synesthetes seems disproportionate to the specific, idiosyncratic nature of the perceptual experiences. The magnitude and widespread nature of hyperconnectivity are an embarrassment of riches. Perhaps the "synesthetic brain" has a wider cognitive phenotype, beyond the synesthetic percepts.

(10) The initial evidence that synesthetic concurrents could provide an advantage in object detection has not been confirmed. Nevertheless, the familial clustering and high prevalence of synesthesia suggest that it conveys some advantage, yet to be defined, and not necessarily related to the conscious experience of concurrents.

ACKNOWLEDGEMENTS

This preparation of this chapter was supported by grants from the Volkswagen-Stiftung and the Silk Charitable Trust. We are very grateful to Megan Steven not only for providing us with data for Figure 47.2b but also for comments on the manuscript.

References

Alvarez, Bryan D., and Lynn C. Robertson. 2013. Synesthesia and binding. In *The Oxford Handbook of Synesthesia*, ed. Julia Simner and Edward M. Hubbard, 317–333. Oxford: Oxford University Press.

Asher, Julian E., Janine A. Lamb, Denise Brocklebank, Jean-Baptiste Cazier, Elena Maestrini, Laura Addis, Mallika Sen, Simon Baron-Cohen, and Anthony P. Monaco. 2009. A whole-genome scan and fine-mapping linkage study of auditory-visual synesthesia reveals evidence of linkage to chromosomes 2q24, 5q33, 6p12, and 12p12. *American Journal of Human Genetics* 84:279–285.

Banissy, Michael J., Vincent Walsh, and Jamie Ward. 2009. Enhanced sensory perception in synaesthesia. *Experimental Brain Research* 196, 4:565–571.

Barnett, Kylie J., Ciara Finucane, Julian E. Asher, Gary Bargary, Aiden P. Corvin, Fiona N. Newell, and Kevin J. Mitchell. 2008. Familial patterns and the origins of individual differences in synaesthesia. *Cognition* 106:871–893.

Barnett, Kylie J., John J. Foxe, Sophie Molholm, Simon P. Kelly, Shani Shalgi, Kevin J. Mitchell, and Fiona N. Newell. 2008. Differences in early sensory-perceptual processing in synesthesia: a visual evoked potential study. *NeuroImage* 43: 605–613.

Barnett, Kylie J., and Fiona N. Newell. 2008. Synaesthesia is associated with enhanced, self-rated visual imagery. *Consciousness and Cognition* 17:1032–1039.

Baron-Cohen, Simon, Lucy Burt, Fiona Smith-Laittan, John Harrison, and Patrick Bolton. 1996. Synaesthesia: prevalence and familiality. *Perception* 25: 1073–1079.

Baron-Cohen, Simon, John Harrison, Laura H. Goldstein, and Maria Wyke. 1993. Coloured speech perception: is synaesthesia what happens when modularity breaks down? *Perception* 22:419–426.

Baron-Cohen, Simon, Maria A. Wyke, and Colin Binnie. 1987. Hearing words and seeing colours: an experimental investigation of a case of synaesthesia. *Perception* 16:761–767.

Beeli, Gian, Michaela Esslen, and Lutz Jäncke. 2007. Frequency correlates in grapheme-color synaesthesia. *Psychological Science* 18:788–792.

Berteletti, Ilaria, Edward M. Hubbard, and Marco Zorzi. 2009. Implicit versus explicit interference effects in a number-color synesthete. *Cortex* 46:170–177.

Block, Ned. 1998. On a confusion about a function of consciousness. In *The Nature of Consciousness: Philosophical Debates*, ed. Ned Block, Owen G, Flanagan, and Güven Güzeldere, 375–415. Cambridge, MA: The MIT Press.

Brang, David, Edward M. Hubbard, Seana Coulson, Minxiong Huang, and Vilayanur S. Ramachandran. 2010. Magnetoencephalography reveals early activation of V4 in grapheme-color synesthesia. *NeuroImage* 53:268–274.

Brang, David, Romke Rouw, Vilayanur S. Ramachandran, and Seana Coulson. 2011. Similarly shaped letters evoke similar colors in grapheme–color synesthesia. Neuropsychologia 49:1355–1358.

Cohen Kadosh, Roi, and Devin B. Terhune. 2012. Redefining synaesthesia? *British Journal of Psychology* 103:20–23.

Cohen Kadosh, Roi, and Vincent Walsh. 2008. Synaesthesia and cortical connections: cause or correlation? *Trends in Neurosciences* 31:549–501.

Cohen Kadosh, Roi, Avishai Henik, Andres Catena, Vincent Walsh, and Luis J. Fuentes. 2009. Induced cross-modal synaesthetic experience without abnormal neuronal connections. *Psychological Science* 20:258–265.

Cutietta, Robert A., and Kelly J. Haggerty. 1987. A comparative study of color association with music at various age levels. *Journal of Research in Music Education* 35:78–91.

Day, Sean. 2005. Some demographic and socio-cultural aspects of synesthesia. In *Synesthesia: Perspectives from Cognitive Neuroscience*, ed. Lynn C. Robertson, and Noam Sagiv, 11–33. New York: Oxford University Press.

———. 2009. Types of synesthesia. <http://home.comcast.net/~sean.day/html/types.htm>.

Dehay, Colette, Henry Kennedy, and Jean Bullier. 1988. Characterization of transient cortical projections from auditory, somatosensory and motor cortices to visual areas 17, 18, and 19 in the kitten. *Journal of Comparative Neurology* 230:576–592.

Dixon, Michael J., Daniel Smilek, and Philip M. Merikle. 2004. Not all synaesthetes are created equal: Projector versus associator synaesthetes. *Cognitive, Affective, and Behavioral Neuroscience* 4:335–343.

Dovern, Anna, Gereon R. Fink, A. Christina B. Fromme, Afra M. Wohlschlager, Peter H. Weiss, and Valentin Riedl. 2012. Intrinsic network connectivity reflects consistency of synesthetic experiences. *The Journal of Neuroscience* 32:7614–7621.

Eagleman, David M. 2012. Synaesthesia in its protean guises. *British Journal of Psychology* 103:16–19.

Edquist, Jessica, Anina N. Rich, Coble Brinkman, and Jason B. Mattingley. 2006. Do synaesthetic colours act as unique features in visual search? *Cortex* 42:222–231.

Elias, Lorin J., Deborah M. Saucier, Colleen Hardie, and Gordon E. Sarty. 2003. Dissociating semantic and perceptual components of synaesthesia: behavioural and functional neuroanatomical investigations. *Cognitive Brain Research* 16:232–237.

Galton, Francis. 1881. Visualised numerals. *The Journal of the Anthropological Institute of Great Britain and Ireland* 10:85–102.

———. 1883. *Inquiries into Human Faculty and its Development*. London: Macmillan.

Gegenfurtner, Karl R. 2003. Cortical mechanisms of colour vision. *Nature Reviews Neuroscience* 4:563–572.

Haack, Paul A. 1980. The behavior of music listeners. In *Handbook of Music Psychology*, ed. Donald A. Hodges, 141–183. Lawrence, KS: National Association for Music Therapy, Inc.

Hancock, Peter. 2006. Monozygotic twins' colour-number association: A case study. *Cortex* 42:147–150.

Hänggi, Jürgen, Diana Wotruba, and Lutz Jäncke. 2011. Globally altered structural brain network topology in grapheme-color synesthesia. *The Journal of Neuroscience* 31: 5816–5828.

Hubbard, Edward M., A. Cyrus. Arman, Vilayanur S. Ramachandran, and Geoffrey M. Boynton. 2005. Individual differences among grapheme-color synesthetes: Brain-behavior correlations. *Neuron* 45:975–985.

Hupé, Jean-Michel, Cécile Bordier, and Michel Dojat. 2012. The neural bases of grapheme-color synesthesia are not localized in real color-sensitive areas. *Cerebral Cortex* 22:1622–1633.

Innocenti, Giorgio M., and David J. Price. 2005. Exuberance in the development of cortical networks. *Nature Reviews Neuroscience* 6:995–965.

Jäncke, Lutz, and Nicolas Langer. 2011. A strong parietal hub in the small-world network of coloured-hearing synaesthetes during resting state EEG. *Journal of Neuropsychology* 5:178–202.

Jewanski, Jörg, Julia Simner, Sean Day, and Jamie Ward. 2011. The development of a scientific understanding of synesthesia from early case studies (1849–1873). *Journal of the History of the Neurosciences: Basic and Clinical Perspectives* 20:284–305.

Johnson, Donielle, Carrie Allison, and Simon Baron-Cohen. 2013. The prevalence of synesthesia: The consistency revolution. In *The Oxford Handbook of Synesthesia*, ed. Julia Simner and Edward M. Hubbard, 3–22. Oxford: Oxford University Press.

Kaiser, Hermann. 1872. *Compendium der physiologischen Optik*. Wiesbaden: C. W. Kreidel's Verlag.

Kennedy, Henry, Alexandre Batardiere, Colette Dehay, and Pascal Barone. 1997. Synesthesia: Implications for developmental neurobiology. In *Synaesthesia: Classic and Contemporary Readings*, ed. Simon Baron-Cohen and John E. Harrison, 243–256. Oxford: Blackwell Publishers.

Laeng, Bruno, Frode Svartdal, and Hella Oelmann. 2004. Does color synesthesia pose a paradox for early-selection theories of attention? *Psychological Science* 15:277–281.

Lewis, Clarence I. 1929. *Mind and the World Order: Outline of a Theory of Knowledge*. New York: Charles Scribner's Sons.

Locke, John. 1690. *An Essay Concerning Human Understanding*. London: T. Basset.

Lynall, Mary-Ellen, Danielle S. Bassett, Robert Kerwin, Peter J. McKenna, Manfred Kitzbichler, Ulrich Muller, and Edward T. Bullmore. 2010. Functional connectivity and brain networks in schizophrenia. *The Journal of Neuroscience* 30:9477–9487.

Marks, Lawrence E. 1987. On cross-modal similarity: Auditory-visual interactions in speeded discrimination. *Journal of Experimental Psychology: Human Perception and Performance* 13:384–394.

——. 2013. Weak synesthesia in perception and language. In *The Oxford Handbook of Synesthesia*, ed. Julia Simner and Edward M. Hubbard, 761–789. Oxford: Oxford University Press.

Maurer, Daphne. 1997. Neonatal synaesthesia: Implications for the processing of speech and faces. *In Synaesthesia: Classic and Contemporary Readings*, ed. Simon Baron-Cohen and John Harrison, 224–242. Oxford: Blackwell Publishers.

McGurk, Harry, and John MacDonald. 1976. Hearing lips and seeing voices. *Nature* 264:746–748.

Meier, Beat, and Nicolas Rothen. 2009. Training grapheme-colour associations produces a synaesthetic Stroop effect, but not a conditioned synaesthetic response. *Neuropsychologia* 47:1208–1211.

Mohr, Christine. 2013. Synesthesia in space versus the "mind's eye": How to ask the right questions. In *The Oxford Handbook of Synesthesia*, ed. Julia Simner and Edward M. Hubbard, 440–458. Oxford: Oxford University Press.

Muggleton, Neil, Elias Tsakanikos, Vincent Walsh, Jamie Ward. 2007. Disruption of synaesthesia following TMS of the right posterior parietal cortex. *Neuropsychologia* 45:1582–1585

Neville, Helen J. 1995. Developmental specificity in neurocognitive development in humans. In *The Cognitive Neurosciences*, ed. Michael S. Gazzaniga, 219–231. Cambridge, MA: The MIT Press.

Niccolai, Valentina, Tessa M. van Leeuwen, Colin Blakemore, and Petra Stoerig. 2012. Synaesthetic perception of colour and visual space in a blind subject: An fMRI case study. *Consciousness and Cognition* 21:889–899.

Novich, Scott, Sherry Cheng, and David M. Eagleman. 2011. Is synaesthesia one condition or many? A large-scale analysis reveals subgroups. *Journal of Neuropsychology* 5:353–371.

Nunn, Julia A., Lloyd J. Gregory, Michael J. Brammer, Steven C. R. Williams, David M. Parslow, Michael J. Morgan, Richard G. Morris, Edward T. Bullmore, Simon Baron-Cohen, and Jeffrey A. Gray. 2002. Functional magnetic resonance imaging of synaesthesia: Activation of V4/V8 by spoken words. *Nature Neuroscience* 5:371–375.

Palmeri, Thomas J., Randoph Blake, Rene Marois, Marci A. Flanery, and William Whetsell, Jr. 2002. The perceptual reality of synesthetic colors. *Proceedings of the National Academy of Sciences of the United States of America* 99:4127–4131.

Perroud, Louis. 1863. De l'hyperchromatopsie. *Memoires de la Société des Sciences Médicales de Lyon* 2:37–41.

Ramachandran, Vilayanur S., and Edward M. Hubbard. 2001a. Synaesthesia—a window into perception, thought and language. *Journal of Consciousness Studies* 8:3–34.

———. 2001b. Psychophysical investigations into the neural basis of synaesthesia. *Proceedings of the Royal Society of London B: Biological Sciences* 268:979–983.

Rich, Anina N., John L. Bradshaw, and Jason B. Mattingley. 2005. A systematic, large-scale study of synaesthesia: Implications for the role of early experience in lexical-colour associations. *Cognition* 98:53–84.

Rich, Anina N., and Jason B. Mattingley. 2002. Anomalous perception in synaesthesia: a cognitive neuroscience perspective. *Nature Reviews Neuroscience* 3:43–52.

———. 2013. The role of attention in synesthesia. In *The Oxford Handbook of Synesthesia*, ed. Julia Simner and Edward M. Hubbard, 265–282. Oxford: Oxford University Press.

Rich, Anina N., Mark A. Williams, Aina Puce, Ari Syngeniotis, Matthew A. Howard, Francis McGlone, and Jason B. Mattingley. 2006. Neural correlates of imagined and synaesthetic colours. *Neuropsychologia* 44:2918–2925.

Rothen, Nicolas, and Beat Meier. 2009. Do synesthetes have a general advantage in visual search and episodic memory? A case for group studies. *PLoS ONE* 4:e5037.

Rouw, Romke. 2013. Synesthesia, hyper-connectivity and diffusion tensor imaging. In *The Oxford Handbook of Synesthesia*, ed. Julia Simner and Edward M. Hubbard, 500–518. Oxford: Oxford University Press.

Rouw, Romke, and H. Steven Scholte. 2007. Increased structural connectivity in grapheme-color synesthesia. *Nature Neuroscience* 10:792–797.

———. 2010. Neural basis of individual differences in synesthetic experiences. *The Journal of Neuroscience* 30:6205–6213.

Sagiv, Noam, Jeffrey Heer, and Lynn Robertson. 2006. Does binding of synesthetic color to the evoking grapheme require attention? *Cortex* 42:232–242.

Sagiv, Noam, Julia Simner, James Collins, Brian Butterworth, and Jamie Ward. 2006. What is the relationship between synaesthesia and visuo-spatial number forms? *Cognition* 101:114–128. doi:10.1016/j.cognition.2005.09.004

Seron, Xavier, Mauro Pesenti, Marie-Pascale Noël, Gérard Deloche, and Jacques-André Cornet. 1992. Images of numbers, or When 98 is upper left and 6 sky blue. *Cognition* 44:159–196.

Simner, Julia. 2012. Defining synaesthesia. *British Journal of Psychology* 103:1–15.

———. 2013. The "rules" of synesthesia. In *The Oxford Handbook of Synesthesia*, ed. Julia Simner and Edward M. Hubbard, 149–164. Oxford: Oxford University Press.

Simner, Julia, Jennifer Harrold, Harriet Creed, Louise Monro, and Louise Foulkes. 2009. Early detection of markers for synaesthesia in childhood populations. *Brain* 132:57–64.

Simner, Julia, and Emma Holenstein. 2007. Ordinal linguistic personification as a variant of synesthesia. *Journal of Cognitive Neuroscience* 19:694–703.

Simner, Julia, and Edward M. Hubbard. 2006. Variants of synesthesia interact in cognitive tasks: Evidence for implicit associations and late connectivity in cross-talk theories. *Neuroscience* 143:805–814.

Simner, Julia, and Robert H. Logie. 2007. Synaesthetic consistency spans decades in a lexical-gustatory synaesthete. *Neurocase* 13:358–365.

Simner, Julia, and Vera U. Ludwig. 2012. The color of touch: A case of tactile-visual synaesthesia. *Neurocase* 18:167–180.

Simner Julia, Catherine Mulvenna, Noam Sagiv, Elias Tsakanikos, S. Athene Witherby, Christine Fraser, Kirsten Scott, and Jamie Ward. 2006. Synaesthesia: The prevalence of atypical cross-modal experiences. *Perception* 35:1024–1033.

Simner Julia, Jamie Ward, Monika Lanz, Ashok Jansari, Krist Noonan, Louise Glover, and David A. Oakley. 2005. Non-random associations of graphemes to colours in synaesthetic and non-synaesthetic populations. *Cognitive Neuropsychology* 22:1069–1085.

Skelton, Richard, Casimir Ludwig, and Christine Mohr. 2009. A novel, illustrated questionnaire to distinguish projector and associator synaesthetes. *Cortex* 45:721–729.

Smilek, Daniel, Mike J. Dixon, Cera Cudahy, and Philip M. Merikle. 2001. Synaesthetic photisms influence visual perception. *Journal of Cognitive Neuroscience* 13:930–936.

Spector, Ferrine and Daphne Maurer. 2009. Synesthesia: a new approach to understanding the development of perception. *Developmental Psychology* 45:175–189.

Spector, Ferrine and Daphne Maurer. 2011. The colors of the alphabet: naturally-biased associations between shape and color. *Journal of Experimental Psychology. Human Perception and Performance* 37:484–495.

Steven, Megan. S. 2004. Neuroimaging of multisensory processing and synaesthesia. DPhil thesis, University of Oxford.

Steven, Megan S., and Colin Blakemore. 2004. Visual synaesthesia in the blind. *Perception* 33:855–868.

Steven, Megan S., Peter C. Hansen, and Colin Blakemore. 2006. Activation of color-selective areas of visual cortex in a blind synesthete. *Cortex* 42:304–8.

Suk, Hyeon-Jeong, Sang-Hoon Jeong, Tae-Heun Yang, and Dong-Soo Kwon. 2009. Tactile sensation as emotion elicitor. *Kansei Engineering International* 8:147–152.

Tomson, Steffie N., Nili Avidan, Kwanghyuk Lee, Anand K. Sarma, Rejnal Tushe, Dianna M. Milewicz, Molly Bray, Suzanne M. Leal, and David M. Eagleman. 2011. The genetics of colored sequence synesthesia: Suggestive evidence of linkage to 16q and genetic heterogeneity for the condition. *Behavioural Brain Research* 223:48–52.

Treisman, Anne. 1986. Features and objects in visual processing. *Scientific American* 255: 114–125.

Treisman, Anne M., and Garry Gelade. 1980. A feature-integration theory of attention. *Cognitive Psychology* 12:97–136.

Treisman, Anne M., and Hilary Schmidt. 1982. Illusory conjunctions in the perception of objects. *Cognitive Psychology* 14:107–141.

Van Leeuwen, Tessa M., Hanneke E. M. den Ouden, and Peter Hagoort. 2011. Effective connectivity determines the nature of subjective experience in grapheme-color synesthesia. *The Journal of Neuroscience* 31:9879–9884.

Vatakis, Argiro. 2013. Cross-modality in speech processing. In *The Oxford Handbook of Synesthesia*, ed. Julia Simner and Edward M. Hubbard, 816–836. Oxford: Oxford University Press.

Wagner, Katie, and Karen R. Dobkins. 2011. Synaesthetic associations decrease during infancy. *Psychological Science* 22:1067–1072.

Ward, Jamie, Brett Huckstep, and Elias Tsakanikos. 2006. Sound-colour synaesthesia: to what extent does it use cross-modal mechanisms common to us all? *Cortex* 42: 264–280.

Ward, Jamie, Clare Jonas, and Anil Seth. 2009. Grapheme-colour synaesthesia improves detection of embedded shapes, but without pre-attentive 'pop-out' of synaesthetic colour. *Proceedings of the Royal Society of London B: Biological Sciences* 277:1021–1026.

Ward, Jamie, Ryan Li, Shireen Salih, and Noam Sagiv. 2007. Varieties of grapheme-colour synaesthesia: A new theory of phenomenological and behavioural differences. *Consciousness
and Cognition* 16:913–931.

Ward, Jamie, and Julia Simner. 2005. Is synaesthesia an X-linked dominant trait with lethality
in males? *Perception* 34:611–623.

Ward, Jamie, Daisy Thompson-Lake, Roxanne Ely, and Flora Kaminski. 2008. Synaesthesia,
creativity and art: What is the link? *British Journal of Psychology* 99 (Pt 1):127–141.

Witthoft, Nathan, and Jonathan Winawer. 2013. Learning, memory, and synaesthesia.
Psychological Science 24:258–265.

CHAPTER 48

FROM MOLECULES TO METAPHOR

Outlooks on synesthesia research

V. S. RAMACHANDRAN AND DAVID BRANG

INTRODUCTION

The march of science usually takes place incrementally, through the slow painstaking process of acquiring new knowledge and insights. This process, which Thomas Kuhn called "normal science" leads to a "paradigm"; a framework of ideas, methodologies, and theories that is widely accepted and zealously guarded by the priesthood of that discipline. These elders regard themselves as the custodians of that paradigm and if a new observation comes along that threatens to topple the edifice, the standard reaction is to brush it under the carpet—engaging in a form of denial. Kuhn called such observations anomalies. This denial is not necessarily as unhealthy or absurd as it seems. Since most anomalies are false alarms (e.g., spoon bending, telekinesis), one can waste a lifetime pursuing them, when it is often a better idea to ignore them. But if every anomaly were ignored scientific progress would be impossible (e.g., X-rays and continental drift were anomalies in their time). Indeed some anomalies can turn our world view topsy-turvy and generate "paradigm shifts"—steering us in a new direction, opening up whole fields of enquiry.

Neurology and psychiatry, it turns out, are disciplines full of oddities ripe for investigation. One has to be careful in choosing the right anomaly to work on though, since the majority of them are bogus. Consider De Clérambault's syndrome, which is officially recognized by psychiatrists: a young woman developing a delusion that a famous, rich older man is in love with her but is in denial about it. This is almost certainly a fabricated syndrome. Ironically the converse syndrome in which an older gentleman develops a delusion that an attractive young woman is irresistibly attracted to him but is in denial is perfectly real and much more common (S. M. Anstis, personal communication) but there is no name for it, undoubtedly because most psychiatrists who name syndromes are men.

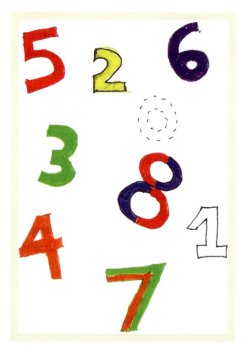

FIGURE 48.1 Number-color associations for one of our synesthetes. Notice that the numbers 7 and 8 are composed of two colors each.

A genuine anomaly is synesthesia. People with this curious "condition"—the subject of this book—experience jumbled sensory experiences. A stimulus (such as a sound) that would normally evoke a sensation in a single modality (hearing) spontaneously and irrepressibly evokes an unrelated sensation—e.g., vision. So, for example, the individual may experience a specific color for every given note ("C sharp is red"), or every grapheme—printed number or letter—may be tinged with a specific hue (e.g., 5 is red and 3 is green; Figure 48.1). The specificity of evoked colors remains stable over time within any given individual (Baron-Cohen et al. 1996) but the same grapheme doesn't necessarily evoke the same color in different people (Cytowic 1989).

Synesthesia seems to defy common sense—although the very phrase "common sense" has synesthetic connotations (and this is discussed also by Keeley, Chapter 46, this volume). Recent research by a number of groups has amply confirmed a suggestion we made a decade ago (Ramachandran and Hubbard 2001a) that far from being just another odd perceptual quirk, synesthesia might hold the key to a treasury of insights into higher mental functions such as the neural and genetic basis of creativity and mathematical talent. This view of synesthesia stands in stark contrast with the notion that it is simply based on associative learning, an explanation that not only begs the question of why only some people make such associations (not to mention the selective nature of the associations, e.g., grapheme-color) but is merely a description masquerading as an explanation, taking us back into the murky waters of classical associationist psychology (that everything the brain does is based on chains of associations—which may well be true but doesn't explain anything).

Although long regarded as a curiosity, following our two publications (Ramachandran and Hubbard 2001a, 2001b); there has been a tremendous resurgence of interest in the phenomenon. (Blakemore et al. 2005; Dixon et al. 2000; Eagleman et al. 2007; Mattingley et al. 2001; Palmeri et al. 2002; Ramachandran and Hubbard, 2003; Robertson and Sagiv 2005; Simner and Ward, 2006).

One of the first forms of synesthesia described is what Galton called "number forms." When asked to imagine or visualize numbers (say 1 to 50) most of us have a vague tendency to imagine the numbers laid out sequentially in space in front of us in a left-to-right manner, but this assignment of numbers to spatial location is by no means obligatory or visually compelling. In some individuals, however, this number line is spontaneously evoked and not easily repressed. In these individuals, each number always occupies a specific location in space and even though they are in proper sequence, the imaginary line on which they lie is often elaborately convoluted—sometimes even doubling back on itself so that (for example) 15 might be closer to 5 in visual/geometric space than it is to 13. Examples of these unconventional yet consistent number-lines as visualized by Francis Galton's synesthetes in 1881 are given in Figure 47.1 (Lynall and Blakemore, Chapter 47, this volume; for other examples see also Figure 7.1, Jonas and Jarick, Chapter 7, this volume).

Beyond identifying this phenomenon as an anomaly worthy of pursuit, Galton also recognized that synesthesia runs in families, providing a 100-year precursor to current genetic work on synesthetes.

Examining this little-studied variant, Ramachandran and Hubbard tried to test the veracity of number lines by measuring reaction times (RTs) on various cognitive tasks pertaining to numbers (such as the "number distance effect"; memory for number locations, etc.). The results were suggestive but not compelling. More recent work has also yielded mixed results (e.g., Brang, Teuscher, et al. 2010; Gertner et al. 2009; Jarick et al. 2009) but, overall, there seems to be a consensus emerging that at least some number-related tasks are indeed influenced by the disposition of the number line, so the phenomenon is perfectly genuine.

Why does the phenomenon arise? No explanation had been proposed since Galton discovered the effect until Ramachandran and Hubbard suggested an evolutionary explanation (Ramachandran and Hubbard 2003) based on the way representation of numbers is mapped on to spatial representations in the brain. Numbers (including concepts of sequence, ordinality, cardinality, magnitude, etc.) are relatively recent inventions in evolution—possibly as recent as a few thousand years. It would have been virtually impossible to evolve a dedicated module in the brain e.g., a "look up table"—to deal with numbers so evolution may have chosen to map numerical concepts such as natural numbers, calendars, etc. on pre-existing *spatial* maps in the brain that are ubiquitous (as we would on a graph paper). Ordinarily the line may be straight left-to-right but if something goes awry in this one-to-one spatial mapping the result might be a Galtonian convoluted number line; as if the graph paper had been genetically coded.

The more common forms of synesthesia (tone color, grapheme color) cry out for similar neurological explanation, based, for example, on cross-activation between brain maps dedicated to different sensory inputs (Ramachandran and Hubbard, 2001b). One recurring theme in synesthesia research, which we will consider in this article, is the extent to which the phenomenon is based on low-level cross-activation between sensory areas versus high-level associations with possible involvements with memory (and the inevitable question of how one goes about operationally distinguishing the two). As we shall see the phenomenon seems to occur in many variants spanning the whole spectrum, from spontaneous sensory cross-wiring to high-level conceptual associations (e.g., associating the letter D with not only the color green, but also with a specific gender and emotional connotation). Our own research has focused mostly on the "sensory cross-activation" variant for three main reasons. First, it is easier to do psychophysical experiments. Second, sensory variants are easier to relate to the known physiology of visual pathways that has been studied in exquisite detail. Third, they lend themselves more readily to brain imaging (e.g., Brang, Hubbard, et al. 2010; Hubbard et al. 2005). With all three in place, the phenomenon became ripe for more extensive studies.

However, "higher" forms of synesthesia have by no means been neglected, having been studied elegantly by several researchers; most notably Jamie Ward and Julia Simner. Indeed, it is precisely the fact that the phenomenon spans the whole spectrum from low-level sensations to higher-order cognitive associations that makes it so fascinating, and at times frustrating, to study (Ramachandran and Hubbard 2006). If the history of science is any guide, such "borderline" phenomena that straddle the boundary between different realms of discourse or levels of analysis can be particularly fruitful in yielding novel insights and this has certainly been shown to be true for synesthesia.

PREVALENCE AND SCOPE OF SYNESTHESIA

Since the time Galton first described it, synesthesia was regarded as a rare condition, but recent estimates suggest an incidence of 4%; one of the most common of which appears to be grapheme-color (Simner et al. 2006). Most individuals report having had the experience for as long back in childhood as they can remember. As Galton himself noted, the condition tends to run in families and recent work suggests a genetic basis (Barnett et al. 2008; Tomson et al. 2011). Synesthesia was previously believed to be six times more common in women than in men according to research that appealed for synesthetes via newspaper ads (Baron-Cohen et al. 1996). However, Simner and colleagues showed no difference between the sexes testing a large population for synesthesia (Simner et al. 2006). Sometimes, sensory deprivation can lead to one sensory input evoking sensations in a different modality. For example, after early visual deprivation due to retinitis pigmentosa, touch stimuli can produce visual phosphenes (Armel and Ramachandran 1999) or after a thalamic lesion leading to a loss of tactile sensation, sounds can elicit touch sensations (Ro et al. 2007). These instances probably occur because the tactile or auditory sensory input now begins to cross-activate the deprived cortical areas. These could be regarded as a form of acquired synesthesia caused, possibly, by pre-existing back projections becoming hyperactive, or through axonal sprouting, especially given the long period of time (on the order of years) between the loss of sensory input and the onset of the synesthetic experiences.

Dozens of strange forms of synesthesia and descriptions of these can be found in several recent books, reviews and edited volumes (Cytowic 1989; Grossenbacher and Lovelace 2001; Robertson and Sagiv 2005; Ramachandran and Hubbard 2001a). Although these will be mentioned in passing, this short review will mainly emphasize grapheme-color synesthesia rather than attempt a comprehensive survey of the entire field. The reason for this is that grapheme-color is one of the most common forms and also the one on which most psychophysical experiments have been done. Equally important, we have now begun to understand the anatomical and physiological basis of grapheme-color synesthesia to an extent that is not yet possible with the other more exotic variants. As such, it might provide a "model" for how we might experimentally approach the less common types.

Bearing all this in mind, we can ask several important questions—some old and some new—regarding the phenomenon.

- Is the phenomenon authentic ("real") and hence worthy of study? Or are synesthete individuals simply making it up?
- Is it an early sensory process or a high-level cognitive process such as a memory association (e.g., formed by having played with refrigerator magnets in early childhood)?
- Do the evoked colors have "quale?"
- Is it based on genes or upbringing?
- Does it have any function? Or could it be the by-product of something else that has function (The answer is Yes; see later).
- What is its neural basis?
- How does one account for the observation that poetry and art are more likely to be pursued by synesthetes? (Domino 1989; Rich, Bradshaw, Mattingley 2005; Rothen and Meier 2010; Yaro and Ward 2007).
- Does the phenomenon have broader implications?
- What are the critical tests necessary for the future of synesthesia research?

SENSORY NATURE OF SYNESTHESIA

Synesthesia is stable (i.e., has test–retest reliability) over several months (Baron-Cohen et al. 1996), which suggests that it is authentic; not confabulatory in origin. The initial evidence that it is an actual sensory process—in some synesthetes at least—rather than a high-level cognitive one, is suggested by five lines of support (Ramachandran and Hubbard 2001a, 2001b, 2003).

First, some simple observations made on synesthetes (without formal psychophysics or brain imaging) had already suggested to us that at least in some synesthetes, the associations are sensory in nature—produced by a hardware "glitch" (whether caused by axonal cross-wiring or disinhibition or transmitter dysfunction or all three) rather than high-level associations. The old adage in clinical medicine that 90% of the diagnosis can be arrived at by simply talking to the patient has, we have found, special force in the case of synesthesia (Ramachandran and Hubbard 2001a). In these interviews we have found:

(1) The same letter can have different portions colored differently, an observation that suggests a "hardware" glitch rather than a cognitive effect.
(2) Intensity of synesthetic color can vary as a function of lower and upper case letters and even font; simple memory association wouldn't be expected to vary based on low-level visual changes that don't change the meaning of the item.
(3) Synesthesia runs in families, and yet the majority of synesthetes report never discussing this condition with anyone in their immediate family.
(4) There is a directional bias: synesthetic associations are typically unidirectional.
(5) There are instances of blindsight for synesthesia: using illusions that render letters and numbers invisible, we have encountered two synesthetes who can nonetheless "guess" what the synesthetically evoked color is.

In addition to these informal observations there is also a wealth of more formal experimental evidence against a mere memory-association account of synesthesia. First, as the luminance contrast of the grapheme is progressively reduced, the perceived saturation of the color decreases monotonically and disappears at less than 10% contrast even though the grapheme is still clearly visible. If the color is a simple memory association there is no reason why it should be less vivid with lower contrast. The physiological basis of this effect was studied by Hubbard, Manohar, and Ramachandran (2006). Second, evidence against a memory account comes from the fact that the evoked color can lead to texture segregation (Figure 48.2). If several 2s are scattered among a random array of 5s, synesthetes can use the evoked color difference to much more rapidly group and segregate the 2s from the 5s than "normal" non-synesthetes (Palmeri et al. 2002; Ramachandran and Hubbard 2001a). Such segregation strongly suggests that the colors are evoked early in sensory processing; this segregation effect has now been elegantly confirmed by Jamie Ward and colleagues in a large population of synesthetes (Ward et al. 2010).

Third, the synesthetically evoked color can provide an input to apparent motion perception (Kim et al. 2003; Ramachandran and Azoulai 2006; Ramachandran and Hubbard, 2002). Fourth, as noted previously even for a single grapheme different regions can be tinged different colors, an observation that suggests a "hardware" glitch rather than a cognitive effect (see Figure 48.1). Fifth, subjects can adapt to synesthetically induced colors and experience McCollough color after effects (Blake et al. 2005). Sixth, there is direct brain imaging evidence for perceptual processes (see later).

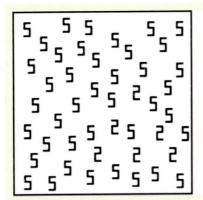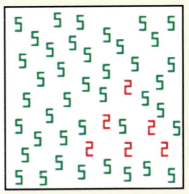

FIGURE 48.2 Display used to test whether synesthetic colors lead to a texture segregation 'pop-out effect' that individuals normally experience from physical colors. Non-synesthetes typically take longer than synesthetes to find a hidden triangle made up of 2 s in the left display, compared to the easy segregation in the right frame. Reprinted from *Journal of Consciousness Studies*, 8 (12), Ramachandran, V. S., and Hubbard, E. M., Synaesthesia: A window into perception, thought and language, pp. 3–34, Copyright (2001), with permission.

There is at least one color blind synesthete on record who reported that she could see colors in numbers that she couldn't see in the real world; referring to them as "Martian colors." Her color anomaly, caused by deficient cone pigments, allowed her to see only a limited range of real colors. But perhaps the color neurons in V4, having been specified genetically, were largely intact and were being indirectly stimulated by cross-activation via graphemes (Ramachandran and Hubbard 2001a). This again negates the memory association theory and supports the sensory cross-activation theory.

These experiments establish the sensory nature of synesthesia but, as we shall see later, this is only true of a subset of synesthetes ("lower synesthetes"). It should also be added that the view that some types of synesthesia are caused by sensory cross-activation is by no means universal. There are people who still believe—in spite of the evidence cited earlier—that all types of synesthesia are the result of higher-level conceptual or linguistic associations. This harks back to the dark ages of classical "associationist" psychology. Taken collectively all these observations support the "early sensory cross-activation" theory, but what is the underlying physiological basis?

PHYSIOLOGICAL BASIS

The visual grapheme area is located in the fusiform gyrus which represents visual appearance and is adjacent to color area V4 in the same gyrus. Since the condition is hereditary, it has been suggested that there is an accidental cross-activation between these areas caused by a gene mutation that causes either defective pruning of axons (Ramachandran and Hubbard 2001a) or disinhibition (Armel and Ramachandran 1999). This has been called the sensory cross-activation hypothesis. This is consistent with the observation that Roman numerals (e.g., V or VI) are ineffective in evoking the color in some synesthetes; for those individuals, it's the visual appearance of the numeral that is critical—not the abstract idea of number. As noted earlier, all this appears to be characteristic of only a subset of synesthetes whom we call "lower synesthetes." A second group called "higher synesthetes" associate the color with more abstract numerical concepts; color is triggered not only by graphemes (visual shapes of numbers) but also by the abstract idea of numerical sequences, even embodied in days of the week or months of the year; so called "calendar synesthetes" or time-space synesthesia (Brang, Teuscher, et al. 2010). It has been suggested that in these higher synesthetes, the cross-wiring occurs higher up in the vicinity of the angular gyrus where more abstract numerical ideas are represented (Ramachandran and Hubbard 2001a). The ratio of "higher" to "lower" synesthesia is not known, but anecdotal evidence suggests that it may be as high as 2:1 reflecting a potentially bimodal distribution (Rouw and Scholte 2010). It should also be noted that in some higher synesthetes the first letter of a word determines the color of that word, suggesting that the grapheme/phoneme-word "package" as a whole evokes the color.

Brain imaging studies (using functional magnetic resonance imaging (fMRI)) which allow precise localization of V4 support the notion that lower synesthetes have cross-activation in the fusiform gyrus between letter and color areas (Hubbard et al. 2005). This result was recently extended using magnetoencephalography (MEG), replicating the activation of V4 color area in synesthetes watching achromatic graphemes (Brang, Hubbard, et al. 2010). Moreover, as magnetoencephalography (MEG) is able to capitalize on temporal aspects of neural processing, Brang and colleagues demonstrated near simultaneous activation of V4 and grapheme regions, beginning as early as 110 ms after stimulus onset.

More compelling evidence for this hypothesis is the recent finding, using diffusion tensor imaging, of an actual increase of connectivity in the fusiform gyrus and the superior parietal lobule of grapheme-color synesthetes (Rouw and Scholte 2007), exactly as we had predicted (Ramachandran and Hubbard 2001a). This finding was also replicated by Jäncke and colleagues (2009), albeit with a more liberal statistical threshold. Such selective "cross-wiring" may be based on transcription factors that lead to selective local expression of the synesthesia gene. Besides studies assessing fractional anisotropy (Rouw and Scholte 2007), voxel-based morphometry (VBM) has also been used to demonstrate that synesthetes have increased gray matter volume compared to non-synesthetes in regions in the inferior temporal lobe, implicated in both grapheme and color processing (Jäncke et al. 2009; Weiss and Fink, 2009). Further, Rouw and Scholte (2010) also demonstrated strong differences in VBM between synesthetes who project the synesthetic colors into the world (projectors) and those who experience the colors only in their minds eye (associators). Critically, projectors relative to associators showed large differences in gray matter volume in the sensory systems (visual cortex, auditory cortex, and motor cortex), consistent with the notion that they experience synesthetic colors as perceptual qualia. Associators, however, differed from projectors in gray matter volume within the hippocampus and parahippocampus, confirming subjective reports from

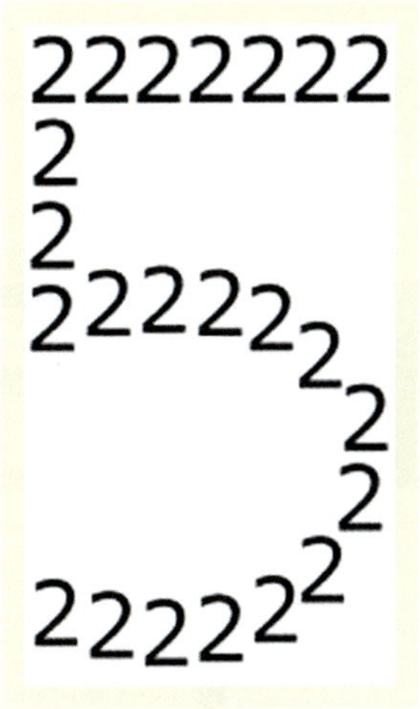

FIGURE 48.3 Classic "Navon" figure in which globally this image is a 5, yet locally it is an array of 2s. Synesthetes experienced the colors changing depending on whether their attention is on the global or local attributes of the image.

synesthetes that the experience is associative in nature, more akin to memory recall than a sensory experience.

Top-Down and Contextual Effects

Saying that synesthesia involves cross-activation (by which one means the spontaneous inevitable activation of neurons in one map by those in another) doesn't imply that the process cannot be influenced by top-down processes. For example, in Figure 48.3 which is a large 5 made up of little 2s one can use a mental zoom lens to focus on the big 5 or the little 2s and for synesthetes the color is seen to switch correspondingly (Ramachandran and Hubbard 2001b) which implies that top-down attentional focus can modulate the cross-modal activation in the fusiform gyrus.

The second experiment (Figure 48.4) used an ambiguous grapheme ("A" or "H") embedded either in between "T" and "E" (as in "THE") or between "C" and "A" ("CAT"). The color of the grapheme then depended on which letters the central letter was grouped with, proving that the linguistic categorization of the grapheme, based on spelling, can determine the induced synesthetic colors (Ramachandran and Hubbard, 2001b). The role of linguistic effects (including phonemic and semantic effects) has since then been shown by several other groups. Simner and Ward (2006) showed that individuals who experience tastes in response to words (lexical-gustatory synesthetes) actually perceive the taste before they can say the associated word (while the word is still on the tip of the tongue)—demonstrating this gustatory sensation arises from semantic meaning. The significance of semantic activation was recently shown in grapheme-color synesthesia

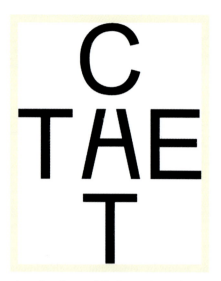

FIGURE 48.4 Synesthetic colors for the middle letter depend on context.

using event-related potentials to record synesthetes' brainwaves (Brang et al. 2008; Brang, Kanai, et al. 2011). In this study, sentences were presented one word at a time, ending with a congruent or incongruent color word ("The sky is BLUE" versus "The sky is RED") OR ending with a congruent or incongruent synesthetic grapheme ("The sky is 4" versus "The sky is 7"). Brainwaves in the grapheme condition showed that synesthetic colors are processed in the brain for semantic meaning and context more quickly (approximately 150 ms) than color words. In addition to semantic effects in grapheme-color synesthesia, the saturation and luminance of the color experienced with each grapheme seems to be modulated by linguistic factors, specifically the frequency of letter and number use in a language (Beeli, Esslen, and Jäncke 2007; Smilek et al. 2007) and similarly by numerical magnitude (Cohen Kadosh, Henik, and Walsh, 2007).

Finally, some synesthetes report that imagined letters (visualized in the mind's eye) are, paradoxically more vividly colored than actual printed ones. For example, when you look at a white printed letter, the bottom-up activity in V4 caused by the white "clashes" with the red color induced by cross-activation; but for top-down imagined letters even though the activity in fusiform number nodes is weaker the final experienced color is stronger because there is no contradictory bottom-up information (Ramachandran and Hubbard 2001a).

LEARNED OR ACQUIRED?

Despite the overwhelming evidence for a role of genes in synesthesia (as discussed later), one still hears the remark that the phenomenon is acquired through learning. Of course learning *must* play a role given that the shapes of numbers vary from culture to culture and we are not born with grapheme coding neurons in the fusiform. What is inherited, however, is the predisposition to link certain brain areas (e.g., number and color regions). If synesthesia is present from birth and the exact pattern of letter-to-color mappings is acquired throughout development, what gives rise to synesthetic colors for a nascent grapheme-color synesthete? One of the most promising models proposes that prior to letter specialization, synesthetic associations begin as colors paired with the basic graphemic features (line segments, curves, basic shapes) present in low-level visual centers (Brang, Hubbard, et al. 2010); it is only after this point during development that synesthetic colors are redefined and tuned to individual graphemes. This is clearly the case with luminance, where synesthetes and non-synesthetes alike pair round objects (including the letter O) with white, and jagged lines (including the letter X) with black (Spector and Maurer, 2011). Furthermore, visually similar letter-forms appear to be associated with similar synesthetic colors (Brang, Rouw, et al. 2011). Moreover, this relationship is expressed more strongly in projectors than associators, consistent with our findings that increased connectivity between V4 and grapheme regions is more likely to be present in projectors (Rouw and Scholte 2007). Our findings are consistent with preliminary work by Hubbard and colleagues (2005), who demonstrated greater synesthetic color similarity within the letter-groups "KVWXY" or "CUDOQ" than when compared across the letter-groups, reflecting the pairing of visually similar letters with similar synesthetic colors.

While familial studies suggest that one is predisposed to having synesthesia based on genetic influences, the notion of how the associations develop and which particular synesthesia emerges within an individual likely involve cultural/behavioral factions on top of predispositions. The latter question is a particularly interesting case, in asking what causes one synesthete to see colors with tones and another synesthete to see colors with numbers. The easiest explanation to this difference is that each form of synesthesia is based on unique and independent genes, but this doesn't fit with the well-established finding that having one form of synesthesia increases the likelihood you will have a second or third form as well, suggesting the genetic undertones only impose a predisposition to having synesthesia in general. If the genetic basis for synesthesia is invariant to the specific form, it is an open question of whether the child of two grapheme-color synesthetes could be "made" into a tone-color synesthete with extensive musical training during childhood. However, recent work by David Eagleman and colleagues suggests that there may in fact be "islands" of synesthetes, such that certain types of synesthesias cluster together within and across individuals (Tomson et al. 2011). But even within these clusters this question remains pertinent. As time-space synesthesia (experiencing a spatial layout or spatial-form for months of the year and other time sequences) is tightly linked with grapheme-color synesthesia (Sagiv et al. 2006), would this shared (latent) underlying mechanism allow individuals with only time-space synesthesia to learn grapheme-color correspondences more easily?

While the majority of the work examining how synesthesia is coded (either through inheritance or development/culture) has focused on grapheme-color synesthesia, preliminary work has extended this research to time-space synesthesia. In time-space synesthesia, months of the year exist in a highly memorable and affect spatial layout, most often in the form of a circle (Brang, Teuscher, et al. 2010; Eagleman, 2009). While the preferred direction may mimic that of a clock, the spatial organization of the months on the circle differs from the pattern on a clock-face (Eagleman 2009). For example, January is no more likely to occur at the 12 or 1 o'clock position than it is to occur at any other position on the clock-face, suggesting that this is not due to imprinting of features from early on in development. Analyzing these circular forms further, however, we find that approximately 75% are arranged in a clockwise direction (with January preceding February according to the layout of a clock) and approximately 25% in a counterclockwise direction. Owing to the strong influence of heredity on this form of synesthesia, Brang and colleagues demonstrated that this difference is mainly driven by the handedness of the individual synesthete, such that 80% of left-handed synesthetes showed a counter-clockwise arrangement, compared to only 17% of right-handed individuals (Brang, Teuscher, et al. 2011).

Consistent with the notion that synesthesia is partially mediated by learning, synesthetes often report that newly acquired languages develop synesthetic colors of their own. While the pattern of this transfer has not been well studied (but see Mills 2002; Witthoft and Winawer 2006), subjective reports suggest that colors transfer due to a combination of phonetic and graphemic similarity. One synesthete who was learning Russian and posted on Sean Day's Synesthesia List exemplifies this idea:

> When there is a letter like P (colored slightly bluish violet), which in Russian is pronounced like R (colored burgundy), the symbol P would take on a reddish-purple tint when in the context of the Cyrillic alphabet. Thus, the same symbol could have a color different from its English look-alike and the English letter it sounds like...

Furthermore, recent research has taken the idea of synesthetic transfer into the laboratory setting and shown that the synesthesia can transfer to novel scripts through visual features by mere experience (Mroczko et al. 2009).

DEFINING THE LIMITS OF SYNESTHESIA

The term synesthesia has been applied liberally throughout the decades, and no clear consensus exists to draw a line between the form of synesthesia of which this book is about, and other similar phenomena and conditions ranging from metaphorical language to vivid drug-induced hallucinations. Conservative boundaries defining synesthesia require the association to be (1) stable over time, (a 7 experienced as green should always be green), (2) involuntary and automatic (experiences do not require effort), and (3) both memorable and affect-laden (a number printed in the "incorrect" color may make a synesthete uncomfortable; Baron-Cohen et al. 1996; Cytowic 1989). However, many phenomena clearly encapsulate one or more of these qualifications, but there is too little evidence to fully classify their relationship to "typical" synesthetic phenomena. Specifically, many phenomena maintained as genuine forms of synesthesia occur from either non-developmental origins or appear largely conceptual, removed from the sensory percepts that originally drew so much interest to synesthesia. Indeed many of these modern forms appear dangerously close to what many would describe as simple metaphor.

Ordinal linguistic personification

At the edge of this boundary is ordinal linguistic personification, a condition in which individuals report specific, highly memorable and affective personified traits for numbers and/or letters (Simner and Holenstein, 2007). The cross-activation (of brain maps) model explains many aspects of synesthesia, but given the complex reports of some synesthetes that each grapheme has a certain personality and sex (Ramachandran and Hubbard 2006), we are unsure whether it can be generalized to all forms of synesthesia, as personality and gender are broadly distributed processes lacking focal modules. One possibility is that as the brain may tend to binarize the world (black/white, male/female, good/evil, ugly/beautiful, yin/yang, etc.) to simplify cognitive processing, and OLP may reflect an enhancement of the connections between numbers and areas responsible for these binarizations. Further, perhaps certain shapes are more feminine (or masculine) through association even in "normals" and these are made explicit by the enhanced connectivity caused by synesthesia genes. While research in this area is scant, Amin and colleagues (2011) have put forward preliminary evidence using fMRI that OLP experiences rely on the precuneus, which past work has implicated in self-referential processes, but also more generally with imagery. One remaining possibility is that while many of us also make such seemingly random associations from time to time, we don't get "stuck" with them. In synesthesia, the proclivity to make such Hebbian associations may have a "self-enhancing" tendency—akin to kindling— once they are set in motion, resulting in the firm belief that, say, "8 is female and has a demanding personality; wants to be a larger number than she is and is difficult for the other numbers to be around."

Mirror neurons and synesthesia

A curious form of acquired synesthesia can be observed in patients with phantom limbs. Such patients have undergone amputation although continue to report sensation or even pain in the lost body part. If a system of mirrors is used to optically resurrect the phantom limb and it is made to appear visually that the phantom is being touched with a pencil, the subjects feels her phantom being touched even though no part of her body is being touched at all. This implies that the visual sensations must be feeding back to activate somatosensory maps in the brain (Ramachandran,

Rogers-Ramachandran, and Cobb 1995). Even more remarkably it was noticed that patients with phantom arms will experience their phantom being touched in a precisely localized manner even if they merely observe another person's intact arm being touched (Ramachandran and Brang 2009). Similarly they experienced their phantom moving if the experimenter put his own hand in the vicinity of the phantom and moved it. Such effects may be mediated by a class of neurons in the premotor cortex and parietal lobes called "mirror neurons" (Rizzolatti et al. 1996). These neurons are activated when a subject moves his hand—as expected. But surprisingly they also fire when the subject watches another person making similar movements. Such activation does not lead a normal observer to experience sensations presumably because the regular somatosensory neurons (i.e., those that are not mirror neurons) signal the absence of real proprioceptive and tactile inputs. When the arm is amputated, however, this normal sensory input is removed, leading the patient to quite literally experience the touch (or proprioceptive) sensations in the phantom (Ramachandran and Brang 2009). The patient also noted that watching another person's intact hand being rubbed caused relief from his phantom pain. There is anecdotal clinical evidence that synesthesia is more common in temporal lobe epilepsy. This can be explained by assuming that the repeated seizure volleys might indiscriminately strengthen certain brain connections through a process known as kindling. This would lead to pathological cross-activation (Ramachandran and Hubbard 2001a).

Touch-emotion synesthesia

Certain rarer forms of "congenital" synesthesia can also be partially explained by the cross-activation model. For example, some people "taste shapes." For these synesthetes, every taste has a shape which they perceive alongside their gustatory experience (i.e., chicken tastes "pointy," Cytowic 1989). It has been suggested that this is caused by cross-activation between taste neurons in the insula and S2 somatosensory cortex involved in discerning tactile texture and shape (Ramachandran and Hubbard 2001a). Similarly, in a newly discovered form of synesthesia, tactile textures evoke highly specific emotions (e.g., velvet = guilt). We postulate that there may be enhancement of connections that already exist between tactile textures (S2 cortex) and adjacent insula (emotion) as well as between the insula and the orbito-frontal cortex (Ramachandran and Brang 2008). Not coincidentally, perhaps similar "touch to emotion" activations are also common in cross-sensory metaphors ("rough day," and "touching remark") suggesting that metaphors may, speaking statistically, respect the same cross-sensory anatomical constraints as "pathological" synesthesia (Ramachandran and Hubbard 2001a). Enhanced cross-activations are most likely to occur between adjacent brain regions given that such regions are most likely to be already partly connected to begin with. But this isn't always true because pre-existing connections can also exist (less frequently) between far-flung brain regions that are functionally linked. The synesthesia gene(s) could enhance these connections.

Bidirectionality in synesthesia

By and large, synesthetes report these experiences are unidirectional, such that numbers may automatically elicit colors, yet colors will not cause the automatic percept of a number. While these subjective reports have been accepted for a number of years, mounting evidence from neuroimaging and behavioral studies suggest that synesthesia may be partially, if not unconsciously, bidirectional in grapheme-color synesthesia. Knoch et al. (2005) elegantly showed that synesthetes, but not controls, implicitly activated numerical representations when randomly generating colors. In addition, synesthetes instructed to choose the numerically larger of two numbers (the 5, when 4 and 5 are presented together) showed slowed reactions times if the numbers were colored with a numerically incongruous synesthetic color (4 printed in the color induced by 8, and 5 printed in the color induced by 2; Cohen Kadosh et al. 2005).

Do drug-induced synesthesias utilize the same mechanisms?

Research stemming from the mid nineteenth century has shown that some drugs (e.g., LSD and mescaline) can cause a blending of the senses in typical individuals (for a review, see Cytowic 1989). While these hallucinations are generally believed to be arbitrary and extant experiences, Klüver (1942) and Simpson and McKellar (1955), among others (e.g., Horowitz 1975; Siegel 1977), have shown that the visual experiences elicited by pharmacological agents tend to follow comparable patterns or themes between individuals. Most notably, subjects report similar "form constants"—visual patterns or shapes that are imbued with movement and color—as opposed to viewing complex landscapes or scenes (Klüver 1942). Critically, Cytowic and Eagleman (2009) point out that the visual sensations and form constants produced by LSD and mescaline are markedly similar to the reports of synesthetes, giving way to the hypothesis that drug induced synesthetic experiences may match the psychophysical definitions and neural mechanisms underlying those of developmental synesthesia.

WHY WAS THE GENE CONSERVED?

While a proven genetic basis for synesthesia remains elusive, the phenomenon tends to run in families, as nearly 50% of synesthetes report a first-degree relative with the phenomenon (Barnett et al. 2008; Baron-Cohen et al. 1996). Importantly, the "type" of synesthesia can vary within families, and the qualitative experience usually differs even between individuals of the same family. Preliminary work by Brang and Ramachandran (2007) suggested previously, based on pharmacological models of synesthesia, that genes on chromosome 13 may be involved in this phenomenon. Two recent genetic studies (Asher et al. 2009; Tomson et al. 2011) on synesthetes have located various non-overlapping hotspots suggesting either a lack of power from the derived sample sizes, or that the phenomenon is due to several genes.

In asking why any synesthesia gene would be maintained through evolution, one first must consider whether synesthesia is merely epiphenomenal, and the related genes serve some totally unrelated purpose and synesthesia operates as simply a by-product. However, as the causality cannot be known at present, we must assume for the time being that this is not (at least not fully) the explanation. To begin to understand why synesthesia would have been maintained, we can ask whether it is a gift or a curse? Most people who have it claim it enriches their lives. For example, if any letter in a word (but especially the first letter) evokes the same color as the referent of that word (say there happen to be blue letters within the word sea, for example), synesthetes report a pleasing harmony between word and letter, which has great aesthetic appeal. However, subjective enjoyment of the experience is not itself a good argument for the conservation of the gene (presuming of course synesthesia is not merely epiphenomenal). What we can point to, however, are the tangible links between synesthesia and more adaptable traits, and specifically what the general consequences of synesthesia are.

Consequences of synesthesia: memory

Many number-form synesthetes have told us (Ramachandran and Hubbard 2006) that they use their number lines to "see hidden relationships" between numbers and numerical calculations, by "wandering the numerical landscape" and adopting multiple allocentric viewpoints of the line. This is most certainly the case for some synesthetes, including Daniel Tammet who, using his synesthesia, memorized pi to 22,514 digits. A clever experiment by Smilek et al. (2002) suggests that synesthesia can enhance memory in all synesthetes, but not to the degree of Tammet's ability. They asked a grapheme-color synesthete to memorize a random selection of letters which were either randomly colored or colored in a manner consistent with their synesthesia. On subsequent testing they found that the letters with concordant colors were more accurately remembered. Luria (1969) described an individual ("S") whose prodigious memory was based largely on using synesthetic associations evoked by the things to be memorized. Enhancements of memory based on synesthesia have also been reported more recently by other groups (Brang and Ramachandran 2010; Yaro and Ward 2007).

Consequences of synesthesia: enhancements in primary sensory processing

Outside the realm of memory research, there is accumulating evidence of generalized processing benefits in synesthesia, providing a provocative evolutionary hypothesis.

Contrary to notions that synesthesia serves no benefit, recent work suggests synesthesia may alter primary sensory processes. Barnett et al. (2008) show differences in early visual perception and there are studies showing increased (unimodal) perceptual sensitivity in synesthetes (Banissy et al. 2009; Yaro and Ward 2007). Furthermore, research from our own laboratory suggests that grapheme-color synesthetes have lower color detection thresholds in a psychophysically low-level visual task (Wagner et al., in preparation). Taken collectively, these data suggest that synesthesia is associated with enhanced primary sensory processing as well as the integration between the senses. If validated, this idea would suggest that synesthesia serves to enhance normal sensory processing at a general level, better utilizing unisensory and multisensory processes.

Consequences of synesthesia: metaphor

If the gene for synesthesia were more diffusely expressed, the result would be an excess of cross-wiring throughout the brain. If abstract concepts are also represented in specific brain regions, then such diffuse cross-wiring would confer a propensity to link seemingly unrelated concepts represented in far-flung brain areas; the basis of metaphor ("sharp cheese" or "Juliet is the sun"). Hence, we would expect a higher incidence of synesthesia in artists, poets and novelists who all have the ability to link unrelated ideas. This "hidden agenda" might explain the high prevalence of the otherwise useless synesthesia gene (Ramachandran and Hubbard 2001a). This is analogous to the manner in which the sickle cell anemia gene survived in the Mediterranean, despite being lethal in the double recessive form, because the single recessive gene confers immunity from malaria. The gene mutation-based cross-wiring hypothesis also receives support from the fact that if you have one type of synesthesia you are also more likely than chance to have one or two other types (again, this would depend the gene being expressed more widely but in a patchy manner; Ramachandran and Hubbard 2001a).

The nature of the link between synesthesia and metaphor remains elusive given that synesthesia involves arbitrarily (in a conceptual sense) connecting two unrelated things (e.g., color and number) whereas there is a non-arbitrary conceptual connection between Juliet and the sun. One potential solution to this problem comes from realizing that any given word only has a *finite* set of strong first order associations (sun = warm, nurturing, radiant, bright) surrounded by a penumbra of weaker second order associations (sun = yellow, flowers, beach, etc.) and third and fourth order associations that fade away like an echo. The overlapping region between two halos of associations (e.g., Juliet and the sun; both are radiant, warm and nurturing)—the basis of metaphor—exists in all of us but may be larger and stronger in synesthesia as a result of the cross-activation gene. In this formulation synesthesia is not synonymous with metaphor but the gene that produces synesthesia confers a propensity towards metaphor. A side effect of this may be that associations that are only vaguely felt in all of us (e.g., masculine or feminine letters or good and bad shapes produced by subliminal associations) may become more explicitly manifest in synesthetes, a prediction that has been tested experimentally (e.g., Ward et al. 2006).

FUTURE DIRECTIONS FOR RESEARCH

As alluded to in the previous sections, some of the most needed research in the field is identifying the relationships between inherited synesthesias (e.g., grapheme-color synesthesia) and other conditions and phenomena that mimic these characteristics. Specifically, what aspects of synesthesia are based on pharmacology (intensity of the experience, numbers of synesthesia, or simply possessing synesthesia in general), and how does altering these neurotransmitters affect the experience of synesthesia in the normal population as well as in synesthetes; i.e., does a synesthete who has taken LSD experience novel forms and/or an enhancement of their current synesthesia? Similarly, what is the relationship between synesthesia and typical cross-modality interactions seen in the general population? As noted throughout the twentieth century, information presented in one sensory modality will alter processing in a second unrelated modality in all individuals (e.g., Hershenson, 1962). Preliminary evidence from our own lab suggests that synesthetes show a generalized increase in communication between the senses, suggesting that synesthesia may have piggy-backed on these phylogenetically old mechanisms (Brang, Williams, and Ramachandran 2012). Lastly, what are the genetic mechanisms underlying synesthesia, and what effect do they promote in the general population (i.e., what is the *normal* purpose of these genes). Do family members of synesthetes who themselves are not synesthetic (i.e., carriers) show latent synesthetic associations or an enhanced ability to make synesthesia-like associations?

CONCLUSION

In summary, these experiments conducted by several groups in the last decade have spawned a new era of investigation into this strange phenomenon that so intrigued Galton. While the topic has been discussed for over a century, the exact definition of synesthesia and what constitutes a "true" form of the phenomenon remains open to debate. Such semantic distinctions aside (as Francis Crick once said its best not to get preoccupied with definitions too early in the game; "That's best left to philosophers"), few would disagree that studies on synesthesia in the last decade have taken us on a journey—not in any particular order—from genes (affecting S2a receptors, perhaps) to anatomy (e.g., fusiform and angular gyri) to psychophysics (texture segregation/contrast effects/apparent motion/McCollough effect/Stroop interference) to metaphor. They suggest that far from being a "fringe" phenomenon as formerly believed (or that it is purely "conceptual" or associative in nature), synesthesia can give us vital clues toward understanding some of the physiological mechanisms underlying some of the most elusive yet cherished aspects of the human mind.

REFERENCES

Amin, Maina, Olufemi Olu-Lafe, Loes E. Claessen, Monika Sobczak-Edmans, Jamie Ward, Adrian L. Williams, and Noam Sagiv. 2011. Understanding grapheme personification: A social synaesthesia? *Journal of Neuropsychology* 5 (2):255–282.

Armel, K. C., and V. S. Ramachandran. 1999. Acquired synesthesia in retinitis pigmentosa. *Neurocase* 5 (4):293–296.

Asher, Julien E., Janine A. Lamb, Denise Brocklebank, Jean-Baptiste Cazier, Elena Maestrini, Laura Addis, Mallika Sen, Simon Baron-Cohen, and Anthony P. Monaco. 2009. A whole-genome scan and fine-mapping linkage study of auditory-visual synesthesia reveals evidence of linkage to chromosomes 2q24, 5q33, 6p12, and 12p12. *The American Journal of Human Genetics* 84 (2):279–285.

Banissy, Michael J., Vincent Walsh, and Jamie Ward. 2009. Enhanced sensory perception in synaesthesia. *Experimental Brain Research* 196 (4):565–571.

Barnett, Kylie J., Ciara Finucane, Julian Asher, Gary Bargary, Aiden P. Corvin, Fiona N. Newell, and Kevin J. Mitchell. 2008. Familial patterns and the origins of individual differences in synaesthesia. *Cognition* 106 (2):871–893.

Barnett, Kylie J., and Fiona N. Newell. 2008. Synaesthesia is associated with enhanced, self-rated visual imagery. *Consciousness and Cognition* 17 (3):1032–1039.

Baron-Cohen, Simon, Lucy Burt, Fiona Smith-Laittan, John J. Harrison, and Patrick Bolton. 1996. Synaesthesia: Prevalence and familiality. *Perception* 25 (9):1073–1079.

Beeli, Gian, Michaela Esslen, and Lutz Jäncke. 2007. Frequency correlates in grapheme-color synaesthesia. *Psychological Science* 18 (9):788–792.

Blake, Randolph, Thomas J. Palmeri, Rene Marois, and Chai-Youn Kim. 2005. On the perceptual reality of synesthetic color. In *Synaesthesia: Perspectives from Cognitive Neuroscience*, ed. Lynn C. Robertson and Noam Sagiv, 47–73. New York: Oxford University Press.

Blakemore, Sarah-Jane, Davina Bristow, Geoffrey Bird, Christopher Frith, and Jamie Ward. 2005. Somatosensory activations during the observation of touch and a case of vision-touch synaesthesia. *Brain* 128 (7):1571.

Brang, David, L. Edwards, Vilayanur S. Ramachandran, and Seana Coulson. 2008. Is the sky 2? Contextual priming in grapheme-color synaesthesia. *Psychological Science* 19 (5):421–428.

Brang, David, Edward M. Hubbard, Seana Coulson, M. Huang, and Vilayanur S. Ramachandran. 2010. Magnetoencephalography reveals early activation of V4 in grapheme-color synesthesia. *NeuroImage* 53 (1):268–274.

Brang, David, Stanley Kanai, Vilayanur S. Ramachandran, and Seana Coulson. 2011. Contextual priming in grapheme–color synesthetes and yoked controls: 400 msec in the life of a synesthete. *Journal of Cognitive Neuroscience* (7):1681–1696.

Brang, David, and Vilayanur S. Ramachandran. 2007. Psychopharmacology of synesthesia; The role of serotonin S2a receptor activation. *Medical Hypotheses* 70 (4):903–934.

——. 2010. Visual field heterogeneity, laterality, and eidetic imagery in synesthesia. *Neurocase* 16 (2):169–174.

Brang, David, Romke Rouw, Vilayanur S. Ramachandran, and Seana Coulson. 2011. Similarly shaped letters evoke similar colors in grapheme-color synesthesia. *Neuropsychologia* 49:1355–1358.

Brang, David, Ursina Teuscher, Luke E. Miller, Vilayanur S. Ramachandran, and Seana Coulson. 2011. Handedness and calendar orientations in time-space synesthesia. *Journal of Neuropsychology* 5 (2):323–332.

Brang, David, Ursina Teuscher, Vilayanur S. Ramachandran, and Seana Coulson. 2010. Temporal sequences, synesthetic mappings, and cultural biases: The geography of time. *Consciousness and Cognition* 19 (1):311–320.

Brang, David, Lisa E. Williams, and Vilayanur S. Ramachandran. 2012. Grapheme-color synesthetes show enhanced crossmodal processing between auditory and visual modalities. *Cortex* 48 (5):630–637.

Cohen Kadosh, R., Henik, A., & Walsh, V. 2007. Small is bright and big is dark in synaesthesia. *Current Biology* 17 (19):R834-R835.

Cohen Kadosh, Roi, Noam Sagiv, David E. J. Linden, Lynn C. Robertson, Gali Elinger, and Avishai Henik. 2005. When blue is larger than red: Colors influence numerical cognition in synesthesia. *Journal of Cognitive Neuroscience* 17 (11):1766–1773.

Cytowic, Richard E. 1989. Synesthesia and mapping of subjective sensory dimensions. *Neurology* 39(6):849–850.

Cytowic, Richard E., and David Eagleman. 2009. *Wednesday is Indigo Blue: Discovering the Brain of Synesthesia*. Cambridge, MA: MIT Press.

Dixon, Mike J., Daniel Smilek, Cera Cudahy, and Philip M. Merikle. 2000. Five plus two equals yellow. *Nature* 406 (6794):365.

Domino, George. 1989. Synesthesia and creativity in fine arts students: An empirical look. *Creativity Research Journal* 2 (1):17–29.

Eagleman, David M. 2009. The objectification of overlearned sequences: A new view of spatial sequence synesthesia. *Cortex* 45 (10):1266–1277.

Eagleman, David M., Arielle D. Kagan, Stephanie S. Nelson, Deepak Sagaram, Anand K. Sarma. 2007. A standardized test battery for the study of synesthesia. *Journal of Neuroscience Methods* 159 (1):139–145.

Galton, Francis. 1881. Visualised numerals. *The Journal of the Anthropological Institute of Great Britain and Ireland* 10:85–102.

Gertner, Limor, Avishai Heni, and Roi Cohen Kadosh. 2009. When 9 is not on the right: Implications from number-form synesthesia. *Consciousness and Cognition* 18 (2):366–374.

Grossenbacher, Peter G., and Christopher T. Lovelace. 2001. Mechanisms of synesthesia: Cognitive and physiological constraints. *Trends in Cognitive Sciences* 5 (1):36–41.

Hershenson, M. 1962. Reaction time as a measure of intersensory facilitation. *Journal of Experimental Psychology* 63 (3):289–293.

Horowitz, M. J. 1975. Hallucinations: An information processing approach. *Hallucinations: Behavior, Experience and Theory*, ed. Ronald K. Seigel, and Louis J. West, 163–195. New York: Wiley.

Hubbard, E. M., P. Ambrosio, S. Azoulai, and V. S. Ramachandran. 2005. Grapheme and letter name based patterns in synesthetic colors. *Cognitive Neuroscience Society Meeting*, April 9-12, 2005, New York City, NY

Hubbard, Edward M., A. Cyrus Arman, Vilayanur S. Ramachandran, and Geoffrey M. Boynton. 2005. Individual differences among grapheme-color synesthetes: Brain-behavior correlations. *Neuron* 45 (6):975–985.

Hubbard, Edward M., Sanjay Manohar, and Vilayanur S. Ramachandran. 2006. Contrast affects the strength of synesthetic colors. *Cortex* 42 (2):184–194.

Jäncke, Lutz, Gian Beeli, Cornelia Eulig, and Jürgen Hänggi. 2009. The neuroanatomy of grapheme-color synesthesia. *European Journal of Neuroscience* 29 (6):1287–1293.

Jarick, Michelle, Mike J. Dixon, Emily C. Maxwell, Mike E. R. Nicholls, and Daniel Smilek. 2009. The ups and downs (and lefts and rights) of synaesthetic number forms: Validation from spatial cueing and SNARC-type tasks. *Cortex* 45 (10):1190–1199.

Jonas, Clare, and Michelle Jarick. 2013. Synesthesia, sequences, and space. In *The Oxford Handbook of Synesthesia*, ed. Julia Simner and Edward M. Hubbard, 123-148. Oxford: Oxford University Press.

Keeley, Bryan L. 2013. What exactly is a sense? In *The Oxford Handbook of Synesthesia*, ed. Julia Simner and Edward M. Hubbard, 941-958. Oxford: Oxford University Press.

Kim, Chai-Youn, Randolph Blake, Thomas J. Palmeri, Rene Marois and William Whetsell. 2003. Synesthetic colors act like real colors and interact with real colors. *Journal of Vision* 3 (9):620.

Klüver, H. 1942. Mechanisms of hallucinations. In *Studies in Personality*, ed. Quinn McNemar and Maude A. Merrill, 175–207. New York: McGraw-Hill.

Knoch, D., L. R. R. Gianotti, C. Mohr, and P. Brugger. 2005. Synesthesia: When colors count. *Cognitive Brain Research* 25 (1):372–374.

Luria, Aleksandr. 1969. *The Mind of a Mnemonist*. Cambridge, MA: Harvard University Press.

Lyall, Mary-Ellen, and Colin Blakemore. 2013. What synesthesia isn't. In *The Oxford Handbook of Synesthesia*, ed. Julia Simner and Edward M. Hubbard, 959-998. Oxford: Oxford University Press.

Mattingley, Jason B., Anina N. Rich, Greg Yelland, and John L. Bradshaw. 2001. Unconscious priming eliminates automatic binding of colour and alphanumeric form in synaesthesia. *Nature* 410 (6828):580–582.

Mills, Carol B., Joanne Innis, Taryn Westendorf, Lauren Owsianiecki, and Angela McDonald. 2002. The color of two alphabets for a multilingual synesthete. *Perception* 31:1371–1394.

Mroczko, Aleksandra, Thomas Metzinger, Wolf Singer, and Danko Nikolić. D. 2009. Immediate transfer of synesthesia to a novel inducer. *Journal of Vision* 9 (12):1–8.

Palmeri, Thomas. J., Randolph Blake, René Marois, Marci A. Flanery, and William Whetsell Jr. 2002. The perceptual reality of synesthetic colors. *Proceedings of the National Academy of Sciences of the United States of America* 99 (6):4127–4131.

Ramachandran, Vilayanur S., and Shai Azoulai. 2006. Synesthetically induced colors evoke apparent-motion perception. *Perception* 35 (1):1557–1560.

Ramachandran, Vilayanur S., and David Brang. (2008). Tactile-emotion synesthesia. *Neurocase* 14 (5):390–399.

Ramachandran, Vilayanur S., and David Brang. 2009. Sensations evoked in patients with amputation from watching an individual whose corresponding intact limb is being touched. *Archives of Neurology* 66 (10):1281–1284.

Ramachandran, Vilayanur S., and Edward M. Hubbard. 2001a. Synaesthesia: A window into perception, thought and language. *Journal of Consciousness Studies* 8 (12):3–34.

——. 2001b. Psychophysical investigations into the neural basis of synaesthesia. *Proceedings of the Royal Society B: Biological Sciences* 268 (1470):979–983.

——. 2002. Synesthetic colors support symmetry perception apparent motion and ambiguous crowding. *Abstracts of the Psychonomic Society* 7:79.

——. 2003. Hearing colors, tasting shapes. *Scientific American* 288 (5):52–59.

——. 2003. The phenomenology of synaesthesia. *Journal of Consciousness Studies* 10 (8):49–57.

——. 2006. Synesthesia: What does it tell us about the emergence of qualia, metaphor, abstract thought, and language? In 23 *Problems in Systems Neuroscience*, ed. J. van Hemmen, and T. J. Sejnowski, 432–473. New York: Oxford University Press.

Ramachandran, Vilayanur S., Diane Rogers-Ramachandran, and Susan Cobb. 1995. Touching the phantom limb. *Nature* 377:489–490.

Rich, Anina N., John L. Bradshaw, and Jason B. Mattingley. 2005. A systematic, large-scale study of synaesthesia: Implications for the role of early experience in lexical-colour associations. *Cognition* 98 (1):53–84.

Rizzolatti, G., L. Fadiga, V. Gallese, and L. Fogassi. 1996. Premotor cortex and the recognition of motor actions. *Cognitive Brain Research* 3 (2):131–141.

Ro, Tony, Alessandro Farnè, Ruth M. Johnson, Van Wedeen, Zili Chu, Zhiyue J. Wang, Jill V. Hunter, and Michael S. Beauchamp. 2007. Feeling sounds after a thalamic lesion. *Annals of Neurology* 62 (5):433–441.

Robertson, Lynn C., and Noam Sagiv, eds. 2005. *Synesthesia: Perspectives from Cognitive Neuroscience*. New York: Oxford University Press.

Rothen, Nicholas, and Beat Meier. 2010. Higher prevalence of synaesthesia in art students. *Perception* 39 (5):718–720.

Rouw, Romke, and H. Steven Scholte. 2007. Increased structural connectivity in grapheme-color synesthesia. *Nature Neuroscience* 10 (6):792–797.

——. 2010. Neural basis of individual differences in synesthetic experiences. *The Journal of Neuroscience* 30 (18):6205–6213.

Sagiv, Noam, Julia Simner, James Collins, Brian Butterworth, and Jamie Ward. 2006. What is the relationship between synaesthesia and visuo-spatial number forms. *Cognition* 101 (1):114–128.

Siegel, R. K. (1977). Hallucinations. *Scientific American* 237 (4):132–140.

Simner, Julia, and Emma Holenstein. 2007. Ordinal linguistic personification as a variant of synesthesia. *Journal of Cognitive Neuroscience* 19 (4):694–703.

Simner, Julia, Catherine Mulvenna, Noam Sagiv, Elias Tsakanikos, S. Athene Witherby, Christine Fraser, Kirsten Scott, and Jamie Ward. 2006. Synaesthesia: The prevalence of atypical cross-modal experiences. *Perception* 35 (8):1024–1033.

Simner, Julia, and Jamie Ward. 2006. Synaesthesia: The taste of words on the tip of the tongue. *Nature* 444 (7118):438.

Simpson, Lorna, and Peter McKellar. 1955. Types of synaesthesia. *British Journal of Psychiatry* 101 (422):141.

Smilek, Daniel, Jonathan S. A. Carriere, Mike J. Dixon, and Philip M. Merikle. 2007. Grapheme frequency and color luminance in grapheme-color synaesthesia. *Psychological Science* 18 (9):793–795.

Smilek, Daniel, Mike J. Dixon, Cera Cudahy, and Philip M. Merikle. 2002. Synesthetic color experiences influence memory. *Psychological Science* 13 (6):548.

Spector, F., and Maurer, D. 2011. The colors of the alphabet: Naturally-biased associations between shape and color. *Journal of Experimental Psychology: Human Perception and Performance* 37 (2):484.

Tomson, Steffie N., Nili Avidan, Kwanghyuk Lee, Anand K. Sarma, Rejnal Tushe, Dianna M. Milewicz, Molly Bray, Suzanne M. Leal, David M. Eagleman. 2011. The genetics of colored sequence synesthesia: Suggestive evidence of linkage to 16q and genetic heterogeneity for the condition. *Behavioural Brain Research* 223 (1):48–52.

Ward, Jamie, Brett Huckstep, and Elias Tsakanikos. 2006. Sound-colour synaesthesia: To what extent does it use cross-modal mechanisms common to us all? *Cortex* 42 (2):264–280.

Ward, Jamie, Clare Jonas, Zoltan Dienes, and Anil Seth. 2010. Grapheme-colour synaesthesia improves detection of embedded shapes, but without pre-attentive 'pop-out' of synaesthetic colour. *Proceedings of the Royal Society B: Biological Sciences* 277 (1684):1021–1026.

Weiss, Peter H., and Gereon R. Fink. 2009. Grapheme-colour synaesthetes show increased grey matter volumes of parietal and fusiform cortex. *Brain* 132 (1):65–70.

Witthoft, Nathan, and Jonathan Winawer. 2006. Synesthetic colors determined by having colored refrigerator magnets in childhood. *Cortex* 42 (2):175–183.

Yaro, Caroline, and Jamie Ward. 2007. Searching for Shereshevskii: What is superior about the memory of synaesthetes? *The Quarterly Journal of Experimental Psychology* 60 (5):681–695.

CHAPTER 49

....

SYNESTHESIA

Where have we been? Where are we going?

....

JAMIE WARD

In this last chapter of the handbook, I'll review where synesthesia research has been and where it is going. I'll consider how we might want to define synesthesia and its relationship to other phenomena and I'll consider the "big questions" that need to be addressed.

THE FIRST 200 YEARS: WHERE HAVE WE BEEN?

....

A short answer to that question could be: round and round in circles. The first convincing case of synesthesia was an autobiographical account by Georg Sachs in 1812 (Jewanski, Day, and Ward 2009). In it Sachs describes colors for letters, numbers, sequences, and tones. However, Sachs' work had very little immediate impact until its rediscovery by an ophthalmologist in 1848 (Cornaz 1848), triggering many more case reports in the following decades (see Jewanski et al. 2011). During this very early period there were interesting debates about the extent to which synesthesia might be a particularly durable form of childhood association or a kind of cross-talk between the nerves. That debate lasted another century without any significant empirical progress that would resolve it.

Galton (1880) independently discovered synesthesia in 1879 after an exchange of letters with George Bidder, the son of a famous mathematician of the same name, who gave Galton a drawing of his own spatial forms of numbers, months, and the Kings and Queens of England (this representing what is also known as "sequence-space synesthesia"). Although Galton also described color associations (e.g., A = red) and personifications (e.g., A = a busy mother) from other synesthetes, these didn't arouse the same interest as the spatial forms for numbers which he regarded as less likely to be learned via tuition. Given that Galton wasn't initially aware of the previous literature in this area he didn't cite it. This led to the preceding period falling into relative obscurity (at least within the English-speaking community), and a mistaken assumption (many years later) that synesthesia research began with Galton.

Up until the 1920s, there was a large and varied literature dealing with synesthesia. Many new forms of synesthesia were discovered. For instance, in their contemporary "discovery" of lexical-gustatory synesthesia, Ward and Simner (2003) acknowledge that this was in fact just a rediscovery of something that had been reported almost 100 years previously in three separate cases (Ferrari 1907, 1910; Pierce 1907). The suggestion that language and color centers of the brain may have unusual anatomical connections (Ramachandran and Hubbard 2001a, 2001b) has a precedent in Lussana (1873). Similarly, the insight that grapheme-color synesthesia could be described in terms of individual differences in the spatial location of the colors (e.g., external versus internal, termed projector and associator respectively; Dixon, Smilek, and Merikle 2004) had several historical precedents (Colman 1894; Flournoy 1893). There was even an early reaction time study of synesthesia conducted in 1890 that was essentially forgotten (Binet 1894).

As such, the modern rediscovery of synesthesia has proceeded almost entirely without an awareness of historical precedents (a notable exception being Marks 1975). In terms of contemporary research that addresses significant historical issues, I'd like to highlight three empirical milestones that I regard as particularly important. First is the attempt to use a statistical approach (or "test of genuineness") to discriminate synesthetes from non-synesthetes which owes its origins to Baron-Cohen and colleagues (Baron-Cohen, Wyke, and Binnie 1987; Baron-Cohen et al. 1993). Second is the finding that most grapheme-color synesthetes do not derive their color associations from alphabet books (Rich, Bradshaw, and Mattingley 2005). This idea had been lurking around since Chabalier (1864) and was effectively taken for granted by the behaviorists (e.g., Howells 1944). Finally, I'd like to highlight the discovery that synesthetes possess structural differences within the brain (Rouw and Scholte 2007). This finding provides convincing evidence that synesthesia is not just associated with functional differences, but is linked to anatomical differences too. Again, this idea had been debated since the earliest days of explorations in synesthesia.

With so many false starts, it is perhaps not surprising that we don't yet have a convincing account of synesthesia. However, with the rapid accumulation of empirical knowledge we are well placed to develop one. The year 2000 to 2001 is surely the year in which synesthesia took off in a big way. Although important groundwork had been laid in the decades before, this was the year in which many different research groups—largely independently from each other—began in-depth explorations of the phenomenon (Dixon et al. 2000; Mattingley, Rich, and Bradshaw 2001; Ramachandran and Hubbard 2001). Many other research groups followed close behind (e.g., Cohen Kadosh et al. 2005; Palmeri et al. 2002; Ward and Simner 2003).

As with the bygone researchers, it remains important to determine where synesthesia begins and ends in terms of its relationship to other phenomena such as mental imagery, hallucinations, learned association, and so forth. This is considered in more detail in the next section.

Defining Synesthesia: Where Does Synesthesia Begin and End?

Many contemporary reviews helpfully start by explaining that the word comes from the Greek "syn" (joining) and "aisthesis" (sensation). But what did the ancient Greeks understand by this term? Aristotle, no less, did use the term (in the form "sunaisthesis") but not to describe the phenomenon we speak of today (Sorabji 2005). In one meaning of the word, it referred to joint attention amongst different perceivers and in another it was used to compare between two or more perceived sensory qualities (e.g., white and fragrant) within one individual (Sorabji 2005). Some contemporary scholars emphasize the role of sunaisthesis in Aristotle's theory of friendship in terms of a "merged selves" or "mirrored selves" approach (Flakne 2005). The term re-entered into medicine in the nineteenth century to explain strange reflex-like sensations such as the "photic sneeze" (sneezing when going into a bright light) and shivers elicited from hearing a blackboard scratched (Vulpian 1866). Neither of these phenomena is generally considered to constitute synesthesia at present (although they could meet certain definitions). In introducing the term into its present day context Calkins (1895) grouped together a variety of phenomena including "colored hearing," spatial forms, and personification. Although there is presently good consensus over the core exemplars of what constitutes synesthesia these days (and it doesn't differ that much from Calkins, 1895) there are some "frilly edges" which are less clear-cut. These are worth exploring as they will shape what an explanation of synesthesia will have to cover.

I have previously suggested three defining features of synesthesia (Ward 2008; Ward and Mattingley 2006):

(1) It is elicited; that is, it requires an inducer (something that triggers it) and a concurrent (the modality in which it is experienced) to use the terminology of Grossenbacher and Lovelace (2001).
(2) It is automatic.
(3) It is percept-like in nature.

Others have suggested different or additional criteria such as extension in space (Cytowic 1989) and consistency over time (Asher et al. 2006), although both these additional criteria have been questioned in recent reports (Simner 2011), as well as the necessity that synesthesia is "percept-like." However, whether or not these are defining qualities, per se (and I believe that the first three at least are), these five features do appear to be key aspects in most forms of synesthesia. With regard to extension in space, this is obviously related to the third criteria listed, but it need not be in externalized space. For instance, some synesthetes see the colors on an "inner screen." This is one of the reasons why I tend to use the term percept-like rather than "just like a percept" or "perceptual reality." With regards to consistency over time, that feature

Table 49.1 Synesthesia is defined here as having three key aspects. Many of these aspects are present in other forms of perception and cognition

	Produces a conscious percept-like experience	Elicited by processing of some other stimulus/attribute	Inevitable and automatic
Synesthesia	Yes	Yes	Yes
Hallucination	Yes	No	No
Cross-modal biases	No	Yes	Yes
Visual imagery	Yes	Yes or No	No
Phantom touch	Yes	No	Yes(?)

may emerge developmentally (Simner et al. 2009) and it is unclear what we would call something that met the three criteria listed but was inconsistent in nature (Ward and Mattingley 2006).

The three features of synesthesia described in the list can be found in other normal or pathological situations. These situations are likely to have over-lapping cognitive and neural mechanisms with synesthesia. Table 49.1 describes a number of situations that share some features with synesthesia. These include hallucinations (perceptual experiences that don't have an obvious trigger), mental imagery (percept-like experiences that are usually voluntarily elicited or under some form of voluntary control), cross-modal biases (when processing of one sensory modality is automatically affected by information in another modality; Marks 2004), and referred phantom limb sensation (in which touch to the face may be simultaneously perceived on the "phantom" hand; Ramachandran, Rogers-Ramachandran, and Cobb 1995).

The problem with defining synesthesia concerns the limits that one might place on the nature of the inducer, the nature of the concurrent, and the relationship between them (Simner 2011). For example, feeling touch to a phantom hand following touch to the ipsilateral face of an amputee *could* be classified as synesthesia if one allowed touch to act as both an inducer and concurrent within the same pairing. Although previous researchers highlighted inter-sensory aspects of synesthesia in its definition, few researchers would strongly endorse such a position these days. The best apparent example of an *intra*-modal synesthesia is grapheme-color synesthesia in which one aspect of vision (shape) elicits another aspect of vision (color). However, even in this instance the inducer could just be regarded as linguistic or supra-modal. If it is to be called vision then it is clearly at the highest levels of visual processing. For instance, meaningless shapes do not tend to elicit colors in grapheme-color synesthetes and "shapes" that are visually very different (e.g., the upper and lower case forms of letters) can elicit the same colors. There is a region of the brain that responds to graphemes more than other visual objects, the so-called visual word form area (e.g., Cohen et al. 2002). However, this region must have evolved for other purposes and only recently in human history has it been used for this purpose. In illiterate people, this region may be used for recognizing faces (Dehaene et al. 2011). In blind people, the region is used for reading Braille characters via touch (Büchel, Price, and Friston 1998; Reich et al. 2011). I have previously argued that if everyone were to read using their fingertips (like the blind) then grapheme-color synesthesia would still exist but it would switch to being a cross-modal tactile-color synesthesia rather than an apparently intra-modal synesthesia (Ward 2008). In other words, the manifestation of (at least some types of) synesthesia is culturally embedded within learned knowledge. We have very little idea about how synesthesia might manifest itself in illiterate cultures. This poses problems for both defining and explaining synesthesia.

It is unclear whether there is any value to placing constraints on the nature of the inducer (e.g., by insisting it is percept-like in nature). Most types of synesthesia are induced by certain forms of conceptual knowledge (e.g., sequences such as days, months) but, again, there is no reason for thinking that this is part of the *definition* of synesthesia. Rather, it is something to be explained. Do we need to impose definitional constraints on the nature of the concurrent? I have argued "yes" but others have argued "no" (Simner 2011). Two possible examples of types of synesthesia which less clearly fit the definition above are spatial forms and personification. The apparent difficulty in classifying spatial forms stems from the fact that "space" is not normally regarded as a sense in its own right (Sagiv et al. 2006). However, most descriptions of spatial forms are *visuo*-spatial. These synesthetes report "seeing" the actual words and digits (e.g., in a particular font of a particular size) and "seeing" blocks on which these are superimposed. For personification, the concurrent is an associated idea of a gender and/or a personality trait that may be assigned to graphemic inducers and other stimuli (e.g., Simner and Holenstein 2007; Smilek et al. 2007). In many respects, it meets the criteria of synesthesia by being automatic and consistent over time. It also appears to be more common in synesthetes than others (Simner and Holenstein 2007). So should we drop the percept-like criteria to include personification? One ramification of broadening the definition of synesthesia in this way is that any type of automatic (and consistent?) association meets the criteria for synesthesia: i.e., the concept becomes very broad indeed. One could argue that when we understand the *causes* of synesthesia then we will be able to distinguish between synesthetic associations and all other associations. That may be true, but it may not be. For instance, personification may have multiple causes (lonely people without other forms of synesthesia may be more likely to do it; Epley et al. 2008) and synesthesia itself is known to have multiple causes (acquired versus developmental synesthesia).

Clearly, any definition of synesthesia is a working definition waiting to be refined. When we have a full understanding of the mechanisms of synesthesia (genetic, neural, and cognitive) and its relationship to other phenomena then the definition won't be worth splitting hairs over. The question for contemporary researchers is whether a broad or narrow definition is going to be the most useful for driving research forwards.

Four Big Things That a Theory of Synesthesia Should Explain

In this section, I'll consider four over-arching issues in synesthesia research: how can science account for the self-reported experiences of synesthetes; what causes it; what are the consequences; and what are the implications for the typical (or "normal") mind and brain.

How can science account for the self-reported experiences of synesthetes?

Studying synesthesia requires the researcher to be open-minded about the nature of other people's experiences. However, synesthetes find it hard to describe their own experiences and, when they do, it is typically not in the language of the scientist. As researchers, we want to translate their experiences into hypotheses about cognitive processes (attention, spatial cognition, etc.), neural mechanisms (connectivity, plasticity, etc.) and experiments that would confirm/disconfirm these suppositions (Smilek and Dixon 2002). Terms such as "mind's eye" can be particularly problematic as it may mean different things to different people. It can also be unclear whether the "mind's eye" that supports synesthesia is the same as the "mind's eye" that supports other imagery as this quote illustrates:

> I realize that I am constantly holding at least three images in my head. Firstly, what I see in front of me. Secondly, in a sort of semi-circle, filling the top part of my head, but definitely inside, perhaps level with my ears, is my synesthetic image. And thirdly, anything I happen to be thinking of, such as my route home etc., which will almost be on a screen at an angle to my synesthetic screen. (Ward 2008, 89)

Consider also the distinction between "knowing" and "seeing" of synesthetic colors. Why would one synesthete claim to "see" their synesthetic colors and another synesthete claim to "know" but not see them? There are two possibilities. Firstly, it could be that both are experiencing the same thing but the latter person just uses a more conservative terminology or tries not to look dumb by implying that synesthesia originates from the eyes. The other possibility is that they are genuinely experiencing different things. If they are experiencing different things then how should we characterize that difference? The most obvious hypothesis is that those who claim to "see" are using perceptual processes whereas those who claim to "know" are using imagery/memory mechanisms.

We have recently conducted a questionnaire study of a large sample (N = 106) of grapheme-color synesthetes that suggests an alternative hypothesis. First of all, synesthetes don't fall neatly into two groups: whereas some claim to "see not know" (55%)

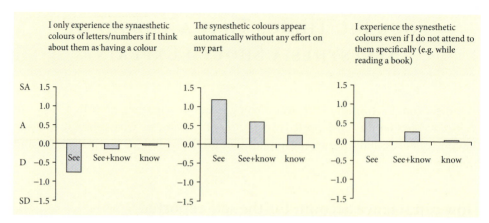

FIGURE 49.1 The phenomenological experiences of "seeing" and "knowing" synesthetic colors, evoked in grapheme-color synesthetes, appears to be related to the extent to which the colors appear effortlessly (more like "seeing") but not the extent to which participants endorse statements about their intensity (data not shown). The relevant three questions about automaticity/effort were answered on a 4-point Likert scale (from Strongly Agree, SA, to Strongly Disagree, SD). In separate questions, synesthetes were asked whether they claim to *see* the synesthetic colors or *know* them.

and others to "know not see" (12%) there are others who claim to "see and know" (31%).[1] We then looked to see what other questions and measures discriminated between these three groups. Interestingly, it was questions about automaticity rather than questions about perceptual intensity that discriminated between them. This is illustrated in Figure 49.1. Specifically, synesthetes who claim to "know" the colors report less automaticity than those who claim to "see." Thus, although researchers may be tempted to cast the distinction between seeing/knowing in terms of perceptual/non-perceptual mechanisms this may be misguided. It may relate instead to the extent to which the colors come to the synesthete ("seeing") or the extent to which the synesthete has to fetch the colors ("knowing").

As another precautionary tale, the distinction above does not map neatly onto the projector-associator distinction suggested by others (Dixon and Smilek 2005; Dixon, Smilek, and Merikle 2004). Projectors claim to experience their colors in the location of the inducer itself (e.g., on the text) and almost invariably describe their experiences as like "seeing." Associators on the other hand either describe their experiences as like "seeing" (e.g., on an inner screen) or "knowing." Using questionnaire measures, such as those described earlier, these appear to be separate. The experience of whether colors claim to be "seen" or "known" may be (at least partly) separable from the issue of *where* the colors are located during the experience. There has been a near-universal trend to group these two concepts (seeing-knowing and external-internal) together but they may

---

[1] The remaining couple of percent respond 'disagree' to both knowing and seeing, and we do not consider them here.

be teased apart using first-person methods (questionnaires, interviews). Both "projec-tors" and "associators" have a tendency to claim to *see* the synesthetic colors (e.g., when given an appropriate questionnaire) but they tend to differ in the location of where the colors are experienced. We would obviously then want to try to corroborate these sub-jective reports using other methods such as behavioral tasks or establishing different neural correlates.

A more fruitful approach to linking the subjective experiences of synesthetes to scien-tific concepts may be to consider the dimensions on which synesthesia varies: automatic-ity, intensity, location, and so on. Some of these dimensions may collapse on to each other; for instance, the automaticity-effort dimension may turn out to be essentially the same as the seeing-knowing dimension. This varying-dimensions approach contrasts with the previously dominant approach of categorizing synesthetes into binary divisions.

Another challenge for synesthesia research is to explain the phenomenology of each particular variant of synesthesia, and not just grapheme-color synesthesia. However, it is possible that a limited number of principles could do the trick. For instance, con-sider again the various possible locations of synesthetic colors. Rather than categorizing them as "internal" or "external," we have proposed an alternative way of thinking about them (Ward 2008; Ward et al. 2007). Namely, in terms of whether they are localized with respect to the inducing stimulus (an object-centered frame of reference), whether they are localized with respect to the observer (an egocentric frame of reference), or whether their location is independent of both observer and stimulus (e.g., on some forms of an "imagined screen"). This may offer a more accurate account of the phenomenology of synesthesia. For instance, experiencing colors "on the page" when viewing text and experiencing a number form in peri-personal space when counting are both examples of externalized visual experiences. However, in this scheme the former is likely to be object-centered (if the text is moved, the colors move with the text) whereas the latter is likely to be observer-centered (if the observer is moved, the spatial form moves with the observer). This can be extended to many other types of synesthesia. For example, audi-tory-visual synesthetes either experience the colors as emanating near the sound source (object-centered) or relative to their own body/head (Goller, Otten, and Ward 2009). Similarly, touch-color synesthetes can experience the color as either "out there" on the felt object or on an inner screen (Ward, Banissy, and Jonas 2008). From a philosophical point of view, research into synesthesia offers a test case as to how one may study a first-person experience from a third-person perspective.

What are the causes of synesthesia?

Within the neurosciences, synesthesia could prove to be an interesting paradigm for exploring the link between various levels of explanation: from the expression of individ-ual genes, to the development of neural pathways and cortical specialization, through to influencing behavior and conscious experience. Synesthesia is known to run in families and, more recently, linkage studies have identified regions on a number of chromosomes that may contain relevant genes (Asher et al. 2009). Most synesthetes cannot recall a time when they didn't have it, although formal testing is now revealing that some forms of synesthesia may not stabilize until school age (Simner et al. 2009). Rather than offering an overview of the causes of synesthesia (which is covered elsewhere in this handbook), I'd like to highlight the problems faced by researchers in *identifying* the causal pathway.

Firstly, there is the recurring problem of measurement. Two areas of research that have been under-explored but should be crucial for understanding the causes of synesthesia are animal models and developmental studies. Progress in both areas is necessarily limited by the fact that there isn't an easy methodology for measuring the presence of synesthesia in animals, human infants, and pre-school children. There have been attempts to consider how synesthesia could be explored in animal models (Bargary and Mitchell 2008). The advantage of this approach is that it is possible to directly alter gene functioning and observe consequences on brain development and behavior, and with development itself occurring much faster in mice than humans. With regards to human developmental studies, there are essentially two kinds of studies that have been brought to bear on this question (Maurer and Mondloch 2006). Firstly, studies establishing that there are "innate" multisensory correspondences in infants that resemble those found in the experiences of adult synesthetes and also found, implicitly, in the behavioral responses of non-synesthetes. For instance, a tendency to associate high pitch with spiky shapes is found in infants at 4 months of age (Walker et al. 2010). The second approach is to demonstrate that infants' brains often show a multisensory response to a unimodal stimulus (e.g., auditory stimuli activating auditory and visual regions), and this tendency decreases developmentally (e.g., Wolff et al. 1974). However, we obviously do not know what the infant experiences. Also, we do not know what differs in the brains of infants destined to become synesthetes versus the brains of typical infants (upon which this body of research is based). To do that would require longitudinal studies which are time-consuming and difficult, although not impossible (given that it tends to run in families one could identify candidates before they are born).

A second issue in establishing the causes of synesthesia is in understanding what role the environment plays. Different types of synesthesia tend to coexist within the same families and the precise associations themselves are not heritable (Barnett et al. 2008; Ward, Simner, and Auyeung 2005). One possibility is that the environmental input is limited to learning sets of inducers (e.g., knowledge of sequences, knowledge of graphemes) or learning sets of concurrents (e.g., knowledge of different flavors) but not necessarily influencing which type of inducer is paired with which type of concurrent. The latter could be set by early differences in connectivity, and the different anatomical locations in the brain of potential inducers and concurrents (Hubbard and Ramachandran 2005). Another possibility is that early experiences or traits unrelated to synesthesia cause certain forms of synesthesia to emerge. For instance, mirror-touch synesthesia is linked to heightened empathy (Banissy and Ward 2007), but does heightened empathy bias the formation of this variety (as opposed to other varieties) of synesthesia, or is heightened empathy a consequence of this particular synesthetic pattern? We have tended to assume the latter, but we can't be sure. To give another anecdote, I recently studied someone who experiences sounds when looking at visual movement/flicker (as first described by Saenz and Koch 2008). This person turned out to be very musically gifted and had been musically trained at a precocious age (3 years). This seems like no coincidence, but it is impossible to be sure. To answer these kinds of research questions convincingly is going to require very large samples, perhaps pooled across research centers, and also a good understanding of what the possible environmental influences could be.

Acquired synesthesia has been largely neglected in the field perhaps because it is considered too different in nature to developmental forms. It certainly is different. The kinds of inducers found in acquired synesthesia are very different from those in developmental synesthesia, and the causal pathway is different. Developmental synesthesia often involves learned inducers particularly of a linguistic nature (Simner 2007), whereas acquired synesthesia is often induced by a non-linguistic perceptual level of processing. For example, the acquisition of auditory-visual synesthesia (Afra, Funke, and Matsuo 2009) and tactile-visual synesthesia (Armel and Ramachandran 1999) has been documented following blindness; the onset of auditory-tactile synesthesia has been documented following a thalamic lesion affecting somatosensation (Ro et al. 2007); and visual-tactile (or mirror touch) synesthesia has been documented as a result of amputation (Fitzgibbon et al. 2011; Goller et al. 2013). Moreover, in acquired synesthesia the cause is environmental: typically, damage to a sensory organ or sensory pathways. However, these differences aren't enough to justify (to me) that we should ignore acquired synesthesia or that we should make no effort to reconcile acquired and developmental synesthesia within the same model. For instance, although we know that the proximate cause of synesthesia in acquired cases is environmental, not all people who suffer the same environmental insult develop these symptoms. One intriguing possibility is that those who tend to acquire synesthesia after injury may have an existing predisposition (e.g., "synesthesia genes"). For instance, we have recently worked with someone who lost her sense of smell (anosmia) in a car accident and subsequently acquired an auditory-olfactory synesthesia. Intriguingly, there was another type of synesthesia present in this person (spatial forms) prior to the injury that lead to the development of an acquired form of synesthesia. Could acquired synesthesia tend to be found in those with a disposition towards the developmental forms of synesthesia?

Like most researchers, I tend to be dismissive of the notion that synesthesia can be *deliberately* learned (whilst readily acknowledging that there are environmental influences of some form). However, there are some interesting potential exceptions to this. These present challenges to any explanation of the causes of synesthesia. The first is hypnosis. It has been claimed that hypnosis can induce synesthesia-like phenomenological and behavioral effects in non-synesthetes (Kadosh et al. 2009). Whether this is "true" synesthesia, vivid imagery, or pure suggestion needs to be established. The second potential example of a learned synesthesia is blind participants who have adapted to a sensory substitution device that, say, converts vision (on a camera) into sound (via headphones). These participants use visual parts of their brain for processing the relevant sounds (Amedi et al. 2007; Merabet et al. 2009). They also report visual experiences from sounds, but did not do so prior to learning to use the device (Ward and Meijer 2010). Is there something special about these individuals (e.g., a latent pre-existing disposition to synesthesia) or could synesthesia be learned by any blind person? We don't yet know.

What are the consequences of synesthesia?

Synesthesia has several possible consequences: for the ability to perceive certain stimuli (Ramachandran and Hubbard 2001; Saenz and Koch 2008), for memory (Rothen and Meier 2010), for engagement in hobbies and creative activities (Rich, Bradshaw, and Mattingley 2005), and so on. Rather than review each of these, I want to instead consider a few conceptual problems in understanding the consequences of synesthesia. Firstly, there is the problem of disentangling what is a cause and what is a consequence. Secondly, there is the problem of knowing whether it is a consequence of synesthesia itself (i.e., the particular inducer-concurrent mappings that synesthetes possess) or a consequence of wider changes that may occur in the brains of synesthetes, not all of which may directly relate to synesthesia.

With regard to disentangling cause from consequence, I have already considered one example: namely, whether heightened empathy in mirror-touch synesthesia is a cause or consequence of that type of synesthesia (Banissy and Ward 2007). Clearly, it cannot be the sole cause (as not everyone who is empathic reports this type of synesthesia) and it doesn't appear to be generally true of synesthetes either; grapheme-color synesthetes don't show heightened empathy (Banissy and Ward 2007). The same problem arises when one comes to consider the finding that synesthetes report increased forms of mental imagery (Barnett and Newell 2007; Price 2009). Is this an enabling condition for (certain forms of) synesthesia to develop, or is it a consequence?

The second problem that should be highlighted is whether the consequences are directly due to synesthesia itself, or due to the changes in the brain that give rise to synesthesia. This is illustrated simplistically in Figure 49.2. Consider the claim that

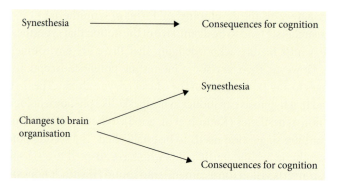

FIGURE 49.2 Synesthesia is linked to a broader cognitive profile affecting perception, imagery, and memory (to name a few). But what is the exact relationship between them? Two simple relationships are considered here.

synesthetes are more creative (Ramachandran and Hubbard 2001, 2003). One possibility is that there is something about the actual experience of synesthesia itself that promotes this. For example, synesthetes who have complex visual experiences (color, texture, shapes, movement) from music are far more likely to play a musical instrument than other types of synesthete (Ward et al. 2008). The link here between synesthesia and consequence appears direct (the top route). These rich and beautiful visual experiences may motivate synesthetes to make music. However, consider this claim: "synesthesia causes excess communication amongst brain maps ... Depending on where and how widely in the brain the trait was expressed, it could lead to both synesthesia and to a propensity towards linking seemingly unrelated concepts and ideas—in short, creativity" (Ramachandran and Hubbard 2003, 58). The proposed link here is more indirect (the bottom route) such that it is the changed brain organization, rather than the synesthesia itself, that leads to the consequences for cognition. Under this account, synesthesia could be regarded as a "colorful sideshow" of its real raison d'être (Ward, 2008).

The same general issue is encountered in the domain of memory. Synesthetes experiencing colors for letters and words often perform better than controls on tests of verbal recognition memory (Radvansky, Gibson, and McNerney 2011) and verbal recall (Yaro and Ward 2007). One logical explanation for this is that the synesthesia itself (i.e., the associated colors) provides an additional cue to memory that is unavailable to other people (i.e., a direct relationship between synesthesia and enhanced memory). However, synesthetes outperform controls on some tests of visual memory that have no direct relationship to their synesthesia (e.g., visual paired associates; Rothen and Meier 2010). Moreover, synesthetes don't perform better than controls on some memory tests involving verbal material (digit span) even though digits elicit colors for that group (Rothen and Meier 2010). An alternative possibility, is that there is a propensity to form certain kinds of associations (e.g., between visual form and color) arising out of differences in connectivity or plasticity and that this gives rise both to synesthesia itself and to enhanced memory on certain tasks.

In summary, there is now convincing evidence that synesthesia is associated with differences in performance across a range of cognitive domains (perception, imagery, memory, etc.). However, we still lack a sophisticated understanding of how they are linked together.

What can synesthesia research reveal about the typical mind and brain?

There are likely to be many different answers to this question and some of them have already been touched upon. Synesthesia is perfectly normal to most synesthetes, and they rarely seek help for it. To some this might make synesthesia rather uninteresting.

However, when tested objectively synesthetes are different on a wide range of measures and it suggests that within the general population there are genuinely different cognitive styles that can be linked back to genetic and neurological differences. As such, synesthesia provides a fascinating model for individual differences in cognition. One general assumption of research into synesthesia is that these individual differences should be explicable in terms of modifications to a model of "normal" sensory and cognitive development and brain function just like other acquired and developmental conditions.

The reference model of "normal" sensory and cognitive development and brain function is likely to have perception at its core, given that, at least in my opinion, percept-like experiences are the hallmark of synesthesia. An understanding of multisensory interactions is likely to be very important. In many forms of synesthesia, the synesthetes are reporting a multisensory experience from a unisensory input. The role of attention and binding processes in the experience are then relevant. Moreover, the actual mappings that determine how inducers and concurrents combine in synesthesia closely relate to the cross-modal and intra-modal associations of non-synesthetes. Synesthesia also provides us with a tool to explore how perception affects cognition more generally. Rather than perception being a mere input-stage into cognition, many theories assume that perceptual representations support "higher"-level functions including imagery, certain forms of memory, empathy, metaphor, and so on. For instance, we have used mirror-touch synesthesia as a model to explore embodied cognition (or simulation theory) accounts of social behavior (Banissy et al. 2011).

At the level of linking mind (i.e., cognitive processes) with brain (i.e., neural pathways), synesthesia may provide important clues into understanding how functional specialization occurs in brain regions. One early metaphor for synesthesia was a breakdown of modularity (Baron-Cohen et al. 1993) and whilst it is not normally cast in those terms now, it remains a broadly accurate description. For instance, functional imaging studies of grapheme-color synesthetes suggest that the "human color area V4" serves a dual function: responding to the color of surfaces, and processing of graphemes/linguistic material (e.g., Nunn et al. 2002; Hubbard et al. 2005). This raises interesting philosophical questions about whether conscious experiences are tied to particular brain regions (irrespective of the function they serve) or whether conscious experiences are tied to particular functions (irrespective of where they are computed in the brain) (Gray 2003; Hurley and Noë 2003). Although the standard neural account of grapheme-color synesthesia is hyperconnectivity (of some sort) between grapheme-sensitive and color-sensitive regions (such that the former activates the latter), an equally plausible explanation is that the response properties of neurons in that region are not differentiated in the same way as normal (i.e., it is both a grapheme-sensitive and color-sensitive region). Thus, functional specialization could breakdown in synesthesia either via changes in connectivity or via changes in the response properties of neurons or both.

Conclusions

If one considers that synesthesia research has been around for 200 years one might reasonably conclude that we haven't come far. However, if one considers that most of our knowledge of synesthesia has been accumulated within only the last 10 years then the picture becomes much healthier. However, there is still much that we don't know. Whilst other chapters have presented the state-of-the-art of what we do know, in this concluding chapter I have attempted to do the opposite by laying out what is still to be learnt. In doing so, I hope to have paved the way for future debate and research.

References

Afra, Pegah, Michael Funke, and Fumisuke Matsuo. 2009. Acquired auditory-visual synesthesia: A window to early cross-modal sensory interactions. *Psychology Research and Behavior Management* 2:31–37.

Amedi, Amir, William Stern, Joan A. Camprodon, Felix Bermpohl, Lotfi Merabet, Stephen Rotman, Christopher Hemond, Peter Meijer, and Alvaro Pascual-Leone. 2007. Shape conveyed by visual-to-auditory sensory substitution activates the lateral occipital complex. *Nature Neuroscience* 10:687–689.

Armel, K. C., and V. S. Ramachandran. 1999. Acquired synaesthesia in retinitis pigmentosa. *Neurocase* 5:293–296.

Asher, Julian E., Michael R. F. Aitken, Nasr Farooqi, Sameer Kurmani, and Simon Baron-Cohen. 2006. Diagnosing and phenotyping visual synaesthesia: A preliminary evaluation of the revised test of genuineness (TOG-R). *Cortex* 42:137–146.

Asher, Julian E., Janine Lamb, Denise Brocklebank, Jean-Baptiste Cazier, Elena Maestrini, Laura Addis, Mallika Sen, Simon Baron-Cohen, and Anthony P. Monaco. 2009. A Whole-Genome Scan and Fine-Mapping Linkage Study of Auditory-Visual Synaesthesia Reveals Evidence of Linkage to Chromosomes 2q24, 5q33, 6p12, and 12p12. *American Journal of Human Genetics* 84 (2):279–285.

Banissy, Michael J., Lúcia Garrido, Flor Kusnir, Bradely Duchaine, Vincent Walsh, and Jamie Ward. 2011. Superior facial expression, but not identity recognition, in mirror-touch synaesthesia. *Journal of Neuroscience* 31:1820–1824.

Banissy, Michael, and Jamie Ward. 2007. Mirror touch synaesthesia is linked with empathy. *Nature Neuroscience* 10:815–816.

Bargary, Gary, and Kevin J. Mitchell. 2008. Synaesthesia and cortical connectivity. *Trends in Neurosciences* 31:335–342.

Barnett, Kylie J., Ciara Finucane, Julian Asher, Gary Bargary, Aiden P. Corvin, Fiona N. Newell, and Kevin J. Mitchell. 2008. Familial patterns and the origins of individual differences in synaesthesia. *Cognition* 106:871–893.

Barnett, Kylie J., and Fiona N. Newell. 2007. Synaesthesia is associated with enhanced, self-rated visual imagery. *Consciousness and Cognition* 17:1032:1039.

Baron-Cohen, Simon, John Harrison, Laura H. Goldstein, and Maria Wyke. 1993. Coloured speech perception: Is synaesthesia what happens when modularity breaks down? *Perception* 22:419–426.

Baron-Cohen, Simon, Maria A. Wyke, and Colin Binnie. 1987. Hearing words and seeing colours: An experimental investigation of a case of synaesthesia. *Perception* 16:761–767.

Binet, Alfred. 1894. *Psychologie des grandes calculateurs et joueurs d'echecs*. Paris: Libraire Hachette.

Büchel, Christian, Cathy Price, and Karl Friston. 1998. A multimodal language region in the ventral visual pathway. *Nature* 6690:274–277.

Calkins, Mary Whiton. 1895. Synaesthesia. *American Journal of Psychology* 7:90–107.

Chabalier. 1864. De la pseudochromesthésie. *Journal de Medicine de Lyon* 1 (2):92–102.

Cohen Kadosh, Roi, Avishai Henik, Andres Catena, Vincent Walsh, and Luis J. Fuentes. 2009. Induced cross-modal synaesthetic experience without abnormal neuronal connections. *Psychological Science* 20 (2):258–265.

Cohen Kadosh, Roi, Noam Sagiv, David E. J. Linden, Lynn C. Robertson, Gali Elinger, and Avishai Henik. 2005. Do colors influence numerical cognition in synaesthesia? *Journal of Cognitive Neuroscience* 17:1766–1773.

Cohen, Laurent, Stéphane Lehéricy, Florence Chochon, Cathy Lemer, Sophie Rivaud, Stanislas Dehaene. 2002. Language-specific tuning of visual cortex functional properties of the visual word form area. *Brain* 125:1054–1069.

Colman, W. S. 1894. Further remarks on colour-hearing. *Lancet* 143:22.

Cornaz, Charles-Auguste-Édouard. 1848. *Des abnormalitiés congénitales de jeux et de leurs annexes*. Lausanne: Bridel.

Cytowic, Richard E. 1989. *Synaesthesia: A Union of the Senses*. New York: Springer.

Dehaene, Stanislas, Felipe Pegado, Lucia W. Braga, Paulo Ventura, Gilberto Nunes Filho, Antoinette Jobert, Ghislaine Dehaene-Lambertz, Régine Kolinsky, José Morais, and Laurent Cohen. 2011. How learning to read changes the cortical networks for vision and language. *Science* 330 (6009):1359–1364.

Dixon, Mike J., and Daniel Smilek. 2005. The importance of individual differences in grapheme-color synesthesia. *Neuron* 45:821–823.

Dixon, Mike J., Daniel Smilek, Cera Cudahy, and Philip M. Merikle. 2000. Five plus two equals yellow. *Nature* 406:365.

Dixon, Mike J., Daniel Smilek, and Philip M. Merikle. 2004. Not all synaesthetes are created equal: Projector vs. associator synaesthetes. *Cognitive, Affective and Behavioral Neuroscience* 4:335–343.

Epley, N., S. Akalis, A. Waytz, and J. T. Cacioppo. 2008. Creating social connection through inferential reproduction—Loneliness and perceived agency in gadgets, gods, and greyhounds. *Psychological Science* 19 (2):114–120.

Ferrari, G. C. 1907. Una varieta nuova di sinestesia. *Rivista di Psicologia* 3:297–317.

——. 1910. Un nuovo caso di sinestesia uditivo-gustativa. *Rivista di Psicologia* 6:101–104.

Fitzgibbon, Bernadette M. Peter G. Enticott, Anina N. Rich, Melita J. Giummarra, Nellie Georgiou-Karistianis, Jack W. Tsao, Sharon R. Weeks, and John L. Bradshaw. 2011. High incidence of 'synaesthesia for pain' in amputees. *Neuropsychologia* 48:3675–3678.

Flakne, April. 2005. Embodied and embedded: Friendship and the sunaisthetic self. *Epoche* 10:37–63.

Flournoy, Théodore. 1893. *Des phénomènes de synopsie*. Paris: Félix Alcan.

Galton, Francis. 1880. Visualised numerals. *Nature* 21:252–256.

Goller, Aviva I., Leun J. Otten, and Jamie Ward. 2009. Seeing sounds and hearing colors: An event-related potential study of auditory-visual synesthesia. *Journal of Cognitive Neuroscience* 21:1869–1881.

Goller, Aviva I., Kerrie Richards, Steven Novak, and Jamie Ward. 2013. Mirror-touch synaes-theisa in the phantom limb of amputees. *Cortex* 49 (1):243–251.

Gray, Jeffrey. 2003. How are qualia coupled to functions? *Trends in Cognitive Sciences* 7:192–194.

Grossenbacher, Peter G., and Christopher T. Lovelace. 2001. Mechanisms of synaesthesia: Cognitive and physiological constraints. *Trends in Cognitive Sciences* 5:36–41.

Howells, T. H. 1944. The experimental development of color-tone synesthesia. *Journal of Experimental Psychology* 34:87–103.

Hubbard, Edward M., A. Cyrus Arman, Vilayanur S. Ramachandran, and Geoffrey M. Boynton. 2005. Individual differences among grapheme-colour synaesthetes: Brain-behavior correla-tions. *Neuron* 45:975–985.

Hubbard, Edward M., and Vilayanur S. Ramachandran. 2005. Neurocognitive mechanisms of synesthesia. *Neuron* 48:509–520.

Hurley, Susan, and Alva Noë. 2003. Neural plasticity and consciousness. *Biology and Philosophy* 18:131–168.

Jewanski, Jörg, Sean A. Day, and Jamie Ward. 2009. A colorful albino: The first documented case of synaesthesia, by Georg Tobias Ludwig Sachs in 1812. *Journal of the History of Neurosciences* 18:293–303.

Jewanski, Jörg, Julia Simner, Sean A. Day, and Jamie Ward. 2011. The development of a scientific understanding of synesthesia during the mid-nineteenth century (1849–1873). *Journal of the History of Neurosciences* 20: 284–305.

Lussana, Filippo. 1873. *Fisiologia dei colori*. Padone: F. Sacchetto.

Marks, Lawrence E. 1975. On coloured-hearing synaesthesia: Cross-modal translations of sen-sory dimensions. *Psychological Bulletin* 82:303–331.

——. 2004. Cross-modal interactions in speeded classification. In *The Handbook of Multisensory Processes*, ed. Gemma Calvert, Charles Spence and Barry E. Stein. Cambridge, MA: MIT Press.

Mattingley, Jason B., Anina N. Rich, and John L. Bradshaw. 2001. Unconscious priming eliminates automatic binding of colour and alphanumeric form in synaesthesia. *Nature* 410:580–582.

Maurer, Daphne, and Catherine J. Mondloch. 2006. The infant as synesthete? *Attention and Performance* XXI:449–471.

Merabet, Lotfi, Lorella Battelli, Souzana Obretenova, Sara Maguire, Peter Meijer, and Alvaro Pascual-Leone. 2009. Functional recruitment of visual cortex for sound encoded object identification in the blind. *NeuroReport* 20:132–138.

Nunn, J. A., L. J. Gregory, M. Brammer, S. C. R. Williams, D. M. Parslow, M. J. Morgan, R. G. Morris, E. T. Bullmore, S. Baron-Cohen, and J. A. Gray. 2002. Functional magnetic reso-nance imaging of synesthesia: Activation of V4/V8 by spoken words. *Nature Neuroscience* 5:371–375.

Palmeri, Thomas J., Randolph Blake, René Marois, Marci A. Flanery, and William Whetsell Jr. 2002. The perceptual reality of synesthetic colors. *Proceedings of the National Academy of Science of the United States of America* 99:4127–4131.

Pierce, Arthur H. 1907. Gustatory audition: A hitherto undescribed variety of synaesthesia. *American Journal of Psychology* 18:341–352.

Price, Mark C. 2009. Spatial forms and mental imagery. *Cortex* 45 (10):1229–1245.

Radvansky, Gabriel A., Bradley S. Gibson, and M. Windy McNerney. 2011. Synesthesia and memory: Color congruency, von Restorff, and false memory effects. *Journal of Experimental Psychology: Learning Memory and Cognition* 37 (1):219–229.

Ramachandran, Vilayanur S., and Edward M. Hubbard. 2001a. Psychophysical investigations into the neural basis of synaesthesia. *Proceedings of the Royal Society of London B: Biological Sciences* 268:979–983.

——. 2001b. Synaesthesia—a window into perception, thought and language. *Journal of Consciousness Studies* 8:3–34.

——. 2003. Hearing colors, tasting shapes. *Scientific American* 288 (5):52–59.

Ramachandran, Vilayanur S., Diane Rogers-Ramachandran, and Susan Cobb. 1995. Touching the phantom limb. *Nature* 377:489–490.

Reich, Lior, Marcin Szwed, Laurent Cohen, and Amir Amedi. 2011. A ventral visual stream reading center independent of visual experience. *Current Biology* 21 (5):363–368.

Rich, Anina N., John L. Bradshaw, and Jason B. Mattingley. 2005. A systematic, large-scale study of synaesthesia: Implications for the role of early experience in lexical-colour associations. *Cognition* 98:53–84.

Ro, Tony, Alessandro Farnè, Ruth M. Johnson, Van Wedeen, Zili Chu, Zhiyue J. Wang, Jill V. Hunter, and Michael S. Beauchamp. 2007. Feeling sounds after a thalamic lesion. *Annals of Neurology* 62:433–441.

Rothen, Nicholas, and Beat Meier. 2010. Grapheme-colour synaesthesia yields an ordinary rather than extraordinary memory advantage: Evidence from a group study. *Memory* 18 (3):258–264.

Rouw, Romke, and H. Steven Scholte. 2007. Increased structural connectivity in grapheme-color synesthesia. *Nature Neuroscience* 10:792–797.

Saenz, Melissa, and Christof Koch. 2008. The sound of change: Visually-induced auditory synesthesia. *Current Biology* 18:R650–R651.

Sagiv, Noam, Julia Simner, James Collins, Brian Butterworth, and Jamie Ward. 2006. What is the relationship between synaesthesia and visuo-spatial number forms? *Cognition* 101:114–128.

Simner, J. 2007. Beyond perception: Synaesthesia as a psycholinguistic phenomenon. *Trends in Cognitive Science* 11:23–29.

——. 2011. Defining synaesthesia. *British Journal of Psychology* 103:1–15.

Simner, Julia, Jenny Harrold, Harriet Creed, Louise Monro, and Louise Foulkes. 2009. Early detection markers for synaesthesia in childhood populations. *Brain* 132:57–64.

Simner, Julia, and Emma Holenstein. 2007. Ordinal linguistic personification as a variant of synesthesia. *Journal of Cognitive Neuroscience* 19:694–703.

Smilek, Daniel, and Mike J. Dixon. 2002. Towards a synergistic understanding of synaesthesia: Combining current experimental findings with synaesthetes' subjective descriptions. *Psyche* 8.

Smilek, Daniel, Kelly A. Malcolmson, Jonathan S. A. Carriere, Meghan Eller, Donna Kwan, and Michael Reynolds. 2007. When '3' is a jerk and 'o' is a king: Personifying inanimate objects in synaesthesia. *Journal of Cognitive Neuroscience* 19:981–992.

Sorabji, Richard. 2005. *The Philosophy of the Commentators 200–600AD*. Cornell, NY: Cornell University Press.

Vulpian, Alfred. 1866. *Leçons sur la physiologie générale et comparée du système nerveux, faites en 1864 au Muséum d'histoire naturelle*. Paris: Gerner-Baillière.

Walker, Peter, J. Gavin Bremner, Ursula Mason, Joanne Spring, Karen Mattock, Alan Slater, and Scott P. Johnson. 2010. Preverbal infants' sensitivity to synaesthetic cross-modality correspondences. *Psychological Science* 21 (1):21–25.

Ward, Jamie. 2008. *The Frog who Croaked Blue: Synesthesia and the Mixing of the Senses*. London: Routledge.

Ward, Jamie, Michael J. Banissy, and Clare N. Jonas. 2008. Haptic perception and synaesthesia. In *Handbook of Haptic Perception*, ed. M. Grunwald, 259–265. Berlin: Springer-Verlag.

Ward, Jamie, Ryan Li, Shireen Salih, and Noam Sagiv. 2007. Varieties of grapheme-colour synaesthesia: A new theory of phenomenological and behavioural differences. *Consciousness and Cognition* 16:913–931.

Ward, Jamie, and Jason B. Mattingley. 2006. Synaesthesia: An overview of contemporary findings and controversies. *Cortex* 42:129–136.

Ward, Jamie, and Peter Meijer. 2010. Visual experiences in the blind induced by an auditory sensory substitution device. *Consciousness and Cognition* 19:492–500.

Ward, Jamie, and Julia Simner. 2003. Lexical-gustatory synaesthesia: Linguistic and conceptual factors. *Cognition* 89:237–261.

Ward, Jamie, Julia Simner, and Vivian Auyeung. 2005. A comparison of lexical-gustatory and grapheme-colour synaesthesia. *Cognitive Neuropsychology* 22:28–41.

Ward, Jamie, Daisy Thompson-Lake, Roxanne Ely, and Flora Kaminski. 2008. Synaesthesia, creativity and art: What is the link? *British Journal of Psychology* 99:127–141.

Wolff, P., Y. Matsumiya, I. F. Abrohms, C. van Velzer, and C. T. Lambroso. 1974. The effect of white noise on the somatosensory evoked responses in sleeping newborn infants. *Electroencephalography and Clinical Neurophysiology* 37:269–274.

Yaro, Caroline, and Jamie Ward. 2007. Searching for Shereshevskii: What is superior about the memory of synaesthetes? *Quarterly Journal of Experimental Psychology* 60:682–696.

Author Index

SUBJECT INDEX